*American & British Genealogy & Heraldry*

# AMERICAN & BRITISH GENEALOGY & HERALDRY

*A Selected List of Books*
*Second Edition*
*Compiled by P. William Filby*

DIRECTOR
MARYLAND HISTORICAL SOCIETY
BALTIMORE, MARYLAND

*American Library Association*
Chicago 1975

Library of Congress Cataloging in Publication Data

Filby, P    William, 1911-
   American & British genealogy & heraldry.

   Includes index.
   1. United States—Genealogy—Bibliography.
   2. Heraldry—United States—Bibliography. 3. Great Britain—Genealogy—Bibliography. 4. Heraldry—Great Britain—Bibliography. I. Title.
   Z5311.F55  [CS47]     016.929′1′097     75-29383
   ISBN 0-8389-0203-0

Copyright © 1975 by the American Library Association

All rights reserved. No part of this publication may be reproduced in any form without permission in writing from the publisher, except by a reviewer who may quote brief passages in a review.

Printed in the United States of America

*To*
# V. R. F.

# Contents

| | | | |
|---|---|---|---|
| Preface | xi | *Areas* | 46 |
| Introduction | xv | New England | 46 |
| Abbreviations | xxi | The South | 48 |
| | | Other Areas | 50 |
| **UNITED STATES** | 1 | Indians | 51 |
| *General Reference* | 1 | *Individual States* | 55 |
| Bibliographies | 1 | Alabama | 55 |
| Records, Guides, Indexes | 4 | Alaska | 58 |
| Periodicals, Series | 9 | Arizona | 59 |
| Biographies | 12 | Arkansas | 60 |
| Censuses | 15 | California | 63 |
| Atlases, Maps, Gazetteers | 16 | Colorado | 68 |
| Place Names | 18 | Connecticut | 69 |
| Surnames | 18 | Delaware | 74 |
| Manuals and Aids | 19 | District of Columbia | 76 |
| Colonial and Precolonial Lists | 22 | Florida | 78 |
| Immigration | 27 | Georgia | 80 |
| Ethnic Groups | 31 | Hawaii | 88 |
| Religions | 33 | Idaho | 89 |
| Military and Pension Lists | 37 | Illinois | 91 |

## Contents

| | | | | |
|---|---|---|---|---|
| Indiana | 95 | LATIN AMERICA | 254 |
| Iowa | 98 | *General* | 254 |
| Kansas | 100 | *Individual Countries* | 256 |
| Kentucky | 103 | Argentine Republic | 256 |
| Louisiana | 110 | Brazil | 257 |
| Maine | 116 | Chile | 257 |
| Maryland | 119 | Colombia | 257 |
| Massachusetts | 126 | Cuba | 258 |
| Michigan | 132 | Dominican Republic | 258 |
| Minnesota | 135 | Ecuador | 258 |
| Mississippi | 138 | Guatemala | 258 |
| Missouri | 140 | Mexico | 258 |
| Montana | 144 | Peru | 260 |
| Nebraska | 145 | Uruguay | 260 |
| Nevada | 147 | Venezuela | 260 |
| New Hampshire | 149 | CANADA | 261 |
| New Jersey | 153 | *General* | 261 |
| New Mexico | 159 | *Loyalists* | 266 |
| New York | 161 | *Provinces* | 268 |
| North Carolina | 172 | Alberta | 268 |
| North Dakota | 178 | British Columbia | 268 |
| Ohio | 180 | Manitoba | 268 |
| Oklahoma | 185 | Maritime Provinces | 268 |
| Oregon | 187 | Northwest Territories | 270 |
| Pennsylvania | 189 | Ontario | 270 |
| Puerto Rico | 203 | Quebec | 272 |
| Rhode Island | 205 | Saskatchewan | 275 |
| South Carolina | 208 | | |
| South Dakota | 214 | ENGLAND | 276 |
| Tennessee | 215 | *Bibliographies* | 276 |
| Texas | 221 | General | 276 |
| Utah | 228 | Local Histories | 278 |
| Vermont | 229 | Pedigrees and Family Histories | 278 |
| Virginia | 232 | *Records* | 280 |
| Washington | 244 | *Paleography* | 283 |
| West Virginia | 246 | *Periodicals and Series* | 284 |
| Wisconsin | 250 | *Chronology* | 286 |
| Wyoming | 253 | *Biographies* | 286 |

## Contents

| | |
|---|---|
| General | 286 |
| Professions | 287 |
| *Parish Registers* | 290 |
| *Vital Statistics* | 291 |
| *Monumental Brasses* | 293 |
| *Wills* | 293 |
| *Topography* | 295 |
| *Names* | 296 |
|    Place | 296 |
|    Personal | 296 |
| *Manuals* | 298 |
| *Royal Family* | 300 |
| *Conqueror and Domesday Book* | 301 |
| *Peerages, Baronetages, Knightages, Gentry* | 301 |
| *Religions* | 307 |
|    General | 307 |
|    Specific | 307 |

## IRELAND 310

| | |
|---|---|
| *Bibliographies* | 310 |
| *Record Guides and Offices* | 311 |
| *Periodicals and Series* | 313 |
| *Biographies* | 313 |
| *Registers* | 313 |
| *Vital Statistics* | 314 |
| *Wills* | 314 |
| *Topography* | 315 |
| *Names* | 316 |
| *Manuals* | 317 |
| *Peerages, Baronetages, Knightages, Gentry* | 318 |
| *Religions* | 320 |

## SCOTLAND 321

| | |
|---|---|
| *Bibliographies* | 321 |
| *Records* | 322 |
| *Paleography* | 322 |
| *Periodicals and Series* | 323 |
| *Biographies* | 323 |
| *Registers* | 324 |
| *Vital Statistics* | 325 |
| *Wills* | 325 |
| *Topography* | 325 |
| *Names* | 326 |
| *Manuals* | 326 |
| *Peerages, Baronetages, Knightages, Gentry* | 327 |
| *Religions* | 329 |

## WALES 330

| | |
|---|---|
| *Bibliographies* | 330 |
| *Records* | 330 |
| *Biographies* | 331 |
| *Registers* | 331 |
| *Vital Statistics* | 331 |
| *Wills* | 331 |
| *Topography* | 332 |
| *Names* | 332 |
| *Manuals* | 332 |
| *Peerages, Baronetages, Knightages, Gentry* | 333 |
| *Religions* | 333 |

## BRITISH ISLAND AREAS 334

## BRITISH DOMINIONS AND FORMER DOMINIONS 336

| | |
|---|---|
| General | 336 |
| Australia | 337 |
| British West Indies | 338 |
| Canada, see pp. 261–75 | |
| India | 339 |
| New Zealand | 339 |

ix

## Contents

| | | | |
|---|---|---|---|
| *South Africa* | 340 | British Island Areas and Dominions | 349 |
| **HERALDRY** | 342 | United States and Canada | 350 |
| *General* | 342 | Latin America | 351 |
| *Manuals* | 344 | *Church, Civic Heraldry, and Flags* | 352 |
| *Rolls of Arms* | 345 | *Periodicals and Series* | 352 |
| General | 345 | *Bibliographies* | 353 |
| Great Britain | 346 | *Foreign Heraldry* | 354 |
| Ireland | 348 | Addresses of Publishers | 355 |
| Scotland | 348 | | |
| Wales | 349 | Index | 367 |

# *Preface to the Second Edition*

In the preface to the first edition of AMERICAN AND BRITISH GENEALOGY AND HERALDRY I stated that the book was the result of a series of fortuitous happenings. I was a librarian in a library containing a very fine genealogy collection, and because of this I had to learn the jargon and familiarize myself with the best books of American and British genealogy and heraldry. I decided then that a book designed specifically to assist other librarians similarly placed, as well as genealogical researchers, would be useful. In general the book received favorable reviews and left me in no doubt that it would serve a useful purpose in the hundreds of libraries which purchased it. And so it has proved; I have spoken at many institutions in the intervening period and almost always have been asked when I intended to update the book. I have in fact kept the book up to date since 1970, first in an interleaved copy and, when this became full, on cards with the entry pasted to each card.

The mode of compilation differed little from that in the 1960s: I compiled lists from various sources and passed them on to librarians, state archivists, professional genealogists and others who have a profound knowledge of genealogy or heraldry, who read the lists and made corrections and additions. Two full drawers of a filing cabinet attest to their assistance.

Because of a continual flow of books, this book has increased in size, and since useful source material cannot be omitted, future editions will get much larger. In six years some 3,000 new or newly noted titles, including over 300 periodical articles, have been added, and the total of almost 2,000 titles in 1968 has grown to over 5,000 titles in the present volume.

*Preface*

The work is longer than I intended. Earlier, I was confronted with the issue of whether I should add only new titles and then update every five years, or include every basic title in the first book and rely on supplements published periodically. I finally decided on the latter course, since genealogy, unlike most other sciences, will never get out of date, so that a basic list is to be favored. For instance, the 1790 census lists cannot be superseded and will always be of great use to genealogists no matter how far into the future research is conducted. I regard this volume as the basic list, and hope to issue supplements perhaps every four years.

My assistants are too numerous to list. The outstanding helper was Dorothy M. Lower, librarian of the Reynolds Historical Genealogy Collection at the Public Library of Fort Wayne and Allen County, Indiana. She has at her fingertips one of the finest genealogical libraries in America, thanks to the wisdom and foresight of the public librarian, Fred J. Reynolds. Dorothy read almost every entry and made suggestions and additions, and I cannot thank her enough for her devotion at all times.

Another small group answered my many questions with enthusiasm. Anthony Camp, Director of Research, Society of Genealogists, London, again revised works concerning England in the light of the many additions; Dr. Edward McLysaght, now retired from the Irish Manuscripts Commission, Dublin; Elizabeth Jenkins and Evelyn Timberlake of the Library of Congress reference division (who incidentally persuaded me to adopt LC headings for all entries), Netti Schreiner-Yantis of Springfield, Virginia, who helped with the addresses of small and private publishers; Anthony W. C. Phelps of the Western Reserve Historical Society, Robert Barnes of the Maryland Historical Society, and Joseph G. Ferrier of Washington, D.C., who fashioned the heraldry division; and Richard Lackey of Forest, Mississippi, who aided my selection in several states.

An enthusiastic "team" acted as advisers on any point which needed a decision: Patricia Chadwell, Fort Worth Public Library; Gunther Pohl, New York Public Library; J. Carlyle Parker, California State College, Stanislaus, Turlock; Jimmy B. Parker of the Research Department of the Church of Jesus Christ of Latter-day Saints; and Dorothy Lower. Much of the advice on Canada came from Roland-J. Auger of Quebec National Archives; Lois S. Neal was a tower of strength with her knowledge drawn from the State of North Carolina, Department of Cultural Resources. George Ely Russell gave me the benefit of his knowledge of serials gained through his *Genealogical Periodical Annual Index,* and if I have added some titles which he did not suggest, I hope he will not mind. Rudecinda Lo Buglio and Nadine Vasquez, both of California, supplied almost all of the Latin America titles, and I wish I could have included every one.

Others providing continual help included G. D. Beauvais and Raymond Gingras (Canada), Willard Heiss and Carolynne L. Miller (Indiana), George E. McCracken (Iowa and Pennsylvania), Raymond B. Clark, Mary K. Meyer and

Robert Barnes (Maryland), Wiley Roger Pope (Minnesota), E. Richard McKinstry (New Jersey), Dr. Kenn Stryker-Rodda (New Jersey and New York), Gerald T. Parsons and James Gregory (New York), Lida Flint Harshman (Ohio), Fernando Labault-Lopez (Puerto Rico), and Lucile A. Boykin and Lloyd D. Bockstruck (Texas).

Questions were answered by: Timothy Field Beard, Helen Marcia Bruner, Vivian Bryan, Pat Bryant, Betty S. Burns, Kendall J. Cram, John D. Cushing, Ruth L. Douthit, Janice Fleming, Pauline Jones Gandrud, Margaret Gleason, Katherine A. Halverson, Collin B. Hamer, Jr., Darlene E. Hamilton, Mary B. Prior, Milton Rubincam, Milton G. Russell, Stella J. Scheckler, Martin F. Schmidt, Mildred V. Schulz, Natalie Seweryn, Mrs. Robert M. Sherman, Alene Simpson, George Stevenson, and Mrs. Huntington Williams. Another two hundred people assisted me when needed and I thank them all.

As before, the Genealogical Publishing Company, Baltimore, gave me the freedom of its shelves and its want lists and answered every query I submitted. To Dr. Michael Tepper and Edgar G. Heyl I offer my heartfelt thanks. Without this company, the Maryland Historical Society, and the Library of Congress I cannot see how this work could have been compiled.

Finally, my thanks are due Mrs. Marian Schori, secretary at the Maryland Historical Society during most of the revision, and Shirley Florie, present secretary, who always was ready to help; and Miss A. Hester Rich, the Society's librarian, who found answers to my bibliographical inquiries. Above all I pay tribute to Alice P. Kriete, my personal assistant. Although I did most of the work at home, I could not have carried it through without her understanding and cooperation.

To Vera Ruth Filby, my wife, must go the ultimate thanks. For much of 1974 and 1975 she nurtured and cosseted me so that most of my waking hours could be devoted to the book.

                P. W. FILBY
                *Director,* Maryland Historical Society
                *Former Chairman,* Genealogical Committee
                History Section, Reference Services Division
                American Library Association

# *Introduction*

Readers and researchers of genealogy and heraldry have increased considerably in the past two decades. Perhaps the affluence of present-day society and the opportunity for earlier retirement have had much to do with this increase. But whatever the reasons, only a few libraries have a staff with sufficient knowledge to cope with the influx. Libraries with large budgets hope to acquire most of the needed books on a broad scale, while smaller libraries want to acquire books which will serve their readers best. AMERICAN AND BRITISH GENEALOGY AND HERALDRY was the first attempt to assist the large library with a staff unversed in the subject and the smaller library with a limited budget or an interest confined to one or a few states, and the attempt was apparently successful.

Since the compilation of that work with its December, 1968, cutoff, interest in genealogy has not diminished, and if the reprint publishers are to be believed, more and more books are avidly sought.

## *Purpose*

The purpose of this volume is to present to American and Canadian libraries a selected list of books needed to meet the wants of genealogists and family searchers. It is: (1) a reference manual to help the librarian show the reader the sources available, (2) a selection aid to the librarian, and (3) a source list for the family searcher who may be embarking on research for the first time in his life. It is also a buying list, with publisher given in the listing for every book in print. Although librarians can find the full addresses for the publishers in various reference tools, such as *Cumulative Book Index, Books in Print,* and *Bowker's*

XV

*Introduction*

*American Book Trade Directory,* there are many genealogical authors and compilers who prefer to publish from their home addresses or from a small, unlisted publisher. In response, therefore, to pleadings from librarians and others, at the end of the book is a list of addresses of those publishers not in general reference works. Publisher names are omitted in the listing for out-of-print books. Because of frequent price changes, prepublication offers, and other variables, no prices are given.

Since this list will often be used by uninitiated researchers and by librarians unfamiliar with genealogy, annotations are provided when they seem needed to give advice, guidance, or supplementary information. Not all the works listed are annotated, partly because some do not require it and partly because the compiler was unable to examine every book listed (and those who assisted were not always able to supply annotations). Many of the books that have appeared in the field contain numerous errors and are therefore unreliable. Nevertheless, some of these are included because they are heavily used and libraries may therefore wish to hold them. The annotations warn librarians and readers of deficiencies, and the phrase "use with care" indicates that if that particular book is used, the information must be checked thoroughly. Now that the Daughters of the American Revolution and other groups demand such complete accuracy in their admissions, the warnings given will prove useful.

## *Scope*

The list is limited to works on genealogy and heraldry. It includes general works of genealogy covering the United States, Latin America, Canada, Great Britain, and finally British Island areas and other former dominions. For every American state there is a selected list of books believed to be the most useful for researchers in that state or peripheral states. Canadian and Latin American works are listed separately, but in view of the great increase in Canadian works the section is split into provinces. Heraldry is international in its extent, and all heraldic works are therefore entered together in a separate division. A few useful European heraldic works have been included.

One innovation requested by readers and reviewers alike was some indication to the smaller library of essential books of reasonable cost. Thanks to a team of librarians, selections have been made for America, Canada, Great Britain, and Heraldry. It should be noted that many excellent books are not marked simply because, although they are definitive and necessary, they are too expensive; it is considered, however, that those so marked will be sufficient for a basic beginning. A listing of the best foreign genealogical and heraldic titles was prepared as well, although its inclusion was not possible because of limits set by the publisher. Perhaps they can become the subject of a separate compilation, since many are vital, written with the specific intention of aiding the American researcher.

Some very expensive titles have been included. While it can be argued that their inclusion will be of little use to the small library with limited funds, the book is intended as a guide for readers as well as for librarians, and the reader should be aware of the existence of expensive sets usually found only in large public libraries. Family histories are not included, nor are general county histories; unlike the first book, however, this edition includes histories such as "western," "eastern," "central," and other area designations, since in their early history some areas were representative of a whole state. Name lists (cemetery surveys and Revolutionary War rolls) are included for North America and for each state.

A few "mug books" *have* been included. A "mug book" is a portrait and biographical history book, a type of book common in early American days. It was produced by publishers with little or no attempt to edit or verify the information. Since the individual usually paid for inclusion and was obligated to order a copy, the selection was not objective. Nevertheless, the present compiler felt obliged to include a number of these books because the family searcher may find a name only in such a work and because, in the later-formed states, the "mug book" is the *only* source of family information in the last half of the nineteenth century. Similarly, many of the Historical Records Survey works compiled in the 1930s and early 1940s in the W.P.A. programs have been added. Many authorities were consulted before this decision was taken, with the consensus that, although over thirty years out of date, the records themselves are reasonably accurate, and if locations are no longer accurate, they are usually easily traced.

The list is limited to printed sources. For the present edition the cutoff date for genealogical information was easier than in the first edition because of the inclusion of Civil War material. Other additions are: Latin America, Alaska, and Puerto Rico; a vastly increased selection for Canada; and, in perhaps the most interesting addition of all, definitive articles of some length which have appeared in the leading genealogical and historical journals. They are included because, in several cases, they are as valuable as many of the books.

## *Closing Date*

The cutoff date for listing new works and new editions was 31 December 1974.

## *Arrangement*

The arrangement is simple: (1) the United States, general works; (2) States in alphabetical order, with authors/titles in alphabetical order under each state; (3) Latin America, with authors/titles in alphabetical order and countries treated separately; (4) Canada, with general titles and provinces in alphabetical order;

*Introduction*

(5) England, Ireland, Scotland, Wales, British Island areas, and British Dominions, again alphabetical; (6) Heraldry, broken down into general, rolls of arms, and foreign selections. In response to requests from the Library of Congress and others, every attempt has been made to follow LC catalog titles; although this system may confuse the genealogist, it will greatly assist a librarian searching for the book. Each work is listed in the comprehensive index under the name of the author, if given, or under the first or key word, if anonymous. Many works have been listed under both author and subject; thus, Ridgely, H. W. *Historic graves of Maryland and the District of Columbia* will be found under Ridgely, Maryland, and District of Columbia.

Each entry is numbered consecutively; occasionally the same title will be found in two places because it relates to more than one subject. When, in the final revision of the manuscript, entries were omitted or added, the numbers were omitted or altered, i.e. small letters—a, b, c, etc.—were added to the previous numbers to accommodate additional entries. The numbers have no other significance than as an aid in finding titles.

## Serial Entries

Annuals and other serials are listed with open entries when still current; if they have ceased publication, the opening and closing date and volume are given. They are entered in their appropriate geographical sections rather than under one heading, in the belief that this arrangement will serve the user best.

## Reprints

Because so many of the important genealogical and heraldic works have been reprinted, every attempt has been made to discover the reprint status of each book in the list as of 31 December 1974.

## Selection and Criteria

This is a selected list of basic works. A number of authorities were asked to assist in making it as useful as possible. In preparing the new edition, the original work was cut up and pasted on cards. Dealers' catalogs and lists, book reviews, and genealogical journals were all studied; anything of value was added to the cards, and new ones prepared for all new books. This process was followed by a thorough study of the Library of Congress catalog, resulting in the addition of many books overlooked in the first edition. Business visits enabled the compiler to examine state library shelves *in situ,* and when these lists were collated, a trial list was prepared for consideration. Lists of general titles were then sent to professional genealogists and manual compilers. State lists were sent to each state archivist, the state historical society, one or two reference librarians in public libraries holding good genealogical collections, and to any-

*Introduction*

one else considered expert in the field. Some few failed to reply; others merely checked the list and returned it without comment. But many carefully considered every title and offered many suggestions. The general American lists were considered by about a dozen authorities, including genealogical bookdealers and publishers. The state lists are based on consideration by two or more authorities in each state as well as by the compiler, and the annotations were often supplied by these authorities. The list could not have been compiled without their help, and with their permission their names or institutions have been gratefully noted at the head of each state. The British lists were fashioned in a similar manner, and here the compiler was fortunate to have genealogical advice from the leading authorities of England and Ireland. Finally, the general lists were reexamined by a team of librarians, who selected the titles suitable for a small library. These selections are marked in the text with an asterisk (*).

# *Abbreviations*

| | | | |
|---|---|---|---|
| A.M.S. Press | Abraham Magazine Service Press | Lib. | Library |
| Assoc. | Associates, Association | ms., mss. | manuscript, manuscripts |
| bull. | bulletin | n.d. | no date |
| ca. | circa | no. | number |
| Co. | Company | n.p. | no place |
| Cong. | Congress | Pr. | Press |
| corr. | corrected, corrections | pr. | printing |
| D.A.R. | Daughters of the American Revolution | pt. | part |
| | | pub. | published, publishing |
| | | publ. | publication, publications |
| Dept. | Department | Repr. | Reprint |
| distr. | distributed | rev. | revised |
| div. | division | ser. | series |
| doc. | document | sess. | session |
| ed. | edited, edition | Soc. | Society |
| enl. | enlarged | St. | Saint |
| Fdn. | Foundation | trans. | translated |
| G.P.C. | Genealogical Publishing Co., Baltimore, Md. | Univ. | University |
| | | v., vol. | volume |
| H.R.S. | Historical Records Survey (W.P.A.) | W.P.A. | Work Projects Administration |
| Inst. | Institute, Institution | | |
| L.D.S. | Genealogical Society of the Church of Jesus Christ of Latter-day Saints, Inc. | | |

*American & British
Genealogy & Heraldry*

# UNITED STATES

## General Reference

### BIBLIOGRAPHIES

**1**   **American genealogical index.** Ed. by Fremont Rider. 48v. Middletown, Conn., 1942–52.
Indexes 1790 census, 43v. of records of soldiers who served in the Revolutionary War, and many family genealogies. Saves endless hours of research. Being superseded by no.2.

**2**   ——— New series. v.1– . Middletown, Conn.: Godfrey Memorial Lib., 1952– .
When the first series (*see* no.1) reached the last entry in the alphabet, the series was recommenced. By December 1974 it had reached v.88, (Ingham). 2v. a year are published, and new works are indexed as work proceeds. Invaluable for beginner. Essential.

*****3**   **Beard, Timothy F.** In v.2 of *Pedigrees of some of the Emperor Charlemagne's descendants* (no.275).
Mr. Beard has a magnificent 100-p. bibliography which informs the readers of the latest works in genealogy available to them. 1974.

**4**   **Besterman, Theodore.** Family history; a bibliography of bibliographies. Totowa, N.J.: Rowman & Littlefield, 1971.
Compiled by the publisher from 4th ed., 1965–66, of Besterman's *A world bibliography of bibliographies*—6,664 columns. Although by a world-renowned bibliographer, the book is of limited usefulness, as it fails to record the best books, and few works are annotated.

**5**   **Bradford, Thomas C.** The bibliographer's manual of American history, containing an account of all states, territories, towns and county histories . . . with verbatim copies of the titles, and useful bibliographical notes. Ed. and rev. by Stan V. Henkels. 1907–10. Repr. in 5v. Detroit, Mich.: Gale Research, 1968.
Although not many genealogical works are listed, the book is an invaluable refer-

1

## 6 United States

ence for use by librarians, historians, and collectors. Some of the 6,056 titles touch on genealogy through local history.

6  **Bremer, Ronald A.** A compendium of American historical sources. Woods Cross, Utah: Gendex Copy Service, 1973.

Bibliography of each state, with sources provided for federal records, state census, maps, ethnic archives, etc.

7  ———— **Blumhagen, H. M.,** and **Williams, K. H.** Selected American historical sources: an annotated bibliography. Rev. Salt Lake City: Gencor, 1974.

Aimed at the genealogist. Gives data on genealogical centers for each state, with full addresses.

8  **Brigham, Clarence S.** History and bibliography of American newspapers, 1690–1820. 2v. Repr. Hamden, Conn.: Archon Books, 1962.

Originally published by the American Antiquarian Soc. in its *Proceedings,* 1923–27. It was revised and published in 2v., and additions and corrections were given in *Proceedings,* v.71, no.1, 1961. The repr. includes the additions. Essential. Gregory covers 1821–1936 (*see* no.11).

8a  **Freemasons and freemasonry:** an extract from The national union catalog. Pre-1956 imprints, v.184; representing holdings of north American libraries reported to the National union catalog in the Library of Congress. London: Mansell Information Pub., 1973.

Entries filed geographically; includes histories, registers.

9  **Furman, Consuelo.** Quaker bibliography for the genealogist; references to biography, genealogy, and records. New York, 1950?

10  **Glenn, Thomas A.** A list of some American genealogies which have been printed in book form. 1897. Repr. Baltimore: G.P.C., 1969.

First comprehensive bibliography of American genealogies, tubular charts and pedigrees; 2,000 references.

11  **Gregory, Winifred.** American newspapers, 1821–36. A union list of files available in the United States and Canada. New York, 1937.

Cover title: *Union list of newspapers.* Brigham (no.8) covers 1690–1820.

12  ———— Alphabetical index to the titles. Arranged by Avis G. Clarke. Oxford, Mass., 1958. Typescript at Library of Congress.

13  **Griffin, Appleton C.** Bibliography of American historical societies (the United States and Dominion of Canada), 2nd ed., rev. and enl. Repr. Detroit, Mich.: Gale Research, 1966.

Repr. of 1907 which was taken from v.2 of *1905 annual report of the American Historical Association.* Excellent list up to 1905.

14  **Hasse, Adelaide R.** Materials for a bibliography of the public archives of the thirteen original states, covering the colonial period and the state period to 1789. New York: Argonaut Pr., 1966.

First published in 1908 from part of v.2 of the *Annual report of the American Historical Assoc.,* 1906. Gives titles of the printed sources, such as charters, laws, records and other official publications, arranged by state.

14a  **Kaganoff, Nathan M.** Judaica Americana. An annotated bibliography of monographic and periodical literature published since 1960. In *American Jewish historical quarterly* v.52– , 1962– .

Continuation of Marcus, no.17a. Judith E. Endelman became compiler in 1972.

*15  **Kaminkow, Marion J.** Genealogies in the Library of Congress: a bibliography of family histories of America and Great Britain. 2nd pr. Baltimore: Magna Carta, 1974.

20,000 entries, including some published in Europe and elsewhere. Covers every entry in the family-name index of the local history and genealogy room in the Library of Congress. Supersedes no.33. Over 25,000 cross references; essential, brings up to date the printed Library of Congress bibliographies of 1910 and 1919 and microcard editions of 1954.

15a  ———— United States local histories in the Library of Congress: a bibliography. 4v. Baltimore: Magna Carta, 1975.

Expensive, but needed in medium and large collections. All books in LC which were cataloged and classified in the local history portion of the Library's classification schedule as of mid-1972.

**16   Lathem, Edward C.** Chronological tables of American newspapers: 1690–1820. Worcester, Mass.: American Antiquarian Soc., 1972.

A tabular guide to holdings of newspapers published in America through 1820. Companion to Brigham (no.8). Vital to genealogists.

**17   Localized history series.** Ed. by Clifford L. Lord. New York: Teachers College Pr., Columbia Univ., various dates.

This series includes most states and many large cities. Good background history and in some cases good bibliographies of works on local history.

**17a   Marcus, Jacob R.** A selected bibliography of American Jewish history. (4th ed.) In *American Jewish historical quarterly* v.51, 1961.

For continuation, see no.14a.

**18   Matthews, William.** American diaries in manuscript 1580–1954; a descriptive bibliography. Athens, Ga.: Univ. of Georgia Pr., 1974.

More than 6,000 items from 350 libraries. Published and unpublished diaries, valuable to historians and genealogists.

**19   ———** (and others). American diaries . . . an annotated bibliography of American diaries written prior to 1861. *Univ. of California publ. in English* 16. 1945. Repr. Boston: Canner, 1959.

**20   Milliken, Elizabeth.** Genealogy and local history: a bibliography. 4th ed. Tallahassee, Fla.: State Library, 1972.

**21   (Munsell's, Joel, Sons)** The American genealogist, being a catalogue of family histories. A bibliography of American genealogy, or a list of the title pages of books and pamphlets on family history, published in America, from 1771 to date (1900). 5th ed. 1900. Repr. Detroit, Mich.: Gale Research, 1967; Baltimore: G.P.C., 1971.

Usually referred to as *Munsell's American genealogist*. Contains about 2,800 entries and thus is comparable to Glenn with its 2,000 references *(see no.10)*.

**22   ———** Index to American genealogies; and to genealogical material contained in all works such as town histories, county histories, etc. 5th ed. (Bound with) *Supplement,* 1900–1908, to the *Index* to genealogies. Baltimore: G.P.C., 1967.

**23   Newberry Library, Chicago.** The genealogical index. 4v. Boston: G. K. Hall, 1960.

Commonly known as the Wall index, these volumes contain more than 500,000 surnames, culled from books on genealogy in the Newberry Library. Although original cards are often difficult to read because of faintness of writing, the work is an essential one. (The Newberry Library conducts no research for correspondents; neither can it answer questions pertaining to the *Index.*) Since locale is provided, it is one of the most useful genealogical references. Additions discontinued about 1918.

**24   New York Public Library.** Dictionary catalog of the local history and genealogy division, the Research Libraries of the New York Public Library, 18v. Boston: G. K. Hall, 1974.

295,000 cards representing 113,000 vols. Much unpublished material. Thousands of analytics and entries for periodical articles. Definitive but expensive. Much on heraldry also included.

**25   ———** United States local history catalog. 2v. Boston: G. K. Hall, 1974.

Supplement to the *Dictionary catalog* (no.24), but can be used separately; 23,400 cards.

**26   Parker, John Carlyle.** Genealogy in the Central Association of Libraries: a union list based on Filby's *American and British Genealogy and Heraldry,* 1970. 2nd preliminary ed. Turlock, Calif.: Stanislaus State College Lib., 1974.

Its chief value is that the books chosen are considered to be those essential to the small/medium collection *(see* asterisks in this book).

## 27 United States

**27** Peterson, Clarence S. Bibliography of local histories in the Atlantic states. (v.1) (Baltimore) 1966.

**28** —— Bibliography of local histories of thirty-five states beyond the Atlantic states. v.2. Baltimore, 1967.

**\*29** —— Consolidated bibliography of county histories in fifty states in 1961. 1935–61. 2nd ed. Repr. Baltimore: G.P.C., 1973.

1973 reprint includes 1935 edition, with supplements for 1944, 1946-47, 1950, 1955, and 1960. Lists 4,000 county histories. Although there are omissions, it is the most comprehensive bibliography in this field. Many errors; work badly needs updating.

**29a** Rosenbach, Abraham S. W. An American Jewish bibliography . . . until 1850. New York, 1926.

Still the best Jewish bibliography.

**30** Rubincam, Milton. Genealogy: a selected bibliography. Prepared for the Institute of Genealogy, Samford University, Ala. Birmingham, Ala.: Banner Pr., 1967.

Of particular value for opinions given about each selection. Also has several references to definitive articles in books and journals. American local histories, genealogical compendiums, and works on royal and noble ancestry which are of uneven value and reliability have been omitted.

**\*31** Schreiner-Yantis, Netti. Genealogical books in print. Springfield, Va.: The Compiler, 1975.

Bibliography of over 2,000 titles from numerous publishers. Information includes author/compiler/editor; usually cost and publisher included as well. Arranged by subject and locality. Surname index to family genealogies included. Since it primarily lists local source records and family genealogies, it complements AMERICAN & BRITISH GENEALOGY & HERALDRY excellently.

**32** Spear, Dorothea N. Bibliography of American directories through 1860. Worcester, Mass.: American Antiquarian Soc., 1961.

1,647 directories described, with locations.

**\*33** U.S. Library of Congress. American and English genealogies in the Library of Congress . . . 2nd ed. 1919. Repr. Baltimore: G.P.C., 1967.

Superseded by Kaminkow (no.15), but useful for libraries with small budgets that cannot afford Kaminkow. Has 7,000 titles.

**33a** Wellauer, Maralyn A. A guide to foreign genealogical research: a selected bibliography of printed material with addresses. Milwaukee, Wisc.: The Compiler, 1974.

51 countries. Fairly comprehensive; will need frequent updating.

### RECORDS, GUIDES, INDEXES

**\*34** American Association of State and Local History. Directory, historical societies and agencies in the United States and Canada. 1956– . Nashville, Tenn.: The Association.

Published biennially. Gives names, addresses and pertinent information about organizations connected with history. Essential.

**35** American blue-book of funeral directors. New York: Kates-Boyleston Pub., 1972 [and various dates].

Lists over 25,000 funeral homes and parlors in the United States and Canada; often the only form of vital records in existence. Most records start after Civil War. Published sporadically.

**36** Bridger, Charles. An index to printed pedigrees contained in county and local histories, the heralds' visitations and in the more important genealogical collections. 1867. Repr. Baltimore: G.P.C., 1969.

British pedigrees. Still not superseded. Other works update to a certain extent, but Bridger still important.

**\*37** Brown, Mary J. Handy index to the holdings of the Genealogical Society of Utah. Logan, Utah: Everton Pub., 1971.

Lists records on microfilm or in printed form available in the library of the Genealogical Society, L.D.S.

**\*38** Child, Sargent B., and Holmes, D. P. Check list of Historical Records Survey publications. *W.P.A. technical ser. Research and records bibliography* 7, 1943. Repr. Baltimore: G.P.C., 1969.

Invaluable tool for record searching. Lists all publications of the H.R.S. projects, 1936–43, plus publications of the Survey of Federal Archives, and Inventory of American Imprints.

**39** ———— and **Hoyt, Max E.** Unpublished Historical Records Survey inventories. *National Genealogical Society. quarterly* v.33, no.2, 1945. Washington, D.C.

Although this article gives details of where unpublished H.R.S. material is stored, an article ("H.R.S. revisited," by L. Rapport) in the *American archivist* v.37, no.2, 1974, suggests that much of the material is no longer available.

*40 **Colket, Meredith B., Jr.,** and **Bridgers, F. E.** Guide to genealogical records in the National Archives. Washington, D.C.: U.S. Govt., 1964.

*NA publ.* 64–68. Lists and describes the genealogical information in the National Archives. Essential.

**41 Crick, Bernard R.,** and **Alman, M.** A guide to manuscripts relating to America in Great Britain and Ireland. Oxford: Univ. Pr. for British Assoc. for American Studies, 1961.

Much family information.

*42 **Crowther, George R., III.** Surname index to sixty-five volumes of colonial and Revolutionary pedigrees. *National Genealogical Soc. special publ.* 27. Washington, D.C.: The Society, 1964.

Some works included are Lawrence (*see* no.303); *Colonial and Revolutionary lineages of America* (no.290); Weis (no.105), 1950 ed.; and *Burke's Prominent families of the U.S.A.* (no.4485). Useful guide, providing leads to family information "buried" in a variety of reference books.

*43 **Cunningham, Ronald,** and **Evans, E.** A handy guide to the Genealogical Library and Church Historical Department (of the Church of Jesus Christ of Latter-day Saints). 2nd ed. Logan, Utah: Everton, 1973.

Because of its immense collections this book should be read before visiting the Library in Salt Lake City. Replaces *A handy guide to the Genealogical Library.*

**44 Cutter, William R.** A consolidated index to Cutter's genealogical sets. Fallbrook, Calif.: Ireland Indexing Service, 1973.

Over 3,150 surnames as found in 33v. of 9 ser. of genealogies by Cutter.

**45 D.A.R.** The catalogue of genealogical and historical works in the library. Washington, D.C.: The Society, 1940.

April, June and December numbers of the *D.A.R. magazine* (*see* no.500) give accessions since 1940. Extremely valuable as it lists many works which exist only in typescript and have never been published.

**45a Directory of United States cemeteries.** San Jose, Calif.: Cemetery Research Inc., 1974.

**46 Gambrill, Georgia.** Genealogical material and local histories in the Saint Louis Public Library. Rev. ed. St. Louis, Mo.: Public Lib., 1965.

**47** ———— 1st suppl. St. Louis: Public Lib., 1971.

**47a Genealogical Society of the Church of Jesus Christ of Latter-day Saints.** A brief guide to the Temple records: index bureau. *Research paper,* ser.F, no.2, rev. Salt Lake City: L.D.S., 1973.

**47b** ———— The Genealogical Society's name extraction programs. *Research paper,* ser.F, no.3. Salt Lake City: L.D.S., 1973.

**48 Greene, Evarts B.,** and **Morris, R. B.** A guide to the principal sources for early American history (1600–1800) in the city of New York. New York, 1929.

Pt.1, printed sources; pt.2, manuscript collections. Directory of the principal libraries and other depositories in New York city, 1800–1900, *see* Carman (no.2435).

**49 Hale, Richard W.** Guide to photocopied historical materials in the United States and Canada. Ithaca, N.Y., [1961].

*50 **Hamer, Philip M.** A guide to archives and manuscripts in the United States. New Haven, Conn.: Yale Univ. Pr., 1961. 3rd pr. 1965. Out-of-date but still useful; 1,300 depositories and 20,000 collections. New ed. in preparation.

*51 **Handy guide to record-searching in the larger cities of the United States.** Logan, Utah: Everton, 1974.
Cities selected by size and historical importance. Information on vital records, indexes to streets, by wards.

52 **Historical Records Survey, Works Projects Administration.** A series of publications appearing during the late 1930s and early 1940s, which concerned primarily the collection of historical records—county, church, vital statistics, and a number of miscellaneous records. In general the reports were the work of scholars, and most showed a high degree of accuracy. They are now over 30 years out-of-date, however, and in some cases may not be useful. Since some are the only records available for the researcher to indicate which records existed and where they are located, many are listed under the appropriate states.

*53 **Ireland, Norma (O.)** Local indexes in American libraries: a union list of unpublished indexes. Boston, 1947.
Compiled by Junior Members Round Table, American Library Assoc., and published by Faxon. Being updated by Kenneth C. Pengelly, Mankato State College, Minnesota.

54 ───── and **Hayes, B. P.** An index to indexes: a subject bibliography of published indexes. Rev. ed. Westwood, Mass.: Faxon, 1974.
Special or general indexes to sets of books, periodicals; bibliographical information given, author-title index, subject headings.

*55 **Jaussi, Laureen R.,** and **Chaston, G. D.** Register of the L.D.S. church records. Salt Lake City: Deseret, 1974.
11,500 Genealogical Society call numbers for microfilmed L.D.S. records.

56 **Jenkins, William S.** A guide to the microfilm collection of early state records. Ed. by Lillian A. Hamrick. Washington, D.C.: Library of Congress, 1950.
Begun in 1941, with 1951 suppl. Includes statutory laws, constitutional, administrative, executive, and court records; some local records, records of American Indians, etc.

*57 **Kirkham, E. Kay.** The land records of America and their genealogical value. Repr. with *Military records of America (see* no.476). Provo, Utah: Stevenson's Genealogical Center, 1972.

*58 ───── A survey of American church records for the period before the Civil War, east of the Mississippi river. 2v. Salt Lake City: Deseret, 1959–60; Logan, Utah: Everton, 1971.
v.1, 2nd ed., rev. and additional material, 1971. Invaluable compilation listing the location of largely inaccessible material.

59 **Lea, James H.,** and **Hutchinson, J. R.** Clues from English archives, contributory to American genealogy. In *New York genealogical and biographical record,* v.40–44, 1909–13.
English public records, 1600–75.

60 **Long Island Historical Society.** Catalogue of the American genealogies in the library. Prepared under the direction of Emma Toedteberg, librarian. 1935. Repr. Baltimore: G.P.C., 1969.
Contains titles of 8,200 printed books and pamphlets and 850 titles in manuscript. One of the richest collections in America.

*61 **McMullin, Phillip W.** Grassroots of America. A computerized index to the *American state papers: land grants and claims* (1789–1837), with other aids to research. Gov. doc. serial set, no.28–36. Salt Lake City: Gendex Corp., 1972.
156,000 entries. Major land grants for Alabama, Arkansas, Florida, Illinois, Louisiana, Michigan, Mississippi, Missouri, Ohio, and Wisconsin. Primarily from territories in the Louisiana Purchase.

*62 **Major genealogical record sources in the United States.** A guide to major sources and their availability. *Genealogical Soc. of the Church of Jesus Christ of Latter-*

*day Saints research paper,* ser.B, no.1, Salt Lake City: The Society, 1967.

63   (Munsell's, Joel, Sons) Index to American genealogies; and to genealogical material contained in all works . . . with (suppl.) 1900–1908 to the index of genealogies, alphabetically arranged. 5th ed. rev., improved, and enl., 1900, and suppl. 1900–1908. Repr. Baltimore: G.P.C., 1967; Detroit, Mich.: Gale Research, 1966.
Standard reference work for locating unknown family histories, i.e., those not cataloged in any library because they are mentioned in books and periodicals, and others missed prior to 1908. 1st–3rd editions, by Daniel S. Durrie, were titled *Bibliographia genealogica Americana;* 4th ed., *Index to American genealogies* . . . 1895; 1899 ed. was titled *List of titles of genealogical articles in American periodicals.* . . . Indexes over 15,000 family histories "buried" in a wide variety of works, with 60,000 references to source materials; mostly New England and mid-Atlantic states.

64   —— Munsell's genealogical index, *Abbe—Dymont.* v.1 (all pub.) South Norwalk, Conn., 1933.
2,900 entries, 1900–32.

*65   Newman, Debra. List of free black heads of families in the first census of the United States 1790. Washington, D.C.: National Archives, 1973.
*Special list* 34. Over 4,000 names.

66   Scotland. Record Office. Source list of manuscripts relating to the United States of America and Canada in private archives preserved in the Scottish Record Office. *List and Index Soc. special ser.* 3. London: The Society, 1970.

67   Scott, Kenneth. Genealogical abstracts from the *American weekly mercury,* 1719–46. Baltimore: G.P.C., 1974.
First newspaper published in Pennsylvania. 3,400 names of persons from Pennsylvania, New Jersey, Delaware, Maryland, South Carolina, and New England.

68   —— Genealogical data from the *New-York (gazette and weekly) mercury* 1752–96. In *New York genealogical and biographical record* v.96– , 1965– (in progress).

69   —— Genealogical data from the *New York weekly post boy,* 1743–73. *National Genealogical Soc. special publ.* 35. Washington, D.C.: The Society, 1970.
More than 5,000 individuals.

70   —— Genealogical data from the *Pennsylvania chronicle,* 1767–74. *National Genealogical Soc. special publ.* 37. Washington, D.C.: The Society, 1971.
3,600 persons primarily from Pennsylvania, but some from Delaware, New Jersey, and Maryland. Full information.

71   ——Rivington's *New York newspaper;* excerpts from a loyalist press, 1773–83. *Collections of the New-York Historical Soc.* 84. New York: The Society, 1973.
Genealogical gleanings from a prominent New York paper, covering the Revolutionary era. Name index has numerous references to American Jews.

72   Sinnott, Mary E. Index to the genealogical and historical queries and answers from the *New York mail and express.* 2v. in 1. Philadelphia, 1911.
An index to a scrapbook in 3v. containing the questions and answers, 1894–1905. Made by Mrs. A. A. Haxtun, and given to the Genealogical Soc. of Pennsylvania by M. E. Sinnott.

*73   Smith, Clifford N. Federal land series.
A calendar of archival materials on the land patents issued by the United States government, with subject tract and name indexes. v.1, 1788–1810. Chicago: American Library Assoc., 1972.
A calendar from records held by National Archives and others. Useful for land-title searcher; American expansion data, migration, Revolutionary War service, and other information. Indispensable basic research tool for the historian, genealogist, librarian, and archivist. Lands in Indiana, Illinois, Tennessee, Louisiana, and Ohio.

*74   —— Revolutionary War bounty-land warrants of the federal government. *Federal land ser.2.* Chicago: American Library Assoc., 1973.

Evidence of Revolutionary War military service antedating by two decades the pension files ordinarily used as proof of service. Indexes all names in summary registers of General Land Office to grants of land (1800-35) in U.S. Military District of Ohio; lists bounty-land warrants exchanged for scrip. Previously unpublished material.

**75  Union list of serials in libraries of the United States and Canada.** Ed. by Edna B. Titus. 3rd ed. 5v. New York: Wilson, 1965.

Mostly referred to as "Gregory" because the editor of the 1st and 2nd eds. was Winifred Gregory.

**76  U.S. Congress.** American state papers, class VIII, Public lands. 8v. Washington, D.C., 1832-61.

From an 18v. set, U.S. House of Representatives. Documents of the U.S. Congress in relation to public lands; with name indexes.

**77  U.S. Dept. of State.** The territorial papers of the United States. Compiled and ed. by Clarence E. Carter (and others). v.1-27. 1934-69. Repr. New York: A.M.S. Press, 1973.

Volumes concern northwest and south of the river Ohio, Missouri, Indiana, Mississippi, Orleans, Louisiana, Illinois, Alabama, Arkansas, Florida, and Wisconsin. Contains many lists of persons signing petitions, memorials, and much correspondence mentioning names, late 18th and early 19th century. Some interest to genealogists.

**78  U.S. Library of Congress.** A guide to the microfilm collections of early state records, prepared by the Library of Congress in association with the Univ. of South Carolina. Collected and compiled under the direction of William S. Jenkins. Washington, D.C.: Library of Congress, 1950- .

**79** ———— The national union catalog of manuscript collections. 1959- . Washington, D.C.: Library of Congress, 1962- .

Based on reports from American repositories of manuscripts. Indexes in alphabetical arrangement for names, places, subjects, and named historical periods.

**80** ———— New serials titles: a union list of serials commencing publication after Dec. 31, 1949. Washington, D.C.: Library of Congress, 1953- .

Cumulation for 1950-60, 1961-65, 1966-69 out of print; cumulation for 1960-70 being published by Bowker, N.Y. Supplement to *Union list of serials,* 3rd ed., no.75.

**81** ———— ———— Subject index to *New serials titles,* 1960-65. Ann Arbor, Mich.: Pierian Pr., 1968.

**82** ———— ———— Classed subject arrangement. 1955- . Washington, D.C.: Library of Congress.

**83** ———— Processing dept. British manuscripts project. A checklist of the microfilms prepared in England and Wales for the American Council of American Learned Societies, 1941-45. Ed. by Lester K. Born. 1955. Repr. New York: Greenwood Pr., 1968.

Makes known contents of 2,652 reels of microfilm containing reproductions of about 5 million pages of manuscripts and rare printed materials in major public and private collections in England and Wales.

**84** ———— Union catalog devision. Newspapers in microform. 1973- . Washington, D.C.: Library of Congress, 1973- .

Earlier editions called *Newspapers on microfilm.*

**85  U.S. National Archives and Record Service.** Preliminary inventories. Washington, D.C.: National Archives, 1942- .

The majority of volumes concern non-genealogical items, but those that do are invaluable; each is listed separately elsewhere in this work.

*****86  U.S. Public Health Service.** Where to write for birth and death records of U.S. citizens. Washington, D.C.: U.S. Govt.

*****87** ———— ———— Birth and death records, U.S. and outlying areas.

*****88** ———— ———— Divorce records: U.S. and outlying areas.

*89 ——— ——— Marriage records: U.S. and outlying areas.
All are available and are revised when necessary.

90   Watkins, Mildred de W. S. Ancestor hunting. Complete reprint of all columns from the *Shreveport journal* during the period 1963–68. With index by J. R. Rembert. Baton Rouge, La.: Claitor's, 1969.
Has 945 pages from weekly column, "Ancestor hunting." General and most useful information not confined to or concerned with Louisiana. Thousands of names.

91   World Conference of Records and Genealogical Seminar, Salt Lake City, Utah, U.S.A., 5–8 August 1969. A series of papers presented. Salt Lake City: L.D.S., 1969–70.
The greatest gathering of authorities on genealogy and heraldry, with some 300 lectures on all aspects of the fields. The papers were printed and published in series:
Area B: Computers and microfilm, technologies, storage, preservation, etc.
Area C: Great Britain: records in England, Ireland, Scotland, Wales, maritime records.
Area D: Central European records: German, Polish, Swiss, Austrian, Netherlands, Yugoslavia—genealogical research in.
Area E: Scandinavian countries: Sweden, Norway, Denmark, Finland, Iceland—genealogical research and records.
Area F: Romance language countries: France, Switzerland, Canada, Huguenots, Italy, Portugal, Spain, South America, Ivory Coast, Jewish records in Israel, Southwestern America, Spanish America —written history as applied to research.
Area H: History and records as they relate to research in East Asia: Japan, China, Korea, Polynesia, Oceania, Pacific, Australasia, South Africa, Egypt, India.
Area I: (a) U.S. records, genealogical research, handwriting, church records, Quakers, migrations; (b) Records in Canada, America, States, Indians, church in Canada.
Areas J,K,L,M: Basic heraldry, international heraldry, lineage societies; publications, book reviews, family organizations.

93   **Yoshpe, Harry P.**, and **Brower, P. P.** Preliminary inventory of the land entry papers of the Government Land Office. *Preliminary inventory* 22. Washington, D.C.: National Archives, 1970.

## PERIODICALS, SERIES

GENERAL

*94   **Annual index to genealogical periodicals and family histories.** By Inez Waldenmaier. Vols. for 1957–63. Washington, D.C.
Fills in gap between Jacobus (no.100) and Rogers (no.99).

95   **Boehm, Erich H.**, and **Adolphus, L.** Historical periodicals: an annotated world list of literary and related serial publications. Santa Barbara, Calif.: Clio Pr., 1961.
Basic list of historical publications, with brief annotations for 4,500 titles.

96   **Cappon, Lester J.** American genealogical periodicals: a bibliography with a chronological finding-list. 2nd pr., with additions including a geographical finding-list. New York: New York Public Lib., 1964.
Needs updating.

97   **Cumulative magazine subject index, 1907–49.** 2v. Boston: G. K. Hall, 1964.
Cumulation of 43 annual vols. of *Faxon's Annual magazine subject index*—a guide to material published in 356 American, Canadian, and English magazines. Provides detailed coverage of U.S. local and state history. 253,000 entries.

*98   **Genealogical periodical annual index.** v.1–8, 1962–69, ed. by George E. Russell, Mitchellville, Md.
v.1–4, ed. by Ellen S. Rogers (no.99); v.5–8, ed. by George E. Russell and he will complete v.9–12, 1970–73; Laird C. Towle (3602 Maureen Lane, Bowie, Md.) will take over from Russell with v.13 (1974). Usually four years in arrears. Continuation of series by Jacobus (no.100), and Inez Waldenmaier (no.94). Now the standard and authoritative topical and author index to genealogical lit-

## 99  United States

erature appearing in over 150 American, Canadian, and British journals. Often referred to as GPAI.

*99  **Genealogical periodical annual index, 1962–65.** Ed. by Ellen S. Rogers. v.1–4, 1962–65. Bladensburg, Md.: The Editor, 1963–67.
Continued by George E. Russell (no.98).

*100  **Jacobus, Donald L.** Index to genealogical periodicals. v.1, 1858–1931; v.2, 1932–46; v.3, 1947–52. 1932–53. Repr. Baltimore: G.P.C., 1973.
Originally repr. by G.P.C. in 1963–65 in 3v.; 1973 repr. 3v. in 1. Cumulative index to articles and references in genealogical material contained in more than 50 genealogical and historical journals. Contains a name index which also gives locale; another index of places and subjects including births, marriages, deaths, military rolls, emigrant lists, church records, etc. v.3 is index of books chiefly relating to families of New England and New York. For later series, see Waldenmaier (no.94), Rogers (no.99), and Russell (no.98). The years 1953–57 have yet to be indexed. Invaluable set. Essential.

100a  **St. Louis Genealogical Society.** Topical index of 1973 genealogical quarterlies, by Geraldine Bailey and I. Rolland. St. Louis: The Society, 1973.
Good coverage. Index to the 125 periodicals exchanged with the Society. Index for 1974 in progress.

101  **Writings on American history, 1903– .** Washington, D.C.: American Historical Assoc., 1905– .
A bibliography of books and articles on United States and Canadian history (from 1948, U.S. only). Good on local history and family history and genealogy until 1940. 1908–1949, ed. by Grace G. Giffen; now compiled by National Historical Publications Commission. Long behind schedule; 1960 appeared in 1972. Always v.2 of *Annual report of the American Historical Association*.

102  ——— Index, 1902–40. Washington, D.C.: The Association, 1956.

SEPARATE

103  **American genealogist.** v.1– , 1922– . Des Moines, Iowa: G. E. McCracken.
Formerly published in New Haven, Conn. v.1–8 appeared as *New Haven genealogical magazine;* v. 9–13, as *American genealogist and New Haven genealogical magazine.* v.1–8 relate almost entirely to families of the original township of New Haven. One of the great genealogical magazines. v.1–8 also known as *Families of ancient New Haven (see also* no.1000). These 8 vols. and cross index by Helen L. Scranton (1939) were reprinted by G.P.C., Baltimore, 1974, 9v. in 3v.

104  **Americana.** v.1–37, 1906–43. New York.
Title varies. Sumptuous magazine; coats of arms in color, family histories, grants, patents, etc. Published by American Historical Co.

105  **The Augustan.** v.16– , 1973– . Harbor City, Calif.: Augustan Soc.
*Bull. of the Augustan Soc.,* v.1–3, 1959–60; *The Royalist magazine* [v.4], 1961 (three issues); *Information bull.,* v.5–6, 1962–63 (22 issues); *Augustan Soc. information bull.,* v.7–10, 1964–67 (48 issues); *The Augustan,* v.11–14, 1968–71 (24 issues); *Forebears,* v.15, 1972 (4 issues); *The Augustan* (omnibus v.), 1973– . Note that the omnibus v. contains *Forebears,* v.16– ; *The colonial genealogist,* v.16– ; *Coat armour,* v.6– ; *Spanish American genealogical helper,* v.3– .
Outstanding journal; monarchy, orders, chivalry, genealogy, history, medals, general heraldry. With *Augustan book* v.2, *Coat-armour* ceased and *Spanish American genealogical helper* was published separately.

106  **Car-del scribe.** v.1– , 1968– . Middleboro, Mass.: Chedwato Service.
The magazine for collectors, genealogists and historians. Called *Ancestral notes* 1954–68; absorbed *Missing links* in 1968. Now covers mainly current books in review.

107  **Detroit Society for Genealogical Research magazine.** v.1– , 1937– . Detroit, Mich.: The Society.

Not confined to Detroit or Michigan; includes several fine works on eastern states. v.1, no.1–10, was published as the Society's *Bulletin*. Index to v.1–26 in 5v. also available.

**108 Family fare.** no.1– , 1961– . Fort Wayne, Ind.: Fort Wayne & Allen County Lib.

Quarterly list of additions to the Historical Library. This library has one of the largest genealogical collections in America, and thus this periodical serves as an excellent bibliography.

**109 Fellowship of Brethren Genealogists newsletter.** v.1– , 1968– . Elgin, Ill.: The Editor.

Good family genealogical journal. Has general coverage.

**110 Forebears.** Quarterly journal of the Augustan Society. v.15– , 1972– . Harbor City, Calif.: Augustan Soc.

Formerly *The Augustan, see* no.105 for data. Dating from v.16, 1973, it is included in the omnibus vol. of *The Augustan*. International journal of things historical, heraldic, and genealogical.

**\*111 The genealogical helper.** v.1– , 1947– . Logan, Utah: Everton.

Good periodical for amateur needing guidance. Contains directory of family associations; directory of genealogical libraries, societies, and professionals; an annual exchange; and a copious surname index. Many book notices. Essential.

**112 Genealogical journal.** v.1– , 1972– . Salt Lake City: Utah Genealogical Assoc.

Professional articles about methods and sources. Some book reviews. Emphasis on L.D.S. (Mormon) sources. One of the best professional journals available. Excellent for overseas guidance.

**113 Genealogical newsletter and research aids.** v.1–9, no.2, 1955–63. By Inez Waldenmaier. Washington, D.C.

**114 Genealogical reference builders.** Newsletter. Ed. by Robertalee Lent. v.1– , 1967– . Post Falls, Idaho.

**115 The genealogist's post.** v.1–8, no.2, 1964–71. Danboro, Pa.

Genealogical records and history of U.S. ancestors. Ceased in 1971 and was incorporated in *The Pennsylvania traveler post* (no.2987).

**116 Genealogy: a journal of American (and British) ancestry,** v.1–15, 1912–29. Ed. by Lyman H. Weeks; later by William M. Clemens. New York [and elsewhere].

Ceased publication in 1929.

**117 Genealogy.** A publication of the Genealogy section, Indiana Historical Soc. By Willard Heiss, no.1– , 1973– . Indianapolis, Ind.: The Soc.

A general periodical not restricted to Indiana. Information on what is going on, publications and reviews of general interest.

**118 Genealogy and History.** v.1–25, no.4 (no.1–158), 1940–64. Ed. by Adrian E. Mount. Washington, D.C. Available from Joseph Ferrier, Box 1717, Washington, D.C. 20013.

Question-and-answer publication.

**119 Genealogy digest.** Genealogy Club of America magazine. v.1– , 1970– . Salt Lake City: The Club.

Slightly L.D.S. oriented. Useful for beginners; many queries, reviews. Good coverage including overseas.

**120 The hereditary register of the United States of America.** 1972– . Washington, D.C.: U.S. Hereditary Register Inc.

Good reference annual; many societies included. Biographical information on several thousand members, current officers, history, etc. A few important societies are omitted. 1000 family associations listed.

**121 Journal of American history.** 29v., 1907–35; index v.1–6, 1907–13. New York, 1907–35.

Has much genealogy and heraldry, including coats of arms.

**\*122 Linkage for ancestral research.** Query index and other data. v.1– , 1967– . Ed. by Mary T. Reeder. Albuquerque, N. Mex.

Lists queries which appear in over 100 genealogical journals.

*123  **The magazine of bibliographies.** v.1– , 1972– . Ed. by Lalla C. Criz. Fort Worth, Tex.

Heavily aimed toward genealogical bibliographies. Parts so far have listed Shenandoah, Kansas, Five Civilized Tribes, American Revolution.

*124  **National Genealogical Society quarterly.** v.1– , 1912– . Washington, D.C.: The Society.

One of the best journals in the field. Excellent general articles and outstanding book reviews.

*125  —— Topical index, v.1–50, 1912–62. By Carleton E. Fisher. *National Genealogical Soc. special publ.* 29. Washington, D.C.: The Society, 1964.

More than a topical index; almost a name index for the first 50v.

126  **Prologue: journal of the National Archives.** v.1– , 1969– . Washington, D.C.: The Archives.

Gives some information about genealogical resources at the Archives in each number.

*127  **Query name index.** A full-name index of queries published in the query sections of numerous genealogical periodicals. v.1–3, no.1, 1973–75. Kenmore, Wash.: Homestead Pr.

Covers 94 periodicals and contains both surnames and given names mentioned, with state of residence. Very useful. No longer published.

128  **Tri-state trader.** v.1– , 1968– . Knightstown, Ind.: R. T. Mayhill.

Strictly a hobby magazine; has many useful articles and details for genealogists.

128a  **Tri-state trader genealogy queries and index.** Knightstown, Ind.: R. T. Mayhill, 1974.

All queries in *Tri-state trader* 1968–73, and complete indexes to surname and county.

129  **World records.** v.4– , 1971– . Salt Lake City: R. T. Obert.

Started as *The genealogical accredited researcher's record round up,* v.1, 1969– . Fine journal, listing records for many sources.

BIOGRAPHIES

130  **Allen, William.** The American biographical dictionary: containing an account of the lives, characters and writing of the most eminent persons deceased in America from its first settlement. 3rd ed. Boston, 1857.

Originally published in 1809 as *An American biographical and historical dictionary.* Many names listed which were dropped from more modern dictionaries.

131  **American biography: a new cyclopedia.** v.1–54, no.1–41. New York, 1916–70.

132  —— Index. v.1–50. New York, 1932.

Became *Encyclopedia of American biography* with n.s. 1934. Has cumulative index at end of each vol. Colored coats of arms. Mug book but very useful.

133  **American families of historic lineage:** being a genealogical, historical and biographical account of representative families of eminent American and foreign ancestry, recognized social standing and distinguished achievements; historic families. By National Americana Society, New York. New York, 19—.

Color portraits. Mug book.

134  **American women, 1,500 biographies with 1,400 portraits.** Newly rev. 2v. New York, 1897.

135  **Appleton's cyclopedia of American biography.** Ed. by J. G. Wilson and J. Fiske. 7v. New York, 1887–1900.

Lists of deaths in v.1–6; includes names of native and adopted citizens of the United States, from the earliest settlement; eminent citizens of Canada, Mexico, and other countries of North and South America. Also names of men of foreign birth closely identified with American history. An edition entitled *Cyclopedia of American biography,* 6v., 1915, called a new enl. ed. of Appleton, adds little to the original.

## Biographies

136   **Bolton, Charles K.** Marriage notices, 1785–94, for the whole United States. Copied from the *Massachusetts centinel* and the *Columbian centinel*. 1900. Repr. Baltimore: G.P.C., 1965.
   3,000 men and women, with fairly complete data.

137   **Burke, Arthur M.** The prominent families of the United States of America. v.1 (all pub.). London, 1908.

138   **Chamberlain, Joshua L.** Universities and their sons . . . with biographical sketches and portraits of alumni and recipients of honorary degrees. 5v. Boston, 1898–1900.
   Biographies of Harvard, Yale, Princeton, and Columbia university graduates.

139   **Columbia University Libraries. Avery Architectural Library.** Avery obituary index of architects and artists. Boston: G. K. Hall, 1963.
   Drawn from information in American and foreign newspapers. Death and birth dates given. 13,500 entries.

140   **Concise dictionary of American biography.** New York: Scribner, 1964.
   Essential facts of every article in *Dictionary of American biography* (*see* no.144), with some revisions. Incorporates contents of two supplements.

140a  **Cutter, William R.** American families, genealogical and heraldic. 3v. New York, 19—.
   American Historical Society. Colored coats of arms.

141   **Dexter, Franklin B.** Biographical notices . . . including those graduated in classes later than 1815 . . . New Haven, Conn., 1913.
   Covers 1815–84.

142   ———— Biographical sketches of the graduates of Yale College. 6v. New York, 1885–1912.
   v.1–6 cover 1701–1815.

143   ———— Obituary record of graduates . . . 1859–1951. New Haven, 1860–1951.
   No more pub. through 1974.

*144  **Dictionary of American biography.** 20v. New York: Scribner, 1928–37; repr. 1943. Index v.1–20. New York: Scribner, 1937. Supplements 1–3, to 1945. New York: Scribner, 1944–73.
   Articles of distinction but narrower in scope than Appleton (*see* no.135) and *National cyclopaedia* (no.153).

145   **Dictionary of national biography.** London, various dates. *See* no.4281–85.

146   **Drake, Francis S.** Dictionary of American biography, including men of the time; containing nearly 10,000 notices of persons . . . 2v. 1872. Repr. Ann Arbor, Mich.: Gryphon Books, 1971.

147   **DuBin, Alexander.** Five hundred first families of America. New York: Historical Pub. Soc., 1967.

148   **Encyclopedia of American biography.** *See* no.131–32.

149   **Groce, George C.** Dictionary of artists in America, 1564–1860. New Haven, Conn.: New-York Historical Soc., 1957.
   About 10,000 painters, sculptors, engravers, etc. who worked in the United States during the 300 years before the Civil War.

150   **Hough, Franklin B.** American biographical notes, being short notices of deceased persons, chiefly those not included in Allen's or in Drake's biographical dictionaries, gathered from many sources. 1875. Repr. Harrison, N.Y.: Harbor Hill Books, 1974.
   Alphabetical, national scope; some items from unusual sources, many are death notices from upstate New York newspapers. 7,000 Americans from late 18th and early 19th centuries.

151   **Ireland, Norma (O.).** Index to women. Westwood, Mass.: Faxon Co., 1970.
   Representative women of all countries from ancient to modern times; their biographies, portraits, and chief contributions. 930 collections covering about 10,000 women.

## United States

**152** **Lanman, Charles.** Biographical annals of the civil government of the United States, during its first century. 2nd ed. New York, 1887.

Alphabetically arranged biographical sketches of about 7,000 individuals. Much historical data.

**153** **The national cyclopaedia of American biography.** v.1– . New York: James T. White Co., 1893– (in progress).

The most comprehensive American work, less limited and more selective than *Dictionary of American biography* (see no.144), and more up-to-date than Appleton's (no.135). Indexes are published from time to time, and since entries are not alphabetical, the indexes are essential. v.1–51, 5th ed. of revised index by H. A. Harvey and R. D. McGill, 1969.

**154** **The New York Times obituary index, 1858–1968.** New York: New York Times, 1970.

Useful key but by no means complete, since notices of pages other than the obituary columns are not listed.

*__155__ **Notable American women, 1607–1950:** a biographical dictionary. Ed. by Edward T. James; prepared under the auspices of Radcliffe College. 3v. Cambridge, Mass.: Belknap Pr., 1971.

1,359 women; biographies excellent and succinct.

**156** **O'Neill, Edward H.** Biography by Americans, 1658–1936. A subject bibliography. Philadelphia, 1939.

*__157__ **Phillips, Lawrence B.** Dictionary of biographical reference; containing over 100,000 names. . . . New ed., rev. and augmented with suppl. to date by Frank Weitenkampf. 3rd ed. London, 1889. Repr. Graz: Akademische Drück u. Verlagsanstalt, 1966.

International in scope. Indexes 40 biographical collections and other works.

*__158__ **Prominent families in America with British ancestry.** New York: British Book Centre, 1971.

Reprint of "American families with British ancestry" which appeared in the 16th ed. of *Burke's Genealogical and heraldic history of the landed gentry of Great Britain and Ireland,* 1939 (see no.4482). Unlike 1939 original; no arms in color.

**159** **Sibley's Harvard graduates:** biographical sketches of those who attended Harvard College. v.1– , 1642– . Boston: Massachusetts Historical Soc., 1873– .

Title varies. From v.4 the set was edited by Clifford K. Shipton. v.1–3, repr. by Johnson Repr., New York; remainder in print.

**160** **Slocum, Robert B.** Biographical dictionaries and related works: an international bibliography of collective biographies. Detroit, Mich.: Gale Research, 1967.

**161** ―――― Supplement. Detroit, Mich.: Gale Research, 1972.

Covers 5,000 who's whos, genealogical works, biographical indexes, etc. Over 100 countries covered. Supplement has 3,500 additional items.

**162** **Sobel, Robert.** Biographical directory of the United States Executive Branch, 1774–1971. Westport, Conn.: Greenwood, 1971.

**163** **The twentieth century biographical dictionary of notable Americans.** 10v. 1904. Repr. Detroit, Mich.: Gale Research, 1968.

30,000 names, often between 1800–50. Complete data on families.

**164** **U.S. Congress.** Biographical directory of the American Congress, 1774–1974, the Continental Congress . . . and the Congress of the United States. Washington: U.S. Govt., 1974.

Almost 2,000 pages; very useful.

**165** **Vincent, Benjamin.** A dictionary of biography, past and present, containing the chief events in the lives of eminent persons of all ages and nations. Preceded by the biographies and genealogies of the chief representatives of the royal houses of the world. 1877. Repr. with addenda. Detroit, Mich.: Gale Research, 1974.

20,000 names, 36 genealogical tables. Rev. and enl. ed. of Haydn's *Universal index of biography.*

**166 White's conspectus of American biography:** a tabulated record of American history and biography. 2nd ed., rev. and enl. 1937. St. Clair Shores, Mich.: Scholarly Pr., 1972.

Rev. ed. of the Conspectus portion of the Conspectus and index v.1. (1906) *National cyclopaedia of American biography* (see no.153). Many lists of office holders, pseudonyms, etc.

**167 Who was who in America:** historical volume, 1607–1896. A component volume of *Who's who in American history.* Chicago: Marquis, 1963.

Sketches of individuals, from America and elsewhere, who have made contributions to, or whose activity was in some manner related to, the history of the United States.

**168 Willard, Frances E.,** and **Livermore, Mary A.** A woman of the century; 1,470 biographical sketches accompanied by portraits of leading American women in all walks of life. 1893. Detroit, Mich.: Gale Research, 1967.

Particularly useful for 19th-century biographies, many of which do not appear elsewhere.

**169 Woman's who's who of America:** a biographical dictionary of contemporary women of the United States and Canada, 1914–15. 1914. Repr. Detroit, Mich.: Gale Research, 1972.

Almost 10,000 entries. Much genealogical information.

CENSUSES

*170 **Brewer, Mary M.** Index to census schedules in printed form: those available and where to obtain them. Huntsville, Ark.: Century Enterprises, 1969.

*171 ——— Suppl. 1970/71. Huntsville, Ark.: Century Enterprises, 1972.

Guide to about 900v. now published or scheduled for publication. A list by state and county of early published censuses, with indication of availability and price. Stemmons (*see* no.177) easier to use, but Brewer gives full title of work.

**172 Franklin, William N.** Federal population and mortality census schedules, 1790–1880, in the National Archives and the States . . . outline of a lecture on their availability, content, and use. Washington, D.C.: U.S. Govt., 1971.

Originally in *National Genealogical Soc. quarterly,* v.50. Reissued as *U.S.N.A. special list* 24.

**173 Gendex census compendium.** Provo, Utah: Gendex Corp., 1972.

Directory of location of about 7,000 census records or records that could be used in their place.

**174 General censuses and vital statistics in the Americas.** An annotated bibliography of the historical censuses and current vital statistics of the 21 American republics. 1943. Repr. Detroit, Mich.: Blaine-Ethridge, 1973.

Includes a historical sketch of the census of each country, and background information on the various census compilations.

**175 Kirkham, E. Kay.** A survey of American census schedules. 1959. Repr. Provo, Utah: Stevenson Genealogical Center, 1972.

Includes enumerations from 1790 to 1950, and a summary of the more common names in the 1790 census.

**176 Newman, Debra L.** List of free black heads of families in the first census of the United States 1790. Washington, D.C.: National Archives, 1973.

Over 4,000 names. *Special N.A. list* 34.

*177 **Stemmons, John "D".** The United States census compendium: a directory of census records, tax lists, poll lists, petitions, directories, etc., which can be used as a census. Logan, Utah: Everton, 1973.

Lists extant census lists or those lists which serve as censuses. Complements Dubester (no.180) and Brewer (no.170), but is somewhat incomplete.

*178 **U.S. Bureau of the Census.** A century of population growth, from the first census of the United States to the twelfth, 1790–1900. U. S. Bureau of the Census, 1909. Repr. Baltimore: G.P.C., 1970; New York: Johnson Repr. Co., 1967.

Contains a detailed analysis of the changes in the population from the early censuses down to the turn of the century. Maps of the first 13 states show changes in county lines; a lengthy table of surnames found in the census schedules of 1790 shows spellings used and in which state the family was most numerous. Especially useful in the variants in spelling of names and in locating families geographically.

*179 ——— Heads of families at the first census, 1790. 12v. 1907-1909. Baltimore: G.P.C., 1952- (reprints when necessary); Spartanburg, S.C.: Reprint Co., 1963, etc.

One of the great genealogical reference series. More than 400,000 families are listed. Volumes are for: Connecticut, Maine, Maryland, Massachusetts, New Hampshire, New York, North Carolina, Pennsylvania, Rhode Island, South Carolina, Vermont, and Virginia (*see also* listings under the various states). *A century of population growth* (see no.178) contains a detailed analysis of the changes in the population and is an important adjunct to the whole series.

**180 U.S. Library of Congress.** Census Library Project. Catalog of United States census publications, 1790-1945. A joint work of the Census Library Project of the Library of Congress and the Bureau of Census. By Henry J. Dubester. 1950. Repr. Westport, Conn.: Greenwood Pr. [1968]; New York: Burt Franklin, 1971; New Haven, Conn.: Research Pub., 1973.

Annotated list of all of the publications of the Bureau of the Census to 1950.

**181** ——— National censuses and vital statistics in Europe, 1918-39; and annotated bibliography, with 1940-48, suppl. 1948. Repr. Detroit, Mich.: Gale Research, 1967; New York: Burt Franklin, 1969.

*182 ——— State censuses; an annotated bibliography of censuses of population taken after the year 1790 by states and territories of the United States. By Henry J. Dubester. 1948. Repr. New York: Burt Franklin, 1967.

Repr. includes supplement published in 1948.

*183 **U.S. National Archives and Records Service.** Federal population censuses, 1790-1890; a catalog of microfilm copies of the schedules. Washington, D.C.: Supt. of Documents, 1971.

Lists censuses by decades for each state and county where a film is available for sale. Price per roll quoted.

**184** ——— Records of the Bureau of the Census, compiled by Katherine H. Davidson and C. M. Ashby. *National Archives preliminary inventory* 161. *Record group* 29. Washington, D.C.: The Archives, 1964.

**185 U.S. decennial census publications, 1790-1960:** a bibliographic guide to the microform collection. New Haven, Conn.: Research Pub., 1973.

The publisher has all U.S. census publications on microform.

ATLASES, MAPS, GAZETTEERS

**186 Adams, James T.** Atlas of American history. New York, 1943.

Concerns exploration, settlements, migrations, land acquisitions, military campaigns, Indians, and many related subjects.

**187 American Geographical Society.** Index to maps in books and periodicals, Map dept. of American Geographical Society, New York. 10v. Boston: G. K. Hall, 1971.

**188** ——— First suppl. Boston: G. K. Hall, 1971.

Map title given, as well as full bibliographic citation of article or book containing the map. About 200,000 entries.

*189 **Bullinger's postal and shippers guide for the United States and Canada.** Westwood, N.J.: Bullinger's Guides, 1897- .

Title varies. One in every decade needed. Bullinger's provides the same information as the post office directory, except that all towns are listed alphabetically rather than by state, and it is not limited to towns with a post office. Good for finding small places.

*189a **The Columbia Lippincott gazetteer of the world.** . . . New York: Columbia Univ. Pr., 1962.

*190 **Everton, George B., Jr.** Genealogical atlas of the United States of

America. 4th pr. Logan, Utah: Everton, 1970.

Good research aid. Contains county map for each state, index to each county, and date of formation; also U.S. and land relief maps.

191    **Friis, Herman R.** A series of population maps of the colonies of the United States, 1625-1790. Rev. ed. New York: American Geographical Soc., 1968.

Modified and brought up-to-date insofar as footnotes are concerned.

192    **Gannett, Henry.** Boundaries of the United States. *See* no.206.

193    **Hayward, John.** A gazetteer of the United States. Hartford, Conn., 1853.
861 pages.

*194    **Heilprin, Angelo,** and **Heilprin, Louis.** A complete pronouncing gazetteer or geographical dictionary of the world . . . containing the most recent and authentic information respecting the countries, cities, towns . . . Philadelphia, 1931.

Binder's title: *Lippincott's gazetteer of the world.*

195    **Lavoisne, C. V.** Lavoisne's complete genealogical, historical, chronological, and geographical atlas . . . exhibiting the origin, descent, and marriages of all the royal families from the earliest records to the year 1829 . . . 4th ed. rev. London, 1830.

Comprehensive and accurate.

196    **Lord, Clifford L.,** and **Lord, E. H.** Historical atlas of the United States. 1953. Rev. ed. 1969. Repr. New York: Johnson Reprint Corp., 1974.

312 maps based on 19th-century censuses; boundary lines, Civil War maps; appendixes useful.

*197    **Shepherd, William R.** Historical atlas. New York: Barnes & Noble, 1964. One of the best atlases available. Easy to use.

198    **Shull, Tressie N.** County atlases for genealogical use. In *National Genealogical Society quarterly.* v.37, 1949.

*199    **U.S. Library of Congress. Map Division.** Land ownership maps: a checklist of 19th century United States county maps in the Library of Congress. By Richard W. Stephenson. Washington, D.C.: Library of Congress, 1967.

1,449 maps relating to 1,041 counties. Mainly northeast and north central states, Virginia, California, and Texas. Essential.

200    ——— A list of geographical atlases in the Library of Congress, with bibliographical notes. 8v., 1909-74. Washington, D.C.: Library of Congress.

v.8 is index. Originally compiled by P. L. Phillips; continued by Clara E. LeGear. Invaluable reference tool for geographers, historians, cartographers, and genealogists. v.1-4 repr. by: Swets & Zeitlinger, Amsterdam, 1971; Theatrum Orbis Terrarum, Amsterdam, 1971; A.M.S. Press, New York, 1972; Western Hemisphere, Boston, 1972. v.5-7 obtainable from Library of Congress.

201    ——— A list of maps of America in the Library of Congress; preceded by a list of works relating to cartography by Philip L. Phillips. 2v in 1. 1901. Repr. New York: Burt Franklin, 1967; Amsterdam: Theatrum Orbis Terrarum. 1967.

202    ——— United States atlases; a list of national, state, county, city, and regional atlases in the Library of Congress, compiled by Clara Le Gear. 2v. Washington, D.C., 1950-53.

v.1 only repr. by Arno Pr., New York, 1971. v.2, out-of-print.

203    **U.S. National Archives and Records Service.** Cartographic records of the Bureau of the Census. By James B. Rhoads and C. M. Ashby. *N.A. preliminary inventory* 103. *Record group* 29. Washington, D.C.: The Archives, 1958.

204    ——— Guide to cartographic records in the National Archives. By Charlotte M. Ashby (and others). Washington, D.C.: Govt. Print. Off., 1971.

Map holdings of the Archives, good for genealogist and local historian.

205    ——— Pre-federal maps in the National Archives: an annotated list. Compiled by Patrick D. McLaughlin.

*N.A. special list* 26. Washington, D.C.: Govt. Print. Off., 1971.

*206   **van Zandt, Franklin K.** Boundaries of the United States and the several states. 1966. Repr. St. Clair Shores, Mich.: Scholarly Pr., 1972.

Revision and updating of Gannett's *Boundaries,* 1904, and Douglas's work in 1930. Explains the various colonial, territorial, and state boundaries.

207   **Wheat, James C.,** and **Brun, Christian F.** Maps and charts published in America before 1800; a bibliography. New Haven, Conn.: Yale Univ. Pr., 1969.

Valuable tool for the historian, researcher, and cartographer.

PLACE NAMES

*208   **Gannett, Henry.** The origin of certain place names in the United States. Dept. of the Interior. *U.S. Geological Survey bull.* 258. 2d ed. 1905 (actually 1906). Repr. Baltimore: G.P.C., 1973.

Repr. in 1947 by Public Affairs Pr., with title, *American names;* repr. by Gale Research in 1972 is of 1st ed., bull.197 (1903) with 2,000 less entries. Contents of 2nd ed. include 10,000 place names, locations in the county or state, and the derivations and meanings of the name. Essential for genealogists.

209   **Holt, Alfred H.** American place names. 1938. Repr. Detroit, Mich.: Gale Research, 1969.

1,700 entries; towns, rivers, lakes, mountains.

*210   **Kane, Joseph N.** The American counties: a record of the origin of the names of the 3,067 counties, dates of establishment and origin, areas, population, historical data, etc. 3rd ed. New York: Scarecrow, 1972.

Not as good as Kirkham *(see* no.211–12), but useful.

*211   **Kirkham, E. Kay.** The counties of the United States and their genealogical value. Salt Lake City, 1965.

*212   ——— The counties of the United States, their derivation and census schedules; a verified and corrected listing that shows parent county, county seat, and census information for each county . . . Salt Lake City, 1961.

*213   **Sealock, Richard B.,** and **Seely, P. A.** Bibliography of place-name literature: United States and Canada. 2nd ed. Chicago: American Library Assoc., 1967.

214   **Stewart, George R.** American place-names. A concise and selective dictionary for the continental United States of America. New York: Oxford Univ. Pr., 1970.

A learned discussion of the origin of names, but very readable. 12,000 entries.

214a   **Street directory of the principal cities of the United States,** embracing letter-carrier offices established to April 30, 1908. 5th ed. 1908. Repr. Detroit, Mich.: Gale Research, 1973.

Streets from 1,280 cities. Useful for unusual street names, but almost useless for commonly named streets.

215   **U.S. Geographic Board.** Sixth report, 1890–1932. 1933. Repr. Detroit, Mich.: Gale Research, 1967.

Gives correct spelling of 32,000 place names. Gives location, indicates rejected forms of its name, provides origin and marks the pronunciation; 14,000 on mainland, 15,000 in Alaska, Hawaii, Puerto Rico, the Philippines, and outlying possessions. Supersedes all previous reports.

216   **U.S. Post Office Dept.** Table of the post offices in the U.S., arranged by states and counties; as they were October 1, 1830. Washington, D.C., 1831.

SURNAMES

217   **American Council of Learned Societies.** Committee on Linguistics and National Stocks in the Population of the U.S. Surnames in the United States census of 1790. 1932. Repr. Baltimore: G.P.C., 1971.

Originally published in *Annual report of the American Historical Assoc.* 1931, v.1. Analysis of national origins of the population; also estimated populations in 1790. 55,000 persons listed.

218   Bardsley, Charles W. E. A dictionary of English and Welsh surnames, with special American instances. Rev. 1901. Repr. Baltimore: G.P.C., 1968.

219   Polk, R. L. and Co. Cross reference to family names. n.p., 1945.
Compiled for the use of business firms, but useful to genealogists.

220   Rule, La Reina, and Hammond, William K. What's in a name? Surnames of America. New York: Pyramid Books, 1973.
Paperback containing over 7,000 surnames, and hundreds of emblems and shields; origins and meanings.

221   Smith, Elsdon C. American surnames. Radnor, Pa.: Chilton, 1969.
Running account of origin of most common American family names, with special attention to social conditions and customs surrounding the adoption of surnames in England and Europe.

*222   —— New dictionary of American family names. New York: Harper & Row, 1972.
Originally published under title *Dictionary of American family names*. Origin and meaning of more than 10,000 names. Dictionary arrangement of all the common names of America, with definition and country or origin.

223   —— Personal names: a bibliography. 1952. Repr. Detroit, Mich.: Gale Research, 1965.
Originally published in *New York Public Library bull.,* 1950/51. Classified bibliography of 3,415 monographs and periodical articles on names, with brief, critical annotations. Library locations given.

224   —— The story of our names. 1950. Repr. Detroit, Mich.: Gale Research, 1970.
The best book on names by an American writer. Contains Christian and surnames.

*225   U.S. Immigration and Naturalization Service. Foreign versions, variations, and diminutives of English names. Foreign equivalents of U.S. military and civilian titles. Rev. Washington: U.S. Govt., 1973.

226   Vallentine, John F. Locality finding aids for U.S. surnames. In *Genealogical journal,* Utah Genealogical Assoc. v. 1–2, 1972–73.
Excellent bibliography of books, microfilms, manuscripts, and private indexes. Full data given. U.S. general, southern, mid-Atlantic, midwestern, and western states. To be published in book form by Everton, Provo, Utah, in 1975.

227   Weidenhan, Joseph L. Baptismal names. 4th ed., enl. 1931. Repr. Detroit, Mich.: Gale Research, 1968.

## MANUALS AND AIDS

✢ The manuals and aids listed here are good, and since each has special facets it would be invidious to single out any one book as the best. However, a team of experts has selected certain manuals for their excellence; these are marked with an asterisk (*).

*228   Babbel, June A. Lest we forget: a guide to genealogical research in the nation's capital. 3rd ed., rev. Annandale, Va.: The Author, 1974.
Guide to research facilities in Washington's institutions, with some discussion of research aids; also government services and publications available. Little mention of material useful for District of Columbia genealogical research.

229   Bennett, Archibald F. Advanced genealogical research. Salt Lake City: Bookcraft, 1959.
Migrations, burned records, use of land records, and changes in family surnames.

230   —— Finding your forefathers in America. Salt Lake City: Bookcraft, 1957.
Particularly good for research in southern New England and middle Atlantic states; also on how to trace families from the east to the west.

231   —— A guide to genealogical research. Salt Lake City, 1951.
Especially important are the appendixes discussing terms used in genealogical research and heraldry; foreign genealogical terms and interpretation of dates.

232  *United States*

232 ―――― Searching with success: a general text. Salt Lake City: Deseret, 1962.

*233 **Cache Branch Genealogical Library, Logan.** Handbook for genealogical correspondence. Rev. ed. Logan, Utah: Everton, 1974.
Much helpful information for the professional and novice.

234 **Criswell, Howard D.** Find your ancestor. Washington, D.C.: The Author, 1973.
Period 1453–1890, arranged in chronological order; answers genealogical and historical facts in the settlement of America. Good maps. Quick and handy method for finding necessary basic facts, genealogical and historical.

*235 **D.A.R. Genealogical Advisory Committee to the Registrar General.** Is that lineage right? A training manual for the examiner of lineage papers, with helpful hints for the beginner in genealogical research. Washington, D.C.: D.A.R., 1965.
Updated sporadically.

*236 **Doane, Gilbert H.** Searching for your ancestors: the how and why of genealogy. 4th ed., rev. New York: Bantam Books, 1974. 3rd ed. also available from Univ. of Minnesota Pr., Minneapolis.
Easy to read and study. Very good bibliography; provides suggestions for Blacks and Indians who wish to trace their ancestry.

*237 **Everton, George B., Jr.** The handy book for genealogists. 6th ed., rev. Logan, Utah: Everton, 1971.
Popular genealogical aid, especially for beginners. Excellent commentary and list of counties. Developmental history and chronology of counties within each state makes it essential.

238 **Fudge, George H.**, and **Smith, F.** L.D.S. genealogist's handbook: modern procedures and systems. Salt Lake City: Bookcraft, 1972.

*239 **Gardner, David E.**, and **Smith, F.** Genealogical research in England and Wales. (v.3: Palaeography) Salt Lake City: Bookcraft, 1964.
Written solely for the genealogist. Virtually all forms of handwriting encountered in early documents are considered. For notes on v.1&2, *see* no.4426.

240 **Genealogical research in England.**
Communicated to the Committee on English Research (of the New-England Historic Genealogical Society.) In *New England historical and genealogical register* v.61–107, 1907–48.
Originally contributed by Joseph G. Bartlett, then Elizabeth French, and finally G. Andrews Moriarty. For a short time it was called "Genealogical research in Germany and England," and later, "Genealogical research in Europe."

*241 **Genealogical research: methods and sources.** Ed. by Milton Rubincam and Jean Stephenson. 6th pr. Washington, D.C., 1966.
General principles of research and source materials; chapters prepared by specialists in all fields of genealogical research. Outstanding manual with excellent chapter on heraldry by Harold Bowditch; other articles deal primarily with the original states.

*242 ―――― v.2. Ed. by Kenn Stryker-Rodda. 2nd pr. Washington, D.C., 1973.
Devoted primarily to genealogical research in the first group of expansion states. Underlying theme is migrations: movement of the people inland as far as the Mississippi. Concerns Ohio, Indiana, Illinois, Wisconsin, Iowa, Kentucky, Tennessee, Alabama, Louisiana, Michigan, Mississippi, and also Ontario, the Huguenots, and Jewish migrations. Constantly out of print; when available, both volumes can be obtained from G.P.C., Baltimore, or Mrs. Donna R. Hotaling, Vienna, Va.

243 **Genealogical Society of the Church of Jesus Christ of Latter-day Saints, Inc.** Research papers. Salt Lake City: The Society, 1966– .
For the major publications the Research Dept. attempted to answer four questions: what types of records exist; for what periods of time; what genealogical information do the records contain; and how available are the records. To September 1974 the following series have been published:

A: Great Britain, no.1–52, 1966–73.
B: North America, no.1–3, 1967–73.
C: Germanic-Slavic, no.1–23, 1967–73.
D: Scandinavia, no.1–15, 1967–71.
E: Pacific, no.1–3, 1967–68.
F: General, no.1–3, 1968–69, no.2 rev. 1973.
G: Romance Europe, no.1–2, 1968–69.
H: Central & South America, no.1–3, 1970–71.
J: Japan, no.1, 1973.

Charts and tables are magnificently compiled and produced; maps (some in color) are perfect for each publication. There is much information on English probate jurisdictions, *see* details under no.4201. From Church Distribution Center, Salt Lake City, Utah.

*244 **Greenwood, Val D.** The researcher's guide to American genealogy. Baltimore: G.P.C., 1973.

Definitive textbook; detailed examination of records in specific areas and times. Unlike some other manuals, it is indispensable and should become the most important manual for American researchers.

245 **Hall, Charles M.** The Atlantic bridge to Germany. v.1, Baden-Wuerttenberg. Logan, Utah: Everton, 1974.

Aids researcher in locating ancestors in the proper places in Germany. Good maps.

246 **Harland, Derek.** Genealogical research standards. Salt Lake City: Bookcraft, 1963.

Scientific approach to research with emphasis on the evaluation of genealogical evidence. Original title: *A basic course in genealogy*, v.2.

247 **Hartwell, Sir Rodney.** Guide to orders of chivalry. A guide for application and research. Harbor City, Calif.: Hartwell Co., 1974.

248 **Jacobus, Donald L.** Genealogy as pastime and profession. 2nd ed. Baltimore: G.P.C., 1971.

Not strictly a manual, but a learned discussion on genealogy by one of the world's leading genealogists.

249 **Jaussi, Laureen R.,** and **Chaston, G. D.** Fundamentals of genealogical research. Salt Lake City: Deseret, 1974.

Description of L.D.S. genealogical sources and how to use them.

250 **Jones, Vincent L., Eakle, A. H.,** and **Christensen, M. H.** Family history for fun and profit. Rev. ed. Salt Lake City: Genealogical Inst., 1972.

Original title was *Genealogical research: a jurisdictional approach*. Primary emphasis is the application of the historical and scientific research methods of genealogy. Well documented, extensive bibliographies but not annotated; inadequate index. Although intended for the beginning amateur and the professional genealogist, it is often confusing.

251 **Kirkham, E. Kay.** A guide to record-searching in the larger cities of the United States, including a guide to their vital records and some maps with street indexes, with other information of genealogical value. Logan, Utah: Everton, 1974.

Good maps.

*252 ———— The handwriting of American records for a period of 300 years. Logan, Utah: Everton, 1973.

Problems of early American handwriting. Techniques of reading old documents, searching original records, etc.

253 ———— Professional techniques and tactics in American genealogical research. Logan, Utah: Everton, 1973.

Very useful for those engaged in genealogical research. Guide to aids, methods in recording genealogical information.

254 ———— Research in American genealogy: a practical approach to genealogical research. 2nd pr. Salt Lake City, 1962.

Particularly valuable for lists of genealogical libraries, archives, etc. State census schedules listed.

255 ———— Simplified genealogy for Americans. 2nd ed. Salt Lake City: Deseret, 1974.

256 **Marsh, Warren L.** Search and retrieval: the application of data processing to genealogical research. Old Saybrook, Conn.: The Author, 1970.

Techniques for modern research.

257 **Morris, Louise E. B.** Advanced primer of genealogical research. 3rd ed. Dallas, Tex.: The Author, 1974.

Updated ed. of *Primer of genealogical research*, 1965. Good bibliography for British and American reference works. Concise guide to research methods and source materials.

*258 **Pine, Leslie G.** American origins. 1960. Repr. Baltimore: G.P.C., 1971.

Handbook of genealogical sources abroad, with addresses to write to for information. Extremely weak on American research, but excellent for British and western Europe research. Out-of-date.

259 ———— The genealogist's encyclopedia. New York: Collier, [1970].

Has details of ancient genealogies, genealogies from 1500; Scottish records, Welsh records and data for Isle of Man, Channel Islands, Ireland, etc.

260 **Poulton, Helen J.** The historian's handbook: a descriptive guide to reference works. Norman, Okla.: Univ. of Oklahoma Pr., 1972.

Guide to the historian and genealogist.

261 **Radewald, Bette (M.).** The library handbook; simplified methods and terms for the genealogist. Riverside, Calif.: RE Genealogy, 1974.

Fresh approach for the advanced or beginning family history researcher in using library resources for genealogical research. Methods, record keeping, and sources augmented by a glossary, bibliography, illustrations, and index.

262 **Special aids to genealogical research in northeastern and central states.** *National Genealogical Soc. special publ.* 16. 2nd pr. Washington, D.C.: The Society, 1962.

Covers Illinois, Indiana, Iowa, Connecticut settlement of Nova Scotia, Ohio, Virginia, West Virginia, and Wisconsin.

263 **Stevenson, Noel C.** Search and research: the researcher's handbook; a guide to official records and library sources for investigators, historians, genealogists, lawyers, and librarians. New ed., rev. Salt Lake City: Deseret, 1973.

Good bibliography and practical advice; chapters on each state.

264 **Wellauer, Maralyn A.** A guide to foreign genealogical research: a selected bibliography of printed material with addresses. Milwaukee, Wisc.: The Compiler, 1973.

*265 **Williams, Ethel W.** Know your ancestors: a guide to genealogical research. 19th ed. Rutland, Vt.: Tuttle, 1972.

Designed for amateur and professional. Has comprehensive bibliography of materials available in the field, and glossary of terms and abbreviations. Oriented to New England and upper midwest states. Constantly updated.

266 **Wright, Norman E.** Building an American pedigree; a study in genealogy. Provo, Utah: Brigham Young Univ. Pr., 1974.

267 ———— and **Pratt, D. H.** Genealogical research essentials. Salt Lake City: Bookcraft, 1967.

Covers all aspects and includes one chapter on the Latter-day Saints' doctrinal outlook on genealogy.

268 **Zabriskie, George O.** Climbing our family tree systematically. Salt Lake City: Parliament Pr., 1969.

Primarily for beginners, but genealogists of all levels will find it useful.

## COLONIAL AND PRECOLONIAL LISTS

✣ It is particularly important that each book in this list be examined with care. Some make unsubstantiated claims, and the researcher must weigh each statement cautiously. All the titles are included because they are in great demand in libraries, but their inclusion is not an endorsement of accuracy.

ROYAL

269 **Angerville, Count Howard H. d'.** Living descendants of Blood Royal

in America. v.1-5 (in progress). London: Tabard, 1959-73.
Pedigrees of Americans who trace their descent from royal families in Europe. Use with care. v.1-2 are out-of-print; v.3-5 from Tabard; some volumes can be obtained from G.P.C. in Baltimore.

270   **Browning, Charles H.** Americans of Royal descent. Collection of genealogies showing the lineal descent from kings of some American families. 7th ed. 1911. Repr. Baltimore: G.P.C., 1969.
As with all Browning works, highly inaccurate.

271   —— Some "Colonial Dames" of Royal descent. 1900. Repr. Baltimore: G.P.C., 1969.
Included are pedigrees showing the lineal descent from kings of some members of the National Society of the Colonial Dames of America, Order of the Crown, etc. Much wishful thinking.

272   **Collins, Carr P., Jr.** Royal ancestors of Magna Charta Barons. Dallas, Tex.: 1959.
Ancestry charts of 12 Magna Charta barons. Chiefly of cross-referenced lineages of a large number of medieval families; fabulous lines included. Many Collins lines included.

273   **Hartwell, Sir Rodney.** Researching your royal ancestry. A guide to individual research. Harbor City, Calif.: Hartwell Co., 1974.

274   **Lainson, Dorothy A. S.** Some Magna Charta barons and other royal lineages. Huntsville, Ark.: Century Enterprises, 1970.
Study of 25 barons and noblemen of the Magna Charta with royal ancestry, and descent to persons living today in America.

275   **Langston, Aileen L.,** and **Buck, J. O.** Pedigrees of some of the Emperor Charlemagne's descendants. v.2. New Orleans, La.: Polyanthos, 1974. (Or from R. G. Cook, 761 Linwood Ave., St. Paul, Minn. 55105).
v.2 has excellent bibliography of modern genealogical works by Timothy F. Beard.

Validity of lines is not supported with evidence. For v.1 by Redlich, *see* no.277. v.3 is being prepared, to be published by the Order of the Crown of Charlemagne in U.S.A.

276   **Order of the Crown of Charlemagne in the United States of America.** Roll of arms. Bridgeport, Pa.: The Order, 1973.
Names and coats of arms.

277   **Redlich, Marcellus D. A. R. von.** Pedigrees of some of the Emperor Charlemagne's descendants. v.1. 1941. Repr. Baltimore: G.P.C., 1972.
Claims that only those pedigrees that can be proved beyond doubt are included. v.2 *see* no.275.

278   **Royalty, peerage and aristocracy of the world.** London, 1966.
English edition of *Annuaire de la noblesse de France*. First published in 1843; 1966 is 90th ed. Present edition contains details for the reigning houses and titled nobility of Europe and a section devoted to "foremost" families of the United States. Depending on the interest, one in every decade is needed; 1966 is the most important for Americans.

279   **Watson, Annah W. (Robinson).** A royal lineage: Alfred the Great, 901-1901. 1901. Repr. Ann Arbor, Mich.: Univ. Microfilms, 1973.
Also has some American descendants of Alfred the Great and other sovereigns.

280   **Wurts, John S.** Magna Charta. 8v. in 7. 1942-54. v.1-6 repr. Philadelphia: Brookfield Pub. Co., 1964.
Pedigrees of representative American families of royal and noble descent. Also lists of living descendants of Magna Charta barons. Must be used with extreme care.

GENERAL

281   **Adams, Arthur,** and **Weis, F. L.** The Magna Charta sureties, 1215: the barons named in the Magna Charta, 1215, and some of their descendants who settled in America, 1607-50. 2nd authorized ed.,

with rev. and corr. by Walter L. Sheppard, Jr. Baltimore: G.P.C., 1968.
Corrects many, but not all, of the errors of the 1955 ed. Traces, generation by generation, the links between the Magna Charta surety barons and a number of early American colonists and their descendants. 1955 ed. indexed by Crowther (no.42).

**282 American ancestry:** giving the name and descent, in the male line, of Americans whose ancestors settled in the United States previous to the Declaration of Independence, A.D. 1776. 12v. 1887–99. Repr. Baltimore: G.P.C., 1968.
v.1–2 are by Thomas P. Hughes. Pedigrees of 7,500 persons resident in the U.S. in the 19th century who could trace their lineage to an ancestor who had settled in America prior to 1776. Establishes the pedigree in the male line for 6 or 7 generations. Virtually a who's who of the colonial families of New England, New York, etc. Sometimes referred to as *Munsell's American ancestry*. Undocumented and not considered authoritative. Indexed in *Index to American genealogies* (no.22).

**283 Bolton, Charles.** The founders; portraits of persons born abroad who came to the colonies in North America before the year 1701, with biographical outlines and comments . . . 3v. Boston, 1919–26.

**284** ——— Magna Charta barons and their [American] descendants. 1898. Repr. Baltimore: G.P.C., 1969.

**285** ——— 1915. Repr. Baltimore: G.P.C., 1969.
Published by the Baronial Order of Runnemede. Lists Americans claiming lineal descent from Magna Charta barons. Readers are warned that there are many false assertions and statements. 1898 and 1915 eds. differ considerably. Membership changed and some members did not renew, etc. The 1915 ed. should be considered as the second "yearbook."

***285a Burke's Distinguished families of America;** the lineages of 1,600 families of British origin now resident in the United States of America. London: Burke's Peerage, 1948, pp.2539–3021.
Has color plates of arms. Descendants in the female line have been included. Repr. with title, *Prominent families in America with British ancestry*, 1971. Has black and white plates of arms. See no.4485.

**286 Burt, Nathaniel.** First families; the making of an American aristocracy. Boston: Little Brown, 1970.

**287 Clemens, William M.** American marriage records before 1699. 1926. Baltimore: G.P.C., 1967.
Some of the earliest marriages recorded: 10,000 entries under brides and grooms. Covers whole of colonial United States. v.14, pt.4 and v.15, pt.3 of *Genealogy* (1929) (no.116) have small suppl. Sources not given.

**288 Clement, John B.** Descent from sureties from the Magna Carta of A.D. 1215. n.p., ca.1930.
A sheet with colored coats of arms.

**289 Coldham, Peter W.** English convicts in colonial America. v.1, Middlesex 1617–1775. New Orleans, La.: Polyanthos, 1974.
In progress. 12,000 individuals in alphabetical order. First time list made public.

**290 Colonial and Revolutionary lineages of America:** a collection of genealogical studies, completely documented, and appropriately illuminated, bearing on notable early American lines and their collateral connections. v.1–25. West Palm Beach, Fla., 1939–68.
Indexed to 1964 in Crowther (no.42). In spite of the subtitle, the work is not completely documented and some claims are not substantiated. Coats of arms.

**291 Colonial Dames of America. Baltimore Chapter.** Ancestral records and portraits, Colonial Dames of America, Chapter I [Baltimore]. 2v. Repr. Baltimore: G.P.C., 1969.
Many portraits; members mostly Maryland residents. Users should treat the pre-American generations with caution.

**292 The colonial genealogist.** v.3– , 1970– . Harbor City, Calif.: Augustan Soc.

Originally *The beetle gazette; The Colonial genealogist,* v.3–5, 1970–72 (10 issues and 2 indexes). As from v.6, it is part of *The Augustan* omnibus vol. *(see* no.105). Well documented and illustrated lineages. Who's who in genealogy, magazine evaluations, colonial families of the Americas, mingling of colonial east coast with South American lines.

**293 Currer-Briggs, Noel.** English wills of colonial families. New Orleans, La.: Polyanthos, 1972.

5,000 name index relating to wills and other documents, concerning people who emigrated to America in 17th century. 7,000 place names.

**294 Daughters of Colonial Wars.** Members and history and index of ancestors.... 1941– . Somerville, Mass.: The National Soc.

**295 Daughters of Founders and Patriots of America.** Lineage book. v.1– , 1910– . Washington, D.C.: The National Soc.

Contained in annual publications; thousands of names.

**296** ——— Index to lineage books, v.1– 25, 1910–37. Somerville, Mass., 1943.

National no.1–3,800. The lineage book is published sporadically.

**297 Daughters of the American Colonists.** Lineage book. v.1– , 1923– . Washington, D.C.: The National Soc.

**298** ——— Supplementals. Book 1– , 1945– . Washington, D.C.: The National Soc.

Out-of-print volumes can be obtained from Bell and Howell, Wooster, Ohio.

**298a Daughters of the American Revolution.** *See* no.496-508.

**299 Daughters of the Barons of Runnemede** ... Members (list of members and their American immigrant ancestors). Athens, Ga., 1937.

Sketches of American immigrant ancestors, royal surety barons from whom proven descent is known.

**300 De Forest, Louis E.** American colonial families; families which do not appear in *Colonial families of America,* by Ruth Lawrence (no.303), and thus a supplement. New York, 1930.

**301 Haxtun, Annie A.** Signers of the Mayflower Compact. 1897–99. Repr. Baltimore: G.P.C., 1968.

Considerable genealogical information of signers and families.

**302 Landis, John T.** Mayflower descendants and their marriages for two generations after the landing. 1922. Repr. Baltimore: G.P.C., 1972.

**303 Lawrence, Ruth.** Colonial families of America. 27v. New York, 1928–48.

Coats of arms. A surname index was made by Crowther (no.42); for families which do not appear in Lawrence, *see* De Forest (no.300).

**303a Lohmann Villena, Guillermo.** Los Americanos en las ordenes nobiliarias, 1529–1900. Madrid, 1947.

Alphabetical list of names of distinguished families from America who were members of some of the most distinguished orders of the nobility. Detailed family information.

**304 Mackenzie, George N.** (and **Rhoades, N. O.).** Colonial families of the United States of America, in which is given the history, genealogy, and armorial bearings of colonial families who settled in the American colonies from ... 1607 to 1775. 7v. 1907–20. Repr. Baltimore: G.P.C., 1966.

Monumental work of more than 5,000p. devoted exclusively to families who trace their ancestry back to the colonial period. More than 125,000 names mentioned. While the work is reasonably accurate, the earlier ancestry is often ludicrous, but the book is used heavily in libraries. Recommended with reservations.

**305 Manross, William W.** The Fulham papers in the Lambeth Palace Library; American colonial section. Calendar and indexes. New York: Oxford Univ. Pr., 1965.

Much 18th-century genealogical information.

**306 The Mayflower quarterly.** v.1– , 1935– . Warwick, R.I.: General Soc. of Mayflower Descendants.

Much information, all pertaining to Mayflower descendants. Good articles with bibliographies.

**307 National Society of Woman Descendants of the Ancient and Honorable Artillery Company [of the U.S.A.].** By Mrs. Wilbur W. Stearns (and others). 3v. Washington, D.C.: The National Soc., 1941–60.

History and lineage book.

**308 National Society, Sons and Daughters of the Pilgrims.** Lineages of members to 1929. Philadelphia, 1929.

**309** ———— 1929–52. Philadelphia, 1953.

**310 The Order of the Founders and Patriots of America.** Register. Rev. New York, 1926.

**311** ———— 1st supplement. New York, 1940.

**312** ———— 2nd supplement. New York: The Order, 1960.

**313 Pittman, Hannah D.** Americans of gentle birth and their ancestors: a genealogical encyclopedia. 2v. 1903–07. Repr. Baltimore: G.P.C., 1970.

Extensive work containing the lineages of the descendants of early American families, with emphasis on the colonial and Revolutionary periods, and including many royal and noble pedigrees. Color plates. Many false assertions.

**314 Plymouth Colony genealogical helper.** no.1– , 1974– . Harbor City, Calif.: Augustan Soc.

**315 Society of Colonial Wars.** General register, 1899–1902. New York, 1902.

**316** ———— Supplement. Boston, 1906.

**317** ———— 2nd supplement. New York, 1911.

See also its index of ancestors (no. 318–19).

**318** ———— An index to ancestors and roll of members . . . New York, 1921.

**319** ———— 1st supplement. 2v. Hartford, 1941.

**320 Society of Mayflower Descendants.** Families of the Pilgrims. By Hubert K. Shaw. Boston, 1956.

A publication of the Massachusetts Society.

**\*321** ———— Mayflower index. rev. ed. of the two volumes of the Mayflower index, which was compiled by the late William A. McAuslan . . . rev. by Lewis E. Neff. 3v. in 2. Boston: The General Soc., 1960; and Tulsa, Okla.: Mayflower Soc.

v.1–2 of the revision is of the old edition; v.3 is by Neff. Alphabetical listing of names from the lineage papers of all members to those dates (1932 and 1960). In these books the numbering system enables the reader to follow any member prior to 1960 back to his Mayflower ancestor.

**322** ———— D.C. Register . . . 1970, in commemoration of the 350th anniversary of the landing of the Pilgrims in Plymouth 1620. Washington, D.C.: The Soc., 1970.

**323 Spooner, Walter W.** Historic families of America, comprehending the genealogical records and representative biography of selected families of early American ancestry. 3v. New York, 1907–08.

Coats of arms in color; all "blue-book" families. Much wishful thinking; treat with extreme caution. Much New York information.

**324 Virkus, Frederick A.** The abridged compendium of American genealogy: first families of America; a genealogical encyclopedia of the U.S. v.1–7, 1925–42. Baltimore: G.P.C., 1968.

Published originally by the Institute of American Genealogy, Chicago. v.4-7 have changed title: *The compendium of American genealogy* . . . v.8 was being prepared when the Institute folded. 54,000 lineages with 425,000 names. One of the first reference sources in American genealogy. It is a major source of information on immigrants to America before 1750. But use with care, since so much of the information was provided by subjects. Often referred to as *Virkus*.

**325   Weis, Frederick L.** Ancestral roots of sixty colonists who came to New England between 1623 and 1650. The lineage of Alfred the Great, Charlemagne, Malcolm of Scotland, Robert the Strong, and some of their descendants. 1950. Repr. with 1952 suppl., 1956 additions and corrections, and 1964 corrections, by Walter L. Sheppard, Jr., 4th ed. rev. and enl. Baltimore: G.P.C., 1969.

Contains all maternal lines, as well as 71 descent charts. Not considered authoritative and must be used with care. New ed. has continuous text and new material. Surname index to 1950 ed. in Crowther (no.42).

**326**   ———— ———— Cross index (to 1964 ed.). Compiled by T. H. Owen. Colorado Springs, Colo., 1964.

**327**   ———— The colonial clergy of the middle colonies, New York, New Jersey, and Pennsylvania, 1628-1776. Worcester, Mass.: American Antiquarian Soc., 1957.

Repr. from *Proceedings of the Soc.*, v.66, 1957. Useful data on each person.

**328   Whittemore, Henry.** Genealogical guide to the early settlers of America, with a brief history of those of the first generation and references to the various local histories and other sources of information where additional data may be found. Baltimore: G.P.C., 1967.

Excerpted from the periodical *The spirit of '76*, Sept. 1898-June 1906, v.5-12. Ran in serial form and ended in the *R*'s, although this excerpt erroneously ends at Prior. With some reservations it takes its place with Savage (*see* no.607). Few complete sets of *The spirit of '76* are recorded.

## IMMIGRATION

BRITISH (settlers and others from Great Britain and Ireland)

*****329   Banks, Charles E.** The planters of the commonwealth. A study of the emigrants and emigration in colonial times: to which are added lists of passengers to Boston and to the Bay Colony; the ships which brought them; their English homes, and the places of their settlement in Massachusetts, 1620-40. Baltimore: G.P.C., 1972.

1,200 passengers; important work on early emigration. Probably the most authentic list in print.

**330**   ———— Topographical dictionary of 2,885 English emigrants to New England, 1620-50. Ed. and indexed by E. E. Brownell. 1937. Repr. Baltimore: G.P.C., 1974.

**331   Bolton, Ethel (Stanwood).** Immigrants to New England, 1700-75. 1931. Repr. Baltimore: G.P.C., 1973.

Not original passenger lists, but combined lists of persons coming to New England. Alphabetical arrangement of 2,250 immigrants with genealogical information.

**332   Boston, Mass. Record Commissioners.** Port arrivals and immigrants to the city of Boston, 1715-16 and 1762-69. Compiled under the direction of William H. Whitmore. 1900. Repr. Baltimore: G.P.C., 1973.

Excerpted from *A volume of records relating to the early history of Boston* . . . 29th in series. Contains names of over 3,000 passengers. Newly indexed.

**333   Cameron, Viola R.** Emigrants from Scotland to America, 1774-75. 1930. Repr. Baltimore: G.P.C., 1965.

About 2,000 names with full data.

**334   Dickson, Robert J.** Ulster emigration to colonial America, 1718-75. *Ulster-Scot historical ser.*1. London: Routledge & Kegan Paul, 1966.

Good background to emigration. Appendixes include lists of ships, data about them, and ports of destination. Good bibliography.

## United States

**335** Drake, Samuel G. Result of some researches among the British archives for information relative to the founders of New England: made in 1858–60. 1860 Repr. Baltimore: G.P.C., 1969.

**336** Erickson, Charlotte. Invisible immigrants; the adaptation of English and Scottish immigrants in nineteenth-century America. Coral Gables, Fla.: Univ. of Miami Pr., 1972.
Treatise based on correspondence of families; genealogical sources.

**337** Farmer, John. A genealogical register of the first settlers of New-England . . . (1620–75). 1829. Repr. with additions and corrections by Samuel G. Drake. Baltimore: G.P.C., 1969.
Invaluable directory to first settlers of New England. Only work of authority prior to Savage (no.607).

**338** Fothergill, Gerald. Emigrants from England, 1773–76. Repr. from *The New England historical and genealogical register*, v.52–55, 1898–1901. 1913. Repr. Baltimore: G.P.C., 1964.
Contains more than 6,000 names, with much useful data.

**339** French, Elizabeth. List of emigrants to America from Liverpool, 1697–1707. Repr. from *The New England historical and genealogical register*, v.64–65, 1910–11. Boston: New England Historic Genealogical Soc., 1913. Repr. by G.P.C., Baltimore, 1972.
Lists over 1,500 indentured servants, with much genealogical data.

**340** Ghirelli, Michael. A list of emigrants from England to America, 1682–92. Transcribed from the original records at the City of London Record Office. Baltimore, 1968. Available from Tuttle, Rutland, Vt.
There were two periods in history when the British government required registration of all indentured servants going to the colonies: 1682–92 and 1718–59. For 1718–59, *see* no.348.

**341** Graham, Ian C. C. Colonists from Scotland: emigration to North America 1707–83. 1956. Repr. Port Washington, N.Y.: Kennikat Pr., 1972.

Also known as *Scottish emigration to North America*.

**342** Hackett, James D., and Early, C. M. Passenger lists from Ireland. Excerpted from *Journal of the American Irish Historical Soc.*, v.28–29, 1929–31. Baltimore: G.P.C., 1973.
5,150 immigrants from Ireland. Covers 109 ships.

**343** Hargreaves-Mawdsley, R. Bristol and America: a record of the first settlers in the colonies of North America, 1654–85, including the names with places of origin of more than 10,000 servants to foreign plantations who sailed from the port of Bristol to Virginia, Maryland, and other parts of the Atlantic coast, and also to the West Indies . . . 1929. Repr. with separate index, 1931, bound in. Baltimore: G.P.C., 1970.
Important and accurate list of servants who came to America. List attributed to William D. Bowman; index is by Marjorie M. Lorenz.

**344** Hartmann, Edward G. Americans from Wales. North Quincy, Mass.: Christopher Pub. House, 1967.
A fine background to the immigration to America. Has chapters on Welsh colonial settlement; church founded by Welsh; Welsh societies.

**\*345** Hotten, John C. Original lists of persons of quality, emigrants, religious exiles, political rebels . . . and others who went from Great Britain to the American plantations. 1874. Repr. Baltimore: G.P.C., 1974.
In spite of its errors and omissions, this title has never been superseded. It is the most important collection of ship passenger lists. There are two versions, one with accurate text and index, and the other with poor text and the good index, which does not entirely match the text. Only the following editions should be used: all 1874 printings; 1931 New York; 1935 New York, and the 1974 reprint.

**346** Jewson, Charles B. Transcript of three registers of passengers from Great Yarmouth to Holland and New England, 1637–39. From *Norfolk Record Soc.*

*publ.* 25, 1954. Repr. Baltimore: G.P.C., 1964.
Full data on emigrants.

347   Johnson, Stanley C. A history of emigration from the United Kingdom to North America, 1763–1912. 1913. Repr. Clifton, N.J.: Kelley, 1966.
Excellent bibliography. Destination of British emigrants; colonization schemes, land systems affecting immigration to North America.

348   Kaminkow, Jack, and Kaminkow, Marion J. A list of emigrants from England to America, 1718–59. Baltimore, 1964. Available from Tuttle, Rutland, Vt.
Transcribed from original records at the Guildhall, London, from "Agreements to serve in America." More than 3,000 names. See note under no.340.

*349   Lancour, Harold. A bibliography of ship passenger lists, 1538–1825. Being a guide to published lists of early immigrants to North America. 3rd ed., rev. and enl. by Richard J. Wolfe, with a list of passenger arrival records in the National Archives, by Frank E. Bridgers. 2nd corr. pr. New York: New York Public Lib., 1966.
Definitive work giving references to the sources of lists. Note that it does *not* contain actual lists. 262 arrivals listed; two indexes and list of ship names.

350   Massachusetts. Superintendent of Alien Passengers. A list of alien passengers, bonded from January 1, 1847, to January 1, 1851, for the use of the Overseers of the Poor, in the Commonwealth. By J. B. Munroe. 1851. Repr. Baltimore: G.P.C., 1971.
Scarce passenger list, containing 5,000 names of immigrants. Primarily from England, Ireland, and Scotland.

351   Miller, Olga K. Migration, emigration, immigration. Logan, Utah: Everton, 1974.
Many reference sources; excellent for all types of research.

352   Nicholson, Cregoe D. P. Some early emigrants to America (and) Early emigrants to American from Liverpool; abstracted by Reginald Sharpe France. Repr. from *Genealogist's magazine,* v.12–13, 1955–58. Baltimore: G.P.C., 1965.
Lists give more than 1,000 names of indentured servants in the 1680s, mainly bound for the South and the West Indies.

353   O'Brien, Michael J. The Irish in America. From *Journal of the American Irish Historical Soc.,* v.13, 1914, retitled with added table of contents. Baltimore: G.P.C., 1974.
500 immigrants to New England, 1716–69, and 1,000 to Virginia, 1623–66.

*354   Sherwood, George [F. T.]. American colonists in English records. A guide to direct references in authentic records, passenger lists not in "Hotten" (*see* no.345). 1932–33. Repr. 2v. in l. Baltimore: G.P.C., 1969.
Record of references to early immigrants to America found in English records but not in Hotten, to which it forms a valuable supplement. Original ed. published as 1st and 2nd series.

*355   Whyte, Donald. A dictionary of Scottish emigrants to the U.S.A. Baltimore, 1972. Available from Tuttle, Rutland, Vt.
Contains only a fraction of emigrants from Scotland between the earliest colonial times and 1855, when registration began in Scotland. But the 6,500 entries with over 5,000 dependents, indexes of names and places of origin, will be a service to genealogists.

OTHER THAN BRITISH

356   Colakovic, Branko M. Yugoslav migrations to America. San Francisco: R. and E. Research Assoc., 1973.
The arrival, distribution, and dispersion of Croatians, Serbians, Slovenes, and other south Slavs to the U.S.

356a   Eterovich, Adam S. Jugoslav immigrant bibliography. San Francisco: R. and E. Research Assoc., 1965.

356b   ——— Yugoslav migrations to the U.S.A. World Conference on Records, area D-13 paper. Salt Lake City: L.D.S., 1969.

**357  Faust, Albert B.** (and **Brumbaugh, Gaius M.**). Lists of Swiss emigrants in the 18th century to the American colonies . . . 2v. 1920-25. Repr. 2v. in 1. Baltimore: G.P.C., 1968.
v.2 was edited by Faust and Brumbaugh. Standard work on Swiss, who emigrated primarily to Pennsylvania and the Carolinas. Also additions to Zurich and Bern lists. Comment and criticism of this work by Leo Schelbert is found in *National Genealogical Soc. quarterly,* v.60, 1972.

**358  Garrett, Christina H.** The Marian exiles. 1938. Repr. New York: Cambridge Univ. Pr., 1966.
Contains 472 biographical sketches of English refugees to Germany during the years 1554-59 during the reign of Mary Tudor. Some descendants later came to America.

**359  Hall, Charles M.** Palatine pamphlet. Midvale, Utah: The Author, 1974.
Origins, place of settlement in U.S., and source of information for one or more families on each of the 324 ships arriving in Philadelphia from 1727-75.

**360  Hansen, Marcus L.** The Atlantic migration, 1607-1860: a history of the continuing settlement of the United States. Cambridge, Mass., 1940. Good background information.

**361  Janeway, William R.** Bibliography of immigration in the U.S., 1900-1930. 1934. Repr. San Francisco: R. and E. Research Assoc., 1972.
Helpful for anyone doing research on America's ethnic groups.

**362  Joseph, Samuel.** Jewish immigration to the United States from 1881 to 1910. 1914. Repr. New York: Arno Pr., 1969; New York: A.M.S. Press, 1967.

***363  Morton Allen directory of European passenger steamship arrivals** for the years 1890-1930 at the port of New York and for the years 1904-26 at the ports of New York, Philadelphia, Boston, and Baltimore. 1931. Repr. Strasburg, Va.: Shenandoah House Pub., 1971.
*See also* no.370.

***364  Neagles, James C.,** and **Lee, L.** Locating your immigrant ancestor: a guide to naturalization records. Logan, Utah: Everton, 1974.
Most useful in locating naturalization records and how to use them.

***365  Olsson, Nils W.** Swedish passenger arrivals in New York, 1820-50. Chicago: Swedish Pioneer Historical Soc., 1967.
4,000 names from 33,000 ships' manifests. Most arrivals are identified. Excellent compilation.

**366  The ridge runners:** a magazine of migration. v.1- , 1972- . Sparta, Mo.: William A. Yates.
Genealogy from Virginia, North Carolina, Tennessee, Indiana, North and South Carolina, Illinois, Missouri, Arkansas, the Ozark region. Much southern genealogical research. Absorbed *Ozark quarterly,* 1969, in 1973.

**367  Tribbeko, John,** and **Ruperti, G.** Lists of Germans from the Palatinate who came to England in 1709. *New York genealogical and biographical record,* 1909-10. Repr. Baltimore: G.P.C., 1965.
List of 6,520 Palatine emigrants from England and elsewhere, many of whom subsequently came to America.

**368  U.S. Dept. of State.** Passenger arrivals 1819-1820: a transcript of the list of passengers who arrived in the U.S. from the 1st October, 1819, to the 30th September, 1820. Repr. of Letter from the Secretary of State, with a transcript of the list of passengers who arrived in the U.S. . . . Repr. Baltimore: G.P.C., 1971.
Senate doc.118, 16th Cong. 2nd sess., ser.45, v.4. Reprint has its own title and has an added index of 54p. More than 10,000 names.

**369  ———** Passengers who arrived in the United States, Sept. 1821-December 1823. From transcripts made by the State Dept., National Archives, Washington, D.C.

Baltimore, 1969. Available from Tuttle, Rutland, Vt.
Over 15,000 names, 1819–20, *see* no.368; October 1820–August 1821 have been lost.

*370 **U.S. Immigration Information Bureau.** Directory relating to record of arrival of passenger steamships at the ports of New York, Philadelphia, Boston, and Baltimore, 1904–26. Repr. 1928. San Francisco: R. and E. Research Assoc., 1972.
Inclusive records of all ships by exact date. *See also* no.363.

371 **University of Minnesota Libraries, St. Paul. Immigrant archives.** Inventory of holdings in the University of Minnesota Libraries. St. Paul, Minn.: Immigration Historical Research Center of the Univ. of Minnesota, 1973.
Holdings pertain to ethnic groups originating in Eastern, Central, and Southern Europe and the Middle East. From the time of immigration to present day; geographical scope of all U.S. and Canada. 20,000 imprints, 2,000 microfilm reels, two million manuscripts. Large quantity in English.

372 **Virkus, Frederick A.** Immigrants to America before 1750; an alphabetical list of immigrants to the colonies, before 1750. Surnames A through BATT (all pub.). Excerpted from *Magazine of American genealogy,* sect.IV, no.1–27, 1929–32. Baltimore: G.P.C., 1965.
Ambitious attempt from all sources, correlating the records of several colonies. Care needed when used.


ETHNIC GROUPS

373 (General) **Wynar, Lubomyr.** Encyclopedic directory of ethnic newspapers and periodicals in the United States. Littleton, Colo.: Libraries Unlimited, 1972.

*374 (Afro-Americans) **Newman, Debra L.**
List of free black heads of families in the first census of the U.S., 1790. Washington, D.C.: National Archives, 1973.
*Special list* 34. Over 4,000 names; original 13 states.

374a (Afro-Americans) **Williams, Ethel L.**
Biographical directory of Negro ministers. 3rd ed. Boston: G. K. Hall, 1974.
Full biographical material about Negro ministers and their achievements. 3rd ed. updates the 643 biographies and contains 799 new biographies. Source list of denominations, churches, and sects included.

375 (Chinese) **Chinn, Thomas W.** Genealogical methods and sources for the Chinese immigrants to the United States. *World Conference of Records,* area H-7 paper. Salt Lake City: Genealogical Soc., 1969.

376 (Croatians) **Markotic, Vladimir.** Biographical directory of Americans and Canadians of Croatian descent. 4v. San Francisco: R. and E. Research Assoc., 1973.
Contains also organizational directory, church and priest directory, newspapers and periodicals.

377 (Danes) **Bille, John H.** A history of the Danes in America. From *Transactions of Wisconsin Academy of Sciences, Arts and Letters* 11, 1896. Repr. San Francisco: R. and E. Research Assoc., 1971.
Begins with settlements of the 1860s.

378 (Dutch) **The Dutch in New Netherland and the United States, 1609–1909.** Repr. San Francisco: R. and E. Research Assoc., 1970.
Colonial settlements and problems of the colonists.

379 (Germans) **Arndt, Karl J.,** and **Olson, M. E.** German-American newspapers and periodicals, 1732–1955: history and bibliography. 2nd ed. rev. 1961. Repr. New York: Johnson Reprint Co., 1965.

380 (Germans) **Lowell, Edward J.** The Hessians: and the other German auxiliaries of Great Britain in the Revolutionary War. 1884. Repr. Port Washington, N.Y.: Kennikat Pr., 1965; Williamstown, Mass.: Corner House, 1970.

381 (Germans) **Stumpp, Karl.** The emigration from Germany to Russia in the years 1763–1862. Lincoln, Neb.: Amer-

## United States

ican Historical Soc. of Germans from Russia, 1974.
Over 1,000 pages of names, places, maps, and charts.

**382** (Irish) **American-Irish Historical Society journal.** v.1-32, 1898-1941.
Has a considerable amount of genealogy concerning the Irish. Michael J. O'Brien was the author of many excellent articles of a genealogical nature.

**383** (Irish) **Early, Charles M.** Passenger lists from the *Shamrock* or *Irish chronicle,* 1815-16 [and list of ships arriving in American ports]. In *Journal of the American-Irish Historical Soc.* v.29, 1938.

**384** (Irish) **Irish in America.** See *American-Irish Historical Soc. journal* (no. 382), and Michael J. O'Brien (no.386-88).

**385** (Irish) **McGee, Thomas D'A.** A history of the Irish settlers in North America from the earliest period to the census of 1850. 1852. Repr. Baltimore: G.P.C., 1974.
Comprehensive survey of the Irish in all phases of their emigration, settlement, and participation in North America. Hundreds of Irish-Americans, from the first emigrants to the Barbados in 1649, to the refugees of 1840.

**386** (Irish) **O'Brien, Michael J.** For almost 20 years, O'Brien wrote many articles about the Irish in America. Each is of considerable importance to the study of Irish genealogy. He wrote of early charters, records (mostly 18th/19th century), mariners, immigrant land administration, property owners, pioneers and settlers, immigrants, and all concern the New England states, Virginia, Georgia, North and South Carolina, Maryland, District of Columbia, Wisconsin, Mexico, and other areas. All articles appeared in the *Journal of the American-Irish Historical Soc.* (no.382) between the years 1912 and 1930.

**387** (Irish) ——— A hidden phase of American history: Ireland's part in America's struggle for liberty. Excerpted from *Journal of the American-Irish Historical Soc.* v.13, 1914. Repr. Baltimore: G.P.C., 1974.
Scholarly work, with list of 5,000 soldiers of the Revolution. Data on settlements in New York, Pennsylvania, Virginia, and the Carolinas and Georgia.

**388** (Irish) ——— The Irish in America. Excerpted from *Journal of the American-Irish Historical Soc.,* v.13, 1914. Repr. Baltimore: G.P.C., 1974.
Retitled by reprint publisher. 500 immigrants to New England, 1716-69, and 1,000 to Virginia,1623-66.

**389** (Italians) **Musmanno, Michael A.** The story of the Italians in America. New York: Doubleday, 1965.
Contributions of Italians to American history.

**390** (Norwegians) **Blegen, Theodore C.** Norwegian migration to America... 2v. 1931-40. Repr. New York: Haskell House, 1969.
Standard reference. Fine history.

**391** (Norwegians) **Haugen, Einar.** The Norwegians in America. A students' guide to localized migration of Norwegians to America. New York: Teachers College Pr., Columbia Univ., 1973.
Good maps and list of reference books.

**392** (Norwegians) **Naeseth, Gerhard B.** Norwegian settlements in the United States: a review of printed and manuscript sources for the study of Norwegian sources in America. *World Conference on Records,* area E-10 paper. Salt Lake City: Genealogical Soc., 1969.

**392a** (Norwegians) **Qualey, Carleton C.** Norwegian settlement in the United States. 1938. Repr. New York: Arno, 1970.

**393** (Norwegians) **Rutt, Anna E. H.** Our Norwegian ancestors and their siblings and descendants. Santa Barbara, Calif.: The Author, 1968.
History of immigration of Norwegians to America. Many families studied in depth.

**394** (Norwegians) **Ulvestad, Martin.** Nordmaendene i Amerika, deres Historie og Rekord. Minneapolis, Minn., 1907.
Norwegian settlements in America. All

states, but principally Wisconsin, Minnesota, the Dakotas, Iowa, and Canada.

395 (Scandinavians) **Nelson, Olof N.** History of the Scandinavians; and successful Scandinavians in the United States. 2v. in 1. 2nd ed. rev. 1900. Repr. New York: Haskell House, 1969.

396 (Scotch) **MacLean, John P.** An historical account of the settlements of Scotch Highlanders in America prior to the peace of 1783, together with notices of the Highland regiments and biographical sketches. 1900. Repr. Baltimore: G.P.C., 1968.

397 (Scotch-Irish) **Bolton, Charles K.** Scotch Irish pioneers in Ulster and America. 1910. Repr. Baltimore: G.P.C., 1972.
Systematic treatment of settlers who came to New England, Pennsylvania, South Carolina, etc. from the north of Ireland.

398 (Scotch-Irish) **Ford, Henry J.** The Scotch-Irish in America. 1915. Repr. Hampden, Conn.: Archon Books, 1966; New York: Arno Pr., 1969.
Description of settlements, settlers, etc.

399 (Scotch-Irish) **Hanna, Charles A.** The Scotch-Irish; or, The Scot in North Britain, North Ireland, and North America. 2v. 1902. Repr. Baltimore: G.P.C., 1968.
Major work containing genealogical and historical materials concerning the part played by the Scotch-Irish in the settlement of America. Good Scotch-Irish bibliography.

400 (Swedes) **Benson, Adolph B.,** and **Hedin, N.** Swedes in America, 1638–1938 . . . 1938. Repr. New York: Haskell House, 1969.
History of the Swedes in America and other contributions. Best study by 2 specialists.

401 (Swedes) **Janson, Florence E.** The background of Swedish immigration, 1840–1930. [1931]. Repr. New York: Arno Pr., 1970.
Good bibliography.

402 (Swedes) **Swedish pioneer historical quarterly.** v.1– , 1950– . Chicago: Swedish Pioneer Historical Soc.

403 (Swiss) **Swiss-American Historical Society.** Prominent Americans of Swiss origin. v.1 (all pub.). New York, 1932.

RELIGIONS

GENERAL

404 **Johnson, Douglas W., Picard, P. R.,** and **Quinn, B.** Churches and church membership in the United States: an enumeration by region, state and county, 1971. Washington, D.C.: Glenmary Research Center, 1974.
53 religious bodies, with membership of over 100 million. Black denominations not included.

404a **Kirkham, E. Kay.** A survey of American church records. 2v. New ed. Logan, Utah: Everton, 1971.
Bibliography of church records available from major and minor denominations for the period prior to the Civil War.

404b **Mead, Frank S.** Handbook of denominations in the United States. New York, 1951.

405 **Mode, Peter G.** Source book and bibliographical guide for American church history. 1921. Repr. Boston: Canner, 1964.
Thorough work, particularly valuable for its extensive annotations.

406 **Society of American Archivists.** Church archives in the United States and Canada: a bibliography by Edmund L. Binsfeld. *American archivist,* v.21, 1958, pp. 311–32. Washington, D.C.: The Society.

407 ——— American church archives: an overview by Mabel E. Deutrich. *American archivist* v.24, 1961, pp.387–402. Washington, D.C. The Society.
Gives the locations of various religious groups, with publications and inventories available.

408 ——— A preliminary guide to church records repositories. Washington, D.C.: The Society, 1969.

409 ——— Church Records Committee. Directory of related archival and historical depositories in America. St. Louis: The Society, 1962.

410 **Sprague, William.** Annals of the American pulpit; or, commemorative notices of distinguished clergymen of various denominations . . . to . . . 1855. 9v. New York, 1857-69.

SEPARATE

411 (Amish) **Cross, Harold E.,** and **Hostetler, B.** Index to selected Amish genealogies. Baltimore: Div. of Medical Genetics, Johns Hopkins Univ. [1970?].
Complete bibliography of old order Amish genealogies. Fine, computerized index to 118 Amish genealogies. Of particular interest to midwest researchers having difficulty with Pennsylvania families.

412 (Anglicans) **Bell, James B.** Anglican clergy in colonial America ordained by bishops in London. *Proc. of the American Antiquarian Soc.,* v.83, pt.1, 1973. Worcester, Mass.: The Society, 1973.
Over 600 clergymen from a list of 1,600 who served in America. Full data given.

413 (Baptists) **Brumbaugh, Martin C.** A history of the German Baptist Brethren in Europe and America. 1899. Repr. N. Manchester, Ind.: L. W. Shultz, 1961.

414 ——— ——— Index. n.p., 1968?

415 (Baptists) **Cathcart, William.** The Baptist cyclopaedia . . . with numerous biographical sketches of distinguished American and foreign Baptists . . . Philadelphia, 1881.

416 ——— ——— Index to names by Elizabeth Hayward. Chester (now Rochester, N.Y.): American Baptist Historical Soc., 1951.

417 (Baptists) **Hayward, Elizabeth.** American vital records from "The Baptist register." 3v. Rochester, N.Y.: American Baptist Historical Soc., 1956-62. v.3: American vital records from "The New York Baptist register." Covers 1824-29.

417a (Baptists) **Encyclopedia of Southern Baptists.** 2v. Nashville, Tenn.: Broadman Pr., 1958.

418 (Baptists) **Historical Records Survey.** Directory of Negro Baptist churches in the United States. 2v. Chicago, 1942.

419 (Baptists) **Lasher, George W.** The ministerial directory of the Baptist churches in the United States. Oxford, 1899.
Concise biographical data of obscure Baptist ministers.

420 (Church of the Brethren) **Eastern Pennsylvania Church of the Brethren history, 1708-1915.** 1915. Repr. N. Manchester, Ind.: L. W. Shultz, 1967.
Contains background and early history of the roots of all the Brethren churches in America. Source material for historical, biographical, and genealogical research. Church of the Brethren Districts, Eastern Pennsylvania.

421 (Church of the Brethren) **History of the Church of the Brethren, Eastern Pennsylvania, 1915-65.** [Lancaster, Pa., 1965.]
Continues the narrative begun in no.420.

422 (Huguenots) **Allen, Cameron.** Records of Huguenots in the United States, Canada, and the West Indies, with some mention of Dutch and German sources. *World Conference on Records,* area F-10 paper. Salt Lake City: Genealogical Soc., L.D.S., 1969.

423 (Huguenots) **Baird, Charles W.** History of the Huguenot emigration to America, 2v. 1885. Repr. 2v. in 1. Baltimore: G.P.C., 1973.
Standard work for Huguenot emigrations. Extensive genealogical information.

424 (Huguenots) **Fosdick, Lucian J.** The French blood in America, 1906.

Repr. Baltimore: G.P.C., 1973.

Traces influence of Huguenots as factor in American life. Has list of some English surnames of French origin, with members of the Huguenot Society of America, 1906.

**425** (Huguenots) **Gilman, Charles M. B.** The Huguenot migration in Europe and America, its cause and effect. 2nd enl. ed. Red Bank, N.J., 1962.

Based on original French sources; also includes an extensive "Index to potential Huguenot ancestors."

**426** (Huguenots) **Huguenot Society of America.** Library catalogue or bibliography of the library. Compiled by Julia P. M. Morand. 1920. Repr. Baltimore: G.P.C., 1971.

Catalog of the works in the largest collection about Huguenots. Carefully analyzed bibliography with dictionary and 15 subdivisions.

**427** (Huguenots) **Huguenot Society of London.** Letters of denization and acts of naturalization for aliens in England and Ireland, 1509-1800. *Huguenot Soc. 4th ser. publ.,* 8, 18, 27. Lymington, England [and elsewhere]: 1893-1923.

**428** ——— ——— Supplement. *Huguenot Soc. 4th ser. publ.*35. Frome, England, 1932. v.1 ed. by William Page, 1509-1603; v.2-3 ed. by William A. Shaw, 1603-1800.

**429** (Huguenots) **Lart, Charles E.** Huguenot pedigrees. 1924-28. Repr. 2v. in 1. Baltimore: G.P.C., 1973.

Bridges gap between the families in France, England, Holland, and America. 1,500 names; many pedigrees.

**430** (Huguenots) **Lee, Hannah, F.** The Huguenots in France and America. 2v. 1843. Repr. 2v. in l. Baltimore: G.P.C., 1973.

History of the Huguenot settlements in New York and elsewhere, with list of names of Huguenot families in America.

**431** (Huguenots) **Reaman, George E.** The trail of the Huguenots in Europe, the United States, South Africa and Canada. [2nd] rev. ed. Repr. Baltimore: G.P.C., 1972.

Repr. of Canadian ed. published in 1963. Mainly devoted to America and Canada: settlements in the Carolinas, Virginia, Pennsylvania, New York, and New England. Included are short biographical sketches. Has addenda and corrigenda by Milton Rubincam, but on the whole is not authoritative.

**432** (Huguenots) **Smiles, Samuel.** The Huguenots: their settlements, their churches, and industries in England and Ireland. 1868. Repr. Baltimore: G.P.C., 1972.

Fine history of the Huguenots. Has 300 biographies of noted refugees who settled in Britain. Section on Huguenots in America, by G. P. Disoway.

**433** (Jews) **Birmingham, Stephen.** The grandees: America's Sephardic elite. New York: Harper & Row, 1971.

Folding genealogical table, portraits, bibliography.

**434** (Jews) **Madison, Charles A.** Eminent American Jews: 1776 to the present. New York: Frederick Ungar, 1970.

Many biographical studies.

**435** (Jews) **Pessin, Deborah.** History of the Jews in America. New York: Abelard-Schuman [1958].

**436** (Jews) **Prominent Jews of America:** a collection of biographical sketches of Jews . . . Toledo, Ohio, 1918.

Also appeared under title, *Eminent Jews of America.*

**437** (Jews) **Rosenbloom, Joseph A.** A biographical dictionary of early American Jews, colonial times through 1800. Lexington, Ky.: Univ. Pr. of Kentucky [1960].

**438** (Jews) **Simonhoff, Harry.** Jewish notables in America, 1776-1865. New York, [1956].

Sequel, 1865-1914, *see* no.439.

**439** ——— Saga of American Jewry 1865-1914; links of an endless chain. New York: Arco Pub. Co., 1959.

Sequel to his *Jewish notables*, 1776–1865, see no.438.

**440** (Jews) **Stern, Malcolm H.** Americans of Jewish descent. A compendium of genealogy. *American-Jewish archives* 3. 1960. Repr. New York: KTAV Pub. House, 1971.
Primarily concerned with settlers prior to 1840. 400 pedigree tables involving over 25,000 persons. Fine index.

**441** (Latter-day Saints) **Early church vital records** . . . In *Utah genealogical and historical magazine*, v.27–28, 1936–37.
All Latter-day Saints records.

**442** (Latter-day Saints) **Genealogical Society of the Church of Jesus Christ of Latter-day Saints.** L.D.S. records and research aids. *Research paper*, ser. F, no.1. Salt Lake City: The Soc., 1968.

*443 (Latter-day Saints) **Jaussi, Laureen R.**, and **Chaston, G. D.** Register of the L.D.S. church records. Classified by the Library of the Genealogical Society of the Church of Jesus Christ. Salt Lake City: Deseret, 1968.
Bibliographical listing of L.D.S. Church records available on microfilm at the library.

**444** (Latter-day Saints) **Jenson, Andrew.** Origin of western geographic names associated with the history of the "Mormon" people. In *Utah genealogical and historical magazine*, v.10–13, 1919–22.

**445** (Latter-day Saints) **Merrill Library, State University of Utah, Special Collections Dept.** Name index to the Library of Congress collection of Mormon diaries. *Western Text Soc.* ser.1, v.2. Logan, Utah: Utah State Univ. Pr., 1971.

**446** (Lutherans) **Bodensieck, Julius.** Encyclopedia of the Lutheran Church. 3v. Minneapolis, Minn.: Augsburg Pub. House, 1965.
Many biographies.

**447** (Lutherans) **Norlie, Olaf M.** Who's who in all the Norwegian Lutheran Synods of America, 1843–1927. 3rd ed. of *Norsk Lutherske prester i Amerika*, 1928. Minneapolis, Minn., 1928.

**448** (Lutherans) **Suelflow, August R.** Microfilm index and bibliography of the Concordia Historical Institute, Dept. of Archives and History, the Lutheran Church —Missouri Synod, St. Louis, Mo., 1954–63. St. Louis, Mo.: Concordia Pr., 1966.

**449** (Mennonites) **Lehman, James O.** Sonnenberg: a haven and a heritage. Kidron, Ohio: Kidron Community Council, Inc., 1974.
150 years of Mennonite history. The story of the Kidron community in Wayne County, Ohio, from 1819 when Swiss Mennonites migrated. 1,000 names.

**450** (Mennonites) **The Mennonite encyclopedia.** 4v. Hillsboro, Kans.: Mennonite Brethren Pub. House, 1955–59.
Has many family histories and much genealogical material. Bibliographical data on published Mennonite genealogies.

**451** (Mennonites) **Mennonite quarterly review.** v.1– , 1927– . Goshen, Ind.: Goshen College.

**452** ——— Indexes by Nelson P. Springer. v.1–40 published in 1952–66.
Available in offprints. Goshen, Ind.: Goshen College.

**453** (Methodists) **Methodist Episcopal Church.** Minutes of the annual conference, 1773–1835. 3v. New York, 1840.
Included because of the yearly personal data on preachers and obituaries.

**454** (Mormons) *See* Latter-day Saints, no. 441–5.

**455** (Presbyterians) **Beecher, Willis J.** Index of Presbyterian ministers, containing the names of all the ministers of the Presbyterian Church in the United States . . . 1706–1881. Philadelphia, 1883.

**456** (Protestants) **Allison, William H.** Inventory of unpublished material for American religious history in Protestant church archives and other repositories . . . *Carnegie Inst. of Washington publ.* 137. Washington, D.C., 1910.

**457** (Protestants) **Giuseppi, Montague S.** Naturalizations of foreign Protestants in the American and West Indian colonies . . . *Huguenot Soc. of London publ.* 24. 1921. Repr. Baltimore: G.P.C., 1969.

Covers the 18th century, mostly in Pennsylvania. 6,500 names of non-British emigrants who were naturalized in the colonies, 1640-1772.

**458** (Protestants) **Kinney, John M.** Bibliography of diocesan histories. In *Historical magazine of the Protestant Episcopal Church,* v.43, 1974.

Contains titles with full data, listing many biographical works.

**459** (Quakers) **Furman, Consuelo,** and **Furman, Robert.** Quaker bibliography for the genealogist; references to biography, genealogy, and records. New York, 1950?

Typescript copies in various libraries.

**460** (Quakers) **Haverford College Library.** Quaker necrology. 2v. Boston: G. K. Hall, 1961.

Index of approximately 59,000 death notices of Quakers in the middle Atlantic region. Entries taken from Quaker periodicals.

**461** (Quakers) **Heiss, Willard C.** Guide to research in Quaker records in the Midwest. Indianapolis, Ind., 1962.

**461a** ———— Quaker genealogies: A preliminary list. Indianapolis, Ind.: The Author, 1974.

Over 500 titles.

**462** (Quakers) **Hinshaw, William W.** Encyclopedia of American Quaker genealogy. v.1-7, pt.4 (in progress). 1936-72. v.1-6 repr. by G.P.C., Baltimore, 1969-73; v.7 available from Indianapolis, Ind.: Indiana Historical Soc.

v.1, North Carolina (no.2598); v.2, Philadelphia (no.2906); v.3, New York City and Long Island (no.2467); v.4-5, Ohio (no. 2713); v.6, Virginia (no.3576); v.7, Indiana (no.1378). The records of the Society of Friends are perhaps the most complete of all church records; few happenings went unrecorded.

**463** (Roman Catholics) **American Catholic Historical Society of Philadelphia.** Records. v.1- , 1886- . Philadelphia: The Society.

**464** ———— Indexes for v.1-31 (1886-1920) pub. in 1920?, and for v.32-41 (1921-30), pub. in 1956.

For the first 40 vols., and less thereafter, there is a wealth of genealogical material; family and church registers and family papers.

**465** (Roman Catholics) **Curry, Cora C.** Records of the Roman Catholic church in the United States as a source for authentic genealogical and historical material. *National Genealogical Soc. special publ.* 5. Washington, D.C., 1935.

**465a** (Shakers) **Pike, Kermit J.** A guide to Shaker manuscripts in the library of the Western Reserve Historical Society. Cleveland: The Society, 1974.

The Shakers were celibate and left no descendants, but since many left the sect there is much genealogical information available. Concerns 19 northeastern U.S. Shaker communities.

## MILITARY AND PENSION LISTS

GENERAL

**466** **Callahan, Edward W.** List of officers of the Navy of the United States and of the Marine Corps, from 1775 to 1900 . . . 1901. Repr. New York: Haskell House, 1969.

Fine reference work.

**467** **Cullum, George W.** Biographical register of the officers and graduates of the U.S. Military Academy at West Point, N.Y., from its establishment, in 1802 to 1890 . . . 3rd ed. 3v. Boston, 1891.

**468** **Ford, Worthington C.** British officers serving in America, 1754-74. Boston, 1894. Repr. from *The New England histori-*

*cal and genealogical register,* 1894. Repr. New York: Burt Franklin, 1969.
Only list in printed form, limited to 100 copies.

**469** ⎯⎯ ⎯⎯ 1775–83. Brooklyn, N.Y., 1897.
Limited to 250 copies.

**470 Hamersly, Thomas H. S.** Complete Army and Navy register of the United States of America, from 1776 to 1887. New York, 1888.
There is also a Washington ed., with slightly different dates. Despite title, the work lists only officers of the army. For the navy, *see* no.471.

**471** ⎯⎯ Complete general Navy register of the United States of America, from 1776–1887 . . . New York, 1888.
Originally appeared in 1v., Washington, D.C., 1880–81. The New York ed. of 1888 was in 2v.

**472** ⎯⎯ Complete regular Army register of the United States for . . . 1779–1879. Together with . . . a register of all appointments by the President of the United States, in the volunteer service during the Rebellion . . . 3rd. Washington, D.C., 1881.

**473** ⎯⎯ General register of the United States Navy and Marine Corps . . . 1782–1882 . . . including volunteer officers . . . Washington, D.C., 1882.

**474 Heitman, Francis B.** Historical register and dictionary of the United States Army, from its organization, September 29, 1789, to March 2, 1903. 2v. 1903. Repr. Urbana, Ill.: Univ. of Illinois Pr., 1965.
Officers only.

***475 Hood, Jennings,** and **Young, C. J.** American orders and societies and their decorations . . . Philadelphia, ca.1917.
Standard work for military, naval, commemorative, and patriotic societies of the U.S. orders. Requirements for membership given. Well illustrated in color.

**476 Kirkham, E. Kay.** Some of the military records of America before 1900. Their use and value in genealogical and historical research. Provo, Utah: Stevenson's Genealogical Center, 1972.
New ed. repr. with Kirkham's *Land records* (no.57).

**477 Leach, Douglas E.** Arms for empire; a military history of the British colonies in North America, 1607–1763. New York: Macmillan, 1973.
Has good maps.

**478 Powell, William H.** List of officers of the Army of the United States from 1779–1900 . . . 1900. Repr. Detroit, Mich.: Gale Research, 1967.

***479 Robles, Philip K.** United States military medals and ribbons. Rutland, Vt.: Tuttle, ca. 1971.
Concise statement on each medal and patriotic society awards.

**480 Rosengarten, Joseph G.** The German soldier in the wars of the United States. 2nd ed. 1890. Repr. San Francisco: R. and E. Research Assoc., 1972.
Includes lists of the Revolutionary and Civil War periods.

**481 Schuon, Karl.** U.S. Navy biographical dictionary. New York: Franklin Watts, 1965.
Leaders and outstanding figures through the ages.

**482 U.S. Adjutant-General's Office.** United States (official) Army register. Washington, D.C.: Adjutant General's Office, 1802– .
Now published annually. Title varies.

**483 U.S. Congress. House.** Digested summary and alphabetical list of private claims which have been presented to the House of Representatives from the First to the 31st Congress, exhibiting the action of Congress on each claim . . . 3v. Washington, D.C., 1853. Repr. Baltimore: G.P.C., 1970.
House Misc. docs., unnumbered, ser.653–55, 32nd Congress, 1st sess. 60,000 names

for 1789-1849. Covers Revolutionary War, War of 1812, and has land title confirmation. One single alphabet.

*484  **U.S. National Archives and Records Service.** Military service records in the National Archives. *General information leaflet* 7. Rev. Washington, D.C.: National Archives, 1974.

485  ———— Preliminary inventory of the records of the Adjutant General's Office. *Preliminary inventory* 17. Compiled by Lucille H. Pendell and E. Bethel. Washington, D.C.: National Archives, 1949.

486  **U.S. Navy Dept.** Report of the Secretary of the Navy with statement showing the operations of the Navy Pension Fund. Washington, D.C., 1828.
Senate doc. 37, 32nd Cong., 1st sess. Alphabetical list of Navy pensioners for each state, giving rank, also list of widow and orphan pensioners.

*487  **U.S. Pension Bureau.** List of pensioners on the roll, January 1, 1883. Senate. Executive doc. 84, 47th Cong., 2nd sess., ser.2078-82. 5v. 1883. Repr. Baltimore: G.P.C., 1970.
Major source for Civil War and War of 1812. Lists regular Army and Navy pensioners. 300,000 names. Seldom shows war involved, but mostly lists War of 1812 soldiers and their widows under the basic acts of 1871 and 1878 for this war. Only Civil War and Mexican War pensions on death or disability in service.

488  ———— Pensioners of Revolutionary War, struck off the roll. 1836. Repr. Baltimore: G.P.C., 1969.
Originally published as *Letter from the Secretary of War, transmitting a list of the names of pensioners . . . whose names were struck off the list . . . and subsequently restored, etc.* 24th Cong., 1st sess., House Misc. doc.127. Over 6,000 entries.

489  **U.S. War Dept.** (Pension list of 1818 [or-1819]). Repr. of Letter from the Secretary of War, transmitting a report of the names, rank, and line, of every person placed on the pension list, in pursuance of Act of 18th March 1818, January 20, 1820. 1820. Repr. Baltimore: G.P.C., 1955.

Senate doc. 55, 16th Cong., 1st sess., ser. 34, v.4. Title on spine of reprint is *Pension list of 1818*, but the list covers 1818-19. This 672p. book is often confused with an earlier publication of 358p. (*see* no.543). In this volume, payments for Sept. 1818-Sept. 1819 are given; no.543 gives payments, etc. for 1818 only.

*490  ———— (Pension roll of 1835) Report from the Secretary of War . . . in relation to the pension establishment of the United States . . . Senate doc. 514, 23rd Cong., 1st sess., ser.249-51. 3v. 1835. Repr. Baltimore: G.P.C., 1968.
Note that the reprint is in 4v.: v.1, New England states; v.2, Mid-Atlantic states; v.3, Southern states; v.4, Mid-Western states. Most complete roll of Revolutionary pensioners. Has service records of 75,000 officers and soldiers.

REVOLUTIONARY WAR

491  **Balch, Thomas.** The French in America during the War of Independence of the United States, 1777-83. 2v. 1891-95. Repr. Boston: Gregg, 1972.
Many names with full data.

492  British mercantile claims, 1775-1803. In *The Virginia genealogist*, v.6- , 1962- (in progress).
From reports in the Public Record Office, London. Claims of British property confiscated in the American Revolution. Many names.

493  **Brunk, Gerald R.,** and **Lehman, J. O.** A guide to select Revolutionary War records pertaining to Mennonites and other pacifist groups in southeastern Pennsylvania and Maryland 1775-1800. Lancaster, Pa.: Mennonite Archives and Libraries, 1974.
A slight but good publication. Deals with Berks, Bucks, Lancaster, and Philadelphia counties militia. Many names.

494  **Coke, Daniel P.** The Royal Commission on the Losses and Services of American Loyalists, 1783-85. Ed. by Hugh E. Egerton. 1915. Repr. New York: Arno Pr., 1969.

## United States

**495** **Dandridge, Danske.** American prisoners of the Revolution. 1911. Repr. Baltimore: G.P.C., 1967.
Lists about 8,000 names: those who were prisoners on board the "Old Jersey," and some from other lists.

**496** **D.A.R.** Annual reports. v.1– , 1899– . Washington, D.C.: The Society.
Much biographical data of Revolutionary War participants, muster rolls, list, graves; 5th report (1903– ) gives full data of graves located by various D.A.R. chapters.

**497** ——— Index to the burials of Revolutionary War soldiers. In the *Annual report of the National Soc. of the D.A.R.*
Brigham Young University Library has card file.

**498** ——— Lineage books. v.1–166, 1890–1921. Washington, D.C., 1895–1939.
Names of 25,000 Revolutionary ancestors and 160,000 Daughters.

**499** ——— Index of the rolls of honor (ancestor's index), in the Lineage books. 1916–40. Repr. 4v. in 2. Baltimore: G.P.C., 1972.
Index covers v.1–160 only. Quickest guide to Revolutionary ancestors and descendants.

**500** ——— Magazine. v.1– , 1892– . Washington, D.C.: D.A.R.
Titled *American monthly magazine,* v.1–42; *Daughters of the American Revolution magazine,* v.43–71; *National historical magazine,* v.71–80.

**501** ——— Genealogical guide: master index of genealogy in the *D.A.R. magazine.* v.1–84, 1892–1950. Compiled by Elizabeth Benton Chapter, D.A.R., Missouri, Kansas City. Washington, D.C., 1951.

**502** ——— Supplement to Genealogical guide: master index of genealogy in the D.A.R. magazine, v.85–89, 1950–55. Compiled by Elizabeth Benton Chapter, D.A.R., Missouri, Kansas City. Washington, D.C., 1956.
Surname indexes refer to the portion of the magazine headed "Genealogical Department," formerly called "Genealogical notes and queries."

**503** ——— ——— v.91–101, 1957–67, indexed by Martha P. Miller and J. F. Dorman. Washington, D.C.: Mary Washington Chapter, Alexandria, 1971.

**504** ——— ——— v.100–104, 1966–70. Compiled by Elaine Walker. Spokane, Wash.: Eastern Washington Genealogical Soc., 1974.

**505** ——— Marked graves of Revolutionary soldiers and patriots, as reported to the office of the Historian General . . . In *Daughters of the American Revolution magazine,* v.103– , 1969– .

**\*506** ——— Patriot index. Washington, D.C.: D.A.R., 1966.

**\*507** ——— ——— 1st supplement. Washington, D.C.: D.A.R., 1969.

**\*508** ——— ——— 2nd supplement. Washington, D.C.: D.A.R., 1973.

**\*509** **Deutrich, Mabel E.** Preliminary inventory of the War Department collection of Revolutionary War records. *Record group* 93, no.144. rev. by Howard H. Wehmann. Washington, D.C.: National Archives, 1970.

**510** **Draper, Lyman C.** King's Mountain and its heroes: history of the Battle of King's Mountain, Oct. 7, 1780, and the events which led to it. 1881. Repr. Baltimore: G.P.C., 1970.
Based on material gathered over a 40-year period from survivors of the engagement, their descendants and contemporary narratives and original documents; *see also* no.546.

**511** **Eardley-Wilmot, John.** Historical view of the Commission for Enquiring into the Losses, Services, and Claims of American Loyalists at the close of the war between England and her colonies in 1783, with an account of the compensation granted to them by Parliament in 1785 and 1788. 1815. Repr. Boston: Gregg, 1972.
Contains the claims of American loyalists

## Military and Pension Lists

at the close of the Revolutionary War, with details of compensation.

**512  Eelking, Max von.** The German allied troops in the North American War of Independence, 1776-83. Transl. and abridged from the German by J. G. Rosengarten. 1893. Repr. Baltimore: G.P.C., 1969; New York: Lenox Hill (Burt Franklin), 1971; New York: Haskell House, 1968.

Original German ed. was published in 2v. in 1863. Haskell repr. is from the 1933 printing. 1,500 names. Standard work on the Hessian officers who were British subsidiary troops during the Revolutionary War.

**513  Ellet, Elizabeth F.** The women of the American Revolution. 3v. 1848-50. Repr. New York: Haskell House, 1968.

Various editions in 2v. and 3v. issues.

**514  France.** Ministère des Affaires Étrangères. Les combattants français de la guerre américaine, 1778-83 . . . Senate doc. 77, 58th Cong., 2nd sess. 1903-4. 1905. Repr. Baltimore: G.P.C., 1969.

French participation in the Revolutionary War. The Government Printing Office published an edition with an index. The French ed. has same title but is unindexed. French officers, sailors, and soldiers.

**515  Godfrey, Carlos E.** The Commander-in-Chief's Guard: Revolutionary War. 1904. Repr. Baltimore: G.P.C., 1972.

Rosters and service records of over 350 officers and men who formed the personal guard of General Washington.

**516  Heitman, Francis B.** Historical register of officers of the Continental Army during the War of the Revolution, April 1775 to December 1783. New rev. enl. ed. 1914. Repr. Baltimore: G.P.C., 1973.

Contains service records and various supplementary lists of 15,000 Revolutionary War officers. Addenda by R. H. Kelby, 1932, are included in the reprint. Standard reference work.

**517  Hessische Truppen im amerikanischen Unabhängigkeitskrieg (Hetrina).** Index nach Familiennamen. Band 1. Marburg: from St. Louis Genealogical Soc., 1972.

no.10 of *Der Archivschule Marburg-Institut für Archivswissenschaft*. Contains details of the four Hessen-Kasse grenadier battalions formed for the American campaign at the request of the British. 10,000 names. 1st of 4v.

**519  Jones, Alexander.** The Cymry of '76. 2nd. ed. 1855. Repr. Baltimore: G.P.C., 1968; San Francisco: R. and E. Research Assoc., 1969.

Welshmen and their descendants of the American Revolution. One of the few printed sources of the part played by Welshmen in the war. Notices also of prominent persons of Welsh ancestry, with a section on surnames.

**520  Kaminkow, Marion J.,** and **Kaminkow, Jack.** Mariners of the American Revolution. Baltimore, 1967. Available from Tuttle, Rutland, Vt.

Primarily concerns the records of men captured by the British. First attempt at collection of the extant manuscript and printed material on privateersmen.

**521  Lossing, Benson J.** The pictorial fieldbook of the Revolution. 2v. 1859. Repr. Rutland, Vt.: Tuttle, 1972; 1851 ed. repr. New York: Books for Libraries Pr., Freeport, N.Y., 1969; New Orleans, La.: Polyanthos, 1973; Spartanburg, S.C.: Reprint Co., 1969.

Extensive index containing thousands of names. Well illustrated. Mostly of 13 original states and Canada.

**522  Lowell, Edward J.** The Hessians: and the other German auxiliaries of Great Britain in the Revolutionary War. 1884. Repr. Port Washington, N.Y.: Kennikat Pr., 1965; Williamstown, Mass.: Corner House, 1970.

**522a  Loyalists.** Those sympathetic to the cause of the Crown during the American Revolution rather than to that of the revolutionaries. Many went to the West Indies and Florida, but four-fifths of the settlers in upper Canada (now Ontario) came from the American colonies. The most useful bibliographies of printed sources on loyalists in the American Revolution will be found in Greenwood (no.244), pp.440-42,

## 523 United States

and in the *American Antiquarian Soc. Proc.,* v.82, pp.245–48 (no.4018), and in Kirkham (no.476), pp.313–15. Loyalist works, *see also* Canada, no.4014–37.

**523 MacLean, John P.** An historical account of the settlements of Scotch Highlanders in America prior to the peace of 1783; together with notices of Highland regiments and biographical sketches. 1900. Repr. Baltimore: G.P.C., 1968.

First study devoted exclusively to Scotch Highlanders from Northern Ireland who came here up to the time of the Revolution. Lists of French and Indian and Revolutionary War soldiers, petitioners, etc.

**524 National Genealogical Society.** Abstracts of Revolutionary War pension applications. In *National Genealogical Soc. quarterly,* v.17–41, 1929–52.

v.17–24, 1929–36 by Mrs. Jessie McC. Casanova; v.25–32, 1936–44, compiler unknown; v.33–40, 1944–51, by Gaius M. Brumbaugh; v.40–41, 1951–52, by Roberta P. Wakefield. Continued desultorily thereafter by Mabel Van D. Baer in later vols. Based wholly on affidavits accepted by U.S. Government and state authorities. An index to the pensions was published in 1966; *see* no.525.

**\*525** ——— Index to Revolutionary War pension applications . . . *National Genealogical Soc. special publ.* 32. Washington, D.C. 1966.

65,000 applicants listed, each with reference to source. Comprehensive work on Revolutionary pension and applications, as distinct from payments granted. Popularly known as "The Hoyt index," because the work was begun by him. Veterans and their widows who applied for pensions and bounty warrants. Rev. ed. being published in 1975.

**526** ——— ——— Corrections by Sadye Giller. *National Genealogical Soc. special publ.* 31. Washington, D.C., 1965.

**527 New-York Historical Society.** Muster and pay rolls of the War of the Revolution, 1775–83. 2v. *Collections of the New-York Historical Soc. fund ser.* 47–48, 1914–15. New York, 1916.

Arranged by artillery, followed by the Continental regiments, line and militia of the various states. Canadian, Connecticut, Maryland, Massachusetts, New York, New Jersey artillery, Continental infantry; New York, North Carolina, Pennsylvania, Rhode Island, South Carolina, Virginia troops.

**528 Newman, Debra L.** List of black servicemen compiled from the War Department collection of Revolutionary War records. *Special list* 36. Washington, D.C.: National Archives, 1974.

Gives name, regiment, rank, roll and card number of the microfilm.

**529 Norton, Mary B.** The British-Americans: the Loyalist exiles in England 1774–89. Boston: Little Brown, 1972.

**530 O'Brien, Michael J.** A hidden phase of American history: Ireland's part in America's struggle for liberty. 1919. Repr. Baltimore: G.P.C., 1973.

Over 5,000 soldiers are named, with details of Irish immigration and separate chapters on Irish settlements in New York, Pennsylvania, Virginia, the Carolinas, and Georgia; Revolutionary War period.

**531 Peterson, Clarence S.** Known military dead during the American Revolutionary War, 1775–83. 1959. Repr. Baltimore: G.P.C., 1967.

Alphabetically arranged list of over 10,000 names, with full military data.

**532 (Revolutionary War, rosters and lists).** A bibliography published in *Magazine of bibliographies* 1973–74 (no. 123). Fort Worth, Tex.

**533 Ryerson, Adolphus E.** The loyalists of America and their times: 1620 to 1816. 2v. 1880. Repr. New York: Haskell House, 1970.

**534 Sabine, Lorenzo.** Biographical sketches of loyalists of the American Revolution. 2nd enl. ed. 2v. 1864. Repr. with new critical introduction by R. A. Brown. Port Washington, N.Y.: Kennikat Pr., 1966.

Much genealogical information.

**535 Saffell, William T. R.** Records of the Revolutionary War; containing the military and financial correspondence of distinguished officers, names of the officers and privates of regiments, companies, and corps, with dates of their commissions and enlistments . . . 3rd ed. 1894. Repr. (Bound with Index to Saffell's *List of Virginia soldiers in the Revolution,* by J. T. McAllister. 1913.) Baltimore: G.P.C., 1969.

Names of officers and privates and lists of distinguished prisoners.

**536   Smith, Clifford N.** Brunswick deserter-immigrants of the American Revolution. *German-American genealogical research monographs* 1. Thomson, Ill.: Heritage House, 1974.

Troops served mainly in Canada and northern New York. 1,500 names with useful data. Gives German birthplace. List of all known deserters from the Braunschweig (Brunswick) contingent of mercenaries serving with British forces.

**537**   ———  Mercenaries from Ansbach and Bayreuth, Germany who remained in America after the Revolution. *German-American genealogical research monographs* 2. Thomson, Ill.: Heritage House, 1974.

List of all known deserters in the U.S. and Canada. List of names taken from Staedtler's: *Die Ansbach-Bayreuth Truppen in amerikanischen Unabhängigkeitskreig, 1777–83.* Names have been taken from alphabetical to a soundex arrangement.

**538   Sons of the American Revolution.**
A national register compiled by Louis H. Cornish, collated and ed. by A. H. Clarke. New York [1902].

**539   U.S. Dept. of the Interior.** Rejected or suspended applications for Revolutionary War pensions. With an added index to states. Senate *Executive doc.* 37: 1–462, 1851–52, 32nd Cong., 1st sess., ser.618, v.7. 1852. Repr. with an added index to states. Baltimore: G.P.C., 1969.

Originally published as *Report of the Secretary of the Interior. With a statement of rejected or suspended applications for pensions.* Title supplied by publisher. Names and residences of 11,000 soldiers or their widows who applied for pensions under the acts of 1832, 1836, 1838.

**540   U.S. Dept. of State.** A census of pensioners for Revolutionary or military services: with their names, ages, and places of residence taken in 1840. 1841. Repr. Baltimore: G.P.C., 1967.

Taken from the 6th census. Over 25,000 living in 1840. Names and heads of families with whom they were residing.

**541**   ——— ——— A general index. Prepared by the Genealogical Soc. of the Church of Jesus Christ of Latter-day Saints, Salt Lake City. Baltimore, 1965.

This and no.540 were repr. in 1v. in 1974 by G.P.C., Baltimore.

**542   U.S. Pay Dept.** (War Dept.) Register of the certificates issued by John Pierce, Esquire, Paymaster General and Commissioner of Army Accounts for the U.S. to officers and soldiers of the Continental Army under Act of July 4, 1783. Contained in *17th report of the D.A.R.,* 1915, pp.147–712. Repr. Baltimore: G.P.C., 1973.

One of the most authoritative Revolutionary lists containing over 93,000 names, with sums owed to them. Sometimes referred to as *Pierce's Register.*

**543   U.S. War Dept.** Revolutionary pensioners (of 1813). A transcript of the pension list of the United States of 1813. Repr. of letter from the Secretary of War, communicating a transcript of the pension list of the U.S. . . . June 1, 1813. 1813. Baltimore: G.P.C., 1959.

Only 47 pp., but invaluable. Title supplied by reprinter. 1,800 pensioners, with data.

**544**   ——— (Revolutionary pensioners of 1818). Message from the President of the United States, transmitting a report of the Secretary of War . . . "to cause to be laid before them a list of all the pensioners of the United States . . ." 1818. Repr. Baltimore: G.P.C., 1959.

Gives payments to 1818 (no.489). Spine and half title supplied by reprinter. 3,814 invalid pensioners, 1,681 widows and orphans listed. Senate doc. 170, 15th Cong., 1st sess., ser.3, v.2.

**545   Waldenmaier, Nellie P.** Some of the earliest oaths of allegiance to the

United States of America. Lancaster, Pa., 1944.
Has alphabetical list.

546   **White, Katherine K.** King's Mountain men. 1924. Repr. Baltimore: G.P.C., 1970.
Story of battle with biographical sketches and records of Revolutionary soldiers who were from the Carolinas, Tennessee, and Virginia; *see also* no.510.

546a  **Wingo, Elizabeth B.** Revolutionary War and War of 1812 applications for pensions, bounty land warrants and heirs of deceased pensioners. Norfolk, Va.: The Author, 1964.
Supplements other pension lists.

WAR OF 1812

547   **General Society of the War of 1812.** Register. Ed. by Frederick I. Ordway, Jr. Washington, D.C., 1972. From Alan Corson, 1034 Nicholson Rd., Winnewood, Pa. 19096.
Complete lineage of each member, name index with over 10,000 entries.

548   **National Society, United States Daughters of 1812.** 1812 ancestor index, 1892-1970. Ed. by Eleanor S. Galvin. Washington, D.C.: The Society, 1970.
Excellent ancestor index giving name of veteran, place and date of birth and death, wife's name, children, with names of their spouses. Rank and military unit given.

549   **Peterson, Clarence S.** Known military dead during the War of 1812. Baltimore, ca. 1955.

550   **Wingo, Elizabeth B.** Revolutionary War and War of 1812 applications for pensions, bounty land warrants and heirs of deceased pensioners. Norfolk, Va.: The Author, 1964.
Supplements other pension lists.

MEXICAN WAR

550a  **Peterson, Clarence S.** Known military dead during the Mexican War, 1846-48. Baltimore, 1957.

550b  **Robarts, William H.** Mexican War veterans. A complete roster of the regular and volunteer troops in the war between the United States and Mexico, from 1846-48. Washington, D.C., 1887.

CIVIL WAR

551   **Bethel, Elizabeth.** War Department collection of Confederate records. *National Archives preliminary inventory* 101. *Record group* 109. Washington, D.C.: National Archives, 1957.

552   **The Confederate veteran.** v.1-40, 1893-1932. Nashville, Tenn.

553   ———— Index, v.1-40. Dayton, Ohio: Morningside Bookshop, 1972.
Contains reminiscences, obituaries, etc. v.1 repr. by Blue and Gray Pr., Nashville, Tenn. Indexes are in each vol. and not composite.

554   **Dornbusch, Charles E.** Regimental publications and personal narratives of the Civil War. v.1-3. New York: New York Public Library, 1961-72.
v.1 was issued in 7pts., and concerned Connecticut, Illinois, Iowa, Kansas, Maine, Massachusetts, Minnesota, Michigan, New Hampshire, New Jersey, New York, Ohio, Pennsylvania, Rhode Island, Vermont, and Wisconsin. v.2 is entitled, *Military bibliography of the Civil War;* v.3, *General references, armed forces, and campaigns and battles.*

555   **Dyer, Frederick H.** A compendium of the War of the Rebellion. 3v. 1908. Repr. New York: Yoseloff, 1959.
Regimental index and regimental histories. Union only; no volume exists for the regiments of the South.

556   **Evans, Clement A.** Confederate military history; a library of Confederate states history . . . 12v. Atlanta, Ga.: 1899.
At end of volumes are additional sketches illustrating the services of officers and privates and patriotic citizens. v.2, Maryland, pp.185-447; West Virginia, pp.139-206; v.3, Virginia, pp.693-1295; v.4, North Carolina, pp.335-813; v.5, South Carolina, pp.425-931.

557 **Groene, Bertram H.** Tracing your Civil War ancestor. Winston-Salem, N.C.: John F. Blair, 1973.
Most useful for nonprofessional genealogists. Good bibliography with locations of records.

558 **Hamersly, Lewis R. and Co.** Officers of the Army and Navy (regular and volunteer) who served in the Civil War. Philadelphia, 1894.

559 **Pompey, Sherman L.** Burial lists of members of Union and Confederate military units. Kingsburg, Calif., 1971.

560 **Powell, William H.,** and **Shippen, E.** Officers of the Army and Navy (regular) who served in the Civil War. Philadelphia, 1892.

561 ——— ——— (volunteer). Philadelphia, 1893.

562 **Ransom, John L.** Andersonville diary; escape, and list of dead, with name, company, regiment, date of death and number of grave in cemetery. 1883. Repr. New York: Haskell House, 1974.

563 **Ulibarri, George S.,** and **Goggin, D. T.** Research relating to Civil War claims, United States and Great Britain. *National Archives preliminary inventory* 135. *Record group* 76. Washington, D.C.: National Archives, 1962.

564 **U.S. Adjutant General's Office.** Official Army register of the volunteer force of the United States Army for the years 1861, '62, '63, '64, '65. 8pts. Washington, D.C., 1865-67.
A roster of volunteer officers of regiments.
Pt.1: New England states (Connecticut, Maine, Massachusetts, New Hampshire, Rhode Island, Vermont.) 1865.
Pt.2: New York and New Jersey. 1865.
Pt.3: Pennsylvania, Delaware, Maryland, District of Columbia. 1865.
Pt.4: Arkansas, Kentucky, Tennessee, Virginia, West Virginia; Federal regiments raised in the South: North and South Carolina, Georgia, Florida, Alabama, Mississippi, Tennessee, Louisiana, Texas. 1865.
Pt.5: Ohio, Michigan. 1865.
Pt.6: Illinois, Indiana. 1865.
Pt.7: Iowa, Kansas, Minnesota, Mississippi, Wisconsin, Missouri, Nevada, Oregon, California. 1865.
Pt.8: Colorado, Dakota, Tennessee, Nebraska, New Mexico, Washington; colored troops, volunteers. 1867.

565 **U.S. Navy War Records Office.** Officers in the Confederate States Navy, 1861-65. 1898. Revised with title, "Register of the Confederate States Navy, 1861-65." Washington, D.C., 1931.

566 **U.S. Quartermaster's Dept.** Roll of honor. Names of soldiers who died in defense of the Union, interred in the National cemeteries [and elsewhere]. no.1-27. Washington, D.C., 1866-71.
Thousands of names with complete data.

567 **U.S. Record and Pension Office.** List of libraries, organizations, and educational institutions in the several states and territories of the United States, supplied with the official records of the Union and Confederate Armies. Washington, D.C., 1903.
Though published over 70 years ago, the list is still useful.

568 **U.S. War Dept.** Official records of the Union and Confederate Armies in the War of the Rebellion. 128v. Washington, D.C., 1901. Repr. 127v. in 69v. Gettysburg, Pa.: National Historical Soc., 1971-72.

569 ——— General index with additions and corrections. Indexed by John S. Moodey. Gettysburg, Pa.: National Historical Soc., 1972.
The reprint has the title, *War of the Rebellion; a compilation . . .*

570 **U.S. War Dept.** Official records of the Union and Confederate Navies in the War of the Rebellion. 31v. Washington, D.C., 1897-1927.

571 ——— Index. 1927. Repr. New York, 1961.

572 **Vasvary, Edmund.** Lincoln's Hungarian heroes, the participation of

Hungarians in the Civil War, 1861-65. Washington, D.C., 1939.
Includes roster.

573   **Wolf, Simon.** The American Jew as patriot, soldier, and citizen. Ed. by L. E. Levy. Philadelphia, 1895.
Lists of Jewish soldiers in the Civil War.

## *Areas*

⁘ This section includes titles which could not be assigned to general reference or to individual states. The divisions are New England; The South; and the remainder of the United States.

NEW ENGLAND

574   **Baker, Mary E.** Bibliography of lists of New England soldiers. *New England historic and genealogical register,* ser.A, 36. Boston, 1911.
Limited to printed books and pamphlets cataloged in the New York state libraries.

575   **Banks, Charles E.** The Winthrop Fleet of 1630. 1930. Repr. Baltimore: G.P.C., 1972.
Background material on early immigrants; also alphabetical list of families on the *Mary and John.* Perhaps those who came with John Winthrop on the *Arabella* and her sister vessels are of more importance than those on the *Mayflower.*

576   **Baxter, James P.** The pioneers of New France in New England, with contemporary letters and documents. Albany, N.Y., 1894.
Period 1720-25; war with eastern Indians, depredation by French and Indians between New England and Nova Scotia.

577   **Bolton, Charles K.** The real founders of New England: stories of their life along the coast, 1602-28. 1929. Repr. Baltimore: G.P.C., 1974.
Data on New England settlers and settlements which predate the *Mayflower* landing. Appendixes especially valuable; tentative list of old planters in New England before 1628; early settlements and their founders, and present place names corresponding to early names mentioned in text.

578   **Bolton, Ethel S.** Immigrants to New England, 1700-75. 1931. Repr. Baltimore: G.P.C., 1973.
2,250 immigrants, with genealogical data.

579   **Coldham, Peter W.** Genealogical gleanings in England. In *National Genealogical Soc. quarterly,* v.59- , 1971- .
English emigrants to America. Similar to Waters (no.610).

580   **Crawford, Mary C.** In the days of the Pilgrim Fathers. 1921. Repr. Detroit, Mich.: Singing Tree Pr., 1973.
Complete study of the Pilgrims.

581   **Currer-Briggs, Noel.** Colonial settlers and English adventurers: Abstracts of legal proceedings in 17th-century English and Dutch courts relating to immigrant families. Baltimore: G.P.C., 1971.
Enables tracing the English and Dutch origins of colonial New England settlers.

582   **Cutter, William R.** New England families, genealogical and memorial ... 4v., 1913; 4v., 1914; 4v.?, 3rd ser., 1915. Paging continuous in each series. New York, 1913-15.
"A record of the achievements of people in the making of a commonwealth and the founding of a nation." 12v. in all, but few libraries appear to hold complete sets. Consolidated index of this and other Cutter works, *see* no.593.

583   **Downs, Winfield S.** Men of New England. 6v. New York, 1941-54.

584   **Eliot, John.** A biographical dictionary, containing a brief account of the first settlers, and other eminent characters, among the magistrates, ministers, literary and worthy men, in New England. Salem, Mass., 1809.

585   **Flagg, Ernest.** Genealogical notes on the founding of New England. 1926. Repr. Baltimore: G.P.C., 1973.
Author demonstrates his connection with 172 New Englanders, each of whom is worked back 5 generations, showing all posterity and collateral connections.

586    Forbes, Harriette (M.) Gravestones of early New England and the men who made them, 1653–1800. 1927. Repr. New York: Da Capo Pr., 1967; Princeton, N.J.: Pyne Pr. (dist. by Scribner, New York), 1973.

587    ——— New England diaries, 1602–1800; a descriptive catalogue of diaries, orderly books and sea journals. 1923. Repr. New York: Russell & Russell, 1967.

588    The genealogical advertiser. A quarterly magazine of family history. Ed. by Lucy H. Greenlaw. v.1–4, 1898–1901. Repr. 4v. in 1. Baltimore: G.P.C., 1974.

Misleading title. Contains vital records, court files, state, county, town, church records, wills, etc., chiefly 17th to 19th centuries. 15,000 names, mainly in New England.

589    Genealogical magazine. v.1–18 (v.1–ser.4, v.4). Salem, Mass., 1893–1917.

Known variously as *Salem Press historical and genealogical record; Putnam's Monthly historical magazine; Putnam's Historical magazine;* and *Genealogical quarterly magazine.* Outstandingly good New England journal.

590    Hayward, John. The New England gazetteer: containing descriptions of all the states, counties, and towns in New England. 14th ed. Boston, 1841.

590a    Hills, Leon C. History and genealogy of the Mayflower planters and first comers to ye olde colonie. 2v. New York, 1936, 1941.

591    Holmes, Frank R. Directory of the ancestral heads of New England families, 1620–1700. 1923. Repr. Baltimore: G.P.C., 1974.

15,000 names of those heads of families who arrived in New England in the seventeenth century.

592    Hühner, Leon. The Jews of New England (other than Rhode Island) prior to 1800. West Cornwall, Conn.: Cornwall Pr., 1973.

Offprinted from *American Jewish Historical Soc. publ.* 11, 1903. Well-supported references.

593    Ireland, Norma (O), and Irving, W. Cutter index. A consolidated index of Cutter's nine genealogy series. Fallbrook, Calif.: Ireland Indexing Service, 1973.

3,150 names as found in 33v. of Cutter books in Massachusetts, New York, Connecticut and New England, all by William R. Cutter.

594    Jeffrey, William, Jr. Early New England court records: a bibliography of published materials on early New England court records. *Boston Public Library quarterly,* 1954. Issued separately for Ames Foundation, Harvard Law School, Cambridge, Mass., 1954.

595    Kuhns, Maude P. The "Mary and John"; a story of the founding of Dorchester, Massachusetts, 1630. 1943. Repr. Rutland, Vt.: Tuttle, 1971. References good; 56 charts; important list.

596    Mayflower descendant: a quarterly magazine of Pilgrim history and genealogy. v.1–34, no.3, 1899–1937. Boston.

597    ——— Index to persons. 3v. Boston: Massachusetts Soc. of Mayflower Descendants, 1959–62.

598    New England Historic Genealogical Society. Memorial biographies. v.1–9, 1845–97. Boston, 1880–1908.

*599    New England historical and genealogical register. v.1– , 1847– . Boston: New England Historic Genealogical Soc.

Oldest continuing American genealogical periodical in existence. Authoritative and respected.

600    ——— Index of persons: v.1–50 (1847–96). 3v. 1907. Repr. Baltimore: G.P.C., 1972.

601    ——— Index of places: v.1–50 (1847–96). 1908–11. Repr. (with no.600). Baltimore: G.P.C., 1972.

602    ——— Index of subjects: v.1–50 (1847–96). 1908. Repr. (with no.601). Baltimore: G.P.C., 1972.

**603** ——— Index to genealogies and pedigrees. v.1-50, 1847-96. Boston, 1896.

**604** ——— Index (abridged). By Margaret W. Parsons. Marlborough, Mass., 1959.
Covers v.51-112 (1897-1958). Not authorized by Society. Genealogy, geography, topography.

**605 Peirce, Ebenezer W.** Peirce's Colonial lists: civil . . . military and professional lists of Plymouth and Rhode Island colonies, etc., 1621-1700. 1881. Repr. Baltimore: G.P.C., 1968.

**605a Plymouth church records, 1620-1859.** 2v. New York, 1920-23.
Original records of First Church in Plymouth.

**606 Sanford, Edwin G.** The Pilgrim Fathers and Plymouth Colony: a bibliographical survey of books and articles published during the past fifty years [1920-70]. A contribution to the 50th anniversary observance of the landing of the Pilgrims at Plymouth, Massachusetts in 1620. Boston: Boston Public Lib., 1970.
The supplement to the bibliography compiled by Mary A. Tenney, entitled *The Pilgrims;* see no.609.

**607 Savage, James.** A genealogical dictionary of the first settlers of New England, showing three generations of those who came before May 1692, on the basis of Farmer's *Register* (no.328). 4v. 1860-62. Repr. with additions. Baltimore: G.P.C., 1969.
Probably the greatest work on genealogy ever compiled for the New England area. Complemented by Whittemore (no.337). v.4 of repr. has *Genealogical notes and errata* . . . by C. H. Dall, 1881; *Genealogical cross index* . . . by O. P. Dexter. 1884.

**608 Talcott, Sebastian V.** Genealogical notes of New York and New England families. 1883. Repr. Baltimore: G.P.C., 1973.
18,000 individuals, taken from Dutch Bible records, and from records of state, county and town archives. Well indexed, but use with care.

**609 Tenney, Mary A.** The Pilgrims: a selected history of works on the Pilgrims of the city of Boston: a contribution to the tercentenary celebration. Boston, 1920.
For supplement, *see* no.606.

**610 Waters, Henry F. G.** Genealogical gleanings in England. 2v. 1901. (With) New series, *A-Anyon* 1901, 1907. Repr. Baltimore: G.P.C., 1969.
Abstracts of wills relating to early American families, with genealogical notes and pedigrees constructed from wills and other records. Originally published in *New England historical and genealogical register,* 1883-99.

**611** ——— ——— Index to testators . . . By William S. Appleton. Boston: The Society, 1898.

**612 Willison, George F.** Saints and strangers, being the lives of the Pilgrim Fathers and their families, with friends and foes. 1945. Repr. North Adams, Mass.: New Englandiana, 1973.
Includes 9 passenger lists, and appendix of officers of the Old Colony and the Pilgrim Church.

**613 Wright, Norman E.** Genealogy in America. v.1. Massachusetts, Connecticut, and Maine. Salt Lake City: Deseret, 1968.
A guide and manual.

**614 Young, Alexander.** Chronicles of the Pilgrim Fathers of the Colony of Plymouth, from 1602-25. 2nd ed. 1844. Repr. Baltimore: G.P.C., 1974.
Taken from documents written by the Fathers.

## THE SOUTH

✣ *See also* specific southern states.

**614a Andrews, Johnnie,** and **Higgins, W. D.** Creole Mobile. A compendium of the families of the Gulf Coast, 1702-1813. Prichard, Ala.: Bienville Historical Soc., 1974.
3,500 names, vital records between Santa

Fe and St. Augustine; priests, Indians, Negroes, mulattoes, and quadroons.

**615 Armstrong, Zella** (and **French, Janie P.C.**). Notable southern families. 6v. 1918-33. Repr. 6v. in 3. Baltimore: G.P.C., 1974; in 6v. Spartanburg, S. C.: Reprint Co., 1974.

v.1-3 treated 57 families; v.4 was devoted solely to the Sevier family; v.5 to the Crockett family (by Armstrong and French); v.6, Doak family, by French. Useful, but not authoritative.

**616 Boddie, John B.** Historical southern families. v.1- (in progress). Redwood City [and elsewhere], 1957- . Dist. by G.P.C., Baltimore.

After Mr. Boddie's death in 1965, Mrs. Boddie continued the work. As each volume goes out of print, the distributors reprint and reissue. More than 700 families have been treated, with thousands of names resulting. v.19 last published in 1974. Useful, but treat with care.

**617 Cheek, John C.** Selected tombstone inscriptions from Alabama, South Carolina, and other southern states. n.p., 1970.

7,000 primarily in Alabama, South Carolina, and Mississippi.

**618 The Christian index.** v.1- , 1822- . Atlanta, Ga.: Baptist Convention of the State of Georgia.

Contains a wealth of southern material. For marriages published in it for 1828-55, *see* no.1219.

**619 Collier, Mary (Wootten).** Biographies of representative women in the South, 1861-1920. 5v. Atlanta, Ga.: 1920-29.

**620 Crozier, William A.** A key to southern pedigrees; being a comprehensive guide to the colonial ancestry of families in the states of Virginia, Maryland, Georgia, North and South Carolina, Kentucky, Tennessee, West Virginia, and Alabama. *Virginia county records* 8. 1911. Repr. Baltimore: G.P.C., 1971.

7,000 references.

**621 Cumming, William P.** The southeast in early maps, with an annotated check list of printed and manuscript regional and local maps of southeastern North America during the colonial period. Chapel Hill, N.C.: Univ. of North Carolina Pr., 1962.

Although not primarily interesting to genealogists, it has some use and it shows cartographic developmental history.

**622 D. A. R. Tennessee. Fort Assumption Chapter, Memphis.** Mid-south Bible records. 2v. Memphis, Tenn.: The Chapter, 1970-73.

Tennessee, Mississippi, North and South Carolina, Alabama, Georgia, Virginia, Kentucky, and Arkansas records.

**623 Deep south genealogical quarterly.** v.1- , 1963- . Mobile, Ala.: Mobile Genealogical Soc.

Covers Alabama, Florida, Arkansas, and Mississippi.

**624 Family puzzlers.** v.1- , 1970- . Danielsville, Ga.: Heritage Papers.

Mainly southern. Queries and answers format genealogical magazine; exchange, workshops, etc.

**625 Francis, Elizabeth W.,** and **Moore, E. S.** Lost links: new recordings of old data from many states. Births, marriages, deaths, census records, deeds and wills from southern states. Nashville, Tenn., 1945.

Valuable book of family clues.

**626 Hardy, Stella P.** Colonial families of the southern states of America. A history and genealogy of colonial families who settled in the colonies prior to the Revolution. Repr. with revisions and additions by the author. Baltimore: G.P.C., 1974.

**627 Henderson, Archibald.** The conquest of the old southwest. 1920. Repr. Spartanburg, S.C.: Reprint Co., 1974.

Story of the pioneers of Virginia, the Carolinas, Tennessee, and Kentucky from 1740 to 1790.

**628 Ladd, Edward J.** Atlas and outline history of the southeastern United

States. Fort Worth, Tex.: Miran, 1973 (or from Author, Box 29, Fort Payne, Ala.)

Outline history of Virginia, North and South Carolina, Tennessee, Kentucky, Georgia, Florida, and Alabama, Indian acquisitions. Maps of various years.

**629 Lester, Memory A.** Old southern Bible records. Transcriptions of births, deaths and marriages from family Bibles, chiefly of the 18th and 19th centuries. Baltimore: G.P.C., 1974.

581 southern family Bibles, 15,000 individuals; originally compiled from family and archival sources and assembled in 7 typescript vols. Ranges all over the South, from Maryland to Mississippi.

**630 McDermott, John F.** The Spanish in the Mississippi Valley 1762–1804. Urbana, Ill.: Univ. of Illinois Pr., 1974.

**631 Menn, Joseph K.** The large slaveholders of the deep South. 2v. Austin, Tex.: Pelican Pub. Co. of New Orleans, La., 1964.

**632 National Genealogical Society.** Special aids to genealogical research on southern families. 2nd pr. *National Genealogical Soc. special publ.* 15. Washington, D.C.: The Society, 1962.

Best feature is that it gives primary and secondary sources for Kentucky, South Carolina and Georgia, from voters, oaths of allegiance, census, jury lists, rent rolls.

**633 Southern genealogist's exchange quarterly.** v.1– , 1957– . Jacksonville, Fla.: Aurora C. Shaw, editor.

All numbers are in print.

**634 Southern Historical Society papers.** v.1–38, 1876–1910; new ser. v.1–14, 1914–59. Richmond, Va.

**635** —— —— Author and subject index, v.1–28 by Kate P. Miner. 1913. Repr. Dayton, Ohio: Morningside Bookshop, 1970.

Index originally in *Virginia State library bull.* 6.

**636 Southern Historical Association.** Publications, v.1–11, 1897–1907. Washington, D.C.

Some family histories, genealogies, etc.

OTHER AREAS

**637 Bowden, Jocelyn.** Private land claims in the southwest. 6v. Houston, Tex., 1969.

**637a Carter, Clarence E.** The territory northwest of the river Ohio, 1787–1803. *Territorial papers of the U.S.* 2–3. 1934. Repr. A.M.S. Press, 1973.

List of persons signing petitions, memorials, etc.

**638 Catholic church records of the Pacific northwest:** Vancouver, v.1–2 (in 1) and Stellamaris Mission. Transl. by Mikell L. W. Warner. Annotated by H. D. Munnick. St. Paul, Ore.: French Prairie Pr., 1972.

Baptisms, marriages and burials made by the first Catholic priests in the West from Red River to Port Vancouver, 1838–60. Valuable, since little is known in this area. Of considerable interest to researchers in Oregon, Idaho, Washington, and Canada. Details of Indians who married whites.

**640 Heiss, Willard C.** Guide to research in Quaker records in the Midwest. Indianapolis, Ind., 1962.

**641 Hemry, Larry H.** Some northwest pioneer families . . . Seattle, Wash.: Sudden Print Co., 1969.

**641a Highsmith, Richard M., Jr.,** and **Bard, R.** Atlas of the Pacific northwest. 5th ed. Corvallis: Oregon State Univ. Pr., 1973.

Well-illustrated section on historical development.

**642 Midwest genealogical register.** v.1– , 1966– . Wichita, Kans.: Midwest Genealogical Soc.

Excellent periodical, with many source records.

**643 Midwestern heritage.** v.1– , 1973– . West Allis, Wisc.: Janlen Enterprises.

Contains sections on Kansas, Wisconsin, Minnesota, Illinois, Iowa, Missouri, and Nebraska. Bible records; 5,000 names per number.

**644 Morgan, Dale L., and Hammond, G. P.** A guide to the manuscript collections of the Bancroft Library. v.1, *Pacific and western manuscripts* (except California). Berkeley, Calif.: Univ. of California Pr., 1963.

**645 Nebraska and midwest genealogical record.** v.1–22, 1923–44. Lincoln, Nebr.
Published by Nebraska Genealogical Soc. Excellent records not found elsewhere.

**646 The "Old northwest" genealogical quarterly.** v.1–15, 1898–1912. Columbus, Ohio.
Vigorous genealogical magazine by the "Old northwest" Genealogical Society. Monumental inscriptions, marriage lists, etc.

**647 Southwestern genealogist.** v.1– , 1963– . El Paso, Tex.: The Editor, (5301 Hanawalt Ave., 79903).
Excellent source for listings of microfilmed out-of-print genealogies and source books.

**648 Stine, Thomas O.** Scandinavians on the Pacific. San Francisco: R. and E. Research Assoc., 1968.

**649 Walden, Blanche L.** Pioneer families of the midwest. 2v. Ann Arbor, Mich. [and elsewhere], 1939–41.

**650 Western States Jewish historical quarterly.** v.1– , 1968– . Santa Monica, Calif.: Southern California Jewish Historical Soc.
Has much family history, with many notes on early Jews.

**651 Winther, Oscar Osborne.** A classified bibliography of the periodical literature of the Trans-Mississippi West (1811–1957). Bloomington, Ind.: Indiana Univ. Pr., 1961.

## INDIANS

**652 American Indian Historical Society.** Index to literature on the American Indian. 2v. San Francisco: Indian Historical Pr., 1970–71.

**653 Barry, Louise.** The Kansa Indians and the census of 1843. In *Kansas historical quarterly,* v.39, 1973, pp.478–90.
Full details of 245 families.

**654 Benedict, John D.** Muskogee northwestern Oklahoma, including Muskogee, McIntosh, Wagoner, Cherokee, Sequoyah, Adair, Delaware, Mayes, Rogers, Washington, Nowata, Craig, and Ottawa counties. 3v. Chicago, 1922.

**655 Bonfanti, Leo.** Biographies and legends of the New England Indians. 3v. Wakefield, Mass.: Pride Pub., 1970–72.
Though not strictly a genealogical work, the author has attempted to identify individual Indians by name, with family information given where possible.

**656 Bossu, Jean B.** Travels through that part of North America formerly called Louisiana . . . 2v. London, 1771.
Transl. of 1768 ed., *Nouveaux voyages.* v.1 has historical and personal sketches of southern Indian tribes.

**657 Brayer, Herbert O.** Pueblo Indian land grants of the "Rio Abajo," New Mexico. Albuquerque, N. Mex., 1939.

**658 Bruner, Joseph.** Who's who among Oklahoma Indians. Oklahoma City, Okla., 1928.

**659 Corbitt, Duvon C., and Corbitt, E.** Papers from the Spanish archives relating to Tennessee and the old southwest, 1783–1800. In *The East Tennessee Historical Society's publ.* 9– , 1937– (in progress).
Much Indian material; many names.

**660 Denig, Edwin T.** Five Indian tribes of the upper Missouri. Ed. by John C. Ewers. Norman, Okla.: Univ. of Oklahoma Pr., 1961.
On Sioux, Arickaras, Assiniboines, Crees, and Crows of lower Canada, Montana,

## United States

North and South Dakota, Wyoming, and Nebraska territories. References to tribal relationships, carrying genealogy in some cases 3 or 4 generations.

661   **Dewitz, Paul W. H.** Notable men of Indian Territory at the beginning of the twentieth century, 1904–1905. Muskogee, Okla., 1905.

662   **Drake, Samuel G.** Biography and history of the Indians in North America... 11th ed. Boston, 1851.
First published in 1832 as *Indian biography;* 8th ed., 1841, *The book of the Indians...*

663   **Ewers, John C.** Indian life on the upper Missouri. Norman, Okla.: Univ. of Oklahoma Pr., 1968.
Deals with the Blackfeet, Crows, and Mandans, from early times to the present.

664   **Foreman, Grant.** Advancing the frontier, 1830-60. Norman, Okla.: Univ. of Oklahoma Pr., 1933.
On the settlement of Oklahoma by the different Indian tribes after their removal from the east. Information on military in areas as well as family relationships of some of the more notable Indians. For continuation, *see* no.695.

665   **Gannett, Henry.** A gazetteer of Indian territories. *U.S. Geological Survey bull.* 248. Washington, D.C., 1905.

665a   **Genealogical Society of the Church of Jesus Christ of Latter-day Saints.**
Major genealogical record sources of Indians in the United States. *Research paper,* ser.B, no.2. Salt Lake City: L.D.S., 1968.

666   **Gideon, D. C.** Indian territory, descriptive, biographical and genealogical, including the landed estates, county seats, etc. New York, 1901.
Lists whites and Indians living in the territory.

667   **Hall, Ted B.** Oklahoma, Indian Territory. Fort Worth, Tex.: Miran Pub., 1971.
History of Oklahoma before statehood; battles, maps, 12,000 names of early settlers and soldiers of early eastern Oklahoma. Good references.

668   **Hanna, Charles A.** The wilderness trail, or The ventures and adventures of the Pennsylvania traders on the Allegheny path, with some new annals of the old west... 2v. 1911. Repr. New York: A.M.S. Pr., 1972.
Mostly Indian history and genealogy: Pennsylvania, Ohio Valley.

669   **Hill, Edward E.** Preliminary inventory of the records of the Bureau of Indian Affairs at the National Archives. 2v. Washington, D.C.: The Archives, 1965.
*Record* G:75. Has brief description of the records and agency responsible for their creation.

670   **Hodge, Frederick W.** The Indian tribes of North America with biographical sketches of the principal chiefs. Repr. St. Clair Shores, Mich.: Scholarly Pr., 1973; Totowa, N.J.: Rowman & Littlefield, 1973.

671   **Kelsay, Laura E.** Cartographic records in the National Archives of the United States relating to American Indians. *Reference information paper* 71. Washington, D.C.: The Archives, 1974.

672   **Morris, John W.** Historical atlas of Oklahoma. Norman, Okla.: Univ. of Oklahoma Pr., 1965.
Useful for Indian research.

673   **Nelson, William.** Personal names of Indians of New Jersey, being a list of 650 such names, gleaned mostly from Indian deeds of the 17th century. Paterson, N.J., 1904.

674   **Read, William A.** Florida place-names of Indian origin, and Seminole personal names. Baton Rouge, La., 1934.

675   —— Indian place names in Alabama. Baton Rouge, La., 1939.

676   **Reference encyclopedia of the American Indian.** 2nd ed. 2v. Rye, N.Y.: Todd Pub., 1973.

v.2 contains biographical sketches of prominent living American Indians, and non-Indians active in Indian affairs. v.1 has fine classified and annotated bibliography of over 2,500 books.

**677**  **Rydjord, John.** Indian place-names, their origin, evolution, and meanings; collected in Kansas . . . Norman, Okla.: Univ. of Oklahoma Pr., 1968.
Good bibliography.

**678**  **Smith, Dwight L. V.** Indians of the United States and Canada. A bibliography. Santa Barbara, Calif.: Clio Pr., 1973.
1,771 abstracts of periodical literature from the last 2 decades.

**679**  **U.S. Dept. of the Interior. Library.** Biographical and historical index of American Indians and persons involved in Indian affairs. A subject index developed in the Library of the Bureau of Indian Affairs. 8v. Boston: G. K. Hall, 1966.
Covers latter half of 19th and first 20 years of the 20th century. 203,000 entries.

**680**  **Wright, Muriel H.** A guide to the Indian tribes of Oklahoma. Norman, Okla.: Univ. of Oklahoma Pr., 1951.
Identifies the 67 Indian tribes who settled in Oklahoma. Biographical data on more prominent members.

FIVE CIVILIZED TRIBES

⁜ Tribes include the Cherokee, Chickasaw, Choctaw, Creek, and Seminole Indians

**681**  **Bell, George M.** Genealogy of "old and new Cherokee Indian families." Bartlesville, Okla.: Leonard Pr., 1972.

**682**  **Browder, Nathaniel C.** The Cherokee Indians and those who came after. Hayesville, N.C.: The Author, 1974.
Covers period 1835–60, and the settlement of the area of land last relinquished by Cherokees east of the Mississippi under the Treaty of 1835. Good history, population schedules, names of earlier inhabitants or their descendants. List of North Carolina volunteers (and a number of Tennessee volunteers) who helped remove the Indians. "Notes for a history of Cherokee county, North Carolina, 1835-60."

**683**  **Campbell, John B.** Campbell's Abstract of Creek freedmen census cards and index. Muskogee, Okla., 1915.

**684**  ——— Campbell's Abstract of Creek Indian census cards and index. Muskogee, Okla., 1915.

**685**  ——— Campbell's Abstract of Seminole Indian census cards and index. Muskogee, Okla., 1915.

**686**  **Carseloway, James M.** Cherokee notes. Fayetteville, Ark.: Washington County Historical Soc., 1960.

**687**  ——— Cherokee pioneers. Adair, Okla.: The Author, 1961.

**688**  ——— Cherokee old timers. Adair, Okla.: The Author, 1972.

**689**  ——— Early settlers. Adair, Okla.: The Author, 1962.

**690**  ——— My journal. Adair, Okla.: The Author, 1962.
Register of births and deaths, Cherokee Indians.

**691**  **Cotterill, Robert S.** The southern Indians: the story of the civilized tribes before removal. Norman, Okla.: Univ. of Oklahoma Pr., 1954.
Story of Cherokees, Choctaws, Creeks, and Chickasaws in the 50 years before 1830. Good sources for reference.

**692**  **Curtis, Mary B.** Bibliography of the Five Civilized Tribes (Cherokee, Chickasaw, Choctaw, Creek, and Seminole Indians). In *Magazine of bibliography*, v.1, no.3, 1972.
Excellent coverage.

**693**  **Cushman, Horatio B.** History of the Choctaw, Chickasaw and Natchez Indians. 1899. Repr. New York: Russell & Russell, 1972.
Many references to white families who intermarried with Indians.

**694**  **Drennen, John.** Drennen roll, 1851, of the Cherokee Indians. Tulsa, Okla.: Indian Nations Pr., 1973.

**695  Foreman, Grant.** The Five Civilized Tribes. Norman, Okla.: Univ. of Oklahoma Pr., 1934.

One of the basic research tools in ancestry and history of the tribes and their westward movement. History of forced migration of tribes from Mississippi, Alabama, Georgia and Florida is also provided. A continuation of *Advancing the frontier,* no.664.

**696** ———— History of the service and list of individuals of the Five Civilized Tribes in the Confederate Army. 2v. Oklahoma City, Okla., 1928.

**697  Hastain, E.** Hastain's Township plats of the Creek nation. Muskogee, Okla., 1910.

**698** ———— Hastain's Township plats of the Seminole nation. Muskogee, Okla., 1913.

**699** ———— Index to Choctaw-Chickasaw deeds and allotments. Muskogee, Okla., 1908.

**700** ———— ———— Supplement. Muskogee, Okla., 1910.

**701  O'Beirne, Harry F.** Leaders and leading men of the Indian Territory, Choctaw-Chickasaws. Chicago, 1891.

Biographical sketches with more than 200 portraits.

**702** ———— and **O'Beirne, E. S.** The Indian Territory: its chiefs, legislators, and leading men. St. Louis, Mo., 1892.

**703  Richardson, Marian M.,** and **Mize, J. J.** 1832 Cherokee land lottery: index to Revolutionary soldiers, their widows and orphans, who were fortunate drawers. Danielsville, Ga.: Heritage Papers, 1969.

Taken from no.705.

**704  Siler, David W.** The eastern Cherokees. A census of the Cherokee nation in North Carolina, Tennessee, Alabama, and Georgia in 1851. Preface by Fred B. Kniffen. New Orleans, La.: Polyanthos, 1972.

Facsimile reproduction of a manuscript preserved in the National Archives, relating to families of eastern Cherokee Indians, as well as those claiming Cherokee ancestry. Enumeration gives places of residence, ages, relationships, sex, blood, and remarks.

**705  Smith, James F.** The Cherokee land lottery, containing a numerical list of the names of fortunate drawers . . . 1832. 1838. Repr. Baltimore: G.P.C., 1969.

With new index and map of original Cherokee county.

**706  Starr, Emmet.** History of the Cherokee Indians and their legends and folk lore. 1921. Repr. Fayetteville, Ark.: Indian Heritage Assoc., Univ. of Arkansas, 1967.

**707** ———— Old Cherokee families: "old families and their genealogy." With a comprehensive index compiled by James J. Hill. 2nd ed. Norman, Okla.: Univ. of Oklahoma Pr., 1972.

Repr. from Starr's *History of the Cherokee Indians* . . . pp.303–476 (no.706). Includes 39 prominent mixed-blood families and individuals of hundreds of affiliated families. Good bibliography, 90p. index.

**708  Tennessee State Library and Archives.** Cherokee collection. v.1: Cherokee Indian claims (all pub.). Nashville, Tenn.: The Archives, 1966.

**709  Tyner, James W.,** and **Timmons, A. T.** Our people and where they rest. v.1– . Norman, Okla.: Univ. of Oklahoma Pr., 1969– (in progress).

Cherokee Indian registers, births, etc., produced by Oklahoma American Indian Institute.

**710  U.S. Commission to the Five Civilized Tribes.** The final rolls of citizens and freedmen of the Five Civilized Tribes in Indian territory . . . Approved by the Secretary of State of the Interior on or prior to March 4, 1907. Washington, D.C., 1907.

**711** ———— ———— Index to the final rolls. Washington, D.C., 1907.

712  **U.S. Dept. of the Interior.** Allotment of the lands of Delaware Indians. Letter from the Secretary of the Interior . . . relative to the allotment of lands in the Cherokee nation to the Delaware Indians, Jan. 19, 1904. Washington, D.C., 1904.

713  **U.S. Senate. Committee on Indian Affairs.** Enrollments, emigration and improvements of the Cherokees residing east of the Mississippi. Washington, D.C., 1836.
Senate doc. Numbers, names of emigrants from 1829 on; value of lands—some homesteads were in Arkansas.

714  **Walker, Homer A.** Cherokee Indian census of 1835 for the state of Tennessee. Washington, D.C., 1958?

715  ——— Cherokee Indian census of 1835 of the state of Georgia, Alabama and North Carolina. Washington, D.C., 1958.

716  **Young, Mary E.** Redskins, ruffleshirts, and rednecks. Indian allotments in Alabama and Mississippi, 1830-60. Norman, Okla.: Univ. of Oklahoma Pr., 1961.
Chickasaw, Choctaw and Creek Indians: land tenures.

## Individual States

✣ The individuals and institutions noted at the heading of each state in the following pages are those who looked over the compiler's list before publication. Some, in returning the list, noted agreement with it; others made additions and corrections. In thanking all those named the compiler wishes to state that the final decisions were not necessarily theirs and that all errors, omissions, and other deficiencies are entirely his. All those credited agreed that their names might accompany the respective state list.

ALABAMA

Settled ca. 1702; entered Union 1819

*Birmingham Public Library*
*State of Alabama Department of Archives and History, Montgomery*
*Mrs. Pauline Jones Gandrud, Tuscaloosa*

717  **Achee, Benjamin E.,** and **Wright, M. D.** Index to compiled service records: Alabama units—Creek War, 1836-37. 2v. Shreveport, La.: The Authors, 1971.
Alphabetical listing of soldiers from Alabama who were in the Creek War. Lists rank and military unit.

718  ——— Florida War. Shreveport, La.: The Authors, 1971.
Alphabetical list of soldiers serving during the Florida War, 1836-43.

719  **Alabama. Dept. of Archives and History.** Alabama census returns, 1820, and an abstract of federal census of Alabama, 1830. From *Alabama historical quarterly,* v.6, no.3, 1944. Repr., reissued. Baltimore: G.P.C., 1971.
The 1820 federal census for Alabama was destroyed by fire, but returns for Baldwin, Conecuh, Dallas, Franklin, Limestone, St. Clair, Shelby, and Wilcox (of 29 counties) were preserved. 4,100 heads of families.

720  **Alabama Baptist.** v.1– , 1874– . Birmingham, Ala.: Alabama Historical Soc. Special Collections, Stamford Univ. Lib.
Much biographical information and notes.

721  **Alabama genealogical register.** v.1–10, 1959-68. Tuscaloosa, Ala.
Contains a vast number of source records and many Revolutionary records not in *Revolutionary soldiers in Alabama* (no.759). Most records stop at 1860. Separate index by Nelle M. Jenkins, ca.1965.

722  **Alabama Genealogical Society, Inc., magazine.** v.1– , 1967– . Leeds and Fort McLellan, Ala.: The Society.

723  **Alabama historical quarterly.** v.1– , 1930– . Montgomery, Ala.: State Dept. of Archives and History.

Considerable amount of genealogy, particularly in the earlier volumes. Excellent for local history.

**724 Brewer, Willis.** Alabama: her history, resources, war record and public men from 1540-1872. 1872. Repr. Tuscaloosa, Ala., 1964.
History of early Alabama, with sketches of prominent citizens and families.

**725 Carter, Clarence E.** The territory of Alabama, 1817–1819. *Territorial papers of the U.S.* 18. 1952. Repr. New York: A.M.S. Press, 1973.
Lists of persons signing petitions, memorials, etc.

**726 D.A.R. Alabama.** Index to Alabama wills, 1808-70. Ann Arbor, Mich., 1955.
Not comprehensive. Location of wills given; useful index.

**727** ——— Some early Alabama churches. Birmingham, Ala.: Mrs. O. B. Wilson, 1701 Fourth Terrace, W., 35208, 1974.
Many give lists of early members, ministers and events of genealogical interest.

**728 Deep South genealogical quarterly.** v.1- , 1963- . Mobile, Ala.: Mobile Genealogical Soc.
Alabama and Gulf Coast areas. Varied information: many cemetery records.

**729 Dodd, Donald B.** Historical atlas of Alabama. University, Ala.: Univ. of Alabama Pr., 1974.
History of the state by means of coordinated text and maps.

**730 DuBose, Joel C.** Notable men of Alabama. 2v. Atlanta, Ga., 1904.
Biographical sketches with portraits. Very scarce.

**731 Elliott, Carl.** Annals of northwest Alabama, including a repr. of Nelson F. Smith's *History of Pickens county,* 1856. 3v. Northport and Tuscaloosa, Ala., 1958-65.
Historical rather than genealogical but has useful index with many names. v.1, 2nd ed., 1965.

**732 England, Flora D.** Alabama notes. 2v. [Marion, Ala., 1970?]
Information of genealogical value from wills, deeds, marriage and probate records of the counties. Has many errors, but useful.

**733** ——— Alabama source book. v.1 (all pub.). Marion, Ala., 1964.
Records for Marengo, Bibb, Dallas, and Wilcox counties; separate indexes.

**734 Foley, Helen S.** Alabama. Ser. 1–3. Fort Worth, Tex.: Miran, 1970.
v.1, marriages; v.2, deaths; v.3, about people, various appointments, settlers, etc. Items from Alabama newspapers, 1846-90.

**735 Gandrud, Pauline Jones.** Alabama: an index to the 1830 U.S. census. Hot Springs, Ark.: Bobbie J. McLane, 1973.
All heads of households in all counties.

**736** ——— Alabama Revolutionary, 1812 and Indian War soldiers surnames. v.1, A–C (in progress). Hot Springs, Ark.: Bobbie J. McLane, 1974.

**737 Gibson-Brittain, Mary N.; Craig, M. B.;** and **Churchill, M. C.** The history and genealogy of some pioneer northern Alabama families . . . Flagstaff, Ariz.: Northland Pr., 1969.
Genealogies of 13 families.

**738 Griffith, Lucille B.** Alabama; a documentary history to 1900. Rev. and enl. ed. University, Ala.: Univ. of Alabama Pr., 1972.
First ed. 1962 was under title *History of Alabama:* 1540-1900.

**739 Historical Records Survey.** Guide to public records in Alabama. Preliminary ed. Birmingham, Ala., 1942.

**740** ——— Guide to public vital statistics in Alabama. Preliminary ed. Birmingham, Ala., 1942.

**741** ——— Guide to vital statistic records in Alabama church archives. Preliminary ed. Birmingham, Ala., 1942.

**742** ——— Inventory of county archives of Alabama. 14v. Birmingham, Ala., 1939-42.

Only the following numbers were published: 14 (Clay), 17 (Colbert), 18 (Conecuh), 22 (Cullman), 32 (Greene), 33 (Hale), 39 (Lauderdale), 43 (Lowndes), 45 (Madison), 46 (Marengo), 60 (Sumter), 61 (Talladega), 66 (Wilcox), and 67 (Winston). Unpublished material deposited in State Dept. of Archives and History, Montgomery, Ala.

**743** ——— Inventory of the church archives of Alabama, Protestant Episcopal Church. Birmingham, Ala., 1939.

**744 Holcombe, Hosea.** A history of the rise and progress of the Baptists in Alabama. 1840. Repr. Bessemer, Ala.: West Jefferson County Historical Soc., 1974.

**745 Jones, Kathleen P.** and **Gandrud, P. J.** Alabama records. v.1- , 1932- . Tuscaloosa, Ala.: Mrs. B. W. Gandrud.

Series had reached v.250 by the end of 1974. Contains all forms of genealogical records. Each volume tends to cover one county, with varying dates. Although in typescript, copies are quickly made available. Useful. Authors maintain a master index.

**746 Lazenby, Marion E.** History of Methodism in Alabama and West Florida [1808-1955]. North Alabama Conference and West Florida Conference of Methodist Church. Philadelphia: Methodist Pub. House, 1960.

Included are brief biographical sketches of over 1,000 ministers, references to thousands of laymen. 90p. index.

**747 Library of Alabama lives.** Hopkinsville, Ky., 1961.

Reference edition recording biographies of contemporary leaders in Alabama. Vanity publication but gives considerable information submitted by biographee.

**748 Lineback, Neal G.,** and **Traylor, C. T.** Atlas of Alabama. University, Ala.: Univ. of Alabama Pr., 1973.

New atlas with colored maps. Up-to-date.

**749 Marks, Henry S.** Who was who in Alabama. Huntsville, Ala.: Strode Pub., 1972. Short biographical sketches, alphabetically arranged.

**750 Mell, Annie R. W.** Revolutionary soldiers buried in Alabama. *Alabama Historical Soc. repr.* 26, from *Transactions* 1899-1903, v.4. Montgomery, Ala., 1904.

Contains 30 sketches of Revolutionary soldiers.

**751 Memorial record of Alabama.** 2v. Madison, Wisc., 1893.

Largely devoted to personal memoirs, some unreliable. Mug book.

**752 Mitchell, Lois D.** Mobile ship news. Mobile, Ala.: The Author, 1964.

Because there is little in print on southern ports and their passengers, this work is valuable.

**753 Moore, Albert B.** History of Alabama and her people. 3v. Chicago, 1927.

v.2-3 biographical. Mug book.

**754 Northern Alabama, historical and biographical.** Birmingham, Ala., 1888.

Town sketches contain much local history; biographical sketches of a few prominent citizens in each town. Sometimes referred to as Smith & DeLand's *Northern Alabama;* Smith and DeLand were publishers.

**755 Owen, Marie (B.).** The story of Alabama: a history of the state. 5v. New York, 1949.

Based on T. McA. Owen's *History of Alabama and dictionary of Alabama biography,* 1921 (no.757).

**756 Owen, Thomas McA.** A bibliography of Alabama. In the *Annual report of the American Historical Assoc. for 1897.* Washington, D.C., 1898. Well-researched and complete to time of publication.

**757** ——— History of Alabama and dictionary of Alabama biography. 4v. Chicago, 1921.

v.3-4 biographical.

758 ——— Deluxe suppl. publ. by S. J. Clarke. Chicago, 1921.

759 ——— Revolutionary soldiers in Alabama; being a list of names of soldiers of the American Revolution who resided in the state of Alabama. *Alabama State Archives bull.* 5, 1911, and in *Alabama historical quarterly,* v.6, no.4, 1944.

Additional material located on Revolutionary soldiers in Alabama since 1911. Much genealogical information.

760 ——— ——— Repr. v.1-2. Tuscaloosa, Ala., 1960-61.

In 1911 Owen compiled his Revolutionary soldiers from records in the State Archives, and it was published as *bull.* 5. By 1944 many new records had been located, and these were published in the *Quarterly* v.6, no.4, 1944. Willo Institute reprinted the 1944 collection as v.1 of a series. Later it published v.2, containing the 1911 list but excluding soldiers in the 1944 ed., and added records from the Mell reprint (no. 750)—not in the 1911 or 1944 eds. *See also* no.767.

761 **Pickett, Albert J.** History of Alabama, and incidentally of Georgia and Mississippi, from the earliest period. 1896. Repr. Birmingham, Ala., 1962.

Good. Has some Georgia and Mississippi history as it relates to Alabama. Arno Pr., N.Y. reprinted the 2v. 1851 set in 1971.

762 **Pike county, Alabama tomb records.** Sponsored by the Pike County Historical Society, 1972. In *Alabama historical quarterly,* v.35, 1973. 15,400 names; 126 cemeteries.

763 **Posey, Betty D.** Alabama 1840 census index. v.1 (in progress). Hattiesburg, Miss.: The Compiler, 1973.

Includes Barbour, Benton, Chambers, Cherokee, Coosa, DeKalb, Macon, Marshall, Randolph, Russell, Talladega, and Tallapoosa counties. These counties were created when Creeks and Cherokees ceded their lands in eastern Alabama in the 1830s. Census is first to be taken in these counties.

764 **Saunders, James E.** Early settlers of Alabama; with notes and genealogies by Elizabeth S. B. Stubbs. Pt.1 (all pub.). 1899. Repr. Baltimore: G.P.C., 1969.

Thousands of names. Encyclopedia of Alabama genealogy.

765 **Settlers of northeast Alabama.** v.1- , 1962- . Gadsden, Ala.: Northeast Alabama Genealogical Soc.

766 **Tap roots.** v.1- , 1963- . Tuskegee, Ala.: Genealogical Soc. of East Alabama.

Mostly cemetery and Bible records.

767 **Thomas, Elizabeth W.** Revolutionary soldiers in Alabama. v.2. Tuscaloosa, Ala., 1961.

v.1 (1960) is reprint of *Alabama historical quarterly,* v.6, no.4, 1944, *see* no.759. v.3 was contemplated in 1962 but it did not materialize.

768 **Valley leaves.** v.1- , 1965- . Huntsville, Ala.: Tennessee Valley Genealogical Soc.

Concerns north Alabama.

769 **West, Anson.** A history of Methodism in Alabama. Nashville, Tenn., 1893.

Some family history but no index.

770 **Wilson, Mabel P.; Woodyerd, D. Y.;** and **Busby, R. L.** Some early Alabama churches. Birmingham, Ala.: Mrs. Wilson (1701 4th Terrace, West, 35208), 1973.

Not a complete record, but much information of location, early members, early pastors and historical information.

ALASKA

Territory established 1912; entered Union 1959

*Coussac Public Library, Anchorage*
*State of Alaska, Alaska Historical Library, Juneau*

✣ The National Archives in Washington, D.C., keeps on file Alaska census reports, Army and Navy rosters, and Coast Guard records.

771   **Alaska place names.** Update of Donald J. Orth's *Dictionary of Alaska place names. U.S. Geological Survey, professional paper* 567, 1969. Rev. 1971. Fairbanks, Alas.: Univ. of Alaska, 1973.

772   **Andrews, Clarence L.** The story of Alaska. Seattle, Wash., 1931 and Caldwell, Id., 1938.
Good background material, but not especially genealogical.

773   **Baker, Marcus.** Geographic dictionary of Alaska. *U.S. Geological Survey bull.* 299. 2nd ed. Washington, D.C., 1906.

774   **Chase, Will H.** Pioneers of Alaska; the trail blazers of bygone days. Kansas City, Kans., 1951.
Gives lists of members of pioneers of Alaska.

775   **De Armond, R. N.** The founding of Juneau. Centennial ed. Gastineau Channel Centennial Assoc., Juneau, Alas., 1967.
pp.135-205 are short stories of people associated with Juneau.

776   **Elmer E. Rasmuson Library, Fairbanks.** The bibliography of Alaskana, 1969-73. 2v. Fairbanks, Alas.: Univ. of Alaska, Rasmuson Library, 1974.
Focused on the Alaska-oriented periodical collection at the library. Monthly updates available.

777   **Harrison, Edward S.** Nome and Seward Peninsula; a book of information about northern Alaska. Seattle, Wash., 1905.
Biographical material on people in Nome gold rush period.

778   **Phillips, James W.** Alaska-Yukon place names. Seattle, Wash.: Univ. of Washington Pr., 1973.
State of Alaska and parts of western Canada.

779   **Polk's Alaska-Yukon gazetteer and business directory.** 1903-24, suppl.1, 1932. Seattle, Wash.

780   **Ricks, Melvin B.** Directory of Alaska post offices and postmasters [1867-1963]. [Ketchikan, Alas., 1965].

781   **Sourdough Stampede Association.**
The Alaska-Yukon gold book; a roster of the progressive men and women who were the Argonauts of the Klondike gold stampede and those who are identified with the pioneer days and subsequent development of Alaska and the Yukon territory. Seattle, Wash., 1930.

782   **Wickersham, James.** A bibliography of Alaskan literature, 1724-1924 . . . Cordova, Alas., 1927.
E. A. Tourville's *Alaska, a bibliography, 1570-1970,* 1974, though later, has only 5,000 entries (against Wickersham's 10,000), and Tourville also omits many official documents.

ARIZONA

Settled ca. 1848; entered Union 1912

*Department of Library and Archives, Phoenix*

783   **Barnes, William C.** Arizona place names. *Univ. of Arizona general bull.* 2. 1935. Rev. and enl. by Byrd H. Granger. Tucson, Ariz.: Univ. of Arizona Pr., 1960.
Thorough treatment of subject; lists all relevant dates; good map and bibliography.

784   **Farish, Thomas E.** History of Arizona. 8v., and index compiled by J. H. McClintock. San Francisco, 1915-18.
Contains results of 1866 census.

785   **Federal census:** territory of New Mexico and territory of Arizona. Washington, D.C.: U.S. Govt., 1965.
Excerpted from decennial federal census 1860 for Arizona county, in the territory of New Mexico; the special territorial census of 1864 taken in Arizona (*see also* no.788); and decennial federal census 1870 for the territory of Arizona. Senate doc.13, 89th Congress, 1st session.

786 **Hinton, Richard J.** The handbook to Arizona; its resources, history, towns, mines, ruins . . . accompanied with a new map . . . Glorieta, N. Mex.: Rio Grande Pr., 1970.
Rio Grande classic first publ. 1878; original title, *Handbook to Arizona.* Index added to reprint.

787 **A historical and biographical record of the territory of Arizona.** Chicago, 1896.
Mug book.

788 **Historical Records Survey.** The 1864 census of Arizona. Phoenix, Ariz., 1938. *See also* no.785.

789 ———— Guide to public vital statistics records in Arizona. Phoenix, Ariz., 1941.

790 ———— Inventory of county archives in Arizona. 3v. Phoenix, Ariz., 1938-41. Only the following numbers were published: 7 (Maricopa), 10 (Pima), 12 (Santa Cruz). Unpublished material deposited in Arizona State Dept. of Library and Archives, Phoenix, Ariz.

791 **Lloyd, Elwood.** Arizonology (knowledge of Arizona); a compilation of more than 2,000 names found on the maps of Arizona, together with information concerning their meaning, history . . . Flagstaff, Ariz., 1933.

792 **Lockwood, Francis C.** Arizona characters. Los Angeles, 1928. Frontier and pioneer life.

793 ———— More Arizona characters. *Univ. of Arizona general bull.* 6. Tucson, Ariz., 1943.

794 ———— Pioneer days in Arizona. New York, 1932.

795 **McClintock, James H.** Arizona: prehistoric, aboriginal, pioneer, modern. 3v. Chicago, 1916.
v.3 biographical.

796 ———— Mormon settlement in Arizona. 1921. Repr. New York: A.M.S. Press, 1971.

796a **Men and women of Arizona, past and present.** Phoenix, Ariz., 1940.

797 **Peplow, Edward H.** History of Arizona. 3v. New York, 1958.
v.3 covers family and personal history.

798 **Pollock, Paul W.** Arizona's men of achievement. 2v. Phoenix, Ariz.: The Author, 1958-64.

799 **Portrait and biographical record of Arizona** commemorating the achievements of citizens who have contributed to the progress of Arizona. Chicago, 1901.
Mug book.

800 **Sloan, Richard E.** History of Arizona. 4v. Phoenix, Ariz., 1930.
v.3-4 biographical.

801 **Southern Arizona Genealogical Society.** Copper state. v.9- , 1973- . Tucson, Ariz.: The Society.
Continuation of Society *bulletin,* v.1-8, 1965-73.

802 **Temple, Thomas W., II.** Sources for tracing Spanish American pedigrees in the southwestern United States: pt.2, California and Arizona. World conference on records, area F-148 paper. Salt Lake City, Genealogical Soc., 1969.

803 **Theobald, John,** and **Theobald, L.** Arizona territory post offices and postmasters. Phoenix, Ariz., 1961.
Contains a chronology of the territory; post offices arranged alphabetically with names of postmasters and brief history and description of the post office.

804 **Wyllys, Rufus K.** Arizona, the history of a frontier state. Phoenix, Ariz., 1950.

## ARKANSAS

Settled ca. 1785; entered Union 1836

*Arkansas History Commission, Little Rock*
*Little Rock Public Library*
*Miss Patricia Chadwell, Fort Worth Public Library*

*Arkansas* 821

805 **Arkansas. Adjutant General's Office.** Report . . . for the late Rebellion, and to November 1, 1866. Washington, D.C., 1867.
Roster of volunteers and militia.

806 **The Arkansas family historian.** v.1- , 1962- . Little Rock, Ark.: Arkansas Genealogical Soc.

807 **The Arkansas genealogical register.** v.1- , 1971- . Quarterly publication of the Northeast Arkansas Genealogical Assoc. Newport, Ark.: The Assoc.
Small periodical reprinting local records.

808 **Arkansas Historical Association.** Publications 1-4. Fayetteville, Ark., 1906-17.
Includes much genealogical information.

809 **The Arkansas records survey.** v.1- , 1972- . Quarterly publication of the Arkansas Records Assoc. Newport, Ark.: The Assoc.
Historical and genealogical source materials.

810 **The backtracker.** v.1- , 1972- . Rogers, Ark.: Northwest Arkansas Genealogical Soc.
Information on the 7 counties which make up the area.

811 **Biographical and historical memoirs of eastern Arkansas.** Chicago, 1890.
Includes considerable amount of family history. no.812-15, 821, and 837 were all published by Goodspeed Pub. Co. and are referred to as *Goodspeed's Arkansas*. Index, *see* no.821 and 836.

812 **Biographical and historical memoirs of northeast Arkansas.** Chicago, 1889.
Goodspeed publication. Biographies of distinguished persons. Index, *see* no.821 and 836.

813 **Biographical and historical memoirs of Pulaski, Jefferson, Lonoke, Faulkner, Grant, Saline, Perry and Hot Spring counties, Arkansas.** Chicago, 1889.
Spine title: *Biographical and historical memoirs of central Arkansas*. Index, *see* no. 821 and 836.

814 **Biographical and historical memoirs of southern Arkansas.** Chicago, 1890.
Includes much family history. Index, *see* no.821 and 836.

815 **Biographical and historical memoirs of western Arkansas.** Chicago, 1891.
Much family history. Southern Book Co.

816 **Carter, Clarence E.** The territory of Arkansas, 1819-36. 3v. *Territorial papers of the U.S.* 19-21. 1953-54. Repr. New York: A.M.S. Press, 1973.
Has lists of persons signing petitions, memorials, etc.

817 **Christensen, Katheren.** Arkansas military bounty grants (War of 1812). Hot Springs, Ark.: Arkansas Ancestors, 1971.
Arranged by counties, giving names of patentees, warrant numbers, patent dates and comments. 6,600 grantees.

818 **County Genealogical Research Pubs.** Arkansas cemetery inscriptions and genealogical records. v.1 (all pub.). North Little Rock, Ark., 1966.

819 **D.A.R. Arkansas.** A roster of the Arkansas Society, 1893-1968. Compiled by Esther Spousta. Rogers, Ark.: D.A.R., 1968.
Impressive list of ancestors, with pertinent genealogical data. Active and inactive members.

820 **Glazner, Capitola H.,** and **McLane, B. J.** 1870 mortality schedules of Arkansas. Hot Springs, Ark.: Arkansas Ancestors, 1971.
Registers of births, etc. Information on all persons in Arkansas who died in the previous year to the decennial census.

821 **(Goodspeed's Histories of Arkansas)** Biographical index to seven Goodspeed's Histories of Arkansas, and also biographical material in a number of early Arkansas newspapers. *Bull. of information, Arkansas History Commission*, no.13-16. Little Rock, Ark., 1912-17.
Very useful for Arkansas genealogical research.

61

**822** **Hallum, John.** Biographical and pictorial history of Arkansas. v.1 (all pub.). Albany, N.Y., 1887.
The first general history of Arkansas. Basically a series of biographies; rich in information about prominent citizens and their families from the earliest times.

**823** **Hempstead, Fay.** Historical review of Arkansas . . . 3v. Chicago, 1911.
v.2-3 biographical.

**824** ———— A pictorial history of Arkansas from earliest times to the year 1890. St. Louis, Mo., 1890.
Includes county histories, histories of the towns and cities, and numerous biographical sketches of prominent citizens.

**825** **Herndon, Dallas T.** Annals of Arkansas, 1947; a narrative historical ed., revised and re-editing and continuing *A centennial history of Arkansas* . . . , and chronicling the genealogical and memorial records of its prominent families and personages. 4v. Hopkinsville, Ky., 1947.

**826** **Historical Records Survey.** A directory of churches and religious organizations in the state of Arkansas. Preliminary ed. Little Rock, Ark., 1942.

**827** ———— Guide to vital statistics records in Arkansas. Church archives. Little Rock, Ark., 1942.

**828** ———— Inventory of county archives of Arkansas. 17v. Little Rock, Ark., 1939-42.
Only the following numbers were published: 3 (Baxter), 4 (Benton), 8 (Carroll), 12 (Cleburne), 13 (Cleveland), 19 (Cross), 23 (Faulkner), 30 (Hot Spring), 33 (Izard), 34 (Jackson), 44 (Madison), 48 (Monroe), 49 (Montgomery), 57 (Polk), 62 (Saline), 63 (Scott), and 65 (Searcy). Unpublished material deposited in Univ. of Arkansas Lib., Fayetteville, Ark.

**829** ———— Union list of newspapers, 1819-1942. A partial inventory of Arkansas newspaper files available in offices of publishers, libraries and private collections in Arkansas. Little Rock, Ark., 1942.

**830** **History of Benton, Washington, Carroll, Madison, Crawford, Franklin, and Sebastian counties.** Chicago, 1889.
Binder's spine title: *History of northwest Arkansas*. Includes much family history. Published by Goodspeed Pub. Co. and referred to as *Goodspeed's Arkansas, see* no.812-15, 821, and 837. Index, *see* no.821 and 836.

**831** **McLane, Bobbie J. (Mrs. Gerald B.)** 1860 mortality schedules of Arkansas. Hot Springs, Ark.: The Compiler, 1970.

**832** ———— An index to fifth census of the United States. 1830 population schedules. Territory of Arkansas. Hot Springs, Ark.: The Author, 1965.

**833** ———— An index to fifth [sic—i.e. sixth] census . . . 1840 . . . Fort Worth, Tex.: Arrow Printing Co., 1963. 13,000 names.

**834** ———— and **Glazner, C. H.** 1850 mortality schedules of Arkansas. Hot Springs, Ark.: The Compilers, 1968.
Registers of births, etc.

**835** **Morgan, James L.** Morgan is the author of several pamphlets on northeast counties of Arkansas: records, marriages, death and other notices, divorces, dates varying from 1809-38. Newport, Ark.: Northeast Arkansas Genealogical Assoc., 1971, and various dates.

**836** **Presley, Cloie (Mrs. Leister E.).** Biographical index to Goodspeed's Biographical and historical memoirs, no.812-15, 821, and 837. Searcy, Ark.: The Author, 1973.

**837** **A reminiscent history of the Ozark region.** 1894. Repr. Cape Girardeau, Mo.: Ramfre Pr., 1966.
Includes biographical sketches of prominent citizens, 27 Missouri and 29 Arkansas counties. Published by Goodspeed Pub. Co. and referred to as *Goodspeed's Arkansas,* no.812-15, 821, and 837.

**838** **Shinn, Josiah H.** Pioneers and makers of Arkansas. 1908. Repr. Baltimore: G.P.C., 1967.

Major work on pioneers, prominent citizens and families. From formation of state in 1819 to latter half of 19th century. Biographies and extensive families.

**839 Thomas, David Y.** Arkansas and its people: a history, 1541–1930. 4v. New York, 1930.
v.3–4 biographical and genealogical.

**840 Waldenmaier, Inez.** Arkansas travelers. Washington, D.C.: The Author, n.d.
Listing of every man from every county in Arkansas who was 60 years old or older in 1850 (7th census excerpt). Originally in *Genealogical newsletter,* 1958–60.

CALIFORNIA

Settled ca. 1769; entered Union 1850

*California State Library, Sacramento*
*Los Angeles Public Library*
*Miss Helen Marcia Bruner, Riverside*
*Mr. J. Carlyle Parker, California State College, Stanislaus*

**841 Antepasados.** v.1– , 1970– . San Francisco: Los Californianos. Devoted to the Spanish (and Mexican) colonial period of Alta (Upper) California.

**842 Bancroft, Hubert H.** California pioneer register and index, 1542–1848. Including inhabitants of California, 1769–1800, and list of pioneers. Extracted from *The history of California,* 1884–90. Baltimore: G.P.C., 1964.
Compilation of genealogical and biographical sketches, extracted from v.2–5 of Bancroft. Virtually the same as no.844.

**843** ———— Chronicles of the builders of the commonwealth. 7v. and index. San Francisco, 1891–92.
Long, laudatory biographical sketches of successful pioneers.

**844** ———— Register of pioneer inhabitants of California, 1542–1848, and index to information concerning them, in Bancroft's *History of California,* v.2–5. Los Angeles: Dawson's Book Shop, 1964.
Virtually the same as no.842.

**845 Barrows, Henry D.** A memorial and biographical history of the coast counties of central California . . . biographical mention of many of its pioneers and prominent citizens . . . Chicago, 1893.
Includes counties of Monterey, San Benito, Santa Cruz, and San Mateo.

**846 Beck, Warren A.,** and **Haase, Y. D.** Historical atlas of California. Norman, Okla.: Univ. of Oklahoma Pr., 1974.
Fine maps. Shows routes of explorers and location of all patented land grants during the Hispano period.

**847 Bowman, Alan P.** Index to the 1850 census of the state of California. Baltimore: G.P.C., 1972.
The California census for 1850 is on 4 microfilm rolls. This is an index to these rolls, and since the rolls were not in alphabetical order, Bowman's work is of inestimable value to California researchers. There is also a table of possible transcription errors in view of the doubtful handwriting occasionally encountered. 92,000 entries.

**848 Bowman, Jacob N.** The parochial books of the California missions. In *The Historical Soc. of Southern California quarterly,* v.43, 1961.
Inventory of many of the mission records and the various mission archives where they are housed.

**849 Burdette, Robert G.** American biography and genealogy. California ed. 2v. Chicago, 191?.

**850 California. Adjutant General.** Records of California men in the War of the Rebellion, 1861–67. Rev. and compiled by Richard H. Orton. Sacramento, Calif., 1890.
Not in alphabetical order and not indexed.

**851 California. State Archives.** Genealogical research in the California State archives. Sacramento, Calif.: Office of State Pr., 1969.
Free pamphlet of contents of archives.

**852 California Historical Society.** Index to *California Society quarterly,* v.1–40, 1922-61. San Francisco: The Society, 1965.
Not much genealogy included, but still useful for genealogist.

**853 Constructive Californians.** Los Angeles, 1926.
Mug book.

**854 Cowan, Robert E.,** and **Cowan, R. G.** A bibliography of the history of California, 1510–1930. 4v. in 1. From R. G. Cowan, 1650 Redcliff St., Los Angeles, Calif. 90026.

**855 Coy, Owen C.** California county boundaries; a study of the division of the state into counties and the subsequent changes in their boundaries. With maps. 1923. Rev. and repr. Fresno, Calif.: Valley Pub., 1973.

**856** ——— Guide to the county archives of California. Sacramento, Calif., 1919.
Published by the California Historical Survey Commission. For genealogists it is much more important than no.855. Includes some archives for the Spanish and Mexican governments. Still essential, though dated.

**857 D.A.R. California.** Index to the vital records from cemeteries in California, 1934-62. California: D.A.R., Berkeley, Calif., 1934-62?

**858** ——— Records of the families of California pioneers. Collections of California Soc., D.A.R., gathered from the various chapters 1925-26. v.2 (all pub.). [Berkeley, Calif., ca.1928.]
Other volumes exist in typescript form; actual records deposited in California State Library; D.A.R. Library, Washington, D.C.; Los Angeles Public Library; and Genealogical Library of the L.D.S.

**859 De Wolfe, Edgar.** Guide to the state of California; an index to more than 10,000 places in the state of California. Los Angeles, 1952.

**860 Dillon, Richard H.** Local indexes in California libraries. In *New notes of California libraries,* v.49, 1954.
List of special indexes, arranged alphabetically by location and subject; includes lists of card indexes of Californians found in county histories, newspapers, etc.

**861 Eminent Californians.** v.1 (all pub.). Palo Alto, Calif., 1953.
Dead and living. 500 biographies and portraits. Mug book.

**862 Eterovich, Adam S.** Jugoslav-America, immigrant-historical ser., 1492–1900. no.1-6. San Francisco: R. and E. Research Assoc., 1966-68.
no.1, Jugoslavs in Los Angeles, 1733-90; no.2, Jugoslavs in San Francisco, 1870-75; no.3, Jugoslav cemetery records of San Francisco, 1849-1930; no.4, Jugoslav-Austria-Bohemia census of population in California, 1850, 1852, 1860, 1870, 1880; no.5, Jugoslav California marriages, 1849-80; no.6, Jugoslavs in the Wild West, 1840-80.

**865 Frickstad, Walter N.** A century of California post offices, 1848-1954. Oakland, Calif., 1955.
Good for locating defunct towns not included in place name literature, *see* no.867, 868, and 908.

**866 Geiger, Maynard J.** Calendar of documents in the Santa Barbara Mission archives. Washington, D.C., 1897.
Published by Academy of American Franciscan History. Includes confirmations for missions Santa Barbara, San Jose, and Soledad.

**867 Gudde, Erwin G.** California place names . . . 3rd ed. Berkeley, Calif.: Univ. of California Pr., 1969.
The origin and etymology of current geographical names. Supplements are in 868 and 908. Additional place name literature in Sealock, no.213.

**868 Guinn, James M.** A history of California and an extended history of its southern coast counties. 2v. Los Angeles, 1907.
Also contains biographies of well-known citizens.

869 ——— Apart from the history of California, Mr. Guinn wrote the following, all of considerable use in family searching: *History and biographical records of southern California,* 1902; *Los Angeles and environs,* 2v., 1915; *Santa Cruz,* etc., 1903; *Sacramento Valley,* 1906; *San Joaquin Valley,* 1905; *The Sierras,* 1906; *Oakland and environs,* 2v., 1907; *California and biographical record of coast counties,* 1902; *Monterey and San Benito counties,* 2v., 1910.

870 **Hager, Anna M.,** and **Hager, E. G.** The Historical Society of Southern California bibliography of all published works, 1884-1957. Los Angeles: The Society, 1958.

871 **Haiman, Miecislaus.** Polish pioneers of California. *Annals* 5, 1940. Repr. San Francisco: R. and E. Research Assoc., 1969.

872 **Hanna, Phil T.** The dictionary of California land names. Los Angeles, 1951.
Rev. and enlarged ed. of 1946 issue.

873 **Haskins, Charles W.** The argonauts of California . . . New York, 1890.
The names were those Haskins was able to learn from passenger lists of vessels bound for California or Panama. Only a few names of overland pioneers. 35,000 1849 emigrants. Index will be published in 1975.

875 **Historical Records Survey.** Directory of churches and religious organizations in Alameda county and San Francisco. 2v. San Francisco, 1940-41.

876 ——— Los Angeles county and San Diego county. 2v. San Francisco, 1940.

877 ——— Guide to public vital statistics records in California. 2v. Births and deaths. San Francisco, 1941.

878 ——— Inventory of the county archives of California. 16v. San Francisco, 1938-43.
Only the following numbers were published: Northern; 1 (Alameda), 10 (Fresno), 15 (Kern), 22 (Marin), 27 (Mono), 29 (Napa), 36 (San Benito), 39 (San Francisco), 41 (San Luis Obispo), 42 (San Mateo), and 44 (Santa Clara). Southern; 20 (Los Angeles), 37 (San Bernardino), 38 (San Diego, v.3), 42 (Santa Barbara), and 57 (Ventura). Unpublished material deposited with State Archives, Sacramento, Calif., and Los Angeles County Museum.

879 ——— Ship registers and enrollments of Eureka, California. San Francisco, 1941.

880 **Historical Society of Southern California quarterly.** v.1- , 1884- . Los Angeles: The Society.
1884-1917 called *Publications.* Has considerable amount of genealogy. Index to v.1-11 (1884-1920) is out of print.

881 **Hunt, Rockwell D.** California and Californians. 5v. Chicago, 1926.
v.3-5 biographical. Other editions with some new material: 4v. 1930, v.3-4 biographical; 4v. 1932, v.3-4 biographical.

882 **Hutchinson, Cecil A.** Frontier settlement in Mexican California: the Híjar-Padrés Colony and its origins, 1769-1835. New Haven, Conn.: Yale Univ. Pr., 1969.
Appendix D lists all members of the settlement colony.

883 **Illustrated history of Southern California,** embracing the counties of San Diego, San Bernardino, Los Angeles and Orange and the peninsula of Lower California. Chicago, 1890.
Mug book.

884 **Irvine, Leigh H.** A history of the new California . . . 2v. New York, 1905.
Last part of v.1 and all of v.2 biographical.

885 **Jensen, Edith G.,** and **Olsen, B. M.** California Mother Lode records. 5v. San Leandro, Calif.: The Authors, 1962-65.
v.5 is entitled "Nevada records." v.1,2,4 are marriages, births, and cemetery records of Calaveras county; v.3 concerns Alpine county.

886 **Kinnaird, Lawrence.** History of the greater San Francisco Bay region. 3v. West Palm Beach, Fla., 1966-67.
v.3 contains family and personal records. Extensive historical bibliography; covers period 1542-1966.

887 **Lingenfelter, Keith,** and **Fulton, R.** Northern California marriages, 1850-1860. In *National Genealogical Soc. quarterly,* v.54, 1956.
Records for 17 counties.

888 **Lopez, Carlos U.** Chilenos in California; a study of the 1850, 1852 and 1860 census. San Francisco: R. and E. Research Assoc., 1973.
Includes bibliographical references.

889 **Meler, Vjekoslav.** The Slavonic pioneers of California . . . 1932. Repr. San Francisco: R. and E. Research Assoc., 1968.
Covers 1849-1932.

890 **Memorial and biographical history of northern California** . . . containing a history . . . from earliest occupation . . . and biographical mention of many of its most eminent pioneers and also of prominent citizens . . . Chicago, 1891.

891 **Memorial and biographical history of the counties of Fresno, Tulare and Kern, California.** Containing a history . . . and biographical mention of many of its pioneers, and also of its prominent citizens. Chicago, 1892.

892 **Memorial and biographical history of the counties of Merced, Stanislaus, Calaveras, Tuolumne and Mariposa, California.** Containing a history . . . and biographical mention of many of its pioneers and also of prominent citizens. Chicago, 1892.

893 ―――― Personal name index. Ed. by J. Carlyle Parker. Stanislaus, Calif.: California State College Library, 1973.

894 **Newmark, Maurice H.,** and **Newmark, M. R.** Sixty years in California, 1853-1915, containing the reminiscences of Harris Newmark. 3rd ed. Boston, 1930.
Much on early settlers; indexed.

895 **Parker, John Carlyle.** Sources of California: from Padron to voter registration. *World Conference on Records and genealogical seminar paper,* area I-34. Salt Lake City: L.D.S., 1969.

896 **Phelps, Alonzo.** Contemporary biography of California's representative men . . . 3v. San Francisco, 1881-82.
Contains about 100 lengthy biographies.

897 **Pompey, Sherman L.** Genealogical records of California. Fresno, Calif., 1968.
Compiled from census, tax, military unit histories, etc.

898 ―――― Miscellaneous northern California cemetery inscriptions. Independence, Calif., 1966.

899 **Prendergast, Thomas F.** Forgotten persons: Irish leaders in early California. San Francisco, 1942.

900 **Questing Heirs Genealogical Society.** Some early southern California burials. Rosemead, Calif.: The Society, 1973.
Long Beach, Wilmington and Sunnyside cemeteries. 5,400 names.

901 **Rasmussen, Louis J.** California wagon train lists. v.1- . San Francisco: The Author, 1971- (in progress).
Will cover 1850-1860s.

902 ―――― Railway passenger lists of overland trains to San Francisco and the West. v.1- . San Francisco: The Author, 1966- (in progress).
Will cover 1870-1890. Lists first class and some second-class overland passengers on the Central Pacific beginning July 1870.

903 ―――― San Francisco ship passenger lists. v.1- . San Francisco: The Author, 1965- (in progress).
Will cover 1850-1875. There will be 15v. and index.

904 **Reed, Lester.** Old-timers of southeastern California. Redlands, Calif.: The Author, 1967.
Family sketches.

905 **Rensch, Hero E.; Hoover, M. B.;** and **Rensch, E. G.** Historic spots in California. Rev. by W. N. Abeloe. 3rd ed. Stanford, Calif.: Stanford Univ. Pr., 1966.
Excellent supplement to no.867 and 868.

906 **Rocq, Margaret M.** California local history. A bibliography and union list of library holdings. 2nd ed., rev. and enlarged. Stanford, Calif.: Stanford Univ. Pr., 1970.
17,000 items, holdings of over 230 libraries. Essential.

907 **Rowland, Leon.** Los fundadores . . . the first families of California and also all other persons with family names that were in California, 1769–85, except those who died at San Diego in 1769. *Acad. of California Church History publ.* 3. Fresno, Calif., 1951.

908 **Sanchez, Nellie (Van de Grift).** Spanish and Indian place names of California, their meaning and romance. San Francisco, 1914.
A supplement to no.867, 868, and 905.

909 **The searcher.** v.1– , 1965– . Long Beach, Calif.: Southern California Genealogical Soc.
Marriages, cemetery inscriptions, Bible records, etc.

910 **Society of Colonial Wars, California.** Register. Los Angeles, 1930.

910a **Society of Mayflower Descendants.** California. Register, San Francisco, 1917.
A record of descendants from passengers on the Mayflower.

911 **Sons of the American Revolution. California Society.** Spirit of patriotism as evidenced by the Revolutionary and ancestral records of the Society, by Orra E. Monnette and L. Le L. French. v.1 (all pub.). Los Angeles, 1915.

Includes lists of Revolutionary soldiers of Maryland and South Carolina. Thousands of names.

912 **Stine, Thomas O.** Scandinavians on the Pacific: Danish, Swedish, Norwegian. 1900. San Francisco: Reprint Research Assoc., 1968.
Covers the first Scandinavian pioneers on the Pacific Coast.

913 **The surname searcher.** v.1– , 1967– . Long Beach, Calif.: Southern California Genealogical Soc.

914 **Temple, Thomas W., II.** Sources for tracing Spanish-American pedigrees in the southwestern United States. pt. 2: California and Arizona. *World Conference on Records,* area F-14B paper. Salt Lake City: L.D.S., 1969.

915 **Thompson and West, publishers.** The following county histories (no.916–922), published by Thompson and West, have been reprinted by Howell-North, Berkeley, Calif., 1973-74.

916 ———— Los Angeles, Orange counties, 1880.

917 ———— Nevada county, 1880.

918 ———— Sacramento county, 1880.

919 ———— San Joaquin county, 1879.

920 ———— San Luis Obispo county, 1883.

921 ———— Santa Barbara, Ventura counties, 1882.

922 ———— Sutter county, 1879.

923 **Valley quarterly.** v.1– , 1961– . San Bernardino, Calif.: San Bernardino Genealogical Soc.
Cumulative index 1961–63.

924 **Vásquez, Nadine M.** Sinaloa roots: an account of the 1781 expedition to Alta California and ancestral records of early California settlers, 1723–1808. Carmichael, Calif.: The Author, 1974.

Mainly concerned with the 1781 Rivera y Moncada expedition; much genealogical information.

**925   A volume of memoirs and genealogy of representative citizens of northern California,** including biographies of many who have passed away . . . Chicago, 1901.

COLORADO

Settled ca. 1858; entered Union 1876

*Denver Public Library*
*State Historical Society of Colorado, Denver*

**926   Baker, James H.** (and **Hafen, Leroy R.**). History of Colorado. 5v. Denver, Colo., 1927.
v.4-5 biographical.

**927   Bromwell, Henrietta E.** Fiftyniners' directory—Colorado argonauts 1858-59; a directory of their arrivals, removals, deaths, marriages, children, property . . . 2v. Denver, Colo., 1926.
v.1, A-LUSB; v.2, LUSE-Z.

**928   Byers, William N.** Encyclopedia of biography of Colorado. v.1 (all pub.). Chicago, 1901.
Standard reference work to the turn of the century.

**929   Chamblin, Thomas S.** Historical encyclopedia of Colorado. 2v. Denver, Colo., 1960.
Short articles on Colorado history and geography, plus articles on the history of each county. Biographies of living Coloradoans in v.2. Published by Colorado Historical Assoc.

**930   Clint, Florence R.** Colorado area key. Castle Rock, Colo.: The Author, 1970.
Court records, maps, condensed histories of counties, cemetery lists, etc.

**931   Colorado. Adjutant-General's Office, Dept. of Military Affairs.** Biennial reports, 1861-65. Denver, Colo., 1866.
Rosters of Civil War participants.

**932   The Colorado genealogist.** v.1- , 1939- . Denver, Colo.: Colorado Genealogical Soc.
Good key to genealogical collections at the Denver Public Library. Society archivist has complete card name index.

**933   ——— Index.** v.1-10, 1939-49. 2v. The Society, 1969.

**934   D.A.R. Colorado.** Sarah Platt Decker Chapter, Durango. Pioneers of the San Juan country. 5v. n.p., 1942.
Reminiscences of Colorado pioneers; much genealogical material on early families.

**935   Early Colorado marriages from the Rocky Mountain news, 1862-1902.** In *The Colorado genealogist,* v.2, 1941.

**936   [Ferril, William C.]** Sketches of Colorado . . . 4v. Denver, Colo., 1911.
Mug book.

**937   Frandsen, Maude L.** Sixty and three on the Flying C: the counties of Colorado. Boulder, Colo.: Johnson Pub. Co., 1960.

**938   Gannett, Henry.** A gazetteer of Colorado. *U.S. Geological Survey bull.* 291. Washington, D.C., 1906.

**939   Griswold, Don,** and **Griswold, J.** Colorado's century of cities, 1858-1958. Denver, Colo., 1958.
Gazetteer of the early settlements.

**940   Hafen, LeRoy R.** Colorado and its people. 4v. New York, 1948.
v.3-4 biographical. Well indexed.

**941   Hall, Frank.** History of the state of Colorado. 4v. Chicago, 1889-97.
Last half of v.4 biographical. There are two editions of v.4: 1890 and 1897. Contents vary, and both are needed for full coverage.

**942   Historical Records Survey.** Guide to vital statistics records in Colorado. 2v. Denver, Colo., 1942.
v.1, Public archives; v.2, Church archives.

943 ——— Inventory of the county archives of Colorado. 16v. Denver, Colo., 1938–41.
Only the following numbers were published: 2 (Alamosa), 3 (Arapahoe), 6 (Bent), 11 (Conejos), 12 (Costilla), 22 (Fremont), 23 (Garfield), 27 (Hinsdale), 35 (Larimer), 38 (Logan), 44 (Morgan), 48 (Phillips), 50 (Prowers), 57 (San Miguel), 61 (Washington), and 63 (Yuma). Unpublished material deposited in State Historical Soc., Denver, Colo.

944 **History of Arkansas Valley, Colorado.** 1881. Repr. Evansville, Ind.: Unigraphic, 1971.
Lake county and the Ten Mile region; El Paso, Chaffee, Fremont, Pueblo and Bent counties.

945 **History of Clear Creek and Boulder Valleys, Colorado** . . . A history of Gilpin, Clear Creek, Boulder and Jefferson counties, and biographical sketches. 1880. Repr. Evansville, Ind.: Unigraphic, 1971.

946 ——— Index. By Sanford C. Gladden. Boulder, Colo.: The Compiler, 1970.

947 **Oehlerts, Donald E.** Guide to Colorado names, 1859–1863. Denver, Colo.: Bibliographical Center for Research, Rocky Mountain Region, 1964.

948 **Perkin, Robert L.** The first hundred years, an informal history of Denver and the Rocky Mountain news. Garden City, N.Y., 1959.

949 **Pompey, Sherman L.** Confederate soldiers buried in Colorado. Independence, Calif., 1965.

950 **Portrait and biographical record of the state of Colorado,** containing portraits and biographies of many well-known citizens of the past and present. Chicago, 1899.
Mug book.

951 **Representative men of Colorado in the nineteenth century** . . . New York, 1902.
Contains over 1,000 portraits, with little attempt to provide biographical information; birth and death dates not given.

952 **Rocky Mountain directory and Colorado gazetteer for 1871** . . . Denver, Colo., 1871.
Contains directories of numerous Colorado communities.

953 **Shaw, Luella.** True history of some of the pioneers of Colorado. Hotchkiss, Colo., 1909.
Contains biographical sketches.

954 **Stone, Wilbur F.** History of Colorado. 6v. Chicago, 1918–19.
v.2–5 and supplement biographical.

955 **University of Colorado historical collections.** Colony ser., v.1–2. Boulder, Colo., 1918–26.
Series contains genealogical information. For v.2 *see also* no.956.

956 **Willard, James F.,** and **Goodykoontz, C. B.** Experiments in Colorado colonization, 1869–72. Selected contemporary records relating to the German Colonization Company and the Chicago colony, St. Louis-Western and Southwestern colonies. *Univ. of Colorado historical collections* 3. *Colony ser.,* v.2. Boulder, Colo., 1926.

## CONNECTICUT

Settled ca. 1635; original state

*Connecticut State Library, Hartford*

957 **Andrews, Frank De W.** Connecticut soldiers in the French and Indian War. Vineland, N.J., 1925.
Bills, receipts and documents printed from original manuscripts.

958 **Bailey, Frederic W.** Early Connecticut marriages as found on ancient church records prior to 1800. 7v. 1896–1906. Repr. with additions, corrections, and introduction by D. L. Jacobus. 7v. in 1. Baltimore, G.P.C., 1968.

959 **Barber, John W.** Connecticut historical collections containing a general collection of interesting facts, traditions, biographical sketches . . . of every town in Connecticut. 2nd ed. New Haven, Conn., [1836].
Serves as an early gazetteer of the state.

960 **Barlow, Claude W.** Sources for genealogical searching in Connecticut and Massachusetts. Syracuse, N.Y.: Central New York Genealogical Soc., 1973.

961 **Bingham, Harold J.** History of Connecticut. 4v. New York, 1962.
v.3-4 personal and family history.

962 **Biographical encyclopedia of Connecticut and Rhode Island of the nineteenth century.** Ed. by Henry C. Williams. New York, 1881.

963 **Buckingham, Thomas.** Roll and journal of Connecticut service in Queen Anne's War, 1710-11. *Acorn Club publ.* 13. New Haven, Conn., 1916.
Reprint of pamphlet of 1825, "The private journals kept by Rev. John Birmingham of the expedition against Canada, 1710-11."

964 **Cameron, Kenneth W.** Historical resources of the Episcopal Diocese of Connecticut. Index by Carolyn Hutchens. Hartford, Conn.: Transcendental Books, 1966.
Based on Historical Records Survey inventory of church archives of Connecticut, v.2 (no.996).

965 **Connecticut (Colony).** Public records of the colony of Connecticut. Transcribed . . . with occasional notes . . . by J. H. Trumbull (v.1-3) and C. J. Hoadly (v.4-15). 15v. 1850-90. Repr. New York: Johnson Repr., 1968; and New York: A.M.S. Press, 1971.
Covers 1636-1776. Excellent indexes; very important to genealogists.

966 ——— Particular Court. Records 1639-1663. *Collections of the Connecticut Historical Soc.* 22. Hartford, Conn., 1928.
Records of Particular (or Civil) Court, as distinguished from the General Court. Extensive index of names.

967 **Connecticut. Public records of the state of Connecticut.** Published in accordance with a resolution of the General Assembly, by C. J. Hoadly (v.1-3), L. W. Labaree (v.4-8), A. E. Van Dusen (v.9-10), and C. Collier (v.11). Hartford, Conn.: Connecticut State Lib., 1894-1967.
Intended primarily as a continuation of the *Public records of the colony of Connecticut* (*see* no.965); this set begins at 1776, and at v.11 (1967) had reached 1803. Important to genealogists. With the exception of v.6 (1785-89), all are in print. Work ceased after v.11.

968 **Connecticut. Adjutant-General's Office.** Catalogue of Connecticut volunteer organizations (infantry, cavalry and artillery) in the service of the United States 1861-65 . . . Hartford, Conn., 1869.

969 ——— Record of service of Connecticut men in the army and navy of the United States during the War of the Rebellion . . . Hartford, Conn., 1936.
Errata list was published in Hartford in 1936.

970 ——— Record of service of Connecticut men in the I, War of the Revolution; II, War of 1812; III, Mexican War. Hartford, Conn., 1889.
War of the Revolution record supplemented by no.976.

971 **Connecticut. Secretary of State.** Register and manual of the State of Connecticut. Published annually by the Secretary of State, Hartford, Conn.
Important to the genealogist for its information on the origins and evolution of Connecticut towns, probate districts; also listings of state, town and other officials.

972 **Connecticut State Library.** Checklist of probate records in the Connecticut State Library. Hartford, Conn.: The Library, 1972.
Useful for locating wills and administrations in the complicated probate system.

**973   Connecticut ancestry.** v.1– , 1972– . Stamford, Conn.: Stamford Genealogical Soc.

Continues the *Stamford Genealogical Society's bulletin,* then in its 90th issue.

**974   Connecticut births before 1730,** taken from the Barbour collection at the Connecticut State Library. In *The Connecticut nutmegger,* v.2– , 1969– (in progress).

**975   Connecticut Historical Society collections.** 1860– . Hartford, Conn.: The Society.

Although mainly historical in content, several genealogical articles and lists of importance are included.

**976   ——— Lists and returns of Connecticut men in the Revolution,** 1775–83. *Collections of the Connecticut Historical Soc.* 12. Hartford, Conn., 1909.

Many important lists, such as Lexington Alarm list, Continental regiments, 1775–76; Connecticut Line, 1777–83 . . . naval records and list of pensioners. Good index. Supplements the Record of service . . . (no.970).

**977   ——— Rolls of Connecticut men in the French and Indian Wars, 1755–62.** 2v. *Collections of the Connecticut Historical Soc.* 9–10. Hartford, Conn., 1903–5.

**978   The Connecticut magazine.** An illustrated monthly devoted to Connecticut . . . v.1–12. Hartford, Conn., 1895–1908.

v.1–4 as *Connecticut quarterly.* Much genealogy.

**979   Connecticut marriages before 1750,** taken from the Barbour collection at the Connecticut State Library. In *The Connecticut nutmegger,* v.2, 1969– (in progress).

**980   The Connecticut nutmegger.** Quarterly of the Connecticut Society of Genealogists, Inc. v.1– , 1968– . West Hartford, Conn.: The Society.

Records and births before 1730, marriages before 1750, headstones before 1800, census records by surnames, family and Bible records, unpublished genealogies, etc.

**982   Cutter, William R.** Genealogical and family history of the state of Connecticut . . . 4v. New York, 1911.

Contains biographical and genealogical sketches of prominent and representative citizens and many of the early settlers. Consolidated index of this and other Cutter books, *see* Ireland and Irving, no.593.

**983   Daughters of Founders and Patriots of America. Connecticut.** Family records (heretofore unpublished). Ed. by Mrs. J. L. (Elizabeth C.) Buel. Derby, Conn., 1935.

Collected in commemoration of the 300th anniversary of the settlement of Connecticut.

**984   Eardeley, William A. D.** Connecticut cemeteries, 1673–1910. 8v. Brooklyn, N.Y., 1914–17.

Has records, with genealogical notes, of 45 Connecticut cemeteries, 27 of which are in Stamford. Typescript copies in many libraries.

**985   Encyclopedia of Connecticut biography, genealogical memorial;** representative citizens . . . 12v. Boston, 1917–23.

v.12 is typed index. Mug book, with coats of arms in color.

**986   Flagg, Charles A.** Reference list on Connecticut local history. *New York State Lib. bull.* 53. Albany, N.Y., 1900.

Good bibliography.

**987   Gannett, Henry.** A geographic dictionary of Connecticut. *U.S. Geological Survey bull.* 117. Washington, D.C., 1894.

**988   Goodwin, Nathaniel.** Genealogical notes, or contributions to the family history of some of the first settlers of Connecticut and Massachusetts. 1856. Repr. Baltimore: G.P.C., 1969.

Partial genealogies of the settlers, often to the 7th generation.

**989   Hale, Charles E.** Connecticut headstone inscriptions before 1800. In *The Connecticut nutmegger,* v.2, 1969– (in progress).

**990  Hart, Samuel.** Representative citizens of Connecticut. Biographical, memorial. New York, 1916.
Many coats of arms.

**991  Harwood, Pliny Le R.** History of eastern Connecticut embracing counties of Tolland, Windham, Middlesex and New London . . . 3v. Chicago, 1931–32.
v.3 biographical.

**992  Hedden, James S.** Roster and graves of, or monuments to, patriots of 1775–83 and of soldiers of colonial wars in and adjacent to New Haven county. 4v. in 3. New Haven, Conn., 1931–34.

**993  Hempstead, Joshua.** The diary of Joshua Hempstead of New London county . . . 1711–58. *New London County Historical Soc. collections* 1. Providence, R.I., 1901.
Contains genealogical material of high quality for the New London area.

**994  Hinman, Royal R.** A catalog of the names of the first Puritan settlers of the Colony of Connecticut, with the time of their arrival in the Colony . . . 1846. Repr. Baltimore: G.P.C., 1968.
Reprint of 1st ed. A 2nd ed. was started but not continued beyond pt.2 (A–Danielson), pub. 1852–56. 2,000 settlers, with genealogical sketches and notices.

**995  Historical Records Survey.** Guide to vital statistics in the church records of Connecticut. New Haven, Conn., 1942.

**996  ———** Inventory of the church archives of Connecticut. 2v. New Haven, Conn., 1940–41.
v.1, Lutheran; v.2, Protestant Episcopal; *see also* no.964.

**997  Hoadly, Charles J.** Records of the colony and jurisdiction of New Haven from May 1653 to the union, together with the New Haven code of 1656. Hartford, Conn., 1858.
Comprises all the records of the jurisdiction of New Haven now known to exist except the few entries in the records of the colony and plantation of New Haven printed in 1857.

**998  ———** Records of the colony and plantation of New Haven from 1638–49. Hartford, Conn., 1857.
Contains records of New Haven while it remained a district, the beginning of jurisdiction and the records to 1650.

**999  Ireland, Norman (O.)** Index to Hartford Times "Genealogical gleanings" in 1912–16. Fallbrook, Calif.: Ireland Indexing Service, 1973.
Index to major surnames, including some long articles.

**1000  Jacobus, Donald L.** Families of ancient New Haven, v.1-8. 1922–32; cross index by Helen L. Scranton, 1939. Repr. 9v. in 3. Baltimore: G.P.C., 1974.
Ancestry and relationships of 35,000 residents of 18th-century New Haven. The continuation was called *American genealogist and New Haven genealogical magazine,* see no.103.

**1001  ———** History and genealogy of the families of Old Fairfield. 3v. New Haven, Conn., 1930–32.
Old Fairfield includes the present towns of Easton, Redding, Weston and Westport and many families in other southwestern Connecticut towns.

**1002  ———** Additions and corrections to the history and genealogy of the families of Old Fairfield. (Supplement to the *American genealogist,* Oct. 1943. Fairfield, Conn., 1943.)

**1003  ———** List of officials, civil, military, and ecclesiastical of Connecticut colony, from March 1636 through 11 October 1677, and of New Haven colony throughout its separate existence; also soldiers in the Pequot War who then or subsequently resided within the present bounds of Connecticut. New Haven, Conn., 1935.
Included are dates of deaths, offices and ranks, and references to printed records of colonies where additional data can be found.

**1004  Manwaring, Charles W.** A digest of the early Connecticut probate records. 3v. Hartford, Conn.: Connecticut Historical Soc., 1904–1906.

Covers Hartford probate district, 1635–1750. Wills, inventories and court records for many towns.

**1005 Mather, Frederic G.** The refugees of 1776 from Long Island to Connecticut. 1913. Repr. Baltimore: G.P.C., 1972.

In the period following the American defeat at the Battle of Long Island (August 27, 1776), more than 5,000 refugees fled Long Island and New York City for the security of Connecticut. 20,000-name index; history of New York in the Revolutionary War; service records. Not up to modern standards of documentation, but useful.

**1006 Middlebrook, Louis F.** History of maritime Connecticut during the American Revolution, 1775–83. 2v. 1925. Repr. Salem, Mass.: Essex Institute, 1973.

**1007 New Haven Colony Historical Society.** Papers. 1–9. New Haven, Conn., 1865–1918.

Mainly historical, but there are several cemetery records and other genealogical materials.

**1008 New Haven genealogical magazine.** *See* no.103 and 1000.

**1009 Pease, John C.,** and **Niles, J. M.** Gazetteer of the states of Connecticut and Rhode Island. Hartford, Conn., 1819.

**1010 Perry, Charles E.** Founders and leaders of Connecticut, 1633–1783 . . . 1934. Repr. Freeport, N.Y.: Books for Libraries Pr., 1971.

**1011 Representative men of Connecticut, 1861–69.** Everett, Mass., 1894. Mug book.

**1012 Sellers, Helen E.** Connecticut town origins, their names, boundaries, early histories and first families. Repr. from *Connecticut register and manual*, 1942 ed. Stonington, Conn., 1964?

**1013 Society of Colonial Wars. Connecticut.** Register of pedigrees and services of ancestors. Hartford, Conn., 1941.

Qualifying ancestors of members or pedigrees, showing descent. Accurate compilation.

**1014 Society of the Cincinnati. Connecticut.** Records 1783–1807. 2v. Hartford, Conn., 1916.

Officers with rank, place of abode, service in the army.

**1015 Spalding, John A.** Illustrated popular biography of Connecticut. 2v. Hartford, Conn., 1891–1900.

Mug book. v.2 compiled by Hartford Post.

**1016 Stevenson, Robert.** Connecticut history makers. Containing sketches and portraits of men who have contributed to the progress of the state. 3v. Waterbury, Conn., 1929–38.

**1017 Teeples, Gary R.,** and **Jackson, R. V.** Connecticut 1800 census. Provo, Utah: Accelerated Indexing Systems, 1974.

Over 40,000 entries. Research aids and maps. Computer listing.

**1018 U.S. Bureau of the Census.** Heads of families at the first census of the United States taken in the year 1790. Connecticut. 1908. Repr. Baltimore: G.P.C., 1966, etc.; Spartanburg, S.C.: Reprint Co., 1965, etc.

**1019 U.S. Pension Bureau.** Pension records of the Revolutionary soldiers from Connecticut. 21st report of the National Society, D.A.R., Washington, D.C., 1919.

Persons who served from Connecticut whose applications are on file in the Pensions Office, Washington, D.C. Copied by Mrs. A. G. Draper.

**1020 Volkel, Lowell M.** An index to the 1800 federal census, State of Connecticut. 3v. in 1. Thomson, Ill.: Heritage House, 1968–69.

Head of each household, with county and page reference of original census records. Counties of Middlesex, New London, Fairfield, Hartford, Litchfield, New Haven, Tolland, and Windham. Complete register.

## DELAWARE

Settled ca. 1638; original state

*Historical Society of Delaware, Wilmington*

**1021** **Beers, Daniel G.** Atlas of the state of Delaware. Philadelphia, 1868.
Includes large-scale plots of hundreds and towns, indicating building and property owners, as well as physical details.

**1022** **Bevan, Wilson L.** History of Delaware past and present. 4v. New York, 1929.
v.3-4 are biographical sketches, many with genealogical data.

**1023** **Biographical and genealogical history of the state of Delaware,** containing sketches of . . . citizens, and many of the early settlers. 2v. Chambersburg, Pa., 1899.
Mug book.

**1024** **Clay, Jehu C.** Annals of the Swedes on the Delaware from their first settlement in 1636 to the present time (1858). 3rd ed. Chicago, 1914.

**1025** **Colonial Dames of Delaware.** A calendar of Delaware wills, New Castle county, 1628-1800. 1911. Repr. Baltimore: G.P.C., 1969.
Full information of contents of wills, but lacks information on intestate estates.

**1026** **Conrad, Henry C.** History of the state of Delaware from the earliest settlements to 1907. 3v. Wilmington, Del., 1908.
Contains a substantial amount of biography and genealogy at scattered points, a civil list, and an acceptable historical account.

**1027** **Delaware. Original land titles in Delaware commonly known as the Duke of York record,** being an authorized transcript from the official archives of the state of Delaware . . . 1646-79. Wilmington, Del., 1903. Obtainable from Public Archives Commission, Dover, Del.
Essential for study of land titles in Delaware; contains many names.

**1028** **Delaware. Public Archives Commission.** Delaware archives. 5v. 1911-19. Repr. New York: A.M.S. Press, 1974.
Contents: v.1, *Colonial and Revolutionary wars, military;* v.2, *Revolutionary War, military and naval;* v.3, *Revolutionary War and index;* v.4, *Military, 1795-1813;* v.5, *Military, 1813-27.*

**1029** ———— Governor's register, state of Delaware. v.1 (all pub.).
Appointments and other transactions by executives of the state, 1674-1851. Ed. by Henry C. Conrad. Wilmington, Del., 1926.
Comprises transcripts of registers dating from 1802 to 1851, with fragmentary lists assembled from various sources disclosing a portion of the earlier appointments. 5,000 names.

**1030** **Delaware history.** v.1- , 1946- . Wilmington, Del.: Historical Soc. of Delaware. v.1-7 repr. New York: Kraus Repr., 1968.
See notation under no.1043. Historical Soc. of Delaware, *Papers. Delaware history* is similar. Has some genealogy.

**1031** **De Valinger, Leon, Jr.** Calendar of Kent county, Delaware probate records, 1680-1800. Dover, Del., 1944.
Includes testate and intestate estates.

**1032** ———— Calendar of Sussex county, Delaware probate records, 1680-1800. Dover, Del., 1964.
Includes testate and intestate estates.

**1033** ———— Court records of Kent county, Delaware, 1680-1705. *American legal records* 8. Washington, D.C.: American Historical Assoc., 1959.
Court records from the original of Kent county, formerly St. Jones county, until the 3 lower counties obtained separate assemblies.

**1034** ———— Reconstructed 1790 census of Delaware. 2nd pr. *National Genealogical Soc. special publ.* 10. Washington, D.C.: The Society, 1962.
Reconstructed from assessment lists of the various hundreds, to replace the missing federal census of 1790 to the best extent possible.

**1035** **Dunlap, Arthur R.** Dutch and Swedish place-names in Delaware. Newark, Del., 1956.

**1036** **Ferris, Benjamin.** A history of the original settlements on the Delaware . . . Wilmington, Del., 1846.

**1037** **Gannett, Henry.** A gazetteer of Delaware. *U.S. Geological Survey bull.* 230. Washington, D.C., 1904.

**1038** **Hancock, Harold B.** The Delaware loyalists. 1940. Repr. Boston: Gregg, 1973.
Authoritative study, in which the author estimates that half of Delaware's inhabitants were loyalists. *Historical Soc. of Delaware papers* 3.

**1039** **Historical and biographical encyclopedia of Delaware.** Wilmington, Del., 1882.

**1040** **Historical Records Survey.** Directory of churches and religious organizations in Delaware. Wilmington, Del., 1942.

**1041** ——— Inventory of church archives of Delaware. Lutheran and Protestant Episcopal. Wilmington, Del., 1938.

**1042** ——— Inventory of the county archives of Delaware. Dover, Del., 1941.
Only the following was published: no.1 (New Castle). Unpublished material deposited with Dept. of Archives, State Univ., Dover, Del.

**1043** **Historical Society of Delaware.** Papers, 1–67, 1879–1922; new ser., 1–3, 1927–40. Wilmington, Del.
Not primarily genealogical, but includes a considerable number of biographical studies with varying amounts of information about the subject's ancestors, descendants, and other relatives. no.7, 9, 9A, 13, 14, 41, 42, and new ser.3 have excellent genealogical matter. Some still available from the Society.

**1044** **Jackson, Ronald V.** Delaware 1800 census. Provo, Utah: Accelerated Indexing Systems, 1972.
Federal census; over 10,000 entries. Includes excerpts from the *Delaware tercentenary almanack and historical repository,* 1938. G. R. Teeples, paleographer.

**1045** **Johnson, Amandus.** The Swedish settlements on the Delaware, 1638–64. 2v. 1st ed. 1911, repr. 1927. 1911 ed. repr. Baltimore: G.P.C., 1969
Thorough and detailed history of the New Sweden settlement on the Delaware, including territory now in Delaware, Pennsylvania and New Jersey. Brief biographies, genealogical notices, and lists of settlers.

**1046** **McCarter, James M.,** and **Jackson, B. F.** Historical and biographical encyclopedia of Delaware. Wilmington, Del., 1882.
Contains biographical sketches with genealogical data.

**1047** **Maddux, Gerald M.,** and **Maddux, D. O.** 1800 census, Delaware. [Montgomery, Ala., 1964.] Distr. by G.P.C., Baltimore.
First census of Delaware available because the 1790 census was destroyed (but *see* no.1034). Includes all three counties, but omits the final columns of the tabulations and all marginal comments. About 8,500 heads of families, with full information.

**1048** **Marvil, James E.** Pilots of the Bayard River, Delaware. Laurel, Del., 1965.
Contains not only lists of pilots and ships, but some captain's ledgers listing passengers.

**1049** **Maryland and Delaware genealogist.** v.1– , 1959– . St. Michael's, Md.: Raymond B. Clark, Jr., and Sara S. Clark, eds. and pubs.
Primarily Maryland. Transcriptions are numerous and accurate.

**1050** **Myers, Albert C.** Walter Wharton's land survey register, 1675–79. West side Delaware river from Newcastle, Delaware into Bucks county, Pennsylvania . . . Wilmington, Del.: Historical Soc. of Delaware, 1955.

**1051** New Castle. Court. Records of the Court of New Castle on Delaware, 1676-99. 2v. Colonial Soc. of Pennsylvania. Lancaster and Meadville, Pa., 1904, 1935.
Earliest legal records for this area. v.1, 1676-81, comprises full transcripts; v.2, 1681-99, has land-probate extracts only.

**1052** Pennsylvania archives. Ser.1 and 2 are important to Delawareans. *See* no.2976.

**1053** Reed, Henry C., and Reed, M. B. A bibliography of Delaware through 1960. Newark, Del.: Univ. of Delaware Pr., 1966.
Has a section on biography and family history.

**1054** ———— Delaware, a history of the first state. 3v. New York, 1947.
v.3 has personal and family records.

**1055** Rogers, Ellen S., and Easter, L. E. 1800 census of Kent county, Delaware. Bladensburg, Md.: Genealogical Recorders, 1959.
Earliest federal census extant. Complete transcription, with good map. 3,100 heads of families with names of slaves.

**1056** ———— 1800 census of New Castle county, Delaware. Bladensburg, Md.: Genealogical Recorders, 1960.

**1057** Runk, J. M., and Co. Biographical and genealogical history of the state of Delaware, containing biographical and genealogical sketches of prominent and representative citizens and many of the early settlers. 2v. Chambersburg, Pa., 1899.

**1058** Scharf, John T. History of Delaware, 1609-1888. 2v. 1888. Repr. Port Washington, N.Y.: Kennikat Pr., 1972.
Contains many biographical sketches with genealogical data; useful histories of hundreds and towns; civil lists. Index very poor.

**1059** Turner, Charles H. B. Rodney's diary and other Delaware records. Philadelphia, 1911.
The diary covers 1813-29, and contains records about Delaware and Delaware people, from archaeological, public, and private sources of Delaware, Maryland, New Jersey, Pennsylvania, and New York, nearly all before 1800. Full index of names. Judge Daniel Rodney (1764-1846) was in a good position to observe and record events of the period.

**1060** Ward, Christopher L. The Delaware continentals, 1776-83. Wilmington, Del., 1941.
History of the Delaware regiment. Roster of officers, 1776 and 1780, and index of persons.

**1061** Whiteley, William G. The Revolutionary soldiers of Delaware . . . Wilmington, Del., 1896.

**1062** Wilmington, Delaware. Holy Trinity Church. The records of Holy Trinity (Old Swedes) Church, 1697-1773. Transl. with an abstract of the English records, 1773-1810, by Horace Burr . . . *Papers of the Historical Soc. of Delaware* 9. Wilmington, Del.: The Society, 1890.

**1063** ———— Catalogue and errata. *Papers* 9A. 1919.

**1064** ———— Communicants records, 1713-56. pts.1-6 in *Delaware history,* v.5-7, 1954-57. Transcribed by Courtland B. and R. L. Springer.

**1065** ———— Burial records, 1713-65. In *Delaware history,* v.5, 1952-53.

DISTRICT OF COLUMBIA

Seat of government established in District of Columbia in 1800 from territory taken from Maryland and Virginia

*Columbia Historical Society, Washington, D.C.*

**1066** American biographical directories, District of Columbia. Concise biographies of its prominent and representative contemporary citizens . . . Washington, D.C., 1908.

**1067** Biographical cyclopedia of representative men of Maryland and the District of Columbia. Baltimore, 1879.

**1068 Bell, Mrs. Alexander H.** Abstracts of wills in the District of Columbia, 1776–1815. 2v. Washington, D.C., 1945–46.

**1069 Brown, Mary R.** An illustrated genealogy of the counties of Maryland and the District of Columbia as a guide to locating records. Baltimore, 1967.
For annotation, see no.1746.

**1070 Bryan, Wilhelmos B.** A history of the National Capital, 1790–1814, 1815–78. 2v. New York, 1914.

**1071 Columbia Historical Society, Washington, D.C.** Records, v.1– , 1897– . Washington, D.C., The Society.
Covers 1894– . Records from v.8 in print. Indexes 1–10, 11–20, 21–30 in print. Index, v.1–34, 1897–1932, by Ella J. Morison, out of print. Contains a wealth of historical and biographical information, and some genealogy.

**1072 Crew, Harvey W.** Centennial history of the city of Washington, D.C. . . . Dayton, Ohio, 1892.

**1073 Delano, Judah.** Washington directory, 1822, showing the name, occupation and residence, of each head of a family and person in business . . . together with other useful information. Washington, D.C., 1822.

**1074 Ely, Selden M.** The District of Columbia in the American Revolution, and patriots of the Revolutionary period who are interred in the District or in Arlington. *Records of the Columbia Historical Soc.* 21. Washington, D.C., The Society, 1918.

**1075 Eminent and representative men of Virginia and the District of Columbia in the nineteenth century . . .** Madison, Wisc., 1893.

**1076 Faehtz, Ernest F. M.,** and **Pratt, F. W.** Washington in embryo, or the national capital from 1791–1800. The original of all rents and titles and property in Washington, D.C. Washington, D.C., 1874.
Plats and many names.

**1077 Gahn, Bessie W.** Original patentees of land at Washington prior to 1700. 1936. Repr. Baltimore: G.P.C., 1969.
Because of the distribution of land when the District was formed, records of Maryland and Virginia are included. 200 family names listed. List of original landowners in D.C.

**1078 Historical Records Survey.** Directory of churches and religious organizations in the District of Columbia. Preliminary ed. Washington, D.C., 1939.

**1079 ———** Inventory of church archives of the District of Columbia . . . 2v. Washington, D.C., 1940.
v.1, Protestant Episcopal church in D.C., Montgomery, Prince George's, and St. Mary's counties, Md.; v.2, Washington Cathedral.

**1080 Huguenot Society of Washington, D.C.** Roster of members, 1940– . Washington, D.C., The Society.
Commenced in 1928 as year book. Lists Huguenot ancestors.

**1081 Jackson, Ronald V.** Washington, D.C. 1800 census. Provo, Utah: Accelerated Indexing Systems, 1972.
About 1,900 entries. Federal census.

**1082 Martenet, Simon J.** New topographical atlas of the state of Maryland and the District of Columbia. Baltimore, 1872.

**1083 Martin, George A.** Vital records from the *National intelligencer* (District of Columbia), 1824–30. In *National Genealogical Society quarterly,* v. 36–49, 1947–60.

**1084 ———** 1831–35. In *National Genealogical Society quarterly,* v.52–61, 1964–73.
1831 in v.55; 1832 in v.52; 1833 in v.56–58; 1834 in v.58–59; 1835 in v.60–61.
For 1805–23 see no.1086.

**1085 Martin, Joseph.** A new and comprehensive gazetteer of Virginia and the District of Columbia. n.p., 1835.

**1086** Metcalf, Frank J. Vital records extracted from the *National intelligencer,* Washington, D. C., 1805-23. In *National Genealogical Society quarterly,* v. 26-35, 1937-46.
For 1824-30, *see* no.1083.

**1087** ——— and **Martin, G. A.** Marriages and deaths, *National intelligencer,* 1800-21. *National Genealogical Soc. publ.* 34. Washington, D.C.: The Society, 1968.
Records of marriages and deaths which occurred in all parts of the country.

**1088** National Genealogical Society quarterly. Topical index. v.1-50, 1912-62, by Carleton E. Fisher. *National Genealogical Soc. special publ.* 29. Washington, D.C.: The Society, 1964.
Has many references to the District of Columbia.

**1089** Proctor, John C. Washington and environs. Privately pr., 1949.
Newspaper articles written for the *Washington Sunday star,* 1928-49. Mostly historical, but some genealogical data.

**1090** ——— Washington, past and present. 4v. Washington, D.C., 1930.
v.3-4 biographical.

**1091** Ridgely, Helen W. Historic graves of Maryland and the District of Columbia, with the inscriptions appearing on the tombstones in most of the counties of Washington and Georgetown. 1908. Repr. Baltimore: G.P.C., 1967.
Primarily on inscriptions on tombstones of the Colonial and Revolutionary areas.

**1092** Society of Colonial Wars, District of Columbia register. Ed. by Frederick L. Ordway. Washington, D.C.: The Society, 1967.
Useful for providing clues for further research, but must not be considered authoritative.

**1093** Society of Mayflower Descendants, District of Columbia. Register 1970. Ed. by Frederick L. Ordway. Washington, D.C.: The Society, 1970.

Over 400 lineages, with biographical information. Complete name index. Suppl. issued in 1973.

**1094** Walker, Homer A. Historical court records of Washington, District of Columbia. Death records of Washington, D.C., 1801-78. As taken from Administration of estates records, group 21 *(OS),* District Court records of Washington, D.C. 2v. Washington, D.C., 1956?

**1095** ——— ——— Miscellaneous marriage records, 1811-58. 14v. Washington, D.C., 1955-56.

## FLORIDA

Settled ca. 1565; entered Union 1845

*Metropolitan Dade Public Library System, Miami*
*Orlando Public Library*
*University of South Florida, Tampa*

**1096** Blackman, Lucy W. Women of Florida. 2v. [Tampa, Fla.], ca. 1940.
v.2 biographical.

**1097** Carter, Clarence E. The territory of Florida, 1821-45. 5v. *Territorial papers of the U.S.* 22-26. 1956-62. Repr. New York: A.M.S. Press, 1973.
Lists of persons signing petitions, memorials, etc.

**1098** Cash, William T. The story of Florida. 4v. New York, 1938.
v.3-4 biographical.

**1099** Chapin, George M. Florida, 1513-1913. 2v. Chicago, 1914.
v.2 biographical.

**1100** Covington, James W. Story of southwestern Florida. 2v. New York, 1957.
v.2 biographical.

**1101** Cutler, Harry G. History of Florida, past and present, historical and biographical. 3v. Chicago, 1923.
v.2-3 biographical.

**1102** **Dovell, Junius E.** Florida: historic, dramatic, contemporary. 4v. New York, 1952.
v.3-4 biographical.

**1103** **Florida. Comptroller's Office.** Report of the Comptroller of the state of Florida, 1882-1906. Tallahassee, Fla.
Lists persons receiving pensions from the state, 1886-1906. Report still issued, but contains no genealogical information. 1886-1906 also have "Lunatics in private hands." 1906 has Confederate soldiers listed.

**1104** **Florida. State Library, Tallahassee.** Genealogy and local history, a bibliography (of the holdings of the library). 4th ed. Tallahassee, Fla.: The Library, 1972.
Over 2,000 titles; some emphasis on Florida.

**1105** **Florida genealogical journal.** v.1- , 1965- . Tampa, Fla.: Florida Genealogical Soc.

**1106** **Florida genealogical research quarterly.** v.1- , 1972- . Pinellas Park, Fla.: Florida Soc. for Genealogical Research, Inc.

**1107** **Fritot, Jessie R.** Pension records of soldiers of the Revolution who removed to Florida, with records of service. Jacksonville, Fla., 1946.

**1108** **Harris, Michael H.** Florida history: a bibliography. Metuchen, N.J.: Scarecrow, 1973.
Church, education, Indians in Florida, local history. 2,932 citations of interest in southern history.

**1109** **Historical Records Survey.** Guide to public vital statistics records in Florida. Jacksonville, Fla., 1941.

**1110** ——— Guide to supplementary vital statistics from church records in Florida. (Preliminary) 3v. Jacksonville, Fla., 1942.
v.1, Aluchua; 2, Gilchrist; 3, Orange.

**1111** ——— Inventory of the church archives of Florida. Baptist bodies. no.3, 12, 17-21, 25, 30, and 32 only pub.

**1112** ——— Inventory of the county archives of Florida. 12v. Jacksonville, Fla., 1938-42.
Only the following numbers were published: 8 (Charlotte), 10 (Clay), 11 (Collier), 16 (Duval), 18 (Flagler), 25 (Hardee), 26 (Hendry), 37 (Leon), 46 (Okaloosa), 54 (Pinellas), 58 (Sarasota), and 65 (Wakulla). Unpublished material deposited in Dept. of Archives, Tallahassee, Fla.

**1113** ——— Preliminary list of religious bodies in Florida. Jacksonville, Fla., 1939.

**1114** ——— Spanish land grants in Florida. Briefed translations . . . for ascertaining claims and titles to land in the territory of Florida. 5v. Tallahassee, Fla., 1940-41.
v.1, Unconfirmed claims; v.2-5, Confirmed claims. v.2 had 2nd ed., 1942.

**1115** ——— Translation and transcription of church archives of Florida; Roman Catholic records, St. Augustine parish: white baptisms, 1784-99. 2v. Tallahassee, Fla., 1941.

**1116** **The Jacksonville Genealogical Society magazine.** v.1- , 1974- . Jacksonville, Fla.: The Society.
Has information on Florida in general; pensioners, censuses of counties, war dead buried in Florida, etc.

**1117** **Lazenby, Marion E.** History of Methodism in Alabama and west Florida. *See* no.746.

**1118** **McKay, Donald B.** Pioneer Florida. 3v. Tampa, Fla., 1959.
v.3 biographical. Personal and family records.

**1119** **Marks, Henry S.** Who was who in Florida. Huntsville, Ala.: Strode Pub., 1973.
Florida notables who have made a contribution to the state's history; short biographical sketches.

**1120** **Morris, Allen C.** Florida place names. Coral Gables, Fla.: Univ. of Miami Pr., 1973.

Comprehensive; includes Indian, Spanish, French, British names, and those of soldiers, settlers, etc.

**1121** **Nance, Ellwood C.** The east coast of Florida. 3v. Delray Beach, Fla., 1962.
v.3 biographical.

**1121a** **Outstanding Floridians..** 1971. Ocala, Fla.: Universal Pub. Co., 1972.
Many portraits.

**1122** **Pierce, Charles W.** Pioneer life in southeast Florida. Ed. by D. W. Curl. Coral Gables, Fla.: Univ. of Miami Pr., 1970.
Palm Beach county history.

**1123** **Rerick, Rowland H.** Memoirs of Florida. 2v. Atlanta, Ga., 1902.
Latter half of each volume has biographies.

**1124** **Robertson, Frederick L.** Soldiers of Florida in the Seminole Indian, Civil and Spanish-American wars. [Live Oak, Fla., 1909?]
Florida in the war between the states, pp.33–338; muster rolls.

**1125** **Rosselli, Bruno.** The Italians in colonial times. A repertory of Italian families who settled in Florida under the Spanish 1513-1762, 1784-1821 and British 1762-1784. Jacksonville, Fla., 1940.
Treats some early residents.

**1126** **Shaw, Aurora C.** 1830 Florida U.S. census. An alphabetical list of all the heads of households enumerated in this census, showing county of residence. Jacksonville, Fla.: *Southern Genealogist's Exchange quarterly,* 1968.

**1127** ———— 1840 Florida U.S. census.
A statewide index of all heads of households in all twenty counties formed by 1840, showing counties in which they resided. Jacksonville, Fla.: The Compiler, 1968.

**1128** **Siebert, Wilbur H.** Loyalists in east Florida, 1774-85. 2v. 1929. Repr. Boston: Gregg, 1973.

East Florida became a haven for loyalists from southern colonies, especially Georgia and the Carolinas.

**1129** **South Florida pioneers quarterly.** v.1– , 1974– . Ft. Ogden, Fla.: Richard Livingston.
Cemetery, court, Bible and census records; early settlers of south Florida.

**1130** **Southern Genealogist's Exchange Society.** 1850 Florida census. v.1– . Jacksonville, Fla.: The Society, 1972– (in progress).
Series of county censuses. Counties published thus far: Duval, Leon, Madison, Alachua, Calhoun, Levy, Putnam, Santa Rosa, Gadsden, Benton, Dade, Orange, St. Lucie, and Nassau.

**1131** **Taylor, Beverly M. (Mrs. Lester E.).**
1840 index to Florida census. Mobile, Ala.: The Compiler, 1974.

**1132** **Tebeau, Charlton W.** A history of Florida. Coral Gables, Fla.: Univ. of Miami Pr., 1971.
General history, indexed, contains extensive bibliography.

**1133** ———— and **Carson, R. L.** Florida from Indian trail to space age. 3v. Delray Beach, Fla.: Southern Pub. Co., 1965.
v.3 biographical.

**1134** **Trinkner, Charles L.** Florida lives. The sunshine state who's who . . . biographies of contemporary leaders . . . Hopkinsville, Ky., 1966.

**1134a** **Warnke, James R.** Ghost towns of Florida. Boynton Beach, Fla.: Star Pub. Co., 1971.
References to settlers in these abandoned communities.

GEORGIA

Settled ca. 1733; original state

*Department of Archives and History, Atlanta*
*Georgia Historical Society, Savannah*

*Surveyor-General Department, Atlanta*
*Mr. Richard S. Lackey, Forest, Mississippi*

**1135** **Averitt, Jack N.** Georgia's coastal plain. 3v. New York, 1964.
v.3 family and personal history.

**1136** **Baker, Pearl R. (Mrs. F. F.)** 'Neath Georgia sod. Georgia cemetery inscriptions. Albany, Ga.: Mary Carter, 1970.
2,000 inscriptions from Columbia, Warren, McDuffie, Lincoln, Wilkes, Richmond, Glascock, and Taliaferro counties.

**1137** **Blair, Ruth.** Some early tax digests of Georgia. 1926. Repr. Easley, S.C.: Southern Historical Pr., 1971.
36,000 names indexed. Full returns for Glynn, Wilkes, Camden, Chatham, Hancock, Lincoln, Pulaski, Richmond, Warren, and Montgomery counties for periods 1790 to 1818.

**1138** **Bonner, James C.** Atlas for Georgia history. 1969. Repr. Fort Worth, Tex.: Miran Pub., 1974.
Essential for genealogical research. 70 maps, some original form, some from Georgia Dept. of Archives; description of the various land lotteries.

**1139** **Brinkley, Hal E.** How Georgia got her names. Rev. Atlanta, Ga.: Educational Supply Co., 1974.
2,000 names; quick reference.

**1140** **Bryan, Mary G.** Passports issued by governors of Georgia, 1785-1820 (and) Index of persons receiving passports, 1785-1820, by William H. Dumont. 2v. *National Genealogical Soc. special publ.* 21, 28. Washington, D.C.: The Society, 1962-64.
Good reference for Mississippi and Alabama settlers.

**1141** **Butts, Sarah H.** The mothers of some distinguished Georgians of the last half of the century. New York, 1902.
Since many biographical sketches ignore wives and mothers, this is useful.

**1142** **Candler, Allen D.** Revolutionary records of the state of Georgia, 1769-84. 3v. 1908. Repr. New York: A.M.S. Press, 1971.

**1143** ——— and **Evans, C. A.** Georgia, comprising sketches of counties, towns, events, institutions, persons, arranged in cyclopedic form. 4v. 1906. Repr. Spartanburg, S.C.: Reprint Co., 1972.
v.4 is supplemental, comprising sketches of representative Georgians for whom special portraits have been prepared. Repr. is titled *Cyclopedia of Georgia.*

**1144** **Cartledge, Groves H.** Historical sketches; Presbyterian churches and early settlers in northeast Georgia. Compiled by J. J. Mize and V. L. Newton. Athens, Ga., 1960.
Good genealogical material.

**1145** **Colonial Dames of America. Georgia.** Abstracts of the colonial wills of the state of Georgia, 1733-77. Ed. by Mary G. Bryan. Atlanta, Ga.: Dept. of Archives and History, 1962.
About 500 wills abstracted. Accurate.

**1146** ——— Register. Baltimore, 1937.

**1147** ——— Some early epitaphs in Georgia, with a foreword and sketches by Frances (Mrs. Peter W.) Meldrim. 1924. Repr. Durham, N.C., 1967.
Mainly old colonial cemetery, Savannah, indexed.

**1148** **The colonial records of the state of Georgia, 1732-82.** Ed. under the supervision of A. D. Candler. 26v. 1904-16. Repr. New York: A.M.S. Press, 1971.
Printed from manuscript originals copied in London. v.20 never published.

**1149** **Cooper, Walter G.** The story of Georgia. 4v. New York, 1938.
v.4 biographical.

**1150** **Coulter, Ellis M.**, and **Saye, A. B.** A list of the early settlers of Georgia. 2nd pr. Athens, Ga.: Univ. of Georgia Pr. [1967].
Details of 2,800 persons living in Georgia 1733-42 as they appeared in the Journal of the Earl of Egmont. Shows those who

came with Oglethorpe, indentured servants, and includes many who went to South Carolina.

**1151 D.A.R. Georgia.** Historical collections of the Georgia chapters. v.1–5, 1926–49. v.1–4 repr. Easley, S. C.: Southern Historical Pr., 1968–69.
v.1, *17 Georgia counties* (1926), with index by Mrs. J. C. Gentry; v.2, *Richmond county* (1927) by Mrs. J. L. Davidson; v.3, *Elbert county* (1930), records abstracted by Mrs. J. L. Davidson; v.4, *Old Bible records and land lotteries* (1932); v.5, *Marriage records, Greene and Oglethorpe counties* (1949) by Mrs. Hershel W. Smith. v.5 not repr.; available from Georgia D.A.R.

**1152** ———— **Joseph Habersham Chapter.** Historical collections. 3v. 1902–10. Repr. Baltimore: G.P.C., 1967–68. v.3 also repr. by Southern Historical Pr., Easley, S.C., 1968.
Volumes contain a variety of genealogical records but with much supporting data omitted; use with reserve.

**1153** ———— Membership roll and register of ancestors, by Nellie (Mrs. J. N.) Brawner. n.p., 1946.

**1154 Davidson, Grace G.** Early records of Georgia: Wilkes county. 2v. 1932. Repr. 2v. in 1. Easley, S.C.: Southern Historical Pr., 1968.
Copies of actual records in Wilkes county courthouse. List of those who petitioned the Land Court commissions for the new ceded lands in 1773, which became Wilkes in 1777. Many did not come to Georgia.

**1155 Davis, Harry A.** Some Huguenot families of South Carolina and Georgia . . . 2nd ed., rev. and enl. Washington, D.C., 1927.
Supplement was published in 1937.

**1156 Delwyn Associates.** 1830 census of Georgia. Albany, Ga.: The Compilers, 1973.
Index of heads of families with all names arranged alphabetically. County of residence and census page reference.

**1157** ———— Substitutes for Georgia's lost 1790 census. Albany, Ga.: The Compilers, 1974.
Arranged alphabetically. Tax digest, jury list, voter list, military rosters, will and deed records and old newspapers used.

**1158 Dumont, William H.** Colonial Georgia genealogical data, 1748–83. National Genealogical Soc. special publ. 36. Washington, D.C.: The Society, 1971.
Marriage agreements, administrations of colonial estates, guardianships, claims, grants, miscellaneous genealogical data.

**1159** ———— Index of persons receiving passports, 1785–1820. *See* no.1140.

**1160 The 1820 land lottery of Georgia.** Easley, S.C.: Southern Historical Pr., 1973.
Over 25,000 names of fortunate drawers covering Walton, Gwinnett, Hall, Habersham, Early, Irwin, Appling, Rabun counties.

**1161 1821 land lottery of Georgia.** Easley, S.C.: Southern Historical Pr., 1973.
Over 17,000 names covering Dooly, Houston, Monroe, Henry and Fayette counties. 1820 and 1821 lotteries also published in 1v.

**1162 Federal census of Atlanta 1850.**
Free inhabitants in Atlanta in the county of DeKalb, state of Georgia . . . Nov. 1850. With index. In *Atlanta historical bull.* 6, no.27, 1944.

**1163 Fries, Adelaide L.** The Moravians in Georgia, 1735–40. 1905. Repr. Baltimore: G.P.C., 1967.
History of first attempt of Moravian Church to establish settlement in Georgia.

**1164 Georgia Dept. of Education, Div. of Public Library Service.** Georgia bibliography: county history. Atlanta, Ga.: The Dept., 1974.
Maps, two lists of the 159 counties, one alphabetically by name, the other in numerical order of creation.

## Georgia

**1165** Georgia. **English Crown grants, 1755-75.** [Atlanta, Ga.: Georgia Dept. of Archives and History, 1972- ] (in progress).

**1166** —— For islands in Georgia. By Pat Bryant. 1972.

**1167** —— In St. Andrew parish. By Pat Bryant. 1972.

**1168** —— In St. Philip parish. By Marion R. Hemperley. 1972.

**1169** —— In St. John parish. By Marion R. Hemperley. 1972.

**1170** —— In the parishes of St. David, St. Patrick, St. Thomas and St. Mary. By Marion R. Hemperley. 1973.

**1171** —— In St. George parish. By Pat Bryant. 1974.

**1172** —— In the parishes of St. Paul's parish. By Pat Bryant. 1974.

Series covers land granted by the King and his officers in Georgia, 1755-75.

**1173** **Georgia genealogical magazine.** v.1- , 1961- . Easley, S.C.: Southern Historical Pr.

no.1-34 out of print; being repr. in 1975. Has supplementary section of South Carolina material, comprising that portion of South Carolina known as "The Old Ninety-Six District." Judge Folks Huxford, former ed.

**1174** —— Index. Issues v.1-46, 1961-72. Easley, S.C., 1973.

v.1-34 contain surname and first name index; 35-36, surname only. Includes a master index, approx. 145,000 names.

**1175** **Georgia Genealogical Society quarterly.** v.1- , 1964- . Atlanta, Ga.: The Society.

Excellent journal.

**1176** **Georgia genealogist.** 1970- . Ed. by Mary G. Warren. Danielsville, Ga.: Heritage Papers.

Good for Georgia ancestors. Marriages prior to 1811, legal records, etc. to 1811. Quarterly.

**1177** **Georgia Historical Society.** The counties of the state of Georgia. Savannah, Ga.: The Society, 1974.

All 159 counties listed alphabetically with dates of creation, etc.

**1178** —— Index to United States census of Georgia for 1820. 2nd ed., with additions and corrections by Mrs. Eugene A. Stanley. Baltimore: G.P.C., 1969.

Since the 1790, 1800, and 1810 censuses are lost, this index is invaluable. 30,000 names, with counties of residence.

**1179** **Georgia pioneers genealogical magazine.** v.1- , 1964- . Albany, Ga.: Mary Carter.

**1180** **Gilmer, George R.** Sketches of some of the first settlers of upper Georgia . . . rev. and corr. ed. 1926. Repr. with added index. Baltimore: G.P.C., 1970.

Added index is to family histories; classic work of genealogy and history.

**1181** **Grice, Warren.** Georgia through two centuries. Ed. by E. M. Coulter. 3v. West Palm Beach, Fla., 1965.

v.2-3 biographical. Covers 1732-1960.

**1182** **Hall Bros., Engineers (B. M.** and **Frank W.).** Hall's Original county map of Georgia. Atlanta, Ga.: Georgia Dept. of Archives and History, 1898.

Reprinted frequently. Shows present (1898) and original counties and land districts. Essential.

**1183** **Hathaway, Beverly W.** Primer for Georgia genealogical research. West Jordan, Utah: Allstates Research Co., 1973.

**1184** **Henderson, Lillian.** Roster of Confederate soldiers of Georgia, 1861-65. 6v. [Hapeville, Ga., 1959-64.]

Compiled for the Georgia Confederate Pension and Record Dept. Roster of infantry regiments only; some questionable information; unindexed.

**1185** **Historical Records Survey.** Guide to public vital statistics records in Georgia. Atlanta, Ga., 1941.

**1186** ———— Inventory of county archives of Georgia. 9v. Atlanta, Ga., 1938-42.

Only the following numbers were published: 25 (Chatham), 32 (Clinch), 37 (Cook), 47 (Dougherty), 50 (Echols), 81 (Jefferson), 88 (Lee, 2v.), 106 (Muscogee), and 121 (Richmond). Unpublished material deposited in Univ. of Georgia, Athens, Ga.

**1187** ———— Inventory of the church and synagogue archives of Georgia. Atlanta Assoc. of Baptist Churches. 2v. Baptists. Atlanta, Ga., 1941.

**1188** **Hitz, Alex M.** Authentic list of all land lottery grants made to veterans of the Revolutionary War by the state of Georgia. 2nd ed. Atlanta, Ga.: Georgia Dept. of Archives and History, 1966.

Guides to these lotteries, compiled by Bertha A. L. (Mrs. Pat) Bryant in 1968 are available free from Surveyor-General Dept., Atlanta. Hitz copied grants marked "R.S." from the 1820, 1827, and 1832 lotteries, showing grantee, which lottery, lot drawn and grant date.

**1189** **Houston, Martha L.** Reprint of official register of land lottery of Georgia, 1827. 1829. Repr. Baltimore: G.P.C., 1967.

Original published in parts. Valuable record of the early settlers of Carroll, Coweta, Lee, Muskogee and Troup counties. About 15,000 listed.

**1190** ———— The Revolutionary soldiers and widows of Revolutionary soldiers living in Georgia, 1827-28. 1965. Repr. Danielsville, Ga.: Heritage Papers, 1965.

List of those entitled to draw who drew blank tickets and so did not receive land. List compiled from "Entitlement lists." no.1189 lists all those who received land.

**1191** **Howell, Clark.** History of Georgia. 4v. Chicago, 1926. v.2-4 have biographical sketches.

**1192** **Huxford, Folks.** Pioneers of wiregrass Georgia. v.1-6. Homerville, Ga.: The Author, 1948-71.

A biographical account of the early settlers of that portion of wiregrass Georgia found in the original counties of Irwin; Appling, Wayne, Camden, and Glynn. Very good.

**1193** **Immigrants from Great Britain to the Georgia Colony.** Morrow, Ga.: Genealogical Enterprises, 1970.

Names of all persons found in the colonial records of Georgia, intending to come to Georgia; arrivals in the Colony; land grants, etc.

**1194** **The index to the headright and bounty grants in Georgia from 1756-1909.** Easley, S.C.: Southern Historical Pr., 1970.

Original work, containing over 61,000 names, arranged alphabetically. Index to all grants made by Georgia from 1756-1909, and shows grantees, county in which grant was made, number of acres, books and page; no lottery grants. Covers Camden, Glynn, Liberty, Chatham, Effingham, Burke, Wilkes, Richmond, Franklin, and Washington counties.

**1195** **Jones, Charles C., Jr.** The dead towns of Georgia. 1878. Repr. Covington, Ga.: Cherokee Pub. Co., 1974; Spartanburg, S.C.: Reprint Co., 1974.

History of the founding, flourishing, and decline of several 18th century towns.

**1196** ———— History of Georgia. 2v. 1883. Repr. Spartanburg, S.C.: Reprint Co., 1965. More historical than genealogical, but useful for genealogists.

**1197** **Knight, Lucian L.** Georgia's landmarks, memorials and legends. 2v. Atlanta, Ga., 1913-14.

Contains hundreds of family histories and thousands of biographies. Over 50,000 entries; both volumes indexed in v.2.

**1198** ———— Georgia's roster of the Revolution . . . 1920. Repr. Baltimore: G.P.C., 1967.

Most comprehensive of Georgia's Revolutionary records, but should be used with reserve, since source of record is not always indicated (*see also* no.1188). 9,000 names.

**1199** ———— A standard history of Georgia and Georgians . . . 6v. Chicago, 1917.

v.4-6 biographical sketches with genealogical tables. Index in v.1.

**1200** **LeMaster, Elizabeth T. (Mrs. Vernon L.)** Abstracts of Georgia death notices from the *Southern Recorder*, 1830-55. Orange, Calif.: Orange County, California Genealogical Soc., 1971.

**1201** —— Abstracts of Georgia marriage notices from the *Southern Recorder*, 1830-55. Orange, Calif.: Orange County, California Genealogical Soc., 1971.

**1202** **Lotteries.** There were six Georgia lotteries; 1805, 1807, 1820, 1821, 1827, and 1832. They were intended to distribute to Georgia citizens only newly acquired land as it was ceded in successive years by Creeks and Cherokees. Citizens of Georgia who had lived in Georgia three years were entitled to draw a maximum of two land lots. But in 1820, 1827, and 1832 lotteries, two "extra" draws were given to Revolutionary veterans, and on the record and in the grant itself they were classified as such by "R.S."

**1203** **Lotteries and grants.** The following cover certain counties only. Headright and bounty land grants (no.1194): Camden, Glynn, Liberty, Chatham.

**1204** —— 1805 land lottery (no.1239): Wayne, Wilkinson, Baldwin.

**1205** —— 1807 land lottery (no.1211): Remainder of Wilkinson, Baldwin.

**1206** —— 1820 land lottery (no.1160): Walton, Gwinnett, Hall, Habersham, Early, Irwin, Appling, Rabun.

**1207** —— 1821 land lottery (no.1161): Dooly, Houston, Monroe, Henry, Fayette.

**1208** —— 1827 land lottery (no.1189): Carroll, Coweta, Troup, Muscogee, Lee.

**1209** —— 1832 land lottery (no.1228, 1220): Cherokee, which was divided into Cass (Bartow), Cherokee, Cobb, Floyd, Forsyth, Gilmer, Lumpkin, Murray, Paulding, Union.

**1210** **Lucas, Silas E.** Some of the lottery volumes are attributed in some dealers' catalogs to him, but *see* lottery information (no.1203-1209) for correct attributions.

**1211** **[Lucas, Silas E.]** The 1807 land lottery of Georgia. Easley, S.C.: Southern Historical Pr., 1968.

Contains names of 12,000 fortunate drawers, indexed. Covers Wilkinson and Baldwin counties.

**1212** **McCall, Etties S. (Tidwell).** Roster of Revolutionary soldiers in Georgia . . . Georgia Society, D.A.R. v.1, 1941. Repr. Baltimore: G.P.C., 1968.

From pension papers, family Bible and tombstone records, grants of land, lottery lists, wills, estates, and official records of military service. Use with reserve.

**1213** —— —— v.2-3. Baltimore: G.P.C., 1968-69.

Use with care; evidence slight in some cases. Majority of entries for Georgia Revolutionary soldiers; some relating to other states.

**1214** **McCay, Betty L.** Index to some early tax digests of Georgia, 1790-1818. Indianapolis, Ind., 1971.

Over 10,000 entries taken from ten early Georgia counties. Important because of loss of 1790, 1800, and 1812 federal censuses.

**1215** **McLendon, Samuel G.** History of the public domain of Georgia. 1924. Repr. Spartanburg, S.C.: Reprint Co., 1974.

Early land grants and records for a definitive history of Georgia lands.

**1216** **North West Georgia Historical and Genealogical Society quarterly.** v.1- , 1969- . Rome, Ga.: The Society.

**1217** **Northen, William J.** Men of mark in Georgia. 7v. 1906-12. Repr.,

with an index prepared by Univ. of Georgia Library. Spartanburg, S.C.: Reprint Co., 1974.
Originally intended to be published in 6v. Sketches of prominent Georgians, 1733–1911.

1218 Otto, Rhea C. 1850 census of Georgia. Savannah, Ga.: The Compiler, 1971– (in progress).
The following counties had been published to end of 1974: Dooly, Early, Effingham, Elbert, Emanuel, Fayette, Floyd, Glynn, Gordon, Greene, Jefferson, Laurens, Lee, Liberty, Lincoln, Lumpkin, Marion, McIntosh, Macon, Talbot, Tattnall, Telfair, and Warren.

1219 Overby, Mary E. (Mrs. James C.). Marriages published in the *Christian index*, 1828–55; abstracts. Indexed by Mrs. E. M. Lancaster. Shady Dale, Ga.: Mrs. E. M. Lancaster, 1971.
Georgia Baptist Historical Soc. at head of title.

1219a ——— Obituaries from the *Christian index*, 1822–79. Washington, Ga.: Baptist Historical Soc., 1974.
Biographical information; over 1,275 names.

1220 Prizes drawn in the Cherokee land lottery of the 1st, 2nd and 3rd quality, with . . . the drawer's name and residence . . . Milledgeville, Ga., 1833.

1220a Register, Alvaretta K. Index to the 1830 census of Georgia. Baltimore: G.P.C., 1974.
The only usable census index of Georgia because of the paucity of earlier records, burned or otherwise destroyed. 52,000 heads of households.

1221 Register, Earldene; McCay, B. L.; and Roth, R. L. Index to [Blair's] *Some early tax digests of Georgia*, 1790–1818. Indianapolis, Ind.: B. L. McCay, 1971.
Made from Blair's 1926 ed. (*see* no.1137). 10,000 entries for ten counties: Camden, Chatham, Glynn, Hancock, Lincoln, Montgomery, Richmond, Warren and Wilkes.

1222 Rigsby, Lewis W. Historic Georgia families. 1925–28. Repr. Baltimore: G.P.C., 1969.
Contains genealogies and lists of settlers near Old Queensboro, and in area now included in the counties of Grady, Decatur, and Seminole.

1223 Rowland, Arthur R. A bibliography of the writings on Georgia history. Hamden, Conn.: Archon Books, 1966.

1224 Shaw, Aurora C. 1850 Georgia mortality census. Jacksonville, Fla.: The Compiler, 1971.
All white persons who died in one year period ending 1 June 1850, prior to the enumeration of the 1850 census. Index from W.P.A. microfilm and slave list; full data.

1225 Sheffield, Eileen, and Woods, B. 1840 index to Georgia census; change of format, names corrected. Baytown, Tex.: The Compilers, 1971.
Replaces the 1969 ed., listed as Woods and Sheffield.

1226 Sherwood, Adiel. A gazetteer of the state of Georgia . . . 4th ed. 1860. Repr. with additions. Covington, Ga.: Cherokee Pub. Co., 1970.
Good for its period; locates place names.

1227 Smith, George G. The story of Georgia and the Georgia people, 1732 to 1860. 2nd ed. 1900. Repr. Baltimore: G.P.C., 1968.
100p. appendix contains valuable genealogical information. Headrights granted, 1754–1800, list of soldiers of the line, list of soldiers paid in money, bounty warrants of Revolutionary War soldiers. Use with reserve.

1228 Smith, James F. The 1832 (Cherokee) land lottery . . . 1838. Repr. with official Georgia Archives index, 1968. Easley, S. C.: Southern Historical Pr., 1968; Baltimore: G.P.C., 1969.
Numerical list of names of the fortunate drawers. 20,000 names.

1229 Southern Historical Association. Memoirs of Georgia, containing historical accounts of the state's civil, military, industrial and professional interests, and personal sketches of many of its people. 2v. Atlanta, Ga., 1895.

**1230** **Stewart, William C.** Gone to Georgia, 1810-20. Jackson and Gwinnett counties and their neighbors in the western migration. *National Genealogical Soc. special publ.* 30. Washington, D.C.: The Society, 1965.

**1231** **Strobel, Philip A.** The Salzburgers and their descendants . . . 1855. Repr. Athens, Ga.: Univ. of Georgia Pr., 1953.
History of a colony of German (Lutheran) Protestants who migrated to Georgia in 1734. Includes lists of the original Salzburg settlers. With appendix and index by E. D. Wells, Sr. Pearl R. Gnann's *Georgia Salzburgers and allied families,* reprinted from the 1956 ed. by Southern Historical Pr., Easley, S.C. gives genealogies of about 75 early German immigrants who settled in Effingham county.

**1232** **Temple, Sarah B.,** and **Coleman, K.** Georgia journeys, being an account of the lives of Georgia's original settlers and many other early settlers from the founding of the colony in 1732 until the institution of royal government in 1754. Athens, Ga.: Univ. of Georgia Pr., 1961.

**1233** **Urlsperger, Samuel.** Detailed reports on the Salzburger emigrants who settled in America. v.1, 1733-34; 2, 1734-35; v.3, 1736. Atlanta, Ga.: Univ. of Georgia Pr., 1968-72.
Daily registers of pastors J. M. Boltzius and I. C. Gronau; also Journal of letters of Lutheran pastors who ministered to the Salzburger exiles and other German settlers in Georgia. v.2-3 ed. by George F. Jones.

**1234** **Waddel, Moses.** A register of marriages celebrated and solemnized by Moses Waddel, D.D. in South Carolina and Georgia, 1795-1836 . . . Danielsville, Ga.: Heritage Papers, 1967.

**1235** **Warren, Mary B.** Marriages and deaths, 1763-1820; abstracted from extant Georgia newspapers. Danielsville, Ga.: Heritage Papers, 1968.
8,000 notices.

**1236** ——— and **White, S. F.** [v.2]. 1820-30. 1972.
10,000 notices.

**1237** **White, Rev. George.** Historical collections of Georgia: containing . . . biographical sketches . . . from its first settlement to the present time. 3rd ed. New York, 1854. Repr. Danielsville, Ga.: Heritage Papers, 1968.
Major collection of biographical sketches, lists of settlers, soldiers, etc. Name index by Alpha C. Dutton. 1920. Repr. Danielsville, Ga.: Heritage Papers, 1968. Contains 7,000 entries. G.P.C., Baltimore repr. both in 1v., 1969.

**1238** **Wilson, Caroline P.** Annals of Georgia: important early records of the state. 3v. 1928-33. v.1-2 repr., rev., corr. and enl. 2v. in 1. Easley, S.C: Southern Historical Pr., 1969.
v.1, Liberty county records and state Revolutionary pay roll; v.2, Effingham county and other records; v.3, Mortuary records of Savannah, 1830-32, and cemetery records.

**1239** **Wood, Virginia S.,** and **Wood, R. V.** The 1805 land lottery of Georgia. Belmont, Mass.: V. S. Wood, 1964.
25,000 names. Acts as substitute for destroyed 1800 census. Only lottery for which the state kept a list of all those who drew, whether or not they got a lot. Covers Wayne, Wilkinson, and Baldwin counties.

**1240** **Wynd, Frances.** "They were here": Georgia genealogical records, 1965- . Albany, Ga.: The Author.
Quarterly magazine; accurate material.

**1241** **Yenawine, Wayne S.** A checklist of source materials for the counties of Georgia. In *Georgia historical quarterly,* v.32, no.3, 1948.

**1242** ——— ——— Supplement. By Carroll Hart. *Georgia Dept. of Archives and History publ.* 5. Atlanta, Ga.: The Dept., 1967.

**1243** **Young, Pauline.** Abstracts of Old Ninety-Six and Abbeville District, South Carolina. Wills, bonds and administrations between 1774 and 1860. 1950. Repr. Easley, S.C.: Southern Historical Pr., 1969.

30,000 names. The Old Ninety-Six District bordered Georgia on its western boundary and was the ancestral home of many early Georgia settlers.

## HAWAII

Territory established 1900; entered Union 1959

*Hawaii Public Library, Honolulu*
*Hawaiian Historical Society, Honolulu*
*State of Hawaii Public Archives, Honolulu*

✣ While basically historical, all these works contain valuable biographical and, in some cases, genealogical data.

**1244** **Atlas of Hawaii.** Honolulu: Univ. Pr. of Hawaii, 1973.

Topography, geography, history, statistics on population.

**1245** **Cartwright, Bruce.** Some aliis of the migratory period. *Bernice P. Bishop Museum occasional papers,* 10, no.7. Honolulu, 1933.

Aliis are Polynesian chiefs or nobles.

**1246** **Char, Tin-Yuke.** The sandalwood mountains: readings and stories of the early Chinese in Hawaii. Honolulu: Univ. Pr. of Hawaii, 1974.

Collection of writings, letters, family histories, genealogies of the oldest generations of Chinese immigrants to Hawaii.

**1247** **Coulter, John W.** A gazetteer of the territory of Hawaii. *Univ. of Hawaii research publ.* 11. Honolulu, 1935.

Consists of a list of place names.

**1248** **Dutton, Meiric K.** The succession of King Kamehameha V to Hawaii's throne. Honolulu, 1957.

**1249** **Fornander, Abraham.** An account of the Polynesian race; its origins and migrations, and the ancient history of the Hawaiian people to the times of Kamehameha I. 3v. 1878–85. Repr. Tuttle, Rutland, Vt., 1969.

v.1–2: Origin and migrations of the Polynesian race; v.3: Comparative vocabulary of the Polynesian and Indo-European languages. An index was compiled by John F. G. Stokes in 1909.

**1250** ———— Fornander collection of Hawaiian antiquities and folk-lore; the Hawaiians' account of the formation of their island and origin of their race . . . 3v. *Bernice P. Bishop Museum memoirs* 4–6. Honolulu, 1916–20.

**1251** **Freitas, Joaquim F. de.** Portuguese-Hawaiian memories. Honolulu, 1930.

Biographical information on Portuguese immigrants.

**1252** **Hawaiian Historical Society, Honolulu.** Annual reports, 1892–1967.

Many reports, as well as other Society publications, contain genealogical information. From 1968 the reports contain only statistics. *Hawaiian journal of history* continues historical material originally in the reports.

**1253** ———— Genealogical series 1–3. Honolulu, 1915–22.

**1254** ———— Papers. 16v. 1892–1940.

Has information on land tenures. Genealogical series contains family history.

**1255** ———— Index to publications of the Hawaiian Historical Society, 1892–1967, by Charles H. Hunter. Honolulu, The Society, 1968.

Complete index of the people, places and subjects, described in the Society's annual reports and papers, with a glossary of Hawaiian words and other tables.

**1256** **Hawaiian Mission Children's Society.** Annual report. no.1– , 1853– . Honolulu, The Society.

Report of society of descendants of the missionaries; early reports give names and addresses of members.

**1257** ———— Missionary album; portraits and biographical sketches of the American Protestant missionaries to the Hawaiian Islands. Sesquicentennial ed. enl. from 1937 ed. Honolulu: The Society, 1969.

1258  Kamaku, Samuel M. Ruling chiefs of Hawaii. Honolulu, 1961.

1259  Kuykendall, Ralph S. The Hawaiian kingdom. 3v. 1938-67. Repr. Honolulu: Univ. Pr. of Hawaii, 1966-68.
v.1, Foundation and transformation, 1788-1854; v.2, Twenty critical years, 1854-74; v.3, Kalakaua dynasty, 1874-93. Little genealogy but only definitive history of Hawaii; it is necessary to study the islands before embarking on genealogical research.

1260  Malo, David. Hawaiian antiquities (Moolelo Hawaii). 2nd ed. *Bernice P. Bishop Museum special publ.* 2. Honolulu, 1951.
Fine biographical data.

1261  Medcalf, Gordon. Hawaiian royal orders. Honolulu, 1962.
Insignia, classes, regulations and members.

1262  Men and women of Hawaii. v.19. Honolulu: *Honolulu Star-Bulletin.* various dates.
Published 1917, 1921, 1925, 1930, 1935, 1940/1, 1954, 1966, and 1972. Many out of print. Biographical reference library of men of achievement in the Hawaiian islands. Various titles: *Story of Hawaii* (no.1268), *Men of Hawaii,* etc.

1263  Paradise of the Pacific. v.1-78, no.3, 1888-1966. Honolulu.
Contains much genealogy.

1264  Polk's directory of city and county of Honolulu. 1880/81- . Richmond, Va.: Polk.
Title varies: *Hawaiian kingdom, Hawaiian directory,* etc.

1265  Pukui, Mary K. (and others). Place names of Hawaii. Honolulu: Univ. Pr. of Hawaii, 1974.
New expanded ed.; 4,000 place names.

1266  Rubincam, Milton. America's only royal family: genealogy of the former Hawaiian ruling house. In *National Genealogical Society quarterly,* v.50, 1962, pp.79-91.
Has excellent bibliography. Comprehensive genealogy from the foundation of the monarchy at the end of 18th century to present time. Members of the family intermarried with Britons and Americans as well as native Hawaiians.

1267  ———— The Hawaiian royal family and its Anglo-American connections... In *American genealogist,* v.32, Apr. 1956.

1268  The Story of Hawaii and its builders, with which is incorporated v.3 of *Men of Hawaii* . . . bibliographical sketches of its men of note . . . past and present . . . Ed. by George F. Nellist. Honolulu, 1925.
Cover title: *Builders of Hawaii.* See also no.1262.

1269  United Chinese Penmen Club, Hawaii. The Chinese of Hawaii. 3v. Honolulu: 1929-57.
Text in Chinese and English. v.1-2 were issued by Club under name *Overseas Penmen Club.*

1270  Women of Hawaii. v.1-2. Ed. by George F. Nellist. Hawaii, 1929-38.

IDAHO

Settled ca. 1842; entered Union 1890

*Boise Public Library*

1271  Beal, Merrill D., and Wells, M. W. History of Idaho. 3v. New York, 1959.
v.3 personal and family history. Mug book.

1272  D.A.R. Idaho. History and register. Ed. by Clara L. Wood. 2v. Caldwell, Id., 1936, 1963.
v.1, 1904-34; v.2, 1935-62.

1273 **Defenbach, Byron.** Idaho: the place and its people . . . 3v. Chicago, 1933. v.2-3 mainly biographical.

1274 **Department of Highway Planning Survey, Boise.** Gazetteer of cities, villages, unincorporated communities . . . in the state of Idaho. 3rd ed. Boise, Id.: The Dept., 1966.

1275 **Donaldson, Thomas.** Idaho of yesterday. Caldwell, Id., 1941.
Chatty history; mainly sketches, some biographical.

1276 **Driggs, Benjamin W.** History of Teton Valley, Idaho. Rexburg, Id., 1970.
Good recent history; some biographical sketches; bibliography.

1277 **Federal Writers' Project, Idaho.** The Idaho encyclopedia . . . Caldwell, Id., 1938.
Includes county histories and short biographical sketches.

1278 **French, Hiram T.** History of Idaho: a narrative account of its historical progress, its people and its principal interests. 3v. Chicago, ca.1914.
v.2-3 have individual biographies.

1279 **Hawley, James H.** History of Idaho. 3v. and suppl. Chicago, ca.1920.
v.2-3 and suppl. consist of individual biographies.

1280 **Historical Records Survey.** Directory of churches and religious organizations of Idaho. Boise, Id., 1940.

1281 ———— Guide to public vital statistics records in Idaho: state and county. Boise, Id., 1942.

1282 ———— Inventory of the county archives of Idaho. 9v. Boise, Id., 1937-42.
Only the following numbers were published: 6 (Bingham), 11 (Boundary), 17 (Clark), 28 (Kootenai), 30 (Lemhi), 34 (Minidoka), 35 (Nez Perce), 39 (Power), and 41 (Teton). Unpublished material deposited with Secretary of State, Boise, Id.

1283 **Idaho Genealogical Society.** First census of Idaho 1870. Indexed, plus mortality schedules. Boise, Id.: The Society, 1973.

1284 ———— Idaho territory: federal population schedules and mortality schedules 1870. Boise, Id.: The Society, 1973.

1285 ———— Quarterly. v.1- , 1958- . Boise, Id.: The Society.

1286 ———— Idaho vital statistics. v.1 (all pub.). Cemetery records from Bingham, Bonneville and Madison counties. Boise, Id.: The Society, 1963.
Contains cemetery records to 1962. Listing not complete for all cemeteries in the area, but it is still an excellent compilation.

1287 **An illustrated history of north Idaho** embracing Nez Perce, Idaho, Latah, Kootenai, and Shoshone counties, state of Idaho. n.p., 1903.
History and biographies. Mug book.

1288 **An illustrated history of the state of Idaho,** containing a history . . . from the earliest period of its discovery to the present time . . . biographical mention of many pioneers and prominent citizens of to-day . . . 1899. Repr. Ann Arbor, Mich.: Xerox Univ. Microfilms, 1973.

1289 **Progressive men of southern Idaho.** Chicago, 1904.
Mug book.

1290 **Rees, John E.** Idaho chronology, nomenclature, bibliography. Chicago, 1918.

1291 **Sons of the American Revolution. Idaho Society.** Lineages of the members, past and present 1909-61. Compiled by John R. Gobble. Idaho Falls, Id.: The Society, 1962.

1292 **State Library, Boise.** Idaho, the Gem State. An Idaho bibliography of books about Idaho and by Idaho authors, selected by M. Shelby and R. Coventry. Boise, Id.: The Library, 1966.

## ILLINOIS

Settled ca. 1720; entered Union 1818

*Detroit Society for Genealogical Research, Inc., Detroit, Mich.*
*Illinois State Historical Library, Springfield*

**1293** **Adams, James N.** Illinois place names. *Illinois State Historical Soc. occasional publ.* 54. Springfield, Ill.: The Society, 1968.
14,000 entries, former names, post office names. Repr. from *Illinois libraries,* April-June 1968 issue. Ed. by W. E. Keller.

**1294** **Bateman, Newton (and others).** Historical encyclopedia of Illinois and biographical memoirs. 2v. Chicago, 1933.
Editions dated 1915, 1917, 1918, and 1926 have same type of information.

**1295** **Beck, Lewis C.** A gazetteer of the state of Illinois and Missouri . . . Albany, N.Y., 1823.

**1296** **Beers, Henry P.** The French and British in the old northwest, a bibliographical guide to archive and manuscript sources. Detroit, Mich.: Wayne State Univ. Pr., 1964.

**1297** **The biographical dictionary and portrait gallery of representative men of Chicago, Minnesota cities . . .** 2v. Chicago, 1892.
Many biographies.

**1298** **The biographical encyclopedia of Illinois of the nineteenth century** . . . Philadelphia, 1875.
Mug book.

**1299** **Bohannan, Larry C.** Fourth census of the United States, 1820: Illinois population schedules. Huntsville, Ark.: Century Enterprises, 1968.
Counties of Alexander, Bond, Clark, Crawford, Edwards, Franklin, Gallatin, Jackson, Jefferson, Johnson, Madison, Monroe, Pope, Randolph, St. Clair, Union, Washington, and Wayne.

**1300** **Carter, Clarence E.** The territory of Illinois, 1809-18. 2v. *Territorial papers of the U.S.* 16-17. 1948-50. Repr. New York: A.M.S. Press, 1973.
Lists of persons signing petitions, memorials, etc.

**1301** **Central Illinois genealogical quarterly.** v.1- , 1965- . Decatur, Ill.: Decatur Genealogical Soc.

**1302** **Chicago Genealogical Society.** Directory of Chicago, 1844. Chicago: The Society, 1970.

**1303** ——— Illinois 1850 census. v.1- , 1970- (in progress). Chicago: The Society.
7v. pub. to end of 1974: Champaign, Franklin, Hamilton, Stark, Wabash, Winnebago, and DeKalb counties.

**1304** ——— List of letters remaining in the post office, Chicago and vicinity, January 1834-July 1836. Chicago: The Society, 1970.
Early northern Illinois residents whose letters remained unclaimed. Post offices of Chicago, DuPage, Juliet (Joliet), Naperville, Ottawa, Pawpaw, and Plainfield.

**1305** ——— Surname index, 1970-73. Chicago: The Society, 1970-74.

**1306** ——— Vital records from Chicago newspapers, 1833- . v.1- . Compiled and ed. by the Newspaper Research Committee. Chicago: The Society, 1971- (in progress).
Seeks to replace records lost in Chicago fire. *Chicago Democrat, Chicago American, Daily Chicago American.* 3v. to end of 1974: 1833-39, 1840-42, 1843-44. Information for Massachusetts, New York, Pennsylvania, and Texas included.

**1307** **Chicago genealogist.** v.1- , 1969- . Chicago: Chicago Genealogical Soc.

**1308** **Clift, Garrett G.** List of officers of the Illinois Regiment and of Crockett's Regiment who have received land for their services. Frankfort, Ill.: Sons of American Revolution, 1962.

**1309** **Conger, John L.** History of the Illinois river valley. 3v. Chicago, 1932.
v.2-3 biographical.

## United States

**1310** **Coulter, O. H.** Roster of Illinois soldiers residing in Kansas. 2v. Topeka, Kans., 1889?
Civil War soldiers.

**1311** **D.A.R. Illinois.** Illinois state directory of members and ancestors. 1957– [Galesburg, Ill.] n.d.
Issued sporadically.

**1312** —— Roster of Revolutionary War soldiers and widows who lived in Illinois counties. Chicago, 1962.

**1313** **Decatur Genealogical Society, Illinois.**
Since 1972 this society has been compiling census returns for 1850, cemetery inscriptions, marriage indexes, etc. Many Illinois counties have been processed, but the following have been recorded in depth: Christian, DeWitt, Fayette, Logan, Macon, Moultrie, and Shelby.

**1314** **Dunne, Edward.** Illinois, the heart of the nation. 5v. Chicago, 1933.
v.3-5 biographical.

**1315** **Edwards, Richard.** Chicago census report . . . embracing a complete directory of the city. Chicago, 1871.
Over 1,200 pages of biographical information.

**1316** **Gill, James V.** Illiana research reports. no.1-5. Thomson, Ill.: Heritage House, 1966.
Original source records, census, military, marriage, inscriptions, landowners, etc. Fine collection of records not found elsewhere in print. Discontinued after no.5.

**1317** —— and **Gill, M. R.** Index to the 1830 federal census of Illinois. 4v. in 1. Thomson, Ill.: Heritage House, 1968-70.
Each volume contains about a dozen counties. Full data given.

**1318** **Gleanings from the heart of the cornbelt.** v.1- , 1967- . [Normal, Ill.]: Bloomington-Normal Genealogical Soc.
Quarterly; queries excellent. Central Illinois.

**1319** **Historical Records Survey.** Guide to church vital statistics records in Illinois. Chicago, 1942.

**1320** —— Guide to public vital statistics records in Illinois. Chicago, 1941.
List of all available official records by counties.

**1321** —— Inventory of the church archives of Illinois. 3v. Chicago, 1941-42.
Cairo, Springfield and Cumberland Presbyteries.

**1322** —— Inventory of the county archives of Illinois. 32v. Chicago, 1939-42.
Only the following numbers were published: 1 (Adams), 5 (Brown), 8 (Carroll), 10 (Champaign), 12 (Clark), 18 (Cumberland), 20 (DeWitt), 21 (Douglas), 25 (Effingham), 26 (Fayette), 28 (Franklin), 39 (Jackson), 43 (Jo Daviess), 48 (Knox), 56 (Macoupin), 65 (Menard), 68 (Montgomery), 69 (Morgan), 70 (Moultrie), 71 (Ogle), 72 (Peoria), 74 (Piatt), 75 (Pike), 81 (Rock Island), 82 (Saline), 83 (Sangamon), 85 (Scott), 86 (Shelby), 88 (St. Clair), 89 (Stephenson), and 92 (Vermilion). Unpublished material deposited in State Archives, Springfield, Ill.

**1323** **Hixson (W. W.) and Co.** Atlas of Illinois. Rockford, Ill., 1934?
Cover: *Plat book of the state of Illinois.*

**1324** —— [Plat books of counties of Illinois.] Rockford, Ill. [192?-193?].

**1325** **The Illiana genealogist.** v.1- , 1965- . Danville, Ill.: Illiana Genealogical and Historical Soc.
Quarterly. Genealogy of Indiana and Illinois, particularly near the border. Bible, cemetery, church and other records.

**1326** **Illinois. Adjutant General's Office.** Record of the burial places of soldiers, sailors, marines, and army nurses of all wars of the United States buried in Illinois. 2v. Springfield, Ill., 1929.

**1327** ———— Military and Naval Dept. Roster of the Adjutant General of the state of Illinois. Rev. by Jasper N. Reece. 9v. Springfield, Ill., 1900-1902.

v.9 entitled, "Record of the services of the soldiers in the Black Hawk War 1831-32 and in the Mexican War 1846-48." v.1-8 concerns Civil War. Has appendix record of militia, rangers, riflemen, 1810-13. Originally published in 1882.

**1328 Illinois. Secretary of State.** Counties of Illinois: their origin and evolution; with 23 maps showing the original and the present boundary lines of each county of the state. Springfield, Ill.: The Secretary.

Published annually.

**1329 Illinois State Genealogical Society quarterly.** v.1- , 1969- . Springfield, Ill.: The Society.

Impressive amount of material presented. Thoroughly professional.

**1330 Illinois State Historical Library.** Index to the Transactions and other publications. By James N. Adams. 2v. Springfield, Ill.: The Library, 1953.

**1331 James, Edmund.** The territorial records of Illinois, 1809-18. *Transactions of the Illinois State Historical Lib.* 3. Springfield, Ill., 1901.

**1332 McCay, Betty L.** Sources for genealogical searching in Illinois. Indianapolis, Ind.: The Compiler, 1970.

Background history, boundaries, maps, census information.

**1333 Norton, Margaret C.** Illinois census returns, 1810 and 1818. *Illinois State Historical Lib. historical collections* 24. 1935. Repr. Baltimore: G.P.C., 1969.

The two censuses contain 5,300 family head names, with names of members.

**1334** ———— ———— 1820. *Illinois State Historical Lib. historical collections* 26. 1934. Repr. Baltimore: G.P.C., 1934.

Contains names of heads of over 11,000 families, with a total of 51,000 persons named.

**1335 Olson, Ernst W.** Swedish element in Illinois. Survey of the past seven decades . . . with life sketches of men of today. Chicago, 1917.

**1336 Pease, Theodore C.** The county archives of the state of Illinois . . . *Illinois State Historical Lib. historical collections* 12. Springfield, Ill.: The Lib., 1915.

Although the only volume covering all Illinois counties, its information is superseded for those counties included in the *Inventory of county records* series (*see* no.1322).

**1337** ———— Illinois election returns 1818-48. *Illinois State Historical Lib. historical collections* 18. Springfield, Ill., 1923.

**1337a Peck, John M.** A gazetteer of Illinois . . . 2nd ed. 1837. Repr. Jacksonville, Ill., 1934.

Very good for the period.

**1338 Perrin, William H.** In the 1880s Mr. Perrin, aided by J. H. Battle and G. C. Kniffin, wrote many local histories of Illinois and Kentucky. The more important are listed under the respective states.

**1339** ———— History of Alexander, Union, and Pulaski counties, Illinois. Chicago, 1883.

**1340** ———— History of Cass county. 1882.

**1341** ———— Effingham county. 1883. Repr. Evansville, Ind.: Unigraphic, 1974. (Surname index added.)

All have biographical sketches.

**1342 Revolutionary heroes honored in Illinois.** Short biographical sketches of Revolutionary soldiers buried in Illinois. In *Journal of the Illinois State Historical Soc.*, v.5-24, 1912-31.

Mostly listed by counties.

**1343 Saga of southern Illinois;** a quarterly by the Genealogical Society of Southern Illinois. 1974- . Flora, Ill.: The Society.

Strong on county records in the area.

**1344 Smith, George W.** A history of Illinois and her people . . . 6v. Chicago, 1927.
v.3–6 biographical.

**1345** ——— A history of southern Illinois. 3v. Chicago, 1912.
v.2–3 biographical.

**1346 Society of Mayflower Descendants. Illinois.** Lineage book, 1962. Northbrook, Ill., 1962.

**1347 Thompson, Jess M.** Pike county history. Pittsfield, Ill. [Pike County Historical Soc., 1967].
193 chapters, being articles printed in the *Pike County Republican,* Pittsfield, Illinois, 1935–39. Primarily concerns history and many families of Pike county, with numerous references to their origins in Kentucky.

**1348 U.S. General Land Office.** [Lands in Illinois to soldiers of the late war (of 1812).] Letter to the Commissioner . . . respecting patents for lands in the military bounty land district in the state of Illinois . . . . House doc.262. 26th Cong. 1st sess. Washington, D.C., 1840.

**1349** ——— Index of the Illinois military patent book by George C. Bestor. Peoria, Ill., 1853.

**1350** ——— Index corrected, etc. by Ephraim S. Green and S. P. Kirkbridge. Bridgeton, Pa., 1855.

**1351 U.S. biographical dictionary and portrait gallery of eminent and self-made men.** Illinois volume. Chicago, 1876.
Mug book.

**1352 U.S. Daughters of 1812. Peoria, Fort Clark Chapter.** Illinois cemetery inscriptions. Compiled by Ruth Crim and M. Herberger. n.p., 1961?
Inscriptions of 58 cemeteries in Knox, Marshall, Peoria, Stark, and Woodford counties, and history of some cemeteries.

**1353 Vogel, Virgil J.** Indian place names. Illinois. Springfield, Ill.: Illinois State Historical Soc., 1963?
Companion to *Illinois place names* (no. 1293). Repr. originally in the Society's *Journal,* v.65, 1962. Authoritative guide to places named for or by Indians.

**1354 Volkel, Lowell M.** Illiana ancestors. 3v. Thomson, Ill.: Heritage House, 1967–69. Queries repr. from the genealogy column in the *Danville Commercial-News* newspaper.

**1355** ——— 1850 Illinois mortality schedule. 3v. in 1. Thomson, Ill.: Heritage House, 1972–73.
Lists deaths between 1 June 1849 and 31 May 1950. v.1, Adams through Iroquois counties; v.2, Jackson through Ogle; v.3, Peoria through Woodford.

**1356** ——— Tracing ancestry in Illinois libraries and archives. In *Treesearcher,* 1973.

**1357** ——— and **Gill, J. V.** 1820 federal census of Illinois. Thomson, Ill.: Heritage House, 1966.
Alphabetical arrangement of 9,700 names.

**1358 Walker, Harriet J.** Revolutionary soldiers buried in Illinois. 1917. Repr. Baltimore: G.P.C., 1967.
Biographical sketches of about 700 soldiers, with much genealogical material.

**1359 Walker, Homer A.** Illinois pensioners lists of the Revolution, 1812, and Indian Wars. Washington, D.C., ca. 1955.
Includes names of soldiers, widows, and heirs.

**1360 Warner and Beer's atlas of the state of Illinois.** 1876. Repr. Knightstown, Ind.: Mayhill Pub., 1972.
All 102 counties. Landowner names, city maps.

**1361 Way, Royal B.** The Rock river valley . . . 3v. Chicago, 1926. v.2–3 biographical.

**1362 Whitney, Ellen M.** The Black Hawk War, 1831–32. v.1: Illinois volunteers. *Illinois State Historical Lib. historical collections* 36. Springfield, Ill.: The Library, 1970.

250 muster rolls, comprehensive listings for counties, towns and battles; 11,000 names on rolls. Further volumes in 1975.

**1363** **Wormer, Maxine.** Illinois 1840 census index. v.1- . Thomson, Ill.: Heritage House, 1973 (in progress).
Lists head of household, residence, and census page reference. v.1, Adams through DuPage counties; v.2, Edgar through Jefferson.

## INDIANA

Settled ca. 1733; entered Union 1816

*Indiana State Library, Indianapolis*
*Public Library of Fort Wayne and Allen County, Fort Wayne*
*Mr. Willard Heiss, Indianapolis*

**1364** **Andreas, Alfred T.** Maps of Indiana counties in 1876, together with the plat of Indianapolis; repr. from *Illustrated historical atlas of the state of Indiana*, publ. by Baskin, Forester & Co., Chicago. Chicago, 1876.
Gives maps of counties showing townships as of 1876; also plans of some cities and towns. Includes county histories and biographical sketches and material on early settlers. The county maps were repr. by Indiana Historical Soc. under title, *Illustrated historical atlas of the state of Indiana*. Indianapolis: The Society, 1968.

**1364a** ———— ———— An index to towns, villages and post offices as shown in county maps from the *Illustrated historical atlas*. By Donald E. Gradeless. 2v. Racine, Wisc.: Gradeless Research, 1974. (1721 Edgewood Ave., Racine, Wisc. 53404)

**1365** **Barnhart, John D.,** and **Carmony, D. F.** Indiana, from frontier to industrial commonwealth. 4v. New York, ca. 1954.
v.3-4 contain family and personal history. Mug book.

**1366** **Biographical and historical souvenir for the counties of Clark, Crawford, Floyd, Harrison, Jefferson, Jennings,** **Scott and Washington, Indiana.** 1889. Repr. with index. Evansville, Ind.: Unigraphic, 1974.

**1367** ———— Index by Betty L. McCay. Indianapolis: The Compiler, 1970. 75,000 names.

**1368** **Biographical history of eminent and self-made men of the state of Indiana** . . . 2v. Cincinnati, Ohio, 1880.
Mug book.

**1369** **Carter, Clarence E.** The territory of Indiana, 1800-16. 2v. *Territorial papers of the U.S.* 7-8. 1939. Repr. New York: A.M.S. Press, 1973.
Contains lists of persons signing petitions, memorials, etc.

**1370** **Commemorative biographical record of prominent and representative men of Indianapolis and vicinity.** Chicago, 1908.

**1370a** **(County atlases of Indiana).** Many county atlases have been reprinted and are available from The Bookmark, Knightstown, Ind. 1974-75.

**1371** **Cox, Evelyn M.** 1820 Indiana federal census. Ellensburgh, Wash.: The Compiler, 1973.

**1372** **D.A.R. Indiana.** Roster of soldiers and patriots of the American Revolution buried in Indiana. 2v. Brookville, Ind., 1938, 1966.
Issued under auspices of Indiana D.A.R. by Mrs. Roscoe C. O'Byrne. v.1 was repr. by G.P.C., Baltimore, in 1968, and v.2 is still in print. Obtainable from Indiana D.A.R., Brookville, Ind.

**1373** **Dunn, Jacob P.** Indiana and Indianans. 5v. Chicago, 1919.

**1374** ———— An index by W.P.A. under the direction of Indianapolis Public Library. Indianapolis, Ind., 1939.
v.3-5 biographical. Comprehensive; by a recognized authority.

**1375 Genealogy.** Ed. by Willard Heiss. v.1- , 1973- . Indianapolis, Ind.: Indiana Historical Soc.

Published 8 times a year, the months in which *Hoosier genealogist* (no.1386) is not. One of the best genealogical periodicals available.

**1376 Hawes (G. W.) and Co.** Indiana state gazetteer and business directory for 1858 and 1859, and 3rd ed., 1862 and 1863. 2v. Indianapolis, Ind., 1860-64.

**1377 Heiss, Willard C.** 1820 federal census for Indiana. Indianapolis, Ind.: Indiana Historical Soc., 1966.

Not merely an index but complete in itself. Over 24,000 names of heads of households arranged alphabetically.

**1378** —— Encyclopedia of American Quaker genealogy. v.7, pt.1- . Abstracts of the records of the Society of Friends in Indiana. Indianapolis, Ind.: Indiana Historical Soc., 1962- .

Edited from Hinshaw material (*see* no. 462). Fine Quaker record. Pts. 1-5 published to 1974; pt.6 being edited; pt.7 will be the index; pt.2 is out of print.

**1379** —— Guide to research in Quaker records in the Midwest. Indianapolis, Ind., 1962. Repr. from Mar. and Apr. 1962 issues of *Indiana history bull.*

**1380** —— A list of all the Friends meetings that exist or ever have existed in Indiana, 1807-1955. Rev. Indianapolis, Ind., 1961.

**1381 Historical Records Survey.** A directory of churches and religious organizations. 3v. Indianapolis, Ind., 1940-41.

Marion county, Calumet region, northern Indiana. Adventist, Mennonite bodies, Methodists.

**1382** —— Guide to public vital statistics records in Indiana. Indianapolis, Ind., 1941.

Gives laws regarding vital statistics; indicated dates of records available at the county office, arranged by county.

**1383** —— Inventory of the county archives of Indiana. 20v. Indianapolis, Ind., 1937-42.

Only the following numbers were published: 2 (Allen), 5 (Blackford), 6 (Boone), 11 (Clay), 18 (Delaware), 25 (Fulton), 28 (Greene), 34 (Howard), 38 (Jay), 46 (LaPorte), 49 (Marion), 50 (Marshall), 53 (Monroe), 55 (Morgan), 65 (Posey), 71 (St. Joseph), 73 (Shelby), 79 (Tippecanoe), 80 (Tipton), 82 (Vanderburgh), 87 (Warwick), and 90 (Wells). Unpublished material deposited in Indiana State Library, Indianapolis, Ind.

**1384 Hixson (W.W.) and Co.** Atlas of Indiana. Rockford, Ill., 1934? Cover: *Plat book of Indiana.*

**1385** —— [Plat books of the counties of Indiana.] Rockford, Ill., [192? and 193?].

**1386 Hoosier genealogist.** v.1- , 1961- . Indianapolis, Ind.: Indiana Historical Soc. Genealogical section.

Small issues; quarterly, containing material pertinent to Indiana.

**1387 Indiana. Adjutant General's Office.** Report. 9v. Indianapolis, Ind., 1865-69.

v.2-8 includes rosters of officers and men of the War of the Rebellion. v.1 repr. by Indiana Historical Bureau. *Indiana historical collections,* 41. Indianapolis: The Bureau, 1960.

Indexed in the Indiana State Archives.

**1388 Indiana. Governor.** Executive proceedings of the state of Indiana, 1816-36. Ed. by Dorothy Riker. *Indiana historical collections* 29. Indianapolis, Ind.: Indiana Historical Soc., 1947.

Lists of commissions; officers in the militia, county officials, judges, and others. Copiously annotated.

**1389 Indiana. State Dept. of Public Welfare, Indianapolis.** List of public and semipublic records available for the verification of age in the respective counties of the state of Indiana. Indianapolis, Ind., 1938.

**1390** The Indiana gazetteer, or topographical dictionary of the state of Indiana. Compiled by E. Chamberlain. 3rd ed. Indianapolis, Ind., 1850.

**1391** Indiana magazine of history. v.1– , 1905– . Bloomington, Ind.: Dept. of History, Indiana Univ.

Had genealogy section, 1936–40, but *see The Hoosier genealogist* (no.1386). Considerable interplay between Canadian and Midwestern history. In 1930, Dorothy Riker compiled a general index for v.1–25, 1905–29. In 1967, Kraus Repr. Corp., New York, reprinted v.1–21 and index for v.1–25.

**1392** Indianapolis Public Library. A consolidated index to thirty-two histories of Indianapolis and Indiana. Indianapolis, Ind., 1939.

**1393** Means, Eloise R. Hoosier ancestors index. 2v. Indianapolis, Ind., 1965–70. From Betty L. McCay, Indianapolis, Ind.

Indexes of the column "Hoosier ancestors" by Pearl Brenton, which appears weekly in the *Indianapolis star*. Index covers: I. June 24, 1963–Dec. 26, 1965. II. Jan. 2, 1966–June 30, 1968. v.1 out of print; v.3 in preparation.

**1394** Memorial record of distinguished men of Indianapolis and Indiana. Chicago, 1912.
Mug book.

**1395** Memorial record of northeastern Indiana. Chicago, 1896.
Mug book.

**1396** Miller, Carolynne L. Aids for genealogical searching in Indiana: a bibliography. Rev. Detroit, Mich.: Detroit Soc. for Genealogical Research, 1970.
A distinguished work.

**1397** Monks, Leander J. Courts and lawyers of Indiana. 3v. Indianapolis, Ind., 1916.

**1398** Morrison, Olin D. Indiana, "Hoosier state": new historical atlas of Indiana. Athens, Ohio, 1958.

Maps showing Indiana at various times between 1679 and 1952.

**1399** Pence, George C. and Armstrong, N. C. Indiana boundaries: territory, state, and county. *Indiana historical collections* 19, 1933. Repr. Indianapolis, Ind.: Indiana Historical Bureau, 1967.

**1400** Reed, George I. Encyclopedia of biography of Indiana. 2v. Chicago, 1895–[99].
Mug book.

**1401** Scott, John. The Indiana gazetteer or topographical dictionary. 1826. Repr. ed. by Gayle Thornbrough. *Publ. of Indiana Historical Soc.* 18, no.1, 1954. Indianapolis, Ind.

**1402** Taylor, Charles W. Biographical sketches and review of the Bench and Bar of Indiana. Indianapolis, Ind., 1895.

**1403** Thompson, Donald E. Indiana authors and their books, 1917–66. A continuation of *Indiana authors and their books, 1816–1916,* and containing additional names from the earlier period. Crawfordsville, Ind.: Wabash College, 1974.
3,000 names with good biographies.

**1404** Volkel, Lowell M. 1850 Indiana mortality schedule. 3v. in 1. Thomson, Ill.: Heritage House, 1971.
v.1 Adams through Harrison; 2, Hendricks through Posey; 3, Pulaski through Whitley. Name of every person who died during year ending 1 June 1850, with other vital information. Essential.

**1405** Walters, Betty L. Furniture makers of Indiana, 1793–1850. *Publ. of Indiana Historical Soc.* 25, no.1. Indianapolis, Ind.: The Soc., 1972.

**1406** Waters, Margaret R. Genealogical sources available at the Indiana State Library for all Indiana counties. Indianapolis, Ind., 1946.
Suppl. published in 1949.

**1407** ——— Indiana land entries. 2v. Indianapolis, Ind., 1948–49.

v.1, Cincinnati district, 1801–40; v.2, Vincennes district, 1807–77.

**1408** ——— Revolutionary soldiers buried in Indiana. 300 names not listed in the D.A.R. *Roster* v.1. 2v. 1949–54. Repr. 2v. in 1. Baltimore: G.P.C., 1970.

Two lists of soldiers, 785 in all, not in *Roster of soldiers and patriots of the American Revolution buried in Indiana* (no.1372). Also contains information on another 352 soldiers who either moved to other states or died in other states.

**1408a** **Woollen, William W.** Biographical and historical sketches of early Indiana. New York, 1883.

## IOWA

Settled ca. 1833; entered Union 1846

*State Department of History and Archives, Des Moines*
*State Historical Society of Iowa, Iowa City*
*Dr. George E. McCracken, Des Moines*

**1409** **Andreas, Alfred T.** Illustrated historical atlas of the state of Iowa. 1875. Repr. Iowa City, Iowa: State Historical Soc. of Iowa, 1970.

**1410** **Annals of Iowa: a historical quarterly.** v.1– , 1863– . Iowa City, Iowa: State Historical Soc. of Iowa.

First series, 1863–74 (called *State Historical Society of Iowa annals*), would be helpful to genealogists if an index existed. Contains early county histories with names that would be found elsewhere only in census or land records. Third series, 1893– , more helpful because there is a cumulative index, containing some references to family backgrounds. The Society has an index in typescript to 1920.

**1411** **Brigham, Johnson.** Iowa, its history and its foremost citizens. 3v. Chicago, 1927.

v.2–3 are biographical.

**1412** **Cheever, Lawrence O.** Newspaper collection of the State Historical Society of Iowa. Iowa City, Iowa: The Soc., 1969.

Complete list to 1969.

**1413** **D.A.R. Iowa.** Iowa pioneers: their ancestors and descendants. v.1– . 1970– . Iowa City, Iowa.

v.6 was published in 1974. Wide variety of information collected from various chapters. No index, making it difficult to use.

**1414** **Gue, Benjamin F.** Biographies and portraits of the progressive men of Iowa . . . 2v. Des Moines, Iowa, 1899.

Mug book.

**1415** ——— History of Iowa from the earliest times to the beginning of the twentieth century . . . 4v. New York, 1903.

Portraits and biographies of notable men and women.

**1416** **Harlan, Edgar R.** A narrative history of the people of Iowa. 5v. Chicago, 1931.

v.3–5 biographical.

**1417** **Harris, Katherine.** Guide to manuscripts (of the State Historical Society of Iowa). Iowa City, Iowa: The Society, 1973.

Guide to documents in typescript, manuscript, and print from 1857. Much genealogy.

**1418** **Hawkeye heritage.** v.1– , 1966– . Des Moines, Iowa: Iowa State Genealogical Society. Local coverage. Much on Jackson county.

**1419** **Headlee, Bettylou.** Heads of families 1840 census of Iowa. Fullerton, Calif.: Mrs. B. M. Stercula, 1968.

**1420** **Historical Records Survey.** Directory of church and religious organizations in Iowa. Iowa City, Iowa, 1941.

**1421** ——— Guide to public vital statistics records in Iowa. Iowa City, Iowa, 1941.

**1422** ——— Inventory of the county archives of Iowa. 11v. Iowa City, Iowa, 1938–42.

Only the following numbers were published: 14 (Carroll), 18 (Cherokee), 25 (Dallas), 31 (Dubuque), 47 (Ida), 50 (Jasper), 69 (Montgomery), 77 (Polk), 81 (Sac), 87 (Taylor), and 97 (Woodbury). Unpublished material deposited in Iowa State Dept. of History & Archives, Des Moines, Iowa.

1423   **Hixson (W. W.) and Co.** Plat book of the state of Iowa. Rockford, Ill., 1933?

1424   **Hughes, Thomas E. (and others).** History of the Welsh in Minnesota, Foreston and Lime Springs, Iowa, gathered by the old settlers. Mankato, Minn., 1895.
Pt.1 in Welsh; pt.2 in English. pp.159–293 biographical sketches.

1425   **Iowa. Adjutant General's Office.** List of ex-soldiers, sailors and marines, living in Iowa. Des Moines, Iowa, 1886.
Occasionally referred to as "Alexander." William L. Alexander was Adjutant General at the time of compilation. Lists almost 40,000 names, including thousands from Illinois, Ohio, and Wisconsin.

1426   ——— Roster and record of Iowa soldiers in the War of the Rebellion . . . 1861–66. 6v. Des Moines, Iowa, 1908–11.
v.6: Roster and record of Iowa soldiers in miscellaneous organizations of the Mexican War, Indian campaigns, War of the Rebellion, Spanish-American, and Philippine wars.

1427   **The Iowa Genealogical Society surname index.** v.1 (all pub.). Des Moines, Iowa: The Society, 1972.
Alphabetical listing of each of the known ancestors, birth, death, marriage dates and places, etc. Numerous New Englanders included. 20,000 names. Spine title: *Iowa genealogical surname index.*

1428   **The Iowa historical record.** v.1–18, 1885–1902. Iowa City, Iowa. Continued as *Iowa journal of history,* which has little genealogy. The record contains extensive biographical material. In-house index compiled by Jacob Swisher in 1925.

1429   **Ivins, Virginia W.** Yesterdays. Reminiscences of long ago. [Keokuk, Iowa, 190?.]

Town sketches; short items on local citizens.

1430   **Jackson, Ronald V.** Iowa territorial census, 1836. Provo, Utah: Accelerated Indexing Systems, 1973.
G. R. Teeples, chief paleographer. About 2,500 entries. Maps, research aids on existing counties; genealogical data.

1431   **Koleda, Elizabeth P.** Some Ohio and Iowa pioneers: their friends and descendants. Prineville, Ore.: The Compiler, 1973. Available from the Compiler, P.O. Box 27, Prineville, Ore. 97754.

1432   **Memorial and biographical record of Iowa.** Chicago, 1896.
Mug book.

1433   **Obert, Rowene T., Blumhagen, H. M.,** and **Adkins, W.** 1840 Iowa census and index. Census of the 18 original counties and several precincts which comprised the area then known as Iowa. Salt Lake City: The Compilers (200 Medical Arts Building, 84111), 1968.
Accurate and invaluable work.

1434   **The palimpsest.** v.1– , 1920– . Iowa City, Iowa: State Historical Soc. of Iowa.
Contains large quantity of local history in earlier volumes; none in later years. Popular rehash of more serious treatments. Cumulative indexes, 1–20, 1920–39.

1435   **Petersen, William J.** Iowa history reference guide. Iowa City, Iowa: State Historical Soc. of Iowa, 1952.
Analyzes all books and periodicals in Iowa history.

1436   ——— The story of Iowa: the progress of an American state. 4v. New York, 1952.
v.3–4 biographical. Mug book.

1437   **Pittman, Edward F.** Index to bound newspapers in Iowa State Department of History and Archives. Des Moines, Iowa, 1947.

1439   **Stiles, Edward H.** Recollections and sketches of notable lawyers and public men of early Iowa, belonging to the first and second generations . . . Des Moines, Iowa, 1916.

**1440 United States biographical dictionary and portrait gallery of eminent and self-made men.** Iowa. Chicago, 1878.
Mug book.

KANSAS

Settled ca. 1854; entered Union 1861

*Kansas Genealogical Society, Dodge City*
*Kansas State Historical Society, Topeka*

**1441 Anderson, Lorene,** and **Farley, A. W.** A bibliography of town and county histories of Kansas. Topeka, Kans.: Kansas State Historical Soc., 1955.
Repr. from *Kansas historical quarterly,* v.21, 1955, pp.513–51.

**1442 Baldwin, Sara M.,** and **Baldwin, R. M.** Illustriana Kansas. Hebron, Nebr., 1933.
Subtitle: Biographical sketches of Kansas men and women of achievement who have been awarded life membership in Kansas Illustriana Society.

**1443 Barry, Louise.** The beginning of the west; annals of the Kansas gateway to the American west, 1540–1854. Topeka, Kans.: Kansas State Historical Soc., 1972.
Story of explorers, trappers, missionaries, soldiers and others.

**1444 Baughman, Robert W.** Kansas post offices, 1828–1961. Topeka, Kans.: Kansas Postal History Soc., 1961.
Contains alphabetical list of every known post office; a territorial list, limited to those established before Kansas became a state, 1861, and including the preterritorial offices created prior to 1854; and a county list including name changes.

**1445 Billdt, Ruth B.** Pioneer Swedish-American culture in central Kansas. Lindsborg, Kans.: Wm. Linder Co., 1964.
Mostly Saline and McPherson counties. Contains data on leading settlers.

**1446 Biographical history of central Kansas.** 2v. Chicago, 1902.
Both large volumes are biographical. Covers counties of Lyon, Pratt, Barton, Reno, Kingman, Ellsworth, Rice, and Barber.

**1447 Blackmar, Frank W.** Kansas: a cyclopedia of state history . . . 3v. in 4. Chicago, 1912.
v.1–2 are arranged A–Z; additional volume designated 3, with arbitrary parts 1–4. All supplements have biographies of prominent persons.

**1448 Bright, John D.** Kansas, the first century. 4v. New York, 1956.
v.2–4 are biographical; Mug book.

**1449 Brower, Jacob V.** Kansas: monumental perpetuation of its earliest history, 1541–1896. St. Paul, Minn., 1903.
Biographies and portraits.

**1450 Carpenter, Thelma,** and **Franklin, H.** 1880 mortality schedules for Kansas. Topeka, Kans.: Helen Franklin, 1973–74.
In 43 booklets, containing details on 92 counties. 15,000 names. Index was published separately in 1974. For 1860 and 1870 schedules, *see* no.1455–56.

**1451 Connelley, William E.** History of Kansas, state and people: Kansas at the first quarter post of the twentieth century . . . 5v. Chicago, 1928.
v.3–5 biographical. 3rd ed. of his *Standard history of Kansas and Kansans,* published in 1918. Same sketches do not appear in each ed. Indian tribes of the area with biographical and genealogical notes.

**1452 Curtis, Mary B.** Bibliography of Kansas: the formative years. In *Magazine of bibliographies,* v.1, no.2, Dec. 1972.
Excellent up-to-the-minute bibliography aimed primarily at genealogists and historians.

**1453 Cutler, William G.** History of the state of Kansas . . . description of its counties, cities, towns and villages . . . to which are added biographical sketches and

portraits of prominent men and early settlers. Chicago, 1883.
Kansas State Historical Soc. has ms. index.

**1454** **Fesler, Myrtle D.** Pioneers of western Kansas. New York: Carlton Pr., 1962.
Biographical and genealogical notes on Rooks, Ellis, Graham, Trego, and Phillips counties.

**1455** **Franklin, Helen.** 1860 mortality schedules for Kansas territory. Topeka, Kans.: Topeka Genealogical Soc., 1972.

**1456** ———— 1870. Topeka, Kans.: Topeka Genealogical Soc., 1974.
Arranged alphabetically, gives county in which death occurred. 1880 schedules, *see* no.1450.

**1457** **Gannett, Henry.** A gazetteer of Kansas. *U.S. Geological Survey bull.* 154. Washington, D.C., 1898.

**1458** **Gazetteer and directory of the state of Kansas** . . . Lawrence, Kans., 1870.

**1459** **Genealogical and biographical record of northeastern Kansas.** Chicago, 1900.
Mug book.

**1460** **Gill, Helen G.** The establishment of counties in Kansas, 1855–1903. [Topeka, Kans., 1904?]
Repr. from v.8 of *Collections of the Kansas State Historical Soc.*

**1461** **Gleed, Charles S.** The Kansas memorial, a report of the Old Settlers' meeting held at Bismarck Grove, Kansas, Sept. 15 and 16, 1879. Kansas City, Mo., 1880.
pp.211–55 list settler's name, place and date of birth, place and date of settlement, "present residence." 3,000 pioneers listed.

**1462** **Green, Charles R.** Early days in Kansas. 5v. Olathe, Kans., 1912–14.

Much history and genealogy, mostly of Osage county.

**1463** **Heiss, Willard C.** and **Mayhill, R. T.** The census of the territory of Kansas, February 1855. Knightstown, Ind.: Eastern Indiana Pub. Co., 1968.
Excerpted from U.S. House of Representatives doc., *Report of the special committee appointed to investigate the trouble in Kansas.* 1856. Has map of Kansas election districts in 1854 and lists voters over 21 years of age. Has alternative title, *Kansas voter list 1855.* Kansas State Historical Soc. has manuscript list.

**1464** **Historical Records Survey.** Guide to public vital statistics records in Kansas. Topeka, Kans., 1942.

**1465** ———— Inventory of the county archives of Kansas. 14v. Topeka, Kans., 1937–41.
Only the following numbers were published: 6 (Bourbon), 11 (Cherokee), 30 (Franklin), 32 (Gove), 33 (Graham), 35 (Gray), 37 (Greenwood), 46 (Johnson), 63 (Montgomery), 64 (Morris), 70 (Osage), 74 (Phillips), 88 (Seward), and 89 (Shawnee). Unpublished material deposited in Kansas State Historical Soc., Topeka, Kans.

**1466** **Kansas.** Special limited ed. Chicago, 1919.
Family histories, coats of arms.

**1467** **Kansas. Adjutant General's Office.** Report, 1861–65. 2v. 1867–70. Repr. Leavenworth, Kans., 1896.
Has rosters of the Kansas regiments, etc., Civil War.

**1468** **Kansas historical quarterly.** v.1– , 1931– . Topeka, Kans.: Kansas State Historical Soc.
Little genealogy. Continuation of no. 1470.

**1469** ———— Subject and author guide-index, v.1–33, 1931–67. By Louise Barry. Topeka, Kans.: The Society, 1967.

**1470** **Kansas State Historical Society collections.** v.1–17. Topeka, Kans., 1881–1928.

Became *Kansas historical quarterly* (no. 1468). Much genealogical information concerning missions, settlements, soldiers, boundaries, religious groups, etc. v.11–17 only still available from the Society.

1471 ——— Comprehensive index, 1875–1930, to *Collections,* biennial reports and publications of the Kansas State Historical Society. Compiled by Louise Barry. Topeka, Kans.: Kansas State Historical Society, 1959.
Wealth of material on early Kansas. Index invaluable.

1472 **Lowry, Mildred.** Who, when, where in Kansas. Pittsburgh, Kans.: The Author, 1973.
Only v.1 published. Other volumes will follow in 1975. Marriages and other data in second half of 19th century.

1473 **Mills, Madeline S.** Relocated cemeteries in Oklahoma and parts of Kansas and Texas. Tulsa, Okla.: The Author, 1974.
Covers cemeteries for all Oklahoma, and a number of counties in southern Kansas. 250 cemeteries, 7,000 graves, 3,000 surnames.

1474 **Official roster of Kansas 1854–1925.** In *Kansas State Historical Soc. collections,* v.16, 1923–25.
Governors, legislators, boards, officials, etc.

1475 **The official state atlas of Kansas.** Philadelphia, 1887.
Publ. by L. H. Everts. Lists of farmers and land owners, description of land, when purchased, and other useful data.

1476 **Owen, Jennie S.** The annals of Kansas, 1886–1925. Ed. by Kirke Mechem. 2v. Topeka, Kans.: Kansas State Historical Soc., 1954–56.
Excellent suppl. to Wilder (no.1485). Information taken from newspapers and official sources.

1477 **Portrait and biographical albums,** published by Chapman Bros. of Chicago. All mug books, as follows: Jackson, Jefferson and Pottawatomie counties. 1890; Marshall county. 1889; Sedgwick county. 1888; Sumner county. 1890; Washington, Clay, and Riley counties. 1890; Dickinson, Saline, McPherson, and Marion counties. 1893; Leavenworth, Douglas, and Franklin counties. 1899.

1478 **Portrait and biographical record of southeastern Kansas,** containing biographical sketches of prominent . . . citizens of the counties . . . Chicago, 1894.
Mug book. Biographical Pub. Co.

1479 **Rydjord, John.** Kansas place-names. Norman, Okla.: Univ. of Oklahoma Pr., 1972.
Concerned more with sources than with perpetuation; includes names no longer used, as well as names currently applied. Good coverage.

1480 **[Shackleton, Bernice C.]** Handbook on the frontier days of southeast Kansas. Kansas centennial, 1861–1961. Pittsburg, Kans.: The Compiler, 1961.
Names many early settlers, but provides little information about them.

1481 **Socolofsky, Homer E.** and **Self, H.** Historical atlas of Kansas. Norman, Okla.: Univ. of Oklahoma Pr., 1972.
Choices arbitrary, and therefore not as much use to genealogists as it could have been.

1482 **Topeka Genealogical Society.** Topeka genealogy workshop textbook. Topeka, Kans., 1971.
Useful for Kansas genealogy.

1483 **The treesearcher.** v.1– , 1959– . Dodge City, Kans.: Kansas Genealogical Soc.
Good quarterly, well written and printed.

1484 **United States biographical dictionary: Kansas vol.** Chicago, 1879.
Mug book.

1485 **Wilder, Daniel W.** The annals of Kansas. New ed. Topeka, Kans., 1886.
Many names, covers period 1541–1885. Continuation *1886–1925, see* no.1476.

**1486  Wilson, Hill P.** Biographical history of eminent men of the state of Kansas. Topeka, Kans., 1901.

**1487  Zornow, William F.** Kansas, a history of the Jayhawk State. 1957. Repr. Norman, Okla.; Univ. of Oklahoma Pr., 1971.
Considerable information on state and settlers.

## KENTUCKY

Settled ca. 1774; entered Union 1792

*Filson Club, Louisville*
*Kentucky Historical Society, Frankfort*

**1488  Allen, William B.** A history of Kentucky and biographical sketches of pioneers, soldiers, jurists, and leading men. 1872. Repr. Ann Arbor, Mich.: Xerox Univ. Microfilms, 1973.

**1489  Ardery, Julia H. (Spencer).** Kentucky [court and other] records, early wills and marriages, old Bible records with tombstone inscriptions. 1926. Repr. Baltimore: G.P.C., 1969.
Covers 1725–1875. Also index of estates, inventories of Revolutionary soldiers.

**1490** ———— Kentucky court and other records: wills, deeds, orders, suits, marriages . . . [v.2]. 1932. Repr. Baltimore: G.P.C., 1972
Records pertinent to Kentucky and that part of Virginia from which Kentucky was formed. Many thousands of Kentucky's earliest inhabitants recorded.

**1491  Beam, Judith A.** Cemetery records of land between the lakes (betwixt the rivers), 1814–1973. Murray, Ky.: The Author, 1974.

**1492  Biographical encyclopedia of Kentucky of the dead and living men of the nineteenth century.** Cincinnati, Ohio, 1878.
Mug book.

**1492a  Bluegrass roots.** v.1– , 1974– . Frankfort, Ky.: Central Kentucky Genealogical Soc.

**1493  Bodley, Temple.** History of Kentucky. 4v. Chicago, 1928.
v.3–4 biographical.

**1494  Burns, Annie (Walker).** Abstracts of pension papers of soldiers of the Revolutionary War, War of 1812, and Indian Wars, who settled . . . in Kentucky. At least 21v. Washington, D.C., 1935, [various dates].
As with the other works, the publishing details of this work are confusing. The names of those soldiers settling in Greenup and other counties and areas were published in 1935 or thereabouts. There were also 2v. published in the 1950s.

**1495** ———— Kentucky genealogies and historical records. Many v. Washington, D.C., ca. 1944.
Published as part of the Historical Records Survey program. Frequent mistakes in copying appear; use with care.

**1496** ———— Record of deaths in Kentucky counties, 1852–59. Washington, D.C. 19??– .

**1497** ———— Records of wills of various counties. Adair, Anderson, Bath, Bracken, Edmonson, Fleming, Garrard, Green, Hardin, Harlan, Laurel, Letcher, Lincoln, Livingston, Logan, Madison, Mercer, Nelson, Ohio, Oldham, Owen, Scott, Shelby, Spencer, Trimble, and Warren. Several vols., n.p., 1932–37.
Mostly from the 1790s to about 1851.

**1498** ———— Third census of the United States (1810). 10v. Washington, D.C., 1934–36. Because of poor transcription, use with care. An alphabetical index to all names was published in 1933.

**1499  Caudhill, Bernice C.** Pioneers of eastern Kentucky; their feuds and settlements. Danville, Ky.: Kentucky Bluegrass Printing Co., 1969.

**1500  Central Kentucky researcher.** v.1– , 1971– . Campbellsville, Ky.: Taylor County Historical Soc.
Monthly; local and county records, cemeteries, queries.

**1501 Clift, Garrett G.** The "Cornstalk" militia of Kentucky, 1792–1811; a brief statutory history of the militia and records of commissions of officers in the organization from the beginning of statehood to the commencement of the War of 1812. Frankfort, Ky.: Kentucky Historical Soc., 1957.

**1502** ——— Guide to the manuscripts of the Kentucky Historical Society. Frankfort, Ky., 1955.

**1503** ——— Kentucky marriages, 1797–1865. In *The Register of the Kentucky Historical Soc.,* v.36–38, 1938–40. Repr. with added index. Baltimore: G.P.C., 1974.

Abstracts listing 8,000 brides and grooms. Clift describes it as "v.1." For v.2, *see* no. 1504. Taken from the files of newspapers in Lexington Public Lib.

**1504** ——— Kentucky marriages and obituaries, 1787–1854. In *The Register of the Kentucky Historical Soc.,* v.39–41, 1941–43.

Called v.2 by Clift. For v.1 *see* no.1503. Taken from the files of newspapers in Lexington Public Lib.

**1505** ——— Remember the Raisin! Kentucky and Kentuckians in the battle and massacres at Frenchtown, Michigan Territory, in the War of 1812. Frankfort, Ky.: Kentucky Historical Soc., 1961.

Raisin river battle was in 1813. Gives War of 1812 regiments and lists.

**1506** ——— "Second census" of Kentucky—1800. A privately compiled and published enumeration of taxpayers appearing in the 79 manuscript columns extant of tax lists of the 42 counties of Kentucky in existence in 1800. Frankfort, Ky.: Kentucky Historical Soc., 1954. Also repr. by G.P.C., Baltimore, 1970.

A reconstructed census. Invaluable; 32,000 names.

**1507 Coleman, John W., Jr.** A bibliography of Kentucky history. Lexington, Ky.: Univ. of Kentucky Pr., 1949.

**1508 Collins, Lewis.** Historical sketches of Kentucky. 1848. Repr. New York: Arno Pr., 1971.

The first comprehensive general history of the state. Some errors.

**1509** ——— History of Kentucky, rev., enl., and brought down to 1874 by Richard H. Collins. 2v. 1874. Repr. Lexington, Ky.: Henry Clay Pr., 1968.

**1510 Connelley, William E., and Coulter, E. M.** History of Kentucky. 5v. 1922. Repr. Ann Arbor, Mich.: Xerox Univ. Microfilms, 1973.

v.3–5 biographical.

**1511 Connor, Seymour V.** Kentucky colonists in Texas. A history of the Peters Colony. In *Register of the Kentucky Historical Soc.,* v.51–52, 1953–54.

**1512 Corbin, John B.** Catalog of genealogical materials in Texas libraries. pt.2, Kentucky. Texas Library and Historical Commission. Austin, Tex.: The Library, 1966.

Most useful bibliography for Texas genealogists working on Kentucky ancestry.

**1513 Cox, Evelyn M., and Culley, L. F. M.** Kentucky records. v.1–5, 10, 12. Madisonville, Ky.: 1960–61.

Volume numbering confusing.

**1514 D.A.R. Kentucky. Records Research Committee.** Kentucky Bible records, from the files of the Genealogical Records Committee. v.1–5. Florence, Ky.: D.A.R., 1962–71.

Compiled by Emma J. Walker and Virginia Wilson.

**1515** ——— ——— Kentucky cemetery records. v.1–4. Florence, Ky.: D.A.R., 1960–72.

v.1–2 by Virginia Wilson and M. B. Coyle; v.3 by Malle B. Coyle and L. C. Mallows; v.4 by M. B. Coyle and I. B. Gaines. County by county listing; much genealogical data.

**1516** ——— Revolution ancestors of Kentucky D.A.R. Compiled and ed. by Clare C. Davis. Frankfort, Ky., 1928.

**1517 Dixon, Norvin,** and **Dixon, N.** Southeastern Kentucky census of 1820. Irvine, Ky.: The Authors, 1974.

Heads of family of Clay, Estill, Floyd, Harlan, Rockcastle, Knox, and Whitley. Since 1820, 20 counties and parts of 8 others have been formed from these 7 counties.

**1518 East Kentuckian.** v.1– , 1965– . Stanville, Ky.: Henry P. Scalf.

Journal of genealogy and history.

**1519 Ellsberry, Elizabeth P.** Kentucky records. Wills, marriage, cemetery, census, probate records. Chillicothe, Mo.: The Author.

Mrs. Ellsberry has published many volumes in the past decade.

**1520 Ely, William.** The Big Sandy Valley: a history of the people and country from the earliest settlement to the present time. 1887. Repr. Baltimore: G.P.C., 1969.

Annals and sketches of settlers in eastern Kentucky, covering 1790–1800.

**1521 Field, Thomas P.** A guide to Kentucky place names . . . *Kentucky Geological Survey, ser.X, special pub. 5.* Lexington, Ky.: College of Arts and Sciences, Univ. of Kentucky, 1961.

**1522 Filson Club history quarterly.** v.1– , 1926– . Louisville, Ky.: The Club.

Has valuable family history material in earlier volumes.

**1523 Fowler, Ila E.** Kentucky pioneers and their descendants. Kentucky Soc. Daughters of Colonial Wars, 1941–50. 1951. Repr. Baltimore: G.P.C., 1967.

15,000 names.

**1523a Fulton Genealogical Society, Kentucky.** Bible records of western Kentucky and Tennessee. Fulton, Ky.: The Society, 1974.

Good index.

**1524 General and field officers of Kentucky militia, 1802–16.** In *The Register of Kentucky State Historical Soc.* v.22, 1924.

**1525 Gray, Frank A.** Gray's new map of Kentucky and Tennessee. 1876. Repr. Murray, Ky.: House of Heather, 1972.

Shows comparative increases in population, 1790–1870. Excellent aid for those working with the 1870 and 1880 federal censuses.

**1526 Green, Thomas M.** Historic families of Kentucky; with special reference to stocks immediately derived from the valley of Virginia. 1889. Repr. Baltimore: Regional Pub. Co., 1966.

Relates to history of Kentucky in the light of accomplishments of its pioneer families.

**1527 Hall, Carl M.** Jenny Wiley country; a history of the Big Sandy Valley in Kentucky's eastern highlands and genealogy of the region's people. 2v. Kingsport, Tenn.: Kingsport Pr., 1972.

Largely Johnson county history; many family lineages, deaths.

**1528 Hathaway, Beverly W.** Inventory of county records of Kentucky. West Jordan, Utah: Allstates Research Co., 1974.

Locations of collections, with details of microfilms of Kentucky court records at the Genealogical Society Library at Salt Lake City.

**1529** ——— Kentucky genealogical research sources. West Jordan, Utah: Allstates Research Co., 1974.

Explains records, court systems, locations of sources, maps, index to State Supreme Court cases; holdings of major collections.

**1530 Heinemann, Charles B.** "First census" of Kentucky. 1790. 1940. Repr. Baltimore: G.P.C., 1971.

Not a federal enumeration; compiled from list of 9,000 taxpayers.

**1531 Historical Records Survey.** Guide to public vital statistics records in Kentucky. Louisville, Ky., 1942.

**1532** ——— Inventory of the county archives in Kentucky. 9v. Louisville, Ky., 1937–41.

Only the following numbers were published: 3 (Anderson), 14 (Breckenridge), 20 (Carlisle), 34 (Fayette), 57 (Jessamine), 61 (Knox), 63 (Laurel), 74 (McCreary), and 82 (Meade). Unpublished material deposited in Univ. of Kentucky Library, Lexington, Ky.

**1533** **Jackson, Ronald V.** (and others). Kentucky 1810 census. Bountiful, Utah: Accelerated Indexing Services, 1974.
Over 50,000 entries.

**1534** **Jillson, Willard R.** The Big Sandy Valley. 1923. Repr. Baltimore: G.P.C., 1970.
History of region prior to 1850; includes lists of settlers, soldiers, etc.

**1535** ———— The Kentucky land grants: a systematic index to all of the land grants recorded in the State Land Office in Frankfort, Kentucky, 1782-1924. *Filson Club publ.* 33. 1925. Repr. 1v. in 2. Baltimore: G.P.C., 1971.
150,000 entries, including some Virginia land grants. Definitive.

**1536** ———— Old Kentucky entries and deeds. A complete index of all of the earliest land entries, military warrants, deeds and wills of the commonwealth of Kentucky. *Filson Club publ.* 34. 1926. Repr. Baltimore: G.P.C., 1972.
45,000 entries, mostly of early Fayette, Lincoln, and Jefferson county records. Also military warrants, 1782-93, grantors 1783-1846, wills 1769-1850.

**1537** **Kentucky. Adjutant General's Office.** Kentucky soldiers of the War of 1812. 1891. Repr. with added index by Minnie S. Wilder, 1931. Baltimore: G.P.C., 1969.
Publisher's title: *Report of the Adjutant General of the state of Kentucky: Soldiers of the War of 1812.* Standard source for names and service records of over 20,000 soldiers and officers, regular and militia.

**1538** ———— Report 1861-66. 2v. Frankfort, Ky., 1866-67.
Roster of officers, Civil War.

**1539** ———— Report. Confederate Kentucky volunteers, war 1861-65. 2v. [Frankfort, Ky., 1915-18.]
Compiled by Abner Harris.

**1540** **Kentucky. State Archives.** Gleanings from the State Archives, Kentucky, recently taken from the basement of the old administration building of the State Capitol, 1780s. In *The register of the Kentucky Historical Soc.,* v.23, 1925.

**1541** ———— Tax lists. In *The register of the Kentucky Historical Soc.,* v.22-29, 1924-31.
v.22, Jefferson; v.23, Lincoln, Logan, Madison; v.24, Christian, Franklin, Shelby; v.25, Floyd, Mercer, Washington; v.26, Nelson; v.27, Wayne; v.28, Mercer; v.29, Knox. All 1780s and 1790s.

**1542** ———— Vital statistics, 1850-1860. In *The register of the Kentucky Historical Soc.,* v.43-63, 1945-65.
v.43, Allen-Boone; v.44, Bourbon-Butler; v.45, Caldwell-Carter; v.46, Casey-Cumberland; v.47, Daviess-Estill; v.48, Fayette-Franklin; v.49, Fulton-Grant; v.50, Graves-Greenup; v.51, Hancock-Harrison; v.52, Hart-Hickman; v.53, Hopkins-Jefferson; v.55, Jefferson-Kenton; v.56, Knox-Lee; v.57, Letcher-Livingston; v.58, Logan-Lyon; v.61, McLean-Madison; v.62, Clay, Magoffin-Marshall; v.63, Mason.

**1543** **Kentucky ancestors.** v.1- , 1965- . Frankfort, Ky.: Genealogical Committee of the Kentucky Historical Soc.

**1544** **Kentucky 1800.** 4v. Thomson, Ill.: Heritage House, 1970.
Head of each household, county and reference to original census records. v.1-4 contain 8 counties.

**1545** **Kentucky family records.** v.1- , 1971- . Owensboro, Ky.: West-Central Kentucky Families Research Assoc.
Bible and cemetery records, pensioners, etc.

**1546** **Kentucky genealogist.** v.1- , 1950- . Ed. by Martha P. Miller. Washington, D.C.
Excellent; source records.

**1547** **Kentucky Historical Society.** Register. v.1- , 1903- . Frankfort, Ky.: The Society.

**1548** ———— General index. 43v., 1903–45. Frankfort, Ky.: The Society.
v.1–53 had considerable amount of genealogy, but from v.54 (1956) genealogy diminished; current volumes have little or no genealogy.

**1549 Kerr, Charles.** History of Kentucky. 5v. Chicago, 1922.
v.3–5 biographical.

**1550 King, June Estelle S.** Abstract of early Kentucky wills and inventories. 1933. Repr. Baltimore: G.P.C., 1969.
Abstracts from 36 counties formed between 1780–1842, with exception of Crittenden.

**1551 Kozee, William C.** Early families of eastern and southeastern Kentucky, and their descendants. 1961. Repr. Baltimore: G.P.C., 1973.
Concerns the section originally comprising Floyd, Knox, Greenup, and Clay counties. 12,000 individuals from late 18th century until 1950.

**1552** ———— Pioneer families of eastern and southeastern Kentucky. 1957. Repr. Baltimore: G.P.C., 1973.
Source record of genealogy, rather than a collection of family histories. Treats same area as *Early families* (no.1551), and refers to 15,000. 16 present-day counties covered, 1789–1865.

**1553 McAdams, Ednah (Wilson).** Kentucky pioneer and court records: abstracts of early wills, deeds and marriages, from court houses and records of old Bibles, churches, grave yards, and cemeteries. 1929. Repr. Baltimore: G.P.C., 1967.
Covers a dozen counties, with index of almost 4,000 names. Also contains a roll of Revolutionary pensioners.

**1554 McCay, Betty L.** Sources for genealogical searching in Kentucky. New ed. Indianapolis, Ind.: The Author, 1973.
Very good list, but confined to sources of genealogy in historical works.

**1555 McDowell, Sam.** Surname index to Kentucky 7th census, 1850. *See* no. 1588.

**1556 McGhee, Lucy K.** Pension abstracts of Maryland soldiers of the Revolution, War of 1812 and Indian Wars who settled in Kentucky. Washington, D.C., n.d.
Note also Mrs. Burns's work (*see* no. 1494).

**1557 Memorial record of western Kentucky.** 2v. Chicago, 1904.
Biographical sketches of men living at that time (late 19th century) in the western half of the state.

**1558 Parrish, Verle H. (Mrs. H. T.).**
1850 census index of eastern Kentucky. Stamping Ground, Ky.: The Author, 1973.
Includes counties of Breathitt, Carter, Clay, Floyd, Harlan, Johnson, Knox, Laurel, Lawrence, Letcher, Morgan, Perry, and Pike.

**1559 Perrin, William H.; Battle, J. H.; and Kniffin, G. C.** Kentucky: a history of the state.... Louisville, 1888.
Between the years 1885 and 1888 there were several editions, and each contained supplemental materials pertaining to various counties in a particular part of the state. Most contained biographical sketches of prominent citizens.

**1560** ———— Kentucky. A history of the state: Ballard, Calloway, Fulton, Graves, Green, Hickman, McCracken, and Marshall. Louisville, Ky., 1885. Repr. Nashville, Tenn.: House of Heather, 1974.
Over 7,000 biographical sketches, thousands of names.

**1561** ———— ———— [2d ed.] Butler, Caldwell, Crittenden, Logan, Hancock, Hopkins, Livingston, Lyon, McLean, Muhlenberg, Ohio, Union, Webster. Louisville, Ky., 1885.

**1562** ———— ———— Biographical sketches. *See* no.1573.

**1563** ———— ———— [3rd ed.] Barren, Simpson, Monroe, Hart, Metcalfe, Allen, Warren, Larue, Hardin, Edmonson, Meade, Grayson, Breckinridge. Louisville, Ky., 1886.

**1564** ——— ——— Biographical sketches. *See* no.1573.

**1565** ——— ——— Index to geographical sketches, by Tessie J. Miller. Pryor, Okla.: The Author, 1972.

**1566** ——— ——— 4th ed. Green, Adair, Boyle, Casey, Garrard, Madison, Mercer, Nelson, Taylor. Louisville, Ky., 1887.

**1567** ——— ——— 5th ed. Franklin, Woodford, Anderson, Jessamine. Louisville, Ky., 1887.

**1568** ——— ——— 6th ed. Henry, Oldham, Shelby, Spencer, Trimble. Louisville, Ky., 1887.

**1569** ——— ——— Index to 6th ed. By Bailey F. Davis. Franklin, Ky., c.1956.

**1570** ——— ——— 7th ed. Boone, Bracken, Campbell, Carroll, Grant, Gallatin, Harrison, Kenton, Owen, Pendleton. Louisville, Ky., 1887.

**1571** ——— ——— Index to 7th ed. By Emma J. Walker. n.p., 1961-63.

**1572** ——— ——— 8th ed. Clay, Laurel, Pulaski, Rockcastle, Wayne, Jefferson. Louisville, Ky., 1888.

**1573** ——— Kentucky genealogy and biography. Sketches from the counties of Kentucky repr. from *Kentucky: a history of the state,* by Perrin, Battle and Kniffin, 2nd and 3rd eds., 1885-86. Compiled by Thomas W. Westerfield. 4v. Owensboro, Ky.: Genealogical Reference Co., 1970-72.
v.1, Hancock, Larue, Hardin, Edmonson, Hart, Breckinridge, Grayson, and Meade; v.2, Allen, Monroe, Metcalfe, Barren, and Warren; v.3, Butler, McLean, Muhlenberg, and Ohio; v.4, Caldwell, Crittenden, Hopkins, Livingston, Logan, Lyon, Simpson, Union, and Webster.

**1574** **Quisenberry, Anderson C.** Kentucky in the War of 1812. 1915. Repr. with index. Baltimore: G.P.C., 1969. Biographical notices and record of services.

**1575** ——— Kentucky officers in the regular army 1789-1900. In *The register of the Kentucky Historical Soc.,* v.23, 1925.

**1576** ——— Revolutionary soldiers in Kentucky . . . also a roster of the Virginia navy. 1896. Repr. Baltimore: G.P.C., 1974.
From *Year book, Kentucky Soc., Sons of the Revolution,* 1896. 3,000 soldiers with military data. Also roll of officers of the Virginia Line who received land bounties, and a roster of the Virginia navy.

**1577** **Rone, Wendell H., Sr.** An historical atlas of Kentucky and her counties. Mayfield, Ky.: Mid-Continent Book Store, 1974.

**1578** **Scalf, Henry P.** Kentucky's last frontier, 2nd ed. Pikeville, Ky.: The Author, 1972.
Though not really genealogical, there are sections on Big Sandy Valley, land titles, Baptists, Methodists, Presbyterians, and other items; many pioneers.

**1579** **Scott, Hattie M.** Scott's papers: Kentucky court and other records. Ed. by Bayless E. Hardin. Frankfort, Ky.: Kentucky Historical Soc., 1953.
Genealogical information abstracted from court and county records, tomb inscriptions, and newspapers.

**1580** **Smith, Dora W.** Kentucky 1830 census index. 6v., v.1-4 in 1. Thomson, Ill.: Heritage House, 1973-74.
v.1, Adair-Campbell; v.2, Casey-Gallatin; v.3, Garrard-Hopkins; v.4, Jefferson-Meade; v.5, Mercer-Russell; v.6, Scott-Woodford.

**1581** **Smith, William T.** A complete index to the names of persons, places, and subjects mentioned in William Littell's *Laws of Kentucky,* Frankfort, 1800-19. A genealogical and historical guide . . . Lexington, Ky., 1931.

1582 **Staples, Charles R.** History in Circuit Court records [Kentucky]. Abstracts. In *The Register of the Kentucky Historical Soc.,* v.28-33, 1930-35.

1583 **Talley, William M.** Talley's Kentucky papers. v.1- . Fort Worth, Tex.: Miran, 1965- (in progress).
v.2 last published in 1974. Marriages, wills, deeds, court orders, cemetery records, from Fleming, Lewis, Rowan, Carter, Bath, Nicholas, Morgan, Montgomery, Greenup, and Mason counties.

1584 ———— Talley's northeastern Kentucky papers. Fort Worth, Tex.: Miran, 1971.
Valuable historical and genealogical data of area little covered hitherto—Fleming, Lewis, Nicholas, Greenup, Carter, Morgan, and Rowan counties; v.2 of series in no. 1583.

1585 **Taylor, Philip F.** A calendar of the warrants for land in Kentucky. Granted for service in the French and Indian War. *Year book of the Society of Colonial Wars of Kentucky,* 1917, pp.64-136. Repr. Baltimore, G.P.C., 1967.
Abstracts of earliest surveys for land grants, 1774-89, as found in Land Office, Frankfort, Ky. Index has over 1,000 names.

1586 **Thompson, Jess M.** Pike county history. Pittsfield, Ill.: [Pike County Historical Soc., 1967].
193 chapters, being articles printed in the *Pike County Republican,* Pittsfield, Illinois, 1935-39. Primarily concerns history and many families of Pike county, with numerous references to their origins in Kentucky.

1587 **Trabue, Alice E.** Kentucky tombstone inscriptions contributed by the Colonial Dames in Kentucky [1700-1800]. In *The register of the Kentucky Historical Soc.,* v.28-33, 1930-35.

1588 **U.S. Census Office.** 7th census, 1850. Population schedules of the 7th census of the U.S., 1850. Surname index compiled by Sam McDowell. Richland, Ind.: The Compiler, 1974.
Indexes are to microfilm rolls, viz.: roll no.192 for Boone, Bourbon, and Boyle counties; roll 202 for Grayson, Green, Greenup, and Hancock; roll 213 for Meade, Mercer and Monroe; 33v. in progress.

1589 **U.S. War Dept.** Kentucky pension roll of 1835. Report from the Secretary of War in relation to the pension establishment of the United States. 1835. Repr. Baltimore: G.P.C., 1959.
2,500 names with military data excerpted from 3v. set.

1590 **Van Meter, Benjamin F.** Genealogies and sketches of some old families who have taken part in the development of Virginia and Kentucky especially . . . Louisville, Ky., 1901.

1591 **Volkel, Lowell M.** An index to the 1810 federal census of Kentucky. 4v. in 1. Thomson, Ill.: Heritage House, 1971-72.
Lists head of household, residence and census page references. v.1, Adair-Cumberland; v.2, Estill-Hopkins; v.3, Jefferson-Muhlenberg; v.4, Nelson-Woodford.

1592 ———— Index to the 1820 federal census of Kentucky. v.1- . Thomson, Ill.: Heritage House, 1974- (in progress).
v.1, Adair-Cumberland; v.2, Daviess-Hopkins.

1593 **Wallis, Frederick A.** A sesquicentennial history of Kentucky . . . and chronicling the genealogies and memorial records of its prominent families and personages . . . 4v. Hopkinsville, Ky., 1945.

1594 **Weaks, Mabel C.** Calendar of the Kentucky Papers of the Draper collection of manuscripts (in the Wisconsin Historical Soc.). Madison, Wisc., 1925.
Calendar with abstracts of cemetery records, certificates, letters, promissory notes, petitions, patents, deeds, bonds, etc. Good index of names.

1595 **Webb, Benjamin J.** Centenary of Catholicity in Kentucky, 1784-1884. 1884. Repr. Evansville, Ind.: Unigraphic, 1973.
Most complete work on Roman Catholic

Church in Kentucky. Brief biographical sketches of priests and pioneer families. Good genealogical data.

1596    **Westerfield, Thomas W.** Kentucky genealogy and biography. *See* no. 1573.

1597    **Wilson, Samuel M.** Catalogue of Revolutionary soldiers and sailors of the commonwealth of Virginia to whom land bounty warrants were granted by Virginia for military services in the War of Independence. Baltimore: G.P.C., 1967.
From *Year book, Kentucky Soc., Sons of the Revolution,* 1913. 4,600 names with complete data. Originally from the official records in the Kentucky State Land Office at Frankfort, Ky.

## LOUISIANA

Settled ca. 1699; entered Union 1812

*Louisiana Genealogical Society, Baton Rouge*
*New Orleans Public Library*

✧ Because many Louisiana and Mississippi families are so closely related and many property owners had estates in both territories, a study should be made of Mississippi entries. For similar reasons, Canada should be checked for French records.

1598    **Achee, Benjamin E.,** and **Wright, M.** Index to Louisiana 1860 mortality schedule. Shreveport, La.: From Achee, 1969.
Full data: large part of population came from German and European states.

1599    **Ardouin, Robert B. L.** Louisiana census records 1810 and 1820. 2v. Baltimore: G.P.C., 1970-72.
v.1, Avoyelles and St. Landry parishes; v.2, Iberville, Natchitoches, Pointe Coupée, and Rapides. Thousands of names.

1600    **Arsenault, Bona.** L'Acadie des ancêtres, avec la généalogie des premières familles acadiennes. Québec, Canada: Conseil de la Vie Française en Amérique, Univ. Laval, 1965.

1601    ——— Histoire et généalogie des Acadiens. 2v. Québec: Conseil de la Vie Française en Amérique, Univ. Laval, 1965.
The history (v.1) was published by the Conseil in 1966.

1602    **Arthur, Stanley C.,** and **Kernion, G. C. H. de.** Old families of Louisiana. 1931. Repr. Baton Rouge, La.: Claitor's, 1971.
Pt.1 contains genealogical series on Louisiana families by Charles P. Dimitry in 1892 and published in a newspaper (*see* no.1674). Though a standard work, it is unreliable. Primarily of aristocratic (by Louisiana standards) families.

1603    **Attakapas gazette.** Official organ of the Attakapas Historical Assoc. v.1- , 1966- . St. Martinville, La.: The Association.

1604    **Attakapas Historical Association.** Special publ.1- . St. Martinville, La.: The Association, 1966- (in progress). v.1, *see* no.1632; v.2-3, *see* no.1610.

1605    **Barron, Bill.** The Vaudreuil papers, 1743-53. A calendar and index. New Orleans, La.: Polyanthos, 1974.
Personal and official records of Pierre de Rigaud de Vaudreuil, Royal Governor of the French Province of Louisiana. 3,000 pages. Census reports, military lists, ship list—over 3,500 names. Fine reference work for the French in the Mississippi Valley.

1606    **Bartlett, Napier.** Military records of Louisiana, including biographical and historical papers relating to the military operations of the state. 1875. Repr. Baton Rouge, La.: Louisiana State Univ., 1964.

1607    **Biographical and historical memoirs of Louisiana** . . . special sketches of early parishes, and a record of the lives of the most worthy and illustrious families and individuals. 2v. Chicago, 1892.

1608    **Biographical and historical memoirs of north-west Louisiana.** Nashville, Tenn., 1890.

**1609** ———— Index to biographical sketches. Natchitoches, La.: Russell Lib., Northwestern State College of Louisiana, 1964.

Standard work, but unreliable.

**1610 Bodin, George A.** Selected Acadian and Louisiana church records. v.1–2. *Attakapas Historical Assoc. special publ.* 2–3. St. Martinville, La.: The Association, 1968–70.

**1611 Booth, Andrew B.** Records of Louisiana Confederate soldiers and Louisiana Confederate commands . . . 3v. in 4. New Orleans, La., 1920.

**1612 Carter, Clarence E.** The territory of Orleans, 1803–12. *Territorial papers of the U.S.* 9. 1940. Repr. New York: A.M.S. Press, 1973.

**1613 Casey, Albert E.** Amite county, Mississippi, and environs, 1699–1890. 4v. Birmingham, Ala.: Amite County Historical Soc., 1948–69.

v.4 contains excellent maps and land plats for the Florida parishes of Louisiana and information on settlers in Louisiana and Mississippi.

**1614 Casey, Powell A.** Louisiana in the War of 1812. Baton Rouge, La.: The Author, 1963.

Includes history about the War of 1812. Roster of soldiers is arranged by companies, regiments, divisions, etc. No index.

**1615 Chambers, Henry E.** A history of Louisiana . . . 3v. Chicago, 1925. v.2–3 biographical.

**1616 Collet, Mathieu B.** The Catholic missions in Canada: 1721; a profile for genealogy and microhistory, based on a procés verbal by procureur-général Collet; ed. and with annotations by Ivanhoe Caron. Index to personal names by Ruth O. Berthelot. Repr. from *Rapport de l'archiviste de la Province de Québec*, 1921-22. New Orleans, La.: Polyanthos, 1972.

2,700 name index to parishioners of the 65 church missions in early 18th-century Canada, during the time when migration to the French Mississippi Valley was at its height. Good for Louisiana and Canada.

**1617 Conrad, Glenn R.** The first families of Louisiana. 2v. Baton Rouge, La.: Claitor's, 1970.

Emphasis on period 1717–51. Includes lists of ship passengers, military, Company of the Indies, census reports, and general roll of Louisiana troops, 1720–70. Supersedes De Ville's *Louisiana troops, 1720–70,* 1965.

**1618 Cooper, J. Wesley.** Louisiana, a treasure of plantation homes. Natchez, Miss., 1961.

**1619 D.A.R. Louisiana.** Louisiana tombstone inscriptions. Indexed by Mrs. Lela Cullon. v.1–11. Shreveport, La.: Louisiana Soc., D.A.R., 1957–60.

**1620 Davis, Edwin A.** The story of Louisiana. 3v. New Orleans, La., 1960. v.2–3 biographical.

**1621 Davis, Ellis A.** The historical encyclopedia of Louisiana. 2v. n.p., 1934.

Has biographical sketches of more than 1,500 leading men. Use with care.

**1622 Deiler, John H.** The settlement of the German coast of Louisiana and the Creoles of German descent. *Americana Germanica* 8, 1909. Repr. San Francisco: R. and E. Research Assoc., 1969; repr. with new index by Jack Belsom. Baltimore: G.P.C., 1970.

Standard reference on German and Swiss settlers in Louisiana.

**1623 De Ville, Winston.** Acadian church records, 1679–1757. v.1 (all pub.). Mobile, Ala., 1964.

Miscellaneous baptismal, marriage, and funeral records from Acadian areas and the Gaspé Peninsula. Contains data not in Arsenault, no.1601.

**1624** ———— Calendar of Louisiana colonial documents. v.1–2. Baton Rouge, La.: Louisiana State Archives and Records Div., 1961–64.

Avoyelles and St. Landry parishes, 1786–1803.

**1625** ——— First settlers of Pointe Coupée: a study based on early Louisiana church records, 1737–50. New Orleans, La.: Polyanthos, 1974.

Basic first reference for one of the earliest settlements in the lower Mississippi Valley.

**1626** ——— Gulf Coast colonials. A compendium of French families in early eighteenth century Louisiana. Baltimore: G.P.C., 1968.

Based on published vital statistics, baptisms, marriages, and funerals in 400 family groups.

**1627** ——— Louisiana colonial marriage contracts. 5v. Baton Rouge, La.: Claitor's, 1960–67.

Some vols. in print. Series includes records for Avoyelles, Natchitoches, Pointe Coupée, and St. Landry.

**1628** ——— Louisiana colonials: soldiers and vagabonds. Mobile, Ala., 1963.

Immigration list. 1719–20. Translated from transcripts in the Library of Congress.

**1629** ——— Louisiana recruits, 1752–58. New Orleans, La.: Polyanthos, 1973.

Ship lists of military recruits. Ancestors who migrated to the Mississippi Valley during the end of the French regime. Index of French colonial soldiers with full details by G. de Villiers and M. Chadbourne.

**1630** ——— The New Orleans French, 1720–33. A collection of marriage records relating to the first colonists of the Louisiana Province. Baltimore: G.P.C., 1973.

One of the definitive statistical works on the French in the Mississippi Valley; relevant data given. Areas covered include Louisiana, Gulf Coast area of Pensacola, Mobile, Biloxi, Natchez region, portions of Illinois and Arkansas.

**1631** ——— Opelousas, the history of a French and Spanish military post in America, 1716–1803. New Orleans, La.: Polyanthos, 1972.

Account of southwest Louisiana in the 18th century.

**1632** ——— (and others). Marriage contracts of the Attakapas Post, 1760–1803 . . . translated and ed. by W. De Ville with Jane G. Bulliard; and the 1774 census of Attakapas Post, annotated and ed. by J. G. Bulliard and L. T. David. *Attakapas Historical Assoc. special publ.* 1. St. Martinville, La.: The Association, 1967.

Two separate works in 1v.

**1633 Fortier, Alcée.** Louisiana; comprising sketches of counties, towns, events, institutions and persons, arranged in cyclopedic form. 2v. 1909. Rev. by Carrigan. Baton Rouge, La.: Claitor's, 1974.

Both volumes biographical. v.3–5 to be published in 1975.

**1634 Genealogical Institute proceedings.** Sponsored by the Dept. of Heraldry and Genealogy Extension Div. of Louisiana State University in cooperation with Louisiana Genealogical and Historical Society. v.1– , 1958– . Baton Rouge, La.: The Society.

Last volume published is 12 (1970). Gives details of research, immigration, colonization, French colonial records, Spanish records, all concerning Louisiana.

**1636 Gianelloni, Elizabeth B.** Calendar of Louisiana colonial documents. v.3, pt.1: St. Charles parish (The D'Arensbourg papers, 1734–69). Louisiana State Archives and Records Commission. Baton Rouge, La.: The Commission, 1966.

Especially useful for German progenitors of the John Law period, i.e. persons who came to Louisiana through the Association of John Law's Company of the Indies.

**1637** ——— Love, honor and betrayal: the notarial acts of Estevan de Quinones, 1778–84. Baton Rouge, La.: The Author, 1964.

Summarizes the first 3 of the 15v. of the notarial acts. *Louisiana ancestry,* ser.1.

**1638** ——— The notarial acts of Estevan de Quinones. Baton Rouge, La.: The Author, 1966.

Summarizes the 4th of the 15 bound vols. containing acts of Estevan de Quinones in the notarial archives of Orleans parish at New Orleans. *Louisiana ancestry,* ser.2.

**1639 Griffin, Harry L.** The Attakapas country: a history of Lafayette parish (New ed.) New Orleans, La.: Pelican Pub. Co., 1974.
History of the Attakapas area, including biographies and genealogies of early settlers.

**1640 Hebert, Donald J.** Southwest Louisiana records; church and civil records of settlers. v.1 (1756–1810). Eunice, La.: The Author, 1974. (in progress).
Records of births, marriages, deaths, and successions, available in churches, courthouses, and library archives. Dictionary listing of ecclesiastical and civil records, v.2 (1811–30).

**1641 Historical Records Survey.** County-parish boundaries in Louisiana. New Orleans, La., 1939.

**1642** ────── Directory of churches and religious organizations in New Orleans. New Orleans, La., 1941.

**1643** ────── Guide to public vital statistics records in Louisiana. New Orleans, La., 1942.

**1644** ────── Guide to vital statistics records of church archives in Louisiana. 2v. New Orleans, La., 1942.
v.1, Protestant and Jewish churches; v.2, Roman Catholic churches.

**1645** ────── Inventory of the church and synagogue archives of Louisiana. New Orleans, La., 1941.
Jewish congregations and organizations.

**1646** ────── Inventory of the parish archives of Louisiana. 21v. New Orleans, La., 1937–42.
Only the following numbers were published: 2 (Allen), 4 (Assumption), 6 (Beauregard), 8 (Bossier), 10 (Calcasieu), 22 (Grant), 26 (Jefferson, 2v.), 28 (Lafayette), 29 (Lafourche), 34 (Morehouse), 35 (Natchitoches), 36 (Orleans), 37 (Ouachita), 38 (Plaquemines), 43 (Sabine), 44 (St. Bernard), 45 (St. Charles), 55 (Terrebonne), 59 (Washington), and 60 (Webster). Unpublished material deposited in Dept. of Archives and History, Louisiana State Univ., Baton Rouge, La.

**1647** ────── Louisiana newspapers, 1794–1940. A union list of Louisiana newspaper files in offices of the publishers, libraries, and private collections. New Orleans, La., 1941.
Updated ed., *see* no.1658.

**1648** ────── Ship registers and enrollments of New Orleans. 6v. 1804–70. New Orleans, La., 1931–42.

**1649 Holmes, Jack D. L.** Honor and fidelity. The Louisiana infantry regiment and the Louisiana militia companies, 1766–1821. *Louisiana collection series of books and documents on colonial Louisiana* 1. Birmingham, Ala.: The Author, 1965.
Spanish officers and soldiers serving in colonial Louisiana. 1,426 names with records; good historical introduction.

**1651 Institut Généalogique Drouin.** Dictionnaire nationale des canadiens français, 1608–1760. 3v. Montréal, Canada: Inst. Drouin, 1958.
v.1–2 devoted to names of persons who were married. Parents are listed, as well as the date and location of marriage. Although the entries disagree somewhat with the Arsenault set (no.1600), the information and sources for particular names are very thorough. Contains mostly entries for individuals. Avant-propos [introduction] par Irénée Lussier. 1965.

**1652 King, Grace E.** Creole families of New Orleans. 1921. Repr. Baton Rouge, La.: Claitor's, 1971.

**1653 Korn, Bertram W.** The early Jews of New Orleans. *American Jewish communal histories* 5. Waltham, Mass.: American Jewish Historical Soc., 1969.
Biographical sketch of every Jew who came to New Orleans before 1815.

**1654 Lonn, Ella.** Foreigners in the Union army and navy. Baton Rouge, La., 1952.

**1654a Louisiana ancestry,** ser.1-2. *See* no. 1637-38.

**1655 Louisiana genealogical register.** v.1- , 1954- . Baton Rouge, La.: Louisiana Genealogical and Historical Soc.
Extensive coverage, most useful for Louisiana researches. Indexes to vital records kept by Louisiana parishes.

**1656 Louisiana historical quarterly.** v.1- , 1917- . New Orleans, La.: Louisiana Historical Soc. Repr. New York: A.M.S. Press, 1968: v.1-10, 1917-27 only.
Formerly *Louisiana Historical Society publications,* v.1-10, 1895-1917. Published sporadically. Has wealth of genealogical material. Some volumes include résumés of selected documents of genealogical and historical interest from the French and Spanish periods.

**1657** —— Index. v.1-33, 1917-50. Compiled by Boyd Cruise. New Orleans, La., 1956.

**1658 McMullan, Theodore N.** Louisiana newspapers 1794-1961. A union list of Louisiana newspaper files available in . . . Louisiana. Baton Rouge, La.: Louisiana State Univ. Lib., 1965.
An updating of the Historical Records Survey work, no.1647.

**1659 Maduell, Charles R., Jr.** The census tables for the French colony of Louisiana from 1699 through 1732. Baltimore: G.P.C., 1972.
Compilation of the 28 earliest census records of Louisiana. 5,000 names; also other lists such as landowners, Negroes. Most of material also in Conrad (no.1617). Good source list and index.

**1660** —— Index of Spanish citizens entering the port of New Orleans between Jan. 1820 and Dec. 1839. New Orleans, La.: The Author, 1968.

**1661** —— —— Jan. 1840 and Dec. 1865. New Orleans, La.: The Author, 1966.
From available passenger lists in New Orleans Public Library.

**1662** —— Marriage contracts, wills and testaments of the Spanish colonial period in New Orleans, 1770-1804. New Orleans, La.: The Author, 1970.
350 marriage contracts and 1,300 wills, with sources. Names of participants, location of material, date of contracts.

**1663** —— Marriages and family relationship of New Orleans, 1820-30. New Orleans, La.: The Author, 1969.
Transactions from the donations records of the mortgage office, marriage contracts, etc. Thousands of names.

**1664** —— —— 1830-40. New Orleans, La.: The Author, 1969.
4,000 personal names, 1,100 donation records transactions; over 600 marriage contracts.

**1665** —— The romance of Spanish surnames. New Orleans, La., 1967.
Only rare and unusual surnames omitted. Short history of each Spanish surname is given together with information about the origin.

**1666 Magee, Zuma F., and Bateman, T. S.** Cemetery records of Louisiana. [Franklinton, La.?]: 1962.

**1667 Marchand, Sidney A., Sr.** Acadian exiles in the golden coast of Louisiana. Donaldsonville, La., 1943.

**1668** —— An attempt to re-assemble the old settlers in family groups. Baton Rouge, La.: Claitor's, 1965.
700 families of the original settlers of Ascension parish.

**1669 Menn, Joseph K.** The large slaveholders of Louisiana—1860. New Orleans, La.: Pelican Pub. Co. [1964].
Based upon returns for Louisiana of the 8th census of the U.S., 1860.

**1670 Morris, Irene.** Be it known and remembered. 4v. Baton Rouge, La.: Louisiana Genealogical and Historical Soc., 1960-69.
Bible records.

1671 **New Orleans, Cabildo.** Spanish census of New Orleans, 1791. New Orleans, La., 193?.

Cabildo was an organization term in the Spanish colonial period, similar to a city council.

1672 **New Orleans genesis.** v.1- , 1962- . New Orleans, La.: Genealogical Research Soc. of New Orleans.

Specializes in indexing local church, cemetery and other hard to locate information. Has good coverage for several parishes around New Orleans.

1673 **Orleans Parish, Louisiana. Civil District Court.** General index of all successions, emancipations, interdictions, and partition proceedings, opened in the Civil District Court, 1805-1903. 5v. in 4. New Orleans, La., 1849-1903.

Inventories for 1800-60 were also published.

1674 **Perrin, William H.** Southwest Louisiana biography and history . . . 1891. Repr. New Orleans, La.: Claitor's, 1971.

Pt.1 contains genealogical series of Louisiana families by Charles P. Dimitry in 1892 and published in New Orleans *Times democrat;* see no.1602.

1675 **Pierson, Marion J. B.** Louisiana soldiers in the War of 1812. Baton Rouge, La.: Louisiana Genealogical and Historical Soc., 1963.

Alphabetical listing giving rank and company of 15,000 names. Standard reference from this war.

1676 **Rieder, Milton P., Jr.,** and **Rieder, N. G.** The crew and passenger registration lists of the seven Acadian expeditions of 1785; a listing of family groups of the refugee Acadians who migrated from France to Spanish Louisiana in 1785. Metairie, La.: The Authors, 1965.

1677 ———— Louisiana: the Acadians in France, 1762-1776. Metairie, La.: The Authors, 1967.

Bridges gap between the 1785 Acadian immigration to Louisiana and those expelled from Acadia in 1755. Acadians listed by towns in which they lived in France. 4,700 names indexed.

1678 ———— New Orleans ship lists. v.1-2. Metairie, La.: The Authors, 1966-68.

Covers 1820-23.

1679 **Robichaux, Albert J.** Louisiana census and militia lists, 1770-89. v.1- . Harvey, La.: Dumag Pr., 1973- (in progress).

v.1, German coast, New Orleans, below New Orleans and Lafourche. Includes militia lists for New Orleans, 1770; a general census of New Orleans, 1777; militia lists for the German coast, 1770; a general census of the second German coast, 1784; militia list of St. Charles parish, 1785; general census below New Orleans, 1770; and a general census of Lafourche.

1680 **Sanders, Mary E.** Records of Attakapas district, Louisiana, 1739-1860. 2v. 1962-63. Fort Worth, Tex.: Miran, 1970.

Takes in much of Louisiana. v.1, 1739-1811; v.2, 1811-60, St. Mary parish.

1681 **Seebold, Herman B. de B.** Old Louisiana plantation homes and family trees. 2v. 1941. Repr. Gretna, La.: The Author, 1972.

v.1, homes; v.2, families.

1682 **Sturtevant, Bruce.** Louisiana 1810 census. R. V. Jackson, ed.; G. R. Teeples, paleographer; R. Moore, computer director. Provo, Utah: Accelerated Indexing Systems, 1973.

Early maps, genealogical data; research aids on existing counties. Over 6,000 entries. Computer index.

1683 **Tanguay, Cyprien.** Dictionnaire généalogique des familles canadiennes depuis la fondation de la colonie jusqu'à nos jours. 7v. 1871-90. Repr. New York: A.M.S. Press, 1970.

Covers period 1608-1763. Does not relate specifically to Louisiana, but because of the state's close connections with Canada the set is invaluable where there were French antecedents.

**1684** ——— Complément au Dictionnaire généalogique Tanguay. ser.1–3. Montréal, Canada: Soc. Généalogique Canadienne-Française, 1957–64.
Its publ. 2, 5, 6.

**1685 Toups, Neil J.** Mississippi Valley pioneers. Lafayette, La.: Neilson Pub. Co., 1970.
37 passenger lists, 1717–21. Emphasis on the French in Louisiana.

**1686 U.S. Census Office.** 3rd census 1810, Territory of Orleans, excluding the parish of Orleans. Baton Rouge, La.: Louisiana Genealogical and Historical Soc., 1961.

**1687 Vidrine, Jacqueline O., and De Ville, W.** Marriage contracts of the Opelousas post, 1766–1803. Villa Platte, La., ca. 1960.
Contracts recorded for the district then comprising all of southwestern Louisiana. Full data.

**1688 Villeré, Sidney L.** The Canary Islands migration to Louisiana, 1778–83. 1971. Repr. Baltimore: G.P.C., 1972.
Passenger lists of eight vessels. List of 2,000 emigrants.

**1689 Villiers, Gladys de.** The Opelousas post. A compendium of church records relating to the first families of southwest Louisiana. New Orleans, La.: Polyanthos, 1972.
Essential reference book for research in French areas in the Mississippi Valley, the colonization and settlement of the Gulf Coast, Catholic Church in America, and studies relating to the westward expansion. Comprises all extant records held in St. Landry Catholic Church in Opelousas.

**1690 Voorhies, Jacqueline K.** Some late eighteenth-century Louisianians; census records, 1758–96. Lafayette, La.: Univ. of Southwestern Louisiana, 1973.
With bibliographical references.

**1691 Vujnovich, Milos M.** Yugoslavs in Louisiana. Gretna, La.: Pelican Pr., 1974; San Francisco: R. and E. Research Assoc., 1974.
Traces first Yugoslav immigrants to Louisiana in early 1830s.

**1692 Williamson, Frederick W., and Goodman, G. T.** Eastern Louisiana: a history of the watershed of the Ouachita river and the Florida parishes ... 3v. Louisville, Ky., 1939.

MAINE

Settled ca. 1624; entered Union 1820

*Maine Historical Society, Portland*
*Maine State Library, Augusta*

✣ Maine and Massachusetts. Since Maine was originally part of Massachusetts, much of the Massachusetts material will contain information pertaining to Maine, particularly concerning the Revolutionary War and War of 1812.

**1692a Attwood, Stanley B.** The length and breadth of Maine. [1946?] Supplement [1949]. Repr. Orono, Me.: Univ. of Maine, 1973.
Gazetteer; should be used in conjunction with Varney (no.1735). Basic data on civil divisions, their designation, date when land was set off from or annexed to, etc.

**1693 Bangor Public Library.** Bibliography of the state of Maine. Boston: G. K. Hall, 1962.
Comprehensive bibliography of books associated with Maine; 16,000 cards from the library catalog. Author-dictionary catalog.

**1694 Banks, Charles E.** History of York, Maine. 2v. 1931–35. Repr. Baltimore: G.P.C., 1967.
Definitive history of area that was political center of province of Maine until 1760. Extensive genealogical and biographical sketches. Indexes have over 3,000 names.

**1695 Beedy, Helen C.** Mothers of Maine. Portland, Me., 1895.
Biographies of prominent women.

**1696 Biographical sketches of representative citizens of the state of Maine.** Boston, 1903.

American series of popular biographies. Mug book.

**1697** **Chadbourne, Ava N.** Maine place names and the peopling of its towns. 1955. Repr. Portland, Me.: Bond Wheelwright, 1970.

**1698** ——— ——— Illustrated county ed. v.1– , 1970– (in progress). Portland, Me.: Bond Wheelwright.

**1699** **Clayton, W. Woodford.** History of York County, Maine, with illustrations and biographical sketches of its prominent men and pioneers. Philadelphia, 1800.
Many names, including roster of Civil War soldiers.

**1700** **Coe, Harris B.** Maine . . . and its people . . . 4v. New York, 1928.
v.3–4 biographical.

**1701** **D.A.R. Maine.** Maine Revolutionary soldiers' graves. Compiled by Ethel R. Houston, n.p., 1940.

**1702** ——— Roster and ancestral roll. Compiled by Mrs. P. L. Tate. n.p., 1948.
Called the "Gold book"; contains listing of 1,700 living members and all ancestors. Being reissued in 1975.

**1703** **Fisher, Carleton E.** Research in Maine. *World Conference of Records,* area I-22 paper. Salt Lake City: L.D.S., 1969.

**1704** **Flagg, Charles A.** An alphabetical index of Revolutionary pensioners living in Maine. 1920. Repr. Baltimore: G.P.C., 1967.
Taken from *Sprague's Journal of Maine history* (no. 1733). Since Maine was part of Massachusetts at the time of the Revolution, this list obviates the necessity of searching through the 17v. of *Massachusetts soldiers and sailors of the Revolutionary War* (no. 1904).

**1705** **Hatch, Lewis C.** Maine, a history. Centennial ed. 5v. New York, 1919.
v.4–5 biographical. Mug book.

**1706** **Hayward, John.** A gazetteer of the United States . . . Maine. Boston, 1843.

**1707** **Hebert, Richard A.** Modern Maine: its history background . . . 4v. New York, 1951.
v.3–4 family and personal records.

**1708** **Herndon, Richard (and others).** Men of progress . . . State of Maine . . . New York, 1916.
Biographies of prominent leaders from the 1897 ed. Mug book.

**1709** **Historical Records Survey.** Counties, cities, towns, and plantations of Maine: a handbook of incorporations and boundary changes. Portland, Me., 1940.

**1710** ——— Ship registers and enrollments. 2v. Portland, Me., 1942.
v.1, Machias 1780–1930; v.2, Saco 1791–1815.

**1711** **House, Charles J.** Names of soldiers of the American Revolution [from Maine] who applied for state bounty . . . as appears of record in Land Office. 1893. Repr. Baltimore: G.P.C., 1967.
Nearly 1,000 soldiers listed.

**1712** **Huston, Almer J.** A check list of Maine local histories Portland, Me., 1915.
Has also genealogical histories of Maine.

**1713** **Jackson, Ronald V., and Teeples, G. R.** Maine 1800 census. Provo, Utah: Accelerated Indexing Systems, 1974.
Computer index with over 25,000 entries, maps and research aids.

**1714** **Letters to Colonel Thomas Westbrook and others relative to Indian affairs in Maine, 1722–26.** In *New-England historical and genealogical register,* v.44–49, 1890–5.
Contains muster rolls and many names.

**1715** **Little, George T.** Genealogical and family history of the state of Maine. 4v. New York, 1909.
Mug book but useful.

**1716  Maine (Colony).** Province and court records of Maine. v.1-2, ed. by Charles T. Libby; v.3, by Robert E. Moody; v.4-5, by Neal W. Allen, Jr. Portland, Me.: Maine Historical Soc., 1928– (in progress).
Covers 1636-1718; v.6 being edited; v.3-5 in print from Somersworth, N.H.: New Hampshire Pub. Co.

**1717  Maine, Adjutant General's Office.** Alphabetical index of Maine volunteers, etc., mustered into the service of the United States during the war of 1861. Augusta, Me., 1867.
Title: *Suppl. to the annual reports of the A.G. of the state of Maine, 1861-66.* Index.

**1718**  ———— Annual reports, 1861-66. 7v. Augusta, Me., 1862-67.
Important for the records of Civil War units and men. The 1866 suppl. contains an alphabetical index of Maine men who served during the war.

**1719**  ———— Records of the Massachusetts volunteer militia called out by the Governor of Massachusetts to suppress a threatened invasion during the War of 1812-14. Boston, 1913.
All of Maine was part of Massachusetts until 1820. Compiled by John Baker. Standard list of service records for War of 1812.

**1720  The Maine genealogical inquirer.** v.1– , 1968– . Oakland, Me.: M. and J. Denis.
Much space given to queries; devoted to Maine and New England genealogy.

**1721  The Maine genealogist and biographer.** A quarterly journal of the Maine Genealogical and Biographical Soc. v.1-3. Augusta, Me., 1875-78.

**1722  Maine historical and genealogical recorder.** Ed. by S. M. Watson. 9v. 1884-98. Repr. 9v. in 3. Baltimore: G.P.C., 1973.
Over 15,000 names mentioned. Articles by many distinguished authors; concerns Massachusetts also.

**1723  The Maine historical magazine.** v.1-9. Bangor, Me., 1885-95.

v.1-6 (1885-91) called *Bangor historical magazine*. Contains fair amount of genealogy.

**1724  Maine Historical Society collections.** 1831-1906. Portland, Me.
Ser.1, v.1-10, 1831-91; ser.2, v.1-10, 1890-99; ser.3, v.1-2, 1904-1906. Ser.2 appeared as *Collections and proceedings*. Contains many valuable lists; mainly historical.

**1725  Noyes, Sybil; Libby, C. T.; and Davis, W. G.** Genealogical dictionary of Maine and New Hampshire. 5pts. 1928-39. Repr. in 1v. Baltimore: G.P.C., 1972.
Hundreds of thousands of entries on births, marriages, and deaths of settlers through the third generation. Other genealogical information includes wills, deeds, court cases, etc.

**1726  Patterson, William D.** Probate records of Lincoln county, Maine, 1760-1800. Portland, Me., 1895.
Aside from those of York county, the records are the oldest surviving.

**1727  Pope, Charles H.** The pioneers of Maine and New Hampshire, 1623-60. 1908. Repr. Baltimore: G.P.C., 1973.
A descriptive list, drawn from records of the colonies, towns, churches, courts, and other contemporary sources. Genealogical notices, dates and places of residence in America, origins, marriages, occupations, estates, and deaths.

**1728  Representative men of Maine . . .** Portland, Me., 1893.
Mug book.

**1729  Ridlon, Gideon T., Sr.** Saco Valley settlements and families; historical, biographical, genealogical . . . 1895. Repr. Rutland, Vt.: Tuttle, 1970.
Saco Valley runs south-east from New Hampshire into Maine. Lists 15,000 names, genealogy of 128 families; good index. A classic of Maine local history.

**1730  Sargent, William M.** Maine wills, 1640-1760. 1887. Repr. Baltimore: G.P.C., 1972.
471 wills with data on several thousand related individuals. Full data.

**1731 Society of Colonial War. Maine.** Register of the officers and members. Portland, Me., 1905.
Also historical notes of Preble's regimental campaigning of 1758.

**1732 Spencer, Wilbur D.** Pioneers on Maine rivers, with lists to 1651. 1930. Repr. Baltimore: G.P.C., 1973.
In 2 pts.: chronological list of European explorers and traders who made first soundings in Maine; second, history and description of each river settlement. Thousands of pioneers and descendants listed.

**1733 Sprague's Journal of Maine history.** 14v. Dover, Del., 1913–26.
Compiled by John F. Sprague. About 40 percent genealogical; includes Revolutionary soldiers, early settlers, families, etc. County of Piscataquis strongly covered.

**1734 U.S. Bureau of the Census.** Heads of families at the first census of the United States taken in the year 1790. Maine. 1908. Repr. Baltimore: G.P.C., 1966 (and later dates); Spartanburg, S.C.: Reprint Co., 1963 (and later dates).

**1735 Varney, George J.** A gazetteer of Maine. Boston, 1881.
Should be used in conjunction with Attwood (no.1692a).

**1736 Williams, Henry C.** Biographical encyclopaedia of Maine of the nineteenth century. Boston, 1885.

**1737 Williamson, Joseph A.** A bibliography of the state of Maine, from the earliest period to 1891. 2v. Portland, Me., 1896.
Over 11,000 books and pamphlets written in or about Maine, or by Maine authors.

**1738 York County, Maine.** York [county] deeds, 1642–1737. 18v. in 19. Portland, Me. [and elsewhere]: Maine Historical Soc., 1887–1910.
Deeds from York county registry including whole of Maine. Full index of grantors, other persons, and places.

MARYLAND

Settled ca. 1634; original state

*Hall of Records, Annapolis*
*Mr. Robert W. Barnes, Perry Hall, Md.*
*Mr. Raymond B. Clark, Jr., St. Michaels, Md.*
*Mrs. Mary Keysor Meyer, Maryland Historical Society*

**1739 Alexander, John H.** Index to the Calendar of Maryland state papers . . . Baltimore, 1861.
This index to *Papers,* compiled by Ethan Allen, liber 88, MSS, Archives of Maryland, is at the Hall of Records.

**1740 Andrews, Matthew P.** Tercentenary history of Maryland. 4v. Baltimore, 1925.
v.2–4 biographical.

**1741 Baldwin, Jane** (and **Henry, Roberta B.**). The Maryland calendar of wills. Wills from 1635 to 1743. 8v. 1904–28. Repr. Baltimore: G.P.C., 1968
Burns (no.1760) covers 1744–73. Abstracts of 8,000 wills; contains valuable genealogical data.

**1742 Baltimore city and county, Maryland.** Marriage licenses, v.1, 1777–99 (in progress). Salt Lake City: Ro'sel Pub., 1974.
Index listing bride and groom with date of license.

**1742a Barnes, Robert W.** Marriages and deaths from the *Maryland gazette,* 1727–1839. Baltimore: G.P.C., 1973.
About 3,000 marriages and deaths fully transcribed.

**1743 The biographical cyclopedia of representative men of Maryland and the District of Columbia.** Baltimore, 1879.
Mug book; use with care.

**1744 Brewer, John M.,** and **Meyer, L.** The laws and rules of the land offices of Maryland. Baltimore, 1871.
Includes list of officers and soldiers en-

titled to lots westward of Fort Cumberland, Allegany county, for Revolutionary service; also list of patented military lots.

**1745 Bromwell, Henrietta E.** Old Maryland families; a collection of charts compiled from public records, wills, family Bibles, tombstone inscriptions, and other original sources. 1916. Repr. Baltimore: G.P.C., 1962.

**1746 Brown, Mary R.** An illustrated genealogy of the counties of Maryland and the District of Columbia as a guide to locating records. Baltimore: Maryland Historical Soc., 1967.
Maps of each county showing sections which came from each parent county or other border change. To these is appended the District of Columbia, showing parts taken from Prince George's and Montgomery counties. Also a survey of Washington, D.C. records with their allocations. A condensed Mathews (no.1808).

**1747 Brumbaugh, Gaius M.** Maryland records, colonial, Revolutionary, county and church, from original sources. 2v. 1915-28. Baltimore: G.P.C., 1967.
Of particular importance because it includes the census of 1776 and early marriage records of many Maryland counties.

**1748** ——— and **Hodges, M. R.** Revolutionary records of Maryland. Pt.1 (all pub.). 1924. Repr. Baltimore: G.P.C., 1967.
Contains unpublished records, including names of those who subscribed to the Oath of Fidelity and Support in early Calvert, Frederick, Montgomery, Prince George's, and Washington counties.

**1749 Burns, Annie (Walker).** Mrs. Burns spent some years in the transcription of Maryland and other state records. Unfortunately some are not too well transcribed, and almost all are difficult to understand. Volume and series numbering are also confusing. Nevertheless, in their mimeographed form on rather poor paper they are still of considerable value to researchers. All must be checked with care.

**1750** ———. Index to Maryland colonial judgments. 7v. Annapolis, Md., 1938-39.

**1751** ——— Maryland account books. no.1-74. Annapolis, Md., 1936-39.

**1752** ——— Maryland balances of final district book. 4v. Annapolis, Md. [1939?].

**1753** ——— Maryland "early settlers" (land records). 14v. Annapolis, Md., 1936-40.

**1754** ——— Maryland genealogies and historical recorder. 3v.? Washington, D.C., [1941-?].

**1755** ——— Maryland inventories and accounts. 5v. Annapolis, Md., 1938.
Titles of all volumes differ slightly.

**1756** ——— Maryland marriage records [1659-1807]. 35v. Washington, D.C., n.d.
Marriage by inference.

**1757** ——— Maryland record of deaths, 1718-77. 2pts. Annapolis, Md., 1936.

**1758** ——— Maryland rent rolls. Annapolis, Md., 1939?

**1759** ——— Maryland soldiers of the Revolutionary, War of 1812, and Indian Wars, who drew pensions while residing in Kentucky. Washington, D.C., n.d.

**1760** ——— Maryland will books, no. 24-38. 1744-73. 15v. Annapolis, Md., [1938-45].
Continuation of Baldwin (no.1741). A few gaps in dates. Indexes to rent rolls, births, marriages, deaths, wills, etc. were compiled by Mrs. Burns for some years. They are difficult to list because of erratic numbering, but a check with the Library of Congress catalogs will establish the general works compiled. All should be used with caution.

**1760a Carothers, Bettie S.** Maryland slave owners and superintendents, 1798.

v.1– , 1974– . Lutherville, Md.: The Compiler.

**1761** ——— 9,000 men who signed the Oath of Allegiance and Fidelity to Maryland during the Revolution. 2v. Lutherville, Md.: The Author, 1972.

**1762** ——— 1778 census of Maryland. Chesterfield, Mo. [1972]. Available from Author, Lutherville, Md.
Arranged by hundred. Name of head of household only; well indexed. Caroline, Charles, and Queen Anne's counties only.

**1763** ——— 1776 census of Maryland. Chesterfield, Mo. [1972]. Available from Author, Lutherville, Md.
Arranged by hundred-name of householder only; well indexed. Anne Arundel, Baltimore, Caroline, Dorchester, Frederick, Harford, Prince George's, Queen Anne's, Talbot counties.

**1764 Carroll, Kenneth.** Joseph Nichols and the Nicholites. Easton, Md.: Easton Pub. Co., 1962.
Book on history of founder of branch of Quakerism. Lists all marriages, births, and deaths.

**1765** ——— Quakerism on the Eastern Shore. Baltimore: Maryland Historical Soc., 1970.
History of the movement, with many lists of members, with birth and death records. Cecil monthly meeting, Third Haven (Tred Avon), Marshy Creek monthly meetings. Chief source on history of Quakers on the Eastern Shore.

**1766 Clark, Charles B.** The Eastern Shore of Maryland and Virginia. 3v. New York [1950].
v.3 personal and family records.

**1767 Clark, Raymond B.,** and **Clark, S. C.** Since 1963 these compilers have published several works pertaining to marriage licenses of Maryland counties, with dates ranging from 1657 through 1850. To date they concern Caroline, Kent, Queen Anne's, and Talbot counties. From the Compilers, St. Michaels, Md.

**1768 Colonial Dames of America. Chapter I, Baltimore.** Ancestral records and portraits: a compilation from the archives. 2v. 1910. Repr. Baltimore: G.P.C., 1969.
Many portraits. Users should treat the pre-American generations with caution. Members mostly Maryland residents. Many coats of arms; no sources given for pedigrees.

**1769 Cordell, Eugene F.** The medical annals of Maryland, 1799–1899. Baltimore, 1903.
Has biographical data on medical profession.

**1770 Cotton, Jane (Baldwin).** See Baldwin, Jane.

**1771 The county court note-book,** v.1–10; and *Ancestral proofs and probabilities,* no.1–4. Ed. by Milnor Ljungstedt. 1921–31, 1935–36. Repr. Baltimore: G.P.C., 1972.
*Ancestral proofs* was intended as a continuation of the *Note-book.* The editor was a Maryland resident, and although much of this periodical concerns Maryland, many other states are treated. The work as a whole is packed with genealogical material from Pennsylvania south to Kentucky. Delaware tax list for 1766 is given.

**1772 Cunz, Dieter.** The Maryland Germans, a history. 1948. Repr. Port Washington, N.Y.: Kennikat Pr., 1972.

**1773 D.A.R. Maryland.** Directory of the Society and their Revolutionary ancestors, 1892–1965. Compiled by Minnie Motsinger. Bel Air, Md.: The Society, 1966.

**1774 Gahn, Bessie W.** Original patentees of land at Washington prior to 1700. 1936. Repr. Baltimore: G.P.C., 1969.
Relates to Maryland, Virginia, and the District of Columbia. 200 family names listed, but limited in scope.

**1775 Gannett, Henry.** A gazetteer of Maryland. *U.S. Geological Survey bull.* 231. Washington, D.C., 1904.

**1776 Genealogical and memorial encyclopedia of the state of Maryland** ... under the editorial supervision of Richard H. Spencer. 2v. New York, 1919.
Good mug book, but use with care.

**1777 Goldsborough, William W.** The Maryland Line in the Confederate Army, 1861-65. 1900. Repr. with index prepared by Louise Q. Lewis. 2nd ed. Port Washington, N.Y.: Kennikat Pr., 1972.
The Hall of Records also published a separate index in 1945. *Commission publ.* 5.

**1778 Hartsook, Elisabeth (Schroeder), and Skordas, Gust.** Land Office and Prerogative Court records of colonial Maryland. *Hall of Records Commission publ.* 4. 1946. Repr. Baltimore: G.P.C., 1968.
History of the land administration with a detailed inventory of patents, warrants, proprietary leases, debt books, etc.

**1779 Hayes, Robert F.** Maryland historical and genealogical bulletin. v.1-24. Baltimore. 1930-50.
Original title: *Maryland genealogical bulletin*. Uneven, but vital for research. Good family histories.

**1780 Historical Records Survey.** Inventory of the church archives in the District of Columbia ... Protestant Episcopal Church, Diocese of Washington. 2v. Washington, D.C., 1940.
Includes 4 Maryland counties: St. Mary's, Charles, Prince George's, and Montgomery; also Washington Cathedral.

**1781** —— Inventory of the church archives of Maryland: Protestant Episcopal Church, Diocese of Maryland. Baltimore, 1940.
No names, but gives lists of sources of county and parish information.

**1782** —— Inventory of the county archives of Maryland. 8v. Baltimore, 1937-41.
Only the following numbers were published: 1 (Allegany), 2 (Anne Arundel), 6 (Carroll), 11 (Garrett), 13 (Howard), 15 (Montgomery), 21 (Washington), and 22 (Wicomico). Unpublished material deposited at Hall of Records, Annapolis, Md.

**1783 Holdcraft, Jacob M.** Names in stone: 75,000 cemetery inscriptions from Frederick county, Maryland. 2v. Ann Arbor, Mich., 1966. From the Author, Baltimore.

**1784** —— More names in stone: cemetery inscriptions from the peripheral areas of Frederick county. Ann Arbor, Mich., 1972. From the Author, Baltimore.

**1785 Hume, Joan.** Index to the wills of Allegany county, 1784-1860. Baltimore, 1970. From Tuttle, Rutland, Vt.

**1786** —— Index to the wills of Garrett county, 1872-1960; Harford, 1774-1960. Baltimore, 1970. From Tuttle, Rutland, Vt.

**1787** —— Maryland: index to the wills of Howard county, 1840-1950; Kent county, 1642-1960. Baltimore, 1970. From Tuttle, Rutland, Vt.

**1788** —— Maryland: index to the wills of St. Mary's county, 1662-1960; Somerset county, 1664-1955. Baltimore, 1970. From Tuttle, Rutland, Vt.
Wills indexed are those preserved in county courthouses, not Hall of Records. Includes some colonial wills not indexed in Magruder (no.1796). Calendars and indexes by Baldwin (no.1741), Burns (no.1760), and Magruder (no. 1797) stop at the Revolution or earlier, but these 4 vols. carry the work to modern days.

**1789 Jacobsen, Phebe R.** Quaker records in Maryland. *Hall of Records Commission publ.* 14. Annapolis, Md.: The Commission, 1966.
Definitive. Excellent guide to locating Friends meetings and their records.

**1790 Kummer, Frederic A.** Free State of Maryland; a history of the state and its people, 1634-1941; also *Contemporary Maryland* by Ferdinand C. Latrobe. 4v. Baltimore, 1941.

1791 **Lantz, Emily E.** Series of genealogical and heraldic articles [Virginia and Maryland families] in the *Baltimore Sun,* 1905-1908.
In 2v. in Maryland Historical Soc. Fairly accurate, with coats of arms delineated. Alton H. Keller published an index to the names of families mentioned.

1792 **Laws of Maryland . . . 1637 (to date).** Title and publishers vary.
Much genealogical information in laws passed for relief of private parties. Includes early naturalizations, Revolutionary pensions, divorces, changes of name, list of insolvent debtors, paupers, business and church incorporation, escheated land, permission to aliens to own land, etc. 19th-century vols. indexed.

1793 **Lewis, Thomas H.** Historical record of the Maryland Annual Conference of the Methodist Protestant Church, 1829-1939. n.p., 1939? 5th ed., rev.
Much biographical data.

1794 **McGhee, Lucy K.** Maryland pension abstracts, Revolutionary, War of 1812, and Indian Wars. Washington, D.C., 1966.
First vol. called v.1, but no more published.

1795 ——— Maryland Revolutionary War pensioners, War of 1812, and Indian Wars. Washington, 1952.

1796 **Magruder, James M.** Index of Maryland colonial wills, 1634-1777, in the Hall of Records, Annapolis, Maryland. 1933. Repr. with additions by Louise E. Magruder. 3v. in 1. Baltimore: G.P.C., 1967.
Exceptionally accurate work, containing 16,000 names with relevant data.

1797 ——— Magruder's Maryland colonial abstracts—wills, accounts and inventories, 1772-77. 5v. 1934-39. Repr. in 1v. Baltimore: G.P.C., 1968.
Includes all genealogical and historical data of value, except that it does not include all inventories and accounts; only those for deceased persons who left a will.

1798 **Marine, William M.** The British invation of Maryland, 1812-15. Ed. with an appendix, containing 11,000 names of participants in the War . . . by Louis H. Dielman. Repr. Hatboro, Pa.: 1965. From Gale Research, Detroit, Mich.

1799 **Martenet, Simon J.** New topographical atlas of the state of Maryland and the District of Columbia, with descriptions historical, scientific and statistical. Baltimore [1872].

1800 **Maryland and Delaware genealogist,** v.1- , 1959- . St. Michael's, Md.: Raymond Clark, Jr. and Sara S. Clark, eds.
Of considerable interest and value. Transcriptions are many and accurate. Little Delaware material.

1801 **Maryland Genealogical Society.** Bulletin. v.1- , 1960- . Baltimore: The Society.
Many useful compilations of Maryland records. Index v.1-5, 1974.

1802 ——— Maryland 1800 census. v.1- , 1965- (in progress). Baltimore: The Society.
Counties of Calvert (1965), Charles (1967), Prince George's (1969), Allegany (1971), Caroline (1972), Cecil (1972), Harford (1972), Montgomery (1972), Queen Anne's (1972), St. Mary's (1972).

1803 **Maryland Hall of Records Commission.** Calendar of Maryland state papers. 5v. in 7. *Hall of Records Commission publ.* 1,5-8, 10, 11. Annapolis, Md., 1943-58.
Some still available from the Commission; others have been repr. by G.P.C., Baltimore. Invaluable guide to the records of the colonial and Revolutionary periods.

1804 **Maryland historical magazine.** v.1- , 1906- . Baltimore: Maryland Historical Soc.
Genealogical information dropped in the 1940s; resumed in 1971. Index being compiled.

1805 **Maryland Historical Society.** Archives of Maryland. v.1- , 1883- . Baltimore: The Society.

123

## 1806 United States

All volumes are in print. Invaluable series; contains the colonial and early state records. Thousands of names.

**1806** ———— Muster rolls and other records of service of Maryland troops in the American Revolution, 1775-83. *Archives of Maryland* 18. 1900. Repr. Baltimore: G.P.C., 1972.

Indexed. Fine source book with more than 20,000 names.

**1807 Maryland Original Research Society of Baltimore.** Bull. 1-3. 1906-13. Repr. in 1v. Baltimore: G.P.C., 1973.

Fine collection of records not reproduced elsewhere. Memorial marbles; much Eastern Shore information and records.

**1808 Mathews, Edward B.** The counties of Maryland, their origin, boundaries, and election districts. Baltimore, 1907.

**1809** ———— Maps and map-makers of Maryland. In *Maryland geological survey,* v.2. Baltimore, 1898.

**1810 Men of mark in Maryland . . .** biographies of leading men of the state . . . 4v. Washington, D.C., 1907-12.

**1811 Meyer, Mary K.** Divorces and names changed in Maryland, 1634-1854. Pasadena, Md.: The Author. 1970.

**1812** ———— Genealogical research in Maryland: a guide. Baltimore: Maryland Historical Soc., 1972.

Good bibliography and description of public records.

**1813 Nead, Daniel W.** The Pennsylvania German in the settlement of Maryland. *Pennsylvania German Soc.* 22. Lancaster, Pa., 1914.

War and tax lists.

**1814 Newman, Harry W.** The flowering of the Maryland Palatinate. Washington, D.C., 1961. Annapolis, Md.: The Author.

Contains biographical sketches and genealogies of the passengers of the "Ark and Dove."

**1815** ———— Heraldic Marylandia. A compilation of Maryland armorial families which used coats of arms in the colonial and early post-Revolutionary records . . . Annapolis, Md.: The Author, 1968.

Completely supersedes Parran's *Register of Maryland's heraldic families* and corrects some of its many errors, but defects still exist.

**1816** ———— Maryland Revolutionary records . . . 1938. Repr. Baltimore: G.P.C., 1967.

Listing of 3,000 pension claims and other records.

**1817 O'Rourke, Timothy J.** Maryland Catholics on the frontier: the Missouri and Texas settlements. Parson, Kans.: Brefney Pr., 1973.

Nucleus of settlers of Perry County, Missouri. Concerns settlement of Catholics from Maryland, with descendants. Over 15,000 names, with many colonial lines from southern Maryland.

**1818 Owings, Donnell M.** His lordship's patronage: offices for profit in colonial Maryland. Baltimore: Maryland Historical Soc., 1953.

Scholarly account of provincial offices of trust in pre-Revolutionary Maryland. The civil list contains biographical data.

**1819 Papenfuse, Edward C. (and others).** Directory of Maryland Legislators, 1635-1789. Annapolis, Md.: Maryland Dept. of Economic & Community Development, 1974.

First comprehensive list of lawmakers from Maryland before 1789. Initial stage of research on a definitive history and biographical dictionary of Maryland legislature, 1635-1789, planned for 1975-76.

**1820 Passano, Eleanor P.** An index of the source records of Maryland: genealogical, historical. 1940. Repr. with new foreword by P. W. Filby. Baltimore: G.P.C., 1974.

Though out of date, still the standard Maryland genealogical source record, 20,000 family names. Has extensive bibliography of Maryland genealogical works.

**1821** **The patriotic Marylander.** Published under the auspices of the Maryland Soc., D.A.R. v.1-3. Baltimore, 1914-17.

Much information on Maryland and Marylanders during the Revolution and War of 1812.

**1822** **Pedley, Avril J. M.** Manuscript collections of the Maryland Historical Society. Baltimore: The Society, 1968.

Lists more than 1,700 collections representing more than 1,500,000 manuscripts. Much genealogy and family papers. v.2 being compiled; will contain additions, Maryland Diocesan Library collections, and the Society's manuscript genealogy collection.

**1823** **Portrait and biographical record of the Eastern Shore of Maryland . . .** New York, 1898.

Example of mug book that contains information not available elsewhere.

**1824** **Radoff, Morris L.; Skordas, G.;** and **Jacobsen, P. R.** The county courthouses and records of Maryland. 2v. *Hall of Records Commission publ.* 12-13. Annapolis, Md.: The Commission, 1960-63.

v.2 lists the records and their locations. Essential.

**1825** ———— (and others). The Old Line State, a history of Maryland; a source edition recounting the early and contemporary history of Maryland through the medium of extensive research and the life histories of its most constructive members, chronicling the backgrounds and achievements of its prominent families and personages . . . 3v. Hopkinsville, Ky., 1956.

v.2-3 biographical.

**1826** **Richardson, Hester D.** Side-lights on Maryland history, with sketches of early Maryland families. 2v. 1913. Repr. Baltimore: G.P.C., 1967; Repr. 2v. in 1. Cambridge, Md.: Tidewater Pub., 1967.

Valuable genealogical and historical work. More than 5,500 names are listed.

**1827** **Ridgely, Helen W.** Historic graves of Maryland and the District of Columbia. 1908. Repr. Baltimore: G.P.C., 1967.

Concerns the colonial and Revolutionary periods; 2,500 entries.

**1828** **Scharf, John T.** History of Baltimore city and county. 2v. 1881. Repr. with a new introduction by Edward G. Howard. Baltimore: G.P.C., 1971.

Comprehensive work with broad coverage. Many biographical sketches; has new index.

**1829** ———— History of Maryland from the earliest period to the present day. 3v. 1879. 3v. Repr. with new index. Hatboro, Pa.: 1967. Available from Gale Research, Detroit, Mich.

New index is available separately.

**1830** ———— History of western Maryland . . . from the earliest period to the present day; including biographical sketches of the representative men. 2v. 1882. Repr. Baltimore: Regional Pub. Co., 1968.

History of Frederick, Montgomery, Carroll, Washington, Allegany, and Garrett counties.

**1831** **Schultz, Edward T.** First settlements of Germans in Maryland. Frederick, Md., 1896.

Contains many names of early German settlers, some land records and a few family genealogies; not indexed.

**1832** **Skirven, Percy G.** The first parishes of the province of Maryland; wherein are given historical sketches of the ten counties and of the thirty parishes in the province at the time of the establishment of the Church of England in Maryland in 1692. Baltimore, 1923.

**1833** **Skordas, Gust.** The early settlers in Maryland: an index to names of immigrants, compiled from records of land patents, 1633-80, in the Hall of Records, Annapolis, Md. Baltimore: G.P.C., 1974.

Valuable census of Maryland emigrants. Taken from a typescript made by Arthur Trader, 1917, and sometimes referred to as the *Trader list*. Library of Congress credits John M. Brewer with starting the list, "Alphabetical list made from 17 manuscript volumes in the Land Office, Annapolis . . ." Essential.

1834 **Society of Colonial Wars. Maryland.** Genealogies of the members and record of services of ancestors. [v.1] Compiled by Christopher Johnston. Baltimore, 1905.

1835 ——— v.2. Ed. by Francis B. Culver. Baltimore, 1940.

1836 **Stewart, Rieman.** The Maryland Line. A history of the Maryland Line in the Revolutionary War, 1775-83. Baltimore: The Author, 1969.

1837 **Teeples, Gary R.** Maryland 1800 census. G. R. Teeples, paleographer and compiler; R. V. Jackson, editor; R. Moore, computer director. Provo, Utah: Accelerated Indexing Systems, 1973.
32,000 entries. State maps and research aids. Best book for 1800 census.

1838 **U.S. Bureau of the Census.** Heads of the families at the first census of the United States taken in the year 1790. Maryland. 1907. Repr. Baltimore: G.P.C., 1952, etc.; Spartanburg, S.C.: Reprint Co., 1965, etc.

1839 **Volkel, Lowell M. (and others).** An index to the 1800 federal census of Maryland. 4v. in 1. Thomson, Ill.: Heritage House, 1967-68.
v.1, Allegany-City of Baltimore; v.2, Caroline-Kent; v.3, Dorchester, Harford, Montgomery-Queen Anne's; v.4, St. Mary's-Worcester. Head of each household, reference to original census.

1840 **Wilmer, Lemuel A., et al.** History and roster of Maryland volunteers, War of 1861-65. 2v. Baltimore, 1898-99.


MASSACHUSETTS

Settled ca. 1620; original state

*Massachusetts Historical Society, Boston*

1841 **Allen, Gardner W.** Massachusetts privateers of the Revolution. *Massachusetts Historical Soc. collections* 77. Boston: The Society, 1927.

1842 **American Antiquarian Society, Worcester.** Index of marriages in the *Massachusetts centinel* and the *Columbian centinel*, 1784-1840. 4v. Boston: G. K. Hall, 1961.
Marriage index contains 87,000 names. Records from the south and west, as well as from the Atlantic seaboard, appear in these papers. Reproduced from cards at the Society.

1843 ——— Index to obituaries in the *Massachusetts centinel* and the *Columbian centinel*, 1784-1840. 5v. Boston: G. K. Hall, 1961.
102,000 obituaries. *See also* note under no.1842.

1844 **Bailey, Frederic W.** Early Massachusetts marriages prior to 1800. 3v. 1897-1914. Repr. with Plymouth county marriages, 1692-1746, in 1v. Baltimore: G.P.C., 1968.
Good collection of marriage records. 21,000 entries.

1845 **Banks, Charles E.** The English ancestry and homes of the Pilgrim Fathers, who came to Plymouth on the *Mayflower* in 1620, the *Fortune* in 1621, and the *Anne* and the *Little James* in 1623. 1929. Repr. Baltimore: G.P.C., 1971.
Thorough work with biographical sketches of the ships' passengers.

1846 ——— The planters of the commonwealth; a study of the emigrants and emigration in colonial times: to which are added lists of passengers to Boston and to the Bay Colony; the ships which brought them; their English homes, and the places of their settlement in Massachusetts, 1620-40. Baltimore: G.P.C., 1972.
1,250 names listed; 96 ships.

1847 ——— Topographical dictionary of 2,885 English emigrants to New England, 1620-50. Ed. by . . . Elijah E. Brownell. 1937. Repr. Baltimore: G.P.C., 1974.

Records of nearly 3,000 emigrants. Errors; treat with caution.

**1848** —— The Winthrop fleet of 1630. An account of the vessels, the voyage, the passengers, etc. 1930. Repr. Baltimore: G.P.C., 1972.
Good background material on the early emigrants.

**1849** **Barlow, Claude W.** Sources for genealogical researching in Connecticut and Massachusetts. Syracuse, N.Y.: Central New York Genealogical Soc., 1973.

**1850** **Belliveau, Pierre.** French neutrals in Massachusetts; the story of Acadians rounded up by soldiers from Massachusetts, and their captivity in the Bay Province 1755-66. Boston: Kirk S. Giffen, 1972.

**1851** **Benton, Josiah H.** Early census making in Massachusetts, 1643-1765, with a reproduction of the lost census of 1765 (recently found) . . . Boston, 1905.

**1852** Biographical encyclopedia of Massachusetts of the nineteenth century. 2v. New York, 1879.
Mug book.

**1853** Biographical sketches of representative citizens of the Commonwealth of Massachusetts . . . Boston, 1901.
Mug book.

**1854** **Bodge, George M.** Soldiers in King Philip's War, being a critical account of that war, with a concise history of the Indian Wars of New England from 1620-77, official lists of the soldiers of Massachusetts colony serving in Philip's War . . . 3rd ed. 1906. Repr. Baltimore: G.P.C., 1967.
Has muster and pay rolls of colonial soldiers, with biographical and genealogical sketches, also lists of grantees and claimants of Massachusetts, Maine, New Hampshire, and Connecticut.

**1855** **Boston. Registry Dept.** Boston births, baptisms, marriages, and deaths, 1630-1800. *Reports* 9 and 24 of Record Commissioners. 2v. Boston, 1833-94.
v.1, 1630-99; v.2, 1700-1800, contains births only.

**1856** —— —— Index to 1630-99 only. By Sanford C. Gladden. Boulder, Colo., 1969.
Excellent index: 9,265 births, 2,736 baptisms, 908 marriages, 1,584 deaths.

**1857** —— Boston marriages from 1700-1809. A volume of records relating to the early history of Boston, Massachusetts. *Reports* 28 and 30 of Record Commissioners. 2v. Boston, 1898-1903.

**1858** —— Lists of tax-payers in the town of Boston, 1674-95. Appendix B to 1st *Report of Record Commissioners*. 2nd ed. Boston, 1881.

**1859** —— Miscellaneous papers. 10th *Report of the Record Commissioners*. Boston, 1886.
Wills, deeds, taxes, 1707 census.

**1860** —— Port arrivals and immigrants to the city of Boston, 1715-16 and 1762-69. Compiled under the direction of William H. Whitmore. Baltimore: G.P.C., 1973.
Excerpted from *A volume of records relating to the early history of Boston* . . . 29, formerly called *Record Commissioners' Reports*, 1900. Unknown ship passenger list, containing over 3,000 names of passengers, with full details of port of embarkation. New reconstructed index.

**1861** —— Records relating to the early history of Boston. v.1-39. Boston, 1876-1909.
v.1-22, 1876-1890 were published as *Report of the Record Commissioners*. Thousands of names from tax lists, wills, deeds, births, marriages, and deaths.

**1862** **Bowen, James L.** Massachusetts in the war, 1861-65. Springfield, Mass., 1889.
Sketches of general officers, pp.875-1010.

**1863** **Bowen, Richard LeB.** Massachusetts records: a handbook for gene-

127

alogists, historians, lawyers, and other researchers. Rehoboth, Mass., 1957.
Contains several misstatements.

1864 **Carlevale, Joseph W.** Leading Americans of Italian descent in Massachusetts. Plymouth, Mass., 1946.

1865 **Codman, Ogden.** Index of obituaries in Boston newspapers, 1704–1800. 3v. Boston: G. K. Hall, 1968.
Since no official record is known to exist on deaths in Massachusetts Bay Colony from 1700 to the mid-1800's, this record from cards in the Boston Athenaeum catalog is important. Index is in 2pts.: deaths within Boston, 1704–1800; v.2–3, outside Boston, 1704–95.

1866 **Colonial Society of Massachusetts.** Publications. v.1– , 1895– . Boston: The Society.
An index, now out-of-print, was issued in 1932, covering v.1–25. Contain a wealth of scholarly and significant material relating to colonial times, bibliography of Massachusetts laws, Suffolk county, Plymouth church and other records. By the end of 1974 the following were out-of-print: v.1, 3, 5–10, 13–14, 22–23, 36–43.

1867 **Crawford, Mary C.** Famous families of Massachusetts. 2v. Boston, 1930.
Should be used with caution.

1868 **Cutter, William R.** Genealogical and personal memoirs relating to Boston and eastern Massachusetts. 4v. New York, 1908.
Mug book. Highly inaccurate but heavily used. Consolidated index of this and other Cutter books, see no.593.

1869 ———— Memorial encyclopedia of the state of Massachusetts. New York, 1918.
Mug book.

1870 ———— and **Adams, W. F.** Genealogical and personal memoirs relating to families of the state of Massachusetts. 4v. New York, 1910.
Mug book.

1871 **D.A.R. Massachusetts.** Directory of members and ancestors. Compiled by Mrs. Leslie Irwin. Newton, Mass.: The Compiler, 1974.
Members and ancestors are indexed with current information.

1872 **Dumont, William H.** A short census of Massachusetts, 1779. In *National Genealogical Soc. quarterly,* v.49–51, 1961–63.

1873 **Eliot, Samuel A.** Biographical history of Massachusetts . . . biographies and autobiographies of the leading men in the state. 10v. Boston, 1909–18.
Mug book.

1874 **Encyclopedia of Massachusetts—biographical and genealogical.** 9v.? New York, ca.1916.
Vols. not numbered; confusing series.

1875 **Essex Institute historical collections.** v.1– , 1859– . Salem, Mass.: The Institute.
Indexes for v.1–22, 23–43, 44–67, 68–85 (1859–1949) and name, place and subject index, v.1–67 (1859–1931) were published from 1954–66. v.1–20 were repr. by Johnson Reprint Corp., New York. Emphasis on history and genealogy of Massachusetts.

1876 **Flagg, Charles A.** A guide to Massachusetts local history, being a bibliographical index to the literature of the towns, cities, and counties of the state . . . Salem, Mass., 1907.

1877 **Forbes, Abner,** and **Greene, J. W.** The rich men of Massachusetts: containing a statement of the reputed wealth of about 2,000 persons, with brief sketches of more than 1,500 characters. 2nd ed. Boston, 1852.

1878 ———— and **Cadman, P. F.** The Boston French; a collection of facts . . . relating to some well known citizens of France who found homes in Boston and New England . . . New Orleans, La.: Polyanthos, 1971.
Originally published as *Boston and some noted emigrés,* 1938. Coats of arms; of particular interest to anyone with French or Huguenot connections.

**1879 Gannett, Henry.** A geographic dictionary of Massachusetts. *U.S. Geological Survey bull.* 116. Washington, D.C., 1894.

**1880 Goodwin, Nathaniel.** Genealogical notes, or contributions to the family history of some of the first settlers of Connecticut and Massachusetts. 1856. Repr. Baltimore: G.P.C., 1969.
Partial genealogies, often to 7th generation.

**1881 Haxtun, Annie A.** Signers of the Mayflower Compact . . . 1896–99. 3pts. in 1. Repr. Baltimore: G.P.C., 1968.
Standard reference on the signers with genealogical data on them and their families.

**1882 Hayward, John.** A gazetteer of Massachusetts: all the counties, towns, and districts in the Commonwealth. Rev. Boston, 1849.

**1883 Hingham, Mass.** History of the town of Hingham, Massachusetts. 3v. in 4. Boston, 1893.
v.2–3 compiled by George Lincoln are genealogical. Hingham was settled in 1638 and therefore important in settling other areas. Genealogies good.

**1884 Historical Records Survey.** Guide to public vital statistics records in Massachusetts. Boston, 1942.

**1885** ———— Index to local news in the *Hampshire gazette,* 1786–1937. 3v. Boston, 1939.
v.1, Northampton *A–M;* v.2, i, *N–Z;* v.2, ii, Hampshire and Franklin counties; v.3, pt.3, personal section.

**1886** ———— Inventory of county archives of Massachusetts. 1v. Boston, 1937.
Only 1v. was published: no.5 (Essex). Unpublished material deposited in Forbes Library, Northampton, Mass.

**1887** ———— Inventory of the church archives of Massachusetts: Universal churches. Boston, 1942.

**1888** ———— Ship registers. 7v. Boston, 1938–42.
Boston and Charlestown, 1789–95; Barnstable, 1814–1913; Plymouth, 1789–1808; Dighton-Fall River, 1789–1938; New Bedford, 3v., 1796–1939.

**1889 Hurd, Charles E.** Genealogy and history of representative citizens of the commonwealth of Massachusetts. Boston, 1902.
Mug book.

**1890 Jones, Edward A.** The loyalists of Massachusetts: their memorials, petitions and claims. 1930. Repr. Baltimore: G.P.C., 1969.
Claims of 501 loyalists, of which almost 300 were of American birth. Mostly from loyalist manuscripts in the Public Record Office, London. Accurate genealogical data.

**1891 Lockwood, John H.** Western Massachusetts: a history, 1636–1925. 4v. New York, 1926.
v.3–4 biographical, with coats of arms.

**1892 McGhee, Lucy K.** Massachusetts pension abstracts of the Revolutionary War, War of 1812, and Indian Wars. Washington, D.C., 1966.

**1893 Massachusetts.** Acts and laws of the commonwealth of Massachusetts. 13v. Boston, 1890–98.
Covers 1780–1804; as valuable as Shurtleff, no.1898.

**1894 Massachusetts (Colony).** The acts and resolves, public and private, of the province of Massachusetts Bay . . . 21v. Boston, 1869–1922.
Covers 1692–1780. As valuable as Shurtleff, no.1898. Running title: *Province laws.*

**1895 Massachusetts (Colony).** County Court (Essex county). Records and files of the quarterly courts of Essex county, Massachusetts, 1636–83. Ed. by George F. Dow. 8v. Salem, Mass., 1911–21.
Courts held at Salem.

**1896** ———— ———— The probate records of Essex county, Massachusetts, 1635–81. Ed. by George F. Dow. 3v. Salem, Mass., 1916–20.

**1897** ———— Probate Court (Suffolk county). Index to the probate records of the county of Suffolk, 1636–1893. 3v. Boston, 1895.

**1898 Massachusetts (Colony and Province).** Records of the governor and company of the Massachusetts Bay in New England. 5v. in 6. Ed. by Nathaniel B. Shurtleff. 1853–54. Repr. New York: A.M.S. Press, 1971.

**1899 Massachusetts. Adjutant General's Office.** Massachusetts soldiers, sailors and marines in the Civil War. 8v. Brookline, Mass., 1931–35.

Index to army records was published in 1937, but names of officers and men who served in the Navy and Marine Corps are not indexed.

**1900** ———— Record of the Massachusetts volunteers, 1861–65. 2v. Boston, 1868–70.

**1901** ———— Records of Massachusetts volunteer militia called out by the Governor of Massachusetts to suppress a threatened invasion during the War of 1812–14. Compiled by John Baker. Boston, 1913.

**1902 Massachusetts. Secretary of the Commonwealth.** Historical data relating to counties, cities and towns in Massachusetts. Boston: The Secretary.
Published sporadically.

**1903** ———— List of persons whose names have been changed in Massachusetts, 1780–1892. Collated and published by the Secretary of the Commonwealth. 2nd ed. 1893. Repr. Baltimore: G.P.C., 1972.

16,000 changes of name. Has two extensive indexes, one to original names, the other to adopted names.

**1904** ———— Massachusetts soldiers and sailors of the Revolutionary War. 17v. Boston: Massachusetts Secretary of State, 1896–1908.

**1905 Massachusetts. Superintendent of Alien Passengers.** A list of alien passengers bonded from January 1, 1847 to January 1, 1851, for the use of the Overseers of the Poor in the Commonwealth. Compiled by J. B. Munroe. 1851. Repr. Baltimore: G.P.C., 1971.

Valuable listing of 5,000 alien passengers, primarily from Great Britain.

**1906 Massachusetts Historical Society.** Catalog of manuscripts. 7v. Boston: G. K. Hall, 1969.

Dictionary catalog with entries under personal and corporate names.

**1907 The Mayflower quarterly.** v.1–, 1935– . Ed. by Ruth W. Sherman. Warwick, R.I.: General Soc. of Mayflower Descendants.

Information on ancestors and descendants of Pilgrims; only regular periodical devoted to Pilgrim families. Excellent.

**1908 Men of progress . . . in the Commonwealth of Massachusetts . . .** Boston, 1896.
Mug book.

**1909 Morse, Abner.** The genealogy of the descendants of several ancient Puritans . . . 4v. Boston, 1837–64.

Genealogy of Massachusetts families. v.2–4 have title: *A genealogical register of the descendants of several ancient Puritans.*

**1910** ———— ———— Index prepared by Clara and Dorothy McCabe. Buffalo, N.Y.: The Authors, 1971.

**1911 Nason, Elias.** A gazetteer of the state of Massachusetts. 2v. Rev. and enl. Boston, 1870.

**1912 [National Society of the] Colonial Dames of America. Massachusetts.** Register . . . 1893–1944. Boston, 1944.
"Entirely the work of Elizabeth F. Bartlett."

**1913 National Society of Women Descendants of the Ancient and Honorable Artillery Company.** History and lineage book, 1940– . Washington, D.C.: The Society.

**1914** ———— Massachusetts heraldica: an illustrated compilation of arms . . . comprising an alphabetical index of 103 armigerous members of the Company . . . 1637-1774. Washington, D.C.: The Society, 1968.
Compiled by Beatrice Kenyon.

**1915** ———— Members in the colonial period. By Maude R. Cowan. Washington, D.C., 1958.

**1916 New England Historic Genealogical Society, Boston.** Massachusetts vital records to 1850. Boston: The Society, various dates.
Records of almost 100 towns of Massachusetts available. Most in print.

**1917 New Plymouth Colony.** Records, 1620-51. 1855-61. Repr. 12v. in 6. New York: A.M.S. Press, 1968.
v.1-8 ed. by Nathaniel B. Shurtleff; 1633-92, v.9-12 ed. by David Pulsifer.
Included are court orders, judicial acts, miscellaneous records, acts of the commissioners.

**1918 Pierce, Richard D.** The records of the First Church of Boston, 1630-1868. 3v. Boston, 1941.
Issued as *Colonial Soc. of Massachusetts collections,* v.39-41.

**1919 Pope, Charles H.** The pioneers of Massachusetts: a descriptive list, drawn from records of the colonies, towns and churches, and other contemporaneous documents. 1900. Repr. with additions and corrections. Reissued. Baltimore: G.P.C., 1969.
Covers 1620-50, with some account until 1720. Lists 5,000 first settlers and their families.

**1920 Quinn, Thomas C.** Massachusetts of today. A memorial of the state, historical and biographical. Boston, 1892.

**1921 Rand, John C.** One of a thousand, a series of biographical sketches of one thousand representative men resident in the Commonwealth of Massachusetts, 1888-89. Boston, 1890.

**1922 Representative men and old families of southeastern Massachusetts** . . . 3v. Chicago, 1912.

**1923 Shaw, Hubert K.** Families of the Pilgrims. Boston: Massachusetts Soc. of Mayflower Descendants, 1956.

**1924 Society of the Cincinnati. Massachusetts.** Members, from the founding in 1783. Boston: The Society, 1964.

**1925 Sons of the Revolution. Massachusetts Society.** Roll of membership with ancestral records, 1893-1923. 12v. n.p., 1923.

**1926 Spofford, Jeremiah.** A historical and statistical gazetteer of Massachusetts. 2nd ed. Haverhill, Mass., 1860.

**1927 Stark, James H.** The loyalists of Massachusetts, and the other side of the American Revolution. 1910. Repr. Clifton, N.J.: A. M. Kelley, 1972.
Extensive biographical sketches.

**1928 Stoddard, Francis R.** The truth about the Pilgrims. 1952. Repr. Baltimore: G.P.C., 1973.
Corrects long-standing misconceptions about the Pilgrims and furnishes authoritative genealogical data on Mayflower passengers. Originally published by the Society of Mayflower Descendants in the State of New York.

**1929 Suffolk county.** Suffolk deeds. Liber I-XIV, 1629-97. Boston, 1850-1906.
Covers Boston area.

**1930 Townsend, Charles D.** Border town cemeteries of Massachusetts . . . Middleboro, Mass.: Chedwato Service, 1953.

**1931 U.S. Bureau of the Census.** Heads of families at the first census of the United States taken in the year 1790. Massachusetts, 1908. Repr. Baltimore: G.P.C., 1966, etc.; Spartanburg, S.C.: Reprint Co., 1964, etc.

**1932 Welch, Laraine.** Massachusetts 1800 census. Mrs. Laraine Welch,

compiler, R. V. Jackson, editor, C. R. Teeples, research director. Provo, Utah: Accelerated Indexing Systems, 1973.
Computer index with 70,000 entries. State maps and research aids.

1933 **Whitmore, William H.** The Massachusetts civil list for the colonial and provincial periods, 1630-1774. Being a list of the names and dates of appointment of all the civil officers constituted by the charters or the local government. 1870. Repr. Baltimore: G.P.C., 1969.
List of over 1,000 names with multiple references.

1934 **Worthley, Harold F.** An inventory of the records of the particular (Congregational) churches of Massachusetts gathered 1620-1805. Cambridge, Mass.: Harvard Univ. Pr., 1970.

1935 **Wright, Harry A.** The story of western Massachusetts. 4v. New York, 1949.
v.3-4 personal and family history.

1936 **Young, Alexander.** Chronicles of the first planters of the Colony of Massachusetts Bay, from 1623 to 1636 . . . 1846. Repr. New York: Da Capo, 1970.

1937 ——— Chronicles of the Pilgrim Fathers of the Colony of Plymouth from 1602 to 1625. 2nd ed. 1844. Repr. Baltimore: G.P.C., 1974; New York: Da Capo, 1971.


MICHIGAN

Settled ca. 1668; entered Union 1837

*Department of Education, State Library Division, Lansing*
*Detroit Public Library*
*Detroit Society for Genealogical Research, Inc.*

1938 **American biographical history of eminent and self-made men . . .** Michigan vol. Cincinnati, Ohio, 1878.
Arranged by Congressional districts. Mug book.

1939 **Blois, John T.** Gazetteer of the state of Michigan . . . and a directory of emigrants. Detroit, Mich., 1839.

1940 **Carter, Clarence E.** The territory of Michigan, 1805-37. 3v. *Territorial papers of the United States* 10-12. 1942-45. Repr. New York: A.M.S. Press, 1973.
Lists of persons signing petitions, memorials, etc.

1941 **Curry, John C.** Michigan Revolutionary War pension payments. In *Michigan heritage*, v.1-2, 1959-60.
Almost 2,000 names of those who lived in Michigan 1818-73.

1942 **Cyclopedia of Michigan;** historical and biographical . . . and biographical sketches of men who have . . . contributed towards its development. New York, 1890.

1943 **D.A.R. Michigan.** Cemetery records from fifteen counties of Michigan. Arranged and indexed by Ruth R. Montieth. Martin, Mich., 1952.

1944 ——— Historical records 1893-1930. Ed. by Emily S. Watkins. Ann Arbor, Mich., 1930.
v.2 concerning genealogy compiled by Mary Howlett.

1945 **The Detroit Society for Genealogical Research magazine.** v.1- , 1937- . Detroit, Mich.: The Society.

1946 ——— Name index. v.1-35. 6v. 1953-72. Detroit, Mich.: The Society.
Not only Michigan genealogy; very fine material on many other states.

1947 **Dunbar, Willis F.** Michigan through the centuries. 4v. New York, 1955.
v.3-4 biographical; index in v.1.

1948 **1820 census of Michigan territory.** Annotated listing. In *Detroit Society for Genealogical Research magazine,* v.12-15, 1948-51.

1949 **Family trails.** v.1- , 1967- . Lansing, Mich.: Michigan Dept. of Education, State Library Services.

Excellent for Michigan sources. Available free.

**1950　Farmer, Silas.** History of Detroit and Wayne County and early Michigan: a chronological cyclopedia of the past and present. 3rd ed. 1890. Repr. Detroit, Mich.: Gale Research, 1969.
Vital Michigan work.

**1951　Frank, Louis F.** German-American pioneers in Wisconsin and Michigan; the Frank-Kerler letters, 1849-64. Transl. from the German by M. Wolff. Ed. by H. H. Anderson. Milwaukee, Wisc.: Milwaukee County Historical Soc., 1971.
Transl. of *Pioneerjahre der deutschamerikanisch Familien Frank-Kerler in Wisconsin und Michigan,* 1911. Good general German material.

**1952　Greeley, Aaron.** Plan of the private claims in Michigan territory . . . 1810. n.p., [1847].
3 sheets. Map issued as part of a report of the Secretary of the Treasury to the Senate, on the surveys of private land claims at Sault Sainte Marie, and in the lower peninsula of Michigan, Feb. 1, 1847. Senate doc. 221, 29th Cong., 2nd sess.

**1953　Harlan, Elizabeth T.; Millbrook, M. D.;** and **Erwin, E. C.** 1830 federal census; territory of Michigan (and) A guide to ancestral trails in Michigan, by Lucy M. Kellogg. 3rd ed. Detroit, Mich.: Detroit Soc. for Genealogical Research, 1970.
Excellent. With maps.

**1954　Historical Records Survey.** Directory of churches and religious organizations: greater Detroit. Detroit, Mich., 1941.

**1955** ———— Inventory of the church and synagogue archives of Michigan. 14v. Detroit, Mich., 1940-42.
Covers most religions.

**1956** ———— Inventory of the county archives of Michigan. 12v. Detroit, Mich., 1938-42.
Only the following numbers were published: 2 (Alger), 4 (Alpena), 7 (Baraga), 9 (Bay), 13 (Calhoun), 16 (Cheboygan), 25 (Genesee), 35 (Iosco), 36 (Iron), 38 (Jackson), 52 (Marquette) and 61 (Muskegon). Unpublished material deposited in Michigan Historical Collecton, Univ. of Michigan, Ann Arbor, Mich.

**1957** ———— Vital statistics holdings by government agencies in Michigan. 4v. Detroit, Mich., 1941-42.
Birth, marriage, death, and divorce records. Information on when marriage records began in each county; aid for locating custodians of death records.

**1958　History of the upper peninsula of Michigan** . . . Chicago, 1883.
Mug book, but good and detailed history of towns.

**1959　Hixson (W. W.) and Co.** Plat books of the counties of Michigan. Rockford, Ill.: [192? – 193?].

**1960　Hudson, J. L., Co., Detroit.** Michigan pioneers, the first hundred years of statehood, 1837-1937. Detroit, Mich., 1937.
In a daily series, Aug. 1–Sept. 5, 1937 in *Detroit Free Press.*

**1961　Kalamazoo family newsletter.** Michigan records. Kalamazoo, Mich., 1973– . From A. H. Kerr, 3628 Market St., 49001.
7 counties published so far in each number of the *Newsletter:* Allegan, Van Buren, Kalamazoo, St. Joseph, Branch, Calhoun, Barry, Eaton, Jackson, and Hillsdale; Steuben, Ind.; Williams, Ohio.

**1962　Michigan. Adjutant General.** Record of service of Michigan volunteers in the Civil War, 1861-65. 46v. [Kalamazoo, Mich., 1905].

**1963** ———— Alphabetical general index to the public library sets, of 85,271 names of Michigan soldiers and sailors individual records . . . Lansing, Mich., 1915.

**1964　Michigan Historical Commission.** Michigan biographies, including members of Congress, officers, justices, etc. 2v. Lansing, Mich., 1924.

1965   **Michigan: a centennial history of the state and its people.** 5v. Chicago, 1939.
v.3-5 biographical; index in v.1.

1966   **Michigan heritage.** v.1-15, 1959-73. Kalamazoo, Mich.: Ethel W. Williams, ed. and publisher.
Quarterly magazine of Michigan biography and local and family history. Index particularly good.

1967   **Michigan Pioneer and Historical Society.** Michigan pioneer and historical collections. v.1-40, 1876-1929. Lansing, Mich.
v.1-38, 1876-1912; v.39-40, 1913, 1929. Originally *Report of the Pioneer Society of Michigan*. Basic tool for Michigan history, consisting of reminiscences and biographical, autobiographical, and historical articles. Mainly historical, but some genealogy.

1968   ——— Indexes. v.1-15, subject and author, 1904; v.16-30, 1907. Classified finding list. Detroit, Mich.: Wayne State Univ. Pr., 1958.

1969   **Michigana.** 1955- . Grand Rapids, Mich.: Western Michigan Genealogical Soc.

1970   **Mid-Michigan Genealogical Society.** Occasional paper, 1- , 1970- . Lansing, Mich.: The Society.

1971   **Miller, Alice T.** Soldiers of the War of 1812 who died in Michigan. Ithaca, Mich., 1962.

1972   **Moore, Charles.** History of Michigan. 4v. Chicago, 1915.
v.2-4 biographical. Index in v.1.

1973   **The pastfinder.** v.1- , 1973- . St. Joseph, Mich.: Genealogical Assoc. Southwestern Michigan.
Registers of births, etc.

1974   **Pioneer Society of Michigan.** *See* no.1967-68.

1975   **Portrait and biographical record of northern Michigan,** containing portraits and biographical sketches of prominent and representative citizens . . . Chicago, 1895.

1976   **Powers, Perry F.** A history of northern Michigan and its people. 3v. Chicago, 1912.
v.2-3 biographical. Index in v.1.

1977   **Quaife, Milo M.** The John Askin papers . . . 1747-1820. 2v. Detroit, Mich., 1928.
Part of the Burton Historical Collection, Detroit Public Library. Good source material for early history of the northwest and Detroit. Many names, well indexed.

1978   **Romig, Walter.** Michigan place names; the history of the founding and the naming of more than 5,000 past and present Michigan communities. Grosse Pointe, Mich.: The Author, 1973.

1979   **Sawyer, Alvah L.** Memorial record of the northern peninsula of Michigan. 3v. Chicago, 1895.
v.2-3 biographical; index in v.1.

1980   **Silliman, Sue I.** Michigan military records. *Michigan Historical Commission bull.* 12. 1920. Repr. Baltimore: G.P.C., 1969.
Standard Michigan Revolutionary reference. The D.A.R. of Michigan historical collections; records of Revolutionary soldiers, etc. buried in Michigan. Lists of pensioners.

1981   **Tuttle, Charles R.** General history of the state of Michigan, with biographical sketches . . . Detroit, Mich., 1873.

1982   **Van Koevering, Adrian.** Legends of the Dutch; the story of a mass movement of 19th century pilgrims. Indianapolis, Ind., 1960.
Fine history of the Dutch in Michigan; appendixes list ships' passenger lists and church members; also an index of family names.

1983   **Wait, Stephen E.,** and **Anderson, W. S.** Old settlers; a historical and chronological record . . . old settlers of the Grand Traverse region . . . Traverse City, Mich., 1918.

Early histories taken from Page's *History of the Grand Traverse region.*

**1984 Wiedeman, Ruby,** and **Bohannan, L.** Fourth census of the United States, 1820 census of Michigan, population schedules. Huntsville, Ark.: Century Enterprises, 1972.
Alphabetically arranged by county.

**1985 Williams, Edwin G.,** and **Williams, E. W.** First land owners of Michigan. Kalamzoo, Mich.: The Compilers, 1964-68.
A series designed to cover the whole of Michigan. Contains, for each county, a list of land patentees, showing residence, exact geographical location, acreage, dates of patent and final proof; also bounty land claimants. Constitutes a directory of the "first families of Michigan." Counties covered: Barry, Eaton, Mason, Wayne, Hillsdale, and Monroe.

**1986 Williams, Ethel W.** The counties and townships of Michigan past and present. Kalamazoo, Mich.: Michigan Heritage, 1972.
Dates of organization or existence given, including the islands. Designed to answer the "when and where" of Michigan research. 4pts. *The counties of Michigan, past and present; The counties and townships of Michigan, past and present; The islands of Michigan; The townships, past and present.*

MINNESOTA

Settled ca. 1805; entered Union 1858

*Minneapolis Public Library*
*Minnesota Historical Society, St. Paul*

**1987 Andreas, Alfred T.** An illustrated atlas of Minnesota. Chicago, 1874.
Contains maps of Minnesota, counties, biographical sketches, portraits, homes, census data, etc. Still the best Minnesota atlas.

**1988 Andrews, Christopher C.** History of St. Paul, Minnesota, with illustrations and biographical sketches of some of its prominent men and pioneers. Syracuse, N.Y., 1890.

**1989 Björnson, Val.** The history of Minnesota. 4v. West Palm Beach, Fla., 1969.
Lewis Historical Pub. Co. v.3-4 have family and personal records.

**1990 Brook, Michael.** Reference guide to Minnesota history; a subject bibliography of books, pamphlets, and articles in English. St. Paul, Minn.: Minnesota Historical Soc., 1974.
Over 3,700 items, divided into 32 subject areas. Selective.

**1991 Burnquist, Joseph A. A.** Minnesota and its people. 4v. Chicago, 1924.
v.3-4 biographical.

**1992 Castle, Henry A.** Minnesota: its story and biography. 3v. Chicago, 1915.
v.2-3 biographical.

**1993 Christianson, Theodore.** Minnesota; a history of the state and its people. 5v. Chicago, 1935.
v.3-5 biographical. Stress is placed on political biographies, although industry is well represented.

**1994 [Clemens, Jeremiah].** The United States biographical dictionary and portrait gallery of eminent and self-made men. Minnesota vol. New York, 1879.

**1995 Commemorative biographical record of the upper lake region** containing biographical sketches of prominent and representative citizens and many of the early settled families. Chicago, 1905.

**1996 Compendium of history and biographies of central and northern Minnesota** . . . biographical sketches of hundreds of prominent old settlers and representative citizens . . . Chicago, 1904.

**1997 Compendium of history and biography of northern Minnesota.** Containing a history of the state of Minnesota . . . an account of early explorations, early settlements, Indian occupancy, etc. Chicago, 1902.
Over 1,000 biographies.

**1998 Folwell, William W.** A history of Minnesota. 4v. 1921–30. Rev. ed., repr. St. Paul, Minn.: Minnesota Historical Soc., 1956–59.
The best single account of the history of the state up to 1857.

**1999 Grönberger, Robert.** Minnesotas historia . . . Minneapolis, Minn., 1889.
Many biographies.

**2000 Harpole, Patricia C., and Nagle, M. D.** Minnesota territorial census, 1850. St. Paul, Minn.: Minnesota Historical Soc., 1972.
Territory also includes parts of present-day North and South Dakota. Over 6,000 persons listed; informative introduction.

**2001 Historical Records Survey.** Directory of churches and religious organizations in Minnesota. St. Paul, Minn. 1942.

**2002** —— Guide to church vital statistics records in Minnesota: baptisms, marriages, funerals. St. Paul, Minn., 1942.

**2003** —— Guide to public vital statistics records in Minnesota. St. Paul, Minn., 1941.

**2004** —— Inventory of the county archives of Minnesota. 44v. St. Paul, Minn., 1937–42.
Only the following numbers were published: 1 (Aitkin), 2 (Anoka), 4 (Beltrami), 5 (Benton), 6 (Big Stone), 7 (Blue Earth), 11 (Cass), 12 (Chippewa), 19 (Dakota), 20 (Dodge), 21 (Douglas), 22 (Farribault), 23 (Fillmore), 24 (Freeborn), 25 (Goodhue), 26 (Grant), 28 (Houston), 29 (Hubbard), 32 (Jackson), 33 (Kanabec), 41 (Lincoln), 45 (Marshall), 46 (Martin), 47 (Meeker), 48 (Mille Lacs), 49 (Morrison), 51 (Murray), 52 (Nicollet), 53 (Nobles), 55 (Olmsted), 56 (Otter Trail), 59 (Pipestone), 64 (Redwood), 65 (Renville), 66 (Rice), 67 (Rock), 70 (Scott), 71 (Sherburne), 73 (Stearns), 78 (Traverse), 79 (Wabasha), 82 (Washington), 86 (Wright), and 87 (Yellow Medicine). Unpublished material deposited in Minnesota Historical Society, St. Paul, Minn.

**2005 Hixson (W. W.) and Co.** Atlas of Minnesota. Rockford, Ill.: [193?].
Cover: *Plat book of the state of Minnesota.*

**2006** —— Plat books of the counties of Minnesota. Rockford, Ill.: [192?, 193?].

**2007 Hughes, Thomas E., and others.** History of the Welsh in Minnesota, Foreston and Lime Springs, Iowa, gathered by the old settlers. Mankato, Minn., 1895.
Pt.1 in Welsh; pt.2 in English. pp.159–293 have biographical sketches.

**2008 Illustrated album of biography of southwestern Minnesota and northwestern Iowa** . . . Chicago, 1889.
Over 600p. of biographies.

**2009 Illustrated album of biography of the famous Valley of the Red River of the north and the park regions of Minnesota and North Dakota,** containing biographical sketches of . . . settlers and representative citizens. Chicago, 1889.
About 800 biographies.

**2010 Kline, George R.** Minnesota Geneaological surname index, 1971. Ed. by Patricia C. Harpole. St. Paul, Minn.: The Society, 1972.

**2011 Marquis, Albert N.** The book of Minnesotans. Chicago, 1907.
Important biographical dictionary of well-known Minnesotans; 4,000 biographies.

**2012 Memorial record of southwestern Minnesota.** Chicago, 1897.

**2012a Minnesota.** Chicago: Lewis Pub. Co., 1917.
Many biographies and portraits.

**2013 Minnesota. Board of Commissioners.** Minnesota in the Civil and Indian Wars, 1861–65. 2nd ed. 2v. St. Paul, Minn., 1891–99.

**2014** —— An index to the rosters, compiled as a W.P.A. project for

the Minnesota Historical Society. St. Paul, Minn., 1936.
v.1 has rosters; v.2 reports and correspondence. 24,000 names.

2015 **Minnesota genealogist.** v.1– , 1970– . St. Paul: Minnesota Genealogical Society.

2016 **Minnesota Historical Society.** Catalog of microfilms for sale. St. Paul, Minn.: The Society, 1970.
The most complete list of Minnesota newspapers published. Alphabetical by town; over 1,000 newspapers listed.

2017 ―――― Guide to the personal papers in the manuscript collections. By Grace L. Nute and G. W. Ackerman. *Guide* 1. St. Paul, Minn., 1935.

2018 ―――― Guide 2 by Lucile M. Kane and K. A. Johnson. St. Paul, Minn., 1955.

2019 **Neill, Edward D.** History of the Minnesota Valley, including the explorers and pioneers of Minnesota; and History of the Sioux Massacre by C. S. Bryant. Minneapolis, Minn. 1882.
Biographies included in the county histories.

2020 **Nelson, Olof N.** History of the Scandinavians and successful Scandinavians in the United States. 2nd ed. 2v. in 1. 1904. Repr. New York: Haskell House, 1969.
v.1 devoted almost entirely to a history of Scandinavians in Minnesota, including brief biographical sketches.

2021 **Northland newsletter.** v.1– , 1969–. Buhl, Minn.: Range Genealogical Soc.
Genealogical material from all parts of Minnesota.

2022 **O'Brien, Frank G.** Minnesota pioneer sketches . . . Minneapolis, Minn., 1904.

2023 **Shutter, Marion D.,** and **McLain, J. S.** Progressive men of Minnesota. Biographical sketches and portraits . . . Minneapolis, Minn., 1897.

2024 **Stevens, John H.** Personal recollection of Minnesota and its people. Minneapolis, Minn., 1890.
One of the best accounts of the people who first settled St. Anthony, which later became part of Minneapolis.

2025 **Strand, Algot E.** A history of the Swedish-Americans of Minnesota. 3v. Chicago, 1910.
v.2–3 biographical. "Concise record of the struggles and achievments of the early settlers, together with a narrative of what is now being done by the Swedish-Americans in Minnesota in the development of their adopted country." Indexed in Upham (no.2027).

2026 **Toensing, Waldemar F.** Minnesota congressmen, legislators, and other elected state officials: an alphabetical check list, 1849–1971. St. Paul, Minn.: Minnesota Historical Soc., 1971.
Full data of 4,628 men and women.

2027 **Upham, Warren.** Minnesota geographic names, their origin and historic significance. *Minnesota Historical Soc. collections.* 17. 1920. Repr. St. Paul, Minn.: Minnesota Historical Soc., 1969.
Still the best such guide for Minnesota. Lists communities incorporated in Minnesota since 1920, and complete list of the 1,167 official decisions on the state's place names by the U. S. Geographic Board.

2028 ―――― and **Dunlap, Rose B.** Minnesota biographies, 1655–1912. *Minnesota Historical Soc. collections* 14. St. Paul, Minn. 1912.
Dictionary type; includes brief biographical sketches of 9,000 individuals. Indexes Strand (no.2025). To be updated, 1820–1970; publication set for 1975.

2029 **Who's who in Minnesota.** Minneapolis, Minn.: 1941, 1958, 1964.
Biographical sketches of thousands of Minnesotans, plus capsule histories of the state and of the counties.

2029a **Winchell, Newton H.** History of the upper Mississippi Valley . . . Explorers and pioneers of Minnesota. Ed. by Edward D. Neill . . . Minneapolis, Minn., 1881.

## MISSISSIPPI

Settled ca. 1699; entered Union 1817

*Department of Archives and History, Jackson*

Mr. Richard S. Lackey, Forest, Miss.

**2030** **Carter, Clarence E.** The territory of Mississippi, 1798–1817. 2v. *Territorial papers of the U.S.* 5–6. 1937–38. Repr. New York: A.M.S. Press, 1973.

Lists of persons signing petitions, memorials, etc.

**2031** **Casey, Albert E.** Amite county, Mississippi, and environs, 1699–1890. 4v. Birmingham, Ala.: Amite County Historical Soc., 1948–69.

Excellent material. Land, church, marriage, and census records. v.4 contains maps and land plats for the Florida parishes of Louisiana, and information on settlers in Louisiana and Mississippi.

**2032** **Claiborne, John F.** Mississippi as a province, territory and state: with biographical notices of eminent citizens. 1880. Repr. Baton Rouge, La.: Louisiana State Univ. Pr., 1964.

Index prepared by C. M. Lagrone, Hattiesburg, Miss., 1939. Claiborne intended a series of publications. This is v.1; v.2 was destroyed by fire in 1884. Primarily history, but considerable biographical and genealogical information.

**2033** **D.A.R. Mississippi.** Family records, Mississippi Revolutionary soldiers, n.p., 1956. Obtainable from Mrs. W. R. Parkes, Box 387, Louisville, Miss.: also from G.P.C., Baltimore.

**2034** ——— Mississippi Daughters and their ancestors. By Mrs. W. R. Parkes. 2v. Madison, Miss.: Mrs. Walter Simmons, 1965–69.

**2035** **Gillis, Irene S.** Mississippi 1850 mortality schedules. Shreveport, La.: The Author, 1973.

All white persons 1 July 1849 through 30 June 1850 as reported in 1850 census. Over 3,000 deaths, showing all relevant data.

**2036** ——— and **Gillis, N. E.** Abstract of Goodspeed's Mississippi memoirs abstracted from Goodspeed's *Biographical and historical memoirs of Mississippi.* 1891. Shreveport, La.: The Authors, 1962.

Goodspeed data (see no.2043) should be used with reserve. 2,400 surnames and 25,000 individual names indexed. Abstracts in alphabetical order. Useful, even if Goodspeed not held by library.

**2037** **Gillis, Norman E.** Early inhabitants of the Natchez district. 4th pr. Shreveport, La.: The Author, 1974.

1792, 1805, 1810, and 1816 censuses of the area. Originally published in 1963.

**2038** ——— Index to Goodspeed's *Biographical memoirs of Mississippi.* 1891. Shreveport, La., 1961.

Alphabetical listing of all names of individuals mentioned, but Goodspeed (no.2043) must be held, otherwise list is useless.

**2039** ——— Mississippi 1820 census. 3rd pr. Shreveport, La.: The Author, 1973.

7,100 family heads arranged alphabetically; thus a study of neighboring families impossible. McEllhiney and Thomas (no. 2056) is better.

**2040** ——— Mississippi 1830 census. 4th pr. Shreveport, La.: The Author, 1965.

More than 10,000 names. Good index, but original census must be consulted because age groups were rearranged by authors.

**2041** ——— and **Gillis, I. S.** Mississippi 1850 census surname index. 2nd pr. Shreveport, La.: The Authors, 1973.

12,000 surnames; facilitates use of 1850 Mississippi census available on microfilm.

**2042** ——— ——— Mississippi genealogical notes. Shreveport, La.: The Authors, 1965.

Notes abstracted from *Mississippi official and statistical register of* 1917, published by Mississippi Dept. of Archives. Considerable genealogical data relating to Mississippi officials.

**2043** **[Goodspeed's] Biographical and historical memoirs of Mississippi.** 2v. Chicago, 1891.
To be used with reserve. For indexes, *see* no.2038. Abstract, *see* no. 2036.

**2043a Henderson, Thomas W.,** and **Tomlin, R. E.** A guide to the official records in The Mississippi Dept. of Archives and History. Jackson, Miss.: The Dept., 1974.
Revises and updates Dunbar Rowland's *Guide to historical materials,* 1911–12.

**2044 Hendrix, Mary L. F.** Mississippi court records from the files of the High Court of Errors and Appeals, 1799–1859. Jackson, Miss.: The Author, 1950.

**2045** ———— Newspaper notices of Mississippians 1820–60. Jackson, Miss.: Mississippi Genealogical Soc., 1960.
Death and estate notices of Hinds, Madison, Noxubee, and Yazoo counties. Originally appeared in *Journal of Mississippi history,* v.18–21, 1956–59.

**2046 Henry, Jeanne H.** 1819–49 abstradex of annual returns, Mississippi Free and Accepted Masons, with 1801, 1816, and 1817 petitioners and first returns through 1851. New Market, Ala.: Southern Genealogical Services, 1969.
Excellent source for geographically locating families prior to 1850.

**2047 Historical Records Survey.** Guide to vital statistics records in Mississippi . . . 2v. Jackson, Miss., 1942.
v.1, public archives; v.2, church archives.

**2048** ———— Inventory of the church and synagogue archives of Mississippi. 2v. Jackson, Miss., 1940.
Jewish congregations; Protestant Episcopal Church, Diocese of Mississippi.

**2049** ———— Inventory of the county archives of Mississippi. 9v. Jackson, Miss., 1937–42.
Only the following numbers were published: 3 (Amite), 18 (Forrest), 22 (Grenada), 27 (Humphreys), 37 (Lamar), 55 (Pearl River), 70 (Tippah), 72 (Tunica), and 74 (Walthall). Humphreys, Tippah and Walthall are in print and these and unpublished material are deposited in Dept. of Archives and History, Jackson, Miss.

**2050** ———— A preliminary union list of Mississippi newspaper files available in county archives, offices and publishers, libraries and private collections in Mississippi, 1805–1940. Jackson, Miss., 1942.

**2051 Jackson, Ronald V.** Mississippi 1820 census. R. V. Jackson, editor, G. R. Teeples, paleographer, R. Moore, computer director. Provo, Utah: Accelerated Indexing Systems, 1973.
About 7,800 entries. A computer index. The best of the 1820 census publications.

**2052 Journal of Mississippi history.** v.1– , 1939– . Jackson, Miss.: Dept. of Archives and History.
Has valuable genealogical information. v.1–19, only a few numbers available; v.20– , all in print.

**2053 King, Junie Estelle S.** Mississippi court records, 1799–1835. 1936. Repr. Baltimore: G.P.C., 1969.
Mostly wills.

**2054 McBee, May W.** Mississippi county court records. 1958. Repr. Baltimore: G.P.C., 1967.
Miscellaneous abstracts of deeds, wills, probate records, and marriage bonds from counties of Wilkinson, Jefferson, Claiborne, Warren, Hinds, Holmes, and Harrison.

**2055** ———— The Natchez court records, 1767–1805, abstracts of early records. Ann Arbor, Mich., 1953.
Published as v.2 of the May Wilson McBee collection. Includes abstracts of court records from Old Natchez district that were translated after 1816 and housed in the Office of the Chancery Clerk of Adams county, Natchez; valuable source for period.

**2056 McEllhiney, Wilda B.,** and **Thomas, E. W.** 1820 census of Mississippi. Tuscaloosa, Ala., 1964.
Copied from original; arranged by counties as on original return. Maps included. Superior to no.2039.

**2057 Mississippi. State Library Commission.** Mississippiana. v.1–2. Jackson, Miss.: The Commission, 1971.
Contains holdings of Mississippi materials of 55 libraries in Mississippi. v.1, union catalog; v.2, newspapers.

**2058 Mississippi Coast Historical and Genealogical Society quarterly.** v.1– , 1968– . Biloxi, Miss.: The Society.
Published records restricted to coastal counties.

**2059 Mississippi genealogical exchange.** v.1– , 1955– . Forest, Miss.: Etoile L. Hopkins and R. S. Lackey, eds.
Quarterly devoted to early families and records. Excellent. Ed. by Katie-Prince W. Esker, 1955–69.

**2060 Mississippi Genealogical Society.** Mississippi cemetery and Bible records. v.1– , 1954– . Jackson, Miss.: The Society.
Tombstone and other records; vols. published every 2 years.

**2061** ────── Survey of records in Mississippi court houses. Jackson, Miss.: The Society.
Excellent.

**2062 Mississippi genealogy and local history.** v.1– , 1969– . Shreveport, La.: Norman E. Gillis.
Suspended with v.3 in 1971; recommenced in March of 1974.

**2063 Mississippi Historical Society.** Publications. v.1–14; Centenary ser., v.1–5, 1898–1925. Jackson, Miss.: Mississippi Dept. of Archives and History.

**2064 Owen, Thomas McA.** A bibliography of Mississippi. *American Historical Association report for 1899,* I. Washington, D.C., 1900.
Some genealogical works listed.

**2065 Platt, Gwen; Lannert, A.;** and **Peer M.** Index to the U.S. census of 1840, Mississippi. 2v. Tustin, Calif.: G. Platt, 1970–72.
v.1, northern district; v.2, southern. Full name index by counties, as names appear in the original schedule.

**2066 Rowland, Dunbar.** Courts, judges, and lawyers of Mississippi, 1798–1935. Jackson, Miss., 1935.

**2067** ────── Encyclopedia of Mississippi history. 3v. Atlanta, Ga., 1907.
Biographical sketches.

**2068** ────── History of Mississippi, the heart of the south. 4v. Chicago, 1925.
v.3–4 biographical; v.1–2 are useful for genealogy.

**2069** ────── Military history of Mississippi, 1803–98. In *The official and statistical register of the state of Mississippi,* 1908, pp.387–943.
Civil War, pp.420–943.

**2070** ────── and **Sanders, E. H.** Mississippi provincial archives, 1763–81. English dominion. 3v. Transcribed from papers in the British Public Record Office. Jackson, Miss., 1911.

**2071** ────── ────── French dominion, 1701–43. 3v. Jackson, Miss., 1927–32.
Earliest records of settlers in the area. Most are still in print, from Mississippi Dept. of Archives and History, Jackson, Miss. They have also been repr. by A.M.S. Press, New York, 1973.

**2072 Rowland, Eron O. (Mrs. Dunbar).** Mississippi territory in the War of 1812. *Mississippi Historical Soc. publ.* 4. 1921. Excerpted and repr. Baltimore: G.P.C., 1968.
Contains rolls of Mississippi commands. Major source for historical and genealogical information on the campaigns and soldiers in the Mississippi territory during the War of 1812. 7,500 soldiers and officers listed.

# MISSOURI

Settled ca. 1764; entered Union 1821.

*Missouri Historical Society, St. Louis*
*St. Louis Genealogical Society*

*State Historical Society of Missouri, Columbia*
*Miss Patricia Chadwell, Fort Worth Public Library*

2074 **Beck, Lewis C.** A gazetteer of the states of Illinois and Missouri . . . Albany, N.Y., 1823.

2075 **Bryan, William S.,** and **Rose, R.** A history of the pioneer families of Missouri. 1876. Repr. with added index. Columbia, Mo., 1935. Distributed by G.P.C., Baltimore.
Much of the book consists of genealogical histories of over 800 families.

2076 **Burns, Annie (Walker).** Missouri genealogical records. 2v. Washington, D.C., 1942.
This and no. 2077 should be used with reservations. Inaccurate.

2077 ——— Missouri pension records of soldiers of the Revolutionary War, War of 1812, and Indian Wars. Washington, D.C., 1937.

2078 **Campbell, Robert A.** Campbell's gazetteer of Missouri . . . St. Louis, Mo., 1875.

2079 **Carter, Clarence E.** The territory of Louisiana-Missouri, 1803–21. 3v. *Territorial papers of the United States* 13–15. 1948–51. Repr. New York: A.M.S. Press, 1973.
Lists of persons signing petitions, memorials, etc.

2080 **Carter, Genevieve L. (Mrs. J. R.).** Early Missouri marriages to and including 1840. 3v. Sedalia, Mo.: The Author, 1969–72.
25 counties. Alphabetical arrangement by bride and groom.

2081 ——— Index to 1830 census for the entire state of Missouri. Sedalia, Mo.: The Author, 1972.

2082 **Conard, Howard L.** Encyclopedia of the history of Missouri . . . 6v. New York, 1901.
Contains many genealogical sketches in each volume.

2083 **Coppage, Arthur M., III.** Missouri cousins. Antioch, Calif.: The Author, 1969. Available from the author, Walnut Creek, Calif.
A genealogical and historical account of some early families, including their migration from east to west.

2084 ——— and **Wulfeck, D. F.** Virginia settlers in Missouri. Naugatuck, Conn.: D. F. Wulfeck, 1964.

2085 **Daughters of American Colonists.** History and lineage book by Mrs. Mellcene T. Smith and J. T. Lewis. St. Louis, 1936.

2086 **D.A.R. Gallatin Chapter, Missouri.** Cemetery records of Missouri. 3v. Chillicothe, Mo.: Elizabeth P. Ellsberry, 1963–67.

2087 ——— Missouri. Missouri state history of the D.A.R. by Mrs. Frank S. (Blanche) Leach. Kansas City, Mo., 1929.
Has biographical sketches.

2088 **Douglass, Robert S.** History of southeast Missouri. 2v. 1912. Repr. with added index by Felix E. Snider. Cape Girardeau, Mo.: Ramfre Pr., 1961.
Repr. 2v. in 1. v.2 biographies.

2089 **Eaton, David W.** How Missouri counties, towns and streams were named. Columbia, Mo.: 1916.
Repr. from *The Missouri historical review,* v.10, no.3, 1916.

2090 **Ellsberry, Elizabeth Prather.** In the past decade Mrs. Ellsberry has compiled hundreds of Missouri county records: marriage, cemetery, wills and administrations, probate, deed, birth, and Bible records. Also 1850 census and mortality records. From the author, Chillicothe, Mo.

2091 **Gambrill, Georgia.** Genealogical materials and local histories in the St. Louis Public Library. Rev. ed. St. Louis, Mo.: The Library, 1966.
Supplement was published in 1971. Excellent genealogical library.

2092　Glazner, Capitola H. and McLane, B. J. An index to the 5th census of the U.S. 1830; population schedules, state of Missouri. Hot Springs, Ark.: Arkansas Ancestors, 1966.

Lists names of the heads of families in the 32 counties existing in 1830 with their county of residence.

2093　Haynes, Shirley, and Conley, A. Missouri obituaries index. v.1–3. Gilliam, Mo.: Saline Sentiments, 1974.

Over 5,000 names.

2094　Historical Records Survey. Early Missouri archives. 3v. St. Louis, Mo., 1941–42.

Ste. Genevieve and St. Charles; New Madrid, Cape Girardeau.

2095　――― Guide to public vital statistics: church records in Missouri. St. Louis, Mo., 1941.

2096　――― Guide to public vital statistics: church records in Missouri. St. Louis, Mo., 1942.

2097　――― Inventory of the county archives of Missouri. 15v. St. Louis, Mo., 1937–42.

Only the following numbers were published: 19 (Cass), 26 (Cole), 30 (Dallas), 42 (Henry), 51 (Johnson), 58 (Linn), 60 (McDonald), 61 (Macon), 64 (Marion), 73 (Jasper), 80 (Pettis), 82 (Pike), 90 (Reynolds), 91 (Ripley), and 102 (Shelby). Unpublished material deposited in Univ. of Missouri, Columbia, Mo.

2098　History of Cole, Moniteau, Morgan, Benton, Miller, Maries, and Osage counties, Missouri . . . Chicago, 1889.

2099　History of Franklin, Jefferson, Washington, Crawford, and Gasconade counties, Missouri, Chicago, 1888.

2100　――― Index compiled Felix E. Snider. Cape Girardeau, Mo.: Ramfre Pr., 1970.

2101　History of Hickory, Polk, Cedar, Dade and Barton counties, Missouri. Chicago, 1889.

2102　History of Lewis, Clark, Knox, and Scotland counties, Missouri . . . St. Louis, Mo., 1887.

2103　History of Newton, Lawrence, Barry, and McDonald counties, Missouri. St. Louis, Mo., 1888.

2104　History of southeast Missouri. Embracing an historical account of the counties of Ste. Genevieve, St. Francois, Perry, Cape Girardeau, Bollinger, Madison, New Madrid, Pemiscot, Dunklin, Scott, Mississippi, Stoddard, Butler, Wayne, and Iron . . . 1888. Repr. Cape Girardeau, Mo.: Ramfre Pr., 1964.

Appendix of 625 pages contains biographical sketches of over 1,100 families, with considerable genealogical data.

2105　Hodges, Nadine. Missouri obituaries. v.1– , 1966– . Kansas City, Mo.: The Author.

Many Missouri pioneers. 23v. to end of 1974.

2106　―――; Vineyard, Mrs. J.; and Woodruff, Audrey (Mrs. Howard). Missouri pioneers, county and genealogical records, v.1– , 1967– . Independence, Mo.: Mrs. Woodruff.

25v. to end of 1974.

2107　Houck, Louis. Memorial sketches of pioneers and early residents of southeast Missouri. Cape Girardeau, Mo., 1915.

2108　Houts, Alice K. (Mrs. Hale), and Eastman, H. Revolutionary soldiers buried in Missouri. Kansas City, Mo.: The Author, 1966.

Contains service records of approximately 1,000 soldiers buried in Missouri. Dates secured from various D.A.R. chapters of the State Society.

2109　The Kansas genealogist. v.1– , 1960– . Kansas City, Mo.: Heart of America Genealogical Soc.

Monthly 1960-62; quarterly thereafter.

2110　McGhee, Lucy K. Missouri Revolutionary soldiers, War of 1812, and Indian Wars pension list. Washington, D.C., 1955.

## Missouri

**2111** **March, David D.** The history of Missouri. 4v. West Palm Beach, Fla., 1967.
v.4 biographical and personal records, 1673–1967.

**2112** **Missouri historical review.** v.1– , 1906– . Columbia, Mo.: State Historical Soc. of Missouri.

**2113** —— Indexes. v.1–25, 1934, out of print; v.26–55, 1955. Columbia, Mo.: The Society.
Early vol. contained some genealogy.

**2114** **O'Rourke, Timothy J.** Maryland Catholics on the frontier: the Missouri and Texas settlements. Parsons, Kans.: Brefney Pr., 1973.
Concerns settlement of Catholics from Maryland, with descendants. Settlers mostly went to Perry county.

**2115** **Pompey, Sherman L.** A partial listing of veterans of the American Revolution, the Civil War, and the Spanish War, that are buried in certain Missouri cemeteries. Warrensburg, Mo.: Johnson County Historical Soc., 1962.

**2116** **The prairie gleaner.** v.1– , 1969– . Warrensburg, Mo.: West Central Missouri Genealogical Soc.

**2117** **Ramsey, Robert L.** Our storehouse of Missouri place names. *Univ. of Missouri bull.* 53, no.24. *Arts and sciences ser.* 7. Columbia, Mo.: State Historical Soc., 1952.

**2118** **A reminiscent history of the Ozark region.** 1894. Repr. Cape Girardeau, Mo.: Ramfre Pr., 1966.
29 Arkansas counties and 25 Missouri Ozark counties included.

**2119** **Revolutionary soldiers and their descendants.** Missouri ed. New York, ca.1900.

**2120** **St. Louis Genealogical Society.** Index to St. Louis marriages. 2v. St. Louis, Mo.: The Society, 1973.
v.1, 1804–59; v.2, 1860–76. Computerized index contains 73,230 marriages and 146,- 246 names of spouses, male and female. All marriages recorded between the time U.S. purchased Louisiana Territory in 1804 and 1876 when the city separated from St. Louis county.

**2121** —— Index of 1850 St. Louis and St. Louis county census. St. Louis, Mo.: The Society, 1968.
Almost 100,000 names.

**2122** —— Quarterly. v.1– , 1968– . St. Louis, Mo.: The Society.

**2123** —— Surname index. Annual supplements. St. Louis, Mo.: The Society, 1968– .

**2125** **Schiavo, Giovanni.** The Italians in Missouri. Chicago [1929].
Numerous short biographical sketches.

**2126** **Selby, Paul O.** A bibliography of Missouri county histories and atlases. 2nd ed. Kirksville, Mo.: Northeast Missouri State Teachers College, 1966.
From its *Bulletin* 66, no.2.

**2127** **Shoemaker, Floyd C.** Missouri and Missourians . . . 5v. Chicago, 1943.
v.3–5 biographical. Good genealogical material.

**2128** **Stercula, Beverly M.** Heads of families, 1830 census of Missouri. Fullerton, Calif.: Genealogems Pub., 1966.
Good name index with county of residence information.

**2129** **Stevens, Walter B.** Centennial history of Missouri . . . 1820–1921. 7v.? St. Louis, Mo., 1921.
Numbering of this series not clear. Stevens apparently edited v.1–4; S. J. Clark, v.5–6; v.7 (unnumbered) was a deluxe supplement. Much biographical material.

**2130** —— —— Biographical index by Cloie (Mrs. Leister E.) Presley. Searcy, Ark.: The Author, 1968.

**2131** **Taft, William H.** Missouri newspapers: when and where, 1808–1963. Columbia, Mo.: State Historical Soc. of Missouri, 1964.

## United States

**2132** **U.S. General Land Office.** Private land claims in Missouri . . . Washington, D.C., 1835.
24th Cong. 1st sess. House doc.59. Includes report of recorder and commissioners for the adjustment of land titles in Missouri. 255 claims going back to French and Spanish times. All pertinent facts.

**2133** **United States biographical dictionary and portrait gallery of eminent and self-made men.** Missouri vol. Chicago, 1878.
Mug book.

**2134** **University of Missouri, Columbia.** Guide to the western historical manuscripts collection, prepared by James N. Primm. *Univ. of Missouri bull.* 53, no.33, 1952. Columbia, Mo.: The University, 1952.

**2135** —————— Supplement by John A. Galloway. *Univ. of Missouri bul.* 58, no. 13. Columbia, Mo.: The University, 1957.

**2136** **Williams, Jacqueline H.,** and **Williams, B. H.** Resources for genealogical research in Missouri. Warrensburg, Mo.: The Authors, 1969.

**2137** **Williams, Walter.** A history of northeast Missouri. 2v. Chicago, 1913.
v.2 (in 2pts.) biographical.

**2138** —————— A history of northwest Missouri. 3v. Chicago, 1915.
v.2–3 biographical.

**2139** —————— and **Shoemaker, Floyd C.** Missouri, mother of the west. 5v. Chicago, 1930.
v.3–5 biographical.

**2140** **Woodruff, Audrey (Mrs. Howard W.).** Central Missouri River counties. 1830 U.S. census. Heads of households . . . 12 pts. Springfield, Mo., 1966.

**2141** —————— Missouri marriages. Pt.1– , 1969– . Kansas City, Mo.: The Author. 17pts.
17 counties to 1974. Covers 1807–93.

**2142** —————— Missouri pioneers, county and genealogical records. v.1– , 1967– . Kansas City, Mo.: The Author.
Some volumes by Audrey Woodruff and Nadine Hodges. 27v. to 1974.

## MONTANA

Settled ca. 1809; entered Union 1889

*Montana Historical Society, Helena*
*Montana State Library, Helena*

**2143** **Burlingame, Merrill G.,** and **O'Toole, K. R.** A history of Montana. 3v. New York, ca.1957.
v.3 contains family and personal history. Sketches deal with individuals whose ancestors (early settlers) are mentioned.

**2144** **Historical Records Survey.** A directory of churches and religious organizations in Montana. Bozeman, Mont., 1941.

**2145** —————— Guide to public vital statistics records in Montana. Bozeman, Mont., 1941.

**2146** —————— Inventory of the county archives of Montana. 16v. Bozeman, 1938–42.
Only the following numbers were published: 1 (Beaverhead), 5 (Carbon, Gallatin, Park, Stillwater, Sweet Grass), 15 (Flathead, Mineral, Lake, Ravalli, Lincoln, Sanders), 16 (Gallatin), 24 (Lake), 27 (Lincoln), 28 (Madison), 31 (Mineral), 32 (Missoula), 34 (Park), 41 (Ravalli), 45 (Sanders), 47 (Silver Bow), 48 (Stillwater), 49 (Sweet Grass), and 51 (Toole). Unpublished material deposited in State College, Bozeman, Mont.

**2147** —————— Inventory of the vital statistics records of churches and religious organizations in Montana. Preliminary ed. Bozeman, Mont., 1942.

**2148** **Historical Society of Montana.** Contributions. v.1–9, 1876–1923; v.10, 1940. Repr. Boston: Canner, 1966.
Source material for history and genealogy.

2149	Hixson (W. W.) and Co. Atlas of Montana. Rockford, Ill.: [193?].
Cover: *Plat book of the state of Montana.*

2150	**An illustrated history of the Yellowstone Valley,** embracing the counties of Park, Sweet Grass, Carbon, Yellowstone, Rosebud, Custer and Dawson, state of Montana. Spokane, Wash., 1907.
281pp. of biographical sketches. Mug book.

2151	Leeson, Michael A. History of Montana, 1739-1885: a history of its discovery and settlement . . . with histories of counties, cities . . . Chicago, 1885.
Better than the usual book of this type.

2152	**Men of affairs and representative institutions of the state of Montana.** 1914. Butte, Mont., 1914.
250 state leaders sketched.

2153	Miller, Joaquin *(i.e.,* Cincinnatus Heine). An illustrated history of the state of Montana, containing . . . biographical mention . . . of its pioneers and prominent citizens. Chicago, 1894.
Mug book.

2154	**Progressive men of the state of Montana** . . . 2nd ed. Chicago, ca.1901.
Mug book.

2155	Sanders, Helen F. History of Montana. 3v. Chicago, 1913.
v.2-3 biographical.

2156	Schoenberg, Wilfred P. Jesuits in Montana, 1840-1960. Portland, Ore., 1960.
Portraits, etc.

2157	Society of Montana Pioneers. Constitution, members and officers with portraits and maps. v.1 (all pub). Helena, Mont., 1899.
Fine, short biographical sketches of several hundred Montana pioneers.

2158	Stout, Tom. Montana: its story and biography. 3v. Chicago, 1921.
v.2-3 biographical.

NEBRASKA

Settled ca. 1847; entered Union 1867

*Nebraska State Historical Society, Lincoln*
*Omaha Public Library*

2159	Baldwin, Sara A., and Baldwin, R. M. Nebraskana. Hebron, Nebr., 1932.
Subtitle: *Biographical sketches of Nebraska men and women of achievement who have been awarded life membership in the Nebraskana Society.* Good biographies, mostly 20th century.

2160	Barns, Cass G. The sod house. 1930. Repr. Lincoln, Nebr.: Univ. of Nebraska Pr., 1970.
Reminiscent, historical, and biographical sketches featuring Nebraska pioneers, 1867-97.

2161	Bengtson, Berndt E. Pen pictures of pioneers, biographical sketches. 2v. Holdrege, Nebr., 1926-31.
Swedes and pioneers in Nebraska.

2162	**Biographical and genealogical history of southeastern Nebraska.** 2v. New York, 1904.
Good biographical sketches.

2163	**Biographical and historical memoirs of Adams, Clay, Hall and Hamilton counties, Nebraska** . . . Chicago, 1890.

2164	Casper, Henry W. History of the Catholic church in Nebraska. 3v. Milwaukee, Wisc., 1960.
Detailed and important biographical information.

2165	**Compendium of history:** reminiscences and biography of western Nebraska containing . . . history of the state of Nebraska . . . and biographical sketches of hundreds of prominent old settlers. Chicago, 1909 and 1912.
1909 ed. contains material different from 1912 ed.; 1909 covers western Nebraska, and 1912 Nebraska as a whole.

2166	Cox, Evelyn M. 1854-1855-1856 Nebraska state census. Ellensburg, Wash.: The Compiler, 1973.
Full data.

2167 ——— 1860 Nebraska territory census. Ellensburg, Wash.: The Compiler, 1973.
Includes unorganized territory, bits of Wyoming, Colorado, and the Dakotas.

2168 **Daughters of Founders and Patriots of America. Nebraska.** Founders and patriots of Nebraska . . . Ed. by Mrs. Charles H. Mullin and others. Omaha, Nebr., 1935.
Unrelated short chapters by various writers.

2169 **D.A.R. Nebraska.** Collection of Nebraska pioneer reminiscences. Cedar Rapids, Iowa, 1916.
Personal reminiscences, not always accurate.

2170 **Edmunds, A. C.** Pen sketches of Nebraskans . . . Lincoln, Nebr., 1871.
Contains biographical material, often difficult to find elsewhere.

2171 **Fitzpatrick, Lilian L.** Nebraska place names . . . Ed. by G. T. Fairclough. Lincoln, Nebr.: Univ. of Nebraska Pr., 1960.
Includes selections from *The origin of the place-names of Nebraska,* by J. T. Link. New ed. of 1925 work, with additions.

2172 **Hagedorn, Eugene.** The Franciscans in Nebraska . . . Norfolk, Nebr., 1931.
Prefaced by historical sketches of mid-Nebraska, and history of individual churches in area. Sketches and reminiscences of mid-Nebraska pioneers and Catholic fathers.

2173 **Haynes, Melda.** Nebraska pioneer. New Orleans, La.: Polyanthos, 1973.
Descendants of William Butler, including important records relating to many Nebraskan families.

2174 **Historical Records Survey.** Guide to public vital statistics records in Nebraska. Lincoln, Nebr., 1941.

2175 ——— Inventory of the county archives of Nebraska. 7v. Lincoln, Nebr., 1939-42.
Only the following numbers were published: 37 (Gosper), 39 (Greeley), 47 (Howard), 58 (Loup), 61 (Merrick), 80 (Seward), and 91 (Webster). Unpublished material deposited in State Historical Soc., Lincoln, Nebr.

2176 **History of the state of Nebraska** . . . biographical sketches . . . 2v. Chicago, 1882.

2177 ——— Index by Raymond E. Dale. Lincoln, Neb.: Nebraska State Historical Soc., 1962.

2178 **Illustrated biographical album of northeastern Nebraska.** Philadelphia, 1893.

2179 **James, Jane E.** Eighth census of the United States 1860 Nebraska territory mortality schedules. Huntsville, Ark.: Century Enterprises, 1972.
Information from schedule 3, deaths, 1860 federal census for Nebraska territory.

2180 **Kučera, Vladimir.** Czech cemeteries in Nebraska . . . Ed. by A. Novacek. San Francisco: R. and E. Research Associates, 1972.

2181 ——— Czechs in Nebraska. Ed. by A. Novacek. Ord, Nebr., 1967.
Available from R. and E. Research Assoc., San Francisco.

2182 **Marquette, David.** A history of Nebraska Methodism: first half-century 1854-1904. Cincinnati, Ohio, 1904.
Good sketches of individuals in the Methodist movement.

2183 **Morton, Julius S.,** and **Watkins, A.** Illustrated history of Nebraska. 3v. Lincoln, Nebr., 1905-13.
v.3 is biographical.

2184 **National Society of the United Daughters of 1812. Nebraska.** Heroes of 1812 . . . Omaha, Nebr., 1930.

**2185 Nebraska. Adjutant General.** Roster of Nebraska volunteers from 1861 to 1869 . . . 1888. [Rev.] Hastings, Nebr. 1908.
Compiled by Edgar S. Dudley.

**2186 Nebraska and midwest genealogical records.** v.1–22. Lincoln, Nebr., 1923–44.
Valuable periodical containing records not found elsewhere; published by Nebraska Genealogical Society.

**2187 Nebraska. Secretary of State.** Roster of soldiers, sailors, and marines of the War of 1812, the Mexican War and the War of the Rebellion, residing in Nebraska, December 1897. Lincoln, Nebr., 1897.

**2188** ———— Roster of soldiers, sailors, and marines of the War of the Rebellion residing in Nebraska . . . 3v. Lincoln, Nebr., 1895–98.

**2189 Olson, James C.** History of Nebraska. 1966. Repr. Lincoln, Nebr.: Univ. of Nebraska Pr., 1974.

**2190 Omaha bee "Nebraskans," 1854–1904.** 2v. Omaha, Nebr., 1904–14.

**2191** ———— Suppl. 1904–14. Omaha, Nebr., 1915.
Portraits of men closely identified with state. Little biographical detail, but pictures valuable and hard to find.

**2192 Rosicky, Rose.** History of Czechs in Nebraska. Omaha, Nebr., 1929.

**2193 Sheldon, Addison E.** Nebraska: the land and the people. 3v. New York, 1931.
v.2–3 biographical.

**2194 Shumway, Grant L.** History of western Nebraska and its people . . . 3v. Lincoln, Nebr., 1921.
v.3 contains biographical material.

**2195 Sutton, Everette G.** Teepee to soddies; southwestern Nebraska and thereabouts. [Republican City, Nebr.: The Author?] 1968.

Informal essays on Nebraska and its pioneers.

NEVADA

Settled ca. 1850; entered Union 1864

*Nevada Historical Society, Reno*
*Washoe County Library, Reno*

**2196 Angel, Myron.** Reproduction of Thompson and West's *History of Nevada, 1881,* with illustrations and biographical sketches of its prominent men and citizens. Berkeley, Calif.: Howell-North, 1958.

**2197** ———— Index by Helen J. Poulton. *Bibliographic ser.* 6. Reno, Nev.: Univ. of Nevada, 1966.
Also repr. by Arno Pr., New York, 1972 under title: *History of Nevada.* Thompson and West were the publishers in 1881.

**2198 Averett, Walter R.** Directory of southern Nevada place-names. Las Vegas, Nev., 1962.
Arthur H. Clark Co., Glendale, Calif., issued *Southern Nevada place-names* in 1963—presumably a rev. ed. of Averett. Special attention given to obscure and forgotten names.

**2199 Dangberg, Grace M.** Carson Valley: historical sketches of Nevada's first settlement. Minden, Nev.: Carson Valley Historical Soc., 1972.
Brief sketches of significant historical events and biographies of people who were important to that area.

**2200 Daughters of the American Colonists, Nevada.** Miscellaneous Bible and family records . . . n.p., 1957?

**2201 Davis, Sam P.** The history of Nevada. 2v. Reno, Nev., 1913.
Good county histories. Covers early territorial and state history; has biographies. v.2 biographical.

**2202 Eterovich, Adam S.** Croatians/Dalmatians, Montenegrins, Hercegavinians in Nevada. San Francisco: R. and E. Research Assoc., 1971.

2203 ——— Yugoslavs in Nevada, 1859–1900 . . . San Francisco: R. and E. Research Associates, 1973.
Some biographies; directory included, quality questionable.

2204 **Folkes, John G.** Nevada's newspapers: a bibliography: a compilation of Nevada history, 1854–1964. Reno, Nev.: Univ. of Nevada Pr., 1964.
*See also* no.2212.

2205 **Frickstad, Walter N.,** and **Thrall, E. W.** A century of Nevada post offices, 1852–1957. Oakland, Calif., 1958.
Listing with dates of establishment and movement.

2206 **Harris, Robert P.** Nevada postal history, 1861–1972. Santa Cruz, Calif.: Bonanza Pr., 1973.
Primarily intended for philatelists, but there is a listing of openings and closings of all official recognized post office branches and stations from 1852–1972. Has good map of locations of all current and discontinued post offices.

2207 **Historical Records Survey.** Guide to public vital statistics records in Nevada. Reno, Nev., 1941.

2208 ——— Inventory of the church archives of Nevada. 2v. Protestant Episcopal Church; Roman Catholic Church. Reno, Nev., 1939–41.

2209 ——— Inventory of the county archives of Nevada. 7v. Reno, 1937–41.
Only the following numbers were published: 3 (Douglas), 4 (Elko), 6 (Eureka), 11 (Mineral), 12 (Nye), 13 (Ormsby), and 16 (Washoe). Unpublished material deposited in Nevada Historical Soc., Reno, Nev.

2210 **Jensen, Edith G.,** and **Olsen, B. M.** Nevada records. *California Mother Lode ser.* 5. San Leandro, Calif.: The Authors, 1965.

2211 **Leigh, Rufus W.** Nevada place names: their origin and significance. Salt Lake City, 1964. From Southern Nevada Historical Soc., Las Vegas.
This and Averett (no.2198) are useful in conjunction.

2212 **Lingenfelter, Richard E.** The newspapers of Nevada, 1858–1958, a history and bibliography. San Francisco, 1964.
*See also* no. 2204.

2213 **Nevada. Adjutant General.** Annual report . . . for the State of Nevada for 1865. Carson City, Nev., 1866.
Rosters of 1st battalion.

2214 **Nevada.** Census of the inhabitants of the state of Nevada. 1875. 2v. Carson City, Nev., 1877.
v.1: Churchill, Ormsby counties; v.2: Storey, White Pine.

2215 **Nevada Historical Society.** Biennial reports. no.1–18, 1907–48. Reno, Nev.

2216 ——— Papers. v.1–5, 1913–26. Reno, Nev.

2217 ——— Quarterlies. v.1– , 1958– . Reno, Nev.: The Society.
Memoirs, journals, letters, and research papers, providing an accurate reference, although the material is not genealogical per se. In view of paucity of Nevada genealogical material, these publications are useful.

2218 **Nevada, the Silver state.** 2v. Carson City, Nev.: Eastern States Historical Pub., 1970.

2219 **Parkin, Nona.** Nevada cemeteries inscriptions from the tombstones of sixteen cemeteries. 17pts. in 1v. Reno, Nev., 1964.

2220 **Ratay, Myra S.** Pioneers of Ponderosa. Sparks, Nev.: Western Printing & Publ. Co., 1972.
Detailed history of Washoe Valley from Mormon Settlement to recent developments.

2221 **Scrugham, James G.** Nevada: a narrative of the conquest of a frontier land. 3v. Chicago, 1935.

Subscription biographies of well-known Nevadans. Well written. v.2-3 biographical.

**2222 Thompson and West,** publishers of *History of Nevada, see* no.2196.

**2223 Wells, J. Kelly.** First directory of Nevada territory containing names of residents in the principal towns . . . Repr. Los Gatos, Calif., 1962.
Nevada Historical Society has editions for 1861-1900 (with a few gaps).

**2224 Who's who in Nevada** . . . Los Angeles, 1907.

**2225 Wren, Thomas.** History of the state of Nevada; its resources and people. Chicago, 1904.
Subscription biographies and portraits. Similar coverage to that of Davis, *see* 2201.

NEW HAMPSHIRE

Settled ca. 1623; original state

*New Hampshire Historical Society, Concord*
*New Hampshire State Library, Concord*

**2226 Belknap, Jeremy.** The history of New-Hampshire. Comprehending the events of one complete century and seventy-five years from the discovery of the river Pascataqua to the year 1790 . . . 1812 and 1831 eds. Repr. of 1831 ed. New York: Johnson Reprint Co., 1970.

**2227** —— —— Repr. of v.3, "Geographical description of New Hampshire," an account of the state in 1792. Ed. by G. T. Lord. New Hampton, N.H.: Peter E. Randall, 1973.

**2228 Biographical sketches of representative citizens of the state of New Hampshire.** Boston, 1902.
Mug book.

**2229 Carter, Nathan F.** The native ministry in New Hampshire. Concord, N.H., 1906.
2,500 ministers with genealogical information.

**2230 Cemetery records of New Hampshire veterans.** 5v. n.p., n.d.
v.1, French and Indian Wars, War of 1812, Mexican War, Indian Wars; v.2, Revolutionary War; v.3-4, Civil War; v.5, Spanish-American War. Typewritten sheets prepared by New Hampshire Veterans Council.

**2231 Chase, Francis.** Gathered sketches from the early history of New Hampshire and Vermont . . . 1856. Somersworth, N.H.: New Hampshire Pub. Co., 1970.

**2232 Colonial Dames of America.** Colonial gravestone inscriptions in the state of New Hampshire. From collections made by Historic Activities Committee. Compiled by Winifred L. Goss. 1942. Repr. Baltimore: G.P.C., 1974.
12,000 names prior to 1770.

**2233** —— Gravestone inscriptions gathered by the Old Burial Grounds Committee. Compiled by Mrs. Josiah Carpenter. Cambridge, Mass., 1913.

**2234 D.A.R. New Hampshire.** Directory of members and ancestors. Littleton, N.H.: D.A.R., 1964.

**2235** —— State history of the D.A.R. Compiled by Elizabeth K. Folsom. [Exeter, N.H., 1930?].
Biographies of officers, etc.

**2236 Dow, Joseph.** History of the town of Hampton, New Hampshire . . . 1638-1892. 2v. Salem, Mass., 1893.
v.2 is all genealogy. Important in settling other areas.

**2237 Draper, Mrs. Amos G.** New Hampshire Revolutionary pensioners. In *National Genealogical Soc. quarterly,* v.11-18, 1922-29.

**2238** —— New Hampshire Revolutionary pensioners omitted from any printed list. In *National Genealogical Soc. quarterly,* v.11-29, 1922-40.

**2239 Driscoll, Mrs. Marion L.** New Hampshire Revolutionary war pension records. In *National Genealogical Soc. quarterly,* v.24–27, 1935–38.

Mrs. Driscoll also compiled Revolutionary War pension abstracts, in v.29, 1940.

**2240** **Ellis, James A.** Memorial encyclopedia of the state of New Hampshire. Boston, 1919.

Good genealogical sketches of prominent citizens

**2241** **Farmer, John,** and **Moore, J. B.** A gazetteer of the state of New Hampshire. Concord, N.H., 1823.

**2242** **Foss, Gerald D.,** and **Adams, W. S.** Three centuries of freemasonry in New Hampshire, with biographical dictionary. Ed. by E. Serafini. Somersworth, N.H.: New Hampshire Pub. Co., 1972.

**2243** **Gill, James V.** (and **Gill, M. R.**). An index to the 1800 federal census of New Hampshire. 3v. in 1. Thomson, Ill.: Heritage House, 1967–73.

v.1, Cheshire; v.2, Grafton and Hillsboro; v.3, Rockingham and Strafford counties. Alphabetized list of head of householders by county with town of residence and census reference page number.

**2244** **Gilmore, George C.** Roll of New Hampshire soldiers at the Battle of Bennington, 1777. Manchester, N.H., 1891.

Appendix has "New Hampshire men who lost their lives from 1775–82."

**2245** **Hammond, Otis G.** Check list of New Hampshire history . . . Ed. by F. J. Hanrahan. 1925. Repr. Somersworth, N.H.: New Hampshire Pub. Co., 1971.

The 1971 ed. updates the 1925 ed.

**2246** —— Notices from the *New Hampshire gazette,* 1765–1800. Lambertville, N.J.: Hunterdon House, 1970.

Full extracts of death and marriage entries, covering New England and Massachusetts. Appeared serially in *The genealogical magazine.* Has index added by publisher. Of general interest, because it covers people who went to other states.

**2247** **Hayward, John.** A gazetteer of New Hampshire: all the counties, towns and districts in the state. Boston, 1849.

**2248** **Historical New Hampshire.** v.1– , 1944– . Concord, N.H.: New Hampshire Historical Soc.

**2249** —— Index 1944–70 compiled by Virginia L. Close. Concord, N.H.: The Society, 1974.

Some genealogy. Index covers v.1–25 with 8,000 entries.

**2250** **Historical Records Survey.** Guide to church vital statistics records in New Hampshire. Manchester, N.H., 1942.

**2251** —— Guide to public vital statistics records in New Hampshire. Manchester, N.H., 1941.

**2252** —— Inventory of the church archives of New Hampshire. Roman Catholic Church. Manchester, N.H., 1939.

**2253** —— Inventory of the county archives of New Hampshire. 6v. Manchester, N.H., 1936–40.

Only the following numbers were published: 1 (Belknap), 2 (Carroll), 3 (Cheshire), 4 (Coos), 5 (Grafton), and 7 (Merrimack). Unpublished material deposited in Univ. of New Hampshire, Manchester, N.H.

**2254** **Hunt, Elmer M.** New Hampshire town names and whence they came. Peterborough, N.H.: Noone House, 1971.

**2255** **Jackson, Ronald V.,** and **Teeples, G. R.** New Hampshire 1800 census. Provo, Utah: Accelerated Indexing Systems, 1974.

Computer index with 26,000 entries. Research aids, early maps, genealogical data, etc.

**2256** **Kidder, Frederic.** History of the First New Hampshire Regiment in the War of the Revolution. 1868. Also New Hampshire at the Battle of Bunker Hill by Henry B. Moore. Repr. with new introduction by Richard F. Upton. Hampton, N.H.: Randall, 1973.

Biographical and historical material.

**2257** **Little, George T.** Genealogical and family history of state of Maine. 4v. New York, 1909.

Contains data on New Hampshire families, but because of many errors should be used with care.

**2258 Merrill, Eliphalet.** Gazetteer of the state of New Hampshire... Exeter, N.H., 1817.

**2259 Metcalf, Henry H.** One thousand New Hampshire notables; brief biographical sketches of New Hampshire men and women, native or resident... Concord, N.H., 1919.

**2260 Moses, George H.** New Hampshire men. A collection of biographical sketches. Concord, N.H., 1893.
Biographies of people living in the 1890s.

**2261 New Hampshire (Colony). Probate Court.** Probate records of the province of New Hampshire, 1635-1771. 9v. Concord, N.H.: New Hampshire Historical Soc., 1907-41.
v.31-39 of New Hampshire state and provincial papers. Some volumes in print.

**2262 New Hampshire.** Documents and records relating to the province (state and towns) of New Hampshire, from the earliest period of its settlement... 1623-1800. 40v. Manchester, N.H. [and elsewhere], 1867-1943.
Known as *New Hampshire state and provincial papers*. Not all are genealogical, but those under no.2261, 2263, 2265, 2266 are essential. Each volume has an index. v.1-7, provincial; v.8-30, province, state, town records; v.31-39, probate records (1635-1771); v.40, early court records.

**2263** ——— Miscellaneous Revolutionary documents of New Hampshire, including the Association Test, the pension rolls, and other important papers. *New Hampshire state and provincial papers,* 30. Manchester, N.H., 1910.

**2264** ——— Provincial and state papers published by the authority of the legislature of New Hampshire. Ed. by Nathaniel Bouton and I. W. Hammond. 18v. 1867-90. Repr. New York: A.M.S. Press, 1970.

**2265** ——— Rolls of the soldiers of the Revolutionary War. 4v. Ed. by Isaac W. Hammond. *New Hampshire state and provincial papers,* 14-17. Manchester, N.H., 1885-89.
v.3 with appendix embracing French and Indian War rolls, 1712-55; v.4, rolls and documents relating to soldiers of the Revolutionary War. For pension rolls, *see* no. 2263; for other rolls, *see* no.2266.

**2266** ——— Rolls of the soldiers of the Revolutionary War, 1775-82. *New Hampshire state and provincial papers,* 30. Manchester, N.H., 1910.
Additional names to those contained in no.2265.

**2266a New Hampshire. Adjutant-General's Office.** Revised register of the soldiers and sailors of New Hampshire in the War of the Rebellion, 1861-66. Concord, N.H., 1895.

**2267 New Hampshire genealogical record.** v.1-7, no.2. 1903-10. Repr. Cleveland, Ohio: Bell & Howell, 1967.
New Hampshire Historical Society has combined index to all volumes.

**2268 New Hampshire Historical Society.** Collections, 1824-1939. Concord, N.H.: The Society.
Many volumes contain genealogical information; some are in print.

**2269** ——— Family names in New Hampshire town histories. A record compiled and indexed by the New Hampshire Historical Society. Concord, N.H:. The Society, 1946.
Appeared in *Historical New Hampshire,* no.3, Dec. 1946. Lists alphabetically 3,000 family names, 85 town histories published.

**2270** ——— Proceedings. v.1-5. Concord, N.H.: The Society, 1872-1912.
Some genealogy.

**2271 New Hampshire loyalists;** transcripts from the records of the Commission for enquiring into the losses and services of American loyalists, 1783-90, preserved in the Public Record Office, London. 5v., n.d.

Typescript at New Hampshire State Library, Concord, N.H.

**2272 New Hampshire state and provincial papers.** *See* no.2261-63, 2265-66.

**2273 Noyes, Sybil; Libby, C. T.;** and **Davis, W. G.** Genealogical dictionary of Maine and New Hampshire. 5pts. 1928-39. Repr. in 1v. Baltimore: G.P.C., 1972.
Hundreds of thousands of births, marriages and deaths of settlers through the 3rd generation. Other genealogical information includes wills, deeds, court cases, etc.

**2274 Pension records for New Hampshire soldiers and sailors who fought in the Revolutionary War.** The records are in the National Archives in Washington. The New Hampshire Historical Society has a name index in 71v. for the New Hampshire men who received pensions.

**2275 Pillsbury, Hobart.** New Hampshire . . . a history. 9v. New York, 1927-29.
v.5-9 biographical.

**2276 Pope, Charles H.** The pioneers of Maine and New Hampshire, 1623-60 . . . 1908. Repr. Baltimore: G.P.C., 1973.
*See* no.1727 for complete listing

**2277 Potter, Chandler E.** The military history of the state of New Hampshire from its settlement in 1623 to the Rebellion in 1861. 2v. Repr. with an added index compiled by New Hampshire Historical Society, in lv. Baltimore: G.P.C., 1972.
Repr. from *Report of Adjutant General 1866,* v.2, pt.1 and 1868, pt.2. The standard work; about 14,000 names and places indexed; index much superior to no.2265-66.

**2278 Ridlon, Gideon T., Sr.** Saco Valley settlements and families; historical, biographical, genealogical . . . 1895. Repr. Rutland, Vt.: Tuttle, 1970.
Saco Valley runs south-east from New Hampshire into Maine. Lists 15,000 names.

**2279 Secomb, Daniel F.** List of the centenarians of New Hampshire who have deceased since 1705. With sketches of many of them. Contoocook, N.H., 1877.

**2280 Sketches of successful New Hampshire men.** Manchester, N.H., 1882.
Many biographies.

**2281 Society of Colonial Wars. New Hampshire.** List of officers . . . list of members and lines of descent, index to ancestors. [Concord, N.H.], 1924.

**2282 Squires, James D.** The Granite state of the United States. A history of New Hampshire from 1623 to the present. 4v. New York, 1956.
v.3-4 has family and personal history.

**2283 Stackpole, Everett S.** History of New Hampshire. 4v. New York, 1916.

**2284 Stearns, Ezra S.** Genealogical and family history of the state of New Hampshire. 4v. New York, 1908.
Mug book.

**2285 Threlfall, John B.** Heads of families at the second census of the United States taken in the year 1800, New Hampshire. Madison, N.H.: The Compiler, 1974.
With notations and index where names are badly misspelled, as in original.

**2286 Towle, Laird C.** New Hampshire genealogical research guide. Bowie, Md.: Prince George's Genealogical Soc., 1973.
Description of records and their location. Good background information. *Prince George's Genealogical Soc. special publ.* 1.

**2287 U.S. Bureau of the Census.** Heads of the families at the first census of the United States taken in the year 1790. New Hampshire. 1907. Repr. Baltimore: G.P.C., 1966, etc.; Spartanburg, S.C.: Reprint Co., 1964, etc.

**2288 Waite, Otis F. R.** New Hampshire in the great rebellion, containing histories of the several New Hampshire regiments, and biographical notices of many of the prominent actors in the Civil War of 1861-65. Claremont, N.H., 1870.

2289 **Walling, Henry F.** Atlas of the state of New Hampshire; including statistics . . . topographical work under H. F. Stalling . . . New York, [1877].

2290 **Wight, Denman B.** The Androscoggin River Valley. Rutland, Vt.: Tuttle, 1967.
Detailed picture of the founding and development of the New England frontier area.

NEW JERSEY

Settled ca. 1660; original state
*New Jersey Historical Society, Newark*
*Public Library of Newark*
*State Library, Archives and History Bureau, Trenton*
*Dr. Kenn Stryker-Rodda, South Orange, N.J.*

2291 **Abstracts of wills.** *See* Calendar of New Jersey wills, no.2366.

2292 **Archives of the state of New Jersey.** 47v. 1880-1949. Trenton, N.J.: New Jersey State Library Archives and History Bureau.
1st ser. 42v.; 2nd ser. v.1-5; 3rd ser. v.1- .
The 3rd series started in 1974 and was called New Jersey archives. Some are in print; not all are genealogical. The most important genealogical works are listed separately. The half-title of this series is: Documents relating to the colonial history of New Jersey.

2293 **Bailey, Rosalie F.** Dutch systems in family naming: New York-New Jersey. *National Genealogical Soc. special publ.* 12. 2nd pr. Washington, D.C.: The Society, 1962.
Fine study of very difficult subject; many tables.

2294 ———— Pre-revolutionary Dutch houses and families in northern New Jersey and southern New York . . . 1936. Repr. New York: Dover, 1968.

2295 **Barber, John W.,** and **Howe, H.** Historical collections of New Jersey past and present. 1868. Repr. Spartanburg, S.C.: Reprint Co., 1966.

New Jersey 2305

1st ed. 1844; 1868 ed. chosen for reprinting because all 21 counties had been formed by 1868. There were subsequent boundary changes.

2296 **Bigelow, Samuel F.,** and **Hagar, J. G.** The biographical cyclopedia of New Jersey. New York, [1909].
Mug book.

2297 **Biographical encyclopaedia of New Jersey of the 19th century** . . . Philadelphia, 1877.

2298 **Board of General Proprietors of the Eastern Division of New Jersey.** Minutes from 1685-1764. 3v. Perth Amboy, N.J.: The Board, 1949.
v.1, 1685-1705; v.2, 1725-44; v.3, 1745-64.

2299 **Brown, William M.** Biographical, genealogical and descriptive history of the state of New Jersey . . . [Newark, N.J.], 1900.

2300 **Burr, Nelson R.** A narrative and descriptive bibliography of New Jersey. *New Jersey historical ser.*, v.21. Princeton, N.J., 1964.
Valuable list of county histories, most of which contain genealogical information, pp.82-99. All index references err by 1p.

2301 **Cape May county magazine of history and genealogy.** v.1- , 1931- .
Cape May, N.J.: Cape May Historical Soc.

2302 **Carlevale, Joseph W.** Americans of Italian descent in New Jersey. Clifton, N.J., 1950.
Contains over 3,000 biographical sketches from all walks of life.

2304 **Chambers, Theodore F.** The early Germans of New Jersey: their history, churches and genealogies. 1895. Repr. with a new introduction by K. Stryker-Rodda. Baltimore: G.P.C., 1969.
Also includes non-German families of Hunterdon, Morris, Somerset, and Sussex counties. Use with care.

2305 **Craig, H. Stanley.** [South Jersey publications, 1926-39. 15v.]

Concern marriage records, wills, genealogical data of Atlantic, Camden, Burlington, Cape May, Cumberland, Gloucester, and Salem counties. Some south Jersey marriages. None in print.

2306 **Cushing, Thomas**, and **Sheppard, C. E.** History of the counties of Gloucester, Salem, and Cumberland, New Jersey, with biographical sketches of their prominent citizens. New York, 1883. Index by Donald A. Sinclair will be published in 1975.

2308 **Cyclopedia of New Jersey biography** . . . 3v. Newark, N.J., 1916.

2309 **D.A.R. New Jersey.** A catalogue of books, pamphlets, typed manuscripts, microfilms, etc. pertaining to the genealogical records and D.A.R. data, contributed by the chapters. Compiled by Margaret E. Borden. Newark, N.J.: D.A.R., 1968.

2310 **Documents relating to the colonial history of New Jersey.** See Archives, no.2292.

2311 **Federal Writers' Project, W.P.A., New Jersey.** The records of the Swedish Lutheran churches at Raccoon and Penns Neck 1713-86. Transl. and compiled by Federal Writers' Project, to "commemorate the 300th anniversary of the settlement by the Swedes and Finns in the Delaware." Elizabeth, N.J., 1938.

2312 **Gannett, Henry.** A geographic dictionary of New Jersey. *Dept. of Interior. Bull. of the U.S. Geological Survey* 118. Washington, D.C., 1894.

2313 **Gardner, Charles C.** A genealogical dictionary of New Jersey. In *Genealogical magazine of New Jersey,* v.10-27, 1935-52.

2314 ———— New Jersey marriage licenses, 1727-34 (with additions to 1751). In *Genealogical magazine of New Jersey,* v.14-23, 1939-48.

2315 **Genealogical magazine of New Jersey.** v.1- , 1925- . New Brunswick, N.J.: Genealogical Soc. of New Jersey.

2316 ———— The first 35 years. The genealogical magazine of New Jersey. A subject and author index . . . to v.1-35, 1925-60. By Donald A. Sinclair. Newark, N.J.: The Society, 1962.

2317 ———— Index. v.1-30, 1925-55. By Kenn Stryker-Rodda. 2v. New Orleans, La: Polyanthos, 1973.
For the most part it supersedes Sinclair's index. Many cross references; a genealogical given-name index.

2318 **Gordon, Thomas F.** A gazetteer of the state of New Jersey. 1834. Repr. New Orleans, La.: Polyanthos, 1973.
Pt.1 explores boundaries; pt.2 has concise accounts of all towns and villages in New Jersey.

2319 **Hartlaub, Robert J.,** and **Miller, G. J.** Colonial conveyances, east and west Jersey, 1664-1794. 2v. Summit, N.J.: The Authors, 1974.
Invaluable to title searchers and historians.

2320 **Heston, Alfred M.** South Jersey, a history, 1664-1924. 5v. New York, 1924.
v.3-5 biographical.

2321 **Hinshaw, William W.** Encyclopedia of American Quaker genealogy. v.2. Containing every item of genealogical value found in all records and minutes . . . of four of the oldest monthly meetings which ever belonged to the Philadelphia yearly meeting of Friends. 1938. Repr. Baltimore: G.P.C., 1969.
Monthly meetings were held at Salem and Burlington (New Jersey) and Philadelphia and Falls (Pennsylvania), 1676-1938. A small fraction of extant Quaker records in New Jersey.

2322 **Historical Records Survey.** Directory of churches in New Jersey, v.1-6, 8-21 (v.7 not published). Newark, N.J., 1940-41.
v.7 was for Gloucester county.

2323 ——— Guide to naturalization records in New Jersey. Newark, N.J., 1941.

2324 ——— Guide to vital statistics records in New Jersey. 2v. Public archives and church archives. Newark, N.J., 1941-42.

2325 ——— Inventory of the church archives of New Jersey. 11v. Newark, N.J., 1938-41.
Includes Baptists, Presbyterians, Protestant Episcopal and other bodies.

2326 ——— Inventory of the county archives of New Jersey. 4v. Newark, N.J., 1937-40.
Only the following numbers were published: 2 (Bergen), 14 (Morris), 15 (Ocean), and 16 (Passaic). Unpublished material deposited in State Library, Trenton, N.J.

2327 ——— Transcriptions of early church records of New Jersey, 2v. Newark, N.J., 1940-41.
American Tract Society (1841-61), and John Brainerd's journals, 1761-62.

2328 **Honeyman, Abraham Van D.** Northwestern New Jersey . . . 4v. Plainfield, N.J., 1927.
History of Somerset, Morris, Hunterdon, Warren, and Sussex counties. v.3-4 biographical; coats of arms.

2329 **Huguenot Society of New Jersey.** Huguenot ancestors represented in the membership of the Huguenot Society of New Jersey. 2nd ed. compiled by Sara M. Koehler. Bloomfield, N.J.: The Society, 1956.
To be superseded in 1975.

2330 **The Jerseyman:** a quarterly magazine of local history and genealogy, principally of Hunterdon county, New Jersey. v.1-11. Flemington, N.J., 1891-1905.
Numerous family genealogies concerning the whole of New Jersey. Church, naturalization, and other records.

2331 **Johnson, Maud E.** Genealogical-index to books, pamphlets, manuscripts, etc. in the New Jersey Historical Society Library. Originally in *Proc. of the New Jersey Historical Soc.* 7, no.2, 1923. Newark, N.J., 1923.

2332 ——— ——— Supplementary list. 1923-29. *Proc.* 14, no.11, 1929.

2333 **Jones, Edward A.** The loyalists of New Jersey; their memorials, petitions, claims, etc. from English records. *New Jersey Historical Soc. collections,* v.10, 1927. Repr. Boston: Gregg, 1973.
Short biographical sketches, occupations, ethnic origins, and military service.

2334 **Knittle, Walter A.** Early eighteenth century Palatine emigration. 1937. Repr. Baltimore: G.P.C., 1970.
Concerns New York primarily and New Jersey. Annotation *see* no.2483.

2335 **Kull, Irving S.** New Jersey, a history. 6v. New York, 1930-32.
v.5-6 biographical and genealogical records.

2336 **Lee, Francis S.** Genealogical and memorial history of the state of New Jersey. 4v. New York, 1910.
Inaccurate; use with care.

2337 **Leiby, Adrian C.** The early Dutch and Swedish settlers of New Jersey. *New Jersey historical ser.* v.10. Princeton, N.J., 1964.
Shows influence of Dutch and Swedes on development of state.

2338 **Littell, John.** Family records; or, genealogies of the first settlers of the Passaic Valley (and vicinity), above Chatham, with their ancestors and descendants. Feltville, N.J., 1851.
No documentation, few dates, but good clues. Covers parts of six counties.

2339 **McKinstry, Edward Richard.** A guide to genealogical sources in the New Jersey Historical Soc. Library. Newark, N.J.: The Society, 1974.
Invaluable for details of manuscript and typescript sources.

2340 **Memorial cyclopedia of New Jersey.** Under the editorial supervision

of Mary D. Ogden. 3v. Newark, N.J., 1915–17.
Mug book.

**2341 Monnette, Orra E.** First settlers of ye plantation of Piscataway and Woodbridge, olde east New Jersey, 1664–1714. 7 pts. Los Angeles, 1930–35.
Head of title, v.4–7: *Colonial and provincial history and genealogy.* Collection of material of varied quality. Coats of arms.

**2342 Myers, William S.** The story of New Jersey; New York. 5v. New York, 1945.
v.4–5 biographical.

**2343 Nelson, William.** Over a period of years William Nelson, of the New Jersey State Archives, edited several works, and they have often become identified with his name. Unless actually compiled or written by Nelson, all official records are under title.

**2344** —— Calendar of records in the office of the Secretary of State, 1664–1703. Documents relating to the colonial history of New Jersey. *Archives of the state of New Jersey,* ser. 1, 21. Paterson, N.J., 1899. Obtainable from State Library, Trenton, N.J.
Mainly concerns patents and deeds prior to the Proprietors' surrender of the government to Queen Anne in 1703.

**2345** —— Church records in New Jersey. Paterson, N.J., 1904.
Originally published in *Journal of the Presbyterian Historical Soc.,* 1904. Notices of character, extent, and condition of original records of about 150 of the old churches and Friends' meetings, with other data.

**2346** —— Extracts from American newspapers relating to New Jersey, 1704–1775. *New Jersey archives,* ser.1, v.11, 12, 19, 20, 24–29, 31. Paterson, N.J. [and elsewhere]: New Jersey Historical Soc., 1894–1923.

**2347** —— —— 1776–82. *New Jersey archives,* ser.2, v.1–5. Trenton, N.J.: New Jersey Historical Soc., 1901–17.
All in print.

**2348** —— Nelson's Biographical cyclopedia of New Jersey. 2v. New York, 1913.

**2349** —— New Jersey biographical and genealogical notes from the volumes of the New Jersey archives, with additions and supplements. *New Jersey Historical Soc. collections,* v.9. Newark, N.J., 1916. Repr. Baltimore: G.P.C., 1973
224 families covered with extensive information.

**2350** —— The New Jersey coast in three centuries; history of the New Jersey coast with genealogical and historic-biographical appendix. 3v. New York, 1902.

**2351** —— New Jersey marriage records, 1665–1800. *Archives of the state of New Jersey,* ser.1, v.22. 1900. Repr. Baltimore: G.P.C., 1973.
Original title: *Documents relating to the colonial history of the state of New Jersey. Marriage records, 1665–1800.*

**2352** —— Personal names of Indians of New Jersey, being a list of 650 such names, gleaned mostly from Indian deeds of the 17th century. Paterson, N.J., 1904.

**2353 New Jersey. Adjutant General's Office.** Records of officers and men of New Jersey in wars, 1791–1815. 1909. Repr. Baltimore: G.P.C., 1970.
Greater portion devoted to War of 1812. Full names and service records of over 10,000 soldiers and officers.

**2354** —— Register of commissioned officers of the New Jersey volunteers in the service of the United States. 2v. Trenton, N.J., 1864–65.
Civil War.

**2355 New Jersey archives.** See *Archives of the state of New Jersey,* no.2292.

**2356 New Jersey (Colony).** The Burlington note book; a record of Quaker jurisprudence in west New Jersey 1680–1709. Ed. by H. C. Reed and G. J. Miller. *American Historical Assoc. American legal records,* 5. Washington, D.C., 1944.

**2357** **New Jersey. Dept. of State.** New Jersey index of wills, inventories, etc., in the office of the Secretary of State prior to 1901. 3v. 1913. Repr. with a foreword by K. Stryker-Rodda. Baltimore: G.P.C., 1969.
Original title: *Index of wills* . . . 185,000 entries. The difference between no.2357 and no.2358 is in name order; 2357 is by county and has fuller information; 2358 has in v.1 (1705-1804) recorded copies of wills for east and west Jersey, not originals as in 2357, which goes to 1900. v.2 (1804-30) of 2358 has name, county, will or intestate, and year.

**2358** ——— Index of wills, 1705-1830. 2v. Trenton, N.J., 1901. *See* note under no.2357.

**2359** **New Jersey. State Library Archives and History Bureau.** Archives of the state of New Jersey. *See Archives of the state of New Jersey*, no.2292.

**2360** ——— Genealogical research: a guide to source materials in the Archives and History Bureau and other agencies. Published by the Genealogical Soc. of New Jersey for the state. Free. Appears sporadically.

**2361** **New Jersey archives.** *See Archives of the State of New Jersey*, no.2292.

**2362** **New Jersey family index:** old New Jersey families and their genealogies. v.1- , 1955- . Ed. by Harold A. Sonn. Short Hills, N.J.

**2363** **New Jersey genesis.** v.1- , 1953- . New York City: Mrs. Carl M. Nissen, editor.
Genealogical and historical data of early New Jersey.

**2364** ——— Index 1953-71. Albuquerque, N. Mex.: Hermosa Pub., 1973. Includes every name mentioned.

**2365** **New Jersey Historical Society collections.** v.1-14, 1846-65. Newark, N.J.: The Society.
Only v.9, 10 (no.2349, 2333) are genealogical.

**2366** ——— Calendar of New Jersey wills and administrations 1670-1817. 13v. *Archives of the State of New Jersey,* ser.1, v.23, 30, 32-42. Paterson, N.J., [and elsewhere], 1901-49.
Series often referred to as *Abstract of wills* and is so marked on the spines. Period covered by whole ser. 1670-1817. Following are in print, from the Society or the State Library, Trenton, N.J.: v.23, 30 (1670-1750), v.32-34 (1751-1800), v.36-41 (1786-1813).

**2367** ——— Proceedings. v.1-84. Newark, N.J.: The Society, 1845-1966.
Continued as *New Jersey history,* which has no genealogy. The proceedings have a fair amount of genealogy up to 1951. ser.1, v.1-10 (1845-66); ser.2, v.1-13 (1867-95); ser.3, v.1-10 (1896-1915); new ser., v.1-16 (1916-31); v.50- . v.1-6 repr. by Kraus, N.Y., 1968; Subject index, v.1-36 (1845-1919) is published in *Proceedings,* 1920; 1920-31 in v.61, 1943.

**2368** **Norton, James S.** New Jersey in 1793. Salt Lake City: Inst. of Family Research, 1973.
Abstract and index of the 1793 militia of men (18-45) who had not served in Revolutionary War or another state militia. 30,000 entries. Tax rateables for the period substituted for missing lists in three counties.

**2369** **Owens, Marguerite D.,** and **Tanco, B. O.** 1850 census of New Jersey. v.1- , 1973- . Arlington, Tex.: The Authors.
v.1, Atlantic, Bergen, Burlington; v.2, Gloucester, Hunterdon, Hudson; v.3, Sussex, Ocean. In progress.

**2370** **Ricard, Frederick W.** Biographical encyclopedia. Successful men of New Jersey. New York, 1896.
Mug book.

**2371** **Rogers, Mrs. Harry,** and **Lane, Mrs. A. H.** Abstracts of New Jersey commissions in the Secretary of State's office at Trenton, 1703-69.
In *Publ. of the Genealogical Soc. of Pennsylvania,* v.6-10, 1917-29.

**2372  Scannell, John J.** Scannell's New Jersey's first citizens and state guide . . . genealogies and biographies of citizens of New Jersey . . . Compiled under the auspices of the New Jersey Genealogical and Biographical Society. 6v. Paterson, N.J., 1917-27.

**2373  Schmidt, Hubert G.** The Germans in colonial New Jersey. In *New Jersey genesis,* v.4-5, 1956-58.
Annotated list of German families and individuals known to have lived in New Jersey before 1801, most of whom arrived there after 1714.

**2374  Shelley, Fred.** A guide to the manuscripts collection of the New Jersey Historical Society. Newark, N. J., 1957.
Originally issued as v.11 of the *Collections of the New Jersey Historical Soc.* Being updated for publication in 1975.

**2375  Shourds, Thomas.** History and genealogy of Fenwick's colony. Bridgeton, N. J., 1876.

**2376**  ———  ——— Index compiled and published privately by Elizabeth Livermore. Ann Arbor, Mich., 1962.
Concerns Salem county.

**2377  Smith, Herbert F.** A guide to the manuscript collections of the Rutgers University Library. New Brunswick, N. J.: The Library, 1964.
Many names.

**2378  Snyder, John P.** The story of New Jersey's civil boundaries, 1606-1968. Trenton, N.J.: Bureau of Geology and Topography, 1969.
Definitive work on New Jersey's boundaries; excellent maps.

**2379  Society of Mayflower Descendants. New Jersey.** Lineages (no.1-1065) from August 15, 1900, date chartered by the General Society of Mayflower Descendants, to February 3, 1973. Compiled by Walter H. Kitchell. Lakewood, N. J.: The Society, 1973.

**2380  Somerset county historical quarterly.** v.1-8. 1912-19. Somerville, N. J.

Many records of Somerset and some of Hunterdon. Transcripts, especially of cemetery inscriptions, somewhat inaccurate.

**2381  Stewart, Frank H.** Stewart's genealogical and historical miscellany. no.1-2. 1918. Repr. Woodbury, N. J.: Gloucester County Historical Soc., 1969-71.
Wealth of information on southern New Jersey. Comprehensive index of names.

**2382  Stillwell, John E.** Historical and genealogical miscellany: data relating to the settlement and settlers of New York and New Jersey. 5v.1903-32. Repr. Baltimore: G.P.C., 1970.
Valuable set. Contains registers not normally known, or available in print; also New Jersey records and families. New York is poorly represented. v.1-2, records relating to Staten Island and New Jersey; 3-5, early families of New Jersey, principally of Monmouth and Burlington counties.

**2383  Stryker, William S.** Official register of the officers and men of New Jersey in the Revolutionary War. 1872. Repr. with James W. S. Campbell's digest and revision . . . 1911. Baltimore: G.P.C., 1967.

**2384**  ———  ——— Index prepared by W.P.A. 1941. Repr.: Baltimore: G.P.C., 1965.
Contains 15,000 names, many with multiple listings.

**2385**  ——— Record of officers and men of New Jersey in the Civil War, 1861-65. 2v. Trenton, N. J., 1876.

**2386  Stryker-Rodda, Kenn.** New Jersey: digging for ancestors in the Garden state. Detroit, Mich.: Detroit Soc. for Genealogical Research, 1970.
Good description and bibliography.

**2387**  ——— New Jersey rateables, 1773-74. In *The genealogical magazine of New Jersey,* v.36-40, 1961-65.

**2388**  ———  ——— 1778-80. In *The genealogical magazine of New Jersey* v.41- , 1966- (in progress).

**2389** ——— Revolutionary census of New Jersey: an index based on rateables, of the inhabitants of New Jersey during the period of the American Revolution. New Orleans, La.: Polyanthos, 1972.

Monumental index to heads of families and single men 1773-84. More comprehensive than any earlier census. Substitute for the missing 1790 census.

**2390 Vineland historical magazine:** devoted to history, biography, genealogy. v.1- , 1916- . Vineland, N. J. Vineland Historical and Antiquarian Soc.

South Jersey information.


NEW MEXICO

Settled ca. 1605; entered Union 1912

*Albuquerque Public Library*

**2391 Abousleman, Michael D.** Who's who in New Mexico. Biographical sketches of contemporary New Mexicans. v.1 (all pub.). Albuquerque, N. Mex., 1937.

**2392 Adams, Eleanor B.,** and **Chavez, A.** The missions of New Mexico, 1776. A description by F. A. Dominguez, with other contemporary documents. [Santa Fe, N. Mex.], 1956.

Important source of early New Mexico genealogy and history.

**2393 Anderson, George B.** History of New Mexico; its resources and people. 2v. Los Angeles, 1907.

v.2 is biographical. Emphasis on American pioneers who came after the Civil War and during the 1800s and 1890s.

**2394 Beck, Warren A.,** and **Haase, Y. D.** Historical atlas of New Mexico. Norman, Okla.: Univ. of Oklahoma Pr., 1969.

Excellent reference tool.

**2395 Bowden, Jocelyn J.** Spanish and Mexican land grants in the Chihuahuan acquisition. El Paso, Tex.: Texas Western Pr., Univ. of Texas at El Paso, 1971.

**2396 Clark, Ann (Nolan).** These were the valiant; a collection of New Mexico profiles. Albuquerque, N. Mex., 1969.

Revision of series of articles published originally in *New Mexico magazine.*

**2397 Coan, Charles F.** A history of New Mexico. 3v. Chicago, 1925. v.2 biographical.

**2398 A comprehensive business directory of New Mexico and gazetteer of the territory for 1882.** Santa Fe, N. Mex., 1882.

**2399 Crocchiola, Stanley F. L.** (or F. Stanley, *pseud.).* [Town histories of New Mexico.] [Nazareth, Tex.] 1962-69.

Almost 100 town histories in pamphlet form, 18-36pp.

**2399a D.A.R. New Mexico State Organization.** History, 1894-1971. v.1-2. Santa Fe, N. Mex.: Mary P. Bonnie (601 W. Mateo Rd., Apt. 28, 87501), 1974.

v.1, 1894-1957, is out of print, so highlights of v.1 are included in v.2.

**2400 Davis, Ellis A.** The historical encyclopedia of New Mexico. Albuquerque, N. Mex., 1945.

**2401 Federal census: territory of New Mexico and territory of Arizona.** Washington, D.C.: U.S. Govt., 1965.

Excerpted from decennial federal census 1860 for Arizona county, in the territory of New Mexico . . . Senate doc.13, 89th Cong. 1st sess.

**2402 Historical Records Survey.** Directory of churches and religious organizations in New Mexico. Albuquerque, N. Mex., 1940.

**2403** ——— Guide to public vital statistics records in New Mexico. Albuquerque, N. Mex., 1942.

**2404** ——— Inventory of the county archives of New Mexico. 15v. Albuquerque, N. Mex., 1937-42.

Only the following numbers were pub-

## United States

lished: 1 (Bernalillo), 4 (Colfax), 7 (Dona Ana), 8 (Eddy), 9 (Grant), 12 (Hidalgo), 15 (Luna), 17 (Mora), 18 (Otero), 23 (Sandoval), 24 (San Miguel), 26 (Sierra), 29 (Torrance), 30 (Union) and 31 (Valencia). Unpublished material deposited in State Museum, Sante Fe., N. Mex.

**2405** **An illustrated history of New Mexico** . . . from the earliest period . . . together with . . . biographical mention of many of its pioneers and prominent citizens of today. Chicago, 1895.

**2406** **Koogler, Clare V.,** and **Whitney, V. K.** Aztec: a story of old Aztec from Anasazi to statehood. Fort Worth, Tex.: Miran, 1972.
Comprehensive history of the early settlement of the early settlement of San Juan county. Biographies of many early settlers.

**2407** **Lee, Susan E.** These also served; brief histories of persons; short stories and pictures relative to Catron, Grant, Sierra, Socorro and Valencia counties of New Mexico. Los Lunas, N. Mex., 1960.

**2408** **New Mexico Folklore Society. Place-name Committee.** New Mexico place-name dictionary. 3pts. Albuquerque, N. Mex., 1949-51.
Each annual collection lists from 138 to 334 names.

**2409** **New Mexico genealogist.** v.1– , 1962– . Albuquerque, N. Mex.: New Mexico Genealogical Soc.
Contains census, cemetery, and other records.

**2410** **Old Santa Fe,** a magazine of history, archives, genealogy, and biography. Ed. by R. E. Twitchell. v.1-3, no.1-12. Santa Fe, N. Mex., 1913-16.

**2411** **Pearce, Thomas M.** New Mexico place names. A geographical dictionary. Albuquerque, N. Mex.: Univ. of New Mexico Pr., 1965.

**2412** **Peterson, Charles S.** Representative New Mexicans. Denver, Colo., 1912.
Who's who of important men of New Mexico at the time of statehood, 1912.

**2413** **Read, Benjamin M.** Illustrated history of New Mexico. Santa Fe, N. Mex., 1912.
Biographies, pp.726-92.

**2414** **Reeve, Franklin D.** History of New Mexico. 3v. West Palm Beach, Fla., 1961.
v.3 biographical. Most recent work of biographical information on many important New Mexicans.

**2415** **Santa Fe, New Mexico (Archdiocese).** Archives, 1678-1900. Compiled by Angelico Chavez. *Academy of American Franciscan History, bibliographical ser.* 3. Washington, D.C., 1957.
Information on Spanish families: official church records, baptisms, marriages, etc. Archives are located in Santa Fe, N. Mex.

**2416** **Sante Fe. Historical Society of New Mexico.** Origins of New Mexico families in the Spanish colonial period. Compiled by Angelico Chavez. 1954. Repr. Albuquerque N. Mex.: Univ. of Albuquerque, 1973.
Supplements published in *El palacio* (Museum of New Mexico, Santa Fe), 1955-57. Most comprehensive study of family information available. Descendants of earliest Spanish colonizers; those who came with Oñate in 1598 and those with De Vargas in 1693. Covers period 1598-1821 in 2 pts.: 1598-1693; 1693-1821. Essential.

**2417** **Sherman, James E.,** and **Sherman, B. H.** Ghost towns and mining camps of New Mexico. Norman, Okla.: Univ. of Oklahoma Pr., 1974.
Brief history of each town and camp, with dates of establishment and abandonment of post offices. Good maps.

**2418** **Simpson, James H.** Navaho expedition: journal of a military reconnaissance from Santa Fe, New Mexico to Navaho county made in 1849. Ed. by Frank McNitt. Norman, Okla.: Univ. of Oklahoma Pr., 1964.
Background on principals, short sketches

on muster roll; family background of more prominent officers and men. Originally pub. in 1850 as a government document.

**2419  Twitchell, Ralph E.** The Spanish archives of New Mexico; compiled and chronologically arranged with historical genealogical notes, etc. Cedar Rapids, Iowa, 1914.
Taken from church and government records from the earliest Spanish times. Very detailed. Archives are in Museum of New Mexico, Santa Fe. Coats of arms.

NEW YORK

Settled ca. 1614; original state
*New York Genealogical and Biographical Society*
*New-York Historical Society*
*New York Public Library*
*New York State Historical Association, Cooperstown*
*Syracuse Public Library*
*University of the State of New York at Albany*
Mrs. Mary K. Meyer, Maryland Historical Society, Baltimore
Dr. Kenn Stryker-Rodda, South Orange, N. J.

**2420  An account of Her Majesty's revenue in the Province of New York, 1701-09.** The customs records of early colonial New York. Ed. by Julius M. Bloch (and others). Boston: Gregg, 1967.

**2421  Albany County, New York.** Early records of the city and county of Albany, and colony of Rensselaerswyck . . . Transl. from the original Dutch by Jonathan Pearson . . . rev. and ed. by Arnold J. F. van Laer. 4v. 1869-1919. Repr. Ann Arbor, Mich.: Xerox Univ. Microfilms, 1973.
v.2-4 known as *Early records of Albany,* 1916-19. Contains deeds, 1678-1704; mortgages, 1658-1660, and wills, 1681-1765.

**2422  ——— Court of Albany.** Minutes of the Court of Albany, Rensselaerswyck, and Schenectady; ed. by Arnold J. F. van Laer. 3v. Albany, N.Y., 1926-32.
A continuation of the minutes of the court of Fort Orange and Beverswyck. v.1, 1675-80; v.2, 1680-85; v.3, 1668-73.

**2423  Bailey, Rosalie F.** Dutch systems in family naming: New-York–New Jersey. *National Genealogical Soc. special publ.* 12. 2nd pr. Washington, D.C.: The Society, 1962.
Fine study of very difficult subject; many tables.

**2424  ———** Guide to genealogical and biographical sources for New York City (Manhattan), 1783-1898. New York, 1954.
Reprinted with revisions from the *New England historical and genealogical register,* v.106-8, 1952-54. Useful as a guide throughout the state.

**2425  ———** Pre-revolutionary Dutch houses and families in northern New Jersey and southern New York . . . 1936. Repr. New York: Dover, 1968.
Much of interest to genealogists.

**2426  Barber, John W.,** and **Howe, H.** Historical collections of the state of New York . . . 1846. Repr. Port Washington, N.Y.: Kennikat Pr., 1970.
Collection of facts, traditions, biographical sketches and geographical description of every township.

**2427  Barck, Dorothy C.** Some references for genealogical searching in New York state. 2nd pr. Detroit, Mich., 1960.
Excellent list, subject-classified.

**2428  Bayer, Henry G.** The Belgians, first settlers in New York and in the middle states . . . New York, 1925.
Walloons in New York. Use with care.

**2429  Beach, Moses T.** Wealth and biography of the wealthy citizens of the city of New York; being . . . the names of the most prominent capitalists . . . and genealogical and biographical notices of the principal persons . . . ed.13 (probably the last). New York, 1855.

**2430  Bergen, Teunis G.** Genealogies of the state of New York—Long Island ed. 3v. New York, 1915.

2431 ———— Register in alphabetical order, of the early settlers of Kings county, Long Island . . . from its first settlement by Europeans to 1700; with contributions to their biographies and genealogies, compiled from various sources. 1881 Repr. with introduction by Harriet M. Stryker-Rodda. New Orleans, La.: Polyanthos, 1973.
Mrs. Stryker-Rodda's introduction is required reading for those studying Dutch families in New York area.

2432 **Berkenmeyer, Wilhelm C.** The Albany Protocol; Wilhelm Christoph Berkenmeyer's chronicle of Lutheran affairs in New York colony, 1731–50 . . . Ed. by John P. Dern. Ann Arbor, Mich.: The Editor, Redwood City, Calif., 1971.
pp.544–643 genealogies, charts, bibliography, indexes.

2433 **Bien, Joseph R.** Atlas of the state of New York. New York, 1895.
Includes locations of the original large land grants.

2434 **Birmingham, Stephen.** "Our crowd"; the great Jewish families of New York. New York: Harper & Row, 1967.
Readable and interesting account, with interrelationships unravelled. Genealogical tables.

2435 **Carman, Harry J.,** and **Thompson, A. W.** A guide to the principal sources for American civilization 1800–1900 in the city of New York—manuscripts. New York: Columbia Univ. Pr., 1970.
Includes records prior to 1800.

2436 **Census of the counties of Orange, Dutches [sic], and Albany, 1702, 1714 and 1720.** 1849. Repr. Philadelphia, 1941.

2437 **Colonial Dames of America. New York.** Catalogue of the genealogical and historical library. Compiled by L. Green. 1912. Repr. Ann Arbor, Mich.: Gryphon Books, 1971.
Little out of date, but it pinpoints family genealogies buried in larger works; 7,500 items.

2438 **Cousin huntin.** v.1– , 1961– . Syracuse, N.Y.: Central New York Genealogical Soc.
From v.13, 1973 issued with *Tree talks,* no.2556.

2439 **Cutter, William R.** The following works on New York state, all pub. in New York, with the title, "Genealogical and family history of . . ." were compiled by Cutter. For a consolidated index of these and other Cutter books, *see* Ireland and Irving, no.593.

2440 ———— Central New York. 3v. 1912.

2441 ———— Northern New York. 3v. 1910.

2442 ———— Southern New York and Hudson River Valley. 3v. 1913.

2443 ———— Western New York. 3v. 1912.
Content often contradictory; use with care.

2444 **Cutts, Dorothy R.** Aids to place names: New York state townships and counties. Orange, Calif.: Orange County California Genealogical Soc., 1973.
Index prepared to assist researchers with locality. Does not supersede French, no.2456a.

2445 **D.A.R. New York.** Master index, genealogical records. Buffalo, N.Y.: R. E. Theobald, D.A.R., 1972.
More than 24,000 names contained in records copied by members. Valuable tool for New York and other researchers.

2446 **Disturnell, John.** A gazetteer of the state of New York . . . 2nd ed. Albany, N.Y., 1843.

2447 **Documents relative to the colonial history of the state of New York.** 15v. 1853–87. Repr. New York: A.M.S. Press, 1969.
v.1–11 ed. by E. B. O'Callaghan; v.12–15 by B. Fernow; v.11 is index to v.1–10. v.12–15 have title *Documents relating to*

... From Dutch, English, and French documents. Major source work for study of colonial times.

**2448** [**Dutch Reformed churches**] Holland Society of New York yearbook, 1912, contains a list of records of 52 in New York state, 20 in New Jersey, and 2 in Pennsylvania; 1 French Reformed; 2 German Reformed; 2 Dutch Lutheran; and 3 German Lutheran churches, transcripts of which are in the Holland Society. Some have been published in *Yearbooks* 1891, 1896-99, 1901, 1903-1908, 1913-16, 1924-28. New York.

**2449** **The Dutch Settlers Society of Albany yearbooks, 1924/5–** . Albany, N.Y.: Harry E. Veeder.
Records and genealogies of early settlers of Albany area. All in print.

**2450** **Evjen, John O.** Scandinavian immigrants in New York, 1630-74, with appendices on some Scandinavians in Mexico and South America, 1532-1640, Scandinavians in Canada, 1619-20, some Scandinavians in New York in the 18th century; German immigrants in New York, 1630-74. 1916. Repr. Baltimore: G.P.C., 1972.
Some transcripts and ascriptions incorrect; use with caution. Biographical articles on Norwegian, Danish, and Swedish immigrants.

**2451** **Federal census, 1800.** New York state. In *New York genealogical and biographical record*.
Dutchess, v.65-69; Kings, v.55; Montgomery, v.49-50; Onondaga, v.53; Orange, v.62-64; Queens, v.54; Richmond, v.60; Rockland, v.61, 63; Steuben, v.60; Suffolk, v.55-57; Tioga, v.59-60; Westchester, v.57-59. The census was published 1918-38.

**2452** **Fernow, Berthold.** New Amsterdam family names and their origin. New York, 1898.

**2453** ——— [New York] Calendar of wills on file and recorded in the offices of the clerk of the Court of Appeals, of the county clerk at Albany, and of the Secretary of State, 1626-1836 . . . 1896. Repr. Baltimore: G.P.C., 1967.
Abstracts of over 2,000 New York wills, mostly of Hudson River Valley. Index has more than 15,000 names.

**2454** ——— New York in the Revolution. v.1 of *New York state archives* and v.15 of *Documents relating to the colonial history of the state of New York.* 1887. Repr. with new introduction by Kenn Stryker-Rodda. New Orleans, La.: Polyanthos, 1972.
Standard work for the history and genealogy of New York state during the Revolution. Fine list of state troops. Contains muster rolls of the New York line, New Yorkers in the Navy, levies and militia and roster of state troops, casualties, state pensioners, etc.

**2455** **Foley, Janet W.** Early settlers of New York state, their ancestors and descendants, 9v. Akron, N.Y., 1934-42.
Title varies. Excellent for western and central New York, but with insufficient documentation. Originally published as a periodical.

**2456** ——— ——— Index to names. Akron, N.Y., 1937-50?

**2456a** **French, John H.** Gazetteer of the state of New York. 1860. Repr. Port Washington, N.Y.: Kennikat Pr., 1969.

**2457** ——— ——— Index to personal names. Compiled by Frank Place II. Cortland, N.Y.: Cortland County Historical Soc., 1962.

**2458** ——— ——— [Supplementary index to places. Albany, N.Y.: Univ. of the State of New York, 1966.]
French, 1860 (no.2456a) is best of five gazetteers published 1813-72. Place (no. 2457) contains a guide to 18,000 personal names, with a 15p. suppl. by D. Raymoure. Gazetteer and indexes indispensable.

**2459** **Greene, Nelson.** History of Mohawk Valley . . . 1614-1925. 4v. Chicago, 1925.
v.3-4 biographical.

**2460** ——— History of Valley of the Hudson . . . 1609–1930 . . . covering sixteen New York State Hudson River counties. 5v. Chicago, 1931.
v.3–5 biographical.

**2461 Haiman, Miecislaus.** Poles in New York in the seventeenth and eighteenth centuries. 1938. Repr. San Francisco: R. and E. Research Assoc., 1970.

**2462 De Halve Maen.** v.1– , 1922– . New York: Holland Soc. of New York. Has items of interest to Dutch in New York.

**2463 Hamm, Margherita A.** Famous families of New York . . . 2v. New York, 1902.
Good mug book. Based on series of articles originally appearing in *New York Evening Post.*

**2464 Harrison, Mitchell C.** New York state's prominent and progressive men. 3v. New York, 1900–1902.
Has many photographs of individuals.

**2465 Hasse, Adelaide R.** Some materials for a bibliography of the official publications of the General Assembly of the Colony of New York, 1693–1775. New York, 1903.
About 1,000 titles. Repr. from the *New York Public Lib. bull.,* 1903.

**2466 Hershkowitz, Leo.** The wills of early New York Jews (1704–99). *Studies in American Jewish history* 4. Waltham, Mass.: American Jewish Historical Soc., 1967.
Covers Jews and Christians and not entirely confined to New York. Concerns also South Carolina, New England, and the British West Indies. Primary research and reference guide.

**2467 Hinshaw, William W.** Encyclopedia of American Quaker genealogy, v.3. Containing every item of genealogical value found in all records and minutes (known to be in existence) of all meetings of all grades ever organized in New York city and on Long Island (1657 to the present time) . . . 1940. Repr. Baltimore: G.P.C., 1969.

**2468 Historical Records Survey.** Guide to depositories of manuscript collections in New York state (exclusive of New York city), with supplement. New York, 1941–44.

**2469** ———Guide to public vital statistics records in New York state, including New York city. 3v. Albany, N.Y., 1942.

**2470** ——— Guide to vital statistics records in the city of New York: churches. 5v. New York, 1942.
For Bronx, Brooklyn, Manhattan, Queens, and Richmond.

**2471** ——— Guide to vital statistics records of churches in New York state (exclusive of New York city). 2v. Albany, N.Y., 1942.
Arranged by counties.

**2472** ——— Inventory of the church archives of New York city. 9v. New York, 1939–41.
Eastern Orthodox, Lutheran, Methodist, Presbyterian, Protestant Episcopal, Roman Catholic, and Society of Friends.

**2473** ——— Inventory of the church archives of New York state. 2v. New York, 1939–41.
Protestant Episcopal, western New York and Rochester.

**2474** ——— Inventory of the county archives, New York city. 3v. New York, 1939–42.
Only the following numbers were published: 1 (Bronx), 2 (Kings), and 5 (Richmond borough and county). Unpublished material deposited in Municipal Reference Library, New York city.

**2475** ——— Inventory of the county archives in New York state. 6v. New York, 1937–40.
Only the following numbers were published: 1 (Albany), 3 (Broome), 4 (Cattaraugus), 6 (Chautauqua), 7 (Chemung), and 51 (Ulster). Unpublished material deposited in State Library, Albany, N.Y.

**2476 Holland Society of New York.** *See* no.2448.

**2477 Hotchkin, James H.** A history of the purchase and settlement of western New York, and of the rise, progress, and present state of the Presbyterian Church . . . New York, 1848.

**2478 Hough, Franklin B.** American biographical notes, being short notices of deceased persons, chiefly those not included in Allen's or in Drake's biographical dictionaries . . . Albany, 1875.
National in scope; many are death notices from upstate New York newspapers.

**2479 Indentures of apprentices,** 1718–27, as contained in *Collections of the New-York Historical Soc.,* v.42. New York, 1909.

**2480** ———— 1694–1707. *New-York Historical Soc. collections publ. fund,* v.18. New York, 1886.
Transcripts complete and verbatim.

**2481 Innes, John H.** New Amsterdam and its people. 1902. Repr. Port Washington, N.Y.: Kennikat Pr., 1969.
Inhabitants street by street as of 1655, some earlier or later.

**2482 Kimball, Francis P.** The capital register of New York state, crossroads of empire. 3v. New York, 1942.
v.3 biographical.

**2483 Knittle, Walter A.** Early eighteenth century Palatine emigration. 1937. Repr. Baltimore: G.P.C., 1970.
Includes ships lists 1709; Simmendinger's register 1717; Roman Catholic Palatines returning to Holland 1709; New York subsistence list 1710–11. Concerns New York primarily and New Jersey slightly. 12,000 names. Knittle and MacWethy (no. 2489) differ in their transcripts of the records; both should be consulted.

**2484 Lamb, Wallace E.** The Lake Champlain and Lake George Valleys. 3v. New York, 1940.
v.3 biographical.

**2485 Landon, Harry F.** The north country. 3v. Indianapolis, Ind. 1932.
v.2–3 biographical. Covers Jefferson, St. Lawrence, Oswego, Lewis, and Franklin counties.

**2486 LeFevre, Ralph.** History of New Paltz, New York, and its old families (from 1678 to 1820). 2nd ed. 1909. Repr. Batimore: G.P.C., 1973.
Definitive history of New Paltz, one of the oldest Huguenot settlements. Has large appendix bringing down the history of certain families to 1850. Several thousand entries.

**2487 Long Island, New York.** Rate lists of Long Island, 1675, 1676, and 1683. In *Documentary history of the state of New-York,* v.2, pp.251–314, 439–542.

**2488 McMullin, Phillip W.** New York in 1800: an index to the federal census schedules of the state of New York, with other aids to research. Provo, Utah, 1971. Available from Everton.
Useful tool which can be studied alone to determine the county of residence, or as index to contents of 8 rolls of microfilm of original census. Charts and maps showing the 30 counties in 1800 and 62 in 1971. 100,000 names.

**2489 MacWethy, Lou D.** The book of names especially relating to the early Palatines and the first settlers in the Mohawk Valley. 1933. Repr. Baltimore: G.P.C., 1969.
Includes Revolutionary War lists. Passenger lists are the Kochertal records, Governor Hunter's ration lists, London lists, etc. MacWethy and Knittle (no.2483) differ in their transcripts of the records; both should be consulted.

**2490 Malone, Harry R.** History of central New York, embracing Cayuga, Seneca, Wayne, Ontario, Tompkins, Schuyler, Yates, Chemung, Steuben, and Tioga counties. 3v. Indianapolis, Ind., 1932.
Mug book, v.2–3 genealogical.

**2491 Mather, Frederic G.** The refugees of 1766 from Long Island to Connecticut. 1913. Repr. Baltimore: G.P.C., 1972.

Service records, complete lists of Long Island militia, and Long Island census of 1776. Genealogies of Long Island families. 20,000 names.

2492 **The men of New York:** a collection of biographies . . . during the last decade of the 19th century. Buffalo, N.Y., 1898.
Concerns New York state.

2493 **Meyers, Carol M.** Early military records of New York, 1689–1738. Ed. and arranged from *Documentary history of New York state,* v.1–4, 1850. Saugus, Calif., 1967. *See* note under no.2529.

2494 ———— Early New York state census records, 1663–1772. 2nd ed. Gardena, Calif., 1965.
From *Documentary history of New York state,* alphabetized in phonetic sequence.

2495 ———— Palatine colonial records of New York. Ed. and rearranged from *Documentary history of New York state,* v.1–4, 1850. Saugus, Calif., 1966.
18th-century lists, but *see* no.2529.

2496 **Nestler, Harold.** A bibliography of New York state communities, counties, towns, villages. Port Washington, N.Y., Kennikat Pr., 1968.

2497 **New York (City).** The burghers of New Amsterdam and the freemen of New York, 1675–1866. *Collections of the New-York Historical Soc.* v.18. New York: The Society, 1886.
Also has indentures of apprenticeship, 1694–1708.

2498 ———— Original book of New York deeds, 1672/3–75, and miscellaneous documents relating to the city of New York and Long Island, 1642–96. *Collections of the New-York Historical Soc.* v.46. New York: The Society, 1914.
Deeds not recorded in the Register's Office of New York county.

2499 ———— **Assessors.** New York tax lists, 1695–99. *Collections of the New-York Historical Soc.* v.43–44. 2v. New York, 1911–12.
Also included is east ward, 1791. Good index.

2500 ———— **Burgomasters and Schepens.** Minutes of the Court of Burgomasters Schepens; the records of New Amsterdam, 1653–74. Ed. by Berthold Fernow. 7v. New York, 1897.
Marginalia omitted; some errors. Helpful index.

2501 ———— **Common Council.** Minutes of the Common Council of the city of New York, 1675–1776; 1784–1831; 1917–30. New York, 1905–30.
1675–1766 in 8v., 1905; 1784–1831 in 21v., 1917–30; last 2v. of 1784–1831 analytical index by David M. Matteson. Thousands of references to individuals.

2502 ————**Orphan Masters.** The minutes of the Orphanmasters of New Amsterdam, 1655–63. Transcribed and ed. . . . by Berthold Fernow. 2v. New York, 1902–1907.
v.2 contains minutes of the executive boards 1661–64, and notarial records of Walewyn van der Veen 1662–64.

2503 **New York Collegiate Church.** Marriages from 1639 to 1801 in the Reformed Dutch Church, New Amsterdam —New York city. *Collections of the New York Genealogical and Biographical Soc.* v.9. New York, 1940.
Records of baptisms and marriages continued in the *New York genealogical and biographical record.* Index, by Samuel S. Purple. New York, 1890.

2504 ———— Records of the Reformed Dutch Church in New Amsterdam and New York. Ed. by Thomas G. Evans. Baptisms . . . 1639–1800. *Collections of the New York Genealogical and Biographical Soc.,* v.2–3. 2v. 1901–1902. Repr. Boston: Gregg, 1968.
Names and dates of baptisms of children, parents and witnesses.

2505 **New York (Colony).** Calendar of New York colonial commissions, 1680–1770. *New-York Historical Soc.* **John**

*Divine Jones Fund ser. of histories and memoirs,* v.7. New York, 1929.
Also appeared under the editorship of Edmund B. O'Callaghan in the *New-York historical quarterly bull.* v.7–12, 1924–29. Digest of 5v. of original commissions, destroyed by fire in 1911.

**2506** ——— 1770–76. Ed. by Kenneth Scott. New York: National Soc. of Colonial Dames, 1972.
Comprises brief abstracts of pardons, commissions, etc.

**2507** ——— Index of conveyances recorded in the Office of Register of the city and county of New York: grantees, 24v. in 9 (1858–64); grantors, 26v. in 11 (1857–58); grantors, corporations (including masters in chancery and sheriffs), 1v. (1857–58). New York.

**2508** ——— Names of persons for whom marriage licenses were issued by the Secretary of Province of New York, previous to 1784. 1860. Repr. Baltimore: G.P.C., 1968.
Supplements included in reprint are: *State Library bull., History,* v.1, 1898, Albany; New York marriage lists, by Robert H. Kelby, *N.Y. genealogical and biographical record,* 1915; *New York marriage licenses, 1639–1706,* by Kenneth Scott, *N.Y. genealogical and biographical record,* 1967; also index by Scott not previously published. Sometimes referred to as "Tucker" because original vol. (1860) was "printed by order of Gideon J. Tucker, Secretary of State." 25,000 entries covering entire period, when licenses were issued under the colonial government.

**2509 New York (County). Surrogate's Court.** Abstracts of wills on file in the Surrogate's Office, 1665–1800. 17v. *New-York Historical Soc. Collections,* v.25–41. 1892–1908. New York, 1893–1909.
v.16–17 are corrections of erroneous readings in v.1–11. Includes Hudson Valley, Long Island, Staten Island, and New Jersey wills. Some inaccurate readings throughout. 90,000 inhabitants mentioned, of whom 30,000 were New York city residents.

**2510 New York (State). Adjutant General's Office.** Index of awards on claims of the soldiers of the War of 1812. 1860. Repr. with added errata list. Baltimore: G.P.C., 1969.
Over 17,000 entries. Standard source for service records of New York militia during War of 1812. Claims made after 1859 for payment for military clothing and equipment provided by militiamen. Includes claims for service by Indians.

**2511** ——— A record of commissioned officers, non-commissioned officers and privates of the regiments which were organized in the state of New York and called into the service of the United States to assist in suppressing the Rebellion . . . 8v. Albany, N.Y., 1864–68.

**2512** ——— **Comptroller's Office.** New York in the Revolution as colony and state . . . 2nd ed. Albany, N.Y., 1898.

**2513** ——— ——— Supplement by Erastus C. Knight . . . Albany, N.Y., 1901. Reissue, 2v. 1904.
v.2 has cover title: *New York in the Revolution: supplement.* Not as full as no.2454 but more names, often regularized. Sometimes referred to as "Roberts" because James A. Roberts was state comptroller. Basic list for New York soldiers in the Revolution.

**2514** ——— **Council of Appointment.** Military minutes, 1783–1821. Ed. by Hugh Hastings. 3v. plus 1 index v. Albany, N.Y., 1901–1902.

**2515** ——— **Court of Appeals.** Genealogical data from administration papers from the New York State Court of Appeals in Albany, New York. Compiled by Kenneth Scott. New York: National Soc. of Colonial Dames of the State of New York, 1972.
Abstracts of documents pertaining to the administration of estates; 17th–19th centuries, with essential genealogical data given. 3,500 decedents, 8,000 names.

**2516** ——— ——— Genealogical data from inventories of New York estates, 1666–1825. Compiled by Kenneth

Scott and J. A. Owre. New York: New York Genealogical and Biographical Soc., 1970.

Abstraction of genealogically significant details from 1,080 inventories and related papers deposited by the Court of Appeals at Albany in Queens College of the City University of New York. 4,700 persons named.

2517 ——— Secretary of State. Calendar of Dutch (and British) historical manuscripts in the office of the Secretary of State. Ed. by Edmund B. O'Callaghan. 2v. 1865-66. Repr. Boston: Gregg, 1967-68.

v.1 contains lists of Dutch records, 1630-64; v.2, English, 1664-1776.

2518 ——— Calendar of New York colonial manuscripts, endorsed land papers, in the Office of the Secretary, New York, 1643-1803. Albany, N.Y., 1864.

pp.669-1025 for 1785-1803 give claims by soldiers, petitions, affidavits, land locations, surveys, etc. re vacant lands.

2519 ——— State Historian. Muster rolls, 1664-1775, printed in appendices to the 2nd and 3rd annual reports of the State Historian . . . *Colonial ser.,* v.1-2. Albany, N.Y., 1897-98.

Rolls actually appear in v.1, *Appendix H,* pp.371-956; v.2, *Appendix M,* pp.437-898; pp.899-1158 contain index to both appendixes.

2520 ——— State Library, Albany. Settlers of Rensselaerswyck, 1630-58. Translated and ed. by Arnold J. F. van Laer. 1908. Repr. from Van Rensselaer Bouwier manuscripts. Baltimore: G.P.C., 1965.

From pp.805-46 of original.

2521 **The New York civil list,** containing the names and origins of the civil divisions, and the names and dates of elections or appointment of the principal state and county officers from the Revolution . . . 1855-60 by Franklin B. Hough; 1861-62 by Stephen C. Hutchins; 1883-88 by Edgar A. Werner.

2522 **The New York genealogical and biographical record.** v.1- , 1870- . New York: New York Genealogical and Biographical Soc.

2523 ——— Indexes. Subject index, v.1-38, by Florence E. Youngs. New York, 1907. v.39-94, 2v., by Gertrude A. Barber. New York, 1946-64. Index for v.39-94 in typescript.

Very fine collection of genealogical records and family studies. One of the best genealogical journals.

2524 **New York Genealogical and Biographical Society.** Genealogical data from New York administration bonds, 1753-99 . . . *Collections of New York Genealogical and Biographical Soc.* v.10. New York: The Society, 1969.

Over 2,000 descendants and 4,000 names. Excellent, complementary volume to no. 2509.

2525 **New-York Historical Society.** Collections. v.1- , 1809- . New York: The Society, 1811- .

Contains important genealogical data: burgesses, freemen, muster rolls, wills, tax lists, etc. *See* no.2505, 2509, 2527.

2526 ———De Lancey's Brigade (Loyalist). Orderly book of the three battalions of loyalists, commanded by Brigadier-General Oliver De Lancey, 1776-78. To which is appended a list of New York city loyalists during the Revolution. By William Kelby. *New-York Historical Soc. John Divine Jones fund ser.* v.3. 1917. Repr. Baltimore: G.P.C., 1972.

Loyalists on Long Island and New York city. 1,500 names.

2527 ——— Muster rolls of New York provincial troops, 1755-64. *Collections of the New-York Historical Soc.,* 1891. ser.24. New York, 1892.

Many of the lists contain age, birthplace, trade and service.

2528 **New York marriages.** *See* no.2508.

2529 **O'Callaghan, Edmund B.** The documentary history of the state of New-York . . . 4v. 1849-51. New impr. New York, 1849-51.

Includes 17th- and 18th-century tax lists,

censuses, 1755 slave census, militia lists, etc. Mostly Long Island and Hudson River Valley. Much of the work has been indexed and newly arranged by Carol M. Meyers (see no.2493-95), but a considerable amount of genealogy has been lost. The 4v. set is needed.

2530 ——— The register of New Netherland; 1626-74. Albany, N.Y., 1865.
Lists of persons by vocation and office.

2531 **Olde Ulster:** an historical and genealogical magazine. Ed. by Benjamin M. Brink. v.1-10. Kingston, N.Y., 1905-14.
Includes the Rev. Mr. Kochertal's Palatine records, family studies, and historical articles. Wealth of genealogical material relative to Ulster county and vicinity.

2532 **Pearson, Jonathan.** Contributions for the genealogies of the descendants of the first settlers of the patent and city of Schenectady, 1662-1800. Albany, N.Y., 1873.
Coats of arms.

2533 ——— Contributions for the genealogies of the first settlers of the ancient county of Albany, 1630-1800. Albany, N.Y., 1872.
Reprinted from Munsell's *Collections on the history of Albany,* v.4, 1871. County was much larger than at present.

2534 **Pelletreau, William S.** Historic homes and institutions and genealogical and family history of New York. 4v. New York, 1907.
New York city only.

2535 **Phisterer, Frederick.** New York in the War of the Rebellion, 1861 to 1865. 3rd ed. 6v. Albany, N.Y., 1912.
v.6 is index.

2536 **Pool, David de S.** Portraits etched in stone: early Jewish settlers, 1682-1831. New York: Columbia Univ. Pr., 1952.
Records of early Jewish settlers in New York city who were buried in Chatham Square cemetery. Genealogical tables.

2537 **Reynolds, Cuyler.** Genealogical and family history of southern New York and Hudson River Valley. 3v. New York, 1914.
Errors, use with care.

2538 ——— Hudson-Mohawk genealogical and family memoirs. 4v. New York, 1911.
Use with care.

2539 **Reynolds, Helen W.** Dutch houses in the Hudson Valley before 1776 .... 1929. Repr. New York: Dover, 1965.
History of houses of the Hudson Valley. Hundreds of names of individuals; emphasis on early Dutch families.

2540 **Robison, Jeannie F.-J.,** and **Bartlett, H. C.** Genealogical records: manuscript entries of births, deaths, and marriages, taken from family Bibles, 1581-1917. 1917. Repr. Baltimore: G.P.C., 1972.
Contains genealogical records of 90 Dutch and English New York families; over 3,000 names. Mostly from 17th century on. Originally a publication of the Colonial Dames of the State of New York.

2541 **Rygg. Andrew N.** Norwegians in New York, 1825-1925. Brooklyn, N.Y., 1941.
Includes biographical accounts.

2542 **Scott, Kenneth.** Chronological data from further New York administration bonds. New York: New York Genealogical and Biographical Soc., 1971.

2543 ——— Genealogical data from the *New-York (gazette and weekly) mercury,* 1752-96; *Rivington's New York newspaper,* 1773-83; and *New York postboy,* 1743-73.
Since each newspaper has items from other colonies, the entries will be found in the General category, no.68.

2544 ——— Marriage bonds of colonial New York 1753-84. New York: Saint Nicholas Soc. in the City of New York (Trumbull Pub. Co.), 1972.
Gives names of persons married, two bondsmen, residence of bride and other important details, many of which are miss-

ing in no.2508. 4,000 bonds which survived the fire of 1911 in whole or in print. Complements no.2508.

**2545** ────── Records of the Chancery Court, Province and state of New York guardianships, 1691–1815 [i.e. 1701–1815]. New York: Holland Soc. of New York, 1971.
Abstracted from manuscript material. Considerable data about Dutch families.

**2546** ────── Ulster county, New York, court records, 1693–1775. Issued serially in *National Genealogical Soc. quarterly* v.60–61, 1972–73.

**2547 Scoville, Joseph A.** (Walter Barrett, *pseud.*) The old merchants of New York city, 5v. New York, 1885. Repr. New York: Greenwood Pr., 1968.
Undocumented but unique source for personal items ca.1790–1850. This is a reprint of 1863–69 ed.

**2548 Seversmith, Herbert F.** Colonial families of Long Island. v.1–4, pt.1; v.5. Washington, D.C., 1939–64.
v.1–4 covered *A* through *L*; v.5 concerns ancestry of Roger Ludlow. Only 25 copies produced. Remainder of notes on microfilm. Originals at East Hampton Free Library, East Hampton, N.Y.

**2549** ────── and **Stryker-Rodda, Kenn.** Long Island genealogical source material (a bibliography). *National Genealogical Soc. special publ.* 24. Washington, D.C., 1962.
Comprehensive bibliography with 845 entries, with holders of the item.

**2550 Society of Old Brooklynites, Brooklyn.** [A] Christmas reminder: being the names of about 8,000 persons, a small portion of the number confined on board the British prison ships during the War of the Revolution. Brooklyn, N.Y., 1888.

**2551 Stevens, John A., Jr.** Colonial records of the New York Chamber of Commerce, 1768–84; with historical and biographical sketches. 1867. Repr. New York: Burt Franklin, 1971.

**2552 Stokes, Isaac N. P.** Iconography of Manhattan Island, 1498–1909. 6v. 1915–28. Repr. New York: Arno Pr., 1967.
Based on land records, maps, many documents destroyed in 1911 fire. Chronology by V. Paltsits. Analytic index. Essential.

**2553 Sullivan, James.** History of New York state, 1523–1927. 6v. New York, 1927.
v.6 biographical.

**2554 Talcott, Sebastian V.** Genealogical notes on New York and New England families. 1883. Repr. Baltimore: G.P.C., 1973.
18,000 individuals, taken from Dutch Bible records, and from state, county, and town archives. Use with care.

**2555 Toler, Henry P.** New Harlem register; a genealogy of the descendants of the 23 original patentees in the town of New Harlem, containing . . . births, baptisms, and marriages from 1630 to date. New York, 1903.
More than 30,000 descendants listed. Use with care.

**2556 Tree talks.** v.1– , 1961– . Syracuse, N.Y.: Central New York Genealogical Soc.
Some records for all counties except those in the Hudson River Valley south of Albany, New York city and Long Island. Absorbed *Cousin huntin* in 1973.

**2557 Tribbeko, John.** Lists of Germans from the Palatinate who came to England in 1709. *See* no. 3022.
Of particular interest to New York and Pennsylvania.

**2558 Trinity church. New York city.** Records. In *New York genealogical and biographical record,* v.79, 81–89, 1948–58.
Marriages 1802–61.

**2559 Turner, Orsamus.** History of the pioneer settlement of Phelps and Gorham's purchase. Rochester, N.Y., 1851.

**2560** ────── ────── Complete name index, by LaVerne C. Cooley. Batavia, N.Y., 1946.

**2560a** ——— and **Lookup, George E.** Index with supplemental material. Lyons, N.Y.: Wayne County Historical Soc., 1973.

**2561** ——— Pioneer history of the Holland purchase of western New York. Buffalo, N.Y., 1850.

**2562** ——— ——— Name index, by LaVerne C. Cooley. Batavia, N.Y., 1946.

**2562a** **U.S. Bureau of the Census.** Heads of families at the first census of the United States taken in the year 1790. New York. 1908. Repr. Baltimore: G.P.C., 1966, etc.; Spartanburg, S.C.: Reprint Co., 1964, etc.

**2563** **Valentine, David T.** History of the city of New York [to 1750]. Newark, N.J., 1853.
Actually compiled by William I. Paulding, but published under Valentine's name.

**2564** ——— Manual of the corporation of the city of New York. 1841/2–1870. New York.
List of current officers, but best known for superb prints and maps, transcripts of records, some no longer extant, back to Dutch period. Usually called "Valentine's manuals."

**2565** ——— ——— Historical index by Otto Hufeland. New York, 1900.
2,325 references.

**2566** **Van Laer, Arnold J. F.** New York historical manuscripts: Dutch. Ed. with added indexes by Kenneth Scott and K. Stryker-Rodda. 4v. Baltimore: G.P.C., 1973.
Carefully annotated translation of earliest extant records pertaining to the administration of New Netherland; important new primary source. *Registers of the Provincial Secretary,* 1638–60 and *Council minutes* 1638–49.

**2567** **Van Rensselaer, Mariana (Mrs. Schuyler).** History of the city of New York in the seventeenth century. 2v. New York, 1909.
v.1, New Amsterdam; v.2, New York under the Stuarts.

**2568** **Weeks, Lyman H.** Prominent families of New York. New ed. New York, 1898.
Representatives of social, professional and civic life of New York city.

**2569** **Wehle, Martin.** Mr. Wehle of 46 Stottle Rd., Churchville, N.Y. 14428, has published reprints of New York atlases. They are reprinted from 19th century classics such as Beers, Stone & Stewart, Evert & Ensign.

**2569a** **Western New York Genealogical Society journal.** v.1– , 1974– . Kenmore, N.Y.: Mrs. H. J. Miller (209 Nassau Ave., 14127).
Records in the 8 western counties: Erie, Niagara, Chautauqua, Cattaraugus, Wyoming, Genesee, Allegany, and Orleans.

**2570** **Wittmeyer, Alfred V.** Registers of the births, marriages, and deaths of the "Eglise Françoise à la Nouvelle York," from 1688 to 1804. 1886. Repr. excerpted from *Collections of the Huguenot Soc. of America,* v.1. Baltimore: G.P.C., 1968.
Has earliest records of Huguenots in New York; covers important period of immigration. In French, but easily understood. Inadequate index.

**2571** **Wright, Albert H.** A check list of New York state county maps published 1779–1945. Ithaca, N.Y.: Cornell Univ., Regional History and Univ. Archives, 1965.
Revision of Wright and Ellis, *Check list of county atlases of New York,* 1943.

**2572** **Yesteryears magazine.** A quarterly magazine for the appreciation and study of New York state regional history and genealogical research. v.1– , 1957– . Aurora, N.Y. (Box 52, 13026).
Censuses, heads of Palatine families, New York settlements. Out-of-print years obtainable from Xerox Univ. Microfilms, Ann Arbor, Mich.

## NORTH CAROLINA

Settled ca. 1650; original state

*Department of Cultural Resources, Division of Archives and Records Management, Raleigh*
*North Carolina State Library, Division of Genealogical Services Branch, Raleigh*
*Pack Memorial Library, Asheville*
*Mrs. Lois S. Neal, Raleigh*

✣ Many works in this book concern both South and North Carolina. Since these will be entered in one or the other state, it is suggested that both Carolinas be consulted.

**2573** **Arthur, John P.** Western North Carolina; a history, 1730–1913. 1914. Repr. Spartanburg, S.C.: Reprint Co., 1973.

**2574** **Ashe, Samuel A'Court (and others).** Biographical history of North Carolina from colonial times to the present. 8v. 1905–17. Repr. Spartanburg, S.C.: Reprint Co., 1971.

Not genealogical, but valuable because of legislative history, 1584–1925.

**2575** **Bernheim, Gotthardt D.** History of the German settlements and of the Lutheran Church in North and South Carolina from the earliest period of the colonization of the Dutch, German, and Swiss settlers to the close of the first half of the present century. 1872. Repr. Spartanburg, S.C.: Reprint Co., 1972.

**2576** **Broughton, Carrie L.** Marriage and death notices from *Raleigh register* and *North Carolina state gazette, Daily sentinel, Raleigh observer* . . . 1799–1893. 6v. Raleigh, N.C.: State Lib., 1944–52.

The notices for 1799–1845 were included in the library's biennial report, 1942–47, and were repr. by G.P.C., Baltimore, 1962–68. The remainder are in print and can be obtained from Raleigh, or are being repr. and can be obtained from Baltimore. Index being prepared by Edith Clark; available in the State archives, Raleigh, N.C.

**2577** **Burns, Annie (Walker).** Abstract of pensions of North Carolina soldiers of the Revolution, War of 1812, and Indian Wars. 15v.? Washington, D.C., 1960–64? Not easy to use. Projected ser., of which 15v. were pub.

**2578** ———— North Carolina genealogical records. 1v.? Washington, D.C., 1943.

Record of abstracts of pension records. Difficult to use.

**2579** Carolina genealogist. v.1– , 1970– . Daniellsville, Ga.: Heritage Papers. Ed. by Mary B. Warren. Legal records, cemetery surveys, Bible and other records.

**2580** **Cartwright, Betty G. C.,** and **Gardiner, L. T.** North Carolina land grants in Tennessee, 1778–91. 1958. Repr. Memphis, Tenn.: The Authors, 1973.

This list of landowners and settlers constitutes the only substitute for a 1790 census of the part of North Carolina which became Tennessee in 1796.

**2581** **Chreitzberg, Abel McKee.** Early Methodism in the Carolinas. 1897. Repr. Spartanburg, S.C.: Reprint Co., 1972.

Extensive information on Methodist preachers but of marginal interest to genealogists.

**2582** **Clemens, William M.** North and South Carolina marriage records, from the earliest colonial days to the Civil War. 1927. Repr. Baltimore: G.P.C., 1973.

Almost 7,500 records. 15,000 names.

**2582a** **Coker, Charles F. W.,** and **Lennon, D. R.** North Carolina's Revolutionary War pay records. *Archives information circular* 1 rev. Raleigh, N.C.: North Carolina Div. of Archives, 1973.

**2582b** ———— North Carolina Civil War records: an introduction to printed and manuscript sources. *Archives information* 4 rev. Raleigh, N.C.: North Carolina Div. of Archives, 1972.

**2583** Colonial records of North Carolina. *See* no.2626, 2618.

**2584** **Connor, Robert D. W.** North Carolina 1584–1929. 4v. Chicago, 1929.

v.1–2 reprint by Reprint Co., Spartanburg, S.C., 1973; v.3–4 biographical.

**2585   Corbitt, David L.** The formation of the North Carolina counties, 1663–1943. 1950. Corr. ed. with supplementary data. Raleigh, N.C.: State Archives, 1969.
Essential tool for genealogical research in North Carolina. Maps 1700–1912.

**2586   Crabtree, Beth G.** Guide to private manuscript collections in the North Carolina State Archives. Raleigh, N.C.: The Archives, 1964.
Supersedes 1942 guide. 1,175 personal collections, diaries, account books, etc.

**2587   Cyclopedia of eminent and representative men of the Carolinas of the nineteenth century . . .** 2v. 1892. Repr. Spartanburg, S.C.: Reprint Co., 1972–73.
v.1, South Carolina; v.2, North Carolina. With portraits, good mug book.

**2588   D.A.R. North Carolina.** Roster of soldiers from North Carolina in the American Revolution . . . 1932. Repr. Baltimore: G.P.C., 1972.
36,000 names. Has appendix containing a collection of miscellaneous records. The standard work.

**2589   DeMond, Robert O.** The loyalists in North Carolina during the Revolution. 1940. Hampden, Conn.: Archon Books, 1964.
Appendices include lists of loyalists, extracts of confiscated grants of lands, loyalists claims and pension rolls.

**2590   Draughon, Wallace R., and Johnson, William P.** North Carolina genealogical reference: a research guide for all genealogists both amateur and professional. New [i.e.] 2nd ed. Durham, N.C.: The Authors, 1966.
A must for any researcher. Good bibliography of printed genealogies and family histories of North Carolina; gives locations of some genealogical collections in North Carolina.

**2591   Foote, William H.** Sketches of North Carolina, historical and biographical . . . 3rd ed. 2nd pr. Dunn, N.C., 1966. Obtainable from Committee on Historical Matters for the Synod of N.C. Presbyterian Church: the U.S. and the N.C. Presbyterian Historical Soc., Raleigh, N.C.
1st ed., 1846, repr. 1912; 2nd, 1872, repr. 1966; 3rd ed. is really a repr. of 1846 ed. with index, new preface, errata, and bibliography, edited by Harold J. Dudley.

**2592   Fries, Adelaide L. (and others).** Records of the Moravians in North Carolina. 11v. Raleigh, N.C.: The Archives, 1922–69.
v.1–7 repr., 1968–70. Records, translated from the German, cover settlement of Piedmont, N.C., 1752–1879.

**2593   Genealogical Society of the Church of Jesus Christ of Latter-day Saints. Research Dept.** Index to individuals born outside the U.S. as enumerated in the 1850 census of North Carolina: Salt Lake City: L.D.S., 1972.

**2594   Hall, Lewis P.** Marriage notices, obituaries, and items of genealogical interest in the *Cape Fear recorder*, the *People's press* and the *Wilmington advertiser*. Wilmington, N.C., 1958.

**2595   Hammer, Carl.** Rhinelanders on the Yadkin. 2nd ed. Salisbury, N.C., 1965.
Yadkin county, northwest North Carolina, and Yadkin river which flows from Blue Ridge through South Carolina, where it is called Pee Dee.

**2596   Henderson, Archibald.** North Carolina, the old state and the new . . . 5v. Chicago, 1941.
v.3–5 biographical.

**2597   Hinshaw, Seth B., and Hinshaw, M. E.** Carolina Quakers . . . tercentenary 1672–1972. Greensboro, N.C.: Yearly Meeting, 1972.
Running account of 3 centuries of progress in the Friends Society of North Carolina yearly meeting. Many biographies.

**2598   Hinshaw, William W.** Encyclopedia of American Quaker genealogy. v.1. Containing every item of genealogical value found in all records and minutes of the

33 oldest monthly meetings which belong, or ever belonged, to the North Carolina yearly meeting of Friends. 1936; suppl. by Thomas W. Marshall issued in Washington, D.C. in 1948. Repr. Baltimore: G.P.C., 1969.

2599   **Historical Records Survey.** The historical records of North Carolina . . . counties. Ed. by Charles C. Crittenden and D. Lacy. 3v. 1938-39. Repr., corr. Raleigh, N.C.: The Archives, 1969.
Inventory of county records, and not a publication of texts of records. v.1, Alamance through Columbus; v.2, Craven through Moore; v.3, Nash through Yancey. Crittenden has in v.1 a 6 chapter authoritative historical introduction. For each county there is considerable descriptive data on types of records not found elsewhere.

2600   ———— Inventory of the church archives of North Carolina. Southern Baptist Convention. 7v. Raleigh, N.C., 1940-42.

2601   **History of North Carolina** . . . 6v. Chicago, 1919.
v.4-6 biographical.

2602   **Hunter, Cyrus L.** Sketches of western North Carolina. 1877, Repr. Baltimore: G.P.C., 1970.
Indexed ed. Illustrates principally the Revolutionary period of Mecklenburg, Rowan, Lincoln, and adjoining counties. 1,500 names.

2603   **Jackson, Ronald V.,** and **Teeples, G. R.** North Carolina 1800 census. Provo, Utah: Accelerated Indexing Systems, 1974.
About 60,000 entries. Computer index; early maps, genealogical data, county research.

2604   **Johnson, William P.** Index to North Carolina wills, 1663-1900. v.1- . Raleigh, N.C.: The Compiler, 1963- .
Projected series of indexes for al! extant counties formed prior to 1900. 4v. to 1974: Alamance through Columbus counties.

2605   **Jones, Roger C.** North Carolina troops, 1861-65. v.4, Infantry series, 4th-8th regiments. Raleigh, N.C.: The Archives, 1973.
For v.1-3 of the series, *see* no.2612.

2606   **Jordan, Weymouth T., Jr.** North Carolina newspapers on microfilm; a checklist. 4th ed. Raleigh, N.C.: The Archives, 1971.
Represents virtually all the newspapers published in North Carolina prior to 1901 and many after that date, with the exception of papers still being published.

2607   **Lambeth, Mary (W.)** Memories and records of eastern North Carolina. [Nashville, Tenn., 1957.]
Greater part of book devoted to genealogies of prominent families; tax lists and other documents.

2608   **Lefler, Hugh T.** History of North Carolina. 4v. New York, 1956.
v.3-4 family and personal histories. Late 19th and early 20th century. Mug book.

2609   ———— and **Newsome, A. R.** North Carolina: the history of a southern state. 3rd ed. Chapel Hill, N.C.: Univ. of North Carolina Pr., 1973.
First appeared in 1954; some parts rewritten to bring history down to 1972. Some genealogy.

2610   **Lonsdale, Richard E.** Atlas of North Carolina. Chapel Hill, N.C.: Univ. of North Carolina Pr., 1967.
Some charts of historical value. Major portion 20th century, social, economic, industrial rather than geographical.

2611   **McCay, Betty L.** Sources for genealogical searching in North Carolina. Indianapolis, Ind.: The Compiler, 1969.
Useful for beginners, county records lost by fire. Maps.

2611a   **McGrew, Ellen Z.** North Carolina census records, 1787-1890. *Archives information circular,* v.2. Rev. Raleigh, N.C.: Office of Archives – History, 1972.

2612   **Manarin, Louis H.** North Carolina troops, 1861-65; a roster, 4v. Raleigh, N.C.: The Archives, 1966-73 (in progress).

v.1, artillery; v.2, cavalry; v.3, 4, infantry, 1st–8th units. Thousands of names; valuable finding aids. v.4 was by Weymouth T. Jordan, Jr., and published by the Archives, *see* no.2605.

**2613    Meyer, Duane G.** The Highland Scots of North Carolina, 1732–36. 1961. Repr. Chapel Hill, N.C.: Univ. of Carolina Pr., 1966.

Origin of Scotch emigration and history of Highlander settlement, the largest in America. Good background reading. Maps of progressive development of settled areas.

**2615    Newsome, Albert R.** Records of emigrants from England and Scotland to North Carolina, 1774–75. *North Carolina historical review,* 1934. Repr. Raleigh, N.C.: The Archives, 1966.

Basic, but contains errors; use with care.

**2616    North Carolina. Adjutant General's Office.** Muster rolls of the soldiers of the War of 1812 and 1814. 1851. Repr. Winston-Salem, N.C., 1926.

Typed index at State Dept. of Archives and History, Raleigh, N.C.

**2617** ———— Roster of North Carolina troops in the war with Mexico. Raleigh, N.C., 1887.

**2618    North Carolina. Colonial Charters.** The colonial records of North Carolina. [2nd ser.] Raleigh, N.C.: The Archives, 1963– .

A projected series of which the following, ed. by Mattie E. E. Parker, have been published: v.[1], 1963, Charters and constitutions, 1578–1698; v.[2], 1968, Higher-court records, 1670–96; v.[3], 1971, Higher-court records, 1697–1701; v.[4], 1974, Higher-court records, 1702–1708, ed. by William S. Price. Important new series; each vol. indexed separately.

**2619    North Carolina Dept. of Cultural Resources. Division of Archives and Records Management.** Archives information circulars, v.1– , 1972– . Raleigh, N.C.: The Archives.

Circulars contain information on Revolutionary War pay records; census records, 1787–1890; Civil War records, map records, etc.

**2620** ———— Guide to Civil War records in the North Carolina state archives. Raleigh, N.C.: The Archives, 1966.

No attempt was made to include mass of records which had no immediate connection with the conflict; military pension and reminiscences with the survivors, have been included.

**2621** ———— Guide to research materials in the North Carolina state archives. Section B: County records. 2nd ed. Raleigh, N.C.: The Archives, 1974.

Essential to effective research in county records held in the state archives.

**2622    North Carolina. General Assembly.** Roster of North Carolina troops in the war between the states. Prepared by John W. Moore. Raleigh, N.C., 1882.

By military unit; no name index. Manarin (no.2612) will supersede this and can now serve as partial index to Moore.

**2623    North Carolina. Historical Commission.** A manual of North Carolina, for the use of members of the General Assembly, session 1913. Compiled and ed. by R. D. W. Connor. Raleigh, N.C., 1913.

General reference tool; has value for genealogy because it has complete lists of legislators, their home counties or districts. Updated ed. in preparation (1974).

**2624    North Carolina. Secretary of State.** Abstract of North Carolina wills on file in the office of the Secretary of State. Ed. by John B. Grimes. 1910. Repr. Baltimore: G.P.C., 1967.

Abstracts, but with relevant data covering 1663–1760. For 1760–1800 *see* Olds, no. 2630. Often referred to as "Grimes." Contains wills only; adds inventories and estates.

**2625** ———— North Carolina wills and inventories in the file of the Secretary of State. Ed. by John B. Grimes. 1912. Baltimore: G.P.C., 1967.

Covers 1663–1760. Full text. Often referred to as "Grimes." Difference between this and the 1910 book (no.2624) is that the 1910 book covers abstracts (about 3,000 entries); 1912 book is complete text of a further 200 wills.

**2626** ——— The state records of North Carolina . . . v.1–30. Goldsboro, N.C., 1886–1907.

v.1–10 appeared as *The colonial records* . . . collected and ed. by William L. Saunders. Repr. by A.M.S. Press, New York, 1967; v.11–26 as *The state records* . . . collected and ed. by Walter Clark; v.27–30 as *Index to colonial and state records,* compiled and ed. by Stephen B. Weeks; v.1–30. Repr. New York: A.M.S. Press, 1971. 2nd ser. entitled, *The colonial records of North Carolina,* 1963, see no.2618.

**2628 North Carolina genealogy** . . . v.1– , 1955– . Ed. by William P. Johnson and Russell E. Bidlack. Raleigh, N.C.: The Editors.

Formerly *The North Carolinian* and *Journal of North Carolina genealogy.*

**2629 North Carolina historical and genealogical register.** v.1–3, no.3 (11 numbers, all pub.). 1900–1903. Repr. Baltimore: G.P.C., 1968–71.

Usually referred to as "Hathaway" because James R. B. Hathaway was editor. Contains more than 50,000 names, land grants, etc. Abstracts of court house records of 11 northeastern North Carolina counties; also Surry and Isle of Wight in Virginia. For index, *see* no.2643.

**2630 Olds, Fred A.** An abstract of North Carolina wills, from about 1760 to about 1800. Supplementing Grimes's *Abstract of North Carolina wills, 1663–1760* (*see* no.2624 and 2625). Repr. with some manuscript corrections. Baltimore: G.P.C., 1972.

Originally published by the D.A.R., North Carolina. Continuation of earlier works by J. B. Grimes (no.2624–25) in abstracting state wills, but it also includes wills before 1760, omitted by Grimes.

**2631** ——— ——— Index by Toni E. Crewe. Mesa, Ariz., 1968.

3,200 names.

**2632 Parker, Mattie E. E.** The colonial records of North Carolina. *See The colonial records of North Carolina,* no.2618.

**2633 Paschal, George W.** History of North Carolina Baptists. 2v. Raleigh, N.C.: Baptist State Convention, 1930–55.

While purely historical, there is a considerable amount of biographical (and sometimes genealogical) information on 18th-century Baptist leaders in North Carolina.

**2634 Peele, William J.** Lives of distinguished North Carolinians . . . Raleigh, N.C., 1898.

**2634a Petty, Gerald M.** Index of the 1840 federal census of North Carolina. Columbus, Ohio: The Compiler, 1974.

**2635 Potter, Dorothy W.** 1820 federal census of North Carolina. v.1–56. Tullahoma, Tenn.: The Author, 1970–74.

**2636** ——— Index, supplemented from tax lists and other records from missing counties. Tullahoma, Tenn.: The Author, 1974.

Series of individual, indexed transcriptions for each of the 56 (of 62) counties, for which censuses exist in 1820.

**2637 Powell, William S.** The North Carolina gazetteer. Chapel Hill, N.C. Univ. of North Carolina Pr., 1968.

20,000 entries.

**2638 Ramsey, Robert W.** Carolina cradle: settlement of the north west Carolina frontier, 1747–62. Chapel Hill, N.C.: Univ. of North Carolina Pr., 1964.

Full name index from Edith Clark, Salisbury, N.C. To be published.

**2639 Ray, Worth S.** Colonial Granville county and its people. Loose leaves from "The lost tribes of North Carolina," pp.193–312. 1945. Repr. Baltimore: G.P.C., 1973.

Pt.2 of *The lost tribes of North Carolina.* Miscellany concerns early records and genealogical notes from counties of Anson, Buncombe, Caswell, Chatham, Cleveland, Duplin, Franklin, and Granville. Thousands of names.

**2640** ——— The lost tribes of North Carolina . . . Where did they come from? Where did they go? Austin, Tex., 1947.

The series contains: v.1, *Index and digest to Hathaway* (no.2643); v.2, *Colonial Granville county* (no.2639); v. 3, *Mecklenburg signers* (no.2641), v.4, *Old Albemarle* (no. 2642). Use with care.

2641 ——— The Mecklenburg signers and their neighbors. 1946. Repr. Baltimore: G.P.C., 1966.

Pt.3 of *The lost tribes of North Carolina*. Genealogical sketches of signers, abstracts from county records, etc. Area covered includes Eastern Shore of Maryland and Virginia, as well as early Mecklenburg county area.

2642 ——— Old Albemarle and its absentee landlords. 1947. Repr. Baltimore: G.P.C., 1968.

Pt.4 of *The lost tribes of North Carolina*. Land grants, marriages, etc. with histories and genealogical notices of families; 1,250 surnames. Albemarle Precinct was original gateway to the state, and home of its first settlers.

2643 ——— Ray's Index and digest to Hathaway's North Carolina historical and genealogical register, with genealogical notes and annotations. 1945. Repr. Baltimore: G.P.C., 1971.

Pt.1 of *The lost tribes of North Carolina*. 7,500 entries. Useful as digest; inadequate as index. The *American genealogical index* (no.1) is better for index. For Hathaway, see no.2629.

2644 **Register, Alvaretta K.** State census of North Carolina, 1784-87. Transcribed and indexed by A. K. Register. 1907. 2nd., rev. 1971. Repr. in new format. Baltimore: G.P.C., 1973.

Based on records in the North Carolina Dept. of Archives and History. Comprehensive index. 14,000 heads of household. A special state enumeration very important, because by 1790 many had left the state.

2645 **Reichel, Levin T.** The Moravians in North Carolina. An authentic history. 1857. Repr. Baltimore: G.P.C., 1968.

Early Moravians, 1782-1856; lists of settlers, heads of families, and relative data.

2646 **Smallwood, Marilu (Burch).** Some colonial and Revolutionary families of North Carolina. v.1-3. St. Augustine, Fla., 1964-73.

2646a **Spence, Wilma C.** Tombstones and epitaphs of northeastern North Carolina. . . . Baltimore: Gateway Pr., 1973.

Consists of Beaufort, Camden, Chowan, Currituck, Gates, Hyde, Pasquotank, Perquimans, and Washington counties.

2647 ——— and **Shannonhouse, E. M.** North Carolina Bible records, dating from the early eighteenth century to the present day, including genealogical notes and letters found in some Bibles. Elizabeth City, N.C.: E. M. Shannonhouse, 1974.

200 Bibles; almost 700 surnames.

2648 **State records of North Carolina.** *See* no.2626.

2649 **Stevenson, George.** Maps and other cartographic records in North Carolina State archives. *Archives information circular*, 12. Raleigh, N.C.: The Archives, 1974.

Discusses the 3,000 maps held; land ownership maps, etc. Valuable to genealogists.

2649a ——— North Carolina Revolutionary War records of primary interest to genealogists. *Archives information circular* 13. Raleigh, N.C.: Div. of Archives & History, 1974.

2650 ——— A select bibliography for genealogical research in North Carolina. *Archives information circular*, 10. Raleigh, N.C.: The Archives, 1973.

Revision of *North Carolina local history*, 1972. Comprehensive coverage of counties and state.

2651 **Stout Map Co.** Historical research maps—North Carolina counties. Greensboro, N.C.: The Company, 1973.

Highly detailed research maps of 68 of the 100 counties, showing historical sites and landmarks, etc. Scale 1 inch to 1 mile.

**2651a** **Tar heel tracks:** genealogical research in North Carolina. Raleigh: Dept. of Cultural Resources, 1974.
12-page brochure for genealogists. Issued free.

**2652** **Thornton, Mary L.** A bibliography of North Carolina, 1598–1956. Repr. Westport, Conn.: Greenwood, 1973.
Publications listed are from the catalog of the North Carolina collection, which includes material dealing with North Carolina and North Carolinians, writing of North Carolinians, and periodicals published. Marginal interest for genealogists.

**2653** **Tilley, Nannie M.,** and **Goodwin, N. L.** Guide to manuscript collections in the Duke University Library, Durham, N.C., 1947. *Historical papers of the Trinity College Historical Soc.,* ser. 27/8. Durham, N.C.: Duke Univ. Pr., 1947.
Dated but useful for genealogists.

**2653a** **Topkins, Robert M.** Marriage and death notices from the *Western Carolinian* (1820–82). Raleigh, N.C.: The Compiler, 1974.
Material covers whole of western Carolina but emphasis on Rowan county.

**2654** **U.S. Bureau of the Census.** Heads of families at the first census of the United States taken in the year 1790. North Carolina. 1908. Repr. Baltimore: G.P.C., 1961, etc.; Spartanburg, S.C.: Reprint Co., 1964, etc.

**2655** **University of North Carolina, Chapel Hill. General alumni Association.** Alumni history of the University of North Carolina. 3rd ed. Durham, N.C., 1974.
3rd ed. includes essential data for all known alumni through 1974.

**2656** ——— Alumni directory. Durham, N.C., 1954.
Covers 1795–1953. Not much biographical data; many inaccuracies.

**2657** **Wheeler, John H.** Historical sketches of North Carolina, from 1584–1851. 2v. in 1. 1851. Repr. ·1925 and 1964. Baltimore: G.P.C., 1974.

v.1, ser.1: *History of the colony;* ser. 2: *History of the state;* v.2, ser.3: *County data, notes on residents.* Sketches of prominent families and early settlers. Emphasis on prominent families and early settlers.

**2658** ——— Reminiscences and memories of North Carolina and eminent North Carolinians. 1884. Repr. Baltimore: G.P.C., 1966.
Extensive genealogies of 65 prominent families. Arrangement by county; biographical sketches of prominent persons and genealogical sketches of families.

**2659** **White, Katherine K.** The King's Mountain men, the story of the battle, with sketches of the American soldiers who took part . . . 1924. Repr. Baltimore: G.P.C., 1970.

NORTH DAKOTA

Settled ca. 1766; entered Union 1889

*North Dakota Library Commission, Bismarck*
*Mrs. William A. Burns, Bismarck*

**2660** **Aberle, George P.** Pioneers and their sons: one hundred and sixty-five family histories. 2v. Hague, N.D.: The Author, [1965–72].
All settlers of North Dakota.

**2661** **Bird, George F.,** and **Taylor, E. J., Jr.** History of the city of Bismarck, North Dakota—the first 100 years 1872–1972. Bismarck, N.D.: Bismarck Centennial Assoc., 1972.
Bibliography, but no index.

**2662** **Bismarck-Mandan Historical and Genealogical Society newsletter.** 1972– . Bismarck, N.D.: The Society.

**2663** **Burns, Betty S.** The historical and genealogical materials in the North Dakota State Historical Society Library 1973. Bismarck, N.D.: Bismarck-Mandan Historical & Genealogical Soc., 1974.

**2664** **Carter, Clarence E.** The territory of the River Ohio, 1790–96. *Territo-*

*rial Papers of the U.S.* 4. 1936. Repr. New York: A.M.S. Press, 1973.
Lists of persons signing petitions, memorials, etc.

2665 **Compendium of history and biography of North Dakota** . . . Chicago, 1909.
Mug book.

2666 **Crawford, Lewis F.** History of North Dakota. 3v. Chicago, 1931.
v.2-3 biographical.

2667 **Hadler, Mabel L.** Towner county, North Dakota families. 6v. Long Beach, Calif., 1958-62.
Excellent; alphabetically indexed.

2668 **Hager, George H.** Index to the journals of the North Dakota State Historical Society, 1906-70; *North Dakota State Historical Society collections,* 1906-25; *North Dakota historical quarterly,* 1926-44; *North Dakota history,* 1945-70. Bismarck, N.C.: State Library Commission, 1973.

2669 **Hennessy, William B.** History of North Dakota . . . including biographies of the builders of the commonwealth . . . Bismarck, N.C., 1910.
Mug book.

2670 **Heritage review.** v.1- , 1971- . Aneta, N.D.: North Dakota Historical Soc. of Germans from Russia, Inc.
Articles about Germans from Russia, customs, migration, etc. Refers mostly to North Dakota, but some information about those who have settled in Canada. Semi-annual.

2671 **Historical Records Survey.** Guide to church vital statistics records in North Dakota. Bismarck, N.C., 1942.

2672 ——— Guide to public vital statistics records in North Dakota. v.1 (all pub.). Bismarck, N.D., 1941.

2673 ——— Inventory of county archives of North Dakota. 3v. Bismarck, N.D., 1938-41.

Only the following numbers were published: 17 (Golden Valley), 29 (Mercer), and 53 (Williams). Unpublished material deposited in State Library Commission, Bismarck, N.D.

2674 **Hixson (W. W.) and Co.** Atlas of North Dakota. Rockford, Ill., [1933?].
Cover: *Plat book of North Dakota.*

2675 **Illustrated album of biography of the famous Valley of the Red River of the north and the park regions of Minnesota and North Dakota.** Containing biographical sketches of . . . settlers and representative citizens. Chicago, 1889.

2676 **Lounsberry, Clement A.** North Dakota history and people . . . 3v. Chicago, 1917.
v.2-3 biographical.

2677 **North Dakota Historical Society of Germans from Russia, Inc.** Work papers 1-4. (Die Historische Gesellschaft der Deutschen von Russland.) Bismarck, N.D.: The Society, 1971-2.
In English.

2678 **North Dakota State Historical Society.** Collections. v.1-7. Bismarck, N.D., 1906-25.
Contains list of members, biographies, gazetteer of old settlers, general and local history.

2679 **Robinson, Elwyn B.** History of North Dakota. Lincoln, Nebr.: Univ. of Nebraska Pr., 1966.
Best and most recent standard work of reference, useful for genealogists.

2680 **Der Stammbaum.** v.1- , 1973- . Aneta, N.D.: North Dakota Historical Soc. of Germans from Russia, Inc.
An annual. Lists of surnames and areas under research. Not limited to North Dakota. In English.

2681 **Williams, Mary A. B.** Origins of North Dakota place names. Washburn, N.D.: Bismarck Tribune, 1966.
No index but useful guide.

**2682** Yarns of pioneers. Minneapolis, Minn., 1953.
Local history of North Dakota.

OHIO

Settled ca. 1788; entered Union 1803
*Ohio Historical Society, Columbus*
*Public Library of Cincinnati and Hamilton County*
*Western Reserve Historical Society, Cleveland*
*Mrs. Lida F. Harshman, Mineral Ridge, Ohio*
*Mrs. Mary Keysor Meyer, Maryland Historical Society, Baltimore*

**2683** Biographical cyclopaedia and portrait gallery, with an historical sketch of the state of Ohio. 6v. Cincinnati, Ohio, 1883[ -95].
Representative of the whole state; pertains only to prominent citizens.

**2684** Biographical cyclopaedia of Ohio in the 19th century. Ed. by Charles Robson. Cincinnati, Ohio, 1876.

**2685** Brennan, Joseph F. A biographical cyclopedia and portrait gallery of distinguished men . . . Cincinnati, Ohio, 1879.

**2686** Brien, Lindsay (Metcalfe). A genealogical index of pioneers in the Miami Valley, Ohio: Miami, Montgomery, Preble, and Warren counties, Ohio. Knightstown, Ind.: Mayhill Pub., 1970.
Cover title: *Miami Valley, Ohio, pioneers.* Rev., corr., and expanded from author's weekly column, "Our forefathers: genealogy of Miami Valley families," published 1933-39 in the *Dayton journal*.

**2687** Cleveland Centennial Committee. Genealogical data relating to women in the Western Reserve before 1840 (1850). Collected and compiled by the Women's Dept., Cleveland Centennial Commission. 13v. Cleveland, Ohio: Western Reserve Historical Soc., 1943-50.
Typescript; also on microfilm.

**2688** Commemorative biographical record of northwestern Ohio, including counties of Henry, Williams, and Fulton, containing biographical sketches of prominent and representative citizens and of many of the early settled families. Chicago, 1899.
Mug book.

**2689** Craig, Robert D. Resident proprietors of the Connecticut Western Reserve. An Ohio tax list of 1804. Cincinnati, Ohio: The Author, 1963.

**2690** Cross, Harold E. Old Amish genealogy, Holmes county and vicinity. Baltimore: Director of Medical Genetics, Johns Hopkins Univ., School of Medicine, 1967.

**2691** D.A.R. Ohio [The D.A.R.'s roster]. The official roster of the soldiers of the American Revolution buried in the state of Ohio . . . 3v. (Columbus, Ohio, 1929-59).
v.1 was given to the state by the D.A.R. and was published by the Adjutant General's Office; v.2 has title *The official roster of the soldiers of the American Revolution who lived in the state of Ohio . . .* compiled by Jane F. Dailey, 1928; v.3 has title *Official register III: soldiers of the American Revolution who lived in the state of Ohio.* 1959. The set is commonly known as *The D.A.R.'s roster.* Many errors; use with caution. Many soldiers listed did not actually serve in the Revolution. Corrections and additions are published in the Ohio D.A.R. news. v.1-2 have been reprinted, 1974, by Trumbull county chapter of Ohio Genealogical Soc., Mineral Ridge, Ohio; v.3 still in print, available from D.A.R., Painesville, Ohio.

**2692** Der Deutsche Pioneer: Errinerungen aus dem Pioneer-Leben der Deutschen in Amerika. v.1-18, 1869-87. Cincinnati, Ohio.
Publ. of Deutscher Pioneerverein von Cincinnati—German Pioneer Club of Cincinnati. Memories from pioneer lives of Germans in America.

**2693** Dickoré, Marie P. Census for Cincinnati, Ohio, 1817 and Hamilton county; Ohio voters' lists, 1798 and 1799. Cincinnati, Ohio, 1960.

**2694** **Diefenbach, Mrs. H. B.** Index to the grave records of soldiers of the War of 1812 buried in Ohio. Assisted by Mrs. C. O. Ross. n.p., 1945.

**2695** **Douthit, Ruth L.** Ohio resources for genealogists with some references for genealogical searching in Ohio. 2nd ed. Detroit, Mich.: Detroit Soc. for Genealogical Research, 1971.

A revision of 2nd ed. of 1962. Ohio genealogical research should begin with this work.

**2696** **Downes, Randolph C.** Evolution of Ohio county boundaries. *Ohio archaeological and historical quarterly,* v.36, no.3, 1927. Columbus, Ohio.

Published in paperback in 1970 by Ohio Historical Soc., Columbus, Ohio.

**2697** ——— History of Lake Shore, Ohio. 3v. New York, 1952.
v.3 biographical.

**2698** **Duff, William C.** History of the north central Ohio embracing Richland, Ashland, Wayne, Medina, Lorain, Huron, and Knox counties. 3v. Topeka, Kans., 1931.

**2699** **Dyer, Albion M.** First ownership of Ohio lands. 1911. Repr. Baltimore: G.P.C., 1969.

Originally published in *New England historical and genealogical register,* v.64–65, 1910–11. Register reprints, ser.A, v.37. Covers only a small part of Ohio: over 1,000 proprietors of the Ohio Company, 1788–92, with full data.

**2700** **Fess, Simeon D.** Ohio . . . 5v. Chicago, 1937.

v.3, gazetteer; v.4, Ohio's 300; v.5, supplementary biographical v.

**2701** **The Firelands pioneer.** v.1–13, 1858–78; new ser., v.1–25, 1882–1937. Norwalk, Ohio: Firelands Historical Soc.

The Firelands area is in the extreme western section of the Western Reserve; it was given to those in Connecticut who suffered at the hands of the British during the Revolution. Some of the volumes are in print.

**2702** ——— Index, 1858–1927. Norwalk, Ohio: The Society, 1939.

Useful for locating Ohio family names. Many reminiscences of original settlers.

**2703** ——— Obituary index, 1857–1909. [1910.]

**2704** **Galbreath, Charles B.** History of Ohio. 5v. Chicago, 1925.
v.3–5 biographical.

**2705** ——— ——— Cross index. By Robertalee Lent. 2v. Post Falls, Id.: Genealogical Reference Builders, 1969.

**2706** ——— ——— Index to v.3. Compiled by Fay Maxwell. Columbus, Ohio: The Author, 1973.

**2707** **Gardner, Frank W.** Central Ohio genealogical notes and queries. In *National Genealogical Soc. quarterly,* v.25–32, 1936–43.

**2708** **Gateway to the west.** v.1– , 1968– . Arcana, Ohio: Anita Short and Ruth Bowers.

Quarterly containing genealogical material taken from early Ohio records at various times. Best Ohio genealogical magazine.

**2708a** **Gutgesell, Stephen.** Ohio newspaper guide, 1793–1973. Columbus: Ohio Historical Soc., 1974.

Listing of over 3,000 Ohio newspapers with holdings coded to 240 Ohio libraries.

**2709** **Hanna, Charles A.** Ohio Valley genealogies relating chiefly to families in Harrison, Belmont, and Jefferson counties, Ohio, and Washington, Westmoreland, and Fayette counties, Pennsylvania. 1900. Repr. Baltimore: G.P.C., 1972.

About 350 genealogies of first settlers in western Pennsylvania and eastern Ohio. Standard work on Ohio Valley area. Use with care.

**2710** Hardesty, H. H., and Co. Historical and geographical encyclopedia . . . maps of each state and territory of the U.S. and the provinces of Canada . . . special history of northwestern Ohio . . . Chicago, 1883.

**2711** Harshman, Lida F. Index to the 1850 federal population census of Ohio. Compiled by the Ohio Family Historians and their friends. Mineral Ridge, Ohio: Lida F. Harshman, 1972.
Only heads of families and any person with a surname differing from that of the head of the household are listed. Over half a million names. Spine: *Index to the 1850 federal population census of Ohio:* Harshman.

**2712** Hildreth, Samuel P. Biographical and historical memoirs of early pioneer settlers of Ohio . . . *Historical and Philosophical Soc. of Ohio publ.* 2. Cincinnati, Ohio, 1852.
Better than 1854 edition.

**2713** Hinshaw, William W. Encyclopedia of American Quaker genealogy. v.4-5. The Ohio Quaker genealogical records. 1946. Repr. Baltimore: G.P.C., 1973.
Ed. by Thomas W. Marshall and H. Lindley, from Hinshaw material. The most complete work on Ohio Quakers.

**2714** Historical Records Survey. Inventory of county archives of Ohio. 27v. Columbus, Ohio, 1936-42.
Only the following numbers were published: 1 (Adams), 2 (Allen), 3 (Ashland), 5 (Athens), 8 (Brown), 15 (Columbiana), 18 (Cuyahoga), 24 (Fayette), 25 (Franklin), 28 (Geauga), 31 (Hamilton), 32 (Hancock), 40 (Jackson), 42 (Knox), 43 (Lake), 47 (Lorain), 48 (Lucas), 49 (Madison), 57 (Montgomery), 66 (Pike), 71 (Ross), 73 (Scioto), 74 (Seneca), 76 (Stark), 77 (Summit), 78 (Trumbull), and 84 (Washington). Unpublished material deposited in Ohio State Archaeological and Historical Society, Columbus, Ohio.

**2715** ———— Roman Catholic Church: Diocese of Cleveland. Columbus, Ohio, 1942.

**2716** History of Hocking Valley, Ohio . . . portraits of prominent persons and biographies of representative citizens. 2v. Chicago, 1883. Embraces counties of Athens, Hocking, and Vinton.

**2717** History of lower Scioto Valley, Ohio. Chicago, 1884.
Portraits of prominent citizens and biographies of representative citizens.

**2718** History of the upper Ohio Valley . . . with family history and biographical sketches. 2v. Madison, Wisc., 1890.
v.1, West Virginia Panhandle; v.2, Jefferson and Belmont counties, Ohio.

**2719** Houck, George F. A history of Catholicity in northern Ohio and in the diocese of Cleveland from 1749 to December 31, 1900. 2v. Cleveland, Ohio, 1903.
v.2 biographical by Michael W. Carr.

**2720** Hover, John C., and Barnes, J. D. Memoirs of the Miami Valley. 3v. Chicago, 1920.
Different editions were printed, each featuring a v.3 which contained biographical sketches of a particular county.

**2721** Howe, Henry. Historical collections of Ohio . . . 3v. Centennial ed. Cincinnati, Ohio, 1901.
Also published in 1v., 1852, and 2v. in 1900. Important Ohio source; histories of each county, biographies, early settlers, etc.

**2722** Jenkins, Warren. The Ohio gazetteer . . . Rev. ed. with a 2nd appendix, containing the census of the state of Ohio . . . Columbus, Ohio, 1841.

**2723** Kilbourn, John. The Ohio gazetteer, or topographical dictionary . . . 11th ed. Columbus, Ohio, 1833.

**2724** Knapp, Horace S. History of the Maumee Valley, commencing . . . 1680. Toledo, Ohio, 1872.
Much on early settlements and settlers in Fort Wayne and Allen counties, Indiana, and Mercer, Allen, Crawford, Wyandot, Seneca, Sandusky, Lucas, Defiance, Paulding, and Putnam counties, Ohio.

2725  **Koleda, Elizabeth P.** Some Ohio and Iowa pioneers; their friends and descendants. Prineville, Ore.: The Compiler, 1973. Available from the Compiler, P.O. Box 27, Prineville, Ore. 97754.

2726  **Lentz, Andrea D.** A guide to manuscripts of the Ohio Historical Society. Columbus, Ohio: The Society, 1972.
Also includes entries for manuscripts at the Hayes Library, Fremont, Ohio.

2727  **Lewis, Thomas W.** History of southeastern Ohio and the Muskingum Valley . . . 3v. Chicago, 1928.
v.3 biographical.

2728  **McCay, Betty L.** Sources for genealogical searching in Ohio. Rev. ed. Indianapolis, Ind.: The Author, 1973.
History, sources, bibliography, and boundaries, 1790–1818.

2729  **Main, Florence (Mrs. Carl).** Ohio genealogical records. Cleveland, Ohio: Genealogical Advisory Committee of the Western Reserve Historical Soc., 1968.

2730  **Maskey, Carle L.** Some early Ohio and Pennsylvania families. Los Angeles, 1945.

2731  **Maxwell, Fay.** Ohio Indian trails, Ohio Revolutionary trails, establishment of Ohio counties. Columbus, Ohio: The Author, 1973.
Township names and other useful information.

2732  **Mercer, James K.,** and **Vallandigham, C. N.** Representative men of Ohio, 1896–97. Columbus, Ohio, 1896.
Mug book.

2733  **Mink, Arthur de W.** Title list of Ohio newspapers. Columbus, Ohio: Ohio State Archaeological and Historical Soc., 1945.

2734  ——— Union list of Ohio newspapers available in Ohio. Columbus, Ohio: Ohio State Archaeological and Historical Soc., 1946.

2735  **National Society, United States Daughters of 1812, Ohio.** Index to the grave records of servicemen of the War of 1812, State of Ohio. n.p., 1969.

2736  **Neely, Ruth.** Women in Ohio . . . 3v. Chicago, n.d.
Mug book.

2737  **Ohio. Adjutant General's Office.** The official roster of Ohio soldiers in the War with Spain 1898–99. Columbus, Ohio, 1916.
Ohio Historical Society has W.P.A. index.

2738  ——— Roster of Ohio soldiers in the War of 1812. 1916. Repr. Baltimore: G.P.C., 1968.

2739  ——— ——— Index compiled by Grace Garner. Spokane, Wash.: Eastern Washington Genealogical Soc., 1974.

2740  **Ohio. Auditor of the State.** A short history of Ohio land grants. Rev. ed. Columbus, Ohio: Blank Book Co., 1971.
Authoritative work by the then state auditor, 1939, Joseph T. Ferguson.

2741  **Ohio. Roster Commission.** Official roster of the soldiers of the state of Ohio in the War of the Rebellion, 1861–66. 12v. Akron, Ohio, 1886–95.
v.12 contains U.S. Navy (Ohio enlistments), and Mexican War soldiers. Ohio Historical Soc. has 4v. W.P.A. typescript index. 1938.

2742  **Ohio. State Library of Ohio.** Ohio genealogy sources by county. Columbus, Ohio: The Library, 1970.
Gives detailed index of histories, marriages, cemetery, and death records and family-church Bible records.

2743  **Ohio Family Historians.** 1830 federal population census. Ohio. Index. 2v. Columbus, Ohio: Ohio Library Fdn., 1964.
First complete census of Ohio.

2744  **Ohio genealogical quarterly.** v.1–8, no.2. Columbus, Ohio, 1937–44.

Published by Columbus Genealogical Society; statewide articles, including 1810 tax lists.

**2745   Ohio Library Foundation.** 1820 federal population census: Ohio. Index. Columbus, Ohio: The Foundation, 1964.

Incomplete; two important counties omitted—Franklin and Wood—as census schedules not extant. Earliest census in Ohio for which records were kept by family name as well as by numerical summary of data collected. First census in 1810 was destroyed by fire.

**2746   Ohio records and pioneer families.** Ed. by Esther W. Powell (1960-69). v.1- , 1960- . Ashland, Ohio: Ohio Genealogical Soc.

Excellent periodical. Source records. Pub. by Society since 1970. v.1-10 still available from E. W. Powell, Akron, Ohio.

**2747   Ohio researcher.** v.1- , 1962- . West Jordan, Utah: Allstates Research Co.

**2748   Ohio's progressive sons . . .** Cincinnati, Ohio, 1905.

Mug book.

**2749   The "Old Northwest" genealogical quarterly.** v.1-15. Columbus, Ohio, 1898-1912.

Vigorous genealogical magazine published by the "Old Northwest" Genealogical Society. Monumental inscriptions, marriage lists, etc.

**2750   Overman, William D.** Ohio town names. Akron, Ohio, 1958.

The origins of the names of over 500 Ohio cities, townships, and villages.

**2751   Peters, William E.** Ohio lands and their history . . . 3rd ed. Athens, Ohio, ca.1930.

**2752   Pike, Kermit J.** A guide to the manuscripts and archive of the Western Reserve Historical Society. Cleveland, Ohio: The Society, 1972.

Primary repository for the study of Ohio and the Western Reserve.

**2753   Portrait and biographical record of the Scioto Valley, Ohio.** Chicago, 1894.

**2755   Powell, Esther W.** Early Ohio tax records. Akron, Ohio: The Compiler, 1971.

130 tax lists, also Virginia Military District tax list in 1801 in Ohio. Substitute for 1810 Ohio census destroyed in War of 1812. Helps to locate earliest landowners, with earliest list for each Ohio county.

**2756   ——— ———** Surname index. Akron, Ohio: The Compiler, 1974.

Includes 74 counties.

**2757   The report.** v.1- , 1970- . Mansfield, Ohio: Ohio Genealogical Soc.

From 1961-69 it was pub. as a newspaper 6 times a year; became quarterly in 1970.

**2758   Rust, Orton G.** History of west central Ohio. 3v. Indianapolis, Ind., 1934.

v.3 biographical.

**2759   Sherman, Christopher E.** Original Ohio land subdivisions. Columbus, Ohio, 1925.

v.3 of *Ohio cooperative topographic survey.*

**2760   Smith, William E.** History of southwestern Ohio: the Miami Valley. 3v. West Palm Beach, Fla., 1964.

v.3 biographical.

**2761   Society of Ohio Archivists.** Guide to manuscripts repositories and institutional records in Ohio. Bowling Green, Ohio: The Society, Bowling Green State Univ. Lib., 1974.

Holdings of 95 manuscripts repositories and 759 institutional records collections.

**2762   Stewart, John S.** History of northeastern Ohio. 3v. Indianapolis, Ind., 1935.

v.2-3 biographical.

**2763   Stille, Samuel H.** Ohio builds a nation; a memoir to the pioneers and the celebrated sons of the "Buckeye" state. 5th ed. Chicago, 1962.

2764 **Summers, Ewing.** Genealogical and family history of eastern Ohio. New York, 1903.

Mug book.

2764a **Swanson, Patricia.** Ohio printed state documents, 1803–1970. Columbus: Ohio Historical Soc., 1973.

Lists 8,000 titles and holdings coded to 18 Ohio libraries.

2765 **Thomson, Peter G.** A bibliography of the state of Ohio; being a catalogue of the books and pamphlets relating to the history of the state . . . 2v. Chicago, 1880–90.

v.1, bibliography; v.2, catalog of books relating to the state of Ohio, the west and northwest. v.1 only repr. by Argonaut Pr., New York, 1966.

2766 **Upton, Harriet (Taylor).** History of the Western Reserve. 3v. Chicago, 1910.

v.2-3 biographical. Counties included: Ashtabula, Cuyahoga, Erie, Geauga, Huron, Lake, Lorain, Mahoning, Medina, Portage, Summit, and Trumbull.

2767 **Van Tassel, Charles S.** Story of the Maumee Valley, Toledo, and the Sandusky region . . . 4v. Chicago, 1929.

v.3-4 biographical.

2768 **Weaver, Clarence L.,** and **Mills, H. M.** County and local historical material in the Ohio State Archaeological and Historical Library. In *Ohio state archaeological and historical quarterly*, v.45, 1936, and updated, v.54, 1945.

2769 **Wickham, Gertrude Van R.** Memorial to the pioneer women of the Western Reserve. 5pts. and index in 2v. Cleveland, Ohio, 1896–1924.

2770 **Wilkens, Cleo G.** Index to 1840 federal population census of Ohio. Alphabetized by J. H. Wilkens. 4v. Fort Wayne, Ind.: The Compiler, 1969–72.

Printed by Fort Wayne Public Lib. Full references.

2771 **William, William W.** History of the Firelands, comprising Huron and Erie counties . . . 1879. Repr. Evansville, Ind.: Unigraphic, 1973.

Basic source on almost any historical subject area of north-central Ohio. Background histories, pioneer memories. Has new 14,500 name index.

2772 **Winter, Nevin O.** A history of northwest Ohio . . . 3v. Chicago, 1917.

v.2-3 biographical. Mug book.

2773 **Wright, George.** Representative citizens of Ohio. Memorial-genealogical. Cleveland, Ohio, 1913.

2774 **Yon, Paul D.** Guide to Ohio county and municipal government records for urban research. Columbus, Ohio: Ohio Historical Soc., 1973.

Lists data on 16 counties and 16 municipalities.

OKLAHOMA

Settled ca. 1889; entered Union 1907

*Oklahoma Historical Society, Oklahoma*
*Tulsa City-County Library System*
*Miss Patricia Chadwell, Fort Worth, Texas*

✢ Many works concerning the Indians of Oklahoma will be found under the Indian section, no.652–716.

2775 **Boren, Lyle H.,** and **Boren, D.** Who is who in Oklahoma: a biographical history of men and women in Oklahoma life today. Guthrie, Okla., 1935.

2776 **D.A.R. Oklahoma.** A roster of the Oklahoma Society, and register of ancestors, 1909–59. Ed. by Lorena Spillers. Tulsa, Okla., 1959.

2777 ———— 1st supplement. Compiled and ed. by Myrtle M. Willson. Tulsa, Okla., 1964.

Both available from Oklahoma Society, D.A.R. Good index.

2778 **Foreman, Grant.** Early post offices of Oklahoma. In *Chronicles of Oklahoma*, v.6–7, 1928–29.

2779　**Harlow, Rex.** Oklahoma leaders: biographical sketches of the foremost living men of Oklahoma City, 1928.
Good sketches, many dating back prior to Civil War.

2780　**Harrell, Mrs. J. B.** Oklahoma and Oklahomans. n.p., 1922.
Contains lists of pioneers.

2781　**Hill, Luther B.** A history of the state of Oklahoma. 2v. New York, 1908.
Pt. of v.1 and all v.2 biographical.

2782　**Historical Records Survey.** Guide to public vital statistics records in Oklahoma. Oklahoma City, Okla., 1941.

2783　――――― Inventory of county archives of Oklahoma. 11v. Oklahoma City, Okla., 1937-41.
Only the following numbers were published: 3 (Atoka), 5 (Beckham), 11 (Cherokee), 13 (Cimarron), 31 (Haskell), 41 (Lincoln), 46 (McIntosh), 49 (Mayes), 51 (Muskogee), 61 (Pittsburgh), and 64 (Pushmataha). Unpublished material deposited in State Library, Oklahoma City, Okla.

2784　――――― Preliminary list of churches and religious organizations in Oklahoma. v.1 (all pub.). Oklahoma City, Okla., 1941.

2785　**Jayne, Bert T.** Who's who in Oklahoma. Oklahoma City, Okla., 1958.

2786　**Litton, Gaston L.** History of Oklahoma at the golden anniversary of statehood. 4v. New York, 1957.
v.3-4 family and personal history.

2787　**Mills, Madeline S.** Relocated cemeteries in Oklahoma and parts of Kansas and Texas. Tulsa, Okla.: The Author, 1974.
Covers cemeteries relocated by Corps of Engineers for flood control, the Arkansas Waterway and enlargement of Fort Sill. Includes all of Oklahoma, a few counties of northern Texas, and a number of counties in southern Kansas. 250 cemeteries, 7,000 graves, 3,000 surnames.

2788　**Morris, John W.,** and **McReynolds, E. C.** Historical atlas of Oklahoma. 2nd pr. Norman, Okla.: Univ. of Oklahoma Pr., 1966.
All pertinent information including tribal locations, missions, battles, county information, etc.

2789　**Oklahoma.** Special limited ed. Chicago, 1916.
Mug book.

2790　**Oklahoma Genealogical Society.**
Index to applications for pensions from the state of Oklahoma submitted by Confederate soldiers, sailors and their widows. *Special publ.* 2. Oklahoma City, Okla.: The Society, 1969.

2791　――――― An index to the 1890 U.S. census of Union veterans and their widows in Oklahoma and Indian territories (including Old Greer county) and soldiers stationed at military installations in their territories. (Section I.) An index to records from the Oklahoma Union Soldiers' Home including Civil War veterans and their dependents, veterans of wars with Spain and Mexico, etc. (Section II.) *Special publ.* 3. Oklahoma City, Okla.: The Society, 1970.

2792　――――― Quarterly. v.1- , 1955- . Oklahoma City, Okla.: The Society.
The Society also published a bulletin from 1955 to 1960.

2793　――――― Surname index. *Special publ.* 1. Oklahoma City, Okla.: The Society, 1969.
Ancestors from 45 states and over 15 foreign countries. Ed. by Jo A. Garrison.

2794　**Portrait and biographical record of Oklahoma** . . . Chicago, 1901.
pp.13-1290 are biographical sketches of early Oklahoma citizens.

2795　**Shirk, George H.** Oklahoma place names. 2nd ed. Norman, Okla.: Univ. of Oklahoma Pr., 1974.
3,600 names. Location of each place, origin, notations of name changes and identification of post offices no longer in existence.

2796 **Smith, James W.** Smith's first directory of Oklahoma territory for . . . 1890. Guthrie, Okla., 1890.
Index of residents, names of all homesteaders, etc.

2797 **Society of Mayflower Descendants. Oklahoma.** Lineages, compiled by Lewis E. Neff. Oklahoma City, Okla.: The Society, 1959.
Cover title: *Mayflower descendants in the state of Oklahoma.*

2798 **Thoburn, Joseph B.** Standard history of Oklahoma. 5v. Chicago, 1916.
v.3–5 biographical.

2799 ——— and **Wright, M. H.** Oklahoma; a history of the state and its people. 4v. New York, 1929.
v.3–4 biographical sketches.

2800 **Toaz, Mildred.** Oklahoma cemetery records. v.1–2. Assembled by Mrs. H. C. Stallings. Oklahoma City, Okla., 1970–74 (in progress). From Author, Stringtown, Okla., 74569.

2800a **Town and place locations.** Oklahoma City, Okla.: Oklahoma Department of Highways, 1974.
Excellent supplement to place name literature. In form of gazetteer with 4,200 entries.

2801 **Tulsa annals.** v.1– , 1966– . Tulsa, Okla.: Tulsa Genealogical Soc.
Quarterly; primarily Oklahoma records.

2802 **West, C. W.** ("Dub"). Persons and places of Indian territory. Muskogee, Okla.: Muskogee Pub. Co., 1974.
Much local and regional history of Oklahoma.

2803 **Woods, Frances.** First census of Oklahoma. Repr. of *Indian lands west of Arkansas (Oklahoma): population schedule of the United States census of 1860.* Fort Worth, Tex.: Arrow Printing Co., 1966.
Concerns whites on Indian lands in Oklahoma.

OREGON

Settled ca. 1811; entered Union 1859

*Genealogical Forum of Portland*
*Oregon Historical Society, Portland*
*Oregon State Library, Salem*
*Seattle Public Library, Seattle, Wash.*

✢ Since much of the material concerns Oregon and Washington states, both states should be considered when researching in these areas.

2804 **Brown, Erma S.** Oregon county boundary change maps, 1843–1916. Lebanon, Ore.: End of Trail Researchers, 1970.

2805 **Canby Historical Society.** Land laws and early settlers of Oregon. 3v. Canby, Ore.: The Society, 1970.

2806 **Carey, Charles H.** General history of Oregon. 3rd ed. Portland, Ore.: Binfords & Mort, 1971.
Prior to 1861.

2807 ——— History of Oregon. 3v. Chicago, 1922.
v.2–3 biographical.

2808 **Corning, Howard McK.** Dictionary of Oregon history. Compiled from the research file of the former Oregon Writer's Project, with much added material. Portland, Ore.: Binfords & Mort, 1956.

2809 **D.A.R. Oregon.** Roster of ancestors. By Mrs. George R. (Louise W.) Goodrich. [Tillamook, Ore.:], D.A.R., 1963.

2810 **Duniway, David C.** Have you an Oregon ancestor? *Oregon state archives bull.* v.5, publ.26. Salem, Ore.: Oregon State Lib., 1962.

2811 **Evans, Elwood** (and others). History of the Pacific northwest: Oregon and Washington. 2v. Portland, Ore., 1889.
v.2 biographical.

2812 **Gaston, Joseph.** The centennial history of Oregon. 1811–1912. 4v. Chicago, 1912.
v.2–4 biographical.

**2813 Genealogical Forum of Portland.** Genealogical material in Oregon donation land claims, abstracted from applications. v.1- , 1957- (in progress). Portland, Ore.: The Forum.
v.4 has ". . . land claims abstracted from rejected applications."

**2813a** ⸺ ⸺ Supplement to v.1 and a new v.5 by Lottie L. Gurley. Portland, Ore.: The Forum, 1974.

**2814** ⸺ Geographical index to v.1- , 1960- . Portland, Ore.: The Forum.

**2815** ⸺ Genealogical research in Oregon. *National Genealogical Soc. quarterly,* v.47, no.3. Washington, D.C.: The Society, 1959.

**2816** ⸺ Index to Oregon donation land claim files in the National Archives. Portland, Ore., 1953-57.
Issued as a separately paged supplement to the *Genealogical Forum of Portland, Oregon, bull.,* 3-7, 1953-57.

**2817** ⸺ Monthly bulletin. v.1- , 1951- . Portland, Ore.: The Forum.
v.1-2, 1951, had title *Forum exchange;* title varies: at times, *Genealogy bulletin;* some vols. have no title.

**2818** ⸺ Year book. v.1- , 1953- . Portland, Ore.: The Forum.

**2819** ⸺ Yesterday's roll call; statistical data and genealogical facts from census in Baker, Sherman and Umatilla counties, Oregon. Portland, Ore.: The Forum.
New roll in progress.

**2820 Hiday, Mrs. Harry I.** United States censuses: Douglas county and Washington county, 1880; Multnomah county and Portland county, 1870. Portland, Ore.: Genealogical Forum, 1972- (in progress).

**2821 Hines, Harvey K.** An illustrated history of the state of Oregon . . . and . . . biographical mention of many of its pioneers and prominent citizens. Chicago, 1893.
Biographies pp.241-1300.

**2822 Historical Records Survey.** Directory of church and religious organizations: state of Oregon. Portland, Ore., 1940.

**2823** ⸺ Guide to public vital statistics records in Oregon. Portland, Ore., 1942.

**2824** ⸺ Inventory of county archives of Oregon. 13v. Portland, Ore., 1937-42.
Only the following numbers were published: 2 (Benton), 4 (Clatsop), 6 (Coos), 14 (Hood River), 17 (Josephine), 18 (Klamath), 22 (Linn), 25 (Morrow), 26 (Multnomah, 2v.), 29 (Tillamook), 30 (Umatilla), 33 (Wasco), and 34 (Washington). Unpublished material deposited in Dept. of History, University of Oregon, Eugene, Ore.

**2825** ⸺ Ship registers and enrollments. 2v. Portland, Ore., 1942.
Marshfield, Ore., 1873-1941; Portland, Ore., 1867-1941.

**2826 Hodgkin, Frank E.** and **Galvin, J. J.** Pen pictures of representative men of Oregon. Portland, Ore., 1882.
Mug book.

**2827 Lang, Herbert O.** History of the Willamette Valley, Oregon. Portland, Ore., 1885.
pp.502-902 biographical.

**2828 McArthur, Lewis A.** Oregon geographic names. 4th ed., rev. and enlarged by L. L. McArthur. Portland, Ore.: Oregon Historical Soc., 1974.
An Oregon classic.

**2829 Oregon genealogical bulletin.** v.1- , 1959- . Eugene, Ore.: Oregon Genealogical Soc.

**2830 Oregon Historical Society manuscripts collections.** *Research and bibliography ser.,* 1. Portland, Ore.: The Society, 1971.

Quarterly supplements began to be issued March 1973; 2,300 collections, 4 million pieces, 8,000 entries. The Oregon Historical Records Survey issued a guide to the collections in 1940.

**2831** ———— Microfilm guide. Portland, Ore.: The Society, 1973.
D.A.R. genealogical records, government, newspapers, Russian-American studies collection, maps and scrapbooks. Much local history.

**2833 Oregon, pictorial and biographical.** De luxe suppl. Chicago, 1912.
Mug book.

**2834 Oregon State Library, Salem.** Pioneer families of the Oregon territory, 1850. *Oregon state archives bull.,* v.3, publ.17. 2nd ed. Salem, Ore.: The Library, 1961.
1st ed. was by Herbert J. Salisbury. Includes Lewis and Clark counties in Washington state also.

**2835 Portrait and biographical record of the Willamette Valley, Oregon . . .** Chicago, 1903.
Mug book.

**2836 Portrait and biographical record of western Oregon,** containing original sketches of many well-known citizens past and present. Chicago, 1904.

**2837 Scott, Harvey W.** History of Portland, Oregon, with illustrations and biographical sketches of prominent citizens and pioneers. Portland, Ore., 1890.

**2838** ———— History of the Oregon country. 6v. Cambridge, Mass., 1924.
v.5 biographical and with obituaries; v.6 is index.

**2839 Walling, Albert C.** History of southern Oregon, comprising Jackson, Josephine, Douglas, Curry and Coos counties. Portland, Ore., 1884.
45p. appendix, "Biographical brevities."

**2840 Youngberg, Elsie.** 1850 Oregon territorial census. Lebanon, Ore.: End of Trail Researchers, 1970.

## PENNSYLVANIA

Settled ca. 1682; original state
*Pennsylvania State Library, Harrisburg*
*Dr. George E. McCracken, Des Moines, Iowa.*

**2841 An account of the donated lands of Pennsylvania.** *Pennsylvania archives,* ser.3, v.3, pp.575–757. Harrisburg, Pa., 1896.

**2842 Bates, Samuel P.** History of Pennsylvania volunteers, 1861-65. 5v. Harrisburg, Pa., 1869-71.
All vital data; 1st to 215 regiments and colored regiments.

**2843 Bell, Raymond M.** Searching in western Pennsylvania. Detroit, Mich.: Detroit Soc. for Genealogical Research, 1968.

**2844 Bentley, Elizabeth P.** Index to the 1850 census of Pennsylvania. Baltimore: G.P.C., 1974– (in progress).
Luzerne and Wyoming counties; Northampton; Lancaster published to end of 1974. Fine surname index.

**2845 The biographical encyclopaedia of Pennsylvania of the nineteenth century.** Ed. by Charles Robson, Philadelphia, 1874.

**2846 Brecht, Samuel K.** The genealogical record of the Schwenkfelder families . . . New York, 1923.
1,752p. "Seekers of religious liberty who fled from Silesia to Saxony and thence to Pennsylvania, 1731-37." Monumental work, well indexed; thousands of names.

**2847 Brossman, Schuyler C.** Our keystone families; genealogical queries published in *Lebanon daily news* from October 1966– . Rehrersburg, Pa., 1971– .
Column still published weekly.

**2848 Browning, Charles H.** Welsh settlement of Pennsylvania. 1912. Repr. Baltimore: G.P.C., 1967.
History of the settlement of "Welsh tract" lands granted by Penn, 1681. Con-

tains names of many early emigrants. Account of early emigration of Welsh Quakers and others.

2849 **Campbell, Jane.** San Domingo refugees in Pennsylvania. Compiled for the original d'Orlic-Rodriguez papers. In *American Catholic Historical Soc. records,* v.28-30, 1917-19.
Family papers of those who sought safety from the Negro insurrections at the end of the 18th century. Mostly d'Orlic and Rodriguez families.

2850 **Clint, Florence R.** Pennsylvania area key. A comprehensive study of the genealogical record sources of the state of Pennsylvania, including genealogical maps and history. Denver, Colo.: Area Keys, 1970- (in progress).
For each county, with exception of Philadelphia and Allegheny counties. 59 counties considered.

2851 **Colonial Dames of America. Pennsylvania.** Register. Philadelphia, 1907.

2852 ———— 1928. Philadelphia, 1928.

2853 **Commemorative biographical record of central Pennsylvania** . . . Chicago, 1898.
Large volume covering Centre, Clarion, Clearfield, and Jefferson counties.

2854 **Commemorative biographical record of northeastern Pennsylvania** . . . Chicago, 1900.
Large volume covering Monroe, Pike, Susquehanna, and Wayne counties.

2855 **Continental line, 1st to 13th Pennsylvania regiments.** *Pennsylvania archives,* ser.5, v.2, pp.607-1,104; and v.3. Harrisburg, Pa., 1906.

2856 **Cross, Harold E.,** and **Hostetler, Beulah.** Index to selected Amish genealogies. Baltimore: Div. of Medical Genetics, Johns Hopkins Univ., 1970?
Complete bibliography (400p.) of old Amish genealogies. Fine, computerized index to 118 Amish genealogies. Of particular interest to midwest researchers having difficulty with Pennsylvania families.

2857 **Crumrine, Boyd.** Virginia court records in southwestern Pennsylvania. Records of the district of West Augusta and Ohio and Yohogania counties, Virginia. Repr. with an index by Inez Waldenmaier. Baltimore: G.P.C., 1974.
Originally published as 5 separate pts. in v.1-3 of *Annals of the Carnegie Museum,* 1902-5. Period 1775-80.

2858 **Cuthbertson, John.** Register of marriages and baptisms performed by Rev. John Cuthbertson, Covenanter minister, 1754-91, with index to locations and persons visited, by S. Helen Fields. Washington, D.C., 1934.
Various parts of Pennsylvania.

2859 **Daly, John.** Descriptive inventory of the archives of the city of Philadelphia. Philadelphia: Dept. of Records, 1970.
Great value to genealogists, historians, and others. Items surveyed include deed books, pleas, petitions for naturalization, divorces, passenger lists, vital records, and some state records also. Replacement pages and additions issued sporadically.

2860 **Daughters of the American Colonists, Pennsylvania.** History of the Pennsylvania state society. Ed. and compiled by Maxim Gubi, Mrs. R. C. Clarke, and Mrs. Herald A. Best. Pittsburgh, Pa.: D.A.C., 1969.

2861 **Day, Sherman.** Historical collections of the state of Pennsylvania, containing a copious selection of the most interesting facts, traditions, biographical sketches, etc. . . . Philadelphia, 1843.

2862 **Dickson, Robert J.** Ulster emigration to colonial America, 1718-75. *Ulster-Scot historical ser.,* v.1. New York: Humanities Pr., 1966.
Good bibliography. Much concerns Pennsylvania, *see* notation under no.334.

2863 **Dinsmore, John W.** The Scotch-Irish in America; their history, traits, institutions, and influences: especially as illustrated in the early settlers of western Pennsylvania and their descendants. Chicago, [1906].

**2864  Doddridge, Joseph.** Notes on the settlement and Indian Wars of the western parts of Virginia and Pennsylvania, 1763-83. 1824. Repr. 1912. Repr. 1960, with new material, rev. by John S. Ritenour and W. T. Lindsey. Parsons, W.Va.: McClain Printing Co., 1960; repr. from 1876 ed. by Burt Franklin, New York, 1973.

**2865  Donehoo, George P.** Pennsylvania—a history. 11v. New York, 1926.

v.5-11 biographical. Very comprehensive history of the state in general, and each county specifically.

**2866  Du Bin, Alexander.** Old Philadelphia families. Philadelphia, 1939.

**2867  Early marriage records of Pennsylvania churches.** Records repr. from *Pennsylvania archives,* 2nd ser. Pub. in 1965 in the *Pennsylvania traveler.* Danboro, Pa.: R.T. and M.C. Williams, 1965.

Presbyterian, First Reformed church, Society of Friends.

**2868  Eddy, Henry H.** Guide to the published archives of Pennsylvania, covering the 138v. of *Colonial records* and ser.1-9 of *Pennsylvania archives.* With alphabetized finding list and 2 special indexes by Martha L. Simonetti. Harrisburg, Pa.: Capitol Book Store, 1949.

Note especially the name indexes to the 3rd ser. of *Pennsylvania archives.*

**2869  Egle, William H.** Draughts of the proprietary manors in the province of Pennsylvania . . . *Pennsylvania archives,* ser.3, v.4. Harrisburg, Pa., 1895.

**2870  ———** Muster rolls of the navy and line, militia and rangers, 1775-83, with list of pensioners, 1818-32. *Pennsylvania archives,* ser.3, v.23. Harrisburg, Pa., 1898.

Has also Cumberland county militia 1777-82.

**2871  ———** Names of foreigners who took the oath of allegiance to the province and state of Pennsylvania, 1727-75, with the foreign arrivals, 1786-1808. *Pennsylvania archives,* 2nd ser. v.17. 1892. Repr. Baltimore: G.P.C., 1967.

Ship passenger lists. 10,000 references. *See also* no.2960, 3031.

**2872  ———** Notes and queries: historical, biographical and genealogical: chiefly relating to interior Pennsylvania. 12v. 1881-1900. Repr. Baltimore: G.P.C., 1970.

**2873  ———** Index to main families, persons, places and subjects, plus introduction and bibliography by A. M. Aurand, Jr. (1893-1901). Repr. Baltimore: G.P.C., 1970.

From Egle's newspaper columns; while important for family histories, it is inaccurate and should be used with extreme care. Concerns central Pennsylvania; data on settlers and soldiers of the French and Indian War, Revolutionary War, and War of 1812. Also church records, early wills, marriages, deaths and tax lists. The annual volume for 1900 contains "Early Swiss settlers," a list of immigrants who arrived in Philadelphia in 1735.

**2874  ———** Old rights, proprietary rights, Virginia entries, and soldiers entitled to lands . . . *Pennsylvania archives,* ser.3, v.3. Harrisburg, Pa., 1896.

**2875  ———** Pennsylvania, genealogies chiefly Scotch-Irish and German. 2nd ed. 1896. Repr. Baltimore: G.P.C., 1969.

An early compilation. 2,500 surnames in index. Use with care.

**2876  ———** Pennsylvania in the War of the Revolution: associated battalions and militia, 1775-83. *Pennsylvania archives,* ser.2, v.13-14. Harrisburg, Pa., 1890-92.

Index to both vol. in v.14.

**2877  ———** Pennsylvania women in the American Revolution. 1898. Repr. New Orleans, La.: Polyanthos, 1972.

Details of families of the women, and families of their husbands. Originally published as *Some Pennsylvania women during the War of the Revolution.* 70 biographical sketches. Data in this work is spread in Egle's *Notes and queries,* no.2872.

2878 ———— Returns of taxables for the counties of Bedford, 1773, 1784; Huntingdon, 1788; Westmoreland, 1783, 1786; Fayette, 1785-86; Allegheny, 1791; Washington, 1886; and census of Bedford, 1784 and Westmoreland, 1783. *Pennsylvania archives,* ser.3, v.22. Harrisburg, Pa., 1898.

2879 ———— York, 1779-83. *Pennsylvania archives,* ser.3, v.21. Harrisburg, Pa., 1898.

2880 **Ellis, Franklin,** and **Evans, S.** History of Lancaster county; with biographical sketches of many of its pioneers and prominent men. 1883. Repr. York, Pa.: Lancaster County Historical Soc., 1973.

Repr. has new extensive name anc subject index.

2881 **Encyclopedia of Pennsylvania biography.** v.1-32. New York, 1914-67.

2882 ———— Index, v.1-20. New York, 1932.

v.1-13, ed. by John W. Jordan; v.14-16 by Thomas L. Montgomery; v.17 by Ernest Spofford; v.18-25 by Frederic A. Godcharles; v.26-32 by Alfred D. Keater. Typical mug book; unreliable. v.32 last pub.

2883 **Eshleman, Henry F.** Historic background and annals of the Swiss and German pioneer settlers of southeastern Pennsylvania, and of their remote ancestors. 1917. Repr. Baltimore: G.P.C., 1969; Detroit, Mich.: Gale Research, 1969.

Standard work for the area, with much on the Palatinate immigration. 2,200 names.

2884 **Espenshade, Abraham H.** Pennsylvania place names. 1925. Repr. Detroit, Mich.: Gale Research, 1969; Baltimore: G.P.C., 1970.

Standard reference. Data on county formation; county histories.

2885 **Fisher, Charles A.** Central Pennsylvania marriages, 1700-1896. 1946. Repr. Baltimore: G.P.C., 1974.

2886 ———— Early central Pennsylvania lineages. Selinsgrove, Pa., ca.1948.

2887 ———— Early Pennsylvania births, 1675-1875. Selinsgrove, Pa., 1947.

2888 **Forfeited estates: inventories and sales.** *Pennsylvania archives,* ser.6, v.12-13. Harrisburg, Pa., 1907.

2889 **Fulton, Eleanore J.,** and **Mylin, B. K.** An index to the will books and intestate records of Lancaster county, Pennsylvania, 1729-1850. 1936. Repr. Baltimore: G.P.C., 1974.

Since Lancaster county comprised a very large area of Pennsylvania, this work provides a great deal of information found in the early records of the state. 15,000 names.

2890 **Geiser, Karl F.** Redemptioners and indentured servants in the colony and commonwealth of Pennsylvania. New Haven, Conn., 1901.

Supplement to *Yale review,* v.10, no.2, August 1901.

2891 **Genealogical Society of Pennsylvania.** Genealogical manuscript material index. Philadelphia: The Society, 1964.

2892 **Gibson, John.** History of York county, Pa. . . . 1886. Repr. Evansville, Ind.: Unigraphic, 1973. Available from Historical Soc. of York county, York, Pa.

Lists of men participating in Revolutionary and Civil Wars. 35,000 references, definitive biographies.

2893 **Giuseppi, Montague S.** Naturalizations of foreign Protestants in the American and West Indian colonies. *Huguenot Soc. of London publ.* 24, 1921. Repr. Baltimore: G.P.C., 1969.

Much of the volume is devoted to Pennsylvania. 6,500 names in all, covering 1740-72.

2894 **Glenn, Thomas A.** Merion in the Welsh tract . . . historical and genealogical collections concerning the Welsh barony in the province of Pennsylvania, settled by the Cymric Quakers in 1682. 1896. Repr. Baltimore: G.P.C., 1970.

Data, pedigrees, genealogies, etc. brought down to the 1800s.

**2895** ——— Welsh founders of Pennsylvania. 2v. 1911, 1913. Repr. 2v. in 1. Baltimore: G.P.C., 1970.
Chiefly genealogical records of Welsh founders; medieval generations must be treated with care. This and no.2894 are based on Dwnn (*see* notation under no. 4871). 300 families, 2,000 individuals, 1682–1700.

**2896** Godcharles, Frederick A. Chronicles of centennial Pennsylvania. 4v. New York, 1944.
Early settlement, Cresap and other wars; proprietary manors, history and formation of cities, counties; over 1,000 biographical sketches.

**2897** Gordon, Thomas F. A gazetteer of the state of Pennsylvania. 1832.
Vital for any study related to the state's early settlement and population.

**2898** The Goshenhoppen registers, 1741–1819. ser.1–5. In *American Catholic Historical Soc. records* 1–11, 61, 1886–1950.
Baptisms at the Pennsylvania Catholic mission at Goshenhoppen (now Bally). Ser. 1–4 were published in v.1–11; ser.5 in v.61.

**2899** Haiman, Miecislaus. Polish pioneers of Pennsylvania. 1941. Repr. San Francisco: R. and E. Research Assoc., 1970.

**2900** Hanna, Charles A. Ohio Valley genealogies relating chiefly to families in Harrison, Belmont and Jefferson counties, Ohio, and Washington, Westmoreland and Fayette counties, Pennsylvania. 1900. Repr. Baltimore: G.P.C., 1972.
About 350 genealogies of first settlers in western Pennsylvania and eastern Ohio. Standard work. Taken from his *Historical collections of Harrison county,* 1900.

**2901** ——— The wilderness trail, or the ventures and adventures of the Pennsylvania traders on the Allegheny path, with some new annals of the Old West . . . 2v. 1911. Repr. New York: A.M.S. Press, 1972.
Pennsylvania and Ohio valley; mostly Indian history and genealogy.

**2902** Harris, Alexander. A biographical history of Lancaster county, Pennsylvania. Being a history of early settlers and eminent men of the county. 1872. Repr. Baltimore: G.P.C., 1974.
2,000 biographies with references to an additional 10,000 people. Included because of size of early Lancaster county.

**2903** Harvey, Oscar J. History of Wilkes-Barre, Pennsylvania. 5v. Wilkes-Barre, Pa., 1909–30.
Harvey died in 1921, and the remaining manuscript was enlarged by Ernest G. Smith; v.5–6 are mug books; remainder excellent work covering the entire northeastern Pennsylvania immigration from Connecticut.

**2904** Heiss, Willard C. Quaker biographical sketches of ministers and elders, and other concerned members of the yearly meeting of Philadelphia, 1682–1800. Indianapolis, Ind., 1972.
600 sketches originally appearing in *The friend* from 1853 to 1863. Primarily concerns Pennsylvania and part of New Jersey.

**2905** Helbron, Father Peter. Registers, 1799–1830. In *American Catholic Historical Soc. records,* v.26–28, 1915–17.
At Sportsman's Hall (now St. Vincent Archabbey) and Greensburg, Pennsylvania. Registers are by Helbron and others, mostly in western Pennsylvania. Mostly baptisms.

**2906** Hinshaw, William W. Encyclopedia of American Quaker genealogy. v.2. Containing every item of genealogical value found in all records and minutes . . . of four of the oldest monthly meetings which ever belonged to the Philadelphia yearly meeting of Friends . . . 1938. Repr. Baltimore: G.P.C., 1969.
Two of the four meetings are New Jersey. Many Pennsylvania meetings, for which records are extant are not included. Extracts not always accurate.

**2907** Historical journal; a quarterly record of local history and genealogy, devoted principally to northwest Pennsylvania. Ed. by John F. Meginness. v.1–2, 1887–94. Williamsport, Pa., 1888–94.
Title varies.

**2908 Historical Records Survey.** *Pennsylvania archives.* 8th ser. Index to votes of Pennsylvania Assembly, page reference to daily sessions of Pennsylvania Assembly, etc. Prepared by W.P.A. Ed. by Joseph L. Rafter. [Harrisburg, Pa.?]: Pennsylvania State Lib., 1967.
Prepared in 1930s. Although some errors it is a useful guide; many names with references of volume concerned. All names and places, 1682-1776 in 8th ser.

**2909** —— Inventories of county archives of Pennsylvania. 17v. Philadelphia, 1938-42.
Only the following numbers were published: 1 (Adams), 4 (Beaver), 6 (Berks), 7 (Blair), 8 (Bradford), 23 (Delaware), 25 (Erie), 26 (Fayette), 27 (Forest), 30 (Greene), 36 (Lancaster), 37 (Lawrence), 40 (Luzerne), 62 (Warren), 63 (Washington), 64 (Wayne), and 65 (Westmoreland). Unpublished material deposited in Historical Commission, Harrisburg, Pa.

**2910** —— Inventory of church and synagogue archives of Pennsylvania: Society of Friends. Philadelphia, 1941.
Historical description of origin and development of Quaker meetings in Pennsylvania, and a checklist of Quaker meeting records. Bibliography, glossary and index.

**2911** —— Maritime records, port of Philadelphia. 190v. Harrisburg, Pa., 1942?
pt.1, 11v. Portwarden's minutes, 1776-83, 1784-1880.
2, 11v. Alphabetical index of naturalization records, 1794-1880.
3, 5v. Arrivals and clearances of vessels, Philadelphia, 1783-1880.
4, 37v. Chronological lists of crews, port of Philadelphia, 1789-1880.
5, 108v. Alphabetical list of masters and crews, 1798-1880.
42v. Index of names and vessels.
6, 12v. Records of wrecks, Philadelphia district, 1874-1937.
lv. Slave manifests, 1800-41.
7, lv. Letters of marque, 1804-15.

**2912** —— Ship registers of port of Philadelphia. v.1, A-D. Philadelphia, 1942.
1762-66, *see* ship registers, no.3011.

**2913 Hoenstine, Floyd G.** 1972 guide to genealogical and historical research in Pennsylvania. 3rd ed. rev. and enl. Hollidaysburg, Pa.: The Author, 1972.
Useful for novices; includes bibliography of central Pennsylvania material and guide to contents of many publications containing Pennsylvania genealogy and history.

**2914 Hull, William I.** William Penn and the Dutch Quaker migration to Pennsylvania. *Swarthmore College monographs on Quaker history,* 2. 1935. Repr. Baltimore: G.P.C., 1970.
Also lists Germantown settlers, 1638-1709, with brief genealogical notices. Study of Dutch and also German emigration to Pennsylvania.

**2915 Indiana State Library. Genealogical section.** Guide to genealogical material in the Pennsylvania archives. Indianapolis, Ind., 1937.
For *Pennsylvania archives, see* no.2976.

**2916 Jackson, Ronald V.** (and others). Computer index to Pennsylvania 1800 census. Butler, Crawford, and Mercer counties. 2v. Provo, Utah: Accelerated Indexing Systems, 1972.
100,000 entries; county research aids, early maps, genealogical data. Cover title: *Accelerated indexing systems computer index to Pennsylvania 1800 census.*

**2917 Johnson, Amandus.** The Swedish settlements on the Delaware, their history and relation to the Indians, Dutch and English, 1638-64. 2v. 1911, repr. 1927. Repr. Baltimore: G.P.C., 1969.
Very good; accurate and authoritative, but not primarily a genealogical work.

**2918 Jordan, John W.** A century and a half of Pittsburgh and her people. 4v. New York, 1908.
v.3-4 genealogical memoirs of leading families.

**2919** ———— Colonial and Revolutionary families of Pennsylvania; genealogical and personal memoirs. 17v. New York, 1911–65.
v.1–3 ed. by John W. Jordan; v.4–15 by Wilfred Jordan; v.16–17 by T. H. Bateman. v.4 on were called new series. First 3v. are vastly superior to the rest, since Jordan had good collaboration; the remaining volumes approach mug book status.

**2920** ———— Colonial families of Philadelphia. 2v. New York, 1911.

**2921** ———— Genealogical and personal history of northern Pennsylvania. 3v. New York, 1913.

**2922** ———— Genealogical and personal history of western Pennsylvania. 3v. New York, 1915.

**2923** ———— Historical homes and institutions and genealogical and personal memoirs. Over a period of 10 years Jordan was a prolific author and compiler of several works on Pennsylvania counties and areas, viz.: Leigh valley, 2v., 1905; Beaver county, 2v., 1914; Fayette, 3v., 1912; Lycoming, 2v., 1906; Allegheny valley, 3v., 1913; Wyoming and Lackawanna valleys, 2v., 1906; Bucks, 3v., 1905; Delaware county, 3v., 1914; Juniata valley, 3v., 1913.

**2924 Jordan, Wilfred.** Colonial and Revolutionary families of Philadelphia. v.1 (all pub.). New York, 1933.
Genealogical and personal memoirs. Intended as a continuation of no.2920.

**2925 Keith, Charles P.** The provincial councillors of Pennsylvania who held office between 1773 and 1776, and their descendants. Philadelphia, 1883.
Reliable work.

**2926 Kellogg, Joseph U.** Tulpehocken-Virginia notes. n.p., 1945.
Five compilations taken from original sources—Pennsylvania German families who migrated to Virginia—mainly Pennsylvania material.

**2927 Kieffer, Henry M.** Some of the first settlers of "The forks of the Delaware" and their descendants; being a translation from the German of the record books of the First Reformed Church of Easton, Pennsylvania, 1760–1852. 1902. Repr. Baltimore: G.P.C., 1973.
20,000 entries but no index.

**2928 Krebs, Friedrich.** Emigrants from the Palatinate to the American colonies in the 18th century. Ed. by Milton Rubincam. Norristown, Pa.: Pennsylvania German Soc., 1953.
The society's *special study* 1.

**2929 Kuhns, Levi Oscar.** The German and Swiss settlements of colonial Pennsylvania. 2nd ed. 1901. Repr. Ann Arbor, Mich.: Gryphon Books, 1971; New York: A.M.S. Press, 1971.
A study of the so-called Pennsylvania Dutch. Historical background of Pennsylvania German families; many names, good bibliography.

**2930 Lambert, Marcus B.** A dictionary of the non-English words of the Pennsylvania German dialect. *Pennsylvania German Soc.,* v.30. Philadelphia, 1924.

**2931 Langguth, Otto.** Pennsylvania German pioneers from the county of Wertheim. Transl. and ed. by Donald H. Yoder. *Pennsylvania German Folklore Soc. yearbook* 12. n.p., 1948.
Alphabetically arranged listing of 272 heads of families who emigrated from Germany to Philadelphia in 17th century.

**2932 Leach, Frank W.** Old Philadelphia families; a series of articles contributed to the *Philadelphia North American*. 3v. Philadelphia, 1908–13.
Indexed in *American genealogist,* v.15 (1939), pp.92–94.

**2933 Leckey, Howard L.** The Tenmile country and its pioneer families. A genealogical history of the upper Monongahela valley. 7v. Waynesburg, Pa., 1950.

**2934** ———— Index to v.1–7. By Hilda Chance. Liberty, Pa.: The Author, [1972].

2935 ——— v.8–9, newspaper columns, supplement to 7v. set. n.d.

2936 **Linn, John B.** Annals of Buffalo valley, Pennsylvania, 1755–1855. Harrisburg, Pa., 1871.

2937 ——— Index compiled by Mary B. Lontz. n.p., 1965.

Area embraces all of present-day Union county and large portions of Snyder, Centre, and Lycoming counties. Assessment lists 1755, muster rolls, etc.

2938 ——— List of officers of the colonies on the Delaware and the provinces of Pennsylvania, 1614–1776. *Pennsylvania archives,* ser.2, v.9, pt.2. Harrisburg, Pa., 1890.

2939 ——— List of "soldiers of the revolutionists who received pay for their services," taken from manuscript records, having neither date nor title, but under "Rangiers on the frontiers, 1778–83." *Pennsylvania archives,* ser.5, v.4, pp.597–777. Harrisburg, Pa., 1906.

2940 ——— List of soldiers who served as rangers on the frontiers, 1778–83. *Pennsylvania archives,* ser.3, v.23, pp. 193–356. Harrisburg, Pa., 1898.

2941 ——— and **Egle, W. H.** Pennsylvania in the War of the Revolution, battalions and line. *Pennsylvania archives,* ser. 2, v.10–11. 1775–83. 2v. Harrisburg, Pa., 1880.

2941a **Lists of persons** pensioned by the United States, residing in Pennsylvania, who served in the War of the Revolution, 1820–25. *Pennsylvania archives,* ser.2, v.15, pp.683–741. Harrisburg, Pa., 1893.

2942 **McAllister, Addams S.** Pennsylvania gravestone inscriptions. In *Publ. of the Genealogical Soc. of Pennsylvania* 7–16, 1919–48.

2943 **McCay, Betty L.** Sources for genealogical searching in Pennsylvania. Rev. Indianapolis, Ind.: The Author, 1973. Historical background and record data.

2944 **Macco, Herman F.** Palatine church visitations 1609. *Publ. of the Genealogical Soc. of Pennsylvania.* special no. Philadelphia, 1930.

2945 **McGhee, Lucy K.** Pennsylvania pension abstracts of soldiers of the Revolutionary War, War of 1812, and Indian Wars. 2v. Washington, D.C., n.d.

2946 **McKirdy, James.** Origin of the names given to the counties in Pennsylvania. n.p., 192?
Many references.

2947 **McKnight, William J.** A pioneer outline history of northwestern Pennsylvania, embracing the counties of Tioga, Potter, McKean, Warren, Crawford, Venango, Forest, Clarion, Elk, Jefferson, Cameron, Butler, Lawrence, and Mercer [and pioneer sketches of several cities]. Philadelphia, 1905.

2948 **Maskey, Carle L.** Some early Ohio and Pennsylvania families. Los Angeles, 1945.

2949 **Mayhill, R. Thomas.** Lancaster county, Pennsylvania, deed abstracts and Revolutionary War oaths of allegiance. Deed books *A* through *M,* through ca.1770, with adjoining landowners and witnesses. Rev. and enl. ed. Knightstown, Ind.: The Author, 1973.

Lancaster covered a large area and some 30 counties can trace their origins to Lancaster county. Many hitherto unknown oaths of allegiance. Pub. in 1965 under title: *Index abstracts of deeds, Lancaster county.*

2950 **Mexican War, 1846–47.** [List of Pennsylvania men who took part, with service records.] *Pennsylvania archives,* ser.6, v.10, pp.247–458. Harrisburg, Pa., 1907.

2951 **Meynen, Emil.** Bibliography on German settlements in colonial North America especially on the Pennsylvania Germans and their descendants, 1683–1933. Tables of contents and captions in German and English. Classified with indexes of authors and surnames. 1937. Repr. Detroit, Mich.: Gale Research, 1966.

Indispensable for research on Pennsylvania Germans. 8,000 titles, and much genealogy and local history.

**2952 Militia rolls, 1783–90.** Bedford, Berks, Bucks, Chester, Cumberland, Dauphin, Franklin, Huntingdon, Lancaster, Montgomery, Northampton, Northumberland, city and county of Philadelphia, Washington, Westmoreland, and York. *Pennsylvania archives,* ser.6, v.3. Harrisburg, Pa., 1907.

**2953 Muster and pay rolls, Pennsylvania militia, 1790–1800.** *Pennsylvania archives,* ser.6, v.5. Harrisburg, Pa., 1907.

**2954 Muster rolls and papers relative to the associators and militia of the counties.** *Pennsylvania archives,* ser.5–6. 6v. Harrisburg, Pa., 1906.
ser.5, v.5, Bedford, Berks, Bucks, Chester; v.6, Cumberland; v.7, Lancaster; v.8, Northampton; ser.6, v.1, city and county of Philadelphia; v.2, Washington, Westmoreland, York.

**2955 Muster rolls of the Pennsylvania Navy, 1776–79.** *Pennsylvania archives,* ser.5, v.1, pp.514–609. Harrisburg, Pa., 1906.
A shorter list is published in ser.3, v.23 of the Archives.

**2956 Muster rolls of the Pennsylvania volunteers in the War of 1812–1814.** *Pennsylvania archives,* ser.2, v.12, 1890. Excerpted and repr. Baltimore: G.P.C., 1967.
15,000 names.

**2957 Myers, Albert C.** Immigration of the Irish Quakers into Pennsylvania, 1628–1750, with their early history in Ireland. 1902. Repr. Baltimore: G.P.C., 1969.
Over 100p. are devoted to certificates of removal, which are evidence of overseas origin.

**2958** ——— Quaker arrivals at Philadelphia, 1682–1750. Being a list of certificates of removal received at Philadelphia monthly meeting of Friends. 1902. Repr. Baltimore: G.P.C., 1969.

**2959 Names of foreigners arriving in Pennsylvania, 1786–1808.** *Pennsylvania archives,* ser.2, v.17, pp.521–667. Harrisburg, Pa., 1892.

**2960 Names of persons who took oath of allegiance to the state of Pennsylvania, 1776–94.** *Pennsylvania archives,* ser. 2, v.3. 1875. Repr. Baltimore: G.P.C., 1967.

**2961 National Society, United States Daughters of 1812.** Lineage book, 1895–1929. Scranton, Pa., [1929].

**2962 Nolan, James B.** Southeastern Pennsylvania, a history of the counties of Berks, Bucks, Chester, Delaware, Montgomery, Philadelphia, and Schuylkill. 3v. Philadelphia, 1943.
Coats of arms, genealogical tables.

**2963 Ohio Family Historians.** Index to 1810 census of Pennsylvania. Columbus, Ohio: Ohio Library Fdn., 1966.

**2964 The Penn Germania:** a popular magazine of biography, history, genealogy, folklore, literature, etc. v.1–15, no.3, 1900–14.
From v.13 until it was discontinued, the title was *The Pennsylvania German.*

**2965 Pennsylvania (Colony).** Officers and soldiers in the service of the province of Pennsylvania, 1744–65. *Pennsylvania archives,* ser.5, v.1, Harrisburg, Pa., 1906.

**2966** ——— **Provincial Council.** Colonial records of Pennsylvania. *See* no.2974.

**2967** ——— **Supreme Court.** Persons naturalized in the province of Pennsylvania, 1740–73. *Pennsylvania archives,* ser.2, v.2, 1876. Excerpted and repr. Baltimore: G.P.C., 1967.
Lists of foreign Protestants naturalized in Pennsylvania, 1740–73. About 3,000 persons, most of whom were Quakers, with place of residence and date of naturalization. Has added index.

**2968 Pennsylvania (Province).** House of Representatives. Votes and proceedings of the House of Representatives of the province of Pennsylvania, 1682-1935. (Votes of assembly.) *Pennsylvania archives,* ser.8, v.1-8. Harrisburg, Pa., 1931-35.

**2969** ———— Index to votes of Pennsylvania Assembly, page reference to daily sessions . . . Prepared by W.P.A. Ed. by Joseph L. Rafter. (Harrisburg, Pa.: Pennsylvania State Lib., 1963.)

Prepared in 1930s; some errors; has all names and places, 1682-1776.

**2970 Pennsylvania Dept. of Internal Affairs.** Incorporation dates of Pennsylvania municipalities. [Harrisburg, Pa.]: The Dept., 1965.

**2971 Pennsylvania. Land Office.** Warrantees of land in the several counties of the state of Pennsylvania, 1730-1898. Ed. by W. H. Egle. 3v. *Pennsylvania archives,* ser.3, v.24-26. Harrisburg, Pa., 1898-99.

Head of title: *Provincial papers.*

**2972** ———— **Navy Board.** List of officers and men of the Pennsylvania Navy, 1775-81. *Pennsylvania archives,* ser.2, v.1, pp.243-434. Harrisburg, Pa., 1896.

**2973** ———— **Treasury Dept.** State of the accounts of the county lieutenants during the War of the Revolution, 1777-89. 3v. *Pennsylvania archives,* ser.3, v.5-7. Harrisburg, Pa., 1896.

**2974 Pennsylvania archives.** Colonial records of Pennsylvania, 1638-1790. 16v. 1838-53. Repr. New York: A.M.S. Press, 1971.

Title of v.1-10, *Minutes of the Provincial Council,* 1682-1776; title of v.11-16, *Minutes of the Supreme Executive Council,* 1776-90. Binder's title: *Colonial records.* This series precedes the *Pennsylvania archives,* no.2976.

**2975** ———— ———— General index. Philadelphia, 1860.

**2976** ———— Pennsylvania archives. Ser. 1, 12v.; ser.2, 19v.; ser.3, 31v.; ser.4, 12v.; ser.5, 8v.; ser.6, 15v.; ser.7, 5v.; ser.8, 8v.; ser.9, 10v. 138v. Harrisburg, Pa., 1852-1935.

The 138v. include *Colonial records* and *Pennsylvania archives,* indexed. Description of series in Eddy (no.2868), Hoenstine (no.2913), and Wilkinson (no.3033). Many of the more important volumes have been reprinted. Essential set, particularly ser.2, 3, 5, 6. Index of names in ser.8, *see* no.2908. *Genealogical research in the Archives, see* Weikel, no.3028.

**2977 Pennsylvania genealogical magazine.** v.1- , 1895- . Philadelphia: Genealogical Soc. of Pennsylvania.

Excellent magazine; scholarly. Emphasis on Philadelphia area but contains articles on Maryland and New Jersey. Publ. of the Genealogical Soc. of Pennsylvania from 1895-1947.

**2978 Pennsylvania German Folklore Society.** Publications. v.1-28, 1963-66. Allentown, Pa.: The Society.

Merged with *Pennsylvania German Society proceedings* (*see* no.2979).

Following volumes are of genealogical value:

v.1, Zweibrücken immigrant list, 1728-49. 1936.

v.3, Newspaper notices by German settlers, 1742-61. 1938.

v.9, Stormblown seed of Schoharie (German immigration from New York to Pennsylvania in colonial period). 1944.

v.10, Emigrants from Württemberg—the Adolf Gerber lists. 1945.

v.11, Pennsylvania Germans in Ontario, Canada, 1946.

v.12, Pennsylvania German pioneers from the county of Wertheim. 1947.

v.15, Pennsylvania German wills. 1950.

v.16, German immigrants from Zweibrücken and Schaffhausen, 1734-71. 1951.

v.19, Pennsylvania Germans in Wisconsin. 1954.

v.26, Pennsylvania Germans of the Shenandoah valley. 1962. *See also* no.3013.

v.1, 10, 12, 16, 26, the most important, are out-of-print.

**2979 Pennsylvania German Society.** Publications. v.1-63, 1891-1966. Philadelphia: The Society.

v.1–53, 1891–1948, appeared as *Proceedings and addresses*. With the merging of *Pennsylvania German Folklore Society publications* (no.2978) it became a new series numbered v.1– , 1968– .

**2980 Pennsylvania Historical Survey.** *See* Historical Records Survey, no. 2908–12.

**2981 Pennsylvania magazine of history and biography.** v.1– , 1877– . Philadelphia: Historical Soc. of Pennsylvania.
Has not published genealogical data per se since v.60, 1936. v.30–67, 1906–1943 repr. by Johnson Reprint Corp., New York, 1969.

**2982** —— Index, v.1–75, 1877–1951. Ed. by Eugene E. Doll. Philadelphia: The Society, 1954.
Index excludes genealogical articles.

**2983 Pennsylvania marriage licenses, 1742–48.** In *Pennsylvania magazine of history and biography,* v.39, 1915.

**2984** —— 1762–68 in v.40, 1916.

**2985** —— 1769–76 in v.41, 1917.

**2986 Pennsylvania marriages prior to 1790.** Names of persons for whom marriage licenses were issued in the province of Pennsylvania previous to 1790. *Pennsylvania archives,* ser.2, v.2, 1876. Repr. Baltimore: G.P.C., 1968.
Original is entitled, *Names of persons* ... Repr. has publisher's title. Records date back to 1742. Public marriage records, as opposed to church marriage records; *see* no.2996.

**2987 The Pennsylvania traveler-post.** v.1– , 1964– . Danboro, Pa.: R. T. and M. C. Williams.
Records, family history, and data relating to Pennsylvania. Incorporated *The genealogist's post* in 1971.

**2988 Penrose, Maryly B.** Heads of families index, 1850 federal census, city of Philadelphia. Franklin Park, N.J.: Liberty Bell Assoc., 1974.

Duopage issue from microfilm, indexed. 19,000 heads of families; 121,376 individuals.

**2989** —— Philadelphia marriages and obituaries, 1857–60, *Philadelphia Saturday bulletin.* Franklin Park, N.J.: Liberty Bell Assoc., 1974.
Since vital records of Philadelphia were not taken before 1860, data prior to this is invaluable.

**2990 Philadelphia. Friends.** (Early) minutes of the Philadelphia monthly meeting (of Friends, 1682–1775). In *Publications of the Genealogical Soc. of Pennsylvania,* v.1–15, 1898–1945.

**2991 Philadelphia. Mayor.** Record of indentures of individuals bound out as apprentices, servants, etc. and of German and other redemptioners in the office of the mayor of the city of Philadelphia, October 3, 1771, to October 3, 1773 ... *Pennsylvania German Soc. publ.,* v.16. 1907. Repr. Baltimore: G.P.C., 1973.
Contains over 5,000 names, mostly from British, Irish, or Dutch ports. Repr. has a new index.

**2992 Proprietary, supply and state tax lists of the city of Philadelphia.** *Pennsylvania archives,* ser.3, v.12–20. Harrisburg, Pa., 1897–98.
v.18, Berks, 1767–85; v.13, Bucks, 1779–86; v.12, Chester, 1774–85; v.20, Cumberland, 1778–85; v.17, Lancaster, 1771–82; v.19, Northampton and Northumberland, 1772, 1787; v.14–16, city and county of Philadelphia, 1769–83.

**2994 Prowell, George R.** History of York county, Pennsylvania. 2v. 1907. Repr. with index as v.3. York, Pa.: York County Historical Soc., 1974.
v.2 biographical.

**2995 Reaman, George E.** The trail of the Black Walnut. Rev. Toronto, Canada: McClelland & Stewart, 1965.
Pennsylvania German "plain folk" who emigrated to Ontario in the latter part of the 18th and early 19th centuries; numerous lists of settlers, township histories with refer-

ences to early settlers; well indexed. Originally v.57, *Publ. of Pennsylvania German Soc.*

**2996 Record of Pennsylvania marriages prior to 1810.** 2v. *Pennsylvania archives,* ser.2, v.8-9, 1880-90. Repr. Baltimore: G.P.C., 1968.
Several Philadelphia churches; Friends' lists in v.2. There is a 1895 ed. with supplementary section of 150p., entitled *Provincial officers of three lower counties, Newcastle, Sussex, and Kent.* Church marriages as opposed to public marriages, see no.2986.

**2996a** —— Index to some Philadelphia marriages, 1745-1806. By Carrie L. T. Lartigue. Spokane, Wash.: Eastern Washington Genealogical Soc., 1974.
To be used in conjunction with ser.2, v.9.

**2997 Richards, Henry M. M.** The Pennsylvania German in the Revolutionary War, 1775-83. *Pennsylvania German Soc. publ.,* 17. Philadelphia, 1908.
Index of surnames, biographies, cemetery lists.

**2998 Riesenman, Joseph, Jr.** History of northwestern Pennsylvania, comprising the counties of Erie, Crawford, Mercer, Venango, Warren, Forest, Clarion, McKean, Elk, Jefferson, Cameron, and Clearfield. 3v. New York, 1943.
v.3 biographical.

**2999 Rolls of soldiers of the Revolution, Pennsylvania line,** found in the Department of State, Washington, D.C. *Pennsylvania archives,* ser.2, v.15, pp.371-560. Harrisburg, Pa., 1893.

**3000 Rupp, Israel D.** A collection of upwards of thirty thousand names of German, Swiss, Dutch, French and other immigrants in Pennsylvania from 1727 to 1776, with a statement of the names of ships . . . also, an appendix containing lists of more than 1,000 German and French names in New York prior to 1712. Repr. of 2nd rev. and enl. ed. with German transl. of 1876; with an added index by Ernst Wecken from the Leipzig ed. of 1931 and an index of ships. Baltimore: G.P.C., 1971.

Considered vastly inferior to Strassburger (*see* no.3020) because Rupp could not read the old script, and hence there are many errors. But Rupp lists movements from Schoharie to Pennsylvania that are not in Strassburger. M. V. Koger compiled an index to Rupp in 1935.

**3001** —— The history and topography of Dauphin, Cumberland, Franklin, Bedford, Adams, and Perry counties; containing a brief history of the first settlers . . . Lancaster, Pa., 1846.

**3002** —— History and topography of Northumberland, Huntingdon, Mifflin, Centre, Union, Columbia, Juniata, and Clinton counties, Pennsylvania. Lancaster, Pa., 1847.

**3003** —— Index by M. B. Lontz. Milton, Pa., [1967?].

**3004** —— History of Lancaster and York counties from the earliest settlements . . . 1709 . . . and 1819 . . . Lancaster, Pa., 1845.

**3005** —— History of Northampton, Lehigh, Monroe, Carbon, and Schuylkyll counties: containing a brief history of the first settlers .. 1845. Repr. New York: Arno Pr., 1971.

**3006 Sachse, Julius F.** The German Pietists of provincial Pennsylvania, 1694-1708. 1895. Repr. New York: A.M.S. Press, 1895.
Very good for early history of "plain" sects. Coats of arms.

**3007** —— The German sectarians of Pennsylvania, 1708-1800. 2v. 1899-1900. Repr. New York: A.M.S. Press, 1971.
v.1, 1708-42; v.2, 1742-1800. Critical history of the Ephrata cloisters and the Dunkers.

**3008 Salisbury, Ruth.** Pennsylvania newspapers: a bibliography and union list. Pittsburgh, Pa.: Pennsylvania Library Assoc., 1969.
Listing of all newspapers ever known to have been published, with locations.

3009 **Scott, Joseph.** A geographical description of Pennsylvania, also of the counties respectively, in the order in which they were established by the Legislature. With an alphabetical list of the townships in each county, and their population in 1800. Philadelphia, 1806.

3010 **Scott, Kenneth.** Genealogical data from the *Pennsylvania chronicle,* 1767-74, and from the *American weekly mercury,* 1719-46. (Since both papers published in Philadelphia contain items from many other colonies, they are entered under the General heading, no.67, 70.)

3011 **Ships' registers, 1762-66.** *Pennsylvania archives,* ser.2, v.2, pp.631-71. Harrisburg, Pa., 1876.
Also published in ser.5, v.1, pp.384-413. Harrisburg, Pa., 1906.

3012 **Siebert, Wilbur H.** The loyalists of Pennsylvania. *Ohio State Univ. bull.,* 24, no.23. 1920. Repr. Boston: Gregg, 1972.
In depth study of state where loyalists abounded.

3013 **Smith, Elmer L.; Stewart, J. G.; and Kyger, M. E.** The Pennsylvania Germans of the Shenandoah valley. From *Yearbook,* v.26 of the Pennsylvania German Folklore Soc. 1964.
Names and family data. *See also* no.2978, v.26.

3014 **Society of the Sons of the American Revolution.** 1955 yearbook. By Floyd G. Hoenstine. Pittsburgh, Pa., 1956.
7,000 Revolutionary ancestors and their descendants, 1893-1956.

3015 **Soldiers who received depreciation pay as per cancelled certificates on file in the Division of Public Records,** Pennsylvania State Library (Continental line). *Pennsylvania archives,* ser.5, v.4, pp.105-496. Harrisburg, Pa., 1906.

3016 **Stapleton, Ammon.** Memorials of the Huguenots in America, with special reference to their emigration to Pennsylvania. 1901. Repr. Baltimore: G.P.C., 1969.

While primarily dealing with Pennsylvania, it also covers New England, New York, Maryland and Virginia. Contains a good list of immigrants. Much unreliable data; particularly confusion between French and German families.

3017 **Stemmons, John D.** Pennsylvania in 1800; a computerized index to the 1800 federal population schedules of the state of Pennsylvania, with other aids to research. Salt Lake City: Institute of Family Research, 1972. Available from Everton Pub., Logan, Utah.
120,000 entries. Index to contents of 8 rolls of microfilm.

3018 **Stocker, Rhamanthus M.** Centennial history of Susquehanna county, Pennsylvania. 1887. Repr. with index of names. Baltimore: G.P.C., 1974.
50,000 entries. Standard genealogy and history for the area; pioneer settlers mainly from Connecticut and other New England states. Muster rolls for all wars up to and including Civil War. Good biographical sketches.

3019 **Stoever, Rev. John C., Jr.** Records of Rev. John Casper Stoever, Jr.: baptisms and marriages, 1730-99. Harrisburg, Pa., 1896.
Covers principally Lebanon, Lancaster, York, and Berks counties.

3020 **Strassburger, Ralph B.** Pennsylvania German pioneers: a publication of the original lists of arrivals in the port of Philadelphia from 1727-1808. Ed. by William J. Hinke. 3v. Philadelphia, 1934. Repr. v.1, 3 only. Baltimore: G.P.C., 1966.
The definitive work on the early German immigrants to Pennsylvania. Supersedes Rupp (no.3000), but see notation. v.2 of the original ed. (signatures in facsimile) was omitted in the reprint as being of little genealogical value, but it is actually of great importance because of the interpretation of the names. Originally published as *Proceedings of Pennsylvania German Society,* v.42, 44.

3021 ———— Annotations by Friedrich Krebs in *Publ. of the Genealogical Soc. of Pennsylvania* 21, 1960, pp.235-48.

3022　**Tribbeko, John.** Lists of Germans from the Palatinate who came to England in 1709, (from original documents in the British Museum, London). Excerpted from *New York genealogical and biographical record,* v.40–41, 1909–10. Baltimore: G.P.C., 1965.

3023　**U.S. Bureau of the Census.** Heads of families at the first census of the United States taken in the year 1790. Pennsylvania. 1908. Repr. Baltimore: G.P.C., 1970; Spartanburg, S.C.: Reprint Co., 1963, etc.

3024　**Virginia claims to land in western Pennsylvania.** *Pennsylvania archives,* ser.3, v.3, pp.483–574. Harrisburg, Pa., 1896.

3025　**Waldenmaier, Inez.** Index to the minute books of the Virginia courts, held wthin the limits of southwestern Pennsylvania, 1775–80, including records of deeds for West Augusta, Virginia 1775–76, and abstract of old Virginia wills proved before the Yohogania county court, 1776–81. Washington, D.C., 1957.

3026　**Walkinshaw, Lewis C.** Annals of southwestern Pennsylvania. 4v. New York, 1939.
v.4 biographical.

3027　**War of 1812–1814. Pennsylvania Volunteers.** Muster rolls, receipt rolls, etc. Miscellaneous papers, accounts, etc. 2v. *Pennsylvania archives,* ser.6, v.7–10, pp.1–246. Harrisburg, Pa., 1907.

3028　**Weikel, Sally A.** Genealogical research in the published Pennsylvania archives. Harrisburg, Pa.: Pennsylvania Dept. of Education, State Library of Pennsylvania, 1974.

3028a　**Weinberg, Allen,** and **Slattery, T. E.** Warrants and surveys of the Province of Pennsylvania including the three lower counties. 1759. 1965. Repr. Knightstown, Ind.: Bookmark, 1974.
Over 4,000 names. "An act for recording of warrants and surveys, and for rendering the real estates and property within this province more secure." The three lower counties are: Philadelphia, Sussex, and York.

3029　**Welcome Society of Pennsylvania.** Passengers and ships prior to 1684 ... Ed. by Walter L. Sheppard. *Publ. of the Welcome Soc. of Pennsylvania* 1. Baltimore: G.P.C., 1970.
A critical examination of passenger lists of persons who arrived in Pennsylvania, 1682–83. Erudite work very useful to genealogists. Scholarly papers. Supersedes entries in Lancour (no.349).

3030　———— The Welcome claimants, proved, disproved and doubtful, with an account of some of their descendants. By George E. McCracken. *Publ. of the Welcome Soc. of Pennsylvania* 2. Baltimore: G. P. C., 1970.
Exhaustive study. Based on original records. 26 lists are indicated for checking but most are very bad. Standard Pennsylvania reference work. Thousands of individuals in 2,000 families listed, 1852–1968.

3031　**Westcott, Thompson.** Names of persons who took the oath of allegiance to the state of Pennsylvania, 1777–89. 1865. Repr. Baltimore: G.P.C., 1965.
Passenger list. Has history of the "test laws" of Pennsylvania. Full data of all listed. *See also* no.2960 and 2871.

3032　**Western Pennsylvania genealogical indexes.** v.1– , 1974– . Saegertown, Pa.: Eugene F. Throop, RD 2, 16433.
Quarterly. Vital statistics, new index in each issue.

3033　**Wilkinson, Norman B.** Bibliography of Pennsylvania history. 2nd ed. of *Writings on Pennsylvania history; a bibliography.* Ed. by S. K. Stevens and D. H. Kent. Harrisburg, Pa.: Pennsylvania Historical and Museum Commission, 1957.
9,198 entries; cut-off date 1952. 7,500 titles since 1952 kept in a card file at Archives building, Harrisburg, Pa., by John B. B. Trussell.

3034　**Williams, Richard T.,** and **Williams, M. C.** Index to Berks county, Penn-

sylvania wills and administrative records, 1752–1850. Danboro, Pa.: The Compilers, 1973.
About 10,000 names.

3035 ——— Bucks county, 1682–1850. Danboro, Pa.: The Compilers, 1971.
About 10,000 names.

3036 ——— Delaware county, Pennsylvania, 1789–1850. Danboro, Pa.: The Compilers, 1974.

3037 ——— Montgomery county, 1784–1850. Danboro, Pa.: The Compilers, 1972.
About 10,000 names.

3038 ——— Northampton county, 1752–1850, and Lehigh county, 1812–50. Danboro, Pa.: The Compilers, 1971.
About 10,000 names.

3039 ——— Philadelphia, 1682–1950. Danboro, Pa.: The Compilers, 1972.
This important series will eventually cover the major counties.

3040 **Williamson, Leland M.** Prominent and progressive Pennsylvanians of the nineteenth century . . . 2v. Philadelphia, 1898.

3041 **Wion, John H.** Deaths in central Pennsylvania. An index to the obituaries appearing in the *Democratic watchman,* Bellefonte, Pa. 2v. New York: The Compiler, 1969.
v.1, 1889–1905; v.2, 1906–20.

3042 **Your family tree.** v.1– , 1948– . Hollidaysburg, Pa.: Floyd G. Hoenstine.
v.1–15, 1948–68, by F. S. Helman and B. Heffelfinger; by F. G. Hoenstine thereafter. Cemetery, church, court and other records, wills, tax lists, concerning western counties of Pennsylvania. Fine set.

PUERTO RICO

Settled 1508; ceded to U.S. from Spain, 1898
*Instituto de Cultura Puertorriqueña, San Juan*
*Sociedad Puertorriqueña de Escritores, San Juan*

3043 **Angelís, María L. de.** Mujeres puertorriqueñas que se han distinguido en el cultivo de las ciencias, las letras y las artes desde el siglo XVII hasta nuestros días. Mexico City, 1908.
Collection of biographies of outstanding women from the 17th century to early nineteen hundreds.

3044 **Archivo Histórico Nacional, Madrid.** Sección de Ultramar. Inventario de la serie gobierno de Puerto Rico, bajo la dirección de M. Teresa de la Pena Marazuela, con la colaboración de José R. Barrasas Ramos, Isabel Echanini Lomo, y M. Angeles Ortega Benaya. 2v. Madrid: Servicio de Pub. del Ministerio de Educación y Ciencia, 1972.
Important documents related to the history of Puerto Rico at the Archivo Histórico Nacional.

3045 **Atiles García, Guillermo.** Kaleidoscopio, prosa y verso. Ponce, P.R., 1905.
A collection of brief biographical details of well-known personalities of the south of the island.

3046 **Carreras, Carlos N.** Hombres y mujeres de Puerto Rico. 2v. Mexico City: Ed. Orión, 1957–61.
Collection of biographies of outstanding men and women.

3047 **Cifre de Loubriel, Estela.** Catálogo de extranjeros residentes en Puerto Rico en el siglo XIX. Río Piedras, P.R., 1962.
Register of foreign residents during the XIXth century arranged by country of origin. Brief biographical information, profession and place of residence.

3048 ——— La inmigración a Puerto Rico durante el siglo XIX. San

Juan: Inst. de Cultura Puertorriqueña, 1964.
Alphabetical listing of immigrants during the 19th century; brief biographical information, profession, etc.

**3049 Coll y Toste, Cayetano.** Puertorriqueños ilustres; primera selección ... New York, 1957.
Appeared originally in *Boletino histórico de Puerto Rico,* 1915-27.

**3050** ——— Segunda selección. New York, 1959.
Distinguished Puertoricans.

**3051 Enciclopedia clásicos de Puerto Rico.** Selección, edición y notas de Lucas Moran Arce. 6v. Barcelona, Spain: Ed. Latinoamericanas, 1971.
v.6 includes a selective list of biographies of personalities of the past and present.

**3052 Farr, Kenneth R.** Historical dictionary of Puerto Rico and U. S. Virgin Islands. Metuchen, N.J.: Scarecrow, 1973.
Fine source book.

**3053 Fernández García, Eugenio.** El libro de Puerto Rico. The book of Porto Rico. San Juan, 1923.
Ch. 18 has a collection of biographies of personalities of the past.

**3054 Figueroa, Sotero.** Ensayo biográfico de los que mas han contribuido al progresso de Puerto Rico. San Juan: Inst. de Cultura Puertorriqueña, 1971.
Biographies of distinguished personalities in the history of Puerto Rico.

**3055 Gannett, Henry.** A gazetteer of Porto Rico. *U.S. Geological Survey bull.* 183. Washington, D.C., 1901.

**3056 Gaudier, Martín.** Genealogías puertorriqueñas partidas de baptismos y biografías. Puerto Rico: Imprenta Aldecoa, 1963-64.
Biographies and baptismal documents related to women of the outstanding families.

**3057 Geigel Zenon, José,** and **Morales Ferrer, A.** Bibliografía puertorriqueña escrita en 1892-1894. Barcelona, Spain, 1934.
Books written and printed in Puerto Rico: by Puerto Ricans and by foreigners about Puerto Rico.

**3058 Gotay, Modesto.** Hombres ilustres de Puerto Rico. Barcelona, Spain: Ed. Rumbos, 1960.

**3059 Hostos, Adoldo de.** Hombres representativos de Puerto Rico. San Juan: Talleres Gráficos, 1961.
Selective biography of most important figures in the 19th and 20th centuries.

**3060 Matos Bernier, Félix.** Muertos y vivos. San Juan, 1905.
The dead and the living.

**3061 Negrón Muñoz, Angela.** Mujeres de Puerto Rico desde el período de colonización hasta el primer tercio del siglo XX. San Juan, 1935.
Women of Puerto Rico from the colonial period to the first third of the 20th century.

**3062 Neumann Gandía, Eduardo.** Benefactores y hombres notables de Puerto Rico: bocetos biograficos-críticos con un estudio sobre nuestros gobernadores generales. 2v. Ponce, 1896-99.
Biographies of outstanding figures of the past, related with the history of Puerto Rico during the Spanish rule.

**3063 Paniagua, Reinaldo.** Puerto Rico roll of honor. San Juan, 1918.
Biographical compilation of outstanding military figures of U.S. and Puerto Rico at the beginning of the 20th century.

**3064 Pedreira, Antonio S.** Bibliografía puertorriqueña (1493-1930). Madrid, 1932.

**3065 Ramirez Brau, Enrique.** Orígenes puertorriqueños, 1658-1853. 2v. San Juan, 1942-43.
The first Puertoricans.

**3066 Rosa-Nieves, Cesáreo,** and **Melón, E. M.** Biografías puertorriqueñas ... Sharon, Conn.: Troutman Pr., 1970.
300 biographies.

3067 **Todd, Roberto H.** Patriotas puertorriqueños; siluetas biográficas. Madrid: Ed. Iberoamericanas S. A., 1965.

RHODE ISLAND

Settled ca. 1636; original state

*Rhode Island Historical Society, Providence*

3068 **Arnold, James N.** Vital record of Rhode Island, 1636-1850. 21v. Providence, R.I., 1891-1912. Repr. Ann Arbor, Mich.: Xerox Univ. Microfilms, 1973.

3069 **Austin, John O.** Ancestry of thirty-three Rhode Islanders . . . Also, Twenty-seven charts of Roger Williams' descendants to the fifth generation. 1889. Repr. Rutland, Vt.: Tuttle, 1970.

3070 ———— Genealogical dictionary of Rhode Island . . . 1887. Repr. with additions and corrections by J. O. Austin and G. A. Moriarty. Baltimore: G.P.C., 1969.
Three generations of settlers who came before 1690. Principal reference tool for Rhode Island genealogy.

3071 ———— One hundred and sixty allied families. Providence, R.I., [1893].

3072 **Bartlett, John R.** Memoirs of the Rhode Island officers who were engaged in the service of their country during the great rebellion of the South. Providence, R.I., 1867.

3073 **Bicknell, Thomas W.** The history of the state of Rhode Island and Providence Plantations. 5v. New York, 1920.
v.4 biographical.

3074 **The biographical cyclopedia of representative men of Rhode Island.** Providence, R.I., 1881.

3075 **Biographical encyclopedia of Connecticut and Rhode Island.** Ed. by Henry C. Williams. New York, 1881.

3076 **Brigham, Clarence S.** Seventeenth century place names of Providence Plantations, 1639-1700. Repr. from *Collections of the Rhode Island Historical Soc.* Providence, R.I., 1903.

3077 **Brownell, Elijah E.** Rhode Island census in 1774. *See* no.3105.

3078 **Carroll, Charles.** Rhode Island, three centuries of democracy. 4v. New York, 1932.
v.3-4 biographical.

3079 **Chapin, Howard M.** Colonial heraldry. *Rhode Island Historical Soc. collections* 20-22, 1927-29. Repr. Providence, R.I.: The Society, 1929.
A roll of arms used in the English colony of Rhode Island in New England, 1636-1776.

3080 ———— Rhode Island in the colonial wars. A list of Rhode Island soldiers and sailors in King George's War, 1740-48. Providence, R.I., 1920.

3081 ———— Rhode Island in the colonial wars. A list of Rhode Island soldiers and sailors in the old French and Indian Wars, 1755-62. Providence, R.I., 1918.

3082 ———— Rhode Island privateers in King George's War, 1739-48. Providence, R.I.: Rhode Island Historical Soc., 1926.
Scholarly account of naval battles and their effect on America's history. Has index that lists owners, captains, and officers.

3083 **Cowell, Benjamin.** Spirit of '76 in Rhode Island. 1901. Repr. with an analytical and explanatory index (excerpted from *Vital record of Rhode Island,* v.12, 1901) by James N. Arnold. Baltimore: G.P.C., 1973.
Authoritative lists of officers and men with references to rank, regiment, dates of service, etc. Best evidence for Revolutionary War participation.

3084 **Historical Records Survey.** Directory of churches and religious organizations of Rhode Island. Providence, R.I., 1939.

3085 ———— Guide to church vital statistics records in the state of Rhode Island and Providence Plantations. 2v. Providence, R.I., 1941-42.

3086 ———— Guide to public statistics records . . . in the state of Rhode Island and Providence Plantations. Providence, R.I., 1941.

3087 ———— Inventory of the church archives of Rhode Island. 2v. Baptist churches; Society of Friends. Providence, R.I., 1939-41.

3088 ———— Ship registers and enrollments. 5v. Providence, R.I., 1941. Providence, 2v., 1773-1939; Bristol-Warren, 1773-1939; Newport, 1790-1939.

3089 **Hopkins, Charles W.** The home lots of the early settlers of the Providence plantations, with notes and plats. Providence, R.I., 1886.

3090 **Jackson, Ronald V.** Rhode Island 1800 census. R. V. Jackson, ed.; R. A. Moore, computer director; G. R. Teeples, paleographer. Provo, Utah: Accelerated Indexing Systems, 1972.
About 13,000 entries. State maps covering a 300-year history of boundary changes (1636-1936). Research aids.

3091 **Mansfield, Helen W.** Block Island cemetery records. Repr. with additions and corrections from *Rhode Island history*. Providence, R.I.: Rhode Island Historical Soc., 1956.
Valuable aid to study of Rhode Island families.

3092 **Men of progress;** biographical sketches and portraits of leaders in business and professional life in the state of Rhode Island and Providence Plantations . . . Boston, 1896.

3093 **The Narragansett historical register,** a magazine devoted to . . . genealogy and historical matter illustrating the history of the state of Rhode Island and Providence Plantations. v.1-9, no.2. Providence, R.I., 1882-91.

3094 **New England families.** Rhode Island ed. New York, 1928.
Mug book.

3095 **Pease, John C.,** and **Niles, J. M.** Gazetteer of the states of Connecticut and Rhode Island. Hartford, Conn., 1819.

3096 **Peirce, Ebenezer W.** Peirce's colonial lists, civil, military and professional lists of Plymouth and Rhode Island colonies . . . 1621-1700. 1881. Repr. Baltimore: G.P.C., 1968.

3097 **Peterson, Edward.** History of Rhode Island . . . New York, 1853.

3098 **Potter, Elisha R.** Memoir concerning the French settlements and French settlers in the colony of Rhode Island. *Rhode Island historical tracts* 5. 1879. Repr. Baltimore: G.P.C., 1968.
Names with genealogical data of band of French emigrants who settled in Narragansett county in 1686.

3099 **Providence, Rhode Island. City Registrar.** Alphabetical index of the births, marriages and deaths recorded in Providence, Rhode Island, 1636-1945. 25v. Providence, R.I., 1879-1946.

3100 **Providence. Record Commissioners.** Early records of the town of Providence. 21v. (1892-1915) and index (1949-50). Providence, R.I.: Rhode Island Historical Soc., 1892-1950.

3101 ———— v.21 together with index by Richard LeB. Bowen. 2v. Providence, R.I.: The Society, 1949-50.
v.21 was reprinted from 1915 ed. One of the finest and complete sets of transcriptions of verbatim early records of any town in New England. 1636-1750. Over 3,000 names.

3102 **Representative men and old families of Rhode Island;** genealogical records and historical sketches of prominent and representative citizens and of many of the old families. 3v. Chicago, 1908.

**3103 Rhode Island (Colony).** Records of the Colony of Rhode Island and Providence Plantations in New England. Ed. by John R. Bartlett. 10v. 1856–65. Repr. New York: A.M.S. Press, 1971.
Spine: *Colonial records of Rhode Island, 1636–1792.*

**3104** ———— Rhode Island court records. 2v. Providence, R.I.: Rhode Island Historical Soc., 1920–22.
v.1, Records of the Court of Trials, 1647–62; v.2, 1662–70.

**3105** ———— **General Assembly.** Census of the inhabitants of the colony of Rhode Island and Providence Plantations, taken by order of the General Assembly in the year of 1774. Arranged by John R. Bartlett. 1858. Repr. [Bound with] *Index of Rhode Island census in 1774,* by Elijah E. Brownell. 1954. 2v. in 1. Baltimore: G.P.C., 1969.
Heads of 9,450 families, representing 54,460 persons.

**3106 Rhode Island. Adjutant General's Office.** Annual report for the year 1865. Corr., rev. and republished by Elisha Dyer. 2v. Providence, R.I., 1893–95.
Added title: *Official register of Rhode Island officers and men who served in the U.S. Army and Navy, from 1861–66.* v.1, Infantry regiments; 2, Cavalry and artillery regiments.

**3107 The Rhode Island historical magazine.** v.1–7, 1880–87. Newport, R.I.
Title varies: v.1–4 were called *Newport historical magazine.*

**3108 Rhode Island Historical Society.** Collections. v.1–34, 1827–1941. Providence, R.I.: The Society.
Superseded by *Rhode Island history,* not a genealogical magazine. Early history of Narragansett, Providence, Rhode Island, Revolutionary affairs, items on Baptists.

**3109** ———— Rhode Island land evidences. v.1, 1921 (all pub.). Repr. Baltimore: G.P.C., 1970.
1648–1696. Abstracted by Dorothy Worthington from official sources. 1,000 entries.

**3110 Rhode Island historical tracts.** 1st ser. v.1–20; 2nd ser. v.1–5. Providence, R.I., 1877–96.

**3111** ———— Additions and corrections to ser.1. Providence, R.I., 1895.
Revolutionary War, Northmen, family information, slaves, Provincial statesmen, laws, etc.

**3112 Smith, Joseph J.** Civil and military list of Rhode Island, 1647–1800. Providence, R.I., 1900.

**3113** ———— ———— 1800–50. Providence, R.I., 1901.

**3114** ———— ———— New index to both volumes. Providence, R.I., 1907.

**3114a Society of Colonial Wars.** Nine muster rolls of Rhode Island troops enlisted during the old French War. Providence, R.I., 1915.

**3114b Society of Mayflower Descendants. Rhode Island. Publications Committee.** Lineages. Providence, R.I.: The Society, 1966.

**3115** ———— Supplement. Providence, R.I.: The Society, 1968.
Mayflower lineages of almost 800 members and index of names with relevant data.

**3116 U.S. Bureau of the Census.** Heads of families at the first census of the United States taken in the year 1790. Rhode Island. 1908. Repr. Baltimore: G.P.C., 1966; Spartanburg, S.C.: Reprint Co., 1963, etc.

**3117 Volkel, Lowell M.** An index to the 1800 federal census of Rhode Island. Thomson, Ill.: Heritage House, 1970.
Alphabetized listing of head of householders with county and residence and census reference number.

**3118 Waterman, Katharine U.** The Rhode Island census of 1782. In *New England historical and genealogical register,* v.127– , 1973– (in progress).

## SOUTH CAROLINA

Settled ca. 1670; original state

*Charleston Library Society*
*South Carolina Historical Society, Charleston*
*University of South Carolina, Columbia*

✠ Many works in this book concern both North and South Carolina. Since they are often entered in one or the other state, it is suggested that when checking titles both North and South Carolina should be consulted.

3119 **Andrea, Leonard O.** South Carolina colonial soldiers and patriots. Columbia, S.C., 1952.
Those who fought in colonial wars. Sponsored by the South Carolina Daughters of Colonial Wars.

3120 **Baldwin, Agnes L.** First settlers of South Carolina, 1670-80. An annotated list. Columbia, S.C.: Univ. of South Carolina Pr., 1969.
*Tricentennial booklet* 1.

3121 **Bernheim, Gotthardt D.** History of the German settlements and of the Lutheran Church in North and South Carolina from the earliest period of the colonization of the Dutch, German and Swiss settlers to the close of the first half of the present century. 1872. Repr. Spartanburg, S.C.: Reprint Co., 1972.

3122 **Boddie, William W.** Marion's men. [Charleston, S.C.], ca.1938.
List of 2,500 volunteers who fought in the Revolution with General Francis Marion. Sources given.

3123 **Brown, Richard L.,** and **Brown, R. E.** Genealogical notes, principally South Carolina and Virginia. West Greenville, S.C., 1937.

3124 **Burns, Annie (Walker).** South Carolina pension abstracts of the Revolutionary War, War of 1812, and Indian Wars. 12v. [Washington, D.C., ca. 193?].
Use with extreme care.

3125 **The Carolina herald.** A quarterly newsletter of South Carolina genealogy and related subjects. v.1- , 1972- . Columbia, S.C.:South Carolina Genealogical Soc.

3126 **Chandler, Marion C.** Colonial and state records in the South Carolina archives: a temporary summary guide. Columbia, S.C.: The Archives, 1973.
List of record series made or maintained by departments of state and provincial government since 1671.

3127 **Charleston Free Library.** Index to wills of Charleston county, South Carolina, 1671-1868. 1950. Repr. Baltimore: G.P.C., 1974.
Originally a W.P.A. typescript. Martha L. Houston's *Indexes to county wills of South Carolina* (no.3152), lacked those for Charleston county.

3128 **Chreitzberg, Abel McK.** Early Methodism in the Carolinas. 1897. Repr. Spartanburg, S.C.: Reprint Co., 1972.
Extensive information on Methodist preachers; of marginal interest to genealogists.

3129 **Clemens, William M.** North and South Carolina marriage records, from the earliest colonial days to the Civil War. 1927. Repr. Baltimore: G.P.C., 1973.
Almost 7,500 records. Excellent list.

3130 **Cohen, Hennig.** The South Carolina gazette, 1732-75. Columbia, S.C.: Univ. of South Carolina Pr., 1953.
Provides a large number of names and identification by profession or occupation.

3131 **Cyclopedia of eminent and representative men of the Carolinas of the nineteenth century** . . . 2v. 1892. Repr. Spartanburg, S.C.: Reprint Co., 1972-73.
With portraits. Good mug book helpful for the period. v.1, South Carolina; v.2, North Carolina.

3132 **D.A.R. South Carolina.** Roster and ancestral roll. Compiled by Mrs. G. Duncan Foxworth. Columbia, S.C., 1954.

3133 **Davis, Harry A.** Some Huguenot families of South Carolina and Georgia . . . 2nd ed., rev. and enl. Washington, D.C., 1927.

3134 ———— Supplement. Washington, D.C., 1937.

3135 **De Saussure, Wilmot G.** The names as far as can be ascertained of the officers who served in the South Carolina regiments of the Continental establishment . . . of the militia . . . 1886. n.p., n.d.
34p. pamphlet containing several hundred names; concerns Revolution.

3136 **Dubose, Samuel,** and **Porcher, F. A.** A contribution to the history of the Huguenots of South Carolina consisting of pamphlets. 1887. Repr. Columbia, S.C.: Bryan Co., 1972.
Includes lists of French refugees.

3137 **Easterby, James H.** Guide to the study and reading of South Carolina history. 2v. 1949-50. Repr. Columbia, S.C.: Univ. of South Carolina Pr., 1965.
*South Carolina bibliographies,* ser.1-2: 1, topical lists; 2, general classified bibliography.

3138 **Elzas, Barnett A.** Jewish marriage notices from the newspaper press of Charleston, S.C., 1775-1906. New York, 1917.

3139 ———— The Jews of South Carolina from the earliest times to the present day. 1905. Repr. Spartanburg, S.C.: Reprint Co., 1972.

3140 **Ervin, Sara S.** South Carolinians in the Revolution. With service records and miscellaneous data. Also abstracts of wills, Laurens county (Ninety-six district), 1775-1855. 1949. Repr. Baltimore: G.P.C., 1971.
Has added index containing extensive index of names. Outstanding record of Revolutionary service; basic genealogical reference for the state.

3141 **Esker, Katie-Prince W.** South Carolina memorials: v.1, 1731-76. Abstracts of selected land records . . . New Orleans, La.: Polyanthos, 1973- (in progress).
From a series of 16v. in the Dept. of Archives and History, Columbia, S.C. Useful in locating individual landowners and in naming adjoining proprietors.

3142 **Faunt, Joan (Reynolds)** and others. Biographical directory of the South Carolina House of Representatives, v.1, session lists, 1692-1973. Columbia, S.C.: Univ. of South Carolina Pr., 1974- (in progress).

3143 **Garlington, J. C.** Men of the time. Sketches of living notables . . . a biographical encyclopedia of contemporaneous South Carolina leaders. 1902. Repr. Spartanburg, S.C.: Reprint Co., 1972.
Mug book.

3144 **Georgia genealogical magazine.** v.1- , 1961- . Easley, S.C.: Southern Historical Pr.
Has some South Carolina source material, particularly concerning the portion formerly known as "The old ninety-six district." Full annotation, *see* no.1173.

3145 **Great Britain. Public Record Office.** Records in the British Public Record Office relating to South Carolina, 1663-90. Indexed by Alexander S. Salley, Jr. 5v. Columbia, S.C., 1928-47.

3146 **Gregg, Alexander.** History of the Old Cheraws. 1867. Repr. Spartanburg, S.C.: Reprint Co., 1965.

3147 ———— 1925 ed. Repr. Baltimore: G.P.C., 1967.
Area is now part of 8 counties along the Pee Dee river. Covers 1730-1810, from the first white settlements. Has family histories. Because the Baltimore reprint is from an expanded ed., with addenda by John I. Dargan, it is preferable.

3147a **Hazelwood, Jean P.; Hazelwood, F. L., Jr.;** and **Smith, T. L.** Index 1830 census South Carolina. Fort Worth, Tex.: Gen Re Put (3624 Guadaloupe Rd., 76116), 1973.
47,570 names. Individual county printouts available.

**3148   Hemphill, James C.** Men of mark in South Carolina . . . 4v. Washington, D.C., 1907–1909.
Good biographical sketches.

**3148a   Hendrix, Ge Lee C.,** and **Lindsay, M. McK.** The jury lists of South Carolina, 1778–79. Greenville, S.C.: Lindsay, 1974.
9,000 names of males; includes districts of Charlestown, Georgetown, Beaufort, Cheraws, Camden, Orangeburg, and Ninety-six.

**3149   Hennig, Helen (Kohn).** Great South Carolinians. 2v. 1940–49. Repr. Freeport, N.Y.: Books for Libraries Pr., 1970.
v.1, from colonial days to the Confederate War; v.2, great South Carolinians of a later date.

**3150   Hirsch, Arthur H.** The Huguenots of colonial South Carolina. 1928. Repr. 1962 and 1973. Hamden, Conn.: Archon Books, 1973.
Reissue of 1962 reprint. Contains details of contributions made in Carolina by French Protestants, with details of Huguenot settlements and of eminent Huguenot families.

**3151   Historical Records Survey.** Inventory of county archives of South Carolina. 14v. Columbia, S.C., 1937–41.
Only the following numbers were published: 1 (Abbeville), 2 (Aiken), 3 (Allendale), 4 (Anderson), 11 (Cherokee), 17 (Dillon), 21 (Florence), 27 (Jasper), 31 (Lee), 35 (McCormick), 37 (Oconee), 39 (Pickens), 40 (Richland), and 41 (Saluda).

**3152   Houston, Martha L.** Indexes to the county wills of South Carolina. 1939. Repr., repaged with added table of contents. Baltimore: G.P.C., 1970.
Copied by Mrs. John D. Rogers. Wills cover 1766 to 1853; transcripts of original W.P.A. work. Lacks Charleston county (*see* no. 3127).

**3153   Huguenot Society of South Carolina.** Transactions. v.1– , 1889– . Charleston, S.C.: The Society.

**3154   Landrum, John B. O.** Colonial and Revolutionary history of upper South Carolina. 1897. Repr. Spartanburg, S.C.: Reprint Co., 1959.
Standard work.

**3155   McCrady, Edward.** The history of South Carolina in the Revolution, 1775–80. 2v. 1901–2. Repr. New York: Russell & Russell, 1969.
Mostly history, but many names given.

**3156   Mills, Robert.** Atlas of the state of South Carolina . . . 1825. Repr. 1938; new ed. 1967. Columbia, S.C., 1967.

**3157   Moore, Caroline T.,** and **Simmons, A. A.** Abstracts of the wills, state of South Carolina, 1670–1760. 2v. Charleston, S.C.: C. T. Moore (307 Stono Dr., 29412), 1960–64.
v.2 is by C. T. Moore only; v.1 is out-of-print.

**3158   ———** v.3–4. Charleston, S.C. C. T. Moore, 1972–74.
v.3, 1760–84; v,4, abstracts of wills of Charleston district, 1783–1800.
Thousands of names. Wills preserved in the journal of the Grand Council, Office of the Secretary of the Province and the Probate Court of Charleston county.

**3159   Moore, John H.** Research materials in South Carolina. A guide . . . Columbia, S.C.: Univ. of South Carolina Pr., 1967.
First survey of contents of all libraries, archives, and files in South Carolina.

**3160   Names in South Carolina.** Ed. by Claude N. Neuffer. v.1– , 1959– . Columbia, S.C.: Dept. of English, Univ. of South Carolina.
Published annually. Invites articles on South Carolina place names. Gives details of county information, post offices, Revolutionary and other information, v.1–12 and index, repr. in 1967; index v.13–18 issued 1973.

**3161   Platt, Gwen.** Index to 1820 federal census, entire state of South Carolina. Tustin, Calif.: G.A.M. Pub., 1972.
Separate name index.

3162 **Pruitt, Jayne C. (G.).** Migration of South Carolinians on Natchez Trace. [Fairfax, Va.?], ca.1949.
Comprises people in the 1850 census of Mississippi listed as having been born in South Carolina.

3163 ——— Revolutionary War pension applicants who served from South Carolina. [Fairfax, Va.?], 1946.

3164 **Rathburn, Thorn.** York county and genealogical records of South Carolina. 2v. Chester, S.C.: The Author, 1973.
Old court records, pioneers from Pennsylvania, North Carolina, and Virginia allied with old South Carolina families.

3165 **Ravenel, Daniel.** "Liste des françois et suisses." From an old manuscript list of French and Swiss Protestants, settled in Charleston, on the Santee and at the Orange Quarter in Carolina who desired naturalization. 1888. Repr. Baltimore: G.P.C., 1968.
Covers ca.1695-96. Published 1868 and later dates, and also in *Transactions of the Huguenot Society* (see no.3153).

3166 **Records of the regiments of the South Carolina Line, Continental establishment.** In *South Carolina historical and genealogical magazine,* v.5-7, 1904-06.

3167 **Revill, Janie.** A compilation of the original lists of Protestant immigrants to South Carolina, 1763-73. 1939. Repr. Baltimore: G.P.C., 1974.
Over 4,000 names; name of immigrant with number of acres allotted him.

3168 ——— Copy of the original index book showing the Revolutionary claims filed in South Carolina, between August 20, 1783 and August 31, 1786. ca.1941. Repr. Baltimore: G.P.C., 1969.

3169 ——— South Carolina counties, districts, parishes and townships; also a list of tax collectors for 1765, a list of justices of the peace for 1765 [and] . . . 1785. Columbia, S.C., ca.193?

3170 ——— South Carolina wills, originally recorded in Charleston, S.C., 1672-1730. Sumter, S.C., 1939.

3171 **Rogers, George C.** History of Georgetown county, South Carolina. Columbia, S.C.: Univ. of South Carolina Pr., 1970.
Full of names, with excellent biographical and genealogical footnotes. Considerable value to genealogical researchers.

3172 **Salley, Alexander S., Jr.** Marriage notices in *Charleston courier,* 1803-1808. 2nd pr. 1919. Repr. Columbia, S.C.: Univ. of South Carolina Pr., [1965].

3173 ——— Marriage notices in the *South-Carolina and American general gazette* . . . 1766-81, and its successor, the *Royal Gazette,* 1781-82. Columbia, S.C., 1914.

3174 ——— Marriage notices in the *South-Carolina gazette;* and *county journal,* 1765-75, and in the *Charleston gazette,* 1778-80.
Columbia, S.C., 1904.

3175 ——— Marriage notices in the *South-Carolina gazette* and its successors, 1732-1801. From files in the Library of Charleston Library Society. 1902. Repr. Baltimore: G.P.C., 1965.

3176 ——— and **Webber, M. L.** Death notices in the *South-Carolina gazette,* 1732-75. 1917. Repr. Columbia, S.C.: Dept. of Archives and History, 1965.

3177 **The Schirmer diary,** 1826- . In *South Carolina historical magazine,* v.67- , 1966- (in progress).
Jacob F. Schirmer (1803-80) wrote a diary of Charleston life from 1826-76. In it he recorded the births, marriages, and deaths of the St. John's Lutheran Church, Charleston, and other Charleston family information. By 1974, the diary had reached the year 1845.

3178 **Smith, Henry A. M.** The baronies of South Carolina. In *South Carolina historical and genealogical magazine,* v.11-15, 18, 1910-14, 1917.
Baronies consisted of 12,000 acres.

3179 **Snowden, Yates.** History of South Carolina. 5v. Chicago, 1920.
v.3-5 biographical.

3180  **South Carolina.** Special limited ed. Chicago, 1920.
Mug book.

3181  **South Carolina (Colony). Assembly.** Colonial records of South Carolina. v.1– , 1736– . Columbia, S.C.: Dept. of Archives and History, 1951– .
Journal of the Commons House of Assembly. Ed. by James H. Easterby. 10v. pub. to 1776 (by 1974).

3182  —— Records of the Secretary of the Province and the register of the Province of South Carolina, 1671–75. Ed. by Alexander S. Salley, Jr. Columbia, S.C., 1944.

3183  —— **Court of Chancery.** Records, 1671–79. Ed. by Anne K. Gregorie. *American legal records,* v.6. Washington, D.C.: American Historical Assoc., 1950.

3184  —— **Court of Ordinary.** Abstracts from the records, 1692–1700. Compiled by Alexander S. Salley, Jr. In *South Carolina historical and genealogical magazine,* v.8–13, 1907–12.
A Court of Ordinary is a court of probate.

3185  —— **Governor and Council.** Warrants for lands in South Carolina, 1672–1711. Ed. by Alexander S. Salley, Jr. 3v. 1910–15. Rev. in 1v. by R. N. Olsberg. Columbia, S.C.: Univ. of South Carolina Pr., 1973.
v.1, 1672–79; v.2, 1680–92; v.3, 1690–1711.

3186  **South Carolina. Council of Safety.** Papers of the first Council of Safety of the Revolutionary party in South Carolina, June-November 1775. In *South Carolina historical and genealogical magazine,* v.1–3, 1900–1902.

3187  —— —— Second Council of Safety, November 1775–March 1776. In *South Carolina historical and genealogical magazine,* v.3–4, 1902–1903.
Many names and much background history.

3188  —— **Dept. of Archives and History.** Ancestor hunting in South Carolina. Columbia, S.C.: The Archives, 1969.

3189  —— Biographical directory of the Senate of the state of South Carolina, 1776–1964. Compiled by Emily B. Reynolds and J. R. Faunt. Columbia, S.C.: Dept. of Archives, 1964.
1,400 biographical sketches.

3190  —— —— South Carolina troops in Confederate service. Compiled by Alexander S. Salley, Jr. 3v. Columbia, S.C.: The Archives, 1913–30.
v.2 is out-of-print. Compiled from photostats made from records in the Office of the Adjutant General of the U.S. Supplementary data from state rolls and elsewhere. No further vols. contemplated because of expense.

3191  —— —— Temporary summary guide to the colonial and state records in the South Carolina Archives. Columbia, S.C.: The Archives, 1973.

3192  **South Carolina. Treasury.** Accounts audited of Revolutionary claims against South Carolina. Compiled by Alexander S. Salley, Jr. 3v. Columbia, S.C.: Dept. of Archives, 1935–43.

3193  —— Stub entries to indents issued in payment of claims against South Carolina, growing out of the Revolution. 12v. 1910–27. Some have been reprinted by Univ. of South Carolina Pr., Columbia, S.C. Books cover: *A* (in progress); *B, C–F, G–H, I, K, L–N, O–Q, R–T, U–W, X* pts. 1–2, *Y–Z*. Some edited by Alexander S. Salley Jr. and Wylma A. Wates.
All available in original or repr. form.

3194  **South Carolina genealogical register.** v.1–6, 1963–68. Pass Christian, Miss.
Contains much source material, including elusive marriage information.

3195  **South Carolina historical and genealogical magazine.** v.1– , 1900– . Charleston, S.C.: South Carolina Historical Soc.

**3196** ———— Consolidated index, v.1–40, 1900–39, with subject index, v.1–61, 1900–60. Charleston, S.C.: The Society.

Contains articles on all phases of South Carolina information, but there is genealogical material still being printed. In 1953 the name was changed to *South Carolina historical magazine.*

**3197 South Carolina Historical Society.** Collections. 1857–1947. Charleston, S.C.: The Society.

Basically historical, but with genealogical applications. Few volumes are in print; none was published after 1947.

**3198 The South Carolina magazine of ancestral research.** v.1– , 1973– . Kingstree, S.C.: Laurence K. Wells, ed., Box 694, 29556.

Study of South Carolina's records and families. Wills, deeds, taxes, tombstone inscriptions, etc.

**3199 Stephenson, Jean.** Scotch-Irish migration to South Carolina, 1772. Vienna, Va.: Donna Hotaling, 2255 Cedar Lane, 22180.

Rev. William Martin and his five shiploads of settlers. Most settlers identified, with place of settlement; gives chapter on variations on spelling of names. Excellent.

**3200 Teeples, Gary R.** South Carolina 1800 census. G. R. Teeples, paleographer and compiler; R. V. Jackson, editor; R. Moore, computer director. Provo, Utah: Accelerated Indexing Systems, 1973.

Computer index, with maps of early days; research aids on existing counties; genealogical data. About 30,000 entries.

**3201 Todd, John R., and Hutson, F. M.** Prince William's parish plantation. Richmond, Va., 1935.

From earliest days to present.

**3202 Townsend, Leah.** South Carolina Baptists, 1670–1805. 1935. Repr. Baltimore: G.P.C., 1974.

7,000 individuals are identified, with full data, from all types of records.

**3203 Turnbull, Robert C.** Bibliography of South Carolina, 1563–1950. 6v. Charlottesville, Va.: Univ. of Virginia Pr., 1956–60.

**3204 U.S. Bureau of the Census.** Heads of families at the first census of the United States taken in the year 1790. South Carolina. 1908. Repr. Baltimore: G.P.C., 1972, etc.; Spartanburg: Reprint Co., 1964, etc.

**3205 Waddel, Moses.** A register of marriages celebrated and solemnized by Moses Waddel, D.D. in South Carolina and Georgia, 1795–1836 . . . Daniellsville, Ga.: Heritage Papers, 1967.

**3206 Wallace, David D.** The history of South Carolina. 4v. New York, 1934.

v.4 biographical.

**3207 Webber, Mabel.** Death notices from the *South Carolina and American general gazette,* and its continuation, the *Royal gazette,* 1766–82. In *South Carolina historical and genealogical magazine,* v.16–17, 1915–16.

**3208** ———— (and others). Marriage and death notices from the *South Carolina weekly gazette,* 1783–1827. In *South Carolina historical and genealogical magazine,* v.18–50, 1917–49; v.52–58, 1951–57; v.60–67, 1959–66.

Through 1783–1827 the newspaper had several titles: *South Carolina weekly gazette, South Carolina gazette, Charleston morning post,* and finally *City gazette of Charleston, South Carolina.*

**3209 Young, Pauline.** Abstracts of Old Ninety-six and Abbeville district, South Carolina. Wills, bonds, and administrations between 1774 and 1860. 1950. Repr. Easley, S.C.: Southern Historical Pr., 1969.

30,000 names. Old ninety-six district bordered Georgia on its western boundary and was the ancestral home of many early Georgia settlers.

**3210** ———— A genealogical collection of South Carolina wills and records. 2v. Greenville and Liberty, S.C.: The Author, 1955.

v.1 repr. by Southern Historical Pr.,

Easley, S.C., 1969. Contains wills, deeds, tombstone inscriptions, etc.

## SOUTH DAKOTA

Settled ca. 1856; entered Union 1889

*South Dakota Historical Resource Center, Pierre*
*South Dakota State Historical Society, Pierre*
*South Dakota State Library, Pierre*

3211   **Bailey, Dana R.** History of Minnehaha county, South Dakota. Sioux Falls, S.D., 1899.

3212   **Black Hills nuggets.** v.1– , 1968– . Rapid City, S.D.: Rapid City Soc. for Genealogical Research.
Quarterly. South Dakota. Queries are general for all states.

3212a   **Brown, Jesse,** and **Willard, A. M.** The Black Hills trails: a history of the struggles of the pioneers in the winning of the Black Hills. New York, 1924.

3213   **The census of 1860** [of South Dakota]. In *South Dakota historical collections,* v.10, 1920.
Names of persons who died in the portion of Minnesota territory that is now South Dakota.

3214   **Clement, Fritz.** Golden anniversary historical book, 1900–50. Selby, S.D., n.d.

3215   **Coursey, Oscar W.** Who's who in South Dakota . . . 3v. Mitchell, S.D., 1913–20.
Historical and biographical.

3216   **Dakota territory.** v.1– , 1969– . Phoenix, Ariz.: Bernice L. Rogers, ed.
Covers South Dakota, Wyoming, and some North Dakota and Montana areas that were in Dakota territory back in formative days when it was cut off from Minnesota. General queries.

3217   **Daughters of Dakota.** In *South Dakota Dept. of History report and historical collections,* v.33, pp.17–438, 1966.
With index to pictures of Pioneer Daughters, pp.439–57. Over 2,000 biographies.

3218   **Ellis, C. H.** History of Faulk county, South Dakota. Faulkton, S.D., 1909.

3219   **Historical Records Survey.** Guide to public vital statistics records in South Dakota. Vermillion, S.D., 1942.

3220   ——— Inventory of county archives of South Dakota. 9v. Vermillion, S.D., 1937–41.
Only the following numbers were published: 3 (Bennett), 8 (Buffalo), 12 (Clark), 24 (Faulk), 27 (Haakon), 35 (Jackson and Washabaugh), 47 (Mellette), 48 (Miner), and 65 (Washabaugh). Unpublished materials deposited in Univ. of South Dakota, Vermillion, S.D.

3221   ——— South Dakota place names. Vermillion, S.D., 1940.
Sponsored by Univ. of South Dakota. Excellent compilation.

3222   **History of southeastern Dakota:** its settlement and growth. Sioux City, Iowa, 1881.
Gives histories of towns and counties, with many lists of early settlers. Biographical sketches of the pioneers and businessmen.

3223   **Honor roll** (of native born South Dakotans). Ed. by William G. Robinson. In *South Dakota historical collections* 22, 1946.

3224   **Jennewein, John L.,** and **Boorman, J.** Dakota panorama. Sioux Falls, S.D., 1961. Obtainable from Dakota Territory Centennial Commission, Pierre, S.D.
Good background material for genealogists. Many names.

3225   **Kingsbury, George W.,** and **Smith, George M.** History of Dakota territory; and South Dakota, its history and its people. 5v. 1915. Repr. Ann Arbor, Mich.: Xerox Univ. Microfilms, 1973.
2v. were by Kingsbury; 1v. by Smith; v.4–5 biographical. Suppl., *see* no.3229.

3226 **McDowell, R. E.** Memorandum and official records concerning Dakota militia, organized 1862, for the protection of the frontier settlements from the hostile Sioux Indians. Compiled for consideration in connection with Senate bill no.5353, doc.241, 58th Cong., 2nd sess. Washington, D.C., 1904.

3227 **Memorial and biographical record.** An illustrated compendium of biography . . . biographical sketches of prominent old settlers and representative citizens of South Dakota . . . Chicago, 1898.
One of the few biographical records of early South Dakotans.

3228 **Parker, Donald D.** Early churches and towns in South Dakota. Brookings, S.D., ca.1964.

3228a **Parker, Watson,** and **Lambert, H. K.** Black Hills ghost towns. Chicago: Swallow Pr., 1974.
Good gazetteer; much local history.

3229 **Peterson, August.** History of the Swedes who settled in South Dakota. n.p., 1947.
Deluxe suppl. to the *History of Dakota territory and South Dakota: its history and its people* (1915), see no.3225.

3230 **Pompey, Sherman L.** The 1870 census records of Deuel, Jayne and Hutchinson, Dakota territory. Independence, Calif., 1965.
Much on early settlers.

3231 **Robinson, Doane.** Encyclopedia of South Dakota. Pierre, S.D., ca.1925.
Has biographies.

3232 ———— History of South Dakota, together with personal mention of citizens of South Dakota. 2v. Chicago, 1904.
v.2 biographical.

3233 ———— South Dakota, sui generis; stressing the unique and dramatic in South Dakota history. (With) South Dakota biography . . . 3v. Chicago, 1930.
v.2-3 biographical.

3234 **Savo Finns Historical Society.** History of the Finnish settlements in Brown and Dickey counties of South and North Dakota, 1881–1955. 2nd ed. Savo, S.D.: The Society, 1956.

3235 **South Dakota historical collections.** v.1– , 1902– . Pierre, S.D.: State Dept. of History.
v.1-6 pub. by State Historical Soc. Some genealogy and much history.

3235a **Stutenroth, Stella M.** Daughters of Dacotah. Mitchell, S.D., 1942.

TENNESSEE

Settled ca. 1757; entered Union 1796

*Public Libary of Knoxville and Knox County (Lawson McGhee)*
*Tennessee State Library and Archives, Nashville*

3236 **Acklen, Jeannette T.** (and others). Tennessee records. 1933. (v.1), Tombstone inscriptions and manuscripts, historical and biographical. (v.2), Bible records and marriage bonds. 1933. Repr. in 2v. Baltimore: G.P.C., 1974.
Collected by chapters of the D.A.R. in Tennessee. Considerable Revolutionary information but much inaccuracy; not comprehensive.

3237 **Allen, Penelope T.** Tennessee soldiers in the Revolution. A roster of soldiers during the Revolutionary War in the counties of Washington and Sullivan, taken from the Revolutionary Army accounts of North Carolina. Bristol, Tenn., 1935.

3238 ———— Tennessee soldiers in the War of 1812: regiments of Col. Allison. v.1 (all pub.). Chattanooga, Tenn., 1947.
Issued by National Society, U.S. Daughters of 1812.

3239 **Allen, Ronald R.** Tennessee books —a preliminary guide. Knoxville, Tenn.: The Author, 1969.
Alphabetical listing of over 1,100 books pertaining to the history and people of Tennessee.

**3240　American historical magazine** (and **Tennessee Historical Society quarterly).** v.1–9, 1896–1904.
Much genealogy.

**3241　Ansearchin' news.** The official publication of the Tennessee Genealogical Society. v.1– , 1954– . Memphis, Tenn.: The Society. Originally *Journal of the Memphis Genealogical Society,* v.1–11.
Source material and genealogical accounts relating to Tennessee.

**3242　Armstrong, Zella.** Notable southern families. 6v. 1918–33. Repr. 6v. in 3. Baltimore: G.P.C., 1974; in 6v. Spartanburg, S.C.: Reprint Co., 1974.
Useful but not authoritative. Southern families, but most have Tennessee connections. Later volumes by Julia P. C. French. Full details, *see* no.615.

**3243　──── Some Tennessee heroes of the Revolution:** compiled from pension statements. 3 pts. Chattanooga, Tenn., 1933–35.
1v. containing 5 pamphlets.

**3244　──── Twenty-four hundred Tennessee pensioners—Revolution, War of 1812.** Chattanooga, Tenn., 1937.

**3245　Arnow, Harriette L.** Seedtime on the Cumberland. New York: Macmillan, 1960.
Excellent background material; many names, well indexed.

**3246　Burns, Annie W.** Major index to wills and inventories of Tennessee at the D.A.R. Library, Washington, D.C. 6v. Washington, D.C., [1962–65].
v.1, 1A, 2, 4–6 (v.3 not published). Covers Bedford through Meigs counties.

**3247　Carpenter, Vera C. (Mrs. V. K.).** Seventh census of the United States, 1850. [Tennessee counties.] Transcribed by Mrs. V. K. Carpenter. Huntsville, Tenn.: Century Enterprises, 1968– (in progress).
Free population schedules. Each volume dealing with separate counties published in series. 11 of 12 counties so far. Contains names of all members of family, age, gender, other data. Not always treated as series by libraries.

**3248　Cartwright, Betty G. C.,** and **Gardiner, L. J.** North Carolina land grants in Tennessee, 1778–91. Memphis, Tenn., 1958.
From 1803 manuscript list. Since census schedules for 1790 and 1800 for Tennessee do not exist, this list of landowners and/or settlers constitutes the only substitute for a census of that part of North Carolina that became Tennessee in 1796. Grants listed were not necessarily taken up.

**3249　Cassell, Charles W.; Finck, W. J.;** and **Henkel, E. O.** History of the Lutheran Church in Virginia and East Tennessee. Strasburg, Tenn., 1930.
Hundreds of names of ministers and laymen.

**3249a　Coker, Charles F. W.** Records relating to Tennessee in the North Carolina State Archives. *Archives information circular* 3, rev. Raleigh, N.C.: North Carolina Div. of Archives, 1973.

**3250　Cram, Kendall J.** Guide to use of genealogical material in the Tennessee State Library and Archives. Nashville, Tenn.: The Library, 1964.

**3251　Curtis, Mary B.** Early east Tennessee tax lists . . . Fort Worth, Tex.: Arrow Press Co., 1964.
Covers 22 east Tennessee counties for which there are no census records prior to 1830. Mostly concerns the early 1800s. Poorly transcribed.

**3252　D.A.R. Tennessee.** Membership roster and soldiers . . . Compiled by Edythe J. Whitley. 2v. Nashville, Tenn.: D.A.R., 1961–70.
Lists soldiers and children of soldiers, and sources for verification of soldiers' service. v.1, 1894–1960; v.2, 1961–70.

**3253　──── Roster of soldiers and patriots of the American Revolution** in Tennessee. Compiled by Lucy E. Bates. n.p., D.A.R., 1974.

**3254　East Tennessee Historical Society.** Publications. no.1– , 1929– . Knoxville, Tenn.: The Society.
Annual publ., mostly historical but some

genealogy, including tax records. Almost all in print. Cumulative index, covering 1929-48, pub. in 1952. Last few years of marginal value.

**3255 Echoes from the East Tennessee Historical Society.** v.1- , 1955- . Knoxville, Tenn.: The Society.
Contains genealogical queries. Useful.

**3256 Edwards, Olga (Jones),** and **Roberts, I. G.** The "connection" in East Tennessee. Washington College, Tenn.: Pioneer Printers, 1969.
Family connections, general information regarding number of east Tennessee families. Compiled in an effort to identify properly families bearing the same surnames, and to trace insofar as possible the complicated "connections" between the families. 7,500 names.

**3257 Family findings.** v.1- , 1969- . Jackson, Tenn.: Mid-west Tennessee Genealogical Soc.

**3258 Folmsbee, Stanley J.; Corlew, R. L.;** and **Mitchell, E. L.** History of Tennessee. 4v. New York, 1960.
v.2 has good bibliography; v.3-4 has family and personal history.

**3259 Foster, Austin P.** Counties of Tennessee. Nashville, Tenn., 1923.
Dates of formation of counties and parent counties. Some errors.

**3259a Fulton Genealogical Society, Kentucky.** Bible records of western Kentucky and Tennessee. Fulton, Ky.: The Society, 1974.
Good index.

**3260 [Gillum, James L.]** Prominent Tennesseans 1796-1928. Lewisburg, Tenn., 1940.

**3261 Goodpasture, Albert V.** A dictionary of distinguished Tennesseans. In *The American historical magazine,* v.8, 1903.

**3262 Goodspeed's Histories of Tennessee.** In the 1880s the Goodspeed Publishing Co., published a number of volumes on the history of Tennessee and its counties, each volume consisting of a fairly comprehensive general history of the state up to the time of publication. The various volumes were supplemented by a history of the county or counties, together with a biographical appendix. The series covered 82 of Tennessee's 95 counties (those not included were the metropolitan county of Davidson and 12 rural Cumberland plateau counties). Within the past few years some have been reprinted, and a few have been indexed separately by Mrs. Leister E. Presley. Those listed below are of importance but a bibliography of Tennessee should be consulted for a complete listing.

**3263 The Goodspeed histories of Cannon, Coffee, DeKalb, Warren, and White counties . . .** Repr. from the 1887 ed. of Goodspeed's *History of Tennessee.* McMinnville, Tenn.: Ben Lomond Pr., 1972.

**3264 Goodspeed histories of Hamilton, Knox and Shelby counties of Tennessee.** Repr. from Goodspeed's 1887 ed. of *History of Tennessee.* Nashville, Tenn.: Elder, 1974.

**3265 The Goodspeed histories of Maury, Williamson, Rutherford, Wilson, Bedford, and Marshall counties of Tennessee.** 1886. Repr. Columbia, Tenn.: Woodward & Stenson Printing Co., 1971.

**3266 The Goodspeed histories of Montgomery, Robertson, Humphreys, Stewart, Dickson, Cheatham, and Houston counties of Tennessee . . .** 1886. Columbia, Tenn.: Woodward & Stenson Printing Co., 1972.

**3267 Goodspeed's general history of Tennessee.** 1887. Repr. Nashville, Tenn.: Elder, 1973.

**3268 Goodspeed's history of Tennessee, containing historical and biographical sketches of thirty east Tennessee counties . . .** 1887. Repr. Nashville, Tenn.: Elder, 1972.

**3269 Goodspeed's History of Tennessee.** Indexes of Eastern, Middle and

Western Tennessee, by Cloie (Mrs. Leister E.) Presley. Searcy, Ark.: The Compiler, 1972-73.

**3270 Gray, Frank A.** Gray's new map of Kentucky and Tennessee. 1876. Repr. Murray, Ky.: Kentucky Repr. Co., 1972.
Shows comparative increases in population, 1790-1870. Excellent aids for genealogists working with the 1870 and 1880 federal censuses.

**3271 Hale, William T.,** and **Merritt, L. M.** A history of Tennessee and Tennesseans . . . 8v. Chicago, 1913.
v.4-8 biographical.

**3272 Hamer, Philip M.** Tennessee, a history, 1673-1922. 4v. New York, 1933.
v.3-4 biographical.

**3273 Hathaway, Beverly W.** Genealogy research sources in Tennessee. West Jordan, Utah: Allstates Research Co., 1972.
Gives location of genealogical sources in Tennessee.

**3274 Historical Records Survey.** Directory of churches, missions and religious institutions of Tennessee. 5v. Nashville, Tenn., 1940-42.
Davidson, Hamilton, Knox, Shelby, and Washington counties.

**3275** ——— Guide to church vital statistics records in Tennessee. Nashville, Tenn., 1942.

**3276** ——— Guide to public vital statistics in Tennessee. Nashville, Tenn., 1941.

**3277** ——— Inventory of county archives of Tennessee. 13v. Nashville, Tenn., 1937-42.
Only the following numbers were published: 1 (Anderson), 2 (Bedford), 5 (Blount), 6 (Bradley), 11 (Cheatham), 17 (Crockett), 33 (Hamilton), 38 (Haywood), 53 (Loudon), 75 (Rutherford), 82 (Sullivan), 84 (Tipton), and 95 (Wilson). Unpublished material deposited in State Planning Commission, Nashville, Tenn.

**3278** ——— Inventory of the church and synagogue archives of Tennessee.
4v. Nashville, Tenn., 1939-42.

**3279 Humes, Thomas W.** The loyal mountaineers of Tennessee. 1888. Repr. Spartanburg, S.C.: Reprint Co., 1974.
Story of the people of east Tennessee who remained loyal to the Union during the Civil War.

**3280 Hunkins, Lillian.** Tombstone inscriptions and marriages of middle Tennessee. Houston, Tex.: The Author, 1965.

**3281 Jackson, Ronald V.,** and **Teeples, G. R.** Tennessee 1820 census. Provo, Utah: Accelerated Indexing Systems, 1974.
About 35,000 computer entries.

**3282 Lindsley, John B.** The military annals of Tennessee. 1886. Repr. Spartanburg, S.C.: Reprint Co., 1974.
Review of military operations in Tennessee from 1861 to 1865, together with regimental histories and memorial rolls of over 9,000 Confederate soldiers who fell in battle or died in service.

**3283 Luttrell, Laura E.,** and **Creekmore, P.** Writings on Tennessee counties. In *Tennessee historical quarterly*. v.2, 1943.
Good bibliography.

**3284 McBride, Robert M.** Tennessee county data for historical and genealogical research. Nashville, Tenn.: State Library, 1966.

**3285 McCay, Betty L.** Sources for genealogical searching in Tennessee. Indianapolis, Ind.: The Author, 1970.
Useful for beginners. Records and maps.

**3286 McCown, Mary (H.),** and **Burns, I. E.** Soldiers of the War of 1812 buried in Tennessee. Memphis, Tenn.: Tennessee Soc., U.S. Daughters of the War of 1812, 1959.

**3287** **McGhee, Lucy K.** Partial census of 1787 to 1791 of Tennessee as taken from the North Carolina land grants. 3v. Washington, D.C., 195?. Invaluable link between North Carolina and the early settlers of Tennessee.

**3288** —— Tennessee military records: pension abstracts of the Revolution, War of 1812 and other wars. v.1 (all pub.?). Washington, D.C., 1965.

**3289** **Memorial and biographical record:** an illustrated compendium of biography . . . including biographical sketches of prominent old settlers and representative citizens of part of the Cumberland region of Tennessee . . . Chicago, 1898.

**3290** **Moore, Mrs. John T.** Record of commissions of officers in the Tennessee militia, 1796-1801, 1807, 1809, 1811-15. In *Tennessee historical quarterly*, v.1-9, 1942-49; v.15, 1956.

**3291** —— and **Foster, A. P.** Tennessee, the volunteer state, 1796-1923. 4v. Nashville, Tenn., 1923.
v.2-4 biographical.

**3292** **Morris, Eastin** (and **Rhea, M.**). Eastin Morris Tennessee gazetteer, 1834, Matthew Rhea's Map of the state of Tennessee, 1832. Ed. by R. M. McBride and O. Meredith. Nashville, Tenn.: Gazetteer Pr., 1971.
Essential adjunct to the study of early Tennessee history.

**3293** **Presley, Cloie (Mrs. Leister E.).** Biographical indexes to Goodspeed's *History of Tennessee*, see no.3262.

**3294** **Ramsey, James G. M.** The annals of Tennessee to the end of the 18th century . . . 1853 ed. with additions and Fain's *Index*, 1920, repr. 1926. Repr. 1967, with new index and annotations and contents of 1926 ed. Knoxville, Tenn.: East Tennessee Historical Soc., 1967.
Standard work on Tennessee. Useful for historians and genealogists. John T. Fain's *Critical and analytical index and genealogical guide* (Nashville, Tenn., 1920) is excellent.

**3295** —— —— Biographies, annotations and index. Repr. East Tennessee Historical Soc., Knoxville, 1972; Repr. Arno Pr., N.Y., 1973.

**3296** **Ray, Worth S.** Tennessee cousins: a history of Tennessee people. 1950. Repr. Baltimore: G.P.C., 1971.
Lists about 6,000 surnames, some with as many as 50 references.

**3297** **Richardson, James D.** Tennessee Templars: a register of names, with biographical sketches of the Knights Templar of Tennessee . . . Nashville, Tenn., 1883.

**3298** **The river counties (of middle Tennessee).** v.1- , 1972- . Columbia, Tenn.: Garrett-McLain.
Periodical containing genealogical and historical material regarding 8 middle Tennessee counties along the Duck river.

**3299** **Rodgers, Ellen D.** The romance of the Episcopal Church in west Tennessee, 1832-1964. Brunswick, Tenn., 1964.
Sketches of early churches and towns, names of settlers and their families from Revolutionary War records, tombstones, etc.

**3300** **Sistler, Byron, and Associates.** U.S. census of Tennessee 1830. 3v. East, middle and west Tennessee. Evanston, Ill.: The Author, 1969-71.
v.1, 2nd printing 1973.
87,000 names of heads of families, with full data.

**3301** —— —— 1850. v.1- (in progress). Evanston, Ill.: The Author, 1974- .
v.1, Aaron through Childress; v.2, Childs through Gary, all published to the end of 1974. The 1850 census was originally published in a series of booklets.

**3301a** **Smith, Sam B.** Tennessee history: a bibliography. Knoxville, Tenn.: Univ. of Tennessee Pr., 1974.
A most comprehensive work: books, articles, theses, etc. with much local history.

**3302** **Speer, William S.** Sketches of prominent Tennesseans; containing biographies and records of many of the families who have attained prominence in Tennessee. Nashville, Tenn., 1888.
Gives fairly long sketches with much family information. Better than Temple's *Notable men of Tennessee* . . . 1912, no. 3303.

**3303** **Temple, Oliver P.** Notable men of Tennessee from 1833 to 1875 . . . New York, 1912.
Mug book.

**3304** **The Tennessee "Bee-hive," or Early 1778–91 North Carolina land grants in the volunteer state,** being an index with some 3,100 names of Revolutionary soldiers and settlers who participated in the distribution of more than five million acres of land . . . With 1837 map. Washington, D.C., 1849.

**3305** **Tennessee Civil War Centennial Commission.** Tennesseans in the Civil War; a military history of Confederate and Union units with available rosters of personnel. 2v. Nashville, Tenn.: Univ. of Tennessee Pr., 1964–65.

**3306** **The Tennessee historical quarterly.** v.1– , 1942– . Nashville, Tenn.: Tennessee Historical Commission and Historical Soc.
Fine journal containing much genealogy until 1960. From v.1 to 19 (1942–60) it had a series, "Notes and documents" with some genealogical interest.

**3307** **Tennessee Historical Society.** Guide to the processed manuscripts. Nashville, Tenn.: Tennessee Historical Commission, 1969.

**3308** **Tennessee marriage records.** v.1–3, 1958–68. Knoxville, Tenn.: Ed. by Pollyanna Creekmore.
Excellent compilation.

**3309** **Tennessee State Library and Archives.** Biographical directory: Tennessee General Assembly, 1796–1973. v.1–41. Nashville, Tenn.: State Library, 1968–73.
Publication ceased in 1973. Unpublished preliminary sketches available at the Library.

**3310** ———— Index to Tennessee Confederate pension applications. Nashville, Tenn.: State Library, 1964.

**3311** ———— Inventories of Tennessee county records on microfilm. Nashville, Tenn.: State Library, 1963– (in progress).
Microfilmed records in the Archives; inventories are published as the county records are made available on film.

**3312** ———— Tennessee diaries, memoirs and church records in the manuscript division. Nashville, Tenn.: State Library, 1965.
Listed by county.

**3313** ———— Writings on Tennessee counties available on interlibrary loan from the Tennessee State Library and Archives. Nashville, Tenn.: The Library, 1971.

**3314** **U.S. Census Office.** Tennessee census reports. no.1–27. Washington, D.C., 1933.
"Done for Martha L. Houston by National Genealogical Society." Transcriptions of 1810 Rutherford county census and all 1820 Tennessee censuses extant.

**3315** **Watauga Association of Genealogists.** Bulletin. v.1– , 1972– . Johnson City, Tenn.: The Assoc.
Excellent for source records of East Tennessee.

**3316** **West Tennessee Historical Society.** Papers. 1– , 1947– . Memphis, Tenn.: The Society.

**3317** **Whitley, Edythe J. (Mrs. E. J. R.)** Tennessee genealogical records. v.1–9, 1932–36. Nashville, Tenn.

**3318** **Williams, Samuel C.** Beginnings of West Tennessee. In the land of the Chickasaws 1541–1841. 1930. Repr. Nashville, Tenn.: Blue and Gray Pr., 1971.

Detailed history with some material on Revolutionary War soldiers and noted citizens.

**3319 Wright, Marcus J.** Tennessee in the war, 1861-65. Lists of military organizations and officers from Tennessee in both the Union and Confederate armies . . . New York, 1908.

## TEXAS

Settled ca. 1691: entered Union 1845
*Dallas Public Library*
*Fort Worth Public Library*

**3320 Austin Genealogical Society quarterly.** v.1- , 1960- . Austin, Tex.: The Society.
Highly professional journal.

**3321 Barton, Henry W.** Texas volunteers in the Mexican War. Wichita Falls, Tex.: Privately pub., 1970. Available from Texian Pr., Waco, Tex.
Historical account of participation of Texan officers. Does not include rosters, but has name index.

**3322 Benjamin, Gilbert G.** The Germans in Texas: a study in immigration. *German American annals,* v.7. 1910. Repr. San Francisco: R. and E. Research Assoc., 1970; Austin, Tex.: Jenkins Pub. Co., 1974.

**3323 Biesele, Rudolph L.** The history of the German settlements in Texas, 1831-61. Austin, Tex., ca.1930.
Contains index, several maps, and bibliography. Well footnoted.

**3324 Biggers, Don H.** German pioneers in Texas: a brief history of their hardships, struggles and achievements . . . Fredericksburg, Tex., 1925.
Marginal genealogical reference work.

**3325 Biggerstaff, Inez (Boswell).** Four thousand tombstone inscriptions from Texas, 1745-1870. Oklahoma City, Okla., 1952.
Under auspices of the Oklahoma Historical Society. Tombs, inscriptions along old San Antonio Road, and the trail of Austin's colonists. Material arranged in cemetery order, well indexed.

**3326 Biographical souvenir of the state of Texas;** containing biographical sketches of the representative public, and many early settled families. Chicago, 1889.
Approximately 1,500 names.

**3327 Bowden, Jocelyn J.** Spanish and Mexican land grants in the Chihuahuan acquisition. El Paso, Tex.: Texas Western Pr., Univ. of Texas at El Paso, 1971.

**3328 Brown, John H.** Indian wars and pioneers of Texas. 2v. Austin, Tex., [1896].
More pioneers than Indians; the book contains biographical sketches and portraits of prominent men from throughout the state.

**3329 Burlage, John,** and **Hollingsworth, J. B.** Abstract of valid land claims of Texas, compiled from the records of the Land Office and Court of Claims of the state of Texas. Austin, Tex., 1859.
Arranged alphabetically in different classifications of land grants.

**3330 Burnett, Arthur C.** Yankees in the republic of Texas . . . Houston, Tex., 1952.
Pub. for the Harris County Historical Society.

**3331 Carpenter, Vera C. (Mrs. V. K.).** The state of Texas federal population schedules, 7th census of the U.S., 1850. v.1-4 and v.5 (index to v.1-4). Huntsville, Ala.: Century Enterprises, 1969.
Gives name, age, gender and place of birth of all persons. Valuable tool; indicates in which counties various families were living in 1850.

**3332 Carroll, Horace B.** Texas county histories. A bibliography. Austin, Tex., 1943.

**3333 Chabot, Frederick C.** With the makers of San Antonio: genealogies of the early Latin, Anglo-American, and

German families, with occasional biographies . . . San Antonio, Tex., 1937.
Half-title: *Genealogies of early San Antonio families.*

**3334 Connor, Seymour V.** The Peters colony in Texas: a history and biographical sketch of the early settlers. 1959. Repr. Fort Worth, Tex.: Arrow/Curtis Printing Co., 1974.
Traces history of colonization of northeast Texas. Short biographies of members of the colony, with vital statistics and land-grant numbers. First and largest empresario grant made by the republic of Texas.

**3335 Crocket, George L.** Two centuries in east Texas: a history of San Augustine county and surrounding territory from 1865 to the present time. 1932. Repr. [San Augustine, Tex.?], 1962.

**3336 Daniell, Lewis E.** Personnel of the Texas state government, with sketches of representative men of Texas. San Antonio, Tex., 1892.
Similar work was published in 1887 and 1889. Mug book.

**3337** —— Texas—the country and its men, historical, biographical, descriptive. Austin, Tex., 1924?
Mug book.

**3338** —— Types of successful men of Texas. Austin, Tex., 1890.

**3339 Daughters of the Republic of Texas. Lineage Book Committee.** Founders and patriots of the republic of Texas: the lineages of the members. Compiled and ed. by L. E. B. Morris. San Antonio, Tex.: The Alamo, The Daughters, 1963.

**3340** —— —— v.2, ed. by Mrs. Murray Ezzell. Austin, Tex.: D.A.R., 1974.
Separate indexes for members and ancestors.

**3341** —— The Texas history collection of the Daughters of the Republic of Texas library. 2v. San Antonio, Tex.: The Library, 1973.

Listing books, manuscripts, maps, documents, newspapers, photographs, special collections and memorabilia spanning 4 centuries.

**3342 Davis, Ellis A.,** and **Grobe, E. H.** The new cyclopedia of Texas. 4v. Dallas, Tex., 1929.
Men of Texas, v.3, p.262– through v.4.

**3343 Day, James M.** Texas almanacs, 1857–73: a compendium of Texas history. Selections from the first 16 eds. of the Texas almanac. Waco, Tex.: Texian Pr., 1967.
63p. index includes hundreds of names from early Texas history.

**3344 Day, James M.,** and **Dunlap, A. B.** Maps of Texas, 1527–1900. Austin, Tex.: Pemberton Pr., 1962.
Map collection of the Texas State archives. Repr. from *Southwestern historical quarterly,* v.65–66, 1962.

**3345 Dixon, Samuel H.,** and **Kemp, L. W.** The heroes of San Jacinto. Houston, Tex., 1932.
Biographies from records of military, Land Office, and state archives. Essential for proof of presence at battle of San Jacinto. Well indexed.

**3346 Dworaczyk, Edward J.** The first Polish colonies of Americans in Texas . . . 1936. Repr. San Francisco: R. and E. Research Assoc., 1969.
Excellent genealogical document. Emphasis on Polish Catholic settlements.

**3347 Ericson, Carolyn R.** Nacogdoches —gateway to Texas. A biographical directory 1773–1849. Fort Worth, Tex.: Arrow/Curtis Printing Co., 1974.
Nacogdoches district was port of entry for many of the early years of Texas. Census records for 1792–1809, 1828–35, and 1847; tax lists 1837, 1839, 1840, 1845, with many other records. Hundreds of biographies.

**3348 Footprints.** Quarterly publication of the Fort Worth Genealogical Soc. v.11– , 1968– . Fort Worth, Tex.: The Society.

Formerly *Genealogical Society bulletin,* v.1-10, 1958-67. Source records pertaining to old northwest Texas.

**3349 Foster, Pearl (O'Donnell).** Trek to Texas, 1770-1870. Fort Worth, Tex.: The Author, 1966.

Coats of arms. History of Texas pioneers. Tarrant, Denton, Cass, and other counties; tax lists, warrants, census records.

**3350 Gannett, Henry.** A gazetteer of Texas. 2nd ed. *U.S. Geological Survey bull.* 224. Washington, D.C., 1904.

**3351 Geue, Chester W.,** and **Geue, E. H.** A new land beckoned: German immigrants to Texas, 1844-47; eleven reports made by Prince Karl of Solms-Braumfels to the director of the Verein in Germany... New ed., enl. Fort Worth, Tex.: The Authors, 1972.

Contains alphabetical list of 7,000 immigrants. A must for students of Texas genealogy. Indexed, with bibliography and the story of the mass immigration of Germans to Texas, giving European residence, on which ship sailed, and (usually) birth and death dates.

**3352 Geue, Ethel H.** New homes in a new land: German immigration to Texas, 1847-61. Waco, Tex.: Texian Pr., 1970.

5,600 names of German immigrants, with complete details. Supplements *A new land beckoned* (no.3351). Based on 105 passenger lists.

**3353 Gracy, Alice D.; Sumner, J.;** and **Gentry, E. G. S.** Early Texas birth records, 1838-78. 2v. Austin, Tex.: Gentry, 1970-72.

v.1 out-of-print 1973; record of births compiled by visits to all 148 counties.

**3354 Grammar, Norma R.** Marriage records of early Texas, 1824-46. Fort Worth, Tex.: Fort Worth Genealogical Soc., 1971.

Surname index. Contains all extant records of Anglo-American marriages celebrated in Texas prior to annexation by the U.S.

**3355 Haiman, Miecislaus.** The Poles in the early history of Texas. *Annals of the Polish Roman Catholic Union, Archives Museum* 1. Chicago, 1936.

**3356 Hardy, Dermot H.,** and **Roberts, I. S.** Historical review of southeast Texas... 2v. Chicago, 1910.

Biographical sketches of pioneers, settlers, founders, leaders, etc. Well-indexed narrative of local history with sketches of towns and counties. Personal data.

**3357 Heart of Texas records.** v.1- , 1958- . Waco, Tex.: Central Texas Genealogical Soc.

Excellent source of transcribed records of central Texas counties. Originally *The Central Genealogical Society's quarterly;* became *Heart of Texas records* in 1972. Contains Bible, court and family records for 25 central Texas counties.

**3358 Hecht, Arthur.** Postal history in the Texas panhandle. Canyon, Tex.: Panhandle-Plains Historical Soc., 1960.

List of the 532 post offices in the 44 counties, with locations, dates of founding and discontinuance, and names of postmasters, 1878-1959.

**3359 Historical Records Survey.** Guide to public vital statistics records in Texas. Austin, Tex., 1941.

Although many of the records have moved from the location given in the *Guide,* this is essential in determining the holdings in cities and counties.

**3360** ———— Inventory of the county archives of Texas. 24v. San Antonio, Tex., 1937-41.

Only the following numbers were published: 10 (Bandera), 11 (Bastrop), 25 (Brown), 28 (Caldwell), 29 (Calhoun), 61 (Denton), 62 (DeWitt), 75 (Fayette), 86 (Gillespie), 92 (Gregg), 94 (Guadalupe), 105 (Hays), 111 (Hood), 120 (Jackson), 158 (Marion), 166 (Milam), 167 (Mills), 181 (Orange), 198 (Robertson), 199 (Rockwall), 202 (Sabine), 213 (Somervell), 232 (Uvalde), and 247 (Wilson). Unpublished material deposited in University of Texas, Austin, Tex.

## 3361 United States

**3361** ——— Texas newspapers, 1813–1939. A union list of newspaper files available in offices of publishers, libraries, and a number of private collections. v.1. San Antonio, Tex., 1941.

**3362** History of Texas, together with a biographical history of Milam, Williamson, Bastrop, Travis, Lee, and Burleson counties ... with portraits and biographies of prominent citizens. Chicago, 1893.

Good mug book, with first-hand biographical information. Binder's title: *Lone star state*.

**3363** History of Texas, together with a biographical history of Tarrant and Parker counties ... with portraits and biographies of prominent citizens ... Chicago, 1895.

Good biographical information. Binder's title: *Lone star state*.

**3364** History of Texas, together with a biographical history of the cities of Houston and Galveston ... Chicago, 1895.

Good biographies. Binder's title: *Lone star state*.

**3365** History of Texas; supplemented with biographical mention of many prominent persons and families of the state ... with biographical sketches of many of the leading families of central Texas. Chicago, 1896.

Binder's title: *Lone star state*.

**3366** Houston Genealogical Forum. Collection of Bible records. Houston, 1963.

**3366a** Hudson, Estelle, and Maresh, H. R. Czech pioneers of the southwest. Dallas, Tex., 1934.

Bohemians in Texas.

**3367** Hunter, John. The trail drivers of Texas. 2v. 1920–23. Repr. (New ed.) New York: Argosy-Antiquarian, 1963.

Narratives are autobiographical and include considerable genealogical data.

**3368** Jenkins, John H. Cracker barrel chronicles: a bibliography of Texas town and county histories. Austin, Tex.: Pemberton Pr., 1965.

Lists 5,000 books; useful guide to local history. Arranged alphabetically by county, with town-county cross index, index of titles, and index of authors. Includes table of county and town populations, 1850–60.

**3369** Johnson, Frank W. A history of Texas and Texans ... 5v. Chicago, 1914. v.3–5 biographical.

**3370** Kemp, Louis W. The signers of the Texas Declaration of Independence. 1944. Repr. Salada, Tex., 1959.

Excellent biographical sketches of the signers, including descendants. Complements Dixon (*see* no.3345). 2,500 names; well footnoted.

**3371** Kielman, Chester V. The University of Texas archives; a guide to the historical manuscripts collections in the University of Texas Library. Austin, Tex.: Univ. of Texas Pr., 1967.

Includes many groups of family papers, as well as many official records of the early governments of the state which were acquired by private collectors and donated to University.

**3372** Knights of Columbus of Texas. Texas State Council. Historical Commission. Our Catholic heritage in Texas, 1519–1936. Austin, Tex., 1936–58.

Compiled by Carlos E. Casteneda. Well-indexed volumes, with essential facts of the Catholic community. Biographical information good.

**3372a** Local History and Genealogical Society. The quarterly. v.1– , 1955– . Dallas: Mrs. H. J. Morris.

**3373** The lone star state. Binder's title for vols. of *The history of Texas*, *see* no.3362–65, 3375–77.

**3374** McLean, Malcolm D. Papers concerning Robertson's Colony in Texas, v.1: 1788–1822: The Texas Association. Fort Worth, Tex.: Texas Christian Univ. Pr., 1974.

Sterling C. Robertson was one of the original stockholders of 1822 Texas settlers. The area discussed occupied most of the territory between Forth Worth and Austin, from which 39 counties were formed. Over 3,000 names. v.1 of projected 7v. set.

**3375  A memorial and biographical history of Johnson and Hill counties.** Chicago, 1892.
Binder's title: *The lone star state.*

**3376  A memorial and biographical history of McLennan, Falls, Bell, and Coryell counties, Texas.** Chicago, 1893.
Binder's title: *Lone star state.*

**3377  Memorial and biographical history of Navarro, Henderson, Anderson, Limestone, Freestone, and Leon counties.** Chicago, 1893.
Binder's title: *Lone star state.*

**3378**  ———  Repr. of biographies by Stephanie Tally-Frost. Corpus Christi, Tex., The Author, 1966.

**3379  Miller, Thomas L.** Bounty and donation land grants of Texas, 1835–88. Austin, Tex.: Univ. of Texas Pr., 1967.
List of men who were granted bounty warrants and donation certificates, from Texas revolution through the Civil War. 7,469 bounty warrants to 1814 veterans.

**3380  Mills, Madeline S.** Relocated cemeteries in Oklahoma and parts of Kansas and Texas. Tulsa, Okla.: The Author, 1974.
Covers cemeteries for all of Oklahoma, and a few counties of northern Texas. 250 cemeteries, 7,000 graves.

**3381  Mullins, Marion D.** The first census of Texas, 1829–36. To which are added Texas citizenship lists, 1821–45, and other early records of the republic of Texas. *National Genealogical Soc. special publ.,* v.22. 2nd pr. Washington, D.C.: The Society, 1962.
Also included are list of certificates of entrance into Texas in 1835 and a muster roll of 1835.

**3382**  ——— Republic of Texas poll lists for 1846. Baltimore: G.P.C., 1974.
18,000 Texas taxpayers. A "poll" tax of one dollar was levied on every white male resident over 21, and on women who were heads of household. This is virtually a census.

**3383  North Texas pioneer.** v.1– , 1966– . Wichita Falls, Tex.: North Texas Genealogical and Historical Assoc.
Excellent concentration of records of north Texas. Quarterly.

**3384  Our heritage.** v.1– , 1959– . San Antonio, Tex.: San Antonio Genealogical and Historical Soc.
Has general Texas material. Quarterly.

**3385  Paddock, Buckley B.** A history of central and western Texas, 2v. 1911. Repr. Ann Arbor, Mich.: Xerox Microfilms, 1967.

**3386**  ——— History of Texas. 4v. Chicago, 1922.
v.2–4 biographical.

**3387**  ——— A twentieth century history and biographical record of north and west Texas. 2v. 1906. Repr. Ann Arbor, Mich.: Xerox Microfilms, 1967.

**3388  Przygoda, Jacek.** Texas pioneers from Poland; a study in the ethnic history . . . Los Angeles, 1971.
Many lists of Polish prisoners; good bibliography and index.

**3388a  Purl, Benjamin F.** Republic of Texas: second class certificates, March 2, 1836–October 1, 1837. Houston: Nettie W. Barnes (Box 6622, 77005), 1974.
Compiled in 1904, transcribed by N. W. Barnes. 5,000 headrights.

**3389  Raines, Cadwell W.** A bibliography of Texas; being a descriptive list of books, pamphlets, and documents relating to Texas in print and manuscript since 1536 . . . 1896. Repr. 1934. Houston, Tex., 1955.

**3390  Ray, Worth S.** Austin colony pioneers, including history of Bastrop, Fayette, Grimes, Montgomery, and Washington counties, Texas, and their earliest settlers. 1949. Repr. Austin, Tex.: Pemberton Pr., 1970. (Also available from joint distributors, G.P.C., Baltimore).
Much information on those who came with Stephen Austin. Tax lists, vital records, etc.

**3391** **Records of East Texas.** v.1– , 1966– . Lufkin, Tex.: John M. Wilkins (1005 Rees, 75901).

**3392** **Richardson, Thomas C.** East Texas, its history and its makers. 4v. New York, 1940.
v.4 biographical.

**3393** **The roadrunner.** v.1– , 1974– . Tomball, Tex.: Chaparral Genealogical Society.
Concerns many counties in Texas; good indexes.

**3394** **Roberts, W. H.** A complete roster of the regular and volunteer troops in the war between the United States and Mexico from 1846 to 1848. Washington, D.C., 1886.
The burning of the Texas Adjutant General's office in 1855 has made the roster more valuable with regard to Texas.

**3395** **Scott, Florence J.** Historical heritage of the lower Rio Grande. A historical record of Spanish exploration, subjugation and colonization of the lower Río Grande valley and the activities of José Escandón, Count of Sierra Gorda together with the development of towns and ranches under Spanish, Mexican and Texas sovereignties 1747–1848. 3rd ed. Rio Grande City, Tex.: La Retama Pr., 1972.
Data on first families.

**3396** ———— Royal land grants north of the Rio Grande, 1777–1821. Waco, Tex., 1969.
Early history of large grants made by Spain to families in jurisdiction of Reynosa which became a part of Texas after the Treaty of Guadalupe Hidalgo.

**3397** **Severin, Ernest.** [Swedes in Texas, 1838–1918] Svenskarne i Texas i ord ochbild 1838–1918 . . . 2v. Austin, Tex., ca.1919.

**3398** **Simpson, Arthur J.** Southwest Texas. San Antonio, Tex., 1952.
Rev. ed. of 1937 issue under title *The centennial of southwest Texas.*

**3399** **Smith, Bennett L.** Marriage by bond in colonial Texas. Fort Worth, Tex.: The Author, 1972.
Discusses process of marriage by bond, incidentally giving a great deal of information about early Texas families. Includes a list of all extant colonial marriage bonds.

**3400** **Society of Mayflower Descendants. Texas.** Lineage books. 2v. San Antonio, Tex., 1967–71. Available from E. K. Zuber, 4501 Druid Lane, Dallas, Tex. 75205.
v.1 by Frankie L. Hauser; v.2 by Edith K. Zuber.

**3401** **South Texas Genealogical and Historical Society quarterly.** v.1– , 1966– . Gonzales, Tex.: The Society.

**3402** **Sowell, Andrew J.** Early settlers and Indian fighters of southwest Texas . . . 2v. 1900. Repr. New York: Argosy-Antiquarian, 1964.

**3403** **Speer, William S.,** and **Brown, J. H.** The encyclopedia of the new West containing full authenticated information of . . . industries . . . also biographical sketches . . . Marshall, Tex., 1881.
Well-indexed narrative of regional history with accompanying biographies.

**3404** **Statewide Records Project, Div. of Professional and Service Projects, W.P.A.** Index to probate cases of Texas. 30v. 1939–42. Repr. Fort Worth, Tex.: Miran, 1972– (in progress).
Good references to unpublished valuable source information in the probate files in various counties, mostly late 1800s–1930s.

**3405** **Stirpes.** Texas State Genealogical Society. v.1– , 1961– . Fort Worth, Tex.: The Society.
Good compilation of records. Representative of the many excellent regional Texas genealogical periodicals.

**3406** **Tally-Frost, Stephanie.** Memorial and biographical histories of Texas. Biographies. *See* no.3377–78.

**3407** **Tarpley, Fred.** Place names of northeast Texas. Commerce, Tex.: East Texas State Univ., 1969.

Arranged alphabetically by the 26 counties in the area, and thereunder by geographical item. Good index.

**3408** **Taylor, Virginia H.** The Spanish archives of the General Land Office of Texas. Austin, Tex., 1955.

**3409** **Texas. General Land Office.** Abstract of all original grants and locations comprising Texas land titles to August 31, 1945. Austin, Tex., 1945.

Constitutes first supplement to the 8 condensed volumes of abstract of land titles now in use, embracing the surveys returned and the action had by this office on those heretofore reported, from Sept. 1, 1941, for v.1–4 and from Sept. 1, 1942 for v.5–8 up to and including Aug. 31, 1945.

**3410** ———— To August 31, 1947. Austin, Tex., 1947.

**3411** ———— Abstract of land claims compiled from the records of the G.L.O. of the State of Texas . . . Galveston, Tex., 1852.

**3412** ———— Austin, Tex., 1860, 1862, 1871. 3v.

**3413** ———— Galveston, Tex., 1878. 2v. and suppl.

There are numerous editions of the land claims; each is arranged by district where claim was made. Galveston editions were compiled by Shaw and Blaylock, and are often referred to by these names.

**3414** ———— An abstract of the original titles of record in the G.L.O. of Texas. 1838. Repr. Austin, Tex.: Pemberton Pr., 1964.

Contains listing, by colony, of every settler granted land in Texas between 1791 and 1836; settlers are given alphabetically. Fundamental source of information on the settlement of Texas.

**3415** ———— Soldiers of the republic of Texas: muster roll of the G.L.O. 3v. Austin, Tex.: G.L.O., 1957.

Photostats copied from manuscript on file at the G.L.O. Gives date of enrollment, name of soldier, period of enlistment, and remarks.

**3416** **Thrall, Homer S.** Pictorial history of Texas. 1879. Repr. Evansville, Ind.: Unigraphic, 1972.

Colonization, biographical sketches of leading historical characters, counties, topical notes, etc.

**3417** **Tiling, Moritz P.** History of the German element in Texas from 1820 to 1850. Houston, Tex., 1913.

**3418** **A twentieth century history of southwest Texas.** 2v. 1907. Repr. Ann Arbor, Mich.: Xerox Microfilms, 1967.

**3419** **Veach, Damon.** Your Texas ancestors. 3v. Fort Worth, Tex.: The author (Box 1870), 1969-73.

Freelance writer's column in *Fort Worth Star telegram.* Mainly queries.

**3420** **Webb, Walter P.** The handbook of Texas. 2v. Austin, Tex.: Texas State Historical Assoc., 1952.

Much information on families and descendants before they came to Texas. Use with care. v.3 in progress.

**3421** **Wheat, James L.** Postmasters and post offices of Texas, 1846-1930. Garland, Tex.: The Author, 1973.

Almost 2,000 pages, over 30,000 postmasters and their post offices, and dates acquired.

**3422** **White, Gifford E.** The 1840 census of the republic of Texas. Austin, Tex.: Pemberton Pr., 1966.

Compilation of tax rolls gathered in 1840. Gives specific names, acreage, facts of township. 10,500 names; 6 counties are missing and some are incomplete. Most detailed and complete census of the Republic of Texas.

**3423** **Woods, Frances.** 1850 [7th census] mortality schedules of Texas. Austin, Tex., 1965.

**3424** ———— 1860 [8th census] mortality schedules of Texas. Austin, Tex., 1966.

**3425** **Yellowed pages.** v.1– , 1971– . Beaumont, Tex.: Southeast Texas Genealogical and Historical Soc.

3426 **Yoakum, Henderson K.** History of Texas, from its first settlement in 1685 to its annexation to the U.S. in 1846. 2v. 1856. Repr. Austin, Tex., 1935.
Indexed and footnoted.

3427 **Young, Louise M.** Peters colonists, their descendants and others who settled in north Texas. 2v. Denton, Tex.: The Author, 1972-73.
Collection of public records, cemetery records, and family records from the north Texas counties which were part of the old Peters Colony.

## UTAH

Settled ca. 1847; entered Union 1896

*Genealogical Society of the Church of Jesus Christ of Latter-day Saints, Inc., Salt Lake City*
*Utah State Historical Society, Salt Lake City*
*Mr. Jimmy B. Parker, Bountiful*

3428 **Alter, J. Cecil,** Utah, the storied domain: a documentary history of Utah's eventful career . . . 3v. Chicago, 1932.
v.2-3 biographical.

3429 **Biographical record of Salt Lake City and vicinity,** containing biographies of well-known citizens of the past and present. Chicago, 1902.

3430 **Burns, Annie W.** First families of Utah, as taken from the 1850 census of Utah. Washington, D.C., 1949.

3431 **Daughters of Utah Pioneers.** Heart throbs of the West . . . Compiled by Kate B. Carter. 12v. Salt Lake City, 1939-51.
Biographical and historical. Official publication of the Daughters.

3432 ———— Our pioneer heritage. v.1-15. Salt Lake City: The Daughters, 1958-72.

3433 ———— Treasures of pioneer history. 6v. Salt Lake City, 1952-57.

3434 **Esshom, Frank.** Pioneers and prominent men of Utah; comprising photographs, genealogies, biographies . . . 1913. Repr. Salt Lake City: Western Epics, 1966.
Covers 1847-68 arrivals. 6,000 photographs and large biographical section.

3435 **Fries, Louis J.** One hundred and fifty years of Catholicity in Utah. Salt Lake City, 1926.

3436 **Gannett, Henry.** Gazetteer of Utah. *U.S. Geological Survey bull.* 166. Washington, D.C., 1900.

3437 **Gates, Susan (Young).** Surname book and racial history. A compilation and arrangement of genealogical and historical data . . . Salt Lake City, 1918.

3438 **Historical Records Survey.** Guide to public vital statistics records in Utah. Salt Lake City, 1941.

3439 ———— Inventory of county archives of Utah. 12v. Salt Lake City, 1938-41.
Only the following numbers were published: 1 (Box Elder), 4 (Carbon), 5 (Daggett), 8 (Emery), 10 (Grand), 15 (Morgan), 20 (Sanpete), 23 (Tooele), 24 (Uintah), 25 (Utah), 26 (Wasatch) and 29 (Weber). Unpublished material deposited in State Historical Soc., Salt Lake City, Utah.

3440 ———— Inventory of the church archives of Utah. 3v. Salt Lake City, 1940-41.
v.2 concerns Baptist church.

3441 ———— Origins of Utah place names. Salt Lake City, 1940.

3442 **Jaussi, Laureen R.,** and **Chaston, G. D.** Genealogical records of Utah. Salt Lake City; Deseret Book Co., 1974.
Rev. and enlarged ed. of chapters 13-19 of 1st ed. of their *Fundamentals of genealogical research.* Explanation of genealogical records of Utah and how to use them.

3443 **Jenson, Andrew.** Latter-day Saint biographical encyclopedia. 4v.

1901-36. Repr. Salt Lake City: Western Epics, 1971.

**3444** **Leigh, Rufus W.** Five hundred Utah place names, their origin and significance. Salt Lake City, 1961.

**3445** **Portrait, genealogical and biographical record of the state of Utah . . .** Chicago, 1902.
Mug book.

**3446** **Sloan, Edward L.** Gazetteer of Utah, and Salt Lake City directory. Salt Lake City, 1884.
Also eds. of 1869 and 1874.

**3447** **Sutton, Wain.** Utah: a centennial history. 3v. New York, 1949.
v.3 biographical.

**3448** **Utah. State Archives.** Veterans with federal service buried in the state of Utah: territorial period to 1865. v.1– . Salt Lake City: The Archives, 1965– (in progress).
Counties thus far completed are Garfield, Wayne, Duchesne and Uintah.

**3449** **Utah genealogical and historical magazine.** v.1-31. 1910-40. Salt Lake City.
Issued by Genealogical Society of Utah; Mormon oriented.

**3450** **Warrum, Noble.** Utah since statehood; historical and biographical. 4v. Chicago, 1919.
v.2-4 biographical.

**3451** **Watters, Leon L.** The pioneer Jews of Utah. *Studies in American Jewish history,* v.2. New York, 1952.

**3452** **Whitney, Orson F.** History of Utah . . . 4v. Salt Lake City, 1892–1904.
v.4 biographical.

**3453** **Zabriskie, George O.,** and **Robinson, D. L.** U.S. census of Utah, 1851. In *The Utah genealogical and historical magazine,* v.28-29, 1937-38.
Not completed.

## VERMONT

Settled ca. 1724; entered Union 1791
*Vermont Historical Society, Montpelier*
*Vermont State Library, Montpelier*

**3454** **Barden, Merritt C.** Vermont: once no man's land. Rutland, Vt., 1928.
Genealogical summary of families who lived along the New York border in Vermont, and their connection with those who lived over the line in New York. Not indexed, and hard to use. Has coats of arms.

**3455** **Benedict, George G.** Vermont in the Civil War, a history of the part taken by Vermont soldiers and sailors in the War of the Union, 1861-65. 2v. Burlington, Vt., 1886-88.

**3456** **Bogart, Walter T.** The Vermont lease lands. Montpelier, Vt.: Vermont Historical Soc., 1950.

**3457** **Branches and twigs.** Newsletter of the Genealogical Soc. of Vermont. v.1– , 1972– . Westminster West, Vt.: The Society.
Contains cemetery records, some family records, many queries.

**3458** **Carleton, Hiram.** Genealogical and family history of the state of Vermont: a record of the achievements of her people . . . 2v. New York, 1903.
Valuable, but limited.

**3459** **Carlisle, Lilian B.** Vermont clock and watchmakers, silversmiths, and jewelers, 1778-1878. Burlington, Vt.: distributed by Stinehour Pr., Lunenberg, Vt., 1970.
Excellent for biographical details.

**3460** **Carpenter, William H.,** and **Arthur, T. S.** The history of Vermont; from its earliest settlement to the present time. Philadelphia, 1856.
Some biographies.

**3461** **Chase, Francis.** Gathered sketches from the early history of New Hampshire and Vermont . . . 1867. Repr. Somersmith, N.H.: New Hampshire Pub. Co., 1970.

**3462** **Clark, Byron N.** A list of pensioners of the War of 1812 [Vermont]. Repr. Baltimore: G.P.C., 1969.
From records of William T. Shaw; contains names primarily from 8 towns in Chittenden county. Used for locations as well as for pensioners; no index.

**3463** **Crockett, Walter H.** Soldiers of the Revolutionary War buried in Vermont . . . Excerpted from *Proc. of Vermont Historical Soc.,* 1903-1904 and 1905-1906. Repr. Baltimore: G.P.C., 1973.
Names of 6,000 Revolutionary soldiers. Gives only name of soldier.

**3464** —— Vermonters; a book of biographies. 2nd ed. Brattleboro, Vt., 1932.
Contains biographies not found elsewhere.

**3465** **Deming, Leonard.** A list of the principal civil officers of Vermont from 1777 to 1918. Being a revision and enlargement of *Deming's Vermont officers . . . 1778-1851, with some biographical notices.* 1851. Ed. by John M. Comstock. St. Albans, Vt., 1918.
Good for locating persons, also for those who held the different offices.

**3466** **Dodge, Prentiss C.** Encyclopedia, Vermont biography; a series of authentic biographical sketches of the representative men of Vermont and sons of Vermont in other states. Burlington, Vt., 1912.

**3467** **Gazetteer of Vermont heritage.** A concise account of the discovery, settlement, and progress of eve.nts in Vermont, including biographical sketches of early notables and historical notes on each town and city in the state. Bicentennial ed. Montpelier, Vt.: Vermont Historical Soc., 1970.

**3468** **Gilman, Marcus D.** The bibliography of Vermont, or, A list of books and pamphlets relating in any way to the state. With biographical notes. Burlington, Vt., 1897.
Over 7,000 titles.

**3469** **Goodrich, John E.** Rolls of the soldiers in the Revolutionary War, 1775-83. Rutland, Vt., 1904.

Would be more useful if place of soldier was given.

**3470** **Hall, Hiland.** The history of Vermont, from its discovery to its admission into the Union in 1791. Albany, Vt., 1868.

**3471** **Hayward, John.** A gazetteer of Vermont: all the counties, towns and districts in the state. Boston, 1849.

**3472** **Historical Records Survey.** Directory of churches and religious organizations in the State of Vermont. Montpelier, Vt., 1939.

**3473** —— Index to the *Burlington free press* in the Billings Library, University of Vermont. 10v. 1848-70. Montpelier, Vt., 1940-42.
Good index.

**3474** —— Inventory of church archives of Vermont. no.1. Protestant Episcopal, Diocese of Vermont. Montpelier, Vt., 1940.
Does not cover whole state.

**3475** —— Inventory of county archives of Vermont. lv. Montpelier, Vt., 1936. Only lv. was published: no.7 (Lamoille). Unpublished material deposited in State Historical Soc., Montpelier, Vt.

**3476** **Kent, Dorman B. E.** Vermonters. Montpelier, Vt., 1937.
Enl. ed. of his "One thousand men, 1914." Published in *Proc. of Vermont Historical Soc.,* 1913-14. Lists Vermonters, their profession, date and location, 1768-1879.

**3477** **Lamb, Wallace E.** The Lake Champlain and Lake George Valleys. 3v. New York, 1940.
v.3 biographical.

**3478** **Men of progress:** the biographical sketches and portraits of leaders in business and professional life in and of the state of Vermont. Compiled under the supervision of R. Herndon; ed. by George G. Benedict. Boston, 1898.

**3479** **New Hampshire Colony. Government and Council.** New Hampshire grants, being transcripts of the charters of townships and minor grants of lands made by the provincial government of New Hampshire, within the present boundaries of the state of Vermont, from 1749 to 1764 ... Also historical and bibliographical notes relative to the towns of Vermont by H. A. Huse, *New Hampshire provincial and state papers*, v.26. Concord, N.H., 1895.

**3480** **Pettengill, Samuel B.** The Yankee pioneers: a saga of courage. Rutland, Vt.: Tuttle, 1971.

33 chapters on a mass of forgotten details about pioneer settlement background on the life of Vermont ancestors.

**3481** **Stone, Arthur F.** The Vermont of today . . . 4v. New York, 1929.

v.3-4 biographical. Contains Vermont residents not found elsewhere.

**3482** **Thompson, John.** A gazetteer of Vermont; containing descriptions of all the counties, towns, and districts in the state . . . Boston, 1849.

**3483** ———— Index by William A. Ellis. In *Proc. of the Vermont Historical Soc.*, 1911-12. Montpelier, Vt., 1913.

**3484** **Ullery, Jacob G.** Men of Vermont: an illustrated biographical history of Vermonters and sons of Vermont. Brattleboro, Vt., 1894.

Useful work and good source book, 3pts. in 1.

**3485** **U.S. Bureau of the Census.** Heads of families at the first census of the United States taken in the year 1790. Vermont. 1907. Repr. Baltimore: G.P.C., 1966; Spartanburg, S.C.: Reprint Co., 1963, etc.

**3486** **Vermont. Adjutant and Inspector General's Office.** Roster of soldiers in the War of 1812-1814. St. Albans, Vt., 1933.

Record of service of about 15,000 men. Used for location as well as for soldiers.

**3487** ———— Revised roster of Vermont volunteers and lists of Vermonters who served in the Army and Navy of the United States during the War of the Rebellion, 1861-66. Montpelier, Vt., 1892.

Would be more useful if place of soldiers was given.

**3488** **Vermont. Council.** Records of the governor and Council of the state of Vermont (1775-1836). 8v. 1873-80. Repr. New York: A.M.S. Press, 1971.

Excellent material, and includes brief biographies.

**3489** **Vermont. Secretary of State.** Charters granted by the state of Vermont, being transcripts of early charters of townships and smaller tracts of land granted by the state of Vermont . . . also historical and bibliographic notes relative to Vermont towns by Hiram A. Huse, and brought up-to-date, [to 1895]. *State papers of Vermont*, v.2. Bellows Falls, Vt., 1922.

Very useful especially when names of towns changed.

**3490** ———— General petitions, 1778-99. 4v. *State papers of Vermont*, v.8-11. Montpelier, Vt., 1952-62.

Petitions to legislature dealing with land claims, etc.

**3491** ———— New York land patents, 1688-1786. Ed. by Mary G. Nye. *State papers of Vermont*, v.7. [Montpelier, Vt., 1947].

Covering land now included in the state of Vermont (not including military patents).

**3492** ———— Petitions for grants of land, 1778-1811. Ed. by Mary G. Nye. *State papers of Vermont*, v.5. Montpelier, Vt., 1939.

Lists of persons to whom grants were made in early charters.

**3493** ———— Population: state of Vermont 1970. Montpelier, Vt.: Secretary of State [1972].

Under each county are listed all towns, villages, date of incorporation or charter date. Changes, mergers, names of towns and villages, dates of changes, etc.

**3494** ———— Sequestration, confiscation and sale of estates. Ed. by Mary

G. Nye. *State papers of Vermont,* v.6. Montpelier, Vt., 1941.
Loyalist material, 1777–1812.

**3495** ——— State papers of Vermont. v.1–11. Montpelier, Vt., 1939–62. See no.3489–92, 3494.

**3496 Vermont historical gazetteer.** Ed. by Abby M. Hemenway. 5v. Burlington, Vt. [and elsewhere], 1867–91.

**3497** ——— Index to the contents, prepared under the direction of George W. Wing. Rutland, Vt., 1923.
Magazine of history with biographical and other information. Often referred to as "Hemenway."

**3498 Vermont Historical Society.** Heads of families at the second census of the United States taken in the year 1800. 1938. Repr. Baltimore: G.P.C., 1972.
25,000 heads of families.

**3499 Vermont marriages** [1791–1852]. v.1 (all pub.). 1903. Repr. Baltimore: G.P.C., 1967.
Covers Burlington, Montpelier, and Berlin only. 2,500 entries. Has some limitations.

**3500 Waite, Otis F. R.** Vermont in the great rebellion, containing historical and biographical sketches, etc. Claremont, N.H., 1869.

**3501 Williams, Henry C.** Biographical encyclopaedia of Vermont of the nineteenth century. Boston, 1885.
Mug book, very limited.

## VIRGINIA

Settled ca. 1607; original state
*Alexandria Public Library*
*Virginia State Library, Richmond*
*Mrs. Netti Schreiner-Yantis, Springfield*

**3502 Ashby, Bernice M.** Shenandoah valley, Virginia, marriage bonds, 1772–1850. Berryville, Va.: Virginia Book Co., 1967.
Has 155p. index of names.

**3503 Bell, Landon C.** The old Free State: a contribution to the history of Lunenburg county and southside Virginia. 1927. Repr. 2v. in 1. Baltimore: G.P.C., 1974.
20,000 southside residents traced, marriage bonds and other records, 1745–1850. The area includes many counties; most important book produced on southside Virginia.

**3504** ——— Sunlight on the southside: lists of tithes, Lunenburg county, Virginia, 1748–83. 1931. Repr. Baltimore: G.P.C., 1974.
Area comprises a substantial portion of the territory lying between North Carolina and the James River—embracing 25 present-day counties. Tithes comprise the earliest census records of the colony of Virginia. 10,000 people named.

**3505 Boddie, John B.** Colonial Surry. 1948. Repr. Baltimore: G.P.C., 1974.
Colonial Surry covered almost the entire southern part of Virginia. Land grants, marriage bonds, censuses and many names.

**3506** ——— Seventeenth century Isle of Wight county, Virginia. 1938. Repr. Baltimore: G.P.C., 1973.
Comprehensive study of early history and inhabitants; deeds, rents, grants. Thousands of name entries.

**3507** ——— Southside Virginia families. v.1–2, 1955–56. Repr. Baltimore: G.P.C., 1966.
Lineages of over 100 families.

**3508** ——— Virginia historical genealogies. 1954. Repr. Baltimore: G.P.C., 1965.
Lineages of families with seats in Virginia, Maryland, and North and South Carolina.

**3509 Boogher, William F.** Gleanings of Virginia history. An historical and genealogical collection largely from original sources. 1903. Repr. Baltimore: G.P.C., 1965.
Early Virginia history and genealogy, 1618–1900, with emphasis on pre-Revolu-

tionary period. Ship passenger lists, militia registers.

**3510  Brock, Robert A.** Documents . . . relating to the Huguenot emigration to Virginia . . . *Collections of Virginia Historical Soc.,* new ser.5, 1886. Repr. Baltimore: G.P.C., 1973.
Definitive work on the wave of Huguenot emigration to Virginia covering 1693-1754. Extensive genealogies, details of settlement at Manakin-Town, and Baptists, 1721-54.

**3511** ———— Virginia and Virginians . . . 2v. 1888. Repr. Spartanburg, S.C.: Reprint Co., 1973.
From 1606-1888. Sketches of eminent Virginians; includes a history of Virginia by Virgil A. Lewis.

**3512  Brown, Alexander.** Genesis of the United States . . . 2v. Boston, 1890.
v.2 contains brief biographies of persons connected with the founding of Virginia, 1605-16. 100 portraits.

**3513  Brown, Richard L.,** and **Brown, R. E.** Genealogical notes, principally of South Carolina and Virginia. West Greenville, S.C., 1937.
Rare work.

**3514  Brown, Stuart E., Jr.** Virginia genealogies: a trial list of printed books and pamphlets. Berryville, Va.: Virginia Book Co., 1967.
Important Virginia book. Although it lists many more titles than Stewart (*see* no.3626), it does not supersede Stewart. Stewart is more analytical, citing counties of residence, etc. 1952 Virginia genealogies, 3,476 families.

**3515  Bruce, Philip A.** Virginia: a rebirth of the Old Dominion . . . 5v. Chicago, 1929.
v.3-5 biographical.

**3516  Brumbaugh, Gaius M.** Revolutionary War records . . . v.1 (all pub.). Virginia. Virginia army and navy forces, with bounty land warrants for Virginia, military district of Ohio, and Virginia military script . . . 1936. Repr. Baltimore: G.P.C., 1967.
10,000 names.

**3517  Brunk, Harry A.** History of Mennonites in Virginia, 1727-1960. 2v. Verona, Va.: McClure Printing Co., 1959-72; or Mennonite Church Office, Harrisonburg, Va.
v.1, 1727-1900; v.2, 1900-60. Extensive history, well documented. Some genealogy and family history.

**3518  Burgess, Louis A.** Virginia soldiers of 1776 . . . 3v. 1927-29. Repr. Baltimore: G.P.C., 1973. Spartanburg, S.C.: Reprint Co., 1973.
Unusual compilation, giving documentary proof of claims to war service of a great many Virginia Revolutionary War veterans. Much genealogy.

**3519  Burns, Annie (Walker).** Virginia genealogies and county records. v.1-11. Washington, D.C., 1941-44.
Contains miscellaneous information at random, inquiries, etc. Pension abstracts of Revolutionary War, War of 1812, and Indian Wars; difficult to use.

**3520  Cannon, Jouett T.** Index to military certificates, 1787, etc. [under the laws of Virginia]. In *Register of Kentucky State Historical Soc.,* v.22, 1924.

**3521  Cappon, Lester J.,** and **Duff, Stella F.** Virginia gazette index, 1736-80. 2v. Williamsburg, Va.: Inst. of Early History and Culture, 1950.
Complete index of articles and advertisements that appeared in Virginia's colonial newspaper.

**3522  Cartmell, Thomas K.** Shenandoah valley pioneers and their descendants; a history of Frederick county, Virginia, from . . . 1738-1908. 1908. Repr. Berryville, Va.: Virginia Book Co., 1972.
Indexed ed. 9,500 names of Virginia and West Virginia residents. Biographical sketches compiled mainly from records of old Frederick county, now Hampshire, Berkeley, Shenandoah, Jefferson, Hardy, Clarke, Warren, Morgan, and Frederick counties.

**3523  Casey, Joseph J.** Personal names in Hening's Statutes. . . . *See* no. 3573.

3524 **Cassell, Charles W.; Finck, W. J.;** and **Henkel, E. O.** History of the Lutheran church in Virginia and East Tennessee. Strasburg, Va., 1930.

Hundreds of names of ministers and laymen.

3525 **Chalkley, Lyman.** Chronicles of the Scotch-Irish settlement in Virginia. Extracted from the original court records of Augusta county, 1745–1800. 3v. 1912. Repr. Baltimore: G.P.C., 1974.

Remarkable collection of information about the early settlement of the valley of Virginia. Includes marriage licenses and bonds, 1748–1801; fee books, 1745–84; Augusta parish vestry book, 1746–60; and records of Revolutionary military service.

3526 **Clemens, William M.** Virginia wills before 1799; a complete abstract register of all names mentioned in over 600 recorded wills . . . 1924. Repr. Baltimore: G.P.C., 1973.

Copied from courthouse records; over 600 wills before 1799.

3527 **Cocke, Charles F.** Parish lines, Diocese of Southern Virginia. *Virginia State Library publ.* 22, Richmond, Va.: The Library, 1964.

3528 —— Diocese of Virginia. *Publ.* 28. Richmond, Va.: The Library, 1967.

3529 —— Diocese of Southwestern Virginia. *Publ.* 14. Richmond, Va., 1960.

History of Episcopal dioceses, Protestant Episcopal church. Maps.

3530 **Corbin, John B.** Catalog of genealogical materials in Texas libraries. Pt.1, Virginia. *Texas State Library and Historical Commission,* monograph 2. Austin, Tex.: The Library, 1965.

Most useful bibliography for Texas genealogists working on Virginia ancestry. Separate title and subject alphabet.

3531 **Crickard, Madeline W.** 1810 census: twenty counties, town of Petersburg and borough of Norfolk, from the original census records. Beverly, W. Va.: 1971.

Out-of-print. Compiler has 95 Virginia-West Virginia census lists, some from 1820 but most from 1810. These are available separately. Supplement to 1810 census, *see* Schreiner-Yantis, no. 3618.

3532 —— Index to the 1810 Virginia census; heads of families listed in the third census of the U.S. Beverly, W. Va.: The Compiler, 1971.

78 counties and 3 cities, made from original census schedules. 80,000 names. First and only index, includes West Virginia. Supplement *see* no.3618.

3533 **Crozier, William A.** Early Virginia marriages. *Virginia county records* ser. 4. 1907. Repr. Baltimore: G.P.C., 1973.

Reprinted in 1953, 1961, 1968. Latest repr. has index by A. M. Cartlidge.

3534 —— Virginia colonial militia, 1651–1776. *Virginia county records* ser. 2. 1905. Repr. Baltimore: G.P.C., 1973.

3535 —— Virginia county records. v.1–10, new ser.1. (all pub.). 1905–13. Repr. Baltimore: G.P.C., 1965–73.

Important set of books on early Virginia counties, with a great deal of accurate material.

3536 —— Virginia heraldica; being a registry of Virginia gentry entitled to coat armor, with genealogical notes of the families. *Virginia county records ser.,* v.5. 1908. Repr. Baltimore: G.P.C., 1965.

3537 **Crumrine, Boyd.** Virginia court records in southwestern Pennsylvania. Records of the district of West Augusta and Ohio and Yohogania counties, Virginia. Repr. with an index by Inez Waldenmaier. Baltimore: G.P.C., 1974.

Originally published as 5 separate pts. in v.1–3 of *Annals of the Carnegie Museum,* 1902–1905. Period covered 1775–80.

3538 **Currer-Briggs, Noel.** English wills of colonial families. New Orleans, La.: Polyanthos, 1972.

Companion volume to his *Virginia settlers* (no.3539). Most families are from Virginia, some New England. All essential information given.

**3539** ———— Virginia settlers and English adventurers: abstracts of wills, 1484–1798, and legal proceedings, 1566–1700, relating to early Virginia families. 3v. in 1. Baltimore: G.P.C., 1970.
Relates to almost 400 Virginia families; over 12,000 names in v.3 alone. British ed. in 3v. was called *English adventurers* . . .

**3540** **D.A.R. Virginia.** Roster, 1890–1958. Richmond, Va., 1959. Available from D.A.R., Pulaski, Va.

**3541** ———— Supplement, 1959–62. From D.A.R., Pulaski, Va.

**3542** **D.A.R. Virginia. Colonel Thomas Hughart Chapter.** First marriage record of Augusta county, Virginia. 1785–1813. 2nd pr. White Marsh, Va.: McClure Pr., 1970.

**3543** ———— Second marriage record, 1813–50. Staunton, Va.: Col. Thomas Hughart Chapter, 1972.

**3544** **Des Cognets, Louis, Jr.** English duplicates of lost Virginia records. [Princeton, N.J., 1960].
Pioneer Virginians from British Public Record Office papers.

**3545** **Dorman, John F.** A guide to the counties of Virginia. In *The Virginia genealogist*, v.3– , 1959– (in progress).
Covers Virginia and West Virginia. Contains extant court records, genealogical materials, and data for use in research.

**3546** ———— Virginia Revolutionary pension applications abstracted. v.1– , 1958– (in progress). Washington, D.C.: The Author.
v.21 to end of 1974.

**3547** **Douglas, William.** The Douglas register. Being a detailed register of births, marriages and deaths, together with other interesting notes as kept by the Rev. William Douglas, from 1750–97. Transcribed and ed. by W. M. Jones. 1928. Repr. Baltimore: G.P.C., 1973.
Vital statistics in St. James Northam parish, Goochland county. Also index of Goochland wills, 1728–40, and notes on the French-Huguenot refugees who lived in Manakin-Town.

**3548** **Dumont, William H.** A short census of Virginia, 1779. In *National Genealogical Soc. quarterly,* v.46, 1957.

**3549** **Eckenrode, Hamilton J.** List of Revolutionary soldiers of Virginia. *Special report of Dept. of Archives,* 1911. *8th annual report of Virginia State Library,* 1910–11. Richmond, Va., 1912.

**3550** ———— ———— Supplement. *Special report,* 1912. *9th annual report.* Richmond, Va., 1913.

**3551** ———— List of the colonial soldiers of Virginia. Virginia State Library. *13th annual report of Dept. of Archives,* 1916. 1917. Repr. Baltimore: G.P.C., 1974.
6,700 soldiers identified.

**3552** **Elliott, Katherine B.** Emigration to other states from southside Virginia. 2v. South Hill, Va.: The Author, ca.1966.
Deeds, wills, marriage, and other records relating to emigrants.

**3553** **Eminent and representative men of Virginia and the District of Columbia in the nineteenth century** . . . Madison, Wisc., 1893.

**3554** **Fishwick, Marshall W.** Gentlemen of Virginia. New York: Dodd Mead, 1971.

**3555** **Fleet, Beverley.** Virginia colonial abstracts. 34v. 1937–49. Repr. Baltimore: G.P.C., 1961–71.
Vital for researcher. 17th and 18th centuries.

**3556** **Foley, Louise P. H.** Early Virginia families along the James River: their deep roots and tangled branches, Henrico county-Goochland county. Richmond, Va.: The Compiler, 1974.

Assists in finding colonial and immigrant ancestors. Abstracts from patent books, quit rent roll, etc.

**3557 Foote, William H.** Sketches of Virginia, historical and biographical. 1st ser. 1850. Repr. Richmond, Va.: John Knox Pr., 1966.
Repr. has added index by Grace M. Pierce, 1916.

**3558** —— 2nd ser. 1855. Repr. Richmond, Va., 1956.

**3559 Fothergill, Augusta B., and Naugle, J. M.** Virginia tax payers, 1782-87, other than those published by the U.S. Census Bureau. 1940. Repr. Baltimore: G.P.C., 1974.
Virtually replaces lost 1790 census for some counties. Fayette and Lincoln counties of the present Kentucky are included; Jefferson is omitted. 34,000 names. With no.3636 it completes the reconstructed 1790 Virginia census.

**3560 Gahn, Bessie W.** Original patentees of land at Washington prior to 1700. 1936. Repr. Baltimore: G.P.C., 1969.
Because of the distribution of land when the District was formed, records of Maryland and Virginia are included.

**3561 Gannett, Henry.** A gazetteer of Virginia. *U.S. Geological Survey bull.* 232. Washington, D.C., 1904.

**3562 Great Britain, Public Record Office.** History, description, record groups, finding aids and materials for American history, with special reference to Virginia. *Virginia State Library publ.* 12. Richmond, Va.: Virginia State Lib., 1960.

**3563 Greer, George C.** Early Virginia immigrants, 1623-66. 1912. Repr. Baltimore: G.P.C., 1973.
25,000 names who were not original patentees of land, collected from the records of the Virginia State Land Office.

**3564 Gwathmey, John H.** Historical register of Virginians in the Revolution: soldiers, sailors, marines, 1775-83. 1938. Repr. Baltimore: G.P.C., 1973.

Over 65,000 names; supersedes Eckenrode, no.3549, and McAllister, no.3597. Names and evidence of service of Virginians who were in the Army and Navy, and Marines in the Revolution.

**3565 Hamlin, Charles H.** They went thataway. v.1-3. 1964-67. Repr. Baltimore: G.P.C., 1974.
Repr. is 3v. in 1. Though primarily concerned with Virginians, England, France, Germany, Scotland, the Barbados, Jamaica, and 22 American states are represented.

**3566** —— Virginia ancestors and adventurers. v.1-3, 1967-73. Powhatan, Va. (being repr. by G.P.C., Baltimore, 1975).
Drawn from migration records, Revolutionary muster rolls, abstracts from the *Virginia gazette* and census records. Authenticated records of all counties of Virginia utilized, 1650-1850.

**3567 Handy, Henry B.** The social recorder of Virginia. Richmond, Va., 1928.

**3568 Hanson, Raus McD.** Virginia place names, derivations, historical uses. White Marsh, Va.: McClure Pr., 1969.
Sources and origins, grouped by counties. Several thousand names.

**3569 Hart, Freeman H.** The valley of Virginia in the American Revolution, 1763-89. 1942. Repr. New York: Russell & Russell, 1971.
Information on availability of records of service in various wars up to Revolution; many private collections cited. Covers religious groups, Indians; excellent history and bibliography. Much Shenandoah information; coats of arms.

**3570 Hayden, Horace E.** Virginia genealogies. 1891. Repr. Baltimore: G.P.C., 1973.
Comprehensive compilation of Virginian genealogies; many families studied in depth. Partially indexed ed.

**3571 Hening, William W.** The statutes at large . . . 1606-1807. 13v. 1819-

23. Repr. Charlottesville, Va.: Univ. Pr. of Virginia, 1969.

**3572** ——— ——— Supplement by Samuel Shepherd. 3v. 1823, etc. Repr. New York: A.M.S. Press, 1967.

**3573** ——— ——— Personal names in Hening's Statutes at large, and Shepherd's Continuation. 1896. By Joseph J. Casey. Repr. Baltimore: G.P.C., 1967.

**3574** ——— ——— The laws of Virginia. Being a supplement to Hening, 1700–1750. By Waverly K. Winfree. Richmond, Va.: Virginia State Lib., 1971.

Hening contains much genealogical information. An important source for historical, legal, and genealogical research. Names in Hening are indexed in Swem (no.3630) and Casey (no.3573). Casey contains 22,500 entries. Winfree's *Laws* has little genealogy.

**3575 Hiden, Martha W.** How justice grew: Virginia counties: an abstract of their formation. *Jamestown 350th anniversary historical booklets* 19. Williamsburg, Va., 1957. Obtainable from Univ. Pr. of Virginia, Charlottesville, Va.

Has charts showing division of shires into the various counties.

**3576 Hinshaw, William W.** Encyclopedia of American Quaker genealogy. v.6. Containing every item of genealogical value found in all records and minutes (known to be in existence) of all meetings of all grades ever organized in Virginia . . . 1950. Repr. Baltimore: G.P.C., 1973.

Because of the death of Hinshaw, this volume was ed. and compiled by Thomas W. Marshall.

**3577 Historical Records Survey.** Guide to the manuscript collections of the Virginia Baptist Society. Suppl. 1, Index to the obituary notices in the *Religious herald,* Richmond, Virginia, 1828–1938. 2v. Richmond, Va., 1941.

**3578** ——— Index to marriage notices in the *Southern churchman,* 1835–1941. 2v. Richmond, Va., 1942.

**3579** ——— Inventory of county archives of Virginia. 9v. Richmond, Va., 1938–43.

Only the following numbers were published: 4 (Amelia), 13 (Brunswick), 21 (Chesterfield), 27 (Dinwiddie), 47 (Isle of Wight), 60 (Middlesex), 73 (Powhatan), 75 (Prince George), and 88 (Southampton). Unpublished material deposited in State Library, Richmond, Va.

**3580 History of Virginia.** 6v. Chicago, 1924.

v.1, by P. A. Bruce; v.2, by L. G. Tyler; v.3, by R. L. Morton; v.4–6, biographies by staff writers.

**3581 Holtzclaw, Benjamin C.** Ancestry and descendants of the Nassau-Siegen immigrants to Virginia, 1714–50. Harrisonburg, Va.: Memorial Foundation of the Germanna Colonies in Virginia. 1964.

**3582 Howe, Henry.** Historical collections of Virginia. Containing . . . facts, traditions, biographical sketches . . . relating to the history and antiquities . . . 1845. Repr. with an added index. Baltimore: G.P.C, 1969.

From early days to 1840. Genealogical data, with about 2,000 names with multiple references.

**3583 The Huguenot.** Publications, v.1–13, 1924–47. Vallejo, Calif., and Richmond, Va.

Published by the Huguenot Society of the Founders of Manakin in the Colony of Virginia. Includes sketches of families, with descriptions of coats of arms.

**3584 Hummel, Ray O., Jr.** A list of places included in nineteenth century Virginia directories. *Virginia State Library publ.* v.11. Richmond, Va.: The Library, 1960.

**3585 Jackson, Ronald V.,** and **Teeples, G. R.** Virginia 1810 census. 2v. Bountiful, Utah: Accelerated Indexing Systems, 1974.

Computer index.

**3586 Jester, Annie L.,** in collaboration with **Martha W. Hiden.** Adventures

*Virginia* 3586

237

of purse and person. Virginia, 1607-25. 2nd ed. Richmond, Va.: Order of First Families of Virginia, 1964.
Unusual and important volume dealing with those who came to Virginia. Three generations of 109 individuals are thoroughly researched.

3587    Kegley, Frederick B. Kegley's Virginia frontier, 1740-83 . . . 3rd pr. Roanoke, Va.: The Author, 1967.
Important compilation dealing with exploration and settlement of the James River and Roanoke sections of colonial Virginia.

3588    Kercheval, Samuel. A history of the valley of Virginia. 4th ed., rev. and new notes added by Oren F. Morton. 1925. Repr. Berryville, Va.: Virginia Book Co., 1973.
Much information on Indians, notes on settlements and Indian wars.

3589    King, George H. S. Copies of extant Virginia wills from counties whose records have been destroyed. In *Tyler's quarterly magazine,* v.20-33, 1939-52.
Unfinished when the magazine ceased publication.

3590    Knorr, Catherine L. (Mrs. H. A.).
Mrs. Knorr has compiled a number of marriage lists of Virginia counties. Many are in print, available from The Compiler, 1401 Linden St., Pine Bluffs, Ark., 71601.

3591    Lancaster, Robert A., Jr. Historic Virginia homes and churches. 1915. Repr. Spartanburg, S.C.: Reprint Co., 1973.
Contains a good deal of genealogical material.

3592    Lantz, Emile E. Series of genealogical and heraldic articles (on Virginia and Maryland families) published in the *Baltimore Sun,* 1905-1908.
In 2v. at Maryland Historical Soc. Fairly accurate, with coats of arms delineated.

3593    ———— Index to the names of families mentioned. By Alton H. Keller.
Typescript copies only.

3594    Latham, Allen, and Leonard, B. G.
A roll of the officers in the Virginia line of the Revolutionary Army who have received land bounty in the states of Ohio and Kentucky . . . 1822. Repr. Chillicothe, Ohio, 1966; Anchorage, Ky., 1962.

3595    Lower Norfolk county Virginia antiquary. Ed. by Edward W. James. 5v., 1895-1906. Repr. 5v. in 2. New York: Peter Smith, 1951.
Lower Norfolk county comprised all of that territory now included within the limits of Norfolk and Princess Anne counties and the cities of Norfolk and Portsmouth. Contains slave records, vital records, and other historical material.

3596    McAllister, Joseph T. Index to Saffell's *List of Virginia soldiers.* See no.3616.

3597    ———— Virginia militia in the Revolutionary War; McAllister's data. Hot Springs, Va., ca.1913.

3598    McCay, Betty L. Sources for genealogical searching in Virginia and West Virginia. Indianapolis, Ind.: The Compiler, 1971.
Published and unpublished material.

3599    McDonald, Cecil D., Jr. Some Virginia marriages, 1700-99. v.1- , 1973- (in progress). Seattle, Wash.: The Author.

3600    ———— ———— 1800-25. v.1- , 1973- (in progress). Seattle, Wash.: The Author.
Marriages found during research on McDonald's own family. Many names other than his kin mentioned.

3601    McGhee, Lucy K. Virginia pension abstracts of the Wars of the Revolution, 1812, and Indian Wars. 35v. Washington, D.C., 1953-66.

3602    McIlhany, Hugh M., Jr. Some Virginia families . . . 1903. Repr. Baltimore: G.P.C., 1962.

3603    McIlwaine, Henry R. Index to obituary notices in the *Richmond enquirer* from May 9, 1804 through 1828, and the *Richmond whig* from January 1824 through 1838. *Bull. of the Virginia State Lib.* 14, no.4, 1921. 1923. Repr. Baltimore: G.P.C., 1974.

Not confined to residents of Virginia, since many had left this state at the time of death. 4,000 notices.

3604    **Martin, Joseph.** A new and comprehensive gazetteer of Virginia and the District of Columbia, n.p., 1835.

3605    **Meade, William.** Old churches, ministers and families of Virginia. 2v. 1857. Repr. with Digested index and genealogical guide, by Jennings C. Wise, 1910. Baltimore: G.P.C., 1966.

Wise's index superior to that of J. M. Toner, 1898. Numerous family histories.

3606    **Men of mark in Virginia** . . . a collection of biographies of the leading men of the state . . . Lyon G. Tyler, ed.-in-chief. 5v. Washington, D.C., 1906–1909.

3607    ———— 2nd ser. v.1 (all pub.). Richmond, Va., 1936.

3608    **Norris, J. E.** History of the lower Shenandoah valley; counties of Frederick, Berkeley, Jefferson, and Clarke, their early settlement . . . a description of their historic . . . localities . . . Portraits of some of the prominent men, and biographies of many of the representative citizens. 1890. Repr. Berryville, Va.: Virginia Book Co., 1973.

The best history of the valley, with the 250 pages of biography outstanding. Repr. has new 112p. index. Several generations of many families.

3609    **Northern Neck (of Virginia) historical magazine.** v.1– , 1951– . Montross, Va.: Northern Neck of Virginia Historical Soc.

Some family histories, cemetery records, deeds, wills, military records. The Northern Neck area is the peninsula between Rappahannock and the Potomac, and includes five Tidewater counties: King George, Westmoreland, Richmond, Northumberland, and Lancaster.

3610    **Nugent, Nell M.** Cavaliers and pioneers: abstracts of Virginia land patents and grants, 1623–66. v.1 (all pub.). 1934. Repr. Baltimore: G.P.C., 1974.

Good record of earliest immigrants; 20,000 names with relevant information and exhaustive index. Superior to Greer's *Early Virginia immigrants* (no.3563) because of numerous errors in the latter. Additional 4-5v. in manuscript at Virginia State Library, Richmond, Va. The Library plans publication.

3611    **Order of the First Families of Virginia 1607–1620.** List of membership, 1912–1971. Washington, D.C. (not for sale).

3612    **Pecquet du Bellet, Louise.** Some prominent Virginia families. 4v. Lynchburg, Va., 1907.

3613    **The researcher.** A magazine of history and genealogical exchange. Ed. by Robert A. Stewart. v.1–2, no.3, 1926–28. Richmond, Va.

A fine Virginian magazine with too short a life span.

3614    **Riggs, Ronald P.** Register of rebel deserters taking the oath of allegiance, Provost Marshall Dept. of Virginia and North Carolina, May 1864 to April 1865. In *Virginia genealogist,* v.17– , 1973– (in progress).

3615    **Robinson, Morgan P.** Virginia counties: those resulting from Virginia legislation. *Virginia State Library bull.* 9, no.1–3. Richmond, Va., 1916.

3616    **Saffell, William T. R.** Records of the Revolutionary War. Bound with Index to Saffell's *List of Virginia soldiers in the Revolution,* by J. T. McAllister. 3rd ed. 1894, 1913. Repr. Baltimore: G.P.C., 1969.

Contains names of officers and privates of regiments, companies and corps, lists of distinguished prisoners, etc.

United States

**3617 Schreiner-Yantis, Netti.** Montgomery county, Virginia—ca. 1790. A comprehensive study, including the 1789 tax lists, abstracts of 800 land surveys and data concerning migration. Springfield, Va.: The Author, 1973.

In 1790 Montgomery county covered a vast area, including some 22 present counties. A thorough study of extant records.

**3618** ——— A supplement to the 1810 census of Virginia. Tax lists of the counties for which the census is missing. Springfield, Va.: Author, 1971.

Supplement to Crickard, no.3531–32. Significant addition to Virginia finding aids. Additional names from other sources. Valuable 70p. index lists complete names of persons mentioned in tax lists, indicating county of residence.

**3619 Schuricht, Herrman.** History of the German element in Virginia. 2v. in 1. Baltimore, 1898–1900.

**3620 Smith, Annie L. W.** The quit rents of Virginia; a copy of the rent rolls of the sevll countys of Virga for the year 1704 . . . and land owners of that section called the Northern Neck [for which] no quit rents exist. [Richmond, Va.], 1957.

**3621 Society of the Sons of the American Revolution.** Genealogy of members compiled by Clayton Torrence. Richmond, Va., 1939.

**3622 Somerby, Horatio G.** Passengers for Virginia, 1635. In *New-England historical and genealogical register* v.2–15, 1848–61.

"A register of the names of all ye passingers wch passed from ye porte of London . . . 1635."

**3623 Stanard, William G.** Some emigrants to Virginia; memoranda in regard to several hundred emigrants to Virginia during the colonial period whose parentage is shown or former residence indicated by authentic records. 2nd ed. enl. 1915. Baltimore: G.P.C., 1972.

**3624** ——— and **Stanard, Mary N.** The colonial Virginia register. A list of . . . officials . . . House of Burgesses, and the Revolutionary conventions of the colony of Virginia. 1902. Repr. Baltimore: G.P.C., 1965.

Register 1607–1776.

**3625 Stewart, Robert A.** The history of Virginia's navy of the Revolution. [Richmond, Va., 1934].

Contains roster of men who served. Half the text is roster of navy; good genealogical study.

**3626** ——— Index to printed Virginia genealogies, including key and bibliography. 1930. Repr. Baltimore: G.P.C., 1970.

750 historical, biographical, and genealogical books indexed. 6,000 family names listed. See also Brown, no.3514.

**3627 Summers, Lewis P.** Annals of southwest Virginia, 1769–1800 . . . 1929. 1v. in 2. Repr. Baltimore: G.P.C., 1970.

Monumental work with comprehensive name index. Covers counties of Botetourt, Fincastle, Montgomery, Washington, and Wythe.

**3628** ——— History of southwest Virginia, 1746–86; Washington county, 1777–1870. 1903. Repr. with rearranged index and table of contents. Baltimore: G.P.C., 1971.

Comprising Botetourt, Fincastle, and Washington counties, now embracing 19 present-day counties of Virginia and 17 of West Virginia, and other areas. Biographical sketches, many lists.

**3629 Swem, Earle G.** Bibliography of Virginia. 5v. *Virginia State Library bull.* 8, 10, 12, 18, 25. Richmond, Va., 1916–55 (i.e. 1956).

Only v.1 contains genealogical material. Later volumes were compiled by Wilmer L. Hall. Pt.4 (*bull.* 18, no.2) and pt.5 (*bull.* 25, no.1–4) in print from Virginia State Library, Richmond, Va.

**3630** ——— Virginia historical index. 2v. in 4. 1934–36. Repr. Northampton, Mass.: Peter Smith, 1965.

Reprinted in 4v. Indexes names in the *Calendar of Virginia state papers* (no.3645); Hening's *Statutes at large* (no.3571); *Tyler's Quarterly historical magazine* (no.3634); *Virginia magazine of history and biography* (no.3660); *William and Mary (College) quarterly,* ser.1-2 (no.3672); *Virginia historical register,* 1845-53 (no.3659); and *Lower Norfolk County Virginia antiquary,* 1895-1906 (no.3595).

**3630a Torrence, Clayton.** A trial bibliography of colonial Virginia [1608-1754]. *Special report of the Dept. of Bibliography,* 1908. 5th annual report of Virginia State Library, 1908. Richmond, Va., 1908.

**3631** ——— ——— 1755-76. *Special report . . . 6th report.* 1909. Richmond, Va., 1910.

*Swem's bibliography* (no.3629) does not supersede Torrence.

**3632** ——— Virginia wills and administrations, 1632-1800. 1930. Repr. Baltimore: G.P.C., 1972.

50,000 names. Administrations on estates shown by inventories of the estates of intestates recorded in will and other books of local courts. Some now in West Virginia.

**3633 Tyler, Lyon G.** Encyclopedia of Virginia biography. 5v. New York, 1915.

A mug book but contains biographies not found elsewhere.

**3634 Tyler's Quarterly historical and genealogical magazine.** v.1-33. Richmond, Va., 1919-52; new ser.1, no.1-2, Nashville, Tenn., 1952.

Exceptionally fine genealogical work, primarily concerned with Virginia. New series under title, *Tyler's Quarterly: a journal of American history, biography, and genealogy,* lasted only 2 numbers. Many vols. are indexed in Swem (no.3630). Whole set repr. by Kraus Reprint Corp., New York, 1966.

**3635 U.S. Board on Geographic Names.** Approved place names in Virginia. An index to Virginia names approved by the Board, through 1969. By Mary Topping (and others). Washington, D.C.: Columbia Historical Soc. [1971]. Also from Univ. Pr. of Virginia, Charlottesville, Va.

**3636 U.S. Bureau of the Census.** Heads of families at the first census of the United States taken in the year 1790. Records of the state enumerations, 1782-85. Repr. Baltimore: G.P.C., 1970; Spartanburg, S.C.: Reprint Co., 1965, etc.

Since original returns for Virginia were destroyed during the War of 1812, taxpayer lists were reconstructed by the Bureau of the Census. Based on state enumerations made in 1782-85; a tax list of Greenbrier county, 1783-86; a list of inhabitants and owners of property in Richmond—represents 39 counties. Supplement, Fothergill, *see* no.3559.

**3637 Valentine, Edward P.** The Edward P. Valentine papers, abstract of records in the local and general archives of Virginia relating to [many] families . . . Ed. by Clayton Torrence. 4v. Richmond, Va., 1927.

Many Virginia families treated.

**3638 Van Meter, Benjamin F.** Genealogies and sketches of some old families who have taken prominent part in the development of Virginia and Kentucky, especially, and later by many other states of this union. Louisville, Ky., 1901.

**3639 VBAPPA:** Virginia books and pamphlets presently available. Berryville, Va.: Virginia Book Co., 1972.

Most useful to librarians wishing to enlarge collections and for researchers to know what is available. Books and pamphlets on Virginia or Virginians or by Virginians.

**3640 Virginia (Colonial). Council.** Minutes of the Council and General Court of Colonial Virginia, 1622-32, 1670-76, with notes and excerpts from original Council and General Court records into 1683, now lost. Ed. by Henry R. McIlwaine. Richmond, Va., 1924.

Extensive index contains many surnames.

**3641 Virginia (Colony). County Court (West Augusta District).** Index to

Virginia court records in Pennsylvania, District of West Augusta. Washington, D.C., 1957.

Index to the minute books of the Virginia courts, held within the limits of southwestern Pennsylvania, 1775-80, including records of deeds for West Augusta, Virginia, 1775-76, and a list of old Virginia wills proved before Yohogania county court, 1776-81.

3642 **Virginia. Auditor's Office.** Muster rolls of the Virginia militia in the War of 1812. Richmond, Va., 1852.

A supplement to *Pay rolls of militia,* no.3643.

3643 —— Pay rolls of militia entitled to land bounty under the Act of Congress of Sept. 28, 1850. Richmond, Va., 1851.

3644 **Virginia. Census.** Records of the state enumeration: 1782-85. Virginia. Washington, D.C., 1908.

3645 **Virginia. Committee on Colonial Records.** Calendar of Virginia state papers . . . 1652-1869. 11v. 1875-93. Repr. New York: Kraus Reprint Corp., 1967.

Much genealogical information.

3646 **Virginia. General Assembly.** Joint Committee on the State Library. Colonial records of Virginia. 1874. Repr. Baltimore: G.P.C., 1973.

Important collection of early documents published by state of Virginia; a partial census of 1623 with 2,000 names, with other records.

3647 **Virginia. Land Commission.** Certificate book, 1779-80. Includes index of names. In *Register of Kentucky State Historical Soc.* 3, 1923.

3648 —— Inventory. Compiled by Daphne Gentry. Richmond, Va.: Virginia State Library, 1973.

Contains a listing of records of the Land Office and history of its activities.

3649 **Virginia State Library.** Genealogical research in the Virginia State Library. Richmond, Va.: The Library, 1971.

3650 —— Virginia local history; a bibliography. Richmond, Va.: The Library, 1971.

3651 **Virginia claims to land in western Pennsylvania.** *Pennsylvania archives,* ser.3, v.3, pp.483-574 Harrisburg, Pa., 1896.

3652 **Virginia Company of London.** Records. The court book from the manuscript in the Library of Congress. Ed. with introduction and bibliography by Susan M. Kingsbury. 4v. Washington, D.C., 1906-35.

3653 —— Introduction published separately. Washington, D.C., 1905.

3654 **Virginia county records.** Ed. by William A. Crozier. v.1-10, new ser.1. New York, 1905-13. Very fine series repr. by G.P.C., Baltimore, 1965-73.

3655 **Virginia Genealogical Society.** Quarterly bulletin. v.1- , 1961- . Richmond, Va.: The Society.

Much good information. Accurate transcriptions.

3656 —— Some marriages in the burned record counties of Virginia. Richmond, Va.: The Society, 1972.

Concerns Hanover, Dinwiddie, Charles City, Nansemond, Elizabeth City, and other sources. 1,500 marriages, fully indexed. *Virginia Genealogical Soc. special publ.* 4.

3657 **Virginia genealogist.** Ed. by John F. Dorman. v.1- , 1957- . Washington, D.C.: The Editor.

Excellent periodical, essential for researchers in Virginia.

3658 **The Virginia historical register.** Ed. by William Maxwell. 6v. 1848-53. Repr. 6v. in 3. Spartanburg, S.C.: Reprint Co., 1973.

Quarterly journal, the forerunner of the Virginia Historical Society's *magazine* (see no.3660).

3659 **Virginia Historical Society.** Virginia historical collections. v.1, 1833; new ser., v.1-11, 1882-92. Richmond, Va.

Fine set published by Virginia Historical Society. Some have been reprinted.

**3660 Virginia magazine of history and biography.** v.1- , 1894- . Richmond, Va.: Virginia Historical Soc.

Much genealogy in earlier volumes; none since the 1940s. v.1-38, 1893/4-1930, repr. by Kraus Reprint Corp., New York, 1966.

**3661 Virginia Place Name Society newsletter.** no.1- , 1973- . Charlottesville, Va.: Univ. of Virginia Lib., Manuscript Dept.

Contains details of work on place names in Virginia.

**3662** ——— Occasional papers. no.1- , 1961-. Charlottesville, Va.: Univ. of Virginia Lib., Manuscript Dept.

Excellent small studies on place names affecting Virginia.

**3663 Waldenmaier, Inez.** Index to the minute books of the Virginia courts, held within the limits of southwestern Pennsylvania, 1775-80, including records of deeds for West Augusta, Virginia 1775-76, and abstract of old Virginia wills proved before the Yohogania county court, 1776-81. Washington, D.C., 1957.

**3664** ——— Virginia marriage records before 1853. 2pts. Washington, D.C., 1956-57?

Pt.2, finding list of the official county court records of marriages in Virginia before 1853.

**3665 Wallace, Lee A., Jr.** A guide to Virginia military organizations, 1861-65. Richmond, Va., 1964. Available from Virginia Book Co., Berryville, Va., with a 48p. added index of personal names.

Lists every company involved and all relevant information.

**3666 Walne, Peter.** English wills: probate records in England and Wales . . . *Virginia State Lib. publ.* 23. Richmond, Va.: The Library, 1964.

With particular reference to Virginia.

**3667 Wayland, John W.** The German element of the Shenandoah valley of Virginia. 1907. Repr. with added index. Bridgewater, Va.: Carrier Co., 1964.

Material on settlers, counties and county records, 1770-86. Also information on Revolutionary War pensioners.

**3668** ——— Virginia valley records. Genealogical and historical materials of Rockingham county, Virginia, and related regions. 1930. Repr. Baltimore: G.P.C., 1973.

**3669 Whichard, Rogers D.** The history of lower Tidewater, Virginia. 3v. New York, 1959.

v.3 family and personal history.

**3670 White, Miles.** Early Quaker records in Virginia. In *Publications of the Southern History Assoc.,* 6-7, 1902-03.

From book containing Friends of Nansemond and Isle of Wight counties, Virginia.

**3671 Whitelaw, Ralph T.** Virginia's Eastern Shore, a history of Northampton and Accomack counties. 2v. 1951. Repr. Magnolia, Mass.: Peter Smith, 1968.

Best work on Virginia's Eastern Shore, historical and genealogical.

**3672 William and Mary (College) quarterly.** v.1-27, 1892-1919; ser.2, v. 1-23, 1921-43; ser.3, v.1- , 1944- . Williamsburg, Va.: The College.

Title varies. No genealogy found after ser.2, v.23, 1943; ser.1-3 reprinted by Kraus Reprint Corp., New York, 1966.

**3673** ——— Index to genealogical data, v.1-16, no.1, 1892-1908. [Richmond, Va., 1908?].

**3674** ——— Index, ser.3, v.1-15, 1944-58 by Stella D. Neiman. Williamsburg, Va.: Inst. of Early American History and Culture, 1960.

**3674a** ——— Index, ser.3, v.16-30, 1959-73 by Donna C. Sheppard. Williamsburg, Va.: Inst. of Early American History and Culture, 1974.

**3675 Wilson, Howard McK.** The Lexington Presbytery heritage; the Presbytery of Lexington and its churches in the Synod of Virginia, Presbyterian Church in the U.S. Verona, Va.: McClure Pr., 1971.

Good maps. Contains over 200p. listing all the churches, ministers, elders, and deacons, from the beginning to 1970, for the entire Synod.

3676 ——— Records of the Synod of Virginia on microfilm, Presbyterian Church, U.S. White Marsh, Va.: McClure Pr., 1970.

Listing of items in 543 reels of official Synod records back to 1740; epitaphs and genealogical data. Reels are available on interlibrary loan, Union Theological Seminary in Richmond, Va.

3677 **Wilson, Samuel M.** Catalogue of Revolutionary soldiers and sailors of the commonwealth of Virginia to whom land bounty warrants were granted by Virginia for military services in the War of Independence. Excerpted from the year book of the Kentucky Soc., D.A.R. 1913. Repr. Baltimore: G.P.C., 1967.

Originally from the official records in the Kentucky State Land Office at Frankfort.

3678 **Woodson, Robert F.,** and **Woodson, I. B.** Virginia tithables from burned record counties. Richmond, Va.: The Compilers, 1970.

Tithable lists of late colonial period for five counties: Buckingham, Gloucester, Hanover, James City, and Stafford, covering 1768–75. Newly acquired Hanover information from British Public Record Office.

3679 **Wulfeck, Dorothy F.** Genealogy notes on Virginia families. Many volumes. Naugatuck, Conn.: The Author, various dates.

Booklets containing miscellaneous notes on families that lived in Virginia before 1850. Notes taken from published and unpublished sources. Families thus treated can be obtained from author, or see VBAPPA, no.3639, p.239–40, for listing.

3680 ——— Marriages of some Virginia residents, 1607–1800. Ser.1, 7v. Naugatuck, Conn.: The Author, 1961–67.

Records from marriage bonds, consent papers, ministers' returns, parish registers, tombstones, etc. and from unpublished manuscripts. Alphabetically by surnames, with index of parents, sureties, and witnesses.

3681 ——— The Virginia gazette genealogy. 4v. 1959–62. Naugatuck, Conn.: The Author, 1960–65.

Reprint of genealogy pages from *The Virginia gazette.*

3682 **Wust, Klaus G.** The Virginia Germans. Charlottesville, Va.: Univ. Pr. of Virginia, 1969.

Comprehensive study of the German settlement by name and origin of many German families in Virginia.

3683 **Yantis, Netti Schreiner-.** See Schreiner-Yantis, Netti, no.31, 3617–18.

WASHINGTON

Settled ca. 1811; entered Union 1889

*Seattle Public Library*
*Washington State Library, Olympia*

✠ Since much of the following material concerns Oregon and Washington states, both states should be considered when researching in these areas.

3684 **Bagley Clarence B.** History of Seattle from the earliest settlement to the present time. 3v. Chicago, 1916.

v.3 and part of v.2 biographical.

3685 **Building a state.** Washington, 1889–1939. *Washington State Historical Soc. publ.,* v.3. [Tacoma, Wash., 1940.]

Has information on donation land claims. Useful for Washington pioneers, 1850–60.

3686 **D.A.R. Washington.** History and register. v.1–3 and suppl. Seattle, Wash., [and elsewhere), 1924–72.

v.1 (1924) and v.2 (1924–41) are out-of-print. v.3 (1941–61) and v.4 (1962–72) can be obtained from D.A.R. Vice-Regent, Puyallup, Wash.

3687 **Durham, Nelson W.** History of the city of Spokane and Spokane county, from its earliest settlement to the

present time. 3v. Spokane, Wash., 1912.
v.2-3 biographical.

3688 **Eastern Washington Genealogical Society bulletin.** v.1- , 1963- . Spokane, Wash.: The Society.

3689 **Evans, Elwood** (and others). History of the Pacific northwest: Oregon and Washington. 2v. Portland, Ore., 1889.
v.2 biographical.

3690 **Hawthorne, Julian.** History of Washington, the evergreen state, from early dawn to daylight, with portraits and biographies. 2v. New York, 1893.
Biographies in both vols.

3691 **Hines, Harvey K.** An illustrated history of the state of Washington. 2 eds. Chicago, 1893, 1894.
1893 and 1894 eds. have different biographical sketches.

3692 **Historical Records Survey.** Guide to church vital statistics records in Washington. Preliminary ed. Seattle, Wash., 1942.

3693 ———— Guide to public vital statistics records in Washington. Seattle, Wash., 1941.

3694 ———— Inventory of county archives of Washington. 15v. Spokane, Wash., 1937-42.
Only the following numbers were published: 1 (Adams), 2 (Asotin), 3 (Benton), 4 (Chelan), 8 (Cowlitz), 12 (Garfield), 17 (King), 21 (Lewis), 22 (Lincoln), 26 (Pend Oreille), 29 (Skagit), 31 (Snohomish), 32 (Spokane), 33 (Stevens), and 39 (Yakima). Unpublished material deposited in State College, Pullman, Wash.

3695 **Hunt, Herbert,** and **Kaytor, F. C.** Washington, west of the cascades; historical and descriptive; the explorers, the Indians, the pioneers, the modern. 3v. Chicago, 1917.
v.2-3 biographical.

3696 **An illustrated history of southeastern Washington,** including Walla Walla, Columbia, Garfield and Asotin counties, Washington. Spokane, Wash., 1906.
Many biographies.

3697 **Landes, Henry.** A geographic dictionary of Washington. *Washington geological survey bull.* 17. Olympia, Wash., 1917.

3698 **Lyman, William D.** History of Yakima Valley, Washington, comprising Yakima, Kittitas and Benton counties. 2v. Chicago, 1919.
v.2 biographical.

3699 ———— Lyman's history of old Walla Walla county, embracing Walla Walla, Columbia, Garfield and Asotin counties. 2v. Chicago, 1918.
v.2 and part of v.1 biographical.

3700 **Meany, Edmond S.** Origin of Washington geographic names. 1923. Repr. Detroit, Mich.: Gale Research, 1968.
Northwest history, lore, and legend found behind more than 2,000 Washington place names.

3701 **Oregon State Library, Salem.** Pioneer families of the Oregon territory, 1850. *Oregon state archives bull.* 3. publ.17. 2nd ed. Salem, Ore.: The Library, 1961.
Includes Lewis and Clark counties in Washington. List of heads of families and of individuals of other surnames recorded in the U.S. census of 1850.

3702 **Phillips, James W.** Washington state place names. Seattle, Wash.: Univ. of Washington Pr., 1971.
1,500 place names; author has drawn on Meany's *Origin of Washington geographic names* (No.3700).

3703 **Pollard, Lancaster,** and **Spencer, Lloyd.** A history of the state of Washington, 4v. New York, 1937.
v.3-4 biographical.

3704 **Prosser, William F.** A history of Puget Sound country . . . 2v. Chicago, 1913.
Half of v.1 and all v.2 biographical. Mug book.

245

3705 **The researcher.** 1969– . Tacoma, Wash.: Tacoma Genealogical Soc.

3706 **Seattle Genealogical Society bulletin.** 1952– . Seattle, Wash.: The Society.

3707 **Sons of the American Revolution, Washington.** Register, 1895–1916. [Seattle, 1917.]

3708 **Steele, Richard F.** An illustrated history of the Big Bend country embracing Lincoln, Douglas, Adams, and Franklin counties, state of Washington. Spokane, Wash., 1904.

3709 **Stewart, Edgar I.** Washington: Northwest frontier. 4v. New York, 1957.
v.3–4 biographical.

3710 **Stine, Thomas O.** Scandinavians on the Pacific, Puget Sound. 1900. Repr. San Francisco: R. and E. Research Assoc., 1968.
Numerous biographical sketches.

3711 **Stucki, J. U.** Index to the first federal census, territory of Washington (1860). Huntsville, Ark.: Century Enterprises, 1972.

3712 **United States. W.P.A. Washington (State).** Told by the pioneers . . . Tales of frontier life as told by those who remember the days of the territory and early statehood of Washington. 3v. Olympia, Wash., 1937–38.
Cover title: *Reminiscences of pioneer life in Washington.*

3713 **A volume of memoirs and geneaology of representative citizens of the city of Seattle and county of King, Washington,** including biographies of many of those who have passed away. New York, 1903.
Mug book, but useful.

3714 **Washington State Library, Olympia.** Washington state and local subscription histories with biographical sketches in the Washington State Library, Olympia. Olympia, Wash., 1969.

2p. list of 30 histories with biographical volumes noted. Concerns state, county, and city; too many to list in this work.

3715 **Yakima Valley Genealogical Society bulletin.** v.1– , 1969– . Yakima, Wash.: The Society.

3716 ———— Records of Yakima county, Washington to 1907 (and Benton) county, Washington, to 1907. 4v. Yakima, Wash.: The Society, 1974.
Benton was formed principally from Yakima in 1905. v.1, births; v.2, deaths; v.3, probates and naturalizations; v.4, marriage records.

## WEST VIRGINIA

Settled 1727; entered Union 1863

*Cabell County Public Library, Huntington
Department of Archives and History,
Charleston*

✠ Originally part of Virginia. Entries for Virginia (no.3502–3683) and, to a certain extent, the western portion of Pennsylvania (no.2841–3042) should be checked when considering list for West Virginia.

3717 **Atkinson, George W.,** and **Gibbens, A. M.** Prominent men of West Virginia: biographical sketches of representative men, the growth and advancement of the state . . . Wheeling, W.Va., 1890.

3718 **Boyd, Peter.** History of northern West Virginia Panhandle, embracing Ohio, Marshall, Brooke, and Hancock counties. 2v. Topeka, Kans., 1927.
Last pt. of v.1 and all v.2 biographical.

3719 **Butcher, Bernard L.** Genealogical and personal history of upper Monongahela valley, West Virginia. 3v. New York, 1912.
v.2–3 biographical.

3720 **Callahan, James M.** History of West Virginia, old and new . . . and West Virginia biography . . . 3v. Chicago, 1923.
v.2–3 biographical.

3721 **Cartmell, Thomas K.** Shenandoah valley pioneers and their descendants; a history of Frederick county, Virginia from . . . 1738-1908. 1908. Berryville, Va.: Virginia Book Co., 1972.
Indexed edition, 9,500 names of Virginia and West Virginia residents. Biographical sketches.

3722 **Conley, Philip.** West Virginia encyclopedia. Charleston, W. Va., 1929.

3722a **D.A.R. West Virginia.** Bibliography of local history and genealogy. Charleston, W. Va.: D.A.R. 1965.
Lists genealogical holdings of many libraries throughout the state.

3723 **Davis, Innis C.** A bibliography of West Virginia. Pts.1-2. Charleston, W.Va., 1939.
A publication of the West Virginia Dept. of Archives: pt.1, Books about West Virginia by West Virginians and printed in West Virginia; pt.2, Printed official documents, etc. relating to the formation of West Virginia.

3724 **DeHass, Wills.** History of the early settlements and Indian Wars of Western Virginia. Parsons, W.Va.: McClain Printing Co., 1960.
Includes biographical sketches of frontiersmen. One of the earliest histories of what is now West Virginia. Carried to 1795.

3725 **Doddridge, Joseph.** Notes on the settlement and Indian Wars of the western parts of Virginia and Pennsylvania, 1763-83. 1824. Repr. 1912. Repr. 1960 with new material. Rev. by John S. Ritenour and W. T. Lindsey. Parsons, W.Va.: McClain Printing Co., 1960.; 1876 ed. repr. by Burt Franklin, New York, 1973.

3726 **Encyclopedia of contemporary biography of West Virginia** . . . New York, 1894.
Large vol.; fine biographical sketches.

3727 **Gannett, Henry.** A gazetteer of West Virginia. *U.S. Geological Survey bull.* 233. Washington, D.C., 1904.

3728 **Hale, John P.** Trans-Allegheny pioneers: historical sketches of the first white settlements west of the Alleghenies, 1748 and after. 3rd ed. Edited by Harold J. Dudley. Raleigh, W.Va.: The Editor, 1971.
3rd ed. is facsimile of 1st ed. plus 2nd supplemental material and editing by H. J. Dudley. One of the most valuable contributions to the biographical history of families in West Virginia.

3729 **Hess, James W.** Guide to manuscripts and archives in the West Virginia collection of West Virginia University Library. Morgantown, W.Va.: The Library, 1974.
Much on Appalachian region. Large collection of court records, but poorly described.

3730 **Historical Records Survey.** Cemetery readings in West Virginia. 3v. Charleston, W.Va., 1939-41.
Cabell and Marion counties.

3731 ———— Guide to church vital statistics records in West Virginia. Charleston, W.Va., 1942.

3732 ———— Inventory of county archives of West Virginia. 13v. Charleston, W.Va., 1937-42.
Only the following numbers were published: 11 (Gilmer), 12 (Grant), 22 (Lincoln), 24 (Marion), 28 (Mineral), 31 (Monroe), 36 (Pendleton), 38 (Pocahontas), 40 (Putnam, 42 (Randolph), 43 (Ritchie), 44 (Roane), and 46 (Taylor). Unpublished material deposited in Dept. of Archives and History, Charleston, W.Va.

3733 ———— Inventory of public vital statistics records in West Virginia. Charleston, W.Va., 1941.

3734 ———— Inventory of the church archives of West Virginia. 2v. Charleston, W.Va., 1939-41.
v.1, Presbyterian churches; v.2, Protestant Episcopal Church.

3735 ———— West Virginia county formations and boundary changes. Charleston, W.Va., 1939.

3736 **History of the upper Ohio valley . . . with family history and biographical sketches.** 2v. Madison, Wisc., 1890.
v.1, West Virginia Panhandle; v.2, Jefferson and Belmont counties, Ohio. Historical and biographical.

3737 **History of the upper Ohio valley . . . with historical account of Columbiana county, Ohio.** 2v. Madison, Wisc., 1891.

3738 **Hixson (W. W.) and Co.** Atlas of the state of West Virginia. Rockford, Ill., [1936?].
Cover: *Plat book of West Virginia.*

3739 **Hughes, Josiah.** Pioneer West Virginia, Charleston, W.Va., 1932.
Principally concise histories of each county.

3740 **Johnston, David E.** A history of Middle New River settlements and contiguous territory. 1906. Repr. Radford, Va.: Commonwealth Pr., 1969.

3741 **Johnston, Ross B.** West Virginia estate settlements (1753-1850). A reprint of West Virginia estate settlements as first published in *West Virginia history,* v.17, 20-24. Ed. and indexed by Mitzi M. Barnett. Fort Worth, Tex.: Miran Pub., 1969.
Extremely useful for West Virginians, but important for those families who passed into the newly opened northwest territory.

3742 ———— West Virginians in the American Revolution. *West Virginia Historical Soc. publ.* 1. Parkersburg, W.Va.: West Augusta Historical and Genealogical Soc., 1959.
Appendix listing Revolutionary War soldiers from various sources, first published in *West Virginia history,* v.1-9, 1939-47.

3743 **Kenny, Hamill T.** West Virginia place names: their origin and meaning including the nomenclature of the streams and mountains. Piedmont, W.Va., 1945.

3744 **Lambert, Oscar D.** Pioneer leaders of western Virginia. Parkersburg, W.Va., 1935.

3745 **Lang, Theodore F.** Loyal West Virginia from 1861 to 1865 . . . Baltimore, 1895.

3746 **Leckey, Howard L.** The Tenmile country and its pioneer families. A genealogical history of the upper Monongahela valley. 7v. Waynesburg, Pa., 1950.

3747 ———— ———— Index, v.1-7 by Hilda Chance, Liberty, Pa. [1972].
v.8-9, newspaper columns, were added as a supplement to original 7v. set. Available in various larger libraries.

3748 **Lewis, Virgil A.** Historical data relating to the formation of West Virginia. 1st-3rd biennial reports, Dept. of Archives and History. Charleston, W.Va., 1906-11.
1st report, *Early explorers of West Virginia* . . . pioneers, settlers, etc.; 2nd report, *West Virginians in Virginia House of Burgesses* . . . West Virginians who helped to form state; 3rd report, *Soldiery of West Virginia,* French and Indian through Spanish-American wars *(see* no.3749).

3749 ———— The soldiery of West Virginia in the French and Indian War; Lord Dunsmore's War; the Revolution; the later Indian Wars . . . 3rd biennial report of Dept. of Archives and History. 1911. Excerpted and repr. Baltimore: G.P.C., 1972.
Most comprehensive compilation of West Virginian soldiers in the wars.

3750 **McCay, Betty L.** Sources for genealogical searching in Virginia and West Virginia. Indianapolis, Ind.: The Compiler, 1971.
Pub. and unpublished materials.

3751 **McWhorter, Lucullus V.** The border settlers of northwestern Virginia, 1768-95 . . . Hamilton, Ohio, 1915.

3752 ———— ———— Index. By H. A. Baumgardner. Tacoma, Wash., 1961.

**3753   Men of West Virginia.** 2v. Chicago, 1903.
Both vols. biographical.

**3754   Miller, Thomas C.,** and **Maxwell, H.** West Virginia and its people. 3v. New York, 1913.
v.2-3 biographical.

**3755   Mockler, William E.** West Virginia surnames: the pioneers. Parsons, W.Va.: McClain Printing Co., 1974.
Survey of family names in use on America's first English-speaking Appalachian frontier.

**3756   Munn, Robert F.** Index to West Virginiana. Charleston, W.Va., 1960.
Index of 13 periodicals of West Virginia.

**3757   Murphy, Robert E.** Progressive West Virginians; some of the men who have built up and developed the state of West Virginia. Wheeling, W.Va., 1905.

**3758   Newton, J. H.; Nichols, G. G.;** and **Sprankle, A. G.** History of the Panhandle . . . counties of Ohio, Brooke, Marshall and Hancock, West Virginia. 1879. Repr. Evansville, Ind.: Unigraphic, 1970.
Large vol. covering section of great importance genealogically.

**3759   Norona, Delf,** and **Shetler, C.** West Virginia imprints, 1790-1863; a checklist of books, newspapers, periodicals and broadsides. Moundsville, W.Va.: West Virginia Library Assoc., 1958.

**3760   Pugh, Maud.** Capon Valley, it's [sic] pioneers and their descendants, 1698-1940. Capon Bridge, W.Va., 1946-48.
Concerns mostly Hampshire county.

**3761   Reddy, Anne W.** West Virginia Revolutionary ancestors whose services were non-military and whose names, therefore, do not appear in Revolutionary indexes of soldiers and sailors. 1930. Baltimore: G.P.C., 1973.
From manuscript public claims of the Revolutionary War in the Virginia State Library.

**3762   A reminiscent history of northern West Virginia.** Chicago, 1895.
Some history; mostly mug book.

**3763   Sage, Clara McC.,** and **Jones L. S.** Early records, Hampshire county Virginia, now West Virginia, including at the start most of known Virginia aside from Augusta District. 1939. Repr. Baltimore: G.P.C., 1969.
Privately printed. Wills, marriage records, state census 1782 and 1784, Revolutionary soldiers pensions 1835. Covers 19th century.

**3764   Shawkey, Morris P.** West Virginia in history, life, literature and industry. 5v. Chicago, 1928.
v.3-5 biographical.

**3765   Shetler, Charles.** Guide to study of West Virginia history. Morgantown, W.Va., 1960.
A must for genealogical researchers.

**3766   Shinedling, Abraham I.** West Virginia Jewry: origins and history, 1850-1958. 3v. Philadelphia, 1963.
Sources for the history of West Virginia Jews, literary and personal. Many names.

**3767   Sims, Edgar B.** Making a state. Charleston, W.Va.: State Auditor's Office, 1956.
Formation of counties; maps; and index to land grants.

**3768   ———** Maps showing development of West Virginia counties. South Charleston, W.Va., 1954.

**3769   ———** Sims' Index to land grants in West Virginia. Charleston, W.Va.: State Auditor's Office, 1952.

**3770   ——— ———** Supplement. Charleston, W.Va.: State Auditor's Office, ca.1963.
50,000 names of persons to whom grants were made in territory now comprising West Virginia. Supplement has grants of Fincastle, Giles, and Rockingham counties, and other counties not on record in Auditor's Office when Sims published his index in 1952. Albion M. Dyer published an index to land grants in 1896, but Sims' is better.

3771　**Tetrick, Willis G.** Obituaries from newspapers of northern West Virginia . . . 2v. Clarksburg, W.Va., 1933.

3772　**Van Voorhis, John S.** The old and new Monongahela. 1893. Repr. with new index of names by Veronica Schofield. Baltimore: G.P.C., 1974.
8,000 names. Embraces territory of the Monongahela Valley, Allegheny and Ohio rivers. Pennsylvania: Washington, Westmoreland, Beaver, Greene, Allegheny, and Fayette counties; West Virginia: Monongalia, Ohio, Brooke, Hancock, Marshall, and Wetzel.

3773　**West Virginia echoer.** v.1– , 1967– Wheeling, W.Va.: Mary F. Warrell, editor, 398 National Rd., 26003.
Census lists, family articles, courthouse records, cemetery records, etc. West Virginia and Pennsylvania information.

3774　**West Virginia historical magazine.** v.1–5, 1901–5. Charleston, W.Va.
Magazine was published by West Virginia Historical Society. Much genealogy and local history.

3775　**West Virginia history.** v.1– , 1939– . Charleston, W.Va.: State Dept. of Archives and History.
Considerable amount of genealogy and local history. Kraus Repr. Corp., New York has reprinted v.1–10, 1939–49.

3776.　**Withers, Alexander S.** Chronicles of border warfare . . . 1831. Repr. of Reuben Thwaites's rev. ed. 1895. Parsons, W.Va.: McClain Printing Co., 1961; also New York: Arno Pr., 1971.
Early explorers, settlers, etc. in what is now West Virginia.

WISCONSIN

Settled ca. 1766; entered Union 1848

*State Historical Society of Wisconsin, Madison*

3777　**Aikens, Andrew J.,** and **Proctor, L. A.** Men of progress: Wisconsin . . . Milwaukee, Wisc., 1897.
Selected list of biographical sketches and portraits.

3778　**Biographical sketches of old settlers and prominent people of Wisconsin.** v.1 (all pub.). Waterloo, Wisc., 1899.

3779　**Bloom, John P.** The territory of Wisconsin . . . 1836–39. *Territorial papers of the U.S.* 27. 1969. Repr. New York: A.M.S. Press, 1973.
Lists of persons signing petitions, memorials, etc.

3780　**Colton, Joseph H.** Colton's township map of Wisconsin. New York, 1855.

3781　**Commemorative biographical record of the upper lake region** containing biographical sketches of prominent and representative citizens and many of the early settled families . . . Chicago, 1905.

3782　**Commemorative biographical record of the upper Wisconsin counties** of Waupaca, Portage, Wood, Marathon, Lincoln, Oneida, Vilas, Langlade, and Shawano . . . Chicago, 1895.
Mug book.

3783　**Commemorative biographical record of the west shore of Green Bay, Wisconsin,** including the counties of Brown, Oconto, Marinette, and Florence . . . Chicago, 1896.
Mug book.

3784　**D.A.R. Wisconsin.** Roster: Revolutionary War ancestors . . . 1891–1964. [Port Washington, Wisc.: D.A.R., 1965?]

3785　**Delgado, David J.** Guide to the Wisconsin state archives. Madison, Wisc.: State Historical Soc., 1966.

3786　**Frank, Louis F.** German-American pioneers in Wisconsin and Michigan: the Frank-Kerler letters, 1849–64. Transl. from the German by M. Wolff. Ed. . . . by Harry H. Anderson. Milwaukee, Wisc.: Milwaukee County Historical Soc., 1971.
Transl. of *Pionierjahre der deutsch-amerikanischen Familien Frank-Kerler in Wisconsin und Michigan,* but considers Germans in general in the 2 states.

3787 **Gard, Robert E., and Sorden, L. G.** The romance of Wisconsin place names. New York: October House, 1968.

3788 **Gleason, Margaret.** Printed resources for general searching in Wisconsin: a selective bibliography. Detroit, Mich.: Detroit Soc. for Genealogical Research, 1964.
Very good; comprehensive.

3789 **Gregory, John G.** Southeastern Wisconsin: a history of old Milwaukee county . . . 4v. Chicago, 1932.
v.3-4 biographical.

3790 —— Southwestern Wisconsin: a history of old Crawford county. 4v. Chicago, 1932.
v.3-4 biographical.

3791 —— West central Wisconsin. A history . . . 4v. Chicago, 1933.
v.3-4 biographical.

3792 **Historical Records Survey.** County government in Wisconsin: inventory. 3v. Madison, Wisc., 1942.

3793 —— Directory of Catholic churches in Wisconsin. Madison, Wisc., 1942.

3794 —— Directory of churches and religious organizations in Wisconsin. Madison, Wisc., 1941.

3795 —— Guide to church vital statistics records in Wisconsin. Madison, Wisc., 1942.

3796 —— Guide to public vital statistics records in Wisconsin. Madison, Wisc., 1941.

3797 —— Inventory of county archives of Wisconsin. 15v. Madison, Wisc., 1939-42.
Only the following numbers were published: 3 (Barron), 6 (Buffalo), 9 (Chippewa), 10 (Clark), 16 (Douglas), 17 (Dunn), 18 (Eau Claire), 22 (Grant), 27 (Jackson), 32 (La Crosse), 37 (Marathon), 41 (Monroe), 43 (Oneida), 46 (Pepin), and 48 (Polk). Unpublished material deposited in State Historical Society, Madison, Wisc.

3798 —— Inventory of the church archives of Wisconsin. 9v. Madison, Wisc., 1938-42.
Evangelical Lutheran Synod of Missouri and other states; Protestant Episcopal Church, Roman Catholic Church (and several other smaller denominations).

3799 —— Wisconsin territorial papers: county ser. 5v. Madison, Wisc., 1941.
Crawford, Iowa and St. Croix counties.

3800 **History of northern Wisconsin . . .** Chicago, 1881.
Many biographical sketches.

3801 **Hixson (W. W.) and Co.** Plat book of Wisconsin. Rockford, Ill. [1934].
Outline map of state, highway map of each county, followed by township maps, several to a page. Also called *Atlas of the state of Wisconsin*. Hixson also publishes other Wisconsin plat books.

3802 **Huffman, A. O.** Biographical sketches of old settlers and prominent people of Wisconsin. v.1 (all pub.). Waterloo, Wisc., 1899.

3803 **Love, William De L.** Wisconsin in the War of the Rebellion: a history of all regiments and batteries . . . Chicago, 1866.

3804 **Nelke, David I.** The Columbian biographical dictionary of the U.S.: Wisconsin volume. Chicago, 1895.

3805 **Oehlerts, Donald E.** Guide to Wisconsin newspapers, 1833-1957. Madison, Wisc.: State Historical Soc. of Wisconsin, 1958.

3806 **Quaife, Milo M.** Wisconsin: its history and its people. 4v. Chicago, 1924.
v.3-4 biographical.

3807 **Quiner, Edwin B.** The military history of Wisconsin: a record of the war . . . for the Union . . . regimental histories—sketches of distinguished officers—rolls—etc. Chicago, 1866.

3807a **Rusk, Jeremiah M.** Roster of Wisconsin volunteers, War of the Rebellion, 1861-65. 2v. Chicago, 1886.

3808 **Schlinkert, Leroy.** Subject bibliography of Wisconsin history. Madison, Wisc., 1947.

3809 **Smith, Alice E.** Guide to the manuscripts of the Wisconsin State Historical Society. Madison, Wisc., 1944.

3810 ———— ———— Supplement 1. By Josephine L. Harper and S. G. Smith. Madison, Wisc.: The Society, 1957.

3811 ———— ———— Supplement 2. By Josephine L. Harper. Madison, Wisc.: The Society, 1966.

3812 ———— The history of Wisconsin. v.1- . Madison, Wisc.: State Historical Soc. of Wisconsin, 1973- (in progress).
Scheduled for publication 1973-78. v.1, from exploration to statehood; v.2, 1848-73; v.3, 1873-93; v.4, 1893-1915; v.5, 1915-40; v.6, 1940-65.
Destined to be definitive work, and therefore of considerable benefit to genealogists.

3813 **Snyder, Van Vechten and Co.** Historical atlas of Wisconsin, embracing complete state and county maps, city and village plats, together with separate state and county histories. Milwaukee, Wisc., 1878.

3814 **Soldiers' and citizens' album of biographical record (of Wisconsin),** containing personal sketches of army men and citizens prominent in loyalty to the United States. 2v. Chicago, 1888-90.

3815 **State Historical Society of Wisconsin. Collections.** 21v., 1855-1915. Madison, Wisc.
v.21 is index for v.1-20. Valuable because of the historical documents, memoirs, and reminiscences from early northwest territory.

3816 ———— Dictionary of Wisconsin biography. Madison, Wisc.: The Society, 1960.

3817 ———— Wisconsin Domesday book: town studies. *Wisconsin State Historical Soc. publ.,* v.1. 1v. (all pub). Madison, Wisc., 1924.

3818 **Titus, William A.** History of the Fox River Valley, Lake Winnebago and the Green Bay region. 3v. Chicago, 1930.
v.3 biographical.

3819 **United States biographical dictionary and portrait gallery of eminent and self-made men.** New York, 1877.

3820 **Usher, Ellis B.** Wisconsin: its history and biography, 1848-1913. 8v. Chicago, 1914.
v.4-8 biographical.

3821 **Wisconsin. Adjutant General's Office.** Wisconsin volunteers, War of the Rebellion, 1861-65, arranged alphabetically. Madison, Wisc., 1914.
Updated edition from 1886 printed, compiled in 1895-99.

3822 **Wisconsin families;** a quarterly published by the Wisconsin Genealogical Society, 1940-41. The Society was incorporated as the Wisconsin State Genealogical Society, which now publishes a newsletter *(see* no.3825). Milwaukee, Wisc.: The Society, 1940-41.
Much information on early Wisconsin pioneers. Only 4 issues pub.

3823 **Wisconsin gazetteers,** containing the names, location . . . of the counties, cities, towns, villages, post offices and settlements, 1853-1927/8. Early editions by John W. Hunt; later editions called *Wisconsin state gazetteers.*

3824 **Wisconsin helper.** v.1-7, 1967-74. Milwaukee, Wisc.: Janlen Enterprises, West Allis, Wis.
Quarterly. Ceased in 1974.

3825 **Wisconsin State Genealogical Society newsletter.** v.1- , 1954- . Milwaukee, Wisc.: The Society.

3826 ——— Index. v.1–10. Milwaukee, Wisc.: The Society, 1972.
Cemetery records, vital statistics, church records, etc.

3827 **Wisconsin territory:** territorial census for 1836. In *Wisconsin State Historical Soc. collections,* v.13, 1895.
Brown, Crawford, Iowa, and Milwaukee counties.

## WYOMING

Settled ca. 1834; entered Union 1890

*Wyoming State Archives and Historical Dept., Cheyenne*

3828 **Annals of Wyoming.** v.1– , 1923– . Cheyenne, Wyo.: State Archives and Historical Dept.
Some genealogy.

3829 **Bartlett, Ichabod S.** History of Wyoming. 4v. Chicago, 1918.
v.2–4 biographical.

3830 **Beard, Frances B.** Wyoming from territorial days to the present. 3v. Chicago, 1933.
v.2–3 biographical.

3831 **Chaffin, Lorah B.** Sons of the west; biographical account of early day Wyoming. Caldwell, Ind., 1941.

3832 **Colonial Dames of America. Wyoming.** Pioneer biographies . . . 2v. n.p., 1959–62.
v.2 has title: *Brides of the open range.*

3833 **Historical encyclopedia of Wyoming.** 2v. Cheyenne, Wyo.: Wyoming Historical Inst., 1970.
Mug book.

3834 **Historical Records Survey.** Guide to public vital statistics records. Cheyenne, Wyo., 1941.

3835 ——— Guide to vital statistics records in Wyoming: church archives. Preliminary ed. Cheyenne, Wyo., 1942.

3836 ——— Inventory of county archives of Wyoming. 6v. Cheyenne, Wyo., 1938–41.
Only the following numbers were published: 1 (Goshen), 11 (Laramie), 12 (Lincoln), 15 (Park), 16 (Platte), and 19 (Sweetwater). Unpublished material deposited in State Library, Cheyenne, Wyo.

3837 **Hixson (W. W.) and Co.** Atlas of Wyoming. Rockford, Ill. [1933?].
Cover: *Plat book of the state of Wyoming.*

3838 **Progressive men of Wyoming.** Chicago, 1903.
Biographies of earlier prominent men.

3839 **U.S. Census Office.** 9th census, 1870. Census of Wyoming, 1870. n.p., 1925.
1st census of Wyoming, copied by members of the D.A.R.

3840 ——— 10th census, 1880. 1880 census of Wyoming territory. Cheyenne, Wyo., 1927. Copied by Cora M. Beach.

3841 **Urbanek, Mae (Bobb).** Wyoming place names. Boulder, Colo., 1967.

# LATIN AMERICA

Mrs. Rudecinda Lo Buglio, Janesville, Calif.
Mrs. Nadine M. Vasquez, Carmichael, Calif.

☩ Under this heading will be found general works pertaining to Latin America, and works which concern the separate countries of Latin America. Heraldic works will be found under Heraldry, no.5082–87.

## General Reference

**3842    Áparicio y Áparicio, Edgar J.**
Genealogical research in Mexico and central America. *World Conference on Records and Genealogical Seminar paper,* area F-15b. Salt Lake City: L.D.S., 1969.

**3843    Bancroft, Hubert H.** History of central America. 3v. 1882–87. Repr. New York: McGraw Hill, 1967.

Researchers should read this work before embarking on genealogical work regardless of which country in Latin America being researched.

**3844    Boyd-Bowman, Peter.** Indice geobiográfico de cuarenta mil pobladores Españoles de América en el siglo XVI. v.1– , 1964– (in progress). Bogotá, Colombia, [and elsewhere].

Excellent lists of colonizers extracted from primary records. Includes parents' names where known; place of origin, date of arrival, etc. Pertains to western hemisphere. v.1, 1493–1519; v.2, 1520–39.

**3845    Chapman, Charles E.** Catalogue of materials in the Archive General de Indias for the History of the Pacific Coast and the American Southwest. Berkeley, Calif., 1919. Available from Univ. Microfilms, Ann Arbor, Mich.

Archive numbering system is obsolete but valuable as reference tool, especially if personal visit to Bancroft Library, Berkeley, Calif., is not possible for viewing the film.

**3846    Enciclopedia universal ilustrada Europeo-Américana.** 70v. and appendixes 10v. Madrid, 1907?–33.

Contains information not generally found anywhere else which will aid genealogical researchers in Spanish America.

**3847    Gosnell, Charles F.** Spanish personal names: principles governing their formation and use which may be pre-

254

sented as a help for catalogers and bibliographers. 1938. Repr. Detroit, Mich.: Blaine Ethridge Books, 1971.
Comprehensive survey of the principles used in establishing Spanish surnames.

**3848 Haggard, Juan Villasana,** and **McLean, M. D.** Handbook for translators of Spanish historical documents. Austin, Tex.: Archives Collections, Univ. of Texas, 1941.

**3849 Hammond, George P.** A guide to the manuscript collections of the Bancroft Library. v.2: Mexican and central American manuscripts. Berkeley, Calif.: Univ. of California Pr., 1972.

**3850 Harrison, John P.** Guide to materials on Latin America in the National Archives. Washington, D.C.: The Archives, 1961.

**3851 Hill, Roscoe R.** The national archives of Latin America: Cambridge, Mass.: Harvard Univ. Pr., 1945.

**3852 The Hispanic Society of America.** Catalogue of the library. 10v. Boston: G. K. Hall, 1962.
Gives a good listing of reference materials for Latin American research.

**3853 Icaza, Francisco A. de.** Diccionario autobiográfico de conquistadores y pobladores de la Nueva España. 2v. Madrid, 1923.

**3854 Jenkins, Myra E.** Tracing Spanish-American pedigrees in the southwestern United States. Pt.1. New Mexico, Texas and Colorado. *World Conference on Records and Genealogical Seminar paper,* area F-14a. Salt Lake City: L.D.S., 1969. Pt.2, *see* Temple, no.3866.

**3855 Jones, Cecil K.** Hispanic American bibliographies. Baltimore, 1922.

**3856 Lohmann, Villena Guillermo.** Genealogical research in South America. *World Conference on Records and Genealogical Seminar paper,* area F-16. Salt Lake City: L.D.S., 1969.

**3857 Maduell, Charles R.** The romance of Spanish surnames. New Orleans, La., 1967.
Helpful finding aid. Spelling of names gives probable location of origin in Europe. 1,500 of the most prominent Spanish surnames.

**3858 Magdaleno, Redondo Ricardo.** Títulos de Indias. Valladolid, Mexico: Archivo de Simancas, 1954.
Lists appointments of officials, civil, military, ecclesiastical, in Spanish America.

**3859 Marchant, Alexander.** Boundaries of the Latin American republics: an annotated list of documents, 1493–1943. Washington, D.C., 1944.

**3860 Mörner, Magnus.** Race mixture in the history of Latin America. Boston: Little, Brown, 1967.
In-depth study; not genealogical, but many definitions. Assists in the understanding of the problems in various areas and in terms used in censuses and register records.

**3861 Peña Camara, José M. de la.** A list of Spanish residencias in the Archives of the Indies, 1516–1775 . . . Washington, D.C., 1955.

**3862 Rubio y Moreno, Luis.** Pasajeros a Indias. Catálogo metodológico de la informaciones y licencias de los que allí pasaron, existentes en el Archivo General de Indias. Siglo primero de la colonización de América, 1492–1592. 2v. Madrid, 1930.
List of passengers that came to America during the years 1492–1592, with personal details.

**3863 Spain, Archivo General de Indias.** Catálogo de pasajeros a Indias durante los siglos XVI, XVII y XVIII. Madrid, 1930.
List of names of the people who came to America during the 16th–18th centuries; with brief biographical information.

**3864 Spanish (American) genealogical helper.** v.1, no. 1– , 1971– . Harbor City, Calif.: Augustan Soc.
*Cuestiones?* v.1, 1971–72 (12 issues); *Spanish genealogical helper,* v.2, 1972 (3 issues); v.3, no. 1–2 included in *Augustan*

*omnibus* volumes (*see* no.105). Resumes original numbering with no.17 in 1974, and published separately thereafter.
Good bibliography, queries, history.

3865    **Taplin, Glen W.** Middle American governors. Metuchen, N.J.: Scarecrow Pr., 1972.
Guide to leaders of middle America (Panama, Mexico, Guatemala, El Salvador, British Honduras, Honduras, Costa Rica, Nicaragua) from earliest times to present.

3866    **Temple, Thomas W., II.** Tracing Spanish-American pedigrees in the southwestern United States. Pt.2, California and Arizona. *World Conference on Records and Genealogical Seminar paper,* area F-14b. Salt Lake City: L.D.S., 1969.
Pt.1, New Mexico, Texas and Colorado, *see* no.3854.

3867    **Tibon, Gutierre.** Onomástica hispanoamericana: indice de siete mil nombres y apellidos castellanos, vascos, árabes, judíos, italianos, indoamericanos, etc., y un índice toponímico. Mexico, 1961.
Listing of names and their origin.

3868    **Toro, Josefina del.** Bibliography of the collective biography of Spanish America. 1938. Repr. Detroit, Mich.: Blaine Ethridge Books, 1971.

3868a   **Who's who in Latin America:** a biographical dictionary of notable living men and women of Latin America. 7v. 3rd ed. 1945–51. Repr. 2v. Detroit, Mich.: Blaine Ethridge Books, 1971.
v.1: Mexico, central America, Panama, Colombia, Ecuador, and Venezuela, Cuba, Dominican Republic, and Haiti; v.2: Brazil, Bolivia, Chile, Peru, Argentina, Paraguay, and Uruguay.

## Individual Countries

ARGENTINE REPUBLIC

3869    **Cutolo, Vicente O.** Nuevo diccionario biográfico argentino, 1750–1930. v.1– , 1968– . Buenos Aires: Editorial Elche.

3870    **Genealogía.** no.1– , 1942– . Buenos Aires: Inst. Argentino Ciencias Genealógicas.

3871    **Instituto Argentino de Ciencias Genealógicas.** Boletín interno. no.1– , 1969– . Buenos Aires: Instituto.

3872    **Levillier, Roberto.** Biografías de conquistadores de la Argentina en el signo XVI; Tucumán. 2nd ed. Madrid, 1933.

3873    **Morales Guiñazú, Fernando.** Genealogía de los conquistadores de Cuyo y fundadores de Mendoz. Buenos Aires, 1932.

3874    **Muzzio, Julio A.** Diccionario histórico y biográfico de la République Argentina. 2v. Buenos Aires, 1920.
Covers all periods; primarily biographical.

3875    **Otárola, Alfredo J.** Antecedentes históricos y genealógicos: el conquistador don Domingo Martínez Irala, símbolo y espina dorsal de la conquista del Río de la Plata, precursor y fundador de la América del Sur, excepto Chile; su numerosa y distinguida descendencia. Buenos Aires: Casa Pardo, 1967.
Biographies, genealogies, coats of arms and good bibliography. 16th century.

3876    ———— Cuñas de ilustres linajes; descendencia de Domingo Martínez de Irala y otras de la época de la conquista, orígenes de primitivas dinastías medievales. Buenos Aires: Casa Pardo [1970].
16th-century genealogy for Argentine Republic and Spain. Good bibliography.

3877    ———— Estudios genealógicos sobre antiguos apellidos del Río de La Plata y remotos orígenes del patriarcado argentino. Buenos Aires: Casa Pardo [1969].

3878    **Udaundo, Enrique.** Diccionario biográfico argentino . . . Buenos Aires, 1938.
3,300 biographies, 1880–1920.

3879    ———— Diccionario biográfico colonial argentino. Obra prologada por G. A. Alfaro . . . Buenos Aires, 1945.

Covers colonial period from the discovery and conquest of the Rio de la Plata to 1810. Companion volume to no.3878.

**3880** ——— Grandes ombres de nuestra patria. Enl. ed. 3v. Buenos Aires: Editorial Pleamar [1968].

BRAZIL

**3881 Anuário genealógico Latino:** revista genealógica latina. v.1- , 1949- . São Paulo.

**3882 Athayde, J. B. de.** Familias fluminenses. Juiz de Flora, Brasil, Esdeva, 1971- .
Rio de Janeiro genealogy.

**3883 Franco, Francisco de A. Carvalho.** Nobiliário colonial. 2nd ed. São Paulo, 1941?
Deals with early Portuguese nobility in colonial Brazil.

**3883a Instituto de Estudos Genealógicos.** Revista. no.1- , 1937- . São Paulo: Institute.

**3884 Instituto genealógico Brasileiro.** Guía das publicaçoes, 1939-46. Ed. by Carlos Fouquet. São Paulo, 1947.
Guide to the publications of the Brazilian Institute of Genealogy; designed for those interested in central and South American genealogy.

**3885 Revista genealogica Brasileira.** Instituto Genealogico Brasileiro. v.1- , 1948- . São Paulo: Institute.
Published in Portuguese; scholarly and useful for researchers into south and central American family histories. Still being published (?).

**3886 Rheingantz, Carlos G.** Primeiras famílias do Rio de Janeiro, séculos XVI e XVII. Rio de Janeiro: Livraria Brasiliana, 1965- .
v.1, A-E (no more pub.?). First families of Rio de Janeiro, 16th and 17th centuries.

CHILE

**3887 Espejo, Juan L.** Nobiliario de la Capitanía General de Chile. Santiago: Editorial Andrés Bello, 1967.
Genealogy and heraldry. Coats of arms.

**3888 Fernández-Pradel, Pedro X.** Linajes Vascos y Montañeses en Chile. Santiago de Chile, 1930.

**3889 Figueroa, Virgilio.** Diccionario histórico, biográfico y bibliográfico de Chile, 1800-1930. 5v. in 4. Santiago, 1925-31.
Title varies. Arranged alphabetically by family name and then by seniority in the family, rather than alphabetically.

**3890 Medina, José T.** Diccionarío biográfico colonial de Chile. Santiago, 1906.

**3891** ——— ——— Muestras de errores y defectos del "Diccionario..." por Luis F. Prieto. Santiago, 1907.
Biographical dictionary covering from the age of discovery through the 18th century, with errors, etc., corrected and noted.

**3892 Roa y Ursua, Luis de.** El reyno de Chile, 1535-1810. Estudio histórico, genealógico y biográfico. Valladolid, Mexico, 1945.

**3893 Thayer Ojeda, Tomas.** Los conquistadores de Chile. 3v. Santiago de Chile, 1908-13.
Repr. from *Anales de la Univ. de Chile,* v.121-22, 125-26, 130-32.

COLOMBIA

**3894 Florez de Ocaríz, Juan.** Genealogías del Nuevo Reinado de Granada. Bogotá: Editorial Kelly, 1955.
List of personalities related with the history of Colombia.

**3895 Ospina, Joaquín.** Diccionario biográfico y bibliográfico de Colombia desde la conquista hasta nuestros dias. 3v. Bogotá, 1927-39.
Covers Spanish conquest to 20th century.

## CUBA

**3896** Calcagno, Francisco. Diccionario biográfico Cubano. New York, 1878–84.

**3896a** Gannett, Henry. A gazetteer of Cuba. *U.S. Geological Survey bull.* 192. Washington, D.C., 1902.

**3897** Nieto y Cortadellas, Rafael. Dignidades nobiliarias en Cuba. Madrid, 1954.
Pedigrees of the noble families of Cuba.

**3898** Suaréz de Tangil y de Angelo, F. Nobiliario Cubano. Las grandes familias isleñas, por el Conde de Vallellano. Prólogo póstumo del Excmo. Sr. Marqués de Laurensin. 2v. Madrid, n.d. [1929].
A selective list of families belonging to the most noble and distinguished families of Cuba, with a detailed account concerning the family and their descendants. Coats of arms.

## DOMINICAN REPUBLIC

**3899** Garcia, José G. Rasgos biográficos de Domínicanos célebres. Santo Domingo: Ed. del Caribe, 1971.
Collection of biographies of distinguished personalities of the Dominican Republic.

**3900** Larrazábal Blanco, Carlos. Familias dominicanas. Santo Domingo: Acad. Dominicana de la Historia, 1967– (in progress).
Biographical compilation of the families of the Dominican Republic; brief information; gives descendants, from 16th century to present.

**3901** Martínez, Rufino. Diccionario biográfico-histórico dominicano, 1821–1930. Santo Domingo: Editora de la Univ. Autónoma de Santo Domingo, 1971.
Alphabetical listing of names of personalities in the history of the Dominican Republic.

**3902** Rodríguez Demorizi, Emilio. Próceres de la restauracíon noticias biográficas. Santo Domingo: Ed. del Caribe, 1963.
Alphabetical listing with brief biographical data of distinguished personalities of the Dominican Republic, during the War of Restauration.

## ECUADOR

**3903** Borrero Crespo, Maximiliano. Orígenes cuencanos. 2v. Cuenca, Ecuador, 1960.
Genealogy of Cuenca, Ecuador city; good bibliography.

**3904** Pérez Marchant, Braulio. Diccionario biográfico del Ecuador. Quito, 1928.
Covers all periods, but primarily 19th century.

## GUATEMALA

**3905** Academia Guatemalteca de Estudios Genealógicos, Heráldicos e Históricos. Revista. no.1– , 1967– . Guatemala: Academia.

**3906** Genealogical Society of the Church of Jesus Christ of Latter-day Saints. Major genealogical record sources in Guatemala. *Research paper,* ser.H, no.1. Salt Lake City: L.D.S., 1970.

## MEXICO

**3907** Almada, Francisco R. Diccionario de historia, geografía y biografía Sonorenses. Chihuahua, México, 1952.
Most dependable and extensive work on Sonora, Mexico.

**3908** Áparicio y Áparicio, Edgar J. Genealogical research in Mexico and central America. *World Conference on Records and Genealogical Seminar paper,* area F-15b. Salt Lake City: L.D.S., 1969.

**3909** Archivo General de la Nación. Boletín. ser.1, v.1–30; ser.2, v.1– , 1930– . México: Archivo.
Contains valuable genealogical information in the form of census records, family

histories, and since 1931 it has listed extracts of land records held by Mexican Archives. Since 1946 extract of records of the Provincias Internas section of the Archives.

**3910  Bravo Ugarte, José.** Diócesis y obispos de la Iglesia Mexicana, 1519–1965. 2nd ed. México: Editorial Jus, 1965.
Guide to formation of the various archdioceses of Mexico; essential for determining where to look for ecclesiastical records held in custody of the bishop of the area, such as dispensations for marriage, etc.

**3911  Cavazos Garza, Israel.** Cedulario autobiográfico y conquistadores de nuevo León. México: Univ. de Nuevo León, 1964.
Much genealogy, as well as history.

**3912  Dahl, Torsten.** Linajes en México. México: Casa Editora de Genealogía Ibero Americana. 1967– (in progress).
Over 100 genealogies of Mexican families in v.1.

**3913  Diccionario Porrúa de historia, biografía y geografía de México.** 2v. 3rd ed. México: Edit Porrúa, 1972.

**3914  Fernández de Recas, Guillermo S.** Cacicazgos y nobiliario indígena de la Nueva España. México: Inst. Bibliográfico Mexicano, 1961.
Includes a selected list of native families and their descendants. Coats of arms.

**3915  ———** Mayorazgos de la Nueva España. México: Inst. Bibliográfico Mexicano, 1965.
A selected list of personalities of Mexico during the colonial days, with extensive documentation concerning each family and their descendants.

**3916  ———** Real y Pontificia Universidad de México. Medicina; nómina de bachilleres. licenciados y doctores, 1607–1780; y guía de méritos y servicios, 1763–1828 ... México: Biblioteca Nacional, Inst. Bibliográfico Mexicana, 1960.
Roster of graduates of the University of Mexico.

**3917  Garcia de Miranda, Enriqueta,** and **Fálcon de Gyves, Z.** Atlas: nuevo atlas Porrúa de la República Mexicana. México: Edit: Porrúa, 1972.
In addition to maps and statistics on all states and territories of Mexico, the atlas includes many topical and historical maps of Mexico.

**3918  Genealogical Society of the Church of Jesus Christ of Latter-day Saints.** Major genealogical record sources in Mexico. *Research paper,* ser.H, no.2. Salt Lake City: L.D.S., 1970.

**3919  Greenleaf, Richard E.,** and **Meyer, M. C.** Research in Mexican history; topics, methodology, sources and a practical guide to field research. Lincoln, Neb.: Univ. of Nebraska Pr., 1973.
Complete manual on how to do research in Mexico, including information on the Archivo General de la Nacion, libraries, newspaper collections, museums, and specialized archives.

**3920  Iguiníz, Juan B.** Bibliografía biográfia Mexicana ... v.1 (all pub.). Enl. ed. of 1930. México: Univ. Nacional, Autónoma de México, Inst. de Investigacíones Históricas, 1969.

**3921  El Libro de la Tasaciones de Pueblos de la Nueva España, siglo XVI.** Prologue by Francisco G. de Cossió. México, 1952.
Assessment of towns of New Spain in 16th century. Contains valuable genealogical data.

**3922  Liebman, Seymour B.** A guide to Jewish references in the Mexican colonial era, 1521–1821. Philadelphia: Univ. of Pennsylvania Pr., 1964.

**3923  ———** The Jews in New Spain: faith, flame, and inquisition. Coral Gables, Fla.: Univ. of Miami Pr., 1970.

**3824  Lo Buglio, Rudecinda L.** A Baja California bibliography. In *The Spanish American genealogical helper,* v.3, no.3, 1974.

Includes only the available books (in print) with sources of supply; compiled with the genealogist in mind (by a genealogist).

3925    **Martínez, Pablo L.** Guía familiar de Baja California 1700-1900. (Vital statistics of Lower California.) México: Edit Baja California, 1965.
Contains over 900p. of primary records: birth registrations, baptisms, marriages and deaths, from the extant ecclesiastical and civil registers of the peninsula. Also many individual genealogies. Text in Spanish with a short guide to easy comprehension.

3926    **O'Gorman, Edmundo.** Historia de las divisiones territoriales de Mexico. 4th ed. México: Editorial Porrúa, 1968.
9 maps, 2 calendars of events. Complete history of boundaries of various areas and states of Mexico under Spanish rule, as well as boundaries of independence. Essential to determine where to seek genealogical records. Of value to researcher of California, Arizona, New Mexico, and Texas history as well. Original title: *Breve historia de las divisiones territoriales.*

3927    **Ortega y Pérez Gallardo, Ricardo.** Historia genealógica de las familias más Antiguas de México. 3v. 3rd ed. corr. México, 1908-10.
Coats of arms.

3928    **Peral, Miguel A.** Diccionario biográfico mexicano. 2v. and apéndice. México, 1944.
Covers 544-1944. Some discrepancies, and not always complete data.

3929    **Rouaix, Pastor.** Diccionario geográfico, histórico y biográfico del estado de Durango. Mexico, 1946.

3930    **Sosa, Francisco.** Biografías de Mexicanos distinguidos. Mexico, 1884.
Covers all periods.

3931    **Vásquez, Nadine M.** Basic research in the parish and civil registers of Mexico. In *The Spanish American genealogical helper,* v.2, no.1, July-Aug., 1972.

PERU

3932    **Crespo Pozo, Jose S.** Linajes de Galicia en el Peru. Bogotá, Colombia, 1953.
Of considerable interest to Spanish genealogists and heraldists. Well-documented account of close connection between Galician and Peruvian families; with coats of arms.

3933    **Instituto Peruano de Investigaciones Genealogicas.** Revista. v.1- , 1946- . Lima: Instituto.

3934    **Mendiburu, Manuel de.** Diccionario histórico-biográfico del Perú. 2nd ed. . . . Por E. San Cristoval. 11v. Lima, 1931-34.

3935    ———— Apendice al diccionario histórico-biográfico del Peru. Por Evaristo San Cristoval. 4v. Lima, 1935.

URUGUAY

3936    **Apolant, Juan A.** Génesis de la familia Uruguaya; los habitantes de Montevideo en sus primeros 40 años, filiaciones, ascendencias, entronques, descendencias. Montevideo: Inst. Histórico y Geografico del Uruguay, [1966].
Repr. of 1937 ed.

VENEZUELA

3937    **Capriles, Alejandro M.** Coronas de Castilla en Venezuela. Madrid, 1967.
Coats of arms, genealogical tables; excellent work on the nobility of Venezuela.

3938    **Iturriza Guillen, Carlos.** Algunas familias caraqueñas. 2v. Caracas, 1967.

3938a    **El Libro parroquial mas antiguo de Caracas.** Caracas: Concejo Municipal del Distrito Federal, 1968.
Registers of births, marriages and deaths, 1579-1615.

# CANADA

*Library of Parliament, Ottawa*
*Public Archives of Canada, Ottawa (Miss G. D. Beauvais)*
*National Archives, Quebec (Mr. Roland-J. Auger)*
*Toronto Public Library*

## General

3939 **Adam, Graeme M.** Prominent men of Canada . . . A collection of persons distinguished in professional, political life . . . Toronto, 1892.

3939a **Allaire, Jean B. A.** Dictionnaire biographique du clergé canadien-français. 2v. Montréal, 1908–10.
There were 2 supplements, in 1910 and 1911.

*3940 **American Association of State and Local History, Nashville.** Directory of historical societies and agencies in the United States and Canada. 1956– . Nashville, Tenn.: The Association.
Published biennially. Gives names, addresses and pertinent information about any historical society of consequence and state archives.

3941 **Armstrong, George H.** The origin and meanings of place names in Canada. Toronto, 1930.

*3942 **Atherton, James J.** Records of genealogical interest in the Public Archives of Canada. Salt Lake City: L.D.S., 1969.

3943 **Bergeron, Roger,** and **Bergeron, Jean.** Parish records of marriages in French Canada. Montreal: The Compilers, 1972– (in progress).
13v. by end of 1974. Good data.

3944 **Bibaud, Maximilien.** Dictionnaire historique des hommes illustrés du Canada et de l'Amérique. Montréal, 1857.

3944a **Bibliographia Canadiana.** Ed. by Claude Thibault. Toronto: Longman, 1973.

Comprehensive bibliography up to 1970; 25,660 items, books and articles.

**3945** **Bibliographie de généalogies et histoire de familles.** In *Rapport de l'archiviste de Québec,* 1940–41, pp.95–332.

**3946** **Biographies canadiennes-français.** 1920–37, 1948, 1952, 1957, 1965, 1968/9– . Ed. by J. A. Fortier and R. Ouimet. Montréal: Public Archives.

**3947** **Bogdan, F.** Dictionary of Ukrainian surnames in Canada: Winnipeg: Onomastic Commission of UVAN and Canadian Inst. of Onomastic Sciences, 1974.
Added title: *Slovnyk ukräins'kykh prizvyschch u Kanadi.* Has bibliographies.

**3948** **Boston Public Library.** Canadian manuscripts in the Boston Public Library: a descriptive catalog. Boston: G. K. Hall, 1971.
Canadiana from the 17th century to the present day. Detailed index by person, place, and subject.

**3949** **Bulletin des recherches historiques, archéologie, histoire, biographie** . . .
Organe de la Société des Études Historiques. v.1–69, 1895–1967. Lévis, Quebec: The Society.
Has 4v. index, 1895–1925, pub. in 1926. Excellent for biographies.

**\*3950** **Bullinger's Postal and shippers guide for the United States and Canada.** Westwood, N.J.: Bullinger's Guides, 1897– .
Title varies. One in every decade needed. Good for finding very small places, since it is not restricted to places with post offices.

**3951** **Campbell, Frank W.** Canada post offices, 1755–1895. Boston: Quarterman Pub., 1972.
Primarily for philatelists, but of considerable value to genealogists since it is a catalog of all post offices for 140 years.

**3952** **Canada. Board on Geographical Names.** Gazetteer of Canada. v.1–10, 1952–62; suppl.1–2, 1963–4. Ottawa: Queen's Pr.

**3952a** **Canada Public Archives.** Checklist of parish registers. Ottawa: Queen's Printer, 1970.

**3953** ——— ——— Checklists of census returns: New Brunswick (1851–71); Nova Scotia (1871); Ontario (1842–71); Quebec (1825–71). 4v. Ottawa: The Archives, 1963.
List of returns in Manuscript div. Lists counties, townships, parishes, and cities, and towns for which census returns are available and provides microfilm references.

**3954** ——— Manuscript division. General inventory: Manuscripts. v.2– . Ottawa: Public Archives, 1972– (in progress).
v.5 to date, but v.1 has yet to appear in 1974. Some family information.

**\*3955** ——— Tracing your ancestors in Canada. Ottawa: Information Canada, 1972.
French ed.: *À la piste de nos ancêtres au Canada.* Very good coverage of Canadian records. Pub. sporadically.

**3957** **Canadiana.** 1950– . Ottawa: National Library of Canada, 1962– .
Publications of Canadian interest received by the National Library. 1921–49, published in 1959 by Toronto Public Libraries, was entitled, *The Canadian catalogue.* Many genealogical titles included. Now published annually.

**3958** **Casgrain, Henri R.** Biographies canadiennes . . . Montréal, 1897.

**3958a** **Charlesworth, Hector W.** A cyclopaedia of Canadian biography . . . Toronto, 1919.

**3959** **Cochrane, William.** Canadian album: men of Canada . . . 5v. Brantford, Ontario, 1891–96.

**\*3960** **Coderre, John E.** Searching in the Public Archives (of Canada). Ottawa: Ontario Genealogical Soc., 1972.

**3961** **Collet, Mathieu B.** The Catholic missions in Canada: 1721; a profile for genealogy and microhistory, based on a procés verbal by procureur-général Collet; ed. with annotations by Ivanhoe Caron. Index to personal names by Ruth O. Berthelot. Repr. from *Rapport de l'archiviste de la Province de Québec,* 1921–22, pp.261–380. New Orleans, La.: Polyanthos, 1972.

2,700 name index to parishioners of the 65 church missions in early 18th-century Canada, during the time when migration to the French Mississippi valley was at its height. Good for Louisiana and Canada genealogy.

3962 **Comité des anciennes familles, Québec.** Le livre d'or de la noblesse rurale canadienne-française. Québec, 1909.

3963 **[Daniel, François]** Histoire des grandes familles françaises du Canada. Montréal, 1867.
Coats of arms. Much Benoist family material.

3964 ——— Nos gloires nationales; ou, histoire des principales familles du Canada. 2v. Montréal, 1867.

3965 **David, Laurent O.** Souvenirs et biographies, 1870–1910. Montréal, 1911.

*3966 **Davin, Nicholas F.** The Irishman in Canada . . . 1877. Repr. Shannon, Ireland: Irish Univ. Pr., 1969.
Emigration to Canada after Irish famine era. Has never been superseded.

3967 **Dent, John C.** The Canadian portrait gallery . . . 4v. Toronto, 1880–81.

*3967a **Dictionary of Canadian biography.** v.1– . Toronto: Univ. of Toronto Pr., 1966– (in progress).
v.1, 1000–1700; v.2, 1701–40; v.10, 1871–80. One of the great new biographical works.

3968 **Dorland, Arthur G.** The Quakers in Canada: a history. 2nd ed. Toronto: Ryerson Pr., 1968.
Not genealogical, but excellent background material for the genealogist. 1st ed. (1927) was called *A history of the Society of Friends (Quakers) in Canada.*

3968a **Epp, Frank H.** Mennonites in Canada 1786–1920: the history of a separate people. Toronto: Macmillan, 1974.
Much useful information in formative years.

*3969 **French Canadian and Acadian genealogical review.** v.1– , 1968– .
Québec: Centre Canadien des Recherches Généalogiques.
One of the best genealogical periodicals available.

3970 **Gellner, John,** and **Smerek, J.** The Czechs and Slovaks in Canada. Toronto: Univ. of Toronto Pr., 1968.
Very good background and bibliography.

*3971 **Genealogical periodical annual index:** index to genealogical literature appearing in over 150 American, Canadian, and British journals. See no.98.

3972 **Genealogical Society of the Church of Jesus Christ of Latter-day Saints.**
Major genealogical record sources for Canada. *Research paper,* ser.B, no.3. Salt Lake City: L.D.S., 1968.

*3973 **Gingras, Raymond.** Précis de généalogiste amateur. Québec: The Author, 1973.
A good manual with bibliography. Entirely in French.

3974 **Grégoire, Jeanne.** À la recherche de nos ancêtres, guide du généalogiste. Montréal: Soc. Généalogique Canadienne-française, 1957.
Excellent manual.

3975 **Gregory, Winifred.** American newspapers, 1821–1936. A union list of files available in the United States and Canada. New York, 1937.
Brigham (*see* no.8) covers 1690–1820.

3976 **Guillet, Edwin C.** The lives and times of the patriots: an account of the rebellion in Upper Canada, 1837–38, and the patriotic agitation in the United States, 1837–42. Toronto, ca.1938.
Fine appendix of selected documents relative to the patriotic movement; many lists of names, well indexed.

3977 Hale, Richard W. Guide to photocopied historical materials in the United States and Canada. Ithaca, N.Y.: Cornell Univ. Pr. for the American Historical Assoc., [1961].
Badly needs revision and updating.

*3978 Hoogenraad, Maureen. Genealogical sources of the Public Archives of Canada. Ottawa: Ontario Genealogical Soc., 1971.

3979 Institut Généalogique Drouin. Dictionnaire nationale des canadiens-français, 1608–1760. 3v. Montréal: Institut, 1958–65.
Cover: *Complément de l'arbre généalogique de tout Canadiens français.* Much information concerning Quebec.

3980 Kaye, Vladimir J. Early Ukrainian settlements in Canada, 1895–1900. Toronto: Univ. of Toronto Pr., 1964.
Has lists of settlers.

3981 Kerr, Donald G. G. A historical atlas of Canada. 2nd ed. Toronto: Nelson, 1966.

3982 Kuczynski, Robert R. Birth registration and birth statistics in Canada . . . 1930. Repr. Toronto, [1967].
Fine summary of legislation and procedure concerning birth statistics in each of the provinces.

3983 Lasseray, André. Les français sous les treize étoiles 1775–1783. 2v. Paris, 1935.
"French under the 13 stars." Biographical sketches of French participants from official and family records.

3983a Lost in Canada? Canadian-American query exchange. v.1– , 1974– . Sparta, Wisc.: Joy Reisinger (1020 Central Ave., 54656).

3984 Lovell, John. Gazetteer of British North America . . . 6,000 cities, towns and villages . . . 2v. in 1. Montreal, 1873.

3985 Loyalists, *see* no.4014–37.

3987 Markovic, Vladimir. Biographical directory of Americans and Canadians of Croatian descent. v.1–4. San Francisco: R. and E. Research Assoc., 1970–73.
Contains also organizational directory, church and priest directory, newspapers and periodicals.

3988 Massicotte, Edouard Z. (and others). Répertoire des engagements pour l'ouest conservés dans les archives judiciaires de Montréal, 1670–1821. *Rapport de l'Archiviste de la Province de Québec.* 1929–33, 1942–47. 6v. Québec, 1930–47.
Index to enlistments for the west preserved in the judicial records: French-speaking Canadians who went west in connection with the fur trade to Wisconsin, Mississippi, Illinois, ports on the northwest coast, Hudson Bay Co., etc. Excellent data for each person.

*3989 ——— and Roy, R. Armorial du Canada français. 1915–18. Repr. 2v. in 1. Baltimore: G.P.C., 1970.

3990 Le mois généalogique. v.1–12, 1948–60. Montréal: Société Généalogique canadienne-française.
Index for v.1–10, 1948–57 was pub. in 1958.

3991 Morgan, Henry J. The Canadian men and women of the time. Toronto, 1898.

3992 ——— Sketches of celebrated Canadians . . . Toronto, 1865.

3992a New-York Historical Society. Muster and pay rolls of the War of the Revolution, 1775–83. 2v. *Collections of the New-York Historical Soc. Fund ser.,* v.47–48, 1914–15. New York, 1916.
v.1 contains data on Canadian troops.

3993 Olivier, Reginald L. Your ancient Canadian family ties. Logan, Utah: Everton Pub., 1972.
Short biographies of Canadian settlers, with full details. Greatest part is of French Canadian families or families from parts of France. Many errors taken word for word from Tanguay (no.4003).

**3994 Pontbriand, Benoit.** M. Pontbriand has compiled many lists of Canadian marriage licenses in the 17th–19th centuries, as early as 1618 and as late as 1973. To date 100v. of marriage information have been issued. From the Author, 2390 Marie-Victorian, Quebec.

**3995 Reaman, George E.** The trail of the Huguenots in Europe, the United States, South Africa and Canada. 2nd rev. ed. Baltimore: G.P.C., 1972.
Canadian ed. pub. in 1963. Mainly devoted to the United States and Canada. Addenda and corrigenda by Milton Rubincam.

**3996 Roy, Antoine.** Bibliographie de généalogies et histoires de familles. *Rapport de l'archiviste de la Province de Québec* 1940-41, pp.95–332. Québec, 1941.

**3997 Scotland. Record Office.** Source list of manuscripts relating to U.S.A. and Canada in private archives preserved in the Scottish Record Office. *List and Index Soc. Special ser.*, v.3. London: The Society, 1970.

**3998 Smith, Clifford N.** German-American genealogical research monographs, v.1– . Thomson, Ill.: Heritage House, 1973– (in progress).
Lists mercenaries and deserters from German regiments who remained in the U.S. and Canada after the Revolution. For full details, *see* no.536–37.

**3999 Smith, Dwight L. V.** Indians of the United States and Canada. A bibliography. Santa Barbara, Calif.: Clio Pr., 1973.
1,771 abstracts of periodical literature of the last 2 decades.

**4000 Society of American Archivists.** Church archives in the United States and Canada: a bibliography. *See* no. 406.

**\*4001 A standard dictionary of Canadian biography**... 2v. Toronto, 1934–38.
Canadians who died 1875–1937.

**4002 Sulte, Benjamin.** Histoire des canadiens-française 1608–1880. 8v. Montréal, 1882–84.

**\*4003 Tanguay, Cyprien.** Dictionnaire généalogique des familles canadiennes depuis la fondation de la colonie jusqu'à nos jours. 7v. 1871–90. Repr. New York: A.M.S. Press, 1969.
Covers period 1608–1763. Genealogical dictionary of Canadian families. Monumental and definitive work, the result of over 30 years of research. Includes information on the French who moved to New England, the Mississippi valley, and especially Louisiana. Essential, but use with care because of errors.

**\*4004** ——— Complément au dictionnaire généalogique Tanguay. ser.1–3. Montréal: Soc. Généalogique Canadienne-Française, 1957–64.
Its publ. 2, 5, 6. Godbout's *Nos ancêtres au XVIIe siècle* is a reedited ed. of Tanguay, *see* no.4113.

**4005 Todd, Herbert G.** Armory and lineages of Canada and North America; comprising the lineage of prominent and pioneer American and Canadian families with descendants and illustrations. New York, 1918.
Many coats of arms. Bibliography is puzzling: evidently there are seven issues (or rather editions) beginning in 1913 and ending in 1919. Title varies slightly.

**4006 Toronto Public Libraries.** A bibliography of Canadiana; being items in the Public Libraries of Toronto, Canada, relating to the early history and development of Canada. Ed. by Frances M. Staton and M. Tremaine. Toronto, 1934.

**4007** ——— suppl. 1 (all pub.?), 1959 includes Newfoundland items.

**4007a Trudel, Marcel.** La population du Canada en 1663. Montreal: Fides, 1973.
Reconstituted census of Canadian population on 30 June 1663.

**4007b** ——— Le terrier du Saint-Laurent en 1663. Ottawa: Ed. de l'Univ. d'Ottawa, 1973.

Record of all land titles in Canada up to 30 June 1663.

**4007c  Union list of manuscripts in Canadian repositories.** Ottawa: Public Archives of Canada, 1968.
Over 11,000 entries from 124 repositories.

**4008  Union list of serials in libraries of the United States and Canada.** Ed. by Edna B. Titus. 3rd ed. 5v. New York: H. W. Wilson, 1965.

**4009  University of Minnesota Libraries, St. Paul.** Immigrant archives. Inventory of holdings in the University of Minnesota Libraries. St. Paul, Minn.: Univ. of Minnesota, 1973.
Ethnic groups originating in Europe and Middle East. Geographical scope—all of U.S. and Canada, see no.371.

*4010  **Varennes, Kathleen M. de.** Annotated bibliography of genealogical works in the Library of Parliament, with locations in other libraries in Canada. Ottawa: Library of Parliament, 1963.

*4011  **Wallace, William S.** The Macmillan dictionary of Canadian biography. 3rd ed., rev. and enl. Toronto, 1963.
Contains no living persons; best general dictionary of Canadian biography.

**4012  Watters, Reginald E.** A checklist of Canadian literature and background materials, 1628–1960. 2nd rev. ed. Toronto: Univ. of Toronto Pr., 1972.

## Loyalists

✣ Loyalists: those sympathetic to the cause of the British Crown during the American Revolution, rather than that of the revolutionaries. Four-fifths of the settlers in upper Canada (now Ontario) came from the American colonies. The most useful bibliography of printed sources on loyalists in the American Revolution will be found in Greenwood (no.244), pp.440–42.

**4014  Bradley, Arthur G.** Colonial Americans in exile: founders of British Canada. Toronto, 1932.
United Empire loyalists.

**4015  Canniff, William.** History of the settlement of upper Canada (Ontario). 1869. Repr. Belleville, Ont.: Mika Pub., 1971.
Has valuable record of individual loyalists.

**4016  Chadwick, Edward M.** Ontarian families: genealogies of United-Empire-loyalists, and other pioneer families of upper Canada. 2v. 1894–98. Repr. Lambertville, N.J.: Hunterdon House, 1970.
v.1 repr. by Mika Pub., Belleville, Ont., 1971. Contains errors.

**4017  Cruikshank, Ernest A.** Settlement of the United Empire loyalists on the upper St. Lawrence and Bay of Quinto in 1784. A documentary record. 1934. Repr. Toronto: Ontario Historical Soc., 1966.
Transcribed from the Haldimand Papers in the Dominion Archives.

**4018  Fellows, Jo-Ann,** and **Calder, K.** A bibliography of loyalist source material in Canada. In *American Antiquarian Soc. proc.,* v.82, pt.1, pp.67–270.
Invaluable for students of the loyalists. "Loyalist imprints printed in America," by J. E. Mooney appeared in the *Proceedings,* v.84, no.1, pp.105–218, 1972.

**4019  Gilroy, Martin.** Loyalists and land settlement in Nova Scotia: a list. *Public archives of Nova Scotia,* v.4. Halifax, N.S., 1937.
Lists thousands of settlers with dates, locations, acreage, origin and rank.

**4020  Great Britain. Commission appointed to enquire into the losses of American loyalists, 1783–89.** United Empire loyalists: enquiry into the losses and services in consequence of their loyalty; evidence in the Canadian claim. 2v. 2nd report of the Bureau of Archives for the Province of Ontario, 1904. [Toronto, 1905.]

*4021  **Kennedy, Patricia.** How to trace your loyalist ancestors: the use of the loyalist sources in the Public Archives of Canada. Ottawa: Ontario Genealogical Soc., 1971.

4022   Kirk, Robert F., and Kirk, A. L. The exodus of British loyalists (royalists) from the U.S. to Canada, England, the Caribbean and Spanish territories. Salt Lake City: L.D.S., 1969.
Paper given at World Conference on Records, 1968. Excellent data on loyalists in Nova Scotia, New Brunswick, upper and lower Canada. Good bibliography.

*4023   ——— Some references and sources for searching for your ancestors in the province of Ontario. Detroit, Mich.: Detroit Soc. for Genealogical Research, 1973.
Loyalist and other records.

4024   Land tenure to 1800; a list of reduced officers, and memorials to Haldimand. In *3rd report of the Dept. of Public Records and Archives, Ontario,* 1906.
Loyalists. Sir Frederick Haldimand was concerned with the settlement of the United Empire Loyalists.

4025   Lapp, Eula C. To their heirs forever. Picton, Ont.: Picton Gazette Pub. Co., 1970.
American loyalists in Canada; Palatines in New York, Canada and Great Britain.

4026   Loyalist gazette. v.1-30, 1931-62; new ser.1- , 1963- . v.1-30 from Empire Loyalists' Assoc. of Canada, Toronto; new ser. pub. by Dominion Council of the United Empire Loyalists' Assoc., Toronto.

4027   Ontario. Bureau of Archives. Reports, 1903-33. 22v. in 23. 1904-34. Toronto: The Bureau.
Invaluable series on early settlers of upper Canada (or Ontario), consisting of records of the United Empire loyalists who emigrated from the U.S. after the close of the Revolutionary War (1784-1824), and including land grant books.

4028   Ontario. Court of Common Pleas. Records, 1789-94. 14th *report of Bureau of Archives,* 1917. Toronto, 1918.
Concerns Empire loyalists who settled in upper Canada or Ontario. Extensive list of names.

4029   Ontario. Dept. of Archives. Grants of crown lands in upper Canada. Land books A-D, 1787-98. 4v. Toronto, 1929-32.
Lands granted to United Empire loyalists of United Empire emigrants who migrated from the U.S. to Ontario after the close of the American Revolution. Good index of names. 17th-20th *Reports of the Dept. of Archives.*

4030   Paterson, Gilbert G. C. Loyalists in upper Canada, 1783-1840. In 16th *Report of the Dept. of Archives for the Province of Canada,* 1921.

4031   Reid, William D. The loyalists in Ontario; the sons and daughters of the American loyalists of upper Canada. Lambertville, N.J.: Hunterdown House, 1973.
Records of land grants to children of loyalists. Comprehensive; lists sons and daughters of loyalists with residence, and daughters' husband's name. Well organized compilation.

4032   Siebert, Wilbur H. The American loyalists in the eastern seignories and townships of the Province of Quebec. *Trans. of the Royal Soc. of Canada,* 3rd ser., v.7-8, 1913.

4033   Tucker, William B. The Camden colony; or The seed of the righteous: a story of the United Empire loyalists, with genealogical tables. Montreal, 1908.

4034   United Empire Loyalist Centennial Committee, Toronto. The centennial of the settlement of upper Canada by the United Empire loyalists, 1784-1884 . . . with an appendix containing a copy of the United Empire list, preserved in the Crown Lands Dept. of Toronto. 1885. Repr. Boston: Gregg, 1973.

4035   ——— The old United Empire loyalist list . . . with a new introduction by Milton Rubincam, Repr. Baltimore: G.P.C., 1969.

This and no.4034 are identical, but no. 4035 has publisher's title. The official list of United Empire loyalists during the American Revolution.

**4036 United Society for the Propagation of the Gospel.** Calendar of letters from Canada, Newfoundland, Pennsylvania, Barbados, and the Bahamas 1721–93, preserved at The United Society . . . *List and Index Soc. special ser.* 5. London: Swift Ltd., 1972.

Published in 2v., the first containing letters from Bahamas, Barbados, Newfoundland, and Pennsylvania. v.2 contains letters between 1738 and 1740, mainly from New England and other original colonies. Considerable loyalist literature.

**4037 Wright, Esther C.** The loyalists of New Brunswick. 1955. Repr. St. John, N.B.: New Brunswick Historical Soc., 1972.

History of the loyalists, why they came, where from, where they settled. List of New Brunswick loyalists; bibliography. Heads of families and men over 18.

# *Provinces*

## ALBERTA

**4038 Alberta past and present, historical and biographical.** 3v. Chicago, 1924.

v.1 by John Blue; v.2–3 biographical.

**4039 Canada. Board on Geographical Names. Alberta.** Its *Gazette,* v.6. Ottawa, 1958.

**4040 Holmgren, Eric J., and Holmgren, P. M.** 2,000 place-names of Alberta. Saskatoon, Sask.: Modern Pr., 1972.

Notes on sources, bibliography, alphabetized list with origins given; good map to aid location.

## BRITISH COLUMBIA

**4041 British Columbia. Provincial Archives Dept. Library.** Dictionary catalogue of the Library of the Provincial Archives of British Columbia (Victoria). 8v. Boston: G. K. Hall, 1971.

176,000 entries, with analytics of periodicals of western Canada, Oregon, Washington, Idaho, Montana, and Alaska. Much local history.

**4042 British Columbia genealogist.** v.1– , 1971– . Richmond, B.C.: British Columbian Genealogical Soc.

Quarterly; directories, cemetery lists, rolls of honor, queries. Surname index as suppl. to v.2.

**4042a Cuddy, Mary L., and Scott, J. J.** British Columbia in books; an annotated bibliography. N. Vancouver, B.C.: Douglas, 1974. Dist. by David & Charles, N. Pomfret, Vt.

Over 1,000 entries.

**4043 Norris, John M.** Strangers entertained: a history of ethnic groups in British Columbia. Vancouver, B.C.: B.C. Centennial Committee Parliament Buildings, Victoria, B.C., 1971.

Good background to ethnic groups; marginal value to genealogists.

**4044 Walbran, John T.** British Columbia coast names, 1592–1906, to which are added a few names . . . adjacent to United States; their origin and history. 1909. Seattle, Wash.: Washington Univ. Pr., 1972.

Fine source book.

## MANITOBA

**4045 Canada. Board on Geographical Names.** Place-names of Manitoba. Ottawa, 1933.

**4046 Harvey, Robert.** Pioneers of Manitoba. Winnipeg: Prairie Pub. Co., [1970].

## MARITIME PROVINCES

☩ Including New Brunswick, Newfoundland, Nova Scotia, Prince Edward Island

**4047** **Acadiensis;** a quarterly devoted to the interests of the Maritime provinces of Canada. v.1–8, 1901–8. Ed. by David R. Jack, St. John, N.S.
Much family history, many registers, etc.

**4048** **Akins, Thomas B.** Acadia and Nova Scotia; documents relating to the Acadian French and the first British colonization of the Province, 1714–58. With translations from the French by Benjamin Curren. 1869. Repr. New Orleans, La.: Polyanthos, 1972.
Original title, *Selections from the public documents of the Province of Nova Scotia.* Lists of settlers, etc.

**4049** **Arsenault, Bona.** L'Acadie des ancêtres; avec la généalogie des premiers familles acadiennes. Québec, 1955.

**4050** ———— Histoire et généalogie des Acadiens. 2v. Québec: Conseil de la Vie Française en Amérique, ca.1965.
Excellent study for genealogists and historians for Canada, France and Louisiana. Good bibliography.

**4051** ———— History of the Acadians. Quebec: Conseil de la Vie Française en Amérique, 1966.
A translation and revision of the historical part of the author's *Histoire et généalogie des Acadiens* (no.4050).

**4052** **Auger, Roland-J.** Tracing ancestors through the Province of Quebec and Acadia to their place of origin in France. In *French Canadian and Acadian genealogical review,* v.2, pp.259–78, 1969.
Also published as a separate in World Conference on Records papers, L.D.S., Salt Lake City, 1969. Very fine and complete study.

**4053** **Bouchette, Joseph.** The British dominions of North America; or A topographical and statistical description of the provinces of lower and upper Canada, New Brunswick, Nova Scotia, the islands of Newfoundland, Prince Edward and Cape Breton. Including considerations of land-granting and emigration; and a topographical dictionary of lower Canada . . . 2v. 1831. Repr. New York: A.M.S. Pr., 1968.

**4054** **Brown, Thomas J.** Place-names of the province of Nova Scotia. [Halifax, N.S., 1922.]

**4055** **Canada. Bureau on Geographical Names.** New Brunswick, Ottawa, 1956.

**4056** **Canada. Public Archives.** Checklists of census returns: New Brunswick (1851–71); Nova Scotia (1871); Ontario (1842–71); Quebec (1825–71). 4v. Ottawa: Public Archives of Canada, 1963.
List of returns in Manuscript div. Lists counties, townships, parishes and cities, and towns for which census returns are available and provides microfilm references.

**4057** **Fergusson, Charles B.** Place names of Nova Scotia. Halifax, N.S.: Public Archives, 1967.
Over 2,300 names, with explanation of derivation of names with brief histories of each community. Names of first settlers given. 18 maps.

**4058** **Gilroy, Marion.** Loyalists and land settlements in Nova Scotia: a list. *Public Archives of Nova Scotia,* 4v. Halifax, N.S., 1937.
Lists thousands of settlers with dates, locations, acreage, origin.

**4059** **Haliburton, Thomas C.** An historical and statistical account of Nova Scotia. 2v. 1829. Repr. Belleville, Ont.: Mika Pub., 1973.
Mika added a new title, *History of Nova Scotia.* Boundaries, counties, militia, churches, etc.

**4060** **Jack, Isaac A.** Biographical review.
This volume contains biographical sketches of leading citizens of the province of New Brunswick. Toronto, 1900.

**4061** **Jehn, Janet B.** Acadian descendants. Covington, Ky.: Acadian Genealogy Exchange, 1972.
450 surnames, with index of thousands of persons. Pioneer French settlers of Aca-

dia (now Nova Scotia), with parts of Canada and Maine, with descendants, especially in Louisiana area.

**4061a Martell, J. S.** Immigation to and emigration from Nova Scotia, 1815-38. *Public Archives of Nova Scotia* 5. Halifax, N.S., 1942.
About 13,000 Irish went to Nova Scotia.

**4062 Men of the soil: century farms.** Truro, N.S.: Nova Scotia Beautification Committee, 1970.
History of family farms in Nova Scotia. Has some genealogy.

**4063 Morley, William F. E.** The Atlantic provinces: Newfoundland, Nova Scotia, New Brunswick, Prince Edward Island. Toronto: Univ. of Toronto Pr., 1967.
Canadian local histories to 1950: a bibliography series.

**4064 Morse, William I.** Gravestones of Acadie and other essays on local history, genealogy and parish records of Annapolis, Nova Scotia. London, England, 1929.

**4065 Nova Scotia Historical Society.** Report and collections. v.1- , 1879- . Armdale, N.S.: The Society.
Became *Collections*. Good for records.

**4066 Piers, Harry.** Biographical review. This volume contains biographical sketches of leading citizens of the province of Nova Scotia. 1900. Repr. Ann Arbor, Mich.: Xerox Univ. Microfilms, 1973.

**4067 Prowse, Daniel W.** History of Newfoundland from the English, colonial, and foreign records. 1895. Belleville, Ont.: Mika Pub., 1972.

**4068 Richard, Bernice C.** 1770 census of Nova Scotia province, Canada. Chicago: Chicago Genealogical Soc., 1973.
Also contains census data from some localities for 1773 and 1787. Gives details of religion and county of birth.

**4069 Wright, Esther C.** The loyalists of New Brunswick. 1955. Repr. St. John, N.B.: New Brunswick Historical Soc., 1972.
Heads of families and men over 18.

NORTHWEST TERRITORIES

⚓ Including the Yukon

**4070 Catholic church records of the Pacific northwest:** Vancouver, v.1-2 (in 1) and Stellamaris Mission. Transl. by Mikell L. W. Warner. Annotated by H. B. Munnick. St. Paul, Ore.: French Prairie Pr., 1972.
Baptisms, marriages, and burials made by the first Catholic priests in the West from Red River to Port Vancouver, 1838-60. Details of Indians who married whites.

**4071 Peel, Bruce B.** A bibliography of the Prairie Provinces to 1953. Toronto, 1956.

**4072** ———— Suppl. Toronto: Univ. of Toronto Pr., 1963.

**4073 Phillips, James W.** Alaska-Yukon place names. Seattle, Wash.: Univ. of Washington Pr., 1973.
State of Alaska and parts of western Canada.

**4074 Wallace, William S.** Documents relating to the north west coast . . . *Champlain Soc. publ.* 22. Toronto, 1934.
Biographical dictionary of northwesterners, pp.425-505.

ONTARIO

**4075 Campeau, Marielle.** Check-list of parish registers. Ottawa: Public Archives of Canada, Manuscripts Div., 1969.
Types of records and dates of coverage. Bilingual.

**4076 Canada. Public Archives.** Checklists of census returns . . . Ontario (1842-71) . . . Ottawa: Public Archives, 1963.
Full annotation, *see* no.3953.

4077 **The Canadian biographical dictionary** and **portrait gallery of eminent and self-made men.** Ontario vol. Toronto, 1880.
Mug book.

4078 **Canniff, William.** History of the province of Ontario . . . including biographies of prominent first setttlers and the census of 1871. Toronto, 1872.

4079 ——— History of the settlement of upper Canada (Ontario). 1869. Repr. Belleville, Ont.: Mika Pub., 1971.
Has valuable record of individual loyalists; includes biographies of prominent citizens.

4080 **Chadwick, Edward M.** Ontarian families; genealogies of United-Empire-loyalist and other pioneer families of upper Canada. 2v. Repr. Lambertville, N.J.: Hunterdon House, 1970.
Contains errors. v.1 repr. 1972 by Mika Pub., Belleville, Ont.

*4081 [**County atlas reprints.**] Owen Sound, Ont.: Mark Cumming, County Atlas Reprints, 1973- .
Reprints of 32 counties of Canada, issued under the auspices of the Ontario Genealogical Soc.

4082 **Families.** v.10- , 1971- . Toronto: Ontario Genealogical Soc. Formerly *Ontario Genealogical Soc. publ.* 1-9 (1962-70).

4083 **Fraser, Alexander.** A history of Ontario . . . 1v. in 2. Toronto, 1907.
History and biography.

*4084 **Kirk, Robert F.,** and **Kirk, A. L.** Some references and sources for searching for your ancestors in the province of Ontario. Detroit, Mich.: Detroit Soc. for Genealogical Research, 1973.
Loyalist, church, local history records, etc.

4085 **London, Ontario. Court of General Quarter Sessions of the Peace for London District.** Minutes, 1800-1809, 1812-18. In 22d *report of the Dept. of Public Records and Archives of Ontario,* 1934.
Thousands of names.

4086 **Middleton, Jesse E.,** and **Landon, F.** The province of Ontario—a history 1615-1927. 4v. Toronto, 1927.
v.3-4 biographical.

4087 **Nadon, Léon.** Répertoire des mariages de Saint-Jean-Baptiste d'Ottawa, Ontario, 1872-1969. Québec: Soc. Canadienne de Généalogie, 1970.
*Contribution* 28.

4088 **Ontarian genealogist and family historian.** 1898-1901 in 1v. (all pub.). Toronto, 1898-1901.

4089 **Ontario. Bureau of Archives.** Reports, 1903-33. 22v. in 23. 1904-34. Toronto: The Bureau.
Invaluable series on early history and settlers of upper Canada (or Ontario), consisting of records of the United Empire loyalists who emigrated from the U.S. after the close of the Revolutionary War (1784-1824), and including land grant books.

4090 [**Ontario atlases.**] Illustrated historical atlases of Ontario originally published by Belden & Co. in the 19th century, are being repr. by Mika Pub. Co., Belleville, Ont., 1970s.

4091 **Ontario history.** v.1- , 1899- . Toronto: Ontario Historical Soc.
1899-1945 called *Papers and records.* Considerable amount of genealogy, particularly in earlier volumes.

4092 **Ontario register.** v.1- , 1968- . Lambertville, N.J.: Thomas B. Wilson, ed.
Quarterly magazine devoted to early settlers of Ontario.

4093 **Ontario since 1867: a bibliography.** *Ontario historical studies,* v.1. Toronto: Ontario Government Bookstore, 1974.

4094 **Pioneer life on the Bay of Quinto,** including genealogies of old families and biographical sketches of representative citizens. Toronto, 190-.

**4095 Reaman, George E.** The trail of the black walnut. Toronto: McClelland & Stewart, 1961. Originally published by Pennsylvania German Soc., Philadelphia, 1957. Settlement of Ontario by Pennsylvania Germans and other smaller related groups, particularly prior to 1812.

**4096 York, Ontario. Court of General Quarter Sessions of the Peace for the Home District (York).** Minutes, 1800-11. In 21st *report of the Dept. of Public Records and Archives of Ontario,* 1932. Thousands of names.

QUEBEC

✠ Since many of the Quebec works are in French, a short word list of the principal words found in the titles is given below:
abrégé—abstract, abridgement
aveu—admission, acknowledgement
cadastre—register of the survey of lands
concession—grant, privilege
dénombrement—enumeration, census
fief—fee
greffe—registry, recording office
insinuation—inscriptions, writings
inventaire—inventory, listing
récensement—census
recueil—collection, selection
répertoire—table, list, catalog
seigneurie—lordship, manor

**4097 Auger, Roland-J.** Tracing ancestors through the province of Quebec and Acadia to their place of origin in France. In *French Canadian and Acadian genealogical review,* v.2, pp.259-78, 1969. Also in World Conference on Records, Salt Lake City, 1969 as a separate work. Fine and complete study.

**4098 Beaulieu, André, and Morley, W. F. E.** La province de Québec. Toronto: Univ. of Toronto Pr., 1971. Canadian local histories to 1950: a bibliography ser.

**4099 Bureau, René; Dumas, J.; and Tessier, G.-R.** Répertoires des mariages de l'île d'Orléans. *Soc. Canadienne de Généalogie de Québec contribution* 20. Québec: The Society, 1966. Revision of Abbé Forgue's "Généalogie des familles de l'île d'Orléans" in *Rapport des Archives canadiennes,* 1905, v.2.

**4100 Campagna, Dominique.** Répertoire des mariages... (Quebec). M. Campagna has compiled many vols. which concern the counties of Champlain, Berthier, Maskinongé, Cap de la Madeleine, Yamachiche, Trois Rivières, covering the years 1673-1966. Quebec: The Author, 1962-68.

**4101 Canada. Commissioners under the Seigniorial Act of 1854.** Cadastres abrégés des seigneuries appartenant à la couronne, déposés au greffe de Québec... Québec, 1863. Abridged register of the surveys of lands of the seigniory belonging to the Crown, deposited at the record office in Quebec. Seigniories abolished in 1854.

**4102 Cadastres abrégés des seigneuries du district de Montréal** ... 3v. Québec, 1863.

**4103 Cadastres abrégés des seigneuries du district de Québec.** 2v. Québec, 1863.

**4104 Cadastres abrégés des seigneuries du district des Trois-Rivières, déposés au greffe des Trois-Rivières** ... Québec, 1863.

**4105 Canada. Public Archives.** Checklists of census returns ... Quebec (1825-71). Ottawa: Public Archives, 1963. Lists of returns in Manuscript div. See no. 3953 for full description.

**4106** —— Preliminary inventory of *Manuscript Group* 8: Quebec provincial and local records; *Manuscript Group* 9: provincial, local and territorial records. Ottawa: Queen's Printer, 1961.

**4107** —— Répertoire des récensements du Québec, 1825-71. *See* no. 3953.

**4107a La Canada militaire:** état provisoire des officiers de milice de 1641-1760.

In *Rapport de l'Archiviste de la province de Québec,* 1949/51, pp.261–527.
Very useful publication, listing all the officers of the militia under the French regime in Canada.

**4108 Carbonneau, Charles A.** Tableau généalogique des mariages célèbres dans les paroisses du diocese de Rimouski, situées dans les comtés de Rimouski, Matane, Matapédia et Témiscouata . . . 2v. in 5. Rimouski, 1936.
Ser.1, 1701–1902; ser.2, 1902–25.

**\*4109 Dionne, Narcisse-F.** Les canadiens-français; origine des familles émigrées de France, d'Espagne, de Suisse, etc. pour venir se fixer au Canada, depuis la fondation de Québec jusqu'a ces derniers temps et signification de leurs noms. 1914. Repr. Baltimore: G.P.C., 1969.
10,000 names, establishing place of family origin in France.

**4110** ———— Inventaire chronologique des ouvrages publiés à l'étranger en diverses langues sur Québec et la Nouvelle France, depuis la découverte du Canada jusqu'à nos jours, 1534–1906. 5v. in 2. 1905–12. Repr. New York: Burt Franklin, 1969.
v.2 has title, *Québec et Nouvelle France.* Set includes supplementary bibliography of works on Quebec and "New France."

**4110a Dumas, Silvio.** Les filles du roi en Nouvelle-France: étude historique avec répertoire biographique. Québec: Soc. Historique de Québec, 1972.
Important study of female French-Canadian settlers.

**4111 Gallant, Patrice.** Les régistrés de la Gaspésie (1752–1850). 6v. Sayabec, Québec, 1968.
Registers of births, etc., Gaspé Peninsula.

**4112 Gingras, Raymond.** Liste des répertoires de mariage. Québec: Ministère des Affaires Culturelles, Hotel du Gouvernement, 1971.
List of parish marriage records available at the National Archives, Quebec. Almost all are Catholic, with a few Protestants included.

**4113 Godbout, Père Archange.** Émigration Rochelaise en Nouvelle-France. From *Rapport des Archives Nationales du Québec,* v.48, 1970, pp.113–367. Québec: Ministère des Affaires Culturelles, Hotel du Governement, 1970.
Also issued as *Familles venues de la Rochelle en Canada.* Genealogical study of all families who left La Rochelle, France for Canada in 17th and 18th centuries; much Catholic and Huguenot information.

**4114** ———— Nos ancêtres au XVIIe siècle: dictionnaire généalogique et bio-bibliographique des familles canadiennes. Liv.1–6. *Extrait du Rapport de l'Archiviste de la Province de Québec,* 1951/53–65.
A reedited ed. of Tanguay (no.4003) on a different plan, designed to give the genealogical origins of Canadians with current-day descendants.

**4115 Institut Généalogique Drouin, Montréal.** Dictionnaire nationale des canadiens-français, 1608–1760. 3v. Montréal, 1958–65.
Cover: *Complément de l'arbre généalogique de tout canadien français.* Concerns much of Quebec.

**4116 Michaud, Adolphe.** Généalogie des familles de la Rivière Oelle, depuis l'origine de la paroisse jusqu'à nos jours. Québec, 1908.

**4117 Montagne, Mme. Pierre.** Tourouvre et les Juchereau; un chapitre de l'émigration percheronne au Canada. Québec: Soc. canadienne de généalogie, 1965.
Coats of arms, excellent genealogical tables. Canadian emigration and immigration, French in Canada. *Contribution* 13.

**4118 Montreal.** Aveu et dénombrement . . . de l'île de Montréal, 1731. In *Rapport de l'Archiviste de la province de Québec* 1941/42, pp.1–178.
Important census.

**4119 Montréal and Trois Rivières.** Le récensement des gouvernements de Montréal et des Trois-Rivières, 1765. In *Rapport de l'Archiviste de la province de Québec,* 1936–37, pp.1–121.

**4120 New France. Conseil Supérieur de Québec.** Lettres de noblesse, généalogies, érections de comtés, et baronnies insinuées par le Conseil souverain de la Nouvelle France, publié par Pierre-G. Roy. 2v. *Archives de la province de Québec*, v.3. Beauceville, Que., 1920.

**4121 Plessis Joseph-O.** Les dénombrements de Québec faits en 1792, 1795, 1798 et 1805. In *Rapport de l'Archiviste de la province de Québec, 1948-49*, pp.1-250.
Extensive index. Important census for city of Quebec.

**4122 Le premier récensement de la Nouvelle France,** état général des habitants du Canada en 1666. In *Rapport de l'Archiviste de la province de Québec*, 1935-36, pp.1-154.

**4123 Proulx, Armand.** Répertoire des mariages . . . (Quebec areas). M. Proulx has compiled many registers of marriages in the Quebec province. From *La Pocatière,* Québec, 1968-71.
The dates are from 1672 to 1969.

**4124 Québec (Province). Archives.** Rapport. v.1- , 1920- . Québec: Archives nationales.
These reports contain thousands of names and much genealogical information. The major series have been recorded in this work separately, but smaller articles (too numerous to list) are of great value to the researcher. Title changed frequently: 1920-60, v.1-40, *Rapport de l'Archiviste de la province de Québec;* v.41-47, 1963-69, *Rapport des archives du Québec;* v.48-51, 1970-73, *Rapport des archives nationales du Québec.*

**4125 Quebec (Province). Judicial Archives.** Inventaires des concessions en fiefs et seigneuries, fois et hommages, et aveux et dénombrements conservés au Archives de la province de Québec, par Pierre-G. Roy. 6v. Beauceville, Que., 1927-29.

**4126** —— Inventaire des contrats de mariage du régime français conservés aux Archives judiciaires de Québec, par Pierre-G. Roy. 6v. Québec, 1927-38.
List of marriage contracts in 17th and 18th centuries, arranged under brides and grooms and date of marriage.

**4127** —— Inventaire des greffes des notaires du régime français. Par Pierre-G. Roy, A. Roy, and others. 1942- (in progress). Québec: Archives.
Probate records in the French regime in Canada. Over 30,000 names. Contains details of marriages, civil contracts, sales of land, and many other transactions. 25v. to 1974. *Rapports de l'Archiviste de la province de Québec,* 1942- .

**4128** —— Inventaire des insinuations de la prévôte . . . de Québec, par Pierre-G. Roy. 3v. Beauceville, Que., 1936-39.
Inventory of the writings of the mayor.

**4129** —— Inventaire d'une collection de pièces judiciaires, notariales, etc. conservées aux Archives de Québec, par Pierre-G. Roy. 2v. Beauceville, Que., 1917.

**4130 Québec.** Le récensement de Québec en 1744. In *Rapport de l'Archiviste de la province de Québec,* 1939-40, pp.1-153.
Important census for the city of Quebec.

**4131** —— —— 1762. In *Rapport de l'Archiviste de la province de Québec,* 1925-26, pp.1-141.

**4132 Roberge, Claude.** Répertoire des mariages . . . (Québec). M. Roberge is compiling a series of marriage and other records as *Contributions of the Soc. Canadienne de Généalogie,* 1973- . Québec: The Society.

**4133 Roy, Pierre-G.** Fils de Québec. 4v. in 2. Lévis, 1933.
All French genealogies. Sons of Quebec. A great and important land record covering Quebec and Trois-Rivières only. Most important archival document. Acts of fidelity and homage avowals and census of the vassals and freeholders of Royal Company of the West Indies, seigniors of New France.

**4133a** —— Papier terrier de la Compagnie des Index Occidentales, 1667-68. Beauceville, Que., 1931.

**4134 Société Canadienne de Généalogie (Québec).** Contributions 1– , 1962– . Québec: The Society.

**4135 Société Généalogique Canadienne-Française.** Mémoires. 1944– . Montréal: The Society.
Excellent material and records.

**4136** ———— Publications. 1955– . Montréal: The Society.
Chiefly marriage registers from records of different parishes in the province of Quebec.

**4137 Talbot, Eloi-Gérard.** Généalogie des familles originaires des comtés de Montmagny, l'Islet, et Bellechasse, province de Québec. v.1– . Chateau-Richer, Québec: Author, 1971– (in progress).
Descendants of pioneer families. Thousands of names.

**4138** ———— Recueil de généalogies des comtés de Beauce-Dorchester-Frontenac 1625–1946. 11v. Beauceville, Que., 1949–55.
Collections of genealogies of the counties of Beauce, Dorchester, and Frontenac. 250 marriages, accurately transcribed.

**4139 Upper Canada Genealogical Society.** Bulletin. 1– , 1951– . Ottawa: The Society.

SASKATCHEWAN

**4140 Canada. Board on Geographical Names.** Saskatchewan. Its *Gazette,* v.5. Ottawa, 1957.

**4141 Hawkes, John.** Saskatchewan and its people. 3v. Chicago, 1924.
v.2–3 biographical. Mug book.

**4142 McDonald, Christine.** Historical directory of Saskatchewan newspapers 1878–1950. Saskatoon, Sask.: Office of the Saskatchewan Archives, Univ. of Saskatchewan, 1951.

**4143 Saskatchewan Genealogical Society.** Bulletin. v.1– , 1970– . Regina, Sask.: The Society.

# ENGLAND

## Bibliographies

### GENERAL

**4144 The British national bibliography cumulated index.** 1950– . British Museum, London: British Library, Bibliographic Service Div., 1955– .

**4145 British union-catalogue of periodicals;** a record of periodicals in the world from the 17th century to the present day, in British libraries. v.1– , 1955– . London: Butterworths Scientific Publ.

**4146 Dexter, Henry M.** The congregationalism of the last three hundred years as seen in its literature. 2v. 1880. Repr. New York: Burt Franklin, 1970.
Has a most extensive bibliography on congregationalism. 7,500 items, 1546–1879.

**4147 Gatfield, George.** Guide to printed books and manuscripts relating to English and foreign heraldry and genealogy; being a classified catalogue of works of those branches of literature. 1892. Repr. Detroit, Mich.: Gale Research, 1966.
Lists more than 17,500 books, periodicals, and manuscripts covering family histories, English counties, pedigrees, etc. Deals primarily with Great Britain, but also covers heraldry and genealogy in Europe. Although not a great work, it has never been superseded because it contains many references to manuscripts in the British Museum and elsewhere.

**4148 Goss, Charles W. F.** The London directories, 1677–1855: a bibliography with notes. London, 1932.

**4149 Harrison, Howard G.** A select bibliography of English genealogy, with brief lists of Wales, Scotland and Ireland. London, 1957.
A manual for students. It is not superseded by Kaminkow (no. 4152).

**4150 Higgs, Audrey H.,** and **Wright, D.** West Midland genealogy: a survey of the local genealogical material available in the public libraries of Hereford, Shropshire, Staffordshire, Warwickshire, and Worcestershire. London: Library Assoc., 1966.

**4151 Kaminkow, Marion J.** Genealogical manuscripts in British libraries: a

descriptive guide. Baltimore, 1967. Available from Tuttle, Rutland, Vt.
Guide to manuscripts, many of which have been unknown to the researcher.

4152 ——— A new bibliography of British genealogy. Baltimore, 1965. Available from Tuttle, Rutland, Vt.
Admirably organized listing of 1,783 primary works of reference available to the genealogical researcher.

4153 The librarian subject guide to books. v.2, Biography, family history, heraldry, genealogy, etc. London: James Clarke [1960].
Carefully compiled guide; has librarian in mind throughout. v.2 in a series; v.1 does not refer to genealogy and need not be acquired.

4154 London University. Institute of Historical Research. Bibliography of historical works issued in the United Kingdom 1946-56. Ed. by Joan C. Lancaster. London: Dawson, 1964.
Almost 8,000 entries. Previous years, see no.4162-63.

4155 ——— ——— 1957-60. Ed. by William Kellaway. 1964. Repr. London: Dawson, 1969; New York: Humanities Pr.

4156 ——— ——— 1961-65. London: The Institute, 1967.

4157 ——— ——— 1966-70. London: The Institute, 1972.
Kept up-to-date in *Annual bulletin of historical literature,* issued by the Historical Association.

*4158 Mullins, Edward L. C. A guide to the historical and archaeological publications of societies in England and Wales, 1901-33. London: Univ. of London, Inst. of Historical Research, 1968.
Since the publications contain much genealogical material, the guide is essential for students of genealogy. Includes England, Wales, Isle of Man, and Channel Isles. More than 400 local and national societies. Continued in *Writings on British history* (no.4166), a more selective publication.

4159 ——— Texts and calendars: an analytical guide to serial publications. *Royal Historical Soc. guides and handbooks* 7. Folkestone, Kent: Dawson's, 1958.
Contains only publications held by the Society; nothing of Ireland or Scotland. Does not include parish register series but is invaluable record for other series and one of the most important bibliographies in the field. See no.4711 for *Handlist of Scottish and Welsh record publications.*

4160 Raven-Hart, Hester E., and Johnston, M. Bibliography of the registers (printed) of the universities, inns of court, colleges, and schools of Great Britain and Ireland. In *London Univ., Inst. of Historical Research bull.,* 1931-32.
Most registers include biographical material.

4161 Royal Historical Society, London. Writings on British history, 1901-33; a bibliography of books and articles on the history of Great Britain from about 400 A.D. to 1914, published during the years 1901-33 inclusive, with an appendix containing a selected list of publications in these years on British history since 1914. Compiled by Alexander T. Milne. 5v. in 7. London: Cape, 1968-70. Repr. see no.4166.
v.3-5 (Tudors to 1914) of more value to genealogists. 1934-45, see no.4162-63.

4162 ——— ——— 1934-39. 6v. London, 1937-53.

4163 ——— ——— 1940-45. 2v. London, 1960.
1946-48, see no.4167. Repr. of 1934-45, see no.4166. 1946-70, see also no.4154-57.

4164 Somerville, Robert. Handlist of record publications. London: British Record Assoc., 1951.
Classified and abbreviated list of publications by 64 English societies. Not superseded by Mullins (no.4158), since some listed are not society publications. Mainly medieval material listed.

4165 Ward, Williams S. Index and finding list of serials published in the

British Isles, 1789–1832. Lexington, Ky.: Univ. of Kentucky Pr., 1953.

Based primarily on the American *Union list of serials* (no.75), and *Union catalogue of the periodical publications in the university libraries of the British Isles* (no.4145). Suppl.1 pub. in *Bull. of the New York Public Lib.*, v.77, no.5, 1974.

**4166  Writings on British history, 1901–45.** Repr. 8v. in 11. New York: Barnes & Noble, 1961.

Details of these *Writings, see* no.4161.

**4167** ———— 1946–48. Compiled by Donald J. Munro. London: Univ. of London, Inst. of Historical Research, 1973.

**4168** ———— 1949–51. Compiled by Donald J. Munro. London: Univ. of London, Inst. of Historical Research, 1974.

Later years, *see* no.4155–57.

**4169  Youings, Joyce.** Local record sources in print and in progress, 1971–72. London: Historical Assoc., 1972.

Compiled for the *Local History Committee for Students of History,* v.85. Contains results of survey of recent and forthcoming publications relating to record sources for study of English and Welsh history. Invaluable for genealogists wishing to know local history publications available and scheduled.

## LOCAL HISTORIES

**4170  Anderson, John P.** The book of British topography: a classified catalogue of the topographical works in the library of the British Museum relating to Great Britain and Ireland. 1881. Repr. Baltimore: G.P.C., 1970.

Still the most comprehensive bibliography on books on the topography of England, Wales, Scotland, and Ireland. 14,000 titles.

**4171  Gross, Charles.** A bibliography of British municipal history including gilds and parliamentary representation. 1897. 2nd ed. Leicester: Leicester Univ. Pr., 1966.

Actually a repr. of the 1897 ed., with an evaluation by G. H. Martin. The 1897 ed. of Gross was reprinted by Burt Franklin, New York, but it lacks Martin's evaluation. Continuation of Gross, *see* no.4175.

**4172  Hotten, John C.** A handbook of topography and family history of England and Wales . . . London, 1863.

7,659 titles.

**4173  Humphreys, Arthur L.** A handbook to county bibliography; being a bibliography of bibliographies relating to the counties and towns of Great Britain and Ireland. 1917. Repr. London: Dawson, 1974.

Still valuable; almost a supplement to Anderson (no.4170).

**4174  Kuhlicke, Frederick W., and Emmison, F. G.** English local history handlist: a short bibliography and list of sources for the study of local history and antiquities. 4th ed., with place and subject indexes. London: Historical Assoc., 1969.

**4175  Martin, Geoffrey H., and McIntyre, S.** A bibliography of British and Irish municipal history. v.1– . Leicester: Leicester Univ. Pr., 1972– (in progress). (Distributed by Humanities Pr., New York.)

Continuation of Gross (no.4171). Comprises printed and published works on the history of municipal government and municipal services in Great Britain and Ireland from the earliest times to the end of 1960. v.1 lists general works.

**4176  Upcott, William.** A bibliographical account of the principal works relating to English topography. 3v. 1818. Repr. New York: Burt Franklin, 1968.

Indispensable work to the collector of topography. 5,000 works arranged under counties from 15th to 19th century, with detailed analysis of contents of each.

## PEDIGREES AND FAMILY HISTORIES

**4177  Bridger, Charles.** An index to printed [English] pedigrees, contained in county and local histories, the heralds' visitations, and in the more important genealogical collections. 1867. Repr. Baltimore: G.P.C., 1969.

16,000 references to pedigrees in county histories and elsewhere. Superseded by Marshall (no.4182), but Bridger's details are often better.

**4178   Campling, Arthur.** East Anglian pedigrees. *Harleian Soc.,* v.91, 97. London, 1939–45.

**4179   Hunter, Joseph.** Familiae minorum gentium; ed. by John W. Clay. *Harleian Soc.,* v.37–40. 4v. London, 1894–96.

**4180   ———** Hunter's pedigrees; a continuation transcribed and ed. by John W. Walker. *Harleian Soc.,* v.88. London, 1936.

Title is misleading. The volumes concern pedigrees chiefly of Yorkshire, Derbyshire, Lancashire, and Cheshire—all north country. Because of Hunter's background, many entries concern Unitarians. George W. Marshall compiled an index to Hunter's manuscript in *The genealogist,* new ser., v.6, 1890.

**\*4181   Kaminkow, Marion J.** Genealogies in the Library of Congress: a bibliography. 2v. Baltimore: Magna Carta Book Co., 1972.

Most comprehensive bibliography of family histories of America and Great Britain available. 20,000 items, including some published in Europe and elsewhere. Covers every entry in the family-name index of the Local history and genealogy room of the Library of Congress. Over 25,000 cross references; brings up-to-date the printed L.C. bibliographies of 1910 and 1919 and microcard editions of 1954. Supersedes 1919 ed. (no.4186).

**\*4182   Marshall, George W.** The genealogist's guide. 4th ed. 1903. Repr. Baltimore: G.P.C., 1973.

This and Whitmore (no.4187) are two of the most valuable source records in British genealogy. They list pedigrees in all printed works and periodicals. Marshall supersedes Coleman's *General index to printed pedigrees,* 1866, and, up to a point, Bridger's *Index to printed pedigrees . . .* (no.4177). The repr. has a new introduction by Anthony J. Camp.

**4183   The Norman people and their existing descendants in the British dominions and the United States of America.** London, 1874.

Contains alphabetical series of Norman names and families from the London postal directory.

**4184   Sims, Richard.** An index to the pedigrees and arms contained in heralds' visitations and other genealogical manuscripts in the British Museum. 1849. Repr. Baltimore: G.P.C., 1970.

Although out-of-date, and although later catalogs of manuscript collections are available, this contains references not found elsewhere. Arranged under counties—a major difficulty because researchers often do not know the county they need. Good for visitations and indexes available for researchers.

**\*4185   Thomson, Theodore R.** A catalogue of British family histories. 2nd ed., much enl. and corr. London, 1935.

Virtually the best book of its kind. Addenda in the *Genealogists' magazine,* v.7, 1937, pp.645–48; and the Society of Genealogists, London, has a manuscript continuation to 1956. From 1951 on, family histories are listed in the *British national bibliography,* no.4144. A revision and updating of work scheduled for 1975.

**4186   U.S. Library of Congress.** American and English genealogies in the Library of Congress, Washington, D.C. 2nd ed. 1919. Repr. Baltimore: G.P.C., 1967.

Although superseded by Kaminkow (no. 4184), it is still useful, and in view of the high cost of Kaminkow, the L.C. ed. is good for the small budget library.

**\*4187   Whitmore, John B.** A genealogical guide: an index to British pedigrees in continuation of Marshall's *Genealogist's guide.* London: Soc. of Genealogists, 1953.

Index to all works on genealogy published in Britain from 1900 to 1950; forms a supplement to Marshall (no.4182). Whitmore also appeared in 4v. in the *Harleian Soc. Visitation publ.* 99, 101, 102, 104, but the 1953 ed. has 50 additional pages and an appendix of families raised to the peerage since 1878. Indexes pedigrees in more than

## Records

**4188** Beresford, Maurice W. The unprinted census returns of 1841, 1851 and 1861. Chichester, England: Phillimore, 1966.

**4189** Bond, Maurice F. Guide to the records of Parliament. London: H.M.S.O., 1971.

**4190** British mercantile claims, 1775–1803. In *The Virginia genealogist,* v.6– , 1962– (in progress).
From reports in the Public Record Office, London. Claims of British property confiscated in the American Revolution. Many names.

**4191** Cam, Helen M. The hundred and the hundred rolls. An outline of Government in medieval England. London, 1930.
Next in importance historically to Domesday inquests are the inquiries made in Edward I's reign, called *Rotuli hundredorum.* In 1274 commissioners toured Britain, enquiring hundred by hundred, by juries of freemen. The results of the hundreds enquiries and the list are important, and simply explained.

**4192** Davis, Godfrey R. C. Medieval cartularies of Great Britain: a short catalogue. London: Longmans, 1958.
A cartulary is a collection or register of charters and deeds relating to a landed estate. This collection is indispensable for finding what exists, where to find it, and what has been printed.

**4192a** Dibben, A. A. Title deeds 13th–19th centuries. London: Historical Assoc., 1971.

**4193** Edwards, L. W. L. A new and revised catalogue of directories and poll books in the possession of the Society of Genealogists. Edited from the original edition by John W. Sims, 1963. Chichester, England: Phillimore, 1974.
Such is the strength of the Society's collection that this catalog may be regarded as the most complete in print. Poll books listed here concern lists of electors, voters, electoral rolls, etc.

**4194** Emmison, Frederick G., and **Gray,** I. County records. *Helps for students of history* 62. Rev. ed. London: Historical Assoc., 1967.

**4195** —— and **Smith, W. J.** Material for theses in some local record offices. Chichester, England: Phillimore, 1973.
Although written primarily for historians, genealogists will find the listings of holdings in each county archives of great value. Archives of church bodies and city offices listed also.

**4196** Ford, Percy, and **Ford, G.** Select list of British Parliamentary papers, 1833–99. Oxford, England, 1953.

**4197** Galbraith, Vivian H. An introduction to the use of the public records. 1952. Repr. New York: Oxford Univ. Pr., 1963.
Original lectures given at Oxford University to those about to start research on public records. Intensely practical handbook.

**4198** Geijer, Eric N. Printed visitation and county pedigrees. In *Genealogists' magazine,* London. v.6–7, 1933–36.
Does not include general works. Majority of printed visitations taken from inaccurate copies.

*****4199** Genealogical Society of the Church of Jesus Christ of Latter-day Saints. Index to 1851 census of England, Wales, Isle of Man and Channel Islands. Salt Lake City: L.D.S., 1965.

*****4200** —— Major genealogical record sources in England and Wales. Salt Lake City: L.D.S., 1966– .

*****4201** —— Pre-1858 English probate jurisdictions. *Research papers,* ser. A, no.7–44. Salt Lake City: L.D.S., 1967–70.

Probate records of England are direct evidence of relationships. This series treats each county separately, and unravels the tortuous journey for the researcher. There were some 300 ecclesiastical courts in which letters of administration were granted. In 1858 all ecclesiastical courts were closed, and England was divided into civil probate districts; thus probate searches were made comparatively simply. Information on the complete *Research papers* series will be found in the notation under no.243.

4202 **Great Britain. General Register Office.** Abstract of arrangements respecting registration of births, marriages and deaths in the United Kingdom, and other countries of the British Commonwealth of Nations, and in the Irish Republic. London: G.R.O., 1952. Available from British Information Services, New York.

States position to 1947. Information regarding dates of commencement and data contained in various registration offices throughout the British Commonwealth. Valuable appendixes of lists of records at Somerset House and at the Bishop of London's Registry (although latter are now in Guildhall Library, London). Also gives details of Church of England records on foreign soil.

4203 **Great Britain. Historical Manuscripts Commission.** Guide to the reports, 1870-1911. Pt.1, Index to places mentioned. London, 1914. Pt.2, index to persons mentioned. 2v. London, 1935-38.

4204 ———— 1911-57. Guide to reports issued. 3v. New York: British Information Services, 1960.

4205 ———— Index to persons by A. C. S. Hall. 3v. New York: British Information Services, 1966.

4206 ———— Index of places. Pt.1, listing places definitely identified; pt.2, those not certainly located. New York: British Information Services, 1974.

4207 ———— (List of) record repositories in Great Britain. 3rd ed. New York: British Information Services, 1969.

Deals almost entirely with manuscript collections. Gives name of archivist, address, opening hours, details of guides in print, etc. Also available from British Records Assoc., London.

4208 ———— National register of archives. Bulletin. no.1-9, 1948-57. London: Historical Manuscripts Commission.

4209 **Great Britain. Parliament. House of Commons.** Hansard's catalogue and breviate of British Parliamentary papers, 1696-1834. 1836. Repr. with an introduction by P. Ford and G. Ford. London, 1953.

Useful for anyone with an ancestor connected with parliamentary activity.

4210 **Great Britain. Public Record Office.** Many of the millions of papers have been printed and are to be found in some of the larger libraries, particularly university libraries. They include records of inquisitions, rolls, warrants, curia regis rolls, calendar, exchequer, and military data.

4211 ———— Calendarium genealogicum, Henry III (1207-72) and Edward I (1272-1307). Ed. by Charles Roberts. 2v. London, 1865.

Index to inquisitiones post mortem (records giving identity of deceased, date of death, land on which he died seized, his heirs and their ages).

4212 ———— A descriptive catalogue of ancient deeds. 6v. London, 1890-1915.

4213 ———— Guide to material relating to American history to 1783 in the Public Record Office. 2v. London, 1912-14.

4214 ———— Guide to the contents. Rev. and extended to 1960 from the *Guide* by Montague S. Giuseppi, 1923-24. 3v. New York: British Information Services, 1963-68.

The most important work for any approach to the Public Record Office. v.1, legal records; v.2, state papers and departmental records; v.3, documents transferred 1960-66.

4215 ——— Lists and indexes. This series began in 1892 and is still being published. The volumes contain many thousands of names and much relevant family data. The more important volumes, genealogically, are listed below. Most are out of print, but the few which are still in print may be obtained from the British Information Services, New York.
- v.1: Index to ancient petitions (16th to 19th century) of the Chancellor of the Exchequer preserved in the Public Record Office, 1892.
- v.2: Index to Chancery proceedings, 1558–1666. 3v. 1896–1909.
- v.9: List of sheriffs from England and Wales from earliest times to 1831. 1898.
- v.12, 16, 20, 29, 38, 48, 50, 51, 54, 56. List of early Chancery proceedings. v.1–10, 1901–36.
- v.21–22. List of proceedings in the Court of Requests. 2v. 1906.
- v.23, 26, 31, 33. Index to inquisitions. v.1, Henry VIII–Philip & Mary; v.2, Elizabeth; 3, James I; v.4, Charles I and later. 1907–09.
- v.39, 42, 44, 45. Index to Chancery proceedings, "Bridges Div.," 1613–1714. 4v. 1911–17.

4216 **Grove, Henry.** Alienated tithes in appropriated and unappropriated parishes . . . together with all Crown grants of tithes from Henry VIII to William III (1591–1702). London, 1896.

Thousands of names of owners, grantees, etc. A tithe was a form of tax generally paid to the church.

4217 **Harcup, Sara.** Historical, archaeological and kindred societies in the British Isles: a list. Rev. ed. London: University of London, Inst. of Historical Research, 1968.

4218 **Houston, Jane.** Index of cases in the records of the Court of Arches at Lambeth Palace Library, 1660–1913. *British Record Soc.,* v.85. Chichester, England: Phillimore, 1972.

Monumental vol. concerning the supreme court of the province of Canterbury. Much testamentary and matrimonial material. Wills figure prominently, and there is a special index of testators. See also no.4221.

4219 **Index library.** *See* British Record Society, Ltd., no.4254.

4220 **Institute of Historical Research, University of London.** For many years the Institute has issued definitive and accurate works of reference; some are listed here, but others can be noted from the list of publications supplied by the Institute.

4221 **London. Court of Arches.** So named from the arches at St. Mary-le-Bow where the ecclesiastical court of appeal for the prerogative of Canterbury formerly met. Records, *see* no.4218.

4222 **London. Guildhall Library.** A handlist of poll books and registers of electors in the Guildhall Library. London: The Library, 1970.

Voting registers for England.

4223 ——— London rate assessments and inhabitants lists in Guildhall Library and Corporation of London Records Office. 2nd ed., rev. London: The Library, 1968.

4224 **Mathias, Peter,** and **Pearsall, A. W. H.** Shipping: a survey of historical records. Newton Abbot, England: David & Charles, 1971.

Shipping records, companies and locations.

4225 **Matthews, William.** British diaries: an annotated bibliography of British diaries written between 1442 and 1942. 1950. Repr. Magnolia, Mass.: Peter Smith, 1959.

Although of marginal value to the average researcher, it contains material not found in other works and can be regarded as a last resort by those who wish to be certain that every piece of ground has been covered.

4226 **Moulton, H. R.** Palaeography, genealogy and topography. 1930 catalogue. Historical documents, ancient charters, leases, court rolls, pedigrees, marriage settlements, etc. Richmond, England, 1936.

One of the finest sale catalogs ever published. Most useful for genealogists. 3pts. Paleography booklet and catalog, 1929; index by Dorothy M. Verrill, 1936. 25,000 entries.

4227   Munby, Lionel M. Short guides to records. See no.4433.

4227a   The names and descriptions of the proprietors of unclaimed dividends on bank stock and on the public funds, transferable at the Bank of England . . . due . . . 1780–88, 1791, 1802, 1812, 1823, 1836, 1838/43, 1845 [and probably other years] . . . and remained unpaid . . . London, 1791, (pub. at intervals).
Each vol. has about 20,000 names listed.

4228   Norton, Jane E. Guide to the national and provincial directories of England and Wales, excluding London, published before 1856. *Royal Historical Soc. guides and handbooks,* v.5. Folkestone, England: Dawson's, 1950.
Chiefly a guide to library holdings. From such sources the researcher may locate unique information. For London directories, *see* no.4148.

4229   Owen, Dorothy M. The records of the Established Church in England, excluding parish records. London: British Record Assoc., 1970.
Parish registers are well known as prime sources, but other sources are often a mystery to most users. This book explains church records and how to use them.

4230   Return of owners of land, 1873; England and Wales . . . 2v. London, 1875.
Shows number and names of owners of land of one acre and more.

4231   Shaw, William A. Letters of denization and acts of naturalization for aliens in England and Ireland, 1603–1800. 3v. *Huguenot Soc. publ.* 18, 27, 35. London: Huguenot Soc., 1911–32.
v.1, 1603–1700; v.2, 1701–1800; v.3, suppl. Full details, *see* no.4542–43.

4232   Squibb, George D. Visitation pedigrees and the genealogist. *Phillimore's handbooks* 4. Chichester, England: Phillimore, 1964.
Evaluation of printed visitations.

4233   Tate, William E. The parish chest: a study of the records of parochial administration in England. 3rd ed., with additions and corr. New York: Cambridge Univ. Pr., 1969.
Deals fully with all classes of parish registers and records, churchwardens' accounts, charity records, vestry minutes, etc.

4234   Tercentenary handlist of English and Welsh newspapers, magazines and reviews, 1620–1920. 1920. Repr. London: Dawson's of Pall Mall, 1966.
section 1, London and suburban; section 2, Provincial.

4235   Wagner, Sir Anthony R. The records and collections of the College of Arms. Repr. New York: Arco, 1974.

*4236   West, John. Village records. New York: St. Martin's Pr., 1962.
Detailed and practical information about materials available for the study of local history and the best way to handle them.

4237   Wright, Donald. Some copy census returns held by West Midland public libraries, 1973. Birmingham, England: West Midland branch of the Library Assoc., 1973.
Extremely useful for researchers dealing with the Midlands area.

# *Paleography*

4238   Buck, William S. B. Examples of handwriting, 1550–1560. 2nd ed. Chichester, England: Phillimore, 1973.
Italic script explained; selected Christian and place names, common spellings and abbreviations. Cheaply priced.

4239   Cornwall, Julian. How to read old title deeds, XVI–XIX centuries. Birmingham, England: Dept. of Extra-Mural Studies, Univ. of Birmingham, 1964.

4240 **Emmison, Frederick G.** How to read local archives, 1550–1700. *Helps for students of history* 82. London: Historical Assoc., 1967.

*4241 **Gardner, David E.,** and **Smith, F.** Genealogical research in England and Wales. v.3. New ed. Salt Lake City: Bookcraft, 1970.
Written solely for the genealogist; all forms of handwriting encountered in early documents are considered. Pt. of a 3v. set (*see* no.4426); can be purchased separately.

*4242 **Gooder, Eileen A.** Latin for local history: an introduction. 2nd impr. London: Longmans, 1963.
Self-teaching manual and guide to the kind of Latin appearing in records.

4243 **Grieve, Hilda E. P.** Examples of English handwriting, 1150–1750. With transcripts and translations . . . 3rd ed. Chelmsford, England: Essex Record Office, 1966.
Includes useful manuscript alphabet.

4244 **Hector, Leonard C.** The handwriting of English documents. 2nd ed. London: Arnold [1966].
Designed to ease the problems of reading handwriting used in English administration, legal, and business documents.

4245 **Latham, Ronald E.** Revised medieval Latin word-list from British and Irish sources. Based on *Medieval Latin word list,* ed. by J. H. Baxter and C. Johnson, 1934. New York: Oxford Univ. Pr., 1965.

4246 **Martin, Charles T.** The record interpreter: a collection of abbreviations, Latin words and names used in English historical manuscripts and records. 2nd ed., 3rd impr. London. Baltimore: G.P.C., 1949.
Lists French and Latin abbreviations, presents an elementary medieval Latin dictionary.

4247 **Newton, Kenneth C.** Medieval local records. A reading aid. London: Historical Assoc., 1971.
Helps for students of history. Facsimiles, transcriptions, and translations.

# *Periodicals and Series*

GENERAL

4248 **Texts and calendars:** an analytical guide to serial publications. *See* no.4159.

SEPARATE

4249 **The ancestor:** a quarterly review of county and family history, heraldry and antiquities of England, Ireland, Scotland, and Wales. 12v. and index. London, 1902–1905.

4250 ——— Index by E. E. Dorling. 3pts. in 1. Repr. London: Heraldry Today, 1970. Distributed in U.S. by G.P.C., Baltimore.
Short-lived but important work. Index has 6,000 names.

4251 **Archives.** v.1– . 1949– . London: British Records Assoc.
no.1–26, 29–30 repr. by Dawson, Folkestone, England, 1973.

4252 **The armorial:** an international quarterly journal of heraldry, genealogy, nobiliary law, heraldic art . . . v.1– , 1959– . Edinburgh, Scotland: The Armorial.
Scholarly articles, every aspect of international heraldry. Sporadic appearance.

4253 **Blackmansbury.** v.1–9, 1964–72. London: Pinhorns.
Journal of notes and queries for the genealogist, local historian, etc. Family lists, parish records, wills, etc.

4254 **British Record Society, Ltd.** The index library; containing indexes, calendars, and abstracts of British records. v.1– , 1888– . Chichester, England: Phillimore.
One of the great record series. Society originally known as the Index Society. Contains wills, deeds, marriage, and other records. Unless the set is complete, researchers will be in difficulties, because several volumes spread over many years.

4255 **Catholic Record Society.** Publications. v.1- , 1905- . London: The Society. Repr. vols. from Dawsons, Folkestone, England.
Several Catholic registers and records of vital importance to the Catholic researcher.

4256 **Coat of arms.** v.1- , 1950- . London: Heraldry Soc.
Attempts to be nontechnical. Most parts are in print. Quarterly. Originally *The escutcheon,* pub. by the Society of Heraldic Antiquaries.

4257 **Collectanea topographica et genealogica.** v.1-8, 1834-43.
Continued as *Topographer and genealogist,* see no.4274. A classic.

4258 **Family history:** the journal of the Institute of Heraldic and Genealogical Studies. Ed. by Cecil R. Humphrey-Smith. v.1- , 1962- . Canterbury, England: The Institute.
Wills, pedigrees, arms, indentures, registers, Morant's additions and corrections to Burke's *General armory* (no.5013). Scholarly and authoritative, but inclined to be irregular in appearance.

4259 **Foster, Joseph.** Collectanea genealogica. 3v. London, 1882-83.
Published material for the admissions to Gray's Inn utilized in Foster's work, *Men at the Bar,* 1885 (no.4317). Also contains, v.1: funeral certificates of noblemen and gentry of Ireland, 1607-1729; v.2, *Musgrave's obituary,* 1665-1880 (*see also* no.4355); v.3, register of admissions to Gray's Inn, 1521-1889 (*see* no.4318); Sims' index to pedigrees contained in the heralds visitations (*see also* no.4184).

4260 **Fragmenta genealogica.** Ed. by Frederick A. Crisp. no.1-13; new ser. no.1. London, 1889-1910.
Coats of arms.

4261 **The genealogical magazine:** a journal of family history, heraldry, and pedigrees. v.1-8, 1897-1904. London.
Full of genealogies; many genealogical references.

4262 **Genealogical quarterly:** notes and queries dealing with British and American family and clan history and biography. v.1-2, 1931-32. Absorbed by *Topographical quarterly, see* no.4275.

4263 **The genealogist.** v.1-7; new ser., v.1-38; 5 suppl. vol.s. London, 1877-1922.
Indexed and referred to in many reference works and genealogies. Fine set.

*4264 **Genealogists' magazine:** official organ of the Society of Genealogists. v.1- , 1925- . (Formerly The quarterly series of the Society of Genealogists, no.1-31, 1917-25.) London: The Society.
Should be considered as a continuation of *The genealogist (see* no.4263), and therefore essential. Many parts still in print.

4265 **Harleian Society.** Publications (Visitation ser.). v.1- , 1869- . London: The Society.
Few volumes in print. The Harleian Society has published 2 series for almost 100 years. The *Visitation series* contains most (but not all) county visitations and other related material. The *Parish register series* contains (with one or two exceptions) only London parish registers. The *Visitation series* is essential, but expensive.

4266 **The herald and the genealogist.** Ed. by John G. Nichols. v.1-8, 1863-74. London.
One of the best literary studies of heraldry and genealogy.

4267 **Jewish Historical Society of England.** Transactions and publications. v.1- , 1893- . London: The Society.
Some in print; other repr. by Dawsons, Folkestone, England.

4268 **The List and Index Society.** Publications. v.1- , 1966- . London: The Public Record Office.
Unpublished Public Record Office search room lists and indexes. Covers last 8 centuries, though much post-1850 material. Available by subscription only. About 12 vols. a year published, many early volumes out-of-print. There is also a special series

which can be purchased by the public. Up to v.108 in 1974.

**4269 The local historian.** v.8– , 1968– . London: Standing Conference for Local History.
Formerly *Amateur historian,* v.1–7, 1952–67. Information and guidance to those interested in local history inquiry. Methods of research, sources of information. Numerous useful and accurate details on archives and genealogical material.

**4270 London Record Society.** Publications. v.1– , 1965– . Leicester: Leicester Univ. Lib.
Transcripts, abstracts, primary sources for the history of London: inhabitants, wills, etc., from 1244.

**4271 London University.** Institute of Historical Research bulletin. v.1– , 1923– . London: The Institute.
Some genealogical works and notes spread throughout the series. Index for v.1–25, 1923–52 published in 1952.

**4272 Miscellanea genealogica et heraldica.** Ser.1, v.1-ser.5, v.10 (31v. in all). London, 1868-1938. Suppl. lv. [1920–25].
Fine series with valuable information not found elsewhere. Indexed in other reference works and therefore essential. Volume numbering confusing in earlier series; volumes often lack title pages in ser.1 and 2. Incorporated *The British archivist* in 1920, and continued as *Miscellanea genealogica et heraldica* and *The British archivist*.

**4273 Recusant history.** v.1– , 1951– . London: Catholic Record Soc. With cumulative index, v.1–5, from Dawson's, Folkestone, England.

**4274 Topographer and genealogist.** v.1–3, 1846–58. London.
Ed. by Sir Frederic Madden, John D. Nichols, and others. A classic. Formerly *Collectanea topographica et genealogica;* see no.4257.

**4275 Topographical quarterly;** notes and queries with British and American local history, antiquity, genealogy . . . v.1–7, 1932–39.
Merged with *Genealogical quarterly,* see no.4262.

# Chronology

**\*4276 Bond, John J.** Handy-book of rules and tables for verifying dates of historical events, and of public and private documents, giving tables of regnal years of English sovereigns . . . 1066–1889. 1889. Repr. New York: Russell & Russell, 1966.

**\*4277 Cheney, Christopher R.** Handbook of dates for students of English history. *Royal Historical Soc. guides and handbooks* 4. Rev. Folkestone, England: Dawsons, 1970.
Establishing dates in England before 1752, and in places like Russia up to the present century, is a complex business. This book is designed to help researchers. Law terms, saints' days, old style/new style are explained.

**4278 Haydn, Joseph T.** Haydn's dictionary of dates and universal information relating to all ages and nations. 25th ed. 1910. Repr. New York: Dover, 1969.
1st ed. appeared in 1850s. Repr. is unabridged and unaltered from 1910 ed.

**4279 Powicke, Sir Frederick M.,** and **Fryde, E. B.** Handbook of British chronology. 2nd ed. *Royal historical Soc. guides and handbooks* 2. Folkestone, England: Dawsons, 1972.
Useful bibliography of published and unpublished list of holders of public office in England. Names and dates of kings, from officers of state and church, dukes, marquesses and earls, parliaments and church synods.

# Biographies

GENERAL

**\*4280 Boase, Frederic.** Modern English biography; containing many thousand concise memoirs of persons who have died between the years 1851–1900 . . . 6v. 1892–1921. Repr. New York: Barnes & Noble, 1965.

Contains more than 40,000 biographies of well-known and lesser-known persons.

*4281  **Dictionary of national biography.** 22v. London, 1908–1909.

*4282  ——— 2nd—6th suppl. New York: Oxford Univ. Pr., 1912–39.

*4283  ——— Index and epitome. 2v. London, 1903–13.

*4284  ——— Corrections and additions . . . cumulated from the *Bulletin of Institute of Historical Research,* Univ. of London, 1923–63. Boston: G. K. Hall, 1966.

The most important reference work for English biography; includes noteworthy Americans of colonial period. Decades added at intervals.

4285  ——— The concise dictionary. 1903. Repr. 2v.: v.1, to 1900; v.2, 1901–50. New York: Oxford Univ. Pr., 1953–61.

4286  **Haydn, Joseph T.** The book of dignities, continued to the present time (1894) and with an index to the entire work by Horace Ockerby. 3rd ed. From G.P.C., Baltimore. Repr. of 1894 ed.

Official personages of the British Empire, sovereigns and rulers of the world and knighthood of United Kingdom and India, etc.

4287  **Phillips, Lawrence B.** Dictionary of biographical reference; containing over 100,000 names, together with a classed index of the biographical literature of Europe and America. 3rd ed., supplemented by F. Weitenkampf. 1889. Repr. Graz, Austria: Akad. Druck u. Verlaganstalt, 1966.

PROFESSIONS

4288  (Apothecaries) **Cameron, Hector C.,** and **Underwood, E. A.** History of the Worshipful Company of Apothecaries. London: The Society, 1963.

Complete list of registered druggists for two centuries.

4289  (Architects) **Colvin, Howard M.** A biographical dictionary of English architects, 1660–1840. London: John Murray, 1954.

4290  (Army) **Army lists.** Apart from those listed below, there are several lists (mostly of officers) of various regiments, e.g. Royal Artillery, 1716–1899; Royal Engineers, 1660–1898; Army Medical Services, 1727–1898.

4291  (Army) **Dalton, Charles.** English army lists and commission registers, 1661–1714. 6v. 1892–1904. Repr. 6v. in 3. London: Edwards, 1960; available only from G.P.C., Baltimore.

12,000 names of commissioned officers, with service records and biographical notes. Irish, Welsh, Scots and lists of troops raised in colonial America also included.

4292  (Army) **Great Britain. War Office.** The army list of 1840. Repr. by the Society for Army Historical Research, with a complete index of names and regiments. Sheffield, England, 1931.

4293  ——— A list of the general and field officers, as they rank in the Army, 1754/1868– . (Now pub. under title *Army list.*) London. Available from British Information Services, New York.

One in every 5 to 10 years needed. Before 1868, not published annually.

4294  (Army) **Peacock, Edward.** The army lists of the Roundheads and Cavaliers, containing the names of the officers in the royal and parliamentary armies of 1642. [New ed.?] London, 1874.

Covers Civil War 1642–49; registers and lists.

4295  (Clergy) **Anstruther, Godfrey.** The seminary priests: a dictionary of the secular clergy of England and Wales. v.1: Elizabethan, 1558–1603. 2v. Woodchester, Glos.: The Author, 1966.

*4296  (Clergy) **Crockford's Clerical directory,** 1858– . New York: Oxford Univ. Pr.

Needed every 5 years. Gives address of every member of the clergy in the Church of England. Lists all parishes of England and Wales, and Anglican parishes of Ireland, Scotland, Canada, and the Commonwealth, but not the Protestant Episcopal Church of the United States of America. Published sporadically until 1870, annually thereafter, and lately biennially.

**4297** (Clergy) **Foster, Joseph.** Index ecclesiasticus; or, Alphabetical lists of all ecclesiastical dignitaries in England and Wales since the Reformation . . . Oxford, England, 1890.

Covers period 1800-40 only; no more published.

**4298** (Clergy) **Hennessy, George L.** Novum repertorium ecclesiasticum parochiale Londinense: or London diocesan clergy succession from the earliest times to the year 1898. London, 1898.

**4299** (Clergy) **Le Neve, John.** Fasti ecclesiae anglicanae, 1066-1300. v.1-, 1968- . Rev. and expanded. New York: Oxford Univ. Pr.

**4300** ———— ———— 1300-1541. 12v. New York: Oxford Univ. Pr., 1962-67.

**4301** ———— 1541-1857. v.1- , 1969- . New York: Oxford Univ. Pr.

Le Neve produced his list of church dignitaries (with dates of tenure) in 1716, and Dufus Hardy brought the list up to date in his 3v. ed. 1845. Standard authority for identification of higher clergy of the Church of England.

**4302** (Clergy) **Matthews, Arnold G.** Calamy revised, being a revision of Edmund Calamy's Account of the ministers and others ejected and silenced, 1660-62. 1702. Oxford, England, 1934.

An alphabetical list of the ejected, with biographical notes. Devoted to dispossessed ministers, with other particulars as given by Calamy in his "Ejected ministers," with new biographical details not available to Calamy. Full and reliable index. A revision of Calamy's account of the ministers and others ejected and silenced.

**4303** (Clergy) **Matthews, Arnold G.** Walker revised, being a revision of John Walker's *Sufferings of the clergy during the Grand Rebellion,* 1642-60. Oxford, England, 1948.

Not a new ed. 1,100 names of parochial clergy added by Matthews. Complementary vol. to *Calamy revised,* no.4302.

**4304** (Clockmakers) **Atkins, Charles E.** Register of apprentices of the Worshipful Company of Clockmakers of the City of London . . . 1631 . . . to 1931. London, 1931.

**4305** (Education) **Emden, Alfred B.** A biographical register of the University of Cambridge to A.D. 1500. New York: Cambridge Univ. Pr., 1963.

**4306** ———— Biographical register of the University of Oxford, to A.D. 1500. 3v. New York: Oxford Univ. Pr., 1957-59.

**4307** ———— ———— 1501-40. New York: Oxford Univ. Pr., 1974.

**4308** (Education) **Foster, Joseph.** Alumni Oxonienses, 1500-1886. 8v. London, 1887-92.

This and Emden (no.4305-06) are authentic lists. *Alumni Oxonienses* was supplemented by Foster's *Oxford men and their colleges,* 1893, but this need only be acquired when it is vital to go up to 1893. The 1500-1886 series gives place of birth and parentage.

**4309** (Education) **Jacobs, Phyllis M.** Registers of the universities, colleges and schools of Great Britain and Ireland: a list. London: Univ. of London, Inst. of Historical Research, 1964.

**4310** (Education) **Venn, John,** and **Venn, J. A.** Alumni Cantabrigienses. Pt.1, (1250)-1751, 4v.; pt.2, 1751-1900, 6v. Cambridge, Eng., 1922-54. From Cambridge Univ. Pr., New York.

Authentic list of members, with place of birth and parentage, of the University of Cambridge.

**4312** (Genealogists) **Phillimore's directory for genealogists and local his-**

torians. Chichester, England: Phillimore, 1963.
Out of date but latest available.

**4313** (Genealogists) **Society of Genealogists, London.** Catalogue of members' interests, 1968-71. London: The Society, 1974.
Supplement to the Society's *Register and directory,* 1966. Useful for discovering current research and researchers in various fields.

**4314** (Government) **Members of Parliament . . . 1213-1874.** London, 1878-91.
v.1, 1213-1702; v.2-3, 1705-96, 1801-74; v.4, Index to name of member of Parliament, 1705-1885.

**4315** (Government) **Sainty, John C.** Office-holders in modern Britain: officials of the Board of Trade, 1660-1870. v.1- . London: Athlone Pr., Univ. of London, Inst. of Historical Research, 1972- (in progress).
Biographies excellent.

**4316** ——— Treasury officials, 1660-1870. London: Athlone Pr., Univ. of London, Inst. of Historical Research, 1972.

**4316a** Unlike lawyers in America, those practicing law in the courts of England barristers must belong to an "Inn," and they are admitted to the Bar through one of the Inns of Court. Therefore, all the following lists are necessary for tracing anyone who was a member of the Bar. On the other hand, solicitors, lawyers who are permitted to appear only in certain lower courts, need not go through the Inns of Court.

**4317** (Law) **Foster, Joseph.** Men at the Bar. London, 1885.
Biographies of all barristers alive in 1885. Much of material came from *Collectanea genealogica* (no.4257), when it ceased in 1883.

**4318** ——— The register of admissions, Gray's Inn, London, 1521-1889. London, 1889.

Contains 16,000 names of members of one of the famous Inns.

**4319** (Law) **Inner Temple, London.** Students admitted, 1547-1660. London, 1878.

**4320** (Law) **Law list.** London, 1841- .
(A continuation of the *New law list,* 1798-1802, and *Clarke's Law list,* 1803-40) London: Stevens.
One in every 5 to 10 years needed. Directory of the legal professions; gives full names of barristers and solicitors and all law officers.

**4321** (Law) **Lincoln's Inn, London.** The records of the Honourable Society of Lincoln's Inn: admissions, 1420-1893, and chapel registers. 2v. London, 1896.

**4322** (Law) **Sturgess, Herbert A. C.** Register of Admissions to the Honourable Society of the Middle Temple, from the 15th century to . . . 1944. 3v. London: Butterworth, 1949.

**4323** (Medicine) **Bloom, James H.,** and **James, R. R.** Medical practitioners in the Diocese of London, licensed under the Act 3 Hen. VIII, cap. II: an annotated list, 1529-1725. Cambridge, England, 1935.

**4324** (Medicine) **Medical directory.** 1845- . London: Churchill.
Because this directory is more inclusive, it is preferred to the *Medical register.* Needed once in every 5 or 10 years.

**4325** (Medicine) **Munk, William.** Roll of the Royal College of Physicians of London, 1518-1825. 2nd ed. rev. and enl. 3v. London: Royal College of Physicians, 1878.
v.1, 1518-1700; v.2, 1701-1800; v.3, 1801-25.

**4326** ——— ——— v.4. Lives of the fellows, 1826-1925. By G. H. Brown. London: Royal College of Physicians, 1955.
Often referred to as *Munk's Roll.* The most authoritative source of biographical information for many physicians. v.4 includes fellows who were elected up to 1925 and who died before 1954.

4327   (Medicine) **Plarr, Victor G.** Plarr's lives of the fellows of the Royal College of Surgeons. 2v. London: College of Surgeons, 1930.

4328   ——— ——— Continued by Sir D'Arcy Power . . . 1930-51. London: Royal College of Surgeons, 1953.

4329   (Medicine) **Raach, John H.** A directory of English country physicians, 1603-43. London: Dawson's, 1962.

4330   (Navy) **Charnock, John.** Biographia navalis. 1660-1797. 6v. London, 1794-98.
Memoirs of officers of the Royal Navy, 1660-1797.

4331   (Navy) **Great Britain. Admiralty.** Navy list, 1749- . London. Available from British Information Services, New York.
Annually since 1749, one in every 5 to 10 years needed. Contains the officers on the active list of the Royal Navy.

4332   (Navy) **Greenwich, England.** National Maritime Museum's commissioned sea officers of the Royal Navy, 1660-1815. 3v. London: The Museum, 1954.

4333   (Navy) **Marshall, John.** Royal naval biography; or, Memoirs of the services of all . . . on the Admiralty list . . . 4v. in 3. and 4v. suppl. (8v. in all). London, 1823-25.
Has supplement in 4v., 1827-30, but is of little genealogical value.

4334   (Navy) **O'Byrne, William R.** A naval biographical dictionary; comprising the life and services of every living officer in Her Majesty's Navy . . . Compiled from authentic and other family documents. London, 1849.
New and enl. ed. was started in 1859, but it was not completed. 1849 ed. gives some account of all naval officers in the 1845 Navy list, and all others alive in 1849.

4335   (Sculptors) **Gunnis, Rupert.** Dictionary of British sculptors, 1660-1851. Cambridge, Mass.: Harvard Univ. Pr., 1954.

4336   (Shipwrights) **Ridge, Cecil H.,** and **Knight, A. C.** Records of the Worshipful Company of Shipwrights, being an alphabetical digest of freemen and apprentices, compiled from the Company's records. 2v. London, 1939-46.
v.1, 1428-1780; v.2, by Ridge and P. E. Jones, 1728-1858.

4337   (Theater) **Highfill, Philip H., Jr.** (and others). A biographical dictionary of actors, actresses, musicians, dancers, managers, and other stage personnel in London, 1660-1800. v.1- . Carbondale, Ill.: Southern Illinois Univ. Pr., 1974- (in progress).
To letter *B* by end of 1974; letters *C* and *D* available early in 1975.

## Parish Registers

*4338  **Burke, Arthur M.** Key to ancient parish registers of England and Wales. 1908. Repr. Baltimore: G.P.C., 1971.
List of parishes with starting date of each register. Annotated index showing date of the earliest pre-1813 entry in every parish register, whether or not it has been published, and if so, where it can be found. Much of the information, particularly as to location, is now wrong, but the book is still useful.

4339   **Cox, John C.** The parish registers of England. 1910. Repr. Totowa, N.J.: Rowman & Littlefield, 1974.
A scholarly study of parish registers, giving details of reasons why registers were scanty at certain periods.

4340   **Genealogical Society of the Church of Jesus Christ of Latter-day Saints.** Computer parish listing, prepared February, 1972. Salt Lake City: L.D.S., 1972.

4341   **Great Britain. Public Record Office.** Parish register abstract . . . 1831. With index. London, 1833.
Registers listed under counties. Includes list of parishes and chapelries with exact periods of each volume of registers from 1538-1812.

**4342  Great Britain. Registrar-General of Births, Deaths, and Marriages.** List of non-parochial registers and records in the custody of the Registrar-General . . . at Somerset House . . . 1841. London, 1859.

More than 6,000 registers listed. For researchers whose forebears were not members of the Church of England, the road is difficult. Catholics, nonconformists, and persons of other religions seldom deposited their registers, and this list does not include Jewish records. Records are now at the Public Record Office.

**4343  London. Guildhall Library.** Parish registers: a handlist. Pt.1, registers of Church of England parishes within the city of London; pt.2, registers of Church of England parishes outside the city of London. Non-parochial registers and registers of foreign denominations. Burial ground records. 3rd ed., rev. London: The Library, 1972.

**4343a  Original parish registers in record offices and libraries.** Matlock, Derbyshire: Local Population Studies, 1974.

Includes original parish registers deposited with institutions; rough books of register entries, duplicate books, early replacement copies; but it does not include registers still in private hands. England, Wales, and Isle of Man. Particularly useful for Welsh registers.

**\*4344  Society of Genealogists.** Catalogue of parish register copies. Pt.1, Society of Genealogists' collection; pt.2, other than in the Society's collection. Rev. Chichester, England: Phillimore, 1972-74.

Has details of about 10,000 registers; pt.2 is useful because it gives location of registers. Contains large numbers of nonconformist registers. Revision of pt.2, 1974 shows Yorkshire to have been completely revised and rearranged.

**\*4345  Steel, Donald J.** National index of parish registers: a guide to Anglican, Roman Catholic and nonconformist registers before 1837, together with information on marriage licences, Bishop's transcripts, and modern copies. London, 1967- . Available from Tuttle, Rutland, Vt.

The following have been published:
v.1, pt. 1. Parish registers, marriage licences, etc. 1968.
v.2. Sources for nonconformist genealogy and family history. 1973.
v.5. South midlands and Welsh border. 1967.
v.12. Sources for Scottish genealogy and family history. 1971.

Those published so far are excellent, and the set will be essential to most libraries. The plan of publication is as follows: v.3, Southeast England; v.3, South-west England; v.6, North and east midlands; v.7, London and home counties north of the Thames; v.8, Eastern England; v. 9, North-east England; v.10, North-west England; v.11, North Wales; v.13, South Wales. The cut-off date, 1837, denotes the fact that from that date all records were deposited in Somerset House, London. Anyone needing information from 1837 on should write to Somerset House.

# Vital Statistics

(Births, Marriages, Deaths)

⊹ Marriage licenses always indicated where the marriage was to take place. But although details of the marriage are to be found in the London, Canterbury, Winchester, York, or other lists, it does not follow that the participants actually came from the area. Searchers would do well to refer to all registers when marriage details are needed. Abbreviated calendars often omit where the marriage was to take place. Also, issuance of the marriage license does not necessarily indicate that the marriage actually took place.

**4346  Bernau, Charles A.** Sixteenth century marriages (1538-1600). London, 1911.

**4347  Canterbury Registry.** Allegations for marriage licenses issued by the Vicar-General of the Archbishop of Canterbury, 1660-1694. 4v. *Harleian Soc. (Visitations),* 30, 31, 33, 34. London, 1890-92.

v.1, 1679-87; v.2, 1687-94; v.3, 1660-68; v.4, 1669-79. The Vicar-General was concerned only with issuing licenses for persons coming from two different dioceses within the province of Canterbury.

**4348 Canterbury (Province). Faculty Office.** Allegations for marriage licenses issued from the Faculty Office of the Archbishop of Canterbury at London, 1543–1869. *Harleian Soc. (Visitations)* 24. London, 1886.

The Faculty Office was similar to the office of the Vicar-General and issued marriage licenses for people from the provinces of Canterbury and York. This volume does not contain any matter other than licenses and marriages.

**4349 Chester, Joseph L.** Allegations for marriage licenses issued by the Dean and Chapter of Westminster, 1558–1699; also for those issued by the Vicar-General of the Archbishop of Canterbury, 1660–79. Compiled and ed. by Joseph L. Chester. *Harleian Soc. (Visitations)* 23. London, 1886.

**4350 Farrar, Robert H.** An index to the biographical and obituary notices in the *Gentleman's magazine*, 1731–80. British Record Soc., 1891. Repr. New York: Kraus, 1970.

The *Gentleman's magazine* was of a high literary character. It ceased in 1907, but to the end it published very accurate birth, marriage, and obituary notices.

**4351 Foster, Joseph.** London marriage licenses, 1521–1869. Ed. by Joseph Foster, from excerpts by Joseph L. Chester. London, 1887.

Extracts only. It represents the alphabetical arrangement of no.4348. Largest collection of marriage licenses in one book.

**4352 Fry, Edward A.** An index to the marriages in the *Gentleman's magazine*, 1731–68. Exeter, England, 1922.

*See* note under no.4350. Originally a suppl. to *The genealogist*, new ser., v.34–38; *see* no.4263.

**4354 Massey, Robert W.** A list of parishes in Boyd's marriage index. Chichester, England: Phillimore, 1974.

An expanded guide of the 2nd ed., 1963. Percival Boyd's *Index* contains more than seven million names. Copies of it, in typescript, are held by the Society of Genealogists, London, and by the Genealogical Society of the Church of Jesus Christ of Latter-day Saints, Salt Lake City. The 2nd ed. lacked the two miscellaneous sections, but this expansion has these series and it also includes marriage indexes of Gloucestershire, Oxfordshire, and Northumberland, not the work of Boyd.

**4355 Musgrave, Sir William.** Obituary prior to 1800 . . . 6v. *Harleian Soc. (Visitations)* 44–49. London, 1899–1901.

Subtitled "A general nomenclature and obituary, as far as relates to England, Scotland, and Ireland." Accurate work, particularly useful for the 18th century. Alphabetical index to a large number of obituaries and biographies, found in 85 works. Many not included in *Dictionary of national biography* (no.4281).

**4355a Pallot's marriage and birth indexes.** Guide to parishes. Canterbury: Inst. of Heraldic & Genealogical Studies, 1974.

Mostly marriages, 1780–1837, with 101 of the 103 London ancient parishes, and details of the county registers of England. Compiled by Pallot & Co., record agents, and purchased by the Institute. This catalog gives periods for which records of each parish are known to be complete in the index. Invaluable.

**4356 Paver's marriage licenses. 1567–1630.** Pts.1–17. From *Yorkshire archaeological journal,* 7, 9–14, 16–17, 20, 1882–1909. York: Yorkshire Archaeological Soc., 1910.

**4357** ——— A consolidated index, 1567–1630. York, 1912.

**4358** ——— 1630–1714. Ed. by John W. Clay. 3v. York, 1909–12. *Yorkshire Archaeological Soc. Record ser.,* v.40, 43, 46. Available from Yorkshire Archaeological Soc., Leeds.

Extracts made by William Paver from original documents in the registry of Yorkshire. The documents are now missing.

**4359 Phillimore's Parish register series (Marriages).** v.1–240. London, 1896–1938.

Invaluable set of marriage registers. Each volume contains several registers; in all, about 1,400. Because there is continuous pagination, the Library of Congress does not catalog each register separately. Details may be found in *A complete alphabetical list* (no.4360). Most volumes are out of print, but some can be obtained from G.P.C., Baltimore, and from Phillimore, Chichester, England.

4360 ———— A complete alphabetical list of over 1,400 parishes included in the *Phillimore's Parish register* series . . . rev. ed. London, 1935.

## Monumental Brasses

4361 **Cooke, Bernard C.** A bibliography of monumental inscriptions in the city and county of London. In *Genealogists' magazine,* v.5-6, 1931-34. London.

4362 **Haines, Herbert.** A manual of monumental brasses. 1861. Repr., with added introduction, biographical notes, and bibliography. 2v. in 1. Baltimore: G.P.C., 1970.

Classic survey of English monumental brasses, or effigies of persons, from the last and expanded ed. Exhaustive list of brasses in the British Isles.

4363 **Monumental Brass Society.** Transactions. v.1- , 1887- . London: The Society.

Available from the Society, Newport, Buckinghamshire, England. Much useful information for genealogists; folding pedigrees, church brasses, genealogical tables.

4364 **Stephenson, Mill.** A list of monumental brasses in the British Isles. (Based upon A manual of monumental brasses, by Herbert Haines.) 1926. Repr. in 2v. with an appendix by Ralph H. Griffin. 1938. London: Monumental Brass Soc., 1965.

Monumental brasses almost invariably contain genealogical information not readily found in printed records. Stephenson has the most complete list of brasses, arranged in county order, with copious index. Bibliographical notes given.

4365 **Suffling, Ernest R.** English church brasses, from the 13th to the 17th century. 1910. Repr. Baltimore: G.P.C., 1970.

237 illustrations of brass memorial effigies, coats of arms, and heraldic devices. Much genealogical and vital statistics information. Has list of churches containing brasses.

## Wills

*4366 **Camp, Anthony.** Wills and their whereabouts; being a thorough revision and extension of the previous work of the same name by B. G. Bouwens. 4th ed., rev. and extended, with several new features. London: The Author, 1974.

Guide to present locations of wills in England, Ireland, Scotland, Wales, the Channel Islands, and the Isle of Man. Bibliography, with exhaustive index.

4367 **Canterbury (Province). Prerogative Court.** Abstracts of probates and sentences, 1620-24. "Year books of probate" by John Matthews and G. F. Matthews. London, 1911.

4368 ———— Abstracts of probate acts. "Year books of probate from 1630 [-1649]." By John Matthews and G. F. Matthews. [v.1]-4. London, 1902-1906.

4369 ———— ———— Extra vol. of "Year books of probate" (from 1630-39). Sentences and complete index nominum. London, 1907.

4370 ———— Abstracts of probate acts. "Commonwealth probates" (1650-55). By John and G. F. Matthews. v.1[-4]. London, 1909-26/7.

4371 ———— Abstracts of wills. "Register Soame" 1620. By J. H. Lea. Boston: New England Historic Genealogical Soc., 1904.

4372 ———— General abstracts of wills proved. Register "Wootton" 1658. 7v. By William Briggs. Leeds, England, 1894-1914.

4373 ———— Index of wills proved 1383-1700. 12v. *British Record Soc.*, v.10, 11, 18, 25, 43, 44, 54, 61, 67, 71, 77, 80. London, 1893-1960. Some available from Kraus Repr. Corp., New York; others from the British Record Soc.
The period 1700-1853 remains unindexed. The Prerogative Court was the court of the Archbishop of Canterbury for granting probates, etc. when the deceased held property in more than one diocese. Thus, wills proved in Canterbury are not necessarily concerned with people from Canterbury, Kent, or even the south of England.

4374 ———— Wills, sentences and probate sets, 1661-70 (inclusive), arranged and numbered in alphabetical order of testators, with separate indexes of places, ships, "stray names," trades and conditions. By John H. Morrison. London, 1935.

4375 **Currer-Briggs, Noel.** English wills of colonial families. New Orleans, La.: Polyanthos, 1972.
434 wills abstracted for the most part to families included in *Virginia settlers* (no. 3539). Few direct references to persons resident in America.

4376 **Genealogical Society of the Church of Jesus Christ of Latter-day Saints.** Pre-1858 English probate jurisdictions. *Research papers,* ser. A, no.7-44. Salt Lake City: L.D.S., 1967-70.
Probate records of England are among the best genealogical sources for direct evidence. For full annotation, *see* no.4201.

*4377 **Gibson, Jeremy S. W.** Wills and where to find them (in England). Baltimore: G.P.C., 1974.
Freshly thought-out guide to the location of wills, admonitions, and inventories in the British Isles. Arranged by county and includes 42 line maps showing testamentary jurisdictions. *British Record Society publ.* Essential.

4378 **Great Britain. Public Record Office.** A list of wills, administrations, etc. in the Public Record Office, London, England, 12th to 19th century . . . Baltimore, 1968. Available from Tuttle, Rutland, Vt.
Gives names and places of testators and stray wills from all over Great Britain; supplements other lists of wills. Approximately 2,000 names.

4379 **London (Diocese). Commissary Court.** Index to testamentary records in the Commissary Court of London, now preserved in the Guildhall Library. Ed. by Marc Fitch. 1374- . v.1- , 1969- (in progress). London: H. M. Stationery Office. From British Information Services, New York.
v.1, 1374-1488; v.2, 1489-1570. Intention is to go to 1700. Alphabetical list of wills registered at the court; also an index to testators' trades and conditions, and a place-name index.

4380 **North country wills;** being abstracts of wills relating to the counties of York, Nottingham, Northumberland, Cumberland, and Westmorland, at Somerset House and Lambeth Palace, 1383-1604. Ed. by J. W. Clay. *Surtees Soc. publ.* 116, 121. Durham, England, 1908-12.
Short abstracts of wills of persons resident in London and the south who had some connection with northern counties.

4381 **Pratt, David H.** A remarkable collection of English-Welsh probate records and aids in using them. World Conference on Records, area C-11 paper. Salt Lake City: L.D.S., 1969.

4382 **York, England.** Index of wills proved in the Prerogative Court of the Archbishop with the Exchequer Court of the Dean of York, 1389-1688. 14v. *Yorkshire Archaeological Soc. record ser.* 6, 11, 14, 19, 22, 24, 25, 28, 32, 35, 49, 60, 68, 89. Leeds, England, 1889-1934.
Some vols. are in print from the Yorkshire Archaeological Soc., Leeds, England.

4383 **York. Registry.** Testamenta Eboracensia; or wills registered at York. 6v. 1300-1551. *Surtees Soc. publ.* 4, 30, 45, 53, 79, 106. Durham, England, 1836-1902.

# Topography

✠ Including maps, atlases, gazetteers

4384   **Anderson, John P.** The book of British topography: a classified catalogue of the topographical works in the library of the British Museum relating to Great Britain and Ireland. 1881. Repr. Baltimore: G.P.C., 1970.
14,000 titles; old but still superior to other titles.

*4385   **Bartholomew, John.** The gazetteer of the British Isles. 9th ed. with supplement of over 2,000 additions and amendments; repr. with surnames of the 1971 census. Edinburgh, Scotland: Bartholomew, 1972.
Useful for determining parish data. The road atlas is best for finding towns and villages. Contains a list of civil parishes and also small localities not found in Lewis (no. 4392). Lewis is useful for details of ecclesiastical parishes.

4386   ———— The handy reference atlas of the British Isles. Edinburgh, Scotland: Bartholomew, 1963.
Useful for determining dates of formation of parishes.

4387   **Census of Great Britain, 1851.** Index to names of parishes, townships, and places in population tables of Great Britain. London, 1852.

*4388   **Gardner, David E.; Harland, D.;** and **Smith, F. A.** A genealogical atlas of England and Wales. Repr. Salt Lake City: Deseret Book Co., 1968.
Designed especially for the American researcher. Rearrangement of an old series originated by Lewis (no.4392) in the 1840s. Superior to the Lewis maps.

4389   **Great Britain. General Register Office.** 1951 census of England and Wales: index of place names. 2v. London, 1955. Available from British Information Services, New York.

4390   ———— 1961. 2v. London, 1965. Available from British Information Services, New York.

Lists all places recorded in census with name of county, borough, urban district, or rural district in which situated. Useful in determining registration district for a given place so that reference can be made to the *List of registration officers,* a government publication which gives addresses of each registration office.

4391   **Institute of Heraldic and Genealogical Studies.** Parish maps of the counties of England and Wales. Canterbury, England: Achievements, 1964.
Large sheets for each county. Counties divided by ancient parishes, boundaries, etc. Dates of commencement of parish registers given; probate jurisdictions shown in color.

4392   **Lewis, Samuel A.** A topographical dictionary of England. 1831, 1833, 1835, 1840, 1842, 1845, 1849. London.
1831 and 1833 editions are considered best, because they contain lists of ecclesiastical parishes and some chapelries, and give information as to ecclesiastical jurisdictions which might be followed in seeking probate records. Although some places are omitted, set is essential; *see also* note under Smith, no.4394. The 1831 and 1833 editions have atlas bound in, but remainder have atlas volume for England and Wales in a separate volume. In general, later editions are reissues and show little, if any, difference.

4393   **Skelton, Raleigh A.** County atlases of the British Isles, 1579–1850: a bibliography. *Map Collectors' Circle ser.* 9, 14. London, 1964–68. Available from British Book Centre, New York.

*4394   **Smith, Frank.** A genealogical gazetteer of England: an alphabetical dictionary of places, with their locations, ecclesiastical jurisdictions, population, and the date of the earliest entry in the registers of every ancient parish in England. Baltimore: G.P.C., 1969.
Compiled from Lewis (no.4392), Burke (no.4338), Wilson (no.4396), and other works. Intended to make all gazetteer references about the ancient parishes available without recourse to books long out-of-print and not generally available in many libraries. Since it succeeds admirably, it is essential in all libraries. 17,000 entries.

**4395** **Victoria history of the counties of England.** By the University of London, Institute of Historical Research. New York: Oxford Univ. Pr., 1900– . Out-of-print vols. from Dawson, London.

Great scholarly work; its aim is "to narrate history of the English counties upon a foundation of original research." Of tremendous value to genealogists because of the large amount of local history, Domesday transcripts, etc. Two counties (Northamptonshire and Hertfordshire) have volumes entirely devoted to genealogy, but in general, every volume contains material vital to the researcher. Most are in two parts: general and topography. Roughly 30 percent of English counties covered so far. For researchers needing additional county information, a list of definitive works can be found in Kaminkow (no.4152). Expensive set, but essential to any library which seeks to assist British research.

**4396** **Wilson, John M.** The imperial gazetteer of England and Wales. 6v. Edinburgh, 1870–72.

There are variant editions. Some professional genealogists prefer Wilson to Lewis (no.4392) because Wilson has many more places listed, but *see* note under Smith, no. 4394.

# Names

PLACE

**4397** **Census of Great Britain, 1851.** Index to the names of parishes, townships, and places in population tables of Great Britain. London, 1852.

**4398** **Copley, Gorden J.** English place-names and their origins. New impr. North Pomfret, Vt.: David & Charles, 1968; New York: Kelley, 1968.

Origin of place-names and how they may be interpreted.

*****4399** **Ekwall, Eilert.** The concise Oxford dictionary of English place-names. 4th ed. New York: Oxford Univ. Pr., 1960.

More than 1,500 place-names given. The standard work.

**4400** ———— Street-names in the city of London. New York: Oxford Univ. Pr., 1954.

**4401** **English Place-Name Society.** [Publications] v.1– , 1924– . Cambridge, Eng. Obtainable from Univ. College, London.

Place-names arranged by hundreds (ancient Saxon administrative division of a county), with derivations. Once a county is known, there is no difficulty in finding the place-names.

**4402** **Genealogical Society of the Church of Jesus Christ of Latter-day Saints.** Index to places in the 1851 census of England, Wales, Isle of Man and the Channel Islands. Salt Lake City: L.D.S., 1965.

**4403** **Great Britain. General Register Office.** 1951 and 1961 censuses of England and Wales: index to place-names, *see* no.4389–90.

**4404** **Reaney, Percy H.** The origin of English place-names. 2nd impr. London: Routledge & Kegan Paul, 1961.

PERSONAL

✠ In this list it is not easy to single out the best source. All have different approaches, and names not in one are sometimes included in others. Most are worth acquiring.

**4405** **Barber, Henry.** British family names: their origin and meaning, with lists of Scandinavian, Frisian, Anglo-Saxon, and Norman names. 2nd ed. enl. 1903. Repr. Baltimore: G.P.C., 1968; Detroit, Mich.: Gale Research, 1968.

Best edition. Some regard Ewen (no.4409) as superior. 8,000 surnames.

*****4406** **Bardsley, Charles W. E.** A dictionary of English and Welsh surnames, with special American instances. Rev. ed. 1901. Repr. Baltimore: G.P.C., 1968; Newton Abbot, England: David & Charles, 1970. North Pomfret, Vt.: David & Charles.

Over 30,000 entries, with origin and meaning.

4407 ——— Our English surnames: their sources and significances. 6th ed. London, 1906. 1873 ed. repr. by Tuttle, Rutland, Vt., 1968; Newton Abbot, England: David & Charles, 1969. North Pomfret, Vt.: David & Charles.

Although the 1906 is the last edition, the earlier editions show little change from this, and some are really reprints. Information on Anglo-Saxon names which still prevail in America.

4408 Dolan, Jack R. English ancestral names: the evolution of the surname for medieval occupations. New York: Potter, distributed by Crown, 1972.

Vast amount of information concerning what the sociologists call "division of labor" in the Middle Ages. Readable social and economic history of Middle Ages with vast amount of information on names. 5,000 names.

4409 Ewen, Cecil H. L'Estrange. A history of surnames of the British Isles: a concise account of their origin . . . 1931. Baltimore: G.P.C., 1968; Detroit, Mich.: Gale Research, 1969.

The G.P.C. reprint includes additions and corrections, etc. Paignton, Eng., 1946, but Gale reprint does not include this addition. Many lists of surnames drawn from sources of the 11th to 17th centuries. Scholarly. Highly regarded by professional genealogists and historians.

4410 Ferguson, Robert. Surnames as a science. 2nd ed., rev. 1884. Repr. New York: Heraldic Pub. Co., 1967.

4411 Guppy, Henry B. Homes of family names in Great Britain. 1890. Repr. Baltimore: G.P.C., 1968.

Useful for locating family names. Still the only book which gives relative distributions according to counties.

4412 Harrison, Henry. Surnames of the United Kingdom. 2v. 1912–18. Repr. in 1v. Baltimore: G.P.C., 1969.

Comprehensive dictionary of 25,000 family names, with language of origin, original and variant forms, and their meanings.

4413 Hitching, Frank K., and Hitching, S. References to English surnames in 1601 (and 1602). 2v. 1911. Repr. in 1v. Baltimore: G.P.C., 1968.

19,650 references in 1601, and 20,500 in 1602. Useful for indicating distribution of various surnames in early 17th century. A total of 778 and 964 parishes represented.

4414 Lower, Mark A. Patronymica Britannica: a dictionary of the family names of the United Kingdom. 1860. Repr. New York: Heraldic Pub. Co., 1967.

4415 Matthews, Constance M. English surnames. New York: Scribner, 1967.

Updates earlier studies but does not supersede them. Has added chapter on American surnames not included in the 1966 British edition. 2,500 English surnames and their origin with index.

4416 Phillimore, William P. W., and Fry, E. A. An index to changes of name . . . 1760–1901. 1905. Repr. Baltimore: G.P.C., 1968; Detroit, Mich.: Gale Research, 1969.

One of the most essential works because of the many changes of name which occurred. 10,000 entries, giving dates, the change and the source.

4417 Pine, Leslie G. The story of surnames. New impr. Rutland, Vt.: Tuttle, 1970.

Norman, English, Scottish, Welsh and Irish surnames, with nicknames. Includes section on foreign names.

*4418 Reaney, Percy H. A dictionary of British surnames. 2nd impr. with some corr. London, 1966. Obtainable from Hillary House, New York.

Useful for finding variants of names. More than 20,000 surnames. Interpreted in the light of modern knowledge of the history of language, this work constitutes the greatest step forward since Bardsley's *Dictionary* (no.4406). Some authorities think that it supersedes Ewen (no.4409).

*4419 ——— The origin of English surnames. New York: Barnes & Noble, 1967.

Sequel to no.4418. Index lists 6,000 names; based largely on no.4418, but with addition of some new material.

*4420 **Smith, Elsdon C.** Personal names: a bibliography. 1952. Repr. Detroit, Mich.: Gale Research, 1965.
Definitive work.

4421 **Withycombe, Elizabeth G.** The Oxford dictionary of English Christian names. 2nd ed. New York: Oxford Univ. Pr., 1950. Paperback, 1973.

## Manuals

✠ The manuals listed are, in the opinion of several authorities, the best available. The compiler prefers Gardner and Smith (no.4426) because it is slanted toward the American researcher and seems to answer all the questions posed, but each one is useful and worth acquiring.

*4422 **American Society of Genealogists.** Genealogical research: methods and sources, Washington, D.C.: The Society, 1960.
pp.291-374 are of particular interest to researchers in America because British research is treated from the American's point of view. v.2, published in 1971, contains nothing on British genealogy.

*4423 **Camp, Anthony J.** Tracing your ancestors: a handbook of English research. New corr. ed. Baltimore: G.P.C., 1971.
Written principally for those trying to search on their own. Many valuable sources given. Highly recommended for library and pocket use. Revision is concise, accurate, and brought up to date.

4424 **Emmison, Frederick G.** Archives and local history. Rev. ed. Chichester, England: Phillimore, 1973.
Concerned with the last four centuries. Practical guide for students and teachers using local records, and deals with problems of Latin and archaic types of handwriting.

4424a ——— Introduction to archives. New ed., rev. Chichester, England: Phillimore, 1973.
Very useful guide and manual for archival users.

4425 **Fines, John.** The history student's guide to the library. Chichester, England: Phillimore, 1973.
Although primarily for historians, genealogists will find the bibliography, works of reference and aids vital to their research. Updates Hepworth (no.4428).

*4426 **Gardner, David E.,** and **Smith, F.** Genealogical research in England and Wales. 3v. v.1, 7th ed., 1967; v.2, 4th pr., 1970; v.3, 2nd ed., 1966. Salt Lake City: Bookcraft.
Work of members of the Church of Jesus Christ of Latter-day Saints. Because the authors are accomplished professionals, the set is one of the best available. v.3, devoted to paleography and the reading of ancient documents, is especially valuable to the genealogist (no.4241).

*4427 **Hamilton-Edwards, Gerald.** Tracing your British ancestors: a guide to genealogical sources, 3rd ed. Baltimore: G.P.C., 1974.
Particularly good for Scotland, the Army, the Navy, and the East India Company. Deals largely with the last 200-300 years. Published in London as *In search of ancestry*. Contains a magnificent bibliography. New chapter, "Searching in the U.S.A." added, with extended bibliography in 3rd ed. Essential.

4428 **Hepworth, Philip.** How to find out in history, a guide to sources of information for all. London: Pergamon, 1966.
Fuller than Fines (no.4425), but Fines updates the items appearing since 1966.

4429 **Hoskins, William G.** Local history in England. 2nd ed. London: Longmans, 1972.
Written by a professional historian; contains valuable information on family mobility, subsidies, and taxation assessments. Many important additions in 2nd ed., some of particular interest to genealogists.

4430 **Humphreys, Dartow W.,** and **Emmison, F. G.** Local history for students. London: National Council of Social Services, 1965.

Contains much of value concerning records useful to the genealogist. Has a good reading list.

4431 **Iredale, David.** Discovering your family tree. A pocket guide to tracing your English ancestors. Rev. Aylesbury, Bucks, England: Shire Pub., 1973.

Although described as a pocket guide, it contains an incredibly large amount of information.

4432 —— Enjoying archives: what they are, where to find them, how to use them. Newton Abbot, England: David & Charles, 1973. From North Pomfret, Vt.: David & Charles.

4433 **Munby, Lionel M.** Short guides to records. London: Historical Assoc., 1962.

Articles in *History,* on rate books, poll books, probate inventories, estate maps and surveys, hearth tax returns, deeds of title, enclosure awards, port books, recusant rolls, tithe apportionments, etc. Offprints available from the Association.

4434 **Pine, Leslie G.** American origins. *See* no.258.

4435 —— Teach yourself heraldry and genealogy. New York: Dover, 1957.

Introductory work; a popular genealogical manual.

4436 —— Your family tree: a guide to genealogical sources. Rev. and expanded. London: Herbert Jenkins, 1962.

Almost an exact reprint of pp.60–202 of Pine's *American origins* (no.258), slanted for English instead of American readers, with a few additional pages on the British Commonwealth.

4437 **Sims, Richard.** A manual for the genealogist, topographer, antiquary, and legal professor . . . new and improved ed. London, 1888.

Still valuable guide to genealogical sources, as it contains more detailed references to archives than any modern work.

*4438 **Society of Genealogists, London.** Genealogists' handbook. 5th ed. rev. by Peter Spufford and A. J. Camp. London: The Society, 1969.

Invaluable guide to all beginners in British genealogy. Contains a remarkable amount of information for its size (under 50p.).

4439 **Steel, Donald J.,** and **Taylor, L.** Family history in schools. Chichester, England: Phillimore, 1973.

Although primarily intended to teach schoolchildren the simple rules of genealogy, the book is also a useful beginning for the amateur.

4440 **Unett, John.** Making a pedigree. 1961. Repr. Baltimore: G.P.C., 1971.

Good manual for the student of local history and genealogy. Particularly useful for earlier period before parish registers began and for the sixteenth century.

4441 **Wagner, Sir Anthony R.** English ancestry. New York: Oxford Univ. Pr., 1961.

Historical picture of the English social framework and the movement of families within it. Abbreviated version of *English genealogy* (no.4442), without footnotes.

4442 —— English genealogy. Repr. with corr. 2nd ed. enl. New York: Oxford Univ. Pr., 1972.

Attempts to give comprehensive picture of known English family pedigrees in relation to English history. Outlines the patterns of English social life from Saxon times and indicates how the knowledge can be procured. Not really a basic genealogical book, but one which should be in most collections. New ed. has been extensively revised and brought up to date.

4443 **Willis, Arthur J.** Genealogy for beginners. 2nd ed., rev. Chichester, England: Phillimore, 1970.

A return to the original arrangement of 1st ed. to replace *Introducing genealogy* (1968).

4444  Wrigley, Edward A. Identifying people in the past. London: Arnold, 1973.

## Royal Family

4445  **Addington, Arthur C.** The Royal house of Stuart, the descendants of King James VI of Scotland, James I of England. v.1– . London: Charles Skilton, 1969– (in progress).
Traces in all lines, male and female, the descendants of James VI–James I; well researched. v.3 will contain corrections and additions and an index to v.1–2. v.4, in preparation, will include illegitimate branches. Coats of arms; 12,500 descendants.

4446  **Anderson, James.** Royal genealogist: or, The genealogical tables of emperors, kings, and princes, from Adam to these times; in two parts . . . 2nd ed. With addenda and corrigenda. 1736. Repr. Ann Arbor, Mich.: Xerox Univ. Microfilms, 1973.

4447  **Burke, Sir John B.** The Royal families of England, Scotland, Wales, with their descendants, sovereigns and subjects. 2v. London, 1848–51.

4448  ——— A complete index to the family names by A. G. C. Fane. Oxford, England, 1932.
Still useful, but some errors.

4449  **Burke's guide to the Royal family.** London: Burke's Peerage, 1973. Available from Arco, New York.
Biographies of present Royal family; royal lineage in narrative pedigree style, pre-Conquest to date; coats of arms and articles on the monarchy. *Burke's genealogical ser.* 1.

4450  **Foster, Joseph.** The royal lineage of our noble and gentle families, together with their paternal ancestry. 3v. London, 1885–91.
Fewer errors than in Burke (no.4447).

4451  **McNaughton, Arnold.** The book of kings: a royal genealogy. 3v. New York: Quadrangle, 1973.
Complete illustrated genealogical record of every descendant of George I of England. v.1, Royal houses; 2, families; 3, plates and indexes. Fine but expensive work.

4452  **Montague-Smith, Patrick W.** The royal line of succession. New ed. London: Pitkin, 1970.

4453  **Ruvigny and Raineval, Melville A. H. D., 9th Marquis of.** The ancestors of King Edward III and Queen Philippa of Hainault. London, 1915.
Exhaustive; plates, many genealogical tables.

4454  ——— The blood royal of Britain; being a roll of the living descendants of Edward IV, and Henry VII, Kings of England and James III, King of Scotland. 1903. Repr. San Francisco: d'Hozier Associates, 1973.

4455  ——— Jacobite peerage, baronetage, knightage, and grants of honor; extracted . . . from the Stuart papers . . . and supplemented by biographical and genealogical notes. Edinburgh, 1904.
Good genealogical tables.

4456  ——— The nobilities of Europe. 1st and 2nd years. London, 1909–10.
Including an alphabetical list of those British families who have received foreign titles.

4457  ——— The Plantaganet roll of the blood royal; being a complete table of all the descendants now living of Edward III, King of England. The Anne of Exeter volume containing the descendants of Anne (Plantaganet) Duchess of Exeter. London, 1907.

4458  ——— ——— The Clarence vol.: George, Duke of Clarence. London, 1905.

4459  ——— ——— The Isabel of Essex volume . . . Isabel (Plantaganet) Countess of Essex and Eu. London, 1908.

**4460** ——— ——— The Mortimer-Percy volume: Lady Elizabeth Percy, née Mortimer, with supplements to Exeter and Essex. London, 1907.

**4461** **Sandford, Francis.** A genealogical history of the kings of England, and monarchs of Great Britain, etc., from the Conqueror, anno 1066 to the year 1677 ... London, 1683.

**4462** **Turton, William H.** The Plantagenet ancestry. 1928. Repr. Baltimore: G.P.C., 1968.

Over 7,000 ancestors of Elizabeth (daughter of Edward IV and wife of Henry VII), the heiress of the Plantaganets. More than 2,700 entries, with reference to each.

## Conqueror and Domesday Book

**4463** **Burke, Sir John B.** The roll of Battle Abbey. 1848. Repr. Baltimore, 1966. Available from Tuttle, Rutland, Vt.

List of companions of William the Conqueror, which once hung in Battle Abbey. Earliest record of the Normans. Biographical and genealogical details of each name on roll.

**4464** **Cleveland, Duchess of.** The Battle Abbey Roll, with some account of the Norman lineages. 3v. London, 1889.

**4465** **Crispin, Mordecai J.,** and **Macary, Leonce.** Falaise Roll, recording prominent companions of William, Duke of Normandy at the Conquest of England. 1938. Repr. Baltimore: G.P.C., 1969.

Has map of Normandy, folding genealogies, biographical list of companions of the Conqueror. Additions and corrections by G. A. Moriarty, which appeared in *The American genealogist,* 1939, are included in the reprint. Excellent reference work for all those with Norman-English ancestry.

**4466** **Ellis, Henry.** A general introduction to Domesday Book. 2v. 1833. Repr. Baltimore: G.P.C., 1973.

Standard genealogical reference work, with index of tenants in time of Edward the Confessor. Biographical and genealogical notices of landowners.

**4467** **Loyd, Lewis C.** The origins of some Anglo-Norman families. Ed. by C. T. Clay and C. Douglas. *Harleian Soc. publ.* 103. London, 1951. 315 families, 1066–1205, are traced. Learned work.

**4468** **Pine, Leslie G.** Sons of the Conqueror: descendants of Norman ancestry. Rutland, Vt.: Tuttle, 1970.

Account of Norman Conquest of England and its effects on the lineage of Britain. Particular emphasis on American connections, written for genealogists.

**4469** **Planché, James R.** The Conqueror and his companions. 2v. London, 1874.

Personal and domestic history of William the Conqueror.

**4470** **Rye, Walter.** An index to six versions of the so-called Roll of Battle Abbey, with especial reference to the corroboration of most of their statements to be obtained from Domesday Book, Wace's Chronicle, and other sources. In *The genealogists' magazine,* London v.1–5, 1925–30.

List compiled from those of Holinshead, Brompton, Duchesne, Leland, and Tailleur, checked carefully and exhaustively, and thus is a comprehensive list of all Norman invaders.

## Peerages, Baronetages, Knightages, Gentry

✠ Note that periodicals concerning British heraldry and the peerage will be found under Periodicals and Series (no.4248–75). Note also that since heraldry and the peerage are closely connected, it is not easy to separate the two, and consequently this chapter should be consulted in conjunction with the entries under Heraldry, no.5012–32.

**4471** **Ashmole, Elias.** The institution, laws and ceremonies of the Most Noble Order of the Garter . . . 1672. Repr. Baltimore: G.P.C., 1971.

The greatest reference work on the history of the highest order of Great Britain. Lists of holders and a definitive study of the background. 475 coats of arms from foundation into the reign of Charles II.

**4472** **Banks, Thomas C.** Baronia Anglica concentrata, or a concentrated account of all the baronies commonly called baronies in fee; deriving their origin from writ of summons, and not from any specific limited creation . . . also a glossary of dormant English, Scotch and Irish peerage titles. 2v. Ripon, 1843–44.

Historical account of the first settlement of Nova Scotia and the foundation of the Order of Nova Scotia Baronets. Barons created by summons to Parliament; contains 74 barons not in Dugdale (no.4496); various pedigree charts carefully documented.

**4473** ——— The dormant and extinct baronage of England; or, An historical and genealogical account of the lives, public employments, and most memorable actions, of the English nobility, who have flourished from the Norman Conquest to 1806 (–1837). With a genealogical history of divers families of the ancient peerage of England . . . forming a suppl. to the . . . Dormant and extinct baronage . . . 5v. London, 1807–37.

A definitive work, often quoted, as a 4v. set, but set is complete in 5v.; the 5th, published 30 years after v.1-4, is very scarce.

**4474** **Bateman, John D.** The great landowners of Great Britain and Ireland. 4th ed. 1883. Repr. Leicester: Univ. Pr., Leicester, 1971.

Lists all owners of 3,000 acres and above.

**4475** **Beltz, George F.** Memorials of the Most Noble Order of the Garter, from its foundation to the present time; including the history of the Order, with biographical notices of the knights in the reigns of Edward III, and Richard II, etc. 1841. Repr. Baltimore: G.P.C., 1971; New York: A.M.S. Press, 1973.

Important book; the only such study of the Garter. Standard historical and genealogical work; includes 668 knights.

**4476** **Betham, William.** The baronetage of England: history of the English baronets and such baronets of Scotland as are of English families. 5v. Ipswich, England, 1801–1805.

Excellent and accurate work.

**4477** **Burke, Ashworth P.** Family records. 1897. Repr. New York: Heraldic Pub. Co., 1965.

More than 350 genealogies and 200 coats of arms of prominent and not-so-well-known armigerous families.

**\*4478** **Burke, John** (1787–1848). Burke's Genealogical and heraldic history of the peerage, baronetage, and knightage. 1826– . London: Burke. Available from Arco, New York. Earlier vols. repr. by Kraus Repr. Corp., New York.

Published sporadically; one in every decade needed. A certain amount of confusion exists as to the relative value of Burke, Debrett (no.4494), and Lodge (no.4507). Burke is complete for the period 1700 to date, but early editions tended to accept information, traditional and often false, supplied by the families themselves. Recent editions are trustworthy, but it is well to note that Burke (possibly to keep the volume within reasonable size) lists sons with full data, but daughters are given without birth and dates. Burke also tends to eliminate males who died young or without issue. Lodge and Debrett concern themselves more with the living and omit the dead except insofar as they are necessary to show present-day connections, but they are useful because they include birth dates of daughters and Debrett includes issue of the daughters. For these reasons, all 3 works are indispensable. To be reprinted in 1975.

With the publication of the 105th ed. in 1970, Burke's *Peerage* ceased, and it will be replaced with *Burke's genealogical series*.

**4479** ——— A genealogical and heraldic history of the commoners of Great Britain and Ireland . . . 3v. London, 1833–35. (And) v.4. A genealogical and heraldic history of the landed gentry. London, 1837. 4v.

**4480** ——— ——— **Ormerod, George.**
Index to the pedigree(s) in Burke's Commoners . . . (ed. by J. R. Magrath). Originally prepared by G. Ormerod. Oxford, 1907.

This was the first appearance of Burke's *Landed gentry* (see no.4482). As with many of Burke's works, the origin is confusing. v.1-3 were reissued in 1837. These volumes were also issued in parts, 1843-49, as v.1-3 of *A genealogical and historical dictionary of the landed gentry of Great Britain and Ireland*. A peerage book for the untitled man of property, originally with "gentle" background, but later with business or professional background.

**\*4481** ——— and **Burke, Sir John Bernard** (1814-92). A genealogical and heraldic history of the extinct and dormant baronetcies of England, Ireland, and Scotland. 2nd ed. 1844. Repr. Baltimore: G.P.C., 1969.

As the various editions of Burke's *Peerage* since the early 19th century dropped titles not currently held, Burke's *Extinct baronetcies* was issued to cover this deficiency.

**\*4482 Burke, Sir John Bernard** (1814-1892). A genealogical and heraldic dictionary of the landed gentry of Great Britain and Ireland. 1846- . (1st ed. was in 2v., 1846, and suppl., 1848). London: Burke. Available from Arco, New York.

All editions are out-of-print with the exception of the 18th, v.1, 1965. The first appearance of the work had another title (no.4479); the 2nd ed., published under the landed gentry title, appeared in 1850-53; and the latest edition appeared as v.1 of a new 4v. edition in 1965. Because this is one of the most important works on the subject, and because of the many changes from edition to edition—some of which were not continued from volume to volume—it is essential to hold all editions, viz.: 2nd, 1850-53; 3rd, 1858; 4th, 1862-63; 4th suppl., 1868; 5th, 1871; 5th, with suppl., 1875; 6th, 1879; 6th, with suppl., 1882; 7th, 1886; 8th, 1894; 9th, 1898; 10th, 1900; 11th, 1906; 12th, 1914; 13th, 1921; 14th, 1925; 15th, 1937; 16th, 1939; 17th, 1952; 17th, suppl., 1957; 18th, in 3v., 1965-72. Some authorities regard the 1952 ed. as the most important, but the 16th, which includes American families with British ancestry—the lineages of 1,600 families of British origin now resident in the United States of America, with color plates of coats of arms —must surely be considered as the most important by American standards (see also no. 4485).

After 9th ed. the Irish families were omitted, and *Landed gentry of Ireland* appeared. With the publication of v.3 of 18th ed. in 1972, *Landed gentry* ceased and it will be replaced by *Burke's genealogical series.*

**4483** ——— A genealogical and heraldic history of the colonial gentry. 2v. 1891-95. Repr. 2v. in 1. Baltimore: G.P.C., 1970.

Contains pedigrees and illustrations of coats of arms of leading families in Canada, Australia, New Zealand, the West Indies, and other parts of the colonies of Great Britain.

**\*4484** ——— A genealogical history of the dormant, abeyant, forfeited and extinct peerages of the British Empire. 1883. Repr. New York: Arco Pr., 1969.

Original edition was published 1831. This reprint from the last edition, although out of date, is an important work. It was (and is) the practice of the author to drop any title which ceased on the death of the holder when there was no issue legally capable of inheriting the title. Thus, those who wish to establish connection with ancestors whose title is no longer current will find this book essential. For the period 1884-1971, see Pine (no.4514).

**\*4485** ——— Prominent families in America with British ancestry. New York: British Book Centre, 1971.

Repr. of the chapter "American families with British ancestry" which appeared in the 16th ed. (1939), pp.2530-3091, of Burke's . . . *landed gentry* (no.4482). Repr. Baltimore: G.P.C., 1975.

**4486** ——— A visitation of the seats and arms of the noblemen and gentlemen of Great Britain. 4v. in 2 series. London, 1852-55.

Fine engravings of houses and arms, pedigrees and genealogical information. Indexes of seats and owners.

**4487 Burke's genealogical series.** This series replaces the publications, Burke's *Landed gentry* (no.4482) and Burke's *Peerage, baronetage and knightage* (no.4478). The first publication in this series was Burke's *Guide to the Royal family* (no.4449).

**4488 Burke's Landed gentry.** 16th ed. London, 1939.
Includes American families with British ancestry—lineage of 1,600 families of British origin now resident in the United States of America. Repr. in 1971 with title, *Prominent families in America with British ancestry* (see no.4485).

**4489 Clay, John W.** The extinct and dormant peerages of the northern counties of England. London, 1913.

**4490 Cokayne, George.** Complete baronetage. 5v. and index. Exeter, England, 1900–1909.
English baronetcies, 1611–1800; Irish, 1619–1800; Scottish, 1625–1707. The standard work on the baronetage.

**4491** ———— The complete peerage; or, A history of the House of Lords and all its members from the earliest times. New ed., rev. and much enl. by Hon. Vicary Gibb (and others). 13v. in 14; v.12 is in 2pts. London, 1910–59.
v.1–5 had title: *Complete peerage of England, Scotland, Ireland, Great Britain, and the United Kingdom, extant, extinct, or dormant.* v.13, *Peerage creations and promotions from 1901–38.* Corrections and additions have been published in *The Genealogists' magazine* and *The American genealogist.*

**4492 (Collins, Arthur)** Collins's Peerage of England: genealogical, biographical, and historical. Greatly augmented and continued to the present time by Sir Egerton Brydges. 9v. London, 1812.
There are other editions, but this is the best.

**4493 Debrett's Baronetage, knightage and companionage, 1809?–** . London: Kelly's Directories; New York: United Press International. Debrett began as *The new baronetage of England,* 1769. Appeared annually from 1864. Knightage was added in 1865; companionage in 1882. One in every decade needed.

**4494 Debrett's Peerage, baronetage, knightage, and companionage, 1784–** . London: Kelly's Directories; New York: United Press International.
First published as *The new peerage* in 1769, then as *Debrett's Correct peerage* in 1802, later under various names; in later years published annually. One in every decade needed. Debrett concerns itself with the living and omits the dead except insofar as they are necessary to show present-day connections; useful since it includes the surviving children of the daughters. (*See also* note under no.4478.)

**4495 Doyle, James W. E.** Official baronage of England. 3v. London, 1886.
Covers the baronage more fully than do other works of the period.

**4496 Dugdale, Sir William.** The baronage of England . . . 3v. London, 1675–76.
The standard work for the period. A monumental work, covering the earlier era of the baronage.

**4497 Farrer, William.** Honours and knights' fees. 3v. London, 1923–24.
For a study of medieval pedigrees in England.

**4498 Fellowes, Edmund H.** The Knights of the Garter, 1348–1939, with a complete list of stall plates in St. George's Chapel. With suppl. to 1963 tipped in. London: Soc. for the Promoting of Christian Knowledge, 1939.

**4499 Foster, Joseph.** Grantees of arms named in docquets and patents between the years 1687–1898 present in various manuscripts . . . collected and alphabetically arranged by J. Foster. Ed. by W. H. Rylands. *Harleian Soc. publ.* 67–68. 2v. London, 1916–17.

**4500** ———— Grantees of arms named in docquets and patents to the end of the 17th century in the British Museum . . .

and elsewhere. Alphabetically arranged by J. Foster. Ed. by W. H. Rylands. *Harleian Soc. publ.* 66. London, 1915.

**4501 Great Britain. Central Office of Information.** Honours and titles in Britain. London: The Office, 1964.

**4502 Hall, Donald.** British orders, decorations and medals. St. Ives, Hunts., England: Balfour Pub., 1973.

**4503 Howard, Joseph J.,** and **Crisp, F. A.** Visitation of England and Wales. 21v., 1893–1921; Notes, v.1–14, 1896–1921. London.

Contains hundreds of pedigrees, with high standard of accuracy. Pedigrees and coats of arms were based on records and grants in the College of Heralds and other sources, and not on visitations conducted by the heralds. v.1–9 ed. by Howard and Crisp; 10–21 by Crisp only.

**4503a Humphery-Smith, Cecil R.** Sources for research into the English in Portugal. In *Family history,* v.8, no. 48, December 1974.

Many entries of value. British subjects who have received Portuguese titles.

**4504 Kelly's Handbook to the titled, landed, and official classes, 1880– .** London: Kelly's Directories; New York: United Press International.

First published as *The upper ten thousand,* 1875–79. One in every decade needed.

**4505 Kinney, Arthur R.** Titled Elizabethans: a directory of Elizabethan state and church officers and knights, with peers of England, Scotland, and Ireland, 1558–1603. Hamden, Conn.: Archon Books, 1973.

Comprehensive and reliable listing drawn from contemporary sources—the first of its kind.

**4506 Littledale, Willoughby A.** A collection of miscellaneous grants, crests, confirmations, augmentations and exemplifications of arms in the manuscripts of the British Museum ... and elsewhere. 2v. *Harleian Soc. publ.* 76–77. London, 1925–26.

**4507 Lodge, Edmund.** Peerage, baronetage, knightage, and companionage of the British Empire. London, 1832–1919.

The title varied from time to time. See also note under no.4478. One in every decade needed.

**4508 Marshall, George W.** An index to pedigrees contained in the printed heralds' visitations. London, 1866.

Valuable index, including Berry's *County genealogies.*

**4509 Metcalfe, Walter C.** A book of Knights Banneret, Knights of the Bath, and Knights Bachelor, made between the 4th year of King Henry VI and the restoration of King Charles II . . . and Knights made in Ireland, between 1566 and 1698, together with index of the names. London, 1885.

Period covered is 1426–1660 for the English holders.

**4510 Montague-Smith, Patrick W.** Debrett's correct form. London: Kelly's 1970; New York: United Press International.

Supersedes all other books on modes of address. Vital to anyone wishing to address nobility and for public occasions.

**4511 Moor, Charles.** Knights of Edward I. Notices collected by C. Moor. *Harleian Soc. publ.* 80–84. 5v. London, 1929–32.

6,000 knights, over 100,000 entries.

**4512 Parry, Colin J.** Index to baronetage creations. 1967. Repr. Baltimore: G.P.C., 1970.

Lists in one alphabetical sequence all the creations from 1611 to 1965, with the designations or seats of the original baronet, the type of title held, the original date of creation and extinction. 4,000 names.

**4513 Pedigree register.** Ed. by George F. T. Sherwood. 3v. London, 1907–16.

Often referred to as Sherwood. Rare work; contains useful information on pedigrees and other genealogical material.

**\*4514 Pine, Leslie G.** The new extinct peerage, 1884–1971: containing ex-

4515  *England*

tinct, abeyant, dormant and suspended peerages with genealogies and arms. Baltimore: G.P.C., 1972.

Forms a continuation of Burke's *A genealogical history of the dormant, . . . peerages of the British Empire,* 1883 (no.4484). Thousands of names in the genealogies and many coats of arms. Concerns peerage creations which became extinct since 1883, but covers all creations prior to 1883 which became extinct since 1884. Essential.

4515 —— The story of the peerage. 1956. Repr. Rutland, Vt.: Tuttle, 1967.

A popular and readable account.

4516 —— The story of titles. Rutland, Vt.: Tuttle, 1970.

Traces the evolution and structure throughout the world against the historical background of the countries concerned.

4517 **Round, John H.** Family origins and other studies. Ed. with a memoir and bibliography by W. Page. 1930. Repr. Baltimore: G.P.C., 1970.

Set of critical studies by one of Britain's foremost genealogy and heraldry scholars. Many traditional pedigrees of distinguished British families are demolished when history and genealogy study combine; many prominent families considered.

4518 —— Peerage and pedigree. Studies in peerage law and family history. 2v. 1910. Repr. Baltimore: G.P.C., 1970.

Brilliant exposition of family history and peerage law. Lengthy chapter on heraldry included.

4519 —— Studies in peerage and family history. 1901. Repr. Baltimore: G.P.C., 1970.

Masterly demonstration of Round's method in genealogical research.

4520 **Sanders, Ivor J.** English baronies . . . New York: Oxford Univ. Pr., 1960.

Traces history of more than 200 baronies, 1086-1327.

4521 **Shaw, William A.** The knights of England: a complete record from the earliest time to the present day of the knights of all orders of chivalry in England, Scotland and Ireland, and of Knights Bachelors . . . incorporating a complete list of Knights Bachelors dubbed in Ireland, compiled by George D. Burtchaell. 2v. 1906. Repr. Baltimore: G.P.C., 1971.

Most complete list available; more complete for period since the civil wars. Over 10,000 names with good data for each person.

4522 **Solly, Edward.** An index of hereditary English, Scottish and Irish titles of honour. *Index Soc.,* v.5. Repr. Baltimore: G.P.C., 1968.

For each peerage and baronetage there is shown the date conferred, changes undergone, and the then current state.

4523 **Squibb, George D.** Founder's kin: privilege and pedigree. New York: Oxford Univ. Pr., 1972.

Details of families which claimed kinship to educational benefactors and thus had right to scholarships in certain English schools and universities. Refers also to large body of unpublished pedigrees.

4524 **Titles and forms of address:** a guide to their correct use. 14th ed. London: Black, 1971.

Useful handbook to correct English usage for titled classes, for church, armed services, the law, etc. Also includes lists of abbreviations, and pronunciation of proper names.

4525 **Visitations:** Visitations were tours of England and Wales by heralds of the College of Arms for the purpose of recording pedigrees and arms. Most works concerning the visitations in the 16th and 17th centuries were issued in the *Harleian series* (no.4265). The Harleian can in no way be described as authentic, as the copies were taken from the "improved" records in the British Museum, and not from the more authentic records in the College of Arms. Several were issued outside of this series, but most are out of print, as is the *Harleian series.*

4526 **Walford, Edward.** The county families of the United Kingdom; or, Royal manual of the titled and untitled aristocracy of England, Wales, Scotland and Ireland. London, 1860–1920.
Issued annually from 1870–71. One in every decade needed. Useful for tracing persons not found in *Landed gentry* (no. 4482).

# Religions

GENERAL

4527 **Garrett, Christina H.** The Marian exiles, a study in the origins of Elizabethan Puritanism. New York: Cambridge Univ. Pr., 1966.
Contains almost 500 biographical sketches of English refugees to Germany during the years 1554–59 in the reign of Mary Tudor. Census of exiles, pp.61–349.

4527a **Owen, Dorothy M.** The records of the Established Church in England, excluding parochial records. *Archives and user,* v.1. London: British Records Assoc., 1974.
Most useful for finding where various records exist and what they mean.

4528 **Purvis, John S.** Dictionary of ecclesiastical terms. New York: Nelson, 1962.
Explanation given in detailed form.

*4529 **Steel, Donald J.** Sources for non-conformist genealogy and family history. *National index of parish registers,* v.2. London: Phillimore, 1973. Available from Tuttle, Rutland, Vt.
Magnificent study of Presbyterians, Unitarians, Congregationalists, Baptists, Society of Friends (Quakers), Moravians, Methodists, foreign churches and other denominations, including Huguenots. Fine bibliographies.

4530 **Turner, George L.** Original records of early nonconformity under persecution and indulgence. 3v. London, 1911–14.
From episcopal reports and state papers covering 1663–76. 3,500 names of teachers, householders, and signatories to petitions. Fine index.

SPECIFIC

4531 (Baptists) **Baptist Historical Society.** Transactions, v.1–7, 1908/9–1921; Baptist quarterly, new ser. v.1– , 1922/23– . London: Baptist Union Pub. Dept.

4532 (Baptists) **General Baptists. General Assembly.** Minutes, 1659–1811, with kindred records . . . introduction and notes by William T. Whitley. 2v. London, 1909–10.
v.1, 1654–1728; v.2, 1731–1811. Many names of ministers and messengers from all over Great Britain.

4533 (Baptists) **Whitley, William T.** A Baptist bibliography; being a register of the chief materials of Baptist history when in manuscript or in print, preserved in Great Britain, Ireland and the colonies. 2v. London, 1916–22.
v.1, 1526–1776; v.2, 1777–1837, and addenda from 1613. Gives date and location of registers, with much biographical information.

4534 (Catholics) **Catholic Record Society.** Publications, v.1– , 1905– . London: The Society.
Most volumes in print. Although some volumes have little or no genealogical information, others are vital to the researcher, since they contain Catholic registers not available in any other form. The *Miscellanea series* is of particular importance; it includes registers of Hampshire and Lancashire Catholics. Out-of-print volumes in the series are reprinted by Dawson, London, when necessary.

4535 (Catholics) **Estcourt, Edgar E.** The English Catholic nonjurors of 1715, being a summary of the register of their estates, with genealogical and other notes . . . 1885. Repr. Farnborough, England: Gregg Pr., 1969. Available from Gregg, Boston.
Registers by Commissions for Forfeited Estates.

**4536** (Catholics) **Gillow, Joseph.** A literary and biographical history; or, Bibliographical dictionary of the English Catholics, from the breach with Rome in 1534, to the present time [1892]. 5v. (1885-1902). Repr. New York: Burt Franklin, 1962.

2,000 biographies. Useful for names not included in *Dictionary of national biography* (no.4281).

**4537** (Catholics) **Lawson, Sir Henry.** Genealogical collections illustrating the history of Roman Catholic families of England. Based on the Lawson manuscript. Ed. by J. J. Howard and Sir H. F. Burke. 4pts. in 1v. London, 1887-92.

Mainly Fermor, Petre, Hunloke, Phillips, Arundel, and Hornyold families.

**4538** (Congregationalists) **Congregational Historical Society.** Transactions. v.1- , 1901- . London: The Society.
Early records and bibliographies.

**4539** ———— Subject index, v.1-15 (1901-48). By P. V. Brunsden. 1948.

**4540** (Friends) *See* Quakers, no.4561-63.

**4541** (Huguenots) **Agnew, David C. A.** Protestant exiles from France, chiefly in the reign of Louis XIV; or, The Huguenot refugees and their descendants in Great Britain and Ireland. 3rd ed. 2v. London, 1886.

Has list of naturalizations, 1681-1701.

**4542** (Huguenots) **Huguenot Society of London.** Shaw, William A. Letters of denization and acts of naturalization for aliens in England and Ireland, 1509-1800. *Publ. of Huguenot Soc. of London,* 4th ser. 8, 18, 27. Lymington, England [and elsewhere], 1893-1923.

v.1, ed. by William Page, 1509-1603; v.2-3, ed. by Shaw, 1603-1800.

**4543** ———— A supplement to W. A. Shaw's Letters of denization . . . *Huguenot Soc. publ.,* 35. Frome, England, 1932.

**4544** (Huguenots) **Huguenot Society of London.** (Quarto) Publications. v.1- , 1887/8- . London: The Society.

The *Quarto series* (as distinct from the *Octavo Proceedings*) contains many valuable registers, also lists of aliens. *Quarto ser.,* v.1-20 available in repr. from Kraus-Thomson, New York; remainder from Society.

**4545** (Huguenots) **Kirk, Richard,** and **Kirk, E. F.** Returns of aliens dwelling in the city and suburbs of London from the reign of Henry VIII to that of James I [1522-1625]. 4v. *Huguenot Soc. pub.* 10, pts.1-4. London, 1900-1908.

Pt.1, 1523-71; pt.2, 1571-97; pt.3, 1598-1625 and additions, 1522-93; pt.4, index.

**4546** (Huguenots) **Lart, Charles E.** Huguenot pedigrees. 1924-28. 2v. Repr. 2v. in 1. Baltimore: G.P.C., 1973.

Bridges gap between families in France, England, Holland, and America. 1,500 names. Many pedigrees.

**4547** (Huguenots) **Smiles, Samuel.** The Huguenots, their settlements, churches, and industries in England and Ireland. 1868. Repr. Baltimore: G.P.C., 1972.

Included are biographies of 300 noted Huguenot refugees in Britain. Unreliable, and few sources given.

**4548** (Jews) **Hyamson, Albert M.** Jewish obituaries in the *Gentleman's magazine.* Index 1731-1868. In the Jewish Historical Soc. of England, *Miscellanies* 4, pp. 33-60. London: The Society, 1942.

850 entries.

**4549** (Jews) **Lehmann, Ruth P.** Anglo-Jewish bibliography, 1937-70. London: Jewish Historical Soc. of England, 1973.

A continuation of Roth's *Magna bibliotheca Anglo-Judaica* . . . (no.4551). Replaces Lehmann's *Nova bibliotheca Anglo-Judaica* (1937-60). *Nova* contained 1,700 items, and the present 4,600.

**4550** (Jews) **London. Spanish and Portuguese Jews' Congregation.** Bevis Marks records, being contributions to the history of the Spanish and Portuguese Congregations of London. Ed. by Lionel D. Barnett. 3pts. New York: Oxford Univ. Pr., 1940-73.

Good family histories. pts.2-3 have abstracts of the Ketuboth or marriage-contracts of the Congregation from earliest times to 1901.

4551 (Jews) **Roth, Cecil.** Magna bibliotheca Anglo-Judaica; a bibliographical guide to Anglo-Jewish history. New ed., rev. London, 1937.

Recommended for any research in Jewish families. Rev. ed. of *Bibliotheca Anglo-Judaica,* compiled by J. Jacobs and L. Wolf. 1888. 2,800 items. Continued by Lehmann (no.4549).

4552 (Jews) **Samuel, Wilfred S.** Sources for Anglo-Jewish genealogy. In *The genealogists' magazine,* v.6, pp.146-59 (1940).

4553 (Methodists) **Beckerlegge, Oliver A.** United Methodist ministers and their circuits: being an arrangement in alphabetical order of the stations of ministers of the Methodist New Connexion, Bible Christians, Arminian Methodists, Protestant Methodists, Wesleyan Methodist Association, Wesleyan Reformers, United Methodist Free Churches, and the United Methodist Church, 1797-1932. London: Epworth Pr., 1968.

4554 (Methodists) **Hall, Joseph.** Hall's circuits and ministers, 1765-1885. An alphabetical list of the circuits of Great Britain, with the names of the ministers stationed in each circuit. 2nd ed. London, 1886.

4555 —— with appendix, 1886-96, rev. and enl. by T. G. Hartley. London, 1914.

4556 —— Supplement . . . 1913-23, ed. by T. G. Hartley. London, 1925.

4557 —— Memorials of Wesleyan Methodist ministers, or the yearly death notices, from 1777-1840. London, 1876.

4558 (Methodists) **Wesley, F.** How to write a local history of Methodism. London: Wesley Methodist Historical Soc., 1964.

Comprehensive account of nature and whereabouts of Methodist archives. Originally in *Proceedings, Wesley Historical Soc.,* v.39.

4559 (Methodists) **Wesley Historical Society.** Proceedings. v.1- , 1896- . London: The Society.

Marginal value to genealogists. Volumes in print from Rev. T. Shaw, St. Keverne, Cornwall, England. An index was published in 1960.

4560 (Presbyterians) **Presbyterian Historical Society of England.** Journal. 1914/1919- . London: The Society.

4561 (Quakers) **Friends' Historical Society journal.** v.1- , 1903- . Supplements, 1907- . London: Obtainable from Friends' Bookstore, Philadelphia, Pa.

Though the Friends are comparatively few in number, the journal contains much of value to genealogists. Other Quaker journals of interest include: *Friends' quarterly examiner,* 1867- ; *The British Friend,* 1843-1913; *Friends intelligencer,* 1844-1955.

4562 (Quakers) **Green, Joseph J.** Quaker records, being an index to "The annual monitor," 1812-92, containing 20,-000 obituaries, notices of members of the Society of Friends alphabetically and chronologically arranged. London, 1894.

4563 (Quakers) **Rowntree, John S.** The Friends' registers of births, deaths and marriages, 1650-1900. London, 1902.

Originally published in *The Friend,* 1902.

4564 (Unitarians) **Unitarian Historical Society.** Transactions, 1917/18- . London: The Society.

4565 (Wesleyan Methodists). *See* Methodists, no. 4553-59.

# IRELAND

## Bibliographies

☧ A separate bibliography of genealogical literature in Ireland has never been published. The following works, however, include excellent Irish bibliographies: Kaminkow (no.4152); Falley (no.4658); McLysaght (no.4649). Genealogical bibliographies of Great Britain, many of which include Ireland, will be found in no.4144–87.

**4565a** **Brefny, Brian de.** Bibliography of Irish family history and genealogy. Cork, Ireland: The Author, 1973.
Comprehensive.

**4566** **Browne, James A.** A history of the Highlands and of the Highland clans. 4v. Glasgow, 1860.
Various editions all similar to this, which is the last. Contains catalog of Gaelic and Irish manuscripts in libraries of Great Britain and Ireland

**4567** **Humphreys, Arthur L.** A handbook of county bibliography . . . of Great Britain and Ireland. 1917. Repr. 1974. *See* no.4173.

**4568** **Martin, Geoffrey H.,** and **McIntyre, S.** A bibliography of British and Irish municipal history . . . *See* no.4175.

**4569** **Pender, Séamus.** A guide to Irish genealogical collections. *Analecta Hibernica,* v.7. 1935. Repr. Folkestone, Kent, England: Dawson, 1972.
Introductory guide to main body of genealogical lore extant in manuscripts of Irish provenance.

**4570** **Raven-Hart, Hester E.,** and **Johnston, M.** Bibliography of the registers (printed) of the universities, inns of court, colleges and schools of Great Britain and Ireland . . . *See* no.4160.

**4571** **Sources for the history of Irish civilization,** articles in Irish periodicals, National Library of Ireland, Dublin. Boston: G. K. Hall, 1970.

All articles in Irish periodicals from about 1800 to 1869. Reviews also given. 271,000 entries.

# Record Guides and Offices

✣ In 1922, during the Civil War, the Public Record Office was burned, and many of the records were destroyed. That year a separate parliament and government were established in Belfast for Northern Ireland, comprising the counties of Antrim, Armagh, Down, Fermanagh, Londonderry, and Tyrone. The remainder of Ireland (26 counties) set up a parliament and government in Dublin, first known as the Irish Free State, later as Eire, and since 1948 as the Republic of Ireland. The partition affected the keeping of vital statistics, and from 1922 on the records pertaining to the 6 separate counties have been kept in Belfast.

There was no official army or navy in Ireland before 1920, and Irishmen therefore served in the British armed forces before that time.

4572 **Ainsworth, John.** Survey of documents in private keeping. *See* no.4590.

4573 **Casey, Albert E.,** and **Dowling, T. E. P.** O'Kief, Coshe, Mang, Slieve Lougher, and Upper Blackwater in Ireland. 15v. Birmingham, Ala.: Amite and Knockagree Historical Fund, 1952-71.

Historical and genealogical items relating to Ireland, especially Cork and Kerry. Abstracts of all types of records, and many leading Irish works.

4574 **Dublin. Municipal Corporation.** Calendar of ancient records of Dublin, in the possession of the Municipal Corporation of that city. Ed. by Sir John T. and Lady Rosa M. Gilbert. 18v. Dublin, 1898-1922, 1944.

Covers 1171-1831; chief emphasis is on rolls, charters, land grants, and other records.

*4575 **Genealogical Society of the Church of Jesus Christ of Latter-day Saints.** Major genealogical record sources in Ireland. *Research paper,* ser. A.2. Salt Lake City: L.D.S., 1966.

4576 **Great Britain. General Register Office.** Abstract of arrangements respecting registration of births, marriages and deaths in the United Kingdom . . . and in the Irish Republic. London, 1952. *See* no.4202.

4577 **Hayes, Richard J.** Manuscript sources for the history of Irish civilisation. 11v. Boston: G. K. Hall, 1965. Fine source for genealogists.

4578 ———— Sources for the history of Irish civilisation; articles in periodicals. 9v. Boston: G. K. Hall, 1970.

v.1-5, persons; v.6-8, persons; v.9, places, dates.

4579 **Henchy, Patrick.** Three centuries of emigration from the British Isles. Irish emigration to North America for the past three centuries. *World Conference on Records,* area C-1C paper. Salt Lake City: L.D.S., 1969.

4580 **Ireland. Irish Manuscripts Commission.** Books of survey and distribution. Ed. by Robert C. Simington. 4v. Dublin: Stationery Office, 1949-67.

v.1, Roscommon; v.2, Mayo; v.3, Galway; v.4, Clare. Valuable records of the Quit Rent Office. With these records details of land ownership can easily be found.

4581 ———— A census of Ireland, ca. 1659, with supplementary material from the Poll money ordinances, (1660-61). Ed. by Séamus Pender. Dublin: Stationery Office, 1939.

Copies of townland census returns of inhabitants of Ireland, arranged geographically in counties, baronies, parishes, and streets. Returns supply names of occupants and comprise only-known actual details prior to first official census in 1821. 1659 census includes more than 12,000 names. Names only the "titulados" and just totals of ordinary people. Counties of Cavan,

Mayo, Wicklow missing in statistical section, but some of their officials are named in the appendix.

**4582** —— The civil survey (A.D. 1654-56). Ed. by Robert C. Simington. 10v. Dublin: Stationery Office, 1931-61.

The survey concerns a descriptive record of the land and of its owners in 1640, written down in 1654-56. Every estate of every proprietor of land in 27 Irish barony maps included.

**4583** —— Patentee officers, 1173-1826, including high sheriffs, 1661-1684 and 1761-1816. Ed. by James L. J. Hughes. Dublin: Stationery Office, 1960.

Extracts from the patent rolls published in *Liber munerum* have been indexed by Hughes, but since the *Liber* is only in large libraries, the alphabetical list is important.

**4584 Ireland. Public Record Office.** Public records in Ireland, 23rd report, 1891. Dublin. This report lists many Anglican Church of Ireland parish registers with those that were in the Public Record Office and subsequently destroyed.

**4585** —— Public records of Ireland before and after 1922. In *Royal Historical Soc. transactions,* 4th ser., v.13. 1930. pp.17-49. London.

Invaluable to the researcher, because it has the authenticity associated with publications of the Royal Historical Society. The destruction in 1922, though serious, is not so serious as commonly thought.

**4586** —— Reports of the Deputy Keeper of the Public Records of Ireland. 1869- . (Until 1924 the reports of Northern Ireland and the Republic of Ireland were published jointly, after which they appeared separately.) Dublin.

Under this somewhat innocuous title are found some of the most valuable Irish genealogical records. Some reports contain merely lists of accessions, but many, particularly those before 1914, contain vast lists of names found in actual records. Unfortunately only those for 1960- are in print, and others seldom appear on the second-hand market. 1960- are obtainable from the Stationery Office, Dublin.

**4587** —— Wood, Herbert, compiler. A guide to the records deposited in the Public Record Office in Ireland. London, 1919.

Indicates what there was *prior* to the fire of 1922.

**4588 MacLysaght, Edward.** Report on documents relating to the wardenship of Galway. *Analecta Hibernia,* v.14. 1944. Repr. Folkestone, Kent, England: Dawson, 1974.

**4589** —— Seventeenth century hearth money rolls, with full transcript for County Sligo. Dublin: Stationery Office, 1967.

From the Irish Manuscripts Commission records.

**4590** —— Survey of documents in private keeping. ser. 1-3. *Analecta Hibernia,* v.15, 20, 25. Dublin: Stationery Office, 1944-67.

Ser.1 by MacLysaght; ser.2 by MacLysaght and John F. Ainsworth; ser.3 by Ainsworth; ser. is now out-of-print. Important because much of the material listed is not public information. Wills, inquisitions, mortgages, exchequer bills, marriage settlements, etc. of various great Irish families. Also family archives in private keeping. Copious index of persons and places.

**4591 McNeill, Charles,** and **Otway-Ruthven, A. J.** Dowdall deeds. Dublin: Stationery Office, 1960.

Mainly family papers of the Douedale (later spelled Dowdall), but many names from other estates and families of the 13th century. *Publ. of Irish Manuscripts Commission.*

**4592 O'Neill, Thomas P.** Sources of Irish local history. 1st ser. Dublin, 1958.

Notes appearing a periodical, *An Leabharlann.*

**4593 Return of owners of land of one acre and upwards, in the several counties of cities, and counties of towns in Ireland . . .** showing the names of such owners arranged alphabetically, addresses, extents, etc. Dublin, 1876.

Though comparatively recent, the work is comprehensive and is useful for anyone wishing to know holders of land. *See also* no.4631.

4594   **Shaw, William A.** Letters of denization and acts of naturalization for aliens in England and Ireland, 1603–1800. 3v. *See* no.4542–43.

## Periodicals and Series

4595   **Analecta Hibernica.** A few of this series are listed under the various headings in Ireland. Some have been reprinted by Dawson, Folkestone, Kent, England.

4596   **The Irish ancestor.** Ed. by Rosemary ffolliott. v.1– , 1969– . Dublin: The Editor.

Wills, names, family histories, book reviews. Admirably edited. Two issues annually. The best Irish periodical.

4597   **Irish genealogical helper.** no.1– , 1974– . Harbor City, Calif.: Augustan Soc.

Queries, book reviews, bibliographies, history. Excellent, but for members of the Augustan Society only.

4598   **Irish genealogist:** official organ of the Irish Genealogical Research Society. v.1– , 1937– . London: The Society.

A learned publication.

## Biographies

4599   **Crone, John S.** A concise dictionary of Irish biography. Rev. and enl. ed. New York: Longmans, 1937.

Brief biographical sketches of notable Irish men and women in every sphere of activity from the early days to the 20th century. Living persons not included.

4600   **D'Alton, John.** Illustrations, historical, genealogical on King James's Irish army list, 1689. 2nd ed., enl. London, 1861.

History of officers' families and account of those who settled in France and Spain after the battle of the Boyne.

4601   **Hayes, Richard J.** Biographical dictionary of Irishmen in France. Dublin, 1949.

Representatives of most of the preplantation families. Some unpublished sources.

4602   **Jacobs, Phyllis M.** Registers of the universities, colleges and schools of Great Britain and Ireland: a list, 1964. *See* no.4309.

4603   **O'Callaghan, John C.** History of the Irish brigades in the service of France, from the Revolution in Great Britain and Ireland under James II to the Revolution in France under Louis XVI. 1870. Repr. Shannon: Irish Univ. Pr., 1969.

4604   **Ryan, Richard.** Biographia Hibernica. A biographical dictionary of the worthies of Ireland, from the earliest periods to the present time. 2v. London, 1819–21.

Sketches of persons known and unknown.

4605   **Webb, Alfred J.** A compendium of Irish biography, comprising sketches of distinguished Irishmen, and of eminent persons connected with Ireland by office or by their country. 1878. Repr. New York: Lemma Pub. Corp., 1970.

Entries are more complete than Crone (no.4599).

## Registers

4606   **Burtchaell, George D.,** and **Sadleir, T. U.** Alumni Dublienses; a register of the students, graduates, professors and provosts of Trinity College in the University of Dublin. 1593–1860. New ed. Dublin, 1935.

Most complete college record extant. Supplies name of father and county, and lists most Irish families of note.

4607 Ireland. Public Record Office. Anglican Church of Ireland parish registers. *See* no.4697.

## Vital Statistics

4608 Association for the Preservation of the Memorials of the Dead in Ireland. Journal. v.1-10. Dublin, 1888-1920. Continued as Irish Memorials Association. Journal. v.11-13, no.2. Suppl. 1907-10. *See* no.4618.

4609 ———— Consolidated index of surnames and place names to v.1-7, 1888-1909. Compiled by Esther A. Vigors (Mrs. S. de O'Grady) and Mrs. P. G. Mahony. Dublin, 1926.
Very scarce and essential work.

4610 Clarke, Richard S. J. Gravestone inscriptions: County Down. v.1- , 1966- . Belfast: Ulster Scot Historical Foundation.
v.13 published in 1974; index to v.1-5 in v.5; v.6-10 in v.10.

4611 Farrar, Henry. Irish marriages, being an index to the marriages in *Walker's Hibernian magazine,* 1771-1812. 2v. 1897. Repr. 2v. in 1. Baltimore: G.P.C., 1972.
Full information on participants. Also 52p. index to births, etc. recorded in *Anthologia Hibernia,* 1793-94.

4612 Gillman, Herbert W. Index to marriage licence bonds of the Diocese of Cork and Ross, Ireland, 1628-1750, preserved in the public records of Ireland. Cork, 1896.
Originally in *Journal of the Cork Historical and Archaeological Society.*

4613 Green, T. G. H. Index to the marriage licence bonds in the Diocese of Cloyne, Ireland, 1630-1800, preserved in the public records of Ireland. Cork, 1899-1900.
Originally in *Journal of the Cork Historical and Archaeological Society.*

4614 Henchion, Richard. The gravestone inscriptions of County Cork. v.1- .
In *Journal of the Cork Historical and Archaeological Society,* v.72- , 1967- .
200p. of inscriptions to 1974.

4615 Ireland. Public Record Office. Testamentary, marriage and ecclesiastical documents salved from the destruction of 1922. 57th *report of the Deputy Keeper of the Public Records of Ireland.* Dublin, 1936.
Thousands of names.

4616 Irish Memorials Association. *See* no.4608.

4617 Jackson, Donald. Intermarriage in Ireland, 1550-1650. Montreal, Wisc.: Cultural and Educational Products, 1970.

4618 Lamacraft, Charles T. Some funeral entries of Ireland. From a manuscript volume in the British Museum. Dublin, 1910?
Suppl. to *Journal of the Association for the Preservation of the Memorials of the Dead in Ireland,* 1907-10. Journal, *see* no. 4608.

## Wills

⚜ Some information on the wills of Ireland will be found in Anthony J. Camp, *Wills and their whereabouts,* no.4366; and Gibson, *Wills and where to find them,* no.4377.

4619 Dublin. Diocese. Register of wills and inventories of the Diocese of Dublin, 1457-83. Ed. by Henry F. Berry. Dublin, 1898.

4620 Eustace, P. Beryl, and Goodbody, O. C. Quaker records, Dublin: abstracts of wills. Dublin: Stationery Office, 1957.
The wills are in the possession of the Dublin and Wexford monthly meetings of the Society of Friends.

4621 Ireland. Irish Manuscripts Commission. Registry of deeds, Dublin:

abstracts of wills, 1708-85. Ed. by P. Beryl Eustace. 2v. Dublin: Stationery Office, 1954-56.

About 1,500 wills, with thousands of names in the indexes, covering the whole of Ireland. v.1, 1708-1845; v.2, 1746-85; v.3 (scheduled), 1786-1827.

4622 ———— Will abstracts in the Genealogical Office, Dublin. *Analecta Hibernica,* v.17, 19. 2v., ed. by P. Beryl Eustace. Dublin: Stationery Office, 1949-57.

7,500 entries, with names and addresses of testators. Excellent index.

4623 **Ireland. Public Record Office.** Index of the wills to 1858: appendix to the 26th and 30th *reports of the Deputy Keeper of the Public Records and Keeper of the State Papers in Ireland.* Dublin, 1895-99.

26th *report* contains index to original wills of the Diocese of Dublin, 1638-1800; 30th *report,* 1800-58.

4624 **Phillimore, William P. W.,** and **Thrift, G.** Indexes to Irish wills. 5v. 1909-20. Repr. 5v. in 1. Baltimore: G.P.C., 1970.

v.1-2 by Phillimore; v.3-5 by Thrift. Indexes to 30,000 diocesan wills proved in the Consistorial Courts, 1536-1857, with full data. Companion to Vicars, no.4624.

4625 **Vicars, Sir Arthur E.** Index to the prerogative wills of Ireland, 1536-1810. 1897. Repr. Baltimore: G.P.C., 1967.

Index to important set of wills. Includes index to Sir William Betham's abstracts to 1800. Over 40,000 wills. Companion to Phillimore and Thrift, no.4624.

# Topography

4626 **Alphabetical index to the townlands and towns of Ireland.** Dublin, 1877.

Not official; published by Alexander Thom.

4627 **Anderson, John P.** The book of British topography . . . works . . . relating to Great Britain and Ireland. *See* no.4384.

*4628 **(Bartholomew's) Quarter-inch map series of Ireland.** Edinburgh: Bartholomew, 1962.

Useful for identifying hamlets and villages.

4629 **Bullock, Leslie G.** Historical map of Ireland. Edinburgh: Bartholomew, 1962.

Shows areas of principal clans, etc. Sheet, 39 by 26 inches, suitable for display.

*4630 **Gardner, David E.; Harland, D.;** and **Smith, F.** A genealogical atlas of Ireland. Salt Lake City: Deseret Book Co., 1964.

Designed especially for the genealogical researcher. Combination of George Philips's *Handy atlas of the counties of Ireland,* 1885, and Lewis's *Atlas of the counties of Ireland,* 1846 (*see* no.4640).

4631 **General valuation of Ireland,** 1849-58. Dublin.

Invaluable work issued as a government publication in 148 pts.; includes the 26 counties now comprising the Republic of Ireland and the 6 counties of Northern Ireland. Compiled for valuation and rating purposes; gives names of tenants, owners, etc. Much superior to no.4593. Always referred to as "Griffith's valuation" because Sir Richard Griffith was Commissioner of Valuations at the time.

4632 **Goblet, Yann M.** A topographical index of the parishes and townlands of Ireland in Sir William Petty's manuscript barony maps ca.1655-59. Dublin, 1932.

Includes more than 2,000 personal names and 25,000 townland names, with variant spellings. Mostly taken from 17th-century maps.

4633 **Hayes-McCoy, Gerard A.** Ulster and other Irish maps ca.1600. Dublin: Stationery Office, 1964.

4634 **Hogan, Edmund.** Onomasticon goedelicum locorum et tribuum Hibernia et Scotiae; an index, with identifications, to the Gaelic names of places and tribes. Dublin, 1910.

Classic work indexing 176 manuscripts and printed sources, some Scottish, but majority Irish, with source of each entry given. 25,000 entries.

**4635  Ireland. Irish Manuscripts Commission.** The civil survey (A.D. 1654–56) . . . a descriptive record of the land and of its owners in 1640. Every estate of every proprietor of land in 27 Irish barony maps included. *See* no.4582.

**4636  Ireland. Registrar-General.** Census of Ireland, 1871. Alphabetical index to the townlands and towns of Ireland; also the areas of the townlands, the county barony . . . in which they are situated . . . Dublin, 1877.

**4637  ———** The census of Ireland, 1901. General topographical index consisting of an alphabetical index to the townlands and topography of Ireland, and indices to the parishes, baronies, etc. Dublin, 1904.
The last townland index published officially for the whole of Ireland; gives acreages. Often referred to simply as "Townland index."

**4638  Joyce, Patrick W., and Sullivan, A. M.** Atlas and cyclopedia of Ireland. Pt.1. A comprehensive delineation of the 32 counties, by P. W. Joyce; pt.2. The general history, by A. M. Sullivan. New York, 1902?
480 arms in color, brief history of every county, illustrations, colored maps, and history of Ireland to 1867.

**4639  Leet, Ambrose.** A directory of the market towns, villages, gentlemen's seats and other noted places in Ireland . . . to which is added a general index of persons' names. 2nd ed. Dublin, 1814.

**4640  Lewis, Samuel.** A topographical dictionary of Ireland . . . 2v. and atlas. London, 1837, 1839, 1842, 1846, 1849. 1837 ed. repr. Port Washington, New York: Kennikat, 1970.
In each edition the atlas is separate. Although 1837 ed. is preferred, other editions will serve the researcher. Much superior to some modern gazetteers, since the smaller places are seldom identified.

**\*4641  MacLysaght, Edward.** Irish families map. Dublin, 1963. Wall sheet showing counties and clan breakdown.

**4642  Simington, Robert C.** The transplantation to Connacht 1654–58. Dublin: Irish Univ. Pr., 1970.
A Cromwellian project for the redistribution of the population. A fine record of 17th-century land ownership. Main value is for personal names, though it has topographical use also. *Publ. of Irish Manuscripts Commission.*

**4643  Taylor, George, and Skinner, A.** Maps of the roads of Ireland. 2nd ed. 1783. Repr. Shannon: Irish Univ. Pr., 1969.
Survey in 1777 and corrected down to 1783. Of considerable genealogical value.

## Names

**4644  Grehan, Ida.** Irish family names— highlights of fifty family histories. New York: British Book Centre, 1974.
Lively sketches, illustrated with family portraits and photographs of ancestral homes. Authentic arms drawn by Myra Maguire.

**4645  Hogan, Edmund.** Onomasticon goedelicum locorum et tribuum Hiberniae et Scotiae; an index, with identifications, to the Gaelic names of places and tribes. Dublin, 1910. *See* no.4634.

**4646  Joyce, Patrick W.** The origin and history of Irish names of places. 3v. 1898–1913. Repr. of 4th ed., 1875. Wakefield, Yorks, England: E. P. Pub., 1972.
Spine: *Irish names of places*. Remains the only comprehensive survey of Irish place names.

**4647  Kelly, Patrick.** Irish family names with origins and meanings, clans, arms, crests and mottoes. 2nd ed. Chicago, 1958.
Collected from the living Gaelic and from authoritative books, manuscripts and public documents.

**4648  MacGiolla-Domhnaigh, Padraic.** Some anglicized surnames in Ireland. Dublin, 1923.

A compilation of English names anglicized from Gaelic origins.

**\*4649  MacLysaght, Edward.** The surnames of Ireland. A compendium of locations and variants. New York: Irish Univ. Pr., 1973.

More than 4,000 Gaelic, Norman and Anglo-Irish surnames listed with wealth of information on historical background and location of the septs and families, and dates and places of settlement of the Anglo-Irish. Supersedes his *Guide to Irish surnames* (1967). Essential.

**4650  Matheson, Sir Robert E.** Special report on surnames in Ireland, with notes as to numerical strength, derivation, ethnology, and distribution based on information extracted from the indexes of the General Register Office, 2nd ed. 1909. Baltimore: G.P.C., 1968.

Previously published in a government report, as appendix to the 29th *annual report of the Registrar General for Ireland,* 1894.

**4651 ———** Varieties and synonymes [sic] of surnames and Christian names in Ireland. 1901. Repr. Baltimore: G.P.C., 1968.

no.4650–51 reprinted in 1v.

**\*4652  Woulfe, Patrick.** Irish names and surnames . . . with explanatory and historical notes. 1923. Repr. Baltimore: G.P.C., 1969.

An outstanding work on Irish names; it should be used in conjunction with MacLysaght's *The surnames of Ireland* (no. 4649). Woulfe's book is also titled *Sloinnte Gaedhael is Gall.*

## Manuals

**4653  Black, J. Anderson.** Your Irish ancestors. Ireland and its people; great Irish families. Tracing your ancestors. New York: Paddington Pr., 1974.

**4654  Campbell, Robert G.** Scotch-Irish family research made simple. Munroe Falls, Ohio: Summit Pub., 1974.

**4655  Clare, Wallace.** A simple guide to Irish genealogy. First compiled by Wallace Clare, 1937. 3rd ed. rev. by Rosemary ffolliott. London: Irish Genealogical Soc., 1966.

Concise guide for research among Irish families.

**4657  Collins, Eleanor J.** Irish family research made simple. Munroe Falls, Ohio: Summit Pub., 1974.

**\*4658  Falley, Margaret D.** Irish and Scotch-Irish ancestral research: a guide to the genealogical records, methods, and sources in Ireland. 2v. Evanston, Ill.: The Author, 1961–62.

Probably the first complete guide to Irish genealogy. Good bibliography and evidence of the wealth of material which exists despite the 1922 destruction during the Civil War. Essential.

**\*4659  Gardner, David E., and Smith, F.** Genealogical research in England and Wales . . . *See* no.4241.

One of the best studies of all forms of handwriting encountered in early documents, and therefore of value to Irish researchers as well.

**4660  Heraldic Artists Ltd., Dublin.** Handbook on Irish genealogy—how to trace ancestors and relatives in Ireland. Enl. ed. Dublin: Heraldic Artists Ltd., 1973.

Incomplete in its treatment, but lists many of the more important genealogical sources, and lists some hitherto unknown passenger lists. Some details of the humbler families of Ireland.

**4661  Irish Touring Board, Dublin.** Tracing your ancestors. Dublin: The Board, various dates.

**4662  Latham, Ronald E.** Revised medieval Latin word-list from British and Irish sources. Based on *Medieval Latin word-list,* ed. by J. H. Baxter and C. Johnson, 1934. New York: Oxford Univ. Pr., 1965.

4663   McCay, Betty L. Seven lesson courses in Irish rescarch and sources. Indianapolis, Ind.: The Author, 1972.
History, source material, bibliography.

4664   Parker, Donald D. Scottish and Scotch-Irish ancestry research. Santa Fe, N. Mex.: The Author, n.d.
Gives historical background of Scots and Scotch-Irish immigration; lists and describes record sources.

# Peerages, Baronetages, Knightages, Gentry

4665   Banks, Sir Thomas C. Baronia Anglica concentrata . . . also a glossary of dormant England, Scotch and Irish peerage titles . . . See no.4472.

4666   Bateman, John D. The great landowners of Great Britain and Ireland. 4th ed. 1883. Repr. Leicester: Univ. Pr., 1971.

4667   Burke, John. A genealogical and heraldic history of the commoners of Great Britain and Ireland . . . See no.4479.

*4668   ——— and Burke, Sir John B. A genealogical and heraldic history of the extinct and dormant baronetcies of England, Ireland and Scotland . . . See no.4481.

*4669   Burke, Sir John Bernard. Burke's Genealogical and heraldic history of the landed gentry of Ireland. 4th ed. London, 1958.
1st ed., 1899; 2nd, 1904; 3rd, 1912. All editions important, because names were dropped from edition to edition. 1st-3rd eds. were called 9th-11th, conforming with the *Landed gentry of Great Britain*. See also note under no.4482.

*4670   ——— A genealogical and heraldic dictionary of the landed gentry of Great Britain and Ireland . . . See no.4482.

4671   Butler, William F. T. Gleanings from Irish history. New York, 1925.
Leading features of the organization of Gaelic portions of Ireland. Good study of some of the notable tribes; maps and pedigree charts; land tenure. Much about MacCarthy family.

4672   Byrne, Francis J. Irish kings and high kings. New York: St. Martin's Pr., 1973.
Appendixes include king lists. 21 genealogical tables, explanation of the pronunciation of old Irish names. Good bibliography. Data corrects many lineages that have been accepted and published. Indispensable for anyone interested in early Irish history and genealogy.

4673   Cokayne, George E. Complete baronetage. 1900-1909. See no.4490.
Irish baronetcies, 1619-1800.

4674   ——— Complete peerage . . . 1910-59.
Had title: *Complete peerage of England, Scotland, Ireland* . . . See no.4491.

4675   Crossly, Aaron. The peerage of Ireland: or, An exact catalogue of the present nobility, both lords spiritual and temporal, with an historical and genealogical account of them . . . with their respective arms, crests, supporters and mottoes . . . Dublin, 1725.

4676   De Courcy, B. W. A genealogical history of the Milesian family of Ireland with . . . chart of armorial bearings of the same families. 1880. Repr. Bridgeport, Conn., 1965.

4677   de Burgh, Ulick H. The landowners of Ireland. Dublin, 1878.

4677a   Herbert, Robert. Worthies of Thomond. 3pts. Limerick, 1944-46.
Short lives of famous people, Limerick and Clare.

4678    **Howard, Joseph J.** and **Crisp, F. A.** Visitation of Ireland. 6v. 1897–1918. Repr. 6v. in 1. Baltimore: G.P.C., 1973.

Contains pedigrees and illustrations of arms, notices of all descendants in 150 pedigrees. All indexed in Whitmore (no.4187). Limited printing, privately issued originally.

*4679   **Irish family names map.** Dublin, 1974. From British Book Centre, New York.

Map of Ireland showing places of origin of the main Irish families. 192 coats of arms drawn by Myra Maguire, artist to the Heraldic Court of Ireland.

4680    **Kinney, Arthur F.** Titled Elizabethans: a directory of Elizabethan state and church officers and knights, with peers of England, Scotland and Ireland, 1558–1603. *See* no.4505.

4682    **Lodge, John.** The peerage of Ireland. Rev. by M. Archdall. 7v. Dublin, 1789.

One of the definitive works on the Irish peerage. Coats of arms.

*4683   **MacLysaght, Edward.** Irish families: their names, arms, and origins. 3rd ed., rev. New York: Crown, 1972.

Origin of over 500 names and 243 coats of arms.

*4684   ——— More Irish families. Galway, Ireland, 1960.

Includes another 600 families and has additional information on more than 150 listed in *Irish families*, no.4683. 2nd ed. being prepared.

*4685   ——— Supplement to Irish families. Dublin, 1964. Obtainable from G.P.C., Baltimore.

This 3rd vol. adds another 550 names and has additional information on families treated in earlier volumes, no.4683–84.

4686    **Metcalfe, Walter C.** A book of Knights Banneret . . . and Knights made in Ireland, between 1566 and 1698, together with index of names. *See* no.4509.

4687    **O'Brien, Michael A.** Corpus genealogiarum Hiberniae. v.1 (all pub.). Dublin: Inst. of Advanced Studies, 1962.

Contains important Irish pedigrees and genealogical material from the earliest literary period down to ca.1500. Large personal name index and index to tribes and families.

4688    **O'Hart, John.** The Irish and Anglo-Irish landed gentry when Cromwell came to Ireland; or, A supplement to Irish pedigrees. 1884. Repr. New York: Barnes and Noble, 1969.

Critical introduction by Edward MacLysaght. Pedigrees are of secondary interest; its value lies in the 370p. section which give précis of a number of important 17th-century source materials now no longer extant.

4689    ——— ——— 2nd ed. Dublin, 1887.

4690    ——— Irish pedigrees; or, The origin and stem of the Irish nation. Dublin, various dates.

2nd ed. 1876–78; 3rd ed., 1881; 4th ed., 2v., 1887–88; 5th ed., 2v., 1892; Limited American ed., 2v. 1915; 2v. 1923.

3rd ed., 1881, is sometimes considered the best. Although O'Hart shows many inaccuracies, it is very useful from 1800 onward. no.4688 is considered superior, but all editions are scarce, and any one is useful. The New York colored-arms edition (1923) is the most prized (and expensive). Colors and charges are often inaccurate.

4691    **O'Toole, E. H.** Decorations and medals of the Republic of Ireland. London: Seaby, 1972.

4692    **Rooney, John.** A genealogical history of Irish families with their crests and armorial bearings. (New York, 1896).

Has more than 350 coats of arms.

4693    **Shaw, William A.** The knights of England: a complete record from the earliest time to the present day of knights of all orders of chivalry in England, Scotland and Ireland and of Knights Bachelors . . . *See* no.4521.

4694  Skey, William. The heraldic calendar... Dublin, 1846.
Contains registers of grants of arms in Ireland.

4695  Solly, Edward. An index of hereditary England, Scottish and Irish titles of honour... See no.4522.

4696  Walsh, Paul. Irish chiefs and leaders. Ed. by Colm O Lochlainn. Dublin, 1960.

## Religions

4697  (Anglican Church of Ireland) Ireland. Public Record Office. Public records of Ireland, 23rd report, 1891. Dublin.
This report lists many Anglican Church of Ireland parish registers with those that were in the Public Record Office and subsequently destroyed.

4698  (Baptists) Whitley, William T. A Baptist bibliography...
Covers 1526–1837 and gives dates and locations of registers. See no.4533.

4699  (Huguenots) Agnew, David C. A. Protestant exiles from France... or, The Huguenot refugees and their descendants in Great Britain and Ireland. See no.4541.

4700  (Huguenots) Lee, Grace L. The Huguenot settlements in Ireland. New York, 1936.
Standard work. Complete and authoritative. Much new information.

4701  (Huguenots) Shaw, William A. Letters of denization and acts of naturalization for aliens in England and Ireland, 1509–1800... See no.4542–43.

4702  (Huguenots) Smiles, Samuel. The Huguenots, their settlements, churches and industries in England and Ireland. See no.4547.

4703  (Quakers) The annual monitor... or, Obituary of the members of the Society of Friends in Great Britain and Ireland... See no.4562.

4704  (Quakers) Eustace, P. Beryl, and Goodbody, O. C. Quaker records, Dublin: abstracts of wills... See no.4620.

4705  (Quakers) Goodbody, Olive C. Guide to Irish Quaker records, 1654–1860. With contribution on Northern Ireland records by B. G. Hutton. Dublin: Stationery Office, 1967.
Calendar, including family collections, diaries, genealogical material, wills, deeds, and other legal documents, with long list of names occurring in Irish Quaker records.

# SCOTLAND

## Bibliographies

☩ Genealogical bibliographies of Great Britain, many of which include Scotland, will be found in no.4144–87.

**4706** **Black, George F.** A list of works relating to Scotland. New York, 1916.
Repr. with additions from *New York Public Library bull.,* 1914.

*****4707** **Ferguson, Joan P. S.** Scottish family histories held in Scottish libraries. Repr. Edinburgh: Scottish Central Lib., 1968.
What exists and where held in Scottish libraries.

**4708** ——— Scottish newspapers held in Scottish libraries. Edinburgh: Scottish Central Lib., 1956.

**4709** **Grant, Sir Francis J.** Index to genealogies, birthbriefs and funeral escutcheons recorded in the Lyon Office, 1908. *Scottish Record Soc.,* pt.40. Edinburgh: The Society, 1908.

**4710** **Hancock, Philip D.** A bibliography of works relating to Scotland, 1916–50. 2v. Edinburgh: Edinburgh Univ. Pr., 1959–60.
Intended as a supplement to no.4713.

**4711** **Handlist of Scottish and Welsh record publications.** Scottish section by Peter Gouldesbrough and A. P. Kup; Welsh section by Idwal Lewis. *British Records Assoc. publ. Pam.* 4. London: The Association, 1954.
Classified and abbreviated list of publications by 46 Scottish and Welsh publishing societies. Note that *Texts and calendars* (no. 4159) does not attempt to cover Scottish and Welsh societies.

321

**4712** **Matheson, Cyril.** A catalogue of the publications of Scottish historical and kindred clubs and societies, and an index of the papers relating to Scotland . . . 1908–27. Aberdeen, 1928.
Prior to 1908, see Terry, no.4715.

**4713** **Mitchell, Sir Arthur,** and **Cash, C. G.** A contribution to the bibliography of Scottish topography. 2v. *Scottish History Soc.,* 2nd ser., v.14–15. Edinburgh, 1916–17.
v.1, alphabetical under county; v.2, alphabetical under subject. For supplement, see no.4710.

*****4714** **Stuart, Margaret.** Scottish family history: a guide to works of reference on the history and genealogy of Scottish families. To which is prefixed an essay on how to write a history of a family, by Sir James B. Paul. Edinburgh, 1930.
Alphabetical references to Scottish families.

**4715** **Terry, Charles S.** A catalogue of the publications of Scottish historical and kindred clubs and societies and of the volumes relative to Scottish history issued by His Majesty's Stationery Office, 1780–1908. With a subject index. Aberdeen, 1909.
1908–27, see no.4712.

**4716** ———— Index of the papers relating to Scotland described and calendared in the *Historical Manuscripts Commission reports.* Glasgow, 1908.

## Records

✠ Many of the records and record guides in the English section (*see* no.4188–4237) concern Scotland as well.

**4717** **Cowan, Ian B.** The parishes of medieval Scotland. *Scottish Record Soc.,* pt. 93. Edinburgh: The Society, 1967.

*****4718** **Genealogical Society of the Church of Jesus Christ of Latter-day Saints.** Major genealogical sources in Scotland. *Research paper,* ser.A, no.3. Salt Lake City: L.D.S., 1967.

**4719** **Handlist of Scottish and Welsh record publications . . .** *See* no.4711.

**4719a** **Livingstone, Matthew.** A guide to the public records of Scotland deposited in H.M.'s General Register House, Edinburgh. Edinburgh, 1905.
Obsolete in some details. Supplements have appeared in the *Scottish historical review,* v.26, 1946, and annually thereafter.

**4720** **Maidment, James.** Collectanea genealogica. Edinburgh, 1883.

**4721** **Owners of land and heritages, 1872–73.** Return of the name and Address of every owner of one acre and upwards . . . Edinburgh, 1874.
Fairly late for genealogists but of inestimable value where necessary to cover this period.

**4722** **Sinclair, Sir John.** The statistical account of Scotland drawn up from the communications of the ministers of the different parishes. 21v. Edinburgh, 1791–99.
Land, rent, and other records; biographies. Concerns also the Scottish Isles, Shetlands, etc.

*****4723** **Steel, Donald J.** Sources for Scottish genealogy and family history. Chichester, England: Phillimore, 1970.

**4724** **Urquhart, R. M.** Scottish burgh and county heraldry. Detroit, Mich.: Gale Research, 1973.
Good bibliography, history and heraldry.

**4725** **Whyte, Donald.** Three centuries of emigration from the British Isles. Scottish emigration to North America. *World Conference of World Records,* area C.1B paper. Salt Lake City: L.D.S., 1969.

## Paleography

**4725a** **Simpson, Grant G.** Scottish handwriting 1150–1650; an introduction to the reading of documents. Edinburgh: Bratton Pub., 1973.

## Periodicals and Series

**4726** The Scottish antiquary, or Northern notes and queries. v.1–17, 1886–1903. Edinburgh, 1888–1903. v.1–4, *Northern notes and queries.*

**4727** Scottish genealogical helper. no.1– , 1974– . Harbor City, Calif.: Augustan Soc.
Balanced publication with queries, family studies, clan and family society listings. Baptismal and other listings. To members of Augustan Society only.

**4728** Scottish genealogist: the quarterly journal of the Scottish Genealogy Society. v.1– , 1954– . Edinburgh: The Society.
Almost all parts still in print.

**4729** Scottish notes and queries. v.1–12, 1887–99; ser.2, v.1–8, 1899–1907; ser.3, v.1–13, 1923–35. General index to ser.1, 1887–99 in v.12, 1901. Aberdeen.

**4730** Scottish Record Society. (Publications) Pt.1– , 1897– . Edinburgh: The Society.
Genealogically the most important Scottish series. Parts contain indexes and calendars, parish registers, testaments, burgess rolls, apprentice registers, etc. Numbering system most confusing, but the Society has issued a list which is intelligible. Many parts still in print.

## Biographies

### GENERAL

**4731** Chambers, Robert. A biographical dictionary of eminent Scotsmen. New ed., rev. and continued by Thomas Thomson. 3v. 1870. Repr. Hildesheim, N.Y.: G. Olms, 1971.

**4732** A list of persons concerned in the Rebellion (of 1745) . . . *Scottish History Soc.,* 2nd ser. v.8. Edinburgh, 1890.
Index to the list of rebels also published separately (originally *Scottish History Soc.,* ser.2, v.8, pp. 405–39); but apparently a new index published also in 1891. 3,000 names.

**4733** Seton, Sir Bruce G., and Arndt, J. G. The prisoners of the '45; ed. from State papers. 3v. *Scottish History Soc.,* 3rd ser. v.13–15. Edinburgh, 1928–29.
3,400 names with good background information.

### PROFESSIONS

**4734** (Advocates) Grant, Sir Francis J. The Faculty of Advocates in Scotland, 1532–1943, with Genealogical notes. *Scottish Record Soc.,* pt. 145. Edinburgh: The Society, 1944.

**4735** (Army) Dalton, Charles. The Scots army, 1661–88: with memoirs of the commanders-in-chief . . . 2pts. London, 1909.
pt.2 has regimental lists and commissioned officers, with index.

**4736** (Army) Forbes-Leith, William. The Scots men-at-arms and life guards in France, 1418–1830. 2v. Edinburgh, 1882.

**4737** (Army) Terry, Charles S. Papers relating to the Army of the Solemn League and Covenant, 1643–47. 2v. *Scottish History Soc.,* ser.2, v.16–17. Edinburgh, 1917.
Has lists, etc.

**4738** (Clergy) Haws, Charles B. Scottish parish clergy at the Reformation, 1540–74. *Scottish Record Soc.,* pt.3, new ser. Edinburgh: The Society, 1972.

**4739** (Clergy) Scott, Hew (and others). Fasti ecclesiae Scoticanae: the succession of ministers in the Church of Scotland from the Reformation. New ed., rev. and continued to 1954. 9v. Edinburgh: Oliver & Boyd, 1915–61.
Gives short biographies of 15,000 ministers, their parents and offspring.

**4740** (Education) (Aberdeen University) Anderson, Peter J. Officers and graduates of University and King's College,

Aberdeen, 1495–1860. New Spalding Club. Aberdeen, 1893.

**4741** (Education) (Aberdeen University) **Watt, Theodore.** Roll of the graduates, 1901–25, with suppl. 1860–1900. Aberdeen: Aberdeen Univ. Pr., 1935.

**4742** (Education) (Edinburgh University) **Laing, David.** A catalogue of the graduates . . . since its foundation, (1587–1858). Bannatyne Club. Edinburgh, 1858.

**4743** (Education) (Edinburgh University) **List of university graduates, 1859–1888.** Edinburgh, 1889.

**4744** (Education) (Glasgow University) **Addison, William I.** The matriculation albums, 1728–1858. Glasgow, 1913.

**4745** —— —— A roll of graduates, 1727–1897, with short biographical notes. Glasgow, 1898.

**4746** (Education) (St. Andrews University) **Anderson, James M.** Early records . . . The graduation roll, 1413–1579 and the matriculation roll, 1473–1579. *Scottish History Soc.,* 3rd ser. v.8. Edinburgh, 1926.

**4747** —— —— Matriculation roll, 1747–1897. Edinburgh, 1905.

**4748** (Lawyers) **Grant, Sir Francis J.** Court of the Lord Lyon: list of His Majesty's officers of arms and other officials, with genealogical notes, 1318–1945. *Scottish Record Soc.,* pt.148. Edinburgh: The Society, 1945.

**4749** (Lawyers) **The Society of Writers to His Majesty's Signet, with a list of members.** Edinburgh, 1936.
Gives biographical details. Replaces 1890 list.

## *Registers*

*****4750** **Bloxham, V. Ben.** Key to the parochial registers of Scotland from the earliest times through 1854 . . . Provo, Utah: Brigham Young Univ. Pr., 1970.

**4751** **Edinburgh.** The roll of burgesses and guild brethren of Edinburgh, 1406–1841. *Scottish Record Soc.* pts.101–5, 108, 109, 112, 114, 115, 124, 125. Edinburgh, 1929–33.

**4752** **Edinburgh (Commissary).** Commissariot records of Edinburgh. Register of testaments, 1601–1800. *Scottish Record Soc.,* pts.1, 2, 4. Edinburgh, 1898–99.

**4753** **Glasgow.** The burgesses and guild brethren of Glasgow, 1573–1846. *Scottish Record Soc.,* pts.93–98, 116, 117, 119–21, 127. Edinburgh, 1925–35.

**4754** **Glasgow (Commissary).** Commissariot records of Glasgow. Register of testaments, 1547–1800. *Scottish Record Soc.,* pts.9–13. Edinburgh, 1901.

**4755** **Karr, Nola M.** Detailed list of the old parochial registers of Scotland. In *National Genealogical Soc. quarterly,* v.44–45, 1955–56.
Appeared originally in 1872.

**4757** **Scotland. Public Record Office.** Now Scottish Public Record Office, *q.v.*

**4757a** **Scottish Public Record Office.** From 1915 to date the Scottish Record Office has published a series of Indexes. Each volume has hundreds of names with much relevant data. Many volumes still in print, available from Her Majesty's Stationery Office, London.
v.1, 4–6, 14, 17, 19, 20, 22–65 (in progress): Index of register of deeds, 1915– .
v.15–16: Index to particular register of sasines in the sheriffdoms of Aberdeen (and other areas), 1630–60. 2v. 1928.
Sasines is the name, designation, date of recording (mostly 17th century) of a city or sheriffdom.

**4758** —— Index to registers of deeds preserved in H.M. General Register House. v.1– , 1915– (in progress). Edinburgh: Her Majesty's Stationery Office.
Fine series. Thousands of names.

**4759** —— Index to secretary's and particularly registers of sasines for sheriffdoms of Inverness, Ross, Cromarty

and Sutherland, preserved in H.M. General Register House, Edinburgh. v.1– , 1966– (in progress). Edinburgh: Her Majesty's Stationery Office.
v.1, 1606–08; 1617–60; v.2, 1661–1721.

**4760 Scottish parish registers.**
Some are published in the Scottish Record Society (publications). *See* no.4730.

## Vital Statistics

**4761 The Scottish Record Society** (*see* no.4730) has published a number of birth, baptism, and marriage registers. Many are in print.

**4761a Edinburgh.** The register of marriages for the parish of Edinburgh, 1595–1800. *The Scottish Record Soc.,* pts. 29–34, 42, 43, 45, 46, 48, 79–81, 84–86, 88–92. Edinburgh, 1905–22.

**4762 Jervise, Andrew.** Epitaphs and inscriptions from burial grounds and old buildings in north east Scotland. 2v. Edinburgh, 1875–79.

**4763 Rogers, Charles.** Monuments and monumental inscriptions in Scotland. 2v. London, 1871–72.
Collection of tombstone and monumental inscriptions arranged church by church and parish by parish. Thousands of entries.

## Wills

**4763a** Some information on the wills of Scotland will be found in Anthony J. Camp, *Wills and their whereabouts* (no. 4366), and Gibson, *Wills and where to find them* (no.4377). The Scottish Record Society (no.4730) has published many indexes to testaments and wills, usually complete down to 1800. Many are in print.

## Topography

**4764 Bartholomew, John.** Philips' Handy atlas of Scotland. London, 1898.
County maps of Scotland in color, showing boundary lines of each parish within each county.

**4765 Bullock, Leslie G.** Historical map of Scotland. rev. Edinburgh: Bartholomew, 1959.
Sheet 39 by 26 inches. Has coats of arms of 129 Scottish clans. Good display piece.

***4766 Gardner, David E.; Harland, D.;** and **Smith, F.** A genealogical atlas of Scotland. rev. Salt Lake City: Deseret Book Co., 1963.
Has complete index to all places on the maps.

**4767 Groome, Francis H.** Ordnance gazetteer of Scotland: a survey of Scottish topography, statistical, biographical and historical. new ed. 6v. Edinburgh (1894).
Each important town has a bibliography. Often preferred to Lewis (no.4770) by Scottish authorities, because it is later and has more details. Both Lewis and Groome are needed, because they supplement each other.

**4768 Hogan, Edmund.** Onomasticon goedelicum locorum et tribuum Hiberniae et Scotiae; an index, with identifications, to the Gaelic names of places and tribes . . . *See* no.4634.

**4769 Johnston (W. and A. K.)** and **G. W. Bacon, Ltd.** Johnston's gazetteer of Scotland. 3rd ed. Rev. by R. W. Munro. Edinburgh: Johnston & Bacon, 1973. Available from British Book Centre, New York.
Includes a glossary of the most common Gaelic names.

**4770 Lewis, Samuel.** A topographical dictionary of Scotland . . . 2v. and atlas. Various editions. London, 1846–51. *See* note under no.4767.

**4771 Mitchell, Sir Arthur,** and **Cash, C. G. A.** A contribution to the bibliography of Scottish topography. *See* no.4713.

**4772 Moncreiffe, Sir Rupert I. K., Bart.,** and **Pottinger, D.** Bartholomew's Map of Scotland of old. Edinburgh: Bartholomew, 1960.

325

Sheet 40 by 30 inches. 174 clan crests with coats of arms of their chiefs.

4773 Munro, Robert W. The gazetteer of Scotland. Rev. ed. Edinburgh, 1974. From British Book Centre, New York.
Lists towns, villages, rivers, and additional topographical information.

*4774 Smith, Frank. A genealogical gazetteer of Scotland. Logan, Utah: Everton Pub., 1972.
Alphabetical dictionary of places with their location. Ecclesiastical jurisdiction, population, and date of earliest entry in the registers of every ancient parish in Scotland. Essential.

4775 Wilson, John M. The imperial gazetteer of Scotland, or dictionary of Scottish topography. 8v. Edinburgh, 1854.
A new edition of 2v. was published in the 1870s.

# Names

*4776 Black, George F. The surnames of Scotland: their origin, meaning, and history. 2nd repr., with amendments and additions. New York: New York Public Lib., 1965.
Variant spellings; shows where names are first listed in ancient charters. Monumental work. Originally published in *New York Public Library bull.*, 1943-46, and later revised. Essential.

4777 Hogan, Edmund. Onomasticon goedelicum locorum et tribuum Hiberniae et Scotiae; an index, with identifications, to the Gaelic names of places and tribes. *See* no.4768.

*4778 Johnston, James B. Place-names of Scotland. Repr. with additional notes on the author. Wakefield, Yorks, England: S. R. Pub., 1970.
Improved color for tartans in this 3rd ed. repr.

4779 McBain, Alexander. Etymology of the principal Gaelic national names, personal names and surnames. Stirling, Scotland, 1911.
Repr. from his *Etymological dictionary of the Gaelic language.*

4780 Mackenzie, William C. Scottish place-names. London, 1931.
Definitive study; comprehensive with fine indexes.

4781 Sims, Clifford S. The origin and signification of Scottish surnames. 1862. Repr. Baltimore: G.P.C., 1968; Rutland, Vt.: Tuttle, 1969.
500 surnames and listing of 300 Christian names with their origins and meanings. Inferior to no.4776, but useful.

4782 Watson, William J. History of Celtic place-names of Scotland. Edinburgh, 1926.

# Manuals

4783 Black, William G. Hints as to how to compile a pedigree in Scotland. In *Transactions of the Glasgow Archaeological Soc.,* v.8, pt.1, 1927.

4784 Eaves-Walton, Patricia M. Tracing your Scottish ancestors. *Transactions,* Hawick Archaeological Soc. Hawick, Scotland: The Society, 1959.

*4785 Genealogical Society of the Church of Jesus Christ of Latter-day Saints. The social, economic, religious and historical background of Scotland as it affects genealogical research. Salt Lake City: L.D.S., 1969.
Useful chronological outline of main events in Scotland affecting genealogical research.

*4786 Hamilton-Edwards, Gerald K. S. In search of Scottish ancestry. Baltimore: G.P.C., 1972.
Comprehensive study on Scottish genealogy. Best book on Scottish genealogy available. Bibliographies and appendixes outstanding. Essential.

4787  **M'Kechnie, Hector.** The pursuit of pedigree. Edinburgh, 1928. In *The juridical review,* v.40, pp.205-34, 304-40.
Slanted toward Scottish researcher.

4788  **Parker, Donald D.** Scottish and Scotch Irish ancestry research. Santa Fe, N.Mex.: The Author, n.d.
Gives historical background of Scots and Scotch-Irish immigration; lists and describes record sources.

4789  **Sandison, Alexander.** Tracing ancestors in Shetland. Lerwick, Scotland: T. & J. Manson, 1972.
Describes in detail the patronymic surnames custom which prevailed until the 19th century. List of parishes; bibliography and guide to local sources.

*4790  **Steel, Donald J.** Sources for Scottish genealogy and family history. Chichester, England: Phillimore, 1970.

# *Peerages, Baronetages, Knightages, Gentry*

⌖ Many works listed under England contain information on Scottish peerages, etc., see no.4471-4526.

*4791  **Adam, Frank.** The clans, septs, and regiments of the Scottish Highlands. Rev. by Sir Thomas Innes of Learney. 8th ed. Baltimore: G.P.C., 1970.
600p. practical encyclopaedia, with colored tartans. Improved color for tartans in latest edition.

4792  **Addington, Arthur C.** The Royal House of Stuarts: the descendants of King James VI of Scotland, James I of England. See no.4445.

4792a  **Anderson, Marjorie O.** Kings and kingship in early Scotland. Totowa, N.J.: Rowman & Littlefield, 1974.
6th to 9th centuries. Pedigree charts; indispensable to the understanding and evaluation of all regnal pedigrees. Table of Pictish kings.

4793  **Anderson, William.** The Scottish nation: or, The surnames, families, literature, honours, and biographical history of the people of Scotland. 3v. Edinburgh, 1882.
Long articles on families and individuals. Coats of arms.

4794  **Bain, Robert.** The clans and tartans of Scotland. London: Collins, 1971.
132 tartans in color; compact and handy guide, with authentic black and white reproductions of the heraldic badges. Glossary of Scottish place names. Several editions prior to this.

4795  **Banks, Sir Thomas C.** Baronia Anglica concentrata . . . also a glossary of dormant English, Scottish and Irish peerage titles. See no.4472.

4796  **Betham, William.** The baronetage of England: history of the English baronets and such baronets of Scotland as are of English families. See no.4476.

4797  **Burke, Sir John B.** The Royal families of England, Scotland, Wales with their descendants, sovereigns and subjects. See no.4447.

4798  **Cokayne, George E.** Complete baronetage. See no.4490.
Scottish, 1625-1707.

4799  ———— The complete peerage . . . See no.4491.
Complete peerage of England, Scotland, Ireland . . . extant, extinct, or dormant.

4800  **Douglas, Sir Robert.** The baronage of Scotland, containing an historical and genealogical account of the gentry of that kingdom . . . v.1 (all pub.). Edinburgh, 1798.
Begun by Douglas and completed by other hands.

4801  ———— The peerage of Scotland, containing an historical and genealogical account of the nobility of that kingdom . . . 2nd ed., continued by John P. Wood. Edinburgh, 1813.

**4802 Dunbar, Sir Archibald H.** Scottish kings: a revised chronology of Scottish history, 1005–1625, with notices of the principal events, tables of regnal years, pedigrees, calendars, etc. 2nd ed. Edinburgh, 1906.

**4803 Fergusson, Sir James.** Lowland lairds. London, 1949.
Landed families of Lowland Scotland.

**4804 Fletcher, William G. D.** Royal descents: Scottish records. How to trace descent from royalty . . . London, 1908.
Pt.1 of v.3 of *The genealogist's pocket library*. Still useful.

**4805 Grant, James.** The tartans of the clans of Scotland. Edinburgh, 1886.
Perhaps the best book on tartans, especially for those seeking authoritative information. Adam (no.4791) is for the majority of researchers, and should be on the regular reference shelf, but Grant should be reserved for scholarly use. Clanships, chiefs, dress, arms, emblazoned arms of chiefs in color.

**4806 Grimble, Ian.** Scottish clans and tartans. New York: Tudor, 1973.
Good study of Highland dress, not confined to Highland clans. 148 Scottish names, excellent colored illustrations.

**\*4806a Innes, Sir Thomas.** The tartans of the clans and families of Scotland. 8th ed., rev. New York: British Book Centre, 1971.
Tartans are in color. Historical and genealogical sketches of clans and families. Definitive, but has poor index.

**4807 Johnston (W. and A. K.) and G. W. Bacon.** Johnston clan map of the Scottish Highlands. Edinburgh: Johnston & Bacon, 1964.
Sheet 40 by 30 inches. Has chiefs, arms, and tartans of 144 clans in full color.

**4808** ———— Johnston's Clan histories, 1943– . Edinburgh: Johnston & Bacon.
Splendid series of inexpensive pocketbooks dealing with 21 clans. Text comprises clan history, maps, etc. Tartans and arms in color. All in print in 1974 and obtainable from British Book Centre, New York.

**4809 Kinney, Arthur F.** Titled Elizabethans . . . with peers of England, Scotland, and Ireland, 1558–1603. *See* no. 4505.

**4810 Logan, James,** and **McIan, R. R.** The clans of the Scottish Highlands. 2v. London, 1845–47.
Perhaps the best work for dress, tartans, armorial insignia; 72 fine colored tartans by McIan. The scarcest work on tartans, very expensive.

**4811 MacFarlane, Walter.** Genealogical collections concerning families in Scotland made in 1750–51. 2v. *Scottish History Soc.,* 1st ser. v.33–34. Edinburgh, 1900.
Authoritative and careful work covering period of considerable importance.

**4812 Moncreiffe of That Ilk, Sir Rupert I. K., Bart.** The Highland clans: the dynastic origins, chiefs and background of the clans connected with Highland history and of some other families. New York: Clarkson N. Potter, 1969.
Although cut by publishers without reference to author, the text and illustrations which remain are good; invaluable for reference.

**4813** ———— and **Pottinger, D.** Bartholomew's Map of Scotland of old. Edinburgh: Bartholomew, 1960.
Sheet 40 by 30 inches. 174 clan crests with coats of arms of their chiefs.

**4814 Munro, Robert W.** Kinsmen and clansmen. Levittown, N.Y.: Transatlantic Arts, 1971.
Story of 93 clans and families. Tartans in color. Good historical background. Not as full as Innes (no.4806a), but less expensive.

**4815 Paul, Sir James B.** The Scots peerage, founded on Wood's ed. of Sir Robert Douglas's *Peerage of Scotland* [no. 4801], containing an historical and genealogical account of the nobility of that kingdom. 8v. and index vol. Edinburgh, 1904–14.

Broader in scope than the *Complete peerage* (no.4491), in that it deals with antecedents of first peer and with a great number of collaterals. Essential and authoritative work.

**4816   Pine, Leslie G.** The Highland clans, their origins and history. Rutland, Vt.: Tuttle, 1973.

Easy-to-understand clan history. Traces origin of clansmen of Scottish Highlands, evolution of their culture; important reference work. A definitive work on the origin and history of the Gael, the Celtic monarchy, clan struggles, life and costumes and systems.

**4817   Rennie, James A.** The Scottish people: their clans, families and origins. London, 1960.

Inexpensive and excellent work, which was soon out-of-print. Has useful clan map.

**4818   Ruvigny and Raineval, Melville A. H. D., 9th Marquis.** The blood royal of Britain; being a roll of the living descendants of . . . James III, King of Scotland . . . See no.4454.

**4819   ———** The Jacobite peerage, baronetage, knightage and grants of honor; extracted . . . from the Stuart Papers . . . See no.4455.

**4820   Scots kith and kin.** Nashville, Tenn.: Nelson, 1973.

Complete guide to the tartans and clans associated with over 4,000 names.

**\*4821   Scottish clans and their tartans.** 40th ed. New York: Transatlantic Arts, 1960.

Important; the Lord Lyon of Scotland, head of the Scottish Office of Arms, has revised the recent editions.

**4822   Shaw, William A.** The knights of England: a complete record from the earliest time to the present day of the knights of all orders of chivalry in England, Scotland and Ireland . . . See no.4521.

**4823   Solly, Edward.** An index of hereditary English, Scottish and Irish titles of honour . . . See no.4522.

**4824   Taylor, James.** The great historic families of Scotland. 2v. Edinburgh, 1887.

Considerable coverage of biographical details of each inheritor of family title.

# *Religions*

**4825   Maxwell, Archibald S.** Records of "Quakers," 1647–1878. Aberdeen: The Author, 1973.

Register of all births, proposals of marriage, deaths and burials of the Society of Friends in Scotland. Chronological and alphabetical order.

**4826   Scottish Public Record Office.** Records of the Church of Scotland; preserved in the Scottish Record Office and General Register Office, Register House, Edinburgh. *Scottish Record Soc.,* pt.94. Edinburgh: The Society, 1967.

# WALES

✠ Genealogical works concerning Wales may appear to be few, but many are to be found under the heading "England," where quite often bibliographies, biographies, etc. include materials pertinent to Wales, as indicated in the titles. A few of the outstanding works on Wales are listed below, with frequent cross references to the full title and annotation.

## Bibliographies

**4827 Blackwell, Henry.** Bibliography of Welsh Americana. Aberystwyth, Wales, 1942.
Books by and about the Welsh in America.

**4828 Mullins, Edward L. C.** A guide to the historical and archaeological publications of societies in England and Wales, 1901–33. See no.4158.

**4829 Norton, Jane E.** Guide to the national and provincial directories of England and Wales . . . before 1856. London, 1950. See no.4228.

**4831 Whitley, William T.** A Baptist bibliography . . . See no.4533.
Covers 1526–1837.

**4832 Youings, Joyce.** Local record sources in print and in progress, 1971–72 . . . Contains results of survey . . . relating to record sources for study of English and Welsh history . . . See no.4169.

## Records

**4833 Bartrum, P. C.** Early Welsh genealogical tracts. Cardiff: Wales Univ. Pr., 1966.
Well documented and good bibliographical references.

4834  Bradney, Sir Joseph A. A history of Monmouthshire, from the coming of the Normans into Wales down to the present time. 5v. in 12. London, 1904–33.
Genealogical tables.

4835  Genealogical Society of the Church of Jesus Christ of Latter-day Saints. Major genealogical record sources in England and Wales. Salt Lake City: L.D.S., 1966.

4836  Handlist of Scottish and Welsh record publications . . . *See* no.4711.

4837  Howells, Brian E. A calendar of letters relating to North Wales, 1533–ca.1700: from . . . collections in the National Library of Wales. Board of Celtic Studies, Univ. of Wales. *History and law ser.* 23. Cardiff: Wales Univ. Pr., 1967.

4838  Return of owners of land, 1873, England and Wales . . . *See* no.4230.

4839  Tercentenary handlist of English and Wales newspapers, magazines and reviews, 1620–1920 . . . *See* no.4234.

4840  West Wales historical records: the annual of the Historical Society of West Wales. v.1–14, 1912–29. Carmarthen, Wales.
Included are many parish registers and other material of genealogical interest. Much family information.

## *Biographies*

4841  Anstruther, Godfrey. The seminary priests: a dictionary of the secular clergy of England and Wales . . . *See* no. 4295.

*4842  Crockford's Clerical directory, 1858– . . . *See* no.4296.

*4843  The dictionary of Welsh biography down to 1940. Under the auspices of the Honourable Society of Cymmrodorion. London: The Society, 1959.
Covers the period 400–1940, with more than 4,000 names. Welsh title is *Y Bywgrafiadur Cymreig hyd 1940.*

4844  Hartmann, Edward G. Americans from Wales. Boston: Christopher Pub. House, 1967.
List of distinguished Welsh Americans, classified bibliography, etc.

4845  Rees, Thomas M. Notable Welshmen (1700–1900), with biographical notes . . . also a complete alphabetical index. Carmarthen, Wales, 1908.

4846  Rowland, E. H. A biographical dictionary of eminent Welshmen who flourished from 1700–1900. Wrexham, Wales, 1907.

## *Registers*

*4847  Burke, Arthur M. Key to ancient parish registers of England and Wales . . . *See* no.4338.

*4848  National index of parish registers . . . *See* no.4345.
Some volumes will concern Wales.

4848a  Original parish registers in record offices and libraries. *See* no.4343a.
Particularly useful for list of registers in institutions.

## *Vital Statistics*

4849  West Wales and Gower. Marriage bonds and fiats of West Wales and Gower, 1612–1799. In *West Wales historical records,* v.3–12, 1913–27.

## *Wills*

⌖ The best books relevant to this section are by Camp (no.4366) and Gibson (no. 4377).

331

*4850 **Genealogical Society of the Church of Jesus Christ of Latter-day Saints.** Welsh probate jurisdictions. *Research papers,* ser.A, no.47–48. 2v. Salt Lake City: L.D.S., 1970.
North and South Wales and Monmouthshire.

4851 **Pratt, David H.** A remarkable collection of English-Welsh probate records and aids in using them . . . *See* no.4381.

## Topography

4853 **Evans, John.** Map of the six counties of North Wales . . . Lwyngyroes, Wales, 1795.
8 engraved maps, 24 by 22 inches.

*4854 **Gardner, David E.; Harland, D.; and Smith, F.** A genealogical atlas of England and Wales . . . *See* no.4388.

4855 **Great Britain. General Register Office.** 1961 census of England and Wales . . . index of place names . . . *See* no.4390.

4856 **Hotten, John C.** A handbook of topography and family history of England and Wales. *See* no.4172.

4857 **Institute of Heraldic and Genealogical Studies, Canterbury.** Parish maps of the counties of England and Wales . . . *See* no.4391.

4858 **Lewis, Samuel.** A topographical dictionary of Wales . . . 2v. Various editions. London, 1833–49.
Dates of editions were 1833, 1840, 1842, 1844, 1845, 1849, 1850. Some have atlases bound in, others have atlas combined with atlas for England (*see* no.4392). The 1833 ed. is best, because it contains the ecclesiastical jurisdictions for Wales.

4859 **Rees, William.** Historical atlas of Wales, from early to modern times. New ed. New York: Faber & Faber, 1959.

4860 **Wilson, John M.** The imperial gazetteer of England and Wales . . . *See* no.4396.

## Names

*4861 **Bardsley, Charles W. E.** A dictionary of English and Welsh surnames . . . *See* no.4406.

4862 **Davies, Trefor R.** A book of Welsh names. London, 1952.
Useful for those having to deal with Welsh pedigrees. English meanings of Welsh names provided.

4863 **Genealogical Society of the Church of Jesus Christ of Latter-day Saints.** Index to places in the 1851 census of England, Wales . . . *See* no.4402.

*4864 ——— Welsh patronymics and place names in Wales and Monmouthshire. *Research paper,* ser.A, no.6. Salt Lake City: L.D.S., 1967.
Research in Wales prior to 1800 is difficult because of the patronymic naming system. This paper helps to explain it.

4865 **Great Britain. General Register Office.** 1961 census of England and Wales: index of place names . . . *See* no.4390.

## Manuals

*4866 **Gardner, David E., and Smith, F.** Genealogical research in England and Wales . . . *See* no.4426.

4867 **Jones, Francis.** An approach to Welsh genealogy. *Cymmrodorion Society transactions,* 1948; pp.303–466. London: The Society, 1949.
Scholarly essay on history of Welsh genealogical research.

4868 ——— The princes and principality of Wales. 1929. Repr. Cardiff: Univ. of Wales Pr., 1969. Distributed by Lawrence Verry, Mystic, Conn.
Jones is Herald Extraordinary of Wales.

Before beginning a study of Welsh genealogy, it would be wise to master this book. Analysis of Welsh monarchial tradition and a review of the English princes, with detailed notes on their creation, investiture, and heraldry, but no index.

## Peerages, Baronetages, Knightages, Gentry

✠ Many works concerning Welsh peerage will be found under no.4465-96.

4869   **Breese, Edward.** Kalendars of Gwynedd; or, Chronological lists of lords-lieutenant, custodes rotulorum [keepers of the rolls], sheriffs, and knights of the shire, for the counties of Anglesey, Caernarvon, and Merioneth . . . London, 1873.
Has other lists also.

4870   **Clark, George T.** Limbus patrum Morganiae et Glamorganiae; being the genealogies of the older families of the Lordships of Morgan and Glamorgan . . . with indexes of names and places. London, 1886.

4871   **Dwnn, Lewys.** Heraldic visitations of Wales and part of the Marches between the years 1586 and 1613 . . . Transcribed from the original manuscripts, and ed. with numerous explanatory notes by Sir Samuel R. Meyrick. 2v. Llandovery, Wales, 1846.
Has errors. Often referred to and listed as "Meyrick."

4872   **Howard, Joseph J.,** and **Crisp, F. A.** Visitation of England and Wales . . . *See* no.4503.

4873   **Lloyd, Howell A.** The gentry of south-west Wales, 1540-1640. Cardiff: Univ. of Wales, 1968.

4874   **Lloyd, Jacob Y. W.** The history of the princes, the Lords Marcher, and the ancient nobility of Powys Fadog, and the ancient lords of Arwystli, Cedewen, and Meirionydd. 6v. London, 1881-87.
Covers ancient families from the 12th century. Owen referred to as "Powys Fadog."

4875   **Nicholas, Thomas.** Annals and antiquities of the counties and county families of Wales. 3rd issue rev. and enl. 2v. London, 1875.
Spines of the 2v. are marked *A-R,* suggesting that the work is incomplete, but there are no counties after *R,* and work is complete in 2v.

4876   **Visitations:** Visitations were tours of England and Wales of the College of Heralds for the purpose of recording pedigrees and arms.
For full annotation, *see* no.4525.

4877   **Williams, John** (fl.1600). Llyfr Baglan; or, The Book of Baglan, 1600-1607. Transcribed from the original manuscript and ed. with explanatory notes by Joseph A. Bradney. London, 1910. Distr. by G.P.C., Baltimore.
Contains many families of landed gentry which do not appear in Dwnn, no.4871. Mainly concerns Glamorgan families.

4878   **Yorke, Philip.** The royal tribes of Wales. Liverpool, 1887.
A valuable account of the 15 regal tribes. The 1798 ed., not so scarce, is less definitive.

## Religions

4879   **Evans, Evan.** National Library of Wales and public record collection of Welsh nonconformists. In *The genealogical helper,* May, 1972, pp. 178-87.

4880   **Foster, Joseph.** Index ecclesiasticus; or, Alphabetical lists of all ecclesiastical dignitaries in England and Wales since the Reformation. *See* no. 4297.
Covers period 1800-40 only.

# BRITISH ISLAND AREAS

4881 (Channel Islands) **Balleine, George R.** A biographical dictionary of Jersey. New York, (1948).
Covers 13th century to the present day, and 300 families. Accurate compilation.

4882 (Channel Islands) **Genealogical Society of the Church of Jesus Christ of Latter-day Saints.** Index to places in the 1851 census of England, Wales, Isle of Man and the Channel Islands. Salt Lake City: L.D.S., 1965.

4883 (Channel Islands) **Livre de percharge du fief:**
des onze bouvées nord-est du fief le comte et dépendances. 1894.
des fouquées dépendance du fief du comte, St. Sauveur. 1853.
le roi en la paroisse de St. Martin. 1861.
de blanchelande en la paroisse de St. Martin. 1911.
le roi en la paroisse de St. Martin. 1902.
St. Michel dans la paroisse de St. Sauveur en l'Île de Guérnsey. **1876.**
Livre de l'entente et percharge du fief des dix quartiers du fief blondil qui est une dépendance du fief St. Michel en la paroisse de St. Sauveur. 1907.
Books of references for fief: Book of scaling or measurement in perche (old agrarian measure).

4884 (Hebrides) **Mackenzie, William C.** The Western Isles, their history, traditions and place-names. Paisley, Scotland, 1932.

4885 (Hebrides) **Minns, George.** Records from the Hebrides Islands. In *Utah genealogical and historical magazine,* v.9–10, 1918–19.

4885a (Hebrides) **Monro, Robert W.** Monro's Western Isles of Scotland and genealogies of the clans. 1549. Edinburgh, 1961.
Gives names of island lords; genealogies trace 5 main branches of clan Donald. Bibliography of Highland sources and glossary.

**4886** (Isle of Man) **Genealogical Society of the Church of Jesus Christ of Latter-day Saints.** Index to places in the 1851 census of England, Wales, Isle of Man and the Channel Islands. Salt Lake City: L.D.S., 1965.

**4887** ———— Major genealogical record sources in the Isle of Man. *Research paper,* ser.A, no.4. Salt Lake City: L.D.S., 1968.

**4888** (Isle of Man) **Kneen, John J.** The personal names of the Isle of Man. London, 1937.
Cover title: *Manx personal names.*

**4889** ———— The place-names of the Isle of Man, with their origin and history. 6v. Douglas, Isle of Man, 1925–29.

**4890** (Orkney Islands) **Minns, George.** Records of Orkney Islands, Scotland. In *Utah genealogical and historical magazine,* v.13, 1922.

**4891** (Western Isles) *See* (Hebrides), no. 4884–4885a.

**4892** (Zetland) **Grant, Sir Francis J.** Zetland family histories . . . a rev. and enl. ed. of Grant's *County families of the Zetland Islands,* 1893. Lerwick, Scotland, 1907.
Genealogies of the local families compiled from public records and other sources.

# BRITISH DOMINIONS & FORMER DOMINIONS

## General

**4893** **Burke, Sir John B.** A genealogical and heraldic history of the colonial gentry... *See* no.4483.

**\*4894** ——— A genealogical history of the dormant, abeyant, forfeited and extinct peerages of the British Empire. *See* no.4484.

**4895** **Haydn, Joseph T.** The book of dignities... *See* no.4286.
Official personages of the British Empire.

**4896** **Hewitt, Arthur R.** Union list of Commonwealth newspapers in London, Oxford and Cambridge. London: Institute of Commonwealth Studies, Athlone Pr., 1960.

**4897** **Lodge, Edmund.** Peerage, baronetage, knightage and companionage of the British Empire. *See* no.4507.

**4898** **Pentin, Herbert.** The Anglican church registers of Lisbon, Portugal. Some extracts of baptisms, marriages, burials, and items of interest, 1721–1867. In *Genealogists' magazine,* v.8, 1938–39, pp.20–278.

**\*4899** **Pine, Leslie G.** The new extinct peerage... *See* no.4514.
Forms a continuation of Burke's *A genealogical history of the dormant abeyant, forfeited, and extinct peerages of the British Empire,* 1883.

**4900** **Pugh, Ralph B.** The records of the Colonial and Dominions Offices. *Public Record Office handbooks* 3. London: Her Majesty's Stationery Office, 1964.
Excellent description of records available and their contents.

**4900a** **Saunders, D. Gail,** and **Carson, E. A.** Guide to the records of the Bahamas. Nassau: Commonwealth of the Bahamas Government Printing Office, 1973.

Excellent guide to records in Public Record Office and elsewhere.

4901   Walford, Edward. The county families of the United Kingdom . . . *See* no.4526.

## Australia

4902   **Ancestor.** v.1– , 1961– . South Oakleigh, Australia: Genealogical Society of Victoria, Melbourne.
Title varies: v.1–2, *Victorian genealogist;* originally the society's *News bulletin.*

4903   **Australian dictionary of biography.** v.1– , 1966– (in progress). Melbourne: Melbourne Univ. Pr.; dist. by Scholarly Book Services, Portland, Ore. 12v. planned.

4904   **Descent: the official organ of the Society of Australian Genealogists.** v.1– , 1961– . Sydney: The Society.
Supersedes *The Australian genealogist,* 1933–59.

4905   **Genealogical Society of the Church of Jesus Christ of the Latter-day Saints.** Major genealogical record sources in Australia. *Research paper,* ser.E, no.2. Salt Lake City: L.D.S., 1968.

4906   **The genealogist.** v.1– , 1974– . Hampton, Victoria: Australian Inst. of Genealogical Studies (P.O. Box 89).

4907   Gray, Nancy. Compiling your family history: a guide to procedure. Sydney: Society of Australian Genealogists, 1965.
Primarily for Australian family searchers; originally published in *Descent,* v.2, pt.3.

4908   Hansen, Niels T. Guide to genealogical sources—Australia and New Zealand. Melbourne: Melbourne Stake Genealogical Committee, 1962.

4909   Heaton, Sir John H., Bart. Australian dictionary of dates and men of the time, containing the history of Australasia from 1542 to 1879. Sydney, 1879.

4910   Johns, Fred. An Australian biographical dictionary. London, 1934.

4911   ——— John's notable Australians; who they are and what they do. Being biographies of men and women of the Commonwealth. Melbourne, 1906.

4911a   Johnson, Keith A., and **Sainty,** **M. R.** Gravestone inscriptions, New South Wales. v.1– , 1974– . Sydney: Genealogical Pub. of Australia (P.O. Box 795).

4912   **Leavitt, Thaddeus W. H.** Australian representative men. Melbourne, 1887.

4913   Mennell, Philip. Dictionary of Australasian biography; comprising notices of eminent colonists from the inauguration of responsible government down to the present time (1855–92) . . . London, 1892.

4914   Mowle, Percival C. A genealogical history of pioneer families of Australia. 4th ed. Sydney: Angus & Robertson, 1948.
Cover titles: *Pioneer families of Australia.*

4914a   Puttock, Arthur G. Tracing your family tree. Adelaide: Rigby, 1973.

4914b   **Sainty, Malcolm R.,** and **Johnson, K. A.** Index to birth, marriage, death and funeral notices in the Sydney herald. v.1– (in progress). Sydney: The Compilers, 1972– .
v.1, 1831–42; v.2, 1842–47; v.3, 1848–51. Also available from Genealogical Publishers of Australia, Sydney.

4915   Serle, Percival. Dictionary of Australian biography. 2v. Sydney: Angus & Robertson, 1949.
1,030 biographies of individuals who died before 1942.

4915a   **The South Australian genealogist.** v.1– , 1974– . Adelaide: South Australian Genealogy and Heraldry Soc.
Quarterly for genealogy and heraldry and related subjects.

4916   **Sydney, Australia. Public Library of New South Wales.** Archives

Dept. Records of the Colonial Secretary of New South Wales; naturalization and denization records, 1834–1904; preliminary inventory. (Sydney), 1959.
Births, etc. Inventory only.

4917 **Who's who in Australia.** 1906. Melbourne: *Herald and Weekly Times.* Published triennially.

# British West Indies
✠ Including Bermuda

4918 **Antigua and the Antiguans:** a full account of the colony and its inhabitants, from the time of the Caribs to the present day . . . 2v. London, 1844.
Biographical notices of the principal families. Attributed to Mrs. Lanaghan.

4919 **Baker, Edward C.** A guide to records in the Leeward Islands. Oxford, England: Blackwell for Univ. of the West Indies, 1965.

4920 ——— A guide to records in the Windward Islands. Oxford, England: Blackwell for Univ. of the West Indies, 1968.

4920a **Caribbean archives.** v.1– , 1973– . St. Thomas, Virgin Islands: Caribbean Historical Assoc. (P.O. Box 390, 00801).
Records and archives in Caribbean and elsewhere.

4921 **Caribbeana;** being miscellaneous papers relating to the history, genealogy, topography and antiquities of the British West Indies. v.1–6, 1909–19. Ed. by Vere L. Oliver. London.
Coats of arms.

4922 **Chandler, Michael J.** A guide to records in Barbados. Oxford, England: Blackwell for Univ. of the West Indies, 1965.
Official, semiofficial, and private archives in Barbados.

4922a **Handler, Jerome S.** A guide to source materials for the study of Barbados history, 1627–1834. Carbondale, Ill.: Southern Illinois Univ. Pr., 1971.
Good bibliography.

4923 **Hotten, John C.** Original lists of persons of quality . . . and others who went from Great Britain to the American plantations . . . *See* no.345.
Includes those who went to Barbados.

4924 **Lawrence-Archer, James H.** Monumental inscriptions of the British West Indies . . . with genealogical and historical annotations . . . London, 1875.
Has numerous coats of arms. Many errors; should be used with care.

4925 **Livingston, Sir Noel B.** Sketch pedigrees of some of the early settlers in Jamaica . . . with a list of the inhabitants in 1670 . . . Kingston, Jamaica, 1909.

4926 **Mercer, Julia E.** Genealogical notes from Bermuda. Ed. by William Zuill. In *Tyler's quarterly magazine,* v.23–28, 1942–47.
To 1700. Deals not only with persons in Bermuda, but also with Bermudan people scattered throughout the United States.

4927 **Oliver, Vere L.** The history of the island of Antiqua, one of the Leeward Caribbees in the West Indies, from the first settlement in 1636 to the present time. 3v. London, 1894–99.
Many biographies.

4928 ——— The monumental inscriptions in the churches and churchyards of the island of Barbados, British West Indies. London, 1915.
Great deal of genealogy.

4929 ——— The monumental inscriptions of the British West Indies. Dorchester, England, 1927.
Since Lawrence-Archer (no.4924) and Oliver have different methods of approach, both are needed. Both have errors. Oliver is strong on Jamaica.

4930 **Shilstone, Eustace M.** Monumental inscriptions in the burial ground of the Jewish synagogue at Bridgetown, Bar-

bados. London: Jewish Historical Society of England, 1958.
Transcriptions date from 1660 to 1907, mostly taken from the cemetery in Bridgetown. 800 personal names.

4931 **Taitt, G. Stewart.** Subscribers to *Mayo's Map of Barbados,* 1722. In *Genealogists' magazine,* v.17, no.9, Mar. 1974.
Lists over 500 names.

4932 **Wright, Philip.** Monumental inscriptions of Jamaica. London: Soc. of Genealogists, 1966.
3,090 monuments from about 1662–1880.

# *India*

4933 **Buckland, Charles E.** Dictionary of Indian biography. 1906. Repr. New York: Haskell House, 1968; Detroit, Mich.: Gale, 1968; New York: Greenwood Pr., 1969; Varansi, India: Indological Book House, 1971.
About 2,600 biographies, English and foreign, noteworthy in the history, service, literature, or science of Indian since 1750.

4934 **Crawford, Dirom G.** History of Indian Medical Service. 2v. London, 1914.

4935 ———— Roll of the Indian Medical Service, 1615–1930. London, 1930.

4935a **Crofton, O. S.** Inscriptions on tombs or monuments in the Central Provinces and Berar, with biographical notes. n.p., 1932.

4936 ———— List of inscriptions on tombs and monuments in H. E. H. the Nizam's dominions, with biographical notes. Hyderabad, India, 1941.

4937 ———— List of inscriptions on tombs or monuments in Rajputana and Central India, with biographical notes. n.p., 1953.

4938 **Derozorario, M.** The complete monumental register containing all the epitaphs, inscriptions, etc. in the different churches and burial grounds in and about Calcutta. Calcutta, 1815.

4939 **Great Britain. India Office.** A guide to the India Office records, 1600–1858. Ed. by Sir William Foster. London, 1919.
Much genealogical information.

4940 **Hodson, Vernon C. P.** List of the officers of the Bengal Army, 1758–1834. 4v. London, 1927–46.
Biographical dictionary, with parentage, place of birth, record of service, marriage, and date of death.

4941 ———— Some families with a long east Indian connexion. In *Genealogists' magazine,* v.6, 1932–33.

4942 **Phillimore, Reginald H.** Historical records of the survey of India. 4v. Dehra Dun, India, 1945–58.
v.1, 1800–15; v.2, 1811–30; v.3, 1815–30; v.4, 1830–43. Contains biographical dictionary.

4943 **United Provinces of Agra and Oudh.** Manual of titles for Oudh; showing all holders of hereditary and personal titles in the Province. Oudh, India, 1889.

# *New Zealand*

4944 **Early Settlers and Historical Association of Wellington.** Newsletter. 1– , 196– .
Material on emigrants and ship passenger lists.

4945 **Family tree:** magazine of the Armorial and Genealogical Institute of New Zealand. v.1– , 1969– . Auckland, N.Zealand: The Society.

4946 **Genealogical Society of the Church of Jesus Christ of Latter-day Saints.** Major genealogical record sources in New Zealand. *Research paper,* ser.E, no.1. Salt Lake City: L.D.S., 1967.

4947 **Hansen, Niels T.** Guide to genealogical sources—Australia and New Zealand ... *See* no.4908.

4948 **The New Zealand genealogist.** Magazine of the New Zealand Society of Genealogists, Inc. v.1– , 1967– . Auckland, N.Zealand: The Society.
Census lists, genealogical news; fair journal.

4949 **Scholefield, Guy H.** A dictionary of New Zealand biography. 2v. Wellington, N.Zealand, 1940.
Persons who have distinguished themselves in history of New Zealand since organized migration began about 1850s.

4950 **Who's who in New Zealand,** 1908– . Wellington: N.Zealand, Reed.

## South Africa

4951 **Botha, Colin G.** The collected works. 3v. Cape Town: Struik, 1962.
Place names and Cape archives and records. By South Africa's leading archivist.

4952 ———— Extracts of marriages at the Cape of Good Hope, 1806–21. In *The genealogist,* London, 1918.

4953 ———— The French refugees at the Cape. 3rd ed. 1919. Repr. Cape Town: Struik, 1970; dist. Lawrence Verry, Mystic, Conn.
Huguenots in Cape of Good Hope.

4954 ———— The published archives of South Africa, 1652–1910. 1928. Repr. New York: Burt Franklin, 1969.

4955 **Cape directory 1800;** with foreword by Eric Rosenthal. Cape Town: Struik, 1969; dist. Lawrence Verry, Mystic, Conn.
Important source book for family research. Record of the earliest census of inhabitants of Cape Town and environs. Afrikaans title: *Almanak van Kaapstad.*

4956 **Dictionary of South African biography.** v.1– , 1968– (in progress). Cape Town: National Council for Social Research, Dept. of Higher Education.
From earliest settlement by Europeans.

4957 **Familia.** v.1– , 1964– . Cape Town: Genealogical Soc. of South Africa.
Text in Afrikaans, Dutch, and English. Quarterly.

4958 **Heese, J. A.** Die herkoms van die Afrikaner, 1657–1867. Kaapstad, S.Africa: Balkema, 1971.
South African genealogy, registers of births, etc. The descent of the Afrikaner.

4959 **Hockly, Harold E.** The story of the British settlers of 1820 in South Africa. 2nd ed., enl. Cape Town: Juta, 1966.
Has list of settlers and their contribution. Also coats of arms and crests.

4960 **Malherbe, David F. du T.** Stamregister van die Suid-Afrikaanse volk: family register of the South African nation. 3rd enl. ed. Stellenbosch, S.Africa: Tegniek, 1966.

4961 **Mitford-Barberton, Ivan, and White, V.** Some frontier families; biographical sketches of 100 Eastern Province families before 1840. Cape Town: Human and Rousseau, 1968.

4962 **Morse-Jones E.** Roll of the British settlers in South Africa.
Published under the auspices of the 1820 Settlers Monument Committee. Cape Town: Balkema, 1969 (in progress?).

4963 **Pama, Cornelis.** Heraldiek en genealogie. Een encyclopedisch vademecum. Utrecht, S.Africa: Het Spectrum, 1969.

4964 **Rosenthal, Eric.** South African surnames. Cape Town: Timmins, 1965.
Surnames and their meanings: information on most common and most famous surnames.

4965 ———— Southern African dictionary of national biography. London: Warne, 1966.
2,000 brief sketches of deceased persons.

**4966** **Villiers, Christoffel C. de,** and **Pama, C.** Genealogies of old South African families. Completely revised ed. augmented and rewritten by C. Pama. 3v. Cape Town: Balkema, 1966.

Added title in Afrikaans, *Geslagsregisters van die ou Kaapse familien*. Original edition appeared in 1893–94. 1,500 genealogies of families who arrived in South Africa before 1795.

# HERALDRY

✠ It is difficult to disassociate the peerages, knightages, and baronetages from heraldry. When using this section, the reader should refer to no.4471–4526. In general, titles are repeated from this earlier section only when heraldry is particularly important in them.

## *General*

**4967** **Brault, Gerald J.** Early blazon; heraldic terminology in the twelfth and thirteenth centuries, with special reference to Arthurian literature. New York: Oxford Univ. Pr., 1972.

Traces the development of blazoning to about 1300 and discusses the semantic evolution of terms. Glossary of heraldic terms and phrases, 276 shields. Students of heraldry, history, and legend will find much of interest. Will provide much help for those studying other works such as Rietstap, no.5120–22.

**4968** **Burke, Ashworth P.** Family records. New York, 1965.

200 coats of arms of prominent and not-so-well-known armigerous families.

**4969** **Edmondson, Joseph.** A complete body of heraldry . . . 2v. London, 1780.

Complete and attractive reference work. 50,000 arms alphabetized. Reflects 18th-century practice.

***4970** **Elvin, Charles N.** Dictionary of heraldry. 1889. London: Heraldry Today, [1969]; dist. by G.P.C., Baltimore.

Good dictionary, with 2,500 illustrations in 19th-century style.

***4971** —————— A hand-book of mottoes borne by the nobility, gentry, cities, public companies, etc. 1860. Repr. Detroit, Mich.: Gale Research, 1971.

Probably the best guide for identification of coats of arms since the mottoes, often untranslatable by the layman, are in alphabetical order with ascriptions. New printing with an added index of names and supplement compiled by Rosemary Pinches. Baltimore: G.P.C., 1971.

**4972** **Fox-Davies, Arthur C.** The art of heraldry: an encyclopedia of armory. 1904. Repr. New York: Benjamin Blom, 1968.

Although the most sumptuous work on heraldry ever produced, it is not authoritative, but important work showing heraldic practice at the end of 19th century. Based on Strohl's *Heraldischer Atlas*.

**4973    Franklin, Charles A. H.** The bearing of coat-armour by ladies. 1923. Repr. Baltimore: G.P.C., 1973.
Covers wider field than its title implies.

**\*4974    Franklyn, Julian.** Shield and crest: an account of the art and science of heraldry. 3rd ed., rev. 2nd pr. London; dist. by G.P.C., Baltimore, 1971.
Some errors.

**4975    ———— and Tanner, J.** An encyclopaedic dictionary of heraldry. New York: Pergamon Pr., 1970.
Some errors; a rehash of *Shield and crest* (no.4974).

**\*4976    Gayre of Gayre and Nigg, Robert.** The nature of arms: an exposition of the meaning and significance of heraldry . . . Edinburgh, 1961.
Covers European heraldry also. Discusses legal aspects especially, as it is illegal to use Scottish arms already owned. Has special reference to Scots practice.

**4977    Godfrey, Walter H., and Wagner, Sir A.** The College of Arms . . . being the sixteenth and final monograph of the London Survey Committee. London: The Committee, 1973.
Authoritative work; over 800 officers listed with biographical and genealogical data by Hugh S. London. Good for scholarly libraries.

**\*4978    Gough, Henry, and Parker, J.** Glossary of terms used in heraldry. New ed. 1894. Repr. Detroit, Mich.: Gale Research, 1966; Rutland, Vt.: Tuttle, 1970.
Has index to 4,000 families whose arms are in the text; more than 1,000 illustrations; lists all terms encountered in the science of heraldry. Many books (Burke, no.5013; Rietstap, no.5120-22, and others) have glossaries, but Gough is more useful, because its primary purpose is to explain the terms. Heraldic Pub. Co., New York also issued a reprint in 1967 from the inferior 1850 ed.

Gough sometimes attributed to Parker. Use with some caution.

**4979    Great Britain. College of Arms.** Heralds' commemorative exhibition, 1484-1934, held at the College of Arms. Enl. and illustrated catalogue. 1936. Repr. London: Tabard Pr., 1970; dist. by G.P.C., Baltimore.
Since the College has the finest collection of rolls of arms and genealogical records in the world, this is an indispensable work for the scholar. Colored plates.

**4980    Guillim, John.** A display of heraldry. 6th ed. London, 1724.
1724 is the best edition. 800p. folio by the leading authority of the day. Important guide to 18th-century practice.

**4981    Lynch-Robinson, Sir Christopher, and Lynch-Robinson, Adrian.** Intelligible heraldry. 1948. Baltimore: G.P.C., 1967.
A well-written account of heraldic practice with illustrations of some Irish armorial displays.

**4982    Nisbet, Alexander.** A system of heraldry . . . 2v. (new ed.) Edinburgh, 1816.

**4983    ———— ————** Heraldic plates. Edinburgh, 1892.
Rare work of historical importance, with information not contained elsewhere. The plates were originally intended to accompany the 1722-42 ed. but were lost and not found until 1890. Only 200 copies were printed.

**4984    Pine, Leslie G.** International heraldry. Rutland, Vt.: Tuttle, 1970.
Special section on American heraldry is not reliable. Popular survey of armorial bearings and heraldic devices, including the Orient and the United States.

**4985    Puttock, Arthur G.** Dictionary of heraldry and related subjects. Baltimore: G.P.C., 1970.
Recently compiled dictionary of heraldry with shorter dictionaries of related subjects. Includes pertinent material on genealogy, arms and armor, and data on celebrated battles, personages, and places.

*4986 **Von Volborth, Carl A.** Heraldry of the world. Ed. by D. H. B. Chesshyre. Translated by Bob Gosney and Inge Gosney. New York: Macmillan, 1974.

Translation of *Alverdens heraldik i farver*. Characteristics of heraldry in different countries where it has flourished. 26 countries covered; also ecclesiastical heraldry. Index of arms, 600 illustrated coats of arms.

4987 **Wagner, Sir Anthony R.** Heralds of England. London, 1967.

History of College of Heralds as seen from records in possession of the College. Erudite work, featuring origins of heraldry with particular reference to heraldry in the 15th century; 18th century is dealt with at length. Because of color plates, an expensive book destined to become a classic.

4988 ———— The records and collections of the College of Arms. New York: Oxford Univ. Pr., 1952.

Useful.

4989 **Woodward, John,** and **Burnett, George.** A treatise on heraldry, British and foreign, with English and French glossaries. 2v. 2nd ed. 1896. Repr., with new introduction by L. G. Pine. Rutland, Vt.: Tuttle, 1969.

Still an important work, but sources frequently absent.

## Manuals

4990 **Allcock, Hubert.** Heraldic design: its origins, ancient forms, and modern usage. New York: Tudor Pub. Co., 1962.

Written primarily for artists. More than 500 crests, shields, devices, and coats of arms.

4991 **Baty, Thomas.** Vital heraldry. Ed. with introduction by Julian Franklyn. Edinburgh: The Armorial, 1962.

Chapters on undifferenced arms, arms in Scotland, tinctures, charges, ordinaries, marshalling, shields, and Episcopal arms. Interesting production of heraldry for the beginner.

4992 **Bergling, John M.** Heraldic designs and engravings: a handbook and dictionary of heraldic terms, rev. and enl. ed. Heraldic terms and technical work by A. T. Hay. Coral Gables, Fla.: V. C. Bergling, 1966.

Illustrated mainly from 18th-century sources. Blazons and heraldic descriptions good.

*4993 **Boutell's heraldry.** Ed. by J. P. Brooke-Little. [Rev. ed.] New York: Frederick Warne, [1973].

Contains additions and revisions, with recent trends and developments in heraldic practice noted.

*4994 **Child, Heather.** Heraldic design: a handbook for students. Corr. ed. Baltimore: G.P.C., 1966.

*4995 **Fox-Davies, Arthur C.** A complete guide to heraldry; illustrated by nearly 800 designs. 1909. Repr. rev. and annotated by J. P. Brooke-Little. New York: Nelson, 1969. Barnes & Noble, New York, 1970, repr. from 1909 also, but not with Brooke-Little's annotations.

1909 ed. somewhat condensed from *Art of heraldry* (no.4972). In a convenient form, provides a comprehensive guide to the practice of heraldry. A well-illustrated book, covering all aspects of British and foreign heraldry. Despite some minor drawbacks, it will remain a standard reference work for many years.

*4996 ———— Heraldry explained. 1925. Repr. Rutland, Vt.: Tuttle, 1971.

One of the best and most easily read explanations of the meaning of heraldry for the beginner.

4997 **Grant, Sir Francis J.** The manual of heraldry: a concise description of the several terms used and containing a dictionary of every designation in the science. Rev. ed. 1914. Edinburgh, 1962. Obtainable from Barnes & Noble, New York, and G.P.C., Baltimore.

Good pocket edition. Includes tables of precedence.

4998 **Hope, Sir William H. St. J.** A grammar of heraldry. 2nd ed., rev. by

Sir Anthony R. Wagner. New York: Cambridge Univ. Pr., 1953.
Good introduction to the subject.

*4999   **Innes, Sir Thomas.** Scots heraldry: a practical handbook on the historical principles and modern application of the art and science. 2nd ed., rev. and enl. 1956. Repr. Baltimore: G.P.C., 1971.
Authoritative reference work on all aspects of heraldry. Innes was a former Lord Lyon of Arms.

*5000   **Johnson, David P.** The American College of Heraldry. A handbook of distinctively American coats of arms. Rev. New Orleans, La.: The College, 1974.
Invaluable for those wishing to acquire coats of arms in U.S. Description of components in American coats.

5001   **London, Hugh S.** The right road for the study of heraldry. 2nd ed., rev. by Cecil R. Humphery-Smith. London: Heraldry Soc., 1960.
Fine manual with survey of books and their value in heraldry.

5002   **Pine, Leslie G.** The story of heraldry. Rutland, Vt.: Tuttle, 1967.
A good account of the growth of use of armorial bearings.

*5003   ———— Teach yourself heraldry and genealogy. 1957. Repr. New York: Dover, 1968.
Introductory work; a popular genealogical manual.

5004   **Reynolds, Jack A.** Heraldry and you: modern heraldic usage in America. New York: Nelson, 1961.
Use with caution. Many arms in color.

*5005   **Stephenson, Jean.** Heraldry for the American genealogist. *National Genealogical Soc. special publ.* 25. Washington, D.C.: The Society, 1959.
More than a manual. Has excellent and sensible consideration of heraldry for Americans. A sound introduction.

5006   **Stevenson, John H.** Heraldry in Scotland, including a recension of "The law and practice of heraldry in Scotland" by George Seton. 2v. Glasgow, 1914.
Scarce and fine work covering every aspect of Scottish heraldry. Limited to 210 copies.

5007   **Von Volborth, Carl A.** Little manual of heraldry; a synoptic approach. 2nd ed., repr. Hermosa Beach, Calif. Available from Augustan Soc., Harbor City, 1973.
Handy manual, with over 600 black-and-white illustrations. The shield, helmet, coronets, crowns, etc. Napoleonic heraldry section good; emphasis on continental heraldry.

5008   **Zieber, Eugene.** Heraldry in America. 2nd ed. 1909. Repr. New York: Haskell House, 1969; New York: Gordon Pr., 1973.
950 illustrations. Handbook from American point of view, with chapters on political seals and society badges.

## *Rolls of Arms*

GENERAL

5009   **The armorial who is who, 1966–69.** 3rd ed. A register of armorial bearings in current use, with the names and addresses of the bearers and the authority for their use. Ed. by Robert Gayre of Gayre and Nigg. Anstruther, Scot.: The Armorial, 1970. Available from G.P.C., Baltimore.
Contains recent grantees of arms with blazons.

5010   **Berry, William.** Encyclopaedia heraldica; or, Complete dictionary of heraldry. 4v. London, (1828–40).
Often advertised as 3v. set, but v.4, very scarce, is required. Berry was one of the greatest authorities on heraldry and specialized in the counties of England. Mainly a rearranged and augmented edition of Edmondson (no.4969). It is the first general armory, followed by Robson (no.5026).

*5011   **Briggs, Geoffrey.** National heraldry of the world. New York: Viking, 1974.

## 5012  Heraldry

Delineations in color of arms of all independent states in the world today. With origins, significance, characteristics and uses.

### GREAT BRITAIN

**5012  Anglo-Jewish notabilities:** their arms and testamentary dispositions. London: Jewish Historical Society of England, 1949.
Dictionary of Anglo-Jewish biography, coats of arms, wills, letters of administration.

**\*5013  Burke, Sir John B.** The general armory of England, Scotland, Ireland and Wales, comprising a registry of armorial bearings from the earliest to the present time. 1884. Repr. Baltimore: G.P.C., 1969.
Earlier editions of this monumental work are entitled *Encyclopedia of heraldry*. 100,000 descriptions of arms. Although more than 80 years old, still holds good for the most important families. Contains many unrecorded and incorrectly described arms, and is therefore misleading; but since it has thousands of arms which were undoubtedly borne, it is essential. Indispensable for the librarian because, although in many cases the American researcher is not really entitled to the arms, it answers most questions. Rietstap (no.5120-22) and Siebmacher (no.5123-24) cover Europe. First reprint was in 1962; later reprints are identical but bound more strongly. The continuation, *General armory two,* is described in no.5022.

**5014  Cleveland, Catherine L. W. P., Duchess of.** The Battle Abbey Roll, with some account of the Norman lineages. 3v. London, 1889.
Biographies of all knights who are believed to have accompanied William the Conqueror at the Battle of Hastings. Most comprehensive account written. Much good genealogy, but use with caution.

**5015  Denholm-Young, Noel.** The country gentry in the fourteenth century, with special reference to the heraldic rolls of arms. New York: Oxford Univ. Pr., 1969.

**\*5016  Fairbairn, James.** Fairbairn's Book of crests of the families of Britain and Ireland. 2v. 1905. 4th ed. Repr. 2v. in 1. Baltimore: G.P.C., 1968.
One of the great books associated with heraldry. Contains 50,000 names with full list of mottoes and covers much that Burke's *General Armory* (no.5013) does not. The significant difference between the shield of arms and a crest is such that Fairbairn is needed in every reference collection. Since many of the 19th-century editions have no date, the bibliography of this work is confusing. Although there have been reprints of the 1911 and 19th-century editions, this one, 1905, 4th and enl. ed., is by far the best reprint.

**5017  Foster, Joseph.** Grantees of arms named in docquets and patents. v.1, To the end of the 17th century; v.2 (in 2 pts.), 1687-1898. 3v. *Harleian Soc. publ.* 66-68. London, 1915-17.

**5018 ——** Some feudal coats of arms from heraldic rolls, 1298-1418. London, 1902.
Not entirely reliable, but indispensable. More than 800 illustrations.

**\*5019  Fox-Davies, Arthur C.** Armorial families: a directory of some gentlemen of coat-armour, showing which arms in use at the moment are borne by legal authority. 7th ed. 2v. 1929. 2v. in 1. Repr. Rutland, Vt.: Tuttle, 1970.
Extensive dictionary of arms in use by several thousand persons, with genealogical notes and illustrations of arms used. Index to quarterings included at end of v.2. Earlier editions, less scarce, are useful, but the 7th (and last) ed. is best. Unlike Burke, *General armory,* (no.5013), Fox-Davies contains only lawfully borne arms.

**5020  Gale, Robert C.** Indexes to quartered coats in *Harleian Society visitation ser.* 1-106. Eltham, England, 1961. Obtainable from Soc. of Genealogists.
Harleian Society publishes a series of *Visitations* (no.4265) and a series of *Parish registers.* Originally an annual volume was available to members, but since World War II, volumes have appeared at less frequent

intervals. This work will save researchers many hours, because it lists all arms in the series.

**5021** ——— Indexes to quartered coats, from various sources not included in the index to the *Harleian visitation ser.* Eltham, England, 1962. Obtainable from Soc. of Genealogists, London.
Companion to no.5020.

***5022** **General armory two.** Alfred Morant's additions and corrections to Burke's *General armory;* ed. and augmented by Cecil R. Humphery-Smith. Baltimore: G.P.C., 1974.
Contains notes and additions on approximately 10,000 arms, some inaccurately described in Burke's *General armory, see* no.5013.

**5023** **Howard, Joseph J.,** and **Crisp, F. A.** Visitation of England and Wales. 21v., 1893-1921; notes, v.1-14, 1896-1921. London.
Pedigrees and coats of arms based on records and grants in the College of Heralds and other sources, and not on visitations conducted by the heralds. v.1-9 ed. by Howard and Crisp; v.10-21 by Crisp only. Pedigrees indexed in Whitmore's *Genealogical guide* (no.4187).

***5024** **Papworth, John W.** An alphabetical dictionary of coats of arms belonging to families in Great Britain and Ireland, forming an extensive ordinary of British armorials, upon an entirely new plan. 2v. 1874. Repr. 2v. in 1. Baltimore: G.P.C., 1965.
The original title was Papworth's *Ordinary of British armorials,* and the 1961 repr. carried this title; the 1965 repr., with the half title as full title, identical with the 1874 and 1961 ed. The heraldic devices are arranged by groups for identification; therefore, perfect for helping to trace owners of unidentified arms. Companion to Burke's *General armory* (no.5013). Has some errors.

**5025** **Pinches, John H.,** and **Pinches, R. V.** The Royal heraldry of Britain. Rutland, Vt.: Tuttle, 1974.
9 color and 258 black-and-white illustrations. First book since the 17th century to give the arms of all the sovereigns of England, with their progeny. Good genealogical tables and index. Many illustrations reproduced for first time. Some errors.

**5026** **Robson, Thomas.** The British herald, or Cabinet of armorial bearings of the nobility and gentry of Great Britain and Ireland, from the earliest to the present time . . . 3v. Sunderland, England, 1830.

**5027** **Rolls of Henry III,** including additions and revisions to Wagner's *Catalogue of English mediaeval rolls of arms* (no.5030). *Aspilogia,* being materials of heraldry, v.2, *Harleian Soc. publ.* v.113/ 14. London, 1967.
Genealogical and heraldic commentaries on the three oldest English rolls *(Matthew Paris shields,* 1244-59; *Glover's Roll,* 1253- 58; *Walford's Roll,* c.1273. Also published by Soc. of Antiquaries, London. *Aspilogia,* v.1, by Sir A. R. Wagner, *see* no.5030.

**5028** **Sims, Richard.** An index to the pedigrees and arms contained in the heralds' visitations and other genealogical manuscripts in the British Museum. London, 1849. *See* note under no.4184.

**5029** **Summers, Peter.** Hatchments in Britain. v.1- , 1973- (in progress). Chichester, England: Phillimore.
Diamond-shaped funeral hatchments from 17th century on. Of interest and importance to students of heraldry, genealogy, and local history. v.1 contains those for Northamptonshire, Warwickshire and Worcestershire; v.2, will contain Norfolk and Suffolk.

**5030** **Wagner, Sir Anthony R.** A catalogue of English mediaeval rolls of arms. New York: Oxford Univ. Pr., 1950. Also published as *Aspilogia,* v.1, being materials of heraldry. *Harleian Soc. publ.* 100.
Invaluable reference for all known medieval rolls of arms, their present whereabouts, etc. Additions and corrections, *see* no.5027 *(Aspilogia,* v.2.)

***5031** ——— Historic heraldry in Britain: an illustrated series of British historical arms, with notes, glossary, and an introduction to heraldry. London: Philli-

5032 *Heraldry*

more, 1972. Dist. by Rowman & Littlefield: Totowa, N.J.
Repr. of 1948 ed.; includes bibliographical references and coats of arms. Describes arms of 142 leading figures in British history. Comprehensive introduction to heraldry, list of medieval rolls of arms. Good introduction to blazons, history and designs.

5032 **Wolf, Lucien.** Anglo-Jewish coats-of-arms. Expanded by Joseph Jacobs for v.4 of the *Jewish Encyclopaedia*. London, [1895]. Originally published in v.2 of the *Jewish Historical Society's transactions*.
162 armigerous Jewish families.

IRELAND

✣ no.4665-96 are all concerned with Irish heraldry. The titles listed below are of particular importance.

*5033 **Burke, Sir John B.** Burke's Genealogical and heraldic history of the landed gentry of Ireland, 1899- . *See* no.4482.

*5034 ——— The general armory of England, Scotland, Ireland and Wales . . . *See* no.5013.

*5035 **Fairbairn, James.** Fairbairn's Book of crests of the families of Great Britain and Ireland. *See* no.5016.

5036 **Howard, Joseph J.,** and **Crisp, F. A.** Visitation of Ireland. 1897-1918. Repr. 6v. in 1. Baltimore: G.P.C., 1973. *See* no.4678.

*5037 **Kennedy, Patrick.** Kennedy's Book of Irish arms. Canterbury, England: Achievements, 1966.
Collected from official records in Dublin Castle from Kennedy's manuscript, 1816.

*5038 **MacLysaght, Edward.** Irish families: their names, arms, and origins. *See* no.4683-85.

*5039 **O'Hart, John.** Irish and Anglo-Irish gentry . . . *See* no.4688-89.

*5040 ——— Irish pedigrees . . . *See* no. 4690.

*5041 **Papworth, John W.** An alphabetical dictionary of coats of arms belonging to families of Great Britain and Ireland . . . *See* no.5024.

5042 **Robson, Thomas.** The British herald; or, Cabinet of armorial bearings of the nobility and gentry of Great Britain and Ireland . . . *See* no.5026.

5043 **Rooney, John.** A genealogical history of Irish families with their crests and armorial bearings. *See* note under no.4692.

5044 **Skey, William.** The heraldic calendar; a list of the nobility and gentry whose arms are registered and pedigree recorded in the Heralds' Office in Ireland. Dublin, 1846.

SCOTLAND

✣ no.4791-4824 are all concerned with Scottish heraldry. The titles listed below are of particular importance.

*5045 **Adam, Frank.** The clans, septs, and regiments of the Scottish Highlands . . . *See* no.4791.

5046 **Grant, James.** The tartans of the clans of Scotland. *See* note under no.4805.

5047 **Innes, Sir Thomas.** Scots heraldry: a practical handbook on the historical principles and modern application of the art and science. 2nd ed., rev. and enl. 1956. Reissue. Baltimore: G.P.C., 1971.
Authoritative reference work by the former Lord Lyon King of Arms.

5048 **Johnston (W. and A. K.).** Johnston's clan histories . . . *See* no.4808.

5049 **Macdonald, William R.** Scottish armorial seals. Edinburgh, 1904.
Describes over 2,800 seals, and since official heraldic records of Scotland date from 1672, earlier references are invaluable.

5050 Moncreiffe, Sir Rupert I. K., Bart., and **Pottinger, D.** Bartholomew's Map of Scotland of old . . . See no.4813.
174 clan crests with coats of arms of their chiefs.

*5051 Paul, Sir James B. An ordinary of arms contained in the public register of all arms and bearings in Scotland (1672-1901). 2nd ed. 1903. Repr. Baltimore: G.P.C., 1969.
Shields of arms are analyzed under their component parts so that it can be ascertained to whom an unnamed coat of arms belongs. Official list of arms recorded in Scotland, with index.

5052 **Roll of Scottish arms.** By Robert Gayre of Gayre and Nigg (and others). Pt.1, A-G; 2, H-Z. 1965-67. Anstruther, Scotland: The Armorial.
Intended to be complete in 6v.; would cover 1672 to present and include bearings recorded in the *Public register of all arms and bearings in Scotland* in H. M. Lyon Court, but no more published after pt.2.

5053 **Scottish clans and their tartans.** See no.4791-4824.

5054 Stevenson, John H. Scottish heraldic seals: royal, official, ecclesiastical, collegiate, burgh, personal. 3v. Glasgow, 1940.
v.1, public; v.2-3, personal.

5055 Stodart, Robert R. Scottish arms; being a collection of armorial bearings, A.D. 1370-1678, reproduced in facsimile from contemporary manuscripts, with heraldic and genealogical notes. 2v. Edinburgh, 1881.
v.1 has colored coats of arms; v.2, descriptions of plates and notes of bearers.

5056 Urquhart, Robert M. Scottish burgh and county heraldry. Detroit, Mich.: Gale Research, 1973.

WALES

✠ no.4869-80 are all concerned with Welsh heraldry. The titles listed below are of particular importance.

5057 Dwnn, Lewys. Heraldic visitations of Wales and part of the Marches; between the years 1586 and 1613 . . . See no.4871.

5058 Howard, Joseph J., and **Crisp, F. A.** Visitation of England and Wales. See no.4872.

5059 Jones, Francis. The princes and principality of Wales . . . See no. 4868.

5060 **Royal and princely heraldry in Wales:** text by Sir Anthony R. Wagner [and others]. London: Tabard Pub., [1969].
Colored coats of arms.

BRITISH ISLAND AREAS AND DOMINIONS

✠ Excluding Canada

5060a Joubert, Joseph. Les armoires de la République Sud-Africaine. Paris, 1903.

5061 Lawrence-Archer, James H. Monumental inscriptions of the British West Indies . . . See no.4924.
Has numerous coats of arms.

5062 Low, Charles. A roll of Australian arms: corporate and personal, borne by lawful authority. Kent Town, S. Australia: Rigby, 1971.
Personal arms section not comprehensive. Use with care.

5063 Pama, Cornelis. Heraldiek in Suid-Afrika: heraldik en genealogie . . . See no.4963.

5064 ———— Heraldry of South African families: coats of arms, crests, ancestry. Cape Town: Balkema, 1972.
1,100 coats of arms; biographies of first settlers.

5065 ———— Lions and virgins: heraldic state symbols, coats of arms, flags, seals and other symbols of authority in South Africa, 1487-1962. Cape Town: Human & Rousseau, 1965.

**5066 Payne, James B.** An armorial of Jersey; being an account, heraldic and antiquarian, of its chief native families. [Jersey], 1859-65.

Has pedigrees, plates, and biographical notices: pp.1-347 only were published. It is believed that pt.2, subscribers' private issue with 112 coats of arms and views, was published in 1860.

UNITED STATES AND CANADA

☩ no.4471-4526 contain much heraldry, but those below are of considerable importance.

**5067 Appleton, William S.** Gore roll of arms, (and) Positive pedigrees and authorized arms. Excerpted from *Heraldic journal,* 1865 and *New England historical and genealogical register,* 1891 and 1898. Repr. Baltimore: G.P.C., 1964.

The *Gore Roll* is a transcript of collection of arms of 99 New England families, 1701-24.

**5068 The Augustan Society roll of arms,** 1967 and addenda for 1968. Ed. by Rodney E. Hartwell and illustrated by Carl Von Volborth. Addenda and illustrations by William W. Bayne. Torrance, Calif., 1968.

Rev. of 1st ed. which contained many text and drawing errors.

**5069** ———— 1969-74. Harbor City, Calif.: Augustan Soc., 1974.

Contains arms registered with the Society, including new sections of the arms of various orders.

**5070 Bolton, Charles K.** Bolton's American armory; a record of coats of arms which have been in use within the present bounds of the United States. 1927. Repr. Baltimore: G.P.C., 1969.

Armorial of more than 2,000 names, with glossary and mottoes. Bolton made no attempt to determine authenticity of arms or use. 1964 repr. was described as "2nd ed.," but the issues for 1927, 1964, and 1969 are identical.

**5071 Canada. Dept. of the Secretary of State.** The arms, flags and floral emblems of Canada—les armoires, drapeaux et emblèmes floraux du Canada. Ottawa: Queen's Printer, 1967.

Magnificent booklet containing blazons in color and text in English and French.

**5072 Crozier, William A.** Crozier's General armory: a registry of American families entitled to coat armor. 2nd ed. 1904. Repr. Baltimore: G.P.C., 1972.

Describes 3,500 names with genealogical data. Not reliable, because despite author's claim that only authentic arms were included, no documentation is given.

**5073 Hoffman, William J.** An armory of American families of Dutch descent. In *The New York genealogical and biographical record,* v.64-72, 1933-41.

Although the last installment in v.72 states, "to be continued," no further articles were published.

**5074 McGivern, James.** Your name and coat of arms. Don Mills, Ont.: General Pub. Co., 1971.

1,250 surnames of Canadian families, based on a column which appears in the *Toronto telegram.* Remarkable coverage of many ethnic groups found in Canada, but few French. Illustrations by Hans D. Birk are outstanding.

**\*5075 Massicotte, Edouard Z.,** and **Roy, R.** Armorial du Canada français. 2v. 1915-18. Repr. 2v. in 1. Baltimore: G.P.C., 1970.

Standard reference work.

**5076 Matthews, John.** Complete American armoury and blue book. 1905-23. Repr. compiled and ed. by L. R. Sosnow. New York: Heraldic Pub. Co., 1965.

Combining 1903, 1907 and suppl. to 1907, and 1911-23 eds. More than 1,000 names of Americans using or displaying coats of arms at time of printing. Unofficial and incomplete compilation of American families; unsourced. Heraldic illustrations contain frequent errors. Caution advised.

5077 **Order of Americans of Armorial Ancestry, Inc.** Complete register of members, with coats of arms (1903–64). Colorado Springs, Colo.: The Order, 1965.

Lists current addresses and name of immigrant ancestor of every accepted member. Prerequisite for membership is ability to prove descent from an immigrant ancestor in colonial America whose forebears in Great Britain or continental Europe had the right to bear arms. Prepared by Ruth R. Ravenscroft.

*5078 **A roll of arms registered by the Committee on Heraldry of the New England Historic Genealogical Society.** Pts. 1–8. Boston: The Society, 1928–58; 1968–71.

Pts.1–2 were corrected reissues of 1928 and 1932 eds., published in 1950; pt.8 commenced in v.122, no.485, 1968 and concluded in v.125, no.3, 1971 of the *New England historical and genealogical register*. Accurate and authentic.

5079 **Spofford, Ernest.** Armorial families of America. 1st. ser. Philadelphia, 1929.

Coats of arms in color. Use with caution.

5080 **Todd, Herbert G.** Armory and lineages of Canada and North America; comprising the lineage of prominent and pioneer American and Canadian families with descendants, and illustrations. New York, 1913–19.

Many coats of arms. Bibliography puzzling: it would seem that there were 7 issues (or rather editions), beginning in 1913 and ending in 1919. Title varies considerably. Pt. (ed.) 1 is called: *Armory and lineages of Canada: comprising pedigrees with historical notes* . . .

5081 **Vermont, E. de V.** America heraldica . . . Repr. of 1886 ed. and later supplements. New York: Heraldic Pub. Co., 1965.

Coats of arms, crests, and mottoes of more than 500 prominent American families settled in America before 1800. Contains Gore's *Roll of arms* and Prince's *List of esquires in 1736*. Not exhaustive, and some information should be treated with caution.

## LATIN AMERICA

✠ Many more titles exist, but the following have been suggested.

5082 **Blasones Mexicanos,** no.126, año XVII, 1970. México: Artes de México, 1970.

Coats of arms, beginning with earliest warriors of Mexico. Text accompanies arms.

5083 **Codazzi Aguirre, Juan A.** Escudo para les Islas Malvinas y adyacencias. Rosario, Argentina: Escuela de Artes Gráficas del Colegio Salesiano San Jose, 1969.

Heraldry of the Falkland Islands. Coats of arms.

5084 **Crespo Pozo, José S.** Blasones y linajes de Galicia. v.1–2. Santiago, 1957–62.

v.1, Heraldry; v.2, genealogy, *A–F* (all pub.?). Useful for Spanish genealogists and heraldists. Well-documented, showing close connection between Galician and Peruvian families. Coats of arms. *See also* no.5086.

5085 **El Escudo de armas de la ciudad de Caracas [por] Arístides Rojas,** [etc.]. [Caracas: Concejo Municipal de Distrito Federal, 1967.]

Heraldry of Caracas, Venezuela. Coats of arms.

5086 **García Carraffa, Alberto,** and **García Carraffa, Arturo.** Diccionario heráldico y genealógica de apellidos Espanoles e Americanos. v.1– , 1920– (in progress). Madrid: Nueva Imprenta Radio.

Also has title *Enciclopedia heráldica y genealógica hispano america*. Magnificent work, profusely illustrated; colored coats of arms. About 100 vols. projected.

5087 **Ortega Ricaurte, Enrique.** Heráldica colombiana. *Publ. del Archivo Nacional de Colombia* 22. Bogotá: Editorial Minerva, 1952.

Selected list of coats of arms of the provincial districts of Colombia.

## Church, Civic Heraldry, and Flags

**5088  Briggs, Geoffrey.** Civic and corporate heraldry. A dictionary of impersonal arms of England, Wales and Northern Ireland. London: Heraldry Today, 1972.

Essential reference book on impersonal arms (i.e. towns, counties, schools, colleges, companies, business, and ecclesiastical bodies that come under the jurisdiction of the English King of Arms). 1,000 coats of arms; to be used in conjunction with Scott-Giles (no.5094).

**5088a  Campbell, Gordon,** and **Evans, I. O.** The book of flags. New ed. New York: Oxford Univ. Pr., 1974.

Definitive; color plates.

**5089  Dorling, Edward E.** Heraldry of the church. A handbook for decorators. London, 1911.

**5090  Evans, Idrisyn O.** Flags of the world. New York: Grosset, 1970.

Past and present flags from all over the world; colored coats of arms.

**5091  Galbreath, Donald L.** Papal heraldry. 2nd ed., rev. by Geoffrey Briggs. London: Heraldry Today, 1972.

Previous edition published as *A treatise on ecclesiastical heraldry*, 1930. Arms and biographical notes of popes; list of popes. Well illustrated, with good bibliographical references.

**\*5092  Gayre of Gayre and Nigg, Robert.** Heraldic standards. Edinburgh: Oliver & Boyd, 1959.

An important work on the heraldic flag. International in scope.

**\*5093  Pedersen, Christian F.** The international flag book in colors. New York: Morrow, 1970.

English-language edition of Danish book; very fine illustrations of 850 flags, mostly in color. Revised periodically.

**5094  Scott-Giles, Charles W.** Civic heraldry of England and Wales. 1953. Repr. brought up to date by Geoffrey Briggs. New York: Blom, 1972.

**\*5095  Smith, Whitney.** The flag book of the United States. New York: Morrow, 1970.

Description of flags of the states and territories of the U.S., and of cities and other organizations by the president of the Vexillological Society.

**5096  Urquhart, Robert M.** Scottish burgh and county heraldry. London: Heraldry Today, 1973.

Blazons and illustrations of all the burgh and county coats of arms and reasons for adoption. Important reference book.

**5097  Woodward, John.** A treatise on ecclesiastical heraldry. Edinburgh, 1894.

One of the few works on church heraldry, but by modern standards lacks a number of references. Papal arms better in Galbreath (no.5091).

## Periodicals and Series

**5098  American College of Heraldry.** Journal. v.1– , 1973– . New Orleans, La.: The College.

**5099  The American heraldic review.** Published by the American Heraldic Association. v.1– , 1973– . Cleveland, Ohio: A. W. C. Phelps (10109 Lake Ave., #304, 44102).

Quarterly. For recording developments and trends in the art and science of heraldry, particularly as they pertain to U.S. Contributions by leading American authorities.

**5100  The ancestor:** a quarterly review of county and family history, heraldry and antiquity. . . . *See* no.4249.

5101  **The armorial:** an international journal of heraldry, genealogy, nobiliary law, heraldic art . . . v.1– , 1959– . Edinburgh: The Armorial.

Scholarly articles, every aspect of international heraldry, but unfortunately its appearance is sporadic.

5102  **Coat-armor.** v.1–6, 1966–73. Hermosa Beach, Calif. Various titles; became part of the omnibus volume of *The Augustan* (no.105).

5103  **Coat of arms.** v.1– , 1950– . London: Heraldry Soc.

For students of genealogy and heraldry. Attempts to be nontechnical. Most parts are in print; those out-of-print are available from Johnson Reprint Corp., New York. Originally *The escutcheon,* published by the Society of Heraldic Antiquaries (1948-50). Excellent publication, well edited.

5104  **The escutcheon.** v.1– , 1966– . Toorak, Australia: Heraldry Soc. of Australia.

Small quarterly journal containing articles on heraldry from an international point of view.

5105  **Family history:** the journal of the Institute of Heraldic and Genealogical Studies. v.1– , 1962– . Ed. by Cecil Humphery-Smith. Canterbury, Kent, England: The Institute.

Wills, pedigrees, arms, indentures, registers, Morant's additions and corrections to Burke's *General armory* (no.5022). Scholarly and authoritative.

5106  **The herald and genealogist.** Ed. by John G. Nichols. v.1–8, 1863–74. London.

One of the very best literary studies of heraldry and genealogy.

5107  **Heraldic journal;** recording the armorial bearings and genealogies of American families. v.1–4, 1865–68. Ed. by William H. Whitmore. Repr. Baltimore: G.P.C., 1972.

Useful for heraldry of early American families. Profusely illustrated; authoritative studies of the ancient families of Virginia, New England, Maryland and New York. Hundreds of heraldic devices; consult with caution.

5108  **The heraldry gazette:** the official newsletter of the Heraldic Society. no.1– , 1957– . London: The Society.

Gives current news on heraldry, books, etc.

5109  **Heraldry in Canada** (Héraldique au Canada). v.1– , 1966– . Ottawa: The Heraldry Society of Canada.

The official journal of the Society. Excellent articles on heraldry, with emphasis on Canadian heraldic practice, charges, and civic heraldry. A few articles in French, but mainly English. Quarterly.

5110  **Journal of American history.** 29v. New York, [and elsewhere], 1907–35.

Has much genealogy and heraldry, including colored coats of arms. Index v.1–7, 1907–13.

5111  **Miscellanea genealogica et heraldica.** London, 1868–1938. *See* no.4272.

5113  **Tabard talk.** v.1– , 1973– . Victoria, Australia: A. Franklin-Jones (48 Russell St., Surrey Hills).

Replaces *The escutcheon.* Published by Heraldry Soc. of Australia. Interesting and informative articles.

## *Bibliographies*

5114  **Cope, Stanley T.** (Bibliography of heraldry) Heraldry, flags, and seals: a select bibliography with annotations, covering the period 1920–45. *Journal of documentation,* v.4, (1948), pp.92–146. London: Assoc. of Special Libraries and Information Bureaus, 1948.

5115  **Gatfield, George.** Guide to printed books and manuscripts relating to English and foreign heraldry and genealogy . . . *See* no.4147.

5116  **The librarian subject guide to books.** v.2, Biography, family history, heraldry . . . *See* no.4153.

*5117 **Moule, Thomas.** Bibliotheca heraldica magnae Britanniae: an analytical catalogue of books on genealogy, heraldry, nobility, knighthood and ceremonies from 1469–1821, and a supplement enumerating the principal foreign genealogical works. 1822. Repr. London: Heraldry Today, 1966; dist. by G.P.C., Baltimore.

An important bibliographic tool for scholarly libraries.

## Foreign Heraldry

⌁ Books on heraldry, particularly in Europe, are numerous. All countries have several very good works. The works listed below are general in nature.

5118 **Almanach de Gotha:** annuaire généalogique, diplomatique et statistique. 1763–1944. Various places of publ.

The "Burke" of Europe. Amazingly accurate, and because of numerous changes from year to year, a complete set is desirable, but almost unobtainable and very expensive. Various volumes can be obtained from bookdealers at a moderate price. The first section is very useful for the genealogies of the royal and princely houses of Europe, up to 1940, and much of this is now continued in *Genealogisches Handbuch des Adels.* Not a strictly heraldic work.

5119 **Renesse, Théodore de, Comte.** Dictionnaire des figures héraldiques . . . 7v. Bruxelles, Belgium, 1894–1903.

Exceptional work analyzing in the form of an ordinary, all of the arms listed in Rietstap *Armorial général* (no.5120). Does for Rietstap what Papworth's *Alphabetical dictionary of coats of arms* (no.5024) does to Burke's *Armory* (no.5013). Helps to trace owners of unidentified arms.

*5120 **Rietstap, Johannes B.** Armorial général; précédé d'un dictionnaire des termes du blason. 2v. Repr. from 1950 ed. Baltimore: G.P.C., 1972.

*5121 ——— Illustrations by Victor and H. V. Rolland. 1903–26. Repr. 6v. in 3. Baltimore: G.P.C., 1967.

*5122 ——— Supplément to the Armorial général, by Victor and H. V. Rolland. 1904–54. Repr. 9v. in 3. Baltimore: G.P.C., 1969–71.

For all practical purposes, the above 3 sets cover all that is needed by the researcher. The work is the most authoritative on standard European and world coats of arms. More than 100,000 families represented. Entire text, including glossary is in French, but recourse to Gough and Parker's *Glossary of terms* (no.4978) should solve most problems. The Rolland illustrations number 85,000 shields of arms in 2,000 plates, in alphabetical sequence and hatched for colors. The present reprints, though a little expensive, are essential in any collection. Earlier editions (with a confusing bibliography) are not as readable as the reprints, but if held will probably suffice.

5123 **Siebmacher, Johann.** Siebmacher's Grosses und allgemeines Wappenbuch in Verbindung mit Mehreren neu hrsg. und mit historischen, genealogischen und heraldischen Notizen begleitet von T. von Hefner. 9v.? (Nürnberg, Germany) 1856–1930.

The complete run from 1605–1961 occupies about 90v., and is almost unobtainable. Complete for the central European countries and, therefore, a companion to Rietstap, no.5120.

5124 ——— Repr. of 1854 ed. under title *Grosses und allgemeines Wappenbuch.* From Neustadt a.d. Aisch, Germany: Bauer & Raspe, 1970– (in progress).

5125 **Stalins, Gaston F. L., Baron, et al.** Vocabulaire-atlas héraldique en six langues: français-English-deutsch-español-italiano-nederlandsch. Paris: Soc. du Grand Armorial de France, 1952.

Clear, concise guide to heraldic terminology. English equivalent of an heraldic term in any one of the other five languages can be seen at a glance.

# Addresses of Publishers

Although many of the publishers' addresses can be readily found in *Bowker's American Book Trade Directory, Books in Print, Directory of the Historical Societies and Agencies of the U.S. and Canada, Literary Market Place,* and *World of Learning,* a number of books issued privately or by the authors/compilers are not listed in any reference work. Every attempt has therefore been made to find the addresses of authors, compilers, private and small publishers, and genealogical societies. Unfortunately, the D.A.R. refused to give addresses for State Chapters, and so it has not always been possible to give details of several D.A.R. books which are of prime importance.

For British publications, the addresses are given where possible, but it is understood that the British Book Centre, New York, will guarantee to supply any British publication within six weeks of the order. British *government* publications are usually readily available from British Information Services, New York. Sources for British Dominions and former Dominions are not easy to obtain, but generally the leading dealers such as Genealogical Publishing Co., Baltimore, Tuttle of Vermont, Goodspeed's of Boston, and Phillimore in England can supply most books. Latin American works will be more difficult to acquire, and the services of a good book dealer must be obtained.

The list which follows includes most of the small publishers and authors/compilers who publish privately. But for the quick servicing of requests for their own publications, the leading reprinters and publishers in the genealogical/heraldic field are also included.

*Addresses of Publishers*

Acadian Genealogy Exchange, 863 Wayman Branch Rd., Covington, KY 41015.
Accelerated Indexing Services, 3346 S. Orchard Dr., Bountiful, UT 84010.
Achee, B., P.O. Box 1414 Fox, Bossier City, LA 71010.
Achievements Ltd., Northgate, Canterbury, Kent, England.
Alabama Genealogical Soc., P.O. Box 35, Epes, AL 35460.
Allen, R. R., 5300 Bluefield Rd., Knoxville, TN 37921.
American College of Heraldry, Box 5007, Tulane Univ., New Orleans, LA 70118.
American Historical Soc. of Germans from Russia, 615 D. St., Lincoln, NE 68502.
Amite and Knockagree Historical Fund, 2011 Southwood Rd., Birmingham, AL 35216.
Anstruther, G., Woodchester, Glos., England.
Archives Nationales de la Province de Québec, 1180 rue Berthelot, Québec, G1R SG3, Canada.
Area Keys, P.O. Box 19465, Denver, CO 80219.
Arkansas Ancestors, *see* McLane, B. J.
Arkansas Genealogical Soc., Mrs. M. B. Cia, Sr., 4200 A St., Little Rock, AR 72205.
Arkansas Records Assoc., *see* Northeast Arkansas Genealogical Assoc.
Armorial, 1 Darnaway St., Edinburgh, Scotland.
Arrow/Curtis Printing Co., 2921 Morton St., Fort Worth, TX 76107.
Augustan Soc., Inc., 1617 W. 261st St., Harbor City, CA 90710.
Austin Genealogical Soc., P.O. Box 774, Austin, TX 78767.
Australian Genealogical Soc., Sydney, N.S.W., Australia.
L'Avant Studios, P.O. Box 1711, Tallahassee, FL 32302.

Babbel, J. A., P.O. Box 89, Annandale, VA 22003.
Balfour Pub., St. Ives, Hunts., England.
Banner Pr., P.O. Box 20180, Birmingham, AL 35216.
Beam, Judith, 145 Riviera Courts, Murray, KY 42071.
Bergeron, R., 9247 24e Ave., Montréal, Québec, Canada.
Bienville Historical Soc., 4559 Old Citronelli Highway, Prichano, AL 36613.

Bismarck Centennial Assoc., North Dakota, Chamber of Commerce, 412 N. 6th St., Bismarck, ND 58501.
Bismarck-Mandan Historical & Genealogical Soc., P.O. Box 485, Bismarck, ND 58501.
Bloomington-Normal Genealogical Soc., P.O. Box 432, Normal, IL 61761.
Bookcraft Inc., 1848 W. 2300 S, Salt Lake City, UT 84119.
Bookmark, *see* Mayhill Pub.
Brefney Pr., 1206 N. 32nd, Parsons, KS 67357.
British Book Centre, 996 Lexington Ave., New York, NY 10021.
British Columbia Genealogical Soc., Miss Jarvis, 6675 Angus Dr., Vancouver, B.C., Canada.
British Information Services, 845 3rd Ave., New York City, NY 10022.
British Record Soc., Dr. P. Spufford, 36 High St., Haddenham, Cambs., England.
Brookfield Pub. Co., P.O. Box 4933, Philadelphia, PA 19119.
Brossman, S. C., P.O. Box 43, Rehrersburg, PA 19550.
Browder, N. C., Route L, Hayesville, NC 28904.
Bullinger's Guides, 63 Woodland Ave., Westwood, NJ 07675.

Los Californianos, P.O. Box 1632, San Francisco, CA 94101.
Cambridge Univ. Pr., 32 E. 57th St., New York, NY 10022.
Camp, Anthony J., 162 Westbourne Grove, London, W. 11, England.
Campagna, Rev. Dominique, Pavillon Coindre, Cap-Rouge, Québec, Canada.
Canby Historical Soc., Canby, OR 97013.
Capitol Book Store, 10th & Market, Harrisburg, PA 17125.
Carlisle, L. B., 117 Lakeview Terrace, Burlington, VT 05401.
Carothers, B. S., 1510 Cranwell Rd., Lutherville, MD 21093.
Carrier Co., P.O. Box 1114, Harrisonburg, VA 22801.
Carter, G. L., 406 E. 5th St., Sedalia, MO 65301.
Carter, M., P.O. Box 1028, Albany, GA 31702.
Cartwright, B. G. C., 1863 Cowden Ave., Memphis, TN 38104.

## Addresses of Publishers

Casey, P. A., 1945 Columbine St., Baton Rouge, LA 70808.
Central Kentucky Genealogical Soc., P.O. Box 153, Frankfort, KY 40601.
Central New York Genealogical Soc., P.O. Box 104, Colvin Station, Syracuse, NY 13205.
Central Texas Genealogical Soc., 1717 Austin Ave., Waco, TX 76701.
Centre Canadian des Recherches Généalogiques Québec, Case Postale 845, Haute Ville, Québec 4, Canada.
Century Enterprises, P.O. Box 312, Huntsville, AR 72740.
Chance, H., Box 141, Route 1, Liberty, PA 16930.
Chaparral Genealogical Soc., P.O. Box 606, Tomball, TX 77375.
Chedwato Service, P.O. Box 120A, Middleboro, MA 02346.
Chicago Genealogical Soc., P.O. Box 1160, Chicago, IL 60690.
Claitor's Pub. Div., P.O. Box 239, Baton Rouge, LA 70821.
Clark, R. B., P.O. Box 352, St. Michaels, MD 21663.
Clint, F. R., P.O. Box 125, Castle Rock, CO 80104.
Colonial Dames of America, New York, 215 E. 71st, New York, NY 10021.
Colonial Soc. of Massachusetts, 87 Mount Vernon St., Boston, MA 02108.
Colorado Genealogical Soc., P.O. Box 9654, Denver, CO 80209.
Concordia Pr., 801 DeMun Ave., St. Louis, MO 63105.
Connecticut Soc. of Genealogists, P.O. Box 305, West Hartford, CT 06107.
Conseil de la Vie Française en Amérique, 75 rue d'Auteuil, Québec, G1R 4C3, Canada.
Cook, M. L., 3318 Wimberg Ave., Evansville, IN 47712.
Coppage, A. M., 707 Wimbledon Rd., Walnut Creek, CA 94598.
Cork Historical & Archaeological Soc., c/o Dept. of History, Univ. College, Cork, Republic of Ireland.
Cornwall Pr., Route 128, W. Cornwall, CT 06796.
Cox, E. M., 708 S. Maple E., Ellensburg, WA 98926.
Crickard, M. W., Route 1, Box 218, Beverly, WV 26253.
Criswell, H. D., 5711 Nebraska Ave., N.W., Washington, DC 20015.
Crocchiola, S.F.L., P.O. Box 107, Nazareth, TX 79036.
Cumming, M., County Atlas Reprints, Owen Sound, Ontario, Canada.

Daughters of the American Colonists, see National Soc., D.A.C.
Daughters of the American Revolution, Kentucky, 407 Foster St., Florence, KY 41042.
——— Missouri, A. K. Houts, 230 W. 61st St., Kansas City, MO 64113.
——— Tennessee, Fort Assumption Chapter, 749 N. Garland, Memphis, TN 38107.
Daughters of the Republic of Texas, 112 E. 11 St., Austin, TX 78701 (also P.O. Box 2599, San Antonio, TX 78299).
Daughters of Utah Pioneers, 300 N. Main St., Salt Lake City, UT 84103.
Decatur Genealogical Soc., P.O. Box 2068, Decatur, IL 62526.
Delwyn Assoc., 717 N. Monroe St., Albany, GA 31701.
Denis, M., P.O. Box 253, Oakland, ME 04963.
Dern, J. P., 950 Palomar Dr., Redwood City, CA 94062.
Deseret Book Co., 44 E. South Temple St., Salt Lake City, UT 84110.
Detroit Soc. for Genealogical Research, c/o Burton Historical Collection, Detroit Public Lib., 5201 Woodward Ave., MI 48202.
Dorman, J. F., P.O. Box 4883, Washington, DC 20008
Draughon, W. R., 1019 Demerius St., Durham, NC 27701.
Dublin, Stationery Office, Government Pub. Sales Office, G.P.O. Arcade, Dublin, Ireland.
Dudley, H. J., 2726 Anderson Dr., Raleigh, NC 27608.
Dutch Settlers Soc. of Albany, H. E. Veeder, P.O. Box 5006, Albany, NY 12205.

E. P. Pub. Ltd., Wakefield, Yorks., England.
Eastern Indiana Pub. Co., see Mayhill Pub.
Eastern Washington Genealogical Soc., P.O. Box 1826, Spokane, WA 99210.
Easton Pub. Co., N. Hanson, Easton, MD 21061.
Educational Supply Co., P.O. Box 11925, Northside Station, Atlanta, GA 30305.
Elliott, K. B., P.O. Box 353, South Hill, VA 23970.

357

Ellsberry, E. P., P.O. Box 206, Chillicothe, MO 64601.
Empire Reproduction and Pr. Co., *see* Gladden, S.C.
End of Trail Researchers (E. Brown), Route 1, Box 138, Lebanon, OR 97337.
Everton Pub., P.O. Box 368, 526 N. Main St., Logan, UT 84321.

Falley, M. D., 999 Michigan Ave., Evanston, IL 60202.
Fellowship of Brethren Genealogists, 318 Perry St., Elgin, IL 60120.
ffolliott, R., Pinton House, Sydenham Villas, Dublin, 14, Ireland.
Florida Genealogical Soc., P.O. Box 18624, Tampa, FL 33609.
Florida Soc. for Genealogical Research, 8461 54th St., Pinellas Park, FL 33565.
Foley, L. P. H., 12 Dahlgren Rd., Richmond, VA 23321.
Fort Worth Genealogical Soc., P.O. Box 864, Fort Worth, TX 76101.
Franklin, H., 2110 N. Topeka Ave., KS 66608.
French Canadian and Acadian Genealogical Review, Case Postale 845, Haute Ville, Québec 4, Canada.
Friends' Bookstore, 302 Arch, Philadelphia, PA 19107.

G.A.M. Pub., 1832 Irvine Blvd., Tustin, CA 92680.
Gale Research, Book Tower, Detroit, MI 48226.
Gandrud, K. P., 311 Caplewood Terrace, Tuscaloosa, AL 35401.
Garrett-McClain, 610 Terrace Dr., Columbia, TN 38401.
Gazetteer Pr., 413 Chesterfield, Nashville, TN 37212.
Gencor, Inc., 322 Crandall Building, 10 W. 1st South, Salt Lake City, UT 84101.
Gendex Corp., *see* Institute of Family Research.
Genealogical Assoc. of Southwestern Michigan, P.O. Box 573, St. Joseph, MI 49085.
Genealogical Enterprises, P.O. Box 232, Morrow, GA 30260.
Genealogical Forum of Portland, Neighbors of Woodcraft Building, 1400 S.W. Morrison, Portland, OR 97204.
Genealogical Institute, 10 S. Main St., Salt Lake City, UT 84101.

Genealogical Pub. Co., 521–523 St. Paul Place, Baltimore, MD 21202.
Genealogical Recorders, P.O. Box 52, Bladensburg, MD 20710.
Genealogical Reference Builders (Robertalee Lent), Post Falls, ID 83854.
Genealogical Reference Co., P.O. Box 1554, Owensboro, KY 42301.
Genealogical Research Soc. of New Orleans, P.O. Box 51791, New Orleans, LA 70150.
Genealogical Soc. of New Jersey, P.O. Box 1291, New Brunswick, NJ 08903.
Genealogical Soc. of South Africa, 40 Haylett St., Strand, Cape Town, S. Africa.
Genealogical Soc. of Southern Illinois, c/o Logan College, Carterville, IL 62918.
Genealogical Soc. of the Church of Jesus Christ of Latter-day Saints, Inc., General Church Distribution Center, P.O. Box 11627, 33 Richards St., Salt Lake City, UT 84111.
Genealogical Soc. of Vermont, Mrs. C. Church, Westminster West, Route 3, Putney, VT 05346.
Genealogical Soc. of Victoria, Block Arcade, Collins St., Melbourne, Australia.
Genealogy Club of America, P.O. Box 15784, Salt Lake City, UT 84115.
General Services Administration, Washington, DC 20405.
General Soc. of Mayflower Descendants, Mrs. R. M. Sherman, 128 Massasoit Dr., Warwick, RI 02888.
——— District of Columbia, Apt. 510N, 5601 Seminary Rd., Falls Church, VA 22041.
——— New Jersey, 381 Creek Bed Rd., Mountainside, NJ 07092.
——— Oklahoma, 1316 S. Trenton, Tulsa, OK 74120.
Gentry, E. G. S., 3311 Clearview, Austin, TX 78703.
Georgia Genealogical Reprints, *see* Southern Historical Pr.
Georgia Genealogical Soc., P.O. Box 4761, Atlanta, GA 30302.
Geue, C. W., 2636 Stadium Dr., Fort Worth, TX 76109.
Gianelloni, Mrs. S. J., Route 3, Box 114, Baton Rouge, LA 70808.
Giffen, K. S., 53 State St., Boston, MA 02109.
Gillis, N. and I., P.O. Box 9114, Shreveport, LA 71109.

*Addresses of Publishers*

Gingras, R., 39 W. St. Cyrille St., app. 5, Québec, Canada.
Gladden, S. C., 1034 Spruce St., Boulder, CO 80302.
Government Printing Office, Washington, DC 20401.
Gregg Pr., 70 Lincoln St., Boston, MA 02111.
Hall, C. M., 7280 Rusty Dr., Midvale, UT 84047.
Hall, G. K., 70 Lincoln St., Boston, MA 02111.
Harbor Hill Books, P.O. Box 407, Harrison, NY 10528.
Harshman, Lida F., P.O. Box 556, Mineral Ridge, OH 44440.
Hartlaub, R. J. Commonwealth Land Title Insurance Co., 24 Beechwood Rd., Summit, NJ 07901.
Hartwell Co., *see* Augustan Soc., Inc.
Heart of America Genealogical Soc., Kansas City Public Lib., 311 E. 12th St., Kansas City, MO 64106.
Hebert, Rev. D. J., P.O. Box 31, Eunice, LA 70535.
Heiss, Willard C., 4828 N. Illinois, Indianapolis, IN 46208.
Hendrix, M. L. F., 408 Dunbar, Jackson, MS 39216.
Heraldry Soc. of Australia, 1 Crusader Crescent, Glen Waverley, Victoria, Australia.
Heraldry Soc. of Canada, 900 Pinecrest Rd., Ottawa 14, Ontario, Canada.
Heraldry Soc. of South Africa, P.O. Box 4839, Cape Town, S. Africa.
Heraldry Today, 10 Beauchamp Place, London, England.
Heritage House, Route 1, Box 211, Thompson, IL 61285.
Heritage Papers, Daniellsville, GA 30633.
Historical Pub. Soc., 1 E. 42nd St., New York, NY 10003.
Hodges, N., 4617 Jefferson, Kansas City, MO 64112.
Hoenstine, F. G., 414 Montgomery St., Hollidaysburg, PA 16648.
Holdcraft, J. M., 5314 Belleville Ave., Baltimore, MD 21207.
Holmes, J. D. L., Univ. College, Univ. of Alabama, Birmingham, AL 35233.
Homestead Pr., Drawer 220, Kenmore, WA 98028.
Hopkins, E. L., P.O. Box 434, Forest, MS 39074.

Hotaling, D., 2255 Cedar Lane, Vienna, VA 22180.
House of Heather, P.O. Box 40204, Nashville, TN 37204.
Houts, A. K., 230 W. 61st St., Kansas City, MO 64113.
Huguenot Soc. of New Jersey, 8 English Village, Crawford, NJ 07016.
Hutchinson Photo & Printing Co., Prineville, OR 97754.
Huxford, Folks, P.O. Box 116, Homerville, GA 31634.

Idaho Genealogical Soc., 610 N. Julia Davis Dr., Boise, ID 83706.
Illiana Genealogical Soc., P.O. Box 207, Danville, IL 61832.
Indian Historian Pr., 1451 Masonic Ave., San Francisco, CA 94117.
Indian Nations Pr., 812 Mayo Building, Tulsa, OK 74113.
Institut Généalogique Drouin, 4184 Saint-Denis, Montréal, Canada.
Institute of Family Research (formerly Gendex Corp.), 1213 E. 2100 S., Salt Lake City, UT 84106.
Institute of Historical Research, London, Senate House, London, England.
Iowa Genealogical Soc., P.O. Box 3815, 6000 Douglas St., Des Moines, IA 50322.
Ireland Indexing Service, 2237 Brooke Rd., Fallbrook, CA 92028.
Irish Genealogical Research Soc., 82 Eaton Square, London, England.
Irish Manuscripts Commission, 73 Merrion Square, Dublin, Ireland.
Irwin, Mrs. L., 26 Saxon Rd., Newton, MA 02161.

Jacksonville Genealogical Soc., 3873 Herschel St., Jacksonville, FL 32205.
Janlen Enterprises, 2236 S. 77th St., West Allis, WI 53219.
Jenkins Garrett Pr., 7111 S. Interregional Highway, P.O. Box 2085, Austin, TX 78767.
Jensen, E., 1335 Graff Ave., San Leandro, CA 94577.
Johnson, W. P., P.O. Box 1770, Raleigh, NC 27602.

Kansas Genealogical Soc., P.O. Box 103, Dodge City, KS 67801.
Kansas Postal History Soc., c/o Kansas State Historical Soc., 120 W. 10th St., Topeka, KS 66612.

359

## Addresses of Publishers

Kegley, G., 2919 Tinker Creek Lane, N.E., Roanoke, VA 24019.

Kentucky Genealogist, Martha P. Miller, P.O. Box 4894, Washington, DC 20008.

Kentucky Reprint Co., *see* House of Heather.

Kidron Community Council, Inc., Kidron, OH 44636.

Latter-day Saints publications, *see* Genealogical Society of the Church of Jesus Christ of Latter-day Saints.

Liberty Bell Associates, P.O. Box 51, Franklin Park, NJ 08823.

Lindsay, W. McK., 139 Seven Oaks Dr., Greenville, SC 29605.

List and Index Soc., Public Record Office, Chancery Lane, London, England.

Livingston, R. M., P.O. Box 166, Ft. Ogden, FL 33842.

Louisiana Genealogical and Historical Soc., P.O. Box 3454, Baton Rouge, LA 70821.

Lowry, M., 311 W. 20th St., Pittsburg, KS 66762.

McCay, B. L., 6702 E. 46th St., Indianapolis, IN 46226.

McClain Printing Co., 212 Main St., Parsons, WV 26287.

McClure Printing Co., P.O. Box 3, White Marsh, VA 23183.

McCracken, G. E., 1232 39th St., Des Moines, IA 50311.

McDonald, C. D., Jr., 1319 N. 167th, Seattle, WA 98133.

McDowell, S., Route 1, Richland, IN 47634.

McLane, B. J., 112 Leach St., Hot Springs, AR 71901.

Maduell, C. R., 6368 Orleans Ave., New Orleans, LA 70124.

Magazine of Bibliographies, 1209 Clover Lane, Fort Worth, TX 76107.

Magna Carta Book Co., 5502 Magnolia Ave., Baltimore, MD 21215.

Maine Genealogical Inquirer, P.O. Box 253, Oakland, ME 04963.

Marsh, W. L., 5 Windsor Court, Old Saybrook, CT 06475.

Maryland Genealogical Soc., 201 W. Monument St., Baltimore, MD 21201.

Maxwell, A. S., 10 Belmont St., Aberdeen, Scotland.

Maxwell, F., P.O. Box 83, Columbus, OH 43216.

Mayhill Pub., P.O. Box 90, Knightstown, IN 46148.

Meyer, M. K., Route 10, Box 138A, Pasadena, MD 21122.

Michigan Enterprises (and Heritage), 730 Parker Ave., Kalamazoo, MI 49008.

Mid-Continent Book Store, N. 15th at Dunbar St., Mayfield, KY 42066.

Mid-Michigan Genealogical Soc., 208 N. Catherine St., Lansing, MI 48917.

Mid-west Tennessee Genealogical Soc., P.O. Box 3179, Jackson, TN 38301.

Midwest Genealogical Soc., 2911 Rivera W., Wichita, KS 67211.

Mika Pub., P.O. Box 536, Belleville, Ontario, Canada.

Mills, M. S., 4041 E. 46th St., Tulsa, OK 74135.

Ministère des Affaires Culturelles du Québec, 955 Chémin Saint-Louis, Québec, Canada.

Minnesota Genealogical Soc., P.O. Box 1120, St. Paul, MN 55105.

Miran Pub., 246–50 Ridgelea Bank, 3327 Winthrop St., Fort Worth, TX 76116.

Mississippi Genealogical Soc., 408 Dunbar, Jackson, MS 39216.

Mitchell, L. D., 2114 Hoppin St., Mobile, AL 36605.

Mobile Genealogical Soc., P.O. Box 6224, Mobile, AL 36608.

Morris, Mrs. Harry J., 2515 Sweetbrier Dr., Dallas, TX 75228.

National Archives & Records Service, Washington, DC 20408.

National Genealogical Soc., 1921 Sunderland Place, NW, Washington, DC 20036.

National Soc., Daughters of the American Colonists, Arizona, Mrs. R. M. James, 3024 E. 6th St., Tucson, AZ 85716.

——— Pennsylvania, 2205 Massachusetts Ave., NW, Washington, DC 20008.

National Soc. U.S. Daughters of the War of 1812, D.C., 1461 Rhode Island Ave., N.W., Washington, D.C.

——— Ohio, Mrs. G. E. Steele, 1215 Smallwood Dr., Columbus, OH 43220.

——— Tennessee, 43 Belleair Dr., Memphis, TN 38104.

National Soc. Women Descendants of the Ancient and Honorable Artillery Co., 141 W. Main St., Norwalk, OH 44857.

Nelson, Thomas., 81 Curlew Dr., Don Mills, 400, Ontario, Canada.

New Englandiana, P.O. Box 787, N. Adams, MA 01247.

*Addresses of Publishers*

New Jersey Genesis, Carl W. Williams, 151 E. 81st, New York, NY 10028.
New Mexico Genealogical Soc., P.O. Box 8734, Albuquerque, NM 87108.
New Zealand Society of Genealogists, P.O. Box 8795, Auckland, New Zealand.
Newman, H. W., 640 Americana Dr., Apt. 202, Annapolis, MD 21403.
Noone House, W. L. Bauhan, Peterborough, NH 03458.
North Carolina Genealogical Soc., P.O. Box 1492, Raleigh, NC 27602.
North Dakota Historical Soc. of Germans from Russia, P.O. Box 41, Dickinson State College, ND 58601.
North Texas Genealogical & Historical Assoc., 2507 Amherst Dr., Wichita Falls, TX 76308.
North West Georgia Historical & Genealogical Soc., P.O. Box 2484, Rome, GA 30161.
Northeast Alabama Genealogical Soc., P.O. Box 674, Gadsden, AL 35902.
Northeast Arkansas Genealogical Assoc., 314 Vine St., Newport, AR 72112.
Northwest Arkansas Genealogical Soc., P.O. Box 362, Rogers, AR 72756.

Obert, R. T., 200 Medical Arts Building, Salt Lake City, UT 84111.
Ohio Genealogical Soc. (Trumbull County Chapter), P.O. Box 556, Mineral Ridge, OH 44440.
——— Route 1, Box 332B, Ashland, OH 44805 *(Ohio records)*.
——— P.O. Box 2625, Mansfield, OH 44906 *(The report)*.
Oklahoma Genealogical Soc., P.O. Box 314, Oklahoma City, OK 73101.
Ontario Genealogical Soc., P.O. Box 66, Station Q, Toronto, Canada.
Orange County California Genealogical Soc., P.O. Box 1587, Orange, CA 92668.
Order of Americans of Armorial Ancestry, G. T. Smallwood, Jr., The Union League, 140 South Rd., Philadelphia, PA 19102.
Order of the Crown of Charlemagne, J. O. Buck, 15 E. 10th St., New York, NY 10003. (*also*) G. R. Cooke, 761 Linwood Ave., St. Paul, MN 55105.
Order of the First Families of Virginia, Mrs. H. D. Forrest, 747 Euclid Ave., Jackson, MS 39202.
Oregon Genealogical Soc., P.O. Box 1214, Eugene, OR 97401.

Otto, R. C., 8816 Ferguson Ave., Savannah, GA 31406.
Owens & Tanco, 1307 Davis Dr., Arlington, TX 76013.
Oxford University Pr., 200 Madison Ave., New York, NY 10016.

Paddington Pr., 30 E. 42nd St., New York, NY 10017.
Parliament Pr., 1848 W. 2300 S., Salt Lake City, UT 84119.
Parrish, Mrs. H. T., Route 2, Seebree Rd., Stamping Ground, KY 40379.
Phillimore, Shopwyke Hall, Chichester, Sussex, England.
Pinhorn, BCM, London, W.C.1, England.
Pioneer Printers, 525 Lake Louise Dr., S.W., Tacoma, WA 98498.
Plantation Book Shop, 301 S. Wall St., Natchez, MS 39150.
Platt, G., *see* G. A. M. Pub.
Polk (Directory Publishers), 2910 W. Clay St., P.O. Box 6874, Richmond, VA 23230.
Pollock, P. W., 4122 N. 3rd Ave., #6, Phoenix, AZ 85013.
Polyanthos, 811 Orleans St., New Orleans, LA 70116.
Pontbriand, B., 2390 Marie-Victorian, Quebec 6, Canada.
Posey, B. D., 2802 Laredo Dr., Hattiesburg, MS 39401.
Potter, D. W., 804 Westwood Dr., Tullahoma, TN 37388.
Powell, E. W., 36 N. Highland Ave., Akron, OH 44303.
Pride Pub., 22 Emerson St., Wakefield, MA 01880.
Prince George's Genealogical Soc., P.O. Box 819, Bowie, MD 20715.
Public Archives of Canada, 395 Wellington St., Ottawa, Canada.
Pyramid Books, 919 3rd Ave., New York, NY 10022.

Queen's Printer, Parliament Building, Ottawa, Canada.
Questing Heirs Genealogical Soc., 4112 Walnut Grove Ave., Rosemead, CA 91770.

R. & E. Research Associates, 4843 Mission St., San Francisco, CA 94112.
RE: Genealogy, 639 Sandalwood Ct., Riverside, CA 92507.

*Addresses of Publishers*

Randall, P. E., 36 Mace Rd., Hampton, NH 03842.
Range Genealogical Soc., P.O. Box 726, Buhl, MN 55713.
Rapid City Soc. for Genealogical Research, P.O. Box 1495, Rapid City, SD 57701.
Rasmussen, L. J., 1204 Nimitz Dr., Colma, CA 94015.
Rathburn, T., 224 Leslie St., Chester, SC 29706.
Reprint Co., P.O. Box 5401, Spartanburg, SC 29301.
La Retama Pr., 801 E. Main St., Rio Grande City, TX 78582.
Rieder, M. P., 1457 Poinsetta Dr., Metairie, LA 70005.
Rigby Ltd., P.O. Box 104, Norwood, S. Australia.
Rogers, Mrs. B. L., 13433 N. 16th Ave., Phoenix, AZ 85029.
Romig, W., 979 Lake Pointe Rd., Grosse Pointe, MI 48236.
Ro'sel Pub., P.O. Box 11457, Salt Lake City, UT 84111.
Russell, G. E., 3800 Enterprise Rd., Mitchellville, MD 20716 (see also Towle, L. C.).
Rutt, A. E. H., 3775 Modoc Rd., Santa Barbara, CA 93105.

S. R. Pub., Wakefield, see E. P. Pub.
St. Louis Genealogical Soc., Rm. 261, 1617 S. Brentwood Blvd., St. Louis, MO 63144.
Saint Nicholas Soc. in the City of New York, 122 E. 58th St., NY 10022.
Saline Sentiments, Route 1, Box 16, Gilliam, MO 65330.
San Antonio Genealogical and Historical Soc., P.O. Box 6383, Alamo Heights Station, San Antonio, TX 78209.
San Bernardino Valley Genealogical Soc., P.O. Box 2505, San Bernardino, CA 92406.
Sanders, J. B., 409 Nacogdoches, Center, TX 75935.
Saskatchewan Genealogical Soc., P.O. Box 1894, 19 Merlin Crescent, Regina, Canada.
Scalf, H. P., P.O. Box 107, Stanville, KY 41659.
Schreiner-Yantis, N., 6818 Lois Dr., Springfield, VA 22150.
Scottish Genealogy Soc., Miss J. P. S. Ferguson, 21 Howard Place, Edinburgh, Scotland.

Scottish Record Soc., c/o Scottish Record Office, Edinburgh, Scotland.
Seattle Genealogical Soc., P.O. Box 549, Seattle, WA 98111.
Shackleton, B., 1016 W. Euclid, Pittsburg, KS 66762.
Shannonhouse, E. M., 402 N. Road St., Elizabeth City, NC 27909.
Shaw, A. C., 2525 Oak St., Jacksonville, FL 32204.
Sheffield, E., 107 Center St., Baytown, TX 77520.
Shire Publications, 12B Temple Square, Aylesbury, Bucks., England.
Short, A., P.O. Box 120, Union City, IN 47390.
Shultz, L. W., P.O. Box 25, 603 College Ave., N. Manchester, IN 46962.
Simmons, Mrs. W., Natchez Trace Village, Madison, MS 39110.
Sistler, Byron, and Associates, 1626 Washington St., Evanston, IL 60202.
Skilton, Charles, 50 Alexandra Rd., London, S.W. 19, England.
Smith, B. L., 2529 Stadium Dr., Fort Worth, TX 76109.
Société Canadienne de Généalogie, 119 Rue Charlotte, Ottawa, Ontario, Canada.
Société Généalogique Canadienne-Française, Case Postale 335, Place d'Armes, Montréal, Québec, Canada.
Society of Australian Genealogists, Heritage House, 413 Riley St., Surry Hills, Sydney, N.S.W., Australia.
Society of Genealogists, 37 Harrington Gardens, London, SW7, England.
Society of Mayflower Descendants, see General Soc. of Mayflower Descendants.
Society of the Cincinnati, Massachusetts, R. C. Storey, 149 Miles River Rd., S. Hamilton, MA 01982.
South Australian Genealogy & Heraldry Soc., P.O. Box 1100, Adelaide, Australia.
South Carolina Genealogical Soc., P.O. Box 11353, Columbia, SC 29221.
South Texas Genealogical and Historical Soc., P.O. Box 40, Gonzales, TX 78629.
Southeast Texas Genealogical & Historical Soc., 2870 Driftwood Lane, Beaumont, TX 77703.
Southern Arizona Genealogical Soc., P.O. Box 6027, Tucson, AZ 85716.
Southern California Genealogical Soc., 401 E. M St., Wilmington, CA 90744.
Southern Genealogical Services, Route 2,

## Addresses of Publishers

Box 123-1, New Market, AL 35761.
Southern Genealogist's Exchange Soc., *see* Shaw, A. C.
Southern Historical Pr., P.O. Box 229, Easley, SC 29640.
Southern Pub. Co., Delray Beach, FL 33444.
Stamford Genealogical Soc., P.O. Box 249, Stamford, CT 06904.
Starke-Verlag, C. A., P.O. Box 310, Limburg-Lahn, Germany.
Stercula, Mrs. B. M., 20602 107th St. E., Sumner, WA 98390.
Steuart, Rieman, 3736 Tudor, 501 W. University Parkway, Baltimore, MD 21210.
Stevens, 11 New Fetter Lane, London, E.C.4, England.
Stevenson's Genealogical Center, 230 W. 1230 North St., Provo, UT 84601.
Stout Map Co., 1209 Hill St., Greensboro, NC 27408.
Struik, Cape Town, distributed by Lawrence Verry, *q.v.*
Summit Pub., P.O. Box 222, Munroe Falls, OH 44262.
Superintendent of Documents, Washington, DC 20401.
Swift Ltd., London, *see* List and Index Soc.

Tabard, *see* E. P. Pub.
Tacoma Genealogical Soc., P.O. Box 11232, Tacoma, WA 98411.
Talbot, Eloi G., 7141 Ave. Royale, Chateau-Richer, Québec, Canada.
Tally-Frost, S., 3909 Live Oak, Corpus Christi, TX 78408.
Taylor, Mrs. L. E., 2706 West Rd., Mobile, AL 36609.
Tennessee Genealogical Soc., P.O. Box 12124, Memphis, TN 38112.
Tennessee Valley Genealogical Soc., P.O. Box 1512, Huntsville, AL 35807.
Texas State Genealogical Soc., 2121 Ashland, Ft. Worth, TX 76107.
Theobald, Mrs. R. E., 721 Parker Blvd., Buffalo, NY 14223.
Threlfall, J. B., 5518 Barton Rd., Madison, WI 53711.
Topeka Genealogical Soc., P.O. Box 4048, Topeka, KS 66604.
Towle, Dr. L. C., 3602 Maureen Lane, Bowie, MD 20715.
Tulsa Genealogical Soc., P.O. Box 585, Tulsa, OK 74101.

Tuttle, Charles E., 28 S. Main St., Rutland, VT 05701.

Ulster-Scot Historical Foundation, Law Courts Building, Chichester St., Belfast, N. Ireland.
Unigraphic, Inc., 4400 Jackson Ave., Evansville, IN 47715.
United Press International, 220 E. 42nd St., New York, NY 10017.
U.S. Government Printing Office, Publ. Documents, Washington, DC 20402.
U.S. Hereditary Register, Inc., 1629 K St. NW, Suite 546, Washington, DC 20006.
University of Minnesota, Immigration Historical Research Center, 826 Berry St., St. Paul, MN 55114.
University of the West Indies, Mona, Kingston 7, Jamaica.
Utah Genealogical Assoc., P.O. Box 1144, Salt Lake City, UT 84110.

Valley Pub., 1759 Fulton St., Fresno, CA 93721.
Vasquez, N. M., 6341 Samoa Way, Carmichael, CA 95608.
Verry, Lawrence, 16 Holmes St., Mystic, CT 06355.
Vineland Historical & Antiquarian Soc., 108 S. 7th St., Vineland, NJ 08360.
Virginia Genealogical Soc., P.O. Box 1397, Richmond, VA 23211.

Waldenmaier, I., 722 N. Birmingham Place, Tulsa, OK 74110.
Watauga Assoc. of Genealogists, Sherrod Lib., E. Tennessee State Univ., Johnson City, TN 37601.
Wellauer, M. A., 3239 N. 58th St., Milwaukee, WI 53216.
West-Central Kentucky Families Research Assoc., Mrs. E. L. Cox, P.O. Box 1465, Owensboro, KY 42301.
West Central Missouri Genealogical Soc., Route 3, Box 102A, Warrensburg, MO 64093.
Western Epics, 254 S. Main, Salt Lake City, UT 84111.
Western Printing & Publishing Co., Sparks, NV 89431.
Wheat, J. L., 1202 Oriole, Garland, TX 75042.
Wilkens, C. G., 450 Rose Lane, Fort Wayne, IN 46807.
Williams, J. H., 410 Eighth St., Warrensburg, MO 64093.

*Addresses of Publishers*

Williams, Mr. & Mrs. R. T., Danbury, PA 18916.
Wilson, T. B., 38 Swan St., Lambertville, NJ 08530.
Wingo, E. B., 5916 Powhatan Ave., Norfolk, VA 23508.
Wion, J. H., 180 Riverside Dr., New York, NY 10024.
Wisconsin State Genealogical Soc., P.O. Box 90068, Milwaukee, WI 53202.
Wood, V. S., 230 Payson Rd., Belmont, MA 02178.
Woodruff, Mrs. H. W., S. Harvard, Independence, MO 64052.
Woodson, R. F., 910 Pine Ridge Rd., Richmond, VA 23226.
Wulfeck, D. F., 51 Park Ave., Naugatuck, CT 06770.
Wynd, F., 2009 Gail Ave., Albany, GA 31705.

Yakima Valley Genealogical Soc., Mrs. F. E. Carver, 924 S. 16th Ave., Yakima, WA 98902.
Yates, W. A., P.O. Box 1867, Rifle, CO 81650.
Yorkshire Archaeological Soc., Mrs. M. Morton, 21 Bedford Garth, Leeds, England.
Young, L. M., Denton, TX 76201.

# Index

# Index

Numbers refer to entries and not to pages, except numbers in parentheses which refer to dates. References to an entry number followed by "n" refer to the notation for that number.

Aberdeen, sasines in sheriffdoms, 4757a
Aberdeen University and King's College, officers and graduates, 4740; roll of graduates, 4741
Aberle, G. P. Pioneers and their sons, 2660
Abousleman, M. D. Who's who in New Mexico, 2391
Abstract of arrangements respecting registration of births, etc., United Kingdom, 4202
Academia Guatemalteca de Estudios Genealógicos, Heráldicos e Históricos. Revista, 3905
Acadians: Canadian, 3969, 4048–4052, 4061, 4064, 4097; church records, 1610, 1623; exiles in Louisiana, 1667; in France (1762–1776), 1677; in Louisiana, 1600–1601; manual, 4097; passenger lists (1785), 1676; rounded up by Massachusetts soldiers (1755–1766), 1850; Acadia and Acadians, *see also* Nova Scotia
Acadiensis; a quarterly, 4047
Account of Her Majesty's revenue in Province of New York, 2420
Account of the donated lands of Pennsylvania, 2841
Achee, B. E., and Wright, M. D. Index to compiled service records, 717–718; Index to Louisiana 1860 mortality schedule, 1598
Acklen, J. T., and others. Tennessee records, 3236
Adam, F. Clans, septs, and regiments of Scottish Highlands, 4791
Adam, G. M. Prominent men of Canada, 3939
Adams, A., and Weis, F. L. Magna Charta sureties, 281
Adams, E. B., and Chavez, A. Missions of New Mexico, 2392
Adams, J. N. Illinois place names, 1293; Index to Transactions and other publications of Illinois State Historical Soc., 1330
Adams, J. T. Atlas of American history, 186
Addington, A. C. Royal house of Stuart, 4445
Addison, W. I. Matriculation, Glasgow University, 4744; Roll of graduates, Glasgow University, 4745
Address, modes of, 4510; titles and forms of, 4524
Administration bonds, New York state, 2524, 2542
Administrations, *see* Wills and probates
Admiralty, *see* Navy (British)

367

*Index*

Afrikaner, *see* South Africa
Agnew, D. C. A. Protestant exiles from France, 4541
Aids, *see* Manuals
Aikens, A. J., and Proctor, L. A. Men of progress, Wisconsin, 3777
Ainsworth, J. F. Survey of documents in private keeping, 4590
Akins, T. B. Acadia and Nova Scotia, 4048
Alabama: 717–770; atlas, 729, 748; Baptists, 744; Bible records, 622; bibliography, 756; census (1820, 1830), 719, (1830), 735, (1840), 763; Cherokee census (1835), 715, 1851), 704; church archives, 741, 743; churches, 727, 770; Civil War, 564; colonial families, 620; county archives, 742; Indians, 675, 704, 715–716; Methodism, 746, 769; records, 732–733, 739, 745; Revolutionary War, 721, 750, 759–760, 767; tombstone inscriptions, 617; vital statistics, 740; wills, 726
Alabama baptist (journal), 720
Alabama genealogical register, 721
Alabama Genealogical Society, Inc. magazine, 722
Alabama historical quarterly, 723
Alaska: 771–782; bibliography, 776, 782, 782n; geographic dictionary, 773; place names, 771, 4073; post offices and postmasters, 780
Alaska-Yukon gold book, 781; place names, 778
Albany, N. Y.: deeds, mortgages, wills, 2421; Dutch settlers, 2449; minutes of Court of, 2422; Protocol, 2432; records, 2421
Alberta, Canada: 4038–4040; gazetteer, 4039; place names, 4040
Alberta past and present, 4038
Alexander, J. H. Index to Calendar of Maryland state papers, 1739
Alfred the Great, 279; 325–326
Aliens: Huguenot, 427–428, 4542–4543, 4545; London, 4545; Massachusetts (1847–1851), 1905
Aliis of Hawaii, 1245
Allaire, J. B. A. Dictionnaire biographique du clergé canadien-français, 3939a
Allcock, H. Heraldic design, 4990
Allegations for marriage licenses, Canterbury, 4347–4348
Allen, C. Records of Huguenots in U.S., 422
Allen, G. W. Massachusetts privateers of the Revolution, 1841
Allen, P. T. Tennessee soldiers in the Revolution, 3237; Tennessee soldiers in War of 1812, 3238
Allen, R. R. Tennessee books, 3239
Allen, W. American biographical dictionary, 130
Allen, W. B. History of Kentucky, 1488
Allison, W. H. Inventory of unpublished material for American religious history in Protestant church archives, 456
Almada, F. R. Diccionario de historia, 3907
Almanach de Gotha, 5118
Almanacs, Texas, 3343
Almanak van Kaapstad, 4955n
Alphabetical index to townlands and towns of Ireland, 4626
Alter, J. C. Utah, 3428
Amateur historian (periodical), 4269n
America, *see* United States
American Antiquarian Soc. Index of marriages in Massachusetts centinel, 1842; Index to obituaries, 1843
American Association of State and Local History. Directory, historical societies and agencies, 34, 3940
American biographical directories, District of Columbia, 1066
American biographical history of eminent and self-made men, Michigan, 1938
American biography, 131–132
American blue-book of funeral directors, 35
American Catholic Historical Soc. of Philadelphia, records, 463–464
American College of Heraldry, 5000, 5098
American families of British origin, 4482n
American families of historic lineage, 133
American families with British ancestry, 158n
American family and clan history, 4262
American genealogical index, 1–2
American genealogist (periodical), 103
American genealogist and New Haven genealogical magazine, 103n
American genealogist (Munsell's), 21–22
American Geographical Society. Index to maps in books and periodicals, 187–188
American heraldic review, 5099
American historical magazine (and Tennessee Historical Soc. quarterly), 3240
American-Irish Historical Soc. journal, 382
American monthly magazine, 500n
American Protestant missionaries in Hawaii, 1256 1257
American Society of Genealogists. Genealogical research, 241–242, 4422
American Tract Soc. records, New Jersey, 2327

*Index*

Americana (magazine), 104
Amish: bibliography, 411; genealogies, 411; Holmes county, Ohio, 2690; Pennsylvania, 2856
Amite county, Mississippi, 1613, 2031
Analecta Hibernica, 4595
Ancestor (The); quarterly review (Great Britain), 4249-4250
Ancestor: Genealogical Soc. of Victoria, 4902
Ancestor hunting in South Carolina, 3188
Ancestral notes, 106n
Ancestral proofs, 1771, 1771n
Anderson, G. B. History of New Mexico, 2393
Anderson, J. Royal genealogist, 4446
Anderson, J. M. Early records, St. Andrews University, 4746; Matriculation roll, St. Andrews University, 4747
Anderson, J. P. Book of British topography, 4170, 4384
Anderson, L., and Farley, A. W. Bibliography of town and county histories of Kansas, 1441
Anderson, M. O. Kings and kingship in early Scotland, 4792a
Anderson, P. J. Officers and graduates of University and King's College, Aberdeen, 4740
Anderson, W. Scottish nation, 4793
Andersonville diary, 562
Andrea, L. South Carolina soldiers and patriots, 3119
Andreas, A. T. Illustrated atlas of Minnesota, 1987; Illustrated historical atlas of Indiana, 1364a, 1364n; Illustrated historical atlas of Iowa, 1409; Maps of Indiana counties in 1876, 1364
Andrews, C. C. History of St. Paul, Minnesota, 1988
Andrews, C. L. Story of Alaska, 772
Andrews, F. De W. Connecticut soldiers in the French and Indian War, 957
Andrews, J., and Higgins, W. D. Creole Mobile, 614a
Andrews, M. P. Tercentenary history of Maryland, 1740
Androscoggin River Valley, N. H., 2290
Angel, M. Reproduction of Thompson and West's History of Nevada, 2196-2197
Angelís, M. L. de. Mujeres puertorriqueñas que se han distinguido en el cultivo de las ciencias, 3043
Angerville, Count H. H. d'. Living descendants of Blood Royal in America, 269
Anglican: Church of Ireland parish registers, 4584, 4697; church registers of Lisbon, Portugal, 4898; colonial America, 412
Anglo-American families, Texas, 3333
Anglo-American marriages, Texas, 3354
Anglo-Irish surnames, 4649
Anglo-Jewish arms, 5012, 5032; bibliography, 4549, 4551; genealogy, sources, 4552; notabilities, 5012
Anglo-Norman families, 4463-4470
Anglo-Saxon family names, 4405; surnames, 4407
Annals of Iowa, 1410
Annals of Wyoming, 3828
Annapolis, Nova Scotia, parish records, 4064
Anne (ship), 1845
Annuaire de la noblesse de France, 278
Annual index to genealogical periodicals, 94
Annual monitor, 4562
Ansearchin news, 3241
Anstruther, G. Seminary priests, 4295
Antepasados, 841
Antigua, 4918, 4927
Anuário genealógico Latino, 3881
Aparicio y Aparicio, E. J. Genealogical research in Mexico and central America, 3842, 3908
Apolant, J. A. Génesis de la familia Uruguaya, 3936
Apothecaries, list, British, 4288
Appalachian region, West Virginia, 3729n
Appleton, W. S. Gore roll of arms, 5067; Positive pedigrees and authorized arms, 5067
Appleton's cyclopedia of American biography, 135
Apprentices: New York city, 2497n; New York state, 2479-2480, 2497n
Arabella (ship), 575
Architects (English): biographies, 4289; obituary index, 139
Archive General de Indias, Catalogue of materials, 3845
Archives (British Records Assoc. journal), 4251
Archives: Maryland, 1805; Missouri, 2094; New Jersey, 2292, 2349; Pennsylvania, 2976; Philadelphia, 2859; U.S., 50
Archivo General de la Nación. Boletín, 3909
Archivo Histórico Nacional, Madrid. Inventario de la serie gobierno de Puerto Rico, 3044
Ardery, J. H. Kentucky records, 1489-1490

369

*Index*

Ardouin, R. B. L. Louisiana census records 1810 and 1820, 1599
Areas (U.S.): 574–651; New England, 574–614; South, 615–636; others, 637–641a
Argentine Republic, 3869–3880
Argonauts: California, 873; Colorado, 927; Klondike gold stampede, 781
Arickaras tribe, 660
Arizona: 783–804; census (1860), 2401; census (1860, 1864, 1870), 785; census (1864), 788; census (1866), 784; county archives, 790; Mormon settlement, 796; place names, 783, 791; post offices and postmasters, 803; Spanish-American pedigrees, 802, 914, 3866; vital statistics records, 789
Ark and Dove passengers, 1814
Arkansas: 805–840; Bible records, 622; cemetery inscriptions, 818; census (1830), 832, (1840), 833, (1850 excerpt), 840; church archives, 827; churches and religious organizations, 826; Civil War, 564, 805; county archives, 828; Indians, 713n; military bounty grants, 817; mortality schedules (1850), 834, (1860), 831, (1870), 820; newspapers, 829; Ozark region, 2118; vital statistics records, 827; War of 1812, 817
Arkansas family historian, 806
Arkansas genealogical register, 807
Arkansas Historical Assoc. Publications, 808
Arkansas records survey, 809
The armorial, 4252, 5101
Armorial, Canada, 3988, 4005
Armorial who is who, 5009
Armstrong, G. H. Origin and meanings of place names in Canada, 3941
Armstrong, Z. Notable southern families, 615, 3242; Some Tennessee heroes of the Revolution, 3243; Twenty-four hundred Tennessee pensioners, 3244
Army (English), 4290–4294
Army (Scottish): 4735–4737; in France, 4736; Solemn League and Covenant, 4737
Army (U.S.): German soldier in wars, 480; history, 477; officers, 478; orders and decorations, 475; pensioners (1883), 487; records, 476, 484, 485; registers, 470, 472, 474, 482
Army of the Solemn League and Covenant, papers, 4737
Arndt, K. J., and Olson, M. E. German-American newspapers and periodicals (1732–1955), 379

Arnold, J. N. Vital records of Rhode Island, 3068
Arnow, H. L. Seedtime on the Cumberland, 3245
Arsenault, B. L'Acadie des ancêtres, 1600, 4049; Histoire et généalogie des Acadiens, 1601, 4050; History of the Acadians, 4051
Arthur, J. P. Western North Carolina, 2573
Arthur, S. C., and Kernion, G. C. H. de. Old families of Louisiana, 1602
Artists, 139, 149
Ashby, B. M. Shenandoah valley, Virginia, 3502
Ashby, C. M. (and others). Guide to cartographic records in National Archives, 204
Ashe, S. A'C. (and others). Biographical history of North Carolina, 2574
Ashmole, E. Institution, laws and ceremonies of . . . Order of the Garter, 4471
Aspilogia, 5027, 5030
Assessors, New York city, 2499
Assiniboines tribe, 660
Association for the Preservation of the Memorials of the Dead in Ireland. Journal, 4608–4609
Association Test, New Hampshire, 2263
Athayde, J. B. de. Familias fluminenses, 3882
Atherton, J. J. Records of genealogical interest in Public Archives of Canada, 3942
Atiles, García, G. Kaleidoscopio, proso y verso, 3045
Atkins, C. E. Register of apprentices of Worshipful Company of Clockmasters, 4304
Atkinson, G. W., and Gibbens, A. M. Prominent men of West Virginia, 3717
Atlanta census (1850), 1162
Atlases: Alabama, 729, 748; America, 186–207; America, south, 628; British Isles, 4386, 4393; California, 846; Canada, 3981; Delaware, 1021; District of Columbia, 1082; England, 4388; Georgia, 1138; Hawaii, 1244; Illinois, 1323, 1360; Indiana, 1364a, 1364n, 1384, 1398; Iowa, 1409; Ireland, 4630, 4638, 4640; Kansas, 1475, 1481; Kentucky, 1577; Maryland, 1799; Mexico, 3917; Minnesota, 1987, 2005; Missouri, 2126; Montana, 2149; New Hampshire, 2289; New Mexico, 2394; New York, 2433, 2569; North Carolina, 2610; North Dakota, 2674; Oklahoma, 672, 2788; Ontario, 4081, 4090; Pacific northwest, 641a; Scotland, 4764, 4766, 4770; South Carolina, 3156; United States, 186–207; Wales, 4388, 4858, 4859;

*Index*

West Virginia, 3738; Wisconsin, 3801n, 3813; Wyoming, 3837
Attakapas country, 1639
Attakapas district, 1680
Attakapas gazette, 1603
Attakapas Historical Assoc. Special publ., 1604
Attwood, S. B. Length and breadth of Maine, 1692a
Auger, R.-J. Tracing ancestors through Quebec, 4052, 4097
Augusta county, Virginia: court records, 3525, 3537, 3663; marriages, 3542-3543
Augustan (The), 105, 292n
Augustan Society: bulletin, 105n; roll of arms, 5068-5069
Aurand, A. M., Index to Egle's Notes and queries, 2873
Austin Genealogical Society quarterly, 3320
Austin, J. O. Ancestry of thirty-three Rhode Islanders, 3069; Genealogical dictionary of Rhode Island, 3070; One hundred and sixty allied families, 3071
Austin's colonists, Texas, 3325n, 3390
Australia: 4902-4917; arms, 5062; birth, marriage, death and funeral notices, 4914b; colonial gentry, 4483n; colonial records, 4916; dictionary of dates, 4909; genealogical sources, 4905, 4908; gravestone inscriptions, 4911a; manual, 4907, 4914a; naturalization and denizen records, 4916
Australian dictionary of biography, 4903
Averett, W. R. Directory of southern Nevada place-names, 2198
Averitt, J. N. Georgia's coastal plain, 1135
Avery obituary index of architects and artists, 139
Aztec, New Mexico, 2406

Babbel, J. A. Lest we forget, 228
The backtracker, 810
Baglan, Book of, 4877
Bagley, C. B. History of Seattle, 3684
Bahamas, records, 4900a
Bailey, D. R. History of Minnehaha county, South Dakota, 3211
Bailey, F. W. Early Connecticut marriages, 958; Early Massachusetts marriages, 1844
Bailey, R. F. Dutch systems in family naming, 2293, 2423; Guide to genealogical and biographical sources for New York City, 2424; Pre-Revolutionary Dutch houses, 2294, 2425
Bain, R. Clans and tartans of Scotland, 4794
Baird, C. W. History of Huguenot emigration to America, 423
Baja California: bibliography, 3924; vital statistics, 3925
Baker, E. C. Guide to records in Leeward Islands, 4919; Windward Islands, 4920
Baker, J. Records of Massachusetts volunteer militia, 1719, 1901
Baker, J. H. (and Hafen, L. R.) History of Colorado, 926
Baker, M. Geographic dictionary of Alaska, 773
Baker, M. E. Bibliography of lists of New England soldiers, 574
Baker, P. R. 'Neath Georgia sod, 1136
Balch, T. French in America, 491
Baldwin, A. L. First settlers of South Carolina, 3120
Baldwin, J. Maryland calendar of wills, 1741
Baldwin, S. M. and R. M. Illustriana Kansas, 1442; Nebraskana, 2159
Balleine, G. R. Biographical dictionary of Jersey, 4881
Baltimore city and county, Maryland. Marriage licenses, 1742
Bancroft, H. H. California pioneer register, 842, 844; Chronicles of the builders of the commonwealth, 843; History of Central America, 3843; Register of pioneer inhabitants of California, 844
Bancroft Library, Berkeley: Archive General de Indias materials, 3845; Manuscript collections, 3849; Mexican and central America manuscripts, 3849
Bangor historical magazine, 1723n
Bangor Public Library. Bibliography of Maine, 1693
Banks, C. E. English ancestry and homes of Pilgrim fathers, 1845; History of York, Maine, 1694; Planters of the commonwealth, 329, 1846; Topographical dictionary of 2,885 English emigrants, 330, 1847; Winthrop Fleet of 1630, 575, 1848
Banks, T. C. Baronia Anglica concentrata, 4472; Dormant and extinct baronage of England, 4473
Baptismal names, 227
Baptisms: Boston, 1855-1856; New York city, 2503-2504, 2555; Pennsylvania, 2858, 3019; Puerto Rico, 3056; Scotland, 4761
Baptist Historical Soc. Transactions, 4531
Baptist quarterly, 4531
Baptists: Alabama, 744; bibliography, 4531-4533; Florida, 1111; genealogy, sources, 4529n; General Assembly, 4532; Geor-

371

*Index*

gia archives, 1187, marriages, 1219, obituaries, 1219a; German Baptist Brethren, 413–414; Ministerial directory, 419; Negro church directory, 418; New Jersey, 2325; New York register, 417; North Carolina, 2600, 2633; Rhode Island, 3087; South, 618; South Carolina, 3202; Southern, 417a; Utah, 3440

Barbados: Irish emigrants, 385; map, 4931; monumental inscriptions, 4928, 4930; records, 4922; source materials, 4922a

Barber, H. British family names, 4405

Barber, J. W. Connecticut historical collections, 959

———— and Howe, H. Historical collections of New Jersey, 2295; Historical collections of New York, 2426

Barck, D. C. Some references for genealogical searching in New York state, 2427

Barden, M. C. Vermont, 3454

Bardsley, C. W. E. Dictionary of English and Welsh surnames, 218; Our English surnames, 4407

Barlow, C. W. Sources for genealogical researching in Connecticut and Massachusetts, 960, 1849

Barnes, R. W. Marriages and deaths from the Maryland Gazette, 1742a

Barnes, W. C. Arizona place names, 783

Barnhart, J. D., and Carmony, D. F. Indiana, 1365

Barns, C. G. Sod house, 2160

Baronetages: British, 4471–4526; creations, 4512; Scottish, 4795–4796, 4798, 4800

Baronial Order of Runnemede, 285n

Baronies of South Carolina, 3178

Barron, B. Vaudreuil papers, 1605

Barrows, H. D. Memorial and biographical history of the coast counties of central California, 845

Barry, L. Beginning of the west, 1443; Kansa Indians and census of 1843, 653

Bartholomew, J. Gazetteer of British Isles, 4385; Handy atlas of Scotland, 4764; Handy reference atlas of British Isles, 4386; Quarter-inch map series of Ireland, 4628

Bartlett, E. F. Register of Colonial Dames of America, Mass., 1912

Bartlett, I. S. History of Wyoming, 3829

Bartlett, J. R. Census of inhabitants of colony of Rhode Island, 3105; Memoirs of Rhode Island officers, 3072; Records of colony of Rhode Island, 3103

Bartlett, N. Military records of Louisiana, 1606

Barton, H. W. Texas volunteers in Mexican War, 3321

Bartrum, P. C. Early Welsh genealogical tracts, 4833

Bateman, J. D. Great landowners of Great Britain and Ireland, 4474, 4666

Bateman, N. (and others). Historical encyclopedia of Illinois, 1294

Bates, L. E. Roster of soldiers and patriots of American Revolution in Tennessee, 3253

Bates, S. P. History of Pennsylvania volunteers, 2842

Battle Abbey roll, 4463–4464, 4470, 5014

Battle of Bennington, N. H., 2244

Baty, T. Vital heraldry, 4991

Baughman, R. W. Kansas post offices, 1828–1961, 1444

Baxter, J. H., and Johnson, C. Medieval Latin wordlist, 4662

Baxter, J. P. Pioneers of New France in New England, 576

Bay Colony: emigrants, 329; passenger lists, 329

Bay of Quinto, Ont., pioneers, 4094

Bayer, H. G. The Belgians, 2428

Beach, M. T. Wealth and biography of wealthy citizens of city of New York, 2429

Beal, M. D., and Wells, M. W. History of Idaho, 1271

Beam, J. A. Cemetery records of land between the lakes, 1491

Beard, F. B. Wyoming from territorial days, 3830

Beard, T. F. (Bibliography of modern genealogical works), 3, 275n

Beaulieu, A., and Morley, W. F. E. Province de Québec, 4098

Beck, L. C. Gazetteer of Illinois and Missouri, 1295, 2074

Beck, W. A., and Haase, Y. D., Historical atlas of California, 846; Historical atlas of New Mexico, 2394

Beckerlegge, O. A. United Methodist ministers, 4553

Beecher, W. J. Index to Presbyterian ministers, 455

Beedy, H. C. Mothers of Maine, 1695

Beers, D. G. Atlas of Delaware, 1021

Beers, H. P. French and British in old northwest, 1296

Beetle gazette, 292n

Belden & Co. Ontario atlases, 4090

Belgians in New York, 2428

Belknap, J. History of New-Hampshire, 2226-2227
Bell, Mrs. A. H. Abstracts of wills in the District of Columbia, 1068
Bell, G. M. Genealogy of "old and new Cherokee Indian families," 681
Bell, J. B. Anglican clergy in colonial America, 412
Bell, L. C. The old Free State, 3503; Sunlight on the southside, 3504
Bell, R. M. Searching in western Pennsylvania, 2843
Belliveau, P. French neutrals in Massachusetts, 1850
Beltz, G. F. Memorials of the Most Noble Order of the Garter, 4475
Benedict, G. G. Vermont in the Civil War, 3455
Benedict, J. D. Muskogee northwestern Oklahoma, 654
Bengal Army officers, 4940
Bengston, B. E. Pen pictures of pioneers, 2161
Benjamin, G. G. Germans in Texas, 3322
Bennett, A. F. Advanced genealogical research, 229; Finding your forefathers in America, 230; Guide for genealogical research, 231; Searching with success, 232
Benson, A. B., and Hedin, N. Swedes in America, 400
Bentley, E. P. Index to 1850 census of Pennsylvania, 2844
Benton, J. H. Early census making in Massachusetts, 1851
Benton county, Washington, records, 3716
Beresford, M. W. Unprinted census returns, 4188
Bergen, T. G. Genealogies of state of New York, 2430; Register of early settlers of Kings county, Long Island, 2431
Bergeron, R. and J. Parish records of marriages in French Canada, 3943
Bergling, J. M. Heraldic designs and engravings, 4992
Berkenmeyer, W. C. Albany Protocol, 2432
Bermuda, 4926
Bernau, C. A. Sixteenth century marriages, 4346
Bernheim, G. D. History of German settlements . . . in North and South Carolina, 2575
Berry, H. F. Register of wills . . . of Diocese of Dublin, 4619
Berry, W. Encyclopaedia heraldica, 5010
Berry's County genealogies, 4508n
Besterman, T. Family history, 4

Bestor, G. C. Index to Illinois military patent book, 1349-1350
Betham, Sir W. Abstracts of Irish wills to 1800, 4625n; Baronetage of England, 4476
Bethel, E. War Department collection of Confederate records, 551
Bevan, W. L. History of Delaware, 1022
Bevis Marks records, 4550
Bibaud, M. Dictionnaire historique des hommes illustrés du Canada, 3944
Bible records: Dutch, 608n, 2540; English New York families, 2540; Georgia, 1151; Kentucky, 1514, 1523a; Louisiana, 1670; mid-south, 622; Mississippi, 2060; Nevada, 2200; North Carolina, 2647; southern, 629; Tennessee, 1523a, 3236, 3259a; Texas, 3366
Bibliographia Canadiana, 3944a
Bibliographies, British: 4144-4169; Anglo-Jewish, 4549, 4551; Baptists, 4533; Catholics, 4536; chronology, 4279; Congregationalism, 4146; counties, 4173; county atlases, 4393; diaries, 4225; English and Welsh societies, 4158; family history, 4153, 4172; flags, 5114; genealogical manuscripts, 4151; genealogies, 15, 21-22, 33; genealogy, 4147, 4149, 4151-4153, 4181, 4186; gilds, 4171; heraldry, 4147; historical and archaeological publications, 4158; historical works, 4154-4157; local histories, 4169-4176; London directories, 4148; monumental inscriptions, 4361; municipal history, 4171, 4175; Norman people, 4183, Parliamentary representation, 4171; pedigrees, 4177-4180, 4182, 4184, 4187; record publications, 4164; seals, 5114; serial publications, 4159, 4165; topography, 4170, 4172, 4176; university registers, 4160; writings on British history, 4161-4163; 4166-4168;

Canadian: 3944a, 3945, 3957, 3996, 3999, 4006, 4007c, 4008, 4010, 4012, 4018; books and articles on history, 101-102; British Columbia, 4041, 4042a; church archives, 406; family history, 3945; Indian literature, 678; New Brunswick, 4063; Newfoundland, 4007, 4063; Nova Scotia, 4063; Ontario, 4093; place-name literature, 213; Prairie Provinces, 4071-4072; Prince Edward Island, 4063; Quebec, 4098, 4110; heraldry, 5114-5117;

Irish: 4566-4571; county, 4567; family history and genealogy, 4565a; genealogical collections, 4569; Highlands, 4566;

*Index*

history of Irish civilization, 4571; municipal history, 4568; sources for history of Irish civilization, 4571; university registers, 4570; Mexican, 3920, 3924;

Scottish: 4706–4716; family histories, 4707, 4714; genealogies, birth briefs, funeral escutcheons, 4709; historical and kindred clubs, 4712, 4715; newspapers, 4708; record publications, 4711; Scotch-Irish, 399n; topography, 4713;

United States: 1–33a; American church history, 405; American diaries, 18, 19; American directories, 32; American genealogical periodicals, 96; American genealogies, 15, 21–22, 33; American historical societies, 13; American history, 5; American newspapers, 8, 11, 12; American states, 6; Amish genealogies, 411; biography by Americans, 156; censuses after 1790, 182; church archives, 406; Civil War, 554; collective biographies, 160–161; county histories, 28–29; ethnic immigration, 361; ethnic newspapers and periodicals, 373; family histories, 4, 15, 21–22; Five Civilized Tribes, 692; foreign genealogical material, 33a; freemasons and freemasonry, 8a; French and British in old northwest, 1296; genealogical books in print, 31; genealogical works, 123n; genealogies in Library of Congress, 15; genealogy, 20, 30; German-American newspapers and periodicals, 379; Hispanic America, 3855; historical censuses, 174; histories in Library of Congress, 15a; history, 101–102; Huguenot books, 426; immigration, 361; indexes, 54; Indian literature, 652, 678; Jewish literature, 14a, 17a, 29a; local histories, 15a, 17, 20, 27; Lutherans, 448; maps, 187–188, 207; New England, 574, 594; passenger lists, 349; personal names, 223; Pilgrim Fathers, 606, 609; place-name literature, 213; Plymouth Colony, 606; printed genealogies, 10; Protestant diocesan histories, 458; public archives, 14; Quakers, 9, 459, 461a; Revolutionary War, 532; Spanish-America, 3868; surnames, 226; Trans-Mississippi West literature, 651; vital statistics, 174; Welsh Americana, 4827;

U.S. states: Alabama, 756; Alaska, 776, 782, 782n; Arkansas, 829; California, 854, 870, 906, 3924; Connecticut, 906, 986, 3924; Delaware, 1053; Florida, 1104, 1108; Georgia, 1164, 1223, 1241–1242; Idaho, 1290, 1292; Indiana, 1403; Iowa, 1435; Kansas, 1441, 1452; Kentucky, 1507, 1512; Maine, 1693, 1712, 1737; Maryland, 1820; Massachusetts, 1876; Minnesota, 1990; Mississippi, 2050, 2057, 2064; Missouri, 2126, 2131; Nevada, 2204, 2212; New Jersey, 2300, 2309, 2331–2332; New York, 2465, 2496, 2571; Long Island, 2549; North Carolina, 2590n, 2652; Ohio, 2764a, 2765, 2768; Pennsylvania, 2913n, 2951, 3008, 3033; Puerto Rico, 3057, 3064; South Carolina, 3137, 3203; Tennessee, 3239, 3283, 3301a; Texas, 3332, 3341, 3361, 3368, 3389; Vermont, 3468; Virginia, 3514, 3530, 3626, 3629–3631, 3639, 3650; West Virginia, 3722a–3723, 3756, 3759; Wisconsin, 3788, 3808;

Welsh: 4827–4832

Bicknell, T. W. History of state of Rhode Island, 3073

Bien, J. R. Atlas of state of New York, 2433

Biesele, R. L. History of German settlements in Texas, 3323

Big Bend country, Washington, 3708

Big Sandy Valley, 1520, 1527, 1534, 1578

Bigelow, S. F., and Hagar, J. G. Biographical cyclopedia of New Jersey, 2296

Biggers, D. H. German pioneers in Texas, 3324

Biggerstaff, I. Four thousand tombstone inscriptions for Texas, 3325

Billdt, R. B. Pioneer Swedish-American culture in central Kansas, 1445

Bille, J. H. History of Danes in America, 377

Bingham, H. J. History of Connecticut, 961

Binsfeld, E. L. Church archives in U.S. and Canada, 406

Biographical and genealogical history of Delaware, 1023; southeastern Nebraska, 2162

Biographical and historical index of American Indians, 679

Biographical and historical memoirs: Adams [and other] counties, Nebraska, 2163; eastern Arkansas, 811; Louisiana, 1607; northeast Arkansas, 812; northwest Louisiana, 1608–1609; Pulaski [and other] counties, Arkansas, 813; southern Arkansas, 814; western Arkansas, 815

Biographical and historical souvenir for counties . . . Indiana, 1366–1367

Biographical cyclopedias: District of Columbia, 1067; Maryland, 1743; Ohio, 2683–2864; Rhode Island, 3074

Biographical dictionaries: Chicago, 1297;

374

*Index*

Illinois, 1351; Iowa, 1440; Kansas, 1484; Missouri, 2133; Wisconsin, 3819
Biographical directory of American Congress, 164
Biographical encyclopedias: Connecticut, 962; Illinois, 1298; Kentucky, 1492; Massachusetts, 1852; New Jersey, 2297; Pennsylvania, 2845; Rhode Island, 3075
Biographical history of central Kansas, 1446
Biographical history of eminent and selfmade men of Indiana, 1368
Biographical record of Salt Lake City, 3429
Biographical sketches of old settlers and prominent people of Wisconsin, 3778
Biographical sketches of representative citizens: Maine, 1696; Massachusetts, 1853; New Hampshire, 2228
Biographical souvenir of the state of Texas, 3326
Biographies: Canadian, 3939–4012; English, 4280–4287, professions, 4288–4337; French Canadian, 3946; Irish, 4599–4605; Latin America, 3842–3868a; Scottish, 4731–4749; United States, 130–169; Welsh, 4841–4846
Bird, G. F., and Taylor, E. J. History of city of Bismarck, 2661
Birmingham, Rev. J. Private journals, expedition against Canada, 963n
Birmingham, S. The grandees, 433; "Our crowd," 2434
Births: Australia, 4914b; Boston, 1855–1856; Canada, 3982; Caracas, 3938a; Cherokee Indians, 690, 709; Connecticut, 974; Gaspé Peninsula, Quebec, 4111; Ireland, 4611n, New York city, 2570; Pallot's, England, 4355a; Pennsylvania, 2887; Scotland, 4761; Texas, 3353; U.S. citizens records, 86–87
Bismarck-Mandan Historical and Genealogical Soc. newsletter, 2662
Bismarck (N.Dak.), history, 2661
Björnson, V. History of Minnesota, 1989
Black, G. F. List of works relating to Scotland, 4706; Surnames of Scotland, 4776
Black, J. A. Your Irish ancestors, 4653
Black, W. G. Hints as to how to compile a pedigree in Scotland, 4783
Black Hawk War, Ill., 1327, 1362
Black Hills ghost towns, 3228a
Black Hills nuggets, 3212
Black Hills trails, 3212a
Blackfeet tribe, 663
Blackman, L. W. Women in Florida, 1096
Blackmansbury, 4253
Blackmar, F. W. Kansas, 1447

Blackwell, H. Bibliography of Welsh Americana, 4827
Blacks: in first census (1790), 176, free, 65, 374; Civil War troops, 564, Pennsylvania, 2842; genealogical aid, 236n; Revolutionary War, 528
Blair, R. Some early tax digests of Georgia, 1137
Blasones Mexicanos, 5082
Blegen, T. C. Norwegian migration to America, 390
Bloch, J. M. (and others). Account of Her Majesty's revenue in Province of New York, 2420
Block Island cemetery records, 3091
Blois, J. T. Gazetteer of Michigan, 1939
Bloom, J. H., and James, R. R. Medical practitioners in London, 4323
Bloom, J. P. Territory of Wisconsin, 3779
Bloxham, V. B. Key to parochial registers of Scotland, 4750
Bluegrass roots, 1492a
Board of General Proprietors of Eastern Division of New Jersey. Minutes, 2298
Boase, F. Modern English biography, 4280
Boddie, J. B. Colonial Surry, 3505; Historical southern families, 616; Seventeenth century Isle of Wight county, Virginia, 3506; Southside Virginia families, 3507; Virginia historical genealogies, 3508
Boddie, W. W. Marion's men, 3122
Bodensieck, J. Encyclopedia of Lutheran Church, 446
Bodge, G. M. Soldiers of King Philip's War, 1854
Bodin, G. A. Selected Acadian and Louisiana church records, 1610
Bodley, T. History of Kentucky, 1493
Boehm, E. H., and Adolphus, L. Historical periodicals, 95
Bogart, W. T. Vermont lease lands, 3456
Bogdan, F. Dictionary of Ukrainian surnames in Canada, 3947
Bohannan, L. C. Fourth census of U.S., 1820: Illinois, 1299
Bohemians, Texas, 3366a
Bolton, C. The founders, 283; Magna Charta barons, 284–285
Bolton, C. K. American armory, 5070; Marriage notices, 136; Real founders of New England, 577; Scotch Irish pioneers in Ulster and America, 397
Bolton, E. Immigrants to New England, 331, 578
Boltzius, J. M., and Gronau, I. C., registers, 1233

375

*Index*

Bond, J. J. Handy-book of rules and tables for verifying dates, 4276
Bond, M. F. Guide to records of Parliament, 4189
Bonfanti, L. Biographies and legends of New England Indians, 655
Bonner, J. C. Atlas for Georgia history, 1138
Bonnie, M. P. History, D.A.R. New Mexico state organization, 2399a
Boogher, W. F. Gleanings of Virginia history, 3509
Books of survey and distribution (Ireland), 4580
Booth, A. B. Records of Louisiana Confederate soldiers, 1611
Borden, M. E. Catalogue of books, D.A.R. data, New Jersey, 2309
Boren, L. H. and D. Who is who in Oklahoma, 2775
Borrero Crespo, M. Orígenes cuencanos, 3903
Bossu, J. B. Travels through part of North America formerly called Louisiana, 656
Boston, Mass.: births, baptisms, marriages, and deaths, 1855–1857; census (1707), 1859; early records, 1861; emigrants, 329; First Church records, 1918; passenger lists, 331–332, 1846; port arrivals, 332, 1860; records, 1861; report of Record Commissioners, 1861; tax-payers, 1858
Boston Public Library. Canadian manuscripts, 3948
Botha, C. G. Collected works, 4951; Extracts of marriages at Cape of Good Hope, 4952; French refugees at Cape, 4953; Published archives of South Africa, 4954
Bouchette, J. British dominions of North America, 4053
Bounty grant, *see* Lotteries
Boutell's heraldry, 4993
Bouton, N., and Hammond, I. W. Rolls of the soldiers of Revolutionary War, 2264
Bouwens, B. G. Wills and their whereabouts, 4366
Bowden, J. J. Private land claims in southwest, 637; Spanish and Mexican land grants, 2395, 3327
Bowen, J. L. Massachusetts in war, 1861–65, 1862
Bowen, R. LeB. Massachusetts records, 1863
Bowman, A. P. Index to 1850 census of California, 847
Bowman, J. N. Parochial books of the California missions, 848

Bowman, W. D. Bristol and America, 343
Boyd, P. History of northern West Virginia Panhandle, 3718
Boyd-Bowman, P. Indice geobiográfico de cuarenta mil pobladores Españoles de America, 3844
Boyd's marriage index, 4354
Bradford, T. C. Bibliographer's manual of American history, 5
Bradley, A. G. Colonial Americans in exile, 4014
Bradney, Sir J. A. History of Monmouthshire, 4834
Brainerd, John, journals (N.J.), 2327
Branches and twigs, 3457
Brasses, 4361–4365
Brault, G. J. Early blazon, 4967
Bravo Ugarte, J. Diócesis y obispos de la Iglesia Mexicana, 3910
Brayer, H. O. Pueblo Indian land grants of the "Rio Abajo," 657
Brazil: 3881–3886; first families, 3886; Portuguese nobility, 3883
Brecht, S. K. Genealogical record of Schwenkfelder families, 2846
Breese, E. Kalendars of Gwynedd, 4869
Brefny, B. de. Bibliography of Irish family history, 4565a
Bremer, R. A. Compendium of American historical sources, 6
——— (and others). Selected American historical sources, 7
Brennan, J. F. Biographical cyclopedia of distinguished men, Ohio, 2685
Brethren churches in America, 420–421
Brewer, J. M. Alphabetical list . . . Land Office (Md.), 1833n
——— and Meyer, L. Laws and rules of the land offices of Maryland, 1744
Brewer, M. M. Index to census schedules in printed form, 170–171
Brewer, W. Alabama, 724
Bridger, C. Index to printed pedigrees, 36, 4177
Bridgetown, Barbados, Jewish synagogue, 4930
Brien, L. Genealogical index of pioneers in the Miami Valley, Ohio, 2686; Miami Valley, Ohio, pioneers, 2686n
Briggs, G. Civic and corporate heraldry, 5088; National heraldry of the world, 5011; Scott-Giles's Civic heraldry of England and Wales, 5094
Briggs, W. General abstracts of wills proved, Register "Wootton," 4372
Brigham, C. S. History and bibliography of

376

American newspapers, 8; Seventeenth century place names of Providence Plantations, 3076
Brigham, J. Iowa, 1411
Bright, J. D. Kansas, 1448
Brinkley, H. E. How Georgia got her names, 1139
Bristol and America, 343
Bristol, England: emigrants, 343; passenger lists, 343
British-American loyalist exiles, 529
British and French in old northwest, 1296
British archivist, 4272n
British Columbia, Canada: 4041–4044; bibliography, 4041, 4042a; coast names, 4044; ethnic groups, 4043
British Columbia genealogist, 4042
British Columbia, Provincial Archives Library. Dictionary catalogue, 4041
British diaries, bibliography, 4225
British Dominions and former Dominions: 4893–4901; Australia, 4902–4917; British West Indies, 4918–4932; India, 4933–4943; New Zealand, 4944–4950; South Africa, 4951–4966; West Indies, 4918–4932
British emigration to America, 329–355
British Empire, dignitaries, 4286
British Friend, 4561n
British historical manuscripts in New York, 2517
British history, bibliography, 4161–4163, 4166–4168
British island areas: 4881–4892; Channel Islands, 4881–4883; Hebrides, 4884–4885a; Isle of Man, 4886–4889; Orkney Islands, 4890; Western Isles, 4884–4885a; Zetland, 4892
British Isles, see England
British mercantile claims (1775–1803), 492, 4190
British Museum, London. Grants, crests, arms, 4506; Index to pedigrees and arms, 4184; topographical works, 4384
British national bibliography cumulated index, 4144
British North America, see Canada
British officers serving in America, 468–469
British prisoners, Revolutionary War, 2550
British property confiscated in Revolutionary War, 492
British Record Soc. Index library, 4254
British settlers of 1820 in South Africa, 4959, 4962
British union-catalogue of periodicals, 4145
British West Indies: 4918–4932; Antigua, 4918, 4927; Barbados, 4922, 4922a, 4923, 4928, 4930, 4931; Bermuda, 4926; coats of arms, 4921n, 4924n; colonial gentry, 4483n; first settlers from England, 343; Huguenots, 422; Jamaica, 4925, 4932; Jews, 4930; Leeward Islands, 4919, 4927; monumental inscriptions, 4924, 4929; naturalizations of foreign Protestants, 2893; Protestants, 457; Virgin Islands, 4920a; Windward Islands, 4920
Brock, R. A. Documents . . . relating to Huguenot emigration to Virginia, 3510; Virginia and Virginians, 3511
Bromwell, H. E. Fiftyniners' directory, 927; Old Maryland families, 1745
Brook, M. Reference guide to Minnesota history, 1990
Brooke-Little, J. P. Boutell's heraldry, 4993; Fox-Davies's Complete guide to heraldry, 4995
Brossman, S. C. Our keystone families, 2847
Broughton, C. L. Marriage and death notices . . . , 2576
Browder, N. C. Cherokee Indians, 682
Brower, J. V. Kansas, 1449
Brown, A. Genesis of the United States, 3512
Brown, E. S. Oregon county boundary change maps, 2804
Brown, G. H. Lives of fellows of Royal College of Physicians of London, 4326
Brown, J., and Willard, A. M. Black Hills trails, 3212a
Brown, J. H. Indian wars and pioneers of Texas, 3328
Brown, M. J. Handy index to holdings of Genealogical Soc. of Utah, 37
Brown, M. R. Illustrated genealogy of the counties of Maryland and the District of Columbia, 1069, 1746
Brown, R. L. and R. E. Genealogical notes, South Carolina and Virginia, 3123, 3513
Brown, S. E., Jr. Virginia genealogies, 3514
Brown, T. J. Place-names of province of Nova Scotia, 4054
Brown, W. M. Biographical . . . history of New Jersey, 2299
Browne, J. A. History of Highlands, 4566
Brownell, E. E. Rhode Island census, 3105
Browning, C. H. Americans of royal descent, 270; Some "colonial dames" of royal descent, 271; Welsh settlement of Pennsylvania, 2848
Bruce, P. A. Virginia, 3515
Brumbaugh, G. M. Maryland records, 1747; Revolutionary War records, 3516
——— and Hodges, M. R. Revolutionary

377

records of Maryland, 1748
Brumbaugh, M. C. History of German Baptist Brethren, 413-414
Bruner, J. Who's who among Oklahoma Indians, 658
Brunk, G. R., and Lehman, J. O. Guide to select Revolutionary War records, 493
Brunk, H. A. History of Mennonites in Virginia, 3517
Bryan, M. G. Abstracts of colonial wills of state of Georgia, 1145; Passports issued by governors of Georgia, 1140
Bryan, W. B. History of the National Capitol, 1070
Bryan, W. S., and Rose, R. History of pioneer families of Missouri, 2075
Bryant, C. S. History of Sioux Massacre, 2019
Brydges, Sir Egerton, Collins's Peerage of England, 4492
Buck, W. S. B. Examples of handwriting, 4238
Buckingham, T. Roll and journal of Connecticut service in Queen Anne's War, 963
Buckland, C. E. Dictionary of Indian biography, 4933
Buffalo Valley, annals, 2936-2937
Builders of Hawaii, 1268n
Building a state, Washington, 3685
Bulletin des recherches historiques, 3949
Bullinger's postal and shippers guide for U.S. and Canada, 189, 3950
Bullock, L. G. Historical map of Ireland, 4629; Historical map of Scotland, 4765
Burdette, R. G. American biography and genealogy, 849
Bureau, R. (and others). Répertoires des mariages de l'île d'Orléans, 4099
Bureau of Indian Affairs, Records in National Archives, 669
Burgess, L. A. Virginia soldiers of 1776, 3518
Burgesses: Edinburgh, 4751; Glasgow, 4753
Burghers, New Amsterdam, 2497; New York city, 2497
Burgomasters and Schepens, minutes, 2500
Burke, A. M. Key to ancient parish registers of England, 4338; Prominent families of the U.S.A., 137
Burke, A. P. Family records, 4477, 4968
Burke, John. Genealogical and heraldic history of commoners, 4479-4480; Genealogical and heraldic history of peerage, 4478
―――― and Sir J. B. Extinct and dormant baronetcies, 4481

Burke, Sir John B. Genealogical and heraldic dictionary of landed gentry of Great Britain, 4482; Genealogical and heraldic history of colonial gentry, 4483; Genealogical and heraldic history of landed gentry of Ireland, 4669; Genealogical history of dormant, abeyant, forfeited and extinct peerages, 4484; General armory of England, 5013, additions and corrections, 4258n, 5105n, 5022; Prominent families in America, 4485; Roll of Battle Abbey, 4463; Royal families of England, 4447-4448; Visitation of seats and arms of noblemen, 4486
Burke's Distinguished families of America, 285a
Burke's Genealogical series, 4478n, 4487
Burke's Guide to Royal family, 4449
Burke's Landed gentry, 4488
Burlage, J., and Hollingsworth, J. B. Abstract of valid land claims of Texas, 3329
Burlingame, M. G., and O'Toole, K. R. History of Montana, 2143
Burlington (Vt.) free press, index to, 3473
Burlington note book, 2356
Burnett, A. C. Yankees in republic of Texas, 3330
Burnquist, J. A. A. Minnesota and its people, 1991
Burns, A. General description of works, 1749; Abstract of pensions of Kentucky, 1494; Abstract of pensions of North Carolina soldiers, 2577; First families of Utah, 3430; Index to Maryland colonial judgements, 1750; Kentucky genealogies, 1495; Major index to wills and inventories of Tennessee, 3246; Maryland account books, 1751; Maryland balances of final district book, 1752; Maryland early settlers, 1753; Maryland genealogies, 1754; Maryland inventories, 1755; Maryland marriage records, 1756; Maryland record of deaths, 1757; Maryland rent rolls, 1758; Maryland soldiers of Revolutionary War, 1759; Maryland will books, 1760; Missouri genealogical records, 2076; Missouri pension records, 2077; North Carolina genealogical records, 2578; Record of deaths in Kentucky counties, 1496; Record of wills . . . Kentucky, 1497; South Carolina pension abstracts, 3124; Third census . . . Kentucky, 1498; Virginia genealogies, 3519
Burns, B. S. Historical and genealogical materials in North Dakota State Historical Soc. Library, 2663

Burr, N. R. Narrative and descriptive bibliography of New Jersey, 2300
Burt, N. First families, 286
Burtchaell, G. D. Knights Bachelors in Ireland, 4521
────── and Sadleir, T. U. Alumni Dublienses, 4521, 4606
Butcher, B. L. Genealogical and personal history of upper Monongahela valley, West Virginia, 3719
Butler, W. F. T. Gleanings from Irish history, 4671
Butts, S. H. Mothers of some distinguished Georgians, 1141
Byers, W. N. Encyclopedia of biography of Colorado, 928
Byrne, F. J. Irish kings, 4672
Bywgrafiadur Cyrmreig hyd 1940, 4843n

C., G. E., *see* Cokayne, G.
Cabildo, New Orleans, 1671
Cache Branch Genealogical Library, Logan. Handbook for genealogical correspondence, 233
Cadastres abrégés des seigneuries: Montréal, 4102; Québec, 4101, 4103; Trois Rivières, 4104
Calamy, E. Ejected ministers, 4302n
Calcagno, F. Diccionario biográfico Cubano, 3896
Calcutta, Monumental register, 4938
Calendar of Virginia state papers, 3645
Calendarium genealogicum, Henry III and Edward I, 4211
California: 841–925; ancestral records, 924; argonauts, 873; atlas, 846; bibliography, 854, 906; cemeteries, 857; census (1850), 847; churches and religious organizations, 875–876; Civil War, 564, 850; county archives, 856, 878; county boundaries, 855; county histories, 915–922; first families, 907; genealogical records, 897; genealogical research, 851; Irish leaders, 899; land names, 872; local indexes in California libraries, 860; missions, 848; northern California cemetery inscriptions, 898; northern California marriages, 887; place names, 859, 867; Polish pioneers, 871; post offices, 865; public vital statistics records, 877; ship registers, Eureka, 879; Slavonic pioneers, 889; sources, 895; Southern California early burials, 900; Spanish-American pedigrees, 3866; Spanish and Indian place names, 908; vital records, 857; Yugoslavs, 862
California Society quarterly, index, 852

Callahan, E. W. List of officers of Navy of U.S., 466
Callahan, J. M. History of West Virginia, 3720
Cam, H. M. Hundred and hundred rolls, 4191; Rotuli hundredorum, 4191n
Cambridge University biographical registers, 4305, 4310
Camden colony (of loyalists), 4033
Cameron, H. C., and Underwood, E. A. History of Worshipful Company of Apothecaries, 4288
Cameron, K. W. Historical sources of Episcopal Diocese of Connecticut, 964
Cameron, V. R. Emigrants from Scotland to America, 333
Camp, A. J. Tracing your ancestors, 4423; Wills and their whereabouts, 4366
Campagna, D. Répertoire des mariages, 4100
Campbell, F. W. Canada post offices, 3951
Campbell, G., and Evans, I. O. Book of flags, 5088a
Campbell, J. San Domingo refugees in Pennsylvania, 2849
Campbell, J. B. Campbell's abstract of Creek freedmen census cards, 683; Campbell's abstract of Creek Indian census cards, 684; Campbell's abstract of Seminole Indian census cards, 685
Campbell, R. A. Campbell's gazetteer of Missouri, 2078
Campbell, R. G. Scotch-Irish family research made simple, 4654
Campeau, M. Check-list of parish registers, 4075
Campling, A. East Anglian pedigrees, 4178
Canada (*see also* United States): 3939–4143; Acadians, 3969, 4048–4052, 4061, 4064, 4097; Alberta, 4038–4040; ancestors, 3955n; Anglican parishes, 4296; armorial, 3988, 4005; arms, flags, floral emblems, 5071; atlas, 3981; bibliographies, 3944a, 3945, 3957, 3996, 3999, births, 3982; British Columbia, 4041–4044; catalogue, 3957n; Catholics, 638, 1616, 3961; census, 3953, 4007a, 4056, 4105, 4107; church archives, 406, 4000; clergy, 3939a; colonial gentry, 4483n; Croatians, 376, 3989; Crown land grants, 4029; Czechs, 3970; enlistments for west, 3988; French Canadians, 3993, 4003, 4004; gazetteer, 3952, 3984; Germans, 3998; Germans from Russia, 2670; heraldry, 3988, 4005; historical materials photocopied, 3977; historical societies,

bibliography, 13, directory, 3940; Huguenots, 422, 431, 3995; immigrant archives, 4009; Indians, 660, 678, 3999; Irish, 3966; land records, 4007b; land tenure (Loyalists), 4024; loyalists, 4014–4037; Manitoba, 4045–4046; manuals, 3955, 3960, 3973, 3974, 4021; manuscripts, 66, 3948, 3954, 4007c; Maritime Provinces, 4047–4069; marriages, 3943, 3994; Mennonites, 3968a; mercenaries and deserters, 3998, military, 4107a; New Brunswick, 4047–4069; Newfoundland, 4047–4069; newspapers, 3975; Northwest territories, 4070–4074; Norwegians, 394; Nova Scotia, 4047–4069; Ontario, 4075–4096; Palatines, 4025n; parish records, 3943, 3952a; periodical annual index, 3971; place names, 213, 3941; post offices, 3951; postal and shippers guide, 3950; Prince Edward's Island, 4047–4069; public archives, 3942, 3978, 4021; Quakers, 3968; Quebec, 4097–4139; Rebellion (1837–1838), 3976; Revolutionary War, 521, 3983, 3992a, 3998, 4025; Saskatchewan, 4140–4143; Scandinavians, 2450; serials, 75, 4008; Slovaks, 3970; Ukrainians, 3947, 3980; United Empire Loyalists, *see* Loyalists

Canada. Library of Parliament, bibliography of genealogical works, 4010

────── Public Archives. A la piste de nos ancêtres au Canada, 3955n; Checklist of census returns, 3953, 4056, 4105; Checklist of parish registers, 3952a; Manuscript inventories, 3954, 4106; Répertoire des récensements du Québec, 4107; Tracing your ancestors, 3955n

Canadiana, 3957

Canary Islands migration to Louisiana, 1688

Canby Historical Soc. Land laws and early settlers of Oregon, 2805

Candler, A. D. Colonial records of state of Georgia, 1148; Revolutionary records of state of Georgia, 1142

────── and Evans, C. A. Georgia, 1143

Canniff, W. History of province of Ontario, 4078; History of settlement of upper Canada (Ontario), 4015, 4079

Cannon, J. T. Index to military certificates, 3520

Canterbury, England: Marriage licenses, 4347–4348; Prerogative Court wills, 4367–4374

Cape Breton, topography, 4053

Cape May county magazine, 2301

Cape of Good Hope, South Africa: archives, 4951; census, 4955n; directory, 4955; French refugees, 4953; Huguenots, 4953n; marriages, 4952

Capon Valley, West Virginia, 3760

Cappon, L. J. American genealogical periodicals, 96

────── and Duff, S. F. Virginia gazette index, 3521

Capriles, A. M. Coronas de Castilla en Venezuela, 3937

Caracas, Venezuela: heraldry, 5085; registers, 3938a

Carbonneau, C. A. Tableau généalogique des mariages célèbres . . . de Rimouski, 4108

Car-del scribe, 106

Carey, C. H. General history of Oregon, 2806; History of Oregon, 2807

Caribbean archives, 4920a; loyalists, 4022

Caribbeana, 4921

Carleton, H. Genealogical and family history of Vermont, 3458

Carlevale, J. W. Americans of Italian descent in New Jersey, 2302; Leading Americans of Italian descent in Massachusetts, 1864

Carlisle, L. B. Vermont clock and watchmakers, 3459

Carman, H. J., and Thompson, A. W. Guide to principal sources for American civilization in city of New York, 2435

Carolina genealogist, 2579

Carolina herald, 3125

Carolinas: Huguenot settlements, 431; Irish immigrants, 387; Swiss immigrants, 357

Carothers, B. S. Maryland slave owners, 1760a; 9,000 men who signed Oath of Allegiance, 1761; 1778 census of Maryland, 1762; 1776 census of Maryland, 1763

Carpenter, Mrs. J. Gravestone inscriptions . . . (New Hampshire), 2233

Carpenter, T., and Franklin, H. 1880 mortality schedules for Kansas, 1450

Carpenter, V. C. Seventh census of U.S., 1850 [Tennessee], 3247; State of Texas federal population schedules, 3331

Carpenter, W. H., and Arthur, T. S. History of Vermont, 3460

Carreras, C. N. Hombres y mujeres de Puerto Rico, 3046

Carroll, C. Rhode Island, 3078

Carroll, H. B. Texas county histories, 3332

Carroll, K. Joseph Nichols and the Nicholites, 1764; Quakerism on Eastern Shore, 1765

Carseloway, J. M. Cherokee notes, 686; Cherokee old timers, 688; Cherokee pioneers, 687; Early settlers, 689; My journal, 690

Carter, C. E. Territorial papers of the U.S., 77: Alabama, 725; Arkansas, 816; Florida, 1097; Illinois, 1300; Indiana, 1369; Louisiana-Missouri, 2079; Michigan, 1940; Mississippi, 2030; Orleans, 1612; River Ohio, 637a, 2664

Carter, G. L. Early Missouri marriages, 2080; Index to 1830 census, 2081

Carter, K. B. Heart throbs of the West, 3431

Carter, N. F. Native ministry in New Hampshire, 2229

Cartledge, G. H. Historical sketches, 1144

Cartmell, T. K. Shenandoah valley pioneers, 3522, 3721

Cartography, *see* Maps

Cartularies, medieval, Great Britain, 4192

Cartwright, B. Some aliis of the migratory period, 1245

Cartwright, B. G. C., and Gardiner, L. T. North Carolina land grants in Tennessee, 2580, 3248

Casey, A. E. Amite county, Mississippi, 1613, 2031

———— and Dowling, T. E. P. O'Kief, Cosh, Mang, Slieve Lougher, and Upper Blackwater in Ireland, 4573

Casey, J. J. Personal names in Hening's Statutes, 3573

Casey, P. A. Louisiana in War of 1812, 1614

Casgrain, H. R. Biographies canadiennes, 3958

Cash, W. T. Story of Florida, 1098

Casper, H. W. History of Catholic church in Nebraska, 2164

Cassell, C. W. (and others). History of Lutheran church in Virginia and East Tennessee, 3249, 3524

Casteneda, C. E. Our Catholic heritage in Texas, 3372

Castle, H. A. Minnesota, 1992

Catalog of U.S. state census publications, 1790-1945, 180

Cathcart, W. Baptist cyclopaedia, 415-416

Catholic Record Soc. Publications, 4255, 4534

Catholics: bibliography, 4536; Canada, missions, 3961; Cleveland, 2715, 2719; English, 4534-4537; Florida, 1115; French Mississippi Valley, 1616; Kentucky, 1595; Louisiana, 1644; Maryland, 1817, 2114; Nebraska, 2164, 2172; Nevada, 2208; New Hampshire, 2252; New York city, 2472; nonjurors (English), 4535; Ohio, 2719; Pacific northwest, 638, 4070; Palatines returning to Holland, 2483; parish registers (English), 4255, 4534n; Pennsylvania, 2898, 2905; Quebec marriages, 4112; recusants (English), 4273; Texas, 3346, 3372; United States, 463-465; Utah, 3435; Wisconsin, 3793, 3798

Caudhill, B. C. Pioneers of eastern Kentucky, 1499

Cavaliers, army lists, 4294

Cavazos, Garza, I. Cedulario autobiográfico y conquistadores de nuevo León, 3911

Celtic place names, 4782

Cemeteries (inscriptions, records): directory, 45a; Arkansas, 818; California, 857, 898; Connecticut, 984; Georgia, 1136; Idaho, 1286; Illinois, 1313, 1352; Kansas, 1473, 2787; Kentucky, 1491, 1515; Louisiana, 1666; Maryland, 1783-1784; Massachusetts, 1930; Michigan, 1943, Mississippi, 2060; Missouri, 2086, 2115; Nebraska, Czech, 2180; Nevada, 2219; New Hampshire veterans, 2230, Oklahoma, 1473, 2787, 2800, 3380; Texas, 1473, 2787, 3380; West Virginia, 3730

Census: United States, 170-185; county schedules, 212; index to schedules, 170-171, 177; locations, 173; surnames in 1790 census, 217

Alabama (1820-1830), 719; (1830); 735, (1840), 763; Arizona (1860, 1864, 1870), 785, (1860), 2401, (1864), 788, (1866), 784; Arkansas (1830), 832, (1840), 833, (1850), 840; Atlanta, Georgia (1850), 1162; Bedford co., Pennsylvania (1784), 2878; Boston, Mass. (1707), 1859; California (1850), 847; Canada (1663), 4007a; Cape Town, South Africa (1800), 4955n; Chicago, Illinois (1870), 1315; Cincinnati, Ohio (1817), 2693; Connecticut (1790), 1018, (1800), 1017, 1020; Delaware (1790), 1044, 1047; District of Columbia (1800), 1081; English, unprinted (1841, 1851, 1861), 4188; Florida (1830), 1126 (1840), 1127, 1131, (1850), 1130; Georgia (1790), 1157, (1800), 1239n, (1820), 1178, (1830), 1156, 1220a, (1840), 1225, (1850), 1218, 1224; Great Britain (1851), 4199, 4387, 4397; Hamilton co., Ohio (1817), 2693; Idaho (1870), 1283-1284; Illinois (1810, 1818), 1333, (1820), 1299, 1334, 1357; (1830), 1317, (1840),

381

*Index*

1363, (1850), 1303, 1313; Indiana (1820), 1371, 1377; Indians: Cherokee, Alabama, Georgia, North Carolina (1835), 715, Cherokees (1851), 704, Creek (n.d.), 683-684, Kansa (1843), 653, Seminole (n.d.), 685; Iowa (1836), 1430, (1840), 1419, 1433; Ireland (ca. 1659), 4581, (1871), 4636, (1901), 4637; Kansas (1855), 1463; Kent co., Delaware (1800), 1055; Kentucky (1790), 1530, (1800), 1506, 1544, (1810), 1498, 1533, 1591, (1820), 1517, 1592, (1830), 1580, (1850), 1555, 1558, 1588; Long Island, N.Y. (1776), 2491n; Louisiana (1743-1753), 1605, (1758-1796), 1690, (1770-1789), 1679, (1810), 1599, 1682, (1820), 1599; Louisiana, French colony (1699-1732), 1659, German coast (1784), 1679; Maine (1790), 1734; Maryland (1776), 1747n, 1763, (1778), 1762, (1790), 1838, (1800), 1802, 1837, 1839; Massachusetts (1643-1765), 1851, (1779), 1872, (1790), 1931, (1800), 1932; Michigan (1820), 1948, 1984, (1830), 1953; Midlands, England (n.d.), 4237; Minnesota (1850), 2000; Mississippi (1820), 2039, 2051, 2056, (1830), 2040, (1840), 2065, (1850), 2041; Missouri (1830), 2081, 2092, 2128, 2140; Montreal (1731), 4118, (1765), 4119; Multnomah and Portland co., Oregon (1870), 2820; Natchez dist., Mississippi (1792, 1805, 1810, 1816), 2037; Nebraska (1854-1856), 2166, (1860), 2167, 2179; Nevada (1875), 2214; New Brunswick, Canada (1851-1871), 3953, 4056; New Castle, Delaware (1800), 1056; New Hampshire (1790), 2287, (1800), 2243, 2255, 2285; New Jersey (1793), 2368, (1850), 2369; New Mexico (1860), 2401; New Orleans (1770), 1679, (1777), 1679: Spanish in, (1791), 1671, Territory of Orleans (1810), 1686; New York (1663-1772), 2494, (1702, 1714, 1720), 2436, (1755, slave), 2529, (1790), 2562a, (1800), 2451, 2488; North Carolina (1787-1890), 2611a, (1790), 2654, 2580a, (1800), 2603, (1820), 2635-2636, (1840), 2634a, (1850), 2593; North Dakota (1850), 2000; Nova Scotia, Canada (1770, 1773, 1787), 4068; (1871), 3953, 4056; Ohio (1810), 2755n, 2756, (1820), 2745, (1830), 2743, (1840), 2722, 2770, (1850), 2711; Oklahoma (1860), 2803, (1890), 2791; Ontario, Canada (1842-1871), 3953, 4056; Oregon (1850), 2840; Pennsylvania (1790), 3023, (1800), 2916, 3017, (1810), 2963; Philadelphia (1850), 2988; Quebec (1666), 4132, (1744), 4130, (1762), 4131, (1792, 1795, 1798, 1805), 4121, (1825-1871), 3953, 4056, 4105; Rhode Island (1774), 3105, (1782), 3118, (1790), 3116, (1800), 3090, 3117; Rutherford co., Tennessee (1810), 3314; South Carolina (1790), 3204, (1800), 3200, (1820), 3161, (1830), 3147a, 1850 (3162); South Dakota (1850), 2000, (1860), 3213, (1870), 3230; Tennessee (1787-1791), 3287, (1790/1800), 3248, (1820), 3281, 3314, (1830), 3300, (1850), 3247, 3301; Texas, (1792-1847), 3347, (1829-1836), 3381, (1840), 3422, (1850), 3331, 3423, (1860), 3424; Trois Rivières, Canada (1765), 4119; Utah (1850), 3430, (1851), 3453; Vermont (1790), 3485, (1800), 3498; Virginia (1623), 3646, (1779), 3548, (1782-1785), 3644, (1790), 3559n, 3636, (1810), 3531-3532, 3585, 3618; Washington (1850), 3701, (1860), 3711; Washington co., Oregon (1880), 2820; West Virginia (1782, 1784), 3763; Westmoreland co., Pennsylvania (1783), 2878; Wisconsin (1836), 3827; Wyoming (1870) 3839, (1880), 3840; Yugoslav-Austria-Bohemia in California (1850-1880), 862

Centennial of the settlement of upper Canada by United Empire loyalists, 4034

Central America, *see* Latin America

Central Association of Libraries (Calif.), genealogy in, 26

Central European records, 91D

Central Genealogical Society's quarterly, 3357n

Central Illinois genealogical quarterly, 1301

Central Kentucky researcher, 1500

Central Provinces and Berar (India) inscriptions, 4935a

Century of population growth, 178

Certificates of entrance, Texas, 3381

Chabot, F. C. With the makers of San Antonio, 3333

Chadbourne, A. N. Maine place names, 1697-1698

Chadwick, E. M. Ontarian families, 4016, 4080

Chaffin, L. B. Sons of the west, 3831

Chalkley, L. Chronicles of Scotch-Irish settlement in Virginia, 3525

Chamberlain, E. Indiana gazetteer, 1390

Chamberlain, J. L. Universities and their sons . . . 138

Chambers, H. E. History of Louisiana, 1615

Chambers, R. Biographical dictionary of eminent Scotsmen, 4731

## Index

Chambers, T. F. Early Germans of New Jersey, 2304
Chamblin, T. S. Historical encyclopedia of Colorado, 929
Chancery proceedings, British, 4215
Chandler, M. C. Colonial and state records in South Carolina archives, 3126
Chandler, M. J. Guide to records in Barbados, 4922
Changes of name, Great Britain, 4416
Channel Islands: place names, 4402; wills, 4366
Chapin, G. M. Florida, 1099
Chapin, H. M. Colonial heraldry, 3079; Rhode Island in the colonial wars, 3080–3081; Rhode Island privateers in King George's War, 3082
Chapman, C. E. Catalogue of materials in Archive General de Indias, 3845
Char, T.-Y. Sandalwood mountains, 1246
Charlemagne, Emperor: 275, 276, 277; lineage, 325–326
Charleston, South Carolina, Free Library: index of wills, 3127; St. John's Lutheran church records, 3177n
Charlesworth, H. W. Cyclopedia of Canadian biography, 3958a
Charnock, J. Biographia navalis, 4330
Charters: medieval British, 4192n, Vermont, 3479, 3489
Chase, F. Gathered sketches from early history of Hampshire and Vermont, 2231, 3461
Chase, W. H. Pioneers of Alaska, 774
Chavez, A. Archives of Archdiocese of New Mexico, 2415; Origins of New Mexico families, 2416
Cheek, J. C. Selected tombstone inscriptions from Alabama . . . 617
Cheever, L. O. Newspaper collection of State Historical Soc. of Iowa, 1412
Cheney, C. R. Handbook of dates, 4277
Cherokees, 1202, 1220, 1228 (all lotteries)
Chester, J. L. Allegations for marriage licenses, London, 4351; Westminster, 4349
Chicago, Illinois: directory (1844), 1302; letters remaining in post office (1834–1836), 1304; vital records from newspapers, 1306
Chicago Genealogical Society. Chicago genealogist, 1307; Directory of Chicago, 1302; Illinois 1850 census, 1303; List of letters remaining in post office, Chicago and vicinity, 1304; Surname index, 1305; Vital records from Chicago newspapers, 1306

Chicago genealogist, 1307
Chickasaws, west Tennessee, 3318
Chihuahuan acquisition, Texas, 3327
Child, H. Heraldic design, 4994
Child, S. B., and Holmes, D. P. Check list of Historical Records Survey publications, 38
Chile: 3887–3893; Coats of arms, 3887
Chilenos in California, 888
Chinese immigrants: to Hawaii, 1246, 1269; to United States, 375
Chinn, T. W. Genealogical methods and sources for Chinese immigrants, 375
Chivalry, orders of, 247
Chreitzberg, A. McK. Early Methodism in the Carolinas, 2581, 3128
Christensen, K. Arkansas military bounty warrants, 817
Christian index, 618
Christian names, English, 4421
Christianson, T. Minnesota, 1993
Chronology, English, 4276–4279
Churches and religious organizations: Greater Detroit, 1954; Idaho, 1280; Indiana, 1381; Iowa, 1420
Church archives and records: American, 404a, 406–409; directory of repositories in America, 409; records, 55, 58, 408; Acadian, 1610; Canada, 4000; Colorado, 1942; greater Detroit, 1954; District of Columbia, 1780; Georgia, 1187; Illinois, 1321; Louisiana, 1610, 1625, 1640, 1644–1645, 1689; Maryland, 1780–1781; Massachusetts, 1887; Mississippi, 2048; Missouri, 2096; Nevada, 2208; New Hampshie, 2252; New Jersey, 2325, 2327; 2345; New York city, 2470, 2472; New York state, 2471, 2473; North Carolina, 2600; Pennsylvania, 2910; Rhode Island, 3087; Tennessee, 3278; Utah, 3440; Vermont, 3474; West Virginia, 3734; Wisconsin, 3798; Wyoming, 3835
Church brasses, 4361–4365
Church heraldry: 5088–5097; designs, 5089; Episcopal, 4991; Papal, 5091
Church history, bibliography, 405
Church of England: clergy, 4296, 4299–4301; in Maryland, 1832; records, 4229; records on foreign soil, 4202
Church of Scotland, records, 4826
Church of the Brethren, Eastern Pennsylvania, *see* Eastern Pennsylvania Church of the Brethren
Church vital statistics records: Illinois, 1319; Minnesota, 2002; New Hampshire, 2250;

*Index*

Rhode Island, 3085; Washington, 3693; West Virginia, 3731

Churches and religious organizations: United States, 404; Arkansas, 826; Minnesota, 2001; Montana, 2144, 2147; New Jersey, 2322; New Mexico, 2402; New Orleans, 1642; Oklahoma, 2784; Oregon, 2822; Pennsylvania, 2867; Philadelphia, 2996; Rhode Island, 3084; South Dakota, 3228; Tennessee, 3274; Vermont, 3472; Wisconsin, 3794

Cifre de Loubriel, E. Catálogo de extranjeros residentes en Puerto Rico, 3047; Inmigración a Puerto Rico, 3048

Cincinnati, Ohio, census (1817), 2693

Cincinnati Society, *see* Society of the Cincinnati

Citizenship lists, Texas, 3381

Civil heraldry: 5088–5097; England, 5094; Scotland, 5096; United Kingdom, 5088; Wales, 5094

Civil list: New York, 2521; Rhode Island, 3112–3114

Civil survey, Ireland, 4582, 4635

Civil War (England) (1642–49), army lists, 4294

Civil War (U.S.): 551–573; Andersonville diary, 562; Army, 558, 560–561, 564, 567–571; bibliography, 554n; burial lists, 559; Confederate military history, 556; Confederate officers, 565; Confederate records, 551; Five Civilized Tribes, 696; Hungarian participation, 572; Jewish participation, 573; Manual for researchers, 557; Navy, 558, 560–561, 565, 570–571; personal narratives, 554; records, 567; regimental publications, 554; Roll of Honor, 566; Union, 555, 566

States: Arkansas, 805; California, 850; Colorado, 931, 949; Connecticut, 968–969; Florida, 1103, 1124; Georgia, 1184; Illinois, 1310, 1327; Indiana, 1387; Iowa, 1426; Kansas, 1467; Kentucky, 1538–1539; Louisiana, 1611; Maine, 1699, 1717–1718; Maryland, 1777, 1840; Massachusetts, 1862, 1899–1900; Michigan, 1962–1963; Minnesota, 2013–2014; Missouri, 2115; Nebraska, 2185, 2187–2188; Nevada, 2213; New Hampshire, 2230, 2266a, 2277, 2288; New Jersey, 2354, 2385; New York, 2511, 2535; North Carolina, 2582b, 2606, 2612, 2620, 2622; Ohio, 2737, 2741; Oklahoma, 2790–2791; Pennsylvania, 2842, 2892n; Rhode Island, 3072, 3106; South Carolina, 3190; Tennessee, 3279, 3282, 3305, 3310, 3319; Vermont, 3455, 3487, 3500; Virginia, 3614, 3665; West Virginia, 3745; Wisconsin, 3803, 3807, 3807a, 3821

Claiborne, J. F. Mississippi as a province territory, 2032

Clans and tartans, 4791, 4794, 4805–4808, 4810, 4812, 4814, 4816–4817, 4820

Clare, W. Simple guide to Irish genealogy, 4655

Clare, Ireland: Books of survey, 4580; worthies, 4677a

Clarence, George, Duke of, descendants, 4458

Clark, A. Those were the valiant, 2396

Clark, B. N. List of pensioners of War of 1812, 3462

Clark, C. B. Eastern Shore of Maryland, 1766

Clark, G. T. Limbus patrum Morganiae, 4870

Clark, R. B. and S. C. List of Maryland works, 1767; Maryland Delaware genealogist, 1049, 1800

Clarke, R. S. J. Gravestone inscriptions: County Down, 4610

Clark, W. State records of North Carolina, 2626n

Clarke's Law list, 4320n

Clay, J. C. Annals of the Swedes on the Delaware, 1024

Clay, J. W. Extinct and dormant peerages of northern counties of England, 4489; North country wills, 4380

Clayton, W. W. History of York county, Maine, 1699

Clemens, J. U.S. Biographical dictionary, 1994

Clemens, W. M. American marriage records before 1699, 287; North and South Carolina marriage records, 2582, 3129; Virginia wills before 1799, 3526

Clement, F. Golden anniversary historical book, 3214

Clement, J. B. Descent from sureties from the Magna Carta, 288

Clergy: British, 4295–4303; Canadian-French, 3939a; middle colonies, U.S., 327; Scottish, 4738–4739; Welsh, 4841–4842

Cleveland, Roman Catholic Church, 2715

Cleveland, Duchess of. Battle Abbey roll, 4464, 5014

Clift, G. G. "Cornstalk" militia of Kentucky, 1501; Guide to manuscripts of Kentucky Historical Soc., 1502; Kentucky marriages, 1503–1504; List of offi-

384

*Index*

cers of Illinois regiment, 1308; Remember the 'Raisin, 1505; "Second census" of Kentucky, 1506

Clint, F. R. Colorado area key, 930; Pennsylvania area key, 2850

Clockmakers, apprentices (Great Britain), 4304

Cloyne, Diocese, marriage licence bonds, 4613

Coan, C. F. History of New Mexico, 2397

Coat-armor (periodical), 5102

Coat armour (periodical), 105n

Coat of arms (periodical), 4256, 5103

Coats of arms, *see* Heraldry

Cochrane, W. Canadian album, 3959

Cocke, C. F. Parish lines, Diocese of Southern Virginia, 3527; Southwestern Virginia, 3529; Virginia, 3528

Codazzi Aguirre, J. A. Escudo para les Islas Malvinas, 5083

Coderre, J. E. Searching in Public Archives (of Canada), 3960

Codman, O. Index of obituaries in Boston newspapers, 1865

Coe, H. B. Maine, 1700

Cohen, H. South Carolina gazette, 3130

Cokayne, G. Complete baronetage, 4490; Complete peerage, 4491; Peerage creations and promotions, 4491n

Coke, D. P. Royal Commission on Losses and Services of American Loyalists, 494

Coker, C. F. W. Records relating to Tennessee in North Carolina State Archives, 3249a

—— and Lennon, D. R. North Carolina Civil War records, 2582b; North Carolina's Revolutionary War pay records, 2582a

Colakovic, B. M. Yugoslav immigrations to America, 356

Coldham, P. W. English convicts in colonial America, 289; Genealogical gleanings in England, 579

Coleman, J. W., Jr. Bibliography of Kentucky history, 1507

Colket, M. B., Jr., and Bridgers, F. E. Guide to genealogical records in the National Archives, 40

Coll y Toste, C. Puertorriqueños, 3049-3050

Collectanea topographica et genealogica, 4257

College of Arms, London: 4977; Heralds' commemorative exhibition, 4979; history, 4987; officers, 4977n; records and collections, 4235, 4988

Collet, M. B. Catholic missions in Canada, 1616, 3961

Collier, M. Biographies of representative women in the South, 619

Collins, C. P., Jr. Royal ancestors of Magna Charta Barons, 272

Collins, E. J. Irish family research made simple, 4657

Collins, L. Historical sketches of Kentucky, 1508; History of Kentucky, 1509

Collins's Peerage of England, 4492

Colombia: 3894-3895; heraldry, 5087

Colonial and Revolutionary lineages of America, 290

Colonial charters, North Carolina, 2618

Colonial clergy, middle colonies, 327

Colonial commissions, New York, 2505-2506

Colonial Dames of America: Baltimore, Ancestral records, 291, 1768; Delaware, New Castle county wills, 1025; Georgia: Abstracts of colonial wills, 1145, Register, 1146; Some early epitaphs in Georgia, 1147; New Hampshire, Gravestone inscriptions, 2232-2233; New York, Library catalogue, 2437; Pennsylvania, Register, 2851-2852; Wyoming: Brides of the open range, 3832n, Pioneer biographies, 3832

Colonial Dames of royal descent, 271

Colonial genealogist (magazine), 105n, 292

Colonial gentry, British Empire, 4483

Colonial lists, general, 281-328; royal, 269-280

Colonial Office, London, records, 4900

Colonial pedigrees, surname index, 42

Colonial records: Georgia, 1148, 1158, 1193; Pennsylvania, 2974-2976; South Carolina, 3181, 3191

Colonial Soc. of Massachusetts. Publications, 1866

Colonial soldiers of Virginia, 3551

Colonies (U.S.), population maps, 191

Colorado: 926-956; argonauts, 927; church archives, 942; Civil War, 564, 931, 949; colonization, 956; county archives, 943; county histories, 929, 937, 944-946; directory, 952; gazetteer, 938, 939, 952; marriages, 935; place names, 947; public archives, 942; Spanish-American pedigrees, 3854; vital statistics records, 942

Colorado genealogist, 932-933

Colored, *see* Blacks

Colton, J. H. Colton's township map of Wisconsin, 3780

385

## Index

Columbia Historical Society, D.C. Records, 1071
Columbia Lippincott gazetteer of world, 189a
Columbia University Libraries. Avery obituary index of architects and artists, 139
Columbian centinel, 1842–1843
Colvin, H. M. Biographical dictionary of English architects, 4289
Combattants français de la guerre américaine, 514
Comité des anciennes familles, Québec. Livre d'or, 3962
Commander-in-Chief's Guard in Revolutionary War, 515
Commemorative biographical record: central Pennsylvania, 2853; Indianapolis, 1370; northeastern Pennsylvania, 2854; northwestern Ohio, 2688; upper lake region of Michigan, 1995; upper lake region of Wisconsin, 3781; upper Wisconsin counties, 3782; west shore of Green Bay, Wisconsin, 3783
Commissariot records: Edinburgh, 4752; Glasgow, 4754
Commissary Court, London. Index to testamentary records, 4379
Commoners, Great Britain and Ireland, 4479–4480
Commonwealth, Anglican parishes: 4296; newspapers, 4896
Companionage, *see* Peerages
Compendium of history and biography: central and northern Minnesota, 1996; North Dakota, 2665; northern Minnesota, 1997; western Nebraska, 2165
Complément de l'arbre généalogique de tout canadien français, 4115n
Comprehensive business directory of New Mexico, 2398
Conard, H. L. Encyclopedia of history of Missouri, 2082
Concise dictionary of American biography, 140
Concise dictionary (of national biography), (British), 4285
Confederate veteran, 552–553
Confederates, *see* Civil War
Conger, J. L. History of the Illinois river valley, 1309
Congregational churches, Massachusetts, 1934
Congregational Historical Soc. Transactions, 4538–4539
Congregationalism, bibliography, 4146
Congregationalist genealogy, sources, 4529n

Conley, P. West Virginia encyclopedia, 3722
Connacht, Ireland, transplantation to, 4642
Connecticut: 957–1020; births, 974; cemeteries, 984; census (1790), 1018, (1800), 1017, 1020; church archives, 964; church records, 995–996; Civil War, 554, 564, 968–969; Episcopal Diocese, 964; French and Indian Wars, 957, 977; gazetteer, 959, 987, 1009; gravestone inscriptions, 989; local history bibliography, 986; manual, 613, 960; marriages, 958, 979; Mexican War, 970; officials, 971, 1003; Particular Court records, 966; Pennsylvania settlers, 2903n, 3018; Pequot War, 1003; probate records, 971–972; public records, 965, 967; Puritans, 994; Queen Anne's War, 963; Revolutionary War, 970, 976, 992, 1005, 1006, 1019; towns, 971, 1012; vital statistics, 995; War of 1812, 970; Western Reserve, 2687, 2689, 2701–2703, 2769; wills, 1004
Connecticut ancestry (magazine), 973
Connecticut Historical Society collections, 975
Connecticut magazine, 978
Connecticut nutmegger (magazine), 980
Connelley, W. E. History of Kansas, 1451; Standard history of Kansas and Kansans, 1451n
—— and Coulter, E. M. History of Kentucky, 1510
Connor, R. D. W. Manual of North Carolina, 2623; North Carolina, 2584
Connor, S. V. Kentucky colonists in Texas, 1511; Peters colony in Texas, 3334
Conqueror (William I), 4463–4470
Conrad, G. R. First families of Louisiana, 1617
Conrad, H. C. History of Delaware, 1026
Constructive Californians, 853
Continental Army, *see* Revolutionary War
Conveyances: New Jersey, 2319; New York city and state, 2507
Cooke, B. C. Bibliography of monumental inscriptions in London, 4361
Cooper, J. W. Louisiana, 1618
Cooper, W. G. Story of Georgia, 1149
Cope, S. T. Heraldry, flags, and seals, 5114
Copley, G. J. English place-names, 4398
Coppage, A. M., III. Missouri cousins, 2083
—— and Wulfeck, D. F. Virginia settlers in Missouri, 2084
Copper state (magazine), 801
Corbin, J. B. Catalog of genealogical materials in Texas libraries, 1512, 3530

*Index*

Corbitt, D. C. and E. Papers from Spanish archives relating to Tennessee, 659
Corbitt, D. L. Formation of North Carolina counties, 2585
Cordell, E. F. Medical annals of Maryland, 1769
Corning, H. McK. Dictionary of Oregon history, 2808
Cornish, L. H. Sons of the American Revolution national register, 538
Cork and Ross Diocese, Ireland. Marriage licence bonds, 4612
Cork, Ireland: gravestone inscriptions, 4614; records, 4573n
Cornwall, J. How to read old title deeds, 4239
Cotterill R. S. Southern Indians, 691
Cotton, Jane, *see* Baldwin, J.
Coulter, E. M., and Saye, A. B. List of early settlers of Georgia, 1150
Coulter, J. W. Gazetteer of the territory of Hawaii, 1247
Coulter, O. H. Roster of Illinois soldiers residing in Kansas, 1310
County atlases, British Isles, bibliography, 4393
County court note-book, 1771
County families of the United Kingdom, 4526
County Genealogical Research Pubs. Arkansas cemetery inscriptions, 818
County histories (U.S.), bibliography, 29
County maps (U.S.), 199
County pedigrees, printed, British, 4198
County records, British, 4194–4195
Coursey, O. W. Who's who in South Dakota, 3215
Court of Arches (London), records, 4218, 4221
Court of Requests, British, 4215
Court of the Lord Lyon (Scotland), list of officers, 4748
Cousin huntin' (magazine), 2438
Covington, J. W. Story of southwestern Florida, 1100
Cowan, I. B. Parishes of medieval Scotland, 4717
Cowan, M. R. National Soc. Women Descendants of the Ancient and Honorable Artillery Co. Members in colonial period, 1915
Cowan, R. E. and R. G. Bibliography of the history of California, 854
Cowell, B. Spirit of '76 in Rhode Island, 3083
Cox, E. M. 1854–1855–1856 Nebraska state census, 2166; 1860 Nebraska territory census, 2167; 1820 Indiana federal census, 1371
——— and Culley, L. F. M. Kentucky records, 1513
Cox, J. C. Parish registers of England, 4339
Coy, O. C. California county boundaries, 855; Guide to county archives of California, 856
Crabtree, B. G. Guide to private manuscript collections in North Carolina State Archives, 2586
Craig, H. S. [South Jersey publications], 2305
Craig, R. D. Resident proprietors of Connecticut Western Reserve, 2689
Cram, K. J. Guide to use of genealogical material in Tennessee State Library, 3250
Crawford county, Wisconsin, 3790
Crawford, D. G. History of Indian Medical Service, 4934; Roll of Indian Medical Service, 4935
Crawford, L. F. History of North Dakota, 2666
Crawford, M. C. Famous families of Massachusetts, 1867; In the days of the Pilgrim Fathers, 580
Creek War, Alabama units, 717
Creekmore, P. Tennessee marriage records, 3308
Creeks, 1202
Crees, 660
Creole Mobile, 614a
Creoles: of German descent in Louisiana, 1622; of New Orleans, 1652
Cresap War, Pennsylvania, 2896
Crespo Pózo, J. S. Blasones y linajes de Galicia, 5084; Linajes de Galicia en el Peru, 3932
Crests: Great Britain, 5016; Ireland, 5016
Crew, H. W. Centennial history of the city of Washington, 1072
Crick, B. R., and Alman, M. Guide to manuscripts relating to America in Great Britain and Ireland, 41
Crickard, M. W. 1810 census, 3531; Index to 1810 Virginia census, 3532
Crim, R., and Herberger, M. Illinois cemetery inscriptions, 1352
Crisp, F. A. Fragmenta genealogica, 4260; Visitation of England and Wales, 4503, 5023; Visitation of Ireland, 4678, 5036
Crispin, M. J., and Macary, L. Falaise roll, 4465
Criswell, H. D. Finding your ancestor, 234
Crittenden, C. C., and Lacy, D. Historical

*Index*

records of North Carolina, 2599
Croatians: America, 3987; Canada, 3989; immigrants, 356; Nevada, 2202
Crocchiola, S. F. L. [Town histories of New Mexico], 2399
Crocket, G. L. Two centuries in east Texas, 3335
Crockett, W. H. Soldiers of Revolutionary War buried in Vermont, 3463; Vermonters, 3464
Crockford's Clerical directory, 4296
Crofton, O. S. Inscriptions . . . in Central Provinces and Berar, 4935a; List of inscriptions . . . in H. E. H. the Nizam's dominions, 4936; List of inscriptions . . . in Rajputana and Central India, 4937
Cromarty, sasines for sheriffdoms, 4759
Crone, J. S. Concise dictionary of Irish biography, 4599
Cross, H. E. Old Amish genealogy, 2690
────── and Hostetler, B. Index to selected Amish genealogies, 411, 2856
Crossly, A. Peerage of Ireland, 4675
Crows tribe, 660, 663
Crowther, G. R., III. Surname index to 65 volumes of colonial and Revolutionary pedigrees, 42
Crozier, W. A. Early Virginia marriages, 3533; General armory, 5072; Key to southern pedigrees, 620; Virginia colonial militia, 3534; Virginia county records, 3535, 3654; Virginia heraldica, 3536
Cruikshank, E. A. Settlement of United Empire loyalists on upper St. Lawrence, 4017
Crumrine, B. Virginia court records in southwestern Pennsylvania, 2857, 3537
Cuba: 3896-3898; gazetteer, 3896a; noble families, 3897-3898
Cuddy, M. L., and Scott, J. J. British Columbia in books, 4042a
Cuenca, Ecuador, genealogy, 3903
Cuestiones (magazine), 3864n
Cullum, G. W. Biographical register of officers and graduates of U.S. Military Academy, 467
Culver, F. B. Society of Colonial Wars, genealogies, 1835
Cumberland region, Tennessee, 3245, 3289
Cumming, M. County atlas reprints (Canada), 4081
Cumming, W. P. Southwest in early maps, 621
Cumulative magazine subject index, 97
Cunningham, R., and Evans, E. Handy guide to Genealogical Library (of L.D.S.), 43
Cunz, D. Maryland Germans, 1772
Currer-Briggs, N. Colonial settlers and English adventurers, 581; English adventurers, 3539n; English wills of colonial families, 293, 3538; Virginia settlers and English adventurers, 3539
Curry, C. C. Records of Roman Catholic church in U.S., 465
Curry, J. C. Michigan Revolutionary War pension payments, 1941
Curtis, M. B. Bibliography of Five Civilized Tribes, 692; Bibliography of Kansas, 1452; Early east Tennessee tax lists, 3251
Cushing, T., and Sheppard, C. E. History of counties of Gloucester [and others], New Jersey, 2306
Cushman, H. B. History of the Choctaw, 693
Customs records, colonial New York, 2420
Cuthbertson, J. Register of marriages, 2858
Cutler, H. G. History of Florida, 1101
Cutler, W. G. History of state of Kansas, 1453
────── and Adams, W. F. Genealogical and personal memoirs relating to families of Massachusetts, 1870
Cutolo, V: O. Nuevo diccionario biográfico argentino, 3869
Cutter, W. R. American families, 140a; Consolidated index to Cutter's genealogical sets, 44; Genealogical and family history of Connecticut, 982; Genealogical and personal memoirs relating to Boston and early Massachusetts; Memorial encyclopedia of Massachusetts, 1869; New England families, 582; New York state genealogies and family histories, 2439-2443
Cutter index, 593
Cutts, D. R. Aids to place names: New York state, 2444
Cyclopedias: American biography, 135n; North and South Carolina, 2587, 3131; Michigan, 1942; New Jersey, 2308
Cymric Quakers, 2894
Cymry of '76, 519
Czechs: Canada, 3970; Nebraska, 2180-2181, 2192; Texas, 3366a

D.A.R., *see* Daughters of the American Revolution
Dahl, T. Linajes en México, 3912
Dailey, J. F. Official roster of soldiers of American Revolution, Ohio, 2691n

*Index*

Dakota territory (magazine), 3216
Dakota Territory, *see* North Dakota and South Dakota
Dalmatians, Nevada, 2202
Dalton, C. English army lists, 4291; Scots army, 4735
D'Alton, J. Illustrations . . . on King James's Irish army list, 4600
Daly, J. Descriptive inventory of archives of Philadelphia, 2859
Dandridge, D. American prisoners of the Revolution, 495
Danes: America, 377; New York, 2450n
Dangberg, G. M. Carson Valley, 2199
Daniel, F. Histoire des grandes familles françaises du Canada, 3963; Nos gloires nationales, 3964
Daniell, L. E. Personnel of Texas state government, 3336; Texas—the country and its men, 3337; Types of successful men of Texas, 3338
Data processing in genealogical research, 256
Dates, 4276-4279
Daughters of Colonial Wars. Members and history and index of ancestors, 294
Daughters of Dacotah, 3235a
Daughters of Dakota, 3217
Daughters of Founders and Patriots of America: Connecticut, Family records, 983; Lineage book, 295-296; Nebraska, Founders and patriots of Nebraska, 2168
Daughters of the American Colonists: Lineage book, 297-298; Missouri, History and lineage book, 2085; Nevada, Miscellaneous Bible and family records, 2200; Pennsylvania, History, 2860
Daughters of the American Revolution. Annual reports, 496; Catalogue of genealogical and historical works in the library, 45; Index to burials of Revolutionary War soldiers, 497; Index of rolls of honor, 499; Lineage books, 498; Magazine, 500; Genealogical guide, 501-504; Marked graves of Revolutionary soldiers, 505; Patriot index, 506-508
―――― Alabama, Index to Alabama wills, 726, Some early Alabama churches, 727; Arkansas, Roster, 819; California, Index to vital records from cemeteries in California, 857; Records of families of California pioneers, 858; Colorado, Pioneers of San Juan country, 934; Georgia, Collections of Georgia chapters, 1151, Historical collections, 1152, Membership roll, 1153; Idaho, History and register, 1272; Illinois, Directory of members, 1311; Roster of Revolutionary War soldiers and widows, 1312; Indiana, Roster of soldiers and patriots of the American Revolution buried in Indiana, 1372; Iowa, Iowa pioneers, 1413; Kentucky, Kentucky Bible records, 1514; Kentucky cemetery records, 1515; Revolution ancestors, 1516; Louisiana, Louisiana tombstone inscriptions, 1619; Maine, Maine Revolutionary soldiers' graves, 1701, Roster and ancestral roll, 1702; Maryland, Directory, 1773; Massachusetts, Directory of members, 1871; Michigan, Cemetery records, 1943, Historical records, 1944; Mississippi, Family records, 2033, Mississippi Daughters and their ancestors, 2043; Missouri, Cemetery records, 2086, Missouri state history, 2087; Nebraska, Collection of Nebraska pioneer reminiscences, 2169; New Hampshire, Directory of members, 2234, State history, 2235; New Jersey, Catalogue of books, 2309; New Mexico, State organization history, 2399a; New York, Master index, 2445; North Carolina, Roster of soldiers, 2588; Ohio, Official roster of soldiers of American Revolution, 2691; Oklahoma, Roster, 2776-2777; Oregon, Genealogical records, 2831n, Roster of ancestors, 2809; South Carolina, Roster and ancestral roll, 3132; Tennessee, Membership roster, 3252; Mid-south Bible records, 622; Roster of soldiers, 3253; Virginia, First (and second) marriage records of Augusta county, 3542-3543, Roster, 3540-3541; Washington, History and register, 3686; West Virginia, Bibliography of local history and genealogy, 3722a; Wisconsin, Roster, Revolutionary War ancestors, 3784

―――― Genealogical Advisory Committee. Is that lineage right? 235
Daughters of the American Revolution Library, Washington, D.C.: catalog, 45; index to Tennessee wills and inventories in the library, 3246
Daughters of the Barons of Runnemede. Members, 299
Daughters of the Republic of Texas: Founders and patriots, 3339-3340; Texas history collection, 3341
Daughters of Utah Pioneers. Heart throbs of the West, 3431; Our pioneer heritage, 3432; Treasures of pioneer history, 3433
David, L. O. Souvenirs et biographies, 3965

*Index*

Davidson, G. G. Early records of Georgia, 1154

Davidson, K. H., and Ashby, C. M. Records of Bureau of the Census, 184

Davies, T. R. Book of Welsh names, 4862

Davin, N. F. Irishmen in Canada, 3966

Davis, C. C. Revolution ancestors of Kentucky DAR, 1516

Davis, Edwin A. Story of Louisiana, 1620

Davis, Ellis A. Historical encyclopedia of Louisiana, 1621; Historical encyclopedia of New Mexico, 2400

—— and Grobe, E. H. New encyclopedia of Texas, 3342

Davis, G. R. C. Medieval cartularies of Great Britain, 4192

Davis, H. A. Some Huguenot families of South Carolina and Georgia, 1155, 3133–3134

Davis, I. C. Bibliography of West Virginia, 3723

Davis, S. P. History of Nevada, 2201

Day, J. M. Texas almanacs, 3343

—— and Dunlap, A B. Maps of Texas, 3344

Day, S. Historical collections of Pennsylvania, 2861

De Armond, R. N. Founding of Juneau, 775

Deaths: Australia, 4914b; Boston, Mass., 1855–1856; Caracas, 3938a; Cherokee Indians, 690; Civil War Union solders, 566; District of Columbia, 1087, 1094; Georgia, 1200, 1224, 1235–1236; Illinois, 1355; Kentucky, 1496; Maryland, 1742a, 1757; Massachusetts, 2246; Mexican War, 550a; Mississippi, 2045; New England, 2246; New Hampshire, 2246; New York city, 2570; North Carolina, 2594; Pennsylvania, 3041; Revolutionary War, 531; South Carolina, 3176, 3207–3208; southern California, 900; U.S. citizens records, 86–87; War of 1812, 549; Wilmington, Delaware, 1065

Debrett's Baronetage, knightage, and companionage, 4493

Debrett's Correct form, 4510

Debrett's Correct peerage, 4494n

Debrett's Peerage, 4494

de Burgh, U. L. Landowners of Ireland, 4677

Decatur Genealogical Soc. publications, 1313

Decorations and medals, Irish Republic, 4691

De Courcy, B. W. Genealogical history of Milesian family, 4676

Deeds: Albany, N.Y., 2421; British, ancient, 4212, medieval, 4192n, 13th-19th centuries, 4192a; 16th-19th centuries, 4239; Choctaw-Chickasaw, 699–700; Dublin, 4621; Lancaster county, Pa., 2949; Long Island, N. Y., 2498; New Jersey, 2344; New York city, 2498; Rensselaerswyck, 2421; Scottish, 4758; Suffolk county, Mass., 1929; West Augusta, Va., 3025, 3663

Deep south genealogical quarterly, 623, 728

Defenbach, B. Idaho, 1273

De Forest, L. E. American colonial families, 300

DeHass, W. History of early settlements and Indian Wars of Western Virginia, 3724

Deiler, J. H. Settlement of German coast of Louisiana, 1622

De Lancey's Brigade (Loyalist), order book, 2526

Delano, J. Washington directory (1822), 1073

Delaware: 1021–1065; archives, 1028; atlas, 1021; bibliography, 1053; census (1790), 1034, (1800), 1044, 1047; Cherokee allotments, 712; church archives, 1041; churches and religious organizations, 1040; Civil War, 564; county archives, 1042; gazetteer, 1037; Governor's register, 1029; Indians, 712; land titles, 1027; loyalists, 1038; original settlements, 1036; Pennsylvania archives, 1052; Revolutionary War, 1028, 1060–1061; Swedes, 1024, 1045; tax list, 1771

Delaware history (magazine), 1030

Delgado, D. J. Guide to Wisconsin state archives, 3785

Delwyn Associates: 1830 census of Georgia, 1156; Substitutes for Georgia's lost 1790 census, 1157

Deming, L. List of principal civil officers of Vermont, 3465

DeMond, R. O. Loyalists in North Carolina, 2589

Denholm-Young, N. Country gentry in fourteenth century, 5015

Denig, E. T. Five Indian tribes of the upper Missouri, 660

Dent, J. C. Canadian portrait gallery, 3967

Denver, history, 948

Denver Public Library, guide to collections, 932–933

Deputy Keeper of Public Records of Ireland. Reports, 4586

Derozorario, M. Complete monumental reg-

*Index*

ister . . . in and about Calcutta, 4938
De Saussure, W. G. Names as far as can be ascertained of officers who served in South Carolina regiments, 3135
Descent (magazine), 4904
Des Cognets, L., Jr. English duplicates of lost Virginia records, 3544
Deserters in Revolutionary War, 536–537
Detroit Society for Genealogical Research magazine, 107, 1945–1946
Deutrich, M. E. American church archives, 407; Preliminary inventory of War Department collection of Revolutionary War records, 509
Der Deutsche Pioneer, 2692
De Valinger, L. Calendar of Kent county, Delaware probate records, 1031; Calendar of Sussex county, Delaware probate records, 1032; Court records of Kent county, 1033; Reconstructed 1790 census of Delaware, 1034
De Ville, W. Acadian church records, 1623; Calendar of Louisiana colonial documents, 1624; First settlers of Pointe Coupée, 1625; Gulf Coast colonials, 1626; Louisiana colonial marriage contracts, 1627; Louisiana colonials, 1628; Louisiana recruits, 1629; New Orleans French, 1630; Opelousas, 1631
———— (and others). Marriage contracts of Attakapas Post, 1632
Dewitz, P. W. H. Notable men of Indian territory, 661
De Wolfe, E. Guide to state of California, 859
Dexter, F. B. Biographical sketches of graduates of Yale College, 141–142; Obituary record of graduates, 143
Dexter, H. M. Congregationalism of last three hundred years, 4146
Diaries: American, annotated bibliography, 19; American, in manuscript, 18; British, 4225; Mormon, 445; New England, 587; Tennessee 3312
Dibben, A. A. Title deeds 13th-19th centturies, 4192a
Diccionario Porrúa de historia . . . de México, 3913
Dickoré, M. P. Census for Cincinnati, 2693
Dickson, R. J. Ulster emigration to colonial America, 334, 2862
Dictionaries: American biography, 144; American surnames, 222; Canadian biography, 3967a; ecclesiastical terms, 4528; English and Welsh surnames, 218; national biography (British), 4281–4284;
New England settlers, 584, 607; South African biography, 4956; Welsh biography, 4843; Welsh surnames, 218
Diefenbach, Mrs. H. B. Index to grave records of soldiers of War of 1812 buried in Ohio, 2694
Digested summary and alphabetical list of private claims, 483
Dignities, book of, 4286
Dillon, R. H. Local indexes in California libraries, 860
Dimitry, C. P. Louisiana families, 1602n, 1674
Dinsmore, J. W. Scotch-Irish in America, 2863
Dionne, N.-F. Canadiens-français, 4109; Inventaire chronologique des ouvrages publiés à l'étranger en diverses langues sur Québec, 4110; Québec et Nouvelle France, 4110n
Directories: American, 32; ancestral heads of New England families, 591; British, 4193; census records (U.S.), 177; Colorado, 952; England and Wales, 4228; Genealogists and local historians (British), 4312; Historical societies and agencies in U.S. and Canada, 34; London, 4148; medical (British), 4324–4329; Nevada territory, 2223; New York city, 2481; Oklahoma, 2796; passenger arrivals (U.S.), 370; petitions (U.S.), 177; poll lists (U.S.), 177; post offices, America and Canada, 189; tax lists (U.S.), 177; U.S. cemeteries, 45a
District of Columbia: 1066–1095; atlas, 1082; census (1800), 1081; church archives, 1079, 1780; churches and religious organizations, 1078; Civil War, 564; counties, 1069, 1746; deaths, 1087, 1094; directory (1822), 1073; gazetteer, 1085; guide to genealogical research in, 228; marriages, 1087, 1095; patentees of land, 1077, 1774; rents and titles, 1076; Revolutionary War, 1074; vital records, 1083–1084, 1086; wills, 1068
Disturnell, J. Gazetteer of state of New York, 2446
Divorces: Maryland, 1811; records, U.S. citizens, 88
Dixon, N. and N. Southeastern Kentucky census of 1820, 1517
Dixon, S. H., and Kemp, L. W. Heroes of San Jacinto, 3345
Doane, G. H. Searching for your ancestors, 236
Documents relating to the colonial history

391

*Index*

of New Jersey, 2292, 2310
Documents relative to colonial history of state of New York, 2447
Dodd, D. B. Historical atlas of Alabama, 729
Doddridge, J. Notes on settlement and Indian Wars of Western parts of Virginia, 2864, 3725
Dodge, P. C. Encyclopedia, Vermont biography, 3466
Dolan, J. R. English ancestral names, 4408
Domesday Book, 4466, 4470
Domesday inquests, 4191n
Dominican Republic, 3899–3902
Dominguez, F. A. Missions of New Mexico, 2392
Dominions Office, London, records, 4900
Donaldson, T. Idaho of yesterday, 1275
Donation land claims, *see* Land
Donehoo, G. P. Pennsylvania, 2865
Dorchester, Mass., founding of, 595
Dorland, A. G. History of Society of Friends in Canada, 3968n; Quakers in Canada, 3968
Dorling, E. E. Heraldry of the church, 5089
Dorman, J. F. Guide to counties of Virginia, 3545; Virginia genealogist, 3657; Virginia Revolutionary pension applications abstracted, 3546
Dornbusch, C. E. Regimental publications ... of Civil War, 554
Douglas, Sir R. Baronage of Scotland, 4800; Peerage of Scotland, 4801
Douglas, W. Douglas register, 3547
Douglass, R. S. History of southeast Missouri, 2088
Douthit, R. L. Ohio resources for genealogists, 2695
Dovell, J. E. Florida, 1102
Dow, G. F. Probate records of Essex county, 1896; Records of quarterly courts of Essex county, 1895
Dow, J. History of town of Hampton, 2236
Dowdall deeds, 4591
Dowdall family papers, Ireland, 4591
Down, Ireland, gravestone inscriptions, 4610
Downes, R. C. Evolution of Ohio county boundaries, 2696; History of Lake Shore, Ohio, 2697
Downs, W. S. Men of New England, 583
Doyle, J. W. E. Official baronage of England, 4495
Drake, F. S. Dictionary of American biography, 146
Drake, S. G. Biography and history of Indians in North America, 662; Book of the Indians, 662n; Indian biography, 662n; Result of some researches among the British archives, 335
Draper, Mrs. A. G. New Hampshire Revolutionary pensioners, 2237; New Hampshire Revolutionary pensioners omitted from any printed list, 2238
Draper, L. C. King's Mountain and its heroes, 510
Draper collection of manuscripts, Kentucky Papers, 1594
Draughon, W. R., and Johnson, W. P. North Carolina genealogical reference, 2590
Drennen, J. Drennen roll, 694
Driggs, B. W. History of Teton Valley, Idaho, 1276
Driscoll, Mrs. M. L. New Hampshire Revolutionary war pension records, 2239; Revolutionary War pension abstracts, 2239n
Druggists (British), list, 4288
Dubester, H. J. Catalog of U.S. census publications, 1790–1945, 180; State censuses, 182
DuBin, A. Five hundred first families of America, 147; Old Philadelphia families, 2866
Dublin: Calendar of ancient records, 4574; deeds, 4622; Quaker records, 4620; Trinity College alumni, 4606; wills, 4619, 4621–4623
Du Bose, J. C. Notable men of Alabama, 730
Dubose, S., and Porcher, F. A. Contribution to history of the Huguenots, 3136
Dudley, E. S. Roster of Nebraska volunteers, 2185
Duff, W. C. History of north central Ohio, 2698
Dugdale, Sir W. Baronage of England, 4496
Duke of York record, 1027
Duke University Library, Durham, N.C. Manuscript collections, 2653
Dumas, S. Les filles du roi en Nouvelle-France, 4110a
Dumont, W. H. Colonial Georgia genealogical data, 1158; Index of persons receiving passports, Georgia, 1140, 1159; Short census of Massachusetts (1779), 1872; Short census of Virginia (1779), 3548
Dunbar, Sir A. H. Scottish kings, 4802
Dunbar, W. F. Michigan through the centuries, 1947
Duniway, D. C. Have you an Oregon ancestor? 2810
Dunkers, Pennsylvania, 3007n

392

*Index*

Dunlap, A. R. Dutch and Swedish place-names in Delaware, 1035
Dunn, J. P. Indiana and Indianans, 1373–1374
Dunne, E. Illinois, 1314
Durham, N. W. History of city of Spokane, 3687
Durrie, D. S. Bibliographia genealogica Americana, 63n
Dutch: Armory of American families, 5073; Bible records, 608n, 2554n; Delaware place names, 1035; Michigan, 1982; New England, 581; New Jersey, 2293, 2294, 2337, 2425, 2448; New Netherland and U.S., 378; New York, 2293, 2294, 2423, 2425, 2448, 2462, 2503–2504, 2517, 2540; North Carolina, 2575; Pennsylvania, 2914, 2917, 3000; Quakers (Pennsylvania), 2914; South Carolina, 3131
Dutch Settlers Society of Albany yearbooks, 2449
Dutton, M. K. Succession of King Kamaheha V to Hawaii's throne, 1248
Dwnn, L. Heraldic visitations of Wales, 2895n, 4871
Dworaczyk, E. J. First Polish colonies of Americans in Texas, 3346
Dyer, A. M. First ownership of Ohio lands, 2699
Dyer, E. Annual report, Adjutant General's Office, Rhode Island, 3106
Dyer, F. H. Compendium of War of the Rebellion, 555

Eardeley, W. A. D. Connecticut cemeteries, 984
Eardley-Wilmot, J. Historical view of the Commission for Enquiring into the Losses . . . of Loyalists, 511
Early, C. M. Passenger lists from the Shamrock or Irish chronicle, 383
Early American history, guide to principal sources in New York city, 48
Early Settlers and Historical Assoc. of Wellington, 4944
East Anglian pedigrees, 4178
East Asia records, 91H
East India Company, genealogical guide, 4427n
East Kentuckian, 1518
East Tennessee Historical Soc. Publications, 3254
Easterby, J. H. Guide to study and reading of South Carolina history, 3137; Journal of Commons House of Assembly, South Carolina, 3181

Eastern Orthodox church, New York city, 2472
Eastern Pennsylvania Church of the Brethren history, 420–421
Eastern Province, South Africa, families, 4961
Eastern Shore, Maryland, Quakers, 1764–1765; records, 1766, 1807
Eastern Shore, Virginia, 3671
Eastern Washington Genealogical Soc. bulletin, 3688
Easton, Pennsylvania, First Reformed Church, record books, 2927
Eaton, D. W. How Missouri counties, towns and streams were named, 2089
Eaves-Walton, P. M. Tracing your Scottish ancestors, 4784
Ecclesiastical heraldry, *see* Church history
Ecclesiastical records, Mexico, 3910
Ecclesiastical terms, dictionary, 4528
Echoes from the East Tennessee Historical Soc., 3255
Eckenrode, H. J. List of colonial soldiers of Virginia, 3551; List of Revolutionary soldiers of Virginia, 3549–3550
Ecuador, 3903–3904
Eddy, H. H. Guide to published archives of Pennsylvania, 2868
Edinburgh, Scotland: commissariot records, 4752; register of marriages, 4761a; roll of burgesses, 4751
Edinburgh University, graduates, 4742–4743
Edmondson, J. Complete body of heraldry, 4969, 5010n
Edmunds, A. C. Pen sketches of Nebraskans, 2170
Edward III, King of England: ancestors, 4453; descendants, 4457
Edward IV, King of England, descendants, 4454
Edward P. Valentine papers, 3637
Edwards, L. W. L. New and revised catalogue of directories, 4193
Edwards, O., and Roberts, I. G. The "connection" in east Tennessee, 3256
Edwards, R. Chicago census report, 1315
Eelking, M. von. German allied troops in North American War of Independence, 512
Effigies, *see* Monumental brasses
Egle, W. H. Draughts of proprietary manors of Pennsylvania, 2869; Muster rolls, 2870; Names of foreigners who took the oath of allegiance, 2871; Notes and queries, 2872–2873; Old rights, 2874; Pennsylvania genealogies, 2875; Pennsylvania in War of

393

*Index*

the Revolution, 2876; Pennsylvania women in the American Revolution, 2877; Return of taxables, 2878; Some Pennsylvania women during Revolutionary War, 2877n; York, Pennsylvania, 2879; Warrantees of land, Pennsylvania, 2971
Eglise Françoise à la Nouvelle York, registers, 2570
Egmont, Earl of, Georgia journal, 1150
1820 land lottery of Georgia, 1160
1821 land lottery of Georgia, 1161
Ekwall, E. Concise Oxford dictionary of English place-names, 4399; Street-names in city of London, 4400
Electors registers, Guildhall Lib., London, 4222
Eliot, J. Biographical dictionary, New England, 584
Eliot, S. A. Biographical history of Massachusetts, 1873
Elizabeth, Queen (of Henry VII), ancestors, 4462
Elizabethans, titled, 4505
Ellet, E. F. Women of the American Revolution, 513
Elliott, C. Annals of northwest Alabama, 731
Elliott, K. B. Emigration to other states from southside Virginia, 3552
Ellis, C. H. History of Faulk county, South Dakota, 3218
Ellis, F., and Evans, S. History of Lancaster county, 2880
Ellis, H. General introduction to Domesday Book, 4466
Ellis, J. A. Memorial encyclopedia of New Hampshire, 2240
Ellsberry, E. P. List of works, 2090; Cemetery records of Missouri, 2086; Kentucky records, 1519
Elmer E. Rasmuson Library, Fairbanks. Bibliography of Alaskana, 776
Elvin, C. N. Dictionary of heraldry, 4970; Hand-book of mottoes, 4971
Ely, S. M. District of Columbia in the American Revolution, 1074
Ely, W. Big Sandy Valley, 1520
Elzas, B. A. Jewish marriage notices, 3138; Jews of South Carolina, 3139
Emden, A. B. Biographical register of Univ. of Cambridge, 4305; Oxford, 4306-4307
Emigration, *see* Immigration
Eminent and representative men of Virginia and the District of Columbia, 1075, 3553
Eminent Californians, 861

Eminent Jews of America, 436n
Emmison, F. G. Archives and local history, 4424; How to read local archives, 4240; Introduction to archives, 4424a
────── and Gray, I. County records, 4194
────── and Smith, W. J. Material for theses in some local record offices, 4195
Enciclopedia clásicos de Puerto Rico, 3051
Enciclopedia universal ilustrada Europeo-Americana, 3846
Encyclopedia of Connecticut biography, 985
Encyclopedia of Pennsylvania biography, 2881-2882
Encyclopedia of southern Baptists, 417a
Encyclopedia of contemporary biography of West Virginia, 3726
Encyclopedia of Massachusetts, 1874
Endelman, J. E. Judaica America, 14a
England, F. D. Alabama notes, 732; Alabama source book, 733
England (*see also* British and Great Britain): 4144-4565; administrations, 4366-4383; apothecaries, 4288; architects, 4289; archives, 2070, 4208; Army, 4290-4294; atlas, 4386, 4388, 4393; Baptists, 4531-4533; bibliographies, general, 4144-4169, local histories, 4170-4176, pedigrees and family history, 4177-4187; biographies, 4153, general, 4280-4287, professions, 4288-4337; births, 4202, 4355a; cartularies, 4192; Catholics, 4255, 4273, 4534-4537; census, (1851) 4199, 4387, 4397, 4402, (1951) 4389, (1961) 4390, copies, 4237, unprinted, 4188, surnames (1971), 4385; chancery proceedings, 4215; charters, medieval, 4192n; chronology, 4276-4279; clergy, 4295-4303; clockmakers, 4304; commoners, 4479; Congregationalists, 4146, 4538-4539; Conqueror and Domesday Book, 4463-4470; convicts in colonial America, 289; county bibliography, 4173; county histories, 4395; county records, 4194-4195; Court of Arches, 4218, 4221; Court of Requests, 4215; crests, 5016; crown grants, 1165-1172; deeds, 4192n, 4212; diaries, 4225; directories, 4193, 4228; Domesday, 4191n, 4463-4470; education, 4305-4310; emigrants to America, 335, 336, 338, 340, 348; emigration to North Carolina, 2613, 2615; Established Church records, 4229, 4527a; Falaise roll, 4465; family history bibliography, 4185; Friends, 4561-4563; gazetteers, 4385, 4394, 4396; genealogical research in, 240; genealogies, 15, 33, 4147, 4181, 4186; genealogists, 4312-

394

4313; gilds, 4171; government, 4314-4316; handwriting, 4226, 4243-4244; heraldry, 4147; historical works bibliography, 4154-4157, 4161-4163, 4166-4168; honors and titles, 4501-4502, 4510, 4516, 4522, 4524; Huguenots, 427-429, 432, 4541-4547; hundreds and hundred rolls, 4191; inventories, 4366-4383; inquisitiones post mortem, 4211, 4215; Jews, 4267, 4548-4552; land owners, 4230, 4474; law, 4316a-4322; local history, 4174, 4424, 4429-4430; Loyalists, 4022; manuals, 4422-4444; manuscript records, 4203-4208; maps, 4391; marriages, 4346-4349, 4351-4354, 4355a, 4356-4360; material relating to American history, 4213; medicine, 4323-4329; medieval local records, 4247; mercantile claims, Revolutionary War, 4190; Methodists, 4553-4559; monumental brasses, 4361-4365; municipal history, 4171, 4175; names, changes, 4416, personal, 4405-4421; places, 4397-4404; national bibliography, 4144, naturalizations of aliens, 4231; Navy, 4330-4334; New England settlers, 581; New York families, 2540; newspapers, 4243; nonconformists, 4529-4530; obituaries, 4350, 4355; Order of Garter, 4471, 4475, 4498; paleography, 4226; parish registers and records, 4233, 4338-4345; Parliamentary records, 4189, 4196, 4209; Parliamentary representation, 4171; pedigrees, 4177, 4182, 4184, 4187, 4198, 4232, 4508, 4513, 4518, 4523; peerages, etc., 4471-4526; periodicals and series, 4145, 4248-4275; petitions, 4215; place names, 4203, 4206, 4387, 4389-4390, 4397-4404; poll books, 4193, 4222; Presbyterians, 4560; probate jurisdictions, 4201; probates, 4366-4383; property confiscated, 4190; Public Record Office works, 4210-4215; public records, 59, 4197; Quakers, 4561-4563; record guides, 4433; records, 4188-4237; records publications, 4164, 4169; refugees to Germany, 358; registers, parish, 4338-4345; religions, general, 4527-4530, specific, 4531-4565; Royal family, 4445-4462; serials, 4159, 4165; sculptors, 4335; sheriffs, 4215; shipping records, 4224; shipwrights, 4336; societies, 4217; stage, 4337; surnames, 218, 4205, 4385, 4405-4415, 4417-4419; testamentary records, 4366-4383; theater, 4337; tithes, 4216; topography, 4170, 4172, 4176, 4384-4396; unclaimed dividends, 4227a; Unitarians, 4564; university registers, 4160;

Virginia records, duplicates of lost, 3544; Virginia wills, 3538; visitation, 4198, 4232, 4486, 4503, 4508, 4525; vital statistics, 4346-4360; Wesleyan Methodists, 4553-4559; wills, 4366-4383

English Place-Name Society publications, 4401

Engravers in America, dictionary, 149

Episcopal Church, Tennessee, 3299

Epitaphs, Georgia, 1147

Epp. F. H. Mennonites in Canada, 3968a

Erickson, C. Invisible emigrants, 336

Ericson, C. R. Nacogdoches, 3347

Ervin, S. S. South Carolinians in the Revolution, 3140

Escudo de armas de la ciudad de Caracas, 5085

The escutcheon (magazine), 4256n, 5103n, 5104, 5113n

Eshleman, H. F. Historic background and annals of Swiss and German pioneer settlers, 2883

Esker, K.-P. W. South Carolina memorials, 3141

Espejo, J. L. Nobiliario de la Capitanía General de Chile, 3887

Espenshade, A. H. Pennsylvania place names, 2884

Essex and Eu, Countess of, descendants, 4459-4560

Essex county, Mass. Records, 1895; Probate records, 1896

Essex Institute historical collections, 1875

Esshom, F. Pioneers and prominent men of Utah, 3434

Established Church in England, records, 4527a

Estate settlements, West Virginia, 3741

Estcourt, E. E. English Catholic nonjurors of 1715, 4535

Eterovich, A. S. Croatians/Dalmatians . . . in Nevada, 2202; Jugoslav-America, 862; Jugoslav immigrant bibliography, 356a; Yugoslav migrations to U.S.A., 356b; Yugoslavs in Nevada, 2203

Ethnic groups, 373-403; *see also* names of specific groups

Ethnic newspapers and periodicals, 373

Europe: Dictionary of biographical reference, 4287; Huguenots, 431; immigration, 363, 371; national censuses and vital statistics, 181; nobilities, 4456; reigning houses and titled nobility, 278

Eustace, P. B., and Goodbody, O. C. Quaker records, Dublin, 4620; Registry of deeds, Dublin, abstracts of wills, 4621; Will ab-

395

stracts in Genealogical Office, Dublin, 4622
Evans, C. A. Confederate military history, 556
Evans, Elwood (and others). History of the Pacific northwest, 2811, 3689
Evans, Evan. National Library of Wales and public record collection of Welsh nonconformists, 4879
Evans, I. O. Flags of the world, 5090
Evans, J. Map of six counties of North Wales, 4853
Evans, T. G. Records of Reformed Dutch Church in New Amsterdam, 2504
Everton, G. B., Jr. Genealogical atlas of U.S.A., 190; Handy book for genealogists, 237
Evjen, J. O. Scandinavian immigrants in New York, 2450
Ewen, C. H. L'E. History of surnames of British Isles, 4409
Ewers, J. C. Indian life on upper Missouri, 663
Exeter, Anne, Duchess of, descendants, 4457, 4460
Ezzell, Murray. Founders and patriots of republic of Texas, 3340

Faculty of Advocates, Scotland, 4734
Faehtz, E. F. M., and Pratt, F. W. Washington in embryo, 1076
Fairbairn, J. Books of crests, 5016
Falaise roll, 4465
Falkland Islands, heraldry, 5083
Falley, M. D. Irish and Scotch-Irish ancestral research, 4658
Familia (periodical), 4957
Families (periodical), 4082
Families of ancient New Haven, 103n
Family fare, 108
Family findings (magazine), 3257
Family histories, bibliography, 15
Family histories, index to, 63–64
Family history (magazine), 4258, 5105
Family names, Polk's cross reference to, 219
Family puzzlers, 624
Family trails, 1949
Family tree, 4945
Farish, T. E. History of Arizona, 784
Farmer J. Genealogical register of the first settlers of New-England, 337
——— and Moore, J. B. Gazetteer of New-Hampshire, 2241
Farmer, S. History of Detroit, 1950
Farr, K. R. Historical dictionary of Puerto Rico, 3052

Farrar, H. Irish marriages, 4611
Farrar, R. H. Index to biographical and obituary notices, 4350
Farrer, W. Honours and knights' fees, 4497
Fasti ecclesiae anglicanae, 4299–4301
Fasti ecclesiae Scoticanae, 4739
Faulk county, South Dakota, 3218
Faunt, J. (and others). Biographical directory of South Carolina House of Representatives, 3142
Faust, A. B. (and Brumbaugh, G. M.). List of Swiss emigrants in 18th century, 357
Faxon's Annual magazine subject index, 97
Federal population censuses, 1790–1890, microfilm copies, 183
Fellowes, E. H. Knights of the Garter, 4498
Fellows, J.-A., and Calder, K. Bibliography of loyalist source material in Canada, 4018
Fellowship of Brethren Genealogists newsletter, 109
Fenwick's colony, New Jersey, 2375–2376
Ferguson, J. P. S. Scottish family histories, 4707; Scottish newspapers, 4708
Ferguson, J. T. Short history of Ohio land grants, 2740
Ferguson, R. Surnames as a science, 4410
Fergusson, C. B. Place names of Nova Scotia, 4057
Fergusson, Sir J. Lowland lairds, 4803
Fernández de Recas, G. S. Cacicazgos y nobiliario indígena de la Nueva España, 3914; Mayorazgos de la Nueva España, 3915; Real y Pontificia Universidad de México, 3916
Fernández García, E. El libro de Puerto Rico, 3053
Fernández-Pradel, P. X. Linajes Vascos y Montañeses en Chile, 3888
Fernow, B. Burgomasters and Schepens, 2500; Calendar of wills, 2453; Documents relative to colonial history of New York, 2447; Minutes of Court of Burgomasters, 2500; Minutes of Orphanmasters of New Amsterdam, 2502; New Amsterdam family names, 2452; New York in the Revolution, 2454
[Ferril, W. C.] Sketches of Colorado, 936
Ferris, B. History of original settlements on the Delaware, 1036
Fesler, M. D. Pionners of western Kansas, 1454
Fess, S. D. Ohio, 2700
ffolliott, R. Irish ancestor, 4596; Simple guide to Irish genealogy, 4655

Field, T. P. Guide to Kentucky place names, 1521
Fiftyniners' directory, 927
Figueroa, S. Ensayo biográfico de los que mas han contribuido al progresso de Puerto Rico, 3054
Figueroa, V. Diccionario histórico, 3889
Filson Club history quarterly, 1522
Fines, J. History student's guide to the library, 4425
Finnish settlements, North and South Dakota, 3234
Firelands area, 2701–2703, 2771
Firelands pioneer, 2701–2703
First Reformed Church, Pennsylvania, 2867
Fisher, C. A. Central Pennsylvania marriages, 2885; Early central Pennsylvania lineages, 2886; Early Pennsylvania births, 2887
Fisher, C. E. National Genealogical Soc. quarterly, topical index, 125, 1088; Research in Maine, 1703
Fishwick, M. W. Gentlemen of Virginia, 3554
Fitch, M. Index to testamentary records in Commissary Court of London, 4379
Fitzpatrick, L. L. Nebraska place names, 2171
Five Civilized Tribes: 681–716; bibliography, 123n
Flagg, C. A. Alphabetical index of Revolutionary pensioners living in Maine, 1704; Guide to Massachusetts local history, 1876; Reference list on Connecticut local history, 986
Flagg, E. Genealogical notes on founding of New England, 585
Flags: bibliography, 5114; heraldic, 5092; U.S., 5095; world 5088a, 5090, 5093
Fleet, B. Virginia colonial abstracts, 3555
Fletcher, W. G. D. Royal descents, 4804
Florez de Ocaríz, J. Genealogías del Nuevo Reinado de Granada, 3894
Florida: 1096–1134a; Baptists, 1111; bibliographies, 1104, 1108; census (1830), 1126, (1840), 1127, (1850), 1130; church archives, 1111, 1115; church records, 1110; Civil War, 564, 718, 1103; county archives, 1112; ghost towns, 1134a; Indian place names, 674; Italians in colonial times, 1125; loyalists, 1128; lunatics in private hands, 1103; Methodism, 746, 1117; parishes of Louisiana land plats, 2031; pension list, 1103; place names, 1120; public vital statistics records, 1109; religious bodies, 1113; Revolutionary War, 1107; Roman Catholics, 1115; Seminole Indian War, 1124; Spanish-American War, 1124; Spanish land grants, 1114; women, 1096
Florida genealogical journal, 1105
Florida genealogical research quarterly, 1106
Foley, H. S. Alabama, 734
Foley, J. W. Early settlers of New York state, 2455–2456
Foley, L. P. H. Early Virginia families along James River, 3556
Folkes, J. G. Nevada's newspapers, 2204
Folmsbee, S. J. (and others). History of Tennessee, 3258
Folsom, E. K. State history of DAR, New Hampshire, 2235
Folwell, W. W. History of Minnesota, 1998
Foote, W. H. Sketches of North Carolina, 2591; Sketches of Virginia, 3557–3558
Footprints (magazine), 3348
Forbes, A., and Cadman, P. F. Boston and some noted emigrés, 1878n; Boston French, 1878
——— and Greene, J. W. Rich men of Massachusetts, 1877
Forbes, H. Gravestones of early New England, 586; New England diaries, 587
Forbes-Leith, W. Scots men-at-arms and life guards in France, 4736
Ford, H. J. Scotch-Irish in America, 398
Ford, P. and G. Select list of British Parliamentary papers, 4196
Ford, W. C. British officers serving in America, 468–469
Forebears, 105n, 110
Foreign denominations, parish registers, 4343
Foreign genealogical research, 33a
Foreign heraldry, 5118–5125
Foreign versions, variations, and diminutives of English names, 225
Foreman, G. Advancing the frontier, 664; Early post offices of Oklahoma, 2778; Five Civilized Tribes, 695; History of the service and list of individuals of Five Civilized Tribes, 696
Forfeited estates, Pennsylvania, 2888
Forgue, Abbé. Généalogie des familles d'ile d'Orléans, 4099n
Fornander, A. Account of the Polynesian race, 1249; Fornander collection of Hawaiian antiquities, 1250
Fortier, A. Louisiana, 1633
Fortier, J. A., and Ouimet, R. Biographies canadiennes-français, 3946

397

*Index*

Fortune (ship), 1845
Fosdick, L. J. French blood in America, 424
Foss, G. D., and Adams, W. S. Three centuries of freemasonry in New Hampshire, 2242
Foster, A. P. Counties of Tennessee, 3259
Foster, J. Alumni Oxonienses, 4308; Collectanea genealogica, 4259; Grantees of arms, 4499–4500, 5017; Index ecclesiasticus, 4297; London marriage licenses, 4351; Men at the Bar, 4259n, 4317; Oxford men and their colleges, 4308n; Register of admissions to Gray's Inn, 4318; Royal lineage of our noble and gentle families, 4450; Some feudal coats of arms, 5018
Foster, P. Trek to Texas, 3349
Foster, Sir W. Guide to India Office records, 4939
Fothergill, A. B., and Naugle, J. M. Virginia tax payers, 3559
Fothergill, G. Emigrants from England, 338
Fowler, I. E. Kentucky pioneers, 1523
Fox-Davis, A. C. Armorial families, 5019; Art of heraldry, 4972, 4995n; Complete guide to heraldry, 4995; Heraldry explained, 4996
Foxworth, Mrs. G. D. Roster and ancestral roll, DAR, South Carolina, 3132
Fragmenta genealogica, 4260
France, R. S. Early emigrants to America from Liverpool, 352
France: ancestors in Nova Scotia, 4050, 4061; emigrants to Canada, 4109, 4117; Huguenots in, 429–430; Scots men-at-arms and life guards in, 4736
Francis, E. W., and Moore, E. S. Lost links, 625
Franciscans in Nebraska, 2172
Franco, F. de A. C. Nobiliário colonial, 3883
Frandsen, M. L. Sixty and three on the Flying C, 937
Frank, L. F. German-American pioneers in Wisconsin and Michigan, 1951, 3786
Frank-Kerler letters, 1951, 3786
Franklin, C. A. H. Bearing of coat-armour by ladies, 4973
Franklin, H. Mortality schedules for Kansas territory (1860), 1455; (1870), 1456
Franklin, W. N. Federal population and mortality census schedules, 1790–1880, 172
Franklyn, J. Shield and crest, 4974, 4975n
—— and Tanner, J. Encyclopaedic dictionary of heraldry, 4975
Fraser, A. History of Ontario, 4083

Frederick county, Maryland, 1783–1784
Frederick county, Virginia, 3522
Freemasons: bibliography, 8a; New Hampshire, 2242
Freitas, J. F. de. Portuguese-Hawaiian memories, 1251
French, E. List of emigrants to America from Liverpool, 339
French, H. T. History of Idaho, 1278
French, J. H. Gazetteer of state of New York, 2456a–2458
French, J. P. C. Notable southern families, 3242n
French and Indian Wars: Connecticut, 957, 977; Kentucky land grants, 1585; New Hampshire, 2230, 2265; Rhode Island, 3081, 3114a; West Virginia, 3749
French: archives, Mississippi, 2071; Canadian migration to Louisiana, 4003–4004, to Mississippi Valley, 4003–4004, to New England, 4003–4004, *see also* Canada; Canadian settlers, 4110a; Canadians, 1651, 1683–1684, 4117, 4127; colony in Louisiana, census (1699–1732), 1659; depredation by in New England, 576; emigrants, Rhode Island, 3098; families in early 18th century Louisiana, 1626; immigrants, New York, 3000, Pennsylvania, 3000; marriage records, New Orleans, 1630; neutrals in Massachusetts, 1850; participants in Revolutionary War, 491, 514; Protestants, South Carolina, 3150, 3165; refugees at the Cape of Good Hope, 4953, in South Carolina, 3136, settlers in old northwest, 1296
French Canadian and Acadian genealogical review, 3969
Frenchtown massacres, Michigan territory, War of 1812, 1505
Frickstad, W. N. Century of California post offices, 865
—— and Thrall, E. W. Century of Nevada post offices, 2205
Friends, *see* Quakers
Friends' Historical Society journal, 4561
Friends' intelligencer, 4561n
Friends' quarterly examiner, 4561n
Fries, A. L. Moravians of Georgia, 1163
—— (and others). Records of Moravians in North Carolina, 2592
Fries, L. J. One hundred and fifty years of Catholicity in Utah, 3435
Friis, H. R. Series of population maps of colonies of U.S., 191
Frisian family names, 4405
Fritot, J. R. Pension records of soldiers of

398

*Index*

the Revolution who removed to Florida, 1107
Fry, E. A. Index to marriages in Gentleman's magazine, 4352
Fudge, G. H., and Smith, F. L.D.S. genealogist's handbook, 238
Fulton, E. J., and Mylin, B. K. Index to will books . . . of Lancaster county, Pennsylvania, 2889
Fulton Genealogical Society, Kentucky. Bible records of western Kentucky and Tennessee, 1523a, 3259a
Funeral directors, United States, 35
Funeral entries, Ireland, 4618
Funeral hatchments, 5029
Funeral homes and parlors, United States, 35
Furman, C. and R. Quaker bibliography for the genealogist, 9, 459

Gaelic and Irish manuscripts in libraries of Great Britain and Ireland, 4566n
Gaelic place names, 4769, 4777; surnames, 4649, 4779
Gahn, B. W. Original patentees of land at Washington (D.C.) prior to 1700, 1077, 1774, 3560
Galbreath, C. B. History of Ohio, 2704–2706
Galbreath, D. L. Papal heraldry, 5091; Treatise on ecclesiastical heraldry, 5091n
Galbraith, V. H. Introduction to use of public records, 4197
Gale, R. C. Indexes to quartered coats in Harleian Soc. visitation ser., 5020; Indexes to quartered coats, not included in Harleian visitation ser., 5021
Galicia: families, 3932; heraldry and genealogy, 5084
Gallant, P. Régistrés de la Gaspésie, 4111
Galway, Ireland: books of survey, 4580; wardenship, 4588
Gambrill, G. Genealogical material and local histories in Saint Louis Public Library, 46–47, 2091
Gandrud, P. J. Alabama: census 1830, 735; Alabama Revolutionary, 1812 and Indian War soldiers surnames, 736
Gannett, H. Boundaries of U.S., 206n; Origin of certain place names in U.S., 208. Gazetteers and geographic dictionaries: Colorado, 938; Connecticut, 987; Cuba, 3896a; Delaware, 1037; Indian territories, 665; Kansas, 1457; Maryland, 1775; Massachusetts, 1879; New Jersey, 2312; Porto Rico, 3055; Texas, 3350; Utah, 3436; Virginia, 3561; West Virginia, 3727
Garcia, J. G. Rasgos biográficos de Dominicanos célebres, 3899
García Carraffa, A. and A. Diccionario heráldico, 5086; Enciclopedia heraldica y genealógica hispano America, 5086n
Garcia de Miranda, E., and Fálcon de Gyves, Z. Atlas Mexicana, 3917
Gard, R. E., and Sorden, L. G. Romance of Wisconsin place names, 3787
Gardner, C. C. Genealogical dictionary of New Jersey, 2313; New Jersey marriage licenses, 2314
Gardner, D. E. (and others). Genealogical atlas of England and Wales, 4388; Genealogical atlas of Ireland, 4630; Genealogical atlas of Scotland, 4766
—— and Smith, F. Genealogical research in England and Wales, 239, 4241, 4426
Gardner, F. W. Central Ohio genealogical notes, 2707
Garlington, J. C. Men of the time, 3143
Garrett, C. H. The Marian exiles, 358, 4527
Garter, Knights of, 4471, 4475, 4498
Gaspé Peninsula, Quebec, births, 4111
Gaston, J. Centennial history of Oregon, 2812
Gates, S. Surname book and racial history, 3437
Gateway to the west, 2708
Gatfield, G. Guide to printed books and manuscripts relating to English and foreign heraldry and genealogy, 4147
Gaudier, M. Genealogías puertorriqueñas partidas de baptismos biografías, 3056
Gayre of Gayre and Nigg, R. Armorial who is who, 5009; Heraldic standards, 5092; Nature of arms, 4976; Roll of Scottish arms, 5052
Gazetteers: U.S., 186–207; Alaska, 773, 779; Alberta, 4039; British Isles, 4385; Canada, 3952, 3984; Colorado, 938, 939, 952; Connecticut, 959, 987, 1009; Cuba, 3896a; Delaware, 1037; District of Columbia, 1085; England, 4394, 4396; Georgia, 1226; Hawaii, 1247; Idaho, 1274; Illinois, 1295, 1337a; Indian territories, 665; Indiana, 1376, 1390, 1401; Ireland, 4640; Kansas, 1457–1458; Maine, 1692a, 1706, 1735; Maryland, 1775; Massachusetts, 1879, 1882, 1911, 1926; Michigan, 1939, 2027; Missouri, 1295, 2074, 2078; New Brunswick, Canada, 4055; New England, 590; New Hampshire, 2241, 2247, 2258; New Jersey, 2312, 2318; New Mexico, 2398; New York, 2446, 2456a–2458;

399

*Index*

North Carolina, 2637; Ohio, 2700, 2722-2723; Oklahoma, 2800a; Oregon, 2828; Pennsylvania, 2897; Porto Rico, 3055; Rhode Island, 3095; Saskatchewan, 4140; Scotland, 4767, 4769-4770, 4773-4775; Tennessee, 3292; Texas, 3350; Utah, 3436, 3446; Vermont, 3467, 3471, 3482-3483, 3493, 3496-3497; Virginia, 3561, 3584, 3604; Wales, 4396; Washington, 3697, 3700; West Virginia, 3727; Wisconsin, 3823; Yukon, 779

Geigel y Zenon, J., and Morales Ferrer, A. Bibliografía puertorriqueña escrita en 1892-1894, 3057

Geiger, M. J. Calendar of documents in the Santa Barbara Mission archives, 866

Geijer, E. N. Printed visitation and county pedigrees, 4198

Geiser, K. F. Redemptioners and indentured servants of Pennsylvania, 2890

Gellner, J., and Smerek, J. Czechs and Slovaks in Canada, 3970

Gendex census compendium, 173

Genealogía, 3870

Genealogical accredited researcher's record round up, 129n

Genealogical advertiser, 588

Genealogical and biographical record of northeastern Kansas, 1459

Genealogical and memorial encyclopedia of Maryland, 1776

Genealogical books in print, 31

Genealogical Forum of Portland. Genealogical material in Oregon donation land claims, 2813-2814; Genealogical research in Oregon, 2815; Index to Oregon donation land claim files in National Archives, 2816; Monthly bulletin, 2817; Year book, 2818; Yesterday's roll call, 2819

Genealogical helper, 111

Genealogical Institute (Louisiana) proceedings, 1634

Genealogical journal, Utah Genealogical Assoc., 112

Genealogical magazine, a journal of family history, 4261

Genealogical magazine (New England), 589

Genealogical magazine of New Jersey, 2315-2317

Genealogical newsletter and research aids, 113

Genealogical Office, Dublin, wills abstracts, 4622

Genealogical periodical annual index, 94, 98-100, 3971

Genealogical quarterly magazine, 589n

Genealogical quarterly: notes and queries, 4262

Genealogical reference builders newsletter, 114

Genealogical research in England, 240

Genealogical research: methods and sources, 241-242

Genealogical Society (Fort Worth) bulletin, 3348n

Genealogical Society of Pennsylvania. Genealogical manuscript material index, 2891

Genealogical Society of the Church of Jesus Christ of Latter-day Saints, Salt Lake City. Brief guide to Temple records, 47a; Computer parish listing (British), 4340; Genealogical sources and how to use them, 249n; Genealogist's handbook, 238; Index to 1851 census (England), 4199, 4402, 4882, 4886; Index to individuals born outside the U. S. . . . , 2593;

Major genealogical record sources: Australia, 4905; Canada, 3972; England, 4200, 4835; Guatemala, 3906; Indians (U.S.), 665a; Ireland 4575; Isle of Man, 4887; Mexico, 3918; New Zealand, 4946; Scotland, 4718; Wales, 4200, 4835;

Name extraction programs, 47b; Pre-1958 English probate jurisdictions, 4201, 4376; Social, economic, religious and historical background to Scotland, 4785; Welsh patronymics and place names, 4864; Welsh probate jurisdictions, 4850; *see also* World Conference of Records and Genealogical Seminar

Genealogical Society of the Church of Jesus Christ of Latter-day Saints: church records, 55; handy guide, 43; holdings, 37; records 442; research aids, 442; research papers, 243

Genealogical Society of Utah, index to holdings, 37

Genealogisches Handbuch des Adels, 5118n

The genealogist (magazine) (London, 1877-1922), 4263

The genealogist (magazine) (Victoria, Australia), 4906

Genealogists, directory of, British, 4312

Genealogists' magazine (Soc. of Genealogists, London), 4264

Genealogist's post (magazine), 115

Genealogy (periodical, ed. by W. Heiss), 117, 1375

Genealogy and history (magazine), 118

Genealogy, bibliography, 10, 20, 30

Genealogy digest (magazine), 119

400

*Index*

Genealogy: journal of American ancestry, 116
General and field officers of Kentucky militia, 1524
General armory two, 5022
General Baptists. General Assembly. Minutes, 4532
General censuses and vital statistics in the Americas, 174
General Land Office, Texas. Land claims and grants, 3408-3414; Soldiers of Texas, 3415
General Register House (Scotland), guide to public records in, 4719a
General Register Office, Great Britain. 1951 census of England and Wales, 4389, (1961), 4390
General Society of Mayflower Descendants, *see* Society of Mayflower Descendants
General Soc. of the War of 1812. Register, 547
General valuation of Ireland, 4631
Gentry, D. Land Commission inventory, 3648
Gentry, *see* Peerages
George I, King of England, descendants of, 4451
Georgetown county, South Carolina, history, 3171
Georgia: 1135-1243; atlas, 1138; Bible records, 622, 1151; bibliographies, 1164, 1223; cemetery inscriptions, 1136; census (1790), 1157, (1820), 1178, (1830), 1156, 1220a, (1840), 1225, (1850), 1218; Cherokee census (1835), 715, (1851), 704; church and synagogue archives, 1187; Civil War, 564, 1184; colonial families, 620; colonial records, 1148, 1158, 1193; colonial wills, 1145; counties, 1177, 1186; deaths, 1200, 1235-1236; English crown grants, 1165-1172; epitaphs, 1147; gazetteer, 1226; Huguenot families, 1155; immigrants from Great Britain, 1193; Irish immigrants, 387; lotteries, 1160, 1161, 1188-1190, 1194, 1202-1211, 1220, 1227-1228, 1239; lottery listing, 1138; manuals, 632, 1183; map, 1182; marriage records, 1151, 1201, 1219, 1234-1236; Moravians, 1163; mortality census (1850), 1224; names, 1139; Old Ninety-Six district, 3209; passports, 1140, 1159; Presbyterian churches, 1144; public vital statistics records, 1185; Revolutionary War, 1142, 1190, 1198, 1212-1213; Salzburgers, 1231, 1233; tax digests, 1137, 1214, 1221; wills, 1145, 1243

Georgia genealogical magazine, 1173-1174, 3144
Georgia Genealogical Society quarterly, 1175
Georgia genealogist, 1176
Georgia Historical Society. Counties of state of Georgia, 1177; Index to U.S. census, Georgia, 1820, 1178
Georgia pioneers, 1179
Gerber, Adolf, lists, 2978 (v.10)
German: Baptist Brethren in Europe and America, 413-414; emigration to Russia, 381; immigration: 367, from Russia, 2670, 2677, 2680; Louisiana, 1598, 1622, 1636; Maryland, 1772, 1813, 1831; Michigan, 1951; New Jersey, 2304, 2373; New York to Pennsylvania, 2978 (v.9); North Carolina, 2575, 3121; Pennsylvania, 2875, 2883, 2914, 2926-2927, 2931, 2951, 2978, 2991, 2995, 2997, 3000, 3006, 3007, 3013, 3020-3022; Philadelphia, 2931; Revolutionary War, 512, 536-537, 3998; South Carolina, 3121; Texas, 3322-3324, 3333, 3351-3352, 3417; U.S. wars, 480; Virginia, 3619, 3667, 3682; Wisconsin, 1951, 3786
German-American newspapers and periodicals, 379
German Colonization Company and the Chicago Colony, 956
German dialect, non-English words, 2930
Germanic-Slavic L.D.S. research papers, 243C
Germantown settlers, Pennsylvania, 2914n
Germany, guide to research in, 245
Geslagsregisters van die ou Kaapse familien, 4966n
Geue, C. W. and E. H. New land beckoned, 3351
Geue, E. H. New homes in a new land, 3352
Ghirelli, M. List of emigrants from England to America, 340
Ghost towns and mining camps of New Mexico, 2417
Gianelloni, E. B. Calendar of Louisiana colonial documents, 1636; Love, honor and betrayal, 1637; Notarial acts of Estavan de Quinones, 1637-1638
Gibb, Hon. Vicary. Complete peerage, 4491
Gibson, J. History of York county, Pennsylvania, 2892
Gibson, J. S. W. Wills and where to find them (in England), 4377
Gibson-Brittain, M. M. (and others). History and genealogy of some pioneer northern Alabama families, 737

401

*Index*

Gideon, D. C. Indian territory, 666
Gilbert, Sir J. T. and Lady R. M. Calendar of ancient records of Dublin, 4574
Gilds (British), bibliography, 4171
Gill, H. G. Establishment of counties in Kansas, 1460
Gill, J. V. Illiana research reports, 1316
────── and Gill, M. R. Index to 1800 federal census of New Hampshire, 2243; Index to 1830 federal census of Illinois, 1317
Gillis, I. S. Mississippi 1850 mortality schedules, 2035
────── and Gillis, N. E. Abstract of Goodspeed's Mississippi memoirs, 2036
Gillis, N. E. Early inhabitants of Natchez district, 2037; Index to Goodspeed's Biographical memoirs of Mississippi, 2038; Mississippi 1830 census, 2040; Mississippi 1820 cenus, 2039
────── and Gillis, I. S. Mississippi 1850 census, 2041; Mississippi genealogical notes 2042
Gillman, H. W. Index to marriage licence bonds, 4612
Gillow, J. Literary and biographical history, 4536
[Gillum, J. L.] Prominent Tennesseans, 3260
Gilman, C. M. B. Huguenot migration in Europe and America, 425
Gilman, M. D. Bibliography of Vermont, 3468
Gilmer, G. R. Sketches of some of the first settlers of upper Georgia, 1180
Gilmore, G. C. Roll of New Hampshire soldiers at Battle of Bennington, 2244
Gilroy, M. Loyalists and land settlement in Nova Scotia, 4019, 4058
Gingras, R. Liste des répertoires de mariage, 4112; Précis de généalogiste amateur, 3973
Giuseppi, M. S. Guide to contents of Public Record Office, 4214; Naturalization of foreign Protestants in American and West Indies colonies, 457, 2893
Glasgow: burgesses, 4753; commissariot records, 4754
Glasgow University: Matriculation albums, 4744; Roll of graduates, 4745
Glazner, C. H., and McLane, B. J. 1870 mortality schedules, Arkansas, 820; Index to 5th census, Missouri (1830), 2092
Gleanings from the heart of the cornbelt, 1318
Gleason, M. Printed resources for general searching in Wisconsin, 3788
Gleed, C. S. Kansas memorial, 1461
Glenn, T. A. Merion in the Welsh tract, 2894; Printed American genealogies, 10; Welsh founders of Pennsylvania, 2895
Glossaries: German dialect, 2930, Hawaiian words, 1255; heraldic terms, 4978, 4989, 4992, 4997; Latin America, 3860
Glover's roll, 5027n
Gnann, P. R. Georgia Salzburgers and allied families, 1231n
Gobble, J. R. Idaho lineages of members, (S.A.R.), 1291
Goblet, Y. M. Topographical index to parishes and townlands of Ireland, 4632
Godbout, A. Emigration Rochelaise en Nouvelle–France, 4113; Familles venues de la Rochelle en Canada, 4113n; Nos ancêtres au XVIIe siecle, 4114
Godcharles, F. A. Chronicles of centennial Pennsylvania, 2896
Godfrey, C. E. Commander-in-Chief's Guard, 515
Godfrey, W. H., and Wagner, Sir A. College of Arms, 4977
Gold book, Maine, 1702n
Goldsborough, W. W. Maryland Line, 1777
Goochland, Virginia, wills, 3547n
Goodbody, O. C. Guide to Irish Quaker records, 4705
Gooder, E. A. Latin for local history, 4242
Goodpasture, A. V. Dictionary of distinguished Tennesseans, 3261
Goodrich, J. E. Rolls of soldiers in Revolutionary War (Vermont), 3469
Goodrich, L. W. Roster of ancestors, D.A.R. (Oregon), 2809
Goodspeed's Arkansas, 811–815, 821, 837; index 821, 836
Goodspeed's Biographical and historical memoirs of Mississippi, 2036, 2038, 2043
Goodspeed's Histories of Tennessee, 3262–3279
Goodwin, N. Genealogical notes . . . Connecticut and Massachusetts, 988, 1880
Gordon, T. F. Gazetteer of New Jersey, 2318; Gazetteer of Pennsylvania, 2897
Gore's Roll of arms, 5067, 5081n
Goshenhoppen registers, 2898
Gosnell, C. F. Spanish personal names, 3847
Goss, C. W. F. London directories, 4148
Goss, W. L. Colonial gravestone inscriptions in New Hampshire, 2232
Gotay, M. Hombres ilustres de Puerto Rico, 3058
Gotha, Almanach de, 5118

Gough, H., and Parker, J. Glossary of terms used in heraldry, 4978

Gouldesbrough, P., and Kup, A. P. Handlist of Scottish record publications, 4711

Government Land Office (U.S.), land entry papers, 93

Government officials, Britain, 4315–4316

Gracy, A. D. (and others). Early Texas birth records, 3353

Gradeless, Donald E. Index to towns . . . from Illustrated historical atlas . . . Indiana, 1364a

Graham, I. C. C. Colonists from Scotland, 341; Scottish emigration to North America, 341n

Grammer, N. R. Marriage records of early Texas, 3354

Grant, Sir F. J. Court of the Lord Lyon, 4748; Faculty of Advocates in Scotland, 4734; Index to genealogies, 4709; Manual of heraldry, 4997; Zetland family histories, 4892

Grant, J. Tartans and clans of Scotland, 4805

Granville county, North Carolina, 2639

Graves: Maryland, 1827; Revolutionary War, 496, 505

Gravestone inscriptions: Connecticut, 989; District of Columbia, 1091; New England, 586; New Hampshire, 2232–2233; New South Wales, Australia, 4911a; Pennsylvania, 2942

Gray, F. A. Gray's new map of Kentucky and Tennessee, 1525, 3270

Gray, N. Compiling your family history, 4907

Gray's Inn, London, admissions, 4259n, 4318

Great Britain (see also England, Ireland, Scotland, Wales): checklist of microfilms, 83; emigrants/immigrants, 345, 347, 350, 352, 354, family history bibliography, 15; L.D.S. research papers, 243A; L.D.S. World Conference, 91C; passenger lists, 345, 354

Great Britain. Historical Manuscripts Commission. Guide to reports, 4203–4206; List of records repositories in Great Britain, 4207; National register of archives, 4208

——— Public Record Office. Calendarium genealogicum, 4211; Descriptive catalogue of ancient deeds, 4212; Guide to contents, 4214; Guide to material relating to American history, 4213; History, description, record groups . . . with special reference to Virginia, 3562; List of wills, 4378; Lists and indexes, 4215; Records . . . relating to South Carolina, 3145

Great Britain, Public Record Office: papers, 4210; unpublished search room lists, 4268n

Great Yarmouth, England: emigrants from, 346; passenger lists, 346

Greeley, A. Plan of private claims in Michigan territory, 1952

Green, C. R. Early days in Kansas, 1462

Green, J. J. Quaker records, 4562

Green, L. Catalogue of genealogical library, Colonial Dames of America, 2437

Green, T. G. H. Index to marriage license bonds, 4613

Green, T. M. Historic families of Kentucky, 1526

Green Bay, Wisconsin, 3783

Greene, E. B., and Morris, R. B. Guide to principal sources for early American history in New York city, 48

Greene, N. History of Mohawk Valley, 2459; History of Valley of the Hudson, 2460

Greenleaf, R. E., and Meyer, M. C. Research in Mexican history, 3919

Greenwood, V. D. Researcher's guide to American genealogy, 244

Greer, G. C. Early Virginia immigrants, 3563

Gregg, A. History of Old Cheraws, 3146–3147

Grégoire, J. À la recherche de nos ancêtres, 3974

Gregorie, A. K. Court of Chancery records, South Carolina, 3183

Gregory, J. G. Southeastern Wisconsin, 3789; Southwestern Wisconsin, 3790; West central Wisconsin, 3791

Gregory, W. American newspapers, 11–12, 3975; Union list of serials, 75

Grehan, I. Irish family names, 4644

Grice, W. Georgia through two centuries, 1181

Grieve, H. E. P. Examples of English handwriting, 4243

Griffin, A. C. Bibliography of American historical societies, 13

Griffin, H. L. Attakapas country, 1639

Griffith, L. B. Alabama, 738; History of Alabama, 738n

Griffith's valuation of Ireland, 4631n

Grimble, I. Scottish clans and tartans, 4806

Grimes, J. B. Abstract of North Carolina wills, 2624–2625

Griswold, D. and J. Colorado's century of cities, 939
Groce, G. C. Dictionary of artists in America, 149
Grönberger, R. Minnesotas historia, 1999
Groene, B. H. Tracing your Civil War ancestor, 557
Groome, F. H. Ordnance gazetteer of Scotland, 4767
Gross, C. Bibliography of British municipal history, 4171
Grove, H. Alienated tithes, 4216
Guardianships, New York, 2545
Guatemala, 3905–3906
Gubi, M. (and others). History of Pennsylvania Society Daughters of the American Colonists, 2860
Gudde, E. G. California place names, 867
Gue, B. F. Biographies and portraits of progressive men of Iowa, 1414; History of Iowa, 1415
Guérnsey, l'Île de, 4881–4883
Guides, *see* Manuals
Guild brethren: Edinburgh, 4751; Glasgow, 4753
Guildhall Library, London: Handlist of poll books, 4222; London rate assessments, 4223; Parish registers, 4343
Guillet, E. C. Lives and times of the patriots, 3976
Guillim, J. Display of heraldry, 4980
Guinn, J. M. Works, 868–869
Gulf Coast: colonials, 1626; colonization and settlement, 1689; families, 614a
Gunnis, R. Dictionary of British sculptors, 4335
Guppy, H. B. Homes of family names in Great Britain, 4411
Gurley, L. L. Genealogical material in Oregon donation land claims, 2813a
Gutgesell, S. Ohio newspaper guide, 2708a
Gwathmey, J. H. Historical register of Virginians in Revolution, 3564
Gwynedd, Kalendars of, 4869

H. R. S., *see* Historical Records Survey
Hackett, J. D., and Early, C. M. Passenger lists from Ireland, 342
Hadler, M. L. Towner County, North Dakota families, 2667
Hafen, L. R. Colorado and its people, 940
Hagedorn, E. Franciscans in Nebraska, 2172
Hager, A. M. and E. G. Historical Society of Southern California bibliography, 870
Hager, G. H. Index to journals of North Dakota State Historical Society, 2668

Haggard, J. V., and McLean, M. D. Handbook for translators of Spanish historical documents, 3848
Haiman, M. Poles in early history of Texas, 3355; Poles in New York, 2461; Polish pioneers of California, 871; Polish pioneers in Pennsylvania, 2899
Haines, H. Manual of monumental brasses, 4362, 4364
Haldimand Papers, 4017, 4020, 4024
Hale, C. E. Connecticut headstone inscriptions before 1800, 989
Hale, J. P. Trans-Allegheny pioneers, 3728
Hale, R. W. Guide to photocopied historical materials in U.S. and Canada, 49, 3977
Hale, W. T., and Merritt, L. M. History of Tennessee, 3271
Haliburton, T. C. Historical and statistical account of Nova Scotia, 4059; History of Nova Scotia, 4059n
Hall, A. C. S. Index to persons in Guide to reports of Historical Manuscripts Commission, 4205
Hall, Carl M. Jenny Wiley country, 1527
Hall, Charles M. Atlantic bridge to Germany, 245; Palatine pamphlet, 359
Hall, D. British orders, 4502
Hall, F. History of the state of Colorado, 941
Hall, H. History of Vermont, 3470
Hall, J. Hall's circuits and ministers, 4554–4556; Memorials of Wesleyan Methodist ministers, 4557
Hall, L. P. Marriage notices, 2594
Hall, T. B. Oklahoma, 667
Hall, W. L. Bibliography of Virginia, 3629n
Hall Bros. Hall's Original county map of Georgia, 1182
Hallum, J. Biographical and pictorial history of Arkansas, 822
De Halve Maen, 2462
Hamer, P. M. Guide to archives and manuscripts in U. S., 50; Tennessee, 3272
Hamersly, L. R., and Co. Officers of Army and Navy in Civil War, 558
Hamersly, T. H. S. Complete Army and Navy register of U.S.A., 470; Complete general Navy register, 471; Complete regular Army register, 472; General register of U.S. Navy, 473
Hamilton county, Ohio, census (1817), 2693
Hamilton-Edwards, G. K. S. In search of ancestry, 4427n; In search of Scottish ancestry, 4786; Tracing your British ancestors, 4427
Hamlin, C. H. They went thataway, 3565;

Virginia ancestors, 3566
Hamm, M. A. Famous families of New York, 2463
Hammer, C. Rhinelanders on the Yadkin, 2595
Hammond, G. P. Guide to manuscript collections of Bancroft Library, 3849
Hammond, I. W. Rolls of soldiers of Revolutionary War, 2265
Hammond, O. G. Check list of New Hampshire history, 2245; Notices from New Hampshire gazette, 2246
Hampshire county, West Virginia, 3760, 3763
Hampton, New Hampshire, 2236
Hancock, H. B. Delaware loyalists, 1038
Hancock, P. D. Bibliography of works relating to Scotland, 4710
Handbook on the frontier days of southeast Kansas, 1480
Handbook to Arizona, 786n
Handler, J. S. Guide to source materials for study of Barbados history, 4922a
Handlist of Scottish and Welsh record publications, 4711
Handwriting, *see* Paleography
Handy, H. B. Social recorder of Virginia, 3567
Handy guide to record-searching in larger cities of U.S., 51
Hanna, C. A. Historical collections of Harrison county, 2900n; Ohio Valley genealogies, 2709, 2900; Scotch-Irish, 399; Wilderness trail, 668, 2901
Hanna, P. T. Dictionary of California land names, 872
Hansard's catalogue and breviate of British Parliamentary papers, 4209
Hansen, M. L. Atlantic migration, 360
Hansen, N. T. Guide to genealogical sources —Australia and New Zealand, 4908
Hanson, R. McD. Virginia place names, 3568
Harcup, S. Historical, archaeological and kindred societies in British Isles, 4217
Hardesty, H. H., and Co. Historical and geographical encyclopedia . . . northwestern Ohio, 2710
Hardy, D. Fasti ecclesiae anglicanae, 4299–4301
Hardy, D. H., and Roberts, I. S. Historical review of southeast Texas, 3356
Hardy, S. P. Colonial families of southern states, 626
Hargreaves-Mawdsley, R. Bristol and America, 343

Harlan, E. R. Narrative history of people of Iowa, 1416
Harlan, E. T. (and others). 1830 federal census, Michigan, 1953
Harland, D. Basic course in genealogy, 246n; Genealogical research standards, 246
Harleian Soc. Indexes to quartered arms in visitations, 5020; Indexes to quartered arms not in visitation, 5021; Publications (Visitation ser.), 4265, 4525
Harlow, R. Oklahoma leaders, 2779
Harpole, P. C., and Nagle, M. D. Minnesota territorial census (1850), 2000
Harrell, Mrs. J. B. Oklahoma and Oklahomans, 2780
Harris, Abner. Confederate Kentucky volunteers, 1539
Harris, Alexander. Biographical history of Lancaster county, 2902
Harris, K. Guide to manuscripts of State Historical Society of Iowa, 1417
Harris, M. H. Florida history, 1108
Harris, R. P. Nevada postal history, 2206
Harrison, E. S. Nome and Seward Peninsula, 777
Harrison, H. Surnames of United Kingdom, 4412
Harrison, H. G. Select bibliography of English genealogy, 4149
Harrison, J. P. Guide to materials on Latin America, in National Archives, 3850
Harrison, M. C. New York state's prominent and progressive men, 2464
Harshman, L. F. Index to 1850 . . . census of Ohio, 2711
Hart, F. H. Valley of Virginia in American Revolution, 3569
Hart, S. Representative citizens of Connecticut, 990
Hartlaub, R. J., and Miller, G. J. Colonial conveyances, east and west Jersey, 2319
Hartley, P. G. Hall's circuits and ministers, 4554–4556
Hartmann, E. G. Americans from Wales, 344, 4844
Hartsook, E., and Skordas, G. Land Office and Prerogative Court records of colonial Maryland, 1778
Hartwell, Sir R. E. Augustan roll of arms, 5068–5069; Guide to orders of chivalry; Researching your royal ancestry, 273
Harvey, O. J. History of Wilkes-Barre, 2903
Harvey, R. Pioneers of Manitoba, 4046
Harwood, P. Le R. History of eastern Connecticut, 991

*Index*

Haskins, C. W. Argonauts of California, 873
Hasse, A. R. Public archives bibliography, original states, 14; Some materials for a bibliography, Colony of New York, 2465
Hastain, E. Hastain's Township plats of Creek nation, 697; Index to Choctaw-Chickasaw deeds, 699–700; Seminole nation, 698
Hastings, H. Military minutes, New York Council of Appointment, 2514
Hatch, L. C. Maine, 1705
Hatchments in Britain, 5029
Hathaway, B. W. Genealogy research sources in Tennessee, 3273; Inventory of county records of Kentucky, 1528; Kentucky genealogical research sources, 1529; Primer for Georgia genealogical research, 1183
Hathaway, J. R. B. North Carolina historical and genealogical register, 2629, 2643
Haugen, E. Norwegians in America, 391
Hauser, F. L. Lineage books, Soc. of Mayflower Descendants (Texas), 3400
Haverford College Library. Quaker necrology, 460
Harvard College graduates, 159
Hawaii: 1244–1270; aliis (Polynesian chief and nobles), 1245; atlas, 1244; Chinese, 1246; directory, 1264n; gazetteer, 1247; glossary of Hawaiian words, 1255; Honolulu directories, 1264; Kalakaua dynasty, 1259; land tenures, 1254; migration, 1245, 1246, 1249; missionaries, 1256–1257; place names, 1247, 1265; Polynesians, 1245, 1249; Portuguese, 1251; royalty, 1248, 1258, 1261, 1266–1267
Hawaiian Historical Society. Annual reports, 1252; Genealogical series, 1253; Index to publications, 1255; Papers, 1254
Hawaiian journal of history, 1252n
Hawaiian kingdom, 1264n
Hawaiian Mission Children's Soc. Annual report, 1256; Missionary album, 1257
Hawes (G. W.) and Co. Indiana state gazetteer, 1376
Hawkes, J. Saskatchewan and its people, 4141
Hawkeye heritage, 1418
Hawley, J. H. History of Idaho, 1279
Haws, C. B. Scottish parish clergy at the Reformation, 4738
Hawthorne, J. History of Washington, 3690
Haxtun, A. A. Signers of the Mayflower Compact, 301, 1881
Hayden, H. E. Virginia genealogies, 3570
Haydn, J. T. Book of dignities, 4286; Dictionary of dates, 4278; Universal index of biography revised, 165n
Hayes, R. F. Maryland historical and genealogical bulletin, 1779
Hayes, R. J. Biographical dictionary of Irishmen in France, 4601; Manuscript sources for history of Irish civilisation, 4577; Sources for history of Irish civilisation, 4578
Hayes Library (Fremont, Ohio) manuscripts, 2726
Hayes-McCoy, G. A. Ulster and other Irish maps, 4633
Haynes, M. Nebraska pioneer, 2173
Haynes, S., and Conley, A. Missouri obituaries index, 2093
Hayward, E. American vital records from "The Baptist register," 417
Hayward, J. Gazetteers: Maine, 1706; Massachusetts, 1882; New England, 590; New Hampshire, 2247; U.S., 193; Vermont, 3471
Hazelwood, J. P. (and others). Index to 1830 census, South Carolina, 3147a
Headlee, B. Heads of families 1840 census of Iowa, 1419
Headright grant, *see* Lotteries
Headrights, Texas, 3388a
Heads of families at first census (1790), 179
Heart of Texas records, 3357
Heaton, Sir J. H. Australian dictionary of dates, 4909
Hebert, D. J. Southwest Louisiana records, 1640
Hebert, R. A. Modern Maine, 1707
Hebrides, Scotland, 4884–4885
Hecht, A. Postal history in Texas panhandle, 3358
Hector, L. C. Handwriting of English documents, 4244
Hedden, J. S. Roster and graves . . . of patriots, 992
Heese, J. A. Herkoms van die Afrikaner, 4958
Heilprin, A. and L. A. Complete pronouncing gazetteer, 194
Heinemann, C. B. "First census" of Kentucky, 1790, 1530
Heiss, W. C. 1820 federal census for Indiana, 1377; Encyclopedia of American Quaker genealogy, 1378; Genealogy (magazine), 117; Guide to Quaker records in the midwest, 640; Guide to research in Quaker records in the midwest, 461, 1379; List of all Friends meetings . . . in Indiana, 1380; Quaker biographical sketches,

2904; Quaker genealogies, 461a
——— and Mayhill, R. T. Census of the territory of Kansas, 1463
Heitman, F. B. Historical register and dictionary of U.S. Army, 474; Historical register of officers of the Continental Army, 516
Helbron, P. Registers, 2905
Hemenway, A. M. Vermont historical gazetteer, 3496-3497
Hemphill, J. C. Men of mark in South Carolina, 3148
Hempstead, F. Historical review of Arkansas, 823; Pictorial history of Arkansas, 824
Hempstead, J. Diary, 993
Hemry, L. H. Some northwest pioneer families, 641
Henchion, R. Gravestone inscriptions of County Cork, 4614
Henchy, P. Three centuries of emigration from British Isles, 4579
Henderson, A. Conquest of old southwest, 627; North Carolina, 2596
Henderson, L. Roster of Confederate soldiers of Georgia, 1184
Henderson, T. W., and Tomlin, R. E. Guide to official records in Mississippi Dept. of Archives, 2043a
Hendrix, G. L. C., and Lindsay, M. McK. Jury lists of South Carolina, 3148a
Hendrix, M. L. F. Mississippi court records, 2044; Newspaper notices of Mississippians, 2045
Hening, W. W. Laws of Virginia, 3574; Statutes at large, 3571-3573
Hennessy, G. L. Novum repertorium ecclesiasticum parochiale Londinense, 4298
Hennessy, W. B. History of North Dakota, 2669
Hennig, H. Great South Carolinians, 3149
Henry, J. H. 1819-49 abstradex of annual returns, Mississippi Free and Accepted Masons, 2046
Henry VII, King of England, descendants of, 4454
Hepworth, P. How to find out in history, 4428
Herald and genealogist (magazine), 4266, 5106
Heraldic Artists Ltd. Handbook on Irish genealogy, 4660
Heraldic journal, 5107
Heraldic visitations, *see* Visitations
Héraldique au Canada (magazine), 5109
Heraldry: general, 4967-4989; bibliographies, 5114-5117; British island areas and dominions, 5060a-5066; Canada, 3988, 4005; Chile, 3887; church, civic and flags, 5088-5097; design, 4990, 4992, 4994-4995, 4997; early blazon, 4967; episcopal arms, 4991n; foreign, 5118-5125; glossary, 4978, 4989, 4992, 4997; Great Britain, 5012-5032; Ireland, 5013, 5016, 5024, 5026, 5033-5044; L.D.S. World Conference of Records, 91J-M; ladies, 4973; Latin America, 5082-5087; manuals, 4435, 4990-5008; Maryland, 1768, 1791, 1815; Massachusetts, 1914; mottoes, 4971; perrage, 4471-4526; periodicals, 5098-5113; Rhode Island, 3079; rolls of arms, 5009-5081; Scotland, 5013, 5045-5056; South Africa, 4963; U.S. and Canada, 5000, 5005, 5008, 5067-5081; Virginia, 3536; Wales, 5013, 5023, 5057-5060
Heraldry gazette, 5108
Heraldry in Canada (magazine), 5109
Heralds' Office in Ireland, arms registered, 5044
Heralds' visitations, *see* Visitations
Herbert, R. Worthies of Thomond, 4677a
Hercegavinians, Nevada, 2202
Hereditary register of the United States of America, 120
Heritage review, 2670
Herndon, D. T. Annals of Arkansas, 825; Centennial history of Arkansas, 825n
Herndon, R. (and others). Men of progress . . . State of Maine, 1708
Hershkowitz, L. Wills of early New York Jews, 2466
Hess, J. W. Guide to manuscripts and archives in West Virginia collection, West Virginia Univ. Library, 3729
Hessians (Revolutionary War): auxiliaries, 380, 522; battalions, 517; officers, 512
Hessische Truppen in amerikanishen Unabhängigkeitskrieg (Hetrina), 517
Heston, A. M. South Jersey, 2320
Hewitt, A. R. Union list of Commonwealth newspapers, 4896
Hiday, Mrs. H. I. United States censuses, 1870/1880 (Oregon), 2820
Hiden, M. W. How justice grew, 3575
Higgs, A. H., and Wright, D. West Midland genealogy, 4150
Highfill, P. H., Jr. (and others). Biographical dictionary of actors, 4337
Highland Scots, North Carolina, 2613
Highsmith, R. M., Jr., and Bard, R. Atlas of Pacific northwest, 641a

407

*Index*

Hijar-Padres Colony, 882
Hildreth, S. P. Biographical . . . memoirs of early pioneer settlers of Ohio, 2712
Hill, E. E. Preliminary inventory of records of Bureau of Indian Affairs in National Archives, 669
Hill, L. B. History of Oklahoma, 2781
Hill, R. R. National archives of Latin America, 3851
Hills, L. C. History and genealogy of Mayflower planters, 590a
Hines, H. K. Illustrated history of Oregon, 2821; Illustrated history of Washington, 3691
Hingham, Massachusetts, 1883
Hinman, R. R. Catalog of names of the first Puritan settlers of . . . Connecticut, 994
Hinshaw, S. B., and M. E. Carolina Quakers, 2597
Hinshaw, W. W. Encyclopedia of American Quaker genealogy, 462, 2598; New York city and Long Island, 2467; Ohio, 2713; Philadelphia, 2321, 2906; Virginia, 3576
Hinton, R. J. Handbook to Arizona, 786
Hirsch, A. R. Huguenots of colonial South Carolina, 3150
Hispanic America, *see* Latin America
Hispanic Soc. of America. Catalogue of library, 3852
Histoire des grandes familles françaises du Canada, 3963
Historical agencies, directory, 34
Historical and biographical encyclopedia of Delaware, 1039
Historical and biographical record of territory of Arizona, 787
Historical encyclopedia of Wyoming, 3833
Historical journal (journal), 2907
Historical New Hampshire (journal), 2248-2249
Historical periodicals, annotated world list, 95
Historical Records Survey (Work Projects Administration): check list of publications, 38; unpublished inventories, 39; directory of Negro Baptist church in U.S., 418;
    United States: Alabama, 739-743; Arizona, 788-790; Arkansas, 826-829; California, 875-879; Colorado, 942-943, Connecticut, 995-996; Delaware, 1040-1042; District of Columbia, 1078-1079; Florida, 1109-1115; Georgia, 1185-1187; Idaho, 1280-1282; Illinois, 1319-1322; Indiana, 1381-1383; Iowa, 1420-1422; Kansas, 1464-1465; Kentucky, 1531-1532; Louisiana, 1641-1648; Maine, 1709-1710; Maryland, 1780-1782; Massachusetts, 1884-1888; Michigan, 1954-1957; Minnesota, 2001-2004; Mississippi, 2047-2050; Missouri, 2094-2097; Montana, 2144-2147; Nebraska, 2174-2175; Nevada, 2207-2209; New Hampshire, 2250-2253; New Jersey, 2322-2327; New Mexico, 2402-2404; New York city, 2469, 2470, 2472, 2474; New York state, 2468-2469, 2471, 2473, 2475; North Carolina, 2599-2600; North Dakota, 2671-2673; Ohio, 2714-2715; Oklahoma, 2782-2784; Pennsylvania, 2909-2912; Oregon, 2822-2825; Rhode Island, 3084-3088; South Carolina, 3151; South Dakota, 3219-3221; Tennessee, 3274-3278; Texas, 3359-3361; Utah, 3438-3441; Vermont, 3472-3475; Virginia, 3577-3579; Washington, 3692-3694; West Virginia, 3730-3735; Wisconsin, 3792-3799; Wyoming, 3834-3836
Historical societies, directory, 34
Historical Society of Delaware. Papers, 1043
Historical Society of Montana. Contributions, 2148
Historical Society of Southern California: bibliography, 870; publications, 880n; quarterly, 880
Historical works, United Kingdom, 4154-4157
History of Arkansas valley, Colorado, 944
History of Benton [and other] counties [Arkansas], 830
History of Clear Creek and Boulder valleys, Colorado, 945-946
History of Cole [and other] counties, Missouri, 2098
History of Franklin [and other] counties, Missouri, 2099-2100
History of Hickory [and other] counties, Missouri, 2101
History of Hocking Valley, Ohio, 2716
History of Lewis [and other] counties, Missouri, 2102
History of lower Scioto Valley, Ohio, 2717
History of Nevada, 2197n
History of Newton [and other] counties, Missouri, 2103
History of North Carolina, 2601
History of northern Wisconsin, 3800
History of southeast Missouri, 2104
History of southeastern Dakota, 3222
History of Texas, 3362-3365
History of the state of Nebraska, 2176-2177
History of the upper Ohio valley, 2718, 3736-3737

408

History of the upper peninsula of Michigan, 1958
History of Virginia, 3580
Hitching, F. E. and S. References to English surnames, 4413
Hitz, A. M. Authentic list of all land lottery grants . . . Georgia, 1188
Hixon (W. W.) and Co. Atlases and platbooks: Illinois, 1323-1324; Indiana, 1384-1385; Iowa, 1423; Michigan, 1959; Minnesota, 2005-2006; Montana, 2149; North Dakota, 2674; West Virginia, 3738; Wisconsin, 3801; Wyoming, 3837
Hoadly, C. J. Records of . . . New Haven, 997-998
——— (and others). Public records of Connecticut, 967
Hocking Valley, Ohio, 2716
Hockly, H. E. Story of British settlers of 1820, 4959
Hodge, F. W. Indian tribes of North America, 670
Hodges, N. Missouri obituaries, 2105; Missouri pioneers, 2142n
——— (and others). Missouri pioneers, 2106
Hodgkin, F. E., and Galvin, J. J. Pen pictures of representative men of Oregon, 2826
Hodson, V. C. P. List of officers of Bengal Army, 4940; Some families with a long east Indian connexion, 4941
Hoenstine, F. G. 1972 guide to genealogical and historical research in Pennsylvania, 2913; Society of the Sons of the American Revolution yearbook, 3014; Your family tree, 3042
Hoffman, W. J. Armory of American families of Dutch descent, 5073
Hogan, E. Onomasticon goedelicum locorum et tribuum Hiberniae, 4634
Holcombe, H. Baptists in Alabama, 744
Holdcraft, J. M. Names in stone, 1783; More names in stone, 1784
Holland, Huguenots in, 429
Holland purchase (New York), 2561-2562
Holland Soc. of New York yearbooks, 2448
Holmes, F. R. Directory of ancestral heads of New England families, 591
Holmes, J. D. L. Honor and fidelity, 1649
Holmgren, E. J. and P. M. 2,000 placenames of Alberta, 4040
Holt, A. H. American place names, 209
Holtzclaw, B. C. Ancestry and descendants of Nassau-Siegen immigrants to Virginia, 3581

Honeyman, A. Van D. Northwestern New Jersey, 2328
Honolulu, Polk's directory, 1264
Honor roll (of native born South Dakotans), 3223
Honorable Society of Lincoln's Inn, admissions, 4321
Honorable Society of the Middle Temple, London, admissions, 4322
Honours and knights' fees, 4497
Honours and titles in Britain, 4501
Hood, J., and Young, C. J. American orders and societies and their decorations, 475
Hoogenraad, M. Genealogical sources of Public Archives of Canada, 3978
Hoosier ancestors index, 1393
Hoosier genealogist, 1386
Hope, Sir W. H. Grammar of heraldry, 4998
Hopkins, C. W. Home lots of early settlers of Providence Plantations, 3089
Hoskins, W. G. Local history in England, 4429
Hostos, A. de. Hombres representativos de Puerto Rico, 3059
Hotchkin, J. H. History of purchase . . . of western New York, 2477
Hotten, J. C. Handbook of topography, 4172; Original lists of persons of quality, 345
Houck, G. F. History of Catholicity in northern Ohio, 2719
Houck, L. Memorial sketches of pioneers . . . of southeast Missouri, 2107
Hough, F. B. American biographical notes, 150, 2478; New York civil list, 2521
House, C. J. Names of soldiers of American Revolution, 1711
House of Lords, members, 4491
Houston, E. R. Maine Revolutionary soldiers' graves, 1701
Houston, J. Index to cases in records of Court of Arches, 4218
Houston, M. L. Index to county wills of South Carolina, 3152; Reprint of official register of land lottery of Georgia, 1189; Revolutionary soldiers and widows living in Georgia, 1190
Houston Genealogical Forum. Collection of Bible records, 3366
Houts, A. E., and Eastman, H. Revolutionary soldiers buried in Missouri, 2108
Hover, J. C., and Barnes, J. D. Memoirs of Miami Valley, 2720
Howard, J. J., and Crisp, F. A. Visitation of England and Wales, 4503, 5023; Visitation of Ireland, 4678, 5036

409

*Index*

Howe, H. Historical collections of Ohio, 2721; Historical collections of Virginia, 3582
Howell, C. History of Georgia, 1191
Howells, B. E., Calendar of letters relating to North Wales, 4837
Hoyt, M. E. Unpublished HRS inventories, 39
Hoyt index, 525n
Hudson, E., and Maresh, H. R. Czech pioneers of the southwest, 3366a
Hudson, J. L. Co. Michigan pioneers, 1960
Hudson River valley, New York: wills, 2453n, history of 16 counties, 2460
Hudson valley (New York), Dutch houses, 2539
Huhner, L. Jews of New England, 592
Huffman, A. O. Biographical sketches of old settlers and prominent people of Wisconsin, 3802
Hughes, J. Pioneer West Virginia, 3739
Hughes, J. L. J. Patentee officers, 4583
Hughes, T. E. (and others). History of Welsh in Minnesota, 1424, 2007
The Huguenot. Publications, 3583
Huguenot Society of America, 424, 426
Huguenot Society of London. (Quarto) Publications, 4544
Huguenot Society of New Jersey. Huguenot ancestors, 2329
Huguenot Society of South Carolina. Transactions, 3153
Huguenot Society of Washington, D.C. Roster of members, 1080
Huguenots: 422–432; acts of naturalization, 427–428; aliens, 4544–4545; ancestors, 425; bibliography, 426; biographies, 432; Canada, 3995; Cape of Good Hope, 4953n; emigration, 423, 425; English surnames of French origin, 424; exiles, 4541; families in America, 430; France and America, 430; French blood in America, 424; genealogy, sources, 4529n; Georgia, 1155; Great Britain, 4541–4547; letters of denization, 427–428, 4542–4543; naturalizations, 4541–4543; New Jersey, 2329; New Paltz, N.Y., 2486; New York, Eglise francoise, 2570; pedigrees, 429, 4546; Pennsylvania, 3016; records, 422; refugees, 4541, 4547; settlements, 4547; settlements in Canada, 431, England, 432, Ireland, 432, 4700, New York, 430, U.S., 431; South Carolina, 1155, 3133–3134, 3136, 3150, 3153; Virginia, 3510, 3547n, 3583
Hull, W. I. William Penn, 2914

Hume, J. Index of wills of: Allegany county, 1785; Garrett county, 1786; Harford county, 1786; Howard county, 1787; Kent county, 1787; St. Mary's county, 1788; Somerset county, 1788
Humes, T. W. Loyal mountaineers of Tennessee, 3279
Hummel, R. O., Jr. List of places included in 19th century Virginia directories, 3584
Humphery-Smith, C. R. Family history, 5105; General armory two, 5022; London's right road for study of heraldry, 5001; Sources for research into English in Portugal, 4503a
Humphreys, A. L. Handbook to county bibliography, 4173
Humphreys, D. W., and Emmison, F. G. Local history for students, 4430
Hundred and hundred rolls, England, 4191
Hungary's participation in the Civil War, 572
Hunkins, L. Tombstone inscriptions and marriages of middle Tennessee, 3280
Hunt, E. M. New Hampshire town names, 2254
Hunt, H., and Kaytor, F. C. Washington, 3695
Hunt, J. W. Wisconsin gazetteers, 3823
Hunt, R. D. California and Californians, 881
Hunter, C. L. Sketches of western North Carolina, 2602
Hunter, John. Trail drivers of Texas, 3367
Hunter, Joseph. Familae minorum gentium, 4179; Pedigrees, 4180
Hunter, Gov. Robert, ration lists (New York), 2489n
Hurd, C. E. Genealogy and history of representative citizens of Massachusetts, 1889
Huse, H. A. Historical and bibliographical notes relative to Vermont towns, 3489
Huston, A. J. Check list of Maine local histories, 1712
Hutchinson, C. A. Frontier settlement in Mexican California, 882
Hutton, B. G. Contribution on Northern Ireland records, 4705
Huxford, F. Pioneers of wiregrass Georgia, 1192
Hyamson, A. M. Jewish obituaries, 4548

Icaza, F. A. de. Diccionario autobiográfico de conquistadores y pobladores de la Nueva España, 3853
Idaho: 1271–1292; bibliographies, 1290,

1292; Catholic church records, 638; cemetery records, 1286; census (1870), 1283; church and religious organizations, 1280; county archives, 1282; federal mortality schedules (1870), 1284; federal population schedules (1870), 1284; gazetteer, 1274; nomenclature, 1290; public statistics, 1281, 1286

Idaho Genealogical Society: census, 1283; Idaho territory, 1284; Idaho vital statistics, 1286; quarterly, 1285

Idaho, the Gem state, 1292

Iguiníz, J. B. Bibliografía Mexicana, 3920

Illiana genealogist (magazine), 1325

Illiana research reports, 1316

Illinois: 1293-1363; atlas, 1323, 1360; Black Hawk War 1327, 1362; burial places in all wars, 1326; cemetery inscriptions, 1352; census (1810), (1818), 1333, (1820), 1299, 1334, 1357, (1830), 1317, (1840), 1363, (1850), 1303, 1313; church archives, 1321; church vital statistics records, 1319; Civil War, 554, 564, 1310, 1327; counties, 1328, 1336; county archives, 1322; election returns, 1337; French and British in northwest, 1296; gazetteer, 1295, 1337a; landowners, 1360; lands, 1348; manual, 1332, 1356; Mexican War, 1327; military patent book, 1349-1350; mortality schedule, 1355; place names, 1293, 1353; plat book, 1323-1324; public vital statistics records, 1320; records, 1316; Revolutionary War, 1308, 1312, 1342, 1358-1359; surname index, 1305; Swedish element, 1335; vital records from Chicago newspapers, 1306; War of 1812, 1348

Illinois State Genealogical Society quarterly, 1329

Illinois State Historical Society Index to publications, 1330

Illustrated album of biography of southwestern Minnesota, 2008

Illustrated album of biography of the famous valley of the Red River, 2009, 2675

Illustrated biographical album of northeastern Nebraska, 2178

Illustrated history of New Mexico, 2405

Illustrated history of north Idaho, 1287

Illustrated history of southeastern Washington, 3696

Illustrated history of southern California, 883

Illustrated history of the state of Idaho, 1288

Illustrated history of Yellowstone Valley, 2150

Immigration: 356-372; Acadians to Louisiana, 1676-1677; archives, Univ. of Minnesota libraries, 371, 4009; bibliography, 361; Boston, 332; British, 329-355, 1846-1848, 1860, 4725; Canada, 4109, 4113, 4117; Canary Islands, 1688; Chinese, 375, 1246; Croatians, 356; Danish, 2450n; early, to North America, 349, 575; English, 336; ethnic bibliography, 361; European, 363, 371; from United Kingdom, 350; Germans, 367, 2450, 2557; Great Britain, 345, 354; Great Britain to Georgia Colony, 1193; Ireland, 342, 353, 383, 385, 386, 388, 4579; Jewish, 362; Marian exiles, 358; Maryland, 1833; Michigan, 1939; New England, 331, 578-579, 581; Norwegians, 390, 393, 2450n; other than British, 356-372; Palatine, 359, 367; Polynesians, 1249; Puerto Rico, 3048; Salzburgers, 1231, 1233; Scandinavian, 2450; Scottish, 336; Serbians, 356; Slovenes, 356; Swedish, 365, 401, 2450n; Swiss, 357; Texas, 3351-3352; Virginia, 3552, 3563, 3610, 3623; Wales, 344; Yugoslavia, 356, 356a, 356b, 862, 1691

Impersonal arms, see Civil heraldry

Indentured servants: from Liverpool, 339, 340, 343, 348; Oglethorpe, South Carolina, 1150; Pennsylvania, 2890, 2991; Philadelphia, 2991

Index library, see British Record Society

Index of Illinois military patent book, 1349-1350

Index of indexes, 54

Index to the headright and bounty grants in Georgia, 1194

Index of the wills to 1858 (Ireland), 4622

Index of wills (Canterbury), 4373

Index of wills (New Jersey), 2357n

Index to American genealogies, Munsell, 63n

Index to probate cases of Texas, W.P.A., 3404

Indexes: American, 34-93; local, unpublished, 53; published, by subject, 54

India (former British Colony): 4933-4943; Bengal Army officers, 4940; India Office records, 4939; Indian Medical Service, 4934-4935; inscriptions on tombs, 4935a-4938; L.D.S. World Conference of Records, 91I; survey records, 4942; titles, 4943

India Office, Great Britain, guide, 4939

Indian Medical Service, 4934-4395

Indian Wars: Alabama, 736; Illinois, 1359; Kentucky, 1494, 1556; Massachusetts, 1854, 1892; Minnesota, 2013-2014; Mis-

411

*Index*

souri, 2077, 2110; New England, 1854; New Hampshire, 2230; North Carolina, 2577; Pennsylvania, 2864, 2945; South Carolina, 3124; Texas, 3328; Virginia, 2864, 3588n, 3601; West Virginia, 3724–3725

Indiana: 1364–1408a; atlas, 1364, 1364a, 1384, 1398; bibliography, 1403; boundaries, 1399; census (1820), 1371, 1377; churches and religious organizations, 1381; Civil War, 564, 1387; county archives, 1383; furniture makers, 1405; gazetteer, 1376, 1390, 1401; Hoosier ancestors, 1393; land entries, 1407; lawyers, 1397, 1402; manual, 1396, 1406; maps, 1364, 1364a; mortality schedule (1850), 1404; officers, 1388; plat books, 1384–1385; public vital statistics, 1382; Quakers, 1378–1380; records, 1389; Revolutionary War, 1372, 1408

Indiana magazine of history, 1391

Indiana State Library. Guide to genealogical material in Pennsylvania archives, 2915

Indianapolis Public Library. Consolidated index to 32 histories of Indianapolis and Indiana, 1392

Indian (American): 652–680; affairs, 679; bibliography, 678; biographical sketches, 670; citizens and freedmen, 710–711; gazetteer, 665; literature on, 652; manual, 236n; maps, 671; place names, 674, 675, 677, 908, 1353; principal chiefs, 670; records, 665a, 669

Indians (American; *see also* Five Civilized Tribes): 652–680; Canadian, 3999; Cherokee, 681–682, 686–692, 694, 703–709, 713–715; Chickasaw, 691–693, 699–701, 716; Choctaw, 691–693, 699–701, 716; during the Civil War, 564; during the War of 1812, 2510; Creek, 683–684, 691–692, 697, 716; Iowa, 1426; Kansa, 653; Kansas, 1451; Louisiana, 656; Maine, 1714; Missouri, 660, 663; New England, 576; New Jersey, 673; Ohio, 2731; Oklahoma, 658, 664, 677, 680, 2802; Pacific northwest, 638, 4070; Pennsylvania, 668, 2901, 2917; Pueblo, 657; Seminole, 685, 692, 698; southern, 691; Texas, 3402; U.S., 56

Inner Temple, London, students admitted, 4319

Innes, J. H. New Amsterdam and its people, 2481

Innes, Sir T. Scots heraldry, 4999, 5047; Tartans and clans and families of Scotland, 4806a

Inquisitions index, Henry VIII–Charles I, 4215

Inquisitiones post mortem (1207–1307), 4211

Inscriptions: Calcutta, 4938; Central Provinces and Berar, India, 4935a; Nizam's dominions, 4936; Rajputana and Central India, 4937

Institut Généalogique Drouin. Dictionnaire nationale des canadiens français, 1651, 3979, 4115

Institute of American Genealogy, Chicago, 324n

Institute of Heraldic and Genealogical Studies. Parish maps of counties of England and Wales, 4391

Institute of Historical Research, *see* London University

Instituto Argentino de Ciencias Genealogicas. Boletín interno, 3871

Instituto de Estudos Genealógicos. Revista, 3883a

Instituto genealógico Brasileiro. Guía das publicaçóes, 3884

Instituto Peruano de Investigaciones Genealogicas, Revista, 3933

Inverness, sasines for sheriffdoms, 4759

Iowa: 1409–1440; atlas, 1409; bibliography, 1435; census (1836), 1430, (1840), 1419, 1433; church and religious organizations, 1420; Civil War, 554, 564, 1426; county archives, 1422; Indian campaigns, 1426; lawyers, 1439; manuscripts, 1417; Mexican War, 1426; military, 1425; New Englanders, 1427; newspapers, 1412, 1437; Norwegians, 394; Philippine War, 1426; pioneers, 2725; plat book, 1423; public vital statistics records, 1421; Spanish American War, 1426; surname index, 1427; Welsh, 1424, 2007

Iowa Genealogical Society surname index, 1427

Iowa historical record (magazine), 1428

Iowa journal of history, 1428n

Iredale, D. Discovering your family tree, 4431; Enjoying archives, 4432

Ireland (*see also* England): 4565a–4705; Anglicans, 4296, 4697; arms, grants of, 4694; atlas, 4630, 4638; Baptists, 4531; baronetcies, 4481, 4490; bibliographies, 4565a–4571; biographies, 4599–4605; births, 4611n; books of survey, 4580; census (1659), 4581; (1871), 4636; (1901), 4637; chiefs and leaders, 4696; civil survey (1654–1656), 4582; commoners, 4479–4480; county families, 4526; crests, 5016;

decorations and medals, 4691; documents in private keeping, 4590; emigration, 342, 353, 385, 4579; family names map, 4679; funeral certificates, 4259n; 4618; Gaelic and Irish manuscripts, 4566n; genealogical collections, 382, 386, 4569; hearth money rolls, 4589; heraldry, 4981n; Huguenots, 427–428, 432, 4541–4543, 4547, 4700; in America, 384; in Barbados, 385; in California, 899; in Canada, 3966; in France, 4600–4601, 4603; in New England, 388; in Nova Scotia, 4061a; in Revolutionary War, 530; King James's army, 4600; kings, 4672; knights, 4509; 4521; knights bachelors, 4521; land ownership, 4474, 4581–4582, 4593, 4642, 4666, 4671, 4677; landed gentry, 4482, 4669, 4688–4689; Latin word list, 4662; local history sources, 4592; manuals, 4653–4664; manuscript sources, 4577; maps, 4628–4629, 4633, 4641, 4643, 4679; marriages, 4611, 4615, 4617; Milesian family, 4676; municipal history, 4175; names, 4644–4652; naturalization of aliens, 4231; nobility and gentry, 5026; obituaries, 4608–4609; passenger lists, 342, 383; patentee officers, 4583; peerages, etc., 4665–4696; periodicals and series, 4595–4598; personal names, 4632, 4639, 4644, 4647–4652; place names, 4634, 4636–4637, 4646; poll money ordinances, 4581; public records, 4584–4587; Quakers, 2957, 4705; record sources, 4575; records guides and offices, 4572–4594; registers, 4606–4607; religions, 4697–4705; Scotch Highlanders in Revolution, 523; surnames, 4644, 4647–4652; titles of honour, 4522; topography, 4642–4643; towns and townlands, 4626, 4632, 4636–4637, 4639; tribes, 4634, 4671; university registers, 4309; valuation, 4631; visitation, 4678, 5036; vital statistics, 4608–4618; wills, 4619–4625
Ireland, N. O. Index to Hartford times "Genealogical gleanings," 999; Index to women, 151; Local indexes in American libraries, 53
────── and Hayes, B. P. Index to indexes, 54
────── and Irving, W. Cutter index, 593
Ireland Indexing Service. Consolidated index to Cutter's genealogical sets, 44
Irish ancestor (magazine), 4596
Irish genealogical helper (magazine), 4597
Irish genealogist (magazine), 4598

Irish Touring Board. Tracing your ancestors, 4661
Irvine, L. H. History of the new California, 884
Irwin, Mrs. L. Directory of members and ancestors of DAR, Massachusetts, 1871
Is that lineage right? 235
Isle of Man, England: 4886–4889; original parish registers, 4343a; personal names, 4888; place names, 4402, 4886, 4889; wills, 4366
Italians: America, 389; Florida, 1125; Massachusetts, 1864; Missouri, 2125; New Jersey, 2302
Iturriza Guillen, C. Algunas familias caraqueñas, 3938
Ivins, V. W. Yesterdays, 1429

Jack, D. R. Acadiensis, 4047
Jack, I. A. Biographical review . . . New Brunswick, 4060
Jackson, D. Intermarriage in Ireland, 4617
Jackson, R. V. Censuses: Delaware (1800), 1044; Iowa (1836), 1430; Mississippi (1820), 2051; Rhode Island (1800), 3090; Washington, D.C. (1800), 1081
────── (and others). Censuses: Kentucky (1810), 1533; Pennsylvania (1800), 2916
────── and Teeples, G. R. Censuses: Maine (1800), 1713; New Hampshire (1800), 2255; North Carolina (1800), 2603; Tennessee (1820), 3281; Virginia (1810), 3585
Jacksonville Genealogical Society magazine, 1116
Jacobite peerage, 4455
Jacobs, P. M. Registers of universities, colleges and schools of Great Britain, 4309
Jacobsen, P. R. Quaker records in Maryland, 1789
Jacobus, D. L. Families of ancient New Haven, 1000; Genealogy as pastime and profession, 248; History and genealogy of families of Old Fairfield, 1001–1002; Index to genealogical periodicals, 100; List of officials . . . of Connecticut colony, 1003
Jamaica, 4925, 4932
James, E. Territorial records of Illinois, 1331
James, E. W. Lower Norfolk county Virginia antiquary, 3595
James, J. E. Eighth census of U.S. (1860) Nebraska territory mortality schedules, 2179
James I, King of England, descendants of, 4445

413

*Index*

James III, King of Scotland, descendants of, 4454
James VI, King of Scotland, descendants, 4445
Janeway, W. R. Bibliography of immigration in U.S., 1900–1930, 361
Janson, F. E. Background of Swedish immigration, 401
Japan, L.D.S. Research papers, 243J
Jaussi, L. R. and Chaston, G. D. Fundamentals of genealogical research, 249, 3442n; Genealogical records of Utah, 3442; Register of L.D.S. church records, 55, 443
Jayne, B. T. Who's who in Oklahoma, 2785
Jeffrey, W., Jr. Early New England court records, 594
Jehn, J. B. Acadian descendants, 4061
Jenkins, J. H. Cracker barrel chronicles, 3368
Jenkins, M. E. Tracing Spanish-American pedigrees in southwestern U.S., 3854
Jenkins, W. Ohio gazetteer, 2722
Jenkins, W. S. Guide to the microfilm collection of early state records, 56
Jennewein, J. L., and Boorman, J. Dakota panorama, 3224
Jensen, E. G., and Olsen, B. M. California Mother Lode records, 885; Nevada records, 885n, 2210
Jenson, A. Latter-day Saint biographical encyclopedia, 3443; Origin of western geographic names associated with Mormons, 444
Jersey, Channel Islands: armorial, 5066; biographical dictionary, 4881; Livre de percharge du fief, 4883; place index, 4882
The Jerseyman (magazine), 2330
Jervise, A. Epitaphs and inscriptions . . . northeast Scotland, 4762
Jester, A. L., and Hiden, M. W. Adventures of purse and person, 3586
Jesuits, Montana, 2156
Jewish, *see* Jews
Jewish Historical Society of England. Transactions, 4267
Jews: American, 433–440; arms, 5012, 5032; bibliography, Great Britain, 4549, 4551, U.S., 14a, 17a, 29a; biographies, 434, 436–440; Bridgetown, Barbados, 4930; California (southern), 650; Civil War soldiers, 573; eminent, 434, 436, 438–439; English, 4548–4552; genealogical sources, 4552; immigration, 362; Louisiana, 1644–1645; Mexico, 3922–3923; Mississippi, 2048; New England, 592; New Orleans, 1653; New York, 2434, 2466, 2536; New York name list, 71; obituaries (British), 4548; settlers, 440; South Carolina, 3138–3139; Spanish and Portuguese Jews' Congregation, 4550; Utah, 3451; West Virginia, 3766
Jewson, C. B. Transcript of three registers of passengers from Great Yarmouth to Holland and New England, 346
Jillson, W. R. Big Sandy Valley, 1534; Kentucky land grants, 1535; Old Kentucky entries and deeds, 1536
John Askin papers, 1977
Johns, F. Australian biographical dictionary, 4910; Notable Australians, 4911
Johnson, A. Swedish settlements on Delaware, 1045, 2917
Johnson, D. P. American College of Heraldry, 5000
Johnson, D. W. (and others). Churches and church membership in U.S., 404
Johnson, F. W. History of Texas, 3369
Johnson, K. A., and Sainty, M. R. Gravestone inscriptions, New South Wales, 4911a
Johnson, M. E. Genealogical-index to books . . . in New Jersey Historical Soc., 2331–2332
Johnson, S. C. History of emigration from the United Kingdom to North America, 347
Johnson, W. P. Index to North Carolina wills, 2604
Johnston, C. Society of Colonial Wars, genealogies, 1834
Johnston, D. E. History of Middle New River settlements, 3740
Johnston, J. B. Place-names of Scotland, 4778
Johnston, R. B. West Virginia estate settlements, 3741; West Virginians in American Revolution, 3742
Johnston (W. and A. K.), and Bacon, G. W. Johnston clan map, 4807; Johnston's Clan histories, 4808; Johnston's gazetteer of Scotland, 4769
Jones, A. Cymry of '76, 519
Jones, C. C., Jr. Dead towns of Georgia, 1195; History of Georgia, 1196
Jones, C. K. Hispanic American bibliographies, 3855
Jones, E. A. Loyalists of Massachusetts, 1890; Loyalists of New Jersey, 2333
Jones, F. Approach to Welsh genealogy, 4867; Princes and principality, 4868

*Index*

Jones, K. P., and Gandrud, P. M. Alabama records, 745
Jones, R. C. North Carolina newspapers on microfilm, 2605
Jones, V. L. (and others). Family history for fun and profit, 250; Genealogical research: a jurisdictional approach, 250n
Jordan, J. W. Century and half of Pittsburgh, 2918; Colonial and Revolutionary families of Pennsylvania, 2919; Colonial families of Philadelphia, 2920; Genealogical and personal history of northern Pennsylvania, 2921; Historical homes..., 2923; Western Pennsylvania, 2922
Jordan, W. Colonial and Revolutionary families of Philadelphia, 2924
Jordan, W. T., Jr. North Carolina troops, 2606
Joseph, S. Jewish immigration to U.S., 362
Joubert, J. Armoires de la Republique Sud-Africaine, 5060a
Journal of American history, 121, 5110
Journal of Mississippi history, 2052
Joyce, P. W. Origin and history of Irish names of places, 4646
——— and Sullivan, A. M. Atlas and cyclopedia of Ireland, 4638
Judaica Americana, 14a
Jugoslavs, *see* Yugoslavs
Juneau, Alaska, founding of, 775

Kaganoff, N. M. Judaica Americana, 14a
Kalamazoo family newsletter, 1961
Kamaku, S. M. Ruling chiefs of Hawaii, 1258
Kamehameha V, King of Hawaii, succession, 1248
Kaminkow, J. and M. J. List of emigrants from England to America, 348; Mariners of American Revolution, 520
Kaminkow, M. J. Genealogical manuscripts in British libraries, 4151; Genealogies in Library of Congress, 15, 4181; New bibliography of British genealogy, 4152; United States histories in Library of Congress, 15a
Kane, J. H. American counties, 210
Kansa Indians census (1843), 653
Kansas: 1441–1487; atlas, 1481; bibliography, 123n, 1441, 1452; cemeteries, 1473; census (1855), 1463; Civil War, 554, 564, 1467; counties, 1460; county archives, 1465; gazetteer, 1457–1458; Indian place names, 677; Indian tribes, 1451; legislators, etc., 1474; mortality schedules (1860), 1455, (1870), 1456, (1880), 1450; official roster, 1474; Old Settlers' meeting, 1461; place names, 1479; post offices, 1444; public vital statistics records, 1464; roster of Illinois soldiers residing in, 1310; voter list, 1463
Kansas genealogist (magazine), 2109
Kansas historical quarterly, 1468–1469, 1470n
Kansas Illustriana Society, 1442
Kansas (special ed.), 1466
Kansas State Historical Society collections, 1470
Karr, N. M. Detailed list of old parochial registers of Scotland, 4755
Kaye, V. J. Early Ukrainian settlements in Canada, 3980
Kegley, F. B. Kegley's Virginia frontier, 3587
Keith, C. P. Provincial counsellors of Pennsylvania, 2925
Kelby, R. H. New York marriage lists, 2508n
Kelby, W. New York city loyalists, 2526
Kellaway, William. Bibliography of historical works, 4155–4157
Kellogg, J. U. Tulpehocken-Virginia notes, 2926
Kellogg, L. M. Guide to ancestral trails in Michigan, 1953
Kelly, P. Irish family names, 4647
Kelly's Handbook to titled, landed, and official classes, 4504
Kelsay, L. E. Cartographic records ... American Indians, 671
Kemp, L. W. Signers of Texas Declaration of Independence, 3370
Kennedy, Patricia. How to trace your loyalist ancestors, 4021
Kennedy, Patrick. Book of Irish arms, 5037
Kenny, H. T. West Virginia place names, 3743
Kent, D. B. E. One thousand men, 3476n; Vermonters, 3476
Kent county, Delaware: census (1800), 1055; probate records, 1031; records, 1033
Kentucky: 1488–1597; atlas, 1577; Bible records, 622, 1514, 1523a; bibliographies, 1507, 1512; Catholics, 1595; cemetery records, 1491, 1515; census (1790), 1530, (1800), 1506, 1544, (1810), 1498, 1533, 1591, (1820), 1517, 1592, (1830), 1580, (1850), 1555, 1558, 1588; Civil War, 564, 1538–1539; colonial families, 620; colonists in Texas, 1511; county archives, 1532; court records, 1489–1490, 1528, 1553, 1582; deaths, 1496; genealogies, 3638;

*Index*

grantors, 1536; land records, 1535–1536, 1576, 1585, 1597; manual, 632, 1529, 1554; manuscripts, 1502; map, 1525; marriages, 1503–1504; military warrants, 1536; militia, 1501, 1524; obituaries, 1504; pensions, 1494, 1589; Peters Colony, 1511; place names, 1521; public vital statistics, 1531, 1542; records, 1489–1490, 1513, 1519, 1528, 1553, 1582–1584, 1594; regular army, 1575; Revolutionary War, 1494, 1516, 1576, 1589, 1597; surname index, 1555, 1588; taxpayers, 1506, 1541; War of 1812, 1494, 1505, 1537, 1574, 1589; wills, 1497, 1536, 1550
Kentucky ancestors (magazine), 1543
Kentucky family records (magazine), 1545
Kentucky genealogist (magazine), 1546
Kentucky Historical Society: manuscripts, 1502; register, 1547–1548
Kenyon, B. Massachusetts heraldica, 1914
Kercheval, S. History of valley of Virginia, 3588
Kerr, C. History of Kentucky, 1549
Kerr, D. G. G. Historical atlas of Canada, 3981
Kidder, F. History of First New Hampshire Regiment, 2256
Kidron Community, Wayne co., Ohio, Mennonites, 449
Kieffer, H. M. Some of the first settlers of "The Forks of the Delaware," 2927
Kielman, C. V. University of Texas archives, 3371
Kilbourn, J. Ohio gazetteer, 2723
Kimball, F. P. Capital register of New York state, 2482
King, G. E. Creole families of New Orleans, 1652
King, G. H. S. Copies of extant Virginia wills from counties whose records have been destroyed, 3589
King, J. E. S. Abstract of early Kentucky wills, 1550; Mississippi court records, 2053
King George's War, Rhode Island list, 3080, 3082
King James's Irish army list, 4600
King Philip's War, soldiers in, 1854
King's Mountain and its heroes, 510
King's Mountain men, 546, 2659
Kingsbury, G. W., and Smith, G. M. History of Dakota territory, 3225
Kingsbury, S. M. Virginia Company of London court book, 3652–3653
Kinnaird, L. History of greater San Francisco Bay region, 886

Kinney, A. R. Titled Elizabethans, 4505
Kinney, J. M. Bibliography of diocesan histories, 458
Kirk, R., and E. F. Returns of aliens . . . of London, 4545
Kirk, R. F., and A. L. Exodus of British loyalists from U.S. to Canada, 4022; Some references and sources for searching for your ancestors in Ontario, 4023, 4084
Kirkham, E. K. Counties of the U.S., 211–212; Guide to record-searching in larger cities of U.S., 251; Handwriting of American records, 252; Land records of America, 57, 476n; Military records of America, 57; Professional techniques and tactics in American genealogical research, 253; Research in American genealogy, 254; Simplified genealogy for Americans, 255; Some of the military records of America, 476; Survey of American church records, 58, 404a
Kitchell, W. H. Lineages, Soc. of Mayflower Descendants, 2379
Kline, G. R. Minnesota Genealogical Soc. surname index, 2010
Klondike gold stampede, 781
Knapp, H. S. History of Maumee Valley, 2724
Kneen, J. J. Personal names of Isle of Man, 4888; Place-names of Isle of Man, 4889
Knight, L. L. Georgia's landmarks, 1197; Georgia's roster of the Revolution, 1198; Standard history of Georgia, 1199
Knightages, *see* Peerages
Knights Bachelor: English, 4509; Irish, 4521
Knights Banneret, 4509
Knights of Columbus of Texas. Our Catholic heritage in Texas, 3372
Knights of Edward I, 4511
Knights of the Bath, 4509
Knights Templar, Tennessee, 3297
Knights who accompanied William the Conqueror, 5014n
Knittle, W. A. Early eighteenth century Palatine emigration, 2334, 2483
Knorr, C. L. Marriage lists, Virginia counties, 3590
Kochertal records, passenger lists, 2489n, 2531n
Koehler, S. M. Huguenot ancestors, New Jersey, 2329
Koleda, E. P. Some Ohio and Iowa pioneers, 1431, 2725
Koogler, C. V., and Whitney, V. K. Aztec, 2406

*Index*

Korn, B. W. Early Jews of New Orleans, 1653
Kozee, W. C. Early families of eastern and southeastern Kentucky, 1551; Pioneer families of eastern and southeastern Kentucky, 1552
Krebs, F. Emigrants from the Palatinate to the American colonies, 2928
Kucera, V. Czech cemeteries in Nebraska, 2180; Czechs in Nebraska, 2181
Kuczynski, R. R. Birth registration and birth statistics in Canada, 3982
Kuhlicke, F. W., and Emmison, F. G. English local history handlist, 4174
Kuhns, L. O. German and Swiss settlements of colonial Pennsylvania, 2929
Kuhns, M. P. The "Mary and John," 595
Kull, I. S. New Jersey, 2335
Kummer, F. A. Free state of Maryland, 1790
Kuykendall, R. S. Hawaiian kingdom, 1259

Ladd, E. J. Atlas and outline history of southeastern U.S., 628
Ladies' heraldry, 4973
Laing, D. Catalogue of the graduates, Edinburgh University, 4742
Lainson, D. A. S. Some Magna Charta barons and other royal lineages, 274
Lake Champlain, New York/Vermont, 2484, 3477
Lake George, New York, 2484, 3477
Lamacraft, C. T. Some funeral entries of Ireland, 4618
Lamb, W. E. Lake Champlain and Lake George Valleys, 2484, 3477
Lambert, M. B. Dictionary of non-English words of Pennsylvania dialect, 2930
Lambert, O. D. Pioneer leaders of western Virginia, 3744
Lambeth, M. Memories and records of eastern North Carolina, 2607
Lanaghan, Mrs. Antigua and the Antiguans, 4918n
Lancaster, Joan C. Bibliography of historical works, 4154
Lancaster, R. A., Jr. Historic Virginia homes, 3591
Lancaster county, Pennsylvania, 2880, 2889, 2902, 2949
Lancour, H. Bibliography of passenger lists, 349
Land (grants, records, warrants, claims, etc.): entry papers of Government Land Office, 93; grants and claims, computerized index, 61; lotteries, *see* Lotteries; ownership maps, 199; patents, 73; state papers, class VIII, 76; Revolutionary War bounty, 74;
  Alabama, Indian allotments, 716; America, 57; California, 872; Canada, 4007b; Canadian loyalists, 4024; Cherokee, 703, 705; Choctaw-Chickasaw, 699–700; Creek, 697; Delaware, 1027, 1050–1051; Delaware Indians, 712; District of Columbia, 1077; England, 4230; English crown grants, 1165–1172; Florida, 1114; Georgia, 1215; Illinois, 1308, 1348, 1360; Indiana, 1407; Kansas, 1475; Kentucky, 1535–1536, 1585; Kentucky-Virginia line, 1576, 1597; Louisiana, 1613, 2031; Maryland, 1744, 1753, 1833; Michigan, 1985; Missouri, 2132; Missouri Indians, 716; Montreal, 4102; New York, 2433n, 2518; North Carolina, 2580, 3248, 3304; Nova Scotia, 4058; Ohio, 2699, 2740, 2751, 2759; Oregon, 2805, 2813–2814, 2816; Pennsylvania, 2841, 2971, 3028a; Pennsylvania-Virginia claims, 3024; Pueblo Indians, 657; Quebec, 4101, 4103, 4133; Rhode Island, 3109; Sault Sainte Marie, 1952; Seminole, 698; South Carolina, 3141, 3185; southwest, 637; Texas, 3327, 3329, 3334, 3379, 3408–3414; Trois Rivières, 4104, 4133a; Vermont, 3456, 3479, 3489–3492, 3494; Vermont-New Hampshire grants, 3479; Vermont-New York land patents, 3491; Virginia, 3560, 3563, 3594, 3610, 3643, 3647, 3651, 3677; Wales, 4230; Washington, 3685; West Virginia, 3767, 3769–3770
Landed gentry, *see* Peerages
Landes, H. Geographic dictionary of Washington, 3697
Landis, J. T. Mayflower descendants and their marriages, 302
Landon, H. F. North country, 2485
Landowners: Great Britain, 4474, 4666; Ireland, 4631, 4635–4636, 4666, 4677; Scotland, 4721
Landrum, J. B. O. Colonial and Revolutionary history of upper South Carolina, 3154
Lang, H. O. History of Willamette Valley, Oregon, 2827
Lang, T. F. Loyal West Virginia, 3745
Langguth, O. Pennsylvania German pioneers from county of Wertheim, 2931
Langston, A. L., and Buck, J. O. Pedigrees of some of Emperor Charlemagne's descendants, 275
Lanman, C. Biographical annals of civil government of U.S., 152

Lantz, E. E. Series of genealogical and heraldic articles, 1791, 3592-3593
Lapp, E. C. To their heirs forever, 4025
Larrazábal Blanco, C. Familias dominicanas, 3900
Lart, C. E. Huguenot pedigrees, 429, 4546
Lartigue, C. L. T. Index to some Philadelphia marriages, 2996a
Lasher, G. W. Ministerial directory of Baptist churches in U.S., 419
Lasseray, A. Les français sous les treize étoiles, 3983
Latham, A., and Leonard, B. G. Roll of officers in Virginia line, 3594
Latham, R. E. Revised medieval Latin word-list, 4245, 4662
Lathem, E. C. Chronological tables of American newspapers, 16
Latin America: 3842-3938a; appointments of officials, 3858; archives, 3851; bibliographies, 3855, 3868; boundaries, 3859; colonizers, 3844; governors, 3865; L.D.S. research papers, 243H; manual, 3842, 3856; manuscript collections, 3849; names, 3867; passenger lists, 3862-3863; pedigrees, 3854, 3866; personal names, 3847; Scandinavians, 2450; Spanish residents, 3861; surnames, 3857
Latin families, Texas, 3333
Latin for local history, 4242
Latin word-list, 4245
Latin words and names, 4246
Latrobe, F. C. Contemporary Maryland, 1790
Latter-day Saints (for genealogical manuals and guides, see Genealogical Society of the Church of Jesus Christ of Latter-day Saints): biographical encyclopedia, 3443; doctrinal outlook on genealogy, 267n; early church vital records, 441; name index to Library of Congress Mormon diaries, 445; origin of western geographic names, 444; register of church records, 443
Lavoisne, C. V. Complete genealogical, historical . . . atlas, 195
Law list, London, 4320
Lawrence, R. Colonial families of America, 300n, 303
Lawrence-Archer, J. H. Monumental inscriptions of British West Indies, 4924
Lawson, Sir H. Genealogical collections illustrating history of Roman Catholic families, 4537
Lazenby, M. E. History of Methodism in Alabama and west Florida, 746, 1117

Lea, J. H. Abstracts of wills, Register Soame, 4371
———— and Hutchinson, J. R. Clues for English archives, contributory to American genealogy, 59
Leach, D. E. Arms for empire, 477
Leach, Mrs. F. S. Missouri state history of DAR, 2087
Leach, F. W. Old Philadelphia families, 2932
Leavitt, T. W. H. Australian representative men, 4912
Leckey, H. L. Tenmile country, 2933-2935, 3746-3747
Lee, F. S. Genealogical and memorial history of New Jersey, 2336
Lee, G. L. Huguenot settlements in Ireland, 4700
Lee, H. F. The Huguenots in France and America, 430
Lee, S. E. These also served, 2407
Leeson, M. A. History of Montana, 2151
Leet, A. Directory of market towns . . . in Ireland, 4639
Leeward Islands, 4919, 4927
LeFevre, R. History of New Paltz, New York, 2486
Lefler, H. T. History of North Carolina, 2608
———— and Newsome, A. R. North Carolina, 2609
LeGear, C. E. List of geographical atlases in Library of Congress, 200; U.S. atlases, 202
Lehman, J. O. Sonnenberg, 449
Lehmann, R. P. Anglo-Jewish bibliography, 4549
Leiby, A. C. Early Dutch and Swedish settlers of New Jersey, 2337
Leigh, R. W. Five hundred Utah place names, 3444; Nevada place names, 2211
LeMaster, E. T. Abstracts of Georgia death notices, 1200; Abstracts of Georgia marriage notices, 1201
Le Neve, J. Fasti ecclesiae anglicanae, 4299-4301
Lentz, A. D. Guide to manuscripts of Ohio Historical Soc., 2726
Lester, M. A. Old southern Bible records, 629
Letter-carrier offices in U.S. 214a
Letter to the Commissioner . . . respecting patents for lands in military bounty land district in Illinois, 1348
Levillier, R. Biografías de conquistadores de la Argentina, 3872

*Index*

Lewis, I. Handlist of Welsh record publications, 4711
Lewis, S. Topographical dictionaries of: England, 4392; Ireland, 4640; Scotland, 4770; Wales, 4858
Lewis, T. H. Historical record of Maryland Annual Conference of Methodist Protestant Church, 1793
Lewis, T. W. History of southeastern Ohio, 2727
Lewis, V. A. Historical data relating to formation of West Virginia, 3748; Soldiery of West Virginia in French and Indian War, 3749
Librarian subject guide to books, 4153
Library of Alabama lives, 747
Library of Congress, *see* U.S. Library of Congress
Library of Parliament, Canada, *see* Canada. Library of Parliament
Libro de la Tasaciones de Pueblos de la Nueva Espana, siglo XVI, 3921
Libro parroquial mas antiguo de Caracas, 3938a
Liebman, S. B. Guide to Jewish references in Mexican colonial era, 3922; Jews in New Spain, 3923
Limerick, Ireland, worthies, 4677a
Lincoln county, Maine, probate records, 1726
Lincoln's Inn, London, Records, 4321
Lindsley, J. B. Military annals of Tennessee, 3282
Lineback, N. G., and Traylor, C. T. Atlas of Alabama, 748
Lingenfelter, K., and Fulton, R. Northern California marriages, 887
Lingenfelter, R. E. Newspapers of Nevada, 2212
Link, J. T. Origin of place-names of Nebraska, 2171n
Linkage for ancestral research, 122
Linn, J. B. Annals of Buffalo Valley, Pennsylvania, 2936-2937; List of officers of colonies on the Delaware, 2938; List of "soldiers of the revolutionists who received pay for their services," 2939; List of soldiers who served as rangers, 2940
────── and Egle, W. H. Pennsylvania in War of the Revolution, 2941
Lippincott's gazetteer of the world, 194n
Lisbon, Portugal, Anglican church registers, 4898
List and Index society. Publications, 4268
List of non-parochial registers (British), 4342

List of persons concerned in the (Scottish) Rebellion (1745), 4732
Littell, J. Family records, 2338
Littell, W. Laws of Kentucky, index, 1581
Little, G. T. Genealogical and family history of Maine, 1715, 2257
Little James (ship), 1845
Littledale, W. A. Collection of miscellaneous grants, 4506
Litton, G. L. History of Oklahoma, 2786
Liverpool, England: emigrants, 339, 352; passenger lists, 352
Livingston, Sir N. B. Sketch pedigrees of settlers in Jamaica, 4925
Livingstone, M. Guide to public records of Scotland, 4719a
Livre de percharge du fief (Channel Islands), 4883
Livre d'or de la noblesse rurale canadienne-française, 3962
Ljungstedt, M. County court note-book, 1771
Lloyd, E. Arizonology, 791
Lloyd, H. A. Gentry of southwest Wales, 4873
Lloyd, J. Y. W. History of princes, Lords Marcher . . . of Arwystli, 4874
Lo Buglio, R. L. Baja California bibliography, 3924
Local historian, 4269
Local histories, bibliography, 27-28; in Library of Congress, 15a
Local History and Genealogical Society. The quarterly, 3372a
Local history bibliography, 17, 20
Local history, dictionary catalog, 24-25
Local indexes in American libraries, 53
Localized history series, 17
Lockwood, F. C. Arizona characters, 792; More Arizona characters, 793; Pioneer days in Arizona, 794
Lockwood, J. H. Western Massachusetts, 1891
Lodge, E. Peerage, baronetage, knightage, and companionage of British Empire, 4507
Lodge, J. Peerage of Ireland, 4682
Logan, J., and McIan, R. R. Clans of Scottish Highlands, 4810
Lohmann Villena, G. Americanos en las ordenes nobiliarias, 303a; Genealogical reach in South America, 3856
London, H. S. College of Arms, biographical and genealogical data, 4977n; Right road to heraldry, 5001
London, England: aliens, 4545; clergy, 4298;

419

*Index*

directories, 4148; Huguenots, aliens, 4545; inhabitants lists, 4223; marriage indexes, 4355a; marriage licenses, 4351; medical practitioners, 4323; monumental inscriptions, 4361; newspapers, 4234n; parishes, Church of England, 4343; passenger lists to New York, 2489n; rate assessments, 4223; records, 4270; Spanish and Portuguese Jews' Congregation, 4550; streetnames, 4400; wills, 4379-4380n

London, Ontario. Court of General Quarter Sessions, Minutes, 4085

London Record Society. Publications, 4270

London University. Institute of Historical Research. Bibliography of historical works, 4154-4157, 4220; bulletin, 4271

Lone star state (histories of Texas), 3362-3365, 3375-3377

Long Island Historical Society. Catalogue of American genealogies, 60

Long Island, New York: bibliography, 2549; census (1776), 2491; colonial families, 2548; deeds, 2498; King's county early settlers, 2431; militia, 2491; Quakers, 2467; rate lists, 2487

Lonn, E. Foreigners in the Union army and navy, 1654

Lonsdale, R. E. Atlas of North Carolina, 2610

Lopez, C. U. Chilenos in California, 888

Lord, C. L. Localized history series, 17

────── and Lord, E. H. Historical atlas of U. S., 196

Lord, G.T. Geographical description of New Hampshire, 2227

Lord Dunsmore's War, W. Va., 3749

Lords Marcher, 4874

Lossing, B. J. Pictorial field-book of Revolution, 521

Lost in Canada? Canadian-American query exchange, 3983a

Lost tribes of North Carolina, W. S. Ray, 2639-2643

Lotteries, Fire Civilized Tribes: (1832), 703, 705; Georgia, history, 1202-1203; (1805), 1204, 1239; (1807), 1205, 1211; (1820), 1160, 1206; (1821), 1161, 1207; (1827), 1189, 1208; (1832), 1209, 1220, 1228

Louisiana (*see also* New Orleans): 1598-1692; Acadian records, 1610, 1623, 1667, 1676-1677; Acadians in Nova Scotia, 4050, 4061; ancestry, 1637-1638; Bible records, 1670; Canadian families, 1683-1684; Canary Islands migration, 1688; Catholic missions, 1616; cemetery records, 1666; census (1699-1732), 1659, (1758-1796), 1690, (1770-1789), 1679, (1810), 1599, 1682, 1686, (1820), 1599; church and synagogue archives, 1645; church records, 1610, 1623, 1625, 1640, 1689; churches and religious organizations, 1642; civil records, 1640; Civil War, 564, 1611, 1654; colonial documents, 1624, 1626, 1628, 1636, 1649; colonial marriages, 1627; county-parish boundaries, 1641; Creoles of German descent, 1622; first families, settlers, 1617, 1625, 1639, 1668, 1689; German settlers, 1622; Gulf Coast colonials, 1626; Indians, 656; infantry regiment and militia companies, 1649; marriages, 1627, 1630, 1632, 1662-1663, 1687; military records, 1606; militia lists, 1649, 1679; Mississippi Valley pioneers, 1685; mortality schedules (1860), 1598; newspapers, 1647, 1658; notarial acts, 1637-1638; old families, 1602, 1689; parish records, 1646, 1680, 1692; passenger lists, 1676, 1678, 1685, 1688; plantation homes, 1618, 1681; plats, 1613; public vital statistics records, 1643; recruits, 1629; ship registers and enrollments, 1648; slave-holders, 1669; Spanish census (1791), 1671; Spanish officers and soldiers, 1649; Spanish surnames, 1665; Swiss settlers, 1622; territorial papers, 1612; tombstone inscriptions, 1619; troops, 1617; Vaudreuil papers, 1605; War of 1812, 1614, 1675; wills, 1662; Yugoslavs, 1691

Louisiana genealogical register (magazine), 1655

Louisiana historical quarterly, 1656-1657

Louisiana Purchase, land grants in, 61

Lounsberry, C. A. North Dakota history, 2676

Love, W. De L. Wisconsin in War of Rebellion, 3803

Lovell, J. Gazetteer of British North America, 3984

Low, C. Roll of Australian arms, 5062

Lowell, E. J. The Hessians, 380, 522

Lower, M. A. Patronymica Britannica, 4414

Lower California, *see* Baja California

Lower Norfolk county, Virginia antiquary, 3595

Lowry, M. Who, when, where in Kansas, 1472

Loyalist gazette, 4026

Loyalists: definition, 522a; American, 494, 533; biographical sketches, 534; British-Americans, 529; Canadians, 4014-4037; Delaware, 1038; East Florida, 1128; historical view of Royal Commission and

*Index*

compensation granted, 511; Massachusetts, 1890, 1927; New Brunswick, Canada, 4037, 4069; New Hampshire, 2271; New Jersey, 2333; New York, 2526; North Carolina, 2589; Nova Scotia, 4058; Old United Empire loyalist list, 4035; Ontario, 4079–4080, 4089; Pennsylvania, 3012; Rivington's New York newspaper and loyalist press, 71; United Empire loyalists, 4020, 4034

Loyd, L. C. Origins of some Anglo-Norman families, 4467

Lucas, S. E. 1807 land lottery of Georgia, 1211; Lottery publications, 1210

Lunenberg county, Virginia, 3503–3504

Lutherans: 446–448; Connecticut, 996; Delaware, 1041; Georgia, 1231, 1233; Missouri, 3798; New York city, 2472; New York colony, 2432; North Carolina, 2575, 3121; South Carolina, 3121; Tennessee, 3249, 3524; Virginia, 3249, 3524; Wisconsin, 3798

Luttrell, L. E., and Creekmore, P. Writings on Tennessee counties, 3283

Lyman, W. D. History of old Walla Walla county, 3699; History of Yakima Valley, 3698

Lynch-Robinson, Sir C. and A. Intelligible heraldry, 4981

Lyon Office, Edinburgh, Index to genealogies, 4709

McAdams, E. Kentucky pioneer and court records, 1553

McAllister, A. S. Pennsylvania gravestone inscriptions, 2942

McAllister, J. T. Index to Saffell's List of Virginia soldiers, 3616; Virginia militia in Revolutionary War, 3597

McArthur, L. A. Oregon geographic names, 2828

McAuslan, W. A. Mayflower index, 321

McBain, A. Etymological dictionary of the Gaelic language, 4779n; Etymology of principal Gaelic national names, 4779

McBee, M. W. Mississippi county court records, 2054; Natchez court records, 2055

McBride, R. M. Tennessee county data for historical and genealogical research, 3284

McCall, E. S. Roster of Revolutionary soldiers in Georgia, 1212–1213

McCarter, J. M., and Jackson, B. F. Historical and biographical encyclopedia of Delaware, 1046

McCay, B. L. Index to some early tax digests of Georgia, 1214; Seven lesson courses in Irish research, 4663; Sources for genealogical searching in: Illinois, 1332; Kentucky, 1554; North Carolina, 2611; Ohio, 2728; Pennsylvania, 2943; Tennessee, 3285; Virginia and West Virginia, 3598, 3750

McClintock, J. H. Arizona, 795; Mormon settlement in Arizona, 796

Macco, H. F. Palatine church visitations, 2944

McCown, M., and Burns, L. E. Soldiers of War of 1812, 3286

McCracken, G. E. Welcome claimants, 3030

McCrady, E. History of South Carolina in Revolution, 3155

McDermott, J. F. Spanish in Mississippi valley, 630

McDonald, C. Historical directory of Saskatchewan newspapers, 4142

McDonald, C. D., Jr. Some Virginia marriages, 3599–3600

Macdonald, W. R. Scottish armorial seals, 5049

McDowell, R. E. Memorandum and official records concerning Dakota militia, 3226

McDowell, S. Surname index to Kentucky 7th census, 1555, 1588

McEllhiney, W. B., and Thomas, E. W. 1820 census of Mississippi, 2056

MacFarlane, W. Genealogical collections concerning families in Scotland, 4811

McGee, T. D'a. History of Irish settlers in North America, 385

McGhee, L. K. Maryland pension abstracts, 1794; Maryland Revolutionary War pensioners, 1795; Massachusetts pension abstracts, 1892; Missouri Revolutionary soldiers, 2110; Partial census of 1787 to 1791 of Tennessee, 3287; Pennsylvania pension abstracts, 2945; Pension abstracts of Maryland soldiers of the Revolution, 1556; Tennessee military records, 3288; Virginia pension abstracts, 3601

MacGiolla-Domhnaigh, P. Some anglicized surnames in Ireland, 4648

McGivern, J. Your name and coat of arms, 5074

McGrew, E. Z. North Carolina census records, 1787–1890, 2611a

McIlhany, H. M., Jr. Some Virginia families, 3602

McIlwaine, H. R. Index to obituary notices in Richmond enquirer, 3603; Minutes of Council and General Court of Colonial Virginia, 3640

McKay, D. B. Pioneer Florida, 1118

421

*Index*

M'Kechnie, H. Pursuit of pedigree, 4787
Mackenzie, G. N. Colonial families of USA, 304
Mackenzie, W. C. Scottish place-names, 4780; Western Isles, 4884
McKinstry, E. R. Guide to genealogical sources in New Jersey Historical Society Library, 2339
McKirdy, J. Origin of names given to counties in Pennsylvania, 2946
McKnight, W. J. Pioneer outline history of northwestern Pennsylvania, 2947
McLane, B. J. 1860 mortality schedules of Arkansas, 831; Index to 5th (1830) census ... Arkansas, 832; Index to 5th [i.e. 6th] (1840) census [Arkansas], 833
——— and Glazner, C. H. 1850 mortality schedules of Arkansas, 834
McLaughlin, P. D. Pre-federal maps in National Archives, 205
MacLean, J. P. Historical account of settlements of Scotch Highlanders in America, 396, 523
McLean, M. D. Papers concerning Robertson's Colony in Texas, 3374
McLendon, S. G. History of the public domain in Georgia, 1215
MacLysaght, E. Irish families, 4683; Irish families map, 4641; More Irish families, 4684; Report on documents relating to wardenship of Galway, 4588; Seventeenth century hearth money rolls, 4589; Supplement to Irish families, 4685; Surnames of Ireland, 4649; Survey of documents in private keeping, 4590
McMullan, T. N. Louisiana newspapers 1794-1961, 1658
McMullin, P. W. Grassroots of America, 61; New York in 1800, 2488
McNaughton, A. Book of kings, 4451
McNeill, C., and Otway-Ruthven, A. J. Dowdall deeds, 4591
MacWethy, L. D. Book of names, 2489
McWhorter, L. V. Border settlers of northwestern Virginia, 3751-3752
Maddux, G. M. and D. O. 1800 census, Delaware, 1047
Madison, C. A. Eminent American Jews, 434
Maduell, C. R., Jr. Census tables for the French colony of Louisiana, 1659; Index to Spanish citizens entering New Orleans, 1660-1661; Marriage contracts ... in New Orleans, 1662; Marriages and family relationships in New Orleans, 1663-1664;
Romance of Spanish surnames, 1665, 3857
Magazine of bibliographies, 123
Magazine subject index, 97
Magdaleno, R. R. Títulos de Indias, 3858
Magee, Z. F., and Bateman, T. S. Cemetery records of Louisiana, 1666
Magna Charta barons: 272, 274, 280, 281, 299; American descendants, 281, 284-285
Magruder, J. M. Index to Maryland colonial wills, 1796; Magruder's Maryland colonial abstracts, 1797
Maidment, J. Collectanea genealogica, 4720
Main, F. Ohio genealogical records, 2729
Maine (*see also* Massachusetts): 1692a-1738; bibliography, 1693, 1712, 1737; boundary changes, 1709; census (1790), 1734, (1800), 1713; Civil War, 554, 564, 1699, 1717-1718; gazetteer, 1692a, 1706, 1735; Indian affairs, 1714; manual, 613; pioneer French settlers, 4061; place names, 1697-1698; probate records, 1726; province and court records, 1716; Revolutionary War, 1701, 1704, 1711; rivers, 1732; Saco Valley settlements, 1729; ship registers, 1710; War of 1812, 1719; wills, 1730; York, 1694, 1699, 1738
Maine genealogical inquirer (magazine), 1720
Maine genealogist and biographer (magazine), 1721
Maine historical and genealogical recorder (magazine), 1722
Maine historical magazine, 1723
Maine Historical Society collections, 1724
Major genealogical record sources in U.S., *see* Genealogical Society of the Church of Jesus Christ of Latter-day Saints
Malcolm of Scotland, lineage, 325-326
Malherbe, D. F. du T. Stamregister van die Suid-Afrikaanse volk, 4960
Malo, D. Hawaiian antiquities, 1260
Malone, H. R. History of central New York, 2490
Manarin, L. H. North Carolina troops, 2612
Mandans, 663
Manhattan Island, iconography, 2552
Manitoba, Canada: 4045-4046; pioneers, 4046; place names, 4045
Manross, W. Fulham papers in Lambeth Palace Library, 305
Mansfield, H. W. Block Island cemetery records, 3091
Manuals: 228-268; Acadia, Nova Scotia, 4097; Australia, 4907, 4914a; Canada,

3955, 3960, 3973, 3974, 4021; Central Americal 2842, 3908; Civil War, 557; Connecticut, 613, 960; English, 4422–4444; Georgia, 1183; heraldry, 4435, 4990–5008; Illinois, 1332, 1356; Indiana, 1396, 1406; Irish, 4653–4664; Kentucky, 1529; Maine, 613; Maryland, 1812, 1820; Massachusetts, 613, 1863; Mexico, 3842, 3908, 3919, 3926; Missouri, 2136; New Hampshire, 2286; New Jersey, 2339, 2360, 2386; New York city and state, 2424, 2427; North Carolina, 2590, 2611, 2651a; Ohio, 2695, 2728; Ontario, 4084; Oregon, 2810, 2815; Pennsylvania, 2843, 2850, 2913, 2943; Quebec, 4052, 4097; Scotch-Irish, 4654, 4658, 4664; Scottish, 4783–4790; South Carolina, 3159, 3188; Tennessee, 3250, 3273, 3284–3285; Utah, 3442; Virginia, 3598, 3649, 3750; Wales, 4866–4868; West Virginia, 3750, 3765

Manuscript collections: Bancroft Library, 644; Boston Public Library, 3948; Canadian repositories, 4007c, Draper collection, papers, 1594; Duke Univ. Library, 2653; Genealogical Society of Pennsylvania, 2891; Hayes Library, 2726; Kentucky Historical Soc., 1502; Maryland Historical Soc., 1822; Massachusetts Historical Soc., 1906; Minnesota Historical Soc., 2017–2018; New Jersey Historical Soc., 2374; New York city and state, 2435, 2468, 2517–2518, 2566; North Carolina archives, 2586; Ohio, 2761; Ohio Historical Soc., 2726; Oregon Historical Soc., 2830; Rutgers Univ. Library, 2377; Santa Barbara Mission archives, 866; State Historical Soc. of Iowa, 1417; Tennessee Historical Soc., 3307; United States, 50; Univ. of Missouri, 2134–2135; Univ. of Texas, 3371; West Virginia Univ. Library, 3729; Western Reserve Historical Soc., 465a, 2752; Wisconsin State Historical Soc., 1594, 3809–3811

Manuscripts: microfilms in England and Wales, 83; National union catalog (U.S.), 79; relating to America in Great Britain and Ireland, 41; source list relating to U.S. and Canada in private archives in Scottish Record Office, 66

Manwaring, C. W. Digest of early Connecticut probate records, 1004

Manx personal names, 4888

Maps: 186–207; America, in Library of Congress, 201; Barbados, 4931; bibliography, 187; Bureau of Census, 203; England, 4391; Georgia, 1138, 1182; Indiana, 1364, 1364a; Indians, 671; Ireland, 4628–4629, 4633, 4641, 4643, 4679; Kansas, 1463; Kentucky, 1525; Maryland, 1809; Mexico, 3917, 3926; National Archives, 204; New York, 2571; North America (southeastern), 621; North Carolina, 2649, 2651; Ohio, 2710; Oregon, 2804; Scotland, 4765, 4772, 4813; Tennessee, 1525, 3270, 3292; Texas, 3344; Wales, 4391, 4853; West Virginia, 3768; Wisconsin, 3801n, 3813

March, D. D. History of Missouri, 2111

Marchand, S. A., Sr. Acadian exiles . . . of Louisiana, 1667; Attempt to re-assemble old settlers in family groups, 1668

Marchant, A. Boundaries of Latin American republics, 3859

Marcus, J. R. Selected bibliography of American Jewish history, 17a

Marian exiles, 358, 4527

Marine, W. M. British invasion of Maryland, 1798

Marine Corps, U. S., 466, 473

Mariners in Revolutionary War, 520

Marion's men, Revolutionary War, South Carolina, 3122

Maritime Provinces, Canada, 4047–4074

Maritime records, Philadelphia, 2911–2912

Markotic, V. Biographical directory of Americans and Canadians of Croatian descent, 376, 3987

Marks, H. S. Who was who in Alabama, 749; Who was who in Florida, 1119

Marquette, D. History of Nebraska Methodism, 2182

Marquis, A. N. Book of Minnesotans, 2011

Marriages: American, 89, 136, 287, 1842; Australia, 4914b; Boston, 1855–1857; British, 4346–4360; California, 887; Cape of Good Hope, 4952; Caracas, 3938a; Colorado, 935; Connecticut, 958, 979; District of Columbia, 1087, 1095; Edinburgh, Scotland, 4761a; French Canada, 3943, 3994; Georgia, 1151, 1201, 1219, 1234–1236; Great Britain, description, 4345, v.1: Illinois, 1313; Ireland, 4611, 4615, 4617; Kentucky, 1503–1504; Louisiana, 1627, 1632, 1662–1664, 1687; Maryland, 1742, 1742a, 1756, 1767; Massachusetts, 1842, 1844, 1855–1857, 2246; Missouri, 2080, 2141; New England, 2246; New Jersey, 2305, 2314, 2351; New Orleans, 1662–1664; New York city and state, 2503, 2508, 2544, 2555, 2570; North Carolina, 2576, 2582, 2594; Ottawa, Ontario, 4087; Pennsylvania, 2858, 2885, 2983-2986, 2996, 3019; Philadelphia, 2989, 2996a; Quebec, 4099-4100, 4108, 4112, 4123, 4126, 4127, 4132, 4136; Scottish, 4761a; South Carolina, 1234, 3129, 3172-3175, 3205, 3208; Tennessee, 3236, 3280, 3308; Texas, 3354, 3399; Vermont, 3499; Virginia, 3502, 3533, 3542-3543; 3578, 3590, 3599-3600, 3656, 3664, 3680; West Wales and Gower, 4849

Marsh, W. L. Search and retrieval, 256

Marshall, G. W. Genealogist's guide, 4182; Index to pedigrees, 4508

Marshall, J. Royal naval biography, 4333

Marshall, T. W. Encyclopedia of American Quaker genealogy, Virginia, 3576n

Martell, J. S. Immigration to and emigration from Nova Scotia, 4061a

Martenet, S. J. New topographical atlas of the state of Maryland and the District of Columbia, 1082, 1799

Martin, C. T. Record interpreter, 4246

Martin, G. A. Vital records from the National intelligencer, 1083, 1084

Martin, G. H., and McIntyre, S. Bibliography of British and Irish municipal history, 4175

Martin, J. A new and comprehensive gazetteer of Virginia and the District of Columbia, 1085, 3604

Martin, Rev. William, and Scotch-Irish migration to South Carolina, 3199

Martínez, P. L. Guía familiar de Baja California, 3925

Martínez, R. Diccionario biográfico-histórico dominicano, 3901

Marvil, J. E. Pilots of the Bayard River, Delaware, 1048

Mary and John (ship), 575, 595

Maryland: 1739-1840; accounts, 1751-1752, 1755, 1778, 1797; archives, 1805; atlas, 1799; border changes, 1746; Catholics, 1817, 2114; cemetery inscriptions, 1783-1784; census (1776), 1747n, 1763, (1778), 1762, (1790), 1838, (1800), 1802, 1837, 1839; Church of England in, 1832; church archives, Protestant Episcopal church, 1780-1781; Civil War, 556, 564, 1777, 1840; colonial families, 291, 620, 1768; colonial judgments, 1750; counties, 1746, 1782, 1808; county courthouses, 1824; deaths, 1742a, 1757; divorces, 1811; Eastern Shore, 1766, 1807, 1823; first settlers, 343; gazetteer, 1775; Germans, 1772, 1813, 1831; graves, 1827; heraldry, 1768, 1791, 1815; immigrants, 1833; Indian Wars, 1759, 1794-1795; inventories, 1755, 1797; land offices, 1744, 1778; land patents, 1833; land records, 1753, 1774; laws, 1792; legislators, 1819; manual, 1812, 1820; manuscript collections, 1822; maps, 1809; marriages, 1742, 1742a, 1756, 1767; Maryland Line, 1836; Mennonites, 493; Methodists, 1793; military land lots, 1744; names changed, 1811; Nicholites, 1764; Oath of Allegiance, 1761; Oath of Fidelity, 1748, 1761; parishes, 1832; passenger list, 1814; pension lists, 1759, 1794-1795, 1816; Prerogative Court records, 1778; Provincial offices, 1818; Quakers, 1764-1765, 1789; records, 1747; rent rolls, 1758; Revolutionary War, 911, 1744, 1747-1748, 1759, 1761, 1773, 1794-1795, 1806, 1816, 1836; slave owners, 1760a; source records, 1820; state papers, 1739, 1803; War of 1812, 1759, 1794-1795, 1798; wills, 1741, 1760, 1785-1788, 1796-1797

Maryland and Delaware genealogist (magazine), 1049, 1800

Maryland genealogical bulletin, 1779n

Maryland Genealogical Soc. bulletin, 1801

Maryland Hall of Records Commission. Calendar of Maryland state papers, 1803

Maryland historical and genealogical bulletin, 1779

Maryland historical magazine, 1804

Maryland Historical Soc. Archives of Maryland, 1805; Manuscript collections, 1822; muster rolls, American Revolution, 1806

Maryland Original Research Soc. of Baltimore, bulletin, 1807

Maskey, C. L. Some early Ohio and Pennsylvania families, 2730, 2948

Massachusetts (see also Maine): 1841-1937; Acadians, 1850; acts and laws, 1893-1894; aliens, 1905; bibliography, 1876; births, 1855-1856; Boston records, 1855-1856; 1865, 1878; cemeteries, 1930; census (1643-1765), 1851, (1779), 1872, (1790), 1931, (1800), 1932; church archives, 1887, 1918, 1934; civil list, 1933; Civil War, 554, 564, 1862, 1899-1900; Congregational churches, 1934; counties, cities, towns, 1902; county archives, 1886, 1902; deaths, 1843, 1855-1856, 1865, 2246; emigrants, 1846, 1847, 1860: first planters, 1936; French, 1850, 1878; gazetteer, 1879, 1882, 1911, 1926; heraldry, 1914; Historical Records Survey, 1884-1888; Indian Wars, 1854, 1892; Italians, 1864; King Philip's War, 1854; local history,

1876; loyalists, 1890, 1927; manual 613, 1849, 1863; manuscripts, 1906; marriages, 1842, 1844, 1855–1857, 2246; Mayflower Compact, 1881; Mayflower passengers, 1928; name changes, 1903; obituaries, 1843, 1865; passenger lists, 1845–1846, 1848, 1860, 1905, 1928; pensions, 1892; Pilgrims, 1845, 1907, 1923, 1928, 1937; port arrivals, 1860; public vital statistics records, 1884; records, 1863, 1898; Revolutionary War, 1841, 1892, 1904, 1927; rich men, 1877; ship registers, 1888; tax-payers, 1858; Universal churches, 1887; vital records, 1916; War of 1812, 1719, 1892, 1901

Massachusetts Bay Colony: deaths, 1865; records of governor and company, 1898

Massachusetts centinel (newspaper) 1842–1843

Massachusetts Historical Society catalog of manuscripts, 1906

Massey, R. W. List of parishes in Boyd's marriage index, 4354

Massicotte, E. Z., and Roy, R. Armorial du Canada français, 3988, 5075

――― (and others). Répertoire des engagements pour l'ouest, 3988

Mather, F. G. Refugees of 1776 from Long Island to Connecticut, 1005, 2491

Matheson, C. Catalogue of publications of Scottish historical and kindred clubs, 4712

Matheson, Sir R. E. Special report on surnames in Ireland, 4650; Varieties and synonymes [sic] of surnames . . . in Ireland, 4651

Mathews, E. B. Counties of Maryland, 1808; Maps and map-makers of Maryland, 1809

Mathias, P., and Pearsall, A. W. H. Shipping, 4224

Matos Bernier, F. Muertos y vivos, 3060

Matthew Paris shields, 5027n

Matthews, A. G. Calamy revised, 4302; Walker revised, 4303

Matthews, C. M. English surnames, 4415

Matthews, John (American). Complete American armoury, 5076

Matthews, John (British), and Matthews, G. F. Abstracts of probates and sentences, 4367; Abstracts of probate acts, 4368–4370

Matthews, W. American diaries in manuscript, 18; British diaries, 4225

――― and others. American diaries, annotated bibliography, 19

Maumee Valley, Ohio, 2724, 2767

Maxwell, A. S. Records of "Quakers," 4825

Maxwell, F. Ohio Indian trails, 2731

Maxwell, W. Virginia historical register 3658

May Wilson McBee collection, 2054–2055

Mayflower: Compact, 301, 1881; descendants and their marriages, 302; index, 321; passengers, 1845, 1928; planters, 590a; Register (District of Columbia), 322; Society of Mayflower descendants, 320–321

Mayflower descendant, 596–597

Mayflower quarterly, 306, 1907

Mayhill, R. T. Lancaster county, Pennsylvania, 2949

Mayo, Ireland, Books of survey, 4580

Mayo's Map of Barbados, 4931

Mead, F. S. Handbook of denominations in U.S., 404b

Meade, W. Old churches . . . of Virginia, 3605

Means, E. R. Hoosier ancestors index, 1393

Meany, E. S. Origin of Washington geographic names, 3700

Mecklenburg signers, 2641

Medals and ribbons of U.S. military, 479

Medcalf, G. Hawaiian royal orders, 1261

Medical annals, Maryland, 1769

Medical directory (British), 4324

Medical practitioners, Britain, 4323–4329

Medina, J. T. Diccionario biográfico colonial de Chile, 3890–3891

Meler, V. The Slavonic pioneers of California, 889

Mell, A. R. W. Revolutionary soldiers buried in Alabama, 750

Members of Parliament (Great Britain), 4314

Memorial and biographical history of counties of: Fresno, etc., California, 891; Johnson and Hill counties, Texas, 3375; McLennan, etc., counties, Texas, 3376; Merced, etc., counties, California, 892–893; Navarro, etc., counties, Texas, 3377–3378; northern California, 890

Memorial and biographical record of: Iowa, 1432; South Dakota, 3227; Tennessee, 3289

Memorial encyclopedia of New Jersey, 2340

Memorial record of: Alabama, 751; northeastern Indiana, 1395; southwestern Minnesota, 2012; western Kentucky, 1557

Memorial record of distinguished men of Indianapolis and Indiana, 1394

Memphis Genealogical Society journal, 3241n

Men and women in Arizona, 796a

Men and women of Hawaii, 1262

*Index*

Men of affairs . . . of Montana, 2152
Men of: Hawaii, 1262n; New York, 2492; West Virginia, 3753
Men of mark in Maryland, 1810; Virginia, 3606-3607
Men of progress . . . in: Massachusetts, 1908; Rhode Island, 3092; Vermont, 3478
Men of the soil, 4062
Mendiburu, M. de. Diccionario histórico-biográfico del Perú, 3934-3935
Menn, J. K. Large slaveholders of deep South, 631; Large slaveholders of Louisiana, 1669
Mennell, P. Dictionary of Australasian biography, 4913
Mennonite encyclopedia, 450
Mennonite quarterly review, 451-452
Mennonites: 449-52; Canada, 3968a; Revolutionary War participation, 493; Virginia, 3517
Mercantile claims, British, Revolutionary War, 4190
Mercer, J. E. Genealogical notes from Bermuda, 4926
Mercer, J. K., and Vallandigham, C. N. Representative men of Ohio, 2732
Merion in the Welsh tract, 2894
Merrill, E. Gazetteer of New Hampshire, 2258
Metcalf, F. J. Vital records extracted from National intelligencer, 1086
―――― and Martin, G. A. Marriages and deaths, National intelligencer, 1087
Metcalf, H. H. One thousand New Hampshire notables, 2259
Metcalfe, W. C. Book of Knights Banneret, 4509
Methodist church, New York city, 2472
Methodist Episcopal Church, Minutes of annual conference, 453
Methodist Protestant Church, Maryland, 1793
Methodists: Alabama, 746, 769; English, 4529n, 4553-4559, Florida (west), 1117; ministers, 4557; Nebraska, 2182; North Carolina, 2581; South Carolina, 3128
Mexican War: 550a-550b; dead, 550a; register, 550b; Connecticut, 970; Illinois, 1327; Iowa, 1426; Nebraska, 2187; New Hampshire, 2230; North Carolina, 2617; Ohio, 2741; Pennsylvania, 2950; Texas, 3321, 3394
Mexico: 3907-3931; archdioceses, 3910; archives, 856n; assessments of towns, 3921; atlas, 3917, 3926; bibliography, 3920, 3924; census records information, 3909n;
coats of arms, 5082; ecclesiastical records, 3910; Jews, 3922-3923; land grants in Chihuahuan acquisition, 3327; land records, 3909n; manual, 3842, 3908, 3919, 3926; manuscripts in Bancroft Libr., 3849; maps, 3917; parish and civil registers, 3931; record sources, 3918; Scandinavians, 2450; vital statistics, 3925
Meyer, D. G. Highland Scots of North Carolina, 2613
Meyer, M. K. Divorce and names changed in Maryland, 1811; Genealogical research in Maryland, 1812
Meyers, C. M. Early military records of New York, 2493; Early New York census records, 2494; Palatine colonial records of New York, 2495
Meynen, E. Bibliography on German settlements, 2951
Meyrick, Sir S. R. Heraldic visitations, Wales, 4871n
Miami Valley, Ohio, 2686, 2720
Michaud, A. Généalogie des familles de la Rivière Oelle, 4116
Michigan: 1938-1986; biographies, 1964; cemetery records, 1943; census (1820), 1948, 1984, (1830), 1953; church and synagogue archives, 1955; churches and religious organizations, 1954; Civil War, 554, 564, 1962-1963; county archives, 1956, 1986; Dutch records, 1982; emigrants, 1939; gazetteer, 1939; German-American pioneers, 1951, 3786; historical records, 1944; land claims, 1952; land owners, 1985; military records, 1980; pensions, 1941; place names, 1978; plat books, 1959; Revolutionary War, 1941, 1980; settlers, 1983; vital statistics, 1957; War of 1812, 1971
Michigan heritage, 1966
Michigan Pioneer and Historical Society collections, 1967-1968
Michigana, 1969
Microfilms: British manuscripts project, 83; L.D.S. records, 55; Minnesota, 2016; Oregon, 2831; population censuses (1790-1890), 183; state records, 56, 78
Microform: newspapers in, 84; U. S. decennial census publications (1790-1960), 185
Mid-Atlantic States, pension roll (1835), 490
Mid-Michigan Genealogical Society. Occasional paper, 1970
Mid-Western states, pension roll (1835), 490
Middle East, immigration, 371
Middle New River settlements, West Virginia, 3740

426

*Index*

Middle Temple, London, admissions, 4322
Middlebrook, L. F. History of maritime Connecticut during American Revolution, 1006
Middlesex, England, English convicts from, 289
Middleton, J. E., and Landon, F. Province of Ontario, 4086
Midwest: Bible records, 643; pioneer families, 649; Quaker records, 461, 640; source records, 642, 645
Midwest genealogical register, 642
Midwestern heritage (magazine), 643
Milesian family of Ireland, 4676
Military lists: general, 57, 466–490; Civil War, 551–573; Mexican War, 550a–550b; National Archives, 484; Revolutionary War, 491–546; War of 1812, 547–550 Arkansas, War of 1812, 817; Illinois, 1349–1350, 1425; Iowa, 1425; Louisiana, 1606, 1629, 1649; Mississippi, 2069; New Hampshire, 2277; New Jersey, 2353–2354, 2368; New Orleans, 1679; New York, 2493, 2514, 2519, 2527, 2529; Ohio, 1425; Rhode Island, 3112–3114; Tennessee, 3288; Virginia, 3520; Wisconsin, 1425
Militia: Canada, 4107a; Dakota, 3226; Kentucky, 1524; Pennsylvania, 2870, 2938, 2952–2954, 2965; Tennessee, 3290
Miller, A. T. Soldiers of War of 1812 who died in Michigan, 1971
Miller, C. L. Aids for genealogical searching in Indiana, 1396
Miller, J. Illustrated history of Montana, 2153
Miller, O. K. Migration, emigration, immigration, 351
Miller, T. C., and Maxwell, H. West Virginia and its people, 3754
Miller, T. L. Bounty and donation land grants of Texas, 3379
Milliken, E. Genealogy and local history, 20
Mills, M. S. Relocated cemeteries in Oklahoma and parts of Kansas and Texas, 1473, 2787, 3380
Mills, R. Atlas of South Carolina, 3156
Milne, A. T. Writings on British history, 4161–4163, 4166–4168
Milwaukee county, Wisconsin, 3789
Ministers, New Hampshire, 2229
Mink, A. de W. Title list of Ohio newspapers, 2733; Union list of Ohio newspapers, 2734
Minnehaha county, South Dakota, 3211
Minnesota: 1987–2029a; atlas, 1987, 2005; bibliography, 1990; biographies, 2012a; census (1850), 2000, (1860), 3213; church vital statistics records, 2002; churches and religious organizations, 2001; Civil War, 554, 564, 2013–2014; county archives, 2004; gazetteer, 2027; Indian Wars, 2013–2014; manuscript collections, 2017–2018; newspapers, 2016; Norwegians, 394; place names, 2027; plat books, 2005–2006; public vital statistics, 2003; Scandinavians, 2020; Sioux massacre, 2019; surname index, 2010; Swedish-Americans, 2025; Welsh, 1424, 2007
Minnesota Genealogical Society surname index, 2010
Minnesota genealogist (magazine), 2015
Minnesota Historical Society. Catalog of microfilms for sale, 2016; Guide to personal papers, 2017–2018
Minns, G. Records from Hebrides Islands, 4885; Records of Orkney Islands, 4890
Miscellanea genealogica et heraldica, 4272
Missing links, 106n
Mississippi: 2030–2072; Bible records, 622; bibliography, 2057, 2064; cemetery and Bible records, 2060; census (1792, 1805, 1810, 1816, Natchez dist.), 2037, (1820), 2039, 2051, 2056, (1830), 2040, (1840), 2065, (1850), 2041, 3162; church and synagogue archives, 2048; church archives, 2047; Cherokees, 713; Civil War, 564; county archives, 2049; court records, 2044, 2053–2054, 2061; death notices, 2045; estate notices, 2045; Florida parishes of Louisiana, 2031; Free and Accepted Masons, 2046; Indian allotments, 716; Jewish congregation, 2048; law, 2066; library holdings, 2057; military history, 2069; mortality schedules, 2035; newspapers, 2045, 2050; official and statistical register, 2042n; Protestant Episcopal church, 2048; Provincial archives, 2070–2071; public archives, 2047; records, 2043a; Revolutionary War, 2033; tombstone inscriptions, 617; vital statistics records, 2047; War of 1812, 2072; wills, 2053
Mississippi Coast Historical and Genealogical Society quarterly, 2058
Mississippi Dept. of Archives. Guide to official records, 2043a
Mississippi Free and Accepted Masons, 2046
Mississippi genealogical exchange (magazine), 2059
Mississippi Genealogical Society. Mississippi cemetery and Bible records, 2060; Survey

427

*Index*

of records in Mississippi court houses, 2061
Mississippi genealogy and local history (magazine), 2062
Mississippi Historical Society. Publications, 2063
Mississippi Valley: French Canadian migration, 4003-4004; French migration, 3961n; Spanish, 630
Mississippiana, 2057
Missouri: 2074-2142; archives, 2094; atlas, 2126; bibliography, 2126, 2131; Catholics, 2114; cemetery records, 2086, 2115; census (1830), 2081, 2092, 2128, 2140, (1850), 2121; church records, 2096; Civil War, 564, 2115; counties, 2089, 2097, 2106, 2142; five Indian tribes, 660, 663; gazetteer, 1295, 2074, 2078; Indian Wars, 2077, 2110; Italians, 2125; land claims, 2132; manual, 2136; manuscripts, 2134-2135; marriages, 2080, 2120, 2141; newspapers, 2131; obituaries index, 2093, 2105; Ozark region, 2118; pension records, 2077, 2110; place names, 2089, 2117; public vital statistics records, 2095-2096; records, 2090, 2095, 2142; Revolutionary War, 2077, 2108, 2110, 2115, 2119; Spanish War, 2115; Virginia settlers, 2084; War of 1812, 2077, 2110
Missouri historical review, 2112-2113
Mitchell, Sir A., and Cash, C. G. Contribution to bibliography of Scottish topography, 4713
Mitchell, L. D. Mobile ship news, 752
Mitford-Barberton, I., and White, V. Some frontier families, 4961
Mobile, Creole, 614a
Mobile ship news, 752
Mockler, W. E. West Virginia surnames, 3755
Mode, P. G. Source book and bibliographical guide for American church history, 405
Mörner, M. Race mixture in history of Latin America, 3860
Mohawk Valley, New York, 2459
Mois généalogique, 3990
Moncreiffe of That Ilk, Sir R. I. K. Highland clans, 4812
——— and Pottinger, D. Bartholomew's map of Scotland of old, 4772, 4813
Monks, L. J. Courts and lawyers of Indiana, 1397
Monmouthshire, Wales: history, 4834; probate jurisdictions, 4850
Monnette, O. E. First settlers of . . . Piscataway and Woodbridge, 2341
——— and French, L. Le L. Spirit of patriotism, 911
Monongahela Valley, West Virginia, 2933-2935, 3719, 3746-3747, 3772
Monro's Western Isles of Scotland, 4885
Montagne, P. Tourouvre et les Juchereau, 4117
Montague-Smith, P. W. Debrett's correct form, 4510; Royal line of succession, 4452
Montana: 2143-2158; atlas, 2149; churches and religious organizations, 2144, 2147; county archives, 2146; Indian tribes, 660; Jesuits, 2156; plat book, 2149; public vital statistics records, 2145
Montenegrins, Nevada, 2202
Montevideo, families, 3936
Montgomery county, Virginia, records, 3617
Montreal, Canada, census (1731), 4118; (1765), 4119
Monumental Brass Society, transactions, 4363
Monumental brasses, 4361-4365
Monumental inscriptions: Barbados, 4928, 4930; bibliography, 4361; British, 4361-4365; British West Indies, 4924, 4929; Jamaica, 4932; Jewish synagogue, Bridgetown, 4930; Scotland, 4762-4763
Mooney, J. E. Loyalist imprints printed in America, 4018n
Moor, C. Knights of Edward I, 4511
Moore, A. D. History of Alabama, 753
Moore, C. History of Michigan, 1972
Moore, C. T., and Simmons, A. A. Abstracts of wills, South Carolina, 3157-3158
Moore, H. B. New Hampshire at the Battle of Bunker Hill, 2256
Moore, J. H. Research materials in South Carolina, 3159
Moore, Mrs. J. T. Record of commissions of officers in Tennessee militia, 3290
——— and Foster, A. P. Tennessee, 3291
Moore, J. W. Roster of North Carolina troops in war between the states, 2622
Morales Guínazú, F. Genealogía de los conquistadores de Curo y fundadores de Mendoz, 3873
Morant, A. Additions and corrections to Burke's General armory, 4258n, 5022, 5105n
Moravians: genealogical sources, 4529n; Georgia, 1163; North Carolina, 2592, 2645
Morgan, D. L., and Hammond, G. P. Guide to manuscript collections of Bancroft Library, 644

*Index*

Morgan, H. J. Canadian men and women, 3991; Sketches of celebrated Canadians, 3992

Morgan, J. L. [Northeast Arkansas publications], 835

Morgan and Glamorgan, Wales, lordships, 4870

Morley, W. F. E. Atlantic provinces, 4063

Mormon settlement in Arizona, 796

Mormons, *see* Genealogical Society of the Church of Jesus Christ of Latter-day Saints *and* Latter-day Saints

Morris, A. C. Florida place names, 1120

Morris, Eastin. Eastin Morris Tennessee gazetteer, 3292

Morris, I. Be it known and remembered, 1670

Morris, J. W. Historical atlas of Oklahoma, 672

——— and McReynolds, E. C. Historical atlas of Oklahoma, 2788

Morris, L. E. B. Advanced primer of genealogical research, 257; Founders and patriots of Republic of Texas, 3339n; Primer for genealogical research, 257n

Morrison, J. H. Wills, sentences, and probate sets, 4374

Morrison, O. D. Indiana, 1398

Morse, A. Genealogical register of descendants, 1909n, 1910; Genealogy of descendants of several ancient Puritans, 1909–1910

Morse, W. I. Gravestones of Acadie, 4064

Morse-Jones, E. Roll of British settlers in South Africa, 4962

Mortality schedules: Arkansas (1850), 834, (1860), 831, (1870), 820; Idaho (1870), 1284; Illinois (1850), 1355; Indiana (1850), 1404; Kansas (1860), 1455; (1870), 1456, (1880), 1450; Louisiana (1860), 1598; Mississippi (1850), 2035; Nebraska (1860), 2179; Texas (1850), 3423, (1860), 3424

Mortgages: Albany, 2421; Rensselaerswyck, 2421

Morton, J. S., and Watkins, A. Illustrated history of Nebraska, 2183

Morton Allen directory of European passenger steamship arrivals for 1890–1930, 363

Moses, G. H. New Hampshire men, 2260

Most Noble Order of the Garter, 4471, 4475, 4498

Motsinger, M. Directory of the D.A.R., Maryland, and their Revolutionary ancestors, 1773

Mottoes, 4971

Moule, T. Bibliotheca heraldica magnae Britanniae, 5117

Moulton, H. R. Palaeography, 4226

Mowle, P. C. Genealogical history of pioneer families of Australia, 4914; Pioneer families of Australia, 4914n

Mullin, Mrs. C. H. (and others). Founders and patriots of Nebraska, 2168

Mullins, E. L. C. Guide to historical and archeological publications, 4158; Texts and calendars, 4159

Mullins, M. D. First census of Texas, 3381; Republic of Texas poll lists, 3382

Munby, L. M. Short guides to records, 4433

Muncipal history, British, 4171, 4175

Munk, W. Royal College of Physicians of London roll, 4325–4326

Munn, R. F. Index to West Virginiana, 3756

Munro, D. J. Writings on British history, 4167–4168

Munro, R. W. Gazetteer of Scotland, 4773; Kinsmen and clansmen, 4814; Monro's Western Isles of Scotland, 4885a

Munroe, J. B. List of alien passengers, 350, 1905

Munsell, Joel, Sons. American ancestry, 282n; The American genealogist, 21; Index to American genealogies, 22, 63–65

Murphy, R. E. Progressive West Virginians, 3757

Musgrave, Sir W. Obituary prior to 1800, 4259n, 4355

Muskingum Valley, Ohio, 2727

Muskogee northwestern Oklahoma, 654

Musmanno, M. A. Story of Italians in America, 389

Muster rolls: New York, 2519, 2527; Texas, 3381n, 3415

Muzzio, J. A. Diccionario histórico y biográfico de la Republica Argentina, 3874

Myers, A. C. Immigration of Irish Quakers into Pennsylvania, 2957; Quaker arrivals at Philadelphia, 2958; Walter Wharton's land survey register, 1050

Myers, W. S. Story of New Jersey, 2342

N. S. D. A. R., *see* Daughters of the American Revolution

Nacogdoches—a gateway to Texas, 3347

Nadon, L. Répertoire des mariages de Saint-Jean-Baptiste d'Ottawa, 4087

Naeseth, G. B. Norwegian settlements in U.S., 392

Name extraction programs, L.D.S., 47b

Names (*see also* Place names; Topography): baptismal, 227; English, personal, 4405–

*Index*

4421; English, place, 4397–4404; foreign versions, variations, and diminutives of English names, 225; Gaelic, 4769; Ireland, personal, 4632; Irish, place, 4645–4646; Irish surnames, 4648–4652; Isle of Man, 4888; Latin America, 3867; Maryland, changes, 1811; Massachusetts, changes, 1903; Mormons, origin of western geographic names associated with, 444; New Hampshire families, 2269; New Hampshire towns, 2254; Pennsylvania counties, 2946; personal, 223; proprietors of unclaimed dividends, Bank of England, 4227a; Scotland, 4776–4782; South Carolina, 3160; Welsh, 4861–4865

Names in South Carolina, 3160

Nance, E. C. East coast of Florida, 1121

Napoleonic heraldry, 5007n

Narragansett historical register, 3093

Nason, E. G. Gazetteer of Massachusetts, 1911

Nassau-Siegen immigrants to Virginia, 3581

Natchez district, Mississippi: censuses, 2037; court records, 2055; early inhabitants, 2037

National Archives, *see* U.S. National Archives and Record Service

National censuses and vital statistics in Europe, 1918–1948, 181

National cyclopaedia of American biography, 153, 166n

National Genealogical Society: abstracts of Revolutionary War pension applications, 524–526; quarterly, 124–125; topical index, 1088

National historical magazine, 500n

National index of parish registers (Great Britain), 4345

National Library of Ireland, Dublin. Articles in Irish periodicals, 4571

National Maritime Museum's commissioned sea officers of Royal Navy, 4332

National origins of U.S. population, 217

National Society of Colonial Dames of America, Mass. Register, 1912

National Society of Women Descendants of the Ancient and Honorable Artillery Company. History and lineage book, 307, 1913; Massachusetts heraldica, 1914; Members in colonial period, 1915

National Society, Sons and Daughters of the Pilgrims. Lineages, 308–309

National Society, U. S. Daughters of 1812, *see* U. S. Daughters of 1812

National union catalog of manuscript collections, 79

Naturalization: aliens in England and Ireland, letters of, 427–428, 4231; foreign Protestants in America and West Indian colonies, 457, 2893, 2967; records, New Jersey, 2323; records, Pennsylvania, 2893, 2911, 2967

Navaho expedition, 2418

Navy (British): biographies, 4330–4334; list, 4331

Navy (U.S.): biographical dictionary, 481; general register, 473; officers, 466, 471; orders and decorations, 475; Pension Fund, report, 486; pensioners on roll, (1883), 487; Pennsylvania, 2955, 2972

Nead, D. W. Pennsylvania German in settlement of Maryland, 1813

Neagles, J. C., and Lee, L. Locating your immigrant ancestor, 364

Nebraska: 2159–2195; Catholic church, 2164, 2172; census (1854–1856), 2166, (1860), 2167; Civil War, 564, 2185, 2187–2188; county archives, 2175; Czech cemeteries, 2180; Czechs, 2181, 2192; Franciscans, 2172; Indian tribes, 660; Methodism, 2182; Mexican War, 2187; mortality schedules (1860), 2179; place names, 2171; public vital statistics records, 2174; records, 645; War of 1812, 2184, 2187

Nebraska and midwest genealogical record, 645, 2186

Nebraskana Society, 2159

Neely, R. Women in Ohio, 2736

Neff, L. E. Mayflower index, 321; Society of Mayflower Descendants, Oklahoma, lineages, 2797

Negro Baptist church in U.S., 418

Negrón Muñoz, A. Mujeres de Puerto Rico, 3061

Neill, E. D. History of Minnesota Valley, 2019

Nelke, D. I. Columbian biographical dictionary, Wisconsin, 3804

Nellist, G. F. Story of Hawaii, 1268; Women of Hawaii, 1270

Nelson, O. N. History of the Scandinavians, 395, 2020

Nelson, William. Introduction to works, 2343; Calendar of records in office of Secretary of State, New Jersey, 2344; Church records in New Jersey, 2345; Extracts from American newspapers, 2346–2347; Nelson's Biographical cyclopedia of New Jersey, 2348; New Jersey biographical . . . notes, 2349; New Jersey coast in three centuries, 2350; New Jersey marriage rec-

ords, 2351; Personal names of Indians of New Jersey, 673, 2352
Nestler, H. Bibliography of New York state communities, 2496
Neumann Gandía, E. Benefactores y hombres notables de Puerto Rico, 3062
Nevada: 2196-2225; Bible records, 2200; bibliography, 2204, 2212; cemeteries inscriptions, 2219; census (1875), 2214; church archives, 2208; Civil War, 564, 2213; county archives, 2209; Croatians, 2202; Dalmatians, 2202; directory, 2223; Hercegavinians, 2202; Montenegrins, 2202; newspapers, 2204, 2212; place names, 2198, 2211; post offices, 2205-2206; Protestant Episcopal church, 2208; public vital statistics records, 2207; records, 885n, 2210; Roman Catholic church, 2208; Yugoslavs, 2203
Nevada Historical Society. Biennial reports, 2215; Papers, 2216; Quarterlies, 2217
New Amsterdam family names, 2452
New baronetage of England, 4493n
New Brunswick, Canada: 4047-4069; bibliography, 4063; census returns (1851-1871), 4056; gazetteer, 4055; geographical names, 4055; loyalists, 4037, 4069; topography, 4053
New Castle county, Delaware: census (1800), 1056; court records, 1051; wills, 1025
New England: 574-614; ancestral heads, 591; bibliography of New England soldiers, 574; biographies, 598; Civil War, 564; colonial lists, 605; court records, 594; deaths, 2246; diaries, 587; emigrants, 330, 337, 579, 1846; English and Dutch colonials, 581; families, 582, 2554, 3094; founding of, 577, 585, 595; French Canadian migration, 4003-4004; gazetteer, 590; genealogical notes, 608, 610-611; gravestones, 586; Huguenot settlements, 431; immigrants, 331, 575, 578; Indians, 655, 1854; Irish immigrants, 388; Jews, 592; manual, 613; marriages, 2246; Massachusetts Bay Company, 1898; New France pioneers, 576; orderly books, 587; passenger lists, 331; pension roll, 490; Pilgrim Fathers, 580, 596-597, 606, 609, 612, 614; records, 588; Scotch-Irish settlers, 397; sea journals, 587; settlers from, in Iowa, 1427, in Pennsylvania, 3018; wills, 610-611
New England Historic Genealogical Soc. Committee on Heraldry. Roll of arms, 5078; Massachusetts vital records, 1916; Memorial biographies, 598

New England historical and genealogical register (magazine), 599-604
New France, *see* Quebec
New Hampshire: 2226-2290; atlas, 2289; Battle of Bennington, 2244; cemetery records, 2230; census (1790), 2287, (1800), 2243, 2255, 2285; centenarians, 2279; church archives, 2252; church vital statistics records, 2250; Civil War, 554, 564, 2230, 2266a, 2277, 2288; county archives, 2253; deaths, 2246; Freemasons, 2242; French and Indian Wars, 2230, 2265, gazetteer, 2241, 2247, 2258; grants, 3479; gravestone inscriptions, 2232-2233; Indian Wars, 2230; loyalists, 2271; manual, 2286; marriages, 2246; Mexican War, 2230; military history, 2277; ministers, 2229; pensioners, 2237-2239, 2256, 2274; probate records, 2261; public vital statistics records, 2251; records, 2262, 2264, 2272; Revolutionary War, 2230, 2237-2239, 2244, 2256, 2263, 2265-2266, 2271, 2274; Roman Catholic church, 2252; Spanish-American War, 2230; state and provincial papers, 2261-2263, 2265-2266; town histories, 2269; town names, 2254; War of 1812, 2230
New Hampshire genealogical record, 2267
New Hampshire Historical Society. Collections, 2268; Family names in New Hampshire town histories, 2269; Proceedings, 2270
New Harlem register, 2555
New Haven, Connecticut: ancient families, 1000; records, 997-998
New Haven Colony Historical Society. Papers, 1007
New Haven genealogical magazine, 103n
New Jersey: 2291-2390; archives, 2292, 2349; Baptists, 2325; bibliography, 2300, 2309, 2331-2332; census (1850), 2369; church archives, 2324-2325, 2327, 2345; churches, 2322; civil boundaries, 2378; Civil War, 554, 564, 2354, 2385; commissions, 2371; conveyances, 2319; county archives, 2326; county histories, 2306, 2328; Dutch houses and families, 2294; Dutch Reformed churches, 2448; Dutch settlers, 2337; Dutch systems of family naming, 2293; Fenwick's colony, 2375-2376; gazetteer, 2312, 2318; Germans, 2304, 2373; Hugucnots, 2329; Indians, 673, 2352; Italians, 2302; John Brainerd's journals, 2327; loyalists, 2333; manual, 2339, 2360, 2386; manuscripts, 2374, 2377; marriages, 2305, 2314, 2351; mili-

*Index*

tary records, 2353-2354, 2368; naturalization records, 2323; newspaper extracts, 2346-2347; Palatines, 2334; patents and deeds, 2344; Presbyterians, 2325, 2345; Protestant Episcopal, 2325; Quakers, 2321, 2345, 2356, 2904, 2906; rateables, 2387-2388; Revolutionary War, 2333, 2383-2384, 2389; Swedish Lutheran churches, 2311; Swedish settlers, 2337; vital statistics records, 2324; War of 1812, 2353; wills, 2305, 2357-2358, 2366, 2509
New Jersey family index (magazine), 2362
New Jersey genesis (magazine), 2363-2364
New Jersey Historical Society: Calendar of New Jersey wills, 2366; collections, 2365; library sources, 2339; manuscripts collection, 2374; proceedings, 2367
New law list, 4320n
New London area, Connecticut, records, 993
New Mexico: 2391-2419; archdiocese archives, 2415; atlas, 2394; Aztec, 2406; census (1860), 2401; churches and religious organizations, 2402; Civil War, 564; county archives, 2404; directory, 2398; gazetteer, 2398; ghost towns and mining camps, 2417; land grants, 2395; missions, 2392; Navaho expedition, 2418; place names, 2408, 2411; post offices, 2417; public vital statistics records, 2403; Pueblo Indian land grants of "Rio Abajo," 657; San Juan county, 2406; Spanish-American pedigrees, 3854; Spanish archives, 2419; Spanish families, 2415-2416; town histories, 2399
New Mexico Folklore Society. New Mexico place-name dictionary, 2408
New Mexico genealogist (magazine), 2409
New Netherland: administration, 2566; Dutch in, 378; register, 2530
New Orleans (*see also* Louisiana): census (1770, 1777), 1679, (1810), 1686; Creole families, 1652; French, 1630; Jews, 1653; marriages, 1663-1664; parish, Civil District Court, 1673; Spanish census (1791), 1671; Spanish citizens entering, 1660-1661
New Orleans genesis (magazine), 1672
New Paltz, New York, 2486
New peerage, 4494n
New Plymouth Colony. Records, 1917, 1937
New serials titles, 80-82
New South Wales: Colonial Secretary's records, 4916; gravestone inscriptions, 4911a; naturalization and denization records, 4916

New Spain, *see* Latin America
New York (city, colony, state): 2420-2572; administration bonds, 2524, 2542; apprentices, 2479-2480, 2497n; atlas, 2433, 2569; baptisms, 2503-2504, 2555; Belgians, 2428; Bible records, 2540; bibliographies, 2465, 2496; births, 2570; British manuscripts, 2517; burghers, 2497; Burgomasters and Scheppens, 2500; census (1663-1772), 2494, (1790), 2562a, (1800), 2451, 2488; church archives, 2472-2473; church records, 2471; civil list, 2521; Civil War, 554, 564, 2511, 2535; Collegiate church, 2503; colonial clergy, 327; colonial records, 2551; commerce, 2551; commissions, 2505-2506; common council minutes, 2501; conveyances, 2507; corporation manual, 2564-2565; county archives, 2474-2475; county census, 2436; county histories, 2439-2443, 2460, 2485, 2490; customs records, 2420; Danish immigration, 2450n; deaths, 2570; deeds, 2498; Dutch, 2462, 2517, 2540, 2554; Dutch houses, 2294, 2425, 2539; Dutch manuscripts, 2517; Dutch Reformed churches, 2448, 2503-2504; Dutch systems in family naming, 2293, 2423; early settlers, 2455-2456; Eastern Orthodox church, 2472; English families, 2540; freemen, 2497; gazetteers, 2446, 2456a-2458; German immigrants, 2450, 2557; grantors and grantees, 2507; guardianships, 2545; Huguenots, 430-431, 2486, 2570; iconography, 2552; inhabitants street by street, 2481; Irish settlements, 387; Jews, 2434, 2466, 2536; land grants, 2433; land patents, 3491; land papers, 2518; loyalists, 2526; Lutherans, 2432, 2472; manuals, 2424, 2427; manuscript collections, 2435, 2468, 2517-2518; 2566; maps, 2571; marriages, 2503-2504, 2508, 2544, 2555, 2570; merchants, 2547; Methodist church, 2472; military records, 2493, 2514, 2519, 2527; militia lists, 2529; muster rolls, 2519, 2527; New Amsterdam family names, 2452; newspaper records, 2543; Norwegians, 2450n, 2451; orphanmasters, 2502; Palatines, 2483, 2489, 2495, 2531, 2557, 4025n; patentees, 2555; personal names, 2457, 2489; place names, 2444, 2458; Poles, 2461; Presbyterian church, 2472, 2477; Protestant Episcopal church, 2472-2473; public vital statistics records, 2470; Quakers, 2472; Reformed Dutch church, 2503-2504; Revolutionary War, 2454, 2489, 2512-2513; 2526, 2550,

432

## Index

3992a; Roman Catholics, 2472; Scandinavians, 2450; ship lists, 2483; slave census, 2529; subsistence list, 2483; Swedish, 2450n; tax lists, 2499, 2529; vital statistics records, 2470; Walloons, 2428; War of 1812, 2510; wills, 2453, 2466, 2509
New York Chamber of Commerce, colonial records, 2551
New York Collegiate Church, marriages, 2503; records, 2504
New-York (gazette and weekly) mercury, genealogical data from, 68
New York genealogical and biographical record (magazine), 2522-2523
New York Genealogical and Biographical Society. Genealogical data from New York administration bonds, 2524
New York Historical Society: Collections, 2525; De Lancey's Brigade, 2526; Muster rolls of New York provincial troops, 2527, 3992a
New York mail and express, Index to genealogical queries and answers, 72
New York Public Library. Dictionary catalog of local history, 24; U.S. local history catalog, 25
New York Times obituary index, 154
New York weekly post boy, genealogical data from, 69
New Zealand: 4944-4950; colonial gentry, 4483n; genealogical record sources, 4908, 4946
New Zealand genealogist (magazine), 4948
Newberry Library, Chicago. Genealogical index, 23
Newfoundland: 4047-4069; bibliography, 4007, 4063; records, 4067; topography, 4053
Newman, D. L. List of black servicemen, Revolutionary War, 528; List of free black heads of families in first census of U.S. (1790), 65, 176, 374
Newman, H. W. Flowering of Maryland Palatinate, 1814; Heraldic Marylandia, 1815; Maryland Revolutionary records, 1816
Newmark, M. H. and M. R. Sixty years in California, 894
Newsome, A. R. Records of emigrants from England and Scotland to North Carolina, 2615
Newspapers: American, bibliography, 8, 11, 12, chronological tables, 16, in microform, 84; Arkansas, 829; Canadian, 3975; Commonwealth, 4896; English, 4234; ethnic, 373; German-American, 379; Iowa, 1412, 1437; London, 4234n; Louisiana, 1647, 1658; Minnesota, 2016; Mississippi, 2045, 2050; Missouri, 2131; Nevada, 2204, 2212; New Jersey extracts, 2346-2347; New York, 2543; North Carolina, 2605; Ohio, 2708a, 2733-2734; Pennsylvania German notices, 2978, v.3; Saskatchewan, 4142; Scottish, 4708; Texas, 3361; Welsh, 4234; Wisconsin, 3805
Newton, J. H. (and others). History of the Panhandle, 3758
Newton, K. C. Medieval local records, 4247
Nicholas, T. Annals of counties and county families of Wales, 4875
Nicholites, Maryland, 1764
Nichols, J. G. Herald and genealogist, 4266, 5106
Nicholson, C. D. Some early emigrants to America, 352
Nieto y Cortadellas, R. Dignidades nobiliarias en Cuba, 3897
Nisbet, A. System of heraldry, 4982-4983
Nizam's dominions, India, inscriptions, 4936
Nolan, J. B. Southeastern Pennsylvania, 2962
Nome gold rush, 777
Nonconformists: genealogy, 4345, 4529; records, 4530; Welsh, 4879
Norlie, O. M. Who's who in all Norwegian Lutheran Synods in America, 447
Norman: 4463-4470; descendants, 4183; family names, 4405; lineages, 5014; surnames, 4649; Welsh, 4834
Normandy, map, 4465
Norona, D., and Shetler, C. West Virginia imprints, 3759
Norris, J. E. History of lower Shenandoah valley, 3608
Norris, J. M. Strangers entertained, 4043
Norsk Lutherske prester i Amerika, 447
North Carolina (see also South Carolina): 2753-2659; atlas, 2610; Baptists, 2600, 2633; Bible records, 622, 2647; bibliography, 2590n, 2650, 2652; census (1787-1890), 2611a, (1784-1787), 2644, (1790 substitute), 2580n, (1790), 2654, (1800), 2603, (1820), 2635-2636, (1840), 2634a, (1850), 2593; Cherokee Indian census, 704, 715; church archives, 2600; Civil War, 556, 564, 2582b, 2606, 2612, 2620, 2622; colonial records, 620, 2618, 2626; counties, 2585, 2599, 2621; deaths, 2576, 2653a; Dutch, 2575; emigrants, English, 2615, Scottish, 2613, 2615; gazetteer, 2637; German settlements, 2575; Highlanders, 2613; Indian Wars, 2577; land

433

*Index*

grants, 2580; land grants, Tennessee, 2580, 3304; land ownership maps, 2649; legislators, 2623; loyalists, 2589; Lutheran church, 2575; manual, 2590, 2611, 2621, 2651a; manuscripts, 2586, 2653; maps, 2649, 2651; marriages, 2576, 2582, 2594, 2653a; Mecklenburg signers, 2641; Methodists, 2581; Mexican War, 2617; Moravians, 2592, 2645; newspapers, 2605; oath of allegiance, 3614; obituaries, 2594; pensions, 2577–2578; pioneers, 627; Quakers, 2597–2598; records information, 2619; records relating to Tennessee, 3249a; Revolutionary War, 2577, 2582a, 2588, 2622, 2649a; Rhinelanders, 2595; Scotch, 2613; Swiss settlers, 2575; tombstones, 2646a; War of 1812, 2577, 2616; wills, 2604, 2624–2625, 2630–2631

North Carolina genealogy (magazine), 2628

North Carolina historical and genealogical register (magazine), 2629, 2643

North Carolina State Archives, records relating to Tennessee, 3249a

North country, England: pedigrees, 4179–4180; wills, 4380

North Dakota (*see also* South Dakota): 2660–2682; atlas, 2674; census (1850), 2000; church vital statistics, 2671; Civil War, 564; county archives, 2673; Finnish settlements, 3234; Germans from Russia, 2670, 2677, 2680; Indian tribes, 660; Norwegians, 394; place names, 2681; plat book, 2674; public vital statistics records, 2672

North Dakota Historical Society of Germans from Russia. Heritage review, 2670; Der Stammbaum, 2680; Work papers, 2677

North Dakota State Historical Society: collections, 2668, 2678; historical and genealogical materials, 2663; index to journals, 2668

North Texas pioneer (magazine), 3383

North West Georgia Historical and Genealogical Society quarterly, 1216

Northen, W. J. Men of mark in Georgia, 1217

Northern Alabama (Smith & Deland's), 754

Northern counties of England, peerages, 4489

Northern Ireland, civic and corporate heraldry, 5088

Northern Neck (Va.) historical magazine, 3609

Northland newsletter, 2021

Northwest: Catholic church records, 638; pioneer families, 641

Norton, J. E. Guide to national and provincial directories of England, 4228

Norton, J. S. New Jersey in 1793, 2368

Norton, M. B. The British-Americans, 529

Norton, M. C. Illinois census returns: (1810, 1820), 1333, (1820), 1334

Norwegian Lutheran Synods of America, who's who, 447

Norwegians: America, 390–394; New York, 2450n, 2541

Notable American women, 155

Nouvelle France, *see* Quebec

Nova Scotia: 4047–4069; Acadia and Acadians, 4047–4052; bibliography, 4063; census (1770, 1773, 1787), 4068, (1871), 4056; colonization, 4048; depredation by French and Indians, 576; farms, 4062; Irish immigration and emigration, 4061a; land settlements, 4019, 4058; loyalists, 4019, 4058; place names, 4054–4057; topography, 4053

Nova Scotia Baronets, Order of, 4472n

Nova Scotia Historical Society. Report and collections, 4065; Collections, 4065n

Noyes, S. T. (and others). Genealogical dictionary of Maine, 1725, 2273

Nugent, N. M. Cavaliers and pioneers, 3610

Nye, M. G. New York land patents, 3491; Petitions for grants of land, 3492; Sequestration, confiscation and sale of estates, 3494

Oath of allegiance: earliest, 545; Maryland, 1761; Pennsylvania, 2871, 2949, 2960, 3031; Virginia, 3614

Oath of fidelity and support, 1748

O'Beirne, H. F. Leaders and leading men of Indian territory, 701

——— and E. S. Indian territory, 702

Obert, R. T. (and others). 1840 Iowa census and index, 1433

Obituaries: America, 150; architects and artists, 139; Farrar's, 4350; Georgia, 1219a; Jews (British), 4548; Kentucky, 1504; Massachusetts, 1843, 1865; Missouri, 2093, 2105; Musgrave's 4355; New York Times index, 154; North Carolina, 2594; Pennsylvania, 3041; Philadelphia, 2989; Quakers, 460, Virginia Baptists, 3577; West Virginia, 3771

O'Brien, F. G. Minnesota pioneer sketches, 2022

O'Brien, M. A. Corpus genealogiarum Hiberniae, 4687

O'Brien, M. J. Articles about Irish in America, 386; Hidden phase of American history, 387, 530; Irish in America, 353, 388

O'Byrne, W. R. Naval biographical dictionary, 4334

O'Callaghan, E. B. Calendar of Dutch historical manuscripts, New York, 2517; Calendar of New York colonial commissions, 2505n; Documentary history of state of New-York, 2529; Documents reative to colonial history of New York, 2447; Register of New Netherland, 2530

O'Callaghan, J. C. History of Irish brigades in service of France, 4603

Oehlerts, D. E. Guide to Colorado names, 947; Guide to Wisconsin newspapers, 3805

Oelle river, Quebec, genealogies, 4116

Official register III: soldiers of American Revolution, Ohio, 2691n

O'Gorman, E. Breve historia de las divisiones territoriales, 3926n; Historia de las divisiones territoriales de México, 3926

O'Hart, J. Irish and Anglo-Irish landed gentry, 4688-4689; Irish pedigrees, 4690

Ohio: 2683-2774; Amish, 2690; bibliography, 2765, 2768; bounty land warrants, 3516; census (substitute for 1810), 2755n, 2756, (1820), 2745, (1830), 2743, (1840), 2722, 2770, (1850), 2711; Civil War, 554, 564, 2741; counties, 2698, 2731; county archives, 2714, 2742, 2774; county boundaries, 2696; families, 2948; Firelands area, 2701-2703, 2771; gazetteer, 2700, 2722-2723; Germans, 2692; lands, 2699, 2740, 2751, 2759; manual, 2695, 2728; manuscripts, 2726, 2752, 2761; maps, 2710; Mexican War, 2741; newspapers, 2708a, 2733-2734; pioneers, 1431; printed state documents, 2764a; Quakers, 2713; Revolutionary War, 2691, 2701-2703; Roman Catholics, 2715, 2719; Spanish-American War, 2737; tax records, 2689, 2744, 2755-2756; town names, 2731, 2750; voters' lists, 2693; War of 1812, 2694, 2735, 2738-2739; Western Reserve, 2687, 2689, 2701-2703, 2766, 2769

Ohio Company, proprietors, 2699n

Ohio Family Historians. 1830 federal population census, 2743; Index to 1850 federal population census, 2711; Index to 1810 Pennsylvania census, 2963

Ohio genealogical quarterly (magazine), 2744

Ohio Historical Society, manuscripts, 2726

Ohio Library Foundation. 1820 federal population census, 2745

Ohio records and pioneer families (magazine), 2746

Ohio researcher (magazine), 2747

Ohio River, territory northwest of, 637a

Ohio Valley, 2709, 2718, 2900-2901, 3736-3737

O'Kief, Cosh, Mang, Slieve Lougher, and Upper Blackwater in Ireland, 4573

Oklahoma: 2775-2803; atlas, 672, 2788; cemeteries, 1473, 2787, 2800, 3380; census (1860), 2803, (1890), 2791; churches and religious organizations, 2784; Civil War, 2790-2791; county archives, 2783; directory, 2796; gazetteer, 2800a; Indians, see nos. 652-716; Mexican War, 2791; pensions, 2790; place names, 2795; post offices, 2778, public vital statistics records, 2782; Spanish American War, 2791; surname index, 2793; town and place locations, 2800a

Oklahoma Genealogical Society. Index to applications for pensions . . . (Civil War), 2790; Index to 1890 U.S. census of Union veterans . . . , 2791; Quarterly, 2792; Surname index, 2793

Oklahoma Union Soldiers' Home, records, 2791

Old Albemarle and its absentee landlords, 2642

Old Cheraws, 3146-3147

Old Fairfield, history and genealogy, 1001-1002

Old Jersey (ship), Revolutionary War prisoners on, 495

Old Ninety-Six and Abbeville district, Abstracts, 1173n, 1243, 3209

"Old northwest" genealogical quarterly, 646, 2749

Old Santa Fe (magazine), 2410

Old Settlers' meeting, Bismarck Grove, Kansas, 1461

Old Swedes church, see Wilmington, Delaware, Holy Trinity church records

Olde Ulster, 2531

Olds, F. A. Abstract of North Carolina wills, 2630-2631

Oliver, V. L., Caribbeana, 4921; History of island of Antigua, 4927; Monumental inscriptions . . . island of Barbados, 4928; Monumental inscriptions of British West Indies, 4929

Olivier, R. L. Your ancient Canadian family ties, 3993

435

*Index*

Olson, E. W. Swedish element in Illinois, 1335
Olson, J. C. History of Nebraska, 2189
Olsson, N. W. Swedish passenger arrivals in New York, 365
Omaha bee "Nebraskans," 2190–2191
O'Neill, E. H. Biography by Americans, 156
O'Neill, T. P. Sources of Irish local history, 4592
Ontarian genealogist and family historian (magazine), 4088
Ontario, Canada: 4075–4096; atlas, 4081, 4090; bibliography, 4093; census returns (1842–1871), 3953, 4056, (1871), 4078; families, 4016; loyalists, 4015–4017, 4023, 4027–4029, 4031, 4079–4080, 4089; manual, 4084; parish registers, 4075; Pennsylvania Germans, 2978, v.11, 2995; references and sources, 4023; since 1867, 4093
Ontario. Bureau of Archives. Reports, 4027, 4089
Ontario. Court of Common Pleas. Records, 4028
Ontario. Dept. of Archives. Grants of crown lands in upper Canada, 4029
Ontario Historical Society. Ontario history, 4091; Papers and records, 4091n
Ontario history (magazine), 4091
Ontario register (magazine), 4092
Opelousas post, 1631, 1687, 1689
Order of Americans of Armorial Ancestry. Register, 5077
Order of the Crown of Charlemagne in the U.S. Roll of arms, 276
Order of the First Families of Virginia (1607–1620), list of membership, 3611
Order of the Founders and Patriots of America, Register, 310–312
Orderly books, New England, 587
Ordinary of arms, for Rietstap, 5119n
Ordway, F. I., Jr. General Society of War of 1812 register, 547; Society of Colonial Wars, D. C. register, 1092; Society of Mayflower Descendants, D. C. register, 1093
Oregon (*see also* Washington): 2804–2840; Catholic church records, 638; census (1850), 2840, (1870, 1880), 2820; church and religious organizations, 2822; Civil War, 564; county archives, 2824; county boundary change maps, 2804; donation land claims, 2813–2814, 2816; geographic names, 2828; land claims, 2813–2814, 2816; land laws, 2805; manual, 2810, 2815; manuscripts, 2830; maps, 2804; microfilm guide, 2831; pioneer families, 2834, 3701; public vital statistics records, 2823; ship registers and enrollments, 2825
Oregon genealogical bulletin, 2829
Oregon Historical Society manuscripts collections, 2830; Microfilm guide, 2831
Oregon State Library. Pioneer families of Oregon territory (1850), 2834, 3701
Original parish registers in record offices and libraries, Great Britain, 4343a
Orkney Islands, 4890
Orleans Island, marriages, 4099
Orleans Parish, Louisiana, Civil District Court, 1673
Ormerod, G. Index to pedigrees in Burke's Commoners, 4480
O'Rourke, T. J. Maryland Catholics on the frontier, 1817, 2114
Orphanmasters of New Amsterdam, 2502
Ortega Ricaurte, E. Heráldica colombiana, 5087
Ortega y Pérez Gallardo, R. Historia genealógica de las familias más Antiguas de México, 3927
Orth, D. J. Dictionary of Alaska place names 771
Orton, R. H. Records of California men in the War of the Rebellion, 850
Ospina, J. Diccionario biográfico y bibliográfico de Columbia, 3895
Otárola, A. J. Antecedentes históricos y genealógicos, 3875; Cuñas de ilustres linajes, 3876; Estudios genealógicos sobre antiguos apellidos del Río de la Plata, 3877
O'Toole, E. H. Decorations and medals of the Republic of Ireland, 4691
Ottawa, Saint-Jean-Baptiste d', marriages, 4087
Otto, R. C. 1850 census of Georgia, 1218
Oudh, India, manual of titles, 4943
Our heritage, 3384
Outstanding Floridians, 1121a
Overby, M. E. Marriages published in Christian index, 1219; Obituaries from Christian index, 1219a
Overman, W. D. Ohio town names, 2750
Owen, D. M. Records of Established Church in England, 4229, 4527a
Owen, J. S. Annals of Kansas, 1476
Owen, M. Story of Alabama, 755
Owen, T. McA. Bibliography of Alabama, 756; Bibliography of Mississippi, 2064; History of Alabama, 757–758; Revolutionary soldiers in Alabama, 759–760
Owens, M. D., and Tanco, B. O. 1850 census of New Jersey, 2369

Owings, D. M. His lordship's patronage, 1818
Owners of land and heritages . . . Scotland, 4721
Oxford University, biographical registers, 4306-4308
Ozark region, 837, 2118

Pacific Coast: Catalog of materials for history of, 3845; L.D.S. research papers, 243E; manuscripts, 644; Scandinavian pioneers, 648, 912
Pacific Northwest: atlas, 641a; Catholic church records, 638, 4070; history, 2811, 3689; Indians who married whites, 4070
Pacifists, southeastern Pennsylvania and Maryland in Revolutionary War, 493
Paddock, B. B. History of central and western Texas, 3385; History of Texas, 3386; Twentieth century history and biographical record of north and west Texas, 3387
Page, W. Letters of denization and acts of naturalization for aliens in England, 4542
Painters in America, dictionary, 149
Palaeography, *see* Paleography
Palatines: Canada, 4025n; Great Britain, 4025n; immigration, 359, 367; New Jersey, 2334; New York, 2483, 2489, 2495, 2521, 2557, 4025n; Pennsylvania, 2883, 2928, 2944
Paleography: England, 4238-4247; manual, 239; Scotland, 4725a
The palimpsest (magazine), 1434
Pallot's marriage and birth indexes, 4355a
Pama, C. Heraldiek en genealogie, 4963; Heraldry of South African families, 5064; Lions and virgins, 5065
Paniagua, R. Puerto Rico roll of honor, 3063
Papal heraldry, 5091, 5097
Papenfuse, E. C. (and others). Directory of Maryland legislators, 1819
Papworth, J. W. Alphabetical dictionary of coats of arms, 5024; Ordinary of British armorials, 5024n
Paradise of the Pacific (magazine), 1263
Parish registers and records: Canada, 3952a; England, 4233, 4338-4345; foreign denominations, 4343; Great Britain, abstract, 4341, description, 4345, v.1; London, 4343; Maryland, 1832; Mexico, 3931; Ontario, 4075; Scotland, 4717, 4760, 4774; Wales, 4847-4848a
Parker, D. D. Early churches and towns in South Dakota, 3228; Scottish and Scotch-Irish ancestry research, 4664; Scottish and Scotch-Irish immigration, 4788

Parker, J. Glossary of terms used in heraldry, 4978n
Parker, J. C. Genealogy in Central Assoc. of Libraries, 26; Sources of California, 895
Parker, M. E. E. Colonial records of North Carolina, 2618, 2632
Parker, W., and Lambert, H. K. Black Hills ghost towns, 3228a
Parkin, N. Nevada cemeteries inscriptions, 2219
Parliament (Great Britain): members, 4314; records guide, 4189
Parliamentary papers (British), 4196, 4209
Parliamentary representation, British, 4171
Parochial registers of Scotland, 4750, 4755
Parrish, V. H. 1850 census index of eastern Kentucky, 1558
Parry, C. J. Index to baronetage creations, 4512
Paschal, G. W. History of North Carolina Baptists, 2633
Passaic Valley, New Jersey, 2338
Passano, E. P. Index of the source records of Maryland, 1820
Passenger lists *(see also* Ship lists): Acadian, 1676; aliens from U.K., 350; aliens into Boston, 329, 332, 1905; arrivals (1819-1820), 368, (1821-1823), 369; Bayard River, Delaware, 1048; bibliography of, 349; California, 901-903; California gold rush, 873; Kochertal, 2489n; Pilgrims, 612n, 1845-1846, 1848, 1928; Scotch-Irish, 3199; Swedish, 365; Virginia, 3622
  from: Bristol, 343; Great Britain, 345, 354; Great Yarmouth, 346; Ireland, 342, 383; Latin America, 3862-3863; Liverpool, 352; London, 2489n; Ulster, 334;
  to: Boston, 1860; New England, 331; New Orleans, 1678; New York, 363, 370; Philadelphia, 359; South Carolina, 3199
Passports, Georgia, 1140, 1159
The pastfinder (magazine), 1973
Patentee officers (of Ireland), 4583
Patentees, New Harlem, N.Y., 2555
Patents, New Jersey, 2344
Paterson, G. G. C. Loyalists in upper Canada, 4030
Patriot index, D.A.R., 506-508
Patriotic Marylander (magazine), 1821
Patriotic societies, orders, 475
Patterson, W. D. Probate records of Lincoln county, Maine, 1726
Paul, Sir J. B. How to write a history of a family, 4714; Ordinary of arms . . . Scotland, 5051; Scots peerage, 4815

437

*Index*

Paulding, W. I. History of city of New York, 2563n
Paver's marriage licenses, 4356–4358
Payne, J. B. Armorial of Jersey, 5066
Peacock, E. Army lists of Roundheads and Cavaliers, 4294
Pearce, T. M. New Mexico place names, 2411
Pearson, J. Contributions for genealogies of descendants of . . . Albany, 2533; Contributions for genealogies of . . . Schenectady, 2532; Early records of Albany, 2421
Pease, J. C., and Niles, J. M. Gazetteer of states of Connecticut and Rhode Island, 1009, 3095
Pease, T. C. County archives of Illinois, 1336; Illinois election returns, 1337
Peck, J. M. Gazetteer of Illinois, 1337a
Pecquet du Bellet, L. Some prominent Virginia families, 3612
Pedersen, C. F. International flag book in colors, 5093
Pedigree register (British), 4513
Pedigrees: British county, 4198; East Anglian, 4178; manuscripts, 4184; North country, England, 4179–4180; printed (English), 36, 4177, 4182, 4187; Welsh, 4862n
Pedley, A. J. M. Manuscript collections of Maryland Historical Society, 1822
Pedreira, A. S. Bibliografía puertorriqueñas, 3064
Peel, B. B. Bibliography of Prairie Provinces, 4071–4072
Peele, W. J. Lives of distinguished North Carolinians, 2634
Peerage creations and promotions (1901–1938), 4491n
Peerages: British, 4471–4526; Irish, 4665–4696; Scottish, 4795, 4799, 4801, 4809, 4815, 4819; Welsh, 4869–4778
Peirce, E. W. Peirce's Colonial lists, 605, 3096
Pelletreau, W. S. Historic homes . . . of New York, 2534
Peña Camara, J. M. de la. List of Spanish residencias in Archives of the Indies, 3861
Pence, G. C., and Armstrong, N. C. Indiana boundaries, 1399
Pender, S. Census of Ireland, ca. 1659, 4581; Guide to Irish genealogical collections, 4569
Penn Germania (magazine), 2964
Pennsylvania (*see also* Philadelphia): 2841–3042; Amish, 2856; archives, 2868, 2915, 2974–2976; Assembly, 2911a, 2968–2969; baptisms, 2858, 3019; bibliographies, 2913n, 2951, 3008, 3003; births, 2887; black regiments, Civil War, 2842; Catholics, 2898, 2905; census, (1790), 3023, (1800), 2916, 3017, (1810), 2963, (1850), 2844; church archives, 2910; churches, 2867; Civil War, 554, 564, 2842, 2892n; colonial clergy, 327; colonial records, 2974–2976; county archives, 2909; county names, 2946; deaths, 3041; deeds, 2949; deeds, Virginia, 3025; Dunkers, 3007n; Dutch, 2917, 3000; Dutch Quakers, 2914; English, 2917; First Reformed Church, 2867; foreigners, 2959; forfeited estates, 2888; French, 3000; gazetteer, 2897; geographical description, 3009; German dialect, 2930; Germans, 2875, 2883, 2914, 2926–2927, 2951, 2991, 2997, 3000, 3020–3021; Germans in Maryland, 1813; Germans in Ontario, 2978, v.11, 2995, 4095; Germans in Shenandoah Valley, 2978, v. 26, 3013; Germans in Virginia, 2926; Germans in Wisconsin, 2978, v.19; Germans from county of Wertheim, 2978, v.12; gravestone inscriptions, 2942; Huguenots, 431, 3016; immigration from Connecticut, 2903n; indentured servants, 2890, 2991; Indian wars, 2864, 2945; Indians, 668, 2901, 2917; Irish immigrants, 387; Irish Quakers, 2957–2958; land claims, Virginia, 3024; lands, 2841, 2971, 3028a; loyalists, 3012; manuals, 2843, 2850, 2913, 2943; manuscripts, 2891; maritime records, 2911; marriages, 2858, 2885, 2983–2986, 2996, 3019;

Mennonites, 493; Mexican War, 2950; militia, 2870, 2938, 2952–2954, 2965; municipalities, 2970; naturalization records, 2893, 2911, 2967; Navy, Revolutionary War, 2955, 2972; newspapers, 3008; oath of allegiance, 2871, 2949, 2960, 3031; Palatines, 2883, 2928, 2944; passenger lists, 2911; pensions, Revolutionary War, 2941a; Pietists, 3006; place names, 2884; Polish, 2899; Presbyterians, 2867n; proprietary manors, 2869; Protestants, 457, 2893, 2967; provincial councillors, 2925; Quakers, 2848, 2867n, 2894, 2904, 2906, 2910, 2914, 2957–2958, 2967, 2990, 2996; rangers, 2939–2940; Redemptioners, 2890, 2991; Revolutionary War, 2855, 2870, 2874, 2876–2877, 2892n, 2939–2941a, 2945, 2949, 2955, 2972–2973, 2997, 2999, 3014–3015; San Domingo refugees, 2849; Scotch-Irish, 397, 2863, 2875; Sectarians, 3007; ship

*Index*

lists, 2871n, 2911, 2959, 3029-3031; ship registers, 2911, 3011, 3029-3030; slave manifests, 2911; Swedes, 2917; Swiss, 357, 2873n, 2883, 2929, 3000; synagogue archives, 2910; taxables, 2878-2879, 2992; Ulster emigration, 2862; Virginia claims to land, 3024, 3651; Virginia court records, 2857; War of 1812, 2945, 2956, 3027; warrantees of land, 2971, 3028a; Welsh settlement, 2848, 2894-2895; wills, 2889, 2978, v.15, 3034-3039; wills, Virginia, 3025; women, Revolution, 2877
Pennsylvania archives, 2974-2976 (also analyzed under Pennsylvania above)
Pennsylvania chronicle, genealogical data from, 70, 3010
Pennsylvania genealogical magazine, 2977
Pennsylvania German (magazine), 2964n
Pennsylvania German Folklore Society. Publications, 2978
Pennsylvania German Society. Publications, 2979
Pennsylvania magazine of history, 2981-2982
Pennsylvania traveler-post (magazine), 115n, 2987
Penrose, M. B. Heads of families index, 1850 census, 2988; Philadelphia marriages, 2989
Pension applications: Confederate (Tennessee), 3310; private claims (1789-1849), 483; rejected or suspended (Rev. War), 539; Revolutionary War, 524-526, 546a; War of 1812, 546a
Pensioners: census of (1840-1841), 540; Navy Pension Fund, 486; Revolutionary War, 488, 543, 544; rolls and lists, 487-490, 543, 544;
    Kentucky, 1494, 1553, 1589; Maryland, 1794-1795; Massachusetts, 1892; Michigan, 1941; Missouri, 2077, 2110; New Hampshire, 2237-2239, 2256, 2274; North Carolina, 2577, 2578; Oklahoma, 2790; Pennsylvania, 2870, 2941a, 2945; South Carolina, 3124; Tennessee, 3244, 3288, 3310; Virginia, 3546, 3601; West Virginia, 3761
Pentin, H. Anglican church registers of Lisbon, 4898
Peplow, E. H. History of Arizona, 797
Pequot War, Connecticut, 1003
Peral, M. A. Diccionario biográfico mexicano, 3928
Percy, Lady Elizabeth (née Mortimer), descendants, 4460

Pérez Marchant, B. Diccionario biográfico del Ecuador, 3904
Periodicals and serials: American, 80-82, 94-129; British Isles, 4165; Canada, 75, 4008; English, 4159, 4248-4275; ethnic, 373; German-American, 379; heraldry, 5098-5113; in British libraries, 4145; Irish, 4595-4598; Scottish, 4726-4730; Welsh, 4159
Perkin, R. L. First hundred years, 948
Perrin, W. H. [Histories of Illinois counties], 1338-1341; Southwest Louisiana biography, 1674
——— (and others). Kentucky, 1559-1573
Perry, C. E. Founders and leaders of Connecticut, 1010
Perry county, Missouri, Catholics, 1817
Personal names (*see also* Names): bibliography, 223; English, 4405-4421; Irish, 4644-4652; Mohawk Valley, New York, 2489; New Jersey Indians, 2352; New York, 2457; Palatines, 2489
Peru: 3932-3935; heraldry and genealogy, 5084
Pessin, D. History of Jews in America, 435
Peters, W. E. Ohio lands, 2751
Peters colony, Texas, 1511, 3334, 3427
Petersen, W. J. Iowa history reference guide, 1435; Story of Iowa, 1436
Peterson, A. History of the Swedes who settled in South Dakota, 3229
Peterson, Charles S. Representative New Mexicans, 2412
Peterson, Clarence S. Bibliography of local histories in Atlantic states, 27; Bibliography of local history of 35 states beyond Atlantic states, 28; Consolidated bibliography of county histories in 50 states, 29; Known military dead during Mexican War, 550a; Known military dead during Revolutionary War, 531; Known military dead during War of 1812, 549
Peterson, E. History of Rhode Island, 3097
Petitions: ancient, British, 4215; U.S. directory, 177
Pettengill, S. B. Yankee pioneers, 3480
Petty, G. M. Index to 1840 federal census of North Carolina, 2634a
Petty, Sir William. Barony maps, 4632
Phelps, A. Contemporary biography of California's representative men, 896
Phelps and Gorham's Purchase, New York, 2559-2560a
Philadelphia (*see also* Pennsylvania): archives, 2859; census (1850), 2988; churches, 2996-2997; colonial and Rev-

439

*Index*

olutionary families, 2924; families, 2866, 2932; Germans, 2931; indentures, 2991; maritime records, 2911–2912; marriages, 2989, 2996a; obituaries, 2989; passenger arrivals, 359, 3020; Quakers, 2904, 2906, 2958, 2990, 2996, 2996a; ship registers, 2912; tax lists, 2992; wills, 3039
Philippa of Hainault, Queen, ancestors of, 4453
Philippine War, Iowa, 1426
Phillimore, R. H. Historical records of survey of India, 4942
Phillimore, W. P. W., and Frye, E. A. Index to changes of name, 4416
―――― and Thrift, G. Indexes to Irish wills, 4624
Phillimore's directory of genealogists and local historians, 4312
Phillimore's Parish register series (Marriages), 4359–4360
Phillips, J. W. Alaska-Yukon place names, 778, 4073; Washington state place names, 3702
Phillips, L. B. Dictionary of biographical reference, 157, 4287
Phillips, P. L. List of geographical atlases in Library of Congress, 200; List of maps of America, 201
Phisterer, F. New York in War of the Rebellion, 2535
Pickett, A. J. History of Alabama, 761
Pictish kings, 4792a
Pierce, C. W. Pioneer life in southeast Florida, 1122
Pierce, John. Register of Revolutionary War certificates, 542
Pierce, R. D. Records of First Church of Boston, 1918
Piers, H. Biographical review, Nova Scotia, 4066
Pierson, M. J. B. Louisiana soldiers in War of 1812, 1675
Pietists of Pennsylvania, 3006
Pike, K. J. Guide to manuscripts . . . Western Reserve Historical Soc., 2752; Guide to Shaker manuscripts, 465a
Pike county, Alabama, tomb records, 762
Pike county, Illinois, 1347, 1586
Pilgrim Fathers, bibliography, 606, 609
Pilgrims (*see also* Mayflower): 580, 596–597, 606, 609, 612, 614, 1845, 1907, 1923, 1928, 1937
Pillsbury, H. New Hampshire, 2275
Pinches, J. H. Handbook of mottoes, 4971n
―――― and R. V. Royal heraldry of Britain, 5025

Pine, L. G. American origins, 258; Genealogist's encyclopedia, 259; Highland clans, 4816; International heraldry, 4984; New extinct peerage, 4514; Sons of the Conqueror, 4468; Story of heraldry 5002; Story of surnames, 4417; Story of the peerage, 4515; Story of titles, 4516; Teach yourself heraldry and genealogy, 4435, 5003; Your family tree, 4436
Pioneer Daughters, South Dakota, 3217, 3235a
Pioneer Society of Michigan, *see* Michigan Pioneer and Historical Society
Pittman, E. F. Index to bound newspapers in Iowa State Dept. of History and Archives, 1437
Pittman, H. D. Americans of gentle birth, 313
Pittsburgh and her people, 2918
Place, F. Personal names, N.Y. state, 2457
Place names: 208–216; British guide to reports of Historical Manuscripts Commission, 4203, 4206; correct spelling, 215; Alabama Indian, 675; Alaska, 771, 778, 4073; Alberta, 4040; Arizona, 783, 791; British Columbia, 4044; California, 859, 867; California Indian and Spanish, 908; Canada, 3941; Celtic, 4782; Channel Islands, 4882; Colorado, 947; Connecticut, 1012; Delaware Dutch and Swedish, 1035; England, 4389–4390, 4397–4404; Florida, 1120; Florida Indian, 674; Georgia, 1139, 1226; Great Britain, 4387, 4397, 4402; Hawaii, 1247, 1265; Hebrides (Western Isles), 4884; Idaho, 1290; Illinois, 1293, 1353; Illinois Indian, 1353; Ireland, 4632, 4634, 4636–4637, 4644–4646; Isle of Man, 4886, 4889; Kansas, 1479; Kansas Indian, 677; Kentucky, 1521; Maine, 1697–1698; Manitoba, 4045; Michigan, 1978; Minnesota, 2027; Missouri, 2089, 2117; Nebraska, 2171; Nevada, 2198, 2211; New Mexico, 2408, 2411; New York, 2444, 2458; North Dakota, 2681; Nova Scotia, 4054, 4057; Oklahoma, 2795; Pennsylvania, 2884; Providence Plantations, 3076; Scotland, 4777–4778, 4780, 4782; South Carolina, 3160; South Dakota, 3221; Texas, 3407; Utah, 3441, 3444; Virginia, 3568, 3584, 3635, 3661–3662; Wales, 4389–4390, 4402, 4863–4865; Washington, 3697, 3700, 3702; West Virginia, 3743; Wisconsin, 3787; Wyoming, 3841; Yukon, 778, 4073
Planché, J. R. Conqueror and his companions, 4469

*Index*

Plantaganet ancestry, 4462
Plantaganet roll of blood royal: Anne of Exeter, 4457; Clarence, 4458; Isabel of Essex, 4459; Mortimer-Percy, 4460
Plarr, V. G. Lives of fellows of Royal College of Surgeons, 4327-4328
Plat books: Illinois, 1323-1324; Indiana, 1384-1385; Iowa, 1423; Michigan, 1959; Minnesota, 2005-2006; Montana, 2149n; North Dakota, 2674n; West Virginia, 3738n; Wisconsin, 3801, 3813; Wyoming, 3837n
Platt, G. Index to 1820 federal census, 3161
—— (and others). Index to U.S. census of 1840, Mississippi, 2065
Plessis, J.-O. Dénombrements de Québec, 4121
Plymouth, Massachusetts: bibliography, 606; colonial lists, 605; First Church records, 605a
Plymouth Colony, colonial lists, 3096
Plymouth Colony genealogical helper (magazine), 314
Plymouth county, Massachusetts, marriages, 1844
Poles: California, 871; New York, 2461; Pennsylvania, 2899; Texas, 3346, 3355, 3388
Polk, R. L., and Co. Cross reference to family names, 219
Polk's Alaska-Yukon gazetteer, 779
Polk's Directory of city and county of Honolulu, 1264
Poll books and lists: British, 4193; Guildhall Libr., London, 4222; Texas, 3382; United States, 177
Poll money ordinances, Ireland, 4581
Pollard, L., and Spencer, L. History of Washington, 3703
Pollock, P. W. Arizona's men of achievement, 798
Polynesian chiefs and nobles, 1245; migrations to Hawaii, 1249
Pompey, S. L. Burial lists of members of Union and Confederate military units, 559; Confederate soldiers buried in Colorado, 949; 1870 census, Dakota territory, 3230; Genealogical records of California, 897; Miscellaneous northern California cemetery inscriptions, 898; Partial listing of veterans of American Revolutions, 2115
Pontbriand, B. Canadian marriage licenses, 3994
Pool, D. de S. Portraits etched in stone, 2536

Pope, C. H. Pioneers of Maine and New Hampshire, 1727, 2276; Massachusetts, 1919
Population, national origins, 217
Portland, Oregon: Genealogical Forum, 2813-2819; history, 2837
Porto Rico, *see* Puerto Rico
Portrait and biographical albums, Kansas counties, 1477
Portrait and biographical record of: Arizona, 799; Colorado, 950; southeastern Kansas, 1478; Eastern Shore of Maryland, 1823; northern Michigan, 1975; Oklahoma, 2794; Scioto Valley, Ohio, 2753; western Oregon, 2836; Willamette Valley, Oregon, 2835
Portrait, genealogical and biographical record of Utah, 3445
Portugal, British subjects with Portuguese titles, 4503a
Portuguese-Hawaiian memories, 1251
Portuguese nobility in Brasil, 3883
Portuguese titles, British subjects with, 4503a
Posey, B. D. Alabama 1840 census, 763
Post offices: Alaska, 780; Arizona, 803; California, 865; Canada, 3951; Illinois, 1293; Kansas, 1444; Nevada, 2205-2206; Oklahoma, 2778; Texas, 3358, 3421; U.S., 216
Potter, C. E. Military history of New-Hampshire, 2277
Potter, D. W. 1820 federal census of North Carolina, 2635-2636
Potter, E. R. Memoir concerning French settlements in Rhode Island, 3098
Poulton, H. J. Historian's handbook, 260
Powell, E. W. Early Ohio tax records, 2755-2756
Powell, W. H. List of officers of Army of U.S., 478
—— and Shippen, E. Officers of Army and Navy, Civil War, 560-561
Powell, W. S. North Carolina gazetteer, 2637
Power, Sir D'A. Plarr's lives of fellows of the Royal College of Surgeons, 4328
Powers, P. F. History of northern Michigan, 1976
Powicke, Sir F. M., and Fryde, E. B. Handbook of British chronology, 4279
Powys Fadog, 4874
Prairie gleaner (magazine), 2116
Prairie provinces, Canada, bibliography, 4071-4072
Pratt, D. H. Remarkable collection of Eng-

441

*Index*

lish-Welsh probate records, 4381
Preble's regimental campaigning, 1731
Precolonial lists: general, 281-328; royal, 269-280
Prendergast, T. F. Forgotten persons, 899
Presbyterian church archives and records: New Jersey, 2325, 2345; New York city, 2472; Pennsylvania, 2867; West Virginia, 3734
Presbyterian churches: northeast Georgia, 1144; Virginia, 3675-3676
Presbyterian Historical Society of England. Journal, 4560
Presbyterian ministers, index to, 455
Presbyterians, English, 4529n, 4560
Presley, C. Biographical index to Goodspeed's Biographical and historical memoirs, 812-814, 836-837; History of Tennessee, 3262
Price, W. S. Colonial records of North Carolina, 2618
Prince Edward Island, Canada: 4047-4069; bibliography, 4063; topography, 4053
Prince William's parish plantation, South Carolina, 3201
Prince's List of esquires in 1736, 5081n
Princes of Wales, 4874
Privateers, Massachusetts, 1841
Privateersmen, 520
Probate records, *see* Wills and probates
Proctor, J. C. Washington and environs, 1089; Washington past and present, 1090
Progressive men of: southern Idaho, 1289; Montana, 2154; Wyoming, 3838
Prologue (magazine), 126
Prominent families in America with British ancestry, 158, 285a
Prominent Jews of America, 436
Prominent Tennesseeans, 3260
Prosser, W. F. History of Puget Sound country, 3704
Protestant Episcopal Church: Alabama, 743; Connecticut, 996; Delaware, 1041; District of Columbia, Washington Diocese, 1780; Maryland Diocese, 1781; Mississippi, 2048; Nevada, 2208; New York city and state, 2472-2473; New Jersey, 2325; Vermont, 3474; West Virginia, 3734; Wisconsin, 3798
Protestants: 456-458; church archives, unpublished material, 456; Louisiana churches, 1644; Pennsylvania, 2893, 2967; South Carolina immigrants, 3167
Proulx, A. Répertoire des mariages (Quebec areas), 4123
Providence Plantations, *see* Rhode Island

Providence, R.I. Alphabetical index of births, 3099; Early records, 3100-3101
Province and court records of Maine, 1716
Provincial and state papers, New Hampshire, 2264
Prowell, G. R. History of York county, 2994
Prowse, D. W. History of Newfoundland, 4067
Pruitt, J. C. Migration of South Carolinians on Natchez Trace, 3162; Revolutionary War pension applicants, 3163
Przygoda, J. Texas pioneers from Poland, 3388
Public archives bibliography, 14
Public Archives of Canada: loyalist sources, 4021; records, 3942
Public Record Office, *see* Great Britain. Public Office
Public register of all arms in Scotland, 5052n
Pueblo Indian land grants of the "Rio Abajo," New Mexico, 657
Puerto Rico: 3043-3067; baptisms, 3056; bibliography, 3057, 3064; foreign residents, 3047; gazetteer, 3055; immigrants, 3048; military figures, 3063; women, 3043, 3056, 3061
Puget Sound, 3704
Pugh, M. Capon Valley, 3760
Pugh, R. B. Records of Colonial and Dominions Offices, 4900
Pukui, M. K. (and others). Place names of Hawaii, 1265
Pulsifer, D. New Plymouth Colony records, 1917
Puritans, Connecticut, 994
Purl, B. F. Republic of Texas, 3388a
Purvis, J. S. Dictionary of ecclesiastical terms, 4528
Putnam's Historical magazine, 589n
Putnam's Monthly historical magazine, 589n
Puttock, A. G. Dictionary of heraldry, 4985; Tracing your family tree, 4914a

Quaife, M. M. John Askin papers, 1977; Wisconsin, 3806
Quakers: Canada, 3968; Dublin wills, 4620; England, 4561-4563, births, deaths, marriages, 4563, genealogy, sources, 4529n, obituaries, 4562, records, 4562; Indiana, 1378, 1380; Irish, 4705; Long Island, 2467; Maryland, 1764-1765, 1789; midwest, 461, 640, 1379; New Jersey, 2321, 2345, 2356; New York city, 2467; North Carolina, 2597-2598; Ohio, 2713; Pennsylvania, 2848, 2867n, 2894, 2904, 2906, 2910, 2914, 2957-2958, 2967, 2990, 2996; Phil-

*Index*

adelphia, 2904, 2906, 2958, 2990, 2996; Rhode Island, 3087; Scotland, 4825; U.S., 459-462, bibliography, 9, 459, encyclopedia, 462, genealogies, 461a, necrology, 460; Virginia, 3576, 3670
Qualey, C. C. Norwegian settlement in the United States, 392a
Quebec: 4097-4139; bibliography, 4098, 4110; births, 4111; Catholics, 4112; census, general, 4105, (1666), 4122, (1744), 4130, (1762), 4131, (1792, 1795, 1798, 1805), 4121, (1825-1871), 4056, 4107; French glossary of terms, 4097; land records, 4101-4104, 4133a; local histories, 4098; loyalists, 4032; manual, 4052, 4097; marriages, 4099-4100, 4108, 4112, 4123, 4126, 4132, 4136; militia, 4107a; noblemen, 4120; pioneers, 576; probate records, 4127
Quebec. Conseil Superieur de Québec. Lettres de noblesse, 4120
Quebec (Province). Archives, rapport, 4124
―――― Judicial Archives. Inventaires des concessions en fiefs et seigneuries ... de Québec, 4125; Inventaire de contrats de mariage ... de Québec, 4126; Inventaire des greffes des notaires, 4127; Inventaire des insinuations de la prévôte ... de Québec, 4128; Inventaire d'une collection de pièces judiciaires ... de Québec, 4129
Queen Anne's War, Connecticut service, 963
Query name index (magazine), 127
Questing Heirs Genealogical Society. Some early southern California burials, 900
Quiner, E. B. Military history of Wisconsin, 3807
Quinn, T. C. Massachusetts of today, 1920
Quinones, Estevan de, notarial acts, 1637-1638
Quisenberry, A. C. Kentucky in War of 1812, 1574; Kentucky officers in regular army 1789-1900, 1575; Revolutionary soldiers in Kentucky, 1576
Quit rents, Virginia, 3620

Raach, J. H. Directory of English country physicians, 4327
Radewald, B. Library handbook, 261
Radoff, M. L. (and others). County courthouses and records of Maryland, 1824; Old Line State, 1825
Rafter, J. L. Index to votes of Pennsylvania Assembly, 2911a, 2969
Raines, C. W. Bibliography of Texas, 3389
Raisin river battle, 1813, 1505

Rajputana and Central India, inscriptions, 4937
Ramirez Brau, E. Orígenes puertorriquénos, 3065
Ramsey, J. G. M. Annals of Tennessee, 3294-3295
Ramsey, R. L. Our storehouse of Missouri place names, 2117
Ramsey, R. W. Carolina cradle, 2638
Rand, J. C. One of a thousand, 1921
Rangers on the frontiers, Pennsylvania, 2939-2940
Ransom, J. L. Andersonville diary, 562
Rasmussen, L. J. California wagon trail lists, 901; Railway passenger lists, 902; San Francisco ship passenger lists, 903
Ratay, M. S. Pioneers of Ponderosa, 2220
Rateables, New Jersey, 2387-2388
Rathburn, T. York county, South Carolina, 3164
Raven-Hart, H. E., and Johnston, M. Bibliography of registers of universities, 4160
Ravenel, D. "Liste des françois et suisses," 3165
Ravenscroft, R. R. Order of Americans of Armorial Ancestry complete register of ancestors, 5077n
Ray, W. S. Austin colony pioneers, 3390; Colonial Granville county, 2639; Lost tribes of North Carolina, 2640; Mecklenburg signers, 2641; Old Albemarle and its absentee landlords, 2642; Ray's Index to Hathaway, 2643; Tennessee cousins, 3296
Read, B. M. Illustrated history of New Mexico, 2413
Read, W. A. Florida place-names of Indian origin, 674; Indian place names of Alabama, 675
Reaman, G. E. Trail of the Black Walnut, 2995, 4095, Trail of the Huguenots in Europe, 431, 3995
Reaney, P. H. Dictionary of British surnames, 4418; Origin of English place-names, 4404; Origin of English surnames, 4419
Records: American, 34-93; English, 4188-4237; Irish, 4572-4594; Scottish, 4717-4725; Welsh, 4833-4840
Recusant history (magazine), 4273
Reddy, A. W. West Virginia Revolutionary ancestors, 3761
Redemptioners, Pennsylvania, 2890, 2991
Redlich, M. D. A. R. von. Pedigrees of some of Emperor Charlemagne's descendants, 277

443

*Index*

Reed, G. I. Encyclopedia of biography of Indiana, 1400
Reed, H. C. and M. B. Bibliography of Delaware, 1053; Delaware, 1054
Reed, L. Old-timers of southeastern California, 904
Rees, J. E. Idaho chronology, 1290
Rees, T. M. Notable Welshmen, 4845
Rees, W. Historical atlas of Wales, 4859
Reeve, F. D. History of New Mexico, 2414
Reference encyclopedia of the American Indian, 676
Reformed Dutch church, New York, 2503–2504
Register, A. K. Index to 1830 census of Georgia, 1220a; State census of North Carolina, 2644
Register, E. (and others). Index to [Blair's] Some early tax digests of Georgia, 1221
Registers: British universities, etc., 4160; parish, English, 4338–4345; Irish, 4606–4607; Scottish, 4750–4760
Reichel, L. T. Moravians in North Carolina, 2645
Reid, W. D. Loyalists in Ontario, 4031
Religions: English, general, 4527–4530, separate, 4531–4565; Irish, 4697–4705; Scottish, 4825–4826; United States, general, 404–410, separate, 411–465a; Wales, 4879–4880
Religious denominations handbook, United States, 404b
Reminiscent history of: northern West Virginia, 3762; Ozark region, Arkansas, 837, 2118
Renesse, T. de. Dictionnaire des figures héraldiques, 5119
Rennie, J. A. Scottish people, 4817
Rensch, H. E. (and others). Historic spots in California, 905
Rensselaerswyck: early records, 2421; minutes of Court, 2422; settlers, 2520
The report (Ohio Genealogical Soc.) (magazine), 2757
Representative men and old families of: Rhode Island, 3102; southeastern Massachusetts, 1922
Representative men of: Colorado, 951; Connecticut, 1011; Maine, 1728
Rerick, R. H. Memoirs of Florida, 1123
The researcher (magazine), 3613
The researcher (Tacoma Genealogical Soc.), 3705
Return of owners of land: England, 4230; Ireland, 4593; Wales, 4230
Revill, J. Compilation of original lists of Protestant immigrants to South Carolina, 3167; Copy of original index book, 3168; South Carolina counties, 3169; South Carolina wills, 3170
Revista genealogica Brasileira, 3885
Revolutionary War: 491–546a; bibliography, 123n, 532; bounty-land warrants, 74; burials, 497; Continental Army officers, 516; dead, 531; graves, 505; lineages, 290; muster and pay rolls, 496, 527, 3992a; oaths of allegiance, 545; participants, 496; pay rolls, 527, 542; pension applications, 524–526, 546a, rejected or suspended, 538–539; pensioners (1813), 543, (1818), 544, census of, (1840), 540–541, struck off roll, 488; pictorial field book, 521; Pierce's certificates, 542; prisoners, 495; records, 509, 535; surname index to pedigrees, 42

Alabama, 721, 736, 750, 759–760, 767; Ansbach Bayreuth mercenaries, 537; black servicemen, 528; British: mercantile claims, 492, 4190, prisoners, 2550, property confiscated, 492, 4190; Brunswick deserter-immigrants, 536; Cherokee land lottery, 703–705; Connecticut, 970, 976, 992, 1005–1006, 1019; D. A. R. publications, 496–508; Delaware, 1028, 1060–1061; District of Columbia, 1074; Florida, 1107; French Canadian participants, 3983; French participation, 491, 514, 523; Georgia, 1142, 1190, 1198, 1212–1213, lotteries, *see* Lotteries; German allied troops, 512; Hessians, 380, 517, 522; Illinois, 1308, 1312, 1342, 1358–1359; Indiana, 1372, 1408; Indians, 523; Ireland, 387, 523, 530; Kentucky, 1489, 1494, 1516, 1553, 1556, 1576; King's Mountain men, 510, 546; loyalists, 494, 511, 522a (definition), 529, 533–534; Maine, 1701, 1704, 1711; mariners, 520; Maryland, 911, 1744, 1747–1748, 1759, 1761, 1773, 1794–1795, 1806, 1816, 1836; Massachusetts, 1841, 1892, 1904, 1927; Mennonites, 493; Michigan, 1941, 1980; Mississippi, 2033; Missouri, 2077, 2108, 2110, 2115, 2119; Mohawk Valley, New York, 2489n; New Hampshire, 2237–2239, 2244, 2256, 2263, 2265–2266, 2271, 2274; New Jersey, 2383–2384, 2389; New York, 2454, 2489, 2512–2513, 2526; North Carolina, 2577, 2582a, 2588, 2649a; Ohio, 2691, 2701–2703; Palatines, 2489n; Pennsylvania, 2855, 2870, 2874, 2876–2877, 2892n, 2939–2941a, 2945, 2949, 2955, 2972–2973, 2997, 2999, 3014–

3015; Rhode Island, 3083; Scotch Highlanders, 396, 523; Sons of the American Revolution, 538; South Carolina, 911, 3122, 3124, 3135, 3140, 3154–3155, 3163, 3166, 3168, 3192–3193; Tennessee, 3236–3237, 3243–3244, 3253, 3288, 3304; Vermont, 3463, 3469; Virginia, 535, 3516, 3518–3519, 3546, 3549–3550, 3564, 3569, 3594, 3597, 3601, 3616, 3621, 3625, 3677; Washington's guard, 515; Welsh, 519; West Virginia, 3742, 3749, 3761; Wisconsin, 3784; women, 513

Reynolds, C. Genealogical and family history of southern New York, 2537; Hudson-Mohawk genealogical and family memoirs, 2538

Reynolds, E. B., and Faunt, J. R. Biographical directory of Senate of South Carolina, 3189

Reynolds, H. W. Dutch houses in Hudson Valley, 2539

Reynolds, J. A. Heraldry and you, 5004

Rhea, M. Map of Tennessee, 3292

Rheingantz, C. G., Primeiras famílias do Rio de Janeiro, 3886

Rhinelanders, North Carolina, 2595

Rhoads, J. B., and Ashby, C. M. Cartographic records of Bureau of Census, 203

Rhode Island: 3068–3118; Baptist churches, 3087; cemetery records, 3091; census (1774), 3105, (1782), 3118, (1790), 3116, (1800), 3090, 3117; church and religious organizations, 3084; church archives, 3087; church vital statistics, 3085; civil and military list, 3112–3114; Civil War, 554, 564, 3072, 3106; colonial lists, 605; colonial records, 3103; court records, 3104; French and Indian Wars, 3081, 3114a; French emigrants, 3098; gazetteer, 3095; heraldry, 3079; King George's War, 3080, 3082; land evidences, 3109; place names, 3076; privateers, 3082; public statistics records, 3086; Quakers, 3087; Revolutionary War, 3083; ship registers and enrollments, 3088; vital record, 3068

Rhode Island historical magazine, 3107

Rhode Island Historical Society. Collections, 3108; Rhode Island land evidences, 3109

Rhode Island historical tracts, 3110–3111

Ricard, F. W. Biographical encyclopedia, New Jersey, 2370

Richard, B. C. 1770 census of Nova Scotia, 4068

Richards, H. M. M. Pennsylvania German in Revolutionary War, 2997

Richardson, H. D. Side-lights on Maryland history, 1826

Richardson, J. D. Tennessee Templars, 3297

Richardson, M. M., and Mize, J. J. 1832 Cherokee land lottery, 703

Richardson, T. C. East Texas, 3392

Ricks, M. B. Directory of Alaska post offices and postmasters, 780

Rider, Fremont. American genealogical index, 1–2

Ridge, C. H., and Knight, A. C. Records of Worshipful Company of Shipwrights, 4336

Ridge runners (magazine), 366

Ridgely, H. W. Historic graves of Maryland and D.C., 1091, 1827

Ridlon, G. T., Sr. Saco Valley settlements, 1729, 2278

Rieder, M. P., Jr., and N. G. Crew and passenger registration lists of seven Acadien expeditions, 1676; Louisiana, 1677; New Orleans ship lists, 1678

Riesenman, J., Jr. History of northwestern Pennsylvania, 2998

Rietstap, J. B. Armorial général, 5120–5122

Riggs, R. P. Register of rebel deserters taking oath of allegiance, 3614

Rigsby, L. W. Historic Georgia families, 1222

Rimouski, diocese of (Quebec), marriages, 4108

Rio de Janeiro: first families, 3886; genealogies, 3882

Rio de la Plata, colonial period, 3879

Rio Grande: Arizona, 786n; Texas, 3395–3396

River counties (of middle Tennessee), 3298

River Ohio, North Dakota Territory, 2664

Rivera y Moncada expedition (1781), 924

Rivington's New York newspaper, excerpts, 71

Roa y Ursua, L. de. Reyno de Chile, 3892

The roadrunner (magazine), 3393

Robarts, W. H. Mexican War veterans, 550b

Roberge, C. Répertoire des mariages . . . (Quebec), 4132

Robert the Strong, lineage, 325–326

Roberts, J. A. New York in Revolution, 2512–2513

Roberts, W. H. Complete roster . . . in war between U.S. and Mexico, 3394

Robertson, F. L. Soldiers of Florida in the Seminole Indian, Civil and Spanish-American wars, 1124

Robertson's colony, Texas, 3374

## Index

Robichaux, A. J. Louisiana census and militia lists, 1679
Robinson, D. Encyclopedia of South Dakota, 3231; History of South Dakota, 3232; South Dakota, 3233
Robinson, E. B. History of North Dakota, 2679
Robinson, M. P. Virginia counties, 3615
Robison, J. F.-J., and Bartlett, H. C. Genealogical records, 2540
Robles, P. K. U.S. military medals and ribbons, 479
Robson, T. British herald, 5026
Rochelle, France, emigration to Quebec, 4113
Rocky Mountain directory (1871), 952
Rocq, M. M. California local history, 906
Rodgers, E. D. Romance of Episcopal church in west Tennessee, 3299
Rodney, Daniel. Diary, 1059
Rodríguez Demorizi, E. Próceres de la restauracíon noticias biográficas, 3902
Rogers, C. Monuments . . . in Scotland, 4763
Rogers, E. S. Genealogical periodical annual index, 99
―――― and Easter, L. E. 1880 census, Kent county, Delaware, 1055; 1800 census, New Castle county, Delaware, 1056
Rogers, G. C. History of Georgetown county, 3171
Rogers, Mrs. H., and Lane, Mrs. A. H. Abstracts of New Jersey commissions, 2371
Rojas, A. (and others). Escudo de armas de la ciudad de Caracas, 5085
Roll of arms registered by Committee on Heraldry of New England Historic Genealogical Soc., 5078
Rolland, V. and H. V. Rietstap's Armorial général, illustrations, 5121; Supplément, 5122
Rolls of arms: general, 5009–5011; Australia, 5062; British West Indies, 4924; Canada: 5071, 5074–5075, 5080, armory and lineages, 5080, ethnic groups, 5074n, flags, 5071, manual, 5074; Colombia, 5087; Falkland Islands, 5083; Galicia, 5084; Great Britain: 5012–5032, Anglo-Jewish, 5012, 5032, Battle Abbey, 5014, crests, 5016, hatchments, 5029, medieval, 5027, 5030–5031, ordinary, 5024, royal heraldry, 5025, visitations, 5020–5021, 5023, 5028; Ireland: 5033–5044, coats of arms, 5024, crests, 5016, gentry, 4688–4689, visitations, 5036; Jersey, 5066;
Latin America, 5082–5087, *see also* names of individual countries; Mexico, 5082; Peru, 5084; Scotland: 4991n, 5045–5056, burgh and county, 5056, maps, 4813, ordinary, 5051, seals, 5049, 5054; South Africa, 4963, 5060a, 5064–5065; Spanish, 5086; United States; 5067–5081, Augustan Society, 5068–5069, Dutch descent, 5073, New England, 5067; Venezuela, 5085; Wales: 5057–5060, princes, 5059–5060, royal, 5060, visitations, 4871–4872, 5023
Rolls of Henry III, 5027
Roman Catholics, *see* Catholics
Romance Europe, L.D.S. research papers, 243G
Romance language countries, L.D.S. World Conference, 91F
Romig, W. Michigan place names, 1978
Rone, W. H., Sr. Historical atlas of Kentucky, 1577
Rooney, J. Genealogical history of Irish families, 4692
Rosa-Nieves, C., and Melón, E. M. Biografías puertorriqueñas, 3066
Roscommon, Ireland, books of survey, 4580
Rosenbach, A. S. W. American Jewish bibliography, 29a
Rosenbloom, J. R. Biographical dictionary of early American Jews, 437
Rosengarten, J. G. German soldier in wars of U.S., 480
Rosenthal, E. South African surnames, 4964; Southern African dictionary, 4965
Rosicky, R. History of Czechs in Nebraska, 2192
Ross, Scotland, sasines for sheriffdoms, 4759
Rosselli, B. Italians in colonial times, 1125
Roth, C. Magna bibliotheca Anglo-Judaica, 4551
Rotuli hundredorum, 4191n
Rouaix, P. Diccionario geográfico, histórico y biográfico del estado de Durango, 3929
Round, J. H. Family origins, 4517; Peerage and pedigree, 4518; Studies in peerage, 4519
Roundheads, army lists, 4294
Rowland, A. R. Bibliography of writings on Georgia history, 1223
Rowland, D. Courts, judges, and lawyers of Mississippi, 2066; Encyclopedia of Mississippi history, 2067; History of Mississippi, 2068; Military history of Mississippi, 2069
―――― and Sanders, E. H. French dominion, 2071; Mississippi provincial archives, 2070

Rowland, E. H. Biographical dictionary of eminent Welshmen, 4846
Rowland, E. O. Mississippi territory in War of 1812, 2072
Rowland, L. Los fundadores, 907
Rowntree, J. S. Friends' registers of births, 4563
Roy, A. Bibliographie de généalogies et histoire de familles, 3996
Roy, P.-G. Fils de Québec, 4133; Invenaire des contrats de mariage du régime français, 4126; Inventaire d'une collection de pièces judiciaires, 4129; Inventaires des concessions en fiefs, 4125; Inventaires des insinuations de la prévôte, 4128; Papier terrier de la Compagnie des Index Occidentales, 4133a
────── (and others). Inventaire des greffes des notaires du régime français, 4127
Royal: families (American), 269–270, 280; family (Great Britain), 4445–4462; family (Hawaiian), 1266–1267; heraldry (Britain), 5025; houses, 165; land grants (Rio Grande), 3396; lineages, 274; pedigrees of Americans, 313; tribes of Wales, 4878
Royal and princely heraldry in Wales, 5060
Royal College of Physicians of London, roll, 4325–4326
Royal College of Surgeons, lives of fellows, 4327–4328
Royal Company of the West Indies, Canadian records, 4133a
Royal Historical Society. Writings on British history, 4161–4163, 4166–4168
Royal Navy, *see* Navy (British)
Royalist magazine, 105n
Royalists, *see* Loyalists
Royalty: Alfred the Great, 279; atlas of, 195; genealogical tables of, 4446; Magna Charta barons, 272; research for, 273
Royalty, peerage, and aristocracy of the world, 278
Rubincam, M. America's only royal family, 1266; Genealogy, 30; Hawaiian royal family, 1267
────── and Stephenson, J. Genealogical research, 241
Rubio y Moreno, L. Pasajeres a Indias, 3862–3863
Rule, La R., and Hammond, W. K. What's in a name, 220
Runk, J. M., and Co. Biographical and genealogical history of Delaware, 1057
Rupp, I. D. Collection of upwards of thirty thousand names of . . . immigrants in Pennsylvania, 3000; History and topography of Dauphin [and other] counties, 3001; History and topography of Northumberland [and other] counties, 3002–3003; History of Lancaster and York counties, 3004; History of Northampton [and other] counties, 3005
Rusk, J. M. Roster of Wisconsin volunteers, War of the Rebellion, 3807a
Russell, G. E. Genealogical periodical annual index, 98
Russia, German emigration to, 381
Rust, O. G. History of west central Ohio, 2758
Rutgers University Library manuscripts, 2377
Rutherford county, Tennessee, census, 3314n
Rutt, A. E. H. Our Norwegian ancestors, 393
Ruvigny and Raineval, M. A. H. D., 9th Marquis of. Ancestors of Edward III, 4453; Blood royal of Britain, 4454; Jacobite peerage, 4455; Nobilities of Europe, 4456; Plantaganet roll of blood royal, 4457–4460
Ryan, R. Biographia Hibernica, 4604
Rydjord, J. Indian place-names, 677; Kansas place-names, 1479
Rye, W. Index to six versions of the so-called Roll of Battle Abbey, 4470
Ryerson, A. E. Loyalists of America, 533
Rygg, A. N. Norwegians in New York, 2541

Sabine, L. Biographical sketches of loyalists, 534
Sachse, J. F. German Pietists, 3006; German sectarians, 3007
Saco Valley, New Hampshire, settlements, 1729, 2278
Saffell, W. T. R. Index to List of Virginia soldiers in Revolutionary War, 535; Records of Revolutionary War, 535, 3616
Saga of southern Illinois, 1343
Sage, C. McC., and Jones, L. S. Early records, Hampshire county, Virginia, 3763
St. Andrews University, Graduation roll and Matriculation roll, 4746–4747
St. George's Chapel, Windsor, stall plates in, 4498
St. Louis Genealogical Society. Index to 1850 St. Louis and St. Louis county census, 2121; Index to St. Louis marriages, 2120; Quarterly, 2122; Surname index, 2123; Topical index of genealogical quarterlies, 100a
Saint Louis Public Library, genealogical

*Index*

material and local histories, 46-47, 2091
St. Paul, Minnesota, 1988
Sainty, J. C. Office-holders in modern Britain, 4315; Treasury officials, 4316
Sainty, M. R., and Johnson, K. A. Index to birth . . . notices in Sydney herald, 4914b
Salem Press historical and genealogical record, 589n
Salisbury, H. J. Pioneer families of Oregon territory, 2834
Salisbury, R. Pennsylvania newspapers, 3008
Salley, A. S., Jr. Abstracts from records, Court of Ordinary, South Carolina, 3184; Accounts audited of Revolutionary claims against South Carolina, 3192; Marriage notices in Charleston courier, 3172; Marriage notices in South Carolina and American general gazette, 3173; Marriage notices in South Carolina gazette, 3174; Marriage notices in South Carolina gazette and its successors, 3175; Records of the secretary of the province [South Carolina] . . . , 3182; South Carolina troops in Confederate service, 3190; Stub entries to indents in payment of claims against South Carolina, 3193; Warrants for lands in South Carolina, 3185
────── and Webber, M. L. Death notices in South Carolina gazette, 3176
Salt Lake City, biographical record, 3429
Salzburgers, 1231, 1233
Samuel, W. S. Sources for Anglo-Jewish genealogy, 4552
San Antonio families, 3333n
San Domingo refugees in Pennsylvania, 2849
San Jacinto, heroes of, 3345
San Juan country, Colorado, pioneers, 934
San Juan county, New Mexico, 2406
Sanchez, N. Spanish and Indian place names of California, 908
Sanders, H. F. History of Montana, 2155
Sanders, I. J. English baronies, 4520
Sanders, M. E. Records of Attakapas district, Louisiana, 1680
Sandford, F. Genealogical history of kings of England, 4461
Sandison, A. Tracing ancestors in Shetland, 4789
Sandusky region, Ohio, 2767
Sanford, E. G. Pilgrim Fathers and Plymouth Colony, 606
Santa Barbara Mission archives, 866
Santa Fe, New Mexico (Archdiocese), archives, 2415

Sargent, W. M. Maine wills, 1730
Saskatchewan: 4140-4143; gazetteer, 4140; geographic names, 4140; newspapers, 4142
Saskatchewan Genealogical Society. Bulletin, 4143
Sault Sainte Marie, land claims, 1952
Saunders, D. G., and Carson, E. A. Guide to records of Bahamas, 4900a
Saunders, J. E. Early settlers of Alabama, 764
Saunders, W. L. Colonial records of North Carolina, 2626n
Savage, J. Genealogical dictionary of first settlers of New England, 607
Savo Finns Historical Society. History of Finnish settlements . . . South and North Dakota, 3234
Sawyer, A. L. Memorial record of northern peninsula of Michigan, 1979
Scalf, H. P. Kentucky's last frontier, 1578
Scandinavians: family names, 4405; L.D.S. research papers, 243D; L.D.S. World Conference on Records, 91E; Minnesota, 2020; New York, 2450; Pacific, 648, 912, 3710; U. S., 395, 2020
Scannell, J. J. Scannell's New Jersey first citizens, 2372
Scharf, J. T. History of: Baltimore city and county, 1828; Delaware, 1058; Maryland, 1829; western Maryland, 1830
Schenectady, New York: first settlers, 2532; minutes of court, 2422
Schiavo, G. Italians in Missouri, 2125
Schirmer diary, 3177
Schlinkert, L. Subject bibliography of Wisconsin history, 3808
Schmidt, H. G. Germans in colonial New Jersey, 2373
Schoenberg, W. P. Jesuits of Montana, 2156
Schoharie immigrants to Pennsylvania, 2978, v.9, 3000
Scholefield, G. H. Dictionary of New Zealand biography, 4949
Schreiner-Yantis, N. Genealogical books in print, 31; Montgomery county, Virginia, 3617; Supplement to 1810 census of Virginia, 3618
Schultz, E. T. First settlements of Germans in Maryland, 1831
Schuon, K. U.S. Navy biographical dictionary, 481
Schuricht, H. History of German element in Virginia, 3619
Schwenkfelder families, 2846
Scioto Valley, Ohio, 2717, 2753

*Index*

Scotch-Irish: bibliography, 399n; in America, 397–399, 2863; 2875; manuals, 4654, 4658, 4664, 4788; migration to South Carolina, 3199; pioneers in Ulster, 397; Virginia, 3525

Scotland (*see also* England, Great Britain): 4706–4771; Anglican parishes, 4296; Army, 4735–4737; atlas, 4764, 4766, 4770; baronetage, 4796, 4798, 4800; baronetcies, 4481, 4490; baronets of English families, 4476; bibliographies, 4706–4716; biographies, general, 4731–4733, professsions, 4734–4749; burgh and county heraldry, 5096; Church of Scotland, 4739, 4826; clans and tartans, 4791, 4794, 4805–4808, 4810, 4812, 4814, 4816–4817, 4820–4821; coats of arms, 4514, 4765n, 4772n; county families, 4526; Court of Lord Lyon, 4748; deeds, 4758; emigration, 333, 341, 355, 2613, 4725; epitaphs and monumental inscriptions, 4762–4763; Faculty of Advocates, 4734; gazetteers, 4767, 4769–4770, 4773–4775; heraldry, 4724, 4794, 5006, 5096; Highlanders, in America, 396, in Revolutionary War, 523; immigrants, 336; kings, 4792, 4797, 4802, 4804, 4818; knights, 4521, 4822; land records, etc., 4722; landowners, 4721; Lowland lairds, 4803; manuals, 4783–4790, 5006; manuscripts, relating to U.S. and Canada, 66, 3997; maps, 4765, 4772, 4807, 4813; names, 4776–4782; newspapers, 4708; paleography, 4725a; parish clergy at the Reformation, 4738; parish registers, 4760; parochial registers, 4750, 4755; peerage, etc., 4791–4824; periodicals and series, 4726–4730; place-names, 4634, 4777–4778, 4780, 4782; public records, 4719a; publications, 4711, 4730; Quakers, 4825; Rebellion of 1745, 4732–4733; records, 4717–4725; registers, 4750–4761; religion, 4825–4826; septs and regiments, 4791; Society of Writers to His Majesty's Signet, 4749; sources for genealogy and family history, 4345, v.12; surnames, 4776, 4779, 4781; tartans, *see* Clans and tartans; titles of honour, 4522, 4823; topography, 4713, 4764–4765; vital statistics, 4761–4763; wills, 4763a

Scott, F. J. Historical heritage of lower Rio Grande, 3395; Royal land grants north of Rio Grande, 3396

Scott, H. (and others). Fasti ecclesiae Scoticanae, 4739

Scott, H. M. Scott's papers, 1579

Scott, H. W. History of Oregon country, 2838; History of Portland, Oregon, 2837

Scott, John. Indiana gazetteer, 1401

Scott, Joseph. Geographical description of Pennsylvania, 3009

Scott, K. Calendar of New York colonial commissions, 2506; Chronological data from further New York administration bonds, 2542; Genealogical abstracts from American weekly mercury, 67; Genealogical data from administration papers, New York state, 2515; Genealogical data from New York mercury, 68, 2543; Genealogical data from New York weekly post boy, 69; Genealogical data from Pennsylvania chronicle, 70, 3010; Genealogical data from Rivington's New York newspaper, 71; Marriage bonds of colonial New York, 2544; New York historical manuscripts, 2566; New York marriage licenses, 2508n; Records of the Chancery Court, province and state of New York, 2545; Ulster county, New York, court records, 2546

——— and Owre, J. A. Genealogical data from inventory of New York estates, 2516

Scott-Giles, C. W. Civic heraldry of England and Wales, 5094

Scottish antiquary (magazine), 4726

Scottish genealogical helper (magazine), 4727

Scottish genealogist (magazine), 4728

Scottish notes and queries (magazine), 4729

Scottish Public Record Office: description, 4757a; index to registers of deeds, 4758; index to secretary's sasines in sheriffdoms of Inverness, 4759; Records of Church of Scotland, 4826; Source list of manuscripts relating to U.S. and Canada, 66, 3997

Scottish Record Society (publications), 4730

Scoville, J. A. Old merchants of New York city, 2547

Script, *see* Paleography

Scrugham, J. G. Nevada, 2221

Sculptors, dictionary of: American, 149; British, 4335

Sea journals, New England, 587

Sealock, R. B., and Seely, P. A. Bibliography of place-name literature, 213

Seals: bibliography, 5114; Scottish, 5049, 5054

The searcher (magazine), 909

Seattle, 3684, 3713

Seattle Genealogical Society bulletin, 3706

449

*Index*

Secomb, D. F. List of centenarians of New Hampshire, 2279
Sectarians of Pennsylvania, 3007
Seebold, H. B. de B. Old Louisiana plantation homes, 1681
Selby, P. O. Bibliography of Missouri county histories, 2126
Sellers, H. E. Connecticut town origins, 1012
Seminole Indian War, Florida, 1124
Septs and regiments of Scottish Highlands, 4791
Serbians, immigrants, 356
Serials, *see* Periodicals and serials
Serle, P. Dictionary of Australian biography, 4915
Seton, Sir B. G., and Arndt, J. G. Prisoners of the '45, 4733
Seton, G. Law and practice of heraldry in Scotland, 5006
1745 Rebellion, Scotland: List of persons, 4732; prisoners, 4733
Severin, E. [Swedes in Texas], 3397
Seversmith, H. F. Colonial families of Long Island, 2548
────── and Stryker-Rodda, K. Long Island genealogical source material, 2549
Seward Peninsula, 777
Shackleton, B. C. Handbook on the frontier days of southeast Kansas, 1480
Shaker genealogy: 465a; manuscripts in Western Reserve Historical Soc., 465a
Shaw, A. C. 1850 Georgia mortality census, 1224; 1840 Florida U.S. census, 1127; 1830 Florida census, 1126
Shaw, H. K. Families of the Pilgrims, 320, 1923
Shaw, L. True history of some of the pioneers of Colorado, 953
Shaw, W. A. Knights of England, 4521; Letters of denization and acts of naturalization for aliens, 4231, 4542-4543
Shaw, W. T. Records, 3462n
Shaw and Blaylock's Abstract of land claims, Galveston, 3413n
Shawkey, M. P. West Virginia in history, 3764
Sheffield, E., and Woods, B. 1840 index to Georgia census, 1225
Sheldon, A. E. Nebraska, 2193
Shelley, F. Guide to manuscripts collection of New Jersey Historical Soc., 2374
Shenandoah Valley: bibliography, 123n; German settlers, 3667; history, 3608; marriage bonds, 3502; Pennsylvania Germans in, 2978, v.26, 3013; pioneers, 3522, 3721
Shepherd, S. Supplement to Hening's Statutes, 3571
Shepherd, W. R. Historical atlas, 197
Sheppard, W. L. Passengers and ships prior to 1684, 3029
Sheriffdoms, Aberdeen, 4757a
Sheriffs from England and Wales to 1831, 4215
Sherman, C. E. Original Ohio land subdivisions, 2759
Sherman, J. E. and B. H. Ghost towns and mining camps of New Mexico, 2417
Sherwood, A. Gazetteer of state of Georgia, 1226
Sherwood, G. F. T. American colonists in English records, 354; Pedigree register, 4513
Shetland: parishes, 4789, patronymic surnames, 4789; ancestors, 4789
Shetler, C. Guide to study of West Virginia history, 3765
Shilstone, E. M. Monumental inscriptions ... at Bridgetown, 4930
Shine, J. H. Pioneers and makers of Arkansas, 838
Shinedling, A. I. West Virginia Jewry, 3766
Ship enrollments, *see* Ship lists
Ship lists, registers: Eureka, California, 879; Maine, 1710; Massachusetts, 1888; Oregon, 2825; Palatine, 2483; Pennsylvania, 2871, 2911, 2959, 3011, 3029-3031; Philadelphia, 2912; Rhode Island, 3088
Ship passenger lists, *see* Passenger lists
Shipping records, British, 4224
Shipwrights, British, records, 4336
Shirk, G. H. Oklahoma place names, 2795
Shoemaker, F. C. Missouri and Missourians, 2127
Shourds, T. History and genealogy of Fenwick's colony, 2375-2376
Shull, T. N. County atlases for genealogical use, 198
Shumway, G. L. History of western Nebraska, 2194
Shurtleff, N. B. New Plymouth Colony records, 1917; Records of governor and company of Massachusetts Bay, 1898
Shutter, M. D., and McLain, J. S. Progressive men of Minnesota, 2023
Sibley's Harvard graduates, 159
Sibmacher, *see* Siebmacher
Siebert, W. H. American loyalists in eastern seignories of Quebec, 4032; Loyalists in

*Index*

east Florida, 1128; Loyalists of Pennsylvania, 3012
Siebmacher, J. Grosses und allgemeines Wappenbuch, 5123–5124
Siler, D. W. Eastern Cherokees, 704
Silliman, S. I. Michigan military records, 1980
Simington, R. C. Books of survey and distribution, 4580; Civil survey, 4582; Transplantation of Connacht, 4642
Simmendinger's register, 2483
Simonhoff, H. Jewish notables in America, 438; Saga of American Jewry, 439
Simpson, A. J. Centennial of southwest Texas, 3398n; Southwest Texas, 3398
Simpson, G. G. Scottish handwriting, 4725a
Simpson, J. H. Navaho expedition, 2418
Sims, C. S. Origin and signification of Scottish surnames, 4781
Sims, E. B. Making a state, 3767; Maps showing development of West Virginia counties, 3768; Sims' Index to land grants in West Virginia, 3769–3770
Sims, R. Index to pedigrees and arms, 4184; Index to pedigrees in heralds visitations, 4259n; Manual for the genealogist, 4437
Sinclair, D. A. Index to Genealogical magazine of New Jersey, 2316
Sinclair, Sir J. Statistical account of Scotland, 4722
Sinnott, M. E. Index to genealogical and historical queries from New York mail, 72
Sioux: massacre, 2019; tribe, 660
Sistler, B., and Associates. U.S. census of Tennessee: (1830), 3300; (1850), 3301
Skelton, R. A. County atlases of British Isles, 4393
Sketches of Colorado [W. C. Ferril], 936
Sketches of successful New Hampshire men, 2280
Skey, W. Heraldic calendar, Ireland, 4694, 5044
Skirven, P. G. First parishes of province of Maryland, 1832
Skordas, G. Early settlers in Maryland, 1833
Slave: census, New York, 2529; manifests, Pennsylvania, 2911
Slaveholders of Louisiana, 1669
Slaveowners of Maryland, 1760a
Slavonic pioneers of California, 889
Sligo, Ireland, hearth money rolls, 4589
Sloan, E. L. Gazetteer of Utah, 3446
Sloan, R. E. History of Arizona, 800
Slocum, R. B. Biographical dictionaries, 160–161
Slovaks, Canada, 3970

Slovenes, immigrants, 356
Smallwood, M. Some colonial and Revolutionary families of North Carolina, 2646
Smiles, S. The Huguenots, 432, 4547
Smith, A. E. Guide to manuscripts of Wisconsin State Historical Soc., 3809–3811; History of Wisconsin, 3812
Smith, A. L. W. Quit rents of Virginia, 3620
Smith, B. L. Marriage by bond in colonial Texas, 3399
Smith, C. N. Brunswick deserter-immigrants of American Revolution, 536; Federal land series, 73–74; German-American genealogical research monographs, 3998; Mercenaries from Ansbach and Bayreuth, 537; Revolutionary War bounty-land warrants, 74
Smith, D. L. V. Indians of the U. S. and Canada, 678, 3999
Smith, D. W. Kentucky 1830 census index, 1580
Smith, E. C. American surnames, 221; Dictionary of American family names, 222n; New dictionary of American family names, 222; Personal names, 223, 4420; Story of our names, 224
Smith, E. L. (and others). Pennsylvania Germans of the Shenandoah Valley, 2978, v. 26, 3013
Smith, F. Genealogical gazetteer: of England, 4394; Scotland, 4774
Smith, G. G. Story of Georgia, 1227
Smith, G. W. History of Illinois, 1344; History of southern Illinois, 1345
Smith, H. A. M. Baronies of South Carolina, 3178
Smith, H. F. Guide to manuscript collections of Rutgers Univ. Library, 2377
Smith, J. F. Cherokee land lottery, 705, 1228
Smith, J. J. Civil and military list of Rhode Island, 3112–3114
Smith, J. W. Smith's first directory of Oklahoma territory, 2796
Smith, Mrs. M. T., and Lewis, J. T. Daughters of American Colonists history and lineage book, 2085
Smith, N. F. History of Pickens county, Alabama, 731
Smith, S. B. Tennessee history, 3301a
Smith, W. Flag book of United States, 5095
Smith, W. E. History of southwestern Ohio, 2760
Smith, W. T. Complete index to names of persons ... in Littell's Laws of Kentucky, 1581

*Index*

Snowden, Y. History of South Carolina, 3179
Snyder, J. P. Story of New Jersey's civil boundaries, 2378
Snyder, Van Vechten and Co. Historical atlas of Wisconsin, 3813
Soame, register of wills, 4371
Sobel, R. Biographical directory of U.S. executive branch, 162
Société Canadienne de Généalogie (Québec). Contributions, 4134
Société Généalogique Canadienne Française. Mémoires, 4135; Publications, 4136
Society of American Archivists, church archives and records, 406–409, 4000
Society of Colonial Dames of America, *see* Colonial Dames of America
Society of Colonial Wars: general register, 315–317; index to ancestors and rolls of members, 318–319; California, register, 910; Connecticut, register of pedigrees, 1013; District of Columbia, register, 1092; Maine, register, 1731; Maryland, genealogies of members, 1834–1835; New Hampshire, lists, 2281; Rhode Island, muster rolls, 3114a
Society of Friends, *see* Quakers
Society of Genealogists, catalog of directories and poll books in the possession of, 4193
Society of Genealogists, London. Catalogue of members' interests, 4313; Catalogue of parish register copies, 4344; Genealogists' handbook, 4438; Genealogists' magazine, 4264; Register and directory, 4313n
Society of Mayflower Descendants. Families of Pilgrims, 320; Mayflower index, 321; Mayflower magazine, 306; California, register, 910a; District of Columbia, register, 322, 1093; Illinois, lineage book, 1346; New Jersey, lineages, 2379; Oklahoma, lineages, 2797; Rhode Island, lineages, 3114b–3115; Texas, lineage book, 3400
Society of Montana Pioneers, constitution, etc., 2157
Society of Ohio Archivists. Guide to manuscripts repositories, Ohio, 2761
Society of Old Brooklynites. Christmas reminder, 2550
Society of the Cincinnati: Connecticut, records, 1014; Massachusetts, members, 1924
Society of the Sons of the American Revolution, *see* Sons of the American Revolution

Society of Writers to His Majesty's Signet, 4749
Socolofsky, H. E., and Self, H. Historical atlas of Kansas, 1481
Soldiers' and citizens' album of biographical record (of Wisconsin), 3814
Soldiers of republic of Texas, General Land Office, 3415
Solly, E. Index to hereditary English, Scottish and Irish titles of honour, 4522
Solms-Braunfels, Prince K. Immigrant reports, Texas, 3351
Some Pennsylvania women during the War of the Revolution, 2877n
Somerby, H. G. Passengers for Virginia (1635), 3622
Somerset county historical quarterly, 2380
Somerville, R. Handlist of record publications, 4164
Sonora, Mexico, 3907n
Sons of the American Revolution: national register, 538; California, records, 911; Idaho, lineages, 1291; Massachusetts, membership roll, 1925; Pennsylvania yearbook, 3014; Virginia, genealogy of members, 3621; Washington, register, 3707
Sosa, F. Biografías de Mexicanos distinguidos, 3930
Sosnow, L. R. Matthews' Complete armoury, 5076
Sources for history of Irish civilization, 4571
Sourdough Stampede Association. Alaska-Yukon gold book, 781
South (area): 615–636; aids, 632; atlas, 628; Baptists, 618; Bible records, 622; Civil War, 564; colonial families, 626; historical southern families, 616; maps, early, 621; notable southern families, 615, 3242; pedigrees, 620; pioneers, 627; records, 625; slaveholders, 631; Spanish in, 630; tombstone inscriptions, 617; women, 619
South Africa: 4951–4966; archives, 4951, 4954; arms, 5060a; British settlers, 4959, 4962; Eastern Province families, 4961; heraldry, 4963, 5064–5065; Huguenots, 431; marriages, 4952; place names, 4951; surnames, 4964
South America, *see* Latin America
South Australian genealogist, 4915a
South Carolina (*see also* North Carolina): 3119–3210; administrations, 3209; aids, 632; Assembly, 3181; atlas, 3156; Baptists, 3202; baronies, 3178; Bible records, 622; bibliography, 3127, 3137, 3203;

bonds, 3209; British records relating to South Carolina, 3145; census (1790), 3204, (1800), 3200, (1820), 3161, (1830), 3147a, (1850), 3162; Civil War, 556, 564, 3190; colonial families, 620; colonial records, 3125, 3181-3187, 3191; colonial soldiers and patriots, 3119; Council of Safety, 3186-3187; counties, 3169; county archives, 3151; Court of Chancery, 3184; Court of Ordinary, 3184; court records, 3164; deaths, 3176, 3207-3208; Dutch settlers, 3121; French Protestants, 3150, 3165; French refugees, 3136n; genealogical notes, 3513; German settlements, 3121; Government and Council, 3185; House of Representatives, 3142; Huguenots, 3133-3134, 3136, 3150, 3153; Indian Wars, 3124; Jewish marriage notices, 3138; Jews, 3139; jury lists, 3148a; land records, 3141; land warrants, 3185; Lutheran church, 3121; manual, 3159, 3188; marriages, 3129, 3172-3175, 3205, 3208; marriages, Jewish, 3138; material in Georgia genealogical magazine, 1173; Methodism, 3128; Mississippians born in South Carolina, 3162; Old Cheraws, 3146-3147; passenger lists, Scotch-Irish, 3199; pensions, 3124, 3163; pioneers, 627; place names, 3160; Protestant immigrants, 3167; Revolutionary War, 911, 3122, 3124, 3135, 3140, 3154-3155, 3163, 3166, 3168, 3192-3193; Scotch-Irish, 397, 3199; Senate, 3189; Swiss, 3121; Swiss Protestants, 3165; tax collectors, 3169; tombstone inscriptions, 617; treasury, 3192-3193; War of 1812, 3124; wills, 3127, 3152, 3157-3158, 3170, 3207-3210

South-Carolina gazette, 3130, 3174-3176

South Carolina genealogical register, 3194

South Carolina historical and genealogical magazine, 3195-3196

South Carolina Historical Society. Collections, 3167

South Carolina magazine of ancestral research, 3198

South Dakota (*see also* North Dakota): 3211-3235a; census (1850), 2000, (1860), 3213, (1870), 3230; churches, 3228; Civil War, 564; county archives, 3220; Finnish settlements, 3234; Indian tribes, 660; militia, 3226; Norwegians, 394; place names, 3221; public vital statistics, 3219; Swedes, 3229; towns, 3228

South Florida pioneers quarterly, 1129

South Midlands, England, parish register index, 4345, v. 5

South Texas Genealogical and Historical Society quarterly, 3401

Southern Arizona Genealogical Society, Copper state, 801

Southern California, Jews, 650

Southern families, special aids to genealogical research, 632

Southern Genealogists' Exchange Society. 1850 Florida census, 1130

Southern genealogist's exchange quarterly, 633

Southern Historical Association. Memoirs of Georgia, 1229; Publications, 636

Southern Historical Society papers, 634-635

Southern states, pension roll (1834), 490

Southwest: materials for history of, 3845; private land claims, 637; source lists, 647

Southwestern genealogist, 647

Southwestern U.S., Spanish-American pedigrees, 3854, 3866

Sowell, A. J. Early settlers and Indian fighters of southwest Texas, 3402

Spalding, J. A. Illustrated popular biography of Connecticut, 1015

Spanish America, *see also* Latin America

Spanish American genealogical helper, 105n, 3864

Spanish-American: heraldry, 5086; pedigrees in southwestern U.S., 802, 914, 3854

Spanish American War: Florida, 1124; Iowa, 1426; Missouri, 2115; New Hampshire, 2230; Ohio, 2737

Spanish and Portuguese Jews' Congregations of London, Bevis Marks records, 4550

Spanish: archives, California, 856n, New Mexico, 2419, Tennessee, 659, Texas, 3408; census of New Orleans, 1671; emigrants to Canada, 4109; exploration, etc.: in Mississippi Valley, 630, of lower Rio Grande, 3395; families, New Mexico, 2415-2416; land grants: in Chihuahuan acquisition, 3327, in Florida, 1114, north of Rio Grande, 3396; officers and soldiers in colonial Louisiana, 1649; personal names, 3847; place names in California, 908; surnames, 1665; territories, loyalists in, 4022

Spear, D. N. Bibliography of American directories, 32

Special aids to genealogical research in northeastern and central states, 262

Speer, W. S. Sketches of prominent Tennesseans, 3302

────── and Brown, J. H. Encyclopedia of new west, 3403

Spence, W. C. Tombstones and epitaphs of

453

*Index*

northeastern North Carolina, 2646a
—— and Shannhouse, E., North Carolina Bible records, 2647
Spencer, W. D. Pioneers on Maine rivers, 1732
Spillers, L. Roster of Oklahoma Society, D. A. R., 2776
The spirit of '76, 328n
Spofford, E. Armorial families of America, 5079
Spofford, J. Historical and statistical gazette of Massachusetts, 1926
Spokane and Spokane county, Washington, history, 3687
Spooner, W. W. Historic families of America, 323
Spousta, E. Roster of Arkansas Society, D. A. R., 819
Sprague, W. Annals of the American pulpit, 410
Sprague's Journal of Maine history, 1733
Spufford, P., and Camp, A. J. Genealogists' handbook, 4438
Squibb, G. D. Founder's kin, 4523; Visitation pedigrees, 4232
Squires, J. D. Granite state of the U.S., 2282
Stackpole, E. S. History of New Hampshire, 2283
Staedtler's Die Ansbach-Bayreuth Truppen in amerikanischen Unabhängigkeitskrieg, 537n
Stage, British, biographical dictionary, 4337
Stalins, G. F. L. (and others). Vocabulaire-atlas héraldique en six langues, 5125
Der Stammbaum, 2680
Stanard, W. G. Some emigrants to Virginia, 3623;
—— and Stanard, M. N. Colonial Virginia register, 3624
Standard dictionary of Canadian biography, 4001
Stanley, F., pseud., *see* Crocchiola, S.F.L.
Staples, C. R. History in Circuit Court records [Kentucky], 1582
Stapleton, A. Memorials to Huguenots in America, 3016
Stark, J. H. Loyalists of Massachusetts, 1927
Starr, E. History of the Cherokee Indians, 706, 707n; Old Cherokee families, 707
State censuses after 1790, bibliography, 182
State Historical Society of Iowa: annals, 1410; manuscripts, 1417; newspaper collection, 1412
State Historical Society of Wisconsin. Collections, 3815; Dictionary of Wisconsin biography, 3816; Wisconsin Domesday book, 3817
State Library of Ohio. Ohio genealogy sources by county, 2742
State records, microfilms, 56, 78
State records of North Carolina, 2626
Stearns, E. S. Genealogical and family history of New Hampshire, 2284
Stearns, Mrs. W. W. (and others). National Society of Woman Descendants of the Ancient and Honorable Artillery Company, 307
Steel, D. J. National index of parish registers, 4345; Sources for nonconformist genealogy, 4529; Sources for Scottish genealogy, 4723, 4790
—— and Taylor L. Family history in schools, 4439
Steele, R. F. Illustrated history of Big Bend country, 3708
Stellamaris Mission, Catholic church records, 638, 4070
Stemmons, J. D. Pennsylvania in 1800, 3017; U.S. census compendium, 177
Stephenson, J. Heraldry for American genealogist, 5005; Scotch-Irish migration to South Carolina, 3199
Stephenson, M. List of monumental brasses in British Isles, 4364
Stephenson, R. W. Land ownership maps, 199
Stercula, B. M. Heads of families, 1830 census of Missouri, 2128
Stern, M. H. Americans of Jewish descent, 440
Stevens, J. A., Jr. Colonial records of New York Chamber of Commerce, 2551
Stevens, J. H. Personal recollection of Minnesota, 2024
Stevens, W. B. Centennial history of Missouri, 2129–2130
Stevenson, G. Maps and other cartographic records in North Carolina State archives, 2649; North Carolina Revolutionary War records, 2649a; Select bibliography for genealogical research in North Carolina, 2650
Stevenson, J. H. Heraldry in Scotland, 5006; Scottish heraldic seals, 5054
Stevenson, N. C. Search and research, 263
Stevenson, R. Connecticut history makers, 1016
Stewart, E. I. Washington, 3709
Stewart, F. H. Stewart's genealogical and historical miscellany, 2381
Stewart, G. R. American place-names, 214

*Index*

Stewart, J. S. History of northeastern Ohio, 2762
Stewart, R. Maryland Line, 1836
Stewart, R. A. History of Virginia's navy of Revolution, 3625; Index to printed Virginia genealogies, 3626; The researcher, 3613
Stewart, W. C. Gone to Georgia, 1230
Stiles, E. H. Recollections and sketches of notable lawyers and public men of Iowa, 1439
Stille, S. H. Ohio builds a nation, 2763
Stillwell, J. E. Historical and genealogical miscellany, 2382
Stine, T. O. Scandinavians on the Pacific, 648, 912, 3710
Stirpes, 3405
Stocker, R. M. Centennial history of Susquehanna county, 3018
Stodart, R. R. Scottish arms, 5055
Stoddard, F. R. Truth about the Pilgrims, 1928
Stoever, J. C. Records, 3019
Stokes, I. N. P. Iconography of Manhattan Island, 2552
Stone, A. F. Vermont of today, 3481
Stone, W. F. History of Colorado, 954
Stormblown seed of Schoharie, 2978, v.9
Story of Hawaii, 1262n, 1268
Stout, T. Montana, 2158
Stout Map Co. Historical research maps—North Carolina counties, 2651
Strand, A. E. History of Swedish-Americans of Minnesota, 2025
Strassburger, R. B. (and Hinke, W. J.). Pennsylvania German pioneers, 3020-3021
Street directory of principal cities of U.S., 214a
Strobel, P. A. Salzburgers and their descendants, 1231
Strohl's Heraldischer Atlas, 4972n
Stryker, W. S. Official register of officers and men of New Jersey in Revolutionary War, 2383-2384; Record of officers and men of New Jersey in Civil War, 2385
Stryker-Rodda, K. Genealogical research, 242; Index to Genealogical magazine of New Jersey, 2317; New Jersey, 2386; New Jersey rateables, 2387-2388; New York historical manuscripts, 2566
Stuart, M. Scottish family history, 4714
Stuart, Royal house of, 4445
Stub entries to indents issued in payment of claims against South Carolina, 3193
Stucki, J. U. Index to first federal census, Washington, 1860, 3711
Stumpp, K. Emigration from Germany to Russia, 381
Sturgess, H. A. C. Register of admissions to . . . Middle Temple, 4322
Sturtevant, B. Louisiana 1810 census, 1682
Stutenroth, S. M. Daughters of Dacotah, 3235a
Suaréz de Tangil y de Angelo, F. Nobiliario Cubano, 3898
Subsistence list, New York, 2483
Suelflow, A. R. Microfilm index and bibliography of Concordia Historical Inst., 448
Suffling, E. R. English church brasses, 4365
Suffolk county, Massachusetts. Deeds, 1929; Probate records, 1897
Sullivan, J. History of New York state, 2553
Sulte, B. Histoire des canadiens-français, 4002
Summers, E. Genealogical and family history of eastern Ohio, 2764
Summers, L. P. Annals of southwest Virginia, 3627; History of southwest Virginia, 3628
Summers, P. Hatchments in Britain, 5029
Surname searcher, 913
Surnames (*see also* Names): American, 217-227; Anglo-Irish, 4649; British, 4403-4421, changes, 4416; Canadian, 3947, 5074; census (1790) spellings, 178, 217; English, 218, 4406; English Huguenots of French origin, 424; Gaelic, 4649, 4779; Illinois, 1305; in Newberry Library collection, 23; Iowa, 1427; Irish, 4644-4652; Kentucky, 1588; Minnesota, 2010; Missouri, 2123; Norman, 4649; Oklahoma, 2793; Scottish, 4776, 4779, 4781; South African, 4964; Spanish, 1665, 3847, 3857; Ukrainian in Canada, 3947; Utah, 3437; Welsh, 218, 519n, 4406, 4863, 4864; West Virginia, 3755
Surry, Virginia, 3505
Survey of Federal Archives, list of publications, 38
Susquehanna county, Pennsylvania, 3018
Sussex county, Delaware, probate records, 1032
Sutherland, sasines for sheriffdoms, 4759
Sutton, E. G. Teepee to soddies, 2195
Sutton, W. Utah, 3447
Swanson, P. Ohio printed state documents, 2764a
Swedish immigration: 365; Delaware, 1024, 1035, 1045; Illinois, 1335; Kansas, 1445;

455

*Index*

Minnesota, 2025; New Jersey, 2337; New York, 2450n; Pennsylvania, 2917; South Dakota, 3229; U.S., 400–402
Swedish Lutheran churches, Raccoon and Penns Neck, New Jersey, 2311
Swedish pioneer historical quarterly, 402
Swem, E. G. Bibliography of Virginia, 3629; Virginia historical index, 3630
Swiss-American Historical Society. Prominent Americans of Swiss origin, 403
Swiss immigration: 357; America, 403; Canada, 4109; Louisiana, 1622; North and South Carolina, 2575, 3121; Pennsylvania, 2873n, 2883, 2929, 3000; Protestants, South Carolina, 3165
Synagogue archives: Georgia, 1187; Louisiana, 1645; Pennsylvania, 2910

Tabard talk, 5113
Taft, W. H. Missouri newspapers, 2131
Taitt, G. S. Subscribers to Mayo's Map of Barbados, 4931
Talbot, E.-G. Généalogie des familles originaires des comtés de Montmagny, 4137; Receuil de généalogies des comtés de Beauce-Dorchester-Frontenac, 4138
Talcott, S. V. Genealogical notes of New York and New England families, 608, 2554
Talley, W. M. Talley's Kentucky papers, 1583; Talley's northeastern Kentucky papers, 1584
Tally-Frost, S. Memorial and biographical histories of Texas, 3377–3378
Tanguay, C. Dictionnaire généalogique des familles canadiennes (1683–1684), 4003–4004, 4114n
Tap roots, 766
Taplin, G. W. Middle American governors, 3865
Tar heel tracks, 2651a
Tarpley, F. Place names of northeast Texas, 3407
Tartans, *see* Clans and tartans
Tate, Mrs. P. L. Maine roster, D.A.R., 1702
Tate, W. E. Parish chest, 4233
Taxes (lists, payers, digests): directory, 177; Georgia, 1137, 1214, 1221; Kentucky, 1541; New York city, 2499; New York state, 2529; Ohio, 2689, 2744, 2755–2756; Pennsylvania, 2878–2879; Philadelphia, 2992; South Carolina, 3169; Texas, 3347, 3382, 3422; Virginia, 3559, 3618;
Taylor, B. M. 1840 index to Florida census, 1131
Taylor, C. W. Biographical sketches and review of the Bench and Bar of Indiana, 1402
Taylor, G., and Skinner, A. Maps of the roads of Ireland, 4643
Taylor, J. Great historic families of Scotland, 4824
Taylor, P. F. Calendar of warrants for land in Kentucky, 1585
Taylor, V. H. Spanish archives of General Land Office of Texas, 3408
Tebeau, C. W. History of Florida, 1132
——— and Carson, R. L. Florida from Indian trail to space age, 1133
Teeples, G. R. Maryland 1800 census, 1837; South Carolina 1800 census, 3200
——— and Jackson, R. V. Connecticut 1800 census, 1017
Temple, O. P. Notable men of Tennessee, 3303
Temple, S. B., and Coleman, K. Georgia journeys, 1232
Temple, T. W. Sources for tracing Spanish American pedigrees in the southwestern U.S., 802, 914, 3866
Tenmile country, West Virginia, 2933–2935, 3746
Tennessee: 3236–3319; Bible records, 622, 1523a, 3236, 3259a; bibliography, 3239, 3283, 3301a; census (1787–1791, partial), 3287, (1790/1800, substitute), 3248, (1810), 3314, (1820), 3281, 3314, (1830), 3300, (1850), 3247, 3301; Cherokee census, 704; Chickasaws, 3318; church and synagogue archives, 3278; church records, 3312; churches, missions and religious institutions, 3274; Civil War, 564, 3279, 3282, 3305, 3310, 3319; colonial families, 620; counties, 3259, 3262–3269, 3284, 3313; county archives, 3277, 3311; diaries, 3312; Episcopal Church, 3299; gazetteer, 3292; Knights Templars, 3297; land grants, 2580, 3248, 3304; Lutheran Church, 3249, 3524; manuals, 3250, 3273, 3284–3285; manuscripts, 3307; maps, 1525, 3270, 3292; marriages, 3236, 3280, 3308; militia records, 3288, 3290; pensions, 3244, 3288, 3310; pioneers, 627; public vital statistics, 3276; records in North Carolina, 3249a; Revolutionary War, 3236–3237, 3243–3244, 3253, 3288, 3304; Spanish archives, 659; tombstone inscriptions, 3236, 3280; War of 1812, 3238, 3286, 3288; wills, 3246
Tennessee "Bee-hive," 3304
Tennessee General Assembly biographical directory, 3309

*Index*

Tennessee historical quarterly, 3306
Tennessee Historical Society. Guide to processed manuscripts, 3307
Tennessee State Library and Archives. Biographical directory: Tennessee General Assembly, 3309; Cherokee collection, 708; Index to Tennessee Confederate pension applications, 3310; Inventories of Tennessee county records on microfilm, 3311; Tennessee diaries, 3312; Writings on Tennessee counties available on interlibrary loan, 3313
Tenney, M. A. The Pilgrims, 609
Tercentenary handlist of English and Welsh newspapers, 4234
Territorial papers of the United States, 77
Terry, C. S. Catalogue of publications of Scottish historical and kindred clubs, 4715; Index to papers relating to Scotland, 4716; Papers relating to Army of the Solemn League and Covenant, 4737
Testamentary records, *see* Wills and probates
Tetrick, W. G. Obituaries from newspapers of northern West Virginia, 3771
Texas: 3320–3427; almanacs, 3343; Anglo-American families, 3333; Anglo-American marriages, 3354; archives, 3371; Austin's colonists, 3325n, 3390; Bible records, 3366; bibliographies, 3332, 3341, 3361, 3368, 3389; births, 3353; Bohemians, 3366a; Catholics, 3346, 3372; cemeteries, 1473, 3380; census (1792–1847), 3347, (1829–1836), 3381, (1840), 3422, (1850), 3331, 3423, (1860), 3424; certificates of entrance, 1835, 3381n; citizen lists, 3381; Civil War, 564; county archives, 3360; Czech pioneers, 3366a; Declaration of Independence, signers, 3370: gazetteer, 3350; Germans, 3322–3324, 3333, 3351–3352, 3417; government personnel, 3336; headrights, 3388a; Indian Wars, 3328; Indians, 3402; Kentucky colonists in, 1511; land claims, 3329, 3408–3414; land grants, 3327, 3329, 3334, 3379, 3408–3414; Latin families, 3333; manuscripts, 3371; maps, 3344; marriages, 3354, 3399; Maryland Catholics in, 2114; Mexican land grants, 3327; Mexican War, 3321, 3394; mortality schedules (1850), 3423, (1860), 3424; muster roll, 3381n, 3415; newspapers, 3361; Peters colony, 1511, 3334, 3427; place names, 3407; Poles, 3346, 3355, 3388; poll lists, 3382; postal records, 3358, 3421; probates, 3404; public vital statistics records, 3359; Robertson's colony, 3374; royal land grants, 3396; signers, 3370; Spanish-American pedigrees, 3854; Spanish archives, 3408; Spanish exploration, 3395; Spanish land grants, 3327, 3396; Swedes, 3397; tax lists, 3347, 3382, 3422; tombstone inscriptions, 3325
Texts and calendars (British), 4159
Thayer Ojeda, T. Conquistadores de Chile, 3893
Theater, British, biographical dictionary, 4337
Theobald, J. and L. Arizona territory post offices and postmasters, 803
Thibault, C. Bibliographia Canadiana, 3944a
Thoburn, J. B. Standard history of Oklahoma, 2798
—— and Wright, M. H. Oklahoma, 2799
Thomas, D. Y. Arkansas and its people, 839
Thomas, E. W. Revolutionary soldiers in Alabama, 767
Thompson, D. E. Indiana authors and their books, 1403
Thompson, J. Gazetteer of Vermont, 3482–3483
Thompson, J. M. Pike county history, Illinois, 147, 1586
Thompson and West, publishers: county histories in California, 915–922; History of Nevada, 2197–2197n
Thomson, P. G. Bibliography of state of Ohio, 2765
Thomson, T. R. Catalogue of British family histories, 4185
Thornton, M. L. Bibliography of North Carolina, 2652
Thrall, H. S. Pictorial history of Texas, 3416
Threlfall, J. B. Heads of families at second census of U.S. (1800), New Hampshire, 2285
Thwaites, Reuben. Chronicles of border warfare, 3776
Tibon, G. Onomástica hispanoamericana, 3867
Tiling, M. P. History of German element in Texas, 3417
Tilley, N. M., and Goodwin, N. L. Guide to manuscript collections in Duke Univ. Library, 2653
Tithes: British, 4216; Virginia, 3504, 3678
Titles, 4516, 4522, 4524, 4823
Titus, E. B. Union list of serials in libraries of U.S. and Canada, 75, 4008
Titus, W. A. History of Fox River Valley, 3818
Toaz, M. Oklahoma cemetery records, 2800
Todd, H. G. Armory and lineages of Can-

457

*Index*

ada and North America, 4005, 5080
Todd, J. R., and Hutson, F. M. Prince William's parish plantation, 3201
Todd, R. H. Patriotas puertorriqueños, 3067
Toedteberg, E. Catalogue of American genealogies in Long Island Historical Soc., 60
Toensing, W. F. Minnesota congressmen, 2026
Told by the pioneers, 3712
Toler, H. P. New Harlem register, 2555
Tombstone inscriptions: District of Columbia, 1091; Kentucky, 1587; Louisiana, 1619; Mississippi, 2061; southern states, 617; Tennessee, 3236, 3280; Texas, 3325
Topeka genealogy workshop textbook, 1482
Topkins, R. M. Marriage and death notices from Western Carolinian, 2653a
Topographer and genealogist, 4274
Topographical quarterly, 4275
Topography: British, 4170, 4172, 4176; Canada, 4053; Cape Breton, 4053; English, 4384–4396; Irish, 4626–4643; New Brunswick, 4053; Newfoundland, 4053; Nova Scotia, 4053; Prince Edward Island, 4053; Scottish, 4713, 4764–4775; Welsh, 4853–4860
Topping, Mary (and others). Approved place names in Virginia, 3635
Toro, J. del. Bibliography of collective biography of Spanish America, 3868
Toronto Public Libraries. Bibliography of Canadians, 4006–4008
Torrence, C. S.A.R. genealogy of members, 3621; Trial bibliography of colonial Virginia, 3630a, 3631; Virginia wills and administrations, 3632
Toups, N. J. Mississippi Valley pioneers, 1685
Tourville, E. A. Alaska, 782n
Towle, L. C. Genealogical periodical annual index, 98; New Hampshire genealogical research guide, 2286
Towner county, North Dakota, families, 2667
Townland index (Ireland), 4637n
Towns: New Spain, 3912; Ohio, 2750; Oklahoma, 2800a; South Dakota, 3228
Townsend, C. D. Border town cemeteries of Massachusetts, 1930
Townsend, L. South Carolina Baptists, 3202
Trabue, A. E. Kentucky tombstone inscriptions, 1587
Trader list, 1833n
Trail of the Black Walnut, 2995
Trans-Allegheny pioneers, West Virginia, 3728

Trans-Mississippi West, bibliography of periodical literature, 651
Tree talks, 2556
The treesearcher (magazine), 1483
Tribbeko, J. Lists of Germans from the Palatinate, 367, 2557, 3022
Trinity church, New York city. Records, 2558
Trinity College, Dublin, alumni, 4606
Trinkner, C. L. Florida lives, 1134
Tri-state trader, 128
Tri-state trader genealogical queries and index, 128a
Trois Rivières, Canada: census, 4119; land records, 4133a
Trudel, M. Population du Canada en 1663, 4007a; Terrier du Saint-Laurent en 1663, 4007b
Trumbull, J. H., and Hoadly, C. J. Public records of the colony of Connecticut, 965
Tucker, G. J. Names of persons for whom marriage licenses were issued, New York, 2508n
Tucker, W. B. Camden colony, 4033
Tulsa annals, 2801
Turnbull, R. C. Bibliography of South Carolina, 3203
Turner, C. H. B. Rodney's diary and other Delaware records, 1059
Turner, G. L. Original records of early nonconformity, 4530
Turner, O. History of pioneer settlement of Phelps and Gorham's purchase, 2559–2560a; Pioneer history of Holland purchase of western New York, 2561–2562
Turton, W. H. Plantaganet ancestry, 4462
Tuttle, C. R. General history of state of Michigan, 1981
Twentieth century biographical dictionary of notable Americans, 163
Twentieth century history of southwest Texas, 3418
Twitchell, R. E. Old Santa Fe, 2410; Spanish archives of New Mexico, 2419
Tyler, L. G. Encyclopedia of Virginia biography, 3633, 3633; Men of mark in Virginia, 3606
Tyler's Quarterly historical and genealogical magazine, 3634
Tyner, J. W., and Timmons, A. T. Our people and where they rest, 709

Udaondo, E. Diccionario biográfico argentino, 3878; Diccionario biográfico colonial argentino, 3879; Grandes ombres de nuestra patria, 3880

*Index*

Ukrainian settlements in Canada: 3980; surnames, 3947
Ulibarri, G. S., and Goggin, D. T. Research relating to Civil War claims, 563
Ullery, J. G. Men of Vermont, 3484
Ulster, Ireland: emigration, 334, 2862; maps, 4633; passenger lists, 334; Scotch-Irish pioneers, 397
Ulster county, New York, 2546
Ulvestad, M. Nordmaendene i Amerika, 394
Unclaimed dividends, Bank of England, names, 4227a
Unett, J. Making a pedigree, 4440
Union, *see* Civil War
Union list of serials in libraries in U.S. and Canada, 75, 4008
Unitarian Historical Society. Transactions, 4564
Unitarians (English), 4529n, 4564
United Chinese Penmen Club, Hawaii. Chinese of Hawaii, 1269
United Empire loyalists, *see* Loyalists
United Kingdom, *see* England and Great Britain
United Methodist ministers, 4553-4556
United Society for the Propagation of the Gospel. Calendar of letters from Canada, 4036
United States: 1-651; archives, 50; Army; 470-485, German soldiers, 480, history, 477, officers, 478, orders and decorations, 475, pensioners, 487, records, 476, 484-485, registers, 467, 470, 472, 482; artists, 149; atlases, 196, 200; bibliographies: diaries, 19, directories, 32, family histories, 15, historical societies, 13, histories, 101-102, place name literature, 213; biographical dictionaries and directories, 155, 162, 164, 481, 1297, 1351, 1440, 1484, 2133, 3819, 4287; biographies, 130-169; boundaries, 206; cartographic records, 203-204, 671; census: publications, 180, 185, (1790), blacks in, 65, surnames in, 217, (1790-1880), 172, 183; church archives, histories, and records, 58, 404-409, 420-421, *see also* names of specific religious denominations; Civil War, 551-573; clergymen, 327, 410, 412;

  colonial families, 292, 300, 303, 304, 328; colonial lists, general, 281-238, royal, 269-280; colonial papers, 305; colonies, English convicts in, 289; counties, 210-213; county maps, 199; diaries, 18; distinguished families, 278, 282, 285a, 303a, 313, 323, 324, 328, 4485; emigrants: British, 329-355, non-British, 356-372;

flag, 5095; gazetteer, 193; genealogical guides and resources, 40, 62, 126n; genealogies, 15, 33, 60, 4181, 4186; heraldry, 5004, 5107n; immigrants: 299, 360-361, 363, 368-372, British, 293, 329-355, non-British, 356-372, *see also* names of specific nationalities; Indian affairs, 669, *see also* Indian and Indians

  land records, 57; Latin American materials, 3850; lineages, 282, 290, 313; local history catalog, 24-25; Magna Charta descendants, 274, 281, 284-285, 288; manuals and aids, 49, 228-268, 5005, 5008; manuscripts, 18, 50, 66, 79; maps, 199, 205, 207; marriage records, 287; Mexican War, 550a-550b; Middle East, 371; military: history of British colonies, 477, medals and ribbons, 479, orders and decorations, 475, pensions and claims, 483, 487-490, records, 57, 476, 484; Navy: pension fund, 486, pensioners, 487, personnel, 466, 481, registers, 471, 473; newspapers, serials, and periodicals, 8, 11, 16, 75, 80-82, 84, 96, 373, 379;

  passenger lists, British, 329-355, non-British, 356-372, pedigrees, royal and noble, 270-280, 313; place names, 208-209, 213-215; post office tables, 216; postal and shippers guide, 189, precolonial lists, 269-328; religious denominations, *see* names of specific groups; Revolutionary War, 491-546a; state records, 78; state papers, 76, index to, 61; street directory, 214a; surnames, 220-222, finding aids, 226; territorial papers, 77; vital records, 86-89; War of 1812, 546a-549

U.S. Adjutant General's Office. Preliminary inventory of records, 485
U.S. Board on Geographic Names. Approved place names in Virginia, 3635
U.S. Bureau of Census: cartographic records, 203; census publications (1790-1945), 180; records, 184; Tennessee census reports, 3314
U.S. Bureau of Indian Affairs, records, 669
U.S. Census Office, *see* U.S. Bureau of Census
U.S. Commission to the Five Civilized Tribes, Final rolls, 710-711
U.S. Daughters of 1812: National Soc. ancester index, 548; Illinois, Illinois cemetery inscriptions, 1352; Nebraska, Heroes of 1812, 2184; Ohio, Index to grave records of servicemen of War of 1812, 2735; Pennsylvania, Lineage book, 2961

459

*Index*

U.S. Geographic Board. Sixth report [on place names], 215

U.S. Library of Congress: American and British genealogies, 15, 33, 4181, 4186; atlases, 202; checklist of microfilms prepared in England and Wales, 83; county maps, 199; genealogies, 15, 4181; geographical atlases, 200; guide to microfilm collections of early state records, 78; land ownership maps, 199; local histories, 15a; maps, 201; Mormon diaries collection, 445; national union catalog of manuscripts collections, 79; new serials titles, 80-82; newspapers in microform, 84; U.S. histories, 15a

U.S. Marine Corps: officers, 466; register, 473

U.S. Military Academy, New York, biographical register, 467

U.S. National Archives and Records Service: American Indian records, 670, 671; cartographic records, Bureau of Census, 203, guide to, 204; censuses (1790–1880), 172; federal population censuses (1790–1890), microfilm copies, 183; genealogical sources, 126n; guide to genealogical records, 40; guide to materials on Latin America, 3850; military service records, 484; pre-federal maps, 205; preliminary inventories, 85; records of Bureau of Indian Affairs, 669

U.S. Public Health Service. Where to write for . . . records, 86–89

Universal churches, Massachusetts, 1887

Universities (American), biographies, 138

University of Colorado historical collections, 955–956

University of London, *see* London University

University of Mexico, roster of graduates, 3916

University of Minnesota Libraries, St. Paul. Immigrant archives, 371, 4009

University of Missouri, Columbia. Guide to western historical manuscripts collection, 2134–2135

University of North Carolina: alumni history, 2655; directory, 2656

University of Texas: archives, 3371; manuscripts, 3371

Unpublished local indexes, American, 53

Upcott, W. Bibliographical account of principal works relating to English topography, 4176

Upham, W. Minnesota geographic names, 2027

———— and Dunlap, R. B. Minnesota biographies, 2028

Upper Canada, *see* Ontario

Upper Canada Genealogical Society. Bulletin, 4139

Upper ten thousand (British), 4504n

Upton, H. History of Western Reserve, 2766

Urbanek, M. Wyoming place names, 3841

Urlsperger, S. Detailed reports on Salzburger emigrants, 1233

Urquhart, R. M. Scottish burgh and county heraldry, 4724, 5056, 5096

Uruguay, 3936

Usher, E. B. Wisconsin, 3820

Utah: 3428–3453; Baptists, 3440; Catholics, 3435; census (1851), 3453; church archives, 3440; county archives, 3439; first families, 3430; gazetteer, 3436, 3446; Jews, 3451; manual, 3442; place names, 3441, 3444; public vital statistics records, 3438; surnames, 3437; veterans, 3448

Utah genealogical and historical magazine, 3449

VBAPPA: Virginia books, 3639

Valentine, D. T. History of city of New York, 2563; Manual of corporation of city of New York, 2564–2565

Valentine, E. P. Papers, 3637

Vallentine, J. F. Locality finding aids for U.S. surnames, 226

Valley leaves, 768

Valley of the Red River, Minnesota and North Dakota, 2675

Valley quarterly, 923

Van Koevering, A. Legends of the Dutch, 1982

Van Laer, A. J. F. Early records of Albany, 2421; Minutes of Court of Albany, 2422; New York historical manuscripts, 2566; Settlers of Rensselaerswyck, 2520

Van Meter, B. F. Genealogies and sketches of some old families . . . of Virginia and Kentucky, 1590, 3638

Van Rensselaer, M. History of city of New York, 2567

Van Rensselaer Bouwier manuscripts, 2520

Van Tassel, C. S. Story of Maumee Valley, Toledo, 2767

Van Voorhis, J. S. Old and new Monongahela, 3772

van Zandt, F. K. Boundaries of U.S., 206

Vancouver, Catholic church records, 638, 4070

Varennes, K. M. de. Annotated bibliography

*Index*

of genealogical works in Library of Parliament, 4010
Varney, G. J. Gazetteer of Maine, 1735
Vásquez, N. M. Basic research in parish and civil registers of Mexico, 3931; Sinaloa roots, 924
Vasvary, E. Lincoln's Hungarian heroes, 572
Vaudreuil papers, 1605
Veach, D. Your Texas ancestors, 3419
Venezuela, 3937–3938a
Venn, J. and J. A. Alumni Cantabrigienses, 4310
Vermont, E. de V. America heraldica, 5081
Vermont: 3454–3501; bibliography, 3468; census (1790), 3485, (1800), 3498; charters, 3479, 3489; church archives, 3474; churches and religious organizations, 3472; civil officers, 3465; Civil War, 554, 564, 3455, 3487, 3500; county archives, 3475; gazetteer, 3471, 3482–3483, 3493, 3496–3497; lands, 3456, 3479, 3489–3492, 3494; marriages, 3499; New Hampshire grants of land, 3479; New York land patents, 3491; pensions, 3462; Protestant Episcopal archives, 3474; records, 3488; Revolutionary War, 3463, 3469; state papers, 3495; War of 1812, 3462, 3486
Vermont historical gazetteer, 3496–3497
Vicars, Sir A. E. Index to prerogative wills of Ireland, 4625
Victoria history of counties of England, 4395
Victorian genealogist, 4902n
Vidrine, J. O., and De Ville, W. Marriage contracts of Opelousas post, 1687
Villeré, S. L. Canary Islands migration to Louisiana, 1688
Villiers, C. C. de, and Pama, C. Genealogies of old South African families, 4966
Villiers, G. de. Opelousas post, 1689
Vincent, B. Dictionary of biography, 165
Vineland historical magazine, 2390
Virginia (see also Kentucky, Pennsylvania, West Virginia): 3502–3683; Baptists, 3577; Bible records, 622; bibliography, 3514, 3530, 3626, 3629, 3630a–3631, 3639, 3650; census (1623), 3646n, (1779), 3548, (1782–1785), 3644, (1790), 3559n, 3636, (1810), 3531–3532, 3585, 3618; Civil War, 556, 564, 3614, 3665; claims to land in western Pennsylvania, 3024, 3651; colonial families, 620; colonial militia, 3534; colonial records, 3555, 3646; colonial register, 3624; colonial soldiers, 3551; Council and General Court minutes, 3640; county formation, 3575; county records, 3535, 3545, 3579, 3615, 3654; court records in Pennsylvaina, 2857, 3025, 3537, 3641, 3663; deeds, 3663; Eastern Shore, 3671; emigration, 3552, 3563, 3610, 3623; English wills, 3538, 3666; first settlers, 343; gazetteer, 3561, 3584, 3604; genealogical notes, 3123; Germans, 3619, 3667, 3682; heraldry, 3536; Huguenots, 431, 3510, 3547n, 3583; index to magazines, 3630; Indian Wars, 2864, 3519, 3588n, 3601; Indians, 3588; Irish immigrants, 353, 387; land, 1774, 2874, 3560, 3563, 3594, 3610, 3643, 3647, 3651, 3677; laws, 3574; Lutheran church, 3524; manuals, 3598, 3649; marriages, 3502, 3533, 3542–3543, 3578, 3590, 3599–3600, 3656, 3664, 3680; marriages in burned record counties, 3656; Mennonites, 3517; military certificates, 3520; military records, 3569; Nassau-Siegen immigrants, 3581; Navy, 1576, 3625; oath of allegiance, 3614; obituaries, 3577, 3603; parish lines, 3527–3529; passenger lists, 3622; pay rolls, 3643; pensions, 3546, 3601; pioneers, 627; place names, 3568, 3584, 3635, 3661–3662; Presbyterians, 3675–3676; Quakers, 3576, 3670; quit rents, 3620; Revolutionary War, 535, 1576, 3516, 3518–3519, 3546, 3549–3550, 3564, 3569, 3594, 3597, 3601, 3616, 3621, 3625, 3677; Scotch-Irish, 3525; settlers in Missouri, 2084; state papers, 3645; statutes, 3571–3573; tax lists, 3618; tax payers, 3559; tithables, 3678; War of 1812, 3519, 3601, 3642; wills, 3025, 3526, 3539, 3589, 3632, 3663
Virginia Baptist Society. Manuscript collections, 3577
Virginia Company of London. Records, 3652–3653
Virginia gazette genealogy, 3681
Virginia gazette index, 3521
Virginia Genealogical Society. Quarterly bull., 3655; Some marriages in burned record counties of Virginia, 3656
Virginia genealogist (magazine), 3657
Virginia historical index, 3630
Virginia historical register (magazine), 3658
Virginia Historical Society. Virginia historical collections, 3659
Virginia magazine of history and biography, 3660
Virginia Place Name Society. Newsletter, 3661; Occasional papers, 3662
Virkus, F. A. Abridged compendium of American genealogy, 324; Compendium

461

*Index*

of American genealogy, 324n; Immigrants to America before 1750, 372
Visitations: explanation, 4525; England, 4503; 5023; Harleian Soc., 4265; heralds, 36; Ireland, 4678, 5036; pedigrees, Great Britain, 4232; printed, 4198; seats, Great Britain, 4486; Wales, 4503, 4871, 4876, 5023
Vital statistics: English, 4346-4360; Irish, 4608-4618; Scottish, 4761-4763
Vital statistics, states, *see* under each state
Vogel, V. J. Indian place names, 1353
Volkel, L. M. Illiana ancestors, 1354; Illinois mortality schedule, 1355; Index to 1800 Connecticut census, 1020; Indiana mortality schedule, 1404; Kentucky 1810 census, 1591; Kentucky 1820 census, 1592; Maryland 1800 census, 1839; Rhode Island 1800 census, 3117; Tracing ancestry in Illinois libraries and archives, 1356
——— and Gill, J. V. 1820 census of Illinois, 1357
Volume of memoirs and genealogy of representative citizens of: northern California, 925; Seattle, 3713
Von Volborth, C. A. Alverdens heraldik i farver, 4986n; Heraldry of the world, 4986; Little manual of heraldry, 5007
Voorhies, J. K. Some late eighteenth-century Louisianians, 1690
Votes and voter lists: Kansas, 1463n; Ohio, 2693; Pennsylvania Assembly, 2911a
Vujnovich, M. M. Yugoslavs in Louisiana, 1691

Waddel, M. Register of marriages celebrated and solemnized in South Carolina, 1234, 3205
Wagner, Sir A. R. Catalogue of English mediaeval rolls of arms, 5030; English ancestry, 4441; English genealogy, 4441n, 4442; Heralds of England, 4987; Historic heraldry in Britain, 5031; Hope's Grammar of heraldry, 4998; Records and collections of College of Arms, 4235, 4988; Rolls of Henry III, 5027
——— (and others). Royal and princely heraldry in Wales, 5060
Wait, S. E., and Anderson, W. S. Old settlers, 1983
Waite, O. F. R. New Hampshire in the great rebellion, 2288; Vermont in the great rebellion, 3500
Walbran, J. T. British Columbia coast names, 4044

Walden, B. L. Pioneer families of midwest, 649
Waldenmaier, I. Annual index to genealogical periodicals, 94; Arkansas travelers, 840; Genealogical newsletter, 113; Index to minute books of Virginia courts, 3025, 3663; Some of the earliest oaths of allegiance, 545; Virginia marriage records, 3664
Wales (*see also* England): 4827-4880; atlas, 4388, 4858-4859; Baptist bibliography, 4531; bibliographies, 4827-4832; biographies, 4841-4846; border genealogy, 4345, v. 5; civic and corporate heraldry, 5088, 5094; clergy, 4295-4297; county families, 4526, 4875; directories, 4228; ecclesiastical dignitaries, 4880; gazetteer, 4396; genealogical atlas, 4388; gentry, 4873, 4875, 4877; handwriting, 4241; heraldic visitations, 4871-4872, 4876; historical and archaeological publications, 4158; immigrants to America, 344, 1424, 2007, 2848, 2894-2895, 4827, 4844, in Revolutionary War, 519; knights, 4869; landowners, 4230; lords-lieutenant, 4869; lords-marcher, 4874; manual, 4426, 4866-4868; maps, 4391, 4853; marriage bonds, 4849; names, 4861-4865; national and provincial directories, 4228; newspapers, 4234; nonconformists, 4879; original parish registers, 4343a; parish list, 4296; parish maps, 4391; parish registers, 4338, 4343a, 4345; patronymics, 4864; peerages, etc., 4869-4878; place names, 4389-4390, 4402, 4863-4865; princes and principality, 4868, 4874; probate records, 4381, 4850-4851; prominent persons, 519n; record publications, 4711, 4836; record sources, 4169, 4836; records, 4833-4840; registers, 4847-4848a; religions, 4879-4880; royal tribes, 4878; secular clergy, 4295; serial publications, 4159; sheriffs, 4215, 4869; surnames, 519n, 4406, 4862, 4864; topography, 4172, 4853-4860; visitations, 4503, 4871, 4876, 5023; vital statistics, 4849; West Wales historical records, 4840; wills, 4850-4851
Walford, E. County families of United Kingdom, 4526
Walford's Roll, 5027n
Walker, E. J., and Wilson, V. Kentucky Bible records, 1514
Walker, H. A. Cherokee Indian census (1835) of: Georgia, Alabama, North Carolina, 715, Tennessee, 714; Historical court

## Index

records of District of Columbia, 1094-1095; Illinois pensioners lists of the Revolution, 1812 and Indian Wars, 1359
Walker, H. J. Revolutionary soldiers buried in Illinois, 1358
Walker, J. Sufferings of the clergy, 4303
Walkinshaw, L. C. Annals of southwestern Pennsylvania, 3026
Wall index, 23
Wallace, D. D. History of South Carolina, 3206
Wallace, L. A., Jr. Guide to Virginia military organizations (1861-65), 3665
Wallace, W. S. Documents relating to north west coasts, 4074; Macmillan dictionary of Canadian biography, 4011
Walling, A. C. History of southern Oregon, 2839
Walling, H. F. Atlas of New Hampshire, 2289
Wallis, F. A. Sesquicentennial history of Kentucky, 1593
Walloons, New York, 2428
Walne, P. English wills, 3666
Walsh, P. Irish chiefs and leaders, 4696
Walters, B. L. Furniture makers of Indiana, 1405
War of 1812: general, 547-550; dead, 549; pension applications, 546a; Alabama, 736; Arkansas, 817; Connecticut, 970; Illinois, 1359; Kentucky, 1494, 1505, 1537, 1556, 1574; Louisiana, 1614, 1675; Maine, 1719; Maryland, 1759, 1794-1795, 1798; Massachusetts, 1719, 1892, 1901; Michigan, 1971; Mississippi, 2072; Missouri, 2077, 2110; Nebraska, 2184, 2187; New Hampshire, 2230; New Jersey, 2353; New York, 2510; North Carolina, 2577, 2616; Ohio, 2694, 2735, 2738-2739; Pennsylvania, 2945, 2956, 3027; South Carolina, 3124; Tennessee, 3238, 3286, 3288; Vermont, 3462, 3486; Virginia, 3519, 3601, 3642
War of the Rebellion, see Civil War (U.S.)
Ward, C. L. Delaware continentals, 1060
Ward, W. S. Index and finding list of serials published in British Isles, 4165
Warner and Beer's atlas of Illinois, 1360
Warnke, J. R. Ghost towns of Florida, 1134a
Warren, M. B. Marriages and deaths, Georgia, 1235-1236
Warrum, N. Utah since statehood, 3450
Washington: 3684-3716; Catholic church records, 638; census (1850), 3701, (1860), 3711; church vital statistics records, 3692; Civil War, 564; county archives, 3694; gazetteer, 3697, 3700; history, 2811; land claims, 3685; place names, 3697, 3700, 3702; Revolutionary War, 515; Scandinavians, 3710; state and local subscription histories, 3714; vital statistics records, 3693
Washington, District of Columbia, see District of Columbia
Washoe Valley, Nevada, 2220
Watauga Association of Genealogists. Bulletin, 3315
Waterman, K. U. Rhode Island census of 1782, 3118
Waters, H. F. G. Genealogical gleanings in England, 610-611
Waters, M. R. Genealogical sources available at Indiana State Library for all Indiana counties, 1406; Indiana land entries, 1407; Revolutionary soldiers buried in Indiana, 1408
Wates, W. A. Stub entries to indents issued in payment of claims against South Carolina, 3193
Watkins, M. de W. S. Ancestor hunting, 90
Watson, A. W. Royal lineage: Alfred the Great (901-1901) 279
Watson, W. J. History of Celtic place-names, 4782
Watt, T. Roll of graduates, Aberdeen University, 4741
Watters, L. L. Pioneer Jews of Utah, 3451
Watters, R. E. Checklist of Canadian literature, 4012
Way, R. B. Rock river valley, 1361
Wayland, J. W. German element of Shenandoah valley, 3667; Virginia valley records, 3668
Weaks, M. C. Calendar of Kentucky Papers of Draper collection of manuscripts, 1594
Weaver, C. L., and Mills, H. M. County and local historical material in Ohio State Archaeological and Historical Library, 2768
Webb, A. J. Compendium of Irish biography, 4605
Webb, B. J. Centenary of Catholicity in Kentucky, 1595
Webb, W. P. Handbook of Texas, 3420
Webber, M. Death notices from South Carolina and American general gazette, 3207
——— (and others). Marriage and death notices from South Carolina weekly gazette, 3208
Weeks, L. H. Prominent families of New York, 2568
Weeks, S. B. Index to colonial and state records, North Carolina, 2626n

## Index

Wehle, M. [Reprints of New York atlases], 2569
Weidenhan, J. L. Baptismal names, 227
Weikel, S. Genealogical research in the published Pennsylvania archives, 3028
Weinberg, A., and Slattery, T. E. Warrants and surveys of Pennsylvania, 3028a
Weis, F. L. Ancestral roots of sixty colonists, 325-326; Colonial clergy of the middle colonies, 327
Welch, L. Massachusetts 1800 census, 1932
Welcome claimants, 3030
Welcome Society of Pennsylvania. Passengers and ships prior to 1864, 3029; Welcome claimants, 3030
Wellauer, M. A. Guide to foreign genealogical research, 33a, 264
Wells, J. K. First directory of Nevada territory, 2223
Welsh, see Wales
Wertheim, county of Germany, 2978, v.12, 2931
Wesley, F. How to write a local history of Methodism, 4558
Wesley Historical Society. Proceedings, 4559
Wesleyan Methodists, see Methodists
West, A. History of Methodism in Alabama, 769
West, C. W. Persons and places of Indian territory, 2802
West, J. Village records, 4236
West Augusta, Virginia, 3025, 3641, 3663
West Indies, see British West Indies
West Midland (England) genealogy, 4150
West Tennessee Historical Society. Papers, 3316
West Virginia (see also Pennsylvania and Virginia): 3717-3776; atlas, 3738; bibliography, 3722a, 3723, 3756, 3759; cemetery readings, 3730; census (1782, 1784), 3763; church archives, 3734; church vital statistics records, 3731; Civil War, 556, 564, 3745; colonial families, 620; counties, 3545; county archives, 3732; county formations, 3735, 3767; estate settlements, 3741; French and Indian Wars, 3749; gazetteer, 3727; Indian Wars, 3724-3725, 3749; Jews, 3766; land grants, 3767, 3769-3770; Lord Dunsmore's War, 3749; manual, 3750, 3765; manuscripts and archives, 3729; maps, 3768; obituaries, 3771; pensions, 3763; place names, 3743; plat book, 3738n; Presbyterian churches, 3734; Protestant Episcopal church, 3734; public vital statistics records, 3733; Revolutionary War, 3742, 3749, 3761; surnames, 3755

West Virginia echoer (magazine), 3773
West Virginia historical magazine, 3774
West Virginia history, 3775
West Virginia Univ. Library, manuscripts and archives, 3729
West Wales and Gower, marriage bonds, 4849
West Wales historical records, 4840
Westbrook, Col. T., letters to, 1714
Westcott, T. Names of persons who took oath of allegiance, Pennsylvania, 3031
Westerfield, T. W. Kentucky genealogy and biography, 1573
Western Isles of Scotland, 4884-4885a
Western Maryland, 1830
Western Massachusetts, 1891
Western New York Genealogical Society journal, 2569a
Western Pennsylvania genealogical indexes, 3032
Western Reserve, Ohio: Firelands area, 2689, 2701-2703, 2766; women in 2687, 2769
Western Reserve Historical Society: manuscripts, 2752; Shaker manuscripts, 465a
Western States Jewish historical quarterly, 650
Westminster, London, marriage licenses (1558-1699), 4349
Wheat, J. C., and Brun, C. F. Maps and charts published in America before 1800, 207
Wheat, J. L. Postmasters and post offices of Texas, 3421
Wheeler, J. H. Historical sketches of North Carolina, 2657; Reminiscences of North Carolina, 2658
Whichard, R. D. History of lower Tidewater, Virginia, 3669
White, Rev. G. Historical collections of Georgia, 1237
White, G. E. 1840 census of Texas, 3422
White, K. K. King's Mountain men, 546, 2659
White, M. Early Quaker records in Virginia, 3670
Whitelaw, R. T. Virginia's Eastern Shore, 3671
Whiteley, W. G. Revolutionary soldiers of Delaware, 1061
White's conspectus of American biography, 166
Whitley, E. J. Membership roster, D.A.R., Tennessee, 3252; Tennessee genealogical records, 3317
Whitley, W. T. Baptist bibliography, 4533
Whitmore, J. B. Genealogical guide, 4187

## Index

Whitmore, W. H. Heraldic journal, 5107; Massachusetts civil list, 1933
Whitney, E. M. Black Hawk War (1831–32), 1362
Whitney, O. F. History of Utah, 3452
Whittemore, H. Genealogical guide to the early settlers of America, 328
Who was who in America, 167
Who's Who in: Australia, 4917; Latin America, 3868a; Minnesota, 2029; Nevada, 2224; New Zealand, 4950
Whyte, D. Dictionary of Scottish emigrants to the U.S.A., 355; Three centuries of emigration, 4725
Wickersham, J. Bibliography of Alaskan litterature, 782
Wickham, G. Van R. Memorial to pioneer women of Western Reserve, 2769
Wiedeman, R., and Bohannon, L. 1820 census of Michigan, 1984
Wight, D. B. Androscoggin River Valley, 2290
Wilder, D. W. Annals of Kansas, 1485
Wilkens, C. G. Index to 1840 federal population census of Ohio, 2770
Wilkes-Barre, Pennsylvania, 2903
Wilkinson, N. B. Bibliography of Pennsylvania history, 3033
Willamette Valley, Oregon, 2827, 2835
Willard, F. E., and Livermore, M. A. Woman of the century, 168
Willard, J. F. and Goodykoontz, C. B. Experiments in Colorado colonization, 956
William and Mary quarterly, 3672–3674a
William the Conqueror, 4463–4470
Williams, E. G. and E. W. First land owners of Michigan, 1985
Williams, E. W. Counties and townships of Michigan, 1986; Know your ancestors, 265
Williams, H. C. Biographical encyclopaedia of: Maine, 1736; Vermont, 3501
Williams, J. Llyfr Baglan, 4877
Williams, J. H. and B. H. Resources for genealogical research in Missouri, 2136
Williams, M. A. B. Origins of North Dakota place names, 2681
Williams, Richard T. and M. C. Index to: Berks county, Pennsylvania, wills, 3034; Bucks county, 3035; Delaware county, 3036; Montgomery county, 3037; Northampton and Lehigh counties, 3038; Philadelphia, 3039
Williams, Roger, descendants, 3069
Williams, S. C. Beginnings of west Tennessee, 3318

Williams, W. History of northeast Missouri, 2137; History of northwest Missouri, 2138
—— and Shoemaker, F. C. Missouri, 2139
Williams, W. W. History of the Firelands, 2771
Williamson, F. W., and Goodman, G. T. Eastern Louisiana, 1692
Williamson, J. A. Bibliography of state of Maine, 1737
Williamson, L. M. Prominent and progressive Pennsylvania, 3040
Willis, A. J. Genealogy for beginners, 4443; Introducing genealogy, 4443n
Willison, G. F. Saints and strangers, 612
Wills and probates: Alabama, 726; American families (early), 610–611; Canada (Quebec), 4127; Connecticut, 972, 1004; Delaware, Kent county, 1031, New Castle county, 1025, Sussex county, 1032; District of Columbia, 1068; English, 4366–4383, Canterbury, 4367–4374, colonial families, 293, 4375, north country, 4380, York, 4382–4383; Georgia, 1145, 1243; Irish, 4619–4625, documents salved (1922), 4615; Kentucky, 1497, 1536, 1550; Maine, 1730; Maryland, 1741, 1760, 1785–1788, 1796–1797; Mississippi, 2053n; New Hampshire, 2261; New Jersey, 2305, 2357–2358, 2366; New York, Albany, 2421; Hudson River valley, 2453n; Jews, 2466; New York county, 2509; Rensselaerswyck, 2421; North Carolina, 2604, 2624–2625, 2630–2631; Pennsylvania, 3034–3039, German, 2978; Lancaster county, 2889, Philadelphia, 3039; Scottish, 4763a, Edinburgh, 4752, Glasgow, 4754; South Carolina, 3152, 3157–3158, 3170, 3209–3210, Charleston county, 3127, 3158; Tennessee, 3246; Texas, 3404; Virginia, 3025, 3526, 3539, 3589, 3632, 3663; Welsh, 4381, 4850–4851
Willson, M. M. Roster of Oklahoma Society, D.A.R., 2777
Wilmer, L. A. (and others). History and roster of Maryland volunteers, 1840
Wilmington, Delaware, Holy Trinity church records, 1062–1065
Wilson, C. T. Annals of Georgia, 1238
Wilson, H. McK. Lexington Presbytery heritage, 3675; Records of Synod of Virginia, 3676
Wilson, H. P. Biographical history of eminent men, Kansas, 1486
Wilson, J. M. Imperial gazetteer of: England and Wales, 4396; Scotland, 4775

## Index

Wilson, M. P. (and others). Some early Alabama churches, 770

Wilson, S. M. Catalogue of Revolutionary soldiers and sailors of Virginia to whom land bounty warrants were granted, 1597, 3677

Winchell, N. H. History of upper Mississippi Valley, 2029a

Windward Islands, 4920

Winfree, W. K. Laws of Virginia, 3574

Wingo, E. B. Revolutionary War and War of 1812 applications for pensions, 546a, 550

Winter, N. O. History of northwest Ohio, 2772

Winther, O. O. Classified bibliography of periodical literature of trans-Mississippi west, 651

Winthrop, John, 575

Winthrop Fleet, 575, 1848

Wion, J. H. Deaths in central Pennsylvania, 3041

Wisconsin: 3777-3827; atlas, 3801n, 3813; bibliography, 3788, 3808; Catholic churches, 3793, 3798; census (1836), 3827; church archives, 3798; church vital statistics records, 3795; churches and religious organizations, 3794; Civil War, 554, 564, 3803, 3807, 3807a, 3821; county archives, 3797; county government, 3792; families, 3822; gazetteers, 3823; Germans, 1951, 3786; Lutherans, 3798; manuscripts, 3809-3811; map, 3801n, 3813; newspapers, 3805; Norwegians, 394; Pennsylvania Germans, 2978, v.19; place names, 3787; plat book, 3801, 3813; Protestant Episcopal church, 3798; public vital statistics records, 3796; Revolutionary War, 3784; state archives, 3785; territory, 3827; town studies, 3817; township map, 3780

Wisconsin helper (magazine), 3824

Wisconsin State Genealogical Society newsletter, 3825-3826

Wisconsin State Historical Society, manuscripts, 3809

Withers, A. S. Chronicles of border warfare, 3776

Withycombe, E. G. Oxford dictionary of English Christian names, 4421

Wittmeyer, A. V. Registers of births . . . of "Eglise Françoise à la Nouvelle York," 2570

Wolf, L. Anglo-Jewish coats-of-arms, 5032

Wolf, S. American Jew as patriot, 573

Woman's who's who in America, 169

Women: biographies of, American, 134, 168, world, 151; notable American, 155; of Hawaii, 1270; of Quebec, 4110a; of the American Revolution, 513, Pennsylvania, 2877

Wood, C. L. Idaho, history and register, D.A.R., 1272

Wood, H. Guide to records deposited in Public Record Office in Ireland, 4587

Wood, J. P. Peerage of Scotland, 4801n

Wood, V. S. and R. 1805 land lottery of Georgia, 1239

Woodruff, A. Central Missouri River counties, 2140; Missouri marriages, 2141; Missouri pioneers, 2142

Woods, F. 1850 mortality schedules of Texas, 3423; 1860 mortality schedules of Texas, 3424; First census of Oklahoma, 2803

Woodson, R. F. and I. B. Virginia tithables, 3678

Woodward, J. Treatise on ecclesiastical heraldry, 5097

——— and Burnett, G. Treatise of heraldry, 4989

Woollen, W. W. Biographical and historical sketches of early Indiana, 1408a

Wootton, register of wills, 4372

Works Projects Administration, see Historical Records Survey

World Conference of Records and Genealogical Seminar, series of papers, 91

World records (magazine), 129

Wormer, M. Illinois 1840 census index, 1363

Worshipful Company of Apothecaries, history, 4288

Worshipful Company of Clockmasters, apprentices, 4304

Worshipful Company of Shipwrights, freemen and apprentices, 4336

Worthington, D. Rhode Island land evidences, 3109

Worthley, H. F. Inventory of records of congregational churches of Massachusetts, 1934

Woulfe, P. Irish names and surnames, 4652

Wren, T. History of the state of Nevada, 2225

Wright, A. H. Check list of New York state county maps, 2571

Wright, D. Some copy census returns, 4237

Wright, E. C. Loyalists of New Brunswick, 4037, 4069

Wright, G. Representative citizens of Ohio, 2773

Wright, H. A. Story of western Massachusetts, 1935

Wright, M. H. Guide to Indian tribes of Oklahoma, 680
Wright, M. J. Tennessee in the War (1861–65), 3319
Wright, N. E. Building an American pedigree, 266; Genealogy in America, 613
———— and Pratt, D. H. Genealogical research essentials, 267
Wright, P. Monumental inscriptions of Jamaica, 4932
Wrigley, E. A. Identifying people in the past, 4444
Writings on: American history, 101–102; British history, 4161–4163, 4166–4168
Wulfeck, D. F. Genealogy notes on Virginia families, 3679; Marriages of some Virginia residents, 3680; Virginia gazette genealogy, 3681
Wurts, J. S. Magna Charta, 280
Wurttemberg, emigrants from, to Pennsylvania, 2978, v.10
Wust, K. Virginia Germans, 3682
Wyllys, R. K. Arizona, 804
Wynar, L. Encyclopedic directory of ethnic newspapers and periodicals in U.S., 373
Wynd, F. "They were here," 1240
Wyoming: 3828–3841; atlas, 3837; census (1870), 3839, (1880), 3840; church archives, 3835; county archives, 3836; Indian tribes, 660; place names, 3841; plat book, 3837n; public vital statistics records, 3834

Yakima Valley, Washington: history, 3698; records, 3716
Yakima Valley Genealogical Society. Bulletin, 3715; Records of Yakima county, 3716
Yale College, biographical sketches, 141–142; obituary record, 143
Yantis, N. S., see Schreiner-Yantis, N.
Yarns of pioneers, 2682
Yellowed pages, 3425
Yenawine, W. S. Checklist of source materials for the counties of Georgia, 1241–1242
Yesteryears magazine, 2572
Yoakum, H. K. History of Texas, 3426
Yohogania county court, Virginia, wills proved, 3663
Yon, P. D. Guide to Ohio county . . . records, 2774
York county: Maine, 1694, 1699, 1738; Pennsylvania, 2892, 2994; South Carolina, 3164
York, England. Index to wills, 4382; Testamenta Eboracensia, 4383
York, Ontario. Court of General Sessions, Minutes, 4096
Yorke, P. Royal tribes of Wales, 4878
Yorkshire, England, marriage licenses, 4356–4358
Yoshpe, H. P., and Brower, P. P. Preliminary inventory of land entry papers of Government Land Office, 93
Youings, J. Local record sources in print, 4169
Young, A. Chronicles of first planters . . . of Massachusetts Bay, 1936; Chronicles of the Pilgrim Fathers, 614, 1937
Young, L. M. Peters colonists, 3427
Young, M. E. Redskins, ruffleshirts, and rednecks, 716
Young, P. Abstracts of Old Ninety-Six and Abbeville district, 1243, 3209; Genealogical collection of South Carolina wills, 3210
Youngberg, E. 1850 Oregon territorial census, 2840
Your family tree, 3042
Yugoslavs: census (1850–1880), 862; California marriages, 862; immigration, 356, 356a, 356b; Los Angeles, 862; Louisiana, 1691; Nevada, 2203; San Francisco, 862; Wild West, 862
Yukon (see also Alaska), place names, 4073

Zabriskie, G. O. Climbing our family tree systematically, 268
———— and Robinson, D. L. U.S. census of Utah (1851), 3453
Zetland family histories, 4892
Zieber, E. Heraldry in America, 5008
Zornow, W. F. Kansas, 1487
Zuber, E. K. Lineage books, Soc. of Mayflower Descendants, Texas, 3400
Zweibrücken immigrant list, 2978, v.1.
Zweibrücken and Schaffhausen, German immigrants from, 2978, v.16